The Works of Browne
Volume I, II, & III

Thomas Browne
Edited by Charles Edward Sayle

Copyright © Thomas Browne & Charles Edward Sayle
All rights reserved.
ISBN-13:9798460393596

**Published in London
1904-1907**

IN THREE VOLUMES

Table of Contents

Volume I											4

Volume II											162

Volume III											316

VOL. I

PREFATORY NOTE

This edition is an endeavour to arrive at a more satisfactory text of the work of Sir Thomas Browne, and to reproduce the principal part of it, as faithfully as seems advisable, in the form in which it was presented to the public at the time of his death. For this purpose, in the first volume, the text of the *Religio Medici* follows more particularly the issue of 1682. The *Pseudodoxia Epidemica* here given is based upon the sixth edition of ten years earlier, with careful revision. In every case in which a spelling or punctuation was dubious, a comparison was made of nearly all the issues printed during the lifetime of the writer, and their merits weighed. By this means it is hoped that the true flavour of the period has been preserved.

The Annotations upon the *Religio Medici*, which were always reprinted with the text during the seventeenth century, are here restored. They will appeal to a certain class of readers which has a right to be considered. It is to be regretted that every quotation given in these pages has not been verified. Several have been corrected; but to have worked through them all, in these busy days, would have been a labour of some years, which it is not possible to devote to the purpose. It has been thought best to leave these passages therefore, in the main, as they stand.[1]

The portrait of Sir Thomas Browne here prefixed is reproduced from the engraving published in 1672 with the edition of the *Religio Medici* and *Pseudodoxia Epidemica*.

C.S.

August, 1903.

Footnotes

[1]The quotation, now corrected, from Montaigne, on p. xxii, is a typical example of the pitfall into which one is liable to stumble. The passage there cited is in chapter xl. of the French author's later arrangement: a clear indication of the edition of the *Essais* used by the author of the Annotations. What is one to make of the readings in Lucretius on p. xxv? No light is thrown upon these difficulties by the edition of Browne's works published in 1686. Wilkin did not reprint the Annotations, except in selection.

ANNOTATIONS UPON RELIGIO MEDICI

Nec satis est vulgasse fidem.—
Pet. Arbit. fragment.

THE ANNOTATOR TO THE READER

A. Gellius (noct. Attic. l. 20. cap. *ult.*) *notes some Books that had strange Titles*; Pliny (Prefat. Nat. Hist.) *speaking of some such, could not pass them over without a jeer: So strange (saith he) are the Titles of some Books,* Ut multos ad vadimonium deferendum compellant. *And* Seneca *saith, some such there are,* Qui patri obstetricem parturienti filiæ accersenti moram injicere possint. *Of the same fate this present Tract* Religio Medici *hath partaken: Exception by some hath been taken to it in respect of its Inscription, which say they, seems to imply that* Physicians *have a Religion by themselves, which is more than Theologie doth warrant: but it is their Inference, and not the Title that is to blame; for no more is meant by that, or endeavoured to be prov'd in the* Book *then that (contrary to the opinion of the unlearned)* Physitians *have Religion as well as other men.*

For the Work it self, the present Age hath produced none that has had better Reception amongst the learned; it has been received and fostered by almost all, there having been but one that I knew of (to verifie that Books have their Fate from the Capacity of the Reader) that has had the face to appear against it; that is Mr. Alexander[2] *Rosse; but he is dead, and it is uncomely to skirmish with his shadow. It shall be sufficient to remember to the* Reader, *that the noble and most learned* Knight, *Sir* Kenelm Digby, *has delivered his opinion of it in another sort, who though in some things he differ from the* Authors *sense, yet hath he most candidly and ingeniously allow'd it to be a very learned and excellent Piece; and I think no Scholar will say there can be an approbation more authentique. Since the time he Published his Observations upon it, one Mr. Jo. Merryweather, a Master of* Arts *of the* University *of* Cambridge, *hath deem'd it worthy to be put into the universal Language, which about the year 1644 he performed; and that hath carried the* Authors *name not only into the* Low-Countries *and* France *(in both which places the Book in* Latin *hath since been printed) but into* Italy *and* Germany; *and in* Germany *it hath since fallen into the hands of a Gentleman of that Nation*[3] *(of his name he hath given us no more than* L.N.M.E.N.) *who hath written learned* Annotations *upon it in* Latin, *which were Printed together with the Book at* Strasbourg 1652. *And for the general good opinion the World had entertained both of the* Work *and Author, this Stranger tells you*[4]: Inter alios Auctores incidi in libruni cui Titulus *Religio Medici,* jam ante mihi innotuerat lectionem istius libri multos præclaros viros delectasse, imo occupasse. Non ignorabam librum in *Anglia, Gallia, Italia, Belgio, Germania,* cupidissime legi; coustabat mihi eum non solum in *Anglia ac Batavia,* sed et *Purisiis* cum præfatione, in qua Auctor magnis laudibus fertur, esse typis mandatum. Compertum mihi erat multos magnos atq; eruditos viros sensere Auctorem (quantum ex hoc scripto perspici potest) sanctitate vitæ ac pietare elucere, etc. *But for the worth of the* Book *it is so well known to every* English-man *that is fit to read it, that this attestation of a* Forrainer *may seem superfluous.*

The German, *to do him right, hath in his* Annotations *given a fair specimen of his learning, shewing his skill in the Languages, as well antient as modern; as also his acquaintance with all manner of Authors, both sacred and profane, out of which he has ammas'd a world of Quotations: but yet, not to mention that he hath not observed some Errors of the Press, and one or two main ones of the Latin Translation, whereby the Author is much injured; it cannot be denyed but he hath pass'd over many hard places untoucht, that might deserve a Note; that he hath made* Annotations *on some, where no need was; in the explication of others hath gone besides the true sense.*

And were he free from all these, yet one great Fault there is he may be justly charg'd with, that is, that he cannot manum de Tabula *even in matters the most obvious: which is an affectation ill-becoming a* Scholar; *witness the most learned Annotator,* Claud. Minos. Divion. in præfat. commentar. Alciat. Emblemat. præfix. Præstat (*saith he*) brevius omnia persequi, et leviter attingere quæ nemini esse ignota suspicari possint, quam quasi ῥαψωδεῖν, perq; locos communes identidem expatiari.

I go not about by finding fault with his, obliquely to commend my own; I am as far from that, as 'tis possible others will be: All I seek, by this Preface, next to acquainting the Reader *with the various entertainment of the Book, is, that he would be advertized that these Notes were collected ten[5] years since, long before the* German's *were written; so that I am no Plagiary (as who peruseth his Notes and mine, will easily perceive): And in the second place, that I made this Recueil meerly for mine own entertainment, and not with any intention to evulge it; Truth is my witness, the publication proceeds meerly from the importunity of the Book-seller (my special friend) who being acquainted with what I had done, and about to set out another Edition of the Book, would not be denied these notes to attex to it; 'tis he (not I) that divulgeth it, and whatever the success be, he alone is concern'd in it; I only say for my self what my Annotations bear in the Frontispiece—*

Nec satis est vulgasse fidem——

That is, that it was not enough to all persons (though pretenders to Learning) that our Physitian *had publish'd his Creed, because it wanted an exposition. I say further, that the* German's *is not full; and that (*——Quicquid sum Ego quamvis infra Lucilli censum ingeniumq;——*) my explications do in many things illustrate the Text of my Author.*

24 Martii, 1654.

Footnotes

[2] In his *Medicus Medicatus*.

[3] That he was a *German* appears by his notes *page* 35, where he useth these words, *Dulcissima nostra Germania*, etc.

[4] In Præfat. Annotat.

[5] Excepting two or three particulars in which reference is made to some Books that came over since that time.

ANNOTATIONS UPON RELIGIO MEDICI
The Epistle to the *READER*

Certainly that man were greedy of life, who should desire to live when all the World were at an end;] This Mr. *Merryweather* hath rendred thus; *Cupidum esse vitæ oportet, qui universo jam expirante mundo vivere cuperet*; and well enough: but it is not amiss to remember, that we have this saying in *Seneca* the *Tragœdian*, who gives it us thus, *Vitæ est avidus quisquis non vult mundo secum pereunte mori.*

There are many things delivered Rhetorically.] The Author herein imitates the ingenuity of St. *Austin*, who in his *Retract.* corrects himself for having delivered some things more like a young Rhetorician than a sound Divine; but though St. *Aug.* doth deservedly acknowledge it a fault in himself, in that he voluntarily published such things, yet cannot it be so in this Author, in that he intended no publication of it, as he professeth in this Epistle, and in that other to Sir *Kenelm Digby.*

THE FIRST PART

Sect. 1. *Pag.* 1.

The general scandal of my Profession.] Physitians (of the number whereof it appears by several passages in this Book the Author is one) do commonly hear ill in this behalf. It is a common speech (but only amongst the unlearn'd sort) *Ubi tres Medici, duo Athei*. The reasons why those of that Profession (I declare my self that I am none, but *Causarum Actor Mediocris*, to use *Horace* his Phrase) may be thought to deserve that censure, the Author rendreth *Sect.* 19.

The natural course of my studies.] The vulgar lay not the imputation of Atheism only upon Physitians, but upon Philosophers in general, who for that they give themselves to understand the operations of *Nature*, they calumniate them, as though they rested in the second causes without any respect to the first. Hereupon it was, that in the tenth Age Pope *Silvester* the second pass'd for a Magician, because he understood Geometry and natural Philosophy. *Baron. Annal.* 990.

And *Apuleius* long before him laboured of the same suspicion, upon no better ground; he was accus'd, and made a learned Apology for himself, and in that hath laid down what the ground is of such accusations, in these words: *Hæc fermè communi quodam errore imperitorum Philosophis objectantur, ut partem eorum qui corporum causas meras et simplices rimantur, irreligiosos putant, eosque aiunt Deos abnuere, ut Anaxagoram, et Lucippum, et Democritum, et Epicurum, cœterosq; rerum naturæ Patronos.* Apul. in Apolog. And it is possible that those that look upon the second Causes scattered, may rest in them and go no further, as my Lord *Bacon* in one of his *Essayes* observeth; but our Author tells us there is a true Philosophy, from which no man becomes an Atheist, Sect. 46.

<u>The indifferency of my behaviour and Discourse in matters of Religion.</u>] Bigots are so oversway'd by a preposterous Zeal, that they hate all moderation in discourse of Religion; they are the men forsooth—*qui solos credant habendos esse Deos quos ipsi colunt. Erasmus* upon this accompt makes a great complaint to Sir *Tho. More* in an Epistle of his, touching one *Dorpius* a Divine of *Lovain*, who because, upon occasion of discourse betwixt them, *Erasmus* would not promise him to write against *Luther*, told *Erasmus* that he was a *Lutheran*, and afterwards published him for such; and yet as *Erasmus* was reputed no very good Catholick, so for certain he was no Protestant.

<u>Not that I meerly owe this Title to the Font</u>] as most do, taking up their Religion according to the way of their Ancestors; this is to be blamed among all persons: It was practised as well amongst Heathens as Christians.

Per caput hoc juro per quod Pater antè solebat, saith *Ascanius* in *Virgil*: and *Apuleius* notes it for an absurdity. *Utrum Philosopho, putas turpe scire ista, an nescire? negligere, an curare? nosse quanta sit etiam in istis providentiæ ratio, an de diis immortalibus Matri et Patri cedere?* saith he in *Apolog.* and so doth *Minutius. Unusquisq; vestrum non cogitat prius se debere deum nosse quam colere, dum inconsulte gestiuntur parentibus obedire, dum fieri malunt alieni erroris accessio, quam sibi credere.* Minut. in Octav.

<u>But having in my ripers examined, etc.</u>] according to the Apostolical Precept, *Omnia probate, quod bonum est tenete.*

Sect. 2, Pag. 8.

<u>There being a Geography of Religion</u>] i.e. of Christian Religion, which you may see described in Mr. *Brerewood's* Enquiries: he means not of the Protestant Religion; for though there be a difference in Discipline, yet the *Anglican, Scotic, Belgic, Gallican,* and *Helvetic* Churches differ not in any essential matter of the Doctrine, as by the *Harmony of Confessions* appears. 5. Epist. Theod. Bezæ Edmundo Grindallo Ep. Londinens.

<u>Wherein I dislike nothing but the Name</u>] that is *Lutheran, Calvinist, Zuinglian,* etc.

<u>Now the accidental occasion wherein, etc.</u>] This is graphically described by *Thuanus* in his History: but because his words are too large for this purpose, I shall give it you somewhat more briefly, according to the relation of the Author of the History of the Council of *Trent*. The occasion was the necessity of Pope *Leo* the Tenth, who by his profusion had so exhausted the Treasure of the *Church*, that he was constrained to have recourse to the publishing of Indulgencies to raise monies: some of which he had destined to his own Treasury, and other part to his Allyes, and particularly to his Sister he gave all the money that should be raised in *Saxony*; and she, that she might make the best profit of the donation, commits it to one *Aremboldus*, a Bishop to appoint Treasurers for these Indulgences. Now the custome was, that whensoever these Indulgences were sent into *Saxony*, they were to be divulged by the Fryars *Eremites* (of which Order *Luther* then was), but *Aremboldus* his Agents thinking with themselves, that the Fryars *Eremites* were so well acquainted with the trade, that if the business should be left to them, they should neither be able to give so good an account of their Negotiation, nor yet get so much themselves by it as they might do in case the business were committed to another Order; they thereupon recommend it to (and the business is undertaken by) the *Dominican* Fryars, who performed it so ill, that the scandal arising both from thence, and from the ill lives of those that set them on work, stirred up *Luther* to write against the abuses of these Indulgences; which was all he did at first; but then, not long after, being provoked by some Sermons and small Discourses that had been published against what he had written, he rips up the *business* from the beginning, and publishes xcv *Theses* against it

at *Wittenberg*. Against these *Tekel* a *Dominican* writes; then *Luther* adds an explication to his. *Eckius* and *Prierius* Dominicans, thereupon take the controversie against him: and now *Luther* begins to be hot; and because his adversaries could not found the matter of Indulgences upon other Foundations then the *Popes* power and infallibility, that begets a disputation betwixt them concerning the Popes power, which *Luther* insists upon as inferiour to that of a *general Council*; and so by degrees he came on to oppose the Popish Doctrine of *Remission of sins*, *Penances*, and *Purgatory*; and by reason of Cardinal *Cajetans* imprudent management of the conference he had with him, it came to pass that he rejected the whole body of Popish doctrine. So that by this we may see what was the accidental occasion wherein, the slender means whereby, and the abject condition of the person by whom, the work of Reformation of Religion was set on foot.

Sect. 3. Pag. 8.

Yet I have not so shaken hands with those, desperate Resolutions, (Resolvers it should be, without doubt) who had rather venture at large their decayed Bottom, than bring her in to be new trimm'd in the Dock; who had rather promiscuously retain all, than abridge any; and obstinately be what they are, than what they have been; as to stand in a diameter and at swords point with them: we have reformed from them, not against them, etc.] These words by Mr. *Merryweather* are thus rendred, sc. *Nec tamen in vecordem illum pertinacium hominum gregem memet adjungo, qui lubefactatum navigium malunt fortunæ committere quam in navale de integro resarciendum deducere, qui malunt omnia promiscuè retinere quam quicquam inde diminuere, et pertinaciter esse qui sunt quam qui olim fuerunt, ita ut iisdem ex diametro repugnent: ab illis, non contra illos, reformationem instituimus*, etc. And the Latine Annotator sits down very well satisfied with it, and hath bestowed some notes upon it; but under the favour both of him and the Translator, this Translation is so far different from the sense of the Author, that it hath no sense in it; or if there be any construction of sense in it, it is quite besides the Author's meaning; which will appear if we consider the context: by that we shall find that the Author in giving an account of his Religion, tells us first, that he is a Christian, and farther, that he is of the reform'd Religion; but yet he saith, in this place, he is not so rigid a Protestant, nor at defiance with Papists so far, but that in many things he can comply with them, (the particulars he afterwards mentions in this Section) for, saith he, we have reform'd from them, not against them, that is, as the *Archbishop* of *Canterbury* against the *Jesuit* discourseth well. We have made no new Religion nor Schism from the old; but in calling for the old, and desiring that which was novel and crept in might be rejected, and the Church of *Rome* refusing it, we have reform'd from those upstart novel Doctrines, but against none of the old: and other sense the place cannot bear; therefore how the *Latine Annotator* can apply it as though in this place the Author intended to note the *Anabaptists*, I see not, unless it were in respect of the expression *Vecordem pertinacium hominum gregem*, which truly is a description well befitting them, though not intended to them in this place: howsoever, I see not any ground from hence to conclude the Author to be any whit inclining to the *Bulk* of Popery (but have great reason from many passages in this Book to believe the contrary,) as he that prefix'd a Preface to the Parisian Edition of this Book hath unwarrantably done.

But for the mistake of the Translator, it is very obvious from whence that arose. I doubt not but it was from mistake of the sense of the English Phrase *Shaken hands*, which he hath rendered by these words, *Memet adjungo*, wherein he hath too much play'd the Scholar, and show'd himself to be more skilful in forraign and antient customs, then in the vernacular practise and usage of the language of his own Country; for although amongst the Latines protension of the Hand were a Symbole and sign of Peace and Concord (as *Alex. ab Alexandro*; *Manum verò protendere, pacem peti significabunt* (saith he) *Gen. Dier. lib. 4. cap. ult.* which also is confirmed by *Cicero pro Dejotaro*; and *Cæsar. l. 2. de Bellico Gallico*) and was used in their first meetings, as appears by the Phrase, *Jungere hospitio Dextras*; and by that of *Virgil*,

Oremus pacem, et Dextras tendamus inermes,

And many like passages that occur in the Poets, to which I believe the Translator had respect; yet in modern practise, especially with us in *England*, that ceremony is used as much in our *Adieu's* as in the *first Congress*; and so the Author meant in this place, by saying he had not *shaken hands*; that is, that he had not so deserted, or bid farewel to the *Romanists*, as to stand at swords point with them: and then he gives his reasons at those words, *For omitting those improperations*, etc. So that instead of *memet adjungo*, the Translator should have used some word or Phrase of a clean contrary signification; and instead of *ex diametro repugnent*, it should be *repugnem*.

Sect. 5. Pag. 11.

Henry the Eighth, who, though he rejected the Pope, refused not the faith of Rome.] So much *Buchanan* in his own life written by himself testifieth, who speaking of his coming into *England* about the latter end of that King's time, saith, *Sed ibi tum omnia adeo erant incerta, ut eodem die, ac eodem igne* (very strange!) *utriusque factionis homines cremarentur, Henrico 8, jam seniore suæ magnis securitati quam Religionis puritati intento*. And for the confirmation of this assertion of the Author, *vide Stat. 31. H. 8, cap. 14*.

And was conceived the state of Venice would have attempted in our dayes.] This expectation was in the time of Pope *Paul* the Fifth, who by excommunicating that Republique, gave occasion to the Senate to banish all such of the Clergy as would not by reason of the Popes command administer the Sacraments; and upon that account the *Jesuits* were cast out, and never since receiv'd into that State.

Sect. 6. Pag. 12.

Or be angry with his judgement for not agreeing with me in that, from which perhaps within a few days I should dissent my self.] I cannot think but in this expression the Author had respect to that of that excellent French Writer *Monsieur Mountaign* (in whom I often trace him). *Combien diversement jugeons nous de choses? Combien de fois changeons nous nos fantasies? Ce que je tien aujourdhuy, ce que je croy, je le tien et le croy de toute ma Creance, mais ne m'est il pas advenu non une fois mais cent, mais mille et tous les jours d'avoir embrasse quelque autre chose?* Mountaign lib. 2. *Des Essais*. Chap. 12.

Every man is not a proper Champion for truth, etc.] A good cause is never betray'd more than when it is prosecuted with much eagerness, and but little sufficiency; and therefore *Zuinglius*, though he were of *Carolostadius* his opinion in the point of the Sacrament of the *Eucharist* against *Luther*, yet he blamed him for undertaking the defence of that cause against *Luther*, not judging him able enough for the encounter: *Non satis habet humerorum*, saith he of *Carolostad*, alluding to that of *Horace, Sumite materiam vestris qui scribitis æquam Viribus, et versate diu quid ferre recusent Quid valeant humeri.*——So *Minutius Fælix; Plerumq; pro disserentium viribus, et eloquentiæ potestate, etiam perspicuæ veritatis conditio mutetur.* Minut. in Octav. And *Lactantius* saith, this truth is verified in *Minutius* himself: for *Him, Tertullian* and *Cyprian*, he spares not to blame (all of them) as if they had not with dexterity enough defended the Christian cause against the *Ethniques. Lactant. de justitia*, cap. 1. I could wish that those that succeeded him had not as much cause of complaint against him: surely he is noted to have many errors *contra fidem*.

Pag. 13.

In Philosophy——there is no man more Paradoxical then my self, but in Divinity I love to keep the Road, etc.] Appositely to the mind of the Author, saith the Publisher of Mr. *Pembel's* Book *de origine formarum, Certe* (saith he) *in locis Theologicis ne quid detrimenti capiat vel Pax. vel Veritas Christi*——*à novarum opinionum pruritu prorsus abstinendum puto, usq; adeo ut ad certam regulam etiam loqui debeamus, quod pie et prudenter monet Augustinus (de Civ. Dei. 1. 10, cap. 23.) [ne verborum licentia impia vi gignat opinionem,] at in pulvere Scholastico ubi in nullius verba, juramus, et in utramvis partem sine dispendio vel pacis, vel salutis ire liceat, major conceditur cum sentiendi tum loquendi libertas*, etc. Capel. *in Ep. Dedicat. Pembel, de origin form. præfix*.

Heresies perish not with their Authors, but like the River Arethusa, though they lose their Currents in one place, they rise again in another.] Who would not think that this expression were taken from Mr. *Mountaigne, l. 2, des Ess. cap. 12*. Where he hath these words, *Nature enserre dans les termes de son progress ordinaire comme toutes autres choses aussi les creances les judgements et opinions des hommes elles ont leur revolutions*; and that *Mountaigne* took his from *Tully. Non enim hominum interitu sententiæ quoque occidunt, Tull. de nat. deorum l. 1*, etc.

Of the River *Arethusa* thus *Seneca. Videbis celebratissimum carminibus fontem Arethusam limpidissimi ac perludicissimi ad imum stagni gelidissimas aquas profundentem, sive illas primum nascentes invenit, sive flumen integrum subter tot maria, et à confusione pejoris undæ servatum reddidit.* Senec. de consolat. ad Martiam.

Sect. 7. Pag. 14.

Now the first of mine was that of the Arabians.] For this Heresie, the Author here sheweth what it was; they are called *Arabians* from the place where it was fostered; and because the *Heresiarch* was not known, *Euseb.* St. *Aug.* and *Nicephorus* do all write of it: the reason of this Heresie was so specious, that it drew Pope *John 22.* to be of the same perswasion. Where then was his infallibility? Why, *Bellarmine* tells you he was nevertheless infallible for that: for, saith he, he maintained this opinion when he might do it without peril of Heresie, for that no definition of the Church whereby 'twas made Heresie, had preceded when he held that opinion. *Bellar. l. 4, de Pontif. Roman. cap. 4.* Now this definition was first made ('tis true) by Pope *Benedict* in the 14 Age: but then I would ask another question, that is, If 'till that time there were nothing defined in the Church touching the beatitude of Saints, what certainty was there touching the sanctity of any man? and upon what ground were those canonizations of Saints had, that were before the 14 Age?

The second was that of Origen.] Besides St. *Augustine*, *Epiphanius*, and also S. *Hierom*, do relate that *Origen* held, that not only the souls of men, but the *Devils* themselves should be discharged from torture after a certain time: but *Genebrard* endeavours to clear him of this. *Vid. Coquæum, in 21. lib. Aug. de. Civ. Dei. cap. 17.*

These opinions though condemned by lawful Councils, were not Heresie in me, etc.] For to make an Heretique, there must be not only *Error in intellectu* but *pertinacia in voluntate.* So St. *Aug. Qui sententiam suam quamvis falsam atque perversam nulla pertinaci animositate defendunt, quærunt autem cauta solicitudine veritatem, corrigi parati cum invenerint, nequaquam sunt inter Hæreticos deputundi.* Aug. cont. Manich. 24, qu. 3.

Sect. 9 Pag. 16.

The deepest mysteries ours contains have not only been illustrated, but maintained by Syllogism and the Rule of Reason,] and since this Book was written, by Mr. *White* in his *Institutiones Sacræ*.

And when they have seen the Red Sea, doubt not of the Miracle.] Those that have seen it, have been better informed then Sir *Henry Blount* was, for he tells us that he desired to view the passage of *Moses* into the Red Sea (not being above three days journey off) but the *Jews* told him the precise place was not known within less than the space of a days journey along the shore; wherefore (saith he) I left that as too uncertain for any Observation. *In his Voyage into the Levant.*

Sect. 10. Pag. 18.

I had as lieve you tell me that *Anima est Angelus hominis, est corpus Dei, as Entelechia; Lux est umbra Dei, as actus perspicui.*] Great variety of opinion there hath been amongst the Ancient Philosophers touching the definition of the Soul. *Thales*, his was, that it is a *Nature without Repose. Asclepiades*, that it is *an Exercitation of Sense. Hesiod*, that it is *a thing composed of Earth and Water; Parmenides* holds, *of Earth and Fire; Galen* that it is *Heat; Hippocrates*, that it is *a spirit diffused through the body*. Some others have held it to be *Light; Plato* saith, 'tis *a Substance moving itself*; after cometh *Aristotle* (whom the Author here reproveth) and goeth a degree farther, and saith it is *Entelechia*, that is, that which naturally makes the body to move. But this definition is as rigid as any of the other; for this tells us not what the *essence, origine* or *nature* of the *soul* is, but only marks an *effect* of it, and therefore signifieth no more than if he had said (as the Author's Phrase is) that it is *Angelus hominis*, or an *Intelligence* that moveth man, as he supposed those other to do the Heavens.

Now to come to the definition of Light, in which the Author is also unsatisfied with the School of *Aristotle*, he saith, It satisfieth him no more to tell him that *Lux est actus perspicui*, than if you should tell him that it is *umbra Dei*. The ground of this definition given by the *Peripateticks*, is taken from a passage in *Aristot. de anima l. 2, cap. 7*, where *Aristotle* saith, That the colour of the thing seen, doth move that which is *perspicuum actu* (i.e. *illustratam naturam quæ sit in aere aliove corpore transparente*) and that that, in regard of its continuation to the eye, moveth the eye, and by its help the internal *sensorium*; and that so vision is perform'd. Now as it is true that the Sectators of *Aristotle* are to blame, by fastening upon him by occasion of this passage, that he meant that those things that made this impress upon the Organs are meer accidents, and have nothing of substance; which is more than ever he meant, and cannot be maintained without violence to Reason, and his own Principles; so for *Aristotle* himself, no man is beholding to him for any Science acquir'd by this definition: for what is any man the near for his telling him that Colour (admitting it to be a body, as indeed it is, and in that place he doth not deny) doth move *actu perspicuum*, when as the perspicuity is in relation to the *eye*; and he doth not say how it comes to be perspicuous, which is the thing enquired after, but gives it that donation before the eye hath perform'd its office; so that if he had said it had been *umbra Dei*, it would have been as intelligible, as what he hath said. He that would be satisfied how Vision is perform'd, let him see Mr. *Hobbs* in *Tract. de nat. human*, cap. 2.

For God hath not caused it to rain upon the Earth.] St. *Aug. de Genes. ad literam*, cap. 5, 6, salves that expression from any inconvenience; but the Author in *Pseudodox. Epidemic.* l. 7, cap. 1, shews that we have no reason to be confident that this Fruit was an *Apple*.

I believe that the Serpent (if we shall literally understand it) from his proper form and figure made his motion on his belly before the curse.] Yet the Author himself sheweth in *Pseudodox. Epidemic.* lib. 7, cap. 1, that the form or kind of the *Serpent* is not agreed on: yet *Comestor* affirm'd it was a *Dragon*, *Eugubinus* a *Basilisk*, *Delrio* a *Viper*, and others a common *Snake*: but of what kind soever it was, he sheweth in the same Volume, *lib. 5, c. 4*, that there was no inconvenience, that the temptation should be perform'd in this proper shape.

I find the tryal of Pucelage and the Virginity of Women which God ordained the Jews, is very fallible.] *Locus extat*, *Deut. c. 22*, the same is affirm'd by *Laurentius* in his *Anatom*.

Whole Nations have escaped the curse of Child-birth, which God seems to pronounce upon the whole sex.] This is attested by M. *Mountaigne*. *Les doleurs de l'enfantiment par les medicins, et par Dieu mesme estimees grandes, et que nous passons avec tant de Ceremonies, il y a des nations entieres qui ne'n fuit nul conte. l. 1, des Ess. c. 14.*

Sect 11. Pag. 19.

Who can speak of Eternity without a Solœcism, or think thereof without an Extasie? Time we may comprehend, etc.] Touching the difference betwixt *Eternity* and *Time*, there have been great disputes amongst Philosophers; some affirming it to be no more than *duration perpetual consisting of parts*; and others (to which opinion, it appears by what follows in this Section, the Author adheres) affirmed (to use the Authors Phrase) that it hath no distinction of Tenses, but is according to *Boetius* (lib. 5, consol. pros. 6), his definition, *interminabilis vitæ tota simul et perfecta possessio*. For me, *non nostrum est tantas componere lites*. I shall only observe what each of them hath to say against the other. Say those of the first opinion against those that follow *Boetius* his definition, That definition was taken by *Boetius* out of *Plato's Timæus*, and is otherwise applyed, though not by *Boetius*, yet by those that follow him, than ever *Plato* intended it; for he did not take it in the Abstract, but in the Concrete, for an *eternal thing*, a *Divine substance*, by which he meant *God*, or his *Anima mundi*: and this he did, to the intent to establish this truth, That no mutation can befal the Divine Majesty, as it doth to things subject to generation and corruption; and that *Plato* there intended not to define or describe any *species* of duration: and they say that it is impossible to understand any such *species* of duration that is (according to the Authors expression) but one *permanent point*.

Now that which those that follow *Boetius* urge against the other definition is, they say, it doth not at all difference *Eternity* from the nature of *Time*; for they say if it be composed of many *Nunc's*, or many instants, by the addition of one more it is still encreased; and by that means *Infinity* or *Eternity* is not included, nor ought more than *Time*. For this, see Mr. *White*, *de dial. mundo*, Dial. 3. Nod. 4.

Indeed he only is, etc.] This the Author infers from the words of God to *Moses*, *I am that I am*; and this to distinguish him from all others, who (he saith) have and shall be: but those that are learned in the *Hebrew*, do affirm that the words in that place (*Exod. 3*) do not signifie, *Ego sum qui sum, et qui est*, etc. but *Ero qui ero, et qui erit*, etc. vid *Gassend. in animad. Epicur. Physiolog.*

Sect. 12. Pag. 20.

I wonder how Aristotle could conceive the World Eternal, or how he could make two Eternities:] (that is, that God, and the World both were eternal.) I wonder more at either the ignorance or incogitancy of the *Conimbricenses*, who in their Comment upon the eighth book of *Aristotle's Physicks*, treating of the matter of Creation, when they had first said that it was possible to know it, and that actually it was known (for *Aristotle* knew it) yet for all this they afterwards affirm, That considering onely the light of Nature, there is nothing can be brought to demonstrate Creation: and yet farther, when they had defined Creation to be the production of a thing *ex nihilo*, and had proved that the World was so created in time, and refused the arguments of the Philosophers to the contrary, they added this, That the World might be created *ab æterno*: for having propos'd this question [*Num aliquid à Deo ex Æternitate procreari potuit?*] they defend the affirmative, and assert that not onely incorporeal substances, as Angels; or permanent, as the celestial Bodies; or corruptible as Men, etc. might be produced and made *ab æterno*, and be conserved by an infinite time, *ex utraq; parte*; and that this is neither repugnant to God the Creator, the things created, nor to the nature of Creation: for proof whereof, they bring instances of the *Sun* which if it had been eternal, had illuminated eternally, (and the virtue of God is not less than the virtue of the Sun.) Another instance they bring of the *divine Word*, which was produced *ab æterno*: in which discourse, and in the instances brought to maintain it, it is hard to say whether the madness or impiety be greater; and certainly if Christians thus argue, we have the more reason to pardon the poor heathen *Aristotle*.

There is in us not three, but a Trinity of Souls.] The *Peripatetiques* held that men had three distinct Souls; whom the Heretiques, the *Anomæi*, and the *Jacobites*, followed. There arose a great dispute about this matter in *Oxford*, in the year 1276, and it was then determined against *Aristotle, Daneus Christ. Eth.* l. 1. c. 4. and *Suarez* in his Treatise *de causa formali, Quest. An dentur plures formæ in uno composito*, affirmeth there was a Synod that did *anathematize* all that held with *Aristotle* in this point.

Sect. 14. Pag. 23.

There is but one first, and four second causes in all things.] In that he saith there is but one first cause, he speaketh in opposition to the *Manichees*, who held there were *Duo principia*; one from whom came all good, and the other from whom came all evil: the reason of *Protagoras* did it seems impose upon their understandings; he was wont to say, *Si Deus non est, unde igitur bona? Si autem est, unde mala?* In that he saith there are but four second Causes, he opposeth *Plato*, who to the four causes, *material, efficient, formal*, and *final*, adds for a fifth *exemplar* or *Idæa*, sc. *Id ad quod respiciens artifex, id quod destinabat efficit*; according to whose mind *Boetius* speaks, *lib. 3. met. 9. de cons. Philosoph.*

O qui perpetua mundum ratione gubernas,
Terrarum Cœliq; sator qui tempus ab ævo
Ire jubes, stabilisq; manens das cuncta moveri:
Quem non externæ pepulerunt fingere causæ
Materiæ fluitantis opus, verum insita summi
Forma boni livore carens: tu cuncta superno
Ducis ab exemplo, pulchrum pulcherrimus ipse
Mundum mente gerens, similique in imagine formans,
Perfectasq; jubens perfectum absolvere partes.

And St. *Augustine l. 83. quest. 46.* where (amongst other) he hath these words, *Restat ergo ut omnia Ratione sint condita, nec eadem ratione homo qua equus; hoc enim absurdum est existimare: singula autem propriis sunt creata rationibus.* But these *ideæ Plato's* Scholar *Aristotle* would not allow to make or constitute a different sort of cause from the *formal* or *efficient*, to which purpose he disputes, *l. 7. Metaphysic.* but he and his Sectators, and the *Ramists* also, agree (as the Author) that there are but the four remembred Causes: so that the Author, in affirming there are but four, hath no Adversary but the *Platonists*; but yet in asserting there are four (as his words imply) there are that oppose him, and the *Schools* of *Aristot.* and *Ramus.* I shall bring for instance Mr. *Nat Carpenter*, who in his *Philosophia Libera* affirmeth, there is no such cause as that which they call the *Final cause*: he argueth thus; Every cause hath an influence upon its effect: but so has not the End, therefore it is not a Cause. The *major* proposition (he saith) is evident, because the influence of a cause upon its effect, is either the causality it self, or something that is necessarily conjoyned to it: and the *minor* as plain, for either the End hath an influence upon the effect immediately, or mediately, by stirring up the Efficient to operate; not immediately, because so it should enter either the *constitution* or *production*, or *conservation* of the things; but the constitution it cannot enter, because the constitution is only of *matter* and *form*; nor the Production, for so it should concur to the production, either as it is *simply the end*, or as *an exciter of the Efficient*; but not simply as the end, because the end *as end* doth not go before, but followeth the thing produced, and therefore doth not concur to its production: if they say it doth so far concur, as it is desired of the agent or efficient cause, it should not so have an immediate influence upon the effect, but should onely first move the efficient. Lastly, saith he, it doth not enter the conservation of a thing, because a thing is often conserved, when it is frustrate of its due end, as when it's converted to a new use and end. Divers other Arguments he hath to prove there is no such cause as the final cause. *Nat. Carpenter Philosoph. liber Decad. 3. Exercitat. 5*. But for all this, the Author and he differ not in substance: for 'tis not the Author's intention to assert that the end is in nature præexistent to the effect, but only that whatsoever God has made, he hath made to some end or other; which he doth to oppose the Sectators of *Epicurus*, who maintain the contrary, as is to be seen by this of *Lucretius* which follows.

Illud in his rebus vitium vehementer et istum,
Effugere errorem vitareque premeditabor
Lumina ne facias oculorum clara creata
Prospicere ut possimus; et, ut proferre viai
Proceros passus, ideo fastigia posse
Surarum ac feminum pedibus fundata plicari:
Brachia tum porro validis ex apta lacertis
Esse, manusq; datas utraq; ex parte ministras,
Vt facere ad vitam possimus, quæ foret usus:
Cætera de genere hoc, inter quæcunq; precantur
Omnia perversa præpostera sunt ratione:
Nil ideo quoniam natum'st in corpore, ut uti
Possemus; sed quod natum'st, id procreat usum,
Nec fuit ante videre oculorum lumina nata,
Nec dictis orare prius, quam lingua creata'st,
Sed potius longe linguæ præcessit origo
Sermonem; multoq: creatæ sunt prius aures
Quam sonus est auditus, et omnia deniq; membra
Ante fuere, ut opinor, eorum quam foret usus:
Haud igitur potuere utendi crescere causa.
Lucret. lib. 4. [822-841.]

Sect. 15. Pag. 24.

There are no Grotesques in nature, etc.] So *Monsr. Montaign, Il n'ya rien d'inutil en nature, non pas l'inutilité mesmes, Rien ne s'est ingeré en cet Univers qui n'y tienne place opportun. Ess.* l. 3. c. 1.

Who admires not Regio-montanus his Fly beyond his Eagle?] Of these *Du Bartas*.
Que diray je de l'aigle,
D'ont un doct Aleman honore nostre siecle
Aigle qui deslogeant de la maistresse main,
Aila loin au devant d'un Empereur Germain;
Et l'ayant recontré suddain d'une aisle accorte,
Se tournant le suit au seuil de la porte
Du fort Norembergois, que lis piliers dorez,
Les tapissez chemins, les arcs elabourez,

Les fourdroyans Canons, in la jeusnesse isnelle,

In le chena Senat, n'honnoroit tant come elle.
Vn jour, que cetominer plus des esbats, que de mets,
En privé fasteyoit ses seignieurs plus amees,
Vne mousche de fer, dans sa main recelee,
Prit sans ayde d'autroy, sa gallard evolee:
Fit une entiere Ronde, et puis d'un cerveau las
Come ayant jugement, se purcha sur son bras.
                            Thus Englished by *Silvester.*
Why should not I that wooden Eagle mention?
(A learned German's *late admir'd invention)*
Which mounting from his Fist that framed her,
Flew far to meet an Almain *Emperour:*
And having met him, with her nimble Train,
And weary Wings turning about again,
Followed him close unto the Castle Gate
Of Noremberg; *whom all the shews of state,*
Streets hang'd with Arras, arches curious built,
Loud thundring Canons, Columns richly guilt,
Grey-headed Senate, and youth's gallantise,
Grac'd not so much as onely this device.
Once as this Artist more with mirth than meat,
Feasted some friends that he esteemed great;
From under's hand an Iron Fly flew out,
Which having flown a perfect round about,
With weary wings, return'd unto her Master,
And (as judicious) on his arm she plac'd her.

<u>Or wonder not more at the operation of two souls in those little bodies, than but one in the Trunk of a Cedar?</u>] That is, the *vegetative*, which according to the common opinion, is supposed to be in *Trees*, though the *Epicures* and *Stoiques* would not allow any Soul in Plants; but *Empedocles* and *Plato* allowed them not only a *vegetative* Soul, but affirm'd them to be *Animals*. The *Manichees* went farther, and attributed so much of the rational Soul to them, that they accounted it *Homicide* to gather either the flowers or fruit, as St. *Aug.* reports.

<u>We carry with us the wonders we seek without us.</u>] So St. *Aug.* l. 10. de civ. c. 3. *Omni miraculo quod fit per hominem majus miraculum est homo.*

Sect. 16. Pag. 25.

<u>Another of his servant Nature, that publique and universal Manuscript that lies expansed, etc.</u>] So is the description of *Du Bartas 7. jour de la sepm.*

Oyes ce Docteur muet estudie en ce livre
Qui nuict et jour ouvert t'apprendra de bien vivre.

<u>All things are artificial, for Nature is the Art of God.</u>] So Mr. *Hobbes* in his *Leviathan (in initio)* Nature is the Art whereby God governs the world.

Sect. 17. Pag. 27.

<u>Directing the operations of single and individual Essences, etc.</u>] Things singular or individuals, are in the opinion of Philosophers not to be known, but by the way of sense, or by that which knows by its Essence, and that is onely God. The Devils have no such knowledge, because whatsoever knows so, is either the cause or effect of the thing known; whereupon *Averroes* concluded that God was the cause of all things, because he understands all things by his Essence; and *Albertus Magnus* concluded, That the inferiour intelligence understands the superiour, because it is an effect of the superiour: but neither of these can be said of the *Devil*; for it appears he is not the effect of any of these inferiour things, much less is he the cause, for the power of Creation onely belongs to God.

<u>All cannot be happy at once, because the Glory of one State depends upon the ruine of another.</u>] This Theme is ingeniously handled by Mr. *Montaigne livr. 1. des Ess.* cap. 22. the title whereof is, *Le profit de l'un est dommage de l'autre.*

Sect. 18. Pag. 29.

'Tis the common fate of men of singular gifts of mind, to be destitute of those of Fortune.] So *Petron. Arbiter. Amor ingenii neminem unquum divitem fecit*, in *Satyric*. And *Apuleius* in Apolog. *Idem mihi etiam* (saith he) *paupertatem opprobravit acceptum Philosopho crimen et ultro profitendum*; and then a little afterwards, he sheweth that it was the common fate of those that had singular gifts of mind: *Eadem enim est paupertas apud Græcos in Aristide justa, in Phocyone benigna, in Epaminonde strenua, in Socrate sapiens, in Homero diserta.*

We need not labour with so many arguments to confute judicial Astrology.] There is nothing in judicial *Astrology* that may render it impious; but the exception against it is, that it is vain and fallible; of which any man will be convinced, that has read *Tully de Divinat.* and St. *Aug.* book 5. *de Civ. dei.*

Sect. 19. Pag. 31.

There is in our soul a kind of Triumvirate——that distracts the peace of our Commonwealth, not less than did that other the State of Rome.] There were two *Triumvirates*, by which the peace of *Rome* was distracted; that of *Crassus, Cæsar* and *Pompey*, of which *Lucan, l.* 1.

——*Tu causam aliorum*——
Facta tribus Dominis communis Roma, nec unquam
In turbam missi feralia fœdera Regni.

And that other of *Augustus, Antonius* and *Lepidus*, by whom, saith *Florus, Respublica convulsa est lacerataque*, which comes somewhat near the Author's words, and therefore I take it that he means this last Triumvirate.

Sect. 19. Pag. 32.

Would disswade my belief from the miracle of the brazen Serpent.] Vid. *Coqueum in, l.* 10. Aug. *de Civ. Dei*, c. 8.

And bid me mistrust a miracle in Elias, etc.] The History is 18. 1 *Reg*. It should be *Elijah*. The Author in 15. *cap. lib.* 7. *Pseudodox*. sheweth it was not perform'd naturally; he was (as he saith) a perfect miracle.

To think the combustion of Sodom might be natural.] Of that opinion was *Strabo*, whereupon he is reprehended by *Genebrard* in these words: *Strabo falsus est*——*dum eversionem addicit sulphuri et bitumini e terra erumpentibus, quæ erat assignanda Cœlo*, i.e. *Deo irato. Tacitus* reports it according to the Bible, *fulminis ictu arsisse.*

Sect. 20. Pag. 33.

Those that held Religion was the difference of man from Beasts, etc.] *Lactantius* was one of those: *Religioni ergo serviendum est, quam qui non suspicit, ipse se prosternit in terram, et vitam pecudum secutus humanitate se abdicat.* Lactant *de fals. Sapientia*, cap. 10.

The Doctrine of Epicurus that denied the providence of God, was no Atheism, but, etc.] I doubt not but he means that delivered in his Epistle to *Menæceus*, and recorded by *Diogenes Laertius*, lib. 10. *Quod beatum æternumque est, id nec habet ipsum negotii quicquam, nec exhibit alteri, itaque neque ira, neque gratia tenetur, quod quæ talia sunt imbecillia sunt omnia*; which the *Epicurean* Poet hath delivered almost in the same words.

Omnis enim per se divum natura necesse 'st
Immortali ævo summa cum pace fruatur,
Semota à nostris rebus sejunctaq; longè:
Nam privata dolore omni, privata periclis
Ipsa suis pollens opibus nihil indiga nostri
Nec bene pro meritis capitur, nec tangitur ira.
Lucret. *lib.* 2.

That Villaine and Secretary of Hell, that composed that miscreant piece of the three Impostors.] It was *Ochinus* that composed this piece; but there was no less a man than the Emperour *Frederick* the Second, that was as lavish of his tongue as the other of his pen; *Cui sæpe in ore, Tres fuisse insignes Impostores, qui genus humanum seduxerunt: Moysem, Christum, Mahumetem.* Lips. *monit. et exempl. Politic.* cap. 4. And a greater than he, Pope *Leo* the Tenth, was as little favourable to our Saviour, when he us'd that speech which is reported of him, *Quantas nobis divitias comparavit ista de Christo fabula.*

Sect. 21. Pag. 34.

There are in Scripture, stories that do exceed the fables of Poets.] So the Author of *Relig. Laici. Certè mira admodum in* S. S. *plus quam in reliquis omnibus Historiis traduntur*; (and then he concludes with the Author) *sed quæ non retundunt intellectum, sed exercent.*

Yet raise no question who shall rise with that Rib *at the Resurrection.*] The Author *cap. 2 l. 7. Pseudodox.* sheweth that it appears in Anatomy, that the Ribs of Man and Woman are equal.

Whether the world were created in Autumn, Summer, or the Spring, etc.] In this matter there is a consent between two learned Poets, *Lucretius* and *Virgil*, that it begins in *Spring*.

At novitas mundi nec frigora dura ciebat,
Nec nimios æstus, nec magnis viribus auras.
Lucretius

Which he would have to be understood of *Autumn*, because that resembles old age rather than Infancy. He speaks expresly of the Fowls.

Principio genus alituum variæq; volucres
Ova relinquebant exclusæ tempore verno.
Lucret.

Then for *Virgil*.

Non alios prima nascentis origine mundi
Illuxisse dies aliumve habuisse tenorem
Crediderim, ver illud erat, ver magnus agebat
Orbis, et hibernis parcebant flatibus Euri.
Virgil 2. Georgic.

But there is a great difference about it betwixt Church-Doctors; some agreeing with these Poets and others affirming the time to be in Autumn: but truly, in strict speaking, it was not created in any one, but all of the seasons, as the Author saith here, and hath shewed at large. *Pseudodox. Epidemic.* lib. 6. cap. 2.

Sect. 22. Pag. 35.

'Tis ridiculous to put off or down the general floud of Noah *in that particular inundation of* Deucalion,] as the Heathens some of them sometimes did: *Confuderunt igitur sæpe Ethnici particularia illa diluvia, quæ longe post secuta sunt, cum illo universali quod præcessit, ut ex fabulis in Diluvio Deucalionæo sparsis colligere licet; non tamen semper nec ubique. Author. Observat. in Mytholog. Nat. Com.* Then amongst those that confound them, he reckons *Ovid* and *Plutarch*.

How all the kinds of Creatures, not onely in their own bulks, but with a competency of food and sustenance, might be preserved in one Ark, and within the extent of 300 Cubits, to a reason that rightly examines it will appear very feasible.] Yet *Apelles* the Disciple of *Mercion*, took upon him to deride the History of *Moses* in this particular, alledging that it must needs be a fable, for that it was impossible so many creatures should be contain'd in so small a space. *Origen* and *St. Aug.* to answer this pretended difficulty, alleadge that *Moses* in this place speakes of Geometrical (and not vulgar) cubits, of which every one was as much as six vulgar ones; and so no difficulty. But *Perer. l. 10. com. in Genes, quest. 5. de arca*, rejects this opinion of *Origen*, as being both against reason and Scripture.

1. Because that sort of Cubit was never in use amongst any people, and therefore absurd to think *Moses* should intend it in this place.

2. If *Moses* should not speak of the same Cubits here, that he mentions in others places, there would be great æquivocation in Scripture: now in another place, *i.e. Exod. 27.* he saith, God commanded him to make an Altar three Cubits high; which if it shall be meant of Geometrical Cubits it will contain 18 vulgar Cubits; which would not only render it useless, but would be contrary to the command which he saith God gave him, *Exod. 20. Thou shall not go up by steps to my Altar*. For without steps what man could reach it. It must therefore be meant of ordinary Cubits; but that being so it was very feasible. I can more easily believe than understand it.

And put the honest Father to the Refuge of a Miracle.] This honest father was St. *Aug.* who delivers his opinion, that it might be miraculously done, *lib. 16. de Civ. Dei, cap. 7.* where having propos'd the question how it might be done, he answers, *Quod si homines eas captas secum adduxerunt, et eo modo ubi habitabant earum genera instituerunt, venandi studio fieri potuisse incredibile non est, quamvis jussu Dei sire permissu etiam opera Angelorum negandum non sit potuisse transferri;* but St. *Aug.* saith not that it could not be done without a miracle.

<u>And 1500 years to people the World, as full a time, etc.</u>]

Pag. 36.

<u>That Methusalem was the longest liv'd of all the children of Adam, etc.</u>] See both these Points cleared by the Author, in *Pseudodox. Epidemic.* the first *lib. 6. cap. 6.* the other *lib. 7. cap. 3.*

<u>That Judas perished by hanging himself, there is no certainty in Scripture, though in one place it seems to affirm it, and by a doubtful word hath given occasion to translate it; yet in another place, in a more punctual description it makes it improbable, and seems to overthrow it.</u>] These two places that seem to contradict one another are *Math. 27. 5.* and *Acts 1. 8.* The doubtful word he speaks of is in the place of *Matthew*; it is ἀπήγξατο, which signifieth suffocation as well as hanging, (ἀπελθὼν ἀπήγξατο, which may signifie literally, after he went out he was choak'd) but *Erasmus* translates it, *abiens laqueo se suspendit*: the words in the *Acts* are, When he had thrown down himself headlong, he burst in the midst, and all his bowels gushed out; which seems to differ much from the expression of *Matthew*; yet the Ancient Writers and Fathers of the Church do unanimously agree that he was hanged. Some I shall cite. *Anastas. Sinaita, l. 7. Anagog. Contempl. Unus latro ingratus cum esset typus Diaboli, et Serpentis, et Judæ, qui se in ligno suffocavit. Gaudentius Brixiens. tract. 13. de natal. Dom. Mortem debitam laqueo sibimet intulit præparato, etc. Droggotoshen. de sacram. dominic. pass. Jamdiu erat quidem quod Christo recesserat, et avaritiæ laqueo se suspenderat, sed quod fecerat in occulto, palam omnibus innotuit. S. Martialis in Ep. ad Tholosanos. Non sustinuit pœnitentiam, donec laqueo mortis seipsum consumpsit. Ignat. ad Philippens. Diabolus laqueum ei ostendit, et suspendium docuit. Leo Serm. 3. de passion.——Ut quia facinus omnem mensuram ultionis excesserat, te haberet impietas tua judicem te pateretur sua pæna Carnificem. Theodoret. lib. 1. hæretic. fabul. Ille protinus strangulatus est, quæ fuit merces ejus proditionis. Chrysostom. Hom. 3. de proditore. Pependit Cœlum Terramque intermedius vago funere suffocatus, et cum flagitio suo tumefacta, viscera crepuerunt, etc. Bernard. Serm. 8. in Psal. 9. Judas in Acre crepuit medius.*

1. There are those that are so particular, that they acquaint us with the manner, as *that it was done with a Cord. Antiochus Laurensis, Spem omnem a se cum abjecisset, insiliente in eum inimico (sc. Diabolo) funiculo sibi præfocavit gulam. Oecumen. in Act. Fracto funiculo quo erat suffocatus decidit in terram præcipitio.* 2. That it was done on a Fig-Tree, *Beda. Portam David egredientibus fons occurrit in Austrum per vallem directus, ad cujus medietatem ab occasu Judas se suspendisse narratur: Nam et ficus magna ibi et vetustissima stat.*

Juvenc. lib. 4. Hist. Evangelic.

Exorsusq; suas laqueo sibi sumere pænas,
Informem rapuit ficus de vertice mortem.

3. Some acquaint us with the time when it was done, *viz.* the next day after he had given the kiss. So *Chrysostom. Homil. 1. de proditor. et Mysterio Cœn. Dominic. Guttur prophanum quod hodie Christo extendis ad osculum, crastino es illud extensurus ad laqueum.* But there are two, that is *Euthymius* and *Oecumenius*, that tell us, *that the hanging did not kill him*, but that either the Rope broke, or that he was cut down, and afterwards cast himself down headlong, as it is related in the before mentioned place of the *Acts*: *Agnitus à quibusdam depositus est ne præfocaretur, denique postquam in secreto quodam loco modico vixisset tempore præceps factus sive præcipitatus, inflatus diruptus, ac diffisus est medius, et effusa sunt omnia viscera ejus; ut in Actis. Euthym.* cap. 67. *in Math. Judas suspendio è vita non decessit, sed supervixit, dejectus est enim prius quam præfocaretur, idque Apotolorum Acta indicant, quod pronus crepuit medius. Oecumen. in Act.* And this may serve to reconcile these two seemingly disagreeing Scriptures.

<u>That our Fathers after the Flood erected the Tower of Babel.</u>] For this see what the Author saith in his *Pseudodox. Epidemic.* l. 7, cap. 6.

Sect. 23. Pag. 37.

<u>And cannot but commend the judgment of Ptolemy.</u>] He means of *Ptolemæus Philadelphus*, who founded the Library of *Alexandria*, which he speaks of in the next Section. He was King

of *Egypt*; and having built and furnish'd that Library with all the choicest Books he could get from any part of the world, and having good correspondence with *Eleazer* the high Priest of the *Jews*, by reason that he had released the *Jews* from Captivity, who were taken by his Predecessor *Ptolemæus Lagi*; he did by the advice of *Demetrius Phalereus* the *Athenian*, whom he had made his Library-Keeper, write to *Eleazer*, desiring him that he would cause the Books of the *Jews*, which contained their Laws, to be translated for him into Greek, that he might have them to put into his Library: to which the Priest consents; and for the King's better satisfaction, sends to him Copies of the Books, and with the same 72 Interpreters skilled both in the Greek and Hebrew Language, to translate them for him into Greek; which afterwards they performed. This is for certain; but whether they translated only the *Pentateuch*, as St. *Jerome* would have it, or together with the Books of the Prophets also, as *Leo de Castro* and *Baronius* contend, I undertake not to determine: but as to that part of the story, that these Interpreters were put into so many several Cells, whilst they were about the work of translation; and notwithstanding they were thus severed, that they all translated it *totidem verbis*; it is but reason to think with St. *Jerome* (notwithstanding the great current of Authority against him) that it is no better than a fable.

The Alcoran of the Turks (I speak without prejudice) is an ill-composed piece, containing in it vain and ridiculous errors in Philosophy, etc.] It is now in every mans hand, having been lately translated into English; I shall therefore observe but these few particulars in it, in regard the book it self is so common; and indeed they are not mine own, but *Lipsius* his observations. He begins, *O nugas, O deliria! primum* (saith he) *commentus est, Deum unum solidumq; (ὁλόσφυρον Græci exprimunt) eundemq; incorporeum esse. Christum non Deum, sed magnum vatem et prophetam; se tamen majorem, et proxime à Deo missum, præmia qui ipsum audient Paradisum, qui post aliquot annorum millia reserabitur, ibi quatuor flumina lacte, vino, melle, aqua fluere, ibi palatia et ædificia gemmata atque aurata esse, carnes avium suavissimarum, fructus omne genus quos sparsi jacentesque sub umbra arborum edent: sed caput fælicitatis, viros fœminasque, majores solito magnis Genitalibus assidua libidine, et ejus usu sine tædio aut fatigatione.* These and some others that are in the Alcoran he reckons up. *Sed et Physica quoq; miranda* (saith he) *nam facit Solem et Lunam in equis vehi, illum autem in aquam calidam vespere mergi, et bene lotum ascendere atque oriri, Stellas in aere è catenis aureis pendere: terram in bovini cornus cuspide stabilitum, et agitante se bove ac succutiente fieri terræ motum; hominem autem ex hirundine aut sanguisuga nasci*, etc. *Just. Lips. Monit. et exempl. Politic.* cap. 3.

Pag. 38.

I believe besides Zoroaster there were divers others that wrote before Moses.] *Zoroaster* was long before *Moses*, and of great name; he was the father of *Ninus, Justin. lib. 1. Si quamlibet modicum emolumentum probaveritis; ego ille sim Carinondas vel Damigeron, vel is Moses, vel Joannes, vel Apollonius, vel ipse Dardanus, vel quicunq; alius post Zoroastrem et Hostanem, inter Magos celebratus est*. Apuleius *in* Apol.

Sect. 24. Pag. 38.

Others with as many groans deplore the combustion of the Library at Alexandria.] This was that Library before spoken of, set up by *Ptolemæus Philadelphus*; in which 'tis reported by *Ammianus Marcellinus* there were 700,000 volumes; it was burnt by *Jul. Cæsar's* means, whose Navy being environed before *Alexandria*, he had no means to keep off the Enemy, but by flinging of fire, which at length caught the Library and consumed it, as *Plutarch* hath it in *Vita Cæsaris*: but notwithstanding we have no reason to believe it was quite consumed, because *Sueton.* in *Claudius*, tells us, that that Emperour added another to it; and there must be somewhat before, if it were an addition; but true it is, too many of the Books perished; to repair which loss, care was taken by *Domitian* the Emperour, as the same *Sueton.* and *Aurel. Victor.* do relate.

I would not omit a Copy of Enoch's Pillars, had they many nearer Authors than Josephus, etc.] For this the Story is, that *Enoch*, or his father, *Seth*, having been inform'd by *Adam*, that the world was to perish once by water, and a second time by fire, did cause two Pillars to be erected, the one of Stone against the water, and another of Brick against the fire; and that upon those Pillars was engraven all such Learning as had been delivered to, or invented by mankind; and that thence it came that all knowledge and learning was not lost by means of the Floud, by reason that one of the Pillars (though the other perished) did remain after the Floud, and *Josephus* witnesseth, till his time, *lib. 1. Antiq. Judaic.* cap. 3.

<u>*Of those three great inventions of* Germany, *there are two which are not without their incommodities.*</u>] Those two he means are *Printing* and *Gunpowder*, which are commonly taken to be *German* Inventions; but Artillery was in *China* above 1500 years since, and Printing long before it was in *Germany*, if we may believe *Juan Concales Mendosa* in his *Hist.* of *China, lib. 3. cap. 15, 16*. The incommodities of these two inventions, are, well described by *Sam. Daniel*, lib. 6. of the Civil Wars.

> *Fierce* Nemesis, *mother of fate and change,*
> *Sword-bearer of th' eternal providence,*
> *Turns her stern look at last into the West,*
> *As griev'd to see on Earth such happy rest;*
> *And for* Pandora *calleth presently,*
> Pandora Jove's *fair gift that first deceived*
> *Poor* Epimetheus *in his imbecility.*
> *That though he had a wondrous boon received,*
> *By means whereof curious mortality*
> *Was of all former quiet quite bereaved.*
> *To whom being come deckt with all qualities,*
> *The wrathful goddess breaks out in this wise:*
> *Dost thou not see in what secure estate,*
> *Those flourishing fair Western parts remain?*
> *As if they had made covenant with fate,*
> *To be exempted free from others pain,*
> *At one with their desires, friends with debate,*
> *In peace with Pride, content with their own gain.*
> *Their bounds contain their mindes, their mindes applyed*
> *To have their bonds with plenty beautified.*
> *Devotion (Mother of Obedience)*
> *Bears such a hand on their credulity,*
> *That it abates the spirit of eminence,*
> *And busies them with humble piety:*
> *For see what works, what infinite expence,*
> *What Monuments of zeal they edifie,*
> *As if they would, so that no stop were found,*
> *Fill all with Temples, make all holy ground.*
> *But we must cool this all-believing zeal,*
> *That hath enjoy'd so fair a turn so long,* etc.
> *Dislike of this first by degrees shall steal,*
> *As upon souls of men perswaded wrong;*
> *And that the sacred power which thus hath wrought,*
> *Shall give her self the sword to cut her throat.*
> *Go therefore thou with all thy stirring train*
> *Of swelling Sciences (the gifts of grief)*
> *Go loose the links of that soul-binding chain,*
> *Enlarge this uninquisitive Belief:*
> *Call up mens spirits, that simpleness retain,*
> *Enter their hearts, and knowledge make the Thief*
> *To open all the Doors to let in Light,*
> *That all may all things see but what is right.*
> *Opinion arm against opinion (grown)*
> *Make new-born contradictions still arise,*
> *As if Thebes Founder* (Cadmus) *tongues had sown*

Indent of teeth, for greater mutinies:
Bring new defended faith against faith known,
Weary the soul with contrarieties,
Till all Religion become Retrograde,
And that fair lye the mask of sin be made:
And better to effect a speedy end,
Let there be found two fatal Instruments,
The one to publish, th' other to defend

> Printing

Impious contention, and proud discontents:
Make that instamped characters may send
Abroad to thousands, thousand mens intents;
And in a moment may dispatch much more,
Than could a world of pens perform before;
Whereby all quarrels, titles, secrecies,
May unto all be presently made known,
Factions prepar'd, parties allur'd to rise,
Seditions under fair pretences sown;
Whereby the vulgar may become so wise
That with a self-presumption overgrown,
They may of deepest mysteries debate,
Controul their betters, censure acts of State.
And then when this dispersed mischief shall
Have brought confusion in each mystery,
Call'd up contempts of State in general,
And ripen'd the humour of impiety,
Then take the other engine wherewithal

> Guns

They may torment their self-wrought misery;
And scourge each other in so strange a wise,
As time or tyrants never could devise, etc.

See *Bellermontan.* in his *Dissertat. politic. dissert.* 29. and 30.

For the other Invention, the Latine Annotator doubts whether the Author means Church-Organs, or Clocks? I suppose he means Clocks, because I find that Invention reckon'd by a *German*, with the other two, as a remarkable one. It is by *Busbequius*, speaking of the Turks, who hath these words: *Testes majores minoresque bombardæ, multaque alia quæ ex nostris excogitata ipsi ad se avertunt; at libros tamen typis excuderent, horologia in publico haberent, nondum adduci potuerunt. Epist. Legat. Turcic.* I suppose if he had known any Invention which next to the other two had been greater than this, he would not have named this, and this being the next considerable, we have no cause to doubt but the Author meant it.

<u>To maintain the Trade and Mystery of Typographers.</u>] Of this *Cunæus* in his *Satyre Sardi vœnates. Qui bis in anno nomen suum ad Germanorum nundinas non transmittit, eruditionem suam in ordinem coactam credit, itaq; nunquam tot fungi una pluvia nascuntur, quot nunc libri uno die.*

Sect. 25. Pag. 40.

<u>The Turk in the bulk that he now stands, is beyond all hope of conversion.</u>] That is, in respect of his great strength, against which it is not probable the Christians will prevail, as it is observed by *Monsieur de Silhon. La Race des Ottomans* (saith he) *quæ oste a Dieu la Religion qu'il a revelee, et aux hommes la liberte que le droit des Gens leur laisse a fait tant de progres depuis trois Cens et quelques annees qu'il semble qu'elle n'ait plus rien a craindre de dehorse, et que son empire ne puisse perir que par la corruption de dedans, et par la dissolution des parties qui composent un corps si vaste. Mr. de Silhon en son Minist. D'Estat. l. 1. c.*

None can more justly boast of persecutions, and glory in the number and valour of martyrs.] Of the fortitude of the Christians in this particular, *Minutius Felix*, in the person of the Ethnique, hath these words, *Per mira stultitia et incredibili audacia spernunt tormenta præsentia, dum incerta metuunt et futura; et dum mori post mortem timent, interim mori non timent.* And afterwards, when he speaks in the person of the Christian, he saith, that Christian women and children have in this surpassed *Scævola* and *Regulus*: *Viros* (saith he) *cum Mutio vel cum Atilio Regulo comparo: pueri et mulierculæ nostræ cruces et Tormenta, feros et omnes suppliciorum terriculas inspirata patientia doloris illudunt.* Minut. in Octav. vide Aug. de Civit. Dei, lib. 1. c. 23, 24.

If we shall strictly examine the circumstances and requisites which Aristotle *requires to true and perfect valour, we shall find the name onely in his Master* Alexander, *(that is, no more than the name) and as little in that Roman worthy* Julius Cæsar.] Aristot. 3. Ethic. cap. 6. amongst other requisites, requires to valour, that it keep a mediocrity betwixt audacity and fear; that we thrust not our selves into danger when we need not; that we spare not to shew our valour when occasion requires: he requires for its proper object, Death; and to any death, he prefers death in War, because thereby a man profits his Country and Friends; and that he calls *mors honesta*, an honest or honourable death: and thereupon he defines a valiant man to be, *Is qui morte honesta proposita, iisq; omnibus quæ cum sint repentina mortem adfuerunt metu vacat*. So that by the Author's saying, there was onely the Name in *Alexander*, he means only that which is rendred in the two last words, *metu vacans*, and not the rest that goes to make up the definition of a valiant man, which is very truly affirmed of *Alexander*, who exposed himself to hazzard many times when there was no cause for it: As you may read in *Curtius*, he did, in the siege of *Tyrus*, and many other ways. *Cettuy-cy semble rechercher et courir à force les dangiers comme un impetueux torrent, qui choque et attaque sans discretion, et sans chois tout ce qu'il rencontre*, saith *Montaign*, speaking of *Alexander, l. 2. des Ess. cap. 34*. And for *Cæsar*, it cannot be denied, but in his Wars he was many times (though not so generally as *Alexander*) more adventrous than reason military could warrant to him; and therefore *Lucan* gives him no better Character than

Acer et indomitus quo spes quoq; ira vocasset
Ferre manum, etc.
Lucan. lib. 1.

To instance in some Particulars: with what an inconsiderable strength did he enterprize the conquest of *Egypt*, and afterwards went to attaque the forces of *Scipio* and *Juba*, which were ten times more than his own? after the Battle of *Pharsalia*, having sent his Army before into *Asia*, and crossing the *Hellespont* with one single Vessel, he there meets *Lucius Cassius* with ten men of War, he makes up to him, summons him to render, and he does it. In the famous and furious siege of *Alexia*, where he had 80,000 men to make defence against him, and an Army of one hundred and nine thousand Horse, and two hundred and forty thousand foot, all marching towards him, to raise his siege; yet for all that he would not quit the siege, but first fought with those without, and obtain'd a great Victory over them, and soon afterwards brought the besieged to his mercy.

Sect. 26. Pag. 41.

The Council of Constance *condemns* John Husse *for an Heretick, the Stories of his own Party style him a Martyr.*] *John Husse* did agree with the Papists against us in the Point of Invocation of Saints, Prayers and Sacrifice for the Dead, free Will, Good Works, confession of Sins, seven Sacraments, etc. *Gordon. Hunt. l. contr. 3. de Sacr. Euch. cap. 17.* Yet was he condemned for maintaining certain Articles said by that Council to be heretical and seditious, and was burnt for Heresie. Now as I will not say he was an Heretick, so can I not maintain that he was a Martyr, if it be but for this one Article, which in the 15. Sess. of that Council was objected against him, which he did acknowledge, but would not recal, *i.e. Nullus est Dominus civilis, dum est in peccato mortali*. If that Doctrine should be believed, we shall have little obedience to Civil Magistrates; and without that, how miserable is humane condition? That which begat compassion towards *Husse* in those of his own Party was, that he had a safe conduct from the Emperour *Sigismund*; and therefore it was, say they, a violation of publick faith in the *Council* and *Emperour* in putting him to death.

That wise heathen Socrates *that suffered on a fundamental point of Religion, the Unity of God.*] That *Socrates* suffered on this Point, divers Christian Writers do object to the Ethniques, as *Justin Martyr*, Apol. 2. *Euseb. l. 5. de præparat. Evangelic. c. 14. Tertul.* in *Apolog.* cap. 14. and *Lactant. de justitia*, cap. 15. whose words are these: *Plato quidem multa de uno Deo locutus est, à quo ait constitutum esse mundum, sed nihil de Religione; somniaverat enim Deum, non cognoverat. Quod si justitiæ defensionem vel ipse vel quilibet alius implere voluisset, imprimis Deorum Religiones evertere debuit, quia contrariæ pietati. Quod quidem Socrates quia facere tentavit in carcerem conjectus est, ut jam tunc appareret quid esset futurum iis hominibus qui justitiam veram defendere Deoque singulari servire cœpissent.*

I have often pitied the miserable Bishop that suffered in the cause of Antipodes.] The suffering was, that he lost his Bishoprick for denying the *Antipodes*. Vid. *Aventin. in Hist. Boio*. Besides him, there were other Church-men of great note, that denyed *Antipodes*, as *Lactantias, Augustin,* and *Bede*.

Sect. 27. Pag. 43.

I hold that God can do all things: How he should work contradictions, I do not understand, yet dare not therefore deny.] Who would not think the Author had taken this from Mr. *Montaign*, whose words are, *Il m'a tousjours semble qu'a un homme Christien, cette sorte de parler est plein d'indiscretion et d'irreverence [Dieu ne se peut disdire,] [Dieu ne peut faire cecy ou cela]. Je ne trouve pas bon d'enfermer ainsi la puissance divine sous les loix de nostre parole. Et l'apparence qui s' offre à nous en ses propositions, il la faudroit representer plus reverement, et plus Religieusement.* Liv. 2. des Ess. c. 12.

I cannot see why the Angel of God should question Esdras *to recal the time past, if it were beyond his own power, or that God should pose mortality in that which he was not able to perform himself.*] Sir *K. Digby* in his Notes upon this place saith, There is no contradiction in this, because he saith it was but putting all things that had motion into the same state they were in at that moment, unto which time was to be reduced back, and from thence letting it travel on again by the same motions, *etc.* which God could do. But under favour, the contradiction remains, if this were done that he mentions; for Time depends not at all upon motion, but has a being altogether independent of it, and therefore the same revolution would not bring back the same time, for that was efflux'd before; as in the time of *Joshua*, when the Sun stood still, we cannot but conceive, though there were no motion of the Sun, but that there was an efflux of Time, otherwise, how could the Text have it, *That there was not any day, before or after, that was so long as that?* for the length of it must be understood in respect of the flux of time. The reasoning of Sir *Kenelme* is founded upon the opinion of *Aristot.* who will needs have it, that Time cannot be without mutation; he gives this for a reason, because when we have slept, and cannot perceive any mutation to have been, we do therefore use to connect the time of our sleeping and of our awaking together, and make but one of it: to which it may be answered, although some mutation be necessary, that we may mark the mix of time, it doth not therefore follow that the mutation is necessary to the flux it self.

Sect. 28. Pag. 43.

I excuse not Constantine *from a fall off his Horse, or a mischief from his enemies, upon the wearing those nails*, etc.] *Hac de re videatur P. Diac. hist. miscell.*

Sect. 29. Pag. 44.

I wonder how the curiosity of wiser heads could pass that great and indisputable miracle, the cessation of Oracles.] There are three opinions touching the manner how the predictions of these Oracles were perform'd: Some say by vapour, some by the intelligences, or influences, of the Heavens, and others say by the assistance of the Devils. Now the indisputable miracle the Author speaks of, is, that they ceas'd upon the coming of Christ; and it is generally so believed; and the Oracle of *Delphos* delivered to *Augustus*, mentioned by the Author in this Section, is brought to prove it, which is this:

Me puer Hebræus divos Deus ipse gubernans
Cedere sede jubet, tristemq; redire sub orcum.
Aris ergo dehinc tacitus discedito nostris.

But yet it is so far from being true that their cessation was miraculous, that the truth is, there never were any predictions given by those Oracles at all.

That their cessation was not upon the coming of Christ, we have luculent testimony out of *Tully*, in his *2. lib. de Divinat.* which he writ many years before Christ was born; who tells us that they were silent (and indeed he never thought they were otherwise) long before that time, insomuch that they were come into contempt: *Cur isto modo jam oracula Delphis non eduntur, non modo nostra œtate, sed jamdiu jam ut nihil possit esse contemptius*. So that for that of *Delphos*, which was the most famous of them all, we see we have no reason to impute the cessation of it to Christ; Why therefore should we do so for any of the rest?

For their predictions, let us consider the three several ways before mentioned, whereby they are supposed to operate; and from thence see whether it be probable that any such Oracles ever were.

The first Opinion is, that it was by exhalation or vapour drawn up from the earth; and gives this for a reason of their being, that they were for a time nourished by those exhalations; and when those ceased, and were exhausted, the Oracles famish'd and died for want of their accustom'd sustenance: this is the far-fetcht reason given by *Plutarch* for their defect; but 'twas not devised by him, but long before, as appears, in that *Tully* scoffs at it, *lib. de divinat. De vino aut salsamento putes loqui* (saith he) *quæ evanescunt vetustate*. This seem'd absurd to others, who do therefore say this was not to be attributed to any power of the Earth, but to the power of the Heavens, or *Intelligences Cœlestial*; to certain aspects whereof, they say, the Statua's of those Oracles were so adapted, that they might divine and foretel future events. But yet to others, this way seemeth as absurd as the others; for, say they, admitting that there were an efficacy in the Heavens, more than in the Earth; yet how can it be that men should come by the skill to fit the Statua's to the Aspects or influences of the Heavens? or if at any time they had such skill, why should not the same continue the rather, because men are more skilled in the motions of the Heavens, of later than in the former time? Again, they do not see how it should be that the cause should be of less excellency than the effect; for if a man (say they) can by his industry make such Oracles, why can he not produce the same effect in another man? for if you affirm that the Heavens influence is requisite, they will tell you that Influence may happen as well to a man, as to a Statue of wood or stone. Therefore the third sort being unsatisfied, which either of the former ways conclude, that this was perform'd by the Devil; but for that it will appear as contrary to Reason and Philosophy, as either of the former; for Philosophy teacheth that things singular, or individual, are to be known only by sense, or by such an Intellect, as doth know by its Essence; and Theology teacheth that God only knoweth the heart, and that the Devil doth not know by sense, nor by essence; and since 'tis admitted by all, that most of the answers that were pretended to be given by those Oracles, were *de rebus singularibus*, or *individuis*; it is evident that these predictions were not perform'd by Devils. How then? why those predictions which the ignorant Heathen took to come from Heaven, and some Christians (not less ignorant) from the Devil, was nothing but the jugling and impostures of the Priests, who from within the Statua's gave the answers; which Princes connived at, that they might upon occasion serve their turns upon the ignorance of the people; and the learned men, for fear of their Princes, durst not speak against it. *Lucian* hath noted it, and so a more Authentick Author, *Minut. Felix.*, in *Octav. Authoritatem quasi præsentis numinis consequuntur dum inspirantur interim vatibus*. But in process of time, the people grew less credulous of their Priests, and so the Oracles became to be silent: *Cum jam* (saith he) *Apollo versus facere desisset, cujus tunc cautum illud et ambiguum deficit oraculum: Cum et politiores homines et minus creduli esse cæperunt*. Sir *H. Blount* in his *Levantine* voyage, saith he saw the Statua of *Memnon* so famous of old; he saith it was hollow at top, and that he was told by the *Egyptians* and Jews there with him, that they had seen some enter there, and come out at the Pyramid, two Bows shoot off; then (saith he) I soon believ'd the Oracle, and believe all the rest to have been such; which indeed, is much easier to imagine than that it was perform'd by any of the three wayes before mentioned. St. *Aug.* hath composed a Book, where he handleth this point at large, and concludeth that the Devils can no more foretel things come, than they are able to discern the thoughts that are within us. *Aug. lib. de Scientia Dæmon.*

Till I laughed my self out of it with a piece of Justin, *where he delivers that the Children of* Israel *for being scabbed were banished out of* Egypt.] These words of *Justin* are, *Sed cum scabiem Ægyptii et pruriginem paterentur, responso moniti, eum (se. Moysen) cum ægris, ne pestis ad plures serperet, terminis Ægypti pellunt. l. 36.* But he is not singular in this, for *Tacitus* tells us, *Hist. lib. 5. Plurimi authores consentiunt orta per Ægyptum tabe quæ corpora fœduret, Regem (Ochirum)* (he means *Pharaoh*) *adito Hammonis oraculo remedium petentem purgare. Regnum et id genus hominum——alias in terras avertere jussum.* Et paulo inferius, *Quod ipsos scabies quondam turpaverat.*

Sect. 30. Pag. 45.

I have ever believed, and do now know that there are Witches.] What sort of Witches they were that the Author knew to be such. I cannot tell; for those which he mentions in the next Section, which proceed upon the principles of Nature, none have denyed that such there are; against such it was, that the *Lex Julia de veneficiis* was made, that is, those, *Qui noxio poculo aut impuris medicuminibus aliquem fuerint insectati. At. ab Alex. Gen. Dier.* l. 5. c. 1. But for the opinion that there are Witches which co-operate with the Devil, there are Divines of great note, and far from any suspition of being irreligious, that do oppose it. Certainly there is no ground to maintain their being from the story of Oracles, as may be seen from what hath been said on the precedent Section.

Nor have the power to be so much as Witches. Pliny saith, so it fared with *Nero*, who was so hot in pursuit of the Magick Arts, that he did dedicate himself wholly to it, and yet could never satisfie himself in that kind, though he got all the cunning men he could from the East, for that purpose. *Plin.* l. 3. *Nat. Hist.* c. 1.

Pag. 46.

By conjunction with the Devil.] Though, as the Author saith, it be without a possibility of Generation, yet there are great men that hold, that such carnality is performed; as *August, in Levit. Aquin.* l. 2. *de qu.* 73. art. ad 2. and *Justin Martyr, Apol.* 1.

Sect. 33. Pag. 48.

It is no new opinion of the Church of Rome, *but an old one of* Pythagoras *and* Plato.] This appears by *Apuleius* a Platonist, in his Book *de Deo Socratis*, and elsewhere. See *Mede's Apostasie of the latter times*, where out of this and other Authors, you shall see collected all the learning *de Geniis*.

Pag. 50.

I cannot with those in that great Father securely interpret the work of the first day, Fiat lux, *to the creation of Angels.*] This great Father is S. *Chrysost. Homil. in Genes*. But yet 'tis his opinion, as also of *Athanasius* and *Theodoret*, that there is express mention of the creation of Angels, so that they need not rest upon this place, which they admit to be somewhat obscure. The place which they take to be express, is that of the 130 *Psalm*, where *David* begins to speak of the Majesty of God, in this manner: *Confessionem sive majestatem et decorem induisti, amictus lumine sicut vestimento*: Next he speaks of the Heavens, saying, *Thou hast stretched them out over us like a Tent*. Then he speaks of the Angels, *Qui facis Angelos tuos spiritus*. Now if it shall be objected, that this expression is onely of the time present, and without relation to the Creation: Answer is given by Divines, that the *Hebrews* have but three Tenses in their Verbs, the Preterperfect, Present, and Future Tense; and have not the use of the Preterimperfect, and Preterpluperfect, as the *Greeks* and *Latines* have; whence it ariseth, that the Present Tense with the *Hebrews*, may, as the sentence will bear it, be translated by the Preterimperfect, as also by the Preterperfect and Preterpluperfect Tense; and this (they say) is practised in this very passage, where the Phrase, as it is in Hebrew, may be rendered as well *qui faciebas*, as *qui facis Angelos*, etc. Vid. *Hieronym. in Ep. ad Titum, et Thom. Aqu.* 1. p. qu. 61. art. 3. The Latine Annotator saith, the Father meant by the Author, is St. *Aug.* and quotes him, *l. II. de Civ. Dei* cap. 9. which place I have perused, and find the expression there used by St. *Aug.* is but hypothetical; for these are his words: *Cum enim dixit Fiat lux, et facta est lux, si rectè in fine luce creatio intelligitur Angelorum*, etc. Where you see 'tis but with a *Si*, and therefore I conceive the Author intends not him, but *Chrysostom*.

Where it subsists alone, 'tis a Spiritual Substance, and may be an Angel.] *Epicurus* was of this opinion, and St. *Aug. in Euchirid. ad Laurentium*.

Sect. 35. Pag. 52.

<u>Moses decided that Question, and all is salved with the new term of Creation.</u>] That is it which *Aristotle* could not understand; he had learned that *ex nihilo nihil fit*, and therefore when he found those that disputed that the World had a beginning, did maintain that it was generated, and he could not understand any generation, but out of matter præ-existent *in infinitum*, therefore he took their opinion to be absurd, and upon that ground principally, concluded the World to be eternal: whereas, if he had understood that there may be such a thing as Creation, he had not done it, for that solves his *processus in infinitum*. Take from *Plato*, that the World had a beginning, and from *Aristot.* that it was not generated, and you have the (true) Christian opinion.

Sect. 36. Pag. 54.

<u>In our study of Anatomy, there is a mass of mysterious Philosophy, and such as reduced the very Heathens to Divinity.</u>] So it did *Galen*, who considering the order, use, and disposition of the parts of the body, brake forth into these words: *Compono hic profecto Canticam in creatoris nostri laudem, quod ultra res suas ornare voluit melius quam ulla arte possent*. Galen, 3. *de usu partium.*

Sect. 37. Pag. 55.

<u>I cannot believe the wisdom of</u> Pythagoras <u>did ever positively, and in a literal sense, affirm his</u> Metempsychosis.] In this the opinion of *Grotius* is contrary to the Author, who saith this opinion was begotten by occasion of the opinion of other Philosophers, who in their discourses of the life that is to be after this, brought such arguments, *Quæ non magis de homine quam de bestiis procedunt*. And therefore, saith he, *mirandum non est, si transitum animarum de hominibus in bestias, de bestiis in homines alii commenti sunt. Lib. 2. de ver. Relig. Christ. (vide etiam Annotat. ejusd.)*. But yet there is a shrewd objection against the opinion of *Pythagoras*, if he did mean it literally, which is cast in by the Sectators of *Democritus* and *Epicurus*, which *Lucretius* remembers in these Verses:

Præterea si immortalis natura animaï
Constat, et in corpus nascentibus insinuatur,
Cur super anteactam ætatem meminisse nequimus?
Nec vestigia gestarum rerum ulla tenemus?
Namsi tantopere 'st animi mutata potestas,
Omnis ut actarum excideret retinentia rerum,
Non ut opinor ea ab læto jam longiter errat.
[Lib. 3.]

This Argument, 'tis true, is *pro falso contra falsum*, but yet holds *ad hominem* so far, that it is not likely (as the Author saith) but *Pythagoras* would observe an absurdity in the consequence of his Metempsychosis; and therefore did not mean it literally, but desired only to express the Soul to be immortal, which he, and the other Philosophers that were of that opinion, who had not heard of Creation, could not conceive, unless it must be taken for truth, that the soul were before the body; so saith *Lactantius* of them. *Non putaverunt aliter fieri posse ut supersint animæ post corpora, nisi videntur fuisse ante corpora. De fals. Sap. c. 18.*

Sect. 41. Pag. 59.

<u>I do not envy the temper of Crows or Daws.</u>] As *Theophrastus* did, who dying, accused Nature for giving them, to whom it could not be of any concernment, so large a life; and to man, whom it much concern'd, so short a one. *Cic. Tusc. quæst. l. 3*. How long Daws live, see in *Not. ad Sect. 41*.

Sect. 42. Pag. 61.

<u>Not upon</u> Cicero's <u>ground, because I have liv'd them well.</u>] I suppose he alludes to an expression in an Epistle of *Cicero*, written in his Exile, to his wife and children, where he hath these words to his wife: *Quod reliquum est, te sustenta mea Terentia ut potes, honestissime viximus, floruimus. Non vitium nostrum sed virtus nos afflixit, peccatum est nullum nisi quod non unà animum cum ornamentis amisimus*, l. 24, Ep. 4.

<u>And stand in need of</u> Eson's <u>bath before threescore.</u>] *Eson* was the Father of *Jason*, and, at his request, was by *Medea*, by the means of this Bath, restored to his youth. Ingredients that went into it, and the description of *Medea's* performance, *Ovid* gives you, *l. 7. Metam.*

Interea calido positum medicamen aheno
Fervet et exultat, spumisq; tumentibus albet.

Illic Æmonia radices valle resectas,
Seminaq; et flores, et succos incoquit atros
Adjicet extremo lapides Oriente petitos,
Et quas Oceani refluum mare lavit arenas:
Addidit exceptas lunæ de nocte pruinas,
Et Strigis infames ipsis cum carnibus alas,
Inq; virum soliti vultus mutare ferinos
Ambigui prosecta lupi, nec defuit illi
Squamea Cinyphei tenuis membrana Chelidri,
Vivacisq; jecur cervi; quibus insuper addit
Ora caputq; novem cornicis secula passæ.
His et mille aliis, postquam sine nomine rebus
Propositum instruxit mortali barbara munus
Arenti ramo jampridem mitis olivæ
Omnia confudit, summisq; immiscuit ima.
Ecce vetus calido versatus stipes aheno
Fit viridis primo, nec longo tempore frondes
Induit, et subito gravidis oneratur olivis.
At quacunq; cavo spumas ejecit aheno
Ignis, et in terram guttæ cecidere calentes,
Vernat humus, floresq; et mollia pabula surgunt.
Quæ simulac vidit, stricto Medea recludit
Ense senis jugulum, veteremq; extare cruorem
Passa replet succis, quos postquam combibit Æson,
Aut ore acceptas, aut vulnere, barba comœq;
Cunitie posita, nigrum rapuere colorem.
Pulsa fugit macies: abeunt pallorq; situsque:
Adjectoq; cavæ supplentur corpore rugæ;
Membraq; luxuriant. Æson miratur, et olim
Ante quater denos hunc se reminiscitur annos,
Dissimilemq; animum subiit, ætate relicta.
[262-293.]

Sect. 44. Pag. 62.

Extol the Suicide of Cato.] As doth *Seneca* in several places; but *Lactantius* saith, he cast away his life, to get the reputation of a *Platonick* Philosopher, and not for fear of *Cæsar*; and 'tis very probable, he was in no great fear of death, when he slept so securely the night before his death, as the story reports of him.

Pag. 63.

Emori nolo, sed me esse mortuum, nihil curo. Were I of Cæsar's Religion.] I doubt not, but here is a fault of the Press, and that instead of *Cæsar* it should be *Cicero*. I meet not with any such saying imputed to *Cæsar*, nor any thing like it, but that he preferr'd a sudden death (in which he had his option) to any other; but I meet with such a saying in *Cicero* quoted out of *Epicharmus* [*Emori nolo, sed me esse mortuum nihili æstimo.*] Where *Cicero* sustaineth the part of the *Epicure* that there is no hurt in being dead, since there remaineth nothing after it. *Cic. 1. Thusc. qu. non procul ab initio.*

Sect. 45. Pag. 64.

Or whence Lucan learn'd to say, Communis mundo superest rogus, etc.] Why, *Lucan* was a *Stoique*, and 'twas an opinion among them almost generally, that the world should perish by fire; therefore without doubt from them he learned it. *Cælum quoque cum omnibus quæ in cælo continentur, ita ut cœpisset desinere, fontium dulci aqua marisve nutriri, in vim ignis abiturum. Stoicis constans opinio est, quod consumpto humore mundus hic omnis ignescat. Minutius in Octav.* But *Minutius* should have excepted *Boetius, Possidonius, Diogenes Babylonius,* and *Zeno Sidonius*, who were *Stoiques*, and yet did not think the world should be destroyed by fire, nor yet by any other means.

Sect. 46. Pag. 65.

How shall we interpret Elias 6000 years, etc.?] *Lactant.* is very positive that the world should last but 6000 years; but his reason for it is somewhat strange; thus it is, *Quoniam sex diebus cuncta Dei opera perfecta sunt, per secula sex,* i.e. *annorum sex millia manere in hoc statu mundum necesse est.* De Divino præmio, cap. 14.

Sect. 47. Pag. 67.

Ipsa sui pretium virtus sibi, is but a cold principle.] It is a Stoical principle. *Quæris enim aliquid supra summum, interrogas quid petam extra virtutem ipsam. Nihil enim habet melius. Pretium sui est.* Senec. *de vit. beat.* c. 19.

That honest artifice of Seneca.] What that article was, is to be seen in *Senec. l. 1. ep. 11. Aliquis vir bonus nobis eligendus est, et semper ante oculos habendus, ut sic tanquam illo spectante vivamus, et omnia tanquam illo vidente faciamus.* Et paulo post; *Elige itaq; Catonem; si hic videtur tibi nimis rigidus, elige remissioris animi virum Lælium,* etc. which though, as the Author saith, it be an honest Artifice, yet cannot I but commend the party, and prefer the direction of him (whoever he were) who in the Margin of my *Seneca*, over against those words, wrote these: *Quin Deo potius qui semper omnibus omnia agentibus non tanquam sed reipsa adest, et videt; ac etiam ut Testis, vindex et punitor est male agentis.*

I have tried, if I could reach that great Resolution of his (that is of Seneca*) to be honest without a thought of Heaven or Hell.*] *Seneca*[6] brags he could do this, in these words: *Si scirem deos peccata ignoscituros, et homines ignoraturos, adhuc propter vilitatem peccati peccare erubescerem. Credat Judæus Appela: non ego.*——

And Atheists have been the onely Philosopher.] That is, if nothing remain after this life. St. *Aug.* was of this opinion. *Disputabam*—— *Epicurum accepturum fuisse palmam in animo meo, nisi ego credidissem post mortem restare animæ vitam,* etc. Aug. *l. 6. conf. cap. 16.*

Sect. 48. Pag. 68.

God by a powerful voice shall command them back into their proper shapes.] So *Minutius. Cæterum quis tam stultus est aut brutus, ut audeat repugnare hominem à Deo ut primum potuit fingi, ita posse denuo reformari, nihil esse post obitum, et ante ortum nihil fuisse; sicut de nihilo nasci licuit, ita de nihilo licere reparari. Porro difficilius est id quod sit incipere, quod quam id quod fuerit iterare. Tu perire Deo credis, si quid nostris oculis hebetibus subtrahitur. Corpus omne sive arescit in pulverem sive in humorem solvitur, vel in cinerem comprimitur vel in nidorem tenuatur, subducitur nobis, sed Deo elementorum custodi inseruntur. In Octav.* Vide Grot. *de veritate Relig. Christian.* ubi (lib. 2.) solvit objectionem, quod dissoluta corpora resititui nequeunt.

Sect. 50. Pag. 71.

Or conceive a flame that can either prey upon, or purifie the substance of a soul.] Upon this ground *Psellus lib 1. de Energia Dæmonum,* c. 7 holds, That Angels have bodies, (though he grants them to be as pure, or more pure than Air is) otherwise he could not apprehend how they should be tormented in Hell; and it may be upon this ground it was, that the Author fell into the error of the *Arabians*, mentioned by him, *Sect. 7.*

Sect. 51. Pag. 73.

There are as many Hells as Anaxagoras *conceited worlds.*] I assure my self that this is false printed, and that instead of *Anaxagoras* it should be *Anaxarchus*; for *Anaxagoras* is reckon'd amongst those Philosophers that maintain'd a Unity of the world, but *Anaxarchus* (according to the opinion of *Epicurus*) held there were infinite Worlds. That is he that caus'd *Alexander* to weep by telling him that there were infinite worlds, whereby *Alexander* it seems was brought out of opinion of his Geography, who before that time thought there remained nothing, or not much beyond his Conquests.

Sect. 54. Pag. 75.

It is hard to place those souls in Hell.] *Lactantius* is alike charitably disposed towards those. *Non sum equidem tam iniquus ut eos putem divinare debuisse, ut veritatem per seipsos invenirent (quod fieri ego non posse confiteor) sed hoc ab eis exigo, quod ratione ipse præstare potuerunt.* Lactant. *de orig. error.* c. 3. which is the very same with Sir *K. Digbie's* expression in his Observations on this place. I make no doubt at all (saith he) but if any follow'd in the whole tenour of their lives, the dictamens of right reason, but that their journey was secure to Heaven.

Sect. 55. Pag. 77.

Aristotle *transgress'd the rule of his own Ethicks.*] And so they did all, as *Lactantius* hath observed at large. *Aristot.* is said to have been guilty of great vanity in his Clothes, of Incontinency, of Unfaithfulness to his Master *Alexander*, etc. But 'tis no wonder in him, if our great *Seneca* be also guilty, whom truely notwithstanding St. *Jerome* would have him inserted in the Catalogue of Saints, yet I think he as little deserv'd it, as many of the Heathens who did not say so well as he did, for I do not think any of them liv'd worse: to trace him a little. In the time of the Emperour *Claudius* we find he was banish'd for suspition of incontinency with *Julia* the daughter of *Germanicus*. If it be said that this proceeded meerly from the spight of *Messalina*, (and that *Lipsius* did not complement with him in that kind *Apostrophe, Non expetit in te hæc culpa, O Romani nominis et Sapientiæ magne. Sol. Not. in Tacit.*) why then did she not cause him to be put to death, as well as she did the other, who was her Husbands Niece? This for certain, whatever his life were, he had *paginam lascivam*, as may appear by what he hath written, *de Speculorum usu, l. 1. Nat. Qu. cap. 16.* Which (admitting it may in a Poet, yet) how it should be excus'd in a Philosopher I know not. To look upon him in his exile, we find that then he wrote his Epistle *De Consolat.* to *Polybius, Claudius* his creature (as honest a man as *Pallas* or *Narcissus*) and therein he extols him and the Emperour to the Skies; in which he did grosly prevaricate, and lost much of his reputation, by seeking a discharge of his exile by so sordid a means. Upon *Claudius* his marriage with *Agrippina*, he was recall'd from Banishment by her means, and made *Prætor*, then he forgets the Emperour, having no need of him, labours all he can to depress him and the hopeful *Brittanicus*, and procured his Pupil *Nero* to be adopted and design'd Successor, and the Emperours own Son to be disinherited; and against the Emperour whom he so much praised when he had need of him, after his death he writes a scurrilous Libel. In *Nero's* Court, how ungratefully doth he behave himself towards *Agrippina*! who although she were a wicked woman, yet she deserv'd well of him, and of her Son too, who yet never was at rest till he had taken away her life, and upon suspition cast in against her by this man. Afterwards not to mention that he made great haste to grow rich, which should not be the business of a Philosopher, towards *Nero* himself, how well did it become his Philosophy to play the Traitor against him, and to become a complice in the conspiracy of *Piso*? And then as good a Tragedian as he was, me thinks he doth in *extremo actu deficere*, when he must needs perswade *Paulina*, that excellent Lady his wife, to die with him: what should move him to desire it? it could in his opinion be no advantage to her, for he believ'd nothing of the immortality of the soul; I am not satisfied with the reason of *Tacitus, Ne sibi unice dilectam ad injurius relinqueret*, because he discredits it himself, in almost the next words, where he saith, *Nero* bore her no ill will at all, (and would not suffer her to die) it must surely be then, because he thought he had not liv'd long enough (being not above 114 years old, so much he was) and had not the fortitude to die, unless he might receive some confirmation in it by her example. Now let any man judge what a precious Legacy it is that he bequeaths by his nuncupative will to his friends in *Tacitus. Conversus ad amicos* (saith he) *quando meritis eorum referre gratiam prohiberetur, quod unum jam tamen et pulcherrimum habebat, imaginem vitæ suæ relinquere testatur*. It cannot be denyed of him, that he hath said very well; but yet it must as well be affirmed, that his Practice hath run counter to his Theory, to use the Author's phrase.

The Scepticks *that affirmed they knew nothing.*] The ancient Philosophers are divided into three sorts, *Dogmatici, Academici, Sceptici*; the first were those that delivered their opinions positively; the second left a liberty of disputing *pro et contra*; the third declared that there was no knowledge of any thing, no not of this very proposition, that there is no knowledge, according to that,

——*Nihil sciri siquis putat, id quoq; nescit*
An sciri possit, quod se nil scire fatetur.

The Duke of Venice *that weds himself to the Sea by a Ring of Gold, etc.*] The Duke and Senate yearly on *Ascension-day* use to go in their best attire to the Haven of *Lido*, and there by throwing a Ring into the water, do take the Sea as their spouse. *Vid. Hist. Ital.* by *Will Thomas Cambrobrit. Busbequius* reports that there is a custom amongst the Turks, which they took from the Greek Priests, not much unlike unto this. *Cum Græcorum sacerdotibus mos sit certo veris tempore aquas consecrando mare clausum veluti reserare, ante quod tempus non facile se committunt fluctibus; ab ea Ceremonia nec Turcæ absunt.* Busb. *Ep. 3. legat. Tursic.*

<u>But the Philosopher that threw his money into the Sea, to avoid avarice, etc.</u>] This was *Apollonius Thyaneus*, who threw a great quantity of Gold into the Sea with these words, *Pessundo divitias, ne pessundarem ab illis*. *Polycrates* the Tyrant of *Samos* cast the best Jewel he had into the Sea, that thereby he might learn to compose himself against the vicissitude of Fortune.

<u>There go so many circumstances to piece up one good action.</u>] To make an action to be good, all the causes that concur must be good; but one bad amongst many good ones, is enough to make it vitious, according to the rule, *Bonum ex causa integra, malum ex partiali.*

Sect. 56. Pag. 78.

<u>The vulgarity of those judgements that wrap the Church of God in</u> Strabo's <u>Cloak, and restrain it unto</u> Europe.] 'Tis *Strabonis tunica* in the translation, but *Chalmydi* would do better, which is the proper expression of the word that *Strabo* useth: it is not *Europe*, but the known part of the world that *Strabo* resembleth to a Cloak, and that is it the Author here alludeth to; but we have no reason to think that the resemblance of *Strabo* is very proper, *Vid.* Sir *Hen. Savil. in not. ad Tac. in vita Agricolæ.*

Sect. 57. Pag. 79.

<u>Those who upon a rigid Application of the Law, sentence</u> Solomon <u>unto damnation, etc.</u>] St. *Aug.* upon *Psal.* 126. and in many other places, holds that *Solomon* is damned. Of the same opinion is *Lyra*, in 2 *Reg.* c. 7. and *Bellarm. 1 Tom. lib. 1. Controv.* c. 5.

THE SECOND PART

Sect. 1. Pag. 83.

<u>I wonder not at the</u> French <u>for their Frogs, Snails and Toad-stools.</u>] Toad-stools are not peculiar to the *French*; they were a great delicacy among the *Romans*, as appears every where in *Martial*. It was conceived the Emperor *Claudius* received his death by Poyson, which he took in Mushroom. *Suet.* and *Tac.*

Sect. 2. Pag. 87.

<u>How among so many millions of faces, there should be none alike.</u>] It is reported there have been some so much alike, that they could not be distinguished; as King *Antiochus*, and one *Antemon*, a Plebeian of *Syria*, were so much alike, that *Laodice*, the Kings widow, by pretending this man was the King, dissembled the death of the King so long, till according to her own mind, a Successor was chosen. *Cn. Pompeius*, and one *Vibius* the Orator; *C. Plancus*, and *Rubrius* the Stage-player; *Cassius Severus* the Orator, and one *Mirmello*; *M. Messala Censorius*, and one *Menogenes*, were so much alike, that unless it were by their habit, they could not be distinguished: but this you must take upon the Faith of *Pliny* (*lib. 7. c. 12.*) and *Solinus*, (*cap. 6.*) who as this Author tells elsewhere, are Authors not very infallible.

Sect. 3. Pag. 89.

<u>What a</u> βατροχομυομαχια <u>and hot skirmish is betwixt</u> S. and T. <u>in Lucian.</u>] In his *Dialog. judicium vocalium*, where there is a large Oration made to the Vowels, being Judges, by *Sigma* against *Tau*, complaining that *Tau* has bereaved him of many words, which should begin with *Sigma*.

<u>Their Tongues are sharper than</u> Actius <u>his razor.</u>] *Actius Navius* was chief Augur, who (as the story saith) admonishing *Tarqu. Priscus* that he should not undertake any action of moment, without first consulting the Augur, the King (shewing that he had little faith in his skill) demanded of him, whether by the rules of his skill, what he had conceived in his mind might be done: to whom when *Actius* had answered it might be done, he bid him take a Whetstone which he had in his hand, and cut it in two with a Razor; which accordingly the Augur did. *Livy*. And therefore we must conceive it was very sharp. Here the Adage was cross'd, ξυρὸς εἰς ἀκόνην, i.e. *novacula in cotem*. *Vid. Erasm. Chiliad.*

Pag. 90.

It is not meer Zeal to Learning, or devotion to the Muses, that wiser Princes Patronize the Arts, etc. but a desire to have their names eterniz'd by the memory of their Writings.] There is a great Scholar, who took the boldness to tell a Prince so much. *Est enim bonorum principum cum viris eruditis tacita quædam naturalisque Societas, ut alteri ab alteris illustrentur, ac dum sibi mutuo suffragantur, et gloria principibus, et doctis authoritas concilietur.* Politian. *Ep. Ludovic. Sfort. quæ extat, lib. 11. Ep. ep. 1.* And to this Opinion astipulates a Country man of our own, whose words are these: *Ignotus esset Lucilius, nisi eum Epistolæ Senecæ illustrarent. Laudibus Cæsareis plus Virgilius et Varus Lucanusq; adjecerunt, quam immensum illud ærarium quo urbem et orbem spoliavit. Nemo prudentiam Ithaci aut Pelidæ vires agnosceret, nisi eas Homerus divino publicasset ingenio: unde nihil mihi videtur consultius viro ad gloriam properanti fidelium favore scriptorum.* Joan. Sarisb. *Polycrat. l 8. c. 14.* And that Princes are as much beholding to the Poets Pens as their own Swords, *Horace* tells *Censorinus* with great confidence. *Od. 8. l. 4. Non incisa notis*, etc.

Sect. 4. Pag. 90.

St. Paul that calls the Cretians Lyars, doth it but indirectly, and upon quotation of one of their own Poets.] That is, *Epimenides*; the place is *Tit. 1. v. 12.* where *Paul* useth this verse, taken out of *Epimenides*.

Κρῆτες ἀεὶ ψεῦσται, κακὰ θηρία, γαστέρες ἀργαί.

It is as bloody a thought in one way, as Nero's was in another. For by a word we wound a thousand.] I suppose he alludes to that passage in *Sueton.* in the life of *Nero*, where he relates that a certain person upon a time, spoke in his hearing these words,

Ἐμοῦ θανόντος γαῖα μιχθήτω πυρί.

i.e. When I am dead let Earth be mingled with Fire. Whereupon the Emperour uttered these words, Ἐμοῦ ζῶντος, *i.e. Yea whilst I live*: there by one word, he express'd a cruel thought, which I think is the thing he meant; this is more cruel than the wish of *Caligula*, that the people of *Rome* had but one Neck, that he might destroy them all at a blow.

Sect. 6. Pag. 95.

I cannot believe the story of the Italian, etc.] It is reported that a certain *Italian* having met with one that had highly provoked him, put a Ponyard to his breast, and unless he would blaspheme God, told him he would kill him, which the other doing to save his life, the *Italian* presently kill'd him, to the intent he might be damned, having no time of Repentance.

Sect. 7. Pag. 97.

I have no sins that want a Name.] The Author in *cap. ult. lib. ult. Pseudodox.* speaking of the Act of carnality exercised by the *Egyptian* Pollinctors with the dead carcasses, saith we want a name for this, wherein neither *Petronius* nor *Martial* can relieve us; therefore I conceive the Author here means a venereal sin.

This was the Temper of that Leacher that carnal'd with a Statua.] The Latine Annotator upon this hath these words: *Romæ refertur de Hispano quodam.* But certainly the Author means the Statue of *Venus Gnidia* made by *Praxiteles*, of which a certain young man became so enamoured, that *Pliny* relates, *Ferunt amore captum cum delituisset nocta simulachro cohæsisse, ejusq; cupiditas esse indicem masculum.* Lucian also has the story in his *Dialog.* [*Amores.*]

And the constitution of Nero in his Spintrian recreations.] The Author doth not mean the last *Nero*, but *Tiberius* the Emperour, whose name was *Nero* too; of whom *Sueton. Secessu vero Capreensi etiam sellariam excogitavit sedem arcanarum libidinum, in quam undique conquisti puellarum et exoletorum greges monstrosiq; concubitus repertores, quos spintrias apellabat, triplici serie connexi invicem incestarent se coram ipso, ut adspectu deficientes libidines excitaret.* Suet. *in Tib. 43.*

Sect. 8 Pag. 98.

I have seen a Grammarian toure and plume himself over a single line in Horace, and shew more pride, etc.] *Movent mihi stomachum Grammatistæ quidam, qui cum duas tenuerint vocabularum origenes ita se ostentant, ita venditant, ita circumferunt jactabundi, ut præ ipsis pro nihilo habendos Philosophos arbitrentur.* Picus Mirand. *in Ep. ad Hermol. Barb. quæ extat lib. nono Epist.* Politian.

Garsio quisq; duas postquam scit jungere partes,

Sic stat, sic loquitur, velut omnes noverit artes.

Pag. 99.

I cannot think that Homer *pin'd away upon the Riddle of the Fishermen.*] The History out of *Plutarch* is thus: Sailing from *Thebes* to the Island *Ion*, being landed and set down upon the shore, there happen'd certain Fishermen to pass by him, and he asking them what they had taken, they made him this Enigmatical answer, That what they had taken, they had left behind them; and what they had not taken, they had with them: meaning, that because they could take no Fish, they went to loose themselves; and that all which they had taken, they had killed, and left behind them, and all which they had not taken, they had with them in their clothes: and that *Homer* being struck with a deep sadness because he could not interpret this, pin'd away, and at last dyed. *Pliny* alludes to this Riddle, in his *Ep.* to his Friend *Fuscus*, where giving an account of spending his time in the Country, he tells him, *Venor aliquando, sed non sine pugilluribus, ut quamvis nihil ceperim, non nihil referam.* Plin. *Ep. lib. 9, Ep. 36.*

Or that Aristot.——*did ever drown himself upon the flux or reflux of* Euripus.] *Laertius* reports that *Aristotle* dyed of a disease at 63 years of age. For this and the last, see the Author in *Pseudodox*.

Aristotle *doth but instruct us as* Plato *did him, to confute himself.*] In the matter of *Idea's*, Eternity of the world, *etc.*

Sec. 9. Pag. 100.

I could be content that we might procreate like trees without conjunction, or that there were any way to perpetuate the world without this trivial and vulgar way of Coition: It is the foolishest act a wise man commits in all his life.] There was a Physitian long before the Author, that was of the same opinion, *Hippocrates*; for which *vide A. Gel. l. 19. Noct. Attic. c. 2.* And so of late time was *Paracelsus*, who did undertake to prescribe a way for the generation of a man without coition. *Vide Campanel. de sensu rerum, in Append. ad cap. 19. l. 4.* Monsieur Montaignes words on this subject, are worth the reading; these they are: *Je trouve apres tout, que l'amour n'est autre chose que la fame de cette jouyssance, et considerant maintes fois la ridicule titillation de ce plaiser par on il nous tient, les absurdes movements escervelez et estourdis deyuoy il agite Zenon et Cratippus, ceste rage indiscrcte, ce visage inflamme de fureur et de cruaute au plus doux effect de l'amour, et puis cette morgue grare severe et extatique en une action si folle, et que la supreme volupte aye du trainsy et du plaintiff commer la douleur, je croye qu'on se joue de nous, et que c'est par industrie que nature nous a laisse la plus trouble de nos actions les plus communes pour nous esgaller par la et apparier les fols et les sayes, et nous et les bestes. Le plus contemplatif et prudent homme quand je l'imagin en cette assiette je le tien pour un affronteur, de faire le prudent et le contemplatif: et sont les pieds du paon qui abbatent son orgueil. Nous mangeons bien et beuvons comme les bestes, mais ce ne sont pas actions, qui empeschent les operations de nostre ame, en celles-la nous gardons nostre advantage sur elles: cettecy met tout autre pensee sous le joug, abrutist et abesiit par son imperieuse authorite toute la Theology et Philosophy, qui est en Platon et si il ne s'en plaint pas. Par tout ailleurs vous pouvez garder quelque decence; toutes autres operations souffrent des Regles d'honestete: cettecy ne se peut sculement imaginer que vitieuse ou ridicule; trouvez y pour voir un proceder sage et discret. Alexander disoit qu'il se cognossoit principalement mortel par cette action et par le dormir: le sommeil suffoque et supprime les facultez de nostre ame, la besoigne les absorbe et dissipe de mesme. Certes c'est une marque non seulement de nostre corruption originelle, mais aussi de nostre vanite et disformite. D'un coste nature nous y pousse ayant attaché à ce desire la plan noble, utile et plaisante de toutes ses operations, et la nous laisse d'autre part accuser et fuyr comme insolent et dishoneste, en rougir et recommander l'abstinence, etc.* Montaign *liv. 3. chapit. 5.*

Sect. 10. Pag. 103.

And may be inverted on the worst.] That is, that there are none so abandoned to vice, but they have some sprinklings of vertue. There are scarce any so vitious, but commend virtue in those that are endued with it, and do some things laudable themselves, as *Plin.* saith in *Panegyric. Machiavel* upon *Livy, lib. 1. cap. 27.* sets down the ensuing relation as a notable confirmation of this truth. *Julius Pontifex ejus nominis secundus, anno salutis 1505. Bononiam exercitus duxit, ut Bentivolorum familiam, quæ ejus urbis imperium centum jam annos tenuerat, loco moveret. Eudemque in expeditione etiam Johannem Pagolum, Bagloneum tyrannum Perusinum sua sede expellere decreverat, ut cæteros item, qui urbes Ecclesiæ per vim tenerent. Ejus rei causa cum ad Perusinam urbem accessisset, et notum jam omnibus esset quid in animo haberet: tamen impatiens moræ, noluit exercitus expectare, sed inermis quasi urbem ingressus est, in quant Johannes Pagolus defendendi sui causa, non exiguas copias contraxerat. Is autem eodem furore, quo res suas administrare solebat, una cum milite, cui custodiam sui corporis demandarat, sese in pontificis potestatem dedidit; à quo abductus est relictusque alius, qui Ecclesiæ nomine urbem gubernaret. Hac ipsu in re magnopere admirati sunt viri sapientes, qui Pontificem comitabantur, cum Pontificis ipsius temeritatem, cum abjectum vilemq; Johannis Pagoli animum: nec causam intelligebant, ob quam permotus idem Pagolus, hostem suum inermem (quod illi cum perpetua nominis sui memoria facere licebat) non subitò oppresserit, et tam pretiosa spolia diripuerit; cum Pontifex urbem ingressus fuisset, Cardinalibus tantum suis stipatus, qui pretiosissimas quasq; suarum rerum secum habebant. Neque enim credebatur Pagolus a tanto facinore vel sua bonitate, vel animi conscientia abstinuisse: quod in hominem sceleratum, qui et propria sorore utebatur, et consobrinos nepotesque dominandi causa e medio sustulerat hujusmodi pii affectus cadere non viderentur. Cum igitur hac de re variæ essent sapientum virorum sententiæ; concluserunt tandem id ei accidisse, quod ita comparatum sit*, ut homines neque plane pravi esse queant, neque perfecte boni. *Pravi perfecte esse nequeant, propterea quod, ubi tale quoddam scelus est, in quo aliquid magnifici ac generosi insit, id patrare non andeant. Nam cum Pagolus neq; incestam prius horraisset, neque patricidio abstinnisset: tamen cnm oblata esset occasio, pravi quidem sed memorabilis, atque æternæ memoriæ facinoris patrandi, id attentare non ausus fuit, cum id sine infamia prestare licuisset, quod rei magnitudo omnia priora scelera obtegere potuisset, et a periculo conservare. Quibus accedit, quod illi gratulati fuissent etiam quam plurimi, si primus ausus esset Pontificibus monstrare rationem dominandi; totiusque humanæ vitæ usum ab illis nimis parei pendi.*

<u>*Poysons contain within themselves their own Antidote.*</u>] The Poyson of a Scorpion is not Poyson to it self, nor the Poyson of a Toad is not Poyson to it self; so that the sucking out of Poyson from persons infected by Psylls, (who are continually nourished with venomous aliment) without any prejudice to themselves, is the less to be wondred at.

<u>*The man without a Navil yet lives in me.*</u>] The Latine Annotator hath explicated this by *Homo non perfectus*, by which it seems he did not comprehend the Author's meaning; for the Author means *Adam*, and by a Metonymie original sin; for the Navil being onely of use to attract the aliment *in utero materno*, and *Adam* having no mother, he had no use of a Navil, and therefore it is not to be conceived he had any; and upon that ground the Author calls him the man without a Navil.

Sect. 11. Pag. 106.

<u>*Our grosser memories have then so little hold of our abstracted understandings, that they forget the story, and can onely relate to our awaked senses a confused and broken tale of that that hath pass'd.*</u>] For the most part it is so. In regard of the Author's expression of forgetting the story, though otherwise it be not very pertinent to this place, I shall set down a relation given by an English Gentleman, of two dreams that he had, wherein he did not forget the story, but (what is more strange) found his dreams verified. This it is.

Whilst I lived at *Prague*, and one night had sit up very late drinking at a feast, early in the morning the Sun beams glancing on my face, as I lay in my bed, I dreamed that a shadow passing by told me that my Father was dead; at which awaking all in a sweat, and affected with this dream, I rose and wrote the day and hour, and all circumstances thereof in a Paper-book, which book with many other things I put into a Barrel, and sent it from *Prague* to *Stode*, thence to be conveyed into *England*. And now being at *Nurenburgh*, a Merchant of a noble Family well acquainted with me and my friends, arrived there, who told me my Father dyed some two months ago. I list not to write any lyes, but that which I write, is as true as strange. When I returned into *England* some four years after, I would not open the Barrel I sent from *Prague*, nor look into the Paper-book in which I had written this dream, till I had called my Sisters and some friends to be witnesses, where my self and they were astonished to see my written dream answer the very day of my Father's death.

I may lawfully swear that which my Kinsman hath heard witnessed by my brother *Henry* whilst he lived, that in my youth at *Cambridge*, I had the like dream of my Mother's death, where my brother *Henry* living with me, early in the morning I dreamed that my Mother passed by with a sad countenance, and told me that she could not come to my Commencement: I being within five months to proceed Master of Arts, and she having promised at that time to come to *Cambridge*. And when I related this dream to my brother, both of us awaking together in a sweat, he protested to me that he had dreamed the very same; and when we had not the least knowledge of our Mother's sickness, neither in our youthful affections were any whit affected with the strangeness of this dream, yet the next Carrier brought us word of our Mother's death. Mr. *Fiennes Morison* in his Itinerary. I am not over-credulous of such relations, but methinks the circumstance of publishing it at such a time, when there were those living that might have disprov'd it, if it had been false, is a great argument of the truth of it.

Sect. 12. Pag. 107.

<u>I wonder the fancy of Lucan and Seneca did not discover it.</u>] For they had both power from *Nero* to chuse their deaths.

Sect. 13. Pag. 108.

<u>To conceive our selves Urinals is not so ridiculous.</u>] *Reperti sunt Galeno et Avicenna testibus qui se vasa fictilia crederent, et ideirco hominum attactum ne confringerentur solicite fugerent.* Pontan. *in Attic. bellar.* (*Hist.* 22.) Which proceeds from extremity of Melancholy.

Pag. 109.

<u>Aristot. is too severe, that will not allow us to be truely liberal without wealth.</u>] Aristot. l. 1. Ethic. c. 8.

Sect. 15. Pag. 112.

<u>Thy will be done though in mine own undoing.</u>] This should be the wish of every man, and is of the most wise and knowing, *Le Christien plus humble et plus sage et mieux recognoissant que c'est que de luy se rapporte a son createur de choisir et ordonner ce qu'il luy faut. Il ne le supplie dautre chose que sa volunte soit faite.* Montaign.

A Letter sent upon the information of Animadversions *to come forth, upon the imperfect and surreptitious copy of* Religio Medici, *whilst this true one was going to Press.*

Honoured Sir, Give your Servant, who hath ever honour'd you, leave to take notice of a Book at present in the Press, intituled (as I am informed) *Animadversions* upon a Treatise lately printed under the name of *Religio Medici*; hereof, I am advertised, you have descended to be the Author. Worthy Sir, permit your Servant to affirm there is contain'd therein nothing that can deserve the Reason of your Contradictions, much less the Candor of your *Animadversions*: and to certifie the truth thereof, That Book (whereof I do acknowledge myself the Author) was penn'd many years past, and (what cannot escape your apprehension) with no intention for the Press, or the least desire to oblige the Faith of any man to its assertions. But what hath more especially emboldened my Pen unto you at present, is, That the same Piece, contrived in my private study, and as an Exercise unto my self, rather than Exercitation for any other, having past from my hand under a broken and imperfect Copy, by frequent transcription it still run forward into corruption, and after the addition of some things, omission of others, & transposition of many, without my assent or privacy, the liberty of these times committed it unto the Press; whence it issued so disguised, the Author without distinction could not acknowledge it. Having thus miscarried, within a few weeks I shall, God willing, deliver unto the Press the true and intended Original (whereof in the mean time your worthy Self may command a view); otherwise when ever that Copy shall be extant, it will most clearly appear how far the Text hath been mistaken, and all Observations, Glosses, or Exercitations thereon, will in a great part impugn the Printer or Transcriber, rather than the Author. If after that, you shall esteem it worth your vacant hours to discourse thereon, you shall but take that liberty which I assume my self, that is, freely to abound in your sense, as I have done in my own. However you shall determine, you shall sufficiently honour me in the Vouchsafe of your Refute, and I oblige the whole World in the occasion of your Pen.

Your Servant.

T. B.

Norwich, *March 3, 1642.*

TO THE READER

Certainly that man were greedy of Life, who should desire to live when all the world were at an end; and he must needs be very impatient, who would repine at death in the society of all things that suffer under it. Had not almost every man suffered by the Press or were not the tyranny thereof become universal, I had not wanted reason for complaint: but in times wherein I have lived to behold the highest perversion of that excellent invention, the name of his Majesty defamed, the Honour of Parliament depraved, the Writings of both depravedly, anticipatively, counterfeitly imprinted; complaints may seem ridiculous in private persons; and men of my condition may be as incapable of affronts, as hopeless of their reparations. And truely had not the duty I owe unto the importunity of friends, and the allegiance I must ever acknowledge unto truth, prevailed with me; the inactivity of my disposition might have made these sufferings continual, and time that brings other things to light, should have satisfied me in the remedy of its oblivion. But because things evidently false are not onely printed, but many things of truth most falsely set forth, in this latter I could not but think my self engaged. For though we have no power to redress the former, yet in the other, reparation being within our selves, I have at present represented unto the world a full and intended Copy of that Piece, which was most imperfectly and surreptitiously published before.

This, I confess, about seven years past, with some others of affinity thereto, for my private exercise and satisfaction, I had at leisurable hours composed; which being communicated unto one, it became common unto many, and was by Transcription successively corrupted, untill it arrived in a most depraved Copy at the Press. He that shall peruse that Work, and shall take notice of sundry particularities and personal expressions therein, will easily discern the intention was not publick: and being a private Exercise directed to my self, what is delivered therein, was rather a memorial unto me, than an Example or Rule unto any other: and therefore if there be any singularity therein correspondent unto the private conceptions of any man, it doth not advantage them: or if dissentaneous thereunto, it no way overthrows them. It was penned in such a place, and with such disadvantage, that (I protest) from the first setting of pen unto paper, I had not the assistance of any good Book, whereby to promote my invention, or relieve my memory; and therefore there might be many real lapses therein, which others might take notice of, and more than I suspected my self. It was set down many years past, and was the sense of my conception at that time, not an immutable Law unto my advancing judgement at all times; and therefore there might be many things therein plausible unto my passed apprehension, which are not agreeable until my present self. There are many things delivered Rhetorically, many expressions therein meerly Tropical, and as they best illustrate my intention; and therefore also there are many things to be taken in a soft and flexible sense, and not to be called unto the rigid test of Reason. Lastly, all that is contained therein is in submission unto maturer discernments; and, as I have declared, shall no further father them than the best and learned judgments shall authorize them: under favour of which considerations I have made its secrecy publick, and committed the truth thereof to every Ingenuous Reader.

THO. BROWNE.

RELIGIO MEDICI

SECT. 1

For my Religion, though there be several Circumstances that might perswade the World I have none at all, as the general scandal of my Profession, the natural course of my Studies, the indifferency of my Behaviour and Discourse in matters of Religion, neither violently Defending one, nor with that common ardour and contention Opposing another; yet, in despight hereof, I dare, without usurpation, assume the honourable Stile of a Christian. Not that I meerly owe this Title to the Font, my Education, or Clime wherein I was born, as being bred up either to confirm those Principles my parents instilled into my Understanding, or by a general consent proceed in the Religion of my Country: But having in my riper years and confirmed Judgment, seen and examined all, I find my self obliged by the Principles of Grace, and the Law of mine own Reason, to embrace no other name but this: Neither doth herein my zeal so far make me forget the general Charity I owe unto Humanity, as rather to hate than pity *Turks, Infidels*, and (what is worse) *Jews*; rather contenting my self to enjoy that happy Stile, than maligning those who refuse so glorious a Title.

SECT. 2

But because the Name of a Christian is become too general to express our Faith, there being a Geography of Religion as well as Lands, and every Clime distinguished not only by their Laws and Limits, but circumscribed by their Doctrines and Rules of Faith; to be particular, I am of that *Reformed* new-cast Religion, wherein I dislike nothing but the Name; of the same belief our Saviour taught, the Apostles disseminated, the Fathers authorized, and the Martyrs confirmed, but by the sinister ends of Princes, the ambition and avarice of Prelates, and the fatal corruption of times, so decayed, impaired, and fallen from its native Beauty, that it required the careful and charitable hands of these times to restore it to its primitive Integrity. Now the accidental occasion whereupon, the slender means whereby the low and abject condition of the Person by whom so good a work was set on foot, which in our Adversaries beget contempt and scorn, fills me with wonder, and is the very same Objection the insolent Pagans first cast at Christ and his Disciples.

SECT.3

Yet have I not so shaken hands with those desperate Resolutions, who had rather venture at large their decayed bottom, than bring her in to be new trimm'd in the Dock; who had rather promiscuously retain all, than abridge any, and obstinately be what they are, than what they have been, as to stand in Diameter and Swords point with them: We have reformed from them, not against them; for omitting those Improperations and Terms of Scurrility betwixt us, which only difference our Affections, and not our Cause, there is between us one common Name and Appellation, one Faith and necessary body of Principles common to us both; and therefore I am not scrupulous to converse and live with them, to enter their Churches in defect of ours, and either pray with them, or for them. I could never perceive any rational Consequence from those many Texts which prohibit the Children of *Israel* to pollute themselves with the Temples of the Heathens; we being all Christians, and not divided by such detested impieties as might prophane our Prayers, or the place wherein we make them; or that a resolved Conscience may not adore her Creator any where, especially in places devoted to his Service; where, if their Devotions offend him, mine may please him; if theirs prophane it, mine may hallow it. Holy-water and Crucifix (dangerous to the common people) deceive not my judgment, nor abuse my devotion at all: I am, I confess, naturally inclined to that which misguided Zeal terms Superstition: my common conversation I do acknowledge austere, my behaviour full of rigour, sometimes not without morosity; yet at my Devotion I love to use the civility of my knee, my hat, and hand, with all those outward and sensible motions which may express or promote my invisible Devotion. I should violate my own arm rather than a Church; nor willingly deface the name of Saint or Martyr. At the sight of a Cross or Crucifix I can dispense with my hat, but scarce with the thought or memory of my Saviour: I cannot laugh at, but rather pity, the fruitless journeys of Pilgrims, or contemn the miserable condition of Fryars; for though misplaced in Circumstances there is something in it of Devotion. I could never hear the *Ave-Mary* Bell[7] without an elevation, or think it a sufficient warrant, because they erred in one circumstance, for me to err in all, that is, in silence and dumb contempt; whilst therefore they directed their Devotions to Her, I offered mine to God, and rectifie the Errors of their Prayers by rightly ordering mine own: At a solemn Procession I have wept abundantly, while my consorts blind with opposition and prejudice, have fallen into an excess of scorn and laughter: There are questionless both in *Greek, Roman,* and *African* Churches, Solemnities and Ceremonies, whereof the wiser Zeals do make a Christian use, and stand condemned by us, not as evil in themselves, but as allurements and baits of superstition to those vulgar heads that look asquint on the face of Truth, and those unstable Judgments that cannot resist in the narrow point and centre of Virtue without a reel or stagger to the Circumference.

SECT.4

As there were many Reformers, so likewise many Reformations; every Country proceeding in a particular way and method, according as their national Interest, together with their Constitution and Clime, inclined them; some angrily, and with extremity; others calmly, and with mediocrity; not rending, but easily dividing the community, and leaving an honest possibility of a reconciliation; which though peaceable Spirits do desire, and may conceive that revolution of time and the mercies of God may effect, yet that judgment that shall continue the present antipathies between the two extreams, their contrarieties in condition, affection, and opinion, may with the same hopes expect an union in the Poles of Heaven.

SECT.5

But to difference my self nearer, and draw into a lesser Circle, There is no Church, whose every part so squares unto my Conscience; whose Articles, Constitutions, and Customs, seem so consonant unto reason, and as it were framed to my particular Devotion, as this whereof I hold my Belief, the Church of *England*, to whose Faith I am a sworn Subject; and therefore in a double Obligation subscribe unto her Articles, and endeavour to observe her Constitutions; whatsoever is beyond, as points indifferent, I observe according to the rules of my private reason, or the humour and fashion of my Devotion; neither believing this, because *Luther* affirmed it, or disproving that, because *Calvin* hath disavouched it. I condemn not all things in the Council of *Trent*, nor approve all in the Synod of *Dort*. In brief, where the Scripture is silent, the Church is my Text; where that speaks, 'tis but my Comment: where there is a joynt silence of both, I borrow not the rules of my Religion from *Rome* or *Geneva*, but the dictates of my own reason. It is an unjust scandal of our adversaries, and a gross errour in our selves, to compute the Nativity of our Religion from *Henry* the Eighth, who, though he rejected the Pope, refus'd not the faith of *Rome*, and effected no more than what his own Predecessors desired and assayed in Ages past, and was conceived the State of *Venice* would have attempted in our days. It is as uncharitable a point in us to fall upon those popular scurrilities and opprobrious scoffs of the Bishop of *Rome*, to whom as a temporal Prince, we owe the duty of good language: I confess there is cause of passion between us; by his sentence I stand excommunicated, Heretick is the best language he affords me; yet can no ear witness I ever returned him the name of Antichrist, Man of Sin, or Whore of *Babylon*. It is the method of Charity to suffer without reaction: Those usual Satyrs and invectives of the Pulpit may perchance produce a good effect on the vulgar, whose ears are opener to Rhetorick than Logick; yet do they in no wise confirm the faith of wiser Believers, who know that a good cause needs not to be pardon'd by passion, but can sustain it self upon a temperate dispute.

SECT.6

I could never divide my self from any man upon the difference of an opinion, or be angry with his judgment for not agreeing with me in that from which perhaps within a few days I should dissent my self. I have no Genius to disputes in Religion, and have often thought it wisdom to decline them, especially upon a disadvantage, or when the cause of truth might suffer in the weakness of my patronage: Where we desire to be informed, 'tis good to contest with men above our selves; but to confirm and establish our opinions, 'tis best to argue with judgments below our own, that the frequent spoils and Victories over their reasons may settle in ourselves an esteem and confirmed Opinion of our own. Every man is not a proper Champion for Truth, nor fit to take up the Gauntlet in the cause of Verity: Many, from the ignorance of these Maximes, and an inconsiderate Zeal unto Truth, have too rashly charged the Troops of Error, and remain as Trophies unto the enemies of Truth: A man may be in as just possession of Truth as of a City, and yet be forced to surrender; 'tis therefore far better to enjoy her with peace, than to hazzard her on a battle: if therefore there rise any doubts in my way, I do forget them, or at least defer them till my better setled judgement and more manly reason be able to resolve them; for I perceive every man's own reason is his best *Œdipus*, and will upon a reasonable truce, find a way to loose those bonds wherewith the subtleties of error have enchained our more flexible and tender judgements. In Philosophy, where Truth seems double-fac'd, there is no man more Paradoxical than my self: but in Divinity I love to keep the Road; and, though not in an implicite, yet an humble faith, follow the great wheel of the Church, by which I move, not reserving any proper Poles or motion from the Epicycle of my own brain; by this means I leave no gap for Heresie, Schismes, or Errors, of which at present I hope I shall not injure Truth to say I have no taint or tincture: I must confess my greener studies have been polluted with two or three, not any begotten in the latter Centuries, but old and obsolete, such as could never have been revived, but by such extravagant and irregular heads as mine: for indeed Heresies perish not with their Authors, but, like the river *Arethusa*, though they lose their currents in one place, they rise up again in another: One General Council is not able to extirpate one single Heresie; it may be cancell'd for the present; but revolution of time, and the like aspects from Heaven, will restore it, when it will flourish till it be condemned again. For as though there were a *Metempsuchosis*, and the soul of one man passed into another; Opinions do find, after certain Revolutions, men and minds like those that first begat them. To see ourselves again, we need not look for Plato's year:[8] every man is not only himself; there hath been many *Diogenes*, and as many *Timons*, though but few of that name; men are liv'd over again, the world is now as it was in Ages past; there was none then, but there hath been some one since that Parallels him, and is, as it were, his revived self.

SECT.7

Now the first of mine was that of the *Arabians*, That the Souls of men perished with their Bodies, but should yet be raised again at the last day: not that I did absolutely conceive a mortality of the Soul; but if that were, which Faith, not Philosophy hath yet throughly disproved, and that both entred the grave together, yet I held the same conceit thereof that we all do of the body, that it should rise again. Surely it is but the merits of our unworthy Natures, if we sleep in darkness until the last Alarm. A serious reflex upon my own unworthiness did make me backward from challenging this prerogative of my Soul; so that I might enjoy my Saviour at the last, I could with patience be nothing almost unto Eternity. The second was that of *Origen*, That God would not persist in his vengeance for ever, but after a definite time of his wrath, he would release the damned Souls from torture: which error I fell into upon a serious contemplation of the great Attribute of God, his Mercy; and did a little cherish it in my self, because I found therein no malice, and a ready weight to sway me from the other extream of despair, whereunto Melancholy and Contemplative Natures are too easily disposed. A third there is which I did never positively maintain or practise, but have often wished it had been consonant to Truth, and not offensive to my Religion, and that is the Prayer for the dead; whereunto I was inclin'd from some charitable inducements, whereby I could scarce contain my Prayers for a friend at the ringing of a Bell, or behold his Corps without an Orison for his Soul: 'Twas a good way, methought, to be remembred by posterity, and far more noble than an History. These opinions I never maintained with pertinacy, or endeavoured to inveagle any mans belief unto mine, nor so much as ever revealed or disputed them with my dearest friends; by which means I neither propagated them in others, nor confirmed them in my self; but suffering them to flame upon their own substance, without addition of new fuel, they went out insensibly of themselves: therefore these Opinions, though condemned by lawful Councels, were not Heresies in me, but bare Errors, and single Lapses of my understanding, without a joynt depravity of my will: Those have not onely depraved understandings, but diseased affections, which cannot enjoy a singularity without an Heresie, or be the Author of an Opinion without they be of a Sect also; this was the villany of the first Schism of *Lucifer*, who was not content to err alone, but drew into his Faction many Legions; and upon this experience he tempted only *Eve*, as well understanding the Communicable nature of Sin, and that to deceive but one, was tacitely and upon consequence to delude them both.

SECT.8

That Heresies should arise, we have the Prophesie of Christ; but that old ones should be abolished, we hold no prediction. That there must be Heresies, is true, not only in our Church, but also in any other: even in doctrines heretical, there will be super-heresies; and Arians not only divided from their Church, but also among themselves: for heads that are disposed unto Schism and complexionally propense to innovation, are naturally disposed for a community; nor will be ever confined unto the order or œconomy of one body; and therefore when they separate from others, they knit but loosely among themselves, nor contented with a general breach or dichotomy with their Church, do subdivide and mince themselves almost into Atoms. 'Tis true, that men of singular parts and humours have not been free from singular opinions and conceits in all Ages; retaining something, not only beside the opinion of his own Church or any other, but also any particular Author; which notwithstanding a sober Judgment may do without offence or heresie; for there is yet, after all the Decrees of Councils and the niceties of Schools, many things untouch'd, unimagin'd, wherein the liberty of an honest reason may play and expatiate with security, and far without the circle of an Heresie.

SECT. 9

As for those wingy Mysteries in Divinity, and airy subtleties in Religion, which have unhing'd the brains of better heads, they never stretched the *Pia Mater* of mine. Methinks there be not impossibilities enough in Religion for an active faith; the deepest Mysteries ours contains have not only been illustrated, but maintained, by Syllogism and the rule of Reason. I love to lose my self in a mystery, to pursue my Reason to an *O altitudo!* 'Tis my solitary recreation to pose my apprehension with those involved Ænigma's and riddles of the Trinity, with Incarnation, and Resurrection. I can answer all the Objections of Satan and my rebellious reason with that odd resolution I learned of *Tertullian, Certum est quia impossibile est*. I desire to exercise my faith in the difficultest point; for to credit ordinary and visible objects is not faith, but perswasion. Some believe the better for seeing Christ's Sepulchre; and when they have seen the Red Sea, doubt not of the Miracle. Now contrarily, I bless my self and am thankful that I lived not in the days of Miracles, that I never saw Christ nor His Disciples; I would not have been one of those *Israelites* that pass'd the Red Sea, nor one of Christ's patients on whom he wrought his wonders; then had my faith been thrust upon me, nor should I enjoy that greater blessing pronounced to all that believe and saw not. 'Tis an easie and necessary belief, to credit what our eye and sense hath examined: I believe he was dead, and buried, and rose again; and desire to see him in his glory, rather than to contemplate him in his Cenotaphe or Sepulchre. Nor is this much to believe; as we have reason, we owe this faith unto History: they only had the advantage of a bold and noble Faith, who lived before his coming, who upon obscure prophesies and mystical Types could raise a belief, and expect apparent impossibilities.

SECT. 10

'Tis true, there is an edge in all firm belief, and with an easie Metaphor we may say, the Sword of Faith; but in these obscurities I rather use it in the adjunct the Apostle gives it, a Buckler; under which I conceive a wary combatant may lye invulnerable. Since I was of understanding to know we knew nothing, my reason hath been more pliable to the will of Faith; I am now content to understand a mystery without a rigid definition, in an easie and Platonick description. That[o] allegorical description of *Hermes*, pleaseth me beyond all the Metaphysical definitions of Divines; where I cannot satisfie my reason, I love to humour my fancy: I had as live you tell me that *anima est angelus hominis, est Corpus Dei*, as *Entelechia; Lux est umbra Dei*, as *actus perspicui*; where there is an obscurity too deep for our Reason, 'tis good to sit down with a description, periphrasis, or adumbration; for by acquainting our Reason how unable it is to display the visible and obvious effects of nature, it becomes more humble and submissive unto the subtleties of Faith; and thus I teach my haggard and unreclaimed reason to stoop unto the lure of Faith. I believe there was already a tree whose fruit our unhappy Parents tasted, though, in the same Chapter when God forbids it, 'tis positively said, the plants of the field were not yet grown, for God had not caus'd it to rain upon the earth. I believe that the Serpent (if we shall literally understand it) from his proper form and figure, made his motion on his belly before the curse. I find the tryal of the Pucellage and virginity of Women, which God ordained the *Jews*, is very fallible. Experience and History informs me, that not onely many particular Women, but likewise whole Nations have escaped the curse of Childbirth, which God seems to pronounce upon the whole Sex; yet do I believe that all this is true, which indeed my Reason would perswade me to be false; and this I think is no vulgar part of Faith, to believe a thing not only above, but contrary to Reason, and against the Arguments of our proper Senses.

SECT. 11

In my solitary and retired imagination (*Neque enim cum porticus, aut me lectulus accepit, desum mihi*) I remember I am not alone, and therefore forget not to contemplate him and his Attributes who is ever with me, especially those two mighty ones, his Wisdom and Eternity; with the one I recreate, with the other I confound my understanding: for who can speak of Eternity without a solœcism, or think thereof without an Extasie? Time we may comprehend; 'tis but five days elder then our selves, and hath the same Horoscope with the World; but to retire so far back as to apprehend a beginning, to give such an infinite start forwards as to conceive an end in an essence that we affirm hath neither the one nor the other, it puts my Reason to *St. Paul's* Sanctuary: my Philosophy dares not say the Angels can do it; God hath not made a Creature that can comprehend him; 'tis a privilege of His own nature. *I am that I am*, was his own definition unto *Moses*; and 'twas a short one, to confound mortality, that durst question God, or ask him what he was; indeed he onely is; all others have and shall be; but in Eternity there is no distinction of Tenses; and therefore that terrible term *Predestination*, which hath troubled so many weak heads to conceive, and the wisest to explain, is in respect to God no prescious determination of our Estates to come, but a definitive blast of his Will already fulfilled, and at the instant that he first decreed it; for to his Eternity which is indivisible and all together, the last Trump is already sounded, the reprobates in the flame, and the blessed in *Abraham's* bosome. *St. Peter* speaks modestly, when he saith, a thousand years to God are but as one day: for to speak like a Philosopher, those continued instances of time which flow into a thousand years, make not to Him one moment; what to us is to come, to his Eternity is present, his whole duration being but one permanent point, without Succession, Parts, Flux, or Division.

SECT.12

There is no Attribute that adds more difficulty to the mystery of the Trinity, where, though in a relative way of Father and Son, we must deny a priority. I wonder how *Aristotle* could conceive the World eternal, or how he could make good two Eternities: his similitude of a Triangle, comprehended in a square, doth somewhat illustrate the Trinity of our Souls, and that the Triple Unity of God; for there is in us not three, but a Trinity of Souls, because there is in us, if not three distinct Souls, yet differing faculties, that can and do subsist apart in different Subjects, and yet in us are thus united as to make but one Soul and substance: if one Soul were so perfect as to inform three distinct Bodies, that were a pretty Trinity: conceive, the distinct number of three, not divided nor separated by the Intellect, but actually comprehended in its Unity, and that is a perfect Trinity. I have often admired the mystical way of *Pythagoras*, and the secret Magick of numbers. Beware of Philosophy, is a precept not to be received in too large a sense; for in this Mass of Nature there is a set of things that carry in their Front, though not in Capital Letters, yet in Stenography and short Characters, something of Divinity, which to wiser Reasons serve as Luminaries in the Abyss of Knowledge, and to judicious beliefs as Scales and Roundles to mount the Pinacles and highest pieces of Divinity. The severe Schools shall never laugh me out of the Philosophy of *Hermes*, that this visible World is but a Picture of the invisible, wherein as in a Pourtraict, things are not truely, but in equivocal shapes, and as they counterfeit some more real substance in that invisible Fabrick.

SECT.13

That other Attribute wherewith I recreate my devotion, is his Wisdom, in which I am happy; and for the contemplation of this only, do not repent me that I was bred in the way of Study: The advantage I have of the vulgar, with the content and happiness I conceive therein, is an ample recompence for all my endeavours, in what part of knowledge soever. Wisdom is his most beauteous Attribute, no man can attain unto it, yet *Solomon* pleased God when he desired it. He is wise, because he knows all things; and he knoweth all things, because he made them all: but his greatest knowledge is in comprehending that he made not, that is, himself. And this is also the greatest knowledge in man. For this do I honour my own profession, and embrace the Counsel even of the Devil himself: had he read such a Lecture in Paradise as he did at *Delphos*,[10] we had better known our selves; nor had we stood in fear to know him. I know he is wise in all, wonderful in what we conceive, but far more in what we comprehend not; for we behold him but asquint, upon reflex or shadow; our understanding is dimmer than *Moses* Eye; we are ignorant of the back-parts or lower side of his Divinity; therefore to prie into the maze of his Counsels is not only folly in man, but presumption even in Angels; like us, they are his Servants, not his Senators; he holds no Counsel, but that mystical one of the Trinity, wherein though there be three Persons, there is but one mind that decrees without Contradiction: nor needs he any; his actions are not begot with deliberation, his Wisdom naturally knows what's best; his intellect stands ready fraught with the superlative and purest *Idea's* of goodness; consultation and election, which are two motions in us, make but one in him; his actions springing from his power at the first touch of his will. These are Contemplations Metaphysical: my humble speculations have another Method, and are content to trace and discover those expressions he hath left in his Creatures, and the obvious effects of

Nature; there is no danger to profound these mysteries, no *sanctum sanctorum* in Philosophy: the World was made to be inhabited by Beasts, but studied and contemplated by Man: 'tis the Debt of our Reason we owe unto God, and the homage we pay for not being Beasts; without this, the World is still as though it had not been, or as it was before the sixth day, when as yet there was not a Creature that could conceive, or say there was a World. The wisdom of God receives small honour from those vulgar Heads that rudely stare about, and with a gross rusticity admire his works; those highly magnifie him, whose judicious inquiry into His Acts, and deliberate research into His Creatures, return the duty of a devout and learned admiration. Therefore,

Search while thou wilt, and let thy reason go,
To ransome truth, even to th' Abyss below;
Rally the scattered Causes; and that line
Which Nature twists, be able to untwine
It is thy Makers will, for unto none,
But unto reason can he e'er be known.
The Devils do know Thee, but those damn'd Meteors
Build not thy Glory, but confound thy Creatures.
Teach my indeavours so thy works to read,
That learning them in thee, I may proceed.
Give thou my reason that instructive flight,
Whose weary wings may on thy hands still light.
Teach me to soar aloft, yet ever so,
When neer the Sun, to stoop again below.
Thus shall my humble Feathers safely hover,
And, though near Earth, more than the Heavens discover
And then at last, when homeward I shall drive,
Rich with the Spoils of nature to my hive,
There will I sit like that industrious Flie,
Buzzing thy praises, which shall never die,
Till death abrupts them, and succeeding Glory
Bid me go on in a more lasting story.

And this is almost all wherein an humble Creature may endeavour to requite and some way to retribute unto his Creator: for if not he that saith, *Lord, Lord*, but *he that doth the will of his Father, shall be saved*; certainly our wills must be our performances, and our intents make out our Actions; otherwise our pious labours shall find anxiety in our Graves, and our best endeavours not hope, but fear a resurrection.

SECT.14

There is but one first cause, and four second causes of all things; some are without efficient, as God; others without matter, as Angels; some without form, as the first matter: but every Essence created or uncreated, hath its final cause, and some positive end both of its Essence and Operation; this is the cause I grope after in the works of Nature; on this hangs the providence of God: to raise so beauteous a structure as the World and the Creatures thereof, was but his Art; but their sundry and divided operations, with their predestinated ends, are from the Treasure of his wisdom. In the causes, nature, and affections of the Eclipses of the Sun and Moon, there is most excellent speculation; but to profound farther, and to contemplate a reason why his providence hath so disposed and ordered their motions in that vast circle as to conjoyn and obscure each other, is a sweeter piece of Reason, and a diviner point of Philosophy; therefore sometimes, and in some things, there appears to me as much Divinity in *Galen* his books *De Usu Partium*, as in *Suarez* Metaphysicks: Had *Aristotle* been as curious in the enquiry of this cause as he was of the other, he had not left behind him an imperfect piece of Philosophy, but an absolute tract of Divinity.

SECT.15

Natura nihil aget frustra, is the only indisputed Axiome in Philosophy; there are no *Grotesques* in nature; not any thing framed to fill up empty Cantons, and unnecessary spaces: in the most imperfect Creatures, and such as were not preserved in the Ark, but having their Seeds and Principles in the womb of Nature, are every where, where the power of the Sun is; in these is the Wisdom of his hand discovered. Out of this rank *Solomon* chose the object of his admiration; indeed what reason may not go to School to the wisdom of Bees, Ants, and Spiders? what wise hand teacheth them to do what reason cannot teach us? ruder heads stand amazed at those prodigious pieces of Nature, Whales, Elephants, Dromidaries and Camels; these, I confess, are the Colossus and Majestick pieces of her hand: but in these narrow Engines there is more curious Mathematicks; and the civility of these little Citizens, more neatly sets forth the Wisdom of their Maker. Who admires not *Regio-Montanus* his Fly beyond his Eagle, or wonders not more at the operation of two Souls in those little Bodies, than but one in the Trunk of a Cedar? I could never content my contemplation with those general pieces of wonder, the Flux and Reflux of the Sea, the increase of *Nile*, the conversion of the Needle to the North; and have studied to match and parallel those in the more obvious and neglected pieces of Nature, which without further trouble I can do in the Cosmography of my self; we carry with us the wonders we seek without us: There is all *Africa* and her prodigies in us; we are that bold and adventurous piece of nature, which he that studies wisely learns in a *compendium* what others labour at in a divided piece and endless volume.

SECT.16

Thus there are two Books from which I collect my Divinity; besides that written one of God, another of his servant Nature, that universal and publick Manuscript, that lies expans'd unto the Eyes of all, those that never saw him in the one, have discovered him in the other: this was the Scripture and Theology of the Heathens: the natural motion of the Sun made them more admire him, than its supernatural station did the Children of *Israel*; the ordinary effects of nature wrought more admiration in them than in the other all his Miracles; surely the Heathens knew better how to joyn and read these mystical Letters than we Christians, who cast a more careless Eye on these common Hieroglyphicks, and disdain to suck Divinity from the flowers of Nature. Nor do I so forget God as to adore the name of Nature; which I define not with the Schools, to be the principle of motion and rest, but that streight and regular line, that settled and constant course the Wisdom of God hath ordained the actions of His creatures, according to their several kinds. To make a revolution every day, is the Nature of the Sun, because of that necessary course which God hath ordained it, from which it cannot swerve but by a faculty from that voice which first did give it motion. Now this course of Nature God seldome alters or perverts, but like an excellent Artist hath so contrived his work, that with the self same instrument, without a new creation, he may effect his obscurest designs. Thus he sweetneth the Water with a Word, preserveth the Creatures in the Ark, which the blast of his mouth might have as easily created; for God is like a skilful Geometrician, who when more easily and with one stroak of his Compass he might describe or divide a right line, had yet rather do this in a circle or longer way; according to the constituted and fore-laid principles of his Art: yet this rule of his he doth sometimes pervert, to acquaint the World with his Prerogative, lest the arrogancy of our reason should question his power, and conclude he could not; and thus I call the effects of Nature the works of God, whose hand and instrument she only is; and therefore to ascribe his actions unto her, is to devolve the honour of the principal agent upon the instrument; which if with reason we may do, then let our hammers rise up and boast they have built our houses, and our pens receive the honour of our writings. I hold there is a general beauty in the works of God, and therefore no deformity in any kind or species of creature whatsoever: I cannot tell by what Logick we call a *Toad*, a *Bear*, or an *Elephant* ugly, they being created in those outward shapes and figures which best express the actions of their inward forms. And having past that general Visitation of God, who saw that all that he had made was good, that is, conformable to his Will, which abhors deformity, and is the rule of order and beauty; there is no deformity but in Monstrosity; wherein, notwithstanding, there is a kind of Beauty. Nature so ingeniously contriving the irregular parts, as they become sometimes more remarkable than the principal Fabrick. To speak yet more narrowly, there was never any thing ugly or mis-shapen, but the Chaos; wherein, notwithstanding, to speak strictly, there was no deformity, because no form; nor was it yet impregnant by the voice of God; now Nature was not at variance with Art, nor Art with Nature, they being both servants of his providence: Art is the perfection of Nature: were the World now as it was the sixth day, there were yet a Chaos: Nature hath made one World, and Art another. In brief, all things are artificial; for Nature is the Art of God.

SECT.17

This is the ordinary and open way of his providence, which Art and Industry have in a good part discovered, whose effects we may foretel without an Oracle: to foreshew these, is not Prophesie, but Prognostication. There is another way, full of Meanders and Labyrinths, whereof the Devil and Spirits have no exact Ephemerides, and that is a more particular and obscure method of his providence, directing the operations of individuals and single Essences: this we call Fortune, that serpentine and crooked line, whereby he draws those actions his wisdom intends, in a more unknown and secret way: This cryptick and involved method of his providence have I ever admired, nor can I relate the History of my life, the occurrences of my days, the escapes of dangers, and hits of chance, with a *Bezo las Manos* to Fortune, or a bare Gramercy to my good Stars: *Abraham* might have thought the *Ram* in the thicket came thither by accident; humane reason would have said, that meer chance conveyed *Moses* in the Ark to the sight of *Pharoh's* daughter: what a Labyrinth is there in the story of *Joseph*, able to convert a Stoick? Surely there are in every man's Life certain rubs, doublings, and wrenches, which pass a while under the effects of chance, but at the last well examined, prove the meer hand of God. 'Twas not dumb chance, that to discover the Fougade or Powder-plot, contrived a miscarriage in the Letter. I like the victory of 88. the better for that one occurrence, which our enemies imputed to our dishonour and the partiality of Fortune, to wit, the tempests and contrariety of Winds. King *Philip* did not detract from the Nation, when he said, he sent his Armado to fight with men, and not to combate with the Winds. Where there is a manifest disproportion between the powers and forces of two several agents, upon a Maxime of reason we may promise the Victory to the Superiour; but when unexpected accidents slip in, and unthought of occurences intervene, these must proceed from a power that owes no obedience to those Axioms; where, as in the writing upon the wall, we may behold the hand, but see not the spring that moves it. The success of that petty province of *Holland* (of which the Grand *Seignour* proudly said, if they should trouble him as they did the *Spaniard*, he would send his men with shovels and pick-axes, and throw it into the Sea,) I cannot altogether ascribe to the ingenuity and industry of the people, but the mercy of God, that hath disposed them to such a thriving Genius; and to the will of his Providence, that disposeth her favour to each Country in their pre-ordinate season. All cannot be happy at once; for, because the glory of one State depends upon the ruine of another, there is a revolution and vicissitude of their greatness, and must obey the swing of that wheel, not moved by Intelligences, but by the hand of God, whereby all Estates arise to their *Zenith* and Vertical points according to their predestinated periods. For the lives, not only of men, but of Commonwealths, and the whole World, run not upon an Helix that still enlargeth; but on a Circle, where arriving to their Meridian, they decline in obscurity, and fall under the Horizon again.

SECT.18

These must not therefore he named the effects of Fortune, but in a relative way, and as we term the works of Nature: it was the ignorance of mans reason that begat this very name, and by a careless term miscalled the Providence of God: for there is no liberty for causes to operate in a loose and stragling way; nor any effect whatsoever, but hath its warrant from some universal or superiour Cause. 'Tis not a ridiculous devotion to say a prayer before a game at Tables; for even in *sortilegies* and matters of greatest uncertainty, there is a setled and preordered course of effects. It is we that are blind, not Fortune: because our Eye is too dim to discover the mystery of her effects, we foolishly paint her blind, and hoodwink the Providence of the Almighty. I cannot justifie that contemptible Proverb, *That fools only are Fortunate*; or that insolent Paradox, *That a wise man is out of the reach of Fortune*; much less those opprobrious epithets of Poets, *Whore, Bawd*, and *Strumpet*. 'Tis, I confess, the common fate of men of singular gifts of mind to be destitute of those of Fortune, which doth not any way deject the Spirit of wiser judgements, who throughly understand the justice of this proceeding; and being inrich'd with higher donatives, cast a more careless eye on these vulgar parts of felicity. It is a most unjust ambition to desire to engross the mercies of the Almighty, not to be content with the goods of mind, without a possession of those of body or Fortune: and it is an error worse than heresie, to adore these complemental and circumstantial pieces of felicity, and undervalue those perfections and essential points of happiness wherein we resemble our Maker. To wiser desires it is satisfaction enough to deserve, though not to enjoy the favours of Fortune; let Providence provide for Fools: 'tis not partiality, but equity in God, who deals with us but as our natural Parents; those that are able of Body and Mind, he leaves to their deserts; to those of weaker merits he imparts a larger portion, and pieces out the defect of one, by the access of the other. Thus have we no just quarrel with Nature, for leaving us naked; or to envy the Horns, Hoofs, Skins, and Furs of other Creatures, being provided with Reason, that can supply them all. We need not labour with so many Arguments to confute Judicial Astrology; for if there be a truth therein, it doth not injure Divinity: if to be born under *Mercury* disposeth us to be witty, under *Jupiter* to be wealthy; I do not owe a Knee unto those, but unto that merciful Hand that hath ordered my indifferent and uncertain nativity unto such benevolous Aspects. Those that hold that all things are governed by Fortune, had not erred, had they not persisted there: The *Romans* that erected a temple to Fortune, acknowledged therein, though in a blinder way, somewhat of Divinity; for in a wise supputation all things begin and end in the Almighty. There is a nearer way to Heaven than *Homer's* Chain; an easy Logick may conjoin heaven and Earth, in one Argument, and with less than a *Sorites* resolve all things into God. For though we christen effects by their most sensible and nearest Causes, yet is God the true and infallible Cause of all, whose concourse though it be general, yet doth it subdivide it self into the particular Actions of every thing, and is that Spirit, by which each singular Essence not only subsists, but performs its operation.

SECT.19

The bad construction, and perverse comment on these pair of second Causes, or visible hands of God, have perverted the Devotion of many unto Atheism; who, forgetting the honest Advisoes of Faith, have listened unto the conspiracy of Passion and Reason. I have therefore always endeavoured to compose those Feuds and angry Dissensions between Affection, Faith and Reason: For there is in our Soul a kind of Triumvirate, or triple Government of three Competitors, which distracts the Peace of this our Common-wealth, not less than did that other the State of *Rome*.

As Reason is a Rebel unto Faith, so Passion unto Reason: As the Propositions of Faith seem absurd unto Reason, so the Theorems of Reason unto Passion, and both unto Reason; yet a moderate and peaceable discretion may so state and order the matter, that they may be all Kings, and yet make but one Monarchy, every one exercising his Soveraignty and Prerogative in a due time and place, according to the restraint and limit of circumstance. There is, as in Philosophy, so in Divinity, sturdy doubts and boisterous Objections, wherewith the unhappiness of our knowledge too nearly acquainteth us. More of these no man hath known than my self, which I confess I conquered, not in a martial posture, but on my Knees. For our endeavours are not only to combat with doubts, but always to dispute with the Devil: the villany of that Spirit takes a hint of Infidelity from our Studies, and by demonstrating a naturality in one way, makes us mistrust a miracle in another. Thus having perused the *Archidoxes* and read the secret Sympathies of things, he would disswade my belief from the miracle of the Brazen Serpent, make me conceit that Image worked by Sympathy, and was but an *Ægyptian* trick to cure their Diseases without a miracle. Again, having seen some experiments of *Bitumen*, and having read far more of *Naphtha*, he whispered to my curiosity the fire of the Altar might be natural; and bid me mistrust a miracle in *Elias*, when he entrenched the Altar round with Water: for that inflamable substance yields not easily unto Water, but flames in the Arms of its Antagonist. And thus would he inveagle my belief to think the combustion of *Sodom* might be natural, and that there was an Asphaltick and Bituminous nature in that Lake before the Fire of *Gomorrah*. I know that *Manna* is now plentifully gathered in *Calabria*; and *Josephus* tells me, in his days it was as plentiful in *Arabia*; the Devil therefore made the *quære*, Where was then the miracle in the days of *Moses*: the *Israelite* saw but that in his time, the Natives of those Countries behold in ours. Thus the Devil played at Chess with me, and yielding a Pawn, thought to gain a Queen of me, taking advantage of my honest endeavours; and whilst I laboured to raise the structure of my Reason, he strived to undermine the edifice of my Faith.

SECT.20

Neither had these or any other ever such advantage of me, as to incline me to any point of Infidelity or desperate positions of Atheism; for I have been these many years of opinion there was never any. Those that held was the difference of Man from Beasts, have spoken probably, and proceed upon a principle as inductive as the other. That doctrine of *Epicurus*, that denied the Providence of God, was no Atheism, but a magnificent and high strained conceit of his Majesty, which he deemed too sublime to mind the trivial Actions of those inferiour Creatures. That fatal Necessity of the Stoicks, is nothing but the immutable Law of his will. Those that heretofore denied the Divinity of the Holy Ghost, have been condemned, but as Hereticks; and those that now deny our Saviour (though more than Hereticks) are not so much as Atheists: for though they deny two persons in the Trinity, they hold as we do, there is but one God.

That Villain and Secretary of Hell, that composed that miscreant piece of the Three Impostors, though divided from all Religions, and was neither Jew, Turk, nor Christian, was not a positive Atheist. I confess every country hath its *Machiavel*, every Age its *Lucian*, whereof common Heads must not hear, nor more advanced Judgments too rashly venture on: It is the Rhetorick of Satan, and may pervert a loose or prejudicate belief.

SECT.21

I confess I have perused them all, and can discover nothing that may startle a discreet belief; yet are there heads carried off with the Wind and breath of such motives. I remember a Doctor in Physick of *Italy*, who could not perfectly believe the immortality of the Soul, because *Galen* seemed to make a doubt thereof. With another I was familiarly acquainted in *France*, a Divine, and a man of singular parts, that on the same point was so plunged and gravelled with [111]three lines of *Seneca*, that all our Antidotes, drawn from both Scripture and Philosophy, could not expel the poyson of his errour. There are a set of Heads, that can credit the relations of Mariners, yet question the Testimonies of St. *Paul*; and peremptorily maintain the traditions of *Ælian* or *Pliny*, yet in Histories of Scripture raise Queries and Objections, believing no more than they can parallel in humane Authors. I confess there are in Scripture Stories that do exceed the Fables of Poets, and to a captious Reader sound like *Garagantua* or *Bevis*: Search all the Legends of times past, and the fabulous conceits of these present, and 'twill be hard to find one that deserves to carry the Buckler unto *Sampson*; yet is all this of an easie possibility, if we conceive a divine concourse, or an influence but from the little Finger of the Almighty. It is impossible that either in the discourse of man, or in the infallible Voice of God, to the weakness of our apprehensions, there should not appear irregularities, contradictions, and antinomies: my self could shew a Catalogue of doubts, never yet imagined nor questioned, as I know, which are not resolved at the first hearing; not fantastick Queries or Objections of Air; for I cannot hear of Atoms in Divinity. I can read the History of the Pigeon that was sent out of the Ark, and returned no more, yet not question how she found out her Mate that was left behind: That *Lazarus* was raised from the dead, yet not demand where in the interim his Soul awaited; or raise a Law-case, whether his Heir might lawfully detain his inheritance bequeathed unto him by his death, and he, though restored to life, have no Plea or Title unto his former possessions. Whether *Eve* was framed out of the left side of *Adam*, I dispute not; because I stand not yet assured which is the right side of a man, or whether there be any such distinction in Nature: that she was edified out of the Rib of *Adam*, I believe, yet raise no question who shall arise with that Rib at the Resurrection. Whether *Adam* was an Hermaphrodite, as the Rabbins contend upon the Letter of the Text, because it is contrary to reason, there should be an Hermaphrodite before there was a Woman; or a composition of two Natures before there was a second composed. Likewise, whether the World was created in Autumn, Summer, or the Spring, because it was created in them all; for whatsoever Sign the Sun possesseth, those four Seasons are actually existent: It is the Nature of this Luminary to distinguish the several Seasons of the year, all which it makes at one time in the whole Earth, and successive in any part thereof. There are a bundle of curiosities, not only in Philosophy, but in Divinity, proposed and discussed by men of most supposed abilities, which indeed are not worthy our vacant hours, much less our serious Studies. *In Rabbelais.* Pieces only fit to be placed in *Pantagruel's* Library, or bound up with Tartaretus, *De modo Cacandi*.

SECT.22

These are niceties that become not those that peruse so serious a Mystery: There are others more generally questioned and called to the Bar, yet methinks of an easie and possible truth.

'Tis ridiculous to put off, or down the general Flood of *Noah* in that particular inundation of *Deucalion*: that there was a Deluge once, seems not to me so great a Miracle, as that there is not one always. How all the kinds of Creatures, not only in their own bulks, but with a competency of food and sustenance, might be preserved in one Ark, and within the extent of three hundred Cubits, to a reason that rightly examines it, will appear very feasible. There is another secret not contained in the Scripture, which is more hard to comprehend, and put the honest Father to the refuge of a Miracle: and that is, not only how the distinct pieces of the World, and divided Islands should be first planted by men, but inhabited by Tigers, Panthers, and Bears. How *America* abounded with Beasts of prey, and noxious Animals, yet contained not in it that necessary Creature, a Horse, is very strange. By what passage those, not only Birds, but dangerous and unwelcome Beasts, came over: How there be Creatures there (which are not found in this Triple Continent); all which must needs be strange unto us, that hold but one Ark, and that the Creatures began their progress from the Mountains of *Ararat*: They who to salve this would make the Deluge particular, proceed upon a principle that I can no way grant; not only upon the negative of holy Scriptures, but of mine own Reason, whereby I can make it probable, that the World was as well peopled in the time of *Noah*, as in ours; and fifteen hundred years to people the World, as full a time for them, as four thousand years since have been to us. There are other assertions and common Tenents drawn from Scripture, and generally believed as Scripture, whereunto notwithstanding, I would never betray the liberty of my Reason. 'Tis a Paradox to me, that *Methusalem* was the longest liv'd of all the Children of *Adam*: and no man will be able to prove it; when from the process of the Text, I can manifest it may be otherwise. That *Judas* perished by hanging himself, there is no certainty in Scripture: though in one place it seems to affirm it, and by a doubtful word hath given occasion to translate it; yet in another place, in a more punctual description, it makes it improbable, and seems to overthrow it. That our Fathers, after the Flood, erected the Tower of *Babel* to preserve themselves against a second Deluge, is generally opinioned and believed, yet is there another intention of theirs expressed in Scripture: Besides, it is improbable from the circumstance of the place, that is, a plain in the Land of *Shinar*: These are no points of Faith, and therefore may admit a free dispute. There are yet others, and those familiarly concluded from the Text, wherein (under favour) I see no consequence: the Church of *Rome*, confidently proves the opinion of Tutelary Angels, from that Answer when *Peter* knockt at the Door; *'Tis not he, but his Angel*; that is, might some say, his Messenger, or some body from him; for so the Original signifies, and is as likely to be the doubtful Families meaning. This exposition I once suggested to a young Divine, that answered upon this point; to which I remember the *Franciscan* Opponent replyed no more, but That it was a new, and no authentick interpretation.

SECT. 23

These are but the conclusions and fallible discourses of man upon the Word of God, for such I do believe the holy Scriptures: yet were it of man, I could not chuse but say, it was the singularest and superlative piece that hath been extant since the Creation: were I a Pagan, I should not refrain the Lecture of it; and cannot but commend the judgment of *Ptolomy*, that thought not his Library compleat without it. The Alcoran of the *Turks* (I speak without prejudice) is an ill composed Piece, containing in it vain and ridiculous Errors in Philosophy, impossibilities, fictions, and vanities beyond laughter, maintained by evident and open Sophisms, the Policy of Ignorance, deposition of Universities, and banishment of Learning, that hath gotten Foot by Arms and violence: This without a blow, hath disseminated it self through the whole Earth. It is not unremarkable what *Philo* first observed, That the Law of *Moses* continued two thousand years without the least alteration; whereas, we see, the Laws of other Common-weals do alter with occasions; and even those, that pretended their Original from some Divinity, to have vanished without trace or memory. I believe besides *Zoroaster*, there were divers that writ before *Moses*, who, notwithstanding, have suffered the common fate of time. Mens Works have an age like themselves; and though they out-live their Authors, yet have they a stint and period to their duration: This only is a work too hard for the teeth of time, and cannot perish but in the general Flames, when all things shall confess their Ashes.

SECT. 24

I have heard some with deep sighs lament the lost lines of *Cicero*; others with as many groans deplore the combustion of the Library of *Alexandria*: for my own part, I think there be too many in the World, and could with patience behold the urn and ashes of the *Vatican*, could I, with a few others, recover the perished leaves of *Solomon*. I would not omit a Copy of *Enoch's* Pillars, had they many nearer Authors than *Josephus*, or did not relish somewhat of the Fable. Some men have written more than others have spoken; [12]*Pineda* quotes more Authors in one work, than are necessary in a whole World. Of those three great inventions in *Germany*, there are two which are not without their incommodities, and 'tis disputable whether they exceed not their use and commodities. 'Tis not a melancholy *Utinam* of my own, but the desires of better heads, that there were a general Synod; not to unite the incompatible difference of Religion, but for the benefit of learning, to reduce it as it lay at first, in a few, and solid Authors; and to condemn to the fire those swarms & millions of *Rhapsodies* begotten only to distract and abuse the weaker judgements of Scholars, and *to maintain the trade and mystery of Typographers*.

SECT. 25

I cannot but wonder with what exception the *Samaritans* could confine their belief to the *Pentateuch*, or five Books of *Moses*. I am ashamed at the Rabbinical Interpretation of the Jews, upon the Old Testament, as much as their defection from the New. And truly it is beyond wonder, how that contemptible and degenerate issue of *Jacob*, once so devoted to Ethnick Superstition, and so easily seduced to the Idolatry of their Neighbours, should now in such an obstinate and peremptory belief adhere unto their own Doctrine, expect impossibilities, and, in the face and eye of the Church, persist without the least hope of Conversion. This is a vice in them, that were a vertue in us; for obstinacy in a bad Cause is but constancy in a good. And herein I must accuse those of my own Religion; for there is not any of such a fugitive Faith, such an unstable belief, as a Christian; none that do so oft transform themselves, not unto several shapes of Christianity and of the same Species, but unto more unnatural and contrary Forms, of Jew and Mahometan; that, from the name of Saviour, can condescend to the bare term of Prophet; and from an old belief that he is come, fall to a new expectation of his coming. It is the promise of Christ to make us all one Flock; but how and when this Union shall be, is as obscure to me as the last day. Of those four Members of Religion we hold a slender proportion; there are, I confess, some new additions, yet small to those which accrew to our Adversaries, and those only drawn from the revolt of Pagans, men but of negative Impieties, and such as deny Christ, but because they never heard of him: but the Religion of the Jew is expressly against the Christian, and the Mahometan against both. For the Turk, in the bulk he now stands, he is beyond all hope of conversion; if he fall asunder, there may be conceived hopes, but not without strong improbabilities. The Jew is obstinate in all fortunes; the persecution of fifteen hundred years hath but confirmed them in their Errour: they have already endured whatsoever may be inflicted, and have suffered, in a bad cause, even to the condemnation of their enemies. Persecution is a bad and indirect way to plant Religion: It hath been the unhappy method of angry Devotions, not only to confirm honest Religion, but wicked Heresies, and extravagant Opinions. It was the first stone and Basis of our Faith; none can more justly boast of Persecutions, and glory in the number and valour of Martyrs; for, to speak properly, those are true and almost only examples of fortitude: Those that are fetch'd from the field, or drawn from the actions of the Camp, are not oft-times so truely precedents of valour as audacity, and at the best attain but to some bastard piece of fortitude: If we shall strictly examine the circumstances and requisites which *Aristotle* requires to true and perfect valour, we shall find the name only in his Master *Alexander*, and as little in that Roman Worthy, *Julius Cæsar*; and if any, in that easie and active way have done so nobly as to deserve that name, yet in the passive and more terrible piece these have surpassed, and in a more heroical way may claim the honour of that Title. 'Tis not in the power of every honest Faith to proceed thus far, or pass to Heaven through the flames; every one hath it not in that full measure, nor in so audacious and resolute a temper, as to endure those terrible tests and trials; who notwithstanding, in a peaceable way do truely adore their Saviour, and have (no doubt) a Faith acceptable in the eyes of God.

SECT. 26

Now as all that dye in the War are not termed Souldiers; so neither can I properly term all those that suffer in matters of Religion, Martyrs. The Council of *Constance* condemns *John Huss* for an Heretick; the Stories of his own Party stile him a Martyr: He must needs offend the Divinity of both, that says he was neither the one nor the other: There are many (questionless) canonised on earth, that shall never be Saints in Heaven; and have their names in Histories and Martyrologies, who in the eyes of God are not so perfect Martyrs, as was that wise Heathen *Socrates*, that suffered on a fundamental point of Religion, the Unity of God. I have often pitied the miserable Bishop that suffered in the cause of *Antipodes*, yet cannot chuse but accuse him of as much madness, for exposing his living on such a trifle; as those of ignorance and folly, that condemned him. I think my conscience will not give me the lye, if I say there are not many extant that in a noble way fear the face of death less than myself; yet, from the moral duty I owe to the Commandment of God, and the natural respects that I tender unto the conservation of my essence and being, I would not perish upon a Ceremony, Politick points, or indifferency: nor is my belief of that untractible temper, as not to bow at their obstacles, or connive at matters wherein there are not manifest impieties: The leaven therefore and ferment of all, not only Civil, but Religious actions, is Wisdom; without which, to commit our selves to the flames is Homicide, and (I fear) but to pass through one fire into another.

SECT.27

That Miracles are ceased, I can neither prove, nor absolutely deny, much less define the time and period of their cessation: that they survived Christ, is manifest upon the Record of Scripture: that they out-lived the Apostles also, and were revived at the Conversion of Nations, many years after, we cannot deny, if we shall not question those Writers whose testimonies we do not controvert in points that make for our own opinions; therefore that may have some truth in it that is reported by the Jesuites of their Miracles in the *Indies*; I could wish it were true, or had any other testimony than their own Pens. They may easily believe those Miracles abroad, who daily conceive a greater at home, the transmutation of those visible elements into the Body and Blood of our Saviour: for the conversion of Water into Wine, which he wrought in *Cana*, or what the Devil would have had him done in the Wilderness, of Stones into Bread, compared to this, will scarce deserve the name of a Miracle. Though indeed to speak properly, there is not one Miracle greater than another, they being the extraordinary effects of the Hand of God, to which all things are of an equal facility; and to create the World as easie as one single Creature. For this is also a Miracle, not onely to produce effects against, or above Nature, but before Nature; and to create Nature as great a Miracle as to contradict or transcend her. We do too narrowly define the Power of God, restraining it to our capacities. I hold that God can do all things; how he should work contradictions, I do not understand, yet dare not therefore deny. I cannot see why the Angel of God should question *Esdras* to recal the time past, if it were beyond his own power; or that God should pose mortality in that, which he was not able to perform himself. I will not say God cannot, but he will not perform many things, which we plainly affirm he cannot: this I am sure is the mannerliest proposition, wherein, notwithstanding, I hold no Paradox. For strictly his power is the same with his will, and they both with all the rest do make but one God.

SECT.28

Therefore that Miracles have been, I do believe; that they may yet be wrought by the living, I do not deny: but have no confidence in those which are fathered on the dead; and this hath ever made me suspect the efficacy of reliques, to examine the bones, question the habits and appurtenances of Saints, and even of Christ himself. I cannot conceive why the Cross that *Helena* found, and whereon Christ himself dyed, should have power to restore others unto life: I excuse not *Constantine* from a fall off his Horse, or a mischief from his enemies, upon the wearing those nails on his bridle, which our Saviour bore upon the Cross in his hands. I compute among *Piæ fraudes*, nor many degrees before consecrated Swords and Roses, that which *Baldwyn*, King of *Jerusalem*, return'd the *Genovese* for their cost and pains in his War, to wit, the ashes of *John* the Baptist. Those that hold the sanctity of their Souls doth leave behind a tincture and sacred faculty on their bodies, speak naturally of Miracles, and do not salve the doubt. Now one reason I tender so little Devotion unto Reliques, is, I think, the slender and doubtful respect I have always held unto Antiquities: for that indeed which I admire, is far before Antiquity, that is, Eternity; and that is, God himself; who, though he be styled the ancient of days, cannot receive the adjunct of Antiquity, who was before the World, and shall be after it, yet is not older than it; for in his years there is no Climacter; his duration is Eternity, and far more venerable than Antiquity.

SECT.29

But above all things I wonder how the curiosity of wiser heads could pass that great and indisputable Miracle, the cessation of Oracles; and in what swoun their Reasons lay, to content themselves, and sit down with such a far-fetch'd and ridiculous reason as *Plutarch* alleadgeth for it. The Jews, that can believe the supernatural Solstice of the Sun in the days of *Joshua*, have yet the impudence to deny the Eclipse, which every Pagan confessed, at his death: but for this, it is evident beyond all contradiction,[13] the Devil himself confessed it. Certainly it is not a warrantable curiosity, to examine the verity of Scripture by the concordance of humane history, or seek to confirm the Chronicle of *Hester* or *Daniel* by the authority of *Megasthenes* or *Herodotus*. I confess, I have had an unhappy curiosity this way, till I laughed my self out of it with a piece of *Justine*, where he delivers that the Children of *Israel* for being scabbed were banished out of *Egypt*. And truely since I have understood the occurrences of the World, and know in what counterfeit shapes, and deceitful vizards times present represent on the stage things past; I do believe them little more then things to come. Some have been of my opinion, and endeavoured to write the History of their own lives; wherein *Moses* hath outgone them all, and left not onely the story of his life, but as some will have it, of his death also.

SECT.30

It is a riddle to me, how this story of Oracles hath not worm'd out of the World that doubtful conceit of Spirits and Witches; how so many learned heads should so far forget their Metaphysicks, and destroy the ladder and scale of creatures, as to question the existence of Spirits: for my part, I have ever believed, and do now know, that there are Witches: they that doubt of these, do not onely deny them, but spirits; and are obliquely and upon consequence a sort not of Infidels, but Atheists. Those that to confute their incredulity desire to see apparitions, shall questionless never behold any, nor have the power to be so much as Witches; the Devil hath them already in a heresie as capital as Witchcraft; and to appear to them, were but to convert them. Of all the delusions wherewith he deceives mortality, there is not any that puzleth me more than the Legerdemain of *Changelings*; I do not credit those transformations of reasonable creatures into beasts, or that the Devil hath a power to transpeciate a man into a Horse, who tempted Christ (as a trial of his Divinity) to convert but stones into bread. I could believe that Spirits use with man the act of carnality, and that in both sexes; I conceive they may assume, steal, or contrive a body, wherein there may be action enough to content decrepit lust, or passion to satisfie more active veneries; yet in both, without a possibility of generation: and therefore that opinion that Antichrist should be born of the Tribe of *Dan*, by conjunction with the Devil, is ridiculous, and a conceit fitter for a Rabbin than a Christian. I hold that the Devil doth really possess some men, the spirit of Melancholly others, the spirit of Delusion others; that as the Devil is concealed and denyed by some, so God and good Angels are pretended by others whereof the late defection of the Maid of *Germany* hath left a pregnant example.

Sect. 31

Again, I believe that all that use sorceries, incantations, and spells, are not Witches, or, as we term them, Magicians; I conceive there is a traditional Magick, not learned immediately from the Devil, but at second hand from his Scholars, who having once the secret betrayed, are able, and do emperically practise without his advice, they both proceeding upon the principles of Nature; where actives, aptly conjoyned to disposed passives, will under any Master produce their effects. Thus I think at first a great part of Philosophy was Witchcraft, which being afterward derived to one another, proved but Philosophy, and was indeed no more but the honest effects of Nature: What invented by us is Philosophy, learned from him is Magick. We do surely owe the discovery of many secrets to the discovery of good and bad Angels. I could never pass that sentence of *Paracelsus*, without an asterisk, or annotation; [14]*Ascendens constellatum multa revelat, quærentibus magnalia naturæ*, i.e. *opera Dei*. I do think that many mysteries ascribed to our own inventions, have been the courteous revelations of Spirits; for those noble essences in Heaven bear a friendly regard unto their fellow Natures on Earth; and therefore believe that those many prodigies and ominous prognosticks, which fore-run the ruines of States, Princes, and private persons, are the charitable premonitions of good Angels, which more careless enquiries term but the effects of chance and nature.

SECT.32

Now, besides these particular and divided Spirits, there may be (for ought I know) an universal and common Spirit to the whole World. It was the opinion of *Plato*, and it is yet of the *Hermetical* Philosophers: if there be a common nature that unites and tyes the scattered and divided individuals into one species, why may there not be one that unites them all? However, I am sure there is a common Spirit that plays within us, yet makes no part of us; and that is the Spirit of God, the fire and scintillation of that noble and mighty Essence, which is the life and radical heat of Spirits, and those essences that know not the vertue of the Sun, a fire quite contrary to the fire of Hell: This is that gentle heat that broodeth on the waters, and in six days hatched the World; this is that irradiation that dispels the mists of Hell, the clouds of horrour, fear, sorrow, despair; and preserves the region of the mind in serenity: Whatsoever feels not the warm gale and gentle ventilation of this Spirit, (though I feel his pulse) I dare not say he lives; for truely without this, to me there is no heat under the Tropick; nor any light, though I dwelt in the body of the Sun.

As when the labouring Sun hath wrought his track
Up to the top of lofty Cancers *back,*
The ycie Ocean cracks, the frozen pole
Thaws with the heat of the Celestial coale;
So when thy absent beams begin t' impart
Again a Solstice on my frozen heart,
My winter 's ov'r; my drooping spirits sing,
And every part revives into a Spring.
But if thy quickening beams a while decline,
And with their light bless not this Orb of mine,
A chilly frost surpriseth every member,
And in the midst of June *I feel December.*
O how this earthly temper doth debase
The noble Soul in this her humble place.
Whose wingy nature ever doth aspire
To reach that place whence first it took its fire.
These flames I feel, which in my heart do dwell,
Are not thy beams, but take their fire from Hell.
O quench them all, and let thy light divine
Be as the Sun to this poor Orb of mine;
And to thy sacred Spirit convert those fires,
Whose earthly fumes choak my devout aspires.

SECT.33

Therefore for Spirits, I am so far from denying their existence, that I could easily believe, that not onely whole Countries, but particular persons, have their Tutelary and Guardian Angels: It is not a new opinion of the Church of *Rome*, but an old one of *Pythagoras* and *Plato*; there is no heresie in it; and if not manifestly defin'd in Scripture, yet is it an opinion of a good and wholesome use in the course and actions of a mans life, and would serve as an *Hypothesis* to salve many doubts, whereof common Philosophy affordeth no solution. Now if you demand my opinion and Metaphysicks of their natures, I confess them very shallow, most of them in a negative way, like that of God; or in a comparative, between our selves and fellow-creatures; for there is in this Universe a Stair, or manifest Scale of creatures, rising not disorderly, or in confusion, but with a comely method and proportion. Between creatures of meer existence and things of life, there is a large disproportion of nature; between plants and animals or creatures of sense, a wider difference; between them and man, a far greater: and if the proportion hold one, between Man and Angels there should be yet a greater. We do not comprehend their natures, who retain the first definition of *Porphyry*, and distinguish them from our selves by immortality; for before his Fall, 'tis thought,

Man also was Immortal; yet must we needs affirm that he had a different essence from the Angels; having therefore no certain knowledge of their Natures, 'tis no bad method of the Schools, whatsoever perfection we find obscurely in our selves, in a more compleat and absolute way to ascribe unto them. I believe they have an extemporary knowledge, and upon the first motion of their reason do what we cannot without study or deliberation; that they know things by their forms, and define by specifical difference what we describe by accidents and properties; and therefore probabilities to us may be demonstrations unto them: that they have knowledge not onely of the specifical, but numerical forms of individuals, and understand by what reserved difference each single *Hypostasis* (besides the relation to its species) becomes its numerical self. That as the Soul hath a power to move the body it informs, so there's a faculty to move any, though inform none; ours upon restraint of time, place, and distance; but that invisible hand that conveyed *Habakkuk* to the Lyons Den, or *Philip* to *Azotus*, infringeth this rule, and hath a secret conveyance, wherewith mortality is not acquainted: if they have that intuitive knowledge, whereby as in reflexion they behold the thoughts of one another, I cannot peremptorily deny but they know a great part of ours. They that to refute the Invocation of Saints, have denied that they have any knowledge of our affairs below, have proceeded too far, and must pardon my opinion, till I can thoroughly answer that piece of Scripture, *At the conversion of a sinner the Angels in Heaven rejoyce*. I cannot with those in that great Father securely interpret the work of the first day, *Fiat lux*, to the creation of Angels, though I confess there is not any creature that hath so neer a glympse of their nature, as light in the Sun and Elements. We stile it a bare accident, but where it subsists alone, 'tis a spiritual Substance, and may be an Angel: in brief, conceive light invisible, and that is a Spirit.

SECT.34

These are certainly the Magisterial and master-pieces of the Creator, the Flower, or (as we may say) the best part of nothing, actually existing, what we are but in hopes and probability; we are onely that amphibious piece between a corporal and spiritual Essence, that middle form that links those two together, and makes good the Method of God and Nature, that jumps not from extreams, but unites the incompatible distances by some middle and participating natures: that we are the breath and similitude of God, it is indisputable, and upon record of holy Scripture; but to call ourselves a Microcosm, or little World, I thought it only a pleasant trope of Rhetorick, till my neer judgement and second thoughts told me there was a real truth therein: for first we are a rude mass, and in the rank of creatures, which onely are, and have a dull kind of being, not yet privileged with life, or preferred to sense or reason; next we live the life of Plants, the life of Animals, the life of Men, and at last the life of Spirits, running on in one mysterious nature those five kinds of existences, which comprehend the creatures not onely of the World, but of the Universe; thus is man that great and true *Amphibium*, whose nature is disposed to live not onely like other creatures in divers elements, but in divided and distinguished worlds: for though there be but one to sense, there are two to reason, the one visible, the other invisible, whereof *Moses* seems to have left description, and of the other so obscurely, that some parts thereof are yet in controversie. And truely for the first chapters of *Genesis*, I must confess a great deal of obscurity; though Divines have to the power of humane reason endeavoured to make all go in a literal meaning, yet those allegorical interpretations are also probable, and perhaps the mystical method of *Moses* bred up in the Hieroglyphical Schools of the Egyptians.

SECT.35

Now for that immaterial world, methinks we need not wander so far as beyond the first moveable; for even in this material Fabrick the spirits walk as freely exempt from the affection of time, place, and motion, as beyond the extreamest circumference: do but extract from the corpulency of bodies, or resolve things beyond their first matter, and you discover the habitation of Angels, which if I call the ubiquitary and omnipresent essence of God, I hope I shall not offend Divinity: for before the Creation of the World God was really all things. For the Angels he created no new World, or determinate mansion, and therefore they are everywhere where is his Essence, and do live at a distance even in himself. That God made all things for man, is in some sense true, yet not so far as to subordinate the Creation of those purer Creatures unto ours, though as ministring Spirits they do, and are willing to fulfil the will of God in these lower and sublunary affairs of man: God made all things for himself, and it is impossible he should make them for any other end than his own Glory; it is all he can receive, and all that is without himself: for honour being an external adjunct, and in the honourer rather than in the person honoured, it was necessary to make a Creature, from whom he might receive this homage; and that is in the other world Angels, in this, Man; which when we neglect, we forget the very end of our Creation, and may justly provoke God, not onely to repent that he hath made the World, but that he hath sworn he would not destroy it. That there is but one World, is a conclusion of Faith. *Aristotle* with all his Philosophy hath not been able to prove it, and as weakly that the world was eternal; that dispute much troubled the Pen of the Philosophers, but *Moses* decided that question, and all is salved with the new term of a Creation, that is, a production of something out of nothing; and what is that? Whatsoever is opposite to something; or more exactly, that which is truely contrary unto God; for he onely is, all others have an existence with dependency, and are something but by a distinction; and herein is Divinity conformant unto Philosophy, and generation not onely founded on contrarieties, but also creation; God being all things, is contrary unto nothing, out of which were made all things, and so nothing became something, and *Omneity* informed *Nullity* into an Essence.

SECT.36

The whole Creation is a Mystery, and particularly that of Man; at the blast of his mouth were the rest of the Creatures made, and at his bare word they started out of nothing: but in the frame of Man (as the Text describes it) he played the sensible operator, and seemed not so much to create, as make him; when he had separated the materials of other creatures, there consequently resulted a form and soul; but having raised the walls of man, he has driven to a second and harder creation of a substance like himself, an incorruptible and immortal Soul. For these two affections we have the Philosophy and opinion of the Heathens, the flat affirmative of *Plato*, and not a negative from *Aristotle*: there is another scruple cast in by Divinity (concerning its production) much disputed in the *Germane* auditories, and with that indifferency and equality of arguments, as leave the controversie undetermined. I am not of *Paracelsus* mind, that boldly delivers a receipt to make a man without conjunction; yet cannot but wonder at the multitude of heads that do deny traduction, having no other argument to confirm their belief, then that Rhetorical sentence, and *Antimetathesis* of *Augustine*, *Creando infunditur, infundendo creatur*: either opinion will consist well enough with Religion; yet I should rather incline to this, did not one objection haunt me, not wrung from speculations and subtilties, but from common sense and observation; not pickt from the leaves of any Author, but bred amongst the weeds and tares of mine own brain: And this is a conclusion from the equivocal and monstrous productions in the copulation of Man with Beast: for if the Soul of man be not transmitted, and transfused in the seed of the Parents, why are not those productions meerly beasts, but have also an impression and tincture of reason in as high a measure, as it can evidence it self in those improper Organs? Nor truely can I peremptorily deny, that the Soul in this her sublunary estate, is wholly, and in all acceptions inorganical, but that for the performance of her ordinary actions, there is required not onely a symmetry and proper disposition of Organs, but a Crasis and temper correspondent to its operations. Yet is not this mass of flesh and visible structure the instrument and proper corps of the Soul, but rather of Sense, and that the hand of Reason. In our study of Anatomy there is a mass of mysterious Philosophy, and such as reduced the very Heathens to Divinity: yet amongst all those rare discourses, and curious pieces I find in the Fabrick of man, I do not so much content my self, as in that I find not, there is no Organ or Instrument for the rational soul: for in the brain, which we term the seat of reason, there is not any thing of moment more than I can discover in the crany of a beast: and this is a sensible and no inconsiderable argument of the inorganity of the Soul, at least in that sense we usually so conceive it. Thus we are men, and we know not how; there is something in us that can be without us, and will be after us, though it is strange that it hath no history, what it was before us, nor cannot tell how it entred in us.

SECT.37

Now for these walls of flesh, wherein the Soul doth seem to be immured, before the Resurrection, it is nothing but an elemental composition, and a Fabrick that must fall to ashes. *All flesh is grass*, is not onely metaphorically, but litterally, true; for all those creatures we behold, are but the herbs of the field, digested into flesh in them, or more remotely carnified in our selves. Nay further, we are what we all abhor, *Anthropophagi* and Cannibals, devourers not onely of men, but of our selves; and that not in an allegory, but a positive truth: for all this mass of flesh which we behold, came in at our mouths; this frame we look upon, hath been upon our trenchers; in brief, we have devour'd our selves. I cannot believe the wisdom of *Pythagoras* did ever positively, and in a literal sense, affirm his *Metempsychosis*, or impossible transmigration of the Souls of men into beasts: of all Metamorphoses, or transmigrations, I believe only one, that is of *Lots* wife; for that of *Nebuchodonosor* proceeded not so far; in all others I conceive there is no further verity than is contained in their implicite sense and morality. I believe that the whole frame of a beast doth perish, and is left in the same state after death as before it was materialled unto life; that the souls of men know neither contrary nor corruption; that they subsist beyond the body, and outlive death by the priviledge of their proper natures, and without a Miracle; that the Souls of the faithful, as they leave Earth, take possession of Heaven: that those apparitions and ghosts of departed persons are not the wandring souls of men, but the unquiet walks of Devils, prompting and suggesting us unto mischief, blood, and villany; instilling and stealing into our hearts that the blessed spirits are not at rest in their graves, but wander sollicitous of the affairs of the World; but that those phantasms appear often, and do frequent Cœmeteries, Charnel-houses, and Churches, it is because those are the dormitories of the dead, where the Devil like an insolent Champion beholds with pride the spoils and Trophies of his Victory over *Adam*.

SECT.38
This is that dismal conquest we all deplore, that makes us so often cry *(O) Adam, quid fecisti?* I thank God I have not those strait ligaments, or narrow obligations to the World, as to dote on life, or be convulst and tremble at the name of death: Not that I am insensible of the dread and horrour thereof, or by raking into the bowels of the deceased, continual sight of Anatomies, Skeletons, or Cadaverous reliques, like Vespilloes, or Gravemakers, I am become stupid, or have forgot the apprehension of Mortality; but that marshalling all the horrours, and contemplating the extremities thereof, I find not any thing therein able to daunt the courage of a man, much less a well-resolved Christian: And therefore am not angry at the errour of our first Parents, or unwilling to bear a part of this common fate, and like the best of them to dye, that is, to cease to breathe, to take a farewel of the elements, to be a kind of nothing for a moment, to be within one instant of a spirit. When I take a full view and circle of my self, without this reasonable moderator, and equal piece of Justice, Death, I do conceive my self the miserablest person extant; were there not another life that I hope for, all the vanities of this World should not intreat a moment's breath from me: could the Devil work my belief to imagine I could never dye, I would not outlive that very thought; I have so abject a conceit of this common way of existence, this retaining to the Sun and Elements, I cannot think this is to be a man, or to live according to the dignity of humanity: in exspectation of a better, I can with patience embrace this life, yet in my best meditations do often defie death: I honour any man that contemns it, nor can I highly love any that is afraid of it: this makes me naturally love a Souldier, and honour those tattered and contemptible Regiments, that will dye at the command of a Sergeant. For a Pagan there may be some motives to be in love with life; but for a Christian to be amazed at death, I see not how he can escape this Dilemma, that he is too sensible of this life, or hopeless of the life to come.

SECT.39
Some Divines count Adam 30 years old at his creation, because they suppose him created in the perfect age and stature of man. And surely we are all out of the computation of our age, and every man is some months elder than he bethinks him; for we live, move, have a being, and are subject to the actions of the elements, and the malice of diseases, in that other world, the truest Microcosm, the Womb of our Mother. For besides that general and common existence we are conceived to hold in our Chaos, and whilst we sleep within the bosome of our causes, we enjoy a being and life in three distinct worlds, wherein we receive most manifest graduations: In that obscure World and womb of our mother, our time is short, computed by the Moon; yet longer then the days of many creatures that behold the Sun, our selves being not yet without life, sense, and reason; though for the manifestation of its actions, it awaits the opportunity of objects, and seems to live there but in its root and soul of vegetation; entring afterwards upon the scene of the World,

we arise up and become another creature, performing the reasonable actions of man, and obscurely manifesting that part of Divinity in us, but not in complement and perfection, till we have once more cast our secondine, that is, this slough of flesh, and are delivered into the last world, that is, that ineffable place of *Paul*, that proper *ubi* of spirits. The smattering I have of the Philosophers Stone (which is something more then the perfect exaltation of Gold) hath taught me a great deal of Divinity, and instructed my belief, how that immortal spirit and incorruptible substance of my Soul may lye obscure, and sleep a while within this house of flesh. Those strange and mystical transmigrations that I have observed in Silk-worms, turned my Philosophy into Divinity. There is in these works of nature, which seem to puzzle reason, something Divine, and hath more in it then the eye of a common spectator doth discover.

SECT.40

I am naturally bashful, nor hath conversation, age or travel, been able to effront, or enharden me; yet I have one part of modesty which I have seldom discovered in another, that is, (to speak truely) I am not so much afraid of death, as ashamed thereof; 'tis the very disgrace and ignominy of our natures, that in a moment can so disfigure us, that our nearest friends, Wife, and Children stand afraid and start at us. The Birds and Beasts of the field, that before in a natural fear obeyed us, forgetting all allegiance, begin to prey upon us. This very conceit hath in a tempest disposed and left me willing to be swallowed up in the abyss of waters; wherein I had perished unseen, unpityed, without wondering eyes, tears of pity, Lectures of mortality, and none had said, *Quantum mutatus ab illo!* Not that I am ashamed of the Anatomy of my parts, or can accuse Nature for playing the bungler in any part of me, or my own vitious life for contracting any shameful disease upon me, whereby I might not call my self as wholesome a morsel for the worms as any.

SECT.41

Some upon the courage of a fruitful issue, wherein, as in the truest Chronicle, they seem to outlive themselves, can with greater patience away with death. This conceit and counterfeit subsisting in our progenies, seems to me a meer fallacy, unworthy the desires of a man, that can but conceive a thought of the next World; who, in a nobler ambition, should desire to live in his substance in Heaven, rather than his name and shadow in the earth. And therefore at my death I mean to take a total adieu of the world, not caring for a Monument, History, or Epitaph, not so much as the memory of my name to be found any where, but in the universal Register of God. I am not yet so Cynical, as to approve the [15]Testament of *Diogenes*, nor do I altogether allow that *Rodomontodo* of Lucan;

——*Cœlo tegitur, qui non habet urnam.*
He that unburied lies wants not his Herse,
For unto him a Tomb's the Universe.

But commend in my calmer judgement, those ingenuous intentions that desire to sleep by the urns of their Fathers, and strive to go the neatest way unto corruption. I do not envy the temper of Crows and Daws, nor the numerous and weary days of our Fathers before the Flood. If there be any truth in Astrology, I may outlive a Jubilee; as yet I have not seen one revolution of Saturn, nor hath my pulse beat thirty years; and yet excepting one, have seen the Ashes, & left under ground all the Kings of *Europe*; have been contemporary to three Emperours, four Grand Signiours, and as many Popes: methinks I have outlived my self, and begin to be weary of the Sun; I have shaken hands with delight: in my warm blood and Canicular days, I perceive I do anticipate the vices of age; the World to me is but a dream or mock-show, and we all therein but Pantalones and Anticks, to my severer contemplations.

SECT.42

It is not, I confess, an unlawful prayer to desire to surpass the days of our Saviour, or wish to outlive that age wherein he thought fittest to dye; yet if (as Divinity affirms) there shall be no gray hairs in Heaven, but all shall rise in the perfect state of men, we do but outlive those perfections in this World, to be recalled unto them by a greater Miracle in the next, and run on here but to be retrograde hereafter. Were there any hopes to outlive vice, or a point to be super-annuated from sin, it were worthy our knees to implore the days of *Methuselah*. But age doth not rectifie, but incurvate our natures, turning bad dispositions into worser habits, and (like diseases) brings on incurable vices; for every day as we grow weaker in age, we grow stronger in sin; and the number of our days doth make but our sins innumerable. The same vice committed at sixteen, is not the same, though it agree in all other circumstances, at forty, but swells and doubles from the circumstance of our ages, wherein, besides the constant and inexcusable habit of transgressing, the maturity of our judgement cuts off pretence unto excuse or pardon: every sin the oftner it is committed, the more it acquireth in the quality of evil; as it succeeds in time, so it proceeds in degrees of badness; for as they proceed they ever multiply, and like figures in Arithmetick, the last stands for more than all that went before it. And though I think no man can live well once, but he that could live twice, yet for my own part I would not live over my hours past, or begin again the thred of my days: not upon *Cicero's* ground, because I have lived them well, but for fear I should live them worse: I find my growing Judgment daily instruct me how to be better, but my untamed affections and confirmed vitiosity makes me daily do worse; I find in my confirmed age the same sins I discovered in my youth; I committed many then because I was a Child, and because I commit them still, I am yet an infant. Therefore I perceive a man may be twice a Child before the days of dotage; and stands in need of *Æsons* Bath before threescore.

SECT.43

And truely there goes a great deal of providence to produce a mans life unto three-score: there is more required than an able temper for those years; though the radical humour contain in it sufficient oyl for seventy, yet I perceive in some it gives no light past thirty: men assign not all the causes of long life, that write whole Books thereof. They that found themselves on the radical balsome, or vital sulphur of the parts, determine not why *Abel* lived not so long as *Adam*. There is therefore a secret glome or bottome of our days: 'twas his wisdom to determine them, but his perpetual and waking providence that fulfils and accomplisheth them; wherein the spirits, our selves, and all the creatures of God in a secret and disputed way do execute his will. Let them not therefore complain of immaturity that die about thirty; they fall but like the whole World, whose solid and well-composed substance must not expect the duration and period of its constitution: when all things are compleated in it, its age is accomplished; and the last and general fever may as naturally destroy it before six thousand, as me before forty; there is therefore some other hand that twines the thread of life than that of Nature: we are not onely ignorant in Antipathies and occult qualities; our ends are as obscure as our beginnings; the line of our days is drawn by night, and the various effects therein by a pensil that is invisible; wherein though we confess our ignorance, I am sure we do not err if we say it is the hand of God.

SECT.44

I am much taken with two verses of *Lucan*, since I have been able not onely as we do at School, to construe, but understand.

Victurosque Dei celant ut vivere durent.
Felix esse mori.
We're all deluded, vainly searching ways
To make us happy by the length of days;
For cunningly to make's protract this breath,
The Gods conceal the happiness of Death.

There be many excellent strains in that Poet, wherewith his Stoical Genius hath liberally supplied him; and truely there are singular pieces in the Philosophy of *Zeno*, and doctrine of the Stoicks, which I perceive, delivered in a Pulpit, pass for current Divinity: yet herein are they in extreams, that can allow a man to be his own *Assassine*, and so highly extol the end and suicide of *Cato*; this is indeed not to fear death, but yet to be afraid of life. It is a brave act of valour to contemn death; but where life is more terrible than death, it is then the truest valour to dare to live; and herein Religion hath taught us a noble example: For all the valiant acts of *Curtius*, *Scevola*, or *Codrus*, do not parallel or match that one of *Job*; and sure there is no torture to the rack of a disease, nor any Ponyards in death it self like those in the way or prologue to it. *Emori nolo, sed me esse mortuum nihil curo*; I would not die, but care not to be dead. Were I of *Cæsar's* Religion, I should be of his desires, and wish rather to go off at one blow, then to be sawed in pieces by the grating torture of a disease. Men that look no farther than their outsides, think health an appurtenance unto life, and quarrel with their constitutions for being sick; but I, that have examined the parts of man, and know upon what tender filaments that Fabrick hangs, do wonder that we are not always so; and considering the thousand doors that lead to death, do thank my God that we can die but once. 'Tis not onely the mischief of diseases, and villany of poysons, that make an end of us; we vainly accuse the fury of Guns, and the new inventions of death; it is in the power of every hand to destroy us, and we are beholding unto every one we meet, he doth not kill us. There is therefore but one comfort left, that, though it be in the power of the weakest arm to take away life, it is not in the strongest to deprive us of death: God would not exempt himself from that, the misery of immortality in the flesh; he undertook not that was immortal. Certainly there is no happiness within this circle of flesh, nor is it in the Opticks of these eyes to behold felicity; the first day of our Jubilee is Death; the Devil hath therefore failed of his desires; we are happier with death than we should have been without it: there is no misery but in himself, where there is no end of misery; and so indeed in his own sense the Stoick is in the right. He forgets that he can dye who complains of misery; we are in the power of no calamity while death is in our own.

SECT.45

Now besides the literal and positive kind of death, there are others whereof Divines make mention, and those I think, not meerly Metaphorical, as mortification, dying unto sin and the World; therefore, I say, every man hath a double Horoscope, one of his humanity, his birth; another of his Christianity, his baptism, and from this do I compute or calculate my Nativity; not reckoning those *Horæ combustæ* and odd days, or esteeming my self any thing, before I was my Saviours, and inrolled in the Register of Christ: Whosoever enjoys not this life, I count him but an apparition, though he wear about him the sensible affections of flesh. In these moral acceptions, the way to be immortal is to dye daily; nor can I think I have the true Theory of death, when I contemplate a skull, or behold a Skeleton with those vulgar imaginations it casts upon us; I have therefore enlarged that common *Memento mori*, into a more Christian memorandum, *Memento quatuor Novissima*, those four inevitable points of us all, Death, Judgement, Heaven, and Hell. Neither did the contemplations of the Heathens rest in their graves, without further thought of Rhadamanth or some judicial proceeding after death, though in another way, and upon suggestion of their natural reasons. I cannot but marvail from what *Sibyl* or Oracle they stole the Prophesie of the worlds destruction by fire, or whence *Lucan* learned to say,

Communis mundo superest rogus, assibus astra Misturus.
There yet remains to th' World one common Fire,
Wherein our bones with stars shall make one Pyre.

I believe the World grows near its end, yet is neither old nor decayed, nor shall ever perish upon the ruines of its own Principles. As the work of Creation was above nature, so its adversary annihilation; without which the World hath not its end, but its mutation. Now what force should be able to consume it thus far, without the breath of God, which is the truest consuming flame, my Philosophy cannot inform me. Some believe there went not a minute to the Worlds creation, nor shall there go to its destruction; those six days, so punctually described, make not to them one moment, but rather seem to manifest the method and Idea of the great work of the intellect of God, than the manner how he proceeded in its operation. I cannot dream that there should be at the last day any such Judicial proceeding, or calling to the Bar, as indeed the Scripture seems to imply, and the literal Commentators do conceive: for unspeakable mysteries in the Scriptures are often delivered in a vulgar and illustrative way; and being written unto man, are delivered, not as they truely are, but as they may be understood; wherein notwithstanding the different interpretations according to different capacities may stand firm with our devotion, nor be any way prejudicial to each single edification.

SECT.46

In those days there shall come lyars and false prophets.

Now to determine the day and year of this inevitable time, is not onely convincible and statute-madness, but also manifest impiety: How shall we interpret *Elias* 6000 years, or imagine the secret communicated to a Rabbi, which God hath denyed unto his Angels? It had been an excellent Quære to have posed the Devil of *Delphos*, and must needs have forced him to some strange amphibology; it hath not onely mocked the predictions of sundry Astrologers in Ages past, but the prophesies of many melancholy heads in these present, who neither understanding reasonably things past or present, pretend a knowledge of things to come; heads ordained onely to manifest the incredible effects of melancholy, and to fulfil old prophecies rather than be the authors of new. In those days there shall come Wars and rumours of Wars, to me seems no prophecy, but a constant truth, in all times verified since it was pronounced: There shall be signs in the Moon and Stars; how comes he then like a Thief in the night, when he gives an item of his coming? That common sign drawn from the revelation of Antichrist, is as obscure as any: in our common compute he hath been come these many years; but for my own part to speak freely, I am half of opinion that Antichrist is the Philosophers stone in Divinity; for the discovery and invention thereof, though there be prescribed rules and probable inductions, yet hath hardly any man attained the perfect discovery thereof. That general opinion that the World grows neer its end, hath possessed all ages past as neerly as ours; I am afraid that the Souls that now depart, cannot escape that lingring expostulation of the Saints under the Altar, *Quousque, Domine? How long, O Lord?* and groan in the expectation of that great Jubilee.

SECT.47

This is the day that must make good that great attribute of God, his Justice; that must reconcile those unanswerable doubts that torment the wisest understandings, and reduce those seeming inequalities, and respective distributions in this world, to an equality and recompensive Justice in the next. This is that one day, that shall include and comprehend all that went before it; wherein, as in the last scene, all the Actors must enter, to compleat and make up the Catastrophe of this great piece. This is the day whose memory hath onely power to make us honest in the dark, and to be vertuous without a witness. *Ipsa sui pretium virtus sibi*, that Vertue is her own reward, is but a cold principle, and not able to maintain our variable resolutions in a constant and setled way of goodness. I have practised that honest artifice of *Seneca*, and in my retired and solitary imaginations, to detain me from the foulness of vice, have fancied to my self the presence of my dear and worthiest friends, before whom I should lose my head, rather than be vitious: yet herein I found that there was nought but moral honesty, and this was not to be vertuous for his sake who must reward us at the last. I have tryed if I could reach that great resolution of his, to be honest without a thought of Heaven or Hell; and indeed I found, upon a natural inclination, and inbred loyalty unto virtue, that I could serve her without a livery; yet not in that resolved and venerable way, but that the frailty of my nature, upon[A] easie temptation, might be induced to forget her. The life therefore and spirit of all our actions, is the resurrection, and a stable apprehension that our ashes shall enjoy the fruit of our pious endeavours: without this, all Religion is a fallacy, and those impieties of *Lucian*, *Euripides*, and *Julian*, are no blasphemies, but subtle verities, and Atheists have been the onely Philosophers.

[A]*Insert* any, 1672.

SECT.48

How shall the dead arise, is no question of my Faith; to believe only possibilities, is not Faith, but meer Philosophy. Many things are true in Divinity, which are neither inducible by reason, nor confirmable by sense; and many things in Philosophy confirmable by sense, yet not inducible by reason. Thus it is impossible by any solid or demonstrative reasons to perswade a man to believe the conversion of the Needle to the North; though this be possible and true, and easily credible, upon a single experiment unto the sense. I believe that our estranged and divided ashes shall unite again; that our separated dust after so many Pilgrimages and transformations into the parts of Minerals, Plants, Animals, Elements, shall at the Voice of God return into their primitive shapes, and joyn again to make up their primary and predestinate forms. As at the Creation there was a separation of that confused mass into its pieces; so at the destruction thereof there shall be a separation into its distinct individuals. As at the Creation of the World, all the distinct species that we behold lay involved in one mass, till the fruitful Voice of God separated this united multitude into its several species: so at the last day, when those corrupted reliques shall be scattered in the Wilderness of forms, and seem to have forgot their proper habits, God by a powerful Voice shall command them back into their proper shapes, and call them out by their single individuals: Then shall appear the fertility of *Adam*, and the magick of that sperm that hath dilated into so many millions. I have often beheld as a miracle, that artificial resurrection and revivification of *Mercury*, how being mortified into a thousand shapes, it assumes again its own, and returns into its numerical self. Let us speak naturally, and like Philosophers, the forms of alterable bodies in these sensible corruptions perish not; nor as we imagine, wholly quit their mansions, but retire and contract themselves into their secret and inaccessible parts, where they may best protect themselves from the action of their Antagonist. A plant or vegetable consumed to ashes, by a contemplative and school-Philosopher seems utterly destroyed, and the form to have taken his leave for ever: But to a sensible Artist the forms are not perished, but withdrawn into their incombustible part, where they lie secure from the action of that devouring element. This is made good by experience, which can from the Ashes of a Plant revive the plant, and from its cinders recal it into its stalk and leaves again. What the Art of man can do in these inferiour pieces, what blasphemy is it to affirm the finger of God cannot do in these more perfect and sensible structures? This is that mystical Philosophy, from whence no true Scholar becomes an Atheist, but from the visible effects of nature grows up a real Divine, and beholds not in a dream, as *Ezekiel*, but in an ocular and visible object the types of his resurrection.

SECT.49

Now, the necessary Mansions of our restored selves, are those two contrary and incompatible places we call Heaven and Hell; to define them, or strictly to determine what and where these are, surpasseth my Divinity. That elegant Apostle which seemed to have a glimpse of Heaven, hath left but a negative description thereof; *which neither eye hath seen, nor ear hath heard, nor can enter into the heart of man*: he was translated out of himself to behold it; but being returned into himself, could not express it. St. *John's* description by Emerals, Chrysolites, and precious Stones, is too weak to express the material Heaven we behold. Briefly therefore, where the Soul hath the full measure and complement of happiness; where the boundless appetite of that spirit remains compleatly satisfied, that it can neither desire addition nor alteration; that I think is truly Heaven: and this can onely be in the injoynient of that essence, whose infinite goodness is able to terminate the desires of it self, and the unsatiable wishes of ours; wherever God will thus manifest himself, there is Heaven though within the circle of this sensible world. Thus the Soul of man may be in Heaven any where, even within the limits of his own proper body; and when it ceaseth to live in the body, it may remain in its own soul, that is, its Creator: and thus we may say that St. *Paul*, whether in the body, or out of the body, was yet in Heaven. To place it in the Empyreal, or beyond the tenth sphear, is to forget the world's destruction; for when this sensible world shall be destroyed, all shall then be here as it is now there, an Empyreal Heaven, a *quasi* vacuity; when to ask where Heaven is, is to demand where the Presence of God is, or where we have the glory of that happy vision. *Moses* that was bred up in all the learning of the *Egyptians*, committed a gross absurdity in Philosophy, when with these eyes of flesh he desired to see God, and petitioned his Maker, that is, truth it self, to a contradiction. Those that imagine Heaven and Hell neighbours, and conceive a vicinity between those two extreams, upon consequence of the Parable, where *Dives* discoursed with *Lazarus* in *Abraham's* bosome, do too grosly conceive of those glorified creatures, whose eyes shall easily out-see the Sun, and behold without a perspective the extreamest distances: for if there shall be in our glorified eyes, the faculty of sight and reception of objects, I could think the visible species there to be in as unlimitable a way as now the intellectual. I grant that two bodies placed beyond the tenth sphear, or in a vacuity, according to *Aristotle's* Philosophy, could not behold each other, because there wants a body or Medium to hand and transport the visible rays of the object unto the sense; but when there shall be a general defect of either Medium to convey, or light to prepare and dispose that Medium, and yet a perfect vision, we must suspend the rules of our Philosophy, and make all good by a more absolute piece of opticks.

SECT.50

I cannot tell how to say that fire is the essence of Hell: I know not what to make of Purgatory, or conceive a flame that can either prey upon, or purifie the substance of a Soul: those flames of sulphur mention'd in the Scriptures, I take not to be understood of this present Hell, but of that to come, where fire shall make up the complement of our tortures, and have a body or subject wherein to manifest its tyranny. Some who have had the honour to be textuary in Divinity, are of opinion it shall be the same specifical fire with ours. This is hard to conceive, yet can I make good how even that may prey upon our bodies, and yet not consume us: for in this material World there are bodies that persist invincible in the powerfullest flames; and though by the action of fire they fall into ignition and liquation, yet will they never suffer a destruction. I would gladly know how *Moses* with an actual fire calcin'd, or burnt the Golden Calf into powder: for that mystical metal of Gold, whose solary and celestial nature I admire, exposed unto the violence of fire, grows onely hot, and liquifies, but consumeth not; so when the consumable and volatile pieces of our bodies shall be refined into a more impregnable and fixed temper, like Gold, though they suffer from the action of flames, they shall never perish, but lye immortal in the arms of fire. And surely if this frame must suffer onely by the action of this element, there will many bodies escape, and not onely Heaven, but Earth will not be at an end, but rather a beginning. For at present it is not earth, but a composition of fire, water, earth, and air; but at that time, spoiled of these ingredients, it shall appear in a substance more like it self, its ashes. Philosophers that opinioned the worlds destruction by fire, did never dream of annihilation, which is beyond the power of sublunary causes; for the last[B] action of that element is but vitrification, or a reduction of a body into glass; and therefore some of our Chymicks facetiously affirm, that at the last fire all shall be christallized and reverberated into glass, which is the utmost action of that element. Nor need we fear this term annihilation, or wonder that God will destroy the works of his Creation: for man subsisting, who is, and will then truely appear, a Microcosm, the world cannot be said to be destroyed. For the eyes of God, and perhaps also of our glorified selves, shall as really behold and contemplate the World in its Epitome or contracted essence, as now it doth at large and in its dilated substance. In the seed of a Plant to the eyes of God, and to the understanding of man, there exists, though in an invisible way, the perfect leaves, flowers, and fruit thereof: (for things that are in *posse* to the sense, are actually existent to the understanding). Thus God beholds all things, who contemplates as fully his works in their Epitome, as in their full volume; and beheld as amply the whole world in that little compendium of the sixth day, as in the scattered and dilated pieces of those five before.

[B]Last and proper, 1672.

SECT.51

Men commonly set forth the torments of Hell by fire, and the extremity of corporal afflictions, and describe Hell in the same method that *Mahomet* doth Heaven. This indeed makes a noise, and drums in popular ears; but if this be the terrible piece thereof, it is not worthy to stand in diameter with Heaven, whose happiness consists in that part that is best able to comprehend it, that immortal essence, that translated divinity and colony of God, the Soul. Surely though we place Hell under Earth, the Devil's walk and purlue is about it: men speak too popularly who place it in those flaming mountains, which to grosser apprehensions represent Hell. The heart of man is the place the Devils dwell in; I feel sometimes a Hell within my self; *Lucifer* keeps his Court in my breast; *Legion* is revived in me. There are as many Hells, as *Anaxagoras* conceited worlds; there was more than one Hell in *Magdalene*, when there were seven Devils; for every Devil is an Hell unto himself; he holds enough of torture in his own *ubi*, and needs not the misery of circumference to afflict him. And thus a distracted Conscience here, is a shadow or introduction unto Hell hereafter. Who can but pity the merciful intention of those hands that do destroy themselves? the Devil, were it in his power, would do the like; which being impossible, his miseries are endless, and he suffers most in that attribute wherein he is impassible, his immortality.

SECT.52

I thank God that with joy I mention it, I was never afraid of Hell, nor never grew pale at the description of that place; I have so fixed my contemplations on Heaven, that I have almost forgot the Idea of Hell, and am afraid rather to lose the Joys of the one, than endure the misery of the other: to be deprived of them is a perfect Hell, and needs methinks no addition to compleat our afflictions; that terrible term hath never detained me from sin, nor do I owe any good action to the name thereof; I fear God, yet am not afraid of him; his mercies make me ashamed of my sins, before his Judgements afraid thereof: these are the forced and secondary method of his wisdom, which he useth but as the last remedy, and upon provocation; a course rather to deter the wicked, than incite the virtuous to his worship. I can hardly think there was ever any scared into Heaven; they go the fairest way to Heaven that would serve God without a Hell; other Mercenaries, that crouch into him in fear of Hell, though they term themselves the servants, are indeed but the slaves of the Almighty.

SECT. 53

And to be true, and speak my soul, when I survey the occurrences of my life, and call into account the Finger of God, I can perceive nothing but an abyss and mass of mercies, either in general to mankind, or in particular to my self: and whether out of the prejudice of my affection, or an inverting and partial conceit of his mercies, I know not; but those which others term crosses, afflictions, judgements, misfortunes, to me who inquire farther into them then their visible effects, they both appear, and in event have ever proved, the secret and dissembled favours of his affection. It is a singular piece of Wisdom to apprehend truly, and without passion, the Works of God, and so well to distinguish his Justice from his Mercy, as not miscall those noble Attributes: yet it is likewise an honest piece of Logick, so to dispute and argue the proceedings of God, as to distinguish even his judgments into mercies. For God is merciful unto all, because better to the worst, than the best deserve; and to say he punisheth none in this world, though it be a Paradox, is no absurdity. To one that hath committed Murther, if the Judge should only ordain a Fine, it were a madness to call this a punishment, and to repine at the sentence, rather than admire the clemency of the Judge. Thus our offences being mortal, and deserving not onely Death, but Damnation; if the goodness of God be content to traverse and pass them over with a loss, misfortune, or disease; what frensie were it to term this a punishment, rather than an extremity of mercy; and to groan under the rod of his Judgements, rather than admire the Scepter of his Mercies? Therefore to adore, honour, and admire him, is a debt of gratitude due from the obligation of our nature, states, and conditions; and with these thoughts, he that knows them best, will not deny that I adore him. That I obtain Heaven, and the bliss thereof, is accidental, and not the intended work of my devotion; it being a felicity I can neither think to deserve, nor scarce in modesty to expect. For these two ends of us all, either as rewards or punishments, are mercifully ordained and disproportionably disposed unto our actions; the one being so far beyond our deserts, the other so infinitely below our demerits.

SECT. 54

There is no Salvation to those that believe not in *Christ*, that is, say some, since his Nativity, and as Divinity affirmeth, before also; which makes me much apprehend the ends of those honest Worthies and Philosophers which dyed before his Incarnation. It is hard to place those Souls in Hell, whose worthy lives do teach us Virtue on Earth: methinks amongst those many subdivisions of Hell, there might have been one Limbo left for these. What a strange vision will it be to see their Poetical fictions converted into Verities, and their imagined and fancied Furies into real Devils? how strange to them will sound the History of *Adam*, when they shall suffer for him they never heard of? when they who derive their genealogy from the Gods, shall know they are the unhappy issue of sinful man? It is an insolent part of reason, to controvert the Works of God, or question the Justice of his proceedings. Could Humility teach others, as it hath instructed me, to contemplate the infinite and incomprehensible distance betwixt the Creator and the Creature; or did we seriously perpend that one simile of St. *Paul*, *Shall the Vessel say to the Potter, Why hast thou made me thus?* it would prevent these arrogant disputes of reason, nor would we argue the definitive sentence of God, either to Heaven or Hell. Men that live according to the right rule and law of reason, live but in their own kind, as beasts do in theirs; who justly obey the prescript of their natures, and therefore cannot reasonably demand a reward of their actions, as onely obeying the natural dictates of their reason. It will therefore, and must at last appear, that all salvation is through *Christ*; which verity I fear these great examples of virtue must confirm, and make it good, how the perfectest actions of earth have no title or claim unto Heaven.

SECT. 55

Nor truely do I think the lives of these or of any other, were ever correspondent, or in all points conformable unto their doctrines. It is evident that *Aristotle* transgressed the rule of his own Ethicks; the Stoicks that condemn passion, and command a man to laugh in *Phalaris* his Bull, could not endure without a groan a fit of the Stone or Colick. The *Scepticks* that affirmed they knew nothing, even in that opinion confute themselves, and thought they knew more than all the World beside. *Diogenes* I hold to be the most vain-glorious man of his time, and more ambitious in refusing all Honours, than *Alexander* in rejecting none. Vice and the Devil put a Fallacy upon our Reasons, and provoking us too hastily to run from it, entangle and profound us deeper in it. The Duke of *Venice*, that weds himself unto the Sea by a Ring of Gold, I will not argue of prodigality, because it is a solemnity of good use and consequence in the State: but the Philosopher that threw his money into the Sea to avoid Avarice, was a notorious prodigal. There is no road or ready way to virtue; it is not an easie point of art to disentangle our selves from this riddle, or web of Sin: To perfect virtue, as to Religion, there is required a *Panoplia*, or compleat armour; that whilst we lye at close ward against one Vice, we lye not open to the venny of another. And indeed wiser discretions that have the thred of reason to conduct them, offend without pardon; whereas, underheads may stumble without dishonour. There go so many circumstances to piece up one good action, that it is a lesson to be good, and we are forced to be virtuous by the book. Again, the Practice of men holds not an equal pace, yea, and often runs counter to their Theory; we naturally know what is good, but naturally pursue what is evil: the Rhetorick wherewith I perswade another, cannot perswade my self: there is a depraved appetite in us, that will with patience hear the learned instructions of Reason, but yet perform no farther than agrees to its own irregular humour. In brief, we all are monsters, that is, a composition of Man and Beast; wherein we must endeavour to be as the Poets fancy that wise man *Chiron*, that is, to have the region of Man above that of Beast, and Sense to sit but at the feet of Reason. Lastly, I do desire with God that all, but yet affirm with men, that few shall know Salvation; that the bridge is narrow, the passage strait unto life: yet those who do confine the Church of God, either to particular Nations, Churches or Families, have made it far narrower then our Saviour ever meant it.

SECT.56

The vulgarity of those judgements that wrap the Church of God in *Strabo's* cloak, and restrain it unto *Europe*, seem to me as bad Geographers as *Alexander*, who thought he had Conquer'd all the World, when he had not subdued the half of any part thereof. For we cannot deny the Church of God both in *Asia* and *Africa*, if we do not forget the Peregrinations of the Apostles, the deaths of the Martyrs, the Sessions of many, and, even in our reformed judgement, lawful Councils, held in those parts in the minority and nonage of ours. Nor must a few differences, more remarkable in the eyes of man than perhaps in the judgement of God, excommunicate from Heaven one another, much less those Christians who are in a manner all Martyrs, maintaining their Faith, in the noble way of persecution, and serving God in the Fire, whereas we honour him in the Sunshine. 'Tis true, we all hold there is a number of Elect, and many to be saved; yet take our Opinions together, and from the confusion thereof there will be no such thing as salvation, nor shall any one be saved. For first, the Church of *Rome* condemneth us, we likewise them; the Sub-reformists and Sectaries sentence the Doctrine of our Church as damnable; the Atomist, or Familist, reprobates all these; and all these, them again. Thus whilst the Mercies of God do promise us Heaven, our conceits and opinions exclude us from that place. There must be, therefore, more than one St. *Peter*: particular Churches and Sects usurp the gates of Heaven, and turn the key against each other: and thus we go to Heaven against each others wills, conceits and opinions; and with as much uncharity as ignorance, do err I fear in points not only of our own, but one an others salvation.

SECT.57

I believe many are saved, who to man seem reprobated; and many are reprobated, who in the opinion and sentence of man, stand elected: there will appear at the Last day, strange and unexpected examples both of his Justice and his Mercy; and therefore to define either, is folly in man, and insolency even in the Devils: those acute and subtil spirits in all their sagacity, can hardly divine who shall be saved; which if they could Prognostick, their labour were at an end; nor need they compass the earth seeking whom they may devour. Those who upon a rigid application of the Law, sentence *Solomon* unto damnation, condemn not onely him, but themselves, and the whole World: for by the Letter and written Word of God, we are without exception in the state of Death; but there is a prerogative of God, and an arbitrary pleasure above the Letter of his own Law, by which alone we can pretend unto Salvation, and through which *Solomon* might be as easily saved as those who condemn him.

SECT.58

The number of those who pretend unto Salvation, and those infinite swarms who think to pass through the eye of this Needle, have much amazed me. That name and compellation of *little Flock*, doth not comfort, but deject my Devotion; especially when I reflect upon mine own unworthiness, wherein, according to my humble apprehensions, I am below them all. I believe there shall never be an Anarchy in Heaven, but as there are Hierarchies amongst the Angels, so shall there be degrees of priority amongst the Saints. Yet is it (I protest) beyond my ambition to aspire unto the first ranks; my desires onely are, and I shall be happy therein, to be but the last man, and bring up the Rere in Heaven.

SECT.59

Again, I am confident and fully perswaded, yet dare not take my oath, of my Salvation: I am as it were sure, and do believe without all doubt, that there is such a City as *Constantinople*; yet for me to take my Oath thereon were a kind of Perjury, because I hold no infallible warrant from my own sense to confirm me in the certainty thereof: And truly, though many pretend an absolute certainty of their Salvation, yet when an humble Soul shall contemplate our own unworthiness, she shall meet with many doubts, and suddenly find how little we stand in need of the Precept of St. *Paul*, *Work out your salvation with fear and trembling*. That which is the cause of my Election, I hold to be the cause of my Salvation, which was the mercy and beneplacit of God, before I was, or the foundation of the World. *Before Abraham was, I am*, is the saying of Christ; yet is it true in some sense, if I say it of myself; for I was not onely before myself, but *Adam*, that is, in the Idea of God, and the decree of that Synod held from all Eternity. And in this sense, I say, the World was before the Creation, and at an end before it had a beginning; and thus was I dead before I was alive: though my grave be *England*, my dying place was Paradise: and *Eve* miscarried of me, before she conceived of Cain.

SECT.60

Insolent zeals that do decry good Works, and rely onely upon Faith, take not away merit: for depending upon the efficacy of their Faith, they enforce the condition of God, and in a more sophistical way do seem to challenge Heaven. It was decreed by God, that only those that lapt in the water like Dogs, should have the honour to destroy the *Midianites*; yet could none of those justly challenge, or imagine he deserved that honour thereupon. I do not deny, but that true Faith, and such as God requires, is not onely a mark or token, but also a means of our Salvation; but where to find this, is as obscure to me, as my last end. And if our Saviour could object unto his own Disciples and Favourites, a Faith, that, to the quantity of a grain of Mustard-seed, is able to remove Mountains; surely that which we boast of, is not any thing, or at the most, but a remove from nothing. This is the Tenor of my belief; wherein, though there be many things singular, and to the humour of my irregular self; yet if they square not with maturer Judgements I disclaim them, and do no further favour them, than the learned and best judgements shall authorize them.

THE SECOND PART

SECT.1

Now for that other Virtue of Charity, without which Faith is a meer notion, and of no existence, I have ever endeavoured to nourish the merciful disposition and humane inclination I borrowed from my Parents, and regulate it to the written and prescribed Laws of Charity; and if I hold the true Anatomy of my self, I am delineated and naturally framed to such a piece of virtue. For I am of a constitution so general, that it comforts and sympathizeth with all things; I have no antipathy, or rather Idio-syncrasie, in dyet, humour, air, any thing: I wonder not at the *French* for their dishes of Frogs, Snails, and Toadstools, nor at the Jews for Locusts and Grasshoppers; but being amongst them, make them my common Viands, and I find they agree with my Stomach as well as theirs. I could digest a Sallad gathered in a Churchyard, as well as in a Garden. I cannot start at the presence of a Serpent, Scorpion, Lizard, or Salamander: at the sight of a Toad or Viper, I find in me no desire to take up a stone to destroy them. I feel not in my self those common Antipathies that I can discover in others: Those National repugnances do not touch me, nor do I behold with prejudice the *French*, *Italian*, *Spaniard*, or *Dutch*; but where I find their actions in balance with my Country-men's, I honour, love, and embrace them in the same degree. I was born in the eighth Climate, but seem for to be framed and constellated unto all: I am no Plant that will not prosper out of a Garden: All places, all airs make unto me one Countrey; I am in *England*, every where, and under any Meridian. I have been shipwrackt, yet am not enemy with the Sea or Winds; I can study, play, or sleep in a Tempest. In brief, I am averse from nothing; my Conscience would give me the lye if I should absolutely detest or hate any essence but the Devil; or so at least abhor any thing, but that we might come to composition. If there be any among those common objects of hatred I do contemn and laugh at, it is that great enemy of Reason, Virtue and Religion, the Multitude; that numerous piece of monstrosity, which taken asunder seem men, and the reasonable creatures of God; but confused together, make but one great beast, and a monstrosity more prodigious than Hydra: it is no breach of Charity to call these Fools; it is the style all holy Writers have afforded them, set down by *Solomon* in Canonical Scripture, and a point of our Faith to believe so. Neither in the name of Multitude do I onely include the base and minor sort of people; there is a rabble even amongst the Gentry, a sort of Plebeian heads, whose fancy moves with the same wheel as these; men in the same Level with Mechanicks, though their fortunes do somewhat guild their infirmities, and their purses compound for their follies. But as in casting account, three or four men together come short in account of one man placed by himself below them: So neither are a troop of these ignorant Doradoes, of that true esteem and value, as many a forlorn person, whose condition doth place him below their feet. Let us speak like Politicians, there is a Nobility without Heraldry, a natural dignity, whereby one man is ranked with another; another filed before him, according to the quality of his Desert, and preheminence of his good parts: Though the corruption of these times, and the byas of present practice wheel another way. Thus it was in the first and primitive Commonwealths, and is yet in the integrity and Cradle of well-order'd Polities, till corruption getteth ground, ruder desires labouring after that which wiser considerations contemn; every one having a liberty to amass and heap up riches, and they a licence or faculty to do or purchase any thing.

SECT.2

This general and indifferent temper of mine doth more neerly dispose me to this noble virtue. It is a happiness to be born and framed unto virtue, and to grow up from the seeds of nature, rather than the inoculation and forced grafts of education: yet if we are directed only by our particular Natures, and regulate our inclinations by no higher rule than that of our reasons, we are but Moralists; Divinity will still call us Heathens. Therefore this great work of charity must have other motives, ends, and impulsions: I give no alms only to satisfie the hunger of my Brother, but to fulfil and accomplish the Will and Command of my God: I draw not *my* purse for his sake that demands it, but his that enjoyned it; I relieve no man upon the Rhetorick of his miseries, nor to content mine own commiserating disposition: for this is still but moral charity, and an act that oweth more to passion than reason. He that relieves another upon the bare suggestion and bowels of pity, doth not this so much for his sake, as for his own: for by compassion we make others misery our own, and so by relieving them, we relieve our selves also. It is as erroneous a conceit to redress other Mens misfortunes upon the common considerations of merciful natures, that it may be one day our own case; for this is a sinister and politick kind of charity, whereby we seem to bespeak the pities of men in the like occasions: and truly I have observed that those professed Eleemosynaries, though in a croud or multitude, do yet direct and place their petitions on a few and selected persons: there is surely a Physiognomy, which those experienced and Master Mendicants observe; whereby they instantly discover a merciful aspect, and will single out a face, wherein they spy the signatures and marks of Mercy: for there are mystically in our faces certain Characters which carry in them the motto of our Souls, wherein he that can read *A. B. C.* may read our natures. I hold moreover that there is a Phytognomy, or Physiognomy, not only of Men but of Plants and Vegetables; and in every one of them, some outward figures which hang as signs or bushes of their inward forms. The Finger of God hath left an Inscription upon all his works, not graphical, or composed of Letters, but of their several forms, constitutions, parts, and operations; which aptly joyned together do make one word that doth express their natures. By these Letters God calls the Stars by their names; and by this Alphabet *Adam* assigned to every creature a name peculiar to its nature. Now there are, besides these Characters in our Faces, certain mystical figures in our Hands, which I dare not call meer dashes, strokes *a la volee*, or at random, because delineated by a Pencil that never works in vain; and hereof I take more particular notice, because I carry that in mine own hand, which I could never read of, nor discover in another. *Aristotle* I confess, in his acute and singular Book of Physiognomy, hath made no mention of Chiromancy; yet I believe the *Egyptians*, who were neerer addicted to those abstruse and mystical sciences, had a knowledge therein; to which those vagabond and counterfeit *Egyptians* did after pretend, and perhaps retained a few corrupted principles, which sometimes might verifie their prognosticks.

It is the common wonder of all men, how among so many millions of faces, there should be none alike: Now contrary, I wonder as much how there should be any. He that shall consider how many thousand several words have been carelesly and without study composed out of 24 Letters; withal, how many hundred lines there are to be drawn in the Fabrick of one Man; shall easily find that this variety is necessary: And it will be very hard that they shall so concur, as to make one portract like another. Let a Painter carelesly limb out a million of Faces, and you shall find them all different; yea let him have his Copy before him, yet after all his art there will remain a sensible distinction; for the pattern or example of every thing is the perfectest in that kind, whereof we still come short, though we transcend or go beyond it, because herein it is wide, and agrees not in all points unto the Copy. Nor doth the similitude of Creatures disparage the variety of Nature, nor any way confound the Works of God. For even in things alike there is diversity; and those that do seem to accord, do manifestly disagree. And thus is man like God; for in the same things that we resemble him, we are utterly different from him. There was never any thing so like another, as in all points to concur; there will ever some reserved difference slip in, to prevent the identity, without which, two several things would not be alike, but the same, which is impossible.

SECT.3

But to return from Philosophy to Charity: I hold not so narrow a conceit of this virtue, as to conceive that to give Alms is onely to be Charitable, or think a piece of Liberality can comprehend the Total of Charity. Divinity hath wisely divided the act thereof into many branches, and hath taught us in this narrow way, many paths unto goodness: as many ways as we may do good, so many ways we may be charitable: there are infirmities, not onely of Body, but of Soul, and Fortunes, which do require the merciful hand of our abilities. I cannot contemn a man for ignorance, but behold him with as much pity as I do *Lazarus*. It is no greater Charity to cloath his body, than apparel the nakedness of his Soul. It is an honourable object to see the reasons of other men wear our Liveries, and their borrowed understandings do homage to the bounty of ours: It is the cheapest way of beneficence, and like the natural charity of the Sun, illuminates another without obscuring it self. To be reserved and caitiff in this part of goodness, is the sordidest piece of covetousness, and more contemptible than pecuniary Avarice. To this (as calling my self a Scholar) I am obliged by the duty of my condition: I make not therefore my head a grave, but a treasure of knowledge; I intend no Monopoly, but a community in learning; I study not for my own sake only, but for theirs that study not for themselves. I envy no man that knows more than my self, but pity them that know less. I instruct no man as an exercise of my knowledge, or with an intent rather to nourish and keep it alive in mine own head, then beget and propagate it in his; and in the midst of all my endeavours, there is but one thought that dejects me, that my acquired parts must perish with my self, nor can be Legacied among my honoured Friends. I cannot fall out, or contemn a man for an errour, or conceive why a difference in Opinion should divide an affection: For Controversies, Disputes, and Argumentations, both in Philosophy and in Divinity, if they meet with discreet and peaceable natures, do not infringe the Laws of Charity: in all disputes, so much as there is of passion, so much there is of nothing to the purpose; for then Reason, like a bad Hound, spends upon a false Scent, and forsakes the question first started. And this is one reason why Controversies are never determined; for though they be amply proposed, they are scarce at all handled, they do so swell with unnecessary Digressions; and the Parenthesis on the party, is often as large as the main discourse upon the subject. The Foundations of Religion are already established, and the Principles of Salvation subscribed unto by all: there remains not many controversies worth a Passion, and yet never any disputed without, not only in Divinity, but inferiour Arts: What a βατραχομυομαχία and hot skirmish is betwixt S. and T. in *Lucian*: How do Grammarians hack and slash for the Genitive case in *Jupiter*? How do they break their own pates to salve that of *Priscian! Si foret in terris, rideret Democritus.* Yea, even amongst wiser militants, how many wounds have been given, and credits slain, for the poor victory of an opinion, or beggerly conquest of a distinction? Scholars are men of Peace, they bear no Arms, but their tongues are sharper than Actus his razor; their Pens carry farther, and give a lowder report than Thunder: I had rather stand the shock of a Basilisco, than the fury of a merciless Pen. It is not meer Zeal to Learning, or Devotion to the Muses, that wiser Princes Patron the Arts, and carry an indulgent aspect unto Scholars; but a desire to have their names eternized by the memory of their writings, and a fear of the revengeful Pen of succeeding ages: for these are the men, that when they have played their parts, and had their *exits*, must step out and give the moral of their Scenes, and deliver unto Posterity an Inventory of their Virtues and Vices. And surely there goes a great deal of Conscience to the compiling of an History: there is no reproach to the scandal of a Story; it is such an authentick kind of falshood, that with authority belies our good names to all Nations and Posterity.

SECT.4

There is another offence unto Charity, which no Author hath ever written of, and few take notice of; and that's the reproach, not of whole professions, mysteries and conditions, but of whole Nations; wherein by opprobrious Epithets we miscal each other, and by an uncharitable Logick, from a disposition in a few, conclude a habit in all.

Le mutin Anglois, & le bravache Escossois;
Le bougre Italian, & le fol François;
Le poultron Romain, le larron de Gascongne,
L'Espagnol superbe, & l'Aleman yurongne.

St. *Paul*, that calls the *Cretians* lyars, doth it but indirectly, and upon quotation of their own Poet. It is as bloody a thought in one way, as *Nero's* was in another. For by a word we wound a thousand, and at one blow assassine the honour of a Nation. It is as compleat a piece of madness to miscal and rave against the times, or think to recal men to reason, by a fit of passion: *Democritus*, that thought to laugh the times into goodness, seems to me as deeply Hypochondriack, as *Heraclitus* that bewailed them. It moves not my spleen to behold the multitude in their proper humours, that is, in their fits of folly and madness, as well understanding that wisdom is not prophan'd unto the World, and 'tis the priviledge of a few to be Vertuous. They that endeavour to abolish Vice, destroy also Virtue; for contraries, though they destroy one another, are yet in life of one another. Thus Virtue (abolish vice) is an Idea; again, the community of sin doth not disparage goodness; for when Vice gains upon the major part, Virtue, in whom it remains, becomes more excellent; and being lost in some, multiplies its goodness in others, which remain untouched, and persist intire in the general inundation. I can therefore behold Vice without a Satyr, content only with an admonition, or instructive reprehension, for Noble Natures, and such as are capable of goodness, are railed into vice, that might as easily be admonished into virtue; and we should be all so far the Orators of goodness, as to protract her from the power of Vice, and maintain the cause of injured truth. No man can justly censure or condemn another, because indeed no man truly knows another. This I perceive in my self; for I am in the dark to all the world, and my nearest friends behold me but in a cloud: those that know me but superficially, think less of me than I do of my self; those of my neer acquaintance think more; God, who truly knows me, knows that I am nothing; for he only beholds me and all the world; who looks not on us through a derived ray, or a trajection of a sensible species, but beholds the substance without the helps of accidents, and the forms of things, as we their operations. Further, no man can judge another, because no man knows himself; for we censure others but as they disagree from that humour which we fancy laudible in our selves, and commend others but for that wherein they seem to quadrate and consent with us. So that in conclusion, all is but that we all condemn, Self-love. 'Tis the general complaint of these times, and perhaps of those past, that charity grows cold; which I perceive most verified in those which most do manifest the fires and flames of zeal; for it is a virtue that best agrees with coldest natures, and such as are complexioned for humility. But how shall we expect Charity towards others, when we are uncharitable to our selves? Charity begins at home, is the voice of the World; yet is every man his greatest enemy, and as it were, his own Executioner. *Non occides*, is the Commandment of God, yet scarce observed by any man; for I perceive every man is his own *Atropos*, and lends a hand to cut the thred of his own days. *Cain* was not therefore the first Murtherer, but *Adam*, who brought in death; whereof he beheld the practice and example in his own son *Abel*, and saw that verified in the experience of another, which faith could not perswade him in the Theory of himself.

SECT.5

There is, I think, no man that apprehends his own miseries less than my self, and no man that so neerly apprehends anothers. I could lose an arm without a tear, and with few groans, methinks, be quartered into pieces; yet can I weep most seriously at a Play, and receive with true passion, the counterfeit grief of those known and professed Impostures. It is a barbarous part of inhumanity to add unto any afflicted parties misery, or indeavour to multiply in any man, a passion, whose single nature is already above his patience: this was the greatest affliction of *Job*; and those oblique expostulations of his Friends, a deeper injury than the down-right blows of the Devil. It is not the tears of our own eyes only, but of our friends also, that do exhaust the current of our sorrows; which falling into many streams, runs more peaceably, and is contented with a narrower channel. It is an act within the power of charity, to translate a passion out of one brest into another, and to divide a sorrow almost out of it self; for an affliction, like a dimension, may be so divided, as if not indivisible, at least to become insensible. Now with my friend I desire not to share or participate, but to engross, his sorrows; that by making them mine own, I may more easily discuss them; for in mine own reason, and within my self, I can command that, which I cannot intreat without my self, and within the circle of another. I have often thought those noble pairs and examples of friendship not so truly Histories of what had been, as fictions of what should be; but I now perceive nothing in them but possibilities, nor any thing in the Heroick examples of *Damon* and *Pythias*, *Achilles* and *Patroclus*, which methinks upon some grounds I could not perform within the narrow compass of my self. That a man should lay down his life for his Friend, seems strange to vulgar affections, and such as confine themselves within that Worldly principle, Charity begins at home. For mine own part I could never remember the relations that I held unto my self, nor the respect that I owe unto my own nature, in the cause of God, my Country, and my Friends. Next to these three I do embrace my self: I confess I do not observe that order that the Schools ordain our affections, to love our Parents, Wives, Children, and then our Friends; for excepting the injunctions of Religion, I do not find in my self such a necessary and indissoluble Sympathy to all those of my blood. I hope I do not break the fifth Commandment, if I conceive I may love my friend before the nearest of my blood, even those to whom I owe the principles of life: I never yet cast a true affection on a woman, but I have loved my friend as I do virtue, my soul, my God. From hence me thinks I do conceive how God loves man, what happiness there is in the love of God. Omitting all other, there are three most mystical unions, two natures in one person; three persons in one nature; one soul in two bodies. For though indeed they be really divided, yet are they so united, as they seem but one, and make rather a duality than two distinct souls.

SECT.6

There are wonders in true affection; it is a body of *Enigma's*, mysteries, and riddles; wherein two so become one, as they both become two: I love my friend before my self, and yet methinks I do not love him enough: some few months hence, my multiplied affection will make me believe I have not loved him at all: when I am from him, I am dead till I be with him; when I am with him, I am not satisfied, but would still be nearer him. United souls are not satisfied with imbraces, but desire to be truly each other; which being impossible, their desires are infinite, and must proceed without a possibility of satisfaction. Another misery there is in affection, that whom we truly love like our own, we forget their looks, nor can our memory retain the Idea of their faces; and it is no wonder, for they are ourselves, and our affection makes their looks our own. This noble affection falls not on vulgar and common constitutions, but on such as are mark'd for virtue: he that can love his friend with this noble ardour, will in a competent degree affect all. Now if we can bring our affections to look beyond the body, and cast an eye upon the soul, we have found out the true object, not only of friendship, but Charity; and the greatest happiness that we can bequeath the soul, is that wherein we all do place our last felicity, Salvation; which though it be not in our power to bestow, it is in our charity and pious invocations to desire, if not procure and further. I cannot contentedly frame a prayer for my self in particular, without a catalogue for my friends; nor request a happiness wherein my sociable disposition doth not desire the fellowship of my neighbour. I never hear the Toll of a passing Bell, though in my mirth, without my prayers and best wishes for the departing spirit: I cannot go to cure the body of my patient, but I forget my profession, and call unto God for his soul: I cannot see one say his prayers, but in stead of imitating him, I fall into a supplication for him, who perhaps is no more to me than a common nature: and if God hath vouchsafed an ear to my supplications, there are surely many happy that never saw me, and enjoy the blessing of mine unknown devotions. To pray for Enemies, that is, for their salvation, is no harsh precept, but the practice of our daily and ordinary devotions. I cannot believe the story of the Italian: our bad wishes and uncharitable desires proceed no further than this life; it is the Devil, and the uncharitable votes of Hell, that desire our misery in the World to come.

SECT.7

To do no injury, nor take none, was a principle, which to my former years, and impatient affections, seemed to contain enough of Morality; but my more setled years, and Christian constitution, have fallen upon severer resolutions. I can hold there is no such thing as injury; that if there be, there is no such injury as revenge, and no such revenge as the contempt of an injury: that to hate another, is to malign himself; that the truest way to love another, is to despise our selves. I were unjust unto mine own Conscience, if I should say I am at variance with any thing like my self. I find there are many pieces in this one fabrick of man; this frame is raised upon a mass of Antipathies: I am one methinks, but as the World; wherein notwithstanding there are a swarm of distinct essences, and in them another World of contrarieties; we carry private and domestick enemies within, publick and more hostile adversaries without. The Devil, that did but buffet St. *Paul*, plays methinks at sharp with me. Let me be nothing, if within the compass of my self I do not find the battail of *Lepanto*, Passion against Reason, Reason against Faith, Faith against the Devil, and my Conscience against all. There is another man within me, that's angry with me, rebukes, commands, and dastards me. I have no Conscience of Marble, to resist the hammer of more heavy offences; nor yet too soft and waxen, as to take the impression of each single peccadillo or scape of infirmity: I am of a strange belief, that it is as easie to be forgiven some sins, as to commit some others. For my Original sin, I hold it to be washed away in my Baptism, for my actual transgressions, I compute and reckon with God, but from my last repentance, Sacrament, or general absolution; and therefore am not terrified with the sins or madness of my youth. I thank the goodness of God, I have no sins that want a name; I am not singular in offences; my transgressions are Epidemical, and from the common breath of our corruption. For there are certain tempers of body, which matcht with an humorous depravity of mind, do hatch and produce vitiosities, whose newness and monstrosity of nature admits no name; this was the temper of that Lecher that fell in love with a Statua, and constitution of *Nero* in his Spintrian recreations. For the Heavens are not only fruitful in new and unheard-of stars, the Earth in plants and animals; but mens minds also in villany and vices: now the dulness of my reason, and the vulgarity of my disposition, never prompted my invention, nor sollicited my affection unto any of those; yet even those common and quotidian infirmities that so necessarily attend me, and do seem to be my very nature, have so dejected me, so broken the estimation that I should have otherwise of my self, that I repute my self the most abjectest piece of mortality. Divines prescribe a fit of sorrow to repentance; there goes indignation, anger, sorrow, hatred, into mine; passions of a contrary nature, which neither seem to sute with this action, nor my proper constitution. It is no breach of charity to our selves, to be at variance with our Vices; nor to abhor that part of us, which is an enemy to the ground of charity, our God; wherein we do but imitate our great selves the world, whose divided Antipathies and contrary faces do yet carry a charitable regard unto the whole by their particular discords, preserving the common harmony, and keeping in fetters those powers, whose rebellions once Masters, might be the ruine of all.

SECT.8

I thank God, amongst those millions of Vices I do inherit and hold from *Adam*, I have escaped one, and that a mortal enemy to Charity, the first and father-sin[C], not onely of man, but of the devil, Pride; a vice whose name is comprehended in a Monosyllable, but in its nature not circumscribed with a World. I have escaped it in a condition that can hardly avoid it. Those petty acquisitions and reputed perfections that advance and elevate the conceits of other men, add no feathers unto mine. I have seen a Grammarian towr and plume himself over a single line in *Horace*, and shew more pride in the construction of one Ode, than the Author in the composure of the whole book. For my own part, besides the *Jargon* and *Patois* of several Provinces, I understand no less than six Languages; yet I protest I have no higher conceit of my self, than had our Fathers before the confusion of *Babel*, when there was but one Language in the World, and none to boast himself either Linguist or Critick. I have not onely seen several Countries, beheld the nature of their Climes, the Chorography of their Provinces, Topography of their Cities, but understood their several Laws, Customs, and Policies; yet cannot all this perswade the dulness of my spirit unto such an opinion of my self, as I behold in nimbler and conceited heads, that never looked a degree beyond their Nests. I know the names, and somewhat more, of all the constellations in my Horizon; yet I have seen a prating Mariner, that could onely name the pointers and the North Star, out-talk me, and conceit himself a whole Sphere above me. I know most of the Plants of my Countrey, and of those about me; yet methinks I do not know so many as when I did but know a hundred, and had scarcely ever Simpled further than *Cheap-side*. For indeed, heads of capacity, and such as are not full with a handful, or easie measure of knowledge, think they know nothing, till they know all; which being impossible, they fall upon the opinion of *Socrates*, and only know they know not any thing. I cannot think that *Homer* pin'd away upon the riddle of the fishermen; or that *Aristotle*, who understood the uncertainty of knowledge, and confessed so often the reason of man too weak for the works of nature, did ever drown himself upon the flux and reflux of *Euripus*. We do but learn to-day, what our better advanced judgements will unteach to-morrow; and *Aristotle* doth but instruct us, as *Plato* did him; that is, to confute himself. I have run through all sorts, yet find no rest in any: though our first studies and *junior* endeavours may style us Peripateticks, Stoicks, or Academicks, yet I perceive the wisest heads prove, at last, almost all Scepticks, and stand like *Janus* in the field of knowledge. I have therefore one common and authentick Philosophy I learned in the Schools, whereby I discourse and satisfie the reason of other men; another more reserved, and drawn from experience, whereby I content mine own. *Solomon*, that complained of ignorance in the height of knowledge, hath not only humbled my conceits, but discouraged my endeavours. There is yet another conceit that hath sometimes made me shut my books, which tells me it is a vanity to waste our days in the blind pursuit of knowledge; it is but attending a little longer, and we shall enjoy that by instinct and infusion, which we endeavour at here by labour and inquisition. It is better to sit down in a modest ignorance, and rest contented with the natural blessing of our own reasons, than buy the uncertain knowledge of this life, with sweat and vexation, which Death gives every fool *gratis*, and is an accessary of our glorification.

[C]Farther-sin, 1682.

SECT.9

I was never yet once, and commend their resolutions who never marry twice: not that I disallow of second marriage; as neither in all cases, of Polygamy, which considering some times, and the unequal number of both sexes, may be also necessary. The whole World was made for man, but the twelfth part of man for woman: Man is the whole World, and the Breath of God; Woman the Rib and crooked piece of man. I could be content that we might procreate like trees, without conjunction, or that there were any way to perpetuate the World without this trivial and vulgar way of coition; it is the foolishest act a wise man commits in all his life; nor is there any thing that will more deject his cool'd imagination, when he shall consider what an odd and unworthy piece of folly he hath committed. I speak not in prejudice, nor am averse from that sweet Sex, but naturally amorous of all that is beautiful; I can look a whole day with delight upon a handsome Picture, though it be but of an Horse. It is my temper, and I like it the better, to affect all harmony; and sure there is musick even in the beauty, and the silent note which *Cupid* strikes, far sweeter than the sound of an instrument. For there is a musick where ever there is a harmony, order or proportion; and thus far we may maintain the musick of the Sphears: for those well-ordered motions, and regular paces, though they give no sound unto the ear, yet to the understanding they strike a note most full of harmony. Whosoever is harmonically composed, delights in harmony; which makes me much distrust the symmetry of those heads which declaim against all Church-Musick. For my self, not only from my obedience, but my particular Genius, I do embrace it: for even that vulgar and Tavern-Musick, which makes one man merry, another mad, strikes in me a deep fit of devotion, and a profound contemplation of the first Composer. There is something in it of Divinity more than the ear discovers: it is an Hieroglyphical and shadowed lesson of the whole

World, and creatures of God; such a melody to the ear, as the whole World well understood, would afford the understanding. In brief, it is a sensible fit of that harmony, which intellectually sounds in the ears of God. I will not say with *Plato*, the soul is an harmony, but harmonical, and hath its nearest sympathy unto Musick: thus some whose temper of body agrees, and humours the constitution of their souls, are born Poets, though indeed all are naturally inclined unto Rhythme. [16]This made *Tacitus* in the very first line of his Story, fall upon a verse, and *Cicero* the worst of Poets, but [17]declaiming for a Poet, falls in the very first sentence upon a perfect [18]Hexameter. I feel not in me those sordid and unchristian desires of my profession; I do not secretly implore and wish for Plagues, rejoyce at Famines, revolve Ephemerides and Almanacks, in expectation of malignant Aspects, fatal Conjunctions, and Eclipses: I rejoyce not at unwholesome Springs, nor unseasonable Winters; my Prayer goes with the Husbandman's; I desire every thing in its proper season, that neither men nor the times be put out of temper. Let me be sick my self, if sometimes the malady of my patient be not a disease unto me; I desire rather to cure his infirmities than my own necessities: where I do him no good, methinks it is scarce honest gain; though I confess 'tis but the worthy salary of our well-intended endeavours. I am not only ashamed, but heartily sorry, that besides death, there are diseases incurable; yet not for my own sake, or that they be beyond my Art, but for the general cause and sake of humanity, whose common cause I apprehend as mine own. And to speak more generally, those three Noble Professions which all civil Commonwealths do honour, are raised upon the fall of *Adam*, and are not exempt from their infirmities; there are not only diseases incurable in Physick, but cases indissolvable in Laws, Vices incorrigible in Divinity: if general Councils may err, I do not see why particular Courts should be infallible; their perfectest rules are raised upon the erroneous reasons of Man; and the Laws of one, do but condemn the rules of another; as *Aristotle* oft-times the opinions of his Predecessours, because, though agreeable to reason, yet were not consonant to his own rules, and Logick of his proper Principles. Again, to speak nothing of the Sin against the Holy Ghost, whose cure not onely, but whose nature is unknown; I can cure the Gout or Stone in some, sooner than Divinity Pride or Avarice in others. I can cure Vices by Physick, when they remain incurable by Divinity; and shall obey my Pills, when they contemn their precepts. I boast nothing, but plainly say, we all labour against our own cure; for death is the cure of all diseases. There is no Catholicon or universal remedy I know but this, which, though nauseous to queasie stomachs, yet to prepared appetites is Nectar, and a pleasant potion of immortality.

SECT.10

For my Conversation, it is like the Sun's with all men, and with a friendly aspect to good and bad. Methinks there is no man bad, and the worst, best; that is, while they are kept within the circle of those qualities, wherein they are good; there is no man's mind of such discordant and jarring a temper, to which a tunable disposition may not strike a harmony. *Magnæ virtutes, nee minora vitia*; it is the posie of the best natures, and may be inverted on the worst; there are in the most depraved and venemous dispositions, certain pieces that remain untoucht, which by an *Antiperistasis* become more excellent, or by the excellency of their antipathies are able to preserve themselves from the contagion of their enemy vices, and persist intire beyond the general corruption. For it is also thus in nature. The greatest Balsomes do lie enveloped in the bodies of most powerful Corrosives; I say moreover, and I ground upon experience, that poisons contain within themselves their own Antidote, and that which preserves them from the venome of themselves, without which they were not deleterious to others onely, but to themselves also. But it is the corruption that I fear within me, not the contagion of commerce without me. 'Tis that unruly regiment within me, that will destroy me; 'tis I that do infect my self; the man without a Navel yet lives in me; I feel that original canker corrode and devour me; and therefore *Defenda me* Dios *de me*, Lord deliver me from my self, is a part of my Letany, and the first voice of my retired imaginations. There is no man alone, because every man is a *Microcosm*, and carries the whole World about him; *Nunquam minus solus quàm cum solus*, though it be the Apothegme of a wise man, is yet true in the mouth of a fool; indeed, though in a Wilderness, a man is never alone, not only because he is with himself and his own thoughts, but because he is with the Devil, who ever consorts with our solitude, and is that unruly rebel that musters up those disordered motions which accompany our sequestred imaginations. And to speak more narrowly, there is no such thing as solitude, nor any thing that can be said to be alone and by itself, but God, who is his own circle, and can subsist by himself; all others, besides their dissimilary and Heterogeneous parts, which in a manner multiply their natures, cannot subsist without the concourse of God, and the society of that hand which doth uphold their natures. In brief, there can be nothing truly alone and by it self, which is not truly one; and such is only God: All others do transcend an unity, and so by consequence are many.

SECT.11

Now for my life, it is a miracle of thirty years, which to relate, were not a History, but a piece of Poetry, and would sound to common ears like a Fable; for the World, I count it not an Inn, but an Hospital; and a place not to live, but to dye in. The world that I regard is my self; it is the Microcosm of my own frame that I cast mine eye on; for the other, I use it but like my Globe, and turn it round sometimes for my recreation. Men that look upon my outside, perusing only my condition and Fortunes, do err in my Altitude, for I am above *Atlas* his shoulders. The earth is a point not only in respect of the Heavens above us, but of that heavenly and celestial part within us: that mass of Flesh that circumscribes me, limits not my mind: that surface that tells the Heavens it hath an end, cannot persuade me I have any: I take my circle to be above three hundred and sixty; though the number of the Ark do measure my body, it comprehendeth not my mind: whilst I study to find how I am a Microcosm, or little World, I find my self something more than the great. There is surely a piece of Divinity in us, something that was before the Elements, and owes no homage unto the Sun. Nature tells me I am the Image of God, as well as Scripture: he that understands not thus much, hath not his introduction or first lesson, and is yet to begin the Alphabet of man. Let me not injure the felicity of others, if I say I am as happy as any: *Ruat cœlum, Fiat voluntas tua*, salveth all; so that whatsoever happens, it is but what our daily prayers desire. In brief, I am content, and what should providence add more? Surely this is it we call Happiness, and this do I enjoy; with this I am happy in a dream, and as content to enjoy a happiness in a fancy, as others in a more apparent truth and realty. There is surely a neerer apprehension of any thing that delights us in our dreams, than in our waked senses; without this I were unhappy: for my awaked judgment discontents me, ever whispering unto me, that I am from my friend; but my friendly dreams in night requite me, and make me think I am within his arms. I thank God for my happy dreams, as I do for my good rest, for there is a satisfaction in them unto reasonable desires, and such as can be content with a fit of happiness. And surely it is not a melancholy conceit to think we are all asleep in this World, and that the conceits of this life are as meer dreams to those of the next, as the Phantasms of the night, to the conceits of the day. There is an equal delusion in both, and the one doth but seem to be the embleme or picture of the other; we are somewhat more than our selves in our sleeps, and the slumber of the body seems to be but the waking of the soul. It is the ligation of sense, but the liberty of reason, and our waking conceptions do not match the Fancies of our sleeps. At my Nativity, my Ascendant was the watery sign of *Scorpius*; I was born in the Planetary hour of *Saturn*, and I think I have a piece of that Leaden Planet in me. I am no way facetious, nor disposed for the mirth and galliardize of company; yet in one dream I can compose a whole Comedy, behold the action, apprehend the jests, and laugh my self awake at the conceits thereof: were my memory as faithful as my reason is then fruitful, I would never study but in my dreams; and this time also would I chuse for my devotions: but our grosser memories have then so little hold of our abstracted understandings, that they forget the story, and can only relate to our awaked souls, a confused and broken tale of that that hath passed. *Aristotle*, who hath written a singular Tract of Sleep, hath not methinks throughly defined it; nor yet *Galen*, though he seem to have corrected it; for those *Noctambuloes* and night-walkers, though in their sleep, do yet injoy the action of their senses: we must therefore say that there is something in us that is not in the jurisdiction of *Morpheus*; and that those abstracted and ecstatick souls do walk about in their own corps, as spirits with the bodies they assume; wherein they seem to hear, and feel, though indeed the Organs are destitute of sense, and their natures of those faculties that should inform them. Thus it is observed, that men sometimes upon the hour of their departure, do speak and reason above themselves; for then the soul beginning to be freed from the ligaments of the body, begins to reason like her self, and to discourse in a strain above mortality.

SECT.12

We term sleep a death, and yet it is waking that kills us, and destroys those spirits that are the house of life. 'Tis indeed a part of life that best expresseth death; for every man truely lives, so long as he acts his nature, or some way makes good the faculties of himself: *Themistocles* therefore that slew his Soldier in his sleep, was a merciful Executioner: 'tis a kind of punishment the mildness of no laws hath invented; I wonder the fancy of *Lucan* and *Seneca* did not discover it. It is that death by which we may be literally said to dye daily; a death which *Adam* dyed before his mortality; a death whereby we live a middle and moderating point between life and death; in fine, so like death, I dare not trust it without my prayers, and an half adieu unto the World, and take my farewell in a Colloquy with God.

The night is come, like to the day;
Depart not thou great God away.
Let not my sins, black as the night,
Eclipse the lustre of thy light.
Keep still in my Horizon; for to me
The Sun makes not the day, but thee.
Thou whose nature cannot sleep,
On my temples centry keep;
Guard me 'gainst those watchful foes,
Whose eyes are open while mine close.
Let no dreams my head infest,
But such as Jacob's *temples blest.*
While I do rest, my Soul advance;
Make my sleep a holy trance.
That I may, my rest being wrought,
Awake into some holy thought;
And with as active vigour run
My course, as doth the nimble Sun.
Sleep is a death; O make me try,
By sleeping, what it is to die;
And as gently lay my head
On my grave, as now my bed.
Howere I rest, great God, let me
Awake again at last with thee.
And this assur'd, behold I lie
Securely, or to awake or die.
These are my drowsie days; in vain
I do now wake to sleep again:
O come that hour, when I shall never
Sleep again, but wake for ever.

This is the Dormative I take to bedward; I need no other *Laudanum* than this to make me sleep; after which, I close mine eyes in security, content to take my leave of the Sun, and sleep unto the resurrection.

SECT.13

The method I should use in distributive Justice, I often observe in commutative; and keep a Geometrical proportion in both; whereby becoming equable to others, I become unjust to my self, and supererogate in that common principle, *Do unto others as thou wouldst be done unto thy self*. I was not born unto riches, neither is it I think my Star to be wealthy; or if it were, the freedom of my mind, and frankness of my disposition, were able to contradict and cross my fates. For to me avarice seems not so much a vice, as a deplorable piece of madness; to conceive ourselves Urinals, or be perswaded that we are dead, is not so ridiculous, nor so many degrees beyond the power of Hellebore, as this. The opinion of Theory, and positions of men, are not so void of reason as their practised conclusions: some have held that Snow is black, that the earth moves, that the Soul is air, fire, water; but all this is Philosophy, and there is no *delirium*, if we do but speculate the folly and indisputable dotage of avarice, to that subterraneous Idol, and God of the Earth. I do confess

I am an Atheist; I cannot perswade myself to honour that the World adores; whatsoever virtue its prepared substance may have within my body, it hath no influence nor operation without: I would not entertain a base design, or an action that should call me villain, for the Indies; and for this only do I love and honour my own soul, and have methinks two arms too few to embrace myself. *Aristotle* is too severe, that will not allow us to be truely liberal without wealth, and the bountiful hand of Fortune; if this be true, I must confess I am charitable only in my liberal intentions, and bountiful well-wishes. But if the example of the Mite be not only an act of wonder, but an example of the noblest Charity, surely poor men may also build Hospitals, and the rich alone have not erected Cathedrals. I have a private method which others observe not; I take the opportunity of my self to do good; I borrow occasion of Charity from mine own necessities, and supply the wants of others, when I am in most need my self; for it is an honest stratagem to make advantage of our selves, and so to husband the acts of vertue, that where they were defective in one circumstance, they may repay their want, and multiply their goodness in another. I have not *Peru* in my desires, but a competence, and ability to perform those good works to which he hath inclined my nature. He is rich, who hath enough to be charitable; and it is hard to be so poor, that a noble mind may not find a way to this piece of goodness. *He that giveth to the poor, lendeth to the Lord*; there is more Rhetorick in that one sentence, than in a Library of Sermons; and indeed if those Sentences were understood by the Reader, with the same Emphasis as they are delivered by the Author, we needed not those Volumes of instructions, but might be honest by an Epitome. Upon this motive only I cannot behold a Beggar without relieving his Necessities with my Purse, or his Soul with my Prayers; these scenical and accidental differences between us, cannot make me forget that common and untouch'd part of us both; there is under these *Cantoes* and miserable outsides, these mutilate and semi-bodies, a soul of the same alloy with our own, whose Genealogy is God as well as ours, and in as fair a way to Salvation as our selves. Statists that labour to contrive a Common-wealth without our poverty, take away the object of charity, not understanding only the Common-wealth of a Christian, but forgetting the prophecie of Christ.

SECT.14

Now there is another part of charity, which is the Basis and Pillar of this, and that is the love of God, for whom we love our neighbour; for this I think charity, to love God for himself, and our neighbour for God. All that is truly amiable is God, or as it were a divided piece of him, that retains a reflex or shadow of himself. Nor is it strange that we should place affection on that which is invisible; all that we truly love is thus; what we adore under affection of our senses, deserves not the honour of so pure a title. Thus we adore virtue, though to the eyes of sense she be invisible: thus that part of our noble friends that we love, is not that part that we imbrace, but that insensible part that our arms cannot embrace. God being all goodness, can love nothing but himself, and the traduction of his holy Spirit. Let us call to assize the loves of our parents, the affection of our wives and children, and they are all dumb shows and dreams, without reality, truth or constancy: for first, there is a strong bond of affection between us and our Parents; yet how easily dissolved? We betake our selves to a woman, forget our mother in a wife, and the womb that bare us, in that that shall bear our Image: this woman blessing us with children, our affection leaves the level it held before, and sinks from our bed unto our issue and picture of Posterity, where affection holds no steady mansion. They, growing up in years, desire our ends; or applying themselves to a woman, take a lawful way to love another better than our selves. Thus I perceive a man may be buried alive, and behold his grave in his own issue.

SECT.15

I conclude therefore and say, there is no happiness under (or as *Copernicus* will have it, above) the Sun, nor any Crambe in that repeated verity and burthen of all the wisdom of *Solomon, All is vanity and vexation of Spirit*. There is no felicity in that the World adores: *Aristotle* whilst he labours to refute the Idea's of *Plato*, falls upon one himself: for his *summum bonum* is a *Chimæra*, and there is no such thing as his Felicity. That wherein God himself is happy, the holy Angels are happy, in whose defect the Devils are unhappy; that dare I call happiness: whatsoever conduceth unto this, may with an easy Metaphor deserve that name: whatsoever else the World terms Happiness, is to me a story out of *Pliny*, a tale of *Boccace* or *Malizspini*; an apparition or neat delusion, wherein there is no more of Happiness, than the name. Bless me in this life with but peace of my Conscience, command of my affections, the love of thy self and my dearest friends, and I shall be happy enough to pity *Cæsar*. These are, O Lord, the humble desires of my most reasonable ambition, and all I dare call happiness on earth; wherein I set no rule or limit to thy Hand or Providence; dispose of me according to the wisdom of thy pleasure. Thy will be done, though in my own undoing.

FINIS

Footnotes

[6]*Tho. Aquin. in com. in Boet. de Consolat. prope finem.*

[7]*A Church Bell that tolls every day at six and twelve of the clock; at the hearing whereof, everyone in what place soever, either of House or Street, betakes himself to his prayer, which is commonly directed to the Virgin.*

[8]*A revolution of certain thousand years, when all things should return unto their former estate, and he be teaching again in his School as when he delivered this Opinion.*

[9]*Sphæra cujus centrum ubique, circumferentia nullibi.*

[10]Γνῶθι σεαυτὸν, *Nosce teipsum.*

[11]*Post Mortem nihil est, ipsaque Mors nihil. Mors individua est, noxia corpori, nec patiens animæ ... Toti morimur, nullaque pars manet nostri.*

[12]*Pineda in his* Monarchica Ecclesiastica *quotes one thousand and forty Authors.*

[13]*In his Oracle to* Augustus.

[14]*Thereby is meant out good Angel appointed us from our Nativity.*

[15]*Who willed his friend not to bury him, but hang him up with a staff in his hand to fright away the crows.*

[16]*Urbem Roman in principio Reges habuere.*

[17]*Pro Archiâ Poëtâ.*

[18]*In qua me non inficior mediocriter esse.*

PSEUDODOXIA EPIDEMICA
OR ENQUIRIES
INTO VERY MANY RECEIVED
TENENTS AND COMMONLY
PRESUMED TRUTHS

TO THE READER

Would Truth dispense, we could be content, with Plato, *that knowledge were but remembrance; that intellectual acquisition were but reminiscential evocation, and new Impressions but the colouring of old stamps which stood pale in the soul before. For what is worse, knowledge is made by oblivion, and to purchase a clear and warrantable body of Truth, we must forget and part with much we know. Our tender Enquiries taking up Learning at large, and together with true and assured notions, receiving many, wherein our reviewing judgments do find no satisfaction. And therefore in this* Encyclopædie *and round of Knowledge, like the great and exemplary Wheels of Heaven, we must observe two Circles: that while we are daily carried about, and whirled on by the swing and rapt of the one, we may maintain a natural and proper course, in the slow and sober wheel of the other. And this we shall more readily perform, if we timely survey our knowledge; impartially singling out those encroachments, which junior compliance and popular credulity hath admitted. Whereof at present we have endeavoured a long and serious* Adviso; *proposing not only a large and copious List, but from experience and reason attempting their decisions.*

And first we crave exceeding pardon in the audacity of the Attempt, humbly acknowledging a work of such concernment unto truth, and difficulty in it self, did well deserve the conjunction of many heads. And surely more advantageous had it been unto Truth, to have fallen into the endeavors of some co-operating advancers, that might have performed it to the life, and added authority thereto; which the privacy of our condition, and unequal abilities cannot expect. Whereby notwithstanding we have not been diverted; nor have our solitary attempts been so discouraged, as to dispair the favourable look of Learning upon our single and unsupported endeavours.

Nor have we let fall our Pen, upon discouragement of Contradiction, Unbelief and Difficulty of disswasion from radicated beliefs, and points of high prescription, although we are very sensible, how hardly teaching years do learn, what roots old age contracteth unto errors, and how such as are but acorns in our younger brows, grow Oaks in our elder heads, and become inflexible unto the powerfullest arm of reason. Although we have also beheld, what cold requitals others have found in their several redemptions of Truth; and how their ingenuous Enquiries have been dismissed with censure, and obloquie of singularities.

Inspection of Urines.

Some consideration we hope from the course of our Profession, which though it leadeth us into many truths that pass undiscerned by others, yet doth it disturb their Communications, and much interrupt the office of our Pens in their well intended Transmissions. And therefore surely in this work attempts will exceed performances; it being composed by snatches of time, as medical vacations, and the fruitless importunity of Uroscopy would permit us. And therefore also, perhaps it hath not found that regular and constant stile, those infallible experiments and those assured determinations, which the subject sometime requireth, and might be expected from others, whose quiet doors and unmolested hours afford no such distractions. Although whoever shall indifferently perpend the exceeding difficulty, which either the obscurity of the subject, or unavoidable paradoxology must often put upon the Attemptor, he will easily discern, a work of this nature is not to be performed upon one legg; and should smel of oyl, if duly and deservedly handled.

Our first intentions considering the common interest of Truth, resolved to propose it unto the Latine republique and equal Judges of Europe, but owing in the first place this service unto our Country, and therein especially unto its ingenuous Gentry, we have declared our self in a language best conceived. Although I confess the quality of the Subject will sometimes carry us into expressions beyond meer English apprehensions. And indeed, if elegancy still proceedeth, and English Pens maintain that stream, we have of late observed to flow from many; we shall within few years be fain to learn Latine to understand English, and a work will prove of equal facility in either. Nor have we addressed our Pen or Stile unto the people (whom Books do not redress, and are this way incapable of reduction), but unto the knowing and leading part of Learning. As well understanding (at least probably hoping) except they be watered from higher regions, and fructifying meteors of Knowledge, these weeds must lose their alimental sap, and wither of themselves. Whose conserving influence, could our endeavours prevent; we should trust the rest unto the sythe of Time, and hopefull dominion of Truth.

We hope it will not be unconsidered, that we find no open tract, or constant manuduction in this Labyrinth; but are oft-times fain to wander in the America and untravelled parts of Truth. For though not many years past, Dr. Primrose hath made a learned Discourse of vulgar Errors in Physick, yet have we discussed but two or three thereof. Scipio Mercurii hath also left an excellent tract in Italian, concerning popular Errors; but confining himself only unto those in Physick, he hath little conduced unto the generality of our doctrine. Laurentius Ioubertus, by the same Title led our expectation into thoughts of great relief; whereby notwithstanding we reaped no advantage; it answering scarce at all the promise of the inscription. περὶ τῶν ψευδῶς πεπιστευμένων, Athenæi, lib. 7. Nor perhaps (if it were yet extant) should we find any farther Assistance from that ancient piece of Andreas, pretending the same Title. And therefore we are often constrained to stand alone against the strength of opinion, and to meet the Goliah and Giant of Authority, with contemptible pibbles, and feeble arguments, drawn from the scrip and slender stock of our selves. Nor have we indeed scarce named any Author whose name we do not honour; and if detraction could invite us, discretion surely would contain us from any derogatory intention, where highest Pens and friendliest eloquence must fail in commendation.

And therefore also we cannot but hope the equitable considerations, and candour of reasonable minds. We cannot expect the frown of Theology herein; nor can they which behold *the present state of things, and controversie of points so long received in Divinity, condemn our sober Enquiries in the doubtfull appertinancies of Arts, and Receptaries of Philosophy. Surely Philologers and Critical Discoursers, who look beyond the shell and obvious exteriors of things, will not be angry with our narrower explorations. And we cannot doubt, our Brothers in Physick (whose knowledge in Naturals will lead them into a nearer apprehension of many things delivered) will friendly accept, if not countenance our endeavours. Nor can we conceive it may be unwelcome unto those honoured Worthies, who endeavour the advancement of Learning: as being likely to find a clearer progression, when so many rubs are levelled, and many untruths taken off, which passing as principles with common beliefs, disturb the tranquility of Axioms, which otherwise might be raised. And wise men cannot but know, that arts and learning want this expurgation: and if the course of truth be permitted unto its self, like that of time and uncorrected computations, it cannot escape many errors, which duration still enlargeth.*

Lastly, we are not Magisterial in opinions, nor have we Dictator-like obtruded our conceptions; but in the humility of Enquiries or disquisitions, have only proposed them unto more ocular discerners. And therefore opinions are free, and open it is for any to think or declare the contrary. And we shall so far encourage contradiction, as to promise no disturbance, or re-oppose any Pen, that shall fallaciously or captiously refute us; that shall only lay hold of our lapses, single out Digressions, Corollaries, or Ornamental conceptions, to evidence his own in as indifferent truths. And shall only take notice of such, whose experimental and judicious knowledge shall solemnly look upon it; not only to destroy of ours, but to establish of his own; not to traduce or extenuate, but to explain and dilucidate, to add and ampliate, according to the laudable custom of the Ancients in their sober promotions of Learning. Unto whom notwithstanding, we shall not contentiously rejoin, or only to justifie our own, but to applaud or confirm his maturer assertions; and shall confer what is in us unto his name and honour; Ready to be swallowed in any worthy enlarger: as having acquired our end, if any way, or under any name we may obtain a work, so much desired, and yet desiderated of Truth.

THOMAS BROWN.

THE POSTSCRIPT

Readers,

To enform you of the Advantages of the present Impression, and disabuse your expectations of any future Enlargements; these are to advertise thee, that this Edition comes forth with very many Explanations, Additions, and Alterations throughout, besides that of one entire Chapter: But that now this Work is compleat and perfect, expect no further Additions.

THE FIRST BOOK
OR GENERAL PART

CHAPTER I
Of the Causes of Common Errors.

The Introduction.

The First and Father-cause of common Error, is, The common infirmity of Human Nature; of whose deceptible condition, although perhaps there should not need any other eviction, than the frequent Errors we shall our selves commit, even in the express declarement hereof: yet shall we illustrate the same from more infallible constitutions, and persons presumed as far from us in condition, as time, that is, our first and ingenerated forefathers. From whom as we derive our Being, and the several wounds of constitution; so, may we in some manner excuse our infirmities in the depravity of those parts, whose Traductions were pure in them, and their Originals but once removed from God. Who notwithstanding (if posterity may take leave to judge of the fact, as they are assured to suffer in the punishment) were grossly deceived, in their perfection; and so weakly deluded in the clarity of their understanding, that it hath left no small obscurity in ours, How error should gain upon them.

Matter of great dispute, how our first parents could be so deceived.

For first, They were deceived by Satan; and that not in an invisible insinuation; but an open and discoverable apparition, that is, in the form of a Serpent; whereby although there were many occasions of suspition, and such as could not easily escape a weaker circumspection, yet did the unwary apprehension of *Eve* take no advantage thereof. It hath therefore seemed strange unto some, she should be deluded by a Serpent, or subject her reason to a beast, which God had subjected unto hers. It hath empuzzled the enquiries of others to apprehend, and enforced them unto strange conceptions, to make out, how without fear or doubt she could discourse with such a creature, or hear a Serpent speak, without suspition of Imposture. The wits of others have been so bold, as to accuse her simplicity, in receiving his Temptation so coldly; and when such specious effects of the Fruit were Promised, as to make them like God; not to desire, at least not to wonder he pursued not that benefit himself. And had it been their own case, would perhaps have replied, If the tast of this Fruit maketh the eaters like *Gods*, why remainest thou a Beast? If it maketh us but *like Gods*, we are so already. If thereby our eyes shall be opened hereafter, they are at present quick enough, to discover thy deceit; and we desire them no opener, to behold our own shame. If to know good and evil be our advantage, although we have Free-will unto both, we desire to perform but one; We know 'tis good to obey the commandement of God, but evil if we transgress it.

Adam *supposed by some to have been the wisest man that ever was.*

They were deceived by one another, and in the greatest disadvantage of Delusion, that is, the stronger by the weaker: For *Eve* presented the Fruit, and *Adam* received it from her. Thus the *Serpent* was cunning enough, to begin the deceit in the weaker, and the weaker of strength, sufficient to consummate the fraud in the stronger. Art and fallacy was used unto her; a naked offer proved sufficient unto him: So his superstruction was his Ruine, and the fertility of his Sleep an issue of Death unto him. And although the condition of Sex, and posteriority of Creation, might somewhat extenuate the Error of the Woman: Yet was it very strange and inexcusable in the Man; especially, if as some affirm, he was the wisest of all men since; or if, as others have conceived, he was not ignorant of the Fall of the Angels, and had thereby Example and punishment to deterr him.

Adam *and* Eve *how they fell*.

They were deceived from themselves, and their own apprehensions; for *Eve* either mistook, or traduced the commandment of God. *Of every Tree of the Garden thou mayest freely eat, but of the Tree of knowledge of good and evil thou shalt not eat: for in the day thou eatest thereof, thou shall surely die*. Now *Eve* upon the question of the *Serpent*, returned the Precept in different terms: *You shall not eat of it, neither shall you touch it, less perhaps you die*. In which delivery, there were no less than two mistakes, or rather additional mendacities; for the Commandment forbad not the touch of the Fruit; and positively said, *Ye shall surely die*: but she extenuating, replied, *ne fortè moriamini, lest perhaps ye die*. For so in the vulgar translation it runneth, and so it is expressed in the *Thargum* or Paraphrase of *Jonathan*. And therefore although it be said, and that very truely, *that the Devil was a lyer from the beginning*, yet was the Woman herein the first express beginner: and falsified twice, before the reply of *Satan*. And therefore also, to speak strictly, the sin of the Fruit was not the first Offence: They first transgressed the Rule of their own Reason; and after the Commandment of God.

They were deceived through the Conduct of their Senses, and by Temptations from the Object it self; whereby although their intellectuals had not failed in the Theory of truth, yet did the inservient and brutal Faculties control the suggestion of Reason: Pleasure and Profit already overswaying the instructions of Honesty, and Sensuality perturbing the reasonable commands of Vertue. For so it is delivered in the Text: That when the Woman saw, *that the Tree was good for food*, and *that it was pleasant unto the eye*, and *a Tree to be desired to make one wise, she took of the fruit thereof and did eat*. Now hereby it appeareth, that *Eve*, before the Fall, was by the same and beaten away of allurements inveigled, whereby her posterity hath been deluded ever since; that is, those three delivered by St. *John*, *The lust of the flesh, the lust of the eye, and the pride of life*: Where indeed they seemed as weakly to fail, as their debilitated posterity, ever after. Whereof notwithstanding, some in their imperfection, have resisted more powerful temptations; and in many moralities condemned the facility of their seductions.

Adam *whence (probably) induced to eat.*
Whether Cain *intended to kill* Abel.

Again, they might, for ought we know, be still deceived in the unbelief of their Mortality, even after they had eat of the Fruit: For, *Eve* observing no immediate execution of the Curse, she delivered the Fruit unto *Adam*: who, after the tast thereof, perceiving himself still to live, might yet remain in doubt, whether he had incurred Death; which perhaps he did not indubitably believe, until he was after convicted in the visible example of *Abel*. For he that would not believe the Menace of God at first, it may be doubted whether, before an ocular example, he believed the Curse at last. And therefore they are not without all reason, who have disputed the Fact of *Cain*: that is, although he purposed to do mischief, whether he intended to kill his Brother; or designed that, whereof he had not beheld an example in his own kind. There might be somewhat in it, that he would not have done, or desired undone, when he brake forth as desperately, as before he had done uncivilly, *My iniquity is greater than can be forgiven me.*

The Thalmudist's *Allegories upon the History of* Adam *and* Eve's *Fall*.

Some nicities I confess there are which extenuate, but many more that aggravate this Delusion; which exceeding the bounds of this Discourse, and perhaps our Satisfaction, we shall at present pass over. And therefore whether the Sin of our First Parents were the greatest of any since; whether the transgression of *Eve* seducing, did not exceed that of *Adam* seduced; or whether the resistibility of his Reason, did not equivalence the facility of her Seduction; we shall refer it to the *Schoolman*; Whether there was not in *Eve* as great injustice in deceiving her husband, as imprudence in being deceived her self; especially, if foretasting the Fruit, her eyes were opened before his, and she knew the effect of it, before he tasted of it; we leave it unto the *Moralist*. Whether the whole relation be not Allegorical, that is, whether the temptation of the Man by the Woman, be not the seduction of the rational and higher parts by the inferiour and feminine faculties; or whether the Tree in the midst of the Garden, were not that part in the Center of the body, in which was afterward the appointment of Circumcision in Males, we leave it unto the *Thalmudist*. Whether there were any Policy in the Devil to tempt them before the Conjunction, or whether the Issue before tentation, might in justice have suffered with those after, we leave it unto the *Lawyer*. Whether *Adam* foreknew the advent of Christ, or the reparation of his Error by his Saviour; how the execution of the Curse should have been ordered, if, after *Eve* had eaten, *Adam* had yet refused. Whether if they had tasted the Tree of life, before that of Good and Evil, they had yet suffered the curse of Mortality: or whether the efficacy of the one had not over-powred the penalty of the other, we leave it unto GOD. For he alone can truly determine these, and all things else; Who as he hath proposed the World unto our disputation, so hath he reserved many things unto his own resolution; whose determination we cannot hope from flesh, but must with reverence suspend unto that great Day, whose justice shall either condemn our curiosities, or resolve our disquisitions.

Lastly, Man was not only deceivable in his Integrity, but the Angels of light in all their Clarity. He that said, He would be like the highest did erre, if in some way he conceived himself so already: but in attempting so high an effect from himself, he mis-understood the nature of God, and held a false apprehension of his own; whereby vainly attempting not only insolencies, but impossibilities, he deceived himself as low as Hell. In brief, there is nothing infallible but GOD, who cannot possibly erre. For things are really true as they correspond unto his conception; and have so much verity as they hold of conformity unto that Intellect, in whose *Idea* they had their first determinations. And therefore being the Rule, he cannot be Irregular; nor, being Truth it self, conceaveably admit the impossible society of Error.

CHAPTER II
A further Illustration of the same.

Being thus deluded before the Fall, it is no wonder if their conceptions were deceitful, and could scarce speak without an Error after. For, what is very remarkable (and no man that I know hath yet observed) in the relations of Scripture before the Flood, there is but one speech delivered by Man, wherein there is not an erroneous conception; and, strictly examined, most hainously injurious unto truth. The pen of *Moses* is brief in the account before the Flood, and the speeches recorded are but six. The first is that of *Adam*, when upon the expostulation of God, he replied; *I heard thy voice in the Garden, and because I was naked I hid my self*. In which reply, there was included a very gross Mistake, and, if with pertinacity maintained, a high and capital Error. For thinking by this retirement to obscure himself from God, he infringed the omnisciency and essential Ubiquity of his Maker, Who as he created all things, so is he beyond and in them all, not only in power, as under his subjection, or in his presence, as being in his cognition; but in his very Essence, as being the soul of their causalities, and the essential cause of their existencies. Certainly, his posterity at this distance and after so perpetuated an impairment, cannot but condemn the poverty of his conception, that thought to obscure himself from his Creator in the shade of the Garden, who had beheld him before in the darkness of his Chaos, and the great obscurity of Nothing; that thought to fly from God, which could not fly himself; or imagined that one tree should conceal his nakedness from Gods eye, as another had revealed it unto his own. Those tormented Spirits that wish the mountains to cover them, have fallen upon desires of minor absurdity, and chosen ways of less improbable concealment. Though this be also as ridiculous unto reason, as fruitless unto their desires; for he that laid the foundations of the Earth, cannot be excluded the secrecy of the Mountains; nor can there any thing escape the perspicacity of those eyes which were before light, and in whose opticks there is no opacity. This is the consolation of all good men, unto whom his Ubiquity affordeth continual comfort and security: And this is the affliction of Hell, unto whom it affordeth despair, and remediless calamity. For those restless Spirits that fly the face of the Almighty, being deprived the fruition of his eye, would also avoid the extent of his hand; which being impossible, their sufferings are desperate, and their afflictions without evasion; until they can get out of *Trismegistus* his Circle, that is, to extend their wings above the Universe, and pitch beyond Ubiquity.

The Second is that Speech of *Adam* unto God; *The woman whom thou gavest me to be with me, she gave me of the Tree, and I did eat*. This indeed was an unsatisfactory reply, and therein was involved a very impious Error, as implying God the Author of sin, and accusing his Maker of his transgression. As if he had said, If thou hadst not given me a woman, I had not been deceived: Thou promisedst to make her a help, but she hath proved destruction unto me: Had I remained alone, I had not sinned; but thou gavest me a Consort, and so I became seduced. This was a bold and open accusation of God, making the fountain of good, the contriver of evil, and the forbidder of the crime an abettor of the fact prohibited. Surely, his mercy was great that did not revenge the impeachment of his justice; And his goodness to be admired, that it refuted not his argument in the punishment of his excusation, and only pursued the first transgression without a penalty of this the second.

The third was that of *Eve; The Serpent beguiled me, and I did eat*. In which reply, there was not only a very feeble excuse, but an erroneous translating her own offence upon another; Extenuating her sin from that which was an aggravation, that is, to excuse the Fact at all, much more upon the suggestion of a beast, which was before in the strictest terms prohibited by her God. For although we now do hope the mercies of God will consider our degenerated integrities unto some minoration of our offences; yet had not the sincerity of our first parents so colourable expectations, unto whom the commandment was but single, and their integrities best able to resist the motions of its transgression. And therefore so heinous conceptions have risen hereof, that some have seemed more angry therewith, than God himself: Being so exasperated with the offence, as to call in question their salvation, and to dispute the eternal punishment of their Maker. Assuredly with better reason may posterity accuse them than they the Serpent or one another; and the displeasure of the *Pelagians* must needs be irreconcilable, who peremptorily maintaining they can fulfil the whole Law, will insatisfactorily condemn the non-observation of one.

The Devill knew not our Saviour to be God when he tempted him.

The fourth, was that speech of *Cain* upon the demand of God, *Where is thy brother?* and he said, *I know not*. In which Negation, beside the open impudence, there was implied a notable Error; for returning a lie unto his Maker, and presuming in this manner to put off the Searcher of hearts, he denied the omnisciency of God, whereunto there is nothing concealable. The answer of Satan in the case of *Job*, had more of truth, wisdom, and Reverence, this; *Whence comest thou Satan?* and he said, *From compassing of the Earth*. For though an enemy of God, and hater of all

Truth, his wisdom will hardly permit him to falsifie with the All-mighty. For well understanding the Omniscience of his nature, he is not so ready to deceive himself, as to falsifie unto him whose cognition is no way deludable. And therefore when in the tentation of Christ he played upon the fallacy, and thought to deceive the Author of Truth, the Method of this proceeding arose from the uncertainty of his Divinity; whereof had he remained assured, he had continued silent; nor would his discretion attempt so unsucceedable a temptation. And so again at the last day, when our offences shall be drawn into accompt, the subtilty of that Inquisitor shall not present unto God a bundle of calumnies or confutable accusations, but will discreetly offer up unto his Omnisciency, a true and undeniable list of our transgressions.

The fifth is another reply of *Cain* upon the denouncement of his curse, *My iniquity is greater then can be forgiven*: For so it is expressed in some Translations. The assertion was not only desperate, but the conceit erroneous, overthrowing that glorious Attribute of God, his Mercy, and conceiving the sin of murder unpardonable. Which how great soever, is not above the repentance of man; but far below the mercies of God, and was (as some conceive) expiated in that punishment he suffered temporally for it. There are but two examples of this error in holy Scripture, and they both for Murder, and both as it were of the same person; for Christ was mystically slain in *Abel*, and therefore *Cain* had some influence on his death as well as *Judas*; but the sin had a different effect on *Cain*, from that it had on *Judas*; and most that since have fallen into it. For they like *Judas* desire death, and not unfrequently pursue it: *Cain* on the contrary grew afraid thereof, and obtained a securement from it. Assuredly, if his despair continued, there was punishment enough in life, and Justice sufficient in the mercy of his protection. For the life of the desperate equalls the anxieties of death; who in uncessant inquietudes but act the life of the damned, and anticipate the desolations of Hell. 'Tis indeed a sin in man, but a punishment only in Devils, who offend not God but afflict themselves, in the appointed despair of his mercies. And as to be without hope is the affliction of the damned, so is it the happiness of the blessed; who having all their expectations present, are not distracted with futurities: So is it also their felicity to have no Faith; for enjoying the beatifical vision, there is nothing unto them inevident; and in the fruition of the object of Faith, they have received the full evacuation of it.

Cain, *as the Rabbins think, was the man slain by* Lamech, *Gen. 4, 23*.

The last speech was that of *Lamech, I have slain a man to my wound, and a young man in my hurt*: If *Cain* be avenged seven fold, truly *Lamech* seventy and seven fold. Now herein there seems to be a very erroneous Illation: from the Indulgence of God unto *Cain*, concluding an immunity unto himself; that is, a regular protection from a single example, and an exemption from punishment in a fact that naturally deserved it. The Error of this offender was contrary to that of *Cain*, whom the *Rabbins* conceive that *Lamech* at this time killed. He despaired in Gods mercy in the same Fact, where this presumed of it; he by a decollation of all hope annihilated his mercy, this by an immoderancy thereof destroyed his Justice. Though the sin were less, the Error was as great; For as it is untrue, that his mercy will not forgive offenders, or his benignity co-operate to their conversions; So is it also of no less falsity to affirm His justice will not exact account of sinners, or punish such as continue in their transgressions.

Thus may we perceive, how weakly our fathers did Erre before the Floud, how continually and upon common discourse they fell upon Errors after; it is therefore no wonder we have been erroneous ever since. And being now at greatest distance from the beginning of Error, are almost lost in its dissemination, whose waies are boundless, and confess no circumscription.

CHAPTER III
Of the second cause of Popular Errors; the erroneous disposition of the People.

Having thus declared the infallible nature of Man even from his first production, we have beheld the general cause of Error. But as for popular Errors, they are more neerly founded upon an erroneous inclination of the people; as being the most deceptable part of Mankind and ready with open armes to receive the encroachments of Error. Which condition of theirs although deducible from many Grounds, yet shall we evidence it but from a few, and such as most neerly and undeniably declare their natures.

How unequal discerners of truth they are, and openly exposed unto Error, will first appear from their unqualified intellectuals, unable to umpire the difficulty of its dissensions. For Error, to speak largely, is a false judgment of things, or, an assent unto falsity. Now whether the object whereunto they deliver up their assent be true or false, they are incompetent judges.

For the assured truth of things is derived from the principles of knowledge, and causes which determine their verities. Whereof their uncultivated understandings, scarce holding any theory, they are but bad discerners of verity; and in the numerous track of Error, but casually do hit the point and unity of truth.

Arguments of sensitive quality most prevailing upon vulgar capacities.

Their understanding is so feeble in the discernment of falsities, and averting the Errors of reason, that it submitteth unto the fallacies of sense, and is unable to rectifie the Error of its sensations. Thus the greater part of Mankind having but one eye of Sense and Reason, conceive the Earth far bigger than the Sun, the fixed Stars lesser than the Moon, their figures plain, and their spaces from Earth equidistant. For thus their Sense informeth them, and herein their reason cannot Rectifie them; and therefore hopelessly continuing in mistakes, they live and die in their absurdities; passing their days in perverted apprehensions, and conceptions of the World, derogatory unto God, and the wisdom of the Creation.

Again, being so illiterate in the point of intellect, and their sense so incorrected, they are farther indisposed ever to attain unto truth; as commonly proceeding in those wayes, which have most reference unto sense, and wherein there lyeth most notable and popular delusion.

For being unable to wield the intellectuall arms of reason, they are fain to betake themselves unto wasters, and the blunter weapons of truth: affecting the gross and sensible ways of Doctrine, and such as will not consist with strict and subtile Reason. *Fable.* Thus unto them a piece of Rhetorick is a sufficient argument of Logick; an Apologue of *Esop*, beyond a Syllogysm in *Barbara*; parables than propositions, and proverbs more powerful than demonstrations. And therefore are they led rather by Example, than Precept; receiving perswasions from visible inducements, before electual instructions. And therefore also they judge of human actions by the event; for being uncapable of operable circumstances, or rightly to judge the prudentiality of affairs, they only gaze upon the visible success, and therefore condemn or cry up the whole progression. And so from this ground in the Lecture of holy Scripture, their apprehensions are commonly confined unto the literal sense of the Text, from whence have ensued the gross and duller sort of Heresies. For not attaining the deuteroscopy, and second intention of the words, they are fain to omit the Superconsequencies, Coherencies, Figures, or Tropologies; and are not sometime perswaded by fire beyond their literalities. And therefore also things invisible, but into intellectual discernments, to humour the grossness of their comprehensions, have been degraded from their proper forms, and God Himself dishonoured into manual expressions. And so likewise being unprovided, or unsufficient for higher speculations, they will always betake themselves unto sensible representations, and can hardly be restrained the dulness of Idolatry: A sin or folly not only derogatory unto God but men; overthrowing their Reason, as well as his Divinity. In brief, a reciprocation, or rather, an inversion of the Creation, making God one way, as he made us another; that is, after our Image, as he made us after His own.

Moreover, their understanding thus weak in it self, and perverted by sensible delusions, is yet farther impaired by the dominion of their appetite; that is, the irrational and brutal part of the soul, which lording it over the soveraign faculty, interrupts the actions of that noble part, and choaks those tender sparks, which *Adam* hath left them of reason. And therefore they do not only swarm with Errors, but vices depending thereon. Thus they commonly affect no man any further than he deserts his reason, or complies with their aberrancies. Hence they imbrace not vertue for it self, but its reward; and the argument from pleasure or Utility is far more powerful, than that from vertuous Honesty: which *Mahomet* and his contrivers well understood, when he set out the felicity of his Heaven, by the contentments of flesh, and the delights of sense, slightly passing over the accomplishment of the Soul, and the beatitude of that part which Earth and visibilities too weakly affect. But the wisdom of our Saviour, and the simplicity of his truth proceeded another way; defying the popular provisions of happiness from sensible expectations; placing his felicity in things removed from sense, and the intellectual enjoyment of God. And therefore the doctrine of the one was never afraid of Universities, or endeavoured the banishment of learning, like the other. And though *Galen* doth sometimes nibble at *Moses*, and, beside the Apostate Christian, *Julian.* some *Heathens* have questioned his Philosophical part, or treaty of the Creation: Yet is there surely no reasonable *Pagan*, that will not admire the rational and well grounded precepts of Christ; whose life, as it was conformable unto his Doctrine, so was that unto the highest rules of Reason; and must therefore flourish in the advancement of learning, and the perfection of parts best able to comprehend it.

Again, Their individual imperfections being great, they are moreover enlarged by their aggregation; and being erroneous in their single numbers, once hudled together, they will be Error it self. For being a confusion of knaves and fools, and a farraginous concurrence of all conditions, tempers, sexes, and ages; it is but natural if their determinations be monstrous, and many wayes inconsistent with Truth. And therefore wise men have alwaies applauded their own judgment, in the contradiction of that of the people; and their soberest adversaries, have ever afforded them the stile of fools and mad men; and, to speak impartially, their actions have made good these *Epithets*. Non sani esse hominis, non sanus juret Orestes. Had *Orestes* been Judge, he would not have acquitted that *Lystrian* rabble of madness, who, upon a visible miracle, falling into so high a conceit of *Paul* and *Barnabas*, that they termed the one *Jupiter*, the other *Mercurius*; that they brought Oxen and Garlands, and were hardly restrained from sacrificing unto them; did notwithstanding suddenly after fall upon *Paul*, and having stoned him drew him for dead out of the City. It might have hazarded the sides of *Democritus*, had he been present at that tumult of *Demetrius*; when the people flocking together in great numbers, some crying one thing, and some another, and the assembly was confused, and the most part knew not wherefore they were come together; notwithstanding, all with one voice for the space of two hours cried out, Great is *Diana* of the *Ephesians*. It had overcome the patience of *Job*, as it did the meekness of *Moses*, and would surely have mastered any, but the longanimity, and lasting sufferance of God; had they beheld the Mutiny in the wilderness, when, after ten great Miracles in *Egypt*, and some in the same place, they melted down their stoln ear-rings into a Calf, and monstrously cryed out; *These are thy Gods*, O Israel, *that brought thee out of the land* of Egypt. It much accuseth the impatience of *Peter*, who could not endure the staves of the multitude, and is the greatest example of lenity in our Saviour, when he desired of God forgiveness unto those, who having one day brought him into the City in triumph, did presently after, act all dishonour upon him, and nothing could be heard but, *Crucifige*, in their Courts. Certainly he that considereth these things in God's peculiar people will easily discern how little of truth there is in the wayes of the Multitude; and though sometimes they are flattered with that *Aphorism*, will hardly believe, The voice of the people to be the voice of God.

Lastly, being thus divided from truth in themselves, they are yet farther removed by advenient deception. For true it is (and I hope I shall not offend their vulgarities,) if I say, they are daily mocked into Error by subtler devisors, and have been expressly deluded by all professions and ages. Thus the *Priests* of Elder time, have put upon them many incredible conceits, not only deluding their apprehensions with Ariolation, South-saying, and such oblique Idolatries, but winning their credulities unto the literal and down right adorement of Cats, Lizzards, and Beetles. And thus also in some Christian Churches, wherein is presumed an irreprovable truth, if all be true that is suspected, or half what is related; there have not wanted many strange deceptions, and some thereof are still confessed by the name of Pious Frauds. Thus *Theudas* an Impostor was able to lead away Four thousand into the Wilderness. and the delusions of *Mahomet* almost the fourth part of Mankind. Thus all Heresies, how gross soever, have found a welcome with the people. For thus, many of the Jews were wrought into belief that *Herod* was the *Messias*; and *David George* of *Leyden and Arden*, were not without a party amongst the people, who maintained the same opinion of themselves almost in our days.

The Author's Censure upon Judgment by Urine.

Physitians (many at least that make profession thereof) beside divers less discoverable wayes of fraud, have made them believe, there is the book of fate, or the power of *Aarons* breast-plate, in Urins. And therefore hereunto they have recourse, as unto the Oracle of life, the great determinator of Virginity, Conception, Fertility, and the Inscrutable infirmities of the whole Body. For as though there were a seminality in Urine, or that, like the Seed, it carried with it the *Idea* of every part, they foolishly conceive, we visibly behold therein the Anatomy of every particle, and can thereby indigitate their Diseases: And running into any demands, expect from us a sudden resolution in things, whereon the Devil of *Delphos* would demurr; and we know hath taken respite of some dayes to answer easier questions.

Places in Venice *and* Paris, *where Mountebanks play their pranks.*

Saltimbancoes, *Quacksalvers*, and *Charlatans*, deceive them in lower degrees. Were *Esop* alive, the *Piazza* and *Pont-Neuf* could not but speak their fallacies; mean while there are too many, whose cries cannot conceal their mischief. For their Impostures are full of cruelty, and worse than any other; deluding not only unto pecuniary defraudations, but the irreparable deceit of death.

Astrologers, which pretend to be of *Cabala* with the Starrs (such I mean as abuse that worthy Enquiry) have not been wanting in their deceptions; who having won their belief unto principles whereof they make great doubt themselves, have made them believe that arbitrary events below, have necessary causes, above; whereupon their credulities assent unto any Prognosticks; and daily swallow the Predictions of men, which, considering the independency of their causes, and contigency in their Events, are only in the prescience of God.

Fortune-tellers, Juglers, Geomancers, and the like incantory Impostors, though commonly men of Inferiour rank, and from whom without Illumination they can expect no more than from themselves, do daily and professedly delude them. Unto whom (what is deplorable in Men and Christians) too many applying themselves, betwixt jest and earnest, betray the cause of Truth, and sensibly make up the legionary body of Error.

The people of Rome, *why never suffered to know the right name of their City.*

Statists and *Politicians*, unto whom *Ragione di Stato*, is the first Considerable, as though it were their business to deceive the people, as a Maxim, do hold, that truth is to be concealed from them; unto whom although they reveal the visible design, yet do they commonly conceal the capital intention. And therefore have they ever been the instruments of great designes, yet seldom understood the true intention of any, accomplishing the drifts of wiser heads, as inanimate and ignorant Agents, the general design of the World; who though in some Latitude of sense, and in a natural cognition perform their proper actions, yet do they unknowingly concurr unto higher ends, and blindly advance the great intention of Nature. Now how far they may be kept in ignorance a greater example there is in the people of *Rome*; who never knew the true and proper name of their own City. For, beside that common appellation received by the Citizens, it had a proper and secret name concealed from them: *Cujus alterum nomen discere secretis Ceremoniarum nefas habetur*, saith *Plinie*; lest the name thereof being discovered unto their enemies, their *Penates* and Patronal God might be called forth by charms and incantations. For according unto the tradition of *Magitians*, the tutelary Spirits will not remove at common appellations, but at the proper names of things whereunto they are Protectors.

Thus having been deceived by themselves, and continually deluded by others, they must needs be stuffed with Errors, and even over-run with these inferiour falsities; whereunto whosoever shall resign their reasons, either from the Root of deceit in themselves, or inability to resist such trivial deceptions from others, although their condition and fortunes may place them many Spheres above the multitude; yet are they still within the line of Vulgarity, and Democratical enemies of truth.

CHAPTER IV
Of the nearer and more Immediate Causes of popular Errors, both in the wiser and common sort, Misapprehension, Fallacy, or false Deduction, Credulity, Supinity, Adherence unto Antiquity, Tradition and Authority.

The belief of Centaures *whence occasioned.*

The first is a mistake, or a misconception of things, either in their first apprehensions, or secondary relations. So *Eve* mistook the Commandment, either from the immediate injunction of God, or from the secondary narration of her Husband. So might the Disciples mistake our Saviour, in his answer unto *Peter* concerning the death of *John*, as is delivered, *John* 21. Peter *seeing* John, *said unto* Jesus, *Lord, and what shall this man do?* Jesus *saith, If I will, that he tarry till I come, what is that unto thee? Then went this saying abroad among the brethren, that that Disciple should not die.* Thus began the conceit and opinion of the *Centaures*: that is, in the mistake of the first beholders, as is declared by *Servius*; when some young *Thessalians* on horseback were beheld afar off, while their horses watered, that is, while their heads were depressed, they were conceived by the first Spectators, to be but one animal; and answerable hereunto have their pictures been drawn ever since.

Equivocation and Amphibologie, how they differ.

And, as simple mistakes commonly beget fallacies, so men rest not in false apprehensions, without absurd and inconsequent deductions; from fallacious foundations, and misapprehended *mediums*, erecting conclusions no way inferrible from their premises. Now the fallacies whereby men deceive others, and are deceived themselves, the Ancients have divided into Verbal and Real. Of the Verbal, and such as conclude from mistakes of the Word, although there be no less than six, yet are there but two thereof worthy our notation, and unto which the rest may be referred; that is the fallacy of Equivocation and Amphibology which conclude from the ambiguity of some one word, or the ambiguous Syntaxis of many put together. From this fallacy arose that calamitous Error of the Jews, misapprehending the Prophesies of their *Messias*, and expounding them always unto literal and temporal expectations. By this way many Errors crept in and perverted the Doctrine of *Pythagoras*, whilst men received his Precepts in a different sense from his intention; converting Metaphors into proprieties, and receiving as literal expressions, obscure and involved truths.

Pythagoras, his Allegorical precepts moralized.

Thus when he enjoyned his Disciples, an abstinence from Beans, many conceived they were with severity debarred the use of that pulse; which notwithstanding could not be his meaning; for as *Aristoxenus*, who wrote his life averreth, he delighted much in that kind of food himself. But herein, as *Plutarch* observeth, he had no other intention than to dissuade men from Magistracy, or undertaking the publick offices of state; for by beans was the Magistrate elected in some parts of *Greece*; and, after his daies, we read in *Thucydides*, of the Councel of the bean in *Athens*. πᾶν δειλοὶ κυαμῶν ἄπο χεῖρας ἔχεσθε. The same word also in Greek doth signifie a Testicle, and hath been thought by some an injunction only of Continency, as *Aul. Gellius* hath expounded, and as *Empedocles* may also be interpreted: that is, *Testiculis miseri dextras subducite*; and might be the original intention of *Pythagoras*; as having a notable hint hereof in Beans, from the natural signature of the venereal organs of both Sexes. Again, his injunction is, not to harbour Swallows in our Houses: Whose advice notwithstanding we do not contemn, who daily admit and cherish them: For herein a caution is only implied, not to entertain ungrateful and thankless persons, which like the Swallow are no way commodious unto us; but having made use of our habitations, and served their own turns, forsake us. So he commands to deface the Print of a Cauldron in the ashes, after it hath boiled. Which strictly to observe were condemnable superstition: But hereby he covertly adviseth us not to persevere in anger; but after our choler hath boiled, to retain no impression thereof. In the like sense are to be received, when he adviseth his Disciples to give the right hand but to few, to put no viands in a Chamber-pot, not to pass over a Balance, not to rake up fire with a Sword, or piss against the Sun. Which ænigmatical deliveries comprehend useful verities, but being mistaken by literal Expositors at the first, they have been mis-understood by most since, and may be occasion of Error to Verbal capacities for ever.

This fallacy in the first delusion Satan put upon *Eve*, and his whole tentation might be the same continued; so when he said, *Ye shall not die*, that was, in his equivocation, ye shall not incurr a present death, or a destruction immediately ensuing your transgression. *Your eyes shall be opened*; that is, not to the enlargement of your knowledge, but discovery of your shame and proper confusion; *You shall know good and evil*; that is, you shall have knowledge of good by its privation, but cognisance of evil by sense and visible experience. And the same fallacy or way of deceit, so well succeeding in Paradise, he continued in his Oracles through all the World. Which had not men more warily understood, they might have performed many acts inconsistent with his intention. *Brutus* might have made haste with *Tarquine* to have kissed his own Mother. The *Athenians* might have built them wooden Walls, or doubled the Altar at *Delphos*.

The circle of this fallacy is very large; and herein may be comprised all Ironical mistakes, for intended expressions receiving inverted significations; all deductions from Metaphors, Parables, Allegories, unto real and rigid interpretations. *De hæresibus.* Whereby have risen not only popular Errors in Philosophy, but vulgar and senseless Heresies in Divinity; as will be evident unto any that shall examine their foundations, as they stand related by *Epiphanius*, *Austin*, or *Prateolus*.

Other wayes there are of deceit; which consist not in false apprehension of Words, that is, Verbal expressions or sentential significations, but fraudulent deductions, or inconsequent illations, from a false conception of things. Of these extradictionary and real fallacies, *Aristotle* and *Logicians* make in number six, but we observe that men are most commonly deceived by four thereof: those are, *Petitio principii, A dicto secundum quid ad dictum simpliciter, A non causa pro causa*; And, *fallacia consequentis*.

The first is, *Petitio principii*. Which fallacy is committed, when a question is made a *medium*, or we assume a *medium* as granted, whereof we remain as unsatisfied as of the question. Briefly, where that is assumed as a Principle to prove another thing, which is not conceded as true it self. By this fallacy was *Eve* deceived, when she took for granted, a false assertion of the Devil; *Ye shall not surely die; for God doth know that in the day ye shall eat thereof, your eyes shall be opened, and you shall be as Gods*. Which was but a bare affirmation of Satan, without proof or probable inducement, contrary unto the command of God, and former belief of her self. And this was the Logick of the *Jews* when they accused our *Saviour* unto *Pilate*; who demanding a reasonable impeachment, or the allegation of some crime worthy of Condemnation; they only replied, *If he had not been worthy of Death, we would not have brought Him before thee*. Wherein there was neither accusation of the person, nor satisfaction of the Judge; who well understood, a bare accusation was not presumption of guilt, and the clamours of the people no accusation at all. The same Fallacy is sometime used in the dispute, between *Job* and his friends; they often taking that for granted which afterward he disproveth.

The second is, *A dicto secundum quid ad dictum simpliciter*, when from that which is but true in a qualified sense, an inconditional and absolute verity is inferred; transferring the special consideration of things unto their general acceptions, or concluding from their strict acception, unto that without all limitation. This fallacy men commit when they argue from a particular to a general; as when we conclude the vices or qualities of a few, upon a whole Nation. Or from a part unto the whole. Thus the Devil argues with our Saviour: and by this, he would perswade Him he might be secure, if he cast himself from the Pinnacle: For, said he, it is written, *He shall give his Angels charge concerning thee, and in their hands they shall bear thee up, lest at any time thou dash thy foot against a stone.* *Psal. 91.* But this illation was fallacious, leaving one part of the Text, *He shall keep thee in all thy wayes*; that is, in the wayes of righteousness, and not of rash attempts: so he urged a part for the whole, and inferred more in the conclusion, than was contained in the premises. By the same fallacy we proceed, when we conclude from the sign unto the thing signified. By this incroachment, Idolatry first crept in, men converting the symbolical use of Idols into their proper Worship, and receiving the representation of things as the substance and thing it self. So the Statue of *Belus* at first erected in his memory, was in after-times adored as a Divinity. *The Original of Idolatry.* And so also in the Sacrament of the *Eucharist*, the Bread and Wine which were but the signals or visible signs, were made the things signified, and worshipped as the Body of Christ. And hereby generally men are deceived that take things spoken in some Latitude without any at all. Hereby the *Jews* were deceived concerning the commandment of the Sabbath, accusing our Saviour *for healing the sick*, and his Disciples *for plucking the ears of Corn upon that day*. And by this deplorable mistake they were deceived unto destruction, upon the assault of *Pompey* the great, made upon that day; by whose superstitious observation they could not defend themselves, or perform any labour whatever.

The Alcoran *endures neither Wine nor Universities.*

The third is, *A non causa pro causa*, when that is pretended for a cause which is not, or not in that sense which is inferred. Upon this consequence the law of *Mahomet* forbids the use of Wine; and his Successors abolished Universities. By this also many Christians have condemned literature, misunderstanding the counsel of Saint *Paul*, who adviseth no further than to beware of Philosophy. On this Foundation were built the conclusions of Southsayers in their Augurial, and Tripudiary divinations; collecting presages from voice or food of Birds, and conjoyning Events unto causes of no connection. Hereupon also are grounded the gross mistakes, in the cure of many diseases: not only from the last medicine, and sympathetical Receipts, but Amulets, Charms, and all incantatory applications; deriving effects not only from inconcurring causes, but things devoid of all efficiency whatever.

The fourth is, the Fallacy of the Consequent; which if strictly taken, may be a fallacious illation in reference unto antecedency, or consequency; as to conclude from the position of the antecedent to the position of the consequent, or from the remotion of the consequent to the remotion of the antecedent. This is usually committed, when in connexed Propositions the Terms adhere contingently. This is frequent in Oratory illations; and thus the *Pharisees*, because He conversed with Publicans and Sinners, accused the holiness of Christ. But if this Fallacy be largely taken, it is committed in any vicious illation, offending the rules of good consequence; and so it may be very large, and comprehend all false illations against the settled Laws of Logick: But the most usual inconsequencies are from particulars, from negatives, and from affirmative conclusions in the second figure, wherein indeed offences are most frequent, and their discoveries not difficult.

CHAPTER V
Of Credulity and Supinity.

A third cause of common Errors is the Credulity of men, that is, an easie assent to what is obtruded, or a believing at first ear, what is delivered by others. This is a weakness in the understanding, without examination assenting unto things, which from their Natures and Causes do carry no perswasion; whereby men often swallow falsities for truths, dubiosities for certainties, feasibilities for possibilities, and things impossible as possibilities themselves. Which, though the weakness of the Intellect, and most discoverable in vulgar heads; yet hath it sometime fallen upon wiser brains, and greater advancers of Truth. Thus many wise *Athenians* so far forgot their Philosophy, and the nature of humane production, that they descended unto belief, that the original of their Nation was from the Earth, and had no other beginning than the seminality and womb of their great Mother. Thus is it not without wonder, how those learned *Arabicks* so tamely delivered up their belief unto the absurdities of the *Alcoran*. How the noble *Geber*, *Avicenna*, and *Almanzor*, should rest satisfied in the nature and causes of Earthquakes, delivered from the doctrine of their *Prophet*; that is, from the motion of a great Bull, upon whose horns all the earth is poised. How their faiths could decline so low, as to concede their generations in Heaven, to be made by the smell of a Citron, or that the felicity of their Paradise should consist in a Jubile of copulation, that is, a coition of one act prolonged unto fifty years. Thus is it almost beyond wonder, how the belief of reasonable creatures, should ever submit unto Idolatry: and the credulity of those men scarce credible (without presumption of a second Fall) who could believe a Deity in the work of their own hands. For although in that ancient and diffused adoration of Idols, unto the *Priests* and subtiler heads, the worship perhaps might be symbolical, and as those Images some way related unto their Deities; yet was the Idolatry direct and down-right in the People; whose credulity is illimitable, who may be made believe that any thing is God; and may be made believe there is no God at all.

Obstinate and irrational Scepticism, justly censured.

And as Credulity is the cause of Error, so Incredulity oftentimes of not enjoying truth; and that not only an obstinate incredulity, whereby we will not acknowledge assent unto what is reasonably inferred, but any Academical reservation in matters of easie truth, or rather sceptical infidelity against the evidence of reason and sense. For these are conceptions befalling wise men, as absurd as the apprehensions of fools, and the credulity of the people which promiscuously swallow any thing. For this is not only derogatory unto the wisdom of God, who hath proposed the World unto our knowledge, and thereby the notion of Himself; but also detractory unto the intellect, and sense of man expressly disposed for that inquisition. And therefore, *hoc tantum scio, quod nihil scio*, is not to be received in an absolute sense, but is comparatively expressed unto the number of things whereof our knowledge is ignorant. Nor will it acquit the insatisfaction of those which quarrel with all things, or dispute of matters, concerning whose verities we have conviction from reason, or decision from the inerrable and requisite conditions of sense. And therefore if any affirm, the earth doth move, and will not believe with us, it standeth still; because he hath probable reasons for it, and I no infallible sense, nor reason against it, I will not quarrel with his assertion. But if, like *Zeno*, he shall walk about, and yet deny there is any motion in Nature, surely that man was constituted for *Anticera*, and were a fit companion for those, who having a conceit they are dead, cannot be convicted into the society of the living.

The fourth is a Supinity, or neglect of Enquiry, even of matters whereof we doubt; rather believing, than going to see; or doubting with ease and *gratis*, than believing with difficulty or purchase. Whereby, either from a temperamental inactivity, we are unready to put in execution the suggestions or dictates of reason; or by a content and acquiescence in every species of truth, we embrace the shadow thereof, or so much as may palliate its just and substantial acquirements. Had our fore-Fathers sat down in these resolutions, or had their curiosities been sedentary, who pursued the knowledge of things through all the corners of nature, the face of truth had been obscure unto us, whose lustre in some part their industries have revealed.

Certainly the sweat of their labours was not salt unto them, and they took delight in the dust of their endeavours. For questionless, in Knowledge there is no slender difficulty; and Truth, which wise men say doth lye in a Well, is not recoverable by exantlation. It were some extenuation of the Curse, if *in sudore vultus tui* were confinable unto corporal exercitations, and there still remained a Paradise, or unthorny place of knowledge. But now our understandings being eclipsed, as well as our tempers infirmed, we must betake our selves to wayes of reparation, and depend upon the illumination of our endeavours. For, thus we may in some measure repair our primary ruines, and build our selves Men again. And though the attempts of some have been precipitous, and their Enquiries so audacious, as to come within command of the flaming swords, and lost themselves in attempts above humanity; yet have the Enquiries of most defected by the way, and tired within the sober circumference of Knowledge.

And this is the reason, why some have transcribed any thing; and although they cannot but doubt thereof, yet neither make Experiment by sense, or Enquiry by reason; but live in doubts of things, whose satisfaction is in their own power; which is indeed the inexcusable part of our ignorance, and may perhaps fill up the charge of the last day. For, not obeying the dictates of Reason, and neglecting the cries of Truth, we fail not only in the trust of our undertakings, but in the intention of man it self. Which although more venial in ordinary constitutions, and such as are not framed beyond the capacity of beaten notions, yet will inexcusably condemn some men, who having received excellent endowments, have yet sate down by the way, and frustrated the intention of their liabilities. For certainly, as some men have sinned in the principles of humanity, and must answer, for not being men, so others offend, if they be not more. *Magis extra vitia, quam cum virtutibus*, would commend those: These are not excusable without an Excellency. For, great constitutions, and such as are constellated unto knowledge, do nothing till they out-do all; they come short of themselves, if they go not beyond others; and must not sit down under the degree of Worthies. God expects no lustre from the minor Stars; but if the Sun should not illuminate all, it were a sin in Nature. *Ultimus bonoram*, will not excuse every man, nor is it sufficient for all to hold the common level: Mens names should not only distinguish them: A man should be something, that men are not, and individual in somewhat beside his proper Name. Thus while it exceeds not the bounds of reason and modesty, we cannot condemn singularity, *Nos numerus sumus*, is the

Motto of the multitude, and for that reason are they Fools. For things as they recede from unity, the more they approach to imperfection, and Deformity; for they hold their perfection in their Simplicities, and as they nearest approach unto God.

Universities why many times full of Scholars, and empty of Learning.
The natural genius or inclination, have much to be regarded in the choice of a Profession.

Now as there are many great Wits to be condemned, who have neglected the increment of Arts, and the sedulous pursuit of knowledge; so are there not a few very much to be pitied, whose industry being not attended with natural parts, they have sweat to little purpose, and rolled the stone in vain. Which chiefly proceedeth from natural incapacity, and genial indisposition, at least, to those particulars whereunto they apply their endeavours. And this is one reason why, though Universities be full of men, they are oftentimes empty of learning: Why, as there are some men do much without learning, so others but little with it, and few that attain to any measure of it. For many heads that undertake it, were never squared, nor timber'd for it. There are not only particular men, but whole Nations indisposed for learning; whereunto is required, not only education, but a pregnant *Minerva*, and teeming Constitution. For the Wisdom of God hath divided the *Genius* of men according to the different affairs of the World: and varied their inclination according to the variety of Actions to be performed therein. Which they who consider not, rudely rushing upon professions and ways of life, unequal to their natures; dishonour, not only themselves and their Functions, but pervert the harmony of the whole World. For, if the World went on as God hath ordained it, and were every one imployed in points concordant to their Natures, Professions; Arts and Commonwealths would rise up of themselves; nor needed we a Lanthorn to find a man in *Athens*.

CHAPTER VI
Of adherence unto Antiquity.

Immoderate respect unto Antiquity, a general cause of Error.

But the mortallest enemy unto Knowledge, and that which hath done the greatest execution upon truth, hath been a peremptory adhesion unto Authority, and more especially, the establishing of our belief upon the dictates of Antiquity. For (as every capacity may observe) most men of Ages present, so superstitiously do look on Ages past, that the Authorities of the one, exceed the reasons of the other: Whose persons indeed being far removed from our times, their works, which seldom with us pass uncontrouled, either by contemporaries, or immediate successors, are now become out of the distance of Envies: and the farther removed from present times, are conceived to approach the nearer unto truth it self. Now hereby methinks we manifestly delude our selves, and widely walk out of the track of Truth.

For first, Men hereby impose a Thraldom on their Times, which the ingenuity of no Age should endure, or indeed, the presumption of any did ever yet enjoyn. Thus *Hippocrates* about 2000 years ago, conceived it no injustice, either to examine or refute the Doctrines of his Predecessors: *Galen* the like, and *Aristotle* the most of any. Yet did not any of these conceive themselves infallible, or set down their dictates as verities irrefragable, but when they deliver their own Inventions, or reject other mens Opinions, they proceed with Judgment and Ingenuity; establishing their assertion, not only with great solidity, but submitting them also unto the correction of future discovery.

Secondly, Men that adore times past, consider not that those times were once present; that is, as our own are at this instant, and we our selves unto those to come, as they unto us at present, as we relye on them, even so will those on us, and magnifie us hereafter, who at present condemn our selves. Which very absurdity is daily committed amongst us, even in the esteem and censure of our own times. And to speak impartially, old Men, from whom we should expect the greatest example of Wisdom, do most exceed in this point of folly; commending the days of their youth, which they scarce remember, at least well understood not; extolling those times their younger years have heard their Fathers condemn, and condemning those times the gray heads of their posterity shall commend. And thus is it the humour of many heads, to extol the days of their Fore-fathers, and declaim against the wickedness of times present. Which notwithstanding they cannot handsomly do, without the borrowed help and Satyrs of times past; condemning the vices of their own times, by the expressions of vices in times which they commend; which cannot but argue the community of vice in both. *Horace* therefore, *Juvenal*, and *Persius* were no Prophets, although their lines did seem to indigitate and point at our times. There is a certain list of vices committed in all Ages, and declaimed against by all Authors, which will last as long as humane nature; which digested into common places, may serve for any Theme, and never be out of date until Dooms-day.

Thirdly, The Testimonies of Antiquity and such as pass oraculously amongst us, were not, if we consider them, always so exact, as to examine the doctrine they delivered. For some, and those the acutest of them, have left unto us many things of falsity; controlable, not only by critical and collective reason, but common and Country observation.

Hereof there want not many examples in *Aristotle*, through all his Book of Animals; we shall instance onely in three of his Problems, and all contained under one Section. The first enquireth, why a Man doth cough, but not an Oxe or Cow; whereas, notwithstanding the contrary is often observed by Husbandmen, and stands confirmed by those who have expressly treated *De Re Rustica*, and have also delivered divers remedies for it. Why Juments, as Horses, Oxen, and Asses, have no eructation or belching, whereas indeed the contrary is often observed, and also delivered by *Columella*. And thirdly, Why Man alone hath gray hairs? whereas it cannot escape the eyes, and ordinary observation of all men, as Horses, Dogs, and Foxes, wax gray with age in our Countries; and in the colder Regions, many other Animals without it. And though favourable constructions may somewhat extenuate the rigour of these concessions, yet will scarce any palliate that in the fourth of his Meteors, that Salt is easiest dissolvable in cold water: Nor that of *Diascorides*, that Quicksilver is best preserved in Vessels of Tin and Lead.

Other Authors write often dubiously even in matters wherein is expected a strict and definite truth; extenuating their affirmations, with *aiunt, ferunt, fortasse*: as *Diascorides, Galen, Aristotle*, and many more. Others by hear-say; taking upon trust most they have delivered, whose Volumes are nicer Collections, drawn from the mouths or leaves of other Authors; as may be observed in *Plinie, Elian, Athenæus*, and many more. Not a few transcriptively, subscribing their Names unto other mens endeavours, and meerly transcribing almost all they have written. The *Latines* transcribing the *Greeks*, the *Greeks* and *Latines*, each other.

The Antiquity, and some notable instances of Plagiarism, that is, of transcribing or filching Authors.

Thus hath *Justine* borrowed all from *Trogus Pompeius*, and *Julius Solinus*, in a manner transcribed *Plinie*. Thus have *Lucian* and *Apuleius* served *Lucius Pratensis*: men both living in the same time, and both transcribing the same Author, in those famous Books, entituled *Lucius* by the one, and *Aureus Asinus* by the other. In the same measure hath *Simocrates* in his Tract De Nilo, dealt with *Diodorus Siculus*, as may be observed in that work annexed unto *Herodotus*, and translated by *Jungermannus*. Thus *Eratosthenes* wholly translated *Timotheus de Insulis*, not reserving the very Preface. The same doth *Strabo* report of *Eudorus*, and *Ariston*, in a Treatise entituled *De Nilo*. *Clemens Alexandrinus* hath observed many examples hereof among the *Greeks*; and *Pliny* speaketh very plainly in his Preface, that conferring his Authors, and comparing their works together, he generally found those that went before *verbatim* transcribed, by those that followed after, and their Originals never so much as mentioned. *His Metamorphosis.* To omit how much the wittiest piece of *Ovid* is beholden unto *Parthenius Chius*; even the magnified *Virgil* hath borrowed, almost in all his Works; his *Eclogues* from *Theocritus*, his *Georgicks* from *Hesiod* and *Aratus*, his *Æneads* from *Homer*, the second Book whereof containing the exploit of *Sinon* and the *Trojan* Horse (as *Macrobius* observeth) he hath *verbatim* derived from *Pisander*. Our own Profession is not excusable herein. Thus *Oribasius, Ætius*, and *Ægineta*, have in a manner transcribed *Galen*. But *Marcellus Empericus*, who hath left a famous Work *De Medicamentis*, hath word for word transcribed all *Scribonius Largus, De Compositione Medicamentorum*, and not left out his very Peroration. Thus may we perceive the Ancients were but men, even like our selves. The practice of transcription in our days, was no Monster in theirs: *Plagiarie* had not its Nativity with Printing, but began in times when thefts were difficult, and the paucity of Books scarce wanted that Invention.

Nor did they only make large use of other Authors, but often without mention of their names. *Aristotle*, who seems to have borrowed many things from *Hippocrates*, in the most favourable construction, makes mention but once of him, and that by the by, and without reference unto his present Doctrine. *In his* Politicks. *Virgil*, so much beholding unto *Homer*, hath not his name in all his Works: and *Plinie*, who seems to borrow many Authors out of *Dioscorides*, hath taken no notice of him. I wish men were not still content to plume themselves with others Feathers. Fear of discovery, not single ingenuity affords Quotations rather than Transcriptions; wherein notwithstanding the Plagiarisme of many makes little consideration, whereof though great Authors may complain, small ones cannot but take notice.

Fourthly, While we so eagerly adhere unto Antiquity, and the accounts of elder times, we are to consider the fabulous condition thereof. *An ancient Author who writ* Περὶ ἀπίστων, *sive de incredibilibus, whereof some part is yet extant.* And that we shall not deny, if we call to mind the Mendacity of *Greece*, from whom we have received most relations, and that a considerable part of ancient Times, was by the *Greeks* themselves termed μυθικόν, that is, made up or stuffed out with Fables. And surely the fabulous inclination of those days, was greater then any since; which swarmed so with Fables, and from such slender grounds, took hints for fictions, poysoning the World ever after; wherein how far they exceeded, may be exemplified from *Palephatus*, in his Book of *Fabulous Narrations*. *The Fable of* Orpheus *his Harp, etc. whence occasioned.* That Fable of *Orpheus* who by the melody of his Musick, made Woods and Trees to follow him, was raised upon a slender foundation; for there were a crew of mad women, retired unto a Mountain from whence being pacified by his Musick, they descended with boughs in their hands, which unto the fabulosity of those times proved a sufficient ground to celebrate unto all posterity the Magick of *Orpheus* Harp, and its power to attract the senseless Trees about it. That *Medea* the famous Sorceress could renew youth, and make old men young again, was nothing else, but that from the knowledge of Simples she had a Receit to make white hair black, and reduce old heads, into the tincture of youth again. The Fable of *Gerion* and *Cerberus* with three heads, was this: *Gerion* was of the City *Tricarinia*, that is, of three heads, and *Cerberus* of the same place was one of his Dogs, which running into a Cave upon pursuit of his Masters Oxen, *Hercules* perforce drew him out of that place, from whence the conceits of those days affirmed no less, then that *Hercules* descended into Hell, and brought up *Cerberus* into the habitation of the living. Upon the like grounds was raised the figment of *Briareus*, who dwelling in a City called *Hecatonchiria*, the fansies of those times assigned him an hundred hands. 'Twas ground enough to fansie wings unto *Dædalus*, in that he stole out of a Window from *Minos*, and sailed away with his son *Icarus*: who steering his course wisely, escaped; but his son carrying too high a sail was drowned. That *Niobe* weeping over her children, was turned into a Stone, was nothing else, but that during her life she erected over their Sepultures a Marble Tomb of her own. When *Acteon* had undone himself with Dogs, and the prodigal attendants of hunting, they made a solemn story how he was devoured by his Hounds. And upon the like grounds was raised the Anthropophagie of *Diomedes* his horses. Eating of Mans flesh. Upon as slender foundation was built the Fable of the *Minotaure*; for one *Taurus* a servant of *Minos* gat his Mistris *Pasiphae* with child, from whence the Infant was named *Minotaurus*. Now this unto the fabulosity of those times was thought sufficient to accuse *Pasiphae* of Beastiality, or admitting conjunction with a Bull; and in succeeding ages gave a hint of depravity unto *Domitian* to act the Fable into reality. In like manner, as *Diodorus* plainly delivereth, the famous Fable of *Charon* had its Nativity; who being no other but the common Ferry-man of *Egypt*, that wafted over the dead bodies from *Memphis*, was made by the *Greeks* to be the Ferry-man of Hell, and solemn stories raised after of him. Lastly, we shall not need to enlarge, if that be true which grounded the generation of *Castor* and *Helen* out of an Egg, because they were born and brought up in an upper room, according unto the Word ὠον, which with the *Lacœdemonians* had also that signification.

Fifthly, We applaud many things delivered by the Ancients, which are in themselves but ordinary, and come short of our own Conceptions. Thus we usually extol, and our Orations cannot escape the sayings of the wise men of *Greece*. *Nosce teipsum*, of *Thales*: *Nosce tempus*, of *Pittacus*: *Nihil nimis*, of *Cleobulus*; which notwithstanding to speak indifferently, are but vulgar precepts in Morality, carrying with them nothing above the line, or beyond the extemporary sententiosity of common conceits with us. Thus we magnifie the Apothegms or reputed replies of Wisdom, whereof many are to be seen in *Laertius*, more in *Lycosthenes*, not a few in the second Book of *Macrobius*, in the salts of *Cicero*, *Augustus*, and the Comical wits of those times: in most whereof there is not much to admire, and are methinks exceeded, not only in the replies of wise men, but the passages of society, and urbanities of our times. And thus we extol their Adages, or Proverbs; and *Erasmus* hath taken great pains to make collections of them, whereof notwithstanding, the greater part will, I believe, unto indifferent Judges be esteemd no extraordinaries: and may be parallel'd, if not exceeded, by those of more unlearned Nations, and many of our own.

A pedantical vanity to quote Authors in matters of common sense or of familiar acknowledgement.

Sixthly, We urge Authorities in points that need not, and introduce the testimony of ancient Writers, to confirm things evidently believed, and whereto no reasonable hearer but would assent without them; such as are, *Nemo mortalium omnibus horis sapit. Virtute nil præastantius, nil pulchrius. Omnia vincit amor. Prœclarum quiddam veritas*. All which, although things known and vulgar, are frequently urged by many men, and though trivial verities in our mouths, yet, noted from *Plato*, *Ovid*, or *Cicero*, they become reputed elegancies. For many hundred to instance but in one we meet with while we are writing. *Antonius Guevara* that elegant *Spaniard*, in his Book entituled, *The Dial of Princes*, beginneth his Epistle thus. *Apolonius Thyancus*, disputing with the Scholars of *Hiarchas*, said, that among all the affections of nature, nothing was more natural, then the desire all have to preserve life. Which being a confessed Truth, and a verity acknowledged by all, it was a superfluous affectation to derive its Authority from *Apolonius*, or seek a confirmation thereof as far as *India*, and the learned Scholars of *Hiarchas*. Which whether it be not all one to strengthen common Dignities and Principles known by themselves, with the Authority of Mathematicians; or think a man should believe, the whole is greater then its parts, rather upon the Authority of *Euclide*, then if it were propounded alone; I leave unto the second and wiser cogitations of all men. 'Tis sure a Practice that savours much of Pedantry; a reserve of Puerility we have not shaken off from School; where being seasoned with Minor sentences, by a neglect of higher Enquiries, they prescribe upon our riper ears, and are never worn out but with our Memories.

Some remarkable mistakes among the Ancients.

Lastly, While we so devoutly adhere unto Antiquity in some things, we do not consider we have deserted them in several others. For they indeed have not onely been imperfect, in the conceit of some things, but either ignorant or erroneous in many more. They understood not the motion of the eighth sphear from West to East, and so conceived the longitude of the Stars invariable. They conceived the torrid Zone unhabitable, and so made frustrate the goodliest part of the Earth. But we now know 'tis very well empeopled, and the habitation thereof esteemed so happy, that some have made it the proper seat of Paradise; and been so far from judging it unhabitable, that they have made it the first habitation of all. Many of the Ancients denied the *Antipodes*, and some unto the penalty of contrary affirmations; but the experience of our enlarged navigations, can now assert them beyond all dubitation. Having thus totally relinquisht them in some things, it may not be presumptuous, to examine them in others; but surely most unreasonable to adhere to them in all, as though they were infallible, or could not err in any way.

CHAPTER VII
Of Authority.

Nor is onely a resolved prostration unto Antiquity a powerful enemy unto knowledge, but any confident adherence unto Authority, or resignation of our judgements upon the testimony of Age or Author whatsoever.

Authority (simply) but a mean argument especially.

For first, to speak generally an argument from Authority to wiser examinations, is but a weaker kind of proof; it being but a topical probation, and as we term it, an inartificial argument, depending upon a naked asseveration: wherein neither declaring the causes, affections or adjuncts of what we believe, it carrieth not with it the reasonable inducements of knowledge. And therefore, *Contra negantem principia, Ipse dixit,* or *Oportet discentem credere,* although Postulates very accommodable unto *Junior* indoctrinations; yet are their Authorities but temporary, and not to be imbraced beyond the minority of our intellectuals. For our advanced beliefs are not to be built upon dictates, but having received the probable inducements of truth, we become emancipated from testimonial engagements, and are to erect upon the surer base of reason.

Secondly, Unto reasonable perpensions it hath no place in some Sciences, small in others, and suffereth many restrictions, even where it is most admitted. *In the Mathematicks.* It is of no validity in the Mathematicks, especially the mother part thereof, Arithmetick and Geometry. For these Sciences concluding from dignities and principles known by themselves: receive not satisfaction from probable reasons, much less from bare and peremptory asseverations. And therefore if all *Athens* should decree, that in every Triangle, two sides, which soever be taken, are greater then the side remaining, or that in rectangle triangles the square which is made of the side that subtendeth the right angle, is equal to the squares which are made of the sides containing the right angle: although there be a certain truth therein, Geometricians notwithstanding would not receive satisfaction without demonstration thereof. 'Tis true, by the vulgarity of Philosophers, there are many points believed without probation; nor if a man affirm from *Ptolomy,* that the Sun is bigger then the Earth, shall he probably meet with any contradiction: whereunto notwithstanding Astronomers will not assent without some convincing argument or demonstrative proof thereof. And therefore certainly of all men a Philosopher should be no swearer; for an oath which is the end of controversies in Law, cannot determine any here; nor are the deepest Sacraments or desperate imprecations of any force to perswade, where reason only, and necessary *mediums* must induce.

In Natural Philosophy more generally pursued amongst us, it carrieth but slender consideration; *And Physick.* for that also proceeding from setled Principles, therein is expected a satisfaction from scientifical progressions, and such as beget a sure rational belief. For if Authority might have made out the assertions of Philosophy, we might have held that Snow was black, that the Sea was but the sweat of the Earth, and many of the like absurdities. Then was *Aristotle* injurious to fall upon *Melissus,* to reject the assertions of *Anaxagoras, Anaximander,* and *Empedocles*; then were we also ungrateful unto himself; from whom our *Junior* endeavours embracing many things on his authority, our mature and secondary enquiries, are forced to quit those receptions, and to adhere unto the nearer account of Reason. And although it be not unusual, even in Philosophical Tractates to make enumeration of Authors, yet are there reasons usually introduced, and to ingenious Readers do carry the stroke in the perswasion. And surely if we account it reasonable among our selves, and not injurious unto rational Authors, no farther to abet their Opinions then as they are supported by solid Reasons: certainly with more excusable reservation may we shrink at their bare testimonies; whose argument is but precarious, and subsists upon the charity of our assentments.

In Morality, Rhetorick, Law and History, there is I confess a frequent and allowable use of testimony; and yet herein I perceive, it is not unlimitable, but admitteth many restrictions. Thus in Law both Civil and Divine: that is onely esteemed a legal testimony, which receives comprobation from the mouths of at least two witnesses; and that not only for prevention of calumny, but assurance against mistake; whereas notwithstanding the solid reason of one man, is as sufficient as the clamor of a whole Nation; and with imprejudicate apprehensions begets as firm a belief as the authority or aggregated testimony of many hundreds. For reason being the very root of our natures, and the principles thereof common unto all, what is against the Laws of true reason, or the unerring understanding of any one, if rightly apprehended; must be disclaimed by all Nations, and rejected even by mankind.

Again, A testimony is of small validity if deduced from men out of their own profession; so if *Lactantius* affirm the Figure of the Earth is plain, or *Austin* deny there are *Antipodes*; though venerable Fathers of the Church, and ever to be honoured, yet will not their Authorities prove sufficient to ground a belief thereon. Whereas notwithstanding the solid reason or confirmed experience of any man, is very approvable in what profession soever. So *Raymund Sebund* a Physitian of *Tholouze*, besides his learned Dialogues *De Natura Humana*, hath written a natural Theologie; demonstrating therein the Attributes of God, and attempting the like in most points of Religion. So *Hugo Grotius* a Civilian, did write an excellent Tract of the verity of Christian Religion. Wherein most rationally delivering themselves, their works will be embraced by most that understand them, and their reasons enforce belief even from prejudicate Readers. Neither indeed have the Authorities of men been ever so awful; but that by some they have been rejected, even in their own professions. Thus *Aristotle* affirming the birth of the Infant or time of its gestation, extendeth sometimes unto the eleventh Month, but *Hippocrates*, averring that it exceedeth not the tenth: *Adrian* the Emperour in a solemn process, determined for *Aristotle*; but *Justinian* many years after, took in with *Hippocrates* and reversed the Decree of the other. Thus have Councils, not only condemned private men, but the Decrees and Acts of one another. So *Galen* after all his veneration of *Hippocrates*, in some things hath fallen from him. *Avicen* in many from *Galen*; and others succeeding from him. And although the singularity of *Paracelsus* be intolerable, who sparing onely *Hippocrates*, hath reviled not onely the Authors, but almost all the learning that went before him; yet is it not much less injurious unto knowledge obstinately and inconvincibly to side with any one. Which humour unhappily possessing many, they have by prejudice withdrawn themselves into parties, and contemning the soveraignty of truth, seditiously abetted the private divisions of error.

Moreover a testimony in points Historical, and where it is of unavoidable use, is of no illation in the negative, nor is it of consequence that *Herodotus* writing nothing of *Rome*, there was therefore no such City in his time; or because *Dioscorides* hath made no mention of Unicorns horn, there is therefore no such thing in Nature. Indeed, intending an accurate enumeration of Medical materials, the omission hereof affords some probability, it was not used by the Ancients, but will not conclude the non-existence thereof. For so may we annihilate many Simples unknown to his enquiries, as *Senna, Rhubarb, Bezoar, Ambregris*, and divers others. Whereas indeed the reason of man hath not such restraint; concluding not onely affirmatively but negatively; not onely affirming there is no magnitude beyond the last heavens, but also denying there is any vacuity within them. Although it be confessed, the affirmative hath the prerogative illation, and *Barbara* engrosseth the powerful demonstration.

Lastly, The strange relations made by Authors, may sufficiently discourage our adherence unto Authority; and which if we believe we must be apt to swallow any thing. Thus *Basil* will tell us, the Serpent went erect like Man, and that that Beast could speak before the Fall. *Tostatus* would make us believe that *Nilus* encreaseth every new Moon. *Leonardo Fioravanti* an Italian Physitian, beside many other secrets, assumeth unto himself the discovery of one concerning Pellitory of the Wall; that is, that it never groweth in the sight of the *North* star. *Doue si possa vedere la stella Tramontana*, wherein how wide he is from truth, is easily discoverable unto every one, who hath but Astronomy enough to know that Star. *Franciscus Sanctius* in a laudable Comment upon *Alciats* Emblems, affirmeth, and that from experience, a Nightingale hath no tongue. *Avem Philomelam lingua carere pro certo affirmare possum, nisi me oculi fallunt*. Which if any man for a while shall believe upon his experience, he may at his leisure refute it by his own. What fool almost would believe, at least, what wise man would relie upon that Antidote delivered by *Pierius* in his Hieroglyphicks against the sting of a Scorpion? that is, to sit upon an Ass with ones face toward his tail; for so the pain leaveth the Man, and passeth into the Beast. It were methinks but an uncomfortable receit for a Quartane Ague (and yet as good perhaps as many others used) to have recourse unto the *Recipe* of *Sammonicus*; that is, to lay the fourth Book of *Homers* Iliads under ones head, according to the precept of that Physitian and Poet, *Mæoniæ Iliados quartum suppone trementi.* *An eye medicine.* There are surely few that have belief to swallow, or hope enough to experiment the Collyrium of *Albertus*; which promiseth a strange effect, and such as Thieves would count inestimable, that is, to make one see in the dark: yet thus much, according unto his receit, will the right eye of an Hedge-hog boiled in oyl, and preserved in a brazen vessel effect. As strange it is, and unto vicious inclinations were worth a nights lodging with *Lais*, what is delivered in *Kiranides*; *Ten thousand drachms.* that the left stone of a Weesel, wrapt up in the skin of a she Mule, is able to secure incontinency from conception.

These with swarms of others have men delivered in their Writings, whose verities are onely supported by their authorities: But being neither consonant unto reason, nor correspondent unto experiment, their affirmations are unto us no axioms: We esteem thereof as things unsaid, and account them but in the list of nothing. I wish herein the *Chymists* had been more sparing: who over-magnifying their preparations, inveigle the curiosity of many, and delude the security of most. For if experiments would answer their encomiums, the Stone and Quartane Agues were not opprobrious unto Physitians: we might contemn that first and most uncomfortable Aphorism of *Hippocrates*, *Ars longa vita brevis.* for surely that Art were soon attained, that hath so general remedies; and life could not be short, were there such to prolong it.

CHAPTER VIII
A brief enumeration of Authors.

Now for as much as we have discoursed of Authority, and there is scarce any tradition or popular error but stands also delivered by some good Author; we shall endeavour a short discovery of such, as for the major part have given authority hereto: who though excellent and useful Authors, yet being either transcriptive, or following common relations, their accounts are not to be swallowed at large, or entertained without all circumspection. In whom the *ipse dixit*, although it be no powerful argument in any, is yet less authentick then in many other, because they deliver not their own experiences, but others affirmations, and write from others, as later pens from them.

The Authors judgement, or a character given of some eminent Authors.

1. The first in order, as also in time shall be *Herodotus* of *Halicarnassus*, an excellent and very elegant Historian; whose Books of History were so well received in his own days, and at their rehearsal in the Olympick games, they obtained the names of the nine Muses; and continued in such esteem unto descending Ages, that *Cicero* termed him, *Historiarum parens*. And *Dionysius* his Countryman, in an Epistle to *Pompey*, after an express comparison, affords him the better of *Thucydides*; all which notwithstanding, he hath received from some, the stile of *Mendaciorum pater*. His Authority was much infringed by *Plutarch*, who being offended with him, as *Polybius* had been with *Philarcus* for speaking too coldly of his Countrymen, hath left a particular Tract, *De malignitate Herodoti*. But in this latter Century, *Camerarius* and *Stephanus* have stepped in, and by their witty Apologies, effectually endeavoured to frustrate the Arguments of *Plutarch*, or any other. Now in this Author, as may be observed in our ensuing discourse, and is better discernable in the perusal of himself, there are many things fabulously delivered, and not to be accepted as truths: whereby nevertheless if any man be deceived, the Author is not so culpable as the Believer. For he indeed imitating the Father Poet, whose life he hath also written, and as *Thucydides* observeth, as well intending the delight as benefit of his Reader, hath besprinkled his work with many fabulosities; whereby if any man be led into error, he mistaketh the intention of the Author, who plainly confesseth he writeth many things by hear-say, and forgetteth a very considerable caution of his; that is, *Ego quæ fando cognovi, exponere narratione mea debeo omnia: credere autem esse vera omnia, non debeo.*

2. In the second place is *Ctesias*: the Cnidian, Physitian unto *Artaxerxes* King of *Persia*, his Books are often recited by ancient Writers, and by the industry of *Stephanus* and *Rhodomanus*, there are extant some fragments thereof in our days; he wrote the History of *Persia*, and many narrations of *India*. In the first, as having a fair opportunity to know the truth, and as *Diodorus* affirmeth the perusal of *Persian* Records, his testimony is acceptable. In his *Indian* Relations, wherein are contained strange and incredible accounts, he is surely to be read with suspension. These were they which weakned his authority with former ages; for as we may observe, he is seldom mentioned, without a derogatory Parenthesis in any Author. *Aristotle* besides the frequent undervaluing of his authority, in his Books of Animals gives him the lie no less then twice, concerning the seed of Elephants. *Strabo* in his eleventh Book hath left a harder censure of him. *Equidem facilius Hesiodo & Homero, aliquis fidem adhibuerit, itémque Tragicis Poetis, quam Ctesiæ, Herodoto, Hellanico & eorum similibus.* But *Lucian* hath spoken more plainer then any. *Scripsit Ctesias de Indorum regione, deque iis quæ apud illos sunt, ea quæ nec ipse vidit, neque ex ullius sermone audivit.* Yet were his relations taken up by some succeeding Writers, and many thereof revived by our Countryman, Sir *John Mandevil*, Knight, and Doctor in Physick; who after thirty years peregrination died at *Liege*, and was there honourably interred. He left a Book of his Travels, which hath been honoured with the translation of many Languages, and now continued above three hundred years; herein he often attesteth the fabulous relations of *Ctesias*, and seems to confirm the refuted accounts of Antiquity. All which may still be received in some acceptions of morality, and to a pregnant invention, may afford commendable mythologie; but in a natural and proper exposition, it containeth impossibilities, and things inconsistent with truth.

3. There is a Book *De mirandis auditionibus*, ascribed unto *Aristotle*; another *De mirabilibus narrationibus*, written long after by *Antigonus*, another also of the same title by *Plegon Trallianus*, translated by *Xilander*, and with the Annotations of *Meursius*, all whereof make good the promise of their titles, and may be read with caution. Which if any man shall likewise observe in the Lecture of *Philostratus*, concerning the life of *Apollonius*, and even in some passages of the sober and learned *Plutarchus*; or not only in ancient Writers, but shall carry a wary eye on *Paulus Venetus*, *Jovius*, *Olaus Magnus*, *Nierembergius*, and many other: I think his circumspection is laudable, and he may thereby decline occasion of Error.

A like opinion there is now of Elder.

4. *Dioscorides Anazarbeus*, he wrote many Books in Physick, but six thereof *De Materia Medica*, have found the greatest esteem: he is an Author of good antiquity and use, preferred by *Galen* before *Cratevas*, *Pamphilus*, and all that attempted the like description before him; yet all he delivereth therein is not to be conceived Oraculous. For beside that, following the wars under *Anthony*, the course of his life would not permit a punctual *Examen* in all; there are many things concerning the nature of Simples, traditionally delivered, and to which I believe he gave no assent himself. It had been an excellent Receit, and in his time when Saddles were scarce in fashion of very great use, if that were true which he delivers, that *Vitex*, or *Agnus Castus* held only in the hand, preserveth the rider from galling. It were a strange effect, and Whores would forsake the experiment of *Savine*, if that were a truth which he delivereth of Brake or female Fearn, that onely treading over it, it causeth a sudden abortion. It were to be wished true, and women would idolize him, could that be made out which he recordeth of *Phyllon*, *Mercury*, and other vegetables, that the juice of the male Plant drunk, or the leaves but applied unto the genitals, determines their conceptions unto males. In these relations although he be more sparing, his predecessors were very numerous; and *Galen* hereof most sharply accuseth *Pamphilus*. Many of the like nature we meet sometimes in *Oribasius*, *Ætius*, *Trallianus*, *Serapion*, *Evax*, and *Marcellus*, whereof some containing no colour of verity, we may at first sight reject them; others which seem to carry some face of truth, we may reduce unto experiment. And herein we shall rather perform good offices unto truth, then any disservice unto their relators, who have well deserved of succeeding Ages; from whom having received the conceptions of former Times, we have the readier hint of their conformity with ours, and may accordingly explore and sift their verities.

Plinius Natural History collected out of 2000 several Authors.

5. *Plinius Secundus of Verona*; a man of great Eloquence, and industry indefatigable, as may appear by his writings, especially those now extant, and which are never like to perish, but even with learning it self; that is, his Natural History. He was the greatest Collector or Rhapsodist of the Latines, and as *Suetonius* observeth, he collected this piece out of two thousand Latine and Greek Authors. Now what is very strange, there is scarce a popular error passant in our days, which is not either directly expressed, or diductively contained in this Work; which being in the hands of most men, hath proved a powerful occasion of their propagation. Wherein notwithstanding the credulity of the Reader, is more condemnable than the curiosity of the Author: for commonly he nameth the Authors from whom he received those accounts, and writes but as he reads, as in his Preface to *Vespasian* he acknowledgeth.

6. *Claudius Ælianus*, who flourished not long after in the reign of *Trajan*, unto whom he dedicated his Tacticks; an elegant and miscellaneous Author, he hath left two Books which are in the hands of every one, his History of Animals, and his *Varia Historia*. Wherein are contained many things suspicious, not a few false, some impossible; he is much beholding unto *Ctesias*, and in many uncertainties writes more confidently then *Pliny*.

7. *Julius Solinus*, who lived also about his time: He left a Work entituled *Polyhistor*, containing great variety of matter, and is with most in good request at this day. But to speak freely what cannot be concealed, it is but *Pliny* varied, or a transcription of his Natural History: nor is it without all wonder it hath continued so long, but is now likely, and deserves indeed to live for ever; not onely for the elegancy of the Text, but the excellency of the Comment, lately performed by *Salmasius*, under the name of *Plinian* Exercitations.

8. *Athenæs*, a delectable Author, very various, and justly stiled by *Casaubon*, *Græcorum Plinius*. There is extant of his, a famous Piece, under the name of *Deipnosophista*, or *Cœna Sapientum*, containing the Discourse of many learned men, at a Feast provided by *Laurentius*. It is a laborious Collection out of many Authors, and some whereof are mentioned no where else. It containeth strange and singular relations, not without some spice or sprinkling of all Learning. The Author was probably a better Grammarian then Philosopher, dealing but hardly with *Aristotle* and *Plato*, and betrayeth himself much in his Chapter *De Curiositate Aristotelis*. In brief, he is an Author of excellent use, and may with discretion be read unto great advantage: and hath therefore well deserved the Comments of *Casaubon* and *Dalecampius*. But being miscellaneous in many things, he is to be received with suspition; for such as amass all relations, must erre in some, and may without offence be unbelieved in many.

That write Hexameters, or long verses.

9. We will not omit the works of *Nicander*, a Poet of good antiquity: that is, his *Theriaca*, and *Alexipharmaca*, Translated and Commented by *Gorræus*: for therein are contained several Traditions, and popular Conceits of venemous Beasts; which only deducted, the Work is to be embraced, as containing the first description of poysons and their antidotes, whereof *Dioscorides*, *Pliny*, and *Galen*, have made especial use in elder times; and *Ardoynus*, *Grevinus*, and others, in times more near our own. We might perhaps let pass *Oppianus*, that famous Cilician Poet. There are extant of his in Greek, four Books of Cynegeticks or Venation, five of Halieuticks or Piscation, commented and published by *Ritterhusius*; wherein describing Beasts of venery and Fishes, he hath indeed but sparingly inserted the vulgar conceptions thereof. So that abating the annual mutation of Sexes in the *Hyæna*, the single Sex of the *Rhinoceros*, the Antipathy between two Drums, of a Lamb and a Wolfes skin, the informity of Cubs, the venation of *Centaures*, the copulation of the *Murena* and the Viper, with some few others, he may be read with great delight and profit. It is not without some wonder his Elegant Lines are so neglected. Surely hereby we reject one of the best Epick Poets, and much condemn the Judgement of *Antoninus*, whose apprehensions so honoured his Poems, that as some report, for every verse, he assigned him a Stater of Gold.

10. More warily are we to receive the relations of *Philes*, who in *Greek Iambicks* delivered the proprieties of Animals, for herein he hath amassed the vulgar accounts recorded by the Ancients, and hath therein especially followed *Ælian*. And likewise *Johannes Tzetzes*, a Grammarian, who besides a Comment upon *Hesiod* and *Homer*, hath left us *Chiliads de Varia Historia*; wherein

delivering the accounts of *Ctesias*, *Herodotus*, and most of the Ancients, he is to be embraced with caution, and as a transcriptive Relator.

11. We cannot without partiality omit all caution even of holy Writers, and such whose names are venerable unto all posterity: not to meddle at all with miraculous Authors, or any Legendary relators, we are not without circumspection to receive some Books even of authentick and renowned Fathers. So are we to read the leaves of *Basil* and *Ambrose*, in their Books entituled *Hexameron*, or *The Description of the Creation*; Wherein delivering particular accounts of all the Creatures, they have left us relations sutable to those of *Ælian*, *Plinie*, and other Natural Writers; whose authorities herein they followed, and from whom most probably they desumed their Narrations. And the like hath been committed by *Epiphanius*, in his Physiologie: that is, a Book he hath left concerning the Nature of Animals. With no less caution must we look on *Isidor* Bishop of *Sevil*; who having left in twenty Books, an accurate work *De Originibus*, hath to the Etymologie of Words, super-added their received Natures; wherein most generally he consents with common Opinions and Authors which have delivered them.

12. *Albertus* Bishop of *Ratisbone*, for his great Learning and latitude of Knowledge, sirnamed *Magnus*. Besides Divinity, he hath written many Tracts in Philosophy; what we are chiefly to receive with caution, are his Natural Tractates, more especially those of Minerals, Vegetables, and Animals, which are indeed chiefly Collections out of *Aristotle*, *Ælian*, and *Pliny*, and respectively contain many of our popular Errors. A man who hath much advanced these Opinions by the authority of his Name, and delivered most Conceits, with strict Enquiry into few. In the same *Classis* may well be placed *Vincentius Belluacensis*, or rather he from whom he collected his *Speculum naturale*, that is, *Guilielmus de Conchis*; and also *Hortus Sanitatis*, and *Bartholomeus Glanvil*, sirnamed *Anglicus*, who writ *De proprietatibus Rerum*. Hither also may be referred *Kiranides*, which is a Collection out of *Harpocration* the Greek, and sundry Arabick Writers; delivering not onely the Natural but Magical propriety of things; a Work as full of Vanity as Variety; containing many relations, whose Invention is as difficult as their Beliefs, and their Experiments sometime as hard as either.

13. We had almost forgot *Jeronimus Cardanus* that famous Physician of *Milan*, a great Enquirer of Truth, but too greedy a Receiver of it. He hath left many excellent Discourses, Medical, Natural, and Astrological; the most suspicious are those two he wrote by admonition in a dream, that is *De Subtilitate & Varietate Rerum*. Assuredly this learned man hath taken many things upon trust, and although examined some, hath let slip many others. He is of singular use unto a prudent Reader; but unto him that onely desireth Hoties, or to replenish his head with varieties; like many others before related, either in the Original or confirmation, he may become no small occasion of Error.

14. Lastly, Authors are also suspicious, not greedily to be swallowed, who pretend to write of Secrets, to deliver Antipathies, Sympathies, and the occult abstrusities of things; in the list whereof may be accounted, *Alexis Pedimontanus*, *Antonius Mizaldus*, *Trinum Magicum*, and many others. Not omitting that famous Philosopher of *Naples*, *Baptista Porta*; in whose Works, although there be contained many excellent things, and verified upon his own Experience; yet are there many also receptary, and such as will not endure the test. Who although he hath delivered many strange Relations in his Phytognomia, and his Villa; yet hath he more remarkably expressed himself in his Natural Magick, and the miraculous effects of Nature. Which containing various and delectable subjects, withall promising wondrous and easie effects, they are entertained by Readers at all hands; whereof the major part sit down in his authority, and thereby omit not onely the certainty of Truth, but the pleasure of its Experiment.

Thus have we made a brief enumeration of these Learned Men; not willing any to decline their Works (without which it is not easie to attain any measure of general Knowledge,) but to apply themselves with caution thereunto. And seeing the lapses of these worthy Pens, to cast a wary eye on those diminutive, and pamphlet Treaties daily published amongst us. Pieces maintaining rather Typography than Verity, Authors presumably writing by Common Places, wherein for many years promiscuously amassing all that makes for their subject, they break forth at last in trite and fruitless Rhapsodies; doing thereby not only open injury unto Learning, but committing a secret treachery upon truth. For their relations falling upon credulous Readers, they meet with prepared beliefs; whose supinities had rather assent unto all, then adventure the trial of any.

Thus, I say, must these Authors be read, and thus must we be read our selves; for discoursing of matters dubious, and many convertible truths; we cannot without arrogancy entreat a credulity, or implore any farther assent, then the probability of our Reasons, and verity of experiments induce.

CHAPTER IX
Of the Same.

There are beside these Authors and such as have positively promoted errors, divers other which are in some way accessory; whose verities although they do not directly assert, yet do they obliquely concur unto their beliefs. In which account are many holy Writers, Preachers, Moralists, Rhetoricians, Orators and Poets; for they depending upon Invention, deduce their mediums from all things whatsoever; and playing much upon the simile, or illustrative argumentation: to induce their Enthymemes unto the people, they took up popular conceits, and from traditions unjustifiable or really false, illustrate matters of undeniable truth. Wherein although their intention be sincere, and that course not much condemnable; yet doth it notoriously strengthen common Errors, and authorise Opinions injurious unto truth.

Expressions of holy Scripture fitted many times rather to popular and common apprehension, then to the exact Nature of things.

Thus have some Divines drawn into argument the Fable of the *Phœnix*, made use of that of the *Salamander*, *Pelican*, *Basilisk*, and divers relations of *Plinie*; deducing from thence most worthy morals, and even upon our Saviour. Now although this be not prejudicial unto wiser Judgments, who are but weakly moved with such arguments, yet it is oft times occasion of Error unto vulgar heads, who expect in the Fable as equal a truth as in the Moral, and conceive that infallible Philosophy, which is in any sense delivered by Divinity. But wiser discerners do well understand, that every Art hath its own circle; that the effects of things are best examined, by sciences wherein are delivered their causes; that strict and definitive expressions, are alway required in Philosophy, but a loose and popular delivery will serve oftentimes in Divinity. As may be observed even in holy Scripture, which often omitteth the exact account of things; describing them rather to our apprehensions, then leaving doubts in vulgar minds, upon their unknown and Philosophical descriptions. Thus it termeth the Sun and the Moon the two great lights of Heaven. Now if any shall from hence conclude, the Moon is second in magnitude unto the Sun, he must excuse my belief; and it cannot be strange, if herein I rather adhere unto the demonstration of *Ptolomy*, then the popular description of *Moses*. Thus is it said, *Chron.* 2. 4. That *Solomon* made a molten Sea of ten Cubits from brim to brim round in compass, and five Cubits the height thereof, and a line of thirty Cubits did compass it round about. Now in this description, the circumference is made just treble unto the Diameter: that is, as 10. to 30. or 7. to 21. But *Archimedes* In his Cyclometria. demonstrates, that the proportion of the Diameter unto the circumference, is as 7. unto almost 22. which will occasion a sensible difference, that is almost a Cubit. Now if herein I adhere unto *Archimedes* who speaketh exactly, rather then the sacred Text which speaketh largely; I hope I shall not offend Divinity: I am sure I shall have reason and experience of every circle to support me.

Thus Moral Writers, Rhetoricians and Orators make use of several relations which will not consist with verity. *Aristotle* in his Ethicks takes up the conceit of the *Bever*, and the divulsion of his Testicles. The tradition of the Bear, the Viper, and divers others are frequent amongst Orators. All which although unto the illiterate and undiscerning hearers may seem a confirmation of their realities; yet is this no reasonable establishment unto others, who will not depend hereon otherwise then common Apologues: which being of impossible falsities, do notwithstanding include wholsome moralities, and such as expiate the trespass of their absurdities.

The Hieroglyphical doctrine of the Ægyptians (which in their four hundred years cohabitation some conjecture they learned from the Hebrews) hath much advanced many popular conceits. For using an Alphabet of things, and not of words, through the image and pictures thereof, they endeavoured to speak their hidden conceits in the letters and language of Nature. In pursuit whereof, although in many things, they exceeded not their true and real apprehensions; yet in some other they either framing the story, or taking up the tradition, conducible unto their intentions, obliquely confirmed many falsities; which as authentick and conceded truths did after pass unto the Greeks, from them unto other Nations, and are still retained by symbolical Writers, Emblematists, Heralds, and others. Whereof some are strictly maintained for truths, as naturally making good their artificial representations; others symbolically intended, are literally received, and swallowed in the first sense, without all gust of the second. Whereby we pervert the profound and mysterious knowledge of Ægypt; containing the Arcana's of Greek Antiquities, the Key of many obscurities and ancient learning extant. Famous herein in former Ages were *Heraiscus*, *Cheremon*, *Epius*, especially *Orus Apollo Niliacus*: who lived in the reign of *Theodosius*, and in Ægyptian language left two Books of Hieroglyphicks, translated into Greek by *Philippus*, and a large collection of all made after by *Pierius*. But no man is likely to profound the Ocean of that Doctrine, beyond that eminent example of industrious Learning, *Kircherus*.

Painters who are the visible representers of things, and such as by the learned sense of the eye endeavour to inform the understanding, are not inculpable herein, who either describing Naturals as they are, or actions as they have been, have oftentimes erred in their delineations. Which being the Books that all can read, are fruitful advancers of these conceptions, especially in common and popular apprehensions: who being unable for farther enquiry, must rest in the draught and letter of their descriptions.

Lastly, Poets and Poetical Writers have in this point exceeded others, trimly advancing the Ægyptian notions of *Harpies*, *Phœnix*, *Gryphins* and many more. Now however to make use of Fictions, Apologues, and Fables, be not unwarrantable, and the intent of these inventions might point at laudable ends; yet do they afford our junior capacities a frequent occasion of error, setling impressions in our tender memories, which our advanced judgments generally neglect to expunge. This way the vain and idle fictions of the Gentiles did first insinuate into the heads of Christians; and thus are they continued even unto our days. Our first and literary apprehensions being commonly instructed in Authors which handle nothing else; wherewith our memories being stuffed, our inventions become pedantick, and cannot avoid their allusions; driving at these as at the highest elegancies, which are but the frigidities of wit, and become not the genius of manly ingenuities. It were therefore no loss like that of *Galens* Library, if these had found the same fate; and would in some way requite the neglect of solid Authors, if they were less pursued. For were a pregnant wit educated in ignorance hereof, receiving only impressions from realities; upon such solid foundations, it must surely raise more substantial superstructions, and fall upon very many excellent strains, which have been jusled off by their intrusions.

CHAPTER X
Of the last and common Promoter of false Opinions, the endeavours of Satan.

The Devils method of propagating Error in the World.

But beside the infirmities of humane Nature, the seed of Error within our selves, and the several ways of delusion from each other, there is an invisible Agent, and secret promoter without us, whose activity is undiscerned, and plays in the dark upon us; and that is the first contriver of Error, and professed opposer of Truth, the Devil. For though permitted unto his proper principles, *Adam* perhaps would have sinned without the suggestion of Satan: and from the transgressive infirmities of himself might have erred alone, as well as the Angels before him: And although also there were no Devil at all, yet there is now in our Natures a confessed sufficiency unto corruption, and the frailty of our own Oeconomie, were able to betray us out of Truth, yet wants there not another Agent, who taking advantage hereof proceedeth to obscure the diviner part, and efface all tract of its traduction. To attempt a particular of all his wiles, is too bold an Arithmetick for man: what most considerably concerneth his popular and practised ways of delusion, he first deceiveth mankind in five main points concerning God and himself.

And first his endeavours have ever been, and they cease not yet to instill a belief in the mind of Man, there is no God at all. And this he principally endeavours to establish in a direct and literal apprehension; that is, that there is no such reality existent, that the necessity of his entity dependeth upon ours, and is but a Political Chymera; that the natural truth of God is an artificial erection of Man, and the Creator himself but a subtile invention of the Creature. Where he succeeds not thus high, he labours to introduce a secondary and deductive Atheism; that although men concede there is a God, yet should they deny his providence. And therefore assertions have flown about, that he intendeth only the care of the species or common natures, but letteth loose the guard of individuals, and single existencies therein: that he looks not below the Moon, but hath designed the regiment of sublunary affairs unto inferiour deputations. To promote which apprehensions, or empuzzel their due conceptions, he casteth in the notions of fate, destiny, fortune, chance, and necessity; terms commonly misconceived by vulgar heads, and their propriety sometime perverted by the wisest. Whereby extinguishing in minds the compensation of vertue and vice, the hope and fear of Heaven or Hell; they comply in their actions unto the drift of his delusions, and live like creatures without the capacity of either.

Now hereby he not onely undermineth the Base of Religion, and destroyeth the principle preambulous unto all belief; but puts upon us the remotest Error from Truth. For Atheism is the greatest falsity, and to affirm there is no God, the highest lie in Nature. And therefore strictly taken, some men will say his labour is in vain; For many there are, who cannot conceive there was ever any absolute *Atheist*; or such as could determine there was no God, without all check from himself, or contradiction from his other opinions. And therefore those few so called by elder times, might be the best of *Pagans*; suffering that name rather in relation to the gods of the Gentiles, then the true Creator of all. A conceit that cannot befal his greatest enemy, or him that would induce the same in us; who hath a sensible apprehension hereof, for he believeth with trembling. To speak yet more strictly and conformably unto some Opinions, no creature can wish thus much; nor can the Will which hath a power to run into velleities, and wishes of impossibilities, have any *utinam* of this. For to desire there were no God, were plainly to unwish their own being; which must needs be annihilated in the substraction of that essence which substantially supporteth them, and restrains them from regression into nothing. And if as some contend, no creature can desire his own annihilation, that Nothing is not appetible, and not to be at all, is worse then to be in the miserablest condition of something; the Devil himself could not embrace that motion, nor would the enemy of God be freed by such a Redemption.

But coldly thriving in this design, as being repulsed by the principles of humanity, and the dictates of that production, which cannot deny its original, he fetcheth a wider circle; and when he cannot make men conceive there is no God at all, he endeavours to make them believe there is not one, but many: wherein he hath been so successful with common heads, that he hath led their belief thorow the Works of Nature.

Areopagus the severe Court of Athens.

Now in this latter attempt, the subtilty of his circumvention, hath indirectly obtained the former. For although to opinion there be many gods, may seem an excess in Religion, and such as cannot at all consist with Atheism, yet doth it deductively and upon inference include the same, for Unity is the inseparable and essential attribute of Deity; and if there be more then one God, it is no Atheism to say there is no God at all. And herein though *Socrates* only suffered, yet were *Plato* and *Aristotle* guilty of the same Truth; who demonstratively understanding the simplicity of perfection, and the indivisible condition of the first causator, it was not in the power of Earth, or Areopagy of Hell to work them from it. For holding an [19]Apodictical knowledge, and assured science of its verity, to perswade their apprehensions unto a plurality of gods in the world, were to make *Euclide* believe there were more than one Center in a Circle, or one right Angle in a Triangle; which were indeed a fruitless attempt, and inferreth absurdities beyond the evasion of Hell. For though Mechanick and vulgar heads ascend not unto such comprehensions, who live not commonly unto half the advantage of their principles; yet did they not escape the eye of wiser *Minerva's*, and such as made good the genealogie of *Jupiters* brains; who although they had divers stiles for God, yet under many appellations acknowledged one divinity: rather conceiving thereby the evidence or acts of his power in several ways and places, then a multiplication of Essence, or real distraction of unity in any one.

Again, To render our errors more monstrous (and what unto miracle sets forth the patience of God,) he hath endeavoured to make the world believe, that he was God himself; and failing of his first attempt to be but like the highest in Heaven, he hath obtained with men to be the same on Earth. And hath accordingly assumed the annexes of Divinity, and the prerogatives of the Creator, drawing into practice the operation of miracles, and the prescience of things to come. Thus hath he in a specious way wrought cures upon the sick: played over the wondrous acts of Prophets, and counterfeited many miracles of Christ and his Apostles. Thus hath he openly contended with God, and to this effect his insolency was not ashamed to play a solemn prize with *Moses*; wherein although his performance were very specious, and beyond the common apprehension of any power below a Deity; yet was it not such as could make good his Omnipotency. For he was wholly confounded in the conversion of dust into lice. An act Philosophy can scarce deny to be above the power of Nature, nor upon a requisite predisposition beyond the efficacy of the Sun. Wherein notwithstanding the head of the old Serpent was confessedly too weak for *Moses* hand, and the arm of his Magicians too short for the finger of God.

The Authors opinion, touching Necromancy and apparitions of the spirits of men departed.

Thus hath he also made men believe that he can raise the dead, that he hath the key of life and death, and a prerogative above that principle which makes no regression from privations. The Stoicks that opinioned the souls of wise men dwelt about the Moon, and those of fools wandered about the Earth, advantaged the conceit of this effect; wherein the Epicureans, who held that death was nothing, nor nothing after death, must contradict their principles to be deceived. Nor could the Pythagoreans or such as maintained the transmigration of souls give easie admittance hereto: for holding that separated souls successively supplied other bodies, they could hardly allow the raising of souls from other worlds, which at the same time, they conceived conjoyned unto bodies in this. More inconsistent with these Opinions, is the Error of Christians, who holding the dead do rest in the Lord, do yet believe they are at the lure of the Devil; that he who is in bonds himself commandeth the fetters of the dead, and dwelling in the bottomless lake, the blessed from *Abrahams* bosome, that can believe the real resurrection of *Samuel*: or that there is any thing but delusion in the practice of [20]Necromancy and popular raising of Ghosts.

How the Devil works his pretended revelations or predictions.

He hath moreover endeavoured the opinion of Deity, by the delusion of Dreams, and the discovery of things to come in sleep, above the prescience of our waked senses. In this expectation he perswaded the credulity of elder times to take up their lodging before his temple, in skins of their own sacrifices: till his reservedness had contrived answers, whose accomplishments were in his power, or not beyond his presagement. Which way, although it had pleased Almighty God, sometimes to reveal himself, yet was the proceeding very different. For the revelations of Heaven are conveyed by new impressions, and the immediate illumination of the soul, whereas the deceiving spirit, by concitation of humours, produceth his conceited phantasms, or by compounding the species already residing, doth make up words which mentally speak his intentions.

But above all he most advanced his Deity in the solemn practice of Oracles, wherein in several parts of the World, he publikely professed his Divinity; but how short they flew of that spirit, whose omniscience, they would resemble, their weakness sufficiently declared. What jugling there was therein, the Orator *Demosthenes.* plainly confessed, who being good at the same game himself, could say that *Pythia* Philippised. Who can but laugh at the carriage of *Ammon* unto *Alexander*, who addressing unto him as a god, was made to believe, he was a god himself? How openly did he betray his Indivinity unto *Crœsus*, who being ruined by his Amphibology, and expostulating with him for so ungrateful a deceit, received no higher answer then the excuse of his impotency upon the contradiction of fate, and the setled law of powers beyond his power to controle! What more then sublunary directions, or such as might proceed from the Oracle of humane Reason, was in his advice unto the Spartans in the time of a great Plague; when for the cessation thereof, he wisht them to have recourse unto a Fawn, that is in open terms, unto one Nebrus, a good Physitian of those days? *Nebros, in Greek, a Fawn.* From no diviner a spirit came his reply unto *Caracalla*, who requiring a remedy for his Gout, received no other counsel then to refrain cold drink; which was but a dietetical caution, and such as without a journey unto *Æsculapius*, culinary prescription and kitchin Aphorisms might have afforded at home. Nor surely if any truth there were therein, of more then natural activity was his counsel unto *Democritus*; when for the Falling sickness he commended the Maggot in a Goats head. For many things secret are true; sympathies and antipathies are safely authentick unto us, who ignorant of their causes may yet acknowledge their effects. Beside, being a natural Magician he may perform many acts in ways above our knowledge, though not transcending our natural power, when our knowledge shall direct it. Part hereof hath been discovered by himself, and some by humane indagation: which though magnified as fresh inventions unto us, are stale unto his cognition. I hardly believe he hath from elder times unknown the verticity of the Loadstone; surely his perspicacity discerned it to respect the North, when ours beheld it indeterminately. Many secrets there are in Nature of difficult discovery unto man, of easie knowledge unto Satan; whereof some his vain glory cannot conceal, others his envy will not discover.

Again, Such is the mysterie of his delusion, that although he labour to make us believe that he is God, and supremest nature whatsoever, yet would he also perswade our beliefs, that he is less then Angels or men; and his condition not onely subjected unto rational powers, but the actions of things which have no efficacy on our selves. Thus hath he inveigled no small part of the world into a credulity of artificial Magick: That there is an Art, which without compact commandeth the powers of Hell; whence some have delivered the polity of spirits, and left an account even to their Provincial Dominions: that they stand in awe of Charms, Spels, and Conjurations; that he is afraid of letters and characters, of notes and dashes, which set together do signifie nothing, not only in the dictionary of man, but the subtiler vocabulary of Satan. That there is any power in *Bitumen*, Pitch, or Brimstone, to purifie the air from his uncleanness; [St. Johns Wort, so called by Magicians.] that any vertue there is in *Hipericon* to make good the name of *fuga Dæmonis*, any such Magick as is ascribed unto the Root *Baaras* by *Josephus*, or *Cynospastus* by *Ælianus*, it is not easie to believe; nor is it naturally made out what is delivered of *Tobias*, that by the fume of a Fishes liver, he put to flight *Asmodeus*. That they are afraid of the pentangle of *Solomon*, though so set forth with the body of man, as to touch and point out the five places wherein our Saviour was wounded, I know not how to assent. [*3 triangles intersected and made of five lines.*] If perhaps he hath fled from holy Water, if he cares not to hear the sound of *Tetragrammaton* [Implying Jehovah, which in Hebrew consisteth of four letters.], if his eye delight not in the sign of the Cross; and that sometimes he will seem to be charmed with words of holy Scripture, and to flie from the letter and dead verbality, who must onely start at the life and animated interiors thereof: It may be feared they are but *Parthian* flights, *Ambuscado* retreats, and elusory tergiversations: Whereby to confirm our credulities, he will comply with the opinion of such powers, which in themselves have no activities. Whereof having once begot in our minds an assured dependence, he makes us relie on powers which he but precariously obeys; and to desert those true and only charms which Hell cannot withstand.

Lastly, To lead us farther into darkness, and quite to lose us in this maze of Error, he would make men believe there is no such creature as himself: and that he is not onely subject unto inferiour creatures, but in the rank of nothing. Insinuating into mens minds there is no Devil at all, and contriveth accordingly, many ways to conceal or indubitate his existency. Wherein beside that he annihilates the blessed Angels and Spirits in the rank of his Creation; he begets a security of himself, and a careless eye unto the last remunerations. And therefore hereto he inveigleth, not only *Sadduces* and such as retain unto the Church of God: but is also content that *Epicurus*, *Democritus*, or any Heathen should hold the same. And to this effect he maketh men believe that apparitions, and such as confirm his existence are either deceptions of sight, or melancholly depravements of phansie. Thus when he had not onely appeared but spake unto *Brutus*; *Cassius* the Epicurian was ready at hand to perswade him, it was but a mistake in his weary imagination, and that indeed there were no such realities in nature. Thus he endeavours to propagate the unbelief of Witches, whose concession infers his co-existency; by this means also he advanceth the opinion of total death, and staggereth the immortality of the soul; for, such as deny there are spirits subsistent without bodies, will with more difficulty affirm the separated existence of their own.

Now to induce and bring about these falsities, he hath laboured to destroy the evidence of Truth, that is the revealed verity and written Word of God. To which intent he hath obtained with some to repudiate the Books of *Moses*, others those of the Prophets, and some both: to deny the Gospel and authentick Histories of Christ; to reject that of *John*, and to receive that of *Judas*; to disallow all, and erect another of *Thomas*. And when neither their corruption by *Valentinus* and *Arrius*, their mutilation by *Marcion*, *Manes*, and *Ebion* could satisfie his design, he attempted the ruine and total destruction thereof; as he sedulously endeavoured, by the power and subtilty of *Julian*, *Maximinus*, and *Dioclesian*.

But the longevity of that piece, which hath so long escaped the common fate, and the providence of that Spirit which ever waketh over it, may at last discourage such attempts; and if not make doubtful its Mortality, at least indubitably declare; this is a stone too big for *Saturns* mouth, and a bit indeed Oblivion cannot swallow.

And thus how strangely he possesseth us with Errors may clearly be observed, deluding us into contradictory and inconsistent falsities; whilest he would make us believe, That there is no God. That there are many. That he himself is God. That he is less then Angels or Men. That he is nothing at all.

Nor hath he onely by these wiles depraved the conception of the Creator, but with such Riddles hath also entangled the Nature of our Redeemer. Some denying his Humanity, and that he was one of the Angels, as *Ebion*; that the Father and Son were but one person, as *Sabellius*. That his body was phantastical, as *Manes*, *Basilides*, *Priscillian*, *Jovinianus*; that he only passed through *Mary*, as *Utyches* and *Valentinus*. Some denying his Divinity; that he was begotten of humane principles, and the seminal Son of *Joseph*; as *Carpocras*, *Symmachus*, *Photinus*: that he was *Seth* the Son of *Adam*, as the *Sethians*: that he was less then Angels, as *Cherinthus*: that he was inferiour unto *Melchisedec*, as *Theodotus*: that he was not God, but God dwelt in him, as *Nicholaus*: and some embroyled them both. So did they which converted the Trinity into a Quaternity, and affirmed two persons in Christ, as *Paulus Samosatenus*: that held he was Man without a Soul, and that the Word performed that office in him, as *Apollinaris*: that he was both Son and Father, as *Montanus*: that *Jesus* suffered, but Christ remained impatible, as *Cherinthus*. Thus he endeavours to entangle Truths: And when he cannot possibly destroy its substance, he cunningly confounds its apprehensions; that from the inconsistent and contrary determinations thereof, consectary impieties, and hopeful conclusions may arise, there's no such thing at all.

Footnotes

[19]*Demonstrative*.
[20]*Divination by the dead*.

CHAPTER XI
A further Illustration.

Now although these ways of delusions most Christians have escaped, yet are there many other whereunto we are daily betrayed, and these we meet with in obvious occurrents of the world, wherein he induceth us, to ascribe effects unto causes of no cognation; and distorting the order and theory of causes perpendicular to their effects, he draws them aside unto things whereto they run parallel, and in their proper motions would never meet together.

Thus doth he sometime delude us in the conceits of Stars and Meteors, beside their allowable actions ascribing effects thereunto of independent causations. Thus hath he also made the ignorant sort believe that natural effects immediately and commonly proceed from supernatural powers: and these he usually drives from Heaven, his own principality the Air, and Meteors therein; which being of themselves the effects of natural and created causes, and such as upon a due conjunction of actives and passives, without a miracle must arise unto what they appear; are always looked on by ignorant spectators as supernatural spectacles, and made the causes or signs of most succeeding contingencies. To behold a Rainbow in the night, is no prodigy unto a Philosopher. Then Eclipses of Sun or Moon, nothing is more natural. Yet with what superstition they have been beheld since the Tragedy of *Nicias* and his Army, many examples declare.

True it is, and we will not deny, that although these being natural productions from second and setled causes, we need not alway look upon them as the immediate hand of God, or of his ministring Spirits; yet do they sometimes admit a respect therein; and even in their naturals, the indifferency of their existencies contemporised unto our actions, admits a further consideration.

That two or three Suns or Moons appear in any mans life or reign, it is not worth the wonder. But that the same should fall out at a remarkable time, or point of some decisive action; that the contingency of the appearance should be confirmed unto that time; that those two should make but one line in the Book of Fate, and stand together in the great Ephemerides of God; beside the Philosophical assignment of the cause, it may admit a Christian apprehension in the signality.

But above all he deceiveth us, when we ascribe the effects of things unto evident and seeming causalities, which arise from the secret and undiscerned action of himself. Thus hath he deluded many Nations in his Augurial and Extispicious inventions, from casual and uncontrived contingencies divining events succeeding. Which *Tuscan* superstition seizing upon *Rome*, hath since possessed all *Europe*. When *Augustus* found two galls in his sacrifice, the credulity of the City concluded a hope of peace with *Anthony*; and the conjunction of persons in choler with each other. Because *Brutus* and *Cassius* met a Blackmore, and *Pompey* had on a dark or sad coloured garment at *Pharsalia*; these were presages of their overthrow. Which notwithstanding are scarce Rhetorical sequels; concluding Metaphors from realities, and from conceptions metaphorical inferring realities again.

Now these divinations concerning events, being in his power to force, contrive, prevent, or further, they must generally fall out conformably unto his predictions. When *Graccus* was slain, the same day the Chickens refused to come out of the Coop: and *Claudius Pulcher* underwent the like success, when he contemned the Tripudiary Augurations: They died not because the Pullets would not feed: but because the Devil foresaw their death, he contrived that abstinence in them. So was there no natural dependence of the event. An unexpected way of delusion, and whereby he more easily led away the incircumspection of their belief. Which fallacy he might excellently have acted before the death of *Saul*; for that being within his power to foretell, was not beyond his ability to foreshew: and might have contrived signs thereof through all the creatures, which visibly confirmed by the event, had proved authentick unto those times, and advanced the Art ever after.

The danger and delusion that is in cures by Charms, Amulets, Ligatures, Characters, etc.

He deludeth us also by Philters, Ligatures, Charms, ungrounded Amulets, Characters, and many superstitious ways in the cure of common diseases: seconding herein the expectation of men with events of his own contriving. Which while some unwilling to fall directly upon Magick, impute unto the power of imagination, or the efficacy of hidden causes, he obtains a bloody advantage: for thereby he begets not only a false opinion, but such as leadeth the open way of destruction. In maladies admitting natural reliefs, making men rely on remedies, neither of real operation in themselves, nor more then seeming efficacy in his concurrence. Which whensoever he pleaseth to withdraw, they stand naked unto the mischief of their diseases: and revenge the contempt of the medicines of the Earth which God hath created for them. And therefore when neither miracle is expected, nor connection of cause unto effect from natural grounds concluded; however it be sometime successful, it cannot be safe to rely on such practises, and desert the known and authentick provisions of God. In which rank of remedies, if nothing in our knowledge or their proper power be able to relieve us, we must with patience submit unto that restraint, and expect the will of the Restrainer.

Now in these effects although he seems oft-times to imitate, yet doth he concur unto their productions in a different way from that spirit which sometime in natural means produceth effects above Nature. For whether he worketh by causes which have relation or none unto the effect, he maketh it out by secret and undiscerned ways of Nature. So when *Caius* the blind, in the reign of *Antoninus*, was commanded to pass from the right side of the Altar unto the left, to lay five fingers of one hand thereon, and five of the other upon his eys; although the cure succeeded and all the people wondered, there was not any thing in the action which did produce it, nor any thing in his power that could enable it thereunto. So for the same infirmity, when *Aper* was counselled by him to make a Collyrium or ocular medicine with the blood of a white Cock and Honey, and apply it to his eyes for three days: When *Julian* for his spitting of blood, was cured by Honey and Pine nuts taken from his Altar: When *Lucius* for the pain in his side, applied thereto the ashes from his Altar with wine; although the remedies were somewhat rational, and not without a natural vertue unto such intentions, yet need we not believe that by their proper faculties they produced these effects.

But the effects of powers Divine flow from another operation; who either proceeding by visible means or not, unto visible effects, is able to conjoin them by his co-operation. And therefore those sensible ways which seem of indifferent natures, are not idle ceremonies, but may be causes by his command, and arise unto productions beyond their regular activities. If *Nahaman* the Syrian had washed in *Jordan* without the command of the Prophet, I believe he had been cleansed by them no more then by the waters of *Damascus*. I doubt if any beside *Elisha* had cast in Salt, the waters of *Jericho* had not been made wholsome. I know that a decoction of wild gourd or Colocynthis (though somewhat qualified) will not from every hand be dulcified unto aliment by an addition of flower or meal. There was some natural vertue in the Plaister of figs applied unto *Ezechias*; we find that gall is very mundificative, and was a proper medicine to clear the eyes of *Tobit*: which carrying in themselves some action of their own, they were additionally promoted by that power, which can extend their natures unto the production of effects beyond their created efficiencies. And thus may he operate also from causes of no power unto their visible effects; for he that hath determined their actions unto certain effects, hath not so emptied his own, but that he can make them effectual unto any other.

Again, Although his delusions run highest in points of practice, whose errors draw on offensive or penal enormities, yet doth he also deal in points of speculation, and things whose knowledge terminates in themselves. Whose cognition although it seems indifferent, and therefore its aberration directly to condemn no man; yet doth he hereby preparatively dispose us unto errors, and deductively deject us into destructive conclusions.

That the Sun, Moon, and Stars are living creatures, endued with soul and life, seems an innocent Error, and an harmless digression from truth; yet hereby he confirmed their Idolatry, and made it more plausibly embraced. For wisely mistrusting that reasonable spirits would never firmly be lost in the adorement of things inanimate, and in the lowest form of Nature; he begat an opinion that they were living creatures, and could not decay for ever.

That spirits are corporeal, seems at first view a conceit derogative unto himself, and such as he should rather labour to overthrow; yet hereby he establisheth the Doctrine of Lustrations, Amulets and Charms, as we have declared before.

That there are two principles of all things, one good, and another evil; from the one proceeding vertue, love, light, and unity; from the other, division, discord, darkness, and deformity, was the speculation of *Pythagoras*, *Empedocles*, and many ancient Philosophers, and was no more then *Oromasdes* and *Arimanius* of *Zoroaster*. Yet hereby he obtained the advantage of Adoration, and as the terrible principle became more dreadful then his Maker; and therefore not willing to let it fall, he furthered the conceit in succeeding Ages, and raised the faction of *Manes* to maintain it.

That the feminine sex have no generative emission, affording no seminal Principles of conception; was *Aristotles* Opinion of old, maintained still by some, and will be countenanced by him forever. For hereby he disparageth the fruit of the Virgin, frustrateth the fundamental Prophesie, nor can the seed of the Woman then break the head of the Serpent.

Nor doth he only sport in speculative Errors, which are of consequent impieties; but the unquietness of his malice hunts after simple lapses, and such whose falsities do only condemn our understandings. Thus if *Xenophanes* will say there is another world in the Moon; If *Heraclitus* with his adherents will hold the Sun is no bigger then it appeareth; If *Anaxagoras* affirm that Snow is black; If any other opinion there are no *Antipodes*, or that Stars do fall, he shall not want herein the applause or advocacy of Satan. For maligning the tranquility of truth, he delighteth to trouble its streams; and being a professed enemy unto God (who is truth it self) he promoteth any Error as derogatory to his nature; and revengeth himself in every deformity from truth. If therefore at any time he speak or practise truth, it is upon design, and a subtile inversion of the precept of God, to do good that evil may come of it. And therefore sometime we meet with wholsome doctrines from Hell; *Nosce teipsum*, the Motto of *Delphos*, was a good precept in morality: That a just man is beloved of the gods, an uncontrolable verity. 'Twas a good deed, though not well done, which he wrought by *Vespasian*, when by the touch of his foot he restored a lame man, and by the stroak of his hand another that was blind, but the intention hereof drived at his own advantage; for hereby he not only confirmed the opinion of his power with the people, but his integrity with Princes; in whose power he knew it lay to overthrow his Oracles, and silence the practice of his delusions.

How spirits understand one another.

But of such a diffused nature, and so large is the Empire of Truth, that it hath place within the walls of Hell, and the Devils themselves are daily forced to practise it; not onely as being true themselves in a Metaphysical verity, that is, as having their essence conformable unto the Intellect of their Maker, but making use of Moral and Logical verities; that is, whether in the conformity of words unto things, or things unto their own conceptions, they practise truth in common among themselves. For although without speech they intuitively conceive each other, yet do their apprehensions proceed through realities; and they conceive each other by species, which carry the true and proper notions of things conceived. And so also in Moral verities, although they deceive us, they lie unto each other; as well understanding that all community is continued by Truth, and that of Hell cannot consist without it.

To come yet nearer the point, and draw into a sharper angle; They do not only speak and practise truth, but may be said well-wishers hereunto, and in some sense do really desire its enlargement. For many things which in themselves are false, they do desire were true; He cannot but wish he were as he professeth, that he had the knowledge of future events; were it in his power, the Jews should be in the right, and the *Messias* yet to come. Could his desires effect it, the opinion of *Aristotle* should be true, the world should have no end, but be as immortal as himself. For thereby he might evade the accomplishment of those afflictions, he now but gradually endureth; for comparatively unto those flames, he is but yet in *Balneo*, then begins his *Ignis Rotæ*, and terrible fire, which will determine his disputed subtilty, and even hazard his immortality.

How the Devils fell.

But to speak strictly, he is in these wishes no promoter of verity, but if considered some ways injurious unto truth; for (besides that if things were true, which now are false, it were but an exchange of their natures, and things must then be false, which now are true) the setled and determined order of the world would be perverted, and that course of things disturbed, which seemed best unto the immutable contriver. For whilest they murmur against the present disposure of things, regulating determined realities unto their private optations, they rest not in their established natures; but unwishing their unalterable verities, do tacitely desire in them a deformity from the primitive Rule, and the Idea of that mind that formed all things best. And thus he offended truth even in his first attempt; For not content with his created nature, and thinking it too low, to be the highest creature of God, he offended the Ordainer, not only in the attempt, but in the wish and simple volition thereof.

THE SECOND BOOK
Of sundry popular Tenets concerning
Mineral, and vegetable bodies, generally
held for truth; which examined, prove
either false, or dubious.

CHAPTER I
Of Crystal.

Hereof the common Opinion hath been, and still remaineth amongst us, that Crystal is nothing else but Ice or Snow concreted, and by duration of time, congealed beyond liquation. Of which assertion, if prescription of time, and numerosity of Assertors, were a sufficient demonstration, we might sit down herein, as an unquestionable truth; nor should there need *ulterior* disquisition. For few Opinions there are which have found so many friends, or been so popularly received, through all Professions and Ages. *Pliny* is positive in this Opinion: *Crystallus sit gelu vehementius concreto*: the same is followed by *Seneca*, elegantly described by *Claudian*, not denied by *Scaliger*, some way affirmed by *Albertus*, *Brasavolus*, and directly by many others. The venerable Fathers of the Church have also assented hereto; As *Basil* in his *Hexameron*, *Isidore* in his Etymologies, and not only *Austin* a Latine Father, but *Gregory* the Great, and *Jerome* upon occasion of that term expressed in the first of *Ezekiel*.

That Crystal is not Ice or Snow congealed.

All which notwithstanding, upon a strict enquiry, we find the matter controvertible, and with much more reason denied then is as yet affirmed. For though many have passed it over with easie affirmatives, yet are there also many Authors that deny it, and the exactest Mineralogists have rejected it. *Diodorus* in his eleventh Book denieth it, (if Crystal be there taken in its proper acception, as *Rhodiginus* hath used it, and not for a Diamond, as *Salmatius* hath expounded it) for in that place he affirmeth; *Crystallum esse lapidem ex aqua pura concretum, non tamen frigore sed divini caloris vi. Solinus* who transcribed *Pliny*, and therefore in almost all subscribed unto him, hath in this point dissented from him. *Putant quidam glaciem coire, et in Crystallum corporari, sed frustra. Mathiolus* in his Comment upon *Dioscorides*, hath with confidence rejected it. The same hath been performed by *Agricola de natura fossilium*; by *Cardan, Bœtius de Boot, Cæsius Bernardus, Sennertus*, and many more.

Now besides Authority against it, there may be many reasons deduced from their several differences which seem to overthrow it. And first, a difference is probable in their concretion. For if Crystal be a stone (as in the number thereof it is confessedly received,) it is not immediately concreted by the efficacy of cold, but rather by a Mineral spirit, and lapidifical principles of its own, and therefore while it lay *in solutis principiis*, and remained in a fluid Body, it was a subject very unapt for proper conglaciation; for Mineral spirits do generally resist and scarce submit thereto. So we observe that many waters and springs will never freeze, and many parts in Rivers and Lakes, where there are Mineral eruptions, will still persist without congelations, as we also observe in *Aqua fortis*, or any Mineral solution, either of Vitriol, Alum, Salt-petre, Ammoniac, or Tartar, which although to some degree exhaled, and placed in cold Conservatories, will Crystallize and shoot into white and glacious bodies; yet is not this a congelation primarily effected by cold, but an intrinsecal induration from themselves; and a retreat into their proper solidities, which were absorbed by the liquor, and lost in a full imbibition thereof before. And so also when wood and many other bodies do putrifie, either by the Sea, other waters, or earths abounding in such spirits; we do not usually ascribe their induration to cold, but rather unto salinous spirits, concretive juices, and causes circumjacent, which do assimilate all bodies not indisposed for their impressions.

But Ice is water congealed by the frigidity of the air, whereby it acquireth no new form, but rather a consistence or determination of its diffluency, and amitteth not its essence, but condition of fluidity. Neither doth there any thing properly conglaciate but water, or watery humidity; for the determination of quick-silver is properly fixation, that of milk coagulation, and that of oyl and unctious bodies, only incrassation; And therefore *Aristotle* makes a trial of the fertility of humane seed, from the experiment of congelation; for that (saith he) which is not watery and improlifical will not conglaciate; which perhaps must not be taken strictly, but in the germ and spirited particles: For Eggs I observe will freeze, in the albuginous part thereof. And upon this ground *Paracelsus* in his Archidoxis, extracteth the magistery of wine; after four moneths digestion in horse-dung, exposing it unto the extremity of cold; whereby the aqueous parts will freeze, but the Spirit retire and be found congealed in the Center.

How to make Ice at any time of the year.

But whether this congelation be simply made by cold, or also by co-operation of any nitrous coagulum, or spirit of Salt the principle of concretion; whereby we observe that ice may be made with Salt and Snow by the fire side; as is also observable from Ice made by Saltpetre and water, duly mixed and strongly agitated at any time of the year, were a very considerable enquiry. For thereby we might clear the generation of Snow, Hail, and hoary Frosts, the piercing qualities of some winds, the coldness of Caverns, and some Cells. We might more sensibly conceive how Saltpetre fixeth the flying spirits of Minerals in Chymical Preparations, and how by this congealing quality it becomes an useful medicine in Fevers.

Again, The difference of their concretion is collectible from their dissolution; which being many ways performable in Ice, is few ways effected in Crystal. Now the causes of liquation are contrary to those of concretion; and as the Atoms and indivisible parcels are united, so are they in an opposite way disjoyned. That which is concreted by exsiccation or expression of humidity, will be resolved by humectation, as Earth, Dirt, and Clay; that which is coagulated by a fiery siccity, will suffer colliquation from an aqueous humidity, as Salt and Sugar, which are easily dissoluble in water, but not without difficulty in oyl, and well rectified spirits of Wine. That which is concreted by cold, will dissolve by a moist heat, if it consist of watery parts, as Gums, Arabick, Tragacanth, Ammoniac and others; in an airy heat or oyl, as all resinous bodies, Turpentine, Pitch, and Frankincense; in both, as gummy resinous bodies, Mastick, Camphire and Storax; in neither, as neutrals and bodies anomalous hereto, as Bdellium, Myrrhe, and others. Some by a violent dry heat, as Metals; which although corrodible by waters, yet will they not suffer a liquation from the powerfullest heat, communicable unto that element. Some will dissolve by this heat although their ingredients be earthy, as Glass, *The original ingredients of Glass.* whose materials are fine Sand, and the ashes of Chali or Fearn; and so will Salt run with fire, although it be concreted by heat. And this way may be effected a liquation in Crystal, but not without some difficulty; that is, calcination or reducing it by Art into a subtle powder; by which way and a vitreous commixture, Glasses are sometime made hereof, and it becomes the chiefest ground for artificial and factitious gemms. But the same way of solution is common also unto many Stones; and not onely Beryls and Cornelians, but Flints and Pebbles, are subject unto fusion, and will run like Glass in fire.

But Ice will dissolve in any way of heat, for it will dissolve with fire, it will colliquate in water, or warm oyl; nor doth it only submit unto an actual heat, but not endure the potential calidity of many waters. For it will presently dissolve in cold *Aqua fortis*, sp. of Vitriol, Salt, or Tartar, nor will it long continue its fixation in spirits of Wine, as may be observed in Ice injected therein.

Again, The concretion of Ice will not endure a dry attrition without liquation; for if it be rubbed long with a cloth, it melteth. But Crystal will calefie unto electricity, that is, a power to attract straws or light bodies, and convert the needle freely placed. Which is a declarement of very different parts, wherein we shall not inlarge, as having discoursed concerning such bodies in the Chap. of Electricks.

They are differenced by supernatation or floating upon water; for Crystal will sink in water, as carrying in its own bulk a greater ponderosity then the space in any water it doth occupy; and will therefore only swim in molten Metal and Quicksilver. But Ice will swim in water of what thinness soever; and though it sink in oyl, will float in spirits of Wine or *Aqua vitæ*. And therefore it may swim in water, not only as being water it self, and in its proper place, but perhaps as weighing somewhat less then the water it possesseth. And therefore as it will not sink unto the bottom, so will it neither float above like lighter bodies, but being near in weight, lie superficially or almost horizontally unto it. And therefore also an Ice or congelation of Salt or Sugar, although it descend not unto the bottom, yet will it abate, and decline below the surface in thin water, but very sensibly in spirits of Wine. For Ice although it seemeth as transparent and compact as Crystal, yet is it short in either; for its atoms are not concreted into continuity, which doth diminish its translucency; it is also full of spumes and bubbles, which may abate its gravity. And therefore waters frozen in Pans, and open Glasses, after their dissolution do commonly leave a froth and spume upon them, which are caused by the airy parts diffused in the congealable mixture which uniting themselves and finding no passage at the surface, do elevate the mass, and make the liquor take up a greater place then before: as may be observed in Glasses filled with water, which being frozen, will seem to swell above the brim. So that if in this condensation any one affirmeth there is also some rarefaction, experience may assert it.

They are distinguished in substance of parts and the accidents thereof, that is, in colour and figure; for Ice is a similary body, and homogeneous concretion, whose material is properly water, and but accidentally exceeding the simplicity of that element. But the body of Crystal is mixed; its ingredients many, and sensibly containeth those principles into which mixt bodies are reduced. For beside the spirit and mercurial principle it containeth a sulphur or inflamable part, and that in no small quantity; for besides its Electrick attraction, which is made by a sulphureous effluvium, it will strike fire upon percussion like many other stones, and upon collision with Steel actively send forth its sparks, not much inferiourly unto a flint. Now such bodies as strike fire have sulphureous or ignitible parts within them, and those strike best, which abound most in them. For these scintillations are not the accension of the air, upon the collision of two hard bodies, but rather the inflamable effluencies or vitrified sparks discharged from the bodies collided. For Diamonds, Marbles, Heliotropes and Agaths, though hard bodies, will not readily strike fire with a steel, much less with one another: Nor a Flint so readily with a Steel, if they both be very wet, for then the sparks are sometimes quenched in their eruption.

It containeth also a salt, and that in some plenty, which may occasion its fragility, as is also observable in Coral. This by the Art of Chymistry is separable, unto the operations whereof it is liable, with other concretions, as calcination, reverberation, sublimation, distillation: And in the preparation of Crystal, *Paracelsus* *de Præparationibus.* hath made a rule for that of Gemms. Briefly, it consisteth of parts so far from an Icie dissolution, that powerful menstruums are made for its emollition; whereby it may receive the tincture of Minerals, and so resemble Gemms, as *Boetius* hath declared in the distillation of Urine; spirits of Wine and Turpentine; and is not only triturable, and reducible into powder, by contrition, but will subsist in a violent fire, and endure a vitrification. Whereby are testified its earthly and fixed parts. *The Physical causes of liquation or melting of Mettals, etc.* For vitrification is the last work of fire, and a fusion of the Salt and Earth, which are the fixed elements of the composition, wherein the fusible Salt draws the Earth and infusible part into one continuum, and therefore ashes will not run from whence the Salt is drawn, as bone ashes prepared for the Test of Metals. Common fusion in Metals is also made by a violent heat, acting upon the volatile and fixed, the dry and humid parts of those bodies; which notwithstanding are so united, that upon attenuation from heat, the humid parts will not fly away, but draw the fixed ones into fluor with them. Ordinary liquation in wax and oily bodies is made by a gentler heat, where the oyl and salt, the fixed and fluid principles will not easily separate. All which, whether by vitrification, fusion or liquation, being forced into fluent consistencies, do naturally regress into their former solidities. Whereas the melting of Ice is a simple resolution, or return from solid to fluid parts, wherein it naturally resteth.

As for colour, although Crystal in his pellucid body seems to have none at all, yet in its reduction into powder, it hath a vail and shadow of blew; and in its courser pieces, is of a sadder hue then the powder of Venice glass; and this complexion it will maintain although it long endure the fire. Which notwithstanding needs not move us unto wonder; for vitrified and pellucid bodies, are of a clearer complexion in their continuities, then in their powders and Atomical divisions. So *Stibium* or glass of *Antimony*, appears somewhat red in glass, but in its powder yellow; so painted glass of a sanguine red will not ascend in powder above a murrey.

As for the figure of Crystal (which is very strange, and forced *Pliny* to despair of resolution) it is for the most part hexagonal or six cornered; being built upon a confused matter, from whence as it were from a root angular figures arise, even as in the Amethyst and Basaltes. Which regular figuration hath made some opinion, it hath not its determination from circumscription, or as conforming unto contiguities, but rather from a seminal root, and formative principle of its own, even as we observe in several other concretions. So the stones which are sometime found in the gall of a man, are most triangular and pyramidal, although the figure of that part seems not to co-operate thereto. So the *Asteria* or *lapis stellaris*; hath on it the figure of a Star, so *Lapis Judaicus* hath circular lines in length all down its body, and equidistant, as though they had been turned by Art. *In Stone-pits and chalk-mines. Which seemeth to be Echinites decima*

Aldrovandi. Musæi Metallici, lib. 4. *Rather Echinometrites, as best resembling the Echinometra found commonly on our Sea-shore.* So that we call a Fayrie stone, and is often found in *gravel pits* amongst us, being of an hemispherical figure, hath five double lines rising from the center of its basis, which if no accretion distract them, do commonly concur, and meet in the pole thereof. The figures are regular in many other stones, as in the Belemnites, *Lapis Anguinus*, *Cornu Ammonis*, and many more; as by those which have not the experience hereof may be observed in their figures expressed by Mineralogists. But Ice receiveth its figure according unto the surface wherein it concreteth, or the circumambiency which conformeth it. So it is plain upon the surface of water, but round in Hayl (which is also a glaciation,) and figured in its guttulous descent from the air, and so growing greater or lesser according unto the accretion or pluvious aggelation about the mother and fundamental Atomes thereof; which seems to be some feathery particle of Snow; although Snow it self be sexangular, or at least of a starry and many-pointed figure.

They are also differenced in the places of their generation; for though Crystal be found in cold countries, and where Ice remaineth long, and the air exceedeth in cold, yet is it also found in regions, where Ice is seldom seen or soon dissolved; as *Pliny* and *Agricola* relate of *Cyprus*, *Caramania* and an Island in the Red sea; *Wherein the Sculptor found a piece of pure Crystal.* It hath been also found in the veins of Minerals, sometimes agglutinated unto lead, sometimes in Rocks, opacous stones, and the marble face of *Octavius* Duke of *Parma*. It hath also constant veins; as beside others, that of mount *Salvino* about the Territory of *Bergamo*; from whence if part be taken, in no long tract of time out of the same place, as from its mineral matrix, others are observed to arise. Which made the learned *Cerautus* to conclude, *Videant hi an sit glacies, an vero corpus fossile.* *Mus. Calceolar.* It is also found in the veins of Minerals, in rocks, and sometime in common earth. But as for Ice, it will not readily concrete but in the approachment of the air, as we have made trial in glasses of water, covered an inch with oyl, which will not easily freeze in hard frosts of our climate. For water commonly concreteth first in its surface, and so conglaciates downward; and so will it do although it be exposed in the coldest metal of lead, which well accordeth with that expression of *Job*, *The waters are hid as with a stone, and the face of the deep is frozen.* *Chap. 38.* But whether water which hath been boiled or heated, doth sooner receive this congelation, as commonly is delivered, we rest in the experiment of *Cabeus*, who hath rejected the same in his excellent discourse of Meteors.

They have contrary qualities elemental, and uses medicinal; for Ice is cold and moist, of the quality of water; but Crystal is cold and dry, according to the condition of earth. The use of Ice is condemned by most Physicians, that of Crystal commended by many. For although *Dioscorides* and *Galen* have left no mention thereof, yet hath *Mathiolus, Agricola*, and many commended it in dysenteries and fluxes; all for the increase of milk, most Chymists for the Stone, and some, as *Brassavolus* and *Bœtius*, as an antidote against poyson. Which occult and specifical operations are not expectable from Ice; for being but water congealed, it can never make good such qualities; nor will it reasonably admit of secret proprieties, which are the affections of forms, and compositions at distance from their elements.

What Crystal is.

Having thus declared what Crystal is not, it may afford some satisfaction to manifest what it is. To deliver therefore what with the judgement of approved Authors, and best reason consisteth, It is a Mineral body in the difference of stones, and reduced by some unto that subdivision, which comprehendeth gemms, transparent and resembling Glass or Ice, made of a lentous percolation of earth, drawn from the most pure and limpid juice thereof, owing unto the coldness of the earth some concurrence or coadjuvancy, but not immediate determination and efficiency, which are wrought by the hand of its concretive spirit, the seeds of petrification and Gorgon of it self. As sensible Philosophers conceive of the generation of Diamonds, Iris, Berils. Not making them of frozen icecles, or from meer aqueous and glaciable substances, condensing them by frosts into solidities, vainly to be expected even from Polary congelations: but from thin and finest earths, so well contempered and resolved, that transparency is not hindred; and containing lapidifical spirits, able to make good their solidities against the opposition and activity of outward contraries, and so leave a sensible difference between the bonds of glaciation, which in the mountains of Ice about the Northern Seas, are easily dissolved by ordinary heat of the Sun, and between the finer ligatures of petrification, whereby not only the harder concretions of Diamonds and Saphirs, but the softer veins of Crystal remain indissolvable in scorching Territories, and the *Negro* land of Congor.

And therefore I fear we commonly consider subterranities, not in contemplations sufficiently respective unto the Creation. For though *Moses* have left no mention of Minerals, nor made any other description then sutes unto the apparent and visible Creation, yet is there unquestionably, a very large Classis of Creatures in the Earth, far above the condition of elementarity. And although not in a distinct and indisputable way of vivency, or answering in all points the properties or affections of Plants, yet in inferiour and descending constitutions, they do like these contain specifical distinctions, and are determined by seminalities, that is, created and defined seeds committed unto the Earth from the beginning. Wherein although they attain not the indubitable requisites of Animation, yet have they a near affinity thereto. And though we want a proper name and expressive appellation, yet are they not to be closed up in the general name of concretions; or lightly passed over as only Elementary and Subterraneous mixtions.

Exact continuity of parts a cause of transparency in things, and why.

The principle and most gemmary affection is its Tralucency: as for irradiancy or sparkling which is found in many gemms, it is not discoverable in this, for it cometh short of their compactness and durity: and therefore requireth not the Emery, as the Saphir, Granate, and Topaz, but will receive impression from Steel, in a manner like the Turchois. As for its diaphanity or perspicuity, it enjoyeth that most eminently; and the reason thereof is its continuity; as having its earthy and salinous parts so exactly resolved, that its body is left imporous and not discreted by atomical terminations. For, that continuity of parts is the cause of perspicuity, it is made perspicuous by two ways of experiment. That is, either in effecting transparency in those bodies which were not so before, or at least far short of the additional degree: So Snow becomes transparent upon liquation, so Horns and Bodies resolvable into continued parts or gelly. The like is observable in oyled paper, wherein the interstitial divisions being continuated by the accession of oyl, it becometh more transparent, and admits the visible rayes with less umbrosity. Or else the same is effected by rendring those bodies opacous, which were before pellucid and perspicuous.

So Glass which was before diaphanous, being by powder reduced into multiplicity of superficies, becomes an opacous body, and will not transmit the light. So it is in Crystal powdered, and so it is also before; for if it be made hot in a crucible, and presently projected upon water, it will grow dim, and abate its diaphanity; for the water entering the body, begets a division of parts, and a termination of Atoms united before unto continuity.

The ground of this Opinion might be, first the conclusions of some men from experience; for as much as Crystal is found sometimes in rocks, and in some places not much unlike the stirious or stillicidious dependencies of Ice. Which notwithstanding may happen either in places which have been forsaken or left bare by the earth, or may be petrifications, or Mineral indurations, like other gemms, proceeding from percolations of the earth disposed unto such concretions.

The second and most common ground is from the name *Crystallus*, whereby in Greek both Ice and Crystal are expressed; which many not duly considering, have from their community of name, conceived a community of nature; and what was ascribed unto the one, not unfitly appliable unto the other. But this is a fallacy of Æquivocation, from a society in name inferring an Identity in nature. By this fallacy was he deceived that drank *Aqua fortis* for strong water. By this are they deluded, who conceive *sperma Cœti* which is found about the head, to be the spawn of the Whale: Or take *sanguis draconis* (which is the gumme of a tree,) to be the blood of a Dragon. By the same Logick we may infer, the Crystalline humour of the eye, or rather the Crystalline heaven above, to be of the substance of Crystal here below; Or that God sendeth down Crystal, because it is delivered in the vulgar translation, Psal. 47. *Mittit Crystallum suum sicut Buccellas.* *Agreement in name.* Which translation although it literally express the Septuagint; yet is there no more meant thereby, than what our translation in plain English expresseth; that is, he casteth forth his Ice like morsels, or what *Tremellius* and *Junius* as clearly deliver, *Deficit gelu suum sicut frusta, coram frigore ejus quis consistet?* which proper and latine expressions, had they been observed in ancient translations, elder Expositors had not been misguided by the Synonomy; nor had they afforded occasion unto *Austin*, the Gloss, *Lyranus*, and many others, to have taken up the common conceit, and spoke of this Text conformably unto the opinion rejected.

CHAPTER II
Concerning the Loadstone.

Of things particularly spoken thereof, evidently or probably true. Of things generally believed, or particularly delivered, manifestly or probably false. In the first of the Magnetical vertue of the Earth, of the four motions of the stone, that is, its Verticity or Direction, its Attraction or Coition, its Declination, its Variation, and also of its Antiquity. In the second a rejection of sundry opinions and relations thereof, Natural, Medical, Historical, Magical.

How the earth is a Magnetical body.

And first we conceive the earth to be a Magnetical body. A Magnetical body, we term not onely that which hath a power attractive, but that which seated in a convenient medium, naturally disposeth it self to one invariable and fixed situation. And such a Magnetical vertue we conceive to be in the Globe of the Earth, whereby as unto its natural points and proper terms, it disposeth it self unto the poles; being so framed, constituted, and ordered unto these points, that those parts which are now at the poles, would not naturally abide under the Æquator, nor *Greenland* remain in the place of *Magellanica*. And if the whole earth were violently removed, yet would it not foregoe its primitive points, nor pitch in the East or West, but return unto its polary position again. For though by compactness or gravity it may acquire the lowest place, and become the center of the universe, yet that it makes good that point, not varying at all by the accession of bodies upon, or secession thereof from its surface, perturbing the equilibration of either Hemisphere (whereby the altitude of the stars might vary) or that it strictly maintains the North and Southern points; that neither upon the motions of the heavens, air, and winds without, large eruptions and division of parts within, its polary parts should never incline or veer unto the Equator (whereby the latitude of places should also vary) it cannot so well be salved from gravity as a Magnetical verticity. *The foundation of the Earths stability.* This is probably, that foundation the wisdom of the Creator hath laid unto the earth; in this sense we may more nearly apprehend, and sensibly make out the expressions of holy Scripture *Psal. 93.*, as *Firmavit orbem terræ qui non commovebitur*, he hath made the round world so sure that it cannot be moved: as when it is said by *Job, Extendit Aquilonem super vacuo, &c.* *Job 38.* He stretcheth forth the North upon the empty place, and hangeth the earth upon nothing. And this is the most probable answer unto that great question. Whereupon are the foundations of the Earth fastened, or who laid the corner stone thereof? Had they been acquainted with this principle, *Anaxagoras, Socrates,* and *Democritus,* had better made out the ground of this stability; *Xenophanes* had not been fain to say the Earth had no bottom; and *Thales Milesius* to make it swim in water.

The magnetical vertue of the Earth diffused extra se *and communicated to bodies adjacent.*

Nor is the vigour of this great body included only in its self, or circumferenced by its surface, but diffused at indeterminate distances through the air, water, and all bodies circumjacent. Exciting and impregnating Magnetical bodies within its surface or without it, and performing in a secret and invisible way what we evidently behold effected by the Loadstone. For these effluxions penetrate all bodies, and like the species of visible objects are ever ready in the medium, and lay hold on all bodies proportionate or capable of their action, those bodies likewise being of a congenerous nature, do readily receive the impressions of their motor; and if not fettered by their gravity, conform themselves to situations, wherein they best unite unto their Animator. And this will sufficiently appear from the observations that are to follow, which can no better way be made out then by this we speak of, the Magnetical vigour of the Earth. Now whether these effluviums do flye by striated Atoms and winding particles as *Renatus des Cartes* conceiveth; or glide by streams attracted from either Pole and Hemisphere of the Earth unto the Equator, as Sir *Kenelm Digby* excellently declareth, it takes not away this vertue of the Earth, but more distinctly sets down the gests and progress thereof, and are conceits of eminent use to salve Magnetical Phenomena's. *Apparencies observations.* And as in Astronomy those hypotheses though never so strange are best esteemed which best do salve apparencies; so surely in Philosophy those principles (though seeming monstrous) may with advantage be embraced, which best confirm experiment, and afford the readiest reason of observation. *The doctrine of effluxions acknowledged by the Author.* And truly the doctrine of effluxions, their penetrating natures, their invisible paths, and insuspected effects, are very considerable; for besides this Magnetical one of the Earth, several effusions there may be from divers other bodies, which invisibly act their parts at any time, and perhaps through any medium; a part of Philosophy but yet in discovery, and will, I fear, prove the last leaf to be turned over in the Book of Nature.

First, Therefore it is true, and confirmable by every experiment, that Steel and good Iron never excited by the Loadstone, discover in themselves a verticity; that is, a directive or polary faculty, whereby, conveniently placed, *Point to the North.* they do Septentrionate at one extream, and Australize at another. *Point to the South.* This is manifestable in long and thin plates of Steel perforated in the middle and equilibrated; or by an easier way in long wires equiponderate with untwisted Silk and soft Wax; for in this manner pendulous, they will conform themselves Meridionally, directing one extream unto the North, another to the South. The same is also manifest in Steel wires thrust through little sphears or globes of Cork and floated on the water, or in naked Needles gently let fall thereon; for so disposed they will not rest, until they have found out the Meridian, and as near as they can lye parallel unto the Axis of the Earth: Sometimes the eye, sometimes the point Northward in divers Needles, but the same point always in most: Conforming themselves unto the whole Earth, in the same manner as they do unto every Loadstone. For if a Needle untoucht be hanged above a Loadstone, it will convert into a parallel position thereto; for in this situation it can best receive its verticity and be excited proportionably at both extreams. Now this direction proceeds not primitively from themselves, but is derivative and contracted from the Magnetical effluxions of the Earth; which they have winded in their hammering and formation; or else by long continuance in one position, as we shall declare hereafter.

It is likewise true what is delivered of Irons heated in the fire, that they contract a verticity in their refrigeration; for heated red hot and cooled in the Meridian from North to South, they presently contract a polary power, and being poised in air or water, convert that part unto the North which respected that point in its refrigeration, so that if they had no sensible verticity before, it may be acquired by this way; or if they had any, it might be exchanged by contrary position in the cooling. For by the fire they omit not onely many drossie and scorious parts, but whatsoever they had received either from the Earth or Loadstone; and so being naked and despoiled of all verticity, the Magnetical Atomes invade their bodies with more effect and agility.

Neither is it only true what *Gilbertus* first observed, that Irons refrigerated North and South acquire a Directive faculty; but if they be cooled upright and perpendicularly, they will also obtain the same. That part which is cooled toward the North on this side the Equator, converting it self unto the North, and attracting the South point of the Needle: the other and highest extream respecting the South, and attracting the Northern, according unto Laws Magnetical: For (what must be observed) contrary Poles or faces attract each other, as the North the South; and the like decline each other, as the North the North. Now on this side of the Equator, that extream which is next the Earth is animated unto the North, and the contrary unto the South; so that in coition it applies it self quite oppositely, the coition or attraction being contrary to the Verticity or Direction. Contrary, If we speak according unto common use, yet alike, if we conceive the vertue of the North Pole to diffuse it self and open at the South, and the South at the North again.

This polarity from refrigeration upon extremity and in defect of a Loadstone might serve to invigorate and touch a Needle any where; and this, allowing variation, is also the readiest way at any season to discover the North or South; *Some conceive that the figure of the Tree or Spread-eagle in the root of Brake or Fern stands North and South, but not truly.* and surely far more certain then what is affirmed of the grains and circles in trees, or the figure in the root of Fern. For if we erect a red hot wire until it cool, then hang it up with wax and untwisted Silk, where the lower end and that which cooled next the earth doth rest, that is the Northern point; and this we affirm will still be true whether it be cooled in the air or extinguished in water, oyl of Vitriol, *Aqua fortis*, or Quicksilver. And this is also evidenced in culinary utensils and Irons that often feel the force of fire, as Tongs, Fire-shovels, Prongs, and Andirons; all which acquire a Magnetical and polary condition, and being suspended, convert their lower extreams unto the North; with the same attracting the Southern point of the Needle. For easier experiment, if we place a Needle touched at the foot of Tongs or Andirons, it will obvert or turn aside its lillie or North point, and conform its cuspis or South extream unto the Andiron. The like verticity though more obscurely is also contracted by Bricks and Tiles, as we have made trial in some taken out of the backs of chimneys. Now to contract this Direction, there needs not a total ignition, nor is it necessary the Irons should be red hot all over. For if a wire be heated only at one end, according as that end is cooled upward or downward, it respectively acquires a verticity, as we have declared in wires totally candent. Nor is it absolutely requisite they should be cooled perpendicularly, or strictly lie in the Meridian; for whether they be refrigerated inclinatorily or somewhat Æquinoxially, that is toward the Eastern or Western points; though in a lesser degree, they discover some verticity.

Nor is this onely true in Irons, but in the Loadstone it self. For if a Loadstone be made red hot, it loseth the magnetical vigour it had before in it self, and acquires another from the Earth in its refrigeration; for that part which cooleth toward the Earth will acquire the respect of the North, and attract the Southern point or cuspis of the Needle. The experiment hereof we made in a Loadstone of a parallelogram or long square figure; wherein onely inverting the extreams, as it came out of the fire, we altered the poles or faces thereof at pleasure.

It is also true what is delivered of the Direction and coition of Irons, that they contract a verticity by long and continued position: that is, not onely being placed from North to South, and lying in the Meridian, but respecting the Zenith and perpendicular unto the Center of the Earth; as is manifest in bars of windows, casements, hinges and the like. For if we present the Needle unto their lower extreams, it wheels about and turns its Southern point unto them. The same condition in long time do Bricks contract which are placed in walls, and therefore it may be a fallible way to find out the Meridian by placing the Needle on a wall; for some Bricks therein by a long and continued position, are often magnetically enabled to distract the polarity of the Needle. And therefore those Irons which are said to have been converted into Loadstones; whether they were real conversions, or onely attractive augmentations, might be much promoted by this position: as the Iron cross of an hundred weight upon the Church of St. *John* in *Ariminum*, *De miner. l. 1.* or that Loadston'd Iron of *Cæsar Moderatus*, set down by *Aldrovandus*.

Lastly, Irons do manifest a verticity not only upon refrigeration and constant situation, but (what is wonderful and advanceth the magnetical Hypothesis) they evidence the same by meer position according as they are inverted, and their extreams disposed respectively unto the Earth. For if an Iron or Steel not firmly excited, be held perpendicularly or inclinatorily unto the Needle, the lower end thereof will attract the *cuspis* or Southern point; but if the same extream be inverted and held under the Needle, it will then attract the lilly or Northern point; for by inversion it changeth its direction acquired before, and receiveth a new and Southern polarity from the Earth, as being the upper extream. Now if an Iron be touched before, it varieth not in this manner; for then it admits not this magnetical impression, as being already informed by the Loadstone, and polarily determined by its preaction.

And from these grounds may we best determine why the Northern Pole of the Loadstone attracteth a greater weight than the Southern on this side the Æquator; why the stone is best preserved in a natural and polary situation; and why as *Gilbertus* observeth, it respecteth that Pole out of the Earth, which it regarded in its Mineral bed and subterraneous position.

It is likewise true and wonderful what is delivered of the Inclination or Declination of the Loadstone; that is, the descent of the Needle below the plain of the Horizon. For long Needles which stood before upon their *axis, parallel* unto the Horizon, being vigorously excited, incline and bend downward, depressing the North extream below the Horizon. That is the North on this, the South on the other side of the Equator; and at the very Line or middle circle stand without deflexion. And this is evidenced not onely from observations of the Needle in several parts of the earth, but sundry experiments in any part thereof, as in a long Steel wire, equilibrated or evenly ballanced in the air; for excited by a vigorous Loadstone it will somewhat depress its animated extream, and intersect the horizontal circumference. It is also manifest in a Needle pierced through a Globe of Cork so cut away and pared by degrees, that it will swim under water, yet sink not unto the bottom, which may be well effected; for if the Cork be a thought too light to sink under the surface, the body of the water may be attenuated with spirits of wine; if too heavy, it may be incrassated with salt; and if by chance too much be added, it may again be thinned by a proportionable addition of fresh water. If then the Needle be taken out, actively touched and put in again, it will depress and bow down its Northern head toward the bottom, and advance its Southern extremity toward the brim. This way invented by *Gilbertus* may seem of difficulty; the same with less labour may be observed in a needled sphere of Cork equally contiguous unto the surface of the water; for if the Needle be not exactly equiponderant, that end which is a thought too light, if touched becometh even; that Needle also which will but just swim under the water, if forcibly touched will sink deeper, and sometime unto the bottom. If likewise that inclinatory vertue be destroyed by a touch from the contrary Pole, that end which before was elevated will then decline, and this perhaps might be observed in some scales exactly ballanced, and in such Needles which for their bulk can hardly be supported by the water. For if they be powerfully excited and equally let fall, they commonly sink down and break the water at that extream whereat they were septentrionally excited: and by this way it is conceived there may be some fraud in the weighing of precious commodities, and such as carry a value in quarter-grains; by placing a powerful Loadstone above or below, according as we intend to depress or elevate one extream.

Now if these Magnetical emissions be onely qualities, and the gravity of bodies incline them onely unto the earth; surely that which alone moveth other bodies to descent, carrieth not the stroak in this, but rather the Magnetical alliciency of the Earth; unto which with alacrity it applieth it self, and in the very same way unto the whole Earth, as it doth unto a single Loadstone. For if an untouched Needle be at a distance suspended over a Loadstone, it will not hang parallel, but decline at the North extream, and at that part will first salute its Director. Again, what is also wonderful, this inclination is not invariable; for just under the line the Needle lieth parallel with the Horizon, but sailing North or South it beginneth to incline, and encreaseth according as it approacheth unto either Pole; and would at last endeavour to erect it self. And this is no more then what it doth upon the Loadstone, and that more plainly upon the Terrella or spherical magnet Cosmographically set out with circles of the Globe. For at the Equator thereof, the Needle will stand rectangularly; but approaching Northward toward the Tropick it will regard the stone obliquely, and when it attaineth the Pole, directly; and if its bulk be no impediment, erect it self and stand perpendicularly thereon. And therefore upon strict observation of this inclination in several latitudes and due records preserved, instruments are made whereby without the help of

Sun or Star, the latitude of the place may be discovered; and yet it appears the observations of men have not as yet been so just and equal as is desirable; for of those Tables of declination which I have perused, there are not any two that punctually agree; though some have been thought exactly calculated, especially that which *Ridley* received from Mr. *Brigs*, in our time Geometry Professor in *Oxford*.

What the variation of the Compass is.

It is also probable what is delivered concerning the variation of the Compass that is the cause and ground thereof, for the manner as being confirmed by observation we shall not at all dispute. The variation of the Compass is an Arch of the Horizon intercepted between the true and Magnetical Meridian; or more plainly, a deflexion and siding East and West from the true Meridian. The true Meridian is a major Circle passing through the Poles of the World, and the Zenith or Vertex of any place, exactly dividing the East from the West. Now on this line the Needle exactly lieth not, but diverts and varieth its point, that is, the North point on this side the Equator, the South on the other; sometimes on the East, sometime toward the West, and in some few places varieth not at all. First, therefore it is observed that betwixt the Shore of *Ireland*, *France*, *Spain*, *Guiny*, and the *Azores*, the North point varieth toward the East, and that in some variety; at *London* it varieth eleven degrees, at *Antwerp* nine, at *Rome* but five: at some parts of the *Azores* it deflecteth not, but lieth in the true Meridian; on the other side of the *Azores*, and this side of the Equator, the North point of the Needle wheeleth to the West; so that in the latitude of 36 near the shore, the variation is about eleven degrees; but on the other side the Equator, it is quite otherwise: for about *Capio Frio* in *Brasilia*, the South point varieth twelve degrees unto the West, and about the mouth of the Straits of *Magellan* five or six; but elongating from the coast of *Brasilia* toward the shore of *Africa* it varieth Eastward, and arriving at *Capo de las Agullas*, it resteth in the Meridian, and looketh neither way.

The cause of the variation of the Compass.

Now the cause of this variation was thought by *Gilbertus* to be the inequality of the Earth, variously disposed, and indifferently intermixed with the Sea: withal the different disposure of its Magnetical vigor in the eminencies and stronger parts thereof. For the Needle naturally endeavours to conform unto the Meridian, but being distracted, driveth that way where the greater and powerfuller part of the Earth is placed. Which may be illustrated from what hath been delivered and may be conceived by any that understands the generalities of Geography. For whereas on this side the Meridian, or the Isles of *Azores*, where the first Meridian is placed, the Needle varieth Eastward; it may be occasioned by that vast Tract of Earth, that is, of *Europe*, *Asia*, and *Africa*, seated toward the East, and disposing the Needle that way. For arriving at some part of the *Azores*, or Islands of Saint *Michael*, which have a middle situation between these Continents, and that vast and almost answerable Tract of *America*, it seemeth equally distracted by both; and diverting unto neither, doth parallel and place it self upon the true Meridian. But sailing farther, it veers its Lilly to the West, and regardeth that quarter wherein the Land is nearer or greater; and in the same latitude as it approacheth the shore augmenteth its variation. And therefore as some observe, if *Columbus* or whosoever first discovered *America*, had apprehended the cause of this variation, having passed more then half the way, he might have been confirmed in the discovery, and assuredly foretold there lay a vast and mighty continent toward the West. The reason I confess and inference is good, but the instance perhaps not so. For *Columbus* knew not the variation of the compass, whereof *Sebastian Cabot* first took notice, who after made discovery in the Northern part of that continent. And it happened indeed that part of *America* was first discovered, which was on this side farthest distant, that is, *Jamaica*, *Cuba*, and the Isles in the Bay of *Mexico*. And from this variation do some new discoverers deduce a probability in the attempts of the Northern passage toward the *Indies*.

Now because where the greater continents are joyned, the action and effluence is also greater; therefore those Needles do suffer the greatest variation which are in Countries which most do feel that action. And therefore hath *Rome* far less variation then *London*; for on the West side of *Rome* are seated the great continents of *France*, *Spain*, *Germany*, which take off the exuperance, and in some way ballance the vigor of the Eastern parts. But unto *England* there is almost no Earth West, but the whole extent of *Europe* and *Asia* lieth Eastward; and therefore at *London* it varieth eleven degrees, that is almost one *Rhomb*. Thus also by reason of the great continent of *Brasilia*, *Peru*, and *Chili*, the Needle deflecteth toward the Land twelve degrees; but at the straits of *Magellan* where the Land is narrowed, and the Sea on the other side, it varieth but five or six. And so likewise, because the Cape *de las Agullas* hath Sea on both sides near it, and other Land remote, and as it were æquidistant from it, therefore at that point the Needle conforms unto the true Meridian, and is not distracted by the vicinity of Adjacencies. This is the general and great cause of variation. But if in certain Creeks and Vallies the Needle prove irregular, and vary beyond expectation, it may be imputed unto some vigorous part of the Earth, or Magnetical eminence not far distant. And this was the invention of *D. Gilbert*, not many years past, a Physician in *London*. And therefore although some assume the invention of its direction, and other have had the glory of the Card; yet in the experiments, grounds, and causes thereof, *England* produced the Father Philosopher, and discovered more in it then *Columbus* or *Americus* did ever by it.

Unto this in great part true the reason of *Kircherus* may be added: That this variation proceedeth not only from terrestrious eminencies, and magnetical veins of the Earth, laterally respecting the Needle, but the different coagmentation of the Earth disposed unto the Poles, lying under the Sea and Waters, which affect the Needle with great or lesser variation, according to the vigour or imbecility of these subterraneous lines, or the entire or broken compagination of the magnetical fabrick under it. As is observable from several Loadstones placed at the bottom of any water, for a Loadstone or Needle upon the surface, will variously conform it self, according to the vigour or faintness of the Loadstones under it.

Thus also a reason may be alledged for the variation of the variation, and why, according to observation, the variation of the Needle hath after some years been found to vary in some places. For this may proceed from mutations of the earth, by subterraneous fires, fumes, mineral spirits, or otherwise; which altering the constitution of the magnetical parts, in process of time, doth vary the variation over the place.

It is also probable what is conceived of its Antiquity, that the knowledge of its polary power and direction unto the North was unknown unto the Ancients; and though *Levinus Lemnius*, and *Cælius Colcagninus*, are of another belief, is justly placed with new inventions by *Pancirollus*. For their *Achilles* and strongest argument is an expression in *Plautus*, a very Ancient author, and contemporary unto *Ennius*. *Hic ventus jam secundus est, cape modo versoriam*. Now this *versoriam* they construe to be the compass, which notwithstanding according unto *Pineda*, who hath discussed the point, *Turnebus*, *Cabeus*, and divers others, is better interpreted the rope that helps to turn the Ship, or as we say, doth make it tack about; the Compass declaring rather the Ship is turned, then conferring unto its conversion. As for the long expeditions and sundry voyages of elder times, which might confirm the Antiquity of this invention, it is not improbable they were performed by the help of Stars; and so might the Phœnicean navigators, and also *Ulisses* sail about the Mediterranean, by the flight of Birds, or keeping near the shore; and so might *Hanno* coast about *Africa*; or by the help of Oars, as is expressed in the voyage of *Jonah*. And whereas it is contended that this verticity was not unknown unto *Solomon*, in whom is presumed an universality of knowledge; it will as forcibly follow, he knew the Art of Typography, Powder and Guns, or had the Philosophers Stone, yet sent unto *Ophir* for Gold. It is not to be denied, that beside his Political wisdom, his knowledge in Philosophy was very large; and perhaps from his works therein, the ancient Philosophers, especially *Aristotle*, who had the assistance of *Alexanders* acquirements, collected great observables. Yet if he knew the use of the Compass, his Ships were surely very slow, that made a three years voyage from *Eziongeber* in the red Sea unto *Ophir*; which is supposed to be *Taprobana* or *Malaca* in the *Indies*, not many moneths sail; and since in the same or lesser time, *Drake* and *Candish* performed their voyage about the Earth.

And as the knowledge of its verticity is not so old as some conceive, so it is more ancient then most believe; nor had its discovery with Guns, Printing, or as many think, some years before the discovery of *America*. For it was not unknown unto *Petrus Peregrinus* a Frenchman, who two hundred years since left a Tract of the Magnet, and a perpetual motion to be made thereby, preserved by *Gasserus*. *Paulus Venetus*, and about five hundred years past *Albertus Magnus* make mention hereof, and quote for it a Book of *Aristotle*, *De Lapide*; which Book although we find in the Catalogue of *Laertius*, yet with *Cabeus* we may rather judge it to be the work of some Arabick Writer, not many years before the days of *Albertus*.

Lastly, It is likewise true what some have delivered of *Crocus Martis*, that is, Steel corroded with Vinegar, Sulphur, or otherwise, and after reverberated by fire. For the Loadstone will not at all attract it, nor will it adhere, but lye therein like Sand. This to be understood of *Crocus Martis* well reverberated, and into a violet colour: for common *chalybs præparatus*, or corroded and powdered Steel, the Loadstone attracts like ordinary filings of Iron; and many times most of that which passeth for *Crocus Martis*. So that this way may serve as a test of its preparation; after which it becometh a very good medicine in fluxes. The like may be affirmed of flakes of Iron that are rusty and begin to tend unto Earth; for their cognation then expireth, and the Loadstone will not regard them.

And therefore this may serve as a trial of good Steel. The Loadstone taking up a greater mass of that which is most pure, it may also decide the conversion of Wood into Iron, as is pretended from some Waters: and the common conversion of Iron into Copper by the mediation of blew Coperose, for the Loadstone will not attract it. Although it may be questioned, whether in this operation, the Iron or Coperose be transmuted, as may be doubted from the cognation of Coperose with Copper; and the quantity of Iron remaining after the conversion. And the same may be useful to some discovery concerning Vitriol or Coperose of Mars, by some called Salt of Steel, made by the spirits of Vitriol or Sulphur. For the corroded powder of Steel will after ablution be actively attracted by the Loadstone, and also remaineth in little diminished quantity. And therefore whether those shooting Salts partake but little of Steel, and be not rather the vitriolous spirits fixed into Salt by the effluvium or odor of Steel, is not without good question.

CHAPTER III
Concerning the Loadstone, therein of sundry common Opinions, and received several relations: Natural, Historical, Medical, Magical.

And first not only a simple Heterodox, but a very hard Paradox, it will seem, and of great absurdity unto obstinate ears, if we say, attraction is unjustly appropriated unto the Loadstone, and that perhaps we speak not properly, when we say vulgarly and appropriately the Loadstone draweth Iron; and yet herein we should not want experiment and great authority. The words of *Renatus des Cartes* in his Principles of Philosophy are very plain. *Præterea magnes trahet ferrum, sive potius magnes & ferrum ad invicem accedunt, neque enim ulla ibi tractio est*. The same is solemnly determined by *Cabeus*. *Nec magnes trahit proprie ferrum, nec ferrum ad se magnetem provocat, sed ambo pari conatu ad invicem confluunt*. Concordant hereto is the assertion of Doctor *Ridley*, Physitian unto the Emperour of *Russia*, in his Tract of Magnetical Bodies, defining Magnetical attraction to be a natural incitation and disposition conforming unto contiguity, an union of one Magnetical Body with another, and no violent haling of the weak unto the stronger. And this is also the doctrine of *Gilbertus*, by whom this motion is termed Coition, and that not made by any faculty attractive of one, but a Syndrome and concourse of each; a Coition alway of their vigours, and also of their bodies, if bulk or impediment prevent not. And therefore those contrary actions which flow from opposite Poles or Faces, are not so properly expulsion and attraction, as *Sequela* and *Fuga*, a mutual flight and following. Consonant whereto are also the determination of *Helmontius, Kircherus*, and *Licetus*.

Attraction reciprocal betwixt the Loadstone and Iron.

The same is also confirmed by experiment; for if a piece of Iron be fastened in the side of a bowl or bason water, a Loadstone swimming freely in a Boot of Cork, will presently make unto it. So if a Steel or Knife untouched, be offered toward the Needle that is touched, the Needle nimbly moveth toward it, and conformeth unto union with the Steel that moveth not. Again, If a Loadstone be finely filed, the Atoms or dust thereof will adhere unto Iron that was never touched, even as the powder of Iron doth also unto the Loadstone. And lastly, if in two Skiffs of Cork, a Loadstone and Steel be placed within the Orb of their activities, the one doth not move the other standing still, but both hoise sail and steer unto each other. So that if the Loadstone attract, the Steel hath also its attraction; for in this action the Alliciency is reciprocal, which joyntly felt, they mutually approach and run into each others arms.

And therefore surely more moderate expressions become this action, then what the Ancients have used, which some have delivered in the most violent terms of their language; so *Austin* calls it, *Mirabilem ferri raptorem: Hippocrates* λίθος τὸν σίδηρον ἁρπάζει, *Lapis qui ferrum rapit. Galen* disputing against *Epicurus* useth the term ἕλκειν, but this also is too violent: among the Ancients *Aristotle* spake most warily, ὅστις τὸν σίδηρον κινεῖ, *Lapis qui ferrum movet*: and in some tolerable acception do run the expressions of *Aquinas, Scaliger* and *Cusanus*.

Many relations are made, and great expectations are raised from the *Magnes Carneus*, or a Loadstone, that hath a faculty to attract not only iron but flesh; but this upon enquiry, and as *Cabeus* also observed, is nothing else but a weak and inanimate kind of Loadstone, veined here and there with a few magnetical and ferreous lines; but consisting of a bolary and clammy substance, whereby it adheres like *Hæmatites*, or *Terra Lemnia*, unto the Lips. And this is that stone which is to be understood, when Physitians joyn it with *Ætites*, or the Eagle stone, and promise therein a vertue against abortion.

There is sometime a mistake concerning the variation of the Compass, and therein one point is taken for another. For beyond that Equator some men account its variation by the diversion of the Northern point, whereas beyond that Circle the Southern point is Soveraign, and the North submits his preheminency. For in the Southern coast either of *America* or *Africa*, the Southern point deflects and varieth toward the Land, as being disposed and spirited that way by the Meridional and proper Hemisphere. And therefore on that side of the Earth the varying point is best accounted by the South. And therefore also the writings of some, and Maps of others, are to be enquired, that make the Needle decline unto the East twelve degrees at *Capo Frio*, and six at the straits of *Magellan*; accounting hereby one point for another, and preferring the North in the Liberties and Province of the South.

That Garlick hinders not the attraction of the Loadstone.

But certainly false it is what is commonly affirmed and believed, that Garlick doth hinder the attraction of the Loadstone, which is notwithstanding delivered by grave and worthy Writers, by *Pliny, Solinus, Ptolemy, Plutarch, Albertus, Mathiolus, Rueus, Langius*, and many more. An effect as strange as that of *Homers Moly*, and the Garlick that *Mercury* bestowed upon *Ulysses*. But that it is evidently false, many experiments declare. For an Iron wire heated red hot and quenched in the juice of Garlick, doth notwithstanding contract a verticity from the Earth, and attracteth the Southern point of the Needle. If also the tooth of a Loadstone be covered or stuck in Garlick, it will notwithstanding attract; and Needles excited and fixed in Garlick until they begin to rust, do yet retain their attractive and polary respects.

Nor yet the Adamant or Diamond.

Of the same stamp is that which is obtruded upon us by Authors ancient and modern, that an Adamant or Diamond prevents or suspends the attraction of the Loadstone: as is in open terms delivered by *Pliny. Adamas dissidet cum Magnete lapide, ut juxta positus ferrum non patiatur abstrahi, aut si admotus magnes, apprehenderit, rapiat atque auferat*. For if a Diamond be placed between a Needle and a Loadstone, there will nevertheless ensue a Coition even over the body of the Diamond. And an easie matter it is to touch or excite a Needle through a Diamond, by placing it at the tooth of a Loadstone; and therefore the relation is false, or our estimation of these gemms untrue; nor are they Diamonds which carry that name amongst us.

De generatione rerum.

It is not suddenly to be received what *Paracelsus* affirmeth, that if a Loadstone be anointed with Mercurial oyl, or onely put into Quicksilver, it omitteth its attraction for ever. For we have found that Loadstones and touched Needles which have laid long time in Quicksilver have not amitted their attraction. And we also find that red hot Needles or wires extinguished in Quicksilver, do yet acquire a verticity according to the Laws of position in extinction. Of greater repugnancy unto reason is that which he delivers concerning its graduation, that heated in fire and often extinguished in oyl of Mars or Iron, it acquires an ability to extract or draw forth a nail fastened in a wall; for, as we have declared before, the vigor of the Loadstone is destroyed by fire, nor will it be re-impregnated by any other Magnete then the Earth.

Nor is it to be made out what seemeth very plausible, and formerly hath deceived us, that a Loadstone will not attract an Iron or Steel red hot. The falsity hereof discovered first by *Kircherus*, we can confirm by iterated experiment; very sensibly in armed Loadstones, and obscurely in any other.

True it is, that besides fire some other wayes there are of its destruction, as Age, Rust; and what is least dreamt on, an unnatural or contrary situation. For being impolarily adjoyned unto a more vigorous Loadstone, it will in a short time enchange its Poles; or being kept in undue position, that is, not lying on the Meridian, or else with its poles inverted, it receives in longer time impair in activity, exchange of Faces; and is more powerfully preserved by position then by the dust of Steel. But the sudden and surest way is fire; that is, fire not onely actual but potential; the one surely and suddenly, the other slowly and imperfectly; the one changing, the other destroying the figure. For if distilled Vinegar or *Aqua fortis* be poured upon the powder of Loadstone, the subsiding powder dryed, retains some Magnetical vertue, and will be attracted by the Loadstone: but if the menstruum or dissolvent be evaporated to a consistence, and afterward doth shoot into Icycles or Crystals, the Loadstone hath no power upon them; and if in a full dissolution of Steel a separation of parts be made by precipitation or exhalation, the exsiccated powder hath lost its wings and ascends not unto the Loadstone. And though a Loadstone fired doth presently omit its proper vertue, and according to the position in cooling contracts a new verticity from the Earth; yet if the same be laid awhile in *aqua fortis* or other corrosive water, and taken out before a considerable corrosion, it still reserves its attraction, and will convert the Needle according to former polarity. And that duly preserved from violent corrosion, or the natural disease of rust, it may long conserve its vertue, beside the Magnetical vertue of the Earth, which hath lasted since the Creation, a great example we have from the observation of our learned friend Mr. *Graves*, | In his learned *Pyramidographia*. | in an Ægyptian Idol cut out of Loadstone, and found among the *Mummies*; which still retains its attraction, though probably taken out of the Mine about two thousand years ago.

It is improbable what *Pliny* affirmeth concerning the object of its attraction, that it attracts not only ferreous bodies, but also *liquorem vitri*; for in the body of Glass there is no ferreous or magnetical nature which might occasion attraction. For of the Glass we use, the purest is made of the finest sand and the ashes of Chali or Glaswort, and the courser or green sort of the ashes of Brake or other plants. True it is that in the making of Glass, it hath been an ancient practice to cast in pieces of magnet, or perhaps manganes: conceiving it carried away all ferreous and earthy parts, from the pure and running portion of Glass, which the Loadstone would not respect; and therefore if that attraction were not rather Electrical then Magnetical, it was a wondrous effect what *Helmont* delivereth concerning a Glass wherein the Magistery of Loadstone was prepared, which after retained an attractive quality.

But whether the Magnet attracteth more then common Iron, may be tried in other bodies. It seems to attract the Smyris or Emery in powder; It draweth the shining or glassie powder brought from the *Indies*, and usually implied in writing-dust. There is also in Smiths Cinders by some adhesion of Iron whereby they appear as it were glazed, sometime to be found a magnetical operation; for some thereof applied have power to move the Needle. But whether the ashes of vegetables which grow over Iron Mines contract a magnetical quality, as containing some mineral particles, which by sublimation ascend unto their Roots, and are attracted together with their nourishment; according as some affirm from the like observations upon the Mines of Silver, Quick silver, and Gold, we must refer unto further experiment.

It is also improbable and something singular what some conceive, and *Eusebius Nierembergius*, a learned Jesuit of *Spain* delivers, that the body of man is magnetical, and being placed in a Boat, the Vessel will never rest untill the head respecteth the North. If this be true, the bodies of Christians do lye unnaturally in their Graves. King *Cheops* in his Tomb, and the *Jews* in their beds have fallen upon the natural position: who reverentially declining the situation of their Temple, nor willing to lye as that stood, do place their Beds from North to South, and delight to sleep Meridionally. This Opinion confirmed would much advance the Microcosmical conceit, and commend the Geography of *Paracelsus*, who according to the Cardinal points of the World divideth the body of man: and therefore working upon humane ordure, and by long preparation rendring it odoriferous, he terms it *Zibeta Occidentalis*, Western *Civet*; making the face the East, but the posteriours the *America* or Western part of his Microcosm. The verity hereof might easily be tried in *Wales*, where there are portable Boats, and made of Leather, which would convert upon the impulsion of any verticity; and seem to be the same whereof in his description of *Britain Cæsar* hath left some mention.

Another kind of verticity, is that which *Angelus doce mihi jus, alias, Anagrammatically. Michael Sundevogis*, in a Tract *De Sulphure*, discovereth in Vegetables, from sticks let fall or depressed under water; which equally framed and permitted unto themselves, will ascend at the upper end, or that which was vertical in their vegetation; wherein notwithstanding, as yet, we have not found satisfaction. Although perhaps too greedy of Magnalities, we are apt to make but favourable experiments concerning welcome Truths, and such desired verities.

It is also wondrous strange what *Lælius Bisciola* reporteth, that if unto ten ounces of Loadstone one of Iron be added, it encreaseth not unto eleven, but weighs ten ounces still. *Horæ subsecivæ.* A relation inexcusable in a work of leisurable hours: the examination being as ready as the relation, and the falsity tried as easily as delivered. Nor is it to be omitted what is taken up by the *Cœsius Bernardus* a late Mineralogist, and originally confirmed by *Porta*, that Needles touched with a *Diamond* contract a verticity, even as they do with a Loadstone, which will not consist with experiment. And therefore, as *Gilbertus* observeth, he might be deceived, in touching such Needles with *Diamonds*, which had a verticity before, as we have declared most Needles to have; and so had he touched them with Gold or Silver, he might have concluded a magnetical vertue therein.

In the same form may we place *Fracastorius* his attraction of silver. *Philostratus* his *Pantarbes*, *Apollodorus* and *Beda* his relation of the Loadstone that attracted onely in the night. But most inexcusable is *Franciscus Rueus*, a man of our own profession; who in his discourse of *Gemms* mentioned in the *Apocalyps*, undertakes a Chapter of the Loadstone. Wherein substantially and upon experiment he scarce delivereth any thing: making long enumeration of its traditional qualities, whereof he seemeth to believe many, and some above convicted by experience, he is fain to salve as impostures of the Devil. But *Bœtius de Boot* Physitian unto *Rodulphus* the second, hath recompenced this defect; and in his Tract *De Lapidibus & Gemmis*, speaks very materially hereof; and his Discourse is consonant unto Experience and Reason.

As for Relations Historical, though many there be of less account, yet two alone deserve consideration: The first concerneth magnetical Rocks, and attractive Mountains in several parts of the Earth. The other the Tomb of *Mahomet* and bodies suspended in the air. Of Rocks magnetical there are likewise two relations; for some are delivered to be in the *Indies*, and some in the extremity of the North, and about the very Pole. The Northern account is commonly ascribed unto *Olaus Magnus* Archbishop of *Upsale*, who out of his Predecessor *Joannes, Saxo*, and others, compiled a History of some Northern Nations; but this assertion we have not discovered in that Work of his which commonly passeth amongst us, and should believe his Geography herein no more then that in the first line of his Book; when he affirmeth that *Biarmia* (which is not seventy degrees in latitude) hath the Pole for its Zenith, and Equinoctial for the Horizon.

Now upon this foundation, how uncertain soever men have erected mighty illations, ascribing thereto the cause of the Needles direction, and conceiving the effluctions from these Mountains and Rocks invite the Lilly toward the North. Which conceit though countenanced by learned men, is not made out either by experience or reason, for no man hath yet attained or given a sensible account of the Pole by some degrees. It is also observed the Needle doth very much vary as it approacheth the Pole; whereas were there such direction from the Rocks, upon a nearer approachment it would more directly respect them. Beside, were there such magnetical Rocks under the Pole, yet being so far removed they would produce no such effect. For they that sail by the Isle of *Ilua* now called *Elba* in the Thuscan Sea which abounds in veins of Loadstone, observe no variation or inclination of the Needle; much less may they expect a direction from Rocks at the end of the Earth. And lastly, men that ascribe thus much unto Rocks of the North, must presume or discover the like magneticals at the South: For in the Southern Seas and far beyond the Equator, variations are large, and declinations as constant as in the Northern Ocean.

(Probably) there be no magnetical Rocks.

The other relation of Loadstone Mines and Rocks, in the shore of *India* is delivered of old by *Pliny*; wherein, saith he, they are so placed both in abundance and vigour, that it proves an adventure of hazard to pass those Coasts in a Ship with Iron nails. *Serapion* the Moor, an Author of good esteem and reasonable Antiquity, confirmeth the same, whose expression in the word *magnes* is this. The Mine of this Stone is in the Sea-coast of *India*, whereto when Ships approach, there is no Iron in them which flies not like a Bird unto those Mountains; and therefore their ships are fastened not with Iron but Wood, for otherwise they would be torn to pieces. But this assertion, how positive soever, is contradicted by all Navigators that pass that way; which are now many, and of our own Nation, and might surely have been controled by *Nearchus* the Admiral of *Alexander*; who not knowing the Compass, was fain to coast that shore.

Mahomet's *tomb of stone, and built upon the ground.*

For the relation concerning *Mahomet*, it is generally believed his Tomb at *Medina Talnabi*, in *Arabia*, without any visible supporters hangeth in the air between two Loadstones artificially contrived both above and below; which conceit is fabulous and evidently false from the testimony of Ocular Testators, who affirm his Tomb is made of Stone, and lyeth upon the ground; as beside others the learned *Vossius* observeth from *Gabriel Sionita*, and *Joannes Hesronita*, two *Maronites* in their relations hereof. Of such intentions and attempt by *Mahometans* we read in some Relators, and that might be the occasion of the Fable, which by tradition of time and distance of place enlarged into the Story of being accomplished. And this hath been promoted by attempts of the like nature; for we read in *Pliny* that one *Dinocrates* began to Arch the Temple of *Arsinoe* in *Alexandria* with Loadstone, that so her Statue might be suspended in the air to the amazement of the beholders. And to lead on our crudelity herein, confirmation may be drawn from History and Writers of good authority. So it is reported by *Ruffinus*, that in the Temple of *Serapis* there was an Iron Chariot suspended by Loadstones in the air; which stones removed, the Chariot fell and dashed into pieces. The like doth *Beda* report of *Bellerophons* Horse, which framed of Iron, was placed between two Loadstones, with wings expansed, pendulous in the air.

The verity of these Stories we shall not further dispute, their possibility we may in some way determine; if we conceive what no man will deny, that bodies suspended in the air have this suspension from one or many Loadstones placed both above and below it; or else by one or many placed only above it. Likewise the body to be suspended in respect of the Loadstone above, is either placed first at a pendulous distance in the medium, or else attracted unto that site by the vigor of the Loadstone. And so we first affirm, that possible it is, a body may be suspended between two Loadstones; that is, it being so equally attracted unto both, that it determineth it self unto neither. But surely this position will be of no duration; for if the air be agitated or the body waved either way, it omits the equilibration, and disposeth it self unto the nearest attractor. Again, It is not impossible (though hardly feasible) by a single Loadstone to suspend an Iron in the air, the Iron being artificially placed and at a distance guided toward the stone, until it find the neutral point, wherein its gravity just equals the magnetical quality, the one exactly extolling as much as the other depresseth. And lastly, Impossible it is that if an Iron rest upon the ground, and a Loadstone be placed over it, it should ever so arise as to hang in the way or medium; for that vigor which at a distance is able to overcome the resistance of its gravity and to lift it up from the Earth, will as it approacheth nearer be still more able to attract it; never remaining in the middle that could not abide in the extreams. Now the way of *Baptista Porta* that by a thred fastneth a Needle to a Table, and then so guides and orders the same, that by the attraction of the Loadstone it abideth in the air, infringeth not this reason; for this is a violent retention, and if the thred be loosened, the Needle ascends and adheres unto the Attractor.

Powder of Loadstones, of what operation.

The third consideration concerneth Medical relations; wherein what ever effects are delivered, they are either derived from its mineral and ferreous condition, or else magnetical operation. Unto the ferreous and mineral quality pertaineth what *Dioscorides* an ancient Writer and Souldier under *Anthony* and *Cleopatra* affirmeth, that half a dram of Loadstone given with Honey and Water, proves a purgative medicine, and evacuateth gross humours. But this is a quality of great incertainty; for omitting the vehicle of Water and Honey, which is of a laxative power it self, the powder of some Loadstones in this dose doth rather constipate and binde, then purge and loosen the belly. And if sometimes it cause any laxity, it is probably in the same way with Iron and Steel unprepared, which will disturb some bodies, and work by Purge and Vomit. And therefore, whereas it is delivered in a Book ascribed unto *Galen*, that it is a good medicine in dropsies, and evacuates the waters of persons so affected: It may I confess by siccity and astriction afford a confirmation unto parts relaxed, and such as be hydropically disposed; and by these qualities it may be useful in *Hernias* or *Ruptures*, and for these it is commended by *Ætius*, *Ægineta*, and *Oribatius*; who only affirm that it contains the vertue of *Hæmatites*, and being burnt was sometimes vended for it. Wherein notwithstanding there is an higher vertue; and in the same prepared, or in rich veins thereof, though crude, we have observed the effects of Chalybeat Medicines; and the benefits of Iron and Steel in strong obstructions. And therefore that was probably a different vein of Loadstone, or infected with other mineral mixture, which the Ancients commended for a purgative medicine, and ranked the same with the violentest kinds thereof: with *Hippophae*, *Cneoron*, and *Thymelæa*, as we find it in *Hippocrates* *De morbis internis.*; and might be somewhat doubtful, whether by the magnesian stone, he understood the Loadstone; did not *Achilles Statius* define the same, the Stone that loveth Iron.

To this mineral condition belongeth what is delivered by some, that wounds which are made with weapons excited by the Loadstone, contract a malignity, and become of more difficult cure; which nevertheless is not to be found in the incision of Chyrurgions with knives and lances touched; which leave no such effect behind them. Hither we also refer that affirmative, which sayes the Loadstone is poison; and therefore in the lists of poisons we find it in many Authors. But this our experience cannot confirm, and the practice of the King of *Zeilan* clearly contradicteth; who as *Garcias ab Horto*, Physitian unto the *Spanish* Viceroy delivereth, hath all his meat served up in dishes of Loadstone, and conceives thereby he preserveth the vigour of youth.

But surely from a magnetical activity must be made out what is let fall by *Ætius*, that a Loadstone held in the hand of one that is podagrical, doth either cure or give great ease in the Gout. Or what *Marcellus Empericus* affirmeth, that as an amulet, it also cureth the headach; which are but additions unto its proper nature, and hopeful enlargements of its allowed attraction. For perceiving its secret power to draw magnetical bodies, men have invented a new attraction, to draw out the dolour and pain of any part. And from such grounds it surely became a philter, and was conceived a medicine of some venereal attraction; and therefore upon this stone they graved the Image of *Venus*, according unto that of *Claudian*, *Venerem magnetica gemma figurat*. Hither must we also ruler what is delivered concerning its power to draw out of the body bullets and heads of arrows, and for the like intention is mixed up in plaisters. Which course, although as vain and ineffectual it be rejected by many good Authors, yet is it not methinks so readily to be denied, nor the Practice of many Physicians which have thus compounded plaisters, thus suddenly to be condemned, as may be observed in the *Emplastrum divinum Nicolai*, the *Emplastrum nigrum* of *Augspurg*, the *Opodeldoch* and *Attractivum* of *Paracelsus*, with several more in the Dispensatory of *Wecker*, and practice of *Sennertus*. The cure also of *Hernias*, or *Ruptures* in *Pareus*: and the method also of curation lately delivered by *Daniel Beckherus*,[D] and approved by the Professors of *Leyden*, that is, of a young man of *Spruceland* that casually swallowed a knife about ten inches long, which was cut out of his stomach, and the wound healed up. In which cure to attract the knife to a convenient situation, there was applied a plaister made up with the powder of Loadstone. Now this kind of practice *Libavius*, *Gilbertus*, and lately *Swickardus* [*In his Ars Magnetica.*] condemn, as vain, and altogether unuseful; because a Loadstone in powder hath no attractive power; for in that form it omits his polarly respects, and loseth those parts which are the rule of attraction.

Wherein to speak compendiously, if experiment hath not deceived us, we first affirm that a Loadstone in powder omits not all attraction. For if the powder of a rich vein be in a reasonable quantity presented toward the Needle freely placed, it will not appear to be void of all activity, but will be able to stir it. Nor hath it only a power to move the Needle in powder and by it self, but this will it also do, if incorporated and mixed with plaisters; as we have made trial in the *Emplastrum de Minia*, with half an ounce of the mass, mixing a dram of Loadstone. For applying the magdaleon or roal unto the Needle, it would both stir and attract it; not equally in all parts, but more vigorously in some, according unto the Mine of the Stone, more plentifully dispersed in the mass. And lastly, In the Loadstone powdered, the polary respects are not wholly destroyed. For those diminutive particles are not atomical or meerly indivisible, but consist of dimensions sufficient for their operations, though in obscurer effects. Thus if unto the powder of Loadstone or Iron we admove the North Pole of the Loadstone, the Powders or small divisions will erect and conform themselves thereto: but if the South Pole approach, they will subside, and inverting their bodies, respect the Loadstone with the other extream. And this will happen not only in a body of powder together, but in any particle or dust divided from it.

Now though we disavow not these plaisters, yet shall we not omit two cautions in their use, that therein the Stone be not too subtilly powdered, for it will better manifest its attraction in a more sensible dimension. That where is desired a speedy effect, it may be considered whether it were not better to relinquish the powdered plaisters, and to apply an entire Loadstone unto the part: And though the other be not wholly ineffectual, whether this way be not more powerful, and so might have been in the cure of the young man delivered by *Beckerus*.

The last consideration concerneth Magical relations; in which account we comprehend effects derived and fathered upon hidden qualities, specifical forms, Antipathies and Sympathies, whereof from received grounds of Art, no reasons are derived. Herein relations are strange and numerous; men being apt in all Ages to multiply wonders, and Philosophers dealing with admirable bodies, as Historians have done with excellent men, upon the strength of their great atcheivements, ascribing acts unto them not only false but impossible; and exceeding truth as much in their relations, as they have others in their actions. Hereof we shall briefly mention some delivered by Authors of good esteem: whereby we may discover the fabulous inventions of some, the credulous supinity of others, and the great disservice unto truth by both: multiplying obscurities in Nature, and authorising hidden qualities that are false; whereas wise men are ashamed there are so many true.

And first, *Dioscorides* puts a shrewd quality upon it, and such as men are apt enough to experiment, who therewith discovers the incontinency of a wife, by placing the Loadstone under her pillow, whereupon she will not be able to remain in bed with her husband. The same he also makes a help unto thievery. For Thieves saith he, having a design upon a house, do make a fire at the four corners thereof, and cast therein the fragments of Loadstone: whence ariseth a fume that so disturbeth the inhabitants, that they forsake the house and leave it to the spoil of the Robbers. This relation, how ridiculous soever, hath *Albertus* taken up above a thousand years after, and *Marbodeus* the Frenchman hath continued the same in Latine Verse, which with the Notes of *Pictorius* is currant unto our dayes. As strange must be the Lithomancy or divination from this Stone, whereby as *Tzetzes* delivers, *Helenus* the Prophet foretold the destruction of *Troy*: and the Magick thereof not safely to be believed, which was delivered by *Orpheus*, that sprinkled with water it will upon a question emit a voice not much unlike an Infant. But surely the Loadstone of *Laurentius Guascus* the Physitian, is never to be matched; wherewith, as *Cardan* delivereth, whatsoever Needles or Bodies were touched, the wounds and punctures made thereby, were never felt at all. And yet as strange is that which is delivered by some, that a Loadstone preserved in the salt of a *Remora*, acquires a power to attract gold out of the deepest Wells. Certainly a studied absurdity, not casually cast out, but plotted for perpetuity: for the strangeness of the effect ever to be admired, and the difficulty of the trial never to be convicted.

These conceits are of that monstrosity that they refute themselves in their recitements. There is another of better notice, and whispered thorow the World with some attention; credulous and vulgar auditors readily believing it, and more judicious and distinctive heads, not altogether rejecting it. The conceit is excellent, and if the effect would follow, somewhat divine; whereby we might communicate like spirits, and confer on earth with *Menippus* in the Moon. And this is pretended from the sympathy of two Needles touched with the same Loadstone, and placed in the center of two Abecedary circles or rings, with letters described round about them, one friend keeping one, and another the other, and agreeing upon an hour wherein they will communicate. For then, saith Tradition, at what distance of place soever, when one Needle shall be removed unto any letter, the other by a wonderful sympathy will move unto the same. But herein I confess my experience can find no truth; for having expressly framed two circles of Wood, and according to the number of the Latine letters divided each into twenty three parts, placing therein two stiles or Needles composed of the same steel, touched with the same Loadstone, and at the same point: of these two, whensoever I removed the one, although but at the distance of half a span, the other would stand like *Hercules* pillars, and if the Earth stand still, have surely no motion at all. Now as it is not possible that any body should have no boundaries, or Sphear of its activity, so it is improbable it should effect that at distance, which nearer hand it cannot at all perform.

Again, The conceit is ill contrived, and one effect inferred, whereas the contrary will ensue. For if the removing of one of the Needles from *A* to *B*, should have any action or influence on the other, it would not intice it from *A* to *B*, but repell it from *A* to *Z*: for Needles excited by the same point of the stone, do not attract, but avoid each other, even as these also do, when their invigorated extreams approach unto one other.

Lastly, Were this conceit assuredly true, yet were it not a conclusion at every distance to be tried by every head: it being no ordinary or Almanack business, but a Problem Mathematical, to finde out the difference of hours in different places; nor do the wisest exactly satisfie themselves in all. For the hours of several places anticipate each other, according unto their Longitudes, which are not exactly discovered of every place; and therefore the trial hereof at a considerable interval, is best performed at the distance of the *Antœci*; that is, such habitations as have the same Meridian and equal parallel, on different sides of the Æquator; or more plainly the same Longitude and the same Latitude unto the South, which we have in the North. For unto such situations it is noon and midnight at the very same time.

And therefore the Sympathy of these Needles is much of the same mould with that intelligence which is pretended from the flesh of one body transmuted by incision into another. *De curtorum Chyrurgia.* For if by the Art of *Taliacotius*, a permutation of flesh, or transmutation be made from one mans body into another, as if a piece of flesh be exchanged from the bicipital muscle of either parties arm, and about them both an Alphabet circumscribed; upon a time appointed as some conceptions affirm, they may communicate at what distance soever. For if the one shall prick himself in *A*, the other at the same time will have a sense thereof in the same part: and upon inspection of his arm perceive what letters the other points out in his. Which is a way of intelligence very strange: and would requite the lost Art of *Pythagoras*, who could read a reverse in the Moon.

Now this magnetical conceit how strange soever, might have some original in Reason; for men observing no solid body, whatsoever did interrupt its action, might be induced to believe no distance would terminate the same; and most conceiving it pointed unto the Pole of Heaven, might also opinion that nothing between could restrain it. Whosoever was the Author, the *Æolus* that blew it about was *Famianus Strada*, that Elegant Jesuit, in his Rhetorical prolusions, who chose out this subject to express the stile of *Lucretius*. But neither *Baptista Porta*, *de Furtivis Literarum notis*; *Trithemius* in his Steganography, *Selenus* in his Cryptography, *Nunc. inanim. by D. Godwin Bishop of Hereford.* *Nuncius inanimatus* make any consideration hereof, although they deliver many ways to communicate thoughts at distance. And this we will not deny may in some manner be effected by the Loadstone; that is, from one room into another; by placing a table in the wall common unto both, and writing thereon the same letters one against another: for upon the approach of a vigorous Loadstone unto a letter on this side, the Needle will move unto the same on the other. But this is a very different way from ours at present; and hereof there are many ways delivered, and more may be discovered which contradict not the rule of its operations.

As for *Unguentum Armarium*, called also *Magneticum*, it belongs not to this discourse, it neither having the Loadstone for its ingredient, nor any one of its actions: but supposeth other principles, as common and universal spirits, which convey the action of the remedy unto the part, and conjoins the vertue of bodies far disjoyned. But perhaps the cures it doth, are not worth so mighty principles; it commonly healing but simple wounds, and such as mundified and kept clean, do need no other hand then that of Nature, and the Balsam of the proper part. Unto which effect there being fields of Medicines, it may be a hazardous curiosity to rely on this; and because men say the effect doth generally follow, it might be worth the experiment to try, whether the same will not ensue, upon the same Method of cure, by ordinary Balsams, or common vulnerary plaisters.

Many other Magnetisms may be pretended, and the like attractions through all the creatures of Nature. Whether the same be verified in the action of the Sun upon inferiour bodies, whether there be *Æolian* Magnets, whether the flux and reflux of the Sea be caused by any Magnetism from the Moon; whether the like be really made out, or rather Metaphorically verified in the sympathies of Plants and Animals, might afford a large dispute; and *Kircherus* in his *Catena Magnetica* hath excellently discussed the same; which work came late unto our hand, but might have much advantaged this Discourse.

Other Discourses there might be made of the Loadstone: as Moral, Mystical, Theological; and some have handsomely done them; as *Ambrose, Austine, Gulielmus Parisiensis*, and many more, but these fall under no Rule, and are as boundless as mens inventions. And though honest minds do glorifie God hereby; yet do they most powerfully magnifie him, and are to be looked on with another eye, who demonstratively set forth its Magnalities; who not from postulated or precarious inferences, entreat a courteous assent; but from experiments and undeniable effects, enforce the wonder of its Maker.

Footnotes

[D]De cultrivoro Prussiaco, 1636. *The cure of the Prussian Knife.*

CHAPTER IV
Of Bodies Electrical.

Bodies Electrical, what?

Having thus spoken of the Loadstone and Bodies Magnetical, I shall in the next place deliver somewhat of Electrical, and such as may seem to have attraction like the other. Hereof we shall also deliver what particularly spoken or not generally known is manifestly or probably true, what generally believed is also false or dubious. Now by Electrical bodies, I understand not such as are Metallical, mentioned by *Pliny*, and the Ancients; for their Electrum was a mixture made of Gold, with the Addition of a fifth part of Silver; a substance now as unknown as true *Aurichalcum*, or *Corinthian* Brass, and set down among things lost by *Pancirollus*. Nor by Electrick Bodies do I conceive such only as take up shavings, straws, and light bodies, in which number the Ancients only placed *Jet* and *Amber*; but such as conveniently placed unto their objects attract all bodies palpable whatsoever. I say conveniently placed, that is, in regard of the object, that it be not too ponderous, or any way affixed; in regard of the Agent, that it be not foul or sullied, but wiped, rubbed, and excitated; in regard of both, that they be conveniently distant, and no impediment interposed. I say, all bodies palpable, thereby excluding fire, which indeed it will not attract, nor yet draw through it; for fire consumes its effluxions by which it should attract.

Now although in this rank but two were commonly mentioned by the Ancients, *Gilbertus* discovereth many more; as *Diamonds, Saphyrs, Carbuncles, Iris, Opalls, Amethysts, Beril, Crystal, Bristol-stones, Sulphur, Mastick*, hard *Wax*, hard *Rosin, Arsenic, Sal-gemm, Roch-Allum*, common Glass, *Stibium*, or Glass of *Antimony*. Unto these Cabeus addeth white Wax, *Gum Elemi, Gum*

Guaici, Pix Hispanica, and *Gipsum*. And unto these we add *Gum Anime, Benjamin, Talcum, China-dishes, Sandaraca, Turpentine, Styrax Liquida*, and *Caranna* dried into a hard consistence. And the same attraction we find, not onely in simple bodies, but such as are much compounded; as in the *Oxycroceum* plaister, and obscurely that *ad Herniam*, and *Gratia Dei*; all which smooth and rightly prepared, will discover a sufficient power to stir the Needle, setled freely upon a well-pointed pin; and so as the Electrick may be applied unto it without all disadvantage.

But the attraction of these Electricks we observe to be very different. Resinous or unctuous bodies, and such as will flame, attract most vigorously, and most thereof without frication; as *Anime, Benjamin*, and most powerfully good hard Wax, which will convert the Needle almost as actively as the Loadstone. And we believe that all or most of this substance if reduced to hardness, tralucency or clearness, would have some attractive quality. But juices concrete, or Gums easily dissolving in water, draw not at all: as *Aloe, Opium, Sanguis Draconis, Lacca, Calbanum, Sagapenum*. Many stones also both precious and vulgar, although terse and smooth, have not this power attractive: as *Emeralds, Pearl, Jaspis, Corneleans, Agathe, Heliotropes, Marble, Alablaster, Touchstone, Flint*, and *Bezoar*. Glass attracts but weakly, though clear; some slick stones and thick Glasses indifferently: *Arsenic* but weakly, so likewise Glass of *Antimony*, but *Crocus Metallorum* not at all. Salts generally but weakly, as *Sal Gemma, Allum*, and also *Talke*; nor very discoverably by any frication, but if gently warmed at the fire, and wiped with a dry cloth, they will better discover their Electricities.

No Metal attracts, nor Animal concretion we know, although polite and smooth; as we have made trial in *Elks* Hoofs, Hawks-Talons, the Sword of a *Sword-fish*, Tortois-shells, *Sea-horse*, and *Elephants* Teeth, in Bones, in *Harts-horn*, and what is usually conceived *Unicorns-horn*. No Wood though never so hard and polished, although out of some thereof Electrick bodies proceed; as *Ebony, Box, Lignum vitæ, Cedar*, etc. And although *Jet* and *Amber* be reckoned among *Bitumens*, yet neither do we find *Asphaltus*, that is, *Bitumens* of *Judea*, nor *Sea-cole*, nor *Camphire*, nor *Mummia* to attract, although we have tried in large and polished pieces. Now this attraction have we tried in straws and paleous bodies, in Needles of Iron, equilibrated, Powders of Wood and Iron, in Gold and Silver foliate. And not only in solid but fluent and liquid bodies, as oyls made both by expression and distillation; in Water, in spirits of Wine, *Vitriol* and *Aquafortis*.

But how this attraction is made, is not so easily determined; that 'tis performed by effluviums is plain, and granted by most; for Electricks will not commonly attract, except they grow hot or become perspirable. For if they be foul and obnubilated, it hinders their effluxion; nor if they be covered, though but with Linen or Sarsenet, or if a body be interposed, for that intercepts the effluvium. If also a powerful and broad Electrick of Wax or *Anime* be held over fine powder, the Atoms or small particles will ascend most numerously unto it; and if the Electrick be held unto the light, it may be observed that many thereof will fly, and be as it were discharged from the Electrick to the distance sometime of two or three inches. Which motion is performed by the breath of the effluvium issuing with agility; for as the Electrick cooleth, the projection of the Atoms ceaseth.

Cabeus his way for attraction in bodies Electrick.

The manner hereof *Cabeus* wittily attempteth, affirming that this effluvium attenuateth and impelleth the neighbor air, which returning home in a gyration, carrieth with it the obvious bodies unto the Electrick. And this he labours to confirm by experiments; for if the straws be raised by a vigorous Electrick, they do appear to wave and turn in their ascents. If likewise the Electrick be broad, and the straws light and chaffy, and held at a reasonable distance, they will not arise unto the middle, but rather adhere toward the Verge or Borders thereof. And lastly, if many straws be laid together, and a nimble Electrick approach, they will not all arise unto it, but some will commonly start aside, and be whirled a reasonable distance from it. Now that the air impelled returns unto its place in a gyration or whirling, is evident from the Atoms or Motes in the Sun. For when the Sun so enters a hole or window, that by its illumination the Atoms or Motes become perceptible, if then by our breath the air be gently impelled, it may be perceived, that they will circularly return and in a gyration unto their places again.

The way of Sir Kenelm Digby.

Another way of their attraction is also delivered; that is, by a tenuous emanation or continued effluvium, which after some distance retracteth into it self; as is observable in drops of Syrups, Oyl, and seminal Viscosities, which spun at length, retire into their former dimensions. Now these effluviums advancing from the body of the Electrick, in their return do carry back the bodies whereon they have laid hold within the Sphere or Circle of their continuities; and these they do not onely attract, but with their viscous arms hold fast a good while after. And if any shall wonder why these effluviums issuing forth impel and protrude not the straw before they can bring it back, it is because the effluvium passing out in a smaller thred and more enlengthened filament, it stirreth not the bodies interposed, but returning unto its original, falls into a closer substance, and carrieth them back unto it self. And this way of attraction is best received, embraced by Sir *Kenelm Digby* in his excellent Treaty of bodies, allowed by *Des Cartes* in his principles of Philosophy, as far and concerneth fat and resinous bodies, and with exception of Glass, whose attraction he also deriveth from the recess of its effluction. And this in some manner the words of *Gilbertus* will bear: *Effluvia illa tenuiora concipiunt & amplectuntur corpora, quibus uniuntur, & electris tanquam extensis brachiis, & ad fontem propinquitate invalescentibus effluviis, deducuntur*. And if the ground were true, that the Earth were an Electrick body, and the air but the effluvium thereof, we might have more reason to believe that from this attraction, and by this effluction, bodies tended to the Earth, and could not remain above it.

Our other discourse of Electricks concerneth a general opinion touching *Jet* and *Amber*, that they attract all light bodies, except *Ocymum* or *Basil*, and such as be dipped in oyl or oyled; and this is urged as high as *Theophrastus*: but *Scaliger* acquitteth him; And had this been his assertion, *Pliny* would probably have taken it up, who herein stands out, and delivereth no more but what is vulgarly known. But *Plutarch* speaks positively in his *Symposiacks*, that *Amber* attracteth all bodies, excepting Basil and oyled substances. With *Plutarch* consent many Authors both Ancient and Modern; but the most inexcusable are *Lemnius* and *Rueus*, whereof the one delivering the nature of Minerals mentioned in Scripture, the infallible fountain of Truth, confirmeth their vertues with erroneous traditions; the other undertaking the occult and hidden Miracles of Nature, accepteth this for one; and endeavoureth to alledge a reason of that which is more then occult, that is, not existent.

Now herein, omitting the authority of others, as the Doctrine of experiment hath informed us, we first affirm, That *Amber* attracts not Basil, is wholly repugnant unto truth. For if the leaves thereof or dried stalks be stripped into small straws, they arise unto *Amber*, *Wax*, and other Electries, no otherwise then those of Wheat and Rye: nor is there any peculiar fatness or singular viscosity in that plant that might cause adhesion, and so prevent its ascension. But that *Jet* and *Amber* attract not straws oyled, is in part true and false. For if the straws be much wet or drenched in oyl, true it is that *Amber* draweth them not; for then the oyl makes the straws to adhere unto the part whereon they are placed, so that they cannot rise unto the Attractor; and this is true, not onely if they be soaked in Oyl, but spirits of Wine or Water. But if we speak of Straws or festucous divisions lightly drawn over with oyl, and so that it causeth no adhesion; or if we conceive an Antipathy between Oyl and *Amber*, the Doctrine is not true. For *Amber* will attract straws thus oyled, it will convert the Needles of Dials made either of Brass or Iron, although they be much oyled; for in these Needles consisting free upon their Center, there can be no adhesion. It will likewise attract Oyl it self, and if it approacheth unto a drop thereof, it becometh conical, and ariseth up unto it, for Oyl taketh not away his attraction, although it be rubbed over it. For if you touch a piece of Wax already excitated with common Oyl, it will notwithstanding attract, though not so vigorously as before. But if you moisten the same with any Chymical Oyl, Water, or spirits of Wine, or only breath upon it, it quite omits its attraction, for either its influencies cannot get through, or will not mingle with those substances.

It is likewise probable the Ancients were mistaken concerning its substance and generation; they conceiving it a vegetable concretion made of the gums of Trees, especially *Pine* and *Poplar* falling into the water, and after indurated or hardened, whereunto accordeth the Fable of *Phaetons* sisters: but surely the concretion is Mineral, according as is delivered by *Boetius*. For either it is found in Mountains and mediterraneous parts; and so it is a fat and unctuous sublimation in the Earth, concreted and fixed by salt and nitrous spirits wherewith it meeteth. Or else, which is most usual, it is collected upon the Sea-shore; and so it is a fat and bituminous juice coagulated by the saltness of the Sea. Now that salt spirits have a power to congeal and coagulate unctuous bodies, is evident in Chymical operations; in the distillations of *Arsenick*, sublimate and *Antimony*; in the mixture of oyl of *Juniper*, with the salt and acide spirit of *Sulphur*, for thereupon ensueth a concretion unto the consistence of *Birdlime*; as also in spirits of salt, or *Aqua fortis* poured upon oyl of Olive, or more plainly in the Manufacture of Soap. And many bodies will coagulate upon commixture, whose separated natures promise no concretion. Thus upon a solution of *Tin* by *Aqua fortis*, there will ensue a coagulation, like that of whites of Eggs. *How the stone is bred in the Kidney or Bladder.* Thus the volatile salt of Urine will coagulate *Aqua vitæ*, or spirits of Wine; and thus perhaps (as *Helmont* excellently declareth) the stones or calculous concretions in Kidney or Bladder may be produced: the spirits or volatile salt of Urine conjoyning with the *Aqua vitæ* potentially lying therein; as he illustrateth from the distillation of fermented Urine. From whence ariseth an *Aqua vitæ* or spirit, which the volatile salt of the same Urine will congeal; and finding an earthy concurrence, strike into a lapideous substance.

Of a Bee and a Viper involved in Amber. Mart. l. 4.

Lastly, We will not omit what *Bellabonus* upon his own experiment writ from *Dantzich* unto *Mellichius*, as he hath left recorded in his Chapter, *De succino*, that the bodies of *Flies*, *Pismires*, and the like, which are said oft-times to be included in *Amber*, are not real but representative, as he discovered in several pieces broke for that purpose. If so, the two famous Epigrams hereof in *Martial* are but Poetical, the *Pismire* of *Brassavolus* imaginary, and *Cardans Mousoleum* for a Flie, a meer phansie. But hereunto we know not how to assent, as having met with some whose reals made good their representments.

CHAPTER V
Compendiously of sundry other common Tenents, concerning Mineral and Terreous Bodies, which examined, prove either false or dubious.

1. And first we hear it in every mouth, and in many good Authors read it, That a *Diamond*, which is the hardest of stones, not yielding unto *Steel*, *Emery*, or any thing but its own powder, is yet made soft, or broke by the blood of a Goat. Thus much is affirmed by *Pliny*, *Solinus*, *Albertus*, *Cyprian*, *Austin*, *Isidore*, and many Christian Writers, alluding herein unto the heart of man and the precious bloud of our Saviour, who was typified by the Goat that was slain, and the scape-Goat in the Wilderness; and at the effusion of whose bloud, not only the hard hearts of his enemies relented, but the stony rocks and vail of the Temple were shattered. But this I perceive is easier affirmed then proved. For *Lapidaries*, and such as profess the art of cutting this stone, do generally deny it; and they that seem to countenance it, have in their deliveries so qualified it, that little from thence of moment can be inferred for it. For first, the holy Fathers, without a further enquiry did take it for granted, and rested upon the authority of the first deliverers. As for *Albertus*, he promiseth this effect, but conditionally, not except the Goat drink wine, and be fed with *Siler montanum, petroselinum*, and such herbs as are conceived of power to break the stone in the bladder. But the words of *Pliny*, from whom most likely the rest at first derived it, if strictly considered, do rather overthrow, then any way advantage this effect. His words are these: *Hircino rumpitur sanguine, nec aliter quam recenti, calidoque macerata, & sic quoque multis ictibus, tunc etiam præterquam eximias incudes malleosque ferreos frangens.* That is, it is broken with Goats blood, but not except it be fresh and warm, and that not without many blows, and then also it will break the best Anvils and Hammers of Iron. And answerable hereto, is the assertion of *Isidore* and *Solinus*. By which account, a Diamond steeped in Goats bloud, rather increaseth in hardness, then acquireth any softness by the infusion; for the best we have are comminuible without it; and are so far from breaking hammers, that they submit unto pistillation, and resist not an ordinary pestle.

Pulvis Lithontripticus.

Upon this conceit arose perhaps the discovery of another; that the bloud of a Goat was soveraign for the Stone, as it stands commended by many good Writers, and brings up the composition in the powder of *Nicolaus*, and the Electuary of the Queen of *Colein*. Or rather because it was found an excellent medicine for the Stone, and its ability commended by some to dissolve the hardest thereof; it might be conceived by amplifying apprehensions, to be able to break a *Diamond*; and so it came to be ordered that the Goat should be fed with saxifragous herbs, and such as are conceived of power to break the stone. However it were, as the effect is false in the one, so is it surely very doubtful in the other. For although inwardly received it may be very diuretick, and expulse the stone in the Kidneys, yet how it should dissolve or break that in the bladder, will require a further dispute; and perhaps would be more reasonably tried by a warm injection thereof, then as it is commonly used. Wherein notwithstanding, we should rather rely upon the urine in a castlings bladder, a resolution of Crabs eyes, or the second distillation of Urine, as *Helmont* hath commended; or rather (if any such might be found) a Chylifactory menstruum or digestive preparation drawn from species or individuals, whose stomacks peculiarly dissolve lapideous bodies.

2. *That Glass is poison*, according unto common conceit, I know not how to grant. Not onely from the innocency of its ingredients, that is, fine Sand, and the ashes of Glass-wort of Fearn, which in themselves are harmless and useful: or because I find it by many commended for the Stone, but also from experience, as having given unto Dogs above a dram thereof, subtilly powdered in Butter and Paste, without any visible disturbance.

Why Glass is commonly held to be poysonous.

The conceit is surely grounded upon the visible mischief of Glass grosly or coursly powdered, for that indeed is mortally noxious, and effectually used by some to destroy Mice and Rats; for by reason of its acuteness and angularity, it commonly excoriates the parts through which it passeth, and solicits them unto a continual expulsion. Whereupon there ensues fearful symptomes, not much unlike those which attend the action of poison. From whence notwithstanding, we cannot with propriety impose upon it that name, either by occult or elementary quality, which he that concedeth will much enlarge the Catalogue or Lists of Poisons. For many things, neither deleterious by substance or quality, are yet destructive by figure, or some occasional activity. So are Leeches destructive, and by some accounted poison; not properly, that is by temperamental contrariety, occult form, or so much as elemental repugnancy; but because being inwardly taken they fasten upon the veins, and occasion an effusion of bloud, which cannot be easily stanched. So a Sponge is mischievous, not in it self, for in its powder it is harmless: but because being received into the stomach it swelleth, and occasioning a continual distension, induceth a strangulation. So Pins, Needles, ears of Rye or Barley may be poison. So *Daniel* destroyed the Dragon by a composition of three things, whereof neither was poison alone, nor properly all together, that is, Pitch, Fat, and Hair, according as is expressed in the History. Then *Daniel* took Pitch, and Fat, and Hair, and did seeth them together, and made lumps thereof, these he put in the Dragons mouth, and so he burst asunder. That is, the Fat and Pitch being cleaving bodies, and the Hair continually extimulating the parts: by the action of the one, Nature was provoked to expell, but by the tenacity of the other forced to retain: so that there being left no passage in or out, the Dragon brake in pieces. It must therefore be taken of grosly-powdered Glass, what is delivered by *Grevinus*: and from the same must that mortal dysentery proceed which is related by *Sanctorius*. And in the same sense shall we only allow a *Diamond* to be poison; and whereby as some relate *Paracelsus* himself was poisoned. So even the precious fragments and cordial gems which are of frequent use in Physick, and in themselves confessed of useful faculties, received in gross and angular Powders, may so offend the bowels, as to procure desperate languors, or cause most dangerous fluxes.

That Glass may be rendred malleable and pliable unto the hammer, many conceive, and some make little doubt, when they read in *Dio*, *Pliny*, and *Petronius*, that one unhappily effected it for *Tiberius*. Which notwithstanding must needs seem strange unto such as consider, that bodies are ductile from a tenacious humidity, which so holdeth the parts together; that though they dilate or extend, they part not from each others. That bodies run into Glass, when the volatile parts are exhaled, and the continuating humour separated: the Salt and Earth, that is, the fixed parts remaining. And therefore vitrification maketh bodies brittle, as destroying the viscous humours which hinder the disruption of parts. Which may be verified even in the bodies of Metals. For Glass of Lead or Tin is fragile, when that glutinous Sulphur hath been fired out, which made their bodies ductile.

He that would most probably attempt it, must experiment upon Gold. Whose fixed and flying parts are so conjoined, whose Sulphur and continuating principle is so united unto the Salt, that some may be hoped to remain to hinder fragility after vitrification. But how to proceed, though after frequent corrosion, as that upon the agency of fire, it should not revive into its proper body before it comes to vitrifie, will prove no easie discovery.

3. That Gold inwardly taken, either in substance, infusion, decoction or extinction, is a cordial of great efficacy, in sundry Medical uses, although a practice much used, is also much questioned, and by no man determined beyond dispute. There are hereof I perceive two extream opinions; some excessively magnifying it, and probably beyond its deserts; others extreamly vilifying it, and perhaps below its demerits. Some affirming it a powerful Medicine in many diseases, others averring that so used, it is effectual in none: and in this number are very eminent Physicians, *Erastus*, *Duretus*, *Rondeletius*, *Brassavolus* and many other, who beside the strigments and sudorous adhesions from mens hands, acknowledge that nothing proceedeth from Gold in the usual decoction thereof. Now the capital reason that led men unto this opinion, was their observation of the inseparable nature of Gold; it being excluded in the same quantity as it was received, without alteration of parts, or diminution of its gravity.

Now herein to deliver somewhat which in a middle way may be entertained; we first affirm, that the substance of Gold is invincible by the powerfullest action of natural heat; and that not only alimentally in a substantial mutation, but also medicamentally in any corporeal conversion. As is very evident, not only in the swallowing of golden bullets, but in the lesser and foliate divisions thereof: passing the stomach and guts even as it doth the throat, that is, without abatement of weight or consistence. So that it entereth not the veins with those electuaries, wherein it is mixed: but taketh leave of the permeant parts, at the mouths of the *Meseraicks*, or Lacteal Vessels, and accompanieth the inconvertible portion unto the siege. Nor is its substantial conversion expectible in any composition or aliment wherein it is taken. And therefore that was truly a starving absurdity, which befel the wishes of *Midas*. And little credit there is to be given to the golden Hen, related by *Wendlerus*. So in the extinction of Gold, we must not conceive it parteth with any of its salt or dissoluble principle thereby, as we may affirm of Iron; for the parts thereof are fixed beyond division, nor will they separate upon the strongest test of fire. This we affirm of pure Gold: for that which is currant and passeth in stamp amongst us, by reason of its allay, which is a proportion of Silver or Copper mixed therewith, is actually dequantitated by fire, and possibly by frequent extinction.

Secondly, Although the substance of Gold be not immuted or its gravity sensibly decreased, yet that from thence some vertue may proceed either in substantial reception or infusion we cannot safely deny. For possible it is that bodies may emit vertue and operation without abatement of weight; as is evident in the Loadstone, whose effluencies are continual, and communicable without a minoration of gravity. And the like is observable in Bodies electrical, whose emissions are less subtile. So will a Diamond or Saphire emit an effluvium sufficient to move the Needle or a Straw, without diminution of weight. Nor will polished Amber although it send forth a gross and corporal exhalement, be found a long time defective upon the exactest scales. Which is more easily conceivable in a continued and tenacious effluvium, whereof a great part retreats into its body.

Thirdly, If amulets do work by emanations from their bodies, upon those parts whereunto they are appended, and are not yet observed to abate their weight; if they produce visible and real effects by imponderous and invisible emissions, it may be unjust to deny the possible efficacy of Gold, in the non-omission of weight, or deperdition of any ponderous particles.

Lastly, Since *Stibium* or Glass of Antimony, since also its *Regulus* will manifestly communicate unto Water or Wine, a purging and vomitory operation; and yet the body it self, though after iterated infusions, cannot be found to abate either vertue or weight: we shall not deny but Gold may do the like, that is, impart some effluences unto the infusion, which carry with them the separable subtilties thereof.

That therefore this Metal thus received, hath any undeniable effect, we shall not imperiously determine, although beside the former experiments, many more may induce us to believe it. But since the point is dubious and not yet authentically decided, it will be no discretion to depend on disputable remedies; but rather in cases of known danger, to have recourse unto medicines of known and approved activity. For, beside the benefit accruing unto the sick, hereby may be avoided a gross and frequent errour, commonly committed in the use of doubtful remedies, conjointly with those which are of approved vertues; that is to impute the cure unto the conceited remedy, or place it on that whereon they place their opinion. Whose operation although it be nothing, or its concurrence not considerable, yet doth it obtain the name of the whole cure: and carrieth often the honour of the capital energie, which had no finger in it.

Herein exact and critical trial should be made by publick enjoinment, whereby determination might be setled beyond debate: for since thereby not only the bodies of men, but great Treasures might be preserved, it is not only an errour of Physick, but folly of State, to doubt thereof any longer.

4. That a pot full of ashes, will still contain as much water as it would without them, although by *Aristotle* in his Problems taken for granted, and so received by most, is not effectable upon the strictest experiment I could ever make. For when the airy intersticies are filled, and as much of the salt of the ashes as the water will imbibe is dissolved, there remains a gross and terreous portion at the bottom, which will possess a space by it self, according whereto there will remain a quantity of Water not receivable; so will it come to pass in a pot of salt, although decrepitated; and so also in a pot of Snow. For so much it will want in reception, as its solution taketh up, according unto the bulk whereof, there will remain a portion of Water not to be admitted. So a Glass stuffed with pieces of Sponge will want about a sixth part of what it would receive without it. So Sugar will not dissolve beyond the capacity of the Water, nor a Metal in *aqua fortis* be corroded beyond its reception. And so a pint of salt of Tartar exposed unto a moist air until it dissolve, will make far more liquor, or as some term it oyl, then the former measure will contain.

Nor is it only the exclusion of air by water, or repletion of cavities possessed thereby, which causeth a pot of ashes to admit so great a quantity of Water, but also the solution of the salt of the ashes into the body of the dissolvent. So a pot of ashes will receive somewhat more of hot Water then of cold, for the warm water imbibeth more of the Salt; and a vessel of ashes more then one of pin-dust or filings of Iron; and a Glass full of Water will yet drink in a proportion of Salt or Sugar without overflowing.

Nevertheless to make the experiment with most advantage, and in which sense it approacheth nearest the truth, it must be made in ashes throughly burnt and well reverberated by fire, after the salt thereof hath been drawn out by iterated decoctions. For then the body being reduced nearer unto Earth, and emptied of all other principles, which had former ingression unto it, becometh more porous, and greedily drinketh in water. He that hath beheld what quantity of Lead the test of saltless ashes will imbibe, upon the refining of Silver, hath encouragement to think it will do very much more in water.

The Ingredients of Gunpowder.

5. Of white powder and such as is discharged without report, there is no small noise in the World: but how far agreeable unto truth, few I perceive are able to determine. Herein therefore to satisfie the doubts of some, and amuse the credulity of others, We first declare, that Gunpowder consisteth of three ingredients, Salt-petre, Small-coal, and Brimstone. Salt-petre although it be also natural and found in several places, yet is that of common use an artificial Salt, drawn from the infusion of salt Earth, as that of Stales, Stables, Dove-houses, Cellers, and other covered places, where the rain can neither dissolve, nor the Sun approach to resolve it. Brimstone is a Mineral body of fat and inflamable parts, and this is either used crude, and called Sulphur Vive, and is of a sadder colour; or after depuration, such as we have in magdeleons or rolls, of a lighter yellow. Small-coal is known unto all, and for this use is made of *Sallow, Willow, Alder, Hazel*, and the like; which three proportionably mixed, tempered, and formed into granulary bodies, do make up that Powder which is in use for Guns.

Now all these, although they bear a share in the discharge, yet have they distinct intentions, and different offices in the composition. From Brimstone proceedeth the piercing and powerful firing; for Small-coal and Petre together will onely spit, nor vigorously continue the ignition. From Small-coal ensueth the black colour and quick accension; for neither Brimstone nor Petre, although in Powder, will take fire like Small-coal, nor will they easily kindle upon the sparks of a Flint; as neither will *Camphire*, a body very inflamable: but Small-coal is equivalent to Tinder, and serveth to light the Sulphur. It may also serve to diffuse the ignition through every part of the mixture; and being of more gross and fixed parts, may seem to moderate the activity of Salt-petre, and prevent too hasty rarefaction. From Salt-petre proceedeth the force and the report; for Sulphur and Small-coal mixed will not take fire with noise, or exilition, and Powder which is made of impure and greasie Petre hath but a weak emission, and giveth a faint report. And therefore in the three sorts of Powder the strongest containeth most Salt-petre, and the proportion thereof is about ten parts of Petre unto one of Coal and Sulphur.

But the immediate cause of the Report is the vehement commotion of the air upon the sudden and violent eruption of the Powder; for that being suddenly fired, and almost altogether, upon this high rarefaction, requireth by many degrees a greater space then before its body occupied; but finding resistance, it actively forceth his way, and by concusion of the air occasioneth the Report. Now with what violence it forceth upon the air, may easily be conceived, if we admit what *Cardan* affirmeth, that the Powder fired doth occupy an hundred times a greater space then its own bulk; or rather what *Snellius* more exactly accounteth; that it exceedeth its former space no less then 12000 and 500 times. *The cause of Thunder.* And this is the reason not only of this fulminating report of Guns, but may resolve the cause of those terrible cracks, and affrighting noises of Heaven; that is, the nitrous and sulphureous exhalations, set on fire in the Clouds; whereupon requiring a larger place, they force out their way, not only with the breaking of the cloud, but the laceration of the air about it. *The greatest distance of the Clouds.* When if the matter be spirituous, and the cloud compact, the noise is great and terrible: If the cloud be thin, and the Materials weak, the eruption is languid, ending in coruscations and flashes without noise, although but at the distance of two miles; which is esteemed the remotest distance of clouds. And therefore such lightnings do seldom any harm. And therefore also it is prodigious to have thunder in a clear sky, as is observably recorded in some Histories.

The cause of Earthquakes.

From the like cause may also proceed subterraneous Thunders and Earthquakes, when sulphureous and nitreous veins being fired, upon rarefaction do force their way through bodies that resist them. Where if the kindled matter be plentiful, and the Mine close and firm about it, subversion of Hills and Towns doth sometimes follow: If scanty, weak, and the Earth hollow or porous, there only ensueth some faint concussion or tremulous and quaking Motion. Surely, a main reason why the Ancients were so imperfect in the doctrine of Meteors, was their ignorance of Gunpowder and Fire-works, which best discover the causes of many thereof.

Now therefore he that would destroy the report of Powder, must work upon the Petre; he that would exchange the colour, must think how to alter the Small-coal. For the one, that is, to make white Powder, it is surely many ways feasible: The best I know is by the powder of rotten Willows, Spunk, or Touch-wood prepared, might perhaps make it Russet: and some, as *Beringuccio* *In his Pyrotechnia.* affirmeth, have promised to make it Red. All which notwithstanding doth little concern the Report, for that, as we have shewed, depends on another Ingredient. And therefore also under the colour of black, this principle is very variable; for it is made not onely by *Willow*, *Alder*, *Hazel*, etc. But some above all commend the coals of *Flax* and *Rushes*, and some also contend the same may be effected with Tinder.

As for the other, that is, to destroy the Report, it is reasonably attempted but two ways; either by quite leaving out, or else by silencing the Salt-petre. How to abate the vigour thereof, or silence its bombulation, a way is promised by *Porta*, not only in general terms by some fat bodies, but in particular by *Borax* and butter mixed in a due proportion; which saith he, will so go off as scarce to be heard by the discharger; and indeed plentifully mixed, it will almost take off the Report, and also the force of the charge. That it may be thus made without Salt-petre, I have met with but one example, that is, of *Alphonsus* Duke of *Ferrara* De examine Salium., who in the relation of *Brassavolus* and *Cardan*, invented such a Powder as would discharge a bullet without Report.

That therefore white Powder there may be, there is no absurdity; that also such a one as may give no report, we will not deny a possibility. But this however, contrived either with or without Salt-petre, will surely be of little force, and the effects thereof no way to be feared: For as it omits of Report so will it of effectual exclusion, and so the charge be of little force which is excluded. For thus much is reported of that famous Powder of *Alphonsus*, which was not of force enough to kill a Chicken, according to the delivery of *Brassavolus*. *Jamque pulvis inventus est qui glandem sine bombo projicit, nec tamen vehementer ut vel pullum interficere possit.*

It is not to be denied, there are ways to discharge a bullet, not only with Powder that makes no noise, but without any Powder at all; as is done by Water and Wind-guns, but these afford no fulminating Report, and depend on single principles. And even in ordinary Powder there are pretended other ways to alter the noise and strength of the discharge; and the best, if not only way, consists in the quality of the Nitre: for as for other ways which make either additions or alterations in the Powder, or charge, I find therein no effect: That unto every pound of Sulphur, an adjection of one ounce of Quick-silver, or unto every pound of Petre, one ounce of *Sal Armoniac* will much intend the force, and consequently the Report, as *Beringuccio* hath delivered, I find no success therein. That a piece of *Opium* will dead the force and blow, as some have promised, I find herein no such peculiarity, no more then in any Gum or viscose body: and as much effect there is to be found from *Scammony*. That a bullet dipped in oyl by preventing the transpiration of air, will carry farther, and pierce deeper, as *Porta* affirmeth, my experience cannot discern. That Quick-silver is more destructive then shot, is surely not to be made out; for it will scarce make any penetration, and discharged from a Pistol, will hardly pierce through a Parchment. That Vinegar, spirits of Wine, or the distilled water of Orange-pills, wherewith the Powder is tempered, are more effectual unto the Report than common Water, as some do promise, I shall not affirm; but may assuredly more conduce unto the preservation and durance of the Powder, as *Cataneo* hath well observed. Cat. avertimenti intorne a un Bombardiero.

That the heads of arrows and bullets have been discharged with that force, as to melt or grow red hot in their flight, though commonly received, and taken up by *Aristotle* in his Meteors, is not so easily allowable by any, who shall consider, that a Bullet of Wax will mischief without melting; that an Arrow or Bullet discharged against Linen or Paper do not set them on fire; and hardly apprehend how an Iron should grow red hot, since the swiftest motion at hand will not keep one red that hath been made red by fire; as may be observed in swinging a red hot Iron about, or fastning it into a Wheel; which under that motion will sooner grow cold then without it. That a Bullet also mounts upward upon the horizontall or point-blank discharge, many Artists do not allow: who contend that it describeth a parabolical and bowing line, by reason of its natural gravity inclining it always downward.

But, Beside the prevalence from Salt-petre, as Master-ingredient in the mixture; Sulphur may hold a greater use in the composition and further activity in the exclusion, then is by most conceived. For Sulphur vive makes better Powder then common Sulphur, which nevertheless is of a quick accension. For Small-coal, Salt-petre, and *Camphire* made into Powder will be of little force, wherein notwithstanding there wants not the accending ingredient. And *Camphire* though it flame well, yet will not flush so lively, or defecate Salt-petre, if you inject it thereon, like Sulphur; as in the preparation of *Sal prunellæ*. And lastly, though many ways may be found to light this Powder, yet is there none I know to make a strong and vigorous Powder of Salt-petre, without the admixtion of Sulphur. *Arsenic* red and yellow, that is *Orpement* and *Sandarach* may perhaps do something, as being inflamable and containing Sulphur in them; but containing also a salt, and mercurial mixtion, they will be of little effect; and white or crystalline *Arsenic* of less, for that being artificial, and sublimed with salt, will not endure flammation.

This Antipathy or contention between Salt-petre and Sulphur upon an actual fire, in their compleat and distinct bodies, is also manifested in their preparations, and bodies which invisibly contain them. Thus in the preparation of *Crocus Metallorum*, the matter kindleth and flusheth like Gunpowder, wherein notwithstanding, there is nothing but *Antimony* and Salt-petre. But this may proceed from the Sulphur of *Antimony*, not enduring the society of Salt-petre; for after three or four accensions, through a fresh addition of Petre, the Powder will flush no more, for the sulphur of the *Antimony* is quite exhaled. Thus Iron in *Aqua fortis* will fall into ebullition, with noise and emication, as also a crass and fumid exhalation, which are caused from this combat of the sulphur of Iron with the acid and nitrous spirits of *Aqua fortis*. So is it also in *Aurum fulminans*, or Powder of Gold dissolved in *Aqua Regis*, and precipitated with oyl of *Tartar*, which will kindle without an actual fire, and afford a report like Gun-powder; that is not as *Crollius* affirmeth from any Antipathy between *Sal Armoniac* Deconsensu Chymicorum, etc. and *Tartar*, but rather between the nitrous spirits of *Aqua Regis*, commixed *per minima* with the sulphur of Gold, as *Sennertus* hath observed.

How Coral of a Plant becomes a Stone.

6. That *Coral* (which is a *Lithophyton* or stone-plant, and groweth at the bottom of the Sea) is soft under Water, but waxeth hard in the air, although the assertion of *Dioscorides*, *Pliny*, and consequently *Solinus*, *Isidore*, *Rueus*, and many others, and stands believed by most, we have some reason to doubt, especially if we conceive with common Believers, a total softness at the bottom, and this induration to be singly made by the air, not only from so sudden a petrifaction and strange induration, not easily made out from the qualities of air, but because we find it rejected by experimental enquiries. In the French Copy. *Johannes Beguinus* in his Chapter of the tincture of *Coral* undertakes to clear the World of this Error, from the express experiment of *John Baptista de Nicole*, who was Overseer of the gathering of *Coral* upon the Kingdom of *Thunis*. This Gentleman, saith he, desirous to find the nature of *Coral*, and to be resolved how it groweth at the bottom of the Sea, caused a man to go down no less then a hundred fathom, with express to take notice whether it were hard or soft in the place where it groweth. Who returning, brought in each hand a branch of *Coral*, affirming it was as hard at the bottom, as in the air where he delivered it. The same was also confirmed by a trial of his own, handling it a fathom under water before it felt the air. *Boetius* in his Tract *De Gemmis*, is of the same opinion, not ascribing its concretion unto the air, but the coagulating spirits of Salt, and lapidifical juice of the Sea, which entring the parts of that Plant, overcomes its vegetability, and converts it into a lapideous substance. And this, saith he, doth happen when the Plant is ready to decay; for all *Coral* is not hard, and in many concreted Plants some parts remain unpetrified, that is the quick and livelier parts remain as Wood, and were never yet converted. Now that Plants and ligneous bodies may indurate under Water without approachment of air, we have experiment in *Coralline*, with many Coralloidal concretions; and that little stony Plant which Mr. *Johnson* nameth, *Hippuris coralloides*, and *Gesner*, *foliis mansu Arenosis*, we have found in fresh water, which is the less concretive portion of that Element. We have also with us the visible petrification of Wood in many waters, whereof so much as is covered with water converteth into stone; as much as is above it and in the air, retaineth the form of Wood, and continueth as before.

Gans *Histor. Coral*.

Now though in a middle way we may concede, that some are soft and others hard; yet whether all *Coral* were first a woody substance, and afterward converted; or rather some thereof were never such, but from the sprouting spirit of Salt, were able even in their stony natures to ramifie and send forth branches; as is observable in some stones, in silver and metallick bodies, is not without some question. And such at least might some of those be, which *Fiaroumti* observed to grow upon Bricks at the bottom of the Sea, upon the coast of *Barbaric*.

Of what matter the China dishes be made.

7. We are not throughly resolved concerning *Porcellane* or *China* dishes, that according to common belief they are made of Earth, which lieth in preparation about an hundred years under ground; for the relations thereof are not onely divers, but contrary, and Authors agree not

herein. *Guido Pancirollus* will have them made of Egg-shells, Lobster-shells, and *Gypsum* laid up in the Earth the space of 80 years: of the same affirmation is *Scaliger*, and the common opinion of most. *Ramuzius* in his Navigations is of a contrary assertion, that they are made out of Earth, not laid under ground, but hardned in the Sun and Wind, the space of forty years. But *Gonzales de Mendoza*, a man imployed into *China* from *Philip* the second King of *Spain*, upon enquiry and ocular experience, delivered a way different from all these. For inquiring into the artifice thereof, he found they were made of a Chalky Earth; which beaten and steeped in water, affordeth a cream or fatness on the top, and a gross subsidence at the bottom; out of the cream or superfluitance, the finest dishes, saith he, are made, out of the residence thereof the courser; which being formed, they gild or paint, and not after an hundred years, but presently commit unto the furnace. This, saith he, is known by experience, and more probable then what *Odoardus Barbosa* hath delivered, that they are made of shells, and buried under earth an hundred years. And answerable in all points hereto, is the relation of *Linschotten*, a diligent enquirer, in his Oriental Navigations. Later confirmation may be had from *Alvarez* the Jesuit, who lived long in those parts, in his relations of *China*. That *Porcellane* Vessels were made but in one Town of the Province of *Chiamsi*: That the earth was brought out of other Provinces, but for the advantage of water, which makes them more polite and perspicuous, they were only made in this. That they were wrought and fashioned like those of other Countries, whereof some were tincted blew, some red, others yellow, of which colour only they presented unto the King.

The latest account hereof may be found in the voyage of the Dutch Embassadors sent from *Batavia* unto the Emperour of *China*, printed in *French* 1665, which plainly informeth, that the Earth whereof *Porcellane* dishes are made, is brought from the Mountains of *Hoang*, and being formed into square loaves, is brought by water, and marked with the Emperours Seal: that the Earth it self is very lean, fine, and shining like Sand: and that it is prepared and fashioned after the same manner which the *Italians* observe in the fine Earthen Vessels of *Faventia* or *Fuenca*: that they are so reserved concerning that Artifice, that 'tis only revealed from Father unto Son: that they are painted with *Indico* baked in a fire for fifteen days together, and with very dry and not smoaking Wood: which when the Author had seen he could hardly contain from laughter at the common opinion above rejected by us.

Now if any enquire, why being so commonly made, and in so short a time, they are become so scarce, or not at all to be had? The Answer is given by these last Relators, that under great penalties it is forbidden to carry the first sort out of the Country. And of those surely the properties must be verified, which by *Scaliger* and others are ascribed unto China-dishes: That they admit no poison, that they strike fire, that they will grow hot no higher then the liquor in them ariseth. For such as pass amongst us, and under the name of the finest, will only strike fire, but not discover *Aconite*, *Mercury*, or *Arsenic*; but may be useful in dysenteries and fluxes beyond the other.

8. Whether a Carbuncle (which is esteemed the best and biggest of Rubies) doth flame in the dark, or shine like a coal in the night, though generally agreed on by common Believers, is very much questioned by many. By *Milius*, who accounts it a Vulgar Error: By the learned *Boetius*, who could not find it verified in that famous one of *Rodulphus*, which was as big as an Egg, and esteemed the best in *Europe*. Wherefore although we dispute not the possibility, and the like is said to have been observed in some Diamonds, yet whether herein there be not too high an apprehension, and above its natural radiancy, is not without just doubt: however it be granted a very splendid *Gem*, and whose sparks may somewhat resemble the glances of fire, and Metaphorically deserve that name. And therefore when it is conceived by some, that this Stone in the Brest-plate of *Aaron* respected the Tribe of *Dan*, who burnt the City of *Laish*; and *Sampson* of the same Tribe, who fired the Corn of the *Philistims*; in some sense it may be admitted, and is no intollerable conception.

As for that *Indian* Stone that shined so brightly in the Night, and pretended to have been shewn to many in the Court of *France*, as *Andreus Chioccus* hath declared out of *Thuanus*, it proved but an imposture, as that eminent Philosopher *Licetus* Licet de quæsit. per Epistolas. hath discovered, and therefore in the revised Editions of *Thuanus*, it is not to be found. Licet de lapide Bononiensi. As for the *Phosphorus* or *Bononian* Stone, which exposed unto the Sun, and then closely shut up, will afterward afford a light in the dark; it is of unlike consideration, for that requireth calcination or reduction into a dry powder by fire, whereby it imbibeth the light in the vaporous humidity of the air about it, and therefore maintaineth its light not long, but goes out when the vaporous vehicle is consumed.

9. Whether the *Ætites* or *Eagle*-stone hath that eminent property to promote delivery or restrain abortion, respectively applied to lower or upward parts of the body, we shall not discourage common practice by our question: but whether they answer the account thereof, as to be taken out of *Eagles* nests, co-operating in Women unto such effects, as they are conceived toward the young *Eagles*: or whether the single signature of one stone included in the matrix and belly of another, were not sufficient at first, to derive this vertue of the pregnant Stone, upon others in impregnation, may yet be farther considered. Many sorts there are of this ratling Stone, beside the *Geodes*, containing a softer substance in it. Divers are found in *England*, and one we met with on the Sea-shore, but because many of eminent use are pretended to be brought from *Iseland*, wherein are divers airies of *Eagles*, we cannot omit to deliver what we received from a learned person in that Country, Theodorus Ionas Hitterdalæ Pastor. *Ætites an in nidis Aquilarum aliquando fuerit repertus, nescio. Nostra certè memoria, etiam inquirentibus non contigit invenisse, quare in fabulis habendum.*

10. Terrible apprehensions and answerable unto their names, are raised of *Fayrie* stones, and *Elves* spurs, found commonly with us in Stone, Chalk, and Marl-pits, which notwithstanding are no more than *Echinometrites* and *Belemnites*, the Sea-Hedge-Hog, and the *Dart*-stone, arising from some siliceous Roots, and softer then that of Flint, the Master-stone, lying more regularly in courses, and arising from the primary and strongest spirit of the Mine. Of the *Echinites*, such as are found in Chalk-pits are white, glassie, and built upon a Chalky inside; some of an hard and flinty substance, are found in Stone-pits and elsewhere. Common opinion commendeth them for the Stone, but are most practically used against Films in Horses eyes.

11. Lastly, He must have more heads than *Rome* had Hills, that makes out half of those vertues ascribed unto stones, and their not only Medical, but Magical proprieties, which are to be found in Authors of great Name. In *Psellus, Serapion, Evax, Albertus, Aleazar, Marbodeus*; in *Maiolus, Rueus, Mylius*, and many more.

That *Lapis Lasuli* hath in it a purgative faculty we know; Against poison. that *Bezoar* is Antidotal, Provoking Urine. *Lapis Judaicus* diuretical, Against the Falling sickness. *Coral* Antepileptical, we will not deny. That *Cornelians, Jaspis, Heliotropes*, and Blood-stones, may be of vertue to those intentions they are implied, experience and visible effects will make us grant. But that an *Amethyst* prevents inebriation, that an *Emerald* will break if worn in copulation. That a *Diamond* laid under the pillow, will betray the incontinency of a wife. That a *Saphire* is preservative against inchantments; that the fume of an *Agath* will avert a tempest, or the wearing of a *Crysoprase* make one out love with Gold; as some have delivered, we are yet, I confess, to believe, and in that infidelity are likely to end our days. And therefore, they which in the explication of the two Beryls upon the *Ephod*, or the twelve stones in the Rational or Brestplate of *Aaron*, or those twelve which garnished the wall of the holy City in the Apocalyps, have drawn their significations from such as these; or declared their symbolical verities from such traditional falsities, have surely corrupted the sincerity of their Analogies, or misunderstood the mystery of their intentions.

Most men conceive that the twelve stones in *Aarons* brestplate made a Jewel surpassing any, and not to be parallel'd; which notwithstanding will hardly be made out from the description of the Text, for the names of the Tribes were engraven thereon, which must notably abate their lustre. Beside, it is not clear made out that the best of Gemms, a Diamond was amongst them; nor is to be found in the list thereof, set down by the *Jerusalem Thargum*, wherein we find the darker stones of *Sardius*, *Sardonix*, and *Jasper*; and if we receive them under those names wherein they are usually described, it is not hard to contrive a more illustrious and splendent Jewel. But being not ordained for meer lustre by diaphanous and pure tralucencies, their mysterious significations became more considerable then their Gemmary substances; and those no doubt did nobly answer the intention of the Institutor. Beside some may doubt whether there be twelve distinct species of noble tralucent Gemms in nature, at least yet known unto us, and such as may not be referred unto some of those in high esteem among us, which come short of the number of twelve; which to make up we must find out some others to match and join with the Diamond, *Beryl*, *Saphyr*, *Emerald*, *Amethyst*, *Topaz*, *Crysolit*, *Jacynth*, *Ruby*, and if we may admit it in this number, the Oriental Gianat.

CHAPTER VI
Of sundry Tenets concerning Vegetables or Plants, which examined, prove either false or dubious.

1. Many Mola's and false conceptions there are of *Mandrakes*, the first from great Antiquity, conceiveth the Root thereof resembleth the shape of Man; which is a conceit not to be made out by ordinary inspection, or any other eyes, then such as regarding the Clouds, behold them in shapes conformable to pre-apprehensions.

Now whatever encouraged the first invention, there have not been wanting many ways of its promotion. The first a Catachrestical and far derived similitude it holds with Man; that is, in a bifurcation or division of the Root into two parts, which some are content to call Thighs; whereas notwithstanding they are oft-times three, and when but two, commonly so complicated and crossed, that men for this deceit are fain to effect their design in other plants; And as fair a resemblance is often found in *Carrots*, *Parsnips*, *Briony*, and many others. There are, I confess, divers Plants which carry about them not only the shape of parts, but also of whole Animals, but surely not all thereof, unto whom this conformity is imputed. Whoever shall peruse the signatures of *Crollius*, or rather the Phytognomy of *Porta*, and strictly observe how vegetable Realities are commonly forced into Animal Representations, may easily perceive in very many, the semblance is but postulatory, and must have a more assimilating phansie then mine to make good many thereof.

Illiterate heads have been led on by the name Μάνδρα, Spelunca., which in the first syllable expresseth its Representation; but others have better observed the Laws of *Etymology*, and deduced it from a word of the same language, because it delighteth to grow in obscure and shady places; which derivation, although we shall not stand to maintain, yet the other seemeth answerable unto the Etymologies of many Authors, who often confound such nominal Notations. Not to enquire beyond our own profession, the Latine Physitians which most adhered unto the *Arabick* way, have often failed herein; particularly *Valescus de Tarranta*, In the old Edition. a received Physitian, in whose *Philonium* or Medical practice these may be observed: *Diarhea*, saith he, *Quia pluries venit in die. Herisepela, quasi hærens pilis, Emorrohis, ab emach sanguis & morrohis quod est cadere. Lithargia à Litos quod est oblivio & Targus morbus, Scotomia à Scotus quod est videre, & mias musca. Opthalmia ab opus Græce quod est succus, & Talmon quod est occulus. Paralisis, quasi læsio partis. Fistula à fos sonus & stolon quod est emissio, quasi emissio soni vel vocis.* Which are derivations as strange indeed as the other, and hardly to be parallel'd elsewhere; confirming not only the words of one language with another, but creating such as were never yet in any.

The received distinction and common Notation by Sexes, hath also promoted the conceit; for true it is, that *Herbalists* from ancient times have thus distinguished them, naming that the Male, whose leaves are lighter, and Fruit and Apples rounder; but this is properly no generative division, but rather some note of distinction in colour, figure or operation. For though *Empedocles* affirm, there is a mixt, and undivided Sex in Vegetables; and *Scaliger* upon *Aristotle* De Plantis., doth favourably explain that opinion; yet will it not consist with the common and ordinary acception, nor yet with *Aristotles* definition. For if that be Male which generates in another, that Female which procreates in it self; if it be understood of Sexes conjoined, all Plants are Female; and if of disjoined and congressive generation, there is no Male or Female in them at all.

The impostures touching the Root of Mandrake.

But the Atlas or main Axis which supported this opinion, was dayly experience, and the visible testimony of sense. For many there are in several parts of *Europe*, who carry about Roots and sell them unto ignorant people, which handsomely make out the shape of Man or Woman. But these are not productions of Nature, but contrivances of Art, as divers have noted, and *Mathiolus* plainly detected, who learned this way of Trumpery from a vagabond cheater lying under his cure for the French disease. His words were these, and may determine the point, *Sed profecto vanum & fabulosum, etc.* But this is vain and fabulous, which ignorant people, and simple women believe; for the roots which are carried about by impostors to deceive unfruitful women, are made of the roots of Canes, Briony and other plants: for in these yet fresh and virent, they carve out the figures of men and women, first sticking therein the grains of Barley or Millet, where they intend the hair should grow; then bury them in sand until the grains shoot forth their roots, which at the longest will happen in twenty days; they afterward clip and trim those tender strings in the fashion of beards and other hairy tegument. All which like other impostures once discovered is easily effected, and in the root of white *Briony* may be practised every spring.

What is therefore delivered in favour thereof, by Authors ancient or modern, must have its root in tradition, imposture, far derived similitude, or casual and rare contingency. So may we admit of the Epithet of *Pythagoras*, who calls it *Anthropomorphus* Orchis Anthropomorphus cujus Icon in Kircheri Magia parastatica.; and that of *Columella*, who terms it *Semihomo*; more appliable unto the Man-*Orchis*, whose flower represents a Man. Thus is *Albertus* to be received when he affirmeth, that *Mandrakes* represent man-kind with the distinction of either Sex. De mandragora. Under these restrictions may those Authors be admitted, which for this opinion are introduced by *Drusius*; nor shall we need to question the monstrous root of *Briony* described in *Aldrovandus* De monstris.

Generations equivocal, are yet commonly regular and of a determinate form or species.

The second assertion concerneth its production. That it naturally groweth under Gallowses and places of execution, arising from fat or urine that drops from the body of the dead; a story somewhat agreeable unto the fable of the Serpents teeth sowed in the earth by *Cadmus*; or rather the birth of *Orion* from the urine of *Jupiter, Mercury*, and *Neptune*. Now this opinion seems grounded on the former, that is, a conceived similitude it hath with man; and therefore from him in some way they would make out its production: Which conceit is not only erroneous in the foundation, but injurious unto Philosophy in the superstruction. Making putrifactive generations, correspondent unto seminal productions, and conceiving in equivocal effects and univocal conformity unto the efficient. Which is so far from being verified of animals in their corruptive mutations into Plants, that they maintain not this similitude in their nearer translation into animals. So when the Oxe corrupteth into Bees, or the Horse into Hornets, they come not forth in the image of their originals. So the corrupt and excrementous humours in man are animated into Lice; and we may observe, that Hogs, Sheep, Goats, Hawks, Hens, and others, have one peculiar and proper kind of vermine; not resembling themselves according to seminal conditions, yet carrying a setled and confined habitude unto their corruptive originals. And therefore come not forth in generations erratical, or different from each other; but seem specifically and in regular shapes to attend the corruption of their bodies, as do more perfect conceptions, the rule of seminal productions.

The third affirmeth the roots of *Mandrakes* do make a noise, or give a shriek upon eradication; which is indeed ridiculous, and false below confute: arising perhaps from a small and stridulous noise, which being firmly rooted, it maketh upon divulsion of parts. A slender foundation for such a vast conception: for such a noise we sometime observe in other Plants, in Parsenips, Liquorish, Eringium, Flags, and others.

The last concerneth the danger ensuing, That there follows an hazard of life to them that pull it up, that some evil fate pursues them, and they live not very long after. Therefore the attempt hereof among the Ancients, was not in ordinary way; but as *Pliny* informeth, when they intended to take up the root of this Plant, they took the wind thereof, and with a sword describing three circles about it, they digged it up, looking toward the *West*. A conceit not only injurious unto truth, and confutable by daily experience, but somewhat derogatory unto the providence of God; that is, not only to impose so destructive a quality on any Plant, but to conceive a Vegetable, whose parts are useful unto many, should in the only taking up prove mortal unto any. To think he suffereth the poison of *Nubia* [Granum Nubiæ.] to be gathered, *Napellus*, *Aconite*, and *Thora*, to be eradicated, yet this not to be moved. That he permitteth Arsenick and mineral poisons to be forced from the bowels of the Earth, yet not this from the surface thereof. This were to introduce a second forbidden fruit, and inhance the first malediction, making it not only mortal for *Adam* to taste the one, but capital unto his posterity to eradicate or dig up the other.

Now what begot, at least promoted so strange conceptions, might be the magical opinion hereof; this being conceived the Plant so much in use with *Circe*, and therefore named *Circea*, as *Dioscorides* and *Theophrastus* have delivered, which being the eminent Sorcerers of elder story, and by the magick of simples believed to have wrought many wonders: some men were apt to invent, others to believe any tradition or magical promise thereof.

Analogous relations concerning other plants, and such as are of near affinity unto this, have made its currant smooth, and pass more easily among us. For the same effect is also delivered by *Josephus*, concerning the root *Baaras*; by *Ælian* of *Cynospastus*; and we read in *Homer* the very same opinion concerning Moly,

Μῶλυ δέ μιν καλέουσι θεοί· χαλεπὸν δέ τ' ὀρύσσειν
Ἀνδράσι γε θνητοῖσι· θεοὶ δέ τε πάντα δύνανται.

The Gods it Moly call, whose Root to dig away,
Is dangerous unto Man; but Gods, they all things may.

Now parallels or like relations alternately relieve each other, when neither will pass asunder, yet are they plausible together; their mutual concurrences supporting their solitary instabilities.

Signaturists have somewhat advanced it; who seldom omitting what Ancients delivered; drawing into inference received distinction of sex, not willing to examine its humane resemblance; and placing it in the form of strange and magical simples, have made men suspect there was more therein, then ordinary practice allowed; and so became apt to embrace whatever they heard or read conformable unto such conceptions.

Lastly, The conceit promoteth it self: for concerning an effect whose trial must cost so dear, it fortifies it self in that invention; and few there are whose experiment it need to fear. For (what is most contemptible) although not only the reason of any head, but experience of every hand may well convict it, yet will it not by divers be rejected; for prepossessed heads will ever doubt it, and timorous beliefs will never dare to trie it. So these Traditions how low and ridiculous soever, will find suspition in some, doubt in others, and serve as tests or trials of Melancholy and superstitious tempers for ever.

That Cinamon, Ginger, Clove, etc., are not of the same tree.

2. That Cinamon, Ginger, Clove, Mace, and Nutmeg, are but the several parts and fruits of the same tree, is the common belief of those which daily use them. Whereof to speak distinctly, Ginger is the root of neither Tree nor Shrub, but of an herbaceous Plant, resembling the Water Flower-

De-luce, as *Garcias* first described; or rather the common Reed, as *Lobelius* since affirmed. Very common in many parts of *India*, growing either from Root or Seed, which in *December* and *January* they take up, and gently dried, roll it up in earth, whereby occluding the pores, they conserve the natural humidity, and so prevent corruption.

Cinamon is the inward bark of a Cinamon Tree, whereof the best is brought from *Zeilan*; this freed from the outward bark, and exposed unto the Sun, contracts into those folds wherein we commonly receive it. If it have not a sufficient isolation it looketh pale, and attains not its laudable colour; if it be sunned too long, it suffereth a torrefaction, and descendeth somewhat below it.

Clove seems to be either the rudiment of a fruit, or the fruit it self growing upon the Clove tree, to be found but in few Countries. The most commendable is that of the Isles of *Molucca*; it is first white, afterward green, which beaten down, and dried in the Sun, becometh black, and in the complexion we receive it.

Nutmeg is the fruit of a Tree differing from all these, and as *Garcias* describeth it, somewhat like a Peach; growing in divers places, but fructifying in the Isle of *Banda*, The fruit hereof consisteth of four parts; the first or outward part is a thick and carnous covering like that of a Walnut. The second a dry and flosculous coat, commonly called Mace. The third a harder tegument or shell, which lieth under the Mace. The fourth a Kernel included in the shell, which is the same we call Nutmeg. All which both in their parts and order of dispusure, are easily discerned in those fruits, which are brought in preserves unto us.

Now if because Mace and Nutmegs proceed from one Tree, the rest must bear them company; or because they are all from the *East Indies*, they are all from one Plant: the Inference is precipitous, nor will there such a Plant be found in the Herbal of Nature.

What the Misseltoe in some Trees is.

3. That Viscus Arboreus or Misseltoe is bred upon Trees, from seeds which Birds, especially Thrushes and Ring-doves let fall thereon, was the Creed of the Ancients, and is still believed among us, is the account of its production, set down by *Pliny*, delivered by *Virgil*, and subscribed by many more. If so, some reason must be assigned, why it groweth onely upon certain Trees, and not upon many whereon these Birds do light. For as Exotick observers deliver, it groweth upon Almond-trees, Chesnut, Apples, Oaks, and Pine-trees. As we observe in *England* very commonly upon Apple, Crabs, and White-thorn; sometimes upon Sallow, Hazel, and Oak: rarely upon Ash, Lime-tree, and Maple; never, that I could observe, upon Holly, Elm, and many more. Why it groweth not in all Countries and places where these Birds are found; for so *Brassavolus* affirmeth, it is not to be found in the Territory of *Ferrara*, and was fain to supply himself from other parts of *Italy*. Why if it ariseth from a seed, if sown it will not grow again, as *Pliny* affirmeth, and as by setting the Berries thereof, we have in vain attempted its production; why if it cometh from seed that falleth upon the tree, it groweth often downwards, and puts forth under the bough, where seed can neither fall nor yet remain. Hereof beside some others, the Lord *Verulam* hath taken notice. And they surely speak probably who make it an arboreous excrescence, or rather superplant, bred of a viscous and superfluous sap which the tree it self cannot assimilate. And therefore sprouteth not forth in boughs and surcles of the same shape, and similary unto the Tree that beareth it; but in a different form, and secondary unto its specified intention, wherein once failing, another form succeedeth: and in the first place that of Misseltoe, in Plants and Trees disposed to its production. And therefore also where ever it groweth, it is of constant shape, and maintains a regular figure; like other supercrescences, and such as living upon the stock of others, are termed parasitical Plants, as Polypody, Moss, the smaller Capillaries, and many more: So that several regions produce several Misseltoes; *India* one, *America* another, according to the law and rule of their degenerations.

Now what begot this conceit, might be the enlargement of some part of truth contained in its story. For certain it is, that some Birds do feed upon the berries of this Vegetable, and we meet in *Aristotle* with one kind of Trush called the Missel Trush Ἰξόβορος., or feeder upon Misseltoe.

But that which hath most promoted it, is a received proverb, *Turdus sibi malum cacat*; appliable unto such men as are authors of their own misfortunes. For according unto ancient tradition and *Plinies* relation, the Bird not able to digest the fruit whereon she feedeth; from her inconverted muting ariseth this Plant, of the Berries whereof Birdlime is made, wherewith she is after entangled. But although Proverbs be popular principles, yet is not all true that is proverbial; and in many thereof, there being one thing delivered, and another intended; though the verbal expression be false, the Proverb is true enough in the verity of its intention.

Paganish superstition about the Misseltoe of the Oak.

As for the Magical vertues in this Plant, and conceived efficacy unto veneficial intentions, it seemeth a *Pagan* relique derived from the ancient *Druides*, the great admirers of the Oak, especially the Misseltoe that grew thereon; which according unto the particular of *Pliny*, they gathered with great solemnity. For after sacrifice the Priest in a white garment ascended the tree, cut down the Misseltoe with a golden hook, and received it in a white coat; the vertue whereof was to resist all poisons, and make fruitful any that used it. Vertues not expected from Classical practice; and did they fully answer their promise which are so commended, in Epileptical intentions, we would abate these qualities. Country practice hath added another, to provoke the after-birth, and in that case the decoction is given unto Cows. That the Berries are poison as some conceive, we are so far from averring, that we have safely given them inwardly; and can confirm the experiment of *Brassavolus*, that they have some purgative quality.

4. The Rose of *Jericho*, that flourishes every year just about Christmas Eve, is famous in Christian reports; which notwithstanding we have some reason to doubt, and are plainly informed by *Bellonius*, it is but a Monastical imposture, as he hath delivered in his observations, concerning the Plants in *Jericho*. That which promoted the conceit, or perhaps begot its continuance, was a propriety in this Plant. For though it be dry, yet will it upon imbibition of moisture dilate its leaves, and explicate its flowers contracted, and seemingly dried up. And this is to be effected not only in the Plant yet growing, but in some manner also in that which is brought exuccous and dry unto us. Which quality being observed, the subtilty of contrivers did commonly play this shew upon the Eve of our Saviours Nativity, when by drying the Plant again, it closed the next day, and so pretended a double mystery: referring unto the opening and closing of the womb of *Mary*.

There wanted not a specious confirmation from a text in *Ecclesiasticus* Cap. 24. Quasi *palma exultata sum in Cades, & quasi plantatio Rosæ in Jericho*: I was exalted like a Palm-tree in *Engaddi*, and as a Rose in *Jericho*. The sound whereof in common ears, begat an extraordinary opinion of the Rose of that denomination. But herein there seemeth a mistake: for by the Rose in the Text, is implied the true and proper Rose, as first the Greek φύτα τοῦ ῥόδου. and ours accordingly rendreth it. But that which passeth under this name, and by us is commonly called the Rose of *Jericho*, is properly no Rose, but a small thorny shrub or kind of Heath, bearing little white flowers, far differing from the Rose; whereof *Bellonius* a very inquisitive *Herbalist*, could not find any in his travels thorow *Jericho*. A Plant so unlike a Rose, it hath been mistaken by some good *Simplist* for *Amomum*; which truly understood is so unlike a Rose, that as *Dioscorides* delivers, the flowers thereof are like the white Violet, and its leaves resemble *Briony*.

Suitable unto this relation almost in all points is that of the Thorn at *Glassenbury*, and perhaps the daughter hereof; herein our endeavours as yet have not attained satisfaction, and cannot therefore enlarge. Thus much in general we may observe, that strange effects are naturally taken for miracles by weaker heads, and artificially improved to that apprehension by wiser. Certainly many precocious Trees, and such as spring in the Winter, may be found in most parts of *Europe*, and divers also in *England*. Such a Thorn there is in Parham Park *in Suffolk, and elsewhere.* For most Trees do begin to sprout in the Fall of the leaf or Autumn, and if not kept back by cold and outward causes, would leaf about the Solstice. Now if it happen that any be so strongly constituted, as to make this good against the power of Winter, they may produce their leaves or blossoms in that season. And perform that in some singles, which is observable in whole kinds; as in *Ivy*, which blossoms and bears at least twice a year, and once in the Winter; as also in *Furz*, which flowereth in that season.

5. That *ferrum Equinum*, or *Sferra Cavallo* hath a vertue attractive of Iron, a power to break locks, and draw off the shoes of a Horse that passeth over it; whether you take it for one kind of *Securidaca*, or will also take in *Lunaria*, we know it to be false: and cannot but wonder at *Mathiolus*, who upon a parallel in *Pliny* was staggered into suspension. Who notwithstanding in the imputed vertue to open things, close and shut up, could laugh himself at that promise from the herb *Æthiopis* or *Æthiopian* mullen; and condemn the judgment of *Scipio*, who having such a picklock, would spend so many years in battering the Gates of *Carthage*. Which strange and Magical conceit, seems to have no deeper root in reason, then the figure of its seed; for therein indeed it somewhat resembles a Horse-shoe; which notwithstanding *Baptista Porta* hath thought too low a signification, and raised the same unto a Lunary representation.

How Beer and Wine come to be spoiled by Lightning.

6. That *Bayes* will protect from the mischief of Lightning and Thunder, is a quality ascribed thereto, common with the Fig-tree, Eagle, and skin of a Seal. Against so famous a quality, *Vicomercatus* produceth experiment of a Bay-tree blasted in *Italy*. And therefore although *Tiberius* for this intent, did wear a Lawrel upon his Temples, yet did *Augustus* take a more probable course, who fled under arches and hollow vaults for protection. And though *Porta* conceive, because in a streperous eruption, it riseth against fire, it doth therefore resist lightning, yet is that no emboldning Illation. And if we consider the threefold effect of *Jupiters* Trisulk, to burn, discuss, and terebrate; and if that be true which is commonly delivered, that it will melt the blade, yet pass the scabbard; kill the child, yet spare the mother; dry up the wine, yet leave the hogshead entire: though it favour the amulet, it may not spare us; it will be unsure to rely on any preservative, 'tis no security to be dipped in Styx, or clad in the armour of *Ceneus*. Now that Beer, Wine, and other liquors, are spoiled with lightning and thunder, we conceive it proceeds not onely from noise and concussion of the air, but also noxious spirits, which mingle therewith, and draw them to corruption; whereby they become not only dead themselves, but sometime deadly unto others, as that which *Seneca* mentioneth; whereof whosoever drank, either lost his life, or else his wits upon it.

How drinks intoxicate or overcome men.

7. It hath much deceived the hope of good fellows, what is commonly expected of bitter Almonds, and though in *Plutarch* confirmed from the practice of *Claudius* his Physitian, that Antidote against ebriety hath commonly failed. Surely men much versed in the practice do err in the theory of inebriation; conceiving in that disturbance the brain doth only suffer from exhalations and vaporous ascensions from the stomack, which fat and oyly substances may suppress. Whereas the prevalent intoxication is from the spirits of drink dispersed into the veins and arteries, from whence by common conveyances they creep into the brain, insinuate into its ventricles, and beget those vertigoes accompanying that perversion. And therefore the same effect may be produced by a Glister, the Head may be intoxicated by a medicine at the Heel. So the poisonous bites of Serpents, although on parts at distance from the head, yet having entered the veins, disturb the animal faculties, and produce the effects of drink, or poison swallowed. And so as the Head may be disturbed by the skin, it may the same way be relieved; as is observable in balneations, washings, and fomentations, either of the whole body, or of that part alone.

CHAPTER VII
Of some Insects, and the properties of several Plants.

1. Few ears have escaped the noise of the Dead-watch, that is, the little clickling sound heard often in many rooms, somewhat resembling that of a Watch; and this is conceived to be of an evil omen or prediction of some persons death: wherein notwithstanding there is nothing of rational presage or just cause of terrour unto melancholy and meticulous heads. For this noise is made by a little sheath-winged gray Insect found often in Wainscot, Benches, and Wood-work, in the Summer. We have taken many thereof, and kept them in thin boxes, wherein I have heard and seen them work and knack with a little *proboscis* or trunk against the side of the box, like *Apicus Martius*, or Woodpecker against a tree. It worketh best in warm weather, and for the most part

giveth not over under nine or eleven stroaks at a time. He that could extinguish the terrifying apprehensions hereof, might prevent the passions of the heart, and many cold sweats in Grandmothers and Nurses, who in the sickness of children, are so startled with these noises.

2. The presage of the year succeeding, which is commonly made from Insects or little Animals in Oak apples, according to the kinds thereof, either Maggot, Fly, or Spider; that is, of Famine, War, or Pestilence; whether we mean that woody excrescence, which shooteth from the branch about *May*, or that round and Apple-like accretion which groweth under the leaf about the latter end of Summer, is I doubt too distinct, nor verifiable from event.

For Flies and Maggots are found every year, very seldom Spiders: And *Helmont* affirmeth he could never find the Spider and the Fly upon the same Trees, that is the signs of War and Pestilence, which often go together: Beside, that the Flies found were at first Maggots, experience hath informed us; for keeping these excrescencies, we have observed their conversions, beholding in Magnifying Glasses the daily progression thereof. As may be also observed in other Vegetable excretions, whose Maggots do terminate in Flies of constant shapes; as in the Nutgalls of the Outlandish Oak, and the Mossie tuft of the wild Briar; which having gathered in *November* we have found the little Maggots which lodged in wooden Cells all *Winter*, to turn into Flies in *June*.

Abundance of Flies, Maggots, etc., what may they naturally signifie.

We confess the opinion may hold some verity in the Analogy, or Emblematical phansie. For Pestilence is properly signified by the Spider, whereof some kinds are of a very venemous Nature. Famine by Maggots, which destroy the fruits of the Earth. And War not improperly by the Fly; if we rest in the phansie of *Homer*, who compares the valiant *Grecian* unto a Fly.

Some verity it may also have in it self, as truly declaring the corruptive constitution in the present sap and nutrimental juice of the Tree; and may consequently discover the disposition of that year, according to the plenty or kinds of these productions. For if the putrifying juices of bodies bring forth plenty of Flies and Maggots, they give forth testimony of common corruption, and declare that the Elements are full of the seeds of putrifaction, as the great number of Caterpillars, Gnats, and ordinary Insects do also declare. If they run into Spiders, they give signs of higher putrifaction, as plenty of Vipers and Scorpions are confessed to do; the putrifying Materials producing Animals of higher mischiefs, according to the advance and higher strain of corruption.

3. Whether all Plants have seed, were more easily determinable, if we could conclude concerning Harts-tongue, Fern, the Caterpillaries, Lunaria, and some others. But whether those little dusty particles, upon the lower side of the leaves, be seeds and seminal parts; or rather, as it is commonly conceived, excremental separations, we have not as yet been able to determine by any germination or univocal production from them when they have been sowed on purpose: but having set the roots of Harts tongue in a garden, a year or two after there came up three or four of the same Plants, about two yards distance from the first. Thus much we observe, that they seem to renew yearly, and come not fully out till the Plant be in his vigour: and by the help of Magnifying Glasses we find these dusty Atoms to be round at first, and fully representing seeds, out of which at last proceed little Mites almost invisible; so that such as are old stand open, as being emptied of some bodies formerly included; which though discernable in Harts-tongue, is more notoriously discoverable in some differencies of Brake or Fern.

But exquisite Microscopes and Magnifying Glasses have at last cleared this doubt, whereby also long ago the noble *Fredericus Cæsius* beheld the dusts of Polypody as bigg as Pepper corns; and as *Johannes Faber* testifieth, made draughts on Paper of such kind of seeds, as bigg as his Glasses represented them: and set down such Plants under the Classis of *Herbæ Tergifætæ*, as may be observed in his notable Botanical Tables.

4. Whether the sap of Trees runs down to the roots in Winter, whereby they become naked and grow not; or whether they do not cease to draw any more, and reserve so much as sufficeth for conservation, is not a point indubitable. For we observe, that most Trees, as though they would be perpetually green, do bud at the Fall of the leaf, although they sprout not much forward untill the Spring, and warmer weather approacheth; and many Trees maintain their leaves all Winter, although they seem to receive very small advantage in their growth. But that the sap doth powerfully rise in the Spring, to repair that moisture whereby they barely subsisted in the Winter,

and also to put the Plant in a capacity of fructification: he that hath beheld how many gallons of water may in a small time be drawn from a Birch-tree in the Spring, hath slender reason to doubt.

5. That *Camphire* Eunuchates, or begets in Men an impotency unto Venery, observation will hardly confirm; and we have found it to fail in Cocks and Hens, though given for many days; which was a more favourable trial then that of *Scaliger*, when he gave it unto a Bitch that was proud. For the instant turgescence is not to be taken off, but by Medicines of higher Natures; and with any certainty but one way that we know, which notwithstanding, by suppressing that natural evacuation, may encline unto Madness, if taken in the Summer.

6. In the History of Prodigies we meet with many showrs of Wheat; how true or probable, we have not room to debate. Only thus much we shall not omit to inform, That what was this year found in many places, and almost preached for Wheat rained from the clouds, was but the seed of Ivy-berries, which somewhat represent it; and though it were found in Steeples and high places, might be conveyed thither, or muted out by Birds: for many feed thereon, and in the crops of some we have found no less then three ounces.

7. That every plant might receive a Name according unto the disease it cureth, was the wish of *Paracelsus*. A way more likely to multiply Empiricks then Herbalists; yet what is practised by many is advantagious unto neither; that is, relinquishing their proper appellations to re-baptize them by the name of Saints, Apostles, Patriarchs, and Martyrs, to call this the herb of *John*, that of *Peter*, this of *James*, or *Joseph*, that of *Mary* or *Barbara*. For hereby apprehensions are made additional unto their proper Natures; whereon superstitious practices ensue, and stories are framed accordingly to make good their foundations.

8. We cannot omit to declare the gross mistake of many in the Nominal apprehension of Plants; to instance but in few. An herb there is commonly called *Betonica Pauli*, or *Pauls Betony*; hereof the People have some conceit in reference to St. *Paul*; whereas indeed that name is derived from *Paulus Ægineta*, an ancient Physitian of *Ægina*, and is no more then Speed-well, or *Fluellen*. The like expectations are raised from *Herba Trinitatis*; which notwithstanding obtaineth that name from the figure of its leaves, and is one kind of Liverwort, or *Hepatica*. In *Milium Solis*, the Epithete of the Sun hath enlarged its opinion; which hath indeed no reference thereunto, it being no more then *Lithospermon*, or *Grummel*, or rather *Milium Soler*; which as *Serapion* from *Aben Juliel* hath taught us, because it grew plentifully in the Mountains of *Soler*, received that appellation. *Why the Jews ear is used for sore Throats.* In Jews-ears something is conceived extraordinary from the Name, which is in propriety but *Fungus sambucinus*, or an excrescence about the Roots of Elder, and concerneth not the Nation of the *Jews*, but *Judas Iscariot*, upon a conceit, he hanged on this Tree; and is become a famous Medicine in Quinsies, sore Throats, and strangulations ever since. And so are they deceived in the name of Horse-Raddish, Horse-Mint, Bull-rush, and many more: conceiving therein some prenominal consideration, whereas indeed that expression is but a Grecism, by the prefix of *Hippos* and *Bous*, that is, Horse and Bull, intending no more then Great. According whereto the great Dock is called *Hippolapathum*; and he that calls the Horse of *Alexander*, *Great-head*, expresseth the same which the *Greeks* do in *Bucephalus*.

9. Lastly, Many things are delivered and believed of other Plants, wherein at least we cannot but suspend. That there is a property in *Basil* to propagate Scorpions, and that by the smell thereof they are bred in the brains of men, is much advanced by *Hollerius*, who found this Insect in the brains of a man that delighted much in this smell. Wherein beside that we find no way to conjoin the effect unto the cause assigned; herein the Moderns speak but timorously, and some of the Ancients quite contrarily. For, according unto *Oribasius*, Physitian unto *Julian*, The *Affricans*, Men best experienced in poisons, affirm, whosoever hath eaten *Basil*, although he be stung with a Scorpion, shall feel no pain thereby: which is a very different effect, and rather antidotally destroying, then seminally promoting its production.

That the leaves of *Catapucia* or Spurge, being plucked upward or downward, respectively perform their operations by Purge or Vomit, as some have written, and old wives still do preach, is a strange conceit, ascribing unto Plants positional operations, and after the manner of the

Loadstone; upon the Pole whereof if a Knife be drawn from the handle unto the point, it will take up a Needle; but if drawn again from the point to the handle, it will attract it no more.

That Cucumbers are no commendable fruits, that being very waterish, they fill the veins with crude and windy serosities; that containing little Salt or spirit, they may also debilitate the vital acidity, and fermental faculty of the Stomach, we readily concede. But that they should be so cold, as be almost poison by that quality, it will be hard to allow, without the contradiction of *Galen* [In his *Anatomia Sambuci*.] who accounteth them cold but in the second degree, and in that Classis have most Physitians placed them.

That Elder Berries are poison, as we are taught by tradition, experience will unteach us. And beside the promises of *Blochwitius*, the healthful effects thereof daily observed will convict us.

That an Ivy Cup will separate Wine from Water, if filled with both, the Wine soaking through, but the Water still remaining, as after *Pliny* many have averred, we know not how to affirm; who making trial thereof, found both the liquors to soak indistinctly through the bowl.

That Sheep do often get the Rot, by feeding in boggy grounds where *Ros-solis* groweth, seems beyond dispute. That this herb is the cause thereof, Shepherds affirm and deny; whether it hath a cordial vertue by sudden refection, sensible experiment doth hardly confirm, but that it may have a Balsamical and resumptive Vertue, whereby it becomes a good Medicine in Catarrhes and Consumptive dispositions, Practice and Reason conclude. That the lentous drops upon it are not extraneous, and rather an exudation from it self, then a rorid concretion from without, beside other grounds, we have reason to conceive; for having kept the Roots moist and earthed in close chambers, they have, though in lesser plenty, sent out these drops as before.

That *Flos Affricanus* is poison, and destroyeth Dogs, in two experiments we have not found.

That Yew and the Berries thereof are harmless, we know.

That a Snake will not endure the shade of an Ash, we can deny. Nor is it inconsiderable what is affirmed by *Bellonius* [*Lib. 1 observat.*]; for if his Assertion be true, our apprehension is oftentimes wide in ordinary simples, and in common use we mistake one for another. We know not the true Thyme; the Savourie in our Gardens is not that commended of old; and that kind of Hysop the Ancients used, is unknown unto us, who make great use of another.

We omit to recite the many Vertues, and endless faculties ascribed unto Plants, which sometime occur in grave and serious Authors; and we shall make a bad transaction for truth to concede a verity in half. To reckon up all, it were employment for *Archimedes*, who undertook to write the number of the Sands. Swarms of others there are, some whereof our future endeavours may discover; common reason I hope will save us a labour in many: Whose absurdities stand naked unto every eye; Errours not able to deceive the Embleme of Justice, and need no *Argus* to descry them. Herein there surely wants expurgatory animadversions, whereby we might strike out great numbers of hidden qualities; and having once a serious and conceded list, we might with more encouragement and safety attempt their Reasons.

THE THIRD BOOK
Of divers popular and received Tenets concerning Animals, which examined, prove either false or dubious.

CHAPTER I
Of the Elephant.

The first shall be of the Elephant, whereof there generally passeth an opinion it hath no joints; and this absurdity is seconded with another, that being unable to lie down, it sleepeth against a Tree; which the Hunters observing, do saw it almost asunder; whereon the Beast relying, by the fall of the Tree, falls also down it self, and is able to rise no more. Which conceit is not the daughter of later times, but an old and gray-headed error, even in the days of *Aristotle*, as he delivereth in his Book, *De incessu Animalium*, and stands successively related by several other authors: by *Diodorus Siculus, Strabo, Ambrose, Cassiodore, Solinus*, and many more. Now herein methinks men much forget themselves, not well considering the absurdity of such assertions.

How progression is made in animals.

For first, they affirm it hath no joints, and yet concede it walks and moves about; whereby they conceive there may be a progression or advancement made in Motion without inflexion of parts. Now all progression or Animals locomotion being (as *Aristotle* teacheth) performed *tractu et pulsu*; that is, by drawing on, or impelling forward some part which was before in station, or at quiet; where there are no joints or flexures, neither can there be these actions. And this is true, not onely in Quadrupedes, Volatils, and Fishes, which have distinct and prominent Organs of Motion, Legs, Wings, and Fins; but in such also as perform their progression by the Trunk, as Serpents, Worms, and Leeches. *Joint-like parts.* Whereof though some want bones, and all extended articulations, yet have they arthritical Analogies, and by the motion of fibrous and musculous parts, are able to make progression. Which to conceive in bodies inflexible, and without all protrusion of parts, were to expect a Race from *Hercules* his pillars; or hope to behold the effects of *Orpheus* his Harp, when trees found joints, and danced after his Musick.

Again, While men conceive they never lie down, and enjoy not the position of rest, ordained unto all pedestrious Animals, hereby they imagine (what reason cannot conceive) that an Animal of the vastest dimension and longest duration, should live in a continual motion, without that alternity and vicissitude of rest whereby all others continue; and yet must thus much come to pass, if we opinion they lye not down and enjoy no decumbence at all. *Extensive or Tonical Motion, what?* For station is properly no rest, but one kind of motion, relating unto that which Physitians (from *Galen*) do name extensive or tonical; that is, an extension of the muscles and organs of motion maintaining the body at length or in its proper figure.

Wherein although it seem to be unmoved, it is not without all Motion; for in this position the muscles are sensibly extended, and labour to support the body; which permitted unto its proper gravity, would suddenly subside and fall unto the earth; as it happeneth in sleep, diseases, and death. From which occult action and invisible motion of the muscles in station (as *Galen* declareth) proceed more offensive lassitudes then from ambulation. And therefore the Tyranny of some have tormented men with long and enforced station, and though *Ixion* and *Sisiphus* which always moved, do seem to have the hardest measure; yet was not *Titius* favoured, that lay extended upon *Caucasus*; and *Tantalus* suffered somewhat more then thirst, that stood perpetually in Hell. Thus *Mercurialis* in his Gymnasticks justly makes standing one kind of exercise; and *Galen* when we lie down, commends unto us middle figures, that is, not to lye directly, or at length, but somewhat inflected, that the muscles may be at rest; for such as he termeth *Hypobolemaioi* or figures, of excess, either shrinking up or stretching out, are wearisome positions, and such as perturb the quiet of those parts. Now various parts do variously discover these indolent and quiet positions, some in right lines, as the wrists: some at right angles, as the cubit: others at oblique angles, as the fingers and the knees: all resting satisfied in postures of moderation, and none enduring the extremity of flexure or extension.

Moreover men herein do strangely forget the obvious relations of history, affirming they have no joints, whereas they dayly read of several actions which are not performable without them. They forget what is delivered by *Xiphilinus*, and also by *Suetonius* in the lives of *Nero* and *Galba*, that Elephants have been instructed to walk on ropes, in publick shews before the people. Which is not easily performed by man, and requireth not only a broad foot, but a pliable flexure of joints, and commandible disposure of all parts of progression. They pass by that memorable place in *Curtius*, concerning the Elephant of King *Porus*, *Indus qui Elephantem regebat, descendere eum ratus, more solito procumbere jussit in genua cæteri quoque (ita enim instituti erant) demisere corpora in terram.* *De rebus gestis Emanuelis.* They remember not the expression of *Osorius*, when he speaks of the Elephant presented to *Leo* the tenth, *Pontificem ter genibus flexis, et demisso corporis habitu venerabundus salutavit.* But above all, they call not to mind that memorable shew of *Germanicus*, wherein twelve Elephants danced unto the sound of Musick, and after laid them down in the *Tricliniums*, or places of festival Recumbency.

They forget the Etymologie of the Knee, Γόνυ *from* γωνία. approved by some Grammarians. They disturb the position of the young ones in the womb: which upon extension of legs is not easily conceivable; and contrary unto the general contrivance of Nature. Nor do they consider the impossible exclusion thereof, upon extension and rigour of the legs.

Lastly, they forget or consult not experience, whereof not many years past, we have had the advantage in *England*, by an Elephant shewn in many parts thereof, not only in the posture of standing, but kneeling and lying down. Whereby although the opinion at present be well suppressed, yet from some strings of tradition, and fruitful recurrence of errour, it is not improbable it may revive in the next generation again. This being not the first that hath been seen in *England*; for (besides some others) as *Polydore Virgil* relateth, *Lewis* the French King sent one to Henry the third, and *Emanuel* of *Portugal* another to *Leo* the tenth into *Italy*, where notwithstanding the errour is still alive and epidemical, as with us.

Round, Pillar-like.

The hint and ground of this opinion might be the gross and somewhat Cylindrical composure of the legs, the equality and less perceptible disposure of the joints, especially in the former legs of this Animal; they appearing when he standeth, like Pillars of flesh, without any evidence of articulation. The different flexure and order of the joints might also countenance the same, being not disposed in the Elephant, as they are in other quadrupedes, but carry a nearer conformity unto those of Man; that is, the bought of the fore-legs, not directly backward, but laterally and somewhat inward; but the hough or suffraginous flexure behind rather outward. Somewhat different unto many other quadrupedes, as Horses, Camels, Deer, Sheep, and Dogs; for their fore-legs bend like our legs, and their hinder legs like our arms, when we move them to our shoulders. But quadrupedes oviparous, as Frogs, Lizards, Crocodiles, have their joints and motive flexures more analogously framed unto ours; and some among viviparous, that is, such thereof as can bring their fore-feet and meat therein unto their mouths, as most can do that have the clavicles or coller-bones: whereby their brests are broader, and their shoulders more asunder, as the Ape, the Monkey, the Squirrel and some others. If therefore any shall affirm the joints of Elephants are differently framed from most of other quadrupedes, and more obscurely and grosly almost then any, he doth herein no injury unto truth. But if *à dicto secundum quid ad dictum simpliciter*, he affirmeth also they have no articulations at all, he incurs the controulment of reason, and cannot avoide the contradiction also of sense.

As for the manner of their venation, if we consult historical experience, we shall find it to be otherwise then as is commonly presumed, by sawing away of Trees. The accounts whereof are to be seen at large in *Johannes*, *Hugo*, *Edwardus Lopez*, *Garcias ab horto*, *Cadamustus*, and many more.

Other concernments there are of the Elephant, which might admit of discourse; and if we should question the teeth of Elephants, that is, whether they be properly so termed, or might not rather be called horns: it were no new enquiry of mine, but a Paradox as old as *Oppianus*. Cyneget. lib. 2. Whether as *Pliny* and divers since affirm it, that Elephants are terrified, and make away upon the grunting of Swine, *Garcias ab horto* may decide, who affirmeth upon experience, they enter their stalls, and live promiscuously in the Woods of *Malavar*. That the situation of the genitals is averse, and their copulation like that which some believe of Camels, as *Pliny* hath also delivered, is not to be received; for we have beheld that part in a different position; and their coition is made by supersaliency, like that of horses, as we are informed by some who have beheld them in that act. That some Elephants have not only written whole sentences, as *Ælian* ocularly testifieth, but have also spoken, as *Oppianus* delivereth, and *Christophorus à Costa* particularly relateth; although it sound like that of *Achilles* Horse in *Homer*, we do not conceive impossible. *Some* Brutes *tolerably well organized for speech and approaching to reason.* Nor beside the affinity of reason in this Animal any such intollerable incapacity in the organs of divers quadrupedes, whereby they might not be taught to speak, or become imitators of speech like Birds. Strange it is how the curiosity of men that have been active in the instruction of Beasts, have never fallen upon this artifice; and among those, many paradoxical and unheard of imitations, should not attempt to make one speak. The Serpent that spake unto *Eve*, the Dogs and Cats that usually speak unto Witches, might afford some encouragement. And since broad and thick chops are required in Birds that speak, since lips and teeth are also organs of speech; from these there is also an advantage in quadrupedes, and a proximity of reason in Elephants and Apes above them all. Since also an Echo will speak without any mouth at all, articulately returning the voice of man, by only ordering the vocal spirit in concave and hollow places; whether the musculous and motive parts about the hollow mouths of Beasts, may not dispose the passing spirit into some articulate notes, seems a query of no great doubt.

CHAPTER II
Of the Horse.

The second Assertion, that an Horse hath no gall, is very general, nor only swallowed by the people, and common Farriers, but also received by good *Veterinarians*, *Veterinarians or Farriers.* and some who have laudably discoursed upon Horses. It seemeth also very ancient; for it is plainly set down by *Aristotle*, an Horse and all solid ungulous or whole hoofed animals have no gall; and the same is also delivered by *Pliny*, which notwithstanding we find repugnant unto experience and reason. For first, it calls in question the providence or wise provision of Nature; who not abounding in superfluities, is neither deficient in necessities. Wherein nevertheless there would be a main defect, and her improvision justly accusable, if such a feeding Animal, and so subject unto diseases from bilious causes, should want a proper conveyance for choler; or have no other receptacle for that humour then the Veins, and general mass of bloud.

It is again controllable by experience, for we have made some search and enquiry herein; encouraged by *Absyrtus* a Greek Author, in the time of *Constantine*, who in his Hippiatricks *Medicina equaria.*, obscurely assigneth the gall a place in the liver; but more especially by *Carlo Ruini* the *Bononian*, who in his *Anatomia del Cavallo*, hath more plainly described it, and in a manner as I found it. For in the particular enquiry into that part, in the concave or simous part of the Liver, whereabout the Gall is usually seated in quadrupedes, I discover an hollow, long and membranous substance, of a pale colour without, and lined with Choler and Gall within; which part is by branches diffused into the lobes and several parcels of the Liver; from whence receiving the fiery superfluity, or cholerick remainder, by a manifest and open passage, it conveyeth it into the *duodenum* or upper gut, thence into the lower bowels; which is the manner of its derivation in Man and other Animals. And therefore although there be no eminent and circular follicle, no round bag or vesicle which long containeth this humour: yet is there a manifest receptacle and passage of choler from the Liver into the Guts: which being not so shut up, or at least not so long detained, as it is in other Animals: procures that frequent excretion, and occasions the Horse to dung more often then many other, which considering the plentiful feeding, the largeness of the guts, and their various circumvolution, was prudently contrived by providence in this Animal. *Choler the natural glister.* For choler is the natural Glister, or one excretion whereby Nature excludeth another; which descending daily into the bowels, extimulates those parts, and excites them unto expulsion. And therefore when this humour aboundeth or corrupteth, there succeeds oft-times a *cholerica passio*, that is, a sudden and vehement Purgation upward and downward: and when the passage of gall becomes obstructed, the body grows costive, and the excrements of the belly white; as it happeneth in the Jaundice.

If any therefore affirm an Horse hath no gall, that is, no receptacle, or part ordained for the separation of Choler, or not that humour at all; he hath both sense and reason to oppose him. But if he saith it hath no bladder of Gall, and such as is observed in many other Animals, we shall oppose our sense, if we gain-say him. Thus must *Aristotle* be made out when he denieth this part, by this distinction we may relieve *Pliny* of a contradiction, who in one place affirming an Horse hath no gall, delivereth yet in another, that the gall of an Horse was accounted poison; and therefore at the sacrifices of Horses in *Rome*, it was unlawful for the *Flamen* Priest. to touch it.

But with more difficulty, or hardly at all is that reconcileable which is delivered by our Countryman, and received *Veterinarian*; whose words in his Master-piece, and Chapter of diseases from the Gall, are somewhat too strict, and scarce admit a Reconciliation. The fallacie therefore of this conceit is not unlike the former; *A dicto secundum quid ad dictum simpliciter*. Because they have not a bladder of gall, like those we usually observe in others, they have no gall at all. Which is a Paralogism not admittible; a fallacy that dwels not in a cloud, and needs not the Sun to scatter it.

CHAPTER III
Of the Dove.

The third assertion is somewhat like the second, that a Dove or Pigeon hath no gall; which is affirmed from very great antiquity; for as *Pierius* observeth, from this consideration the Egyptians did make it the Hieroglyphick of Meekness. It hath been averred by many holy Writers, commonly delivered by *Postillers* and *Commentators*, who from the frequent mention of the Dove in the *Canticles*, the precept of our Saviour, to be wise as Serpents, and innocent as Doves: and especially the appearance of the Holy Ghost in the similitude of this Animal, have taken occasion to set down many affections of the Dove, and what doth most commend it, is, that it hath no gall. And hereof have made use not only Minor Divines, but *Cyprian, Austin, Isidore, Beda, Rupertus, Jansenius*, and many more.

Whereto notwithstanding we know not how to assent, it being repugnant unto the Authority and positive determination of ancient Philosophy. The affirmative of *Aristotle* in his History of Animals is very plain, *Fel aliis ventri, aliis intestino jungitur*: Some have the gall adjoined to the guts, as the Crow, the Swallow, Sparrow, and the Dove; the same is also attested by *Pliny*, and not without some passion by *Galen*, who in his Book *De Atra bile*, accounts him ridiculous that denies it.

It is not agreeable to the constitution of this Animal, nor can we so reasonably conceive there wants a Gall: that is, the hot and fiery humour in a body so hot of temper, which Phlegm or Melancholy could not effect. Salubrium, 31° Now of what complexion it is, *Julius Alexandrinus* declareth, when he affirmeth that some upon the use thereof, have fallen into Feavers and Quinsies. The temper of their Dung and intestinal Excretions do also confirm the same; which Topically applied become a *Phænigmus* or Rubifying Medicine, and are of such fiery parts, that as we read in *Galen*, they have of themselves conceived fire, and burnt a house about them. And therefore when in the famine of *Samaria* (wherein the fourth part of a Cab of Pigeons dung was sold for five pieces of silver,) it is delivered by *Josephus*, that men made use hereof in stead of common Salt: although the exposition seem strange, it is more probable then many other. For that it containeth very much Salt, as beside the effects before expressed, is discernable by taste, and the earth of Columbaries or Dove-houses, so much desired in the artifice of Salt-petre. And to speak generally, the Excrement of Birds hath more of Salt and acrimony, then that of other pissing animals. Now if because the Dove is of a mild and gentle nature, we cannot conceive it should be of an hot temper; our apprehensions are not distinct in the measure of constitutions, and the several parts which evidence such conditions. *Whence the irascible, whence the concupiscible Passions do most arise.* For the Irascible passions do follow the temper of the heart, but the concupiscible distractions the crasis of the liver. Now many have hot livers, which have but cool and temperate hearts; and this was probably the temper of *Paris*, a contrary constitution to that of *Ajax*, and both but short of *Medea*, who seemed to exceed in either.

Lastly, it is repugnant to experience, for Anatomical enquiry discovereth in them a gall: and that according to the determination of *Aristotle*, not annexed unto the liver, but adhering unto the guts: nor is the humour contained in smaller veins, or obscurer capillations, but in a vescicle, or little bladder, though some affirm it hath no bag at all. And therefore the Hieroglyphick of the Ægyptians, though allowable in the sense, is weak in the foundation: who expressing meekness and lenity by the portract of a Dove with a tail erected, affirmed it had no gall in the inward parts, but only in the rump, and as it were out of the body. And therefore also if they conceived their gods were pleased with the sacrifice of this Animal, as being without gall, the ancient Heathens were surely mistaken in the reason, and in the very oblation. Whereas in the holocaust or burnt offering of *Moses*, the gall was cast away: for as *Ben Maimon* instructeth Levit. 1., the inwards whereto the gall adhereth were taken out with the crop, according unto the Law: which the Priest did not burn, but cast unto the East, that is, behind his back, and readiest place to be carried out of the Sanctuary. Doves, the Birds of Venus, why? And if they also conceived that for this reason they were the Birds of *Venus*, and wanting the furious and discording part, were more acceptable unto the Deity of Love, they surely added unto the conceit, which was at first venereal: and in this Animal may be sufficiently made out from that conception.

The ground of this conceit is partly like the former, the obscure situation of the gall, and out of the liver, wherein it is commonly enquired. But this is a very injust illation, not well considering with what variety this part is seated in Birds. In some both at the stomach and the liver, as in the Capriceps; in some at the liver only, as in Cocks, Turkeys, and Pheasants; in others at the guts and liver, as in Hawks and Kites, in some at the guts alone, as Crows, Doves, and many more. And these perhaps may take up all the ways of situation, not only in Birds, but also other Animals; for what is said of the Anchovie, Ἐγκρασίχολος. that answerable unto its name, it carrieth the gall in the head, is farther to be enquired. And though the discoloured particles in the skin of an Heron be commonly termed Galls, yet is not this Animal deficient in that part, but containeth it in the Liver. And thus when it is conceived that the eyes of *Tobias* were cured by the gall of the fish *Callyonimus*, or *Scorpius marinus*, commended to that effect by *Dioscorides*, although that part were not in the liver, yet there were no reason to doubt that probability. And whatsoever Animal it was, it may be received without exception, when it's delivered, the married couple as a testimony of future concord, did cast the gall of the sacrifice behind the Altar.

A strict and literal acception of a loose and tropical expression was a second ground hereof. For while some affirmed it had no gall, intending only thereby no evidence of anger or fury; others have construed it anatomically, and denied that part at all. By which illation we may infer, and that from sacred Text, a Pigeon hath no heart; according to that expression, Hosea 7. *Factus est Ephraim sicut Columba seducta non habens Cor*. And so from the letter of the Scripture we may conclude it is no mild, but a fiery and furious animal, according to that of *Jeremy*, Cap. 25. *Facta est terra in desolationem à facie iræ Columbæ*: and again, *Revertamur ad terram nativitatis nostræ à facie gladii Columbæ*. Cap. 46. Where notwithstanding the Dove is not literally intended; but thereby may be implied the *Babylonians*, whose Queen *Semiramis* was called by that name, and whose successors did bear the Dove in their Standard. So is it proverbially said, *Formicæ sua bilis inest, habet et musca splenem*; whereas we know Philosophy doubteth these parts, nor hath *Anatomy* so clearly discovered them in those insects.

If therefore any affirm a Pigeon hath no gall, implying no more thereby then the lenity of this Animal, we shall not controvert his affirmation. Thus may we make out the assertions of Ancient Writers, and safely receive the expressions of Divines and worthy Fathers. But if by a transition from Rhetorick to Logick, he shall contend, it hath no such part or humour, he committeth an open fallacy, and such as was probably first committed concerning *Spanish* Mares, whose swiftness tropically expressed from their generation by the wind; might after be grosly taken, and a real truth conceived in that conception.

CHAPTER IV
Of the Bever.

That a Bever to escape the Hunter, bites off his testicles or stones, is a Tenet very ancient; and hath had thereby advantage of propagation. *Æsops Apologues, of what antiquity.* For the same we find in the Hieroglyphicks of the Egyptians in the Apologue of *Æsop*, an Author of great Antiquity, who lived in the beginning of the *Persian* Monarchy, and in the time of *Cyrus*: the same is touched by *Aristotle* in his Ethicks, but seriously delivered by *Ælian, Pliny*, and *Solinus*: the same we meet with in *Juvenal*, who by an handsome and Metrical expression more welcomly engrafts it in our junior Memories:

——*imitatus Castora, qui se*
Eunuchum ipse facit, cupiens evadere damno
Testiculorum, adeo medicatum intelligit inguen.

It hath been propagated by Emblems: and some have been so bad Grammarians as to be deceived by the Name, deriving *Castor à castrando*, whereas the proper Latine word is *Fiber*, and *Castor* but borrowed from the Greek, so called *quasi* γάστωρ, that is, *Animal ventricosum*, from his swaggy and prominent belly.

Herein therefore to speak compendiously, we first presume to affirm that from strict enquiry, we cannot maintain the evulsion or biting off any parts, and this is declarable from the best and most professed Writers: for though some have made use hereof in a Moral or Tropical way, yet have the professed Discoursers by silence deserted, or by experience rejected this assertion. Thus was it in ancient times discovered, and experimentally refuted by one *Sestius* a Physitian, as it stands related by *Pliny*; by *Dioscorides*, who plainly affirms that this tradition is false; by the discoveries of Modern Authors, who have expressly discoursed hereon, as *Aldrovandus, Mathiolus, Gesnerus, Bellonius*; by *Olaus Magnus, Peter Martyr*, and others, who have described the manner of their Venations in *America*; they generally omitting this way of their escape, and have delivered several other, by which they are daily taken.

The original of the conceit was probably Hieroglyphical, which after became Mythological unto the Greeks, and so set down by *Æsop*; and by process of tradition, stole into a total verity, which was but partially true, that is in its covert sense and Morality. Now why they placed this invention upon the Bever (beside the Medicable and Merchantable commodity of *Castoreum*, or parts conceived to be bitten away) might be the sagacity and wisdom of that Animal, which from the works it performs, and especially its Artifice in building, is very strange, and surely not to be matched by any other. Omitted by *Plutarch, De solertia Animalium*, but might have much advantaged the drift of that Discourse.

If therefore any affirm a wise man should demean himself like the Bever, who to escape with his life, contemneth the loss of his genitals, that is in case of extremity, not strictly to endeavour the preservation of all, but to sit down in the enjoyment of the greater good, though with the detriment and hazard of the lesser; we may hereby apprehend a real and useful Truth. In this latitude of belief, we are content to receive the Fable of *Hippomanes*, who redeemed his life with the loss of a Golden Ball; and whether true or false, we reject not the Tragœdy of *Absyrtus*, and the dispersion of his Members by *Medea*, to perplex the pursuit of her Father. But if any shall positively affirm this act, and cannot believe the Moral, unless he also credit the Fable; he is surely greedy of delusion, and will hardly avoid deception in theories of this Nature. The Error therefore and Alogy in this opinion, is worse then in the last; that is, not to receive Figures for Realities, but expect a verity in Apologues; and believe, as serious affirmations, confessed and studied Fables.

Again, If this were true, and that the Bever in chase makes some divulsion of parts, as that which we call *Castoreum*; yet are not the same to be termed Testicles or Stones; for these Cods or Follicles are found in both Sexes, though somewhat more protuberant in the Male. There is hereto no derivation of the seminal parts, nor any passage from hence, unto the Vessels of Ejaculation: some perforations onely in the part it self, through which the humour included doth exudate: as may be observed in such as are fresh, and not much dried with age. And lastly, The Testicles properly so called, are of a lesser magnitude, and seated inwardly upon the loins: and therefore it were not only a fruitless attempt, but impossible act, to Eunuchate or castrate themselves: and might be an hazardous practice of Art, if at all attempted by others.

Now all this is confirmed from the experimental Testimony of five very memorable Authors: *Bellonius*, *Gesnerus*, *Amatus*, *Rondeletius*, and *Mathiolus*: who receiving the hint hereof from *Rondeletius* in the Anatomy of two Bevers, did find all true that had been delivered by him, whose words are these in his learned Book *De Piscibus*: *Fibri in inguinibus geminos tumores habent, utrinque vnicum, ovi Auscrini magnitudine, inter hos est mentula in maribus, in fæminis pudendum, hi tumores testes non sunt, sed folliculi membrana contecti, in quorum medio sunguli sunt meatus è quibus exudat liquor pinguis et cerosus, quem ipse Castor sæpe admoto ore lambit et exugit, postea veluti oleo, corporis partes oblinit: Hos tumores testes non esse hinc maxime colligitur, quod ab illus nulla est ad mentulam via neque ductus quo humor in mentulæ meatum derivitur, et foras emittatur; præterea quod testes intus reperiuntur, eosdem tumores Moscho animali inesse puto, è quibus odoratum illud plus emanat.* Then which words there can be no plainer, nor more evidently discovering the impropriety of this appellation. That which is included in the cod or visible bag about the groin, being not the Testicle, or any spermatical part; but rather a collection of some superfluous matter deflowing from the body, especially the parts of nutrition as unto their proper emunctories; and as it doth in Musk and Civet Cats, though in a different and offensive odour; proceeding partly from its food, that being especially Fish; whereof this humour may be a garous excretion and olidous separation.

Most therefore of the Moderns before *Rondeletius*, and all the Ancients excepting *Sestius*, have misunderstood this part, conceiving *Castoreum* the Testicles of the *Bever*; as *Dioscorides*, *Galen*, *Ægineta*, *Ætius*, and others have pleased to name it. The Egyptians also failed in the ground of their Hieroglyphick, when they expressed the punishment of Adultery by the Bever depriving himself of his testicles, which was amongst them the penalty of such incontinency. Nor is *Ætius* perhaps, too strictly to be observed, when he prescribeth the stones of the Otter, or River-dog, as succedaneous unto *Castoreum*. But most inexcusable of all is *Pliny*, who having before him in one place the experiment of *Sestius* against it, sets down in another, that the *Bevers* of *Pontus* bite off their testicles: and in the same place affirmeth the like of the *Hyena*. Which was indeed well joined with the Bever, as having also a bag in those parts; if thereby we understand the *Hyena odorata*, or Civet Cat, as is delivered and graphically described by *Castellus*. Castellus de Hyena odorifera.

Now the ground of this mistake might be the resemblance and situation of these tumours about those parts, wherein we observe the testicles in other animals. Which notwithstanding is no well founded illation, for the testicles are defined by their office, and not determined by place or situation; they having one office in all, but different seats in many. For beside that, no Serpent, or Fishes oviparous, that neither biped nor quadruped oviparous have testicles exteriourly, or prominent in the groin; some also that are viviparous contain these parts within, as beside this Animal, the Elephant and the Hedg-hog.

If any therefore shall term these testicles, intending metaphorically, and in no strict acception; his language is tolerable, and offends our ears no more then the Tropical names of Plants: when we read in Herbals, of Dogs, Fox, and Goat-stones. But if he insisteth thereon, and maintaineth a propriety in this language: our discourse hath overthrown his assertion, nor will Logic permit his illation; that is, from things alike, to conclude a thing the same; and from an accidental convenience, that is a similitude in place or figure, to infer a specifical congruity or substantial concurrence in Nature.

CHAPTER V
Of the Badger.

That a Brock or Badger hath the legs on one side shorter then of the other, though an opinion perhaps not very ancient, is yet very general; received not only by Theorists and unexperienced believers, but assented unto by most who have the opportunity to behold and hunt them daily. Which notwithstanding upon enquiry I find repugnant unto the three Determinators of Truth, Authority, Sense, and Reason. For first, *Albertus Magnus* speaks dubiously, confessing he could not confirm the verity hereof; but *Aldrovandus* plainly affirmeth, there can be no such inequality observed. And for my own part, upon indifferent enquiry, I cannot discover this difference, although the regardable side be defined, and the brevity by most imputed unto the left.

Again, It seems no easie affront unto Reason, and generally repugnant unto the course of Nature; for if we survey the total set of Animals, we may in their legs, or Organs of progression, observe an equality of length, and parity of Numeration; that is, not any to have an odd legg, or the supporters and movers of one side not exactly answered by the other. Although the hinder may be unequal unto the fore and middle legs, as in Frogs, Locusts, and Grasshoppers; or both unto the middle, as in some Beetles and Spiders, as is determined by *Aristotle*, *De incessu Animalium*. **De incessu Animalium.** Perfect and viviparous quadrupeds, so standing in their position of proneness, that the opposite joints of Neighbour-legs consist in the same plane; and a line descending from their Navel intersects at right angles the axis of the Earth. It happeneth often I confess that a Lobster hath the Chely or great claw of one side longer then the other; but this is not properly their leg, but a part of apprehension, and whereby they hold or seiz upon their prey; for the legs and proper parts of progression are inverted backward, and stand in a position opposite unto these.

Lastly, The Monstrosity is ill contrived, and with some disadvantage; the shortness being affixed unto the legs of one side, which might have been more tolerably placed upon the thwart or Diagonial Movers. **Diagonion, a line drawn from the cross angles.** For the progression of quadrupeds being performed *per Diametrum*, that is the cross legs moving or resting together, so that two are always in motion, and two in station at the same time; the brevity had been more tolerable in the cross legs. For then the Motion and station had been performed by equal legs; whereas herein they are both performed by unequal Organs, and the imperfection becomes discoverable at every hand.

CHAPTER VI
Of the Bear.

That a Bear brings forth her young informous and unshapen, which she fashioneth after by licking them over, is an opinion not only vulgar, and common with us at present: but hath been of old delivered by ancient Writers. Upon this foundation it was an Hieroglyphick with the Egyptians: *Aristotle* seems to countenance it; *Solinus*, *Pliny*, and *Ælian* directly affirm it, and *Ovid* smoothly delivereth it:

Nec catulus partu quem reddidit ursa recenti
Sed male viva caro est, lambendo mater in artus
Ducit, et in formam qualem cupit ipsa reducit.

Which notwithstanding is not only repugnant unto the sense of every one that shall enquire into it, but the exact and deliberate experiment of three Authentick Philosophers. The first of *Mathiolus* in his Comment on *Dioscorides*, whose words are to this effect. In the Valley of *Anania* about *Trent*, in a Bear which the Hunters eventerated or opened, I beheld the young ones with all their parts distinct: and not without shape, as many conceive; giving more credit unto *Aristotle* and *Pliny*, then experience and their proper senses. Of the same assurance was *Julius Scaliger* in his Exercitations, *Ursam fœtus informes potius ejicere, quam parere, si vera dicunt, quos postea linctu effingat: Quid hujusce fabulæ authoribus fidei habendum ex hac historia cognosces; In nostris Alpibus venatores fætum Ursam cepere, dissecta ea fætus plane formatus intus inventus est*. And lastly, Aldrovandus who from the testimony of his own eyes affirmeth, that in the Cabinet of the Senate of *Bononia*, there was preserved in a Glass a Cub taken out of a Bear perfectly formed, and compleat in every part.

It is moreover injurious unto Reason, and much impugneth the course and providence of Nature, to conceive a birth should be ordained before there is a formation. For the conformation of parts is necessarily required, not onely unto the pre-requisites and previous conditions of birth, as Motion and Animation: but also unto the parturition or very birth it self: Wherein not only the Dam, but the younglings play their parts; and the cause and act of exclusion proceedeth from them both. For the exclusion of Animals is not meerly passive like that of Eggs, nor the total action of delivery to be imputed unto the Mother: but the first attempt beginneth from the Infant: which at the accomplished period attempteth to change his Mansion: and strugling to come forth, dilacerates and breaks those parts which restrained him before.

Beside (what few take notice of) Men hereby do in an high measure vilifie the works of God, imputing that unto the tongue of a Beast, which is the strangest Artifice in all the acts of Nature; that is the formation of the infant in the Womb, not only in Mankind, but all viviparous Animals. *Formation in the Matrix, the admirable work of Nature.* Wherein the plastick or formative faculty, from matter appearing Homogeneous, and of a similary substance, erecteth Bones, Membranes, Veins, and Arteries: and out of these contriveth every part in number, place, and figure, according to the law of its species. Which is so far from being fashioned by any outward agent, that once omitted or perverted by a slip of the inward *Phidias*, it is not reducible by any other whatsoever. And therefore *Mirè me plasmaverunt manus tuæ*, though it originally respected the generation of Man, yet is it appliable unto that of other Animals; who entring the Womb in bare and simple Materials, return with distinction of parts, and the perfect breath of life. He that shall consider these alterations without, must needs conceive there have been strange operations within; which to behold, it were a spectacle almost worth ones beeing, a sight beyond all; except that Man had been created first, and might have seen the shew of five dayes after.

Now as the opinion is repugnant both unto sense and Reason, so hath it probably been occasioned from some slight ground in either. Thus in regard the Cub comes forth involved in the Chorion, a thick and tough Membrane obscuring the formation, and which the Dam doth after bite and tear asunder; the beholder at first sight conceives it a rude and informous lump of flesh, and imputes the ensuing shape unto the Mouthing of the Dam; which addeth nothing thereunto, but only draws the curtain, and takes away the vail which concealed the Piece before. And thus have some endeavoured to enforce the same from Reason; that is, the small and slender time of the Bears gestation, or going with her young; which lasting but few days (a Month some say) the exclusion becomes precipitous, and the young ones consequently informous; according to that of *Solinus, Trigesimus dies uterum liberat ursæ; unde evenit ut præcipitata fæcunditas informes creet partus*. But this will overthrow the general Method of Nature in the works of generation. For therein the conformation is not only antecedent, but proportional unto the exclusion; and if the period of the birth be short, the term of conformation will be as sudden also. There may I confess from this narrow time of gestation ensue a Minority or smalness in the exclusion; but this however inferreth no informity, and it still receiveth the Name of a natural and legitimate birth; whereas if we affirm a total informity, it cannot admit so forward a term as an Abortment, for that supposeth conformation. So we must call this constant and intended act of Nature, a slip or effluxion Ἔκρυσις, that is an exclusion before conformation: before the birth can bear the name of the Parent, or be so much as properly called an *Embryon*.

CHAPTER VII
Of the Basilisk.

Many Opinions are passant concerning the Basilisk or little King of Serpents, commonly called the Cockatrice: some affirming, others denying, most doubting the relations made hereof. What therefore in these incertainties we may more safely determine: that such an Animal there is, if we evade not the testimony of Scripture and humane Writers, we cannot safely deny. So it is said *Psalm* 91. *Super Aspidem et Basiliscum ambulabis*, wherein the Vulgar Translation retaineth the Word of the Septuagint, using in other places the Latine expression *Regulus*, as *Proverbs* 23. *Mordebit ut coluber, et sicut Regulus venena diffundet*: and *Jeremy* 8. *Ecce ego mittam vobis serpentes Regulos, etc.* That is, as ours translate it, *Behold I will send Serpents, Cockatrices among you which will not be charmed, and they shall bite you.* And as for humane Authors, or such as have discoursed of Animals, or Poisons, it is to be found almost in all: in *Dioscorides, Galen, Pliny, Solinus, Ælian, Ætius, Avicen, Ardoynus, Grevinus*, and many more. In *Aristotle* I confess we find no mention thereof, but *Scaliger* in his Comment and enumeration of Serpents, hath made supply; and in his Exercitations delivereth that a Basilisk was found in *Rome*, in the days of *Leo* the fourth. The like is reported by *Sigonius*; and some are so far from denying one, that they have made several kinds thereof: for such is the *Catoblepas* of *Pliny* conceived to be by some, and the *Dryinus* of *Ætius* by others.

But although we deny not the existence of the Basilisk, yet whether we do not commonly mistake in the conception hereof, and call that a Basilisk which is none at all, is surely to be questioned. For certainly that which from the conceit of its generation we vulgarly call a Cockatrice, and wherein (but under a different name) we intend a formal Identity and adequate conception with the Basilisk; is not the Basilisk of the Ancients, whereof such wonders are delivered. For this of ours is generally described with legs, wings, a Serpentine and winding tail, and a crist or comb somewhat like a Cock. But the Basilisk of elder times was a proper kind of Serpent, not above three palms long, as some account; and differenced from other Serpents by advancing his head, and some white marks or coronary spots upon the crown, as all authentick Writers have delivered.

Nor is this Cockatrice only unlike the Basilisk, but of no real shape in Nature; and rather an Hieroglyphical fansie, to express different intentions, set forth in different fashions. Sometimes with the head of a Man, sometime with the head of an Hawk, as *Pierius* hath delivered; and as with addition of legs the Heralds and Painters still describe it. Nor was it only of old a symbolical and allowable invention, but is now become a manual contrivance of Art, and artificial imposure; whereof besides others, *Scaliger* hath taken notice: *Basilici formam mentiti sunt vulgo Gallinacco similem, et pedibus binis; neque enim absimiles sunt cæteris serpentibus, nisi macula quasi in vertice candida, unde illi nomen Regium*; that is, men commonly counterfeit the form of a Basilisk with another like a Cock, and with two feet; whereas they differ not from other serpents, but in a white speck upon their Crown. Now although in some manner it might be counterfeited in *Indian* Cocks, and flying Serpents, yet is it commonly contrived out of the skins of Thornbacks, Scaits, or Maids, as *Aldrovand* hath observed, [*By way of figure.*] and also graphically described in his excellent Book of Fishes; and for satisfaction of my own curiosity I have caused some to be thus contrived out of the same Fishes.

Nor is onely the existency of this animal considerable, but many things delivered thereof, particularly its poison and its generation. Concerning the first, according to the doctrine of the Ancients, men still affirm, that it killeth at a distance, that it poisoneth by the eye, and by priority of vision. *Destructive.* Now that deleterious it may be at some distance, and destructive without corporal contaction, what uncertainty soever there be in the effect, there is no high improbability in the relation. For if Plagues or pestilential Atoms have been conveyed in the Air from different Regions, if men at a distance have infected each other, if the shadows of some trees be noxious, if *Torpedoes* deliver their opium at a distance, and stupifie beyond themselves; we cannot reasonably deny, that (beside our gross and restrained poisons requiring contiguity unto their actions) there may proceed from subtiller seeds, more agile emanations, which contemn those Laws, and invade at distance unexpected.

That this venenation shooteth from the eye, and that this way a Basilisk may empoison, although thus much be not agreed upon by Authors, some imputing it unto the breath, others unto the bite, it is not a thing impossible. For eyes receive offensive impressions from their objects, and may have influences destructive to each other. *Effluxion of corporeal species.* For the visible species of things strike not our senses immaterially, but streaming in corporal raies, do carry with them the qualities of the object from whence they flow, and the medium through which they pass. *How the Basilisk kills at distance.* Thus through a green or red Glass all things we behold appear of the same colours; thus sore eyes affect those which are sound, and themselves also by reflection, as will happen to an inflamed eye that beholds it self long in a Glass; thus is fascination made out, and thus also it is not impossible, what is affirmed of this animal, the visible rayes of their eyes carrying forth the subtilest portion of their poison, which received by the eye of man or beast, infecteth first the brain, and is from thence communicated unto the heart.

But lastly, That this destruction should be the effect of the first beholder, or depend upon priority of aspection, is a point not easily to be granted, and very hardly to be made out upon the principles of *Aristotle*, *Alhazen*, *Vitello*, and others, who hold that sight is made by Reception, and not by extramission; by receiving the raies of the object into the eye, and not by sending any out. For hereby although he behold a man first, the Basilisk should rather be destroyed, in regard he first receiveth the rayes of his Antipathy, and venomous emissions which objectively move his sense; but how powerful soever his own poison be, it invadeth not the sense of man, in regard he beholdeth him not. And therefore this conceit was probably begot by such as held the opinion of sight by extramission; as did *Pythagoras*, *Plato*, *Empedocles*, *Hipparrchus*, *Galen*, *Macrobius*, *Proclus*, *Simplicius*, with most of the Ancients, and is the postulate of *Euclide* in his Opticks, but now sufficiently convicted from observations of the Dark Chamber.

The generation of the Cocks egg.

As for the generation of the Basilisk, that it proceedeth from a Cocks egg hatched under a Toad or Serpent, it is a conceit as monstrous as the brood it self. For if we should grant that Cocks growing old, and unable for emission, amass within themselves some seminal matter, which may after conglobate into the form of an egg, yet will this substance be unfruitful. As wanting one principle of generation, and a commixture of both sexes, which is required unto production, as may be observed in the eggs of Hens not trodden; and as we have made trial in some which are termed Cocks eggs. *Ovum Centeninum, or the last egg which is a very little one.* It is not indeed impossible that from the sperm of a Cock, Hen, or other Animal, being once in putrescence, either from incubation or otherwise, some generation may ensue, not univocal and of the same species, but some imperfect or monstrous production, even as in the body of man from putrid humours, and peculiar ways of corruption, there have succeeded strange and unseconded shapes of worms; whereof we have beheld some our selves, and read of others in medical observations. And so may strange and venomous Serpents be several ways engendered; but that this generation should be regular, and alway produce a Basilisk, is beyond our affirmation, and we have good reason to doubt.

Again, It is unreasonable to ascribe the equivocacy of this form unto the hatching of a Toad, or imagine that diversifies the production. For Incubation alters not the species, nor if we observe it, so much as concurs either to the sex or colour: as appears in the eggs of Ducks or Partridges hatched under a Hen, there being required unto their exclusion only a gentle and continued heat: and that not particular or confined unto the species or parent. So have I known the seed of Silk-worms hatched on the bodies of women: and *Pliny* reports that *Livia* the wife of *Augustus* hatched an egg in her bosome. Nor is only an animal heat required hereto, but an elemental and artificial warmth will suffice: for as *Diodorus* delivereth, the Ægyptians were wont to hatch their eggs in Ovens, and many eye-witnesses confirm that practice unto this day. And therefore this generation of the Basilisk, seems like that of *Castor* and *Helena*; he that can credit the one, may easily believe the other: that is, that these two were hatched out of the egg which *Jupiter* in the form of a Swan, begat on his Mistress *Leda*.

The occasion of this conceit might be an Ægyptian tradition concerning the Bird *Ibis*: which after became transferred unto Cocks. For an opinion it was of that Nation, that the *Ibis* feeding upon Serpents, that venomous food so inquinated their oval conceptions, or eggs within their bodies, that they sometimes came forth in Serpentine shapes, and therefore they always brake their eggs, nor would they endure the Bird to sit upon them. But how causeless their fear was herein, the daily incubation of Ducks, Pea-hens, and many other testifie, and the Stork might have informed them; which Bird they honoured and cherished, to destroy their Serpents.

That which much promoted it, was a misapprehension of holy Scripture upon the Latine translation in *Esa.* 51, *Ova aspidum ruperunt et telas Arenearum texuerunt, qui comedent de ovis corum morietur, et quod confotum est, erumpet in Regulum.* From whence notwithstanding, beside the generation of Serpents from eggs, there can be nothing concluded; and what kind of Serpents are meant, not easie to be determined, for Translations are here very different: *Tremellius* rendering the Asp Hæmorrhous, and the Regulus or Basilisk a Viper, and our translation for the Asp sets down a Cockatrice in the Text, and an Adder in the margin.

Another place of *Esay* doth also seem to countenance it, Chap. 14. *Ne læteris Philistæa quoniam diminuta est virga percussoris tui, de radice enim colubri egredietur Regulus, et semen ejus absorbens volucrem*, which ours somewhat favourably rendereth: *Out of the Serpents Root shall come forth a Cockatrice, and his fruit shall be a fiery flying Serpent.* But *Tremellius, è radice Serpentis prodit Hæmorrhous, et fructus illius præster volans*; wherein the words are different, but the sense is still the same; for therein are figuratively intended *Uzziah* and *Ezechias*; for though the Philistines had escaped the minor Serpent *Uzziah*, yet from his stock a fiercer Snake should arise, that would more terribly sting them, and that was *Ezeckias*.

But the greatest promotion it hath received from a misunderstanding of the Hieroglyphical intention. For being conceived to be the Lord and King of Serpents, to aw all others, nor to be destroyed *by any*; the Ægyptians hereby implied Eternity, and the awful power of the supreme Deitie: and therefore described a crowned Asp or Basilisk upon the heads of their gods. As may be observed in the Bembine Table, and other Ægyptian Monuments.

CHAPTER VIII
Of the Wolf.

Such a Story as the Basilisk is that of the Wolf concerning priority of vision, that a man becomes hoarse or dumb, if a Wolf have the advantage first to eye him. And this is a plain language affirmed by *Plyny*: *In Italia ut creditur, Luporum visus est noxius, vocemque homini, quem prius contemplatur adimere*; so is it made out what is delivered by *Theocritus*, and after him by *Virgil*:

——*Vox quoque Mœrim*
Jam fugit ipsa, Lupi Mœrim videre priores.

Thus is the Proverb to be understood, when during the discourse, if the party or subject interveneth, and there ensueth a sudden silence, it is usually said, *Lupus est in fabula.* Which conceit being already convicted, not only by *Scaliger, Riolanus*, and others; but daily confutable almost every where out of *England*, we shall not further refute.

The ground or occasional original hereof, was probably the amazement and sudden silence the unexpected appearance of Wolves do often put upon Travellers; not by a supposed vapour, or venomous emanation, but a vehement fear which naturally produceth obmutescence; and sometimes irrecoverable silence. Thus Birds are silent in presence of an Hawk, and *Pliny* saith that Dogs are mute in the shadow of an Hiæna. But thus could not the mouths of worthy Martyrs be silenced, who being exposed not onely unto the eyes, but the merciless teeth of Wolves, gave loud expressions of their faith, and their holy clamours were heard as high as Heaven.

That which much promoted it beside the common Proverb, was an expression in *Theocritus*, a very ancient Poet, οὐ φθέγξῃ λύκον εἶδες *Edere non poteris vocem, Lycus est tibi visus*; which *Lycus* was Rival unto another, and suddenly appearing stopped the mouth of his Corrival: now *Lycus* signifying also a Wolf, occasioned this apprehension; men taking that appellatively, which was to be understood properly, and translating the genuine acception. Which is a fallacy of Æquivocation, and in some opinions begat the like conceit concerning *Romulus* and *Remus*, that they were fostered by a Wolf, the name of the Nurse being *Lupa*; and founded the fable of *Europa*, and her carriage over Sea by a Bull, because the Ship or Pilots name was *Taurus*. And thus have some been startled at the Proverb, *Bos in lingua*, confusedly apprehending how a man should be said to have an Oxe in his tongue, that would not speak his mind; which was no more then that a piece of money had silenced him: for by the Oxe was onely implied a piece of coin stamped with that figure, first currant with the *Athenians*, and after among the *Romans*.

CHAPTER IX
Of the Deer.

The common Opinion concerning the long life of Animals, is very ancient, especially of Crows, Choughs and Deer; in moderate accounts exceeding the age of man, in some the days of *Nestor*, and in others surmounting the years of *Artephius* or *Methuselah*. From whence Antiquity hath raised proverbial expressions, and the real conception of their duration, hath been the Hyperbolical expression of many others. From all the rest we shall single out the Deer, upon concession a long-lived Animal, and in longævity by many conceived to attain unto hundreds; wherein permitting every man his own belief, we shall our selves crave liberty to doubt, and our reasons are these ensuing.

The first is that of *Aristotle*, drawn from the increment and gestation of this Animal, that is, its sudden arrivance unto growth and maturity, and the small time of its remainder in the Womb. His words in the translation of *Scaliger* are these, *De ejus vitæ longitudine fabulantur; neque enim aut gestatio aut incrementum hinnulorum ejusmodi sunt ut præstent argumentum longævi animalis*; that is, Fables are raised concerning the vivacity of Deer; for neither are their gestation or increment, such as may afford an argument of long life. And these, saith *Scaliger*, are good Mediums conjunctively taken, that is, not one without the other. For of Animals viviparous such as live long, go long with young, and attain but slowly to their maturity and stature. So the Horse that liveth above thirty, arriveth unto his stature about six years, and remaineth above ten moneths in the womb: so the Camel that liveth unto fifty, goeth with young no less then ten moneths, and ceaseth not to grow before seven; and so the Elephant that liveth an hundred, beareth its young above a year, and arriveth unto perfection at twenty. On the contrary, the Sheep and Goat, which live but eight or ten years, go but five moneths, and attain to their perfection at two years; and the like proportion is observable in Cats, Hares, and Conies. And so the Deer that endureth the womb but eight moneths, and is compleat at six years, from the course of Nature, we cannot expect to live an hundred; nor in any proportional allowance much more then thirty. As having already passed two general motions observable in all animations, that is, its beginning and encrease; and having but two more to run thorow, that is, its state and declination; which are proportionally set out by Nature in every kind: and naturally proceeding admit of inference from each other.

The other ground that brings its long life into question, is the immoderate salacity, and almost unparallel'd excess of venery, which every *September* may be observed in this Animal: and is supposed to shorten the lives of Cocks, Partridges, and Sparrows. Certainly a confessed and undeniable enemy unto longævity, and that not only as a sign in the complexional desire and impetuosity, but also as a cause in the frequent act, or iterated performance thereof. For though we consent not with that Philosopher, who thinks a spermatical emission unto the weight of one drachm, is æquivalent unto the effusion of sixty ounces of bloud; yet considering the exolution and languor ensuing that act in some, the extenuation and marcour in others, and the visible acceleration it maketh of age in most: we cannot but think it much abridgeth our days. Although we also concede that this exclusion is natural, that Nature it self will find a way hereto without either act or object: And although it be placed among the six Non-naturals, that is, such as neither naturally constitutive, nor meerly destructive, do preserve or destroy according unto circumstance: yet do we sensibly observe an impotency or total privation thereof, prolongeth life: and they live longest in every kind that exercise it not at all. *Eunuchs and gelded creatures generally longer lived.* And this is true not only in Eunuchs by Nature, but Spadoes by Art: for castrated Animals in every species are longer lived then they which retain their virilities. For the generation of bodies is not meerly effected as some conceive, of souls, that is, by Irradiation, or answerably unto the propagation of light, without its proper diminution: but therein a transmission is made materially from some parts, with the Idea of every one: and the propagation of one, is in a strict acception, some minoration of another. *From the parts of generation.* And therefore also that axiom in Philosophy, that the generation of one thing, is the corruption of another: although it be substantially true concerning the form and matter, is also dispositively verified in the efficient or producer.

As for more sensible arguments, and such as relate unto experiment: from these we have also reason to doubt its age, and presumed vivacity: for where long life is natural, the marks of age are late: and when they appear, the journey unto death cannot be long. Now the age of Deer (as *Aristotle* not long ago observed) is best conjectured, by view of the horns and teeth. From the horns there is a particular and annual account unto six years: they arising first plain, and so successively branching: after which the judgment of their years by particular marks becomes uncertain. But when they grow old, they grow less branched, and first do lose their ἀμυντῆρες or *propugnacula*; that is, their brow-antlers, or lowest furcations next the head, which *Aristotle* saith the young ones use in fight: and the old as needless, have them not at all. The same may be also collected from the loss of their Teeth, whereof in old age they have few or none before in either jaw. Now these are infallible marks of age, and when they appear, we must confess a declination: which notwithstanding (as men inform us in *England*, where observations may well be made), will happen between twenty and thirty. As for the bone, or rather induration of the Roots of the arterial vein and great artery, which is thought to be found only in the heart of an old Deer, and therefore becomes more precious in its Rarity; it is often found in Deer much under thirty, and we have known some affirm they have found it in one of half that age. And therefore in that account of *Pliny*, of a Deer with a Collar about his neck, put on by *Alexander* the Great, and taken alive an hundred years after, with other relations of this nature, we much suspect imposture or mistake. And if we grant their verity, they are but single relations, and very rare contingencies in individuals, not affording a regular deduction upon the species. For though *Ulysses* his Dog lived unto twenty, and the *Athenian* Mule unto fourscore, yet do we not measure their days by those years, or usually say, they live thus long. Nor can the three hundred years of *John* of times *Psalm 90.*, or *Nestor*, overthrow the assertion of *Moses*, or afford a reasonable encouragement beyond his septuagenary determination.

The ground and authority of this conceit was first Hierogliphical, the *Ægyptians* expressing longævity by this Animal; but upon what uncertainties, and also convincible falsities they often erected such Emblems, we have elsewhere delivered. And if that were true which *Aristotle* delivers of his time *Histor. animal. lib. 8.*, and *Pliny* was not afraid to take up long after, the *Ægyptians* could make but weak observations herein; for though it be said that *Æneas* feasted his followers with Venison, yet *Aristotle* affirms that neither Deer nor Boar were to be found in *Africa*. And how far they miscounted the lives and duration of Animals, is evident from their conceit of the Crow, which they presume to live five hundred years; and from the lives of Hawks, which (as *Ælian* delivereth) the *Ægyptians* do reckon no less then at seven hundred.

The second which led the conceit unto the *Grecians*, and probably descended from the Egyptians was Poetical; and that was a passage of *Hesiod*, thus rendered by *Ausonius*.

Ter binos deciesque novem super exit in annos,
Justa senescentum quos implet vita virorum.
Hos novies superat vivendo gorrula cornix,
Et quater egreditur cornicis sæcula cervus,
Alipidem cervum ter vincit corvus.——
To ninety six the life of man ascendeth,
Nine times as long that of the Chough extendeth,
Four times beyond the life of Deer doth go,
And thrice is that surpassed by the Crow.

So that according to this account, allowing ninety six for the age of Man, the life of a Deer amounts unto three thousand four hundred fifty six. A conceit so hard to be made out, that many have deserted the common and literal construction. So *Theon* in *Aratus* would have the number of nine not taken strictly, but for many years. In other opinions the compute so far exceedeth the truth, that they have thought it more probable to take the word *Genea*, that is, a generation consisting of many years, but for one year, or a single revolution of the Sun; which is the remarkable measure of time, and within the compass whereof we receive our perfection in the womb. So that by this construction, the years of a Deer should be but thirty six, as is discoursed at large in that Tract of *Plutarch*, concerning the cessation of Oracles; and whereto in his discourse of the Crow, *Aldrovandus* also inclineth. Others not able to make it out, have rejected the whole account, as may be observed from the words of *Pliny*, *Hesiodus qui primus aliquid de longævitate vitæ prodidit, fabulose (reor) multa de hominum ævo referens, cornici novem nostras attribuit ætates, quadruplum ejus cervis, id triplicatum corvis, et reliqua fabulosius de Phœnice et nymphis*. And this how slender soever, was probably the strongest ground Antiquity had for this longævity of Animals; that made *Theophrastus* expostulate with Nature concerning the long life of Crows; that begat that Epithete of Deer τετρακόρωνος. in *Oppianus*, and that expression of *Juvenal*,

——*Longa et cervina senectus.*

The third ground was Philosophical, and founded upon a probable Reason in Nature, that is, the defect of a Gall, which part (in the opinion of *Aristotle* and *Pliny*) this Animal wanted, and was conceived a cause and reason of their long life: according (say they) as it happeneth unto some few men, who have not this part at all. But this assertion is first defective in the verity concerning the Animal alledged: for though it be true, a Deer hath no Gall in the Liver like many other Animals, yet hath it that part in the Guts, as is discoverable by taste and colour: and therefore *Pliny* doth well correct himself, when having affirmed before it had no Gall, he after saith, some hold it to be in the guts; and that for their bitterness, dogs will refuse to eat them. The assertion is also deficient in the verity of the Induction or connumeration of other Animals conjoined herewith, as having also no Gall; that is, as *Pliny* accounteth, *Equi, Muli*, etc. Horses, Mules, Asses, Deer, Goats, Boars, Camels, Dolphins, have no Gall. In Dolphins and Porpoces I confess I could find no Gall. But concerning Horses, what truth there is herein we have declared before; as for Goats we find not them without it; what Gall the Camel hath, *Aristotle* declareth: that Hogs also have it, we can affirm; and that not in any obscure place, but in the Liver, even as it is seated in man.

That therefore the Deer is no short-lived Animal, we will acknowledge: that comparatively, and in some sense long-lived we will concede; and thus much we shall grant if we commonly account its days by thirty six or forty: for thereby it will exceed all other cornigerous Animals. But that it attaineth unto hundreds, or the years delivered by Authors, since we have no authentick experience for it, since we have reason and common experience against it, since the grounds are false and fabulous which do establish it: we know no ground to assent.

Concerning Deer there also passeth another opinion, that the Males thereof do yearly lose their pizzel. For men observing the decidence of their horns, do fall upon the like conceit of this part, that it annually rotteth away, and successively reneweth again. Now the ground hereof was surely the observation of this part in Deer after immoderate venery, and about the end of their Rut, which sometimes becomes so relaxed and pendulous, it cannot be quite retracted: and being often beset with flies, it is conceived to rot, and at last to fall from the body. But herein experience will contradict us: for Deer which either die or are killed at that time, or any other, are always found to have that part entire. And reason will also correct us: for spermatical parts, or such as are framed from the seminal principles of parents, although homogeneous or similary, will not admit a Regeneration, much less will they receive an integral restauration, which being organical and instrumental members, consist of many of those. Now this part, or Animal of *Plato*, containeth not only sanguineous and reparable particles: but is made up of veins, nerves, arteries, and in some Animals, of bones: whose reparation is beyond its own fertility, and a fruit not to be expected from the fructifying part it self. Which faculty were it communicated unto Animals, whose originals are double, as well as unto Plants, whose seed is within themselves: we might abate the Art of *Taliacotius*, and the new in-arching of Noses. And therefore the fancies of Poets have been so modest, as not to set down such renovations, even from the powers of their deities: for the mutilated shoulder of *Pelops* was pieced out with Ivory, and that the limbs of *Hippolitus* were set together, not regenerated by *Æsculapius*, is the utmost assertion of Poetry.

CHAPTER X
Of the King-fisher.

That a King-fisher hanged by the bill, sheweth in what quarter the wind is by an occult and secret propriety, converting the breast to that point of the Horizon from whence the wind doth blow, is a received opinion, and very strange; introducing natural Weather-cocks, and extending Magnetical positions as far as Animal Natures. A conceit supported chiefly by present practice, yet not made out by Reason or Experience.

Whence it is, that some creatures presage the weather.

Unto Reason it seemeth very repugnant, that a carcass or body disanimated, should be so affected with every wind, as to carry a conformable respect and constant habitude thereto. For although in sundry Animals we deny not a kind of natural Meteorology or innate presention both of wind and weather, yet that proceeding from sense receiving impressions from the first mutation of the air, they cannot in reason retain that apprehension after death, as being affections which depend on life, and depart upon disanimation. And therefore with more favourable Reason may we draw the same effect or sympathie upon the Hedg-hog, whose presention of winds is so exact, that it stoppeth the North or Southern hole of its nest, according to the prenotion of these winds ensuing: which some men observing, have been able to make predictions which way the wind would turn, and been esteemed hereby wise men in point of weather. Now this proceeding from sense in the creature alive, it were not reasonable to hang up an Hedg-hogs head, and to expect a conformable motion unto its living conversion. And though in sundry Plants their vertues do live after death, and we know that Scammony, Rhubarb and Senna will purge without any vital assistance; yet in Animals and sensible creatures, many actions are mixt, and depend upon their living form, as well as that of mistion; and though they wholly seem to retain unto the body, depart upon disunion. Thus Glow-worms alive, project a lustre in the dark, which fulgour notwithstanding ceaseth after death; and thus the Torpedo which being alive stupifies at a distance, applied after death, produceth no such effect; which had they retained in places where they abound, they might have supplied Opium, and served as frontals in Phrensies.

As for experiment, we cannot make it out by any we have attempted; for if a single King-fisher be hanged up with untwisted silk in an open room, and where the air is free, it observes not a constant respect unto the mouth of the wind, but variously converting, doth seldom breast it right. If two be suspended in the same room, they will not regularly conform their breasts, but oft-times respect the opposite points of Heaven. And if we conceive that for exact exploration, they should be suspended where the air is quiet and unmoved, that clear of impediments, they may more freely convert upon their natural verticity; we have also made this way of inquisition, suspending them in large and capacious glasses closely stopped; wherein nevertheless we observed a casual station, and that they rested irregularly upon conversion. Wheresoever they rested, remaining inconverted, and possessing one point of the Compass, whilst the wind perhaps had passed the two and thirty.

Commonly mistaken for the true Halcion, ours being rather the Ispida.

The ground of this popular practice might be the common opinion concerning the vertue prognostick of these Birds; as also the natural regard they have unto the winds, and they unto them again; more especially remarkable in the time of their nidulation, and bringing forth their young. For at that time, which happeneth about the brumal Solstice, it hath been observed even unto a proverb, that the Sea is calm, and the winds do cease, till the young ones are excluded; and forsake their nest which floateth upon the Sea, and by the roughness of winds might otherwise be overwhelmed. But how far hereby to magnifie their prediction we have no certain rule; for whether out of any particular prenotion they chuse to sit at this time, or whether it be thus contrived by concurrence of causes and providence of Nature, securing every species in their production, is not yet determined. Surely many things fall out by the design of the general motor, and undreamt of contrivance of Nature, which are not imputable unto the intention or knowledge of the particular Actor. So though the seminality of Ivy be almost in every earth, yet that it ariseth and groweth not, but where it may be supported; we cannot ascribe the same unto the distinction of the seed, or conceive any science therein which suspends and conditionates its eruption. So if, as *Pliny* and *Plutarch* report, the Crocodiles of *Ægypt* so aptly lay their Eggs, that the Natives thereby are able to know how high the floud will attain; it will be hard to make out, how they should divine the extent of the inundation depending on causes so many miles remote; that is, the measure of showers in *Æthiopia*; and whereof, as *Athanasius* in the life of *Anthony* delivers, the Devil himself upon demand could make no clear prediction. So are there likewise many things in Nature, which are the fore runners or signs of future effects, whereto they neither concur in causality or prenotion, but are secretly ordered by the providence of causes, and concurrence of actions collateral to their signations.

It was also a custome of old to keep these Birds in chests, upon opinion that they prevented Moths; whether it were not first hanged up in Rooms to such effects, is not beyond all doubt. Or whether we mistake not the posture of suspension, hanging it by the bill, whereas we should do it by the back; that by the bill it might point out the quarters of the wind; for so hath *Kircherus* described the Orbis and the Sea Swallow. But the eldest custome of hanging up these birds was founded upon a tradition that they would renew their feathers every year as though they were alive: In expectation whereof four hundred years ago *Albertus Magnus* was deceived.

VOL. II
PREFATORY NOTE

The frontispiece to this volume is reproduced from a photograph kindly lent to me for the purpose by Mr. Charles Williams, F.R.C.S.E., of Norwich, whose note upon the measurements of Sir Thomas Browne's skull appeared as Appendix II. in the edition of Browne's *Hydriotaphia* and *Garden of Cyrus*, published in the 'Golden Treasury Series,' by Messrs. Macmillan and Co., in 1896.

The identification of the author quoted in the margin of page 233 (Book v. Chapter x.). I owe to Mr. W. Aldis Wright.

C.S.

May 1, 1904.

PSEUDODOXIA EPIDEMICA

THE THIRD BOOK—*continued*

CHAPTER XI
Of Griffins.

That there are Griffins in Nature, that is a mixt and dubious Animal, in the fore-part resembling an Eagle, and behind, the shape of a Lion, with erected ears, four feet and a long tail, many affirm, and most, I perceive, deny not. The same is averred by *Ælian*, *Solinus*, *Mela*, and *Herodotus*, countenanced by the Name sometimes found in Scripture, and was an Hieroglyphick of the Egyptians.

Notwithstanding we find most diligent enquirers to be of a contrary assertion. For beside that *Albertus* and *Pliny* have disallowed it, the learned *Aldrovandus* hath in a large discourse rejected it; *Mathias Michovius* who writ of those Northern parts wherein men place these Griffins, hath positively concluded against it; and if examined by the Doctrine of Animals, the invention is monstrous, nor much inferiour unto the figment of Sphynx, Chimæra, and Harpies, for though there be some flying Animals of mixed and participating Natures, that is, between Bird and quadruped, yet are their wings and legs so set together, that they seem to make each other; there being a commixtion of both, rather then an adaptation or cement of prominent parts unto each other, as is observable in the Bat, whose wings and fore-legs are contrived in each other. For though some species there be of middle and participating Natures, that is, of Bird and Beast, as Bats and some few others, yet are their parts so conformed and set together, that we cannot define the beginning or end of either; there being a commixtion of both in the whole, rather then an adaptation or cement of the one unto the other.

Now for the word γρὺπς or *Gryps*, sometimes mentioned in Scripture *Levit. 11.*, and frequently in humane Authors, properly understood, it signifies some kind of Eagle or Vulture, from whence the Epithete *Grypus* for an hooked or Aquiline Nose. Thus when the Septuagint makes use of this word, *Tremellius* and our Translation hath rendred it the Ossifrage, which is one kind of Eagle. And although the Vulgar Translation, and that annexed unto the Septuagint, retain the word *Gryps*, which in ordinary and school construction is commonly rendred a Griffin, yet cannot the Latine assume any other sense then the Greek, from whence it is borrowed. And though the Latine *Gryphes* be altered somewhat by the addition of an *h*, or aspiration of the letter π, yet is not this unusual; so what the Greeks call τρόπαιον, the Latine will call *Trophæum*; and that person which in the Gospel is named Κλέοπας, the Latines will render *Cleophas*. And therefore the quarrel of *Origen* was unjust, and his conception erroneous, when he conceived the food of Griffins forbidden by the law of *Moses*: that is, Poetical Animals, and things of no existence. And therefore when in the Hecatombs and mighty Oblations of the Gentiles, it is delivered they sacrificed Gryphes or Griffins; hereby we may understand some stronger sort of Eagles. And therefore also when its said in *Virgil* of an improper Match, or *Mopsus* marrying *Nysa*, *Jungentur jam gryphes equis*; we need not hunt after other sense, then that strange unions shall be made, and different Natures be conjoined together.

As for the testimonies of ancient Writers, they are but derivative, and terminate all in one *Aristeus* a Poet of *Proconesus*; who affirmed that near the *Arimaspi*, or one-eyed Nation, Griffins defended the Mines of Gold. But this, as *Herodotus* delivereth, he wrote by hear-say; and *Michovius* who hath expresly written of those parts, plainly affirmeth, there is neither Gold nor Griffins in that Country, nor any such Animal extant; for so doth he conclude, *Ego vero contra veteres authores, Gryphes nec in illa septentrionis, nec in aliis orbis partibus inveniri affirmarim*.

Lastly, Concerning the Hieroglyphical authority, although it nearest approach the truth, it doth not infer its existency. The conceit of the *Griffin* properly taken being but a symbolical phansie, in so intollerable a shape including allowable morality. So doth it well make out the properties of a *Guardian*, or any person entrusted; the ears implying attention, the wings celerity of execution, the Lion-like shape, courage and audacity, the hooked bill, reservance and tenacity. It is also an Emblem of valour and magnanimity, as being compounded of the Eagle and Lion, the noblest Animals in their kinds; and so is it appliable unto Princes, Presidents, Generals, and all heroick Commanders; and so is it also born in the Coat-arms of many noble Families of *Europe*.

But the original invention seems to be Hieroglyphical, derived from the Egyptians, and of an higher signification. By the mystical conjunction of Hawk and Lion, implying either the Genial or the sydereous Sun, the great celerity thereof, and the strength and vigour in its operations. And therefore under such Hieroglyphicks *Osyris* was described; and in ancient Coins we meet with Gryphins conjointly with *Apollo's*, *Tripodes* and Chariot wheels; and the marble Gryphins at Saint *Peters* in *Rome*, as learned men conjecture, were first translated from the Temple of *Apollo*. Whether hereby were not also mystically implied the activity of the Sun in Leo, the power of God in the Sun, or the influence of the Cœlestial *Osyris*, by *Moptha* the Genius of Nilus, might also be considered. And then the learned *Kircherus*, no man were likely to be a better *Oedipus*.

CHAPTER XII
Of the Phœnix.

That there is but one Phœnix in the World, which after many hundred years burneth it self, and from the ashes thereof ariseth up another, is a conceit not new or altogether popular, but of great Antiquity; not only delivered by humane Authors, but frequently expressed also by holy Writers; by *Cyril*, *Epiphanius*, and others, by *Ambrose* in his Hexameron, and *Tertullian* in his Poem *De Judicio Domini*; but more agreeably unto the present sense, in his excellent Tract, *De Resurrectione carnis. Illum dico alitem orientis peculiarem, de singularitate famosum, de posteritate monstruosum; qui semetipsum libenter funerans renovat, natali fine decedens, atque succedens iterum Phœnix. Ubi jam nemo, iterum ipse; quia non jam, alius idem*. The Scripture also seems to favour it, particularly that of *Job* 21. In the interpretation of *Beda, Dicebam in nidulo meo moriar, et sicut Phœnix multiplicabo dies*: and *Psal*. 31. δίκαιος ὥσπερ φοῖνιξ ἀνθήσει, *vir justus ut Phœnix florebit*, as *Tertullian* renders it, and so also expounds it in his Book before alledged.

Against the story of the Phœnix.

All which notwithstanding, we cannot presume the existence of this Animal; nor dare we affirm there is any Phœnix in Nature. For, first there wants herein the definitive confirmator and test of things uncertain, that is, the sense of man. For though many Writers have much enlarged hereon, yet is there not any ocular describer, or such as presumeth to confirm it upon aspection. And therefore *Herodotus* that led the story unto the *Greeks*, plainly saith, he never attained the sight of any, but only in the picture.

Again, Primitive Authors, and from whom the stream of relations is derivative, deliver themselves very dubiously; and either by a doubtful parenthesis, or a timorous conclusion overthrow the whole relation. Thus *Herodotus* in his *Euterpe*, delivering the story hereof, presently interposeth, ἐμοὶ μὲν οὐ πιστὰ λέγοντες; that is, which account seems to me improbable. *Tacitus* in his annals affordeth a larger story, how the Phœnix was first seen at *Heliopolis* in the reign of *Sesostris*, then in the reign of *Amasis*, after in the days of *Ptolomy*, the third of the *Macedonian* race; but at last thus determineth, *Sed Antiquitas obscura, et nonnulli falsum esse hunc Phœnicem neque Arabum è terris crediere*. *Pliny* makes yet a fairer story, that the Phœnix flew into *Egypt* in the Consulship of *Quintus Plancius*, that it was brought to

Rome in the Censorship of *Claudius*, in the eight hundred year of the City, and testified also in their records; but after all concludeth, *Sed quæ falsa nemo dubitabit*, As we read it in the fair and ancient impression of *Brixia*; as *Aldrovandus* hath quoted it, and as it is found in the manuscript Copy, as *Dalechampius* hath also noted.

Moreover, Such as have naturally discoursed hereon, have so diversly, contrarily, or contradictorily delivered themselves, that no affirmative from thence can reasonably be deduced. For most have positively denied it, and they which affirm and believe it, assign this name unto many, and mistake two or three in one. So hath that bird been taken for the Phœnix which liveth in *Arabia*, and buildeth its nest with Cinnamon; by *Herodotus* called *Cinnamulgus*, and by *Aristotle*, *Cinnamomus*; and as a fabulous conceit is censured by *Scaliger*. Some have conceived that bird to be the Phœnix, which by a *Persian* name with the *Greeks* is called *Rhyntace*; but how they made this good we find occasion of doubt; whilest we read in the life of *Artaxerxes*, that this is a little bird brought often to their Tables, and wherewith *Parysatis* cunningly poisoned the Queen. The *Manucodiata* or Bird of Paradise, hath had the honour of this name, and their feathers brought from the *Molucca's* do pass for those of the Phœnix. Which though promoted by rarity with us, the *Eastern* Travellers will hardly admit; who know they are common in those parts, and the ordinary plume of *Janizaries* among the *Turks*. And lastly, the Bird *Semenda* hath found the same appellation, for so hath *Scaliger* observed and refuted; nor will the solitude of the Phœnix allow this denomination; for many there are of that species, and whose trifistulary bill and crany we have beheld our selves. Nor are men only at variance in regard of the Phœnix it self, but very disagreeing in the accidents ascribed thereto: for some affirm it liveth three hundred, some five, others six, some a thousand, others no less then fifteen hundred years; some say it liveth in *Æthiopia*, others in *Arabia*, some in *Egypt*, others in *India*, and some in *Utopia*; for such a one must that be which is described by *Lactantius*; that is, which neither was singed in the combustion of *Phaeton*, or overwhelmed by the innundation of *Deucalion*.

Lastly, Many Authors who have discoursed hereof, have so delivered themselves, and with such intentions, that we cannot from thence deduce a confirmation. For some have written Poetically, as *Ovid, Mantuan, Lactantius, Claudian,* and others: Some have written mystically, as *Paracelsus* in his Book *De Azoth*, or *De ligno et linea vitæ*; and as several Hermetical Philosophers, involving therein the secret of their Elixir, and enigmatically expressing the nature of their great work. Some have written Rhetorically, and concessively, not controverting, but assuming the question, which taken as granted, advantaged the illation. So have holy men made use hereof as far as thereby to confirm the Resurrection; for discoursing with Heathens who granted the story of the Phœnix, they induced the Resurrection from principles of their own, and positions received among themselves. Others have spoken Emblematically and Hieroglyphically; and so did the *Egyptians*, unto whom the Phœnix was the Hieroglyphick of the Sun. And this was probably the ground of the whole relation; succeeding Ages adding fabulous accounts, which laid together built up this singularity, which every Pen proclaimeth.

As for the Texts of Scripture, which seem to confirm the conceit, duly perpended, they add not thereunto. For whereas in that of *Job*, according to the Septuagint or Greek Translation we find the word Phœnix, yet can it have no animal signification; for therein it is not expressed φοῖνιξ, but στέλεχος φοίνικος, the trunk of the Palm-tree, which is also called Phœnix; and therefore the construction will be very hard, if not applied unto some vegetable nature. Nor can we safely insist upon the Greek expression at all; for though the Vulgar translates it *Palma*, and some retain the word Phœnix, others do render it by a word of a different sense; for so hath *Tremellius* delivered it: *Dicebam quod apud nidum meum expirabo, et sicut arena multiplicabo dies*; so hath the *Geneva* and ours translated it, *I said I shall die in my Nest, and shall multiply my days as the sand.* As for that in the Book of Psalms, *Vir justus ut Phœnix florebit*, as *Epiphanius* and *Tertullian* render it, it was only a mistake upon the Homonymy of the Greek word Pœnix, which signifies also a Palm-tree. | Consent of names. | Which is a fallacy of equivocation, from a community in name inferring a common nature; and whereby we may as firmly conclude, that Diaphœnicon a purging Electuary hath some part of the Phœnix for its ingredient; which receiveth that name from Dates, or the fruit of the Palm-tree, from whence, as *Pliny* delivers, the Phœnix had its name.

Nor do we only arraign the existence of this Animal, but many things are questionable which are ascribed thereto, especially its unity, long life, and generation. As for its unity or conceit there should be but one in nature, it seemeth not only repugnant unto Philosophy, but also holy Scripture; which plainly affirms, there went of every sort two at least into the Ark of *Noah*, according to the Text, Gen. 7. *Every Fowl after his kind, every bird of every sort, they went into the Ark, two and two of all flesh, wherein there is the breath of life, and they that went in, went in both male and female of all flesh.* It infringeth the benediction of God concerning multiplication. God blessed them, saying, Gen. 1. *Be fruitful and multiply, and fill the waters in the seas, and let fowl multiply in the earth:* And again Chap. 8. *, Bring forth with thee every living thing, that they may breed abundantly in the earth, and be fruitful and multiply upon the earth:* which terms are not appliable unto the Phœnix, whereof there is but one in the world, and no more now living then at the first benediction. For the production of one, being the destruction of another, although they produce and generate, they encrease not; and must not be said to multiply, who do not transcend an unity.

As for longævity, that it liveth a thousand years or more; beside that from imperfect observations and rarity of appearance, no confirmation can be made; there may be probable a mistake in the compute. For the tradition being very ancient and probably Egyptian, the *Greeks* who dispersed the Fable, might summ up the account by their own numeration of years; whereas the conceit might have its original in times of shorter compute. For if we suppose our present calculation, the Phœnix now in nature will be the sixth from the Creation, but in the middle of its years; and if the *Rabbins* Prophecie That the World should last but six thousand years. succeed, shall conclude its days not in his own but the last and general flames, without all hope of Reviviction.

Concerning its generation, that without all conjunction it begets and reseminates it self, hereby we introduce a vegetable production in Animals, and unto sensible natures, transfer the propriety of Plants; that is, to multiply within themselves, according to the Law of the Creation Gen. 1. , *Let the earth bring forth grass, the herb yielding seed, and the tree yielding fruit, whose seed is in it self*. Which is indeed the natural way of Plants, who having no distinction of sex, and the power of the species contained in every *individuum*, beget and propagate themselves without commixtion; and therefore their fruits proceeding from simpler roots, are not so unlike, or distinguishable from each other, as are the off-springs of sensible creatures and prolifications descending from double originals. But Animal generation is accomplished by more, and the concurrence of two sexes is required to the constitution of one. And therefore such as have no distinction of sex, engender not at all, as *Aristotle* conceives of Eels, and testaceous animals. And though Plant-animals do multiply, they do it not by copulation, but in a way analogous unto Plants. So *Hermaphrodites* although they include the parts of both sexes, and may be sufficiently potent in either; yet unto a conception require a separated sex, and cannot impregnate themselves. And so also though *Adam* included all humane nature, or was (as some opinion) an *Hermaphrodite*, yet had he no power to propagate himself; and therefore God said, *It is not good that man should be alone, let us make him an help meet for him*; that is, an help unto generation; for as for any other help, it had been fitter to have made another man.

Now whereas some affirm that from one Phœnix there doth not immediately proceed another, but the first corrupteth into a worm, which after becometh a Phœnix, it will not make probable this production. *Irregularities.* For hereby they confound the generation of perfect animals with imperfect, sanguineous with exanguious, vermiparous with oviparous, and erect Anomalies, disturbing the laws of Nature. Nor will this corruptive production be easily made out in most imperfect generations; for although we deny not that many animals are vermiparous, begetting themselves at a distance, and as it were at the second hand (as generally Insects, and more remarkably Butter-flies and Silkworms) yet proceeds not this generation from a corruption of themselves, but rather a specifical and seminal diffusion, retaining still the Idea of themselves, though it act that part a while in other shapes. And this will also hold in generations equivocal, and such as are not begotten from Parents like themselves; so from Frogs corrupting, proceed not Frogs again; so if there be anatiferous Trees, whose corruption breaks forth into Bernacles, yet if they corrupt, they degenerate into Maggots, which produce not them again. For this were a confusion of corruptive and seminal production, and a frustration of that seminal power committed to animals at the Creation. The problem might have been spared, *Why we love not our lice as well as our children? Noah's* Ark had been needless, the graves of Animals would be the fruitful'st wombs; for death would not destroy, but empeople the world again.

Since therefore we have so slender grounds to confirm the existence of the Phœnix, since there is no ocular witness of it, since as we have declared, by Authors from whom the story is derived, it rather stands rejected; since they who have seriously discoursed hereof, have delivered themselves negatively, diversly, or contrarily; since many others cannot be drawn into Argument, as writing Poetically, Rhetorically, Enigmatically, Hieroglyphically; since holy Scripture alledged for it duly perpended, doth not advantage it; and lastly, since so strange a generation, unity and long life, hath neither experience nor reason to confirm it, how far to rely on this tradition, we refer unto consideration.

But surely they were not well-wishers unto parable Physick εὐπόριστα, or remedies easily acquired, who derived medicines from the Phœnix; as some have done, and are justly condemned by *Pliny*; *Irridere est vitæ remedia post millesimum annum reditura monstrare*; It is a folly to find out remedies that are not recoverable under a thousand years; or propose the prolonging of life by that which the twentieth generation may never behold. More veniable is a dependance upon the Philosophers stone, potable gold, or any of those Arcana's whereby *Paracelsus* that died himself at forty-seven, gloried that he could make other men immortal. Which, although extreamly difficult, and *tantum non* infesible, yet are they not impossible, nor do they (rightly understood) impose any violence on Nature. And therefore if strictly taken for the Phœnix, very strange is that which is delivered by *Plutarch* De sanitate tuenda, That the brain thereof is a pleasant bit, but that it causeth the head-ach. Which notwithstanding the luxurious Emperour Heliogabalus. could never taste, though he had at his Table many a Phœnicopterus, yet had he not one Phœnix; for though he expected and attempted it, we read not in *Lampridius* that he performed it; and considering the unity thereof, it was a vain design, that is, to destroy any species, or mutilate the great accomplishment of six days. And although some conceive, and it may seem true, that there is in man a natural possibility to destroy the world in one generation, that is, by a general conspire to know no woman themselves, and disable all others also: yet will this never be effected. And therefore *Cain* after he had killed *Abel*, were there no other woman living, could not have also destroyed *Eve*: which although he had a natural power to effect, yet the execution thereof, the providence of God would have resisted: for that would have imposed another creation upon him, and to have animated a second Rib of *Adam*.

CHAPTER XIII
Of Frogs, Toads, and Toad-stone.

Concerning the venomous Urine of Toads, of the stone in the Toads head, and of the generation of Frogs, conceptions are entertained which require consideration. And first, that a Toad pisseth, and this way diffuseth its venome, is generally received, not only with us, but also in other parts; for so hath *Scaliger* observed in his Comment, *Aversum urinam reddere ob oculos persecutoris perniciosam ruricolis persuasum est*; and *Mathiolus* hath also a passage, that a Toad communicates its venome, not only by Urine, but by the humidity and slaver of its mouth; which notwithstanding strictly understood, may admit of examination: for some doubt may be made whether a Toad properly pisseth, that is distinctly and separately voideth the serous excretion: for though not only birds, but oviparous quadrupeds and Serpents have kidneys and ureters, and some Fishes also bladders: yet for the moist and dry excretion they seem at last to have but one vent and common place of exclusion: and with the same propriety of language, we may ascribe that action unto Crows and Kites. And this not onely in Frogs and Toads, but may be enquired in Tortoyses: that is, whether that be strictly true, or to be taken for a distinct and separate miction, when *Aristotle* affirmeth, that no oviparous animal, that is, which either spawneth or layeth Eggs, doth Urine except the Tortois.

The ground or occasion of this expression might from hence arise, that Toads are sometimes observed to exclude or spit out a dark and liquid matter behind: which we have observed to be true, and a venomous condition there may be perhaps therein, but some doubt there may be, whether this is to be called their urine: not because it is emitted aversly or backward, by both sexes, but because it is confounded with the intestinal excretions and egestions of the belly: and this way is ordinarily observed, although possible it is that the liquid excretion may sometimes be excluded without the other.

As for the stone commonly called a Toad-stone, which is presumed to be found in the head of that animal, we first conceive it not a thing impossible: nor is there any substantial reason why in a Toad there may not be found such hard and lapideous concretions. For the like we daily observe in the heads of Fishes, as Cods, Carps, and Pearches: the like also in Snails, a soft and exosseous animal, whereof in the naked and greater sort, as though she would requite the defect of a shell on their back, Nature near the head hath placed a flat white stone, or rather testaceous concretion. Which though *Aldrovandus* affirms, that after dissection of many, he found but in some few: yet of the great gray Snails, I have not met with any that wanted it: and the same indeed so palpable, that without dissection it is discoverable by the hand.

Again, though it be not impossible, yet it is surely very rare: as we are induced to believe from some enquiry of our own, from the trial of many who have been deceived, and the frustrated search of *Porta*, who upon the explorement of many, could scarce find one. Nor is it only of rarity, but may be doubted whether it be of existencie, or really any such stone in the head of a Toad at all. For although *Lapidaries* and questuary enquirers affirm it, yet the Writers of Minerals and natural speculators, are of another belief: conceiving the stones which bear this name, to be a Mineral concretion; not to be found in animals, but in fields. And therefore *Bœtius* refers it to *Asteria* or some kind of *Lapis stellaris*, and plainly concludeth, *reperiuntur in agris, quos tamen alii in annosis ac qui diu in Arundinetis inter rubos sentesque delituerunt bufonis capitibus generari pertinaciter affirmant*.

Lastly, If any such thing there be, yet must it not, for ought I see, be taken as we receive it, for a loose and moveable stone, but rather a concretion or induration of the crany it self; for being of an earthy temper, living in the earth, and as some say feeding thereon, such indurations may sometimes happen. Thus when *Brassavolus* after a long search had discovered one, he affirms it was rather the forehead bone petrified, then a stone within the crany; and of this belief was *Gesner*. Which is also much confirmed from what is delivered in *Aldrovandus*, upon experiment of very many Toads, whose cranies or sculs in time grew hard, and almost of a stony substance. All which considered, we must with circumspection receive those stones which commonly bear this name, much less believe the traditions, that in envy to mankind they are cast out, or swallowed down by the Toad; which cannot consist with *Anatomy*, and with the rest, enforced this censure from *Bœtius*, *Ab eo tempore pro nugis habui quod de Bufonio lapide, ejusque origine traditur*.

What therefore best reconcileth these divided determinations, may be a middle opinion; that of these stones some may be mineral, and to be found in the earth; some animal, to be met with in Toads, at least by the induration of their cranies. The first are many and manifold, to be found in *Germany* and other parts; the last are fewer in number, and in substance not unlike the stones in Crabs heads. This is agreeable unto the determination of *Aldrovandus* De Mineral. lib. 4. Musæi Calceolariani, Sect. 3., and is also the judgment of learned *Spigelius* in his Epistle unto *Pignorius*.

But these Toadstones, at least very many thereof, which are esteemed among us, are at last found to be taken not out of Toads heads, but out of a Fishes mouth, being handsomely contrived out of the teeth of the *Lupus Marinus*, a Fish often taken in our Northern Seas, as was publickly declared by an eminent and learned Physitian. Sir *George Ent*. But because men are unwilling to conceive so low of their Toadstones which they so highly value, they may make some trial thereof by a candentorned hot Iron applied unto the hollow and unpolished part thereof, whereupon if they be true stones they will not be apt to burn or afford a burnt odour, which they may be apt to do, if contrived out of animal parts or the teeth of fishes.

Concerning the generation of Frogs, we shall briefly deliver that account which observation hath taught us. By Frogs I understand not such as arising from putrefaction, are bred without copulation, and because they subsist not long, are called *Temporariæ*; nor do I mean the little Frog of an excellent Parrat green, that usually sits on Trees and Bushes, and is therefore called *Ranunculus viridis*, or *arboreus*; but hereby I understand the aquatile or Water-Frog, whereof in ditches and standing plashes we may behold many millions every Spring in *England*. Now these do not as *Pliny* conceiveth, exclude black pieces of flesh, which after become Frogs; but they let fall their spawn in the water, of excellent use in Physick, and scarce unknown unto any. In this spawn of a lentous and transparent body, are to be discerned many specks, or little conglobulations, which in a small time become of deep black, a substance more compacted and terrestrious then the other; for it riseth not in distillation, and affords a powder when the white and aqueous part is exhaled. Now of this black or dusky substance is the Frog at last formed; as we have beheld, including the spawn with water in a glass, and exposing it unto the Sun. For that black and round substance, in a few days began to dilate and grow longer, after a while the head, the eyes, the tail to be discernable, and at last to become that which the Ancients called *Gyrinus*, we a *Porwigle* or Tadpole. This in some weeks after becomes a perfect Frog, the legs growing out before, and the tail wearing away, to supply the other behind; as may be observed in some which have newly forsaken the water; for in such, some part of the tail will be seen, but curtailed and short, not long and finny as before. A part provided them a while to swim and move in the water, that is, untill such time as Nature excluded legs, whereby they might be provided not only to swim in the water, but move upon the land, according to the amphibious Amphibious Animals, such as live in both elements of land and water. and mixt intention of Nature, that is, to live in both. So that whoever observeth the first progression of the seed before motion, or shall take notice of the strange indistinction of parts in the Tadpole, even when it moveth about, and how successively the inward parts do seem to discover themselves, until their last perfection; may easily discern the high curiosity of Nature in these inferiour animals, and what a long line is run to make a Frog.

And because many affirm, and some deliver, that in regard it hath lungs and breatheth, a Frog may be easily drowned; though the reason be probable, I find not the experiment answerable; for fastning one about a span under water, it lived almost six days. Nor is it only hard to destroy one in water, but difficult also at land: for it will live long after the lungs and heart be out; how long it will live in the seed, or whether the spawn of this year being preserved, will not arise into Frogs in the next, might also be enquired: and we are prepared to trie.

CHAPTER XIV
Of the Salamander.

That a Salamander is able to live in flames, to endure and put out fire, is an assertion, not only of great antiquity, but confirmed by frequent, and not contemptible testimony.

The *Egyptians* have drawn it into their Hieroglyphicks, *Aristotle* seemeth to embrace it; more plainly *Nicander, Sarenus Sammonicus, Ælian* and *Pliny*, who assigns the cause of this effect: An Animal (saith he) so cold that it extinguisheth the fire like Ice. All which notwithstanding, there is on the negative, Authority and Experience; *Sextius* a Physitian, as *Pliny* delivereth, denied this effect; *Dioscorides* affirmed it a point of folly to believe it; *Galen* that it endureth the fire a while, but in continuance is consumed therein. For experimental conviction, *Mathiolus* affirmeth, he saw a Salamander burnt in a very short time; and of the like assertion is *Amatus Lusitanus*; and most plainly *Pierius*, whose words in his Hieroglyphicks are these: *Whereas it is commonly said that a Salamander extinguisheth fire, we have found by experience, that it is so far from quenching hot coals, that it dieth immediately therein.* As for the contrary assertion of *Aristotle*, it is but by hear say, as common opinion believeth, *Hæc enim (ut aiunt) ignem ingrediens, eum extinguit*; and therefore there was no absurdity in *Galen*, when as a Septical medicine [A corruptive Medicine destroying the parts like Arsenike.] he commended the ashes of a Salamander; and *Magicians* in vain from the power of this Tradition, at the burning of Towns or Houses expect a relief from Salamanders.

The ground of this opinion, might be some sensible resistance of fire observed in the Salamander: which being, as *Galen* determineth, cold in the fourth, and moist in the third degree, and having also a mucous humidity above and under the skin, by vertue thereof it may a while endure the flame: which being consumed, it can resist no more. Such an humidity there is observed in Newtes, or Water-Lizards, especially if their skins be perforated or pricked. Thus will Frogs and Snails endure the Flame: thus will whites of Eggs, vitreous or glassie flegm extinguish a coal: thus are unguents made which protect a while from the fire: and thus beside the *Hirpini* there are later stories of men that have passed untoucht through the fire. And therefore some truth we allow in the tradition: truth according unto *Galen*, that it may for a time resist a flame, or as *Scaliger* avers, extinguish or put out a coal: for thus much will many humid bodies perform: but that it perseveres and lives in that destructive element, is a fallacious enlargement. Nor do we reasonably conclude, because for a time it endureth fire, it subdueth and extinguisheth the same, because by a cold and aluminous moisture, it is able a while to resist it: from a peculiarity of Nature it subsisteth and liveth in it.

It hath been much promoted by Stories of incombustible napkins and textures which endure the fire, whose materials are called by the name of Salamanders wool. Which many too literally apprehending, conceive some investing part, or tegument of the Salamander: wherein beside that they mistake the condition of this Animal (which is a kind of Lizard, a quadruped corticated and depilous, that is, without wool, fur, or hair) they observe not the method and general rule of nature; whereby all Quadrupeds oviparous, as Lizards, Frogs, Tortois, Chamelions, Crocodiles, are without hair, and have no covering part or hairy investment at all. And if they conceive that from the skin of the Salamander, these incremable pieces are composed; beside the experiments made upon the living, that of *Brassavolus* will step in, who in the search of this truth, did burn the skin of one dead.

Nor is this Salamanders wooll desumed from any Animal, but a Mineral substance Metaphorically so called from this received opinion. For beside *Germanicus* his heart [Suetonius.], and *Pyrrhus* his great Toe, [Plutarch.] which would not burn with the rest of their bodies, there are in the number of Minerals some bodies incombustible; more remarkably that which the ancients named *Asbeston*, and *Pancirollus* treats of in the Chapter of *Linum vivum*. Whereof by art were weaved Napkins, Shirts, and Coats, inconsumable by fire; and wherein in ancient times to preserve their ashes pure, and without commixture, they burnt the bodies of Kings. A Napkin hereof *Pliny* reports that *Nero* had, and the like saith *Paulus Venetus* the Emperour of *Tartary* sent unto Pope *Alexander*; and also affirms that in some part of *Tartary* there were Mines of Iron whose filaments were weaved into incombustible cloth. Which rare Manufacture, although delivered for lost by *Pancirollus*, yet *Salmuth* his Commentator affirmeth, that one *Podocaterus* a Cyprian, had shewed the same at *Venice*; and his materials were from *Cyprus*, where indeed *Dioscorides* placeth them; the same is also ocularly confirmed by *Vives* upon *Austin*, and *Maiolus* in his Colloquies. And thus in our days do men practise to make long-lasting Snasts for Lamps out of Alumen plumosum; and by the same we read in *Pausanius*, that there always burnt a Lamp before the Image of *Minerva*.

CHAPTER XV
Of the Amphisbæna.

That the Amphisbæna, that is, a smaller kind of Serpent, which moveth forward and backward, hath two heads, or one at either extream, was affirmed first by *Nicander*, and after by many others, by the Author of the Book *De Theriaca ad Pisonem*, ascribed unto *Galen*; more plainly *Pliny*, *Geminum habet caput, tanquam parum esset uno ore effundi venenum*: but *Ælian* most confidently, who referring the conceit of *Chimera* and *Hydra* unto Fables, hath set down this as an undeniable truth.

Whereunto while men assent, and can believe a bicipitous conformation in any continued species, they admit a gemination of principle parts, not naturally discovered in any Animal. True it is that other parts in Animals are not equal; for some make their progression with many legs, even to the number of an hundred, as *Juli, Scolopendræ*; or such as are termed *Centipedes*: some fly with two wings, as Birds and many Insects, some with four, as all farinaceous or mealy-winged Animals, as Butterflies, and Moths: all vaginipennous or sheath-winged Insects, as Beetles and Dorrs. Some have three Testicles, as *Aristotle* speaks of the Buzzard; and some have four stomachs, as horned and ruminating Animals; but for the principle parts, the Liver, Heart, and especially the brains; regularly they are but one in any kind or species whatsoever.

And were there any such species or natural kind of animal, it would be hard to make good those six positions of body, which according to the three dimensions are ascribed unto every Animal: that is, *infra, supra, ante, retro, dextrosum, sinistrosum*: for if (as it is determined) that be the anterior and upper part, wherein the senses are placed, and that the posterior and lower part which is opposite thereunto, there is no inferiour or former part in this Animal; for the senses being placed at both extreams, doth make both ends anterior, which is impossible; the terms being Relative, which mutually subsist, and are not without each other. And therefore this duplicity was ill contrived to place one head at both extreams, and had been more tolerable to have setled three or four at one. And therefore also Poets have been more reasonable then Philosophers, and *Geryon* or *Cerberus* less monstrous than *Amphisbæna*.

Again, if any such thing there were, it were not to be obtruded by the name of *Amphisbæna*, or as an Animal of one denomination; for properly that Animal is not one, but multiplicious or many, which hath a duplicity or gemination of principal parts. And this doth *Aristotle* define, when he affirmeth a monster is to be esteemed one or many, according to its principle, which he conceived the heart, whence he derived the original of Nerves, and thereto ascribed many acts which Physitians assign unto the brain: and therefore if it cannot be called one, which hath a duplicity of hearts in his sense, it cannot receive that appellation with a plurality of heads in ours. And this the practice of Christians hath acknowledged, who have baptized these geminous births, and double connascencies with several names, as conceiving in them a distinction of souls, upon the divided execution of their functions; that is, while one wept, the other laughing; while one was silent, the other speaking; while one awaked, the other sleeping; as is declared by three remarkable examples in *Petrarch, Vincentius* and the *Scottish* History of *Buchanan*.

It is not denied there have been bicipitous Serpents with the head at each extream, for an example hereof we find in *Aristotle*, and of the like form in *Aldrovandus* we meet with the Icon of a Lizzard; and of this kind perhaps might that *Amphisbæna* be, the picture whereof *Cassianus Puteus* shewed unto the learned *Faber*. Which double formations do often happen unto multiparous generations, more especially that of Serpents; whose productions being numerous, and their Eggs in chains or links together (which sometime conjoin and inoculate into each other) they may unite into various shapes and come out in mixed formations. But these are monstrous productions, beside the intention of Nature, and the statutes of generation, neither begotten of like parents, nor begetting the like again, but irregularly produced, do stand as Anomalies in the general Book of Nature. Which being shifts and forced pieces, rather then genuine and proper effects, they afford us no illation; nor is it reasonable to conclude, from a monstrosity unto a species, or from accidental effects, unto the regular works of Nature.

Lastly, The ground of the conceit was the figure of this Animal, and motion oft-times both ways; for described it is to be like a worm, and so equally framed at both extreams, that at an ordinary distance it is no easie matter to determine which is the head; and therefore some observing them to move both ways, have given the appellation of heads unto both extreams, which is no proper and warrantable denomination; for many Animals with one head, do ordinarily perform both different and contrary Motions; Crabs move sideling, Lobsters will swim swiftly backward, Worms and Leeches will move both ways; and so will most of those Animals, whose bodies consist of round and annulary fibers, and move by undulation; that is, like the waves of the Sea, the one protruding the other, by inversion whereof they make a backward Motion.

Upon the same ground hath arisen the same mistake concerning the Scolopendra or hundred-footed Insect, as is delivered by *Rhodiginus* from the Scholiast of *Nicander*: *Dicitur à Nicandro, ἀμφικαρὴς, id est dicephalus aut biceps fictum vero, quoniam retrorsum* (ut scribit Aristoteles), arrepit, observed by *Aldrovandus*, but most plainly by *Muffetus*, who thus concludeth upon the Text of *Nicander*: *Tamen pace tanti authoris dixerim, unicum illi duntaxat caput licet pari facilitate, prorsum capite, retrorsum ducente cauda, incedat, quod Nicandro aliisque imposuisse dubito*: that is, under favour of so great an Author, the Scopolendra hath but one head, although with equal facility it moveth forward and backward, which I suspect deceived *Nicander*, and others.

And therefore we must crave leave to doubt of this double-headed Serpent until we have the advantage to behold or have an iterated ocular testimony concerning such as are sometimes mentioned by *American* relators; and also such as *Cassianus Puteus* shewed in a picture to *Johannes Faber*; and that which is set down under the name of *Amphisbæna Europæa* in his learned discourse upon *Hernandez* his History of *America*.

CHAPTER XVI
Of the Viper.

That the young Vipers force their way through the bowels of their Dam, or that the female Viper in the act of generation bites off the head of the male, in revenge whereof the young ones eat through the womb and belly of the female, is a very ancient tradition. In this sense entertained in the Hieroglyphicks of the *Egyptians*; affirmed by *Herodotus, Nicander, Pliny, Plutarch, Ælian, Jerome, Basil, Isidore,* seems countenanced by *Aristotle,* and his Scholar *Theophrastus*: from hence is commonly assigned the reason why the *Romans* punished *Parricides* by drowning them in a Sack with a Viper. And so perhaps upon the same opinion the men of *Melita* when they saw a Viper upon the hand of *Paul*, said presently without conceit of any other sin, *No doubt this man is a murderer, who though he have escaped the Sea, yet vengeance suffereth him not to live*: that is, he is now paid in his own way, the parricidous Animal and punishment of murderers is upon him. And though the tradition were currant among the Greeks, to confirm the same the Latine name is introduced, *Vipera quasi vi pariat*; That passage also in the Gospel, *O ye generation of Vipers!* hath found expositions which countenance this conceit. Notwithstanding which authorities, transcribed relations and conjectures, upon enquiry we find the same repugnant unto experience and reason.

And first, it seems not only injurious unto the providence of Nature, to ordain a way of production which should destroy the producer, or contrive the continuation of the species by the destruction of the Continuator; but it overthrows and frustrates the great Benediction of God, [Gen. 1.] *God blessed them, saying, Be fruitful and multiply*. Now if it be so ordained that some must regularly perish by multiplication, and these be the fruits of fructifying in the Viper; it cannot be said that God did bless, but curse this Animal: *Upon thy belly shalt thou go, and dust shalt thou eat all thy life*, was not so great a punishment unto the Serpent after the fall, as *encrease, be fruitful and multiply*, was before. This were to confound the Maledictions of God, and translate the curse of the Woman upon the Serpent: that is, *in dolore paries*, in sorrow shalt thou bring *forth*; which being proper unto the Woman, is verified best in the Viper, whose delivery is not only accompanied with pain, but also with death it self. And lastly, it overthrows the careful course, and parental provision of Nature, whereby the young ones newly excluded are sustained by the Dam, and protected until they grow up to a sufficiency for themselves. All which is perverted in this eruptive generation: for the Dam being destroyed, the younglings are left to their own protection: which is not conceivable they can at all perform, and whereof they afford us a remarkable continuance many days after birth. For the young one supposed to break through the belly of the Dam, will upon any fright for protection run into it; for then the old one receives them in at her mouth, which way the fright being past, they will return again, which is a peculiar way of refuge; and although it seem strange, is avowed by frequent experience and undeniable testimony.

As for the experiment, although we have thrice attempted it, it hath not well succeeded; for though we fed them with Milk, Bran, Cheese, etc., the females always died before the young ones were mature for this eruption; but rest sufficiently confirmed in the experiments of worthy enquirers. Wherein to omit the ancient conviction of *Apollonius*, we shall set down some few of Modern Writers. *That Vipers exclude their young ones by an ordinary passage, as other viviparous creatures.* The first, of *Amatus Lusitanus* in his Comment upon *Dioscorides*, *Vidimus nos viperas prægnantes inclusas pixidibus parere, quæ inde ex partu nec mortuæ, nec visceribus perforatæ manserunt.* The second is that of *Scaliger*, *Viperas ab impatientibus moræ fœtibus numerosissimis rumpi atque interire falsum esse scimus, qui in Vincentii Camerini circulatoris lignea theca vidimus, enatas viperellas, parente salva.* The last and most plain of *Franciscus Bustamantinus*, a *Spanish* Physitian of *Alcala de Henares*, whose words in his third *de Animantibus Scripturæ*, are these: *Cum vero per me et per alios hæc ipsa disquisissem servata Viperina progenie, etc.*: that is, when by my self and others I had enquired the truth hereof, including Vipers in a glass, and feeding them with Cheese and Bran, I undoubtedly found that the Viper was not delivered by the tearing of her bowels; but I beheld the young ones excluded by the passage of generation, near the orifice of the seidge. Whereto we might also add the ocular confirmation of *Lacuna* upon *Dioscorides*, *Ferdinandus Imperatus*, and that learned Physician of *Naples*, *Aurelius Severinus*.

Now although the Tradition be untrue, there wanted not many grounds which made it plausibly received. The first was a favourable indulgence and special contrivance of Nature; which was the conceit of *Herodotus*, who thus delivereth himself. Fearful Animals, and such as serve for food, Nature hath made more fruitful; but upon the offensive and noxious kind, she hath not conferred fertility. So the Hare that becometh a prey unto Man, unto Beasts, and Fowls of the air, is fruitful even to superfætation; but the Lion, a fierce and ferocious Animal hath young ones but seldom, and also but one at a time; Vipers indeed although destructive are fruitful; but lest their number should increase, Providence hath contrived another way to abate it: for in copulation the female bites off the head of the male, and the young ones destroy the mother. But this will not consist with reason, as we have declared before. And if we more nearly consider the condition of Vipers and noxious Animals we shall discover an higher provision of Nature: how although in their paucity she hath not abridged their malignity, yet hath she notoriously effected it by their secession or latitancy. For not only offensive insects, as Hornets, Wasps, and the like; but sanguineous corticated Animals, as Serpents, Toads and Lizzards, do lie hid and betake themselves to coverts in the Winter. Whereby most Countries enjoying the immunity of *Ireland* and *Candie*, there ariseth a temporal security from their venoms; and an intermission of their mischiefs, mercifully requiting the time of their activities.

A second ground of this effect, was conceived the justice of Nature, whereby she compensates the death of the father by the matricide or murder of the mother: and this was the expression of *Nicander*. But the cause hereof is as improbable as the effect; and were indeed an improvident revenge in the young ones, whereby in consequence, and upon defect of provision they must destroy themselves. And whereas he expresseth this decollation of the male by so full a term as ἀποκόπτειν, that is, to cut or lop off, the act is hardly conceiveable; for the Viper hath but two considerable teeth, and those so disposed, so slender and needle-pointed, that they are apter for puncture then any act of incision. And if any like action there be, it may be only some fast retention or sudden compression in the *Orgasmus* or fury of their lust; according as that expression of *Horace* is construed concerning *Lydia* and *Telephus*.

––*Sive puer furens,*
Impressit memorem dente labris notam.

Others ascribe this effect unto the numerous conception of the Viper; and this was the opinion of *Theophrastus*. Who though he denieth the exesion or forcing through the belly, conceiveth nevertheless that upon a full and plentiful impletion there may perhaps succeed a disruption of the matrix, as it happeneth sometimes in the long and slender fish *Acus*. Needle-fish, found sometimes upon the Sea-shore, consisting of four lines unto the vent, and six from thence unto the head. Now although in hot Countries, and very numerous conceptions, in the Viper or other Animals, there may sometimes ensue a dilaceration of the genital parts; yet is this a rare and contingent effect, and not a natural and constant way of exclusion. For the wise Creator hath formed the organs of Animals unto their operations, and in whom he ordaineth a numerous conception, in them he hath prepared convenient receptacles, and a sutable way of exclusion.

Others do ground this disruption upon their continued or protracted time of delivery, presumed to last twenty days; whereat excluding but one a day, the latter brood impatient, by a forcible proruption anticipate their period of exclusion; and this was the assertion of *Pliny*, *Cæteri tarditatis impatientes prorumpunt latera, occisâ parente*; which was occasioned upon a mistake of the Greek Text in *Aristotle*, τίκτει δὲ ἐν μίᾳ ἡμέρᾳ καθ' ἕν, τίκτει δὲ πλείω ἤε εἴκοσιν, which are literally thus translated, *Parit autem una die secundum unum, parit autem plures quam viginti*, and may be thus Englished, *She bringeth forth in one day, one by one, and sometimes more than twenty*: and so hath *Scaliger* rendered it, *Sigillatim parit absolvit, una die, interdum plures quam viginti*: But *Pliny*, whom *Gaza* followeth, hath differently translated it, *Singulos diebus singulis parit, numero ferè viginti*; whereby he extends the exclusion unto twenty days, which in the textuary sense is fully accomplished in one.

But what hath most advanced it, is a mistake in another text of *Aristotle*, which seemeth directly to determine this disruption, τίκτει μικρὰ ἐχίδια ἐν ὑμέσιν, ἃι περιρρήγνυνται τριταῖοι, ἐνίοτε δὲ καὶ ἔσωθεν διαφαγόντα αὐτὰ ἐξέρχεται, which *Gaza* hath thus translated, *Parit catulos abvolutos membranis quæ tertio die rumpuntur, evenit interdum ut qui in utero adhuc sunt abrosis membranis prorumpant*. Now herein probably *Pliny*, and many since have been mistaken; for the disruption of the membranes or skins, which include the young ones, conceiving a dilaceration of the matrix and belly of the Viper: and concluding from a casual dilaceration, a regular and constant disruption.

As for the Latine word *Vipera*, which in the Etymologie of *Isidore* promoteth this conceit; more properly it may imply *vivipera*. For whereas other Serpents lay Eggs, the Viper excludeth living Animals; and though the *Cerastes* be also viviparous, and we have found formed Snakes in the belly of the *Cicilia* or Slow-worm; yet may the Viper emphatically bear the name. For the notation or Etymology is not of necessity adequate unto the name; and therefore though animal be deduced from *anima*, yet are there many animations beside, and Plants will challenge a right therein as well as sensible Creatures.

As touching the Text of Scripture, and compellation of the *Pharisees*, by Generation of Vipers, although constructions be made hereof conformable to this Tradition; and it may be plausibly expounded, that out of a viperous condition, they conspired against their Prophets, and destroyed their spiritual parents; yet (as *Jansenius* observeth) *Gregory* and *Jerome*, do make another construction; apprehending thereby what is usually implied by that Proverb, *Mali corvi, malum ovum*; that is, of evil parents, an evil generation, a posterity not unlike their majority; of mischievous progenitors, a venomous and destructive progeny.

And lastly, Concerning the Hieroglyphical account, according to the Vulgar conception set down by *Orus Apollo*, the Authority thereof is only Emblematical; for were the conception true or false, to their apprehensions, it expressed filial impiety. Which strictly taken, and totally received for truth, might perhaps begin, but surely promote this conception.

More doubtful assertions have been raised of no Animal then the Viper, as we have dispersedly noted: and *Francisco Redi* hath amply discovered in his noble observations of Vipers; from good reasons and iterated experiments affirming, that a Viper containeth no humour, excrement, or part which either dranke or eat, is able to kill any: that the *remorsores* or dog-teeth, are not more than two in either sex: that these teeth are hollow, and though they bite and prick therewith, yet are they not venomous, but only open a way and entrance unto the poyson, which notwithstanding is not poysonous except it touch or attain unto the bloud. And that there is no other poison in this Animal, but only that almost insipid liquor like oyl of Almonds, which stagnates in the sheaths and cases that cover the teeth; and that this proceeds not from the bladder of gall, but is rather generated in the head, and perhaps demitted and sent from thence into these cases by salival conducts and passages, which the head communicateth unto them.

CHAPTER XVII
Of Hares.

The double sex of single Hares, or that every Hare is both male and female, beside the vulgar opinion, was the affirmative of *Archelaus*, of *Plutarch*, *Philostratus*, and many more. Of the same belief have been the Jewish *Rabbins*; The same is likewise confirmed from the Hebrew word; *Arnabeth.* which, as though there were no single males of that kind, hath only obtained a name of the feminine gender. As also from the symbolical foundation of its prohibition in the law, *Levit.* 11. and what vices therein are figured; that is, not only pusillanimity and timidity from its temper, feneration or usury from its fœcundity and superfetation; but from this mixture of sexes, unnatural venery and degenerous effemination. Nor are there hardly any who either treat of mutation or mixtion of sexes, who have not left some mention of this point; some speaking positively, others dubiously, and most resigning it unto the enquiry of the Reader. Now hereof to speak distinctly, they must be male and female by mutation and succession of sexes; or else by composition, mixture or union thereof.

Transmutation of Sexes, viz. *of Women into Men, granted.*

As for the mutation of sexes, or transition into one another, we cannot deny it in Hares, it being observable in Man. For hereof beside *Empedocles* or *Tiresias*, there are not a few examples: and though very few, or rather none which have emasculated or turned women, yet very many who from an esteem or reality of being Women have infallibly proved Men. Some at the first point of their menstruous eruptions, some in the day of their marriage, others many years after: which occasioned disputes at Law, and contestations concerning a restore of the dowry. And that not only mankind, but many other Animals may suffer this transexion, we will not deny, or hold it at all impossible: although I confess by reason of the postick and backward position of the feminine parts in quadrupedes, they can hardly admit the substitution of a protrusion, effectual unto masculine generation; except it be in Retromingents, and such as couple backward.

Nor shall we only concede the succession of sexes in some, but shall not dispute the transition of reputed species in others; that is, a transmutation, or (as *Paracelsians* term it) Transplantation of one into another. Hereof in perfect Animals of a congenerous seed, or near affinity of natures, examples are not unfrequent, as in Horses, Asses, Dogs, Foxes, Pheasants, Cocks, etc. but in imperfect kinds, and such where the discrimination of sexes is obscure, these transformations are more common; and in some within themselves without commixtion, as particularly in Caterpillars or Silkworms, wherein there is a visible and triple transfiguration. But in Plants, wherein there is no distinction of sex, these transplantations are conceived more obvious then any; as that of Barley into Oats, of Wheat into Darnel; and those grains which generally arise among Corn, as Cockle, Aracus, Ægilops, and other degenerations; which come up in unexpected shapes, when they want the support and maintenance of the primary and master-forms. And the same do some affirm concerning other Plants in less analogy of figures; as the mutation of Mint into Cresses, Basil into

Serpoile, and Turneps into Radishes. In all which, as *Severinus* conceiveth, In Idea Medicinæ Philosophicæ. there may be equivocal seeds and Hermaphroditical principles, which contain the radicality and power of different forms; thus in the seed of Wheat there lieth obscurely the seminality of Darnel, although in a secondary or inferiour way, and at some distance of production; which nevertheless if it meet with convenient promotion, or a conflux and conspiration of causes more powerful then the other, it then beginneth to edifie in chief, and contemning the superintendent form, produceth the signatures of its self.

Now therefore although we deny not these several mutations, and do allow that Hares may exchange their sex, yet this we conceive doth come to pass but sometimes, and not in that vicissitude or annual alteration as is presumed. That is, from imperfection to perfection, from perfection to imperfection; from female unto male, from male to female again, and so in a circle to both without a permansion in either. For beside the inconceivable mutation of temper, which should yearly alternate the sex, this is injurious unto the order of nature, whose operations do rest in the perfection of their intents; which having once attained, they maintain their accomplished ends, and relapse not again into their progressional imperfections. So if in the minority of natural vigor, the parts of seminality take place; when upon the encrease or growth thereof the masculine appear, the first design of nature is atchieved, and those parts are after maintained.

But surely it much impeacheth this iterated transexion of Hares, if that be true which *Cardan* and other Physicians affirm, that Transmutation of sex is only so in opinion; and that these transfeminated persons were really men at first; although succeeding years produced the manifesto or evidence of their virilities. Which although intended and formed, was not at first excluded: and that the examples hereof have undergone no real or new transexion, but were Androgynally born, and under some kind of *Hermaphrodites*. For though *Galen* do favour the opinion, that the distinctive parts of sexes are only different in Position, that is, inversion or protrusion; yet will this hardly be made out from the Anatomy of those parts. The testicles being so seated in the female, that they admit not of protrusion; and the neck of the matrix wanting those parts which are discoverable in the organ of virility.

The second and most received acception, is, that Hares are male and female by conjunction of both sexes; and such as are found in mankind, Poetically called Hermaphrodites; supposed to be formed from the equality, or *non victorie* of either seed; carrying about them the parts of Man and Woman; although with great variety in perfection, site and ability; not only as *Aristotle* conceived, with a constant impotency in one; but as later observers affirm, sometimes with ability of either venery. And therefore the providence of some Laws have thought good, that at the years of maturity they should elect one sex, and the errors in the other should suffer a severer punishment. Whereby endeavouring to prevent incontinency, they unawares enjoyned perpetual chastity; for being executive in both parts, and confined unto one, they restrained a natural power, and ordained a partial virginity. *Plato* and some of the Rabbins proceeded higher; who conceived the first Man an Hermaphrodite; and *Marcus Leo* the learned *Jew*, in some sense hath allowed it; affirming that *Adam* in one suppositum without division, contained both Male and Female. And therefore whereas it is said in the text, That God created man in his own Image, in the Image of God created he him, male and female created he them: applying the singular and plural unto *Adam*, it might denote, that in one substance, and in himself he included both sexes, which was after divided, and the female called Woman. The opinion of *Aristotle* extendeth farther, from whose assertion all men should be Hermaphrodites; for affirming that Women do not spermatize, and confer a place or receptacle rather then essential principles of generation, he deductively includes both sexes in mankind; for from the father proceed not only males and females, but from him also must Hermaphroditical and masculo-feminine generations be derived, and a commixtion of both sexes arise from the seed of one. But the Schoolmen have dealt with that sex more hardly then any other; who though they have not much disputed their generation, yet have they controverted their Resurrection, and raisen a querie, whether any at the last day should arise in the sex of Women; as may be observed in the supplement of *Aquinas*.

Now as we must acknowledge this Androgynal condition in Man, [*Consisting of man and woman.*] so can we not deny the like doth happen in beasts. Thus do we read in *Pliny*, that *Neroes* Chariot was drawn by four Hermaphroditical Mares, and *Cardan* affirms he also beheld one at *Antwerp*. And thus may we also concede, that Hares have been of both sexes, and some have ocularly confirmed it; but that the whole species or kind should be bisexous or double-sexed, we cannot affirm, who have found the parts of male and female respectively distinct and single in any wherein we have enquired: And the like success had *Bacchinus* [*Bacch. De Hermaphroditis.*] in such as he dissected. And whereas it is conceived, that being an harmless Animal and delectable food unto man, nature hath made them with double sexes, that actively and passively performing they might more numerously increase; we forget an higher providence of nature whereby she especially promotes the multiplication of Hares, which is by superfetation; that is, a conception upon a conception, or an improvement of a second fruit before the first be excluded; preventing hereby the usual intermission and vacant time of generation; which is very common and frequently observable in Hares, mentioned long ago by *Aristotle*, *Herodotus*, and *Pliny*; and we have often observed, that after the first cast, there remain successive conceptions, and other younglings very immature, and far from their term of exclusion.

Superfetation possible in women, and that unto a perfect birth.

Nor need any man to question this in Hares, for the same we observe doth sometime happen in Women; for although it be true, that upon conception the inward orifice of the matrix exactly closeth, so that it commonly admitteth nothing after; yet falleth it out sometime, that in the act of coition, the avidity of that part dilateth it self, and receiveth a second burden; which if it happen to be near in time unto the first, they do commonly both proceed unto perfection, and have legitimate exclusions, periodically succeeding each other. But if the superfetation be made with considerable intermission, the latter most commonly proves abortive; for the first being confirmed, engrosseth the aliment from the other. However therefore the project of *Julia* seem very plausible, and that way infallible, when she received not her passengers, before she had taken in her lading, yet was there a fallibility therein: nor indeed any absolute security in the policy of adultery after conception. For the Matrix (which some have called another Animal within us, and which is not subjected unto the law of our will) after reception of its proper Tenant, may yet receive a strange and spurious inmate. As is confirmable by many examples in *Pliny*; by *Larissæa* in *Hippocrates* and that merry one in *Plautus* urged also by *Aristotle*: that is, of *Iphicles* and *Hercules*, the one begat by *Jupiter*, the other by *Amphitryon* upon *Alemæna* as also in those super-conceptions, where one child was like the father, the other like the adulterer, the one favoured the servant, the other resembled the master.

Now the grounds that begat, or much promoted the opinion of a double sex in Hares, might be some little bags or tumours, at first glance representing stones or Testicles, to be found in both sexes about the parts of generation; which men observing in either sex, were induced to believe a masculine sex in both. But to speak properly, these are no Testicles or parts official unto generation, but glandulous substances that seem to hold the nature of Emunctories. For herein may be perceived slender perforations, at which may be expressed a black and fæculent matter. If therefore from these we shall conceive a mixtion of sexes in Hares, with fairer reason we may conclude it in Bevers; whereof both sexes contain a double bag or Tumour in the groin, commonly called the Cod of *Castor*, as we have delivered before.

Another ground were certain holes or cavities observable about the siedge; which being perceived in Males, made some conceive there might be also a fœminine nature in them. And upon this very ground, the same opinion hath passed upon the Hyæna, and is declared by *Aristotle*, and thus translated by *Scaliger*; *Quod autem aiunt utriusque sexus habere genitalia, falsum est, quod videtur esse fœmineum sub cauda est simile figura fœminino, verum pervium non est*; and thus is it also in Hares, in whom these holes, although they seem to make a deep cavity, yet do they not perforate the skin, nor hold a community with any part of generation: but were (as *Pliny* delivereth) esteemed the marks of their age, the number of those deciding their number of years. In which opinion what truth there is we shall not contend; for if in other Animals there be authentick notations, if the characters of years be found in the horns of Cows, or in the Antlers of Deer; if we conjecture the age of Horses from joints in their docks, and undeniably presume it from their teeth; we cannot affirm, there is in this conceit, any affront unto nature; although who ever enquireth shall find no assurance therein.

The last foundation was Retromingency or pissing backward; for men observing both sexes to urine backward, or aversly between their legs, they might conceive there was a fœminine part in both; wherein they are deceived by the ignorance of the just and proper site of the Pizzel, or part designed unto the Excretion of urine; which in the Hare holds not the common position, but is aversly seated, and in its distention enclines unto the Coccix or Scut. Now from the nature of this position, there ensueth a necessity of Retrocopulation, which also promoteth the conceit: for some observing them to couple without ascension, have not been able to judge of male or female, or to determine the proper sex in either. And to speak generally, this way of copulation is not appropriate unto Hares, nor is there one, but many ways of coition: according to divers shapes and different conformations. For some couple laterally or sidewise, as Worms: some circularly or by complication, as Serpents: some pronely, that is, by contaction of the ventral parts in both, as Apes, Porcupines, Hedgehogs, and such as are termed Mollia, as the Cuttle-fish and the Purple; some mixtly, that is, the male ascending the female, or by application of the ventral parts of the one, unto the postick parts of the other, as most Quadrupeds: Some aversly, as all Crustaceous Animals, Lobsters, Shrimps, and Crevises, and also Retromingents, as Panthers, Tygers, and Hares. This is the constant Law of their Coition, this they observe and transgress not: onely the vitiosity of man hath acted the varieties hereof; nor content with a digression from sex or species, hath in his own kind run thorow the Anomalies of venery; and been so bold, not only to act, but represent to view, the irregular ways of Lust.

CHAPTER XVIII
Of Moles, or Molls.

That Moles are blind and have no eyes, though a common opinion, is received with much variety; some affirming only they have no sight, as *Oppianus*, the Proverb *Talpa Cæcior*, and the word σπαλαχία, or *Talpitas*, which in *Hesychius* is made the same with *Cæcitas*: some that they have eyes, but no sight, as the text of *Aristotle* seems to imply; some neither eyes nor sight, as *Albertus*, *Pliny*, and the vulgar opinion; some both eyes and sight, as *Scaliger*, *Aldrovandus*, and some others. Of which opinions the last with some restriction, is most consonant unto truth: for that they have eyes in their head is manifest unto any, that wants them not in his own: and are discoverable, not only in old ones, but as we have observed in young and naked conceptions, taken out of the belly of the Dam. And he that exactly enquires into the cavity of their cranies, may perhaps discover some propagation of nerves communicated unto these parts. But that the humours together with their coats are also distinct (though *Galen* seem to affirm it) transcendeth our discovery; for separating these little Orbs, and including them in magnifying Glasses, we discerned no more then *Aristotle* mentions, τῶν ὀφθαλμῶν μέλαινα, that is, a black humour, nor any more if they be broken. That therefore they have eyes we must of necessity affirm; but that they be comparatively incomplete we need not to deny: So *Galen* affirms the parts of generation in women are imperfect, in respect of those of men, as the eyes of Moles in regard of other Animals; So *Aristotle* terms them πηρουμένους, which *Gaza* translates *Oblæsos*, and *Scaliger* by a word of imperfection *inchoatos*.

Now as that they have eyes is manifest unto sense, so that they have sight not incongruous unto reason; if we call not in question the providence of this provision, that is, to assign the Organs, and yet deny the Office, to grant them eyes and withhold all manner of vision. For as the inference is fair, affirmatively deduced from the action to the Organ, that they have eyes because they see; so is it also from the organ to the action, that they have eyes, therefore some sight designed, if we take the intention of Nature in every species, and except the casual impediments, or morbosities in individuals. But as their eyes are more imperfect then others, so do we conceive of their sight or act of vision, for they will run against things, and hudling forwards fall from high places. So that they are not blind, nor yet distinctly see; there is in them no Cecity, yet more then a Cecutiency; they have sight enough to discern the light, though not perhaps to distinguish of objects or colours; so are they not exactly blind, for light is one object of vision. And this (as *Scaliger* observeth) might be as full a sight as Nature first intended, for living in darkness under the earth, they had no further need of eyes then to avoid the light; and to be sensible when ever they lost that darkness of earth, which was their natural confinement. And therefore however Translators do render the word of *Aristotle* or *Galen*, that is, *imperfectos oblæsos* or *inchoatos*, it is not much considerable; for their eyes are sufficiently begun to finish this action, and competently perfect for this imperfect Vision.

And lastly, although they had neither eyes nor sight, yet could they not be termed blind. For blindness being a privative term unto sight, this appellation is not admittible in propriety of speech, and will overthrow the doctrine of privations; which presuppose positive forms or habits, and are not indefinite negations, denying in all subjects, but such alone wherein the positive habits are in their proper Nature, and placed without repugnancy. So do we improperly say a Mole is blind, if we deny it the Organs or a capacity of vision from its created Nature; so when the text of *John* had said, that person was blind from his nativity, whose cecity our Saviour cured, it was not warrantable in *Nonnus* to say he had no eyes at all, as in the judgment of *Heinsius*, he describeth in his paraphrase; and as some ancient Fathers affirm, that by this miracle they were created in him. And so though the sense may be accepted, that Proverb must be candidly interpreted, which maketh fishes Mute; and calls them silent which have no voice in Nature.

Now this conceit is erected upon a misapprehension or mistake in the symtomes of vision; men confounding abolishment, diminution and depravement, and naming that an abolition of sight, which indeed is but an abatement. For if vision be abolished, it is called *cæcitas*, or blindness; if depraved and receive its objects erroneously, Hallucination; if diminished, *hebetudo visus*, *caligatio*, or dimness. Now instead of a diminution or imperfect vision in the Mole, we affirm an abolition or total privation; instead of a caligation or dimness, we conclude a cecity or blindness. Which hath been frequently inferred concerning other Animals; so some affirm the Water-Rat is blind, so *Sammonicus* and *Nicander* do call the Mus-Araneus the shrew or Ranny, blind: And because darkness was before light, the *Ægyptians* worshipped the same. So are *Cæciliæ* or Slow-worms accounted blind, and the like we affirm proverbially of the Beetle; although their eyes be evident, and they will flye against lights, like many other Insects, and though also *Aristotle* determines, that the eyes are apparent in all flying Insects, though other senses be obscure, and not perceptible at all. And if from a diminution we may infer a total privation, or affirm that other Animals are blind which do not acutely see, or comparatively unto others, we shall condemn unto blindness many not so esteemed; for such as have corneous or horney eyes, as Lobsters and crustaceous Animals, are generally dim-sighted; all Insects that have *antennæ*, or long horns to feel out their way, as Butterflyes and Locusts; or their forelegs so disposed, that they much advance before their heads, as may be observed in Spiders; and if the Eagle were judge, we might be blind our selves. The expression therefore of Scripture in the story of *Jacob* is surely with circumspection: And it came to pass when *Jacob* was old, and his eyes were dim, *quando caligarunt oculi*, saith *Jerome* and *Tremellius*, which are expressions of diminution, and not of absolute privation.

Other concerns there are of Molls, which though not commonly opinioned are not commonly enough considered: As the peculiar formation of their feet, the slender *ossa Iugalia*, and Dogteeth, and how hard it is to keep them alive out of the Earth: As also the ferity and voracity of these animals; for though they be contented with Roots, and stringy parts of Plants, or Wormes under ground, yet when they are above it will sometimes tear and eat one another, and in a large glass wherein a Moll, a Toad, and a Viper were inclosed, we have known the Moll to dispatch them and to devour a good part of them both.

CHAPTER XIX
Of Lampries.

Whether Lampries have nine eyes, as is received, we durst refer it unto *Polyphemus*, who had but one, to judge it. An error concerning eyes, occasioned by the error of eyes; deduced from the appearance of diverse cavities or holes on either side, which some call eyes that carelessly behold them; and is not only refutable by experience, but also repugnant unto Reason. For beside the monstrosity they fasten unto Nature, in contriving many eyes, who hath made but two unto any Animal, that is, one of each side, according to the division of the brain; it were a superfluous inartificial act to place and settle so many in one plane; for the two extreams would sufficiently perform the office of sight without the help of the intermediate eyes, and behold as much as all seven joyned together. For the visible base of the object would be defined by these two; and the middle eyes, although they behold the same thing, yet could they not behold so much thereof as these; so were it no advantage unto man to have a third eye between those two he hath already; and the fiction of *Argus* seems more reasonable then this; for though he had many eyes, yet were they placed in circumference and positions of advantage, and so are they placed in several lines in Spiders.

Again, These cavities which men call eyes are seated out of the head, and where the Gils of other fish are placed; containing no Organs of sight, nor having any Communication with the brain. *All sense is from the brain.* Now all sense proceeding from the brain, and that being placed (as *Galen* observeth) in the upper part of the body, for the fitter situation of the eyes, and conveniency required unto sight; it is not reasonable to imagine that they are any where else, or deserve that name which are seated in other parts. And therefore we relinquish as fabulous what is delivered of *Sternopthalmi*, or men with eyes in their breast, and when it is said by *Solomon*, A wise mans eyes are in his head, it is to be taken in a second sense, and affordeth no objection. True it is that the eyes of Animals are seated with some difference, but in sanguineous animals in the head, and that more forward then the ear or hole of hearing. In quadrupedes, in regard of the figure of their heads, they are placed at some distance; in latirostrous and flat-bill'd birds they are more laterally seated, and therefore when they look intently they turn one eye upon the object, and can convert their heads to see before and behind, and to behold two opposite points at once. But at a more easie distance are they situated in man, and in the same circumference with the ear; for if one foot of the compass be placed upon the Crown, a circle described thereby will intersect, or pass over both the ears.

To what use the nine eyes in a Lamprie do serve.

The error in this conceit consists in the ignorance of these cavities, and their proper use in nature; for this is a particular dispourse of parts, and a peculiar conformation whereby these holes and sluces supply the defect of Gils, and are assisted by the conduit in the head; for like cetaceous Animals and Whales, the Lamprie hath a fistula, spout or pipe at the back part of the head, whereat it spurts out water. Nor is it only singular in this formation, but also in many other; as in defect of bones, whereof it hath not one; and for the spine or backbone, a cartilaginous substance without any spondyles, processes or protuberance whatsoever. As also in the provision which Nature hath made for the heart; which in this Animal is very strangely secured, and lies immured in a cartilage or gristly substance. And lastly, in the colour of the liver: which is in the Male of an excellent grass-green: but of a deeper colour in the Female, and will communicate a fresh and durable verdure.

CHAPTER XX
Of Snayls.

Whether *Snayls* have eyes some Learned men have doubted. For *Scaliger* terms them but imitations of eyes; and *Aristotle* upon consequence denyeth them, when he affirms that *Testaceous* Animals have no eyes. But this now seems sufficiently asserted by the help of exquisite Glasses, which discover those black and atramentous spots or globales to be their eyes.

That they have two eyes is the common opinion, but if they have two eyes, we may grant them to have no less than four, that is, two in the larger extensions above, and two in the shorter and lesser horns below, and this number may be allowed in these inferiour and exanguious animals;

since we may observe the articulate and latticed eyes in Flies, and nine in some Spiders: And in the great *Phalangium* Spider of *America*, we plainly number eight.

But in sanguineous animals, quadrupeds, bipeds, or man, no such number can be regularly verified, or multiplicity of eyes confirmed. And therefore what hath been under this kind delivered, concerning the plurality, paucity or anomalous situation of eyes, is either monstrous, fabulous, or under things never seen includes good sense or meaning. And so may we receive the figment of *Argus*, who was an Hieroglyphick of heaven, in those centuries of eyes expressing the stars; and their alternate wakings, the vicissitude of day and night. Which strictly taken cannot be admitted; for the subject of sleep is not the eye, but the common sense, which once asleep, all eyes must be at rest. And therefore what is delivered as an Embleme of vigilancy, that the Hare and Lion do sleep with one eye open, doth not evince they are any more awake then if they were both closed. For the open eye beholds in sleep no more then that which is closed; and no more one eye in them then two in other Animals that sleep with both open; as some by disease, and others naturally which have no eye-lids at all.

How things happen to be seen as double.

As for Polyphemus, although the story be fabulous, the monstrosity is not impossible. For the act of Vision may be performed with one eye; and in the deception and fallacy of sight, hath this advantage of two, that it beholds not objects double, or sees two things for one. For this doth happen when the axis of the visive cones, diffused from the object, fall not upon the same plane; but that which is conveyed into one eye, is more depressed or elevated then that which enters the other. So if beholding a Candle, we protrude either upward or downward the pupill of one eye, the object will appear double; but if we shut the other eye, and behold it with one, it will their appear but single; and if we abduce the eye unto either corner, the object will not duplicate: for in that position the axis of the cones remain in the same plane, as is demonstrated in the opticks, and delivered by *Galen*, in his tenth *De usu partium*.

Relations also there are of men that could make themselves invisible, which belongs not to this discourse: but may serve as notable expressions of wise and prudent men, who so contrive their affairs, that although their actions be manifest, their designs are not discoverable. In this acception there is nothing left of doubt, and *Giges* Ring remaineth still amongst us: for vulgar eyes behold no more of wise men then doth the Sun: they may discover their exteriour and outward ways, but their interiour and inward pieces he only sees, that sees into their beings.

CHAPTER XXI
Of the Chameleon.

Concerning the *Chameleon* there generally passeth an opinion that it liveth only upon air, and is sustained by no other aliment: Thus much is in plain terms affirmed by *Solinus*, *Pliny*, and others, and by this periphrasis is the same described by *Ovid*. All which notwithstanding, upon enquiry I find the assertion mainly controvertible, and very much to fail in the three inducements of belief.

And first for its verity, although asserted by some, and traditionally delivered by others, yet is it very questionable. For beside *Ælian*, who is seldom defective in these accounts; *Aristotle* distinctly treating hereof, hath made no mention of this remarkable propriety: which either suspecting its verity, or presuming its falsity, he surely omitted: for that he remained ignorant of this account it is not easily conceiveable: it being the common opinion, and generally received by all men. Some have positively denied it, as *Augustinus*, *Niphus*, *Stobæus*, *Dalechampius*, *Fortunius Licetus*, with many more; others have experimentally refuted it, as namely *Johannes Landius*, who in the relation of *Scaliger*, observed a *Chameleon* to lick up a fly from his breast: But *Bellonius* *Comment. in Ocell.* Lucan. hath been more satisfactorily experimental, not only affirming they feed on Flies, Caterpillars, Beetles and other Insects, but upon exenteration he found these Animals in their bellies: whereto we might also add the experimental decisions of the worthy *Peireschius* and learned *Emanuel Vizzanius*, in that *Chameleon* which had been often observed to drink water, and delight to feed on Meal-worms.

And although we have not had the advantage of our own observation, yet have we received the like confirmation from many ocular spectators.

As touching the verisimility or probable truth of this relation, several reasons there are which seem to overthrow it. For first, there are found in this Animal, the guts, the stomack, and other parts official unto nutrition; which were its aliment the empty reception of air, their provisions had been superfluous. Now the wisdom of nature abhorring superfluities, and effecting nothing in vain, unto the intention of these operations, respectively contriveth the Organs; and therefore where we find such Instruments, we may with strictness expect their actions; and where we discover them not, we may with safety conclude the non-intention of their operations. So when we perceive that Bats have teats, it is not unreasonable to infer they suckle their younglings with milk; but whereas no other flying Animal hath these parts, we cannot from them expect a viviparous exclusion; but either a generation of eggs, or some vermiparous separation, whose navel is within it self at first, and its nutrition after not connexedly depending of its original.

Again, Nature is so far from leaving any one part without its proper action, that she oft-times imposeth two or three labours upon one, so the Pizel in Animals is both official unto Urine and to generation, but the first and primary use is generation; for some creatures enjoy that part which urine not. So the nostrils are useful both for respiration and smelling, but the principal use is smelling; for many have nostrils which have no lungs, as fishes, but none have lungs or respiration, which have not some shew, or some analogy of nostrils. *Nature provides no part without its proper function or office.* Thus we perceive the providence of Nature, that is, the wisdom of God, which disposeth of no part in vain, and some parts unto two or three uses, will not provide any without the execution of its proper office, nor where there is no digestion to be made, make any parts inservient to that intention.

Beside the remarkable teeth, the tongue of this animal is a second argument to overthrow this airy nutrication: and that not only in its proper nature, but also its peculiar figure. For of this part properly taken there are two ends; that is, the formation of the voice, and the execution of tast; for the voice, it can have no office in *Chameleons*, for they are mute Animals; as beside fishes, are most other sorts of Lizards. As for their tast, if their nutriment be air, neither can it be an Instrument thereof; for the body of that element is ingustible, void of all sapidity, and without any action of the tongue, is by the rough artery or wezon conducted into the lungs. And therefore *Pliny* much forgets the strictness of his assertion, when he alloweth excrements unto that Animal, that feedeth only upon Air; which notwithstanding with the urine of an Ass, he commends as a magicall Medicine upon our enemies.

The figure of the tongue seems also to overthrow the presumption of this aliment, which according to exact delineation, is in this Animal peculiar, and seemeth contrived for prey. For in so little a creature it is at the least a palm long, and being it self very slow in motion, hath in this part a very great agility; withall its food being flies and such as suddenly escape, it hath in the tongue a mucous and slimy extremity, whereby upon a sudden emission it inviscates and tangleth those Insects. And therefore some have thought its name not unsuitable unto its nature; the nomination in Greek is a little Lion; χαμαιλέων. not so much for the resemblance of shape, as affinity of condition; that is for vigilancy in its prey, and sudden rapacity thereof, which it performeth not like the Lion with its teeth, but a sudden and unexpected ejaculation of the tongue. This exposition is favoured by some, especially the old gloss upon *Leviticus*, whereby in the Translation of *Jerome* and the Septuagint, this Animal is forbidden; what ever it be, it seems as reasonable as that of *Isidore*, who derives this name *à Camelo et Leone*, as presuming herein resemblance with a Camell.

As for the possibility hereof, it is not also unquestionable; and wise men are of opinion, the bodies of Animals cannot receive a proper aliment from air; for beside that tast being (as *Aristotle* terms it) a kind of touch; it is required the aliment should be tangible, and fall under the palpable affections of touch; beside also that there is some sapor in all aliments, as being to be distinguished and judged by the gust; which cannot be admitted in air: Beside these, I say, if we consider the nature of aliment, and the proper use of air in respiration, it will very hardly fall under the name hereof, or properly attain the act of nutrication.

Requisites unto Nutrition.

And first concerning its nature, to make a perfect nutrition into the body nourished, there is required a transmutation of the nutriment, now where this conversion or aggeneration is made, there is also required in the aliment a familiarity of matter, and such a community or vicinity unto a living nature, as by one act of the soul may be converted into the body of the living, and enjoy one common soul. Which cannot be effected by air, it concurring only with our flesh in common principles, which are at the largest distance from life, and common also unto inanimated constitutions. And therefore when it is said by *Fernelius*, and asserted by divers others, that we are only nourished by living bodies, and such as are some way proceeding from them, that is, the fruits, effects, parts, or seeds thereof; they have laid out an object very agreeable unto assimilation; for these indeed are fit to receive a quick and immediate conversion, as holding some community with our selves, and containing approximate dispositions unto animation.

Secondly, (as is argued by *Aristotle* against the *Pythagoreans*) whatsoever properly nourisheth before its assimilation, by the action of natural heat it receiveth a corpulency or incrassation progressional unto its conversion; which notwithstanding cannot be effected upon air; for the action of heat doth not condense but rarifie that body, and by attenuation, rather then for nutrition, disposeth it for expulsion.

Thirdly, (which is the argument of *Hippocrates*) all aliment received into the body, must be therein a considerable space retained, and not immediately expelled. Now air but momentarily remaining in our bodies, it hath no proportionable space for its conversion; only of length enough to refrigerate the heart; which having once performed, lest being it self heated again, it should suffocate that part, it maketh no stay, but hasteth back the same way it passed in.

Fourthly, The use of air attracted by the lungs, and without which there is no durable continuation in life, is not the nutrition of parts, but the contemperation and ventilation of that fire always maintained in the forge of life; whereby although in some manner it concurreth unto nutrition, yet can it not receive the proper name of nutriment. And therefore by *Hippocrates* De Alimento. it is termed *Alimentum non Alimentum*, a nourishment and no nourishment. That is, in a large acception, but not in propriety of language; conserving the body, not nourishing the same; nor repairing it by assimilation, but preserving it by ventilation; for thereby the natural flame is preserved from extinction, and so the individuum supported in some way like nutrition.

And though the air so entreth the Lungs, that by its nitrous Spirit doth affect the heart, and several ways qualifie the blood; and though it be also admitted into other parts, even by the meat we chew, yet that it affordeth a proper nutriment alone, it is not easily made out.

Again, Some are so far from affirming the air to afford any nutriment, that they plainly deny it to be any Element, or that it entreth into mixt bodies as any principle in their compositions, but performeth other offices in the Universe; as to fill all vacuities about the earth or beneath it, to convey the heat of the sun, to maintain fires and flames, to serve for the flight of volatils, respiration of breathing Animals, and refrigeration of others. And although we receive it as an Element, yet since the transmutation of Elements and simple bodies, is not beyond great question, since also it is no easie matter to demonstrate that air is so much as convertible into water; *Wherein Vapour is commonly mistaken for air.* how transmutable it is into flesh, may be of deeper doubt.

And although the air attracted may be conceived to nourish the invisible flame of life, in as much as common and culinary flames are nourished by the air about them; we make some doubt whether air is the pabulous supply of fire, much less that flame is properly air kindled. And the same before us, hath been denied by the Lord of *Verulam*, in his Tract of Life and Death, and also by Dr. *Jorden* in his book of Mineral waters. *What the matter of Culinary or Kitchin fire is.* For that which substantially maintaineth the fire, is the combustible matter in the kindled body, and not the ambient air, which affordeth exhalation to its fuliginous atomes; nor that which causeth the flame properly to be termed air, but rather as he expresseth it, the accension of fuliginous exhalations, which contain an unctuosity in them, and arise from the matter of fuel, which opinion will salve many doubts, whereof the common conceit affordeth no solution.

As first, How fire is stricken out of flints? that is, not by kindling the air from the collision of two hard bodies; for then Diamonds should do the like better than Flints: but rather from sulphureous inflamed and even vitrified effluviums and particles, as hath been observed of late. The like saith *Jorden* we observe in canes and woods, that are unctuous and full of oyl, which will yield fire by frication, or collision, not by kindling the air about them, but the inflamable oyl within them. *Why fire goes out commonly wanting air, and why sometimes continued many ages in flame without fuel.* Why the fire goes out without air? that is, because the fuliginous exhalations wanting evaporation recoil upon the flame and choak it, as is evident in cupping glasses; and the artifice of charcoals, where if the air be altogether excluded, the fire goes out. Why some lamps included in those bodies have burned many hundred years, as that discovered in the Sepulchre of *Tullia*, the sister of *Cicero*, and that of *Olibius* many years after, near *Padua*? because whatever was their matter, either a preparation of gold, or *Naptha*, the duration proceeded from the purity of their oyl which yielded no fuliginous exhalations to suffocate the fire; For if air had nourished the flame, it had not continued many minutes, for it would have been spent and wasted by the fire. Why a piece of flax will kindle, though it touch not the flame? because the fire extendeth further, then indeed it is visible, being at some distance from the week, a pellucide and transparent body, and thinner then the air it self. Why Mettals in their liquation, although they intensly heat the air above their surface, arise not yet into a flame, nor kindle the air about them? because their sulphur is more fixed, and they emit not inflamable exhalations. And lastly, why a lamp or candle burneth only in the air about it, and inflameth not the air at a distance from it? because the flame extendeth not beyond the inflamable effluence, but closely adheres unto the original of its inflamation; and therefore it only warmeth, not kindleth the air about it. Which notwithstanding it will do, if the ambient air be impregnate with subtile inflamabilities, and such as are of quick accension; as experiment is made in a close room; upon an evaporation of spirits of wine and Camphire; as subterraneous fires do sometimes happen, and as *Creusa* and *Alexanders* boy in the bath were set on fire by *Naptha*.

Lastly, The Element of air is so far from nourishing the body, that some have questioned the power of water; many conceiving it enters not the body in the power of aliment, or that from thence there proceeds a substantial supply. For beside that some creatures drink not at all; Even unto our selves, and more perfect Animals, though many ways assistent thereto, it performs no substantial nutrition, serving for refrigeration, dilution of solid aliment, and its elixation in the stomack; which from thence as a vehicle it conveys through less accessible cavities, and so in a rorid substance through the capillary cavities, into every part; which having performed, it is afterward excluded by Urine, sweat and serous separations. And this opinion surely possessed the Ancients; for when they so highly commended that water which is suddenly hot and cold, which is without all savour, the lightest, the thinnest, and which will soonest boil Beans or Pease, they had no consideration of nutrition; whereunto had they had respect, they would have surely commended gross and turbid streams, in whose confusion at least, there might be contained some nutriment; and not jejune or limped water, nearer the simplicity of its Element. Although, I confess, our clearest waters and such as seem simple unto sense, are much compounded unto reason, as may be observed in the evaporation of large quantities of water; wherein beside a terreous residence some salt is also found, as is also observable in rain water; which appearing pure and empty, is full of seminal principles, and carrieth vital atomes of plants and Animals in it, which have not perished in the great circulation of nature; *A seed of plants and animals contained in rainwater. Zibavius, tom. 4. Chym.* as may be discovered from several Insects generated in rain water, from the prevalent fructification of plants thereby; and (beside the real plant of *Cornerius*) from vegetable figurations, upon the sides of glasses, so rarely delineated in frosts.

All which considered, severer heads will be apt enough to conceive the opinion of this Animal, not much unlike that of the Astomi, or men without mouths, in *Pliny*; sutable unto the relation of the Mares in *Spain*, and their subventaneous conceptions, from the Western wind; and in some way more unreasonable then the figment of *Rabican* the famous horse in *Ariosto*, which being conceived by flame and wind, never tasted grass, or fed on any grosser provender then air; for this way of nutrition was answerable unto the principles of his generation. Which being not airy, but gross and seminal in the *Chameleon*; unto its conservation there is required a solid pasture, and a food congenerous unto the principles of its nature.

The grounds of this opinion are many; the first observed by *Theophrastus*, was the inflation or swelling of the body, made in this Animal upon inspiration or drawing in its breath; which people observing, have thought it to feed upon air. But this effect is rather occasioned upon the greatness of its lungs, which in this Animal are very large, and by their backward situation, afford a more observable dilation; and though their lungs be less, the like inflation is also observable in Toads, but especially in Sentortoises.

A second is the continual hiation or holding open its mouth, which men observing, conceive the intention thereof to receive the aliment of air; but this is also occasioned by the greatness of its lungs; for repletion whereof not having a sufficient or ready supply by its nostrils; it is enforced to dilate and hold open the jaws.

The third is the paucity of blood observed in this Animal, scarce at all to be found but in the eye, and about the heart; which defect being observed, inclined some into thoughts, that the air was a sufficient maintenance for these exanguious parts. But this defect or rather paucity of blood, is also agreeable unto many other Animals, whose solid nutriment we do not controvert; as may be observed in other sorts of Lizards, in Frogs and divers Fishes; and therefore an Horse-leech will not readily fasten upon every fish; and we do not read of much blood that was drawn from Frogs by Mice, in that famous battel of *Homer*.

The last and most common ground which begat or promoted this opinion, is the long continuation hereof without any visible food, which some observing, precipitously conclude they eat not at all. It cannot be denied it is (if not the most of any) a very abstemious Animal, and such as by reason of its frigidity, paucity of blood, and latitancy in the winter (about which time the observations are often made) will long subsist without a visible sustentation. But a like condition may be also observed in many other Animals; for Lizards and Leeches, as we have made trial, will live some months without sustenance; and we have included Snails in glasses all winter, which have returned to feed again in the spring. Now these notwithstanding, are not conceived to pass all their lives without food; for so to argue is fallacious, and is moreover sufficiently convicted by experience. And therefore probably other relations are of the same verity, which are of the like affinity; as is the conceit of the *Rhintace* in *Persia*, the *Canis Levis* of *America*, and the *Manucodiata* or bird of Paradise in *India*.

To assign a reason of this abstinence in Animals, or declare how without a supply there ensueth no destructive exhaustion, exceedeth the limits and intention of my discourse. *Fortunius Licetus* in his excellent Tract, *de his qui diu vivunt sine alimento*, hath very ingeniously attempted it; deducing the cause hereof from an equal conformity of natural heat and moisture, at least no considerable exuperancy in either; which concurring in an unactive proportion, the natural heat consumeth not the moisture (whereby ensueth no exhaustion) and the condition of natural moisture is able to resist the slender action of heat (whereby it needeth no reparation) and this is evident in Snakes, Lizards, Snails, and divers Insects latitant many months in the year; which being cold creatures, containing a weak heat in a crass or copious humidity, do long subsist without nutrition. For the activity of the agent, being not able to overmaster the resistance of the patient, there will ensue no deperdition. And upon the like grounds it is, that cold and phlegmatick bodies, and (as *Hippocrates* determineth) that old men will best endure fasting. Now the same harmony and stationary constitution, as it happeneth in many species, so doth it fall out sometime in Individuals. For we read of many who have lived long without aliment; and beside deceits and impostures, there may be veritable Relations of some, who without a miracle, and by peculiarity of temper, have far out fasted *Elias*. Which notwithstanding doth not take off the miracle; for that may be miraculously effected in one, which is naturally causable in another. Some naturally living unto an hundred; unto which age, others notwithstanding could not attain without a miracle.

CHAPTER XXII
Of the Ostrich.

The common opinion of the *Ostrich, Struthiocamelus* or *Sparrow-Camel* conceives that it digesteth Iron; and this is confirmed by the affirmations of many; beside swarms of others, *Rhodiginus* in his prelections taketh it for granted, *Johannes Langius* in his Epistles pleadeth experiment for it; the common picture also confirmeth it, which usually describeth this Animal with an horshoe in its mouth. Notwithstanding upon enquiry we find it very questionable, and the negative seems most reasonably entertained; whose verity indeed we do the rather desire, because hereby we shall relieve our ignorance of one occult quality; for in the list thereof it is accounted, and in that notion imperiously obtruded upon us. For my part, although I have had the sight of this Animal, I have not had the opportunity of its experiment, but have received great occasion of doubt, from learned discourses thereon.

For *Aristotle* and *Oppianus* who have particularly treated hereof are silent in this singularity; either omitting it as dubious, or as the Comment saith, rejecting it as fabulous. *Pliny* speaketh generally, affirming only, the digestion is wonderful in this Animal; *Ælian* delivereth, that it digesteth stones without any mention of Iron; *Leo Africanus*, who lived in those Countries wherein they most abound, speaketh diminutively, and but half way into this assertion: *Surdum ac simplex animal est, quicquid invenit, absque delectu, usque ad ferrum devorat*: *Fernelius* in his second *De abditis rerum causis*, extenuates it, and *Riolanus* in his Comment thereof positively denies it. Some have experimentally refuted it, as *Albertus Magnus*; and most plainly *Ulysses Aldrovandus*, whose words are these: *Ego ferri frusta devorare, dum Tridenti essem, observavi, sed quæ incocta rursus excerneret*, that is, at my being at Trent, I observed the *Ostrich* to swallow Iron, but yet to exclude it undigested again.

Now beside experiment, it is in vain to attempt against it by Philosophical argument, it being an occult quality, which contemns the law of Reason, and defends it self by admitting no reason at all. *How (possibly) the stomack of the Ostrich may alter Iron.* As for its possibility we shall not at present dispute; nor will we affirm that Iron ingested, receiveth in the stomack of the *Ostrich* no alteration at all; but if any such there be, we suspect this effect rather from some way of corrosion, then any of digestion; not any liquid reduction or tendance to chilification by the power of natural heat, but rather some attrition from an acide and vitriolous humidity in the stomack, which may absterse and shave the scorious parts thereof. So rusty Iron crammed down the throat of a Cock, will become terse and clear again in its gizzard: So the Counter which according to the relation of *Amatus* remained a whole year in the body of a youth, and came out much consumed at last; might suffer this diminution, rather from sharp and acide humours, then the strength of natural heat, as he supposeth. So silver swallowed and retained some time in the body, will turn black, as if it had been dipped in *Aqua fortis*, or some corrosive water, but Lead will remain unaltered; for that mettal containeth in it a sweet salt or sugar, whereby it resisteth ordinary corrosion, and will not easily dissolve even in *Aqua fortis*. So when for medical uses, we take down the filings of Iron or Steel, we must not conceive it passeth unaltered from us; for though the grosser parts be excluded again, yet are the dissoluble parts extracted, whereby it becomes effectual in deopilations; and therefore for speedier operation we make extinctions, infusions, and the like, whereby we extract the salt and active parts of the Medicine; which being in solution, more easily enter the veins. *What the Chymists would have by their Aurum Potabile.* And this is that the Chymists mainly drive at in the attempt of their *Aurum Potabile*; that is, to reduce that indigestible substance into such a form as may not be ejected by siege, but enter the cavities, and less accessible parts of the body, without corrosion.

The ground of this conceit is its swallowing down fragments of Iron, which men observing, by a froward illation, have therefore conceived it digesteth them; which is an inference not to be admitted, as being a fallacy of the consequent, that is, concluding a position of the consequent, from the position of the antecedent. For many things are swallowed by Animals, rather for condiment, gust or medicament, then any substantial nutriment. So Poultrey, and especially the Turkey, do of themselves take down stones; and we have found at one time in the gizzard of a Turkey no less then seven hundred. Now these rather concur unto digestion, then are themselves digested; for we have found them also in the guts and excrements; but their descent is very slow, for we have given them stones and small pieces of Iron, which eighteen days after we have found remaining in the gizzard. And therefore the experiment of *Langius* and others might be fallible, whilst after the taking they expected it should come down within a day or two after. *How Cherry-stones may be thought to prevent surfets upon eating Cherries.* Thus also we swallow Cherry-stones, but void them unconcocted, and we usually say they preserve us from surfet; for being hard bodies they conceive a strong and durable heat in the stomack, and so prevent the crudities of their fruit: And upon the like reason do culinary operators observe, that flesh boiles best, when the bones are boiled with it. Thus dogs will eat grass, which they digest not: Thus Camels to make the water sapid, do raise the mud with their feet: Thus horses will knable at walls, Pigeons delight in salt stones. Rats will gnaw iron, and *Aristotle* saith the Elephant swalloweth stones. And thus may also the *Ostrich* swallow Iron; not as his proper aliment, but for the ends above expressed, and even as we observe the like in other Animals.

And whether these fragments of Iron and hard substances swallowed by the *Ostrich*, have not also that use in their stomacks, which they have in other birds; that is, in some way to supply the use of teeth, by commolition, grinding and compression of their proper aliment, upon the action of the strongly conformed muscles of the stomack; as the honor'd Dr. *Harvey* discourseth, may also be considered.

What effect therefore may be expected from the stomack of an *Ostrich* by application alone to further digestion in ours, beside the experimental refute of *Galen*, we refer it unto considerations above alledged; Or whether there be any more credit to be given unto the Medicine of *Ælian*, who affirms the stones they swallow have a peculiar vertue for the eyes, then that of *Hermolaus* and *Pliny* drawn from the urine of this Animal; let them determine who can swallow so strange a transmission of qualities, or believe that any Bird or flying Animal doth separately and distinctly urine beside the Bat.

That therefore an *Ostrich* will swallow and take down Iron, is easily to be granted: that oftimes it pass entire away, if we admit of ocular testimony not to be denied. And though some experiment may also plead, that sometimes they are so altered, as not to be found or excluded in any discernable parcels: yet whether this be not effected by some way of corrosion, from sharp and dissolving humidities, rather then any proper digestion, chilifactive mutation, or alimental conversion, is with good reason doubted.

CHAPTER XXIII
Of Unicorns Horn.

Great account and much profit is made of *Unicorns horn*, at least of that which beareth the name thereof; wherein notwithstanding, many I perceive suspect an Imposture, and some conceive there is no such Animal extant. Herein therefore to draw up our determinations; beside the several places of Scripture mentioning this Animal (which some may well contend to be only meant of the Rhinoceros *Some doubt to be made what* ראם *signifieth in Scripture.*) we are so far from denying there is any *Unicorn* at all, that we affirm there are many kinds thereof. In the number of Quadrupedes, we will concede no less then five; that is, the *Indian* Ox, the *Indian* Ass, the Rhinoceros, the Oryx, and that which is more eminently termed *Monoceros,* or *Unicornis.* Some of the list of fishes; as that described by *Olaus, Albertus* and others: and some Unicorns we will allow even among Insects; as those four kinds of nasicornous Beetles described by *Muffetus.*

Secondly, Although we concede there may be many *Unicorns,* yet are we still to seek; for whereunto to affix this Horn in question, or to determine from which thereof we receive this magnified Medicine, we have no assurance, or any satisfactory decision. For although we single out one, and eminently thereto assign the name of the *Unicorn;* yet can we not be secure what creature is meant thereby; what constant shape it holdeth, or in what number to be received. For as far as our endeavours discover, this animal is not uniformly described, but differently set forth by those that undertake it. *The Unicorn, how variously reported by Authors.* Pliny affirmeth it is a fierce and terrible creature; *Vartomannus* a tame and mansuete Animal: those which *Garcias ab Horto* described about the cape of good hope, were beheld with heads like horses; those which *Vartomannus* beheld, he described with the head of a Deer; *Pliny, Ælian, Solinus,* and after these from ocular assurance, *Paulus Venetus* affirmeth, the feet of the *Unicorn* are undivided, and like the Elephants: But those two which *Vartomannus* beheld at *Mecha,* were as he describeth, footed like a Goat. As *Ælian* describeth, it is in the bigness of an Horse, as *Vartomannus,* of a Colt; that which *Thevet* speaketh of was not so big as an Heifer; but *Paulus Venetus* affirmeth, they are but little less then Elephants. Which are discriminations very material, and plainly declare, that under the same name Authors describe not the same Animal: so that the *Unicorns* Horn of one, is not that of another, although we proclaim an equal vertue in all.

Thirdly, Although we were agreed what Animal this was, or differed not in its description, yet would this also afford but little satisfaction; for the Horn we commonly extol, is not the same with that of the Ancients. For that in the description of *Ælian* and *Pliny* was black: this which is shewed amongst us is commonly white, none black; and of those five which *Scaliger* beheld, though one spadiceous, or of a light red, and two enclining to red, yet was there not any of this complexion among them.

Fourthly, What Horns soever they be which pass amongst us, they are not surely the Horns of any one kind of Animal, but must proceed from several sorts of *Unicorns.* For some are wreathed, some not: That famous one which is preserved at St. *Dennis* near *Paris,* hath wreathy spires, and chocleary turnings about it, which agreeth with the description of the *Unicorns* Horn in *Ælian.* Those two in the treasure of St. *Mark* are plain, and best accord with those of the *Indian* Ass, or the descriptions of other *Unicorns:* That in the Repository of the electour of Saxone is plain and not hollow, and is believed to be a true Land *Unicorns* Horn. *Albertus Magnus* describeth one ten foot long, and at the base about thirteen inches compass: And that of *Antwerp* which *Goropius Becanus* describeth, is not much inferiour unto it; which best agree unto the descriptions of the *Sea-Unicorns;* for these, as *Olaus* affirmeth, are of that strength and bigness, as able to penetrate the ribs of ships. The same is more probable, because it was brought from Island, from whence, as *Becanus* affirmeth, three other were brought in his days: And we have heard of some which have been found by the Sea-side, and brought unto us from *America.* So that while we commend the *Unicorns* Horn, and conceive it peculiar but unto one animal; under apprehension of the same vertue, we use very many; and commend that effect from all, which every one confineth unto some one he hath either seen or described.

Fifthly, Although there be many *Unicorns,* and consequently many Horns, yet many there are which bear that name, and currantly pass among us, which are no Horns at all. Such are those fragments and pieces of *Lapis Ceratites,* commonly termed *Cornu fossile,* whereof *Bœtius* had no less than twenty several sorts presented him for *Unicorns* Horn. Hereof in subterraneous cavities, and under the earth there are many to be found in several parts of *Germany;* which are but the lapidescencies and petrifactive mutations of hard bodies; sometimes of Horn, of teeth, of bones, and branches of trees, whereof there are some so imperfectly converted, as to retain the odor and qualities of their originals; as he relateth of pieces of Ash and Walnut. Again, in most, if not all which pass amongst us, and are extolled for precious Horns, we discover not an affection common unto other Horns; that is, they mollifie not with fire, they soften not upon decoction or infusion, nor will they afford a jelly, or mucilaginous concretion in either; which notwithstanding we may effect in Goats horns, Sheeps, Cows and Harts-horn, in the Horn of the *Rhinoceros*, the horn of the Pristis or Sword fish. Nor do they become friable or easily powderable by Philosophical calcination, that is, from the vapor or steam of water, but split and rift contrary to others horns. Unicorns *Horn commonly used in* England, *what it is.* Briefly, many of those commonly received, and whereof there be so many fragments preserved in *England*, are not only no Horn, but a substance harder then a bone, that is, parts of the tooth of a Morse or Sea-horse; in the midst of the solider part contained a curdled grain, which is not to be found in Ivory. This in Northern Regions is of frequent use for hafts of knives or hilts of swords, and being burnt becomes a good remedy for fluxes: but Antidotally used, and exposed for *Unicorns* Horn, it is an insufferable delusion; and with more veniable deceit, it might have been practised in Harts-horn.

The like deceit may be practised in the teeth of other Sea-animals; in the teeth also of the *Hippopotamus*, or great Animal which frequenteth the River *Nilus*: For we read that the same was anciently used instead of Ivory or Elephants tooth. Nor is it to be omitted, what hath been formerly suspected, but now confirmed by *Olaus Wormius*, and *Thomas Bartholinus* and others, that those long Horns preserved as pretious rarities in many places, are but the teeth of Narhwales, to be found about Island, Greenland and other Northern regions; of many feet long, commonly wreathed, very deeply fastned in the upper jaw, and standing directly forward, graphically described in *Bartholinus* De Unicornu., according unto one sent from a Bishop of Island, not separated from the crany. Hereof *Mercator* hath taken notice in his description of Island: some relations hereof there seem to be in *Purchas*, who also delivereth that the Horn at *Windsor*, was in his second voyage brought hither by *Frobisher*. These before the Northern discoveries, as unknown rarities, were carried by Merchants into all parts of *Europe*; and though found on the Sea-shore, were sold at very high rates; but are now become more common, and probably in time will prove of little esteem; and the bargain of *Julius* the third, be accounted a very hard one, who stuck not to give many thousand crowns for one.

Nor is it great wonder we may be so deceived in this, being daily gulled in the brother Antidote Bezoar; whereof though many be false, yet one there passeth amongst us of more intollerable delusion; somewhat paler then the true stone, and given by women in the extremity of great diseases, which notwithstanding is no stone, but seems to be the stony seed of some Lithospermum or greater Grumwell; or the Lobus Echinatus of *Clusius*, called also the Bezoar Nut; for being broken, it discovereth a kernel of a leguminous smell and tast, bitter like a Lupine, and will swell and sprout if set in the ground, and therefore more serviceable for issues, then dangerous and virulent diseases.

Sixthly, Although we were satisfied we had the *Unicorns* Horn, yet were it no injury unto reason to question the efficacy thereof, or whether those vertues pretended do properly belong unto it. For what we observe, (and it escaped not the observation of *Paulus Jovius* many years past) none of the Ancients ascribed any medicinal or antidotal vertue unto the *Unicorns* Horn; and that which *Ælian* extolleth, who was the first and only man of the Ancients who spake of the medical vertue of any *Unicorn*, was the Horn of the *Indian* Ass; whereof, saith he, the Princes of those parts make bowls and drink therein, as preservatives against Poyson, Convulsions, and the Falling-sickness. Now the description of that Horn is not agreeable unto that we commend; for that (saith he) is red above, white below, and black in the middle; which is very different from ours, or any to be seen amongst us. And thus, though the description of the *Unicorn* be very ancient, yet was there of old no vertue ascribed unto it; and although this amongst us receive the opinion of the same vertue, yet is it not the same Horn whereunto the Antients ascribed it.

Lastly, Although we allow it an Antidotal efficacy, and such as the Ancients commended, yet are there some vertues ascribed thereto by Moderns not easily to be received; and it hath surely faln out in this, as other magnified medicines, whose operations effectual in some diseases, are presently extended unto all. That some Antidotal quality it may have, we have no reason to deny; for since Elks Hoofs and Horns are magnified for Epilepsies, since not only the bone in the heart, but the Horn of a Deer is Alexipharmacal, and ingredient into the confection of Hyacinth, and the Electuary of Maximilian; we cannot without prejudice except against the efficacy of this. *Expulsive of Poisons.* But when we affirm it is not only Antidotal to proper venoms, and substances destructive by qualities we cannot express; but that it resisteth also Sublimate, Arsenick, and poysons which kill by second qualities, that is, by corrosion of parts; I doubt we exceed the properties of its nature, and the promises of experiment will not secure the adventure. And therefore in such extremities, whether there be not more probable relief from fat oyly substances, which are the open tyrants over salt and corrosive bodies, then precious and cordial medicines which operate by secret and disputable proprieties; or whether he that swallowed Lime, and drank down Mercury water, did not more reasonably place his cure in milk, butter or oyl, then if he had recurred unto Pearl and Bezoar, common reason at all times, and necessity in the like case would easily determine.

Since therefore there be many *Unicorns*; since that whereto we appropriate a Horn is so variously described, that it seemeth either never to have been seen by two persons, or not to have been one animal; Since though they agreed in the description of the animal, yet is not the Horn we extol the same with that of the Ancients; Since what Horns soever they be that pass among us, they are not the Horns of one, but several animals; Since many in common use and high esteem are no Horns at all; Since if there were true Horns, yet might their vertues be questioned; Since though we allowed some vertues, yet were not others to be received; with what security a man may rely on this remedy, the mistress of fools hath already instructed some, and to wisdom (which is never to wise to learn) it is not too late to consider.

CHAPTER XXIV
That all Animals of the Land, are in their
kind in the Sea.

That all Animals of the Land, are in their kind in the Sea, although received as a principle, is a tenent very questionable, and will admit of restraint. For some in the Sea are not to be matcht by any enquiry at Land, and hold those shapes which terrestrious forms approach not; as may be observed in the Moon-fish, or Orthragoriscus, the several sorts of Raia's, Torpedo's, Oysters, and many more, and some there are in the Land which were never maintained to be in the Sea, as Panthers, Hyæna's, Camels, Sheep, Molls, and others, which carry no name in Icthyology *History of fishes.*, nor are to be found in the exact descriptions of *Rondoletius*, *Gesner*, or *Aldrovandus*.

Again, Though many there be which make out their nominations, as the Hedg-hog, Sea-serpents and others; yet are there also very many that bear the name of animals at Land, which hold no resemblance in corporal configuration; in which account we compute *Vulpecula, Canis, Rana, Passer, Cuculus, Asellus, Turdus, Lepus*, etc. Wherein while some are called the Fox, the Dog, the Sparrow or Frog-fish: and are known by common names with those at Land; yet as their describers attest, they receive not these appellations from a total similitude in figure, but any concurrence in common accidents, in colour, condition or single conformation. As for Sea-horses which much confirm this assertion; in their common descriptions, they are but Crotesco deliniations which fill up empty spaces in Maps, and meer pictorial inventions, not any Physical shapes: sutable unto those which (as *Pliny* delivereth) *Praxiteles* long ago set out in the Temple of *Domitius*. For that which is commonly called a Sea-horse, is properly called a Morse, and makes not out that shape. That which the Ancients named *Hippocampus* is a little animal about six inches long, and not preferred beyond the classis of Insects. That which they termed *Hippopotamus* an amphibious animal, about the River *Nile*, so little resembleth an horse, that as *Mathiolus* observeth, in all except the feet, it better makes out a swine. That which they termed a Lion, was but a kind of Lobster: that which they called the Bear, was but one kind of Crab: and that which they named *Bos marinus*, was not as we conceive a fish resembling an Ox, but a Skait or Thornback, so named from its bigness, expressed by the Greek word *Bous*, which is a prefix of augmentation to many words in that language.

And therefore although it be not denied that some in the water do carry a justifiable resemblance to some at Land, yet are the major part which bear their names unlike; nor do they otherwise resemble the creatures on earth, then they on earth the constellations which pass under animal names in heaven: nor the Dog fish at Sea much more make out the Dog of the Land, then that his cognominal or name-sake in the heavens. Now if from a similitude in some, it be reasonable to infer a correspondence in all, we may draw this analogy of animals upon plants; for vegetables there are which carry a near and allowable similitude unto animals. [Fab. column. de stirp. rarioribus, Orchis, Cercopithecophora, Anthropophora.] We might also conclude that animal shapes were generally made out in minerals: for several stones there are that bear their names in relation to animals or their parts, as *Lapis anguinus, Conchites, Echinites, Encephalites, Ægopthalmus*, and many more; as will appear in the Writers of Minerals, and especially in *Bœtius* and *Aldrovandus*.

Moreover if we concede, that the animals of one Element, might bear the names of those in the other, yet in strict reason the watery productions should have the prenomination: and they of the land rather derive their names, then nominate those of the Sea. For the watery plantations were first existent, and as they enjoyed a priority in form, had also in nature precedent denominations: but falling not under that Nomenclature of *Adam*, which unto terrestrious animals assigned a name appropriate unto their natures: from succeeding spectators they received arbitrary appellations: and were respectively denominated unto creatures known at Land; who in themselves had independent names and not to be called after them, which were created before them.

Lastly, By this assertion we restrain the hand of God, and abridge the variety of the creation; making the creatures of one Element, but an acting over those of another, and conjoyning as it were the species of things which stood at distance in the intellect of God; and though united in the Chaos, had several seeds of their creation. For although in that indistinguisht mass, all things seemed one; yet separated by the voice of God, according to their species, they came out in incommunicated varieties, and irrelative seminalities, as well as divided places; and so although we say the world was made in six days, yet was there as it were a world in every one; that is, a distinct creation of distinguisht creatures; a distinction in time of creatures divided in nature, and a several approbation and survey in every one.

CHAPTER XXV
Concerning the common course of Diet, in making choice of some Animals, and abstaining from eating others.

Why we confine our food unto certain Animals, and totally reject some others; how these distinctions crept into several Nations; and whether this practice be built upon solid reason, or chiefly supported by custom or opinion; may admit consideration.

For first there is no absolute necessity to feed on any; and if we resist not the stream of Authority, and several diductions from holy Scripture: there was no *Sarcophagie* before the flood; [Eating of Flesh.] and without the eating of flesh, our fathers from vegetable aliments, preserved themselves unto longer lives, then their posterity by any other. For whereas it is plainly said [Gen. 1. 29.], I have given you every herb which is upon the face of all the earth, and every tree, to you it shall be for meat; [*The natural vertue of vegetables impaired by the deluge.*] presently after the deluge, when the same had destroyed or infirmed the nature of vegetables, by an expression of enlargement, it is again delivered: [Gen. 9. 3.] Every moving thing that liveth, shall be meat for you, even as the green herb, have I given you all things.

And therefore although it be said that *Abel* was a Shepherd, and it be not readily conceived, the first men would keep sheep, except they made food thereof: great Expositors will tell us, that it was partly for their skins, wherewith they were cloathed, partly for their milk, whereby they were sustained; and partly for Sacrifices, which they also offered.

And though it may seem improbable, that they offered flesh, yet eat not thereof; and *Abel* can hardly be said to offer the firstlings of his flock, and the fat or acceptable part, if men used not to tast the same, whereby to raise such distinctions: some will confine the eating of flesh unto the line of *Cain*, who extended their luxury, and confined not unto the rule of God. That if at any time the line of *Seth* eat flesh, it was extraordinary, and only at their sacrifices; or else (as *Grotius* hinteth) if any such practice there were, it was not from the beginning; but from that time when the waies of men were corrupted, and whereof it is said, that the wickedness of mans heart was great; the more righteous part of mankind probably conforming unto the diet prescribed in Paradise, and the state of innocency. *Eating of Flesh (probably) not so common before the flood.* And yet however the practice of men conformed, this was the injunction of God, and might be therefore sufficient, without the food of flesh.

That they fed not on flesh, at least the faithful party before the flood, may become more probable, because they refrained the same for some time after. For so was it generally delivered of the golden age and reign of *Saturn*; which is conceived the time of *Noah*, before the building of *Babel*. And he that considereth how agreeable this is unto the traditions of the *Gentiles*; that that age was of one tongue: that *Saturn* devoured all his sons but three; that he was the son of *Oceanus* and *Thetis*; that a Ship was his Symbole; that he taught the culture of vineyards, and the art of husbandry, and was therefore described with a sickle, may well conceive, these traditions had their original in *Noah*. Nor did this practice terminate in him, but was continued at least in many after: as (beside the *Pythagoreans* of old, *Bannyans* now in *India*, who upon single opinions refrain the food of flesh) ancient records do hint or plainly deliver. Although we descend not so low, as that of *Æsclepiades* delivered by *Porphyrius*, περὶ ἀποχῆς. that men began to feed on flesh in the raign of *Pygmaleon* brother of *Dido*, who invented several torments, to punish the eaters of flesh.

Nor did men only refrain from the flesh of beasts at first, but as some will have it, beasts from one another. And if we should believe very grave conjecturers, carnivorous animals now, were not flesh devourers then, according to the expression of the divine provision for them. Gen. 1. 36. To every beast of the earth, and to every fowl of the air, I have given every green herb for meat, and it was so. As is also collected from the store laid up in the Ark; wherein there seems to have been no fleshly provision for carnivorous Animals. For of every kind of unclean beast there went but two into the Ark: and therefore no stock of flesh to sustain them many days, much less almost a year.

But when ever it be acknowledged that men began to feed on flesh, yet how they betook themselves after to particular kinds thereof, with rejection of many others, is a point not clearly determined. As for the distinction of clean and unclean beasts, the original is obscure, and salveth not our practice. For no Animal is naturally unclean, or hath this character in nature; and therefore whether in this distinction there were not some mystical intention: *How* Moses *might distinguish beasts into clean and unclean before the flood.* whether *Moses* after the distinction made of unclean beasts, did not name these so before the flood by anticipation: whether this distinction before the flood, were not only in regard of sacrifices, as that delivered after was in regard of food: (for many were clean for food, which were unclean for sacrifice) or whether the denomination were but comparative, and of beasts less commodious for food, although not simply bad, is not yet resolved.

And as for the same distinction in the time of *Moses*, long after the flood, from thence we hold no restriction, as being no rule unto Nations beside the *Jews* in dietetical consideration, or natural choice of diet, they being enjoyned or prohibited certain foods upon remote and secret intentions. Especially thereby to avoid community with the Gentiles upon promiscuous commensality: or to divert them from the Idolatry of *Egypt* whence they came, they were enjoyned to eat the Gods of *Egypt* in the food of Sheep and Oxen. Withall in this distinction of Animals the consideration was hieroglyphical; in the bosom and inward sense implying an abstinence from certain vices symbolically intimated from the nature of those animals; as may be well made out in the prohibited meat of Swine, Cony, Owl, and many more.

At least the intention was not medical, or such as might oblige unto conformity or imitation; For some we refrain which that Law alloweth, as Locusts and many others; and some it prohibiteth, which are accounted good meat in strict and Medical censure: as (beside many fishes which have not finns and scales,) the Swine, Cony and Hare, a dainty dish with the Ancients; as is delivered by *Galen*, testified by *Martial*, Inter quadrupedes mattya prima Lepus. as the popular opinion implied, that men grew fair by the flesh thereof: by the diet of *Cato*, that is Hare and Cabbage; and the *Jus nigrum*, or Black broath of the *Spartans*, which was made with the blood and bowels of an Hare.

And if we take a view of other Nations, we shall discover that they refrained many meats upon the like considerations. For in some the abstinence was symbolical; so *Pythagoras* enjoyned abstinence from fish: that is, luxurious and dainty dishes; So according to *Herodotus*, some *Egyptians* refrained swines flesh, as an impure and sordid animal: which whoever but touched, was fain to wash himself.

Some abstained superstitiously or upon religious consideration: So the *Syrians* refrained Fish and Pigeons; the *Egyptians* of old, Dogs, Eeles and Crocodiles; though Leo *Africanus* delivers, that many of late, do eat them with good gust: and *Herodotus* also affirmeth, that the *Egyptians* of *Elephantina* (unto whom they were not sacred,) did eat thereof in elder times: and Writers testify, that they are eaten at this day in *India* and *America*. And so, as *Cæsar* reports, Lib. 3. de bello Gall. unto the ancient *Britains* it was piaculous to tast a Goose, which dish at present no table is without.

Unto some Nations the abstinence was political and for some civil advantage: So the *Thessalians* refrained Storks, because they destroyed their Serpents; and the like in sundry animals is observable in other Nations.

And under all these considerations were some animals refrained: so the *Jews* abstained from swine at first symbolically, as an Emblem of impurity; and not for fear of the Leprosie, as *Tacitus* would put upon them. The *Cretians* superstitiously, upon tradition that *Jupiter* was suckled in that countrey by a Sow. Some *Egyptians* politically, because they supplyed the labour of plowing by rooting up the ground. And upon like considerations perhaps the *Phœnicians* and *Syrians* fed not on this Animal: and as *Solinus* reports, the *Arabians* also and *Indians*. Aul. Gell. lib. 4. A great part of mankind refraining one of the best foods, and such as *Pythagoras* himself would eat; who, as *Aristoxenus* records, refused not to feed on Pigs.

Certain dishes in great request with the Ancients, not so much esteemed now.

Moreover while we single out several dishes and reject others, the selection seems but arbitrary, or upon opinion; for many are commended and cryed up in one age, which are decryed and nauseated in another. Thus in the dayes of *Mecenas*, no flesh was preferred before young Asses; which notwithstanding became abominable unto succeeding appetites. At the table of *Heliogabalus* the combs of Cocks were an esteemed service; which country stomacks will not admit at ours. The Sumen or belly and dugs of swine with Pig, and sometimes beaten and bruised unto death: the womb of the same Animal, especially that was barren, or else had cast her young ones, though a tough and membranous part, was magnified by Roman Palats; whereunto nevertheless we cannot perswade our stomacks. How *Alec*, *Muria*, and *Garum*, would humour our gust I know not; but surely few there are that could delight in their *Cyceon*; that is, the common draught of Honey, Cheese, parcht Barley-flower, Oyl and Wine; which notwithstanding was commended mixture, and in high esteem among them. We mortifie our selves with the diet of fish, and think we fare coursly if we refrain from the flesh of other animals. But antiquity held another opinion hereof: When *Pythagoras* in prevention of luxury advised, not so much as to tast on fish. Since the *Rhodians* were wont to call them clowns that eat flesh: and since *Plato* to evidence the temperance of the noble *Greeks* before *Troy*, observed, that it was not found they fed on fish, though they lay so long near the *Hellespont*; Odyss. 4º. and was only observed in the companions of *Menelaus*, that being almost starved, betook themselves to fishing about *Pharos*.

Nor will (I fear) the attest or prescript of Philosophers and Physitians, be a sufficient ground to confirm or warrant common practice, as is deducible from ancient Writers, from *Hippocrates*, *Galen*, *Simeon*, *Sethi*: and the later tracts of *Nonnus* Non de re cibaria. and *Castellanus*. Cast. de esu carnium. So *Aristotle* and *Albertus* commend the flesh of young Hawks: *Galen* Gal. Alim. fac. lib. 3. when they feed on Grapes: but condemneth Quails, and ranketh Geese but with Ostriches; which notwithstanding, present practice and every table extolleth. Men think they have fared hardly, if in times of extremity they have descended so low as Dogs: but *Galen* delivereth Gal. Simpl. fac. lib. 3. were the food of many Nations: and *Hippocrates* Hip. de morbis de superfit. ranketh the flesh of Whelps with that of Birds: who also commends them against the Spleen, and to promote conception. The opinion in *Galens* time, which *Pliny* also followeth, deeply condemned Horse-flesh, and conceived the very blood thereof destructive; but no diet is more common among the *Tartars*, who also drink their blood. And though this may only seem an adventure of *Northern* stomacks, yet as *Herodotus* tells us, in the hotter clime of *Persia*, the same was a convivial dish, and solemnly eaten at the feasts of their nativities: whereat they dressed whole Horses, Camels and Asses; contemning the Poverty of *Grecian* feasts, as unfurnish'd of dishes sufficient to fill the bellies of their guests.

Again, While we confine our diet in several places, all things almost are eaten, if we take in the whole earth: for that which is refused in one country, is accepted in another, and in the collective judgment of the world, particular distinctions are overthrown. Thus were it not hard to shew, that Tigers, Elephants, Camels, Mice, Bats and others, are the food of several countries; and *Lerius* with others delivers, that some *Americans* eat of all kinds, not refraining Toads and Serpents: and some have run so high, as not to spare the flesh of man: a practise inexcusable, nor to be drawn into example, a diet beyond the rule and largest indulgence of God.

As for the objection against beasts and birds of prey, it acquitteth not our practice, who observe not this distinction in fishes: nor regard the same in our diet of Pikes, Perches and Eels; Nor are we excused herein, if we examine the stomacks of Mackerels, Cods, and Whitings. Nor is the foulness of food sufficient to justifie our choice; for (beside that their natural heat is able to convert the same into laudable aliment) we refuse not many whose diet is more impure then some which we reject; as may be considered in hogs, ducks, puets, and many more.

Thus we perceive the practice of diet doth hold no certain course, nor solid rule of selection or confinement; Some in an indistinct voracity eating almost any, others out of a timorous pre-opinion, refraining very many. Wherein indeed necessity, reason and Physick, are the best determinators. Surely many animals may be fed on, like many plants; though not in alimental, yet medical considerations: Whereas having raised Antipathies by prejudgement or education, we often nauseate proper meats, and abhor that diet which disease or temper requireth.

A problem.

Now whether it were not best to conform unto the simple diet of our fore-fathers; whether pure and simple waters were not more healthfull then fermented liquors; whether there be not an ample sufficiency without all flesh, in the food of honey, oyl, and the several parts of milk: in the variety of grains, pulses, and all sorts of fruits; since either bread or beverage may be made almost of all?

whether nations have rightly confined unto several meats? or whether the common food of one countrey be not more agreeable unto another? how indistinctly all tempers apply unto the same, and how the diet of youth and old age is confounded: were considerations much concerning health, and might prolong our days, but must not this discourse.

CHAPTER XXVI
Of Sperma-Ceti, and the Sperma-Ceti Whale.

What Sperma-Ceti is, men might justly doubt, since the learned *Hofmannus* in his work of Thirty years *De medicamentis officin.*, saith plainly, *Nescio quid sit*. And therefore need not wonder at the variety of opinions; while some conceived it to be *flos maris*, and many, a bituminous substance floating upon the sea.

That it was not the spawn of the Whale, according to vulgar conceit, or nominal appellation Phylosophers have always doubted, not easily conceiving the Seminal humour of Animals, should be inflamable; or of a floating nature.

That it proceedeth from a Whale, beside the relation of *Clusius* and other learned observers, was indubitably determined, not many years since by a Sperma-Ceti Whale, Near Wells. cast on our coast of *Norfolk*. Which, to lead on further inquiry, we cannot omit to inform. It contained no less then sixty foot in length, the head somewhat peculiar, with a large prominency over the mouth; teeth only in the lower Jaw, received into fleshly sockets in the upper. The Weight of the largest about two pound: No gristly substances in the mouth, commonly called Whale-bones; Only two short finns seated forwardly on the back; the eyes but small, the pizell large, and prominent. Near Hunstanton. A lesser Whale of this kind above twenty years ago, was cast upon the same shore.

The discription of this Whale seems omitted by *Gesner*, *Rondeletius*, and the first Editions of *Aldrovandus*; but describeth the latin impression of *Pareus*, in the Exoticks of *Clusius*, and the natural history of *Nirembergius*; but more amply in Icons and figures of *Johnstonus*.

Mariners (who are not the best Nomenclators) called it a *Jubartas*, or rather *Gibbartas*. Of the same appellation we meet with one in *Rondeletius*, called by the *French* Gibbar, from its round and Gibbous back. The name *Gibbarta* we find also given unto one kind of *Greenland* Whales: But this of ours seemed not to answer the Whale of that denomination; but was more agreeable unto the *Trumpa* or Sperma-Ceti Whale: according to the account of our *Greenland* describers in *Purchas*. And maketh the third among the eight remarkable Whales of that Coast.

Out of the head of this Whale, having been dead divers days, and under putrifaction, flowed streams of oyl and Sperma-Ceti; which was carefully taken up and preserved by the Coasters. But upon breaking up, the Magazin of Sperma-Ceti, was found in the head lying in folds and courses, in the bigness of goose eggs, encompassed with large flakie substances, as large as a mans head, in form of hony-combs, very white and full of oyl.

Some resemblance or trace hereof there seems to be in the *Physiter* or *Capidolio* of *Rondeletius*; while he delivers, that a fatness more liquid then oyl, runs from the brain of that animal; which being out, the Reliques are like the scales of *Sardinos* pressed into a mass; which melting with heat, are again concreted by cold. And this many conceive to have been the fish which swallowed *Jonas*. Although for the largeness of the mouth, and frequency in those seas, it may possibly be the *Lamia*.

Some part of the Sperma-Ceti found on the shore was pure, and needed little depuration; a great part mixed with fetid oyl, needing good preparation, and frequent expression, to bring it to a flakie consistency. And not only the head, but other parts contained it. For the carnous parts being roasted, the oyl dropped out, an axungious and thicker parts subsiding; the oyl it self contained also much in it, and still after many years some is obtained from it.

Greenland Enquirers seldom meet with a Whale of this kind: and therefore it is but a contingent Commodity, not reparable from any other. It flameth white and candent like Camphire, but dissolveth not in *aqua fortis*, like it. Some lumps containing about two ounces, kept ever since in water, afford a fresh and flosculous smell. Well prepared and separated from the oyl, it is of a substance unlikely to decay, and may out last the oyl required in the Composition of *Mathiolus*.

Of the large quantity of oyl, what first came forth by expression from the Sperma-Ceti, grew very white and clear, like that of Almonds or Ben. What came by decoction was red. It was found to spend much in the vessels which contained it: It freezeth or coagulateth quickly with cold, and the newer soonest. It seems different from the oyl of any other animal, and very much frustrated the expectation of our soap-boylers, as not incorporating or mingling with their lyes. But it mixeth well with painting Colours, though hardly drieth at all. Combers of wooll made use hereof, and Country people for cuts, aches and hard tumors. It may prove of good Medical use; and serve for a ground in compounded oyls and Balsams. Distilled, it affords a strong oyl, with a quick and piercing water. Upon Evaporation it gives a balsame, which is better performed with Turpentine distilled with Sperma-Ceti.

Had the abominable scent permitted, enquiry had been made into that strange composure of the head, and hillock of flesh about it. Since the Work-men affirmed, they met with *Sperma-Ceti* before they came to the bone, and the head yet preserved, seems to confirm the same. The Sphincters inserving unto the Fistula or spout, might have been examined, since they are so notably contrived in other cetaceous Animals; as also the Larynx or Throtle, whether answerable unto that of Dolphins and Porposes in the strange composure and figure which it maketh. What figure the stomack maintained in this Animal of one jaw of teeth, since in Porposes, which abound in both, the ventricle is trebly divided, and since in that formerly taken nothing was found but Weeds and a Loligo. The heart, lungs, and kidneys had not escaped; wherein are remarkable differences from Animals of the land, likewise what humor the bladder contained, but especially the seminal parts, which might have determined the difference of that humour; from this which beareth its name.

In vain it was to rake for Ambergreece in the panch of this *Leviathan*, as *Greenland* discoverers, and attests of experience dictate, that they sometimes swallow great lumps thereof in the Sea; insufferable fetour denying that enquiry. And yet if, as *Paracelsus* encourageth, Ordure makes the best Musk, and from the most fetid substances may be drawn the most odoriferous Essences; all that had not *Vespasians* Nose Cui dulcis odor lucri ex re qualibet., might boldly swear, here was a subject fit for such extractions.

CHAPTER XXVII
Compendiously of sundry Tenents concerning other Animals, which examined, prove either false or dubious.

1. And first from great Antiquity, and before the Melody of *Syrens*, the Musical note of Swans hath been commended, and that they sing most sweetly before their death. For thus we read in *Plato*, that from the opinion of *Metempsuchosis*, or transmigration of the souls of men into the bodies of beasts most sutable unto their humane condition, after his death, *Orpheus* the Musician became a Swan. Thus was it the bird of *Apollo* the god of Musick by the *Greeks*; and an Hieroglyphick of musick among the *Egyptians*, from whom the *Greeks* derived the conception; hath been the affirmation of many Latines, and hath not wanted assertors almost from every Nation.

Of swans, and their singing before death.

All which notwithstanding, we find this relation doubtfully received by *Ælian*, as an hear-say account by *Bellonius*, as a false one by *Pliny*, expresly refuted by *Myndius* in *Athenæus*; and severely rejected by *Scaliger*; whose words unto *Cardan* are these: *De Cygni vero cantu suavissimo quem cum parente mendaciorum Græcia jactare ausus est, ad Luciani tribunal, apud quem novi aliquid dicas, statuo.* Authors also that countenance it, speak not satisfactorily of it. Some affirming they sing not till they die; some that they sing, yet die not. Some speak generally, as though this note were in all; some but particularly, as though it were only in some; some in places remote, and where we can have no trial of it; others in places where every experience can refute it; as *Aldrovandus* upon relation delivered, concerning the Musick of the Swans on the river of *Thames* near *London*.

The figuration to be found in Elks, and not in common Swans.

Now that which countenanceth, and probably confirmeth this opinion, is the strange and unusual conformation of the wind pipe, or vocal organ in this animal; observed first by *Aldrovandus*, and conceived by some contrived for this intention. For in its length it far exceedeth the gullet; and hath in the chest a sinuous revolution, that is, when it ariseth from the lungs, it ascendeth not directly unto the throat, but descending first into a capsulary reception of the breast bone; by a Serpentine and Trumpet recurvation it ascendeth again into the neck; and so by the length thereof a great quantity of air is received, and by the figure thereof a Musical modulation effected. But to speak indifferently, this formation of the Weazon, is not peculiar unto the Swan, but common also unto the Platea or Shovelard, a bird of no Musical throat; And as *Aldrovandus* confesseth, may thus be contrived in the Swan to contain a larger stock of air, whereby being to feed on weeds at the bottom, they might the longer space detain their heads under water. But were this formation peculiar, or had they unto this effect an advantage from this part: yet have they a known and open disadvantage from another; that is, a flat bill. For no Latirostrous animal (whereof nevertheless there are no slender numbers) were ever commended for there note, or accounted among those animals which have been instructed to speak.

When therefore we consider the dissention of Authors, the falsity of relations, the indisposition of the Organs, and the immusical note of all we ever beheld or heard of; if generally taken and comprehending all Swans, or of all places, we cannot assent thereto. Surely he that is bit with a Tarantula, shall never be cured by this Musick; and with the same hopes we expect to hear the harmony of the Spheres.

Of the Peacock.

2. That there is a special propriety in the flesh of Peacocks, roast or boiled, to preserve a long time incorrupted, hath been the assertion of many; stands yet confirmed by *Austin, De Civitate Dei*; by *Gygas Sempronius*, in *Aldrovandus*; and the same experiment we can confirm our selves, in the brawn or fleshly parts of Peacoks so hanged up with thred, that they touch no place whereby to contract a moisture; and hereof we have made trial both in summer and winter. The reason, some, I perceive, attempt to make out from the siccity and driness of its flesh, and some are content to rest in a secret propriety thereof. As for the siccity of the flesh, it is more remarkable in other animals, as Eagles, Hawks, and birds of prey; That it is a propriety or agreeable unto none other, we cannot with reason admit: for the same preservation, or rather incorruption we have observed in the flesh of Turkeys, Capons, Hares, Partridge, Venison, suspended freely in the air, and after a year and a half, dogs have not refused to eat them.

As for the other conceit, that a Peacok is ashamed when he looks on his legs, as is commonly held, and also delivered by *Cardan*; beside what hath been said against it by *Scaliger*; let them believe that hold specificial deformities; or that any part can seem unhandsome to their eyes, which hath appeared good and beautiful unto their makers. The occasion of this conceit, might first arise from a common observation, that when they are in their pride, that is, advance their train, if they decline their neck to the ground, they presently demit, and let fall the same: which indeed they cannot otherwise do; for contracting their body, and being forced to draw in their foreparts to establish the hinder in the elevation of the train; if the foreparts depart and incline to the ground, the hinder grow too weak, and suffer the train to fall. And the same in some degree is also observable in Turkeys.

Of the Stork.

3. That Storks are to be found, and will only live in Republikes or free States, is a petty conceit to advance the opinion of popular policies, and from Antipathies in nature, to disparage Monarchical government. But how far agreeable unto truth, let them consider who read in *Pliny*, that among the *Thessalians* who were governed by Kings, and much abounded with Serpents, it was no less then capital to kill a Stork. That the Ancient *Egyptians* honoured them, whose government was from all times Monarchical. That *Bellonius* affirmeth, men make them nests in *France*. That relations make them common in *Persia*, and the dominions of the great *Turk*. And

lastly, how *Jeremy* the Prophet delivered himself Ier. 8. 7. unto his countreymen, whose government was at that time Monarchical. The Stork in the heaven knowing her appointed time, the Turtle, Crane and Swallow observe the time of their coming, but my people know not the judgment of the Lord. Wherein to exprobate their stupidity, he induceth the providence of Storks. Now if the bird had been unknown, the illustration had been obscure, and the exprobation not so proper.

Of the Bittor.

4. That a Bittor maketh that mugient noise, or as we term it Bumping, by putting its bill into a reed as most believe, or as *Bellonius* and *Aldrovandus* conceive, by putting the same in water or mud, and after a while retaining the air by suddenly excluding it again, is not so easily made out. For my own part, though after diligent enquiry, I could never behold them in this motion; Notwithstanding by others whose observations we have expressly requested, we are informed, that some have beheld them making this noise on the shore, their bills being far enough removed from reed or water; that is, first strongly attracting the air, and unto a manifest distention of the neck, and presently after with great contention and violence excluding the same again. As for what others affirm of putting their bill in water or mud, it is also hard to make out. For what may be observed from any that walketh the Fens, there is little intermission, nor any observable pawse, between the drawing in and sending forth of their breath. And the expiration or breathing forth doth not only produce a noise, but the inspiration or hailing in of the air, affordeth a sound that may be heard almost a flight-shot.

Now the reason of this strange and peculiar noise, is deduced from the conformation of the wind-pipe, which in this bird is different from other volatiles. For at the upper extream it hath no fit Larinx, or throttle to qualify the sound, and at the other end, by two branches deriveth it self into the lungs. Which division consisteth only of Semicircular fibers, and such as attain but half way round the part; By which formation they are dilatable into larger capacities, and are able to contain a fuller proportion of air; which being with violence sent up the weazon, and finding no resistance by the Larinx, it issueth forth in a sound like that from caverns, and such as sometimes subterraneous eruptions, from hollow rocks afford. As *Aristotle* observeth in a Problem Sect. 15., and is observable in pitchers, bottles, and that instrument which *Aponensis* upon that Problem describeth, wherewith in *Aristotles* time Gardiners affrighted birds.

Whether the large perforations of the extremities of the weazon, in the *abdomen*, admitting large quantity of ayr within the cavity of its membrans, as it doth in Frogs; may not much assist this mugiency or boation, may also be considered. For such as have beheld them making this noise out of the water, observe a large distention in their bodies; and their ordinary note is but like that of a Raven.

Of Whelps.

5. That whelps are blind nine days and then begin to see, is the common opinion of all, and some will be apt enough to descend unto oaths upon it. But this I find not answerable unto experience, for upon a strict observation of many, I have scarce found any that see the ninth day, few before the twelfth, and the eyes of some not open before the fourteenth day. And this is agreeable unto the determination of *Aristotle*: who computeth the time of their anopsie or non-vision by that of their gestation. For some, saith he, do go with their young the sixt part of a year, two days over or under, that is, about sixty days or nine weeks; and the whelps of these see not till twelve days. Some go the fifth part of a year, that is, seventy-one days, and these, saith he, see not before the fourteenth day. Others do go the fourth part of the year, that is, three whole months, and these, saith he, are without sight no less then seventeen days. Wherein although the accounts be different, yet doth the least thereof exceed the term of nine days, which is so generally received. And this compute of *Aristotle* doth generally overthrow the common cause alleadged for this effect, that is, a precipitation or over-hasty exclusion before the birth be perfect, according unto the vulgar Adage, *Festinans canis cæcos parit catulos*: for herein the whelps of longest gestation,

are also the latest in vision. The manner hereof is this. At the first littering, their eyes are fastly closed, that is, by coalition or joining together of the eyelids, and so continue untill about the twelfth day; at which time they begin to separate, and may be easily divelled or parted asunder; they open at the inward Canthis or greater Angle of the eye, and so by degrees dilate themselves quite open. An effect very strange, and the cause of much obscurity, wherein as yet mens enquiries are blind, and satisfaction not easily acquirable. What ever it be, thus much may we observe, those animals are only excluded without sight, which are multiparous and multifidous, that is, which have many at a litter, and have also their feet divided into many portions. For the Swine, although multiparous, yet being bisulcous, and only cloven hoofed, is not excluded in this manner, but farrowed with open eyes, as other bisulcous animals.

Of a Toad and a Spider.

6. The Antipathy between a Toad and a Spider, and that they poisonously destroy each other, is very famous, and solemn stories have been written of their combats; wherein most commonly the victory is given unto the Spider. Of what Toads and Spiders it is to be understood would be considered. For the Phalangium and deadly Spiders, are different from those we generally behold in *England*. However the verity hereof, as also of many others, we cannot but desire; for hereby we might be surely provided of proper Antidotes in cases which require them; But what we have observed herein, we cannot in reason conceal; who having in a Glass included a Toad with several Spiders, we beheld the Spiders without resistance to sit upon his head and pass over all his body; which at last upon advantage he swallowed down, and that in few hours, unto the number of seven. And in the like manner will Toads also serve Bees, and are accounted enemies unto their Hives.

Of a Lion and a Cock.

7. Whether a Lion be also afraid of a Cock, as is related by many, and believed by most, were very easie in some places to make trial. Although how far they stand in fear of that animal, we may sufficiently understand, from what is delivered by *Camerarius*, whose words in his Symbola are these: *Nostris temporibus in Aula serenissimi Principis Bavariæ, unus ex Leonibus miris saltibus in vicinam cujusdam domus aream sese dimisit, ubi Gallinaceorum cantum aut clamores nihil reformidans, ipsos unà cum plurimis gallinis devoravit.* That is, In our time in the Court of the Prince of *Bavaria*, one of the Lions leaped down into a Neighbours yard, where nothing regarding the crowing or noise of the Cocks, he eat them up with many other Hens. And therefore a very unsafe defensative it is against the fury of this animal (and surely no better then Virginity or bloud Royal) which *Pliny* De sacrificiis et magia. doth place in Cock broth: For herewith, saith he, whoever is anointed (especially if Garlick be boiled therein) no Lion or Panther will touch him. But of an higher nature it were, and more exalted Antipathy, if that were certain which *Proclus* delivers, that solary *Dæmons*, and such as appear in the shape of Lions, will disappear and vanish, if a Cock be presented upon them.

8. It is generally conceived, an Ear-wig hath no Wings, and is reckoned amongst impennous insects by many; but he that shall narrowly observe them, or shall with a needle put aside the short and sheathy cases on their back, may extend and draw forth two wings of a proportionable length for flight, and larger then in many flies. The experiment of *Pennius* is yet more perfect, who with a Rush or Bristle so pricked them as to make them flie.

Of Worms.

9. That Worms are exanguious Animals, and such as have no bloud at all, is the determination of Philosophy, the general opinion of Scholars, and I know not well to dissent from thence my self. If so, surely we want a proper term whereby to express that humour in them which so strictly resembleth bloud: and we refer it unto the discernment of others what to determine of that red and sanguineous humor, found more plentifully about the Torquis or carneous Circle of great Worms in the Spring, affording in Linnen or Paper an indiscernable tincture from bloud. Or wherein that differeth from a vein, which in an apparent blew runneth along the body, and if dexterously pricked with a lancet, emitteth a red drop, which pricked on either side it will not readily afford.

In the upper parts of Worms, there are likewise found certain white and oval Glandulosities, which Authors term Eggs, and in magnifying Glasses, they also represent them; how properly, may also be enquired; since if in them there be distinction of Sexes, these Eggs are to be found in both. For in that which is presumed to be their coition, that is, their usual complication, or lateral adhesion above the ground, dividing suddenly with two Knives the adhering parts of both, I have found these Eggs in either.

10. That Flies, Bees, etc. do make that noise or humming sound by their mouth, or as many believe with their wings only, would be more warily asserted, if we consulted the determination of *Aristotle*, who as in sundry other places, so more expresly in his book of respiration, affirmeth this sound to be made by the illision of an inward spirit upon a pellicle or little membrane about the precinct or pectoral division of their body. If we also consider that a Bee or Flie, so it be able to move the body, will buz, though its head be off; that it will do the like if deprived of wings, reserving the head, whereby the body may be the better moved. And that some also which are big and lively will hum without either head or wing.

Nor is it only the beating upon this little membrane, by the inward and con-natural spirit as *Aristotle* determines, or the outward air as *Scaliger* conceiveth, which affordeth this humming noise, but most of the other parts may also concur hereto; as will be manifest, if while they hum we lay our finger on the back or other parts; for thereupon will be felt a serrous or jarring motion like that which happeneth while we blow on the teeth of a comb through paper; and so if the head or other parts of the trunk be touched with oyl, the sound will be much impaired, if not destroyed: for those being also dry and membranous parts, by attrition of the spirit do help to advance the noise: And therefore also the sound is strongest in dry weather, and very weak in rainy season, and toward winter; for then the air is moist, and the inward spirit growing weak, makes a languid and dumb allision upon the parts.

Of a Tainct.

11. There is found in the Summer a kind of Spider called a Tainct, of a red colour, and so little of body that ten of the largest will hardly outway a grain; this by Country people is accounted a deadly poison unto Cows and Horses; who, if they suddenly die, and swell thereon, ascribe their death hereto, and will commonly say, they have licked a Tainct. Now to satisfie the doubts of men we have called this tradition unto experiment; we have given hereof unto Dogs, Chickens, Calves and Horses, and not in the singular number; yet never could find the least disturbance ensue. There must be therefore other causes enquired of the sudden death and swelling of cattle; and perhaps this insect is mistaken, and unjustly accused for some other. For some there are which from elder times have been observed pernicious unto cattle, as the Buprestis or Burstcow, the Pityocampe or Eruca Pinuum, by *Dioscorides, Galen* and *Ætius*, the Staphilinus described by *Aristotle* and others, or those red Phalangious Spiders like Cantharides mentioned by *Muffetas*. Now although the animal may be mistaken and the opinion also false, yet in the ground and reason which makes men most to doubt the verity hereof, there may be truth enough, that is, the inconsiderable quantity of this insect. For that a poison cannot destroy in so small a bulk, we have no reason to affirm. For if, as *Leo Africanus* reporteth, the tenth part of a grain of the poison of *Nubia* [granum Nubiæ.], will dispatch a man in two hours; if the bite of a Viper and sting of a Scorpion, is not conceived to impart so much; if the bite of an Asp will kill within an hour, yet the impression scarce visible, and the poison communicated not ponderable; we cannot as impossible reject this way of destruction; or deny the power of death in so narrow a circumscription.

Of the Glow-worm.

12. Wondrous things are promised from the Glow-worm; from thence perpetual lights are pretended, and waters said to be distilled which afford a lustre in the night; and this is asserted by *Cardan, Albertus, Gaudentinus, Mizaldus*, and many more. But hereto we cannot with reason assent: for the light made by this animal depends much upon its life. For when they are dead they shine not, nor alwaies while they live; but are obscure or light, according to the protrusion of their luminous parts, as observation will instruct us. For this flammeous light is not over all the body, but only visible on the inward side; in a small white part near the tail. When this is full and seemeth protruded, there ariseth a flame of a circular figure and Emerald green colour; which is discernable in any dark place in the day; but when it falleth and seemeth contracted, the light disappeareth, and the colour of the part only remaineth. Now this light, as it appeareth and disappeareth in their

life, so doth it go quite out at their death. As we have observed in some, which preserved in fresh grass have lived and shined eighteen days; but as they declined, and the luminous humor dryed, their light grew languid, and at last went out with their lives. Thus also the *Torpedo*, which alive hath a power to stupifie at a distance, hath none upon contaction being dead, as *Galen* and *Rondeletius* particularly experimented. And this hath also disappointed the mischief of those intentions, which study the advancement of poisons; and fancy destructive compositions from Asps or Vipers teeth, from Scorpions or Hornet stings. For these omit their efficacy in the death of the individual, and act but dependantly on their forms. And thus far also those Philosophers concur with us, which held the Sun and Stars were living creatures, for they conceived their lustre depended on their lives; but if they ever died, their light must also perish.

It were a Notable piece of Art to translate the light from the *Bononian* Stone into another Body; he that would attempt to make a shining Water from *Glow-worms*, must make trial when the Splendent part is fresh and turgid. For even from the great *American Glow-worms*, and Flaming *Flies*, the light declineth as the luminous humor dryeth.

Now whether the light of animals, which do not occasionally shine from contingent causes, be of Kin unto the light of Heaven; whether the invisible flame of life received in a convenient matter, may not become visible, and the diffused ætherial light make little Stars by conglobation in idoneous parts of the compositum: whether also it may not have some original in the seed and spirit analogous unto the Element of Stars, whereof some glympse is observable in the little refulgent humor, at the first attempts of formation: Philosophy may yet enquire.

True it is, that a Glow-worm will afford a faint light, almost a days space when many will conceive it dead; but this is a mistake in the compute of death, and term of disanimation; for indeed, it is not then dead, but if it be distended will slowly contract it self again, which when it cannot do, it ceaseth to shine any more. And to speak strictly, it is no easie matter to determine the point of death in Insects and Creatures who have not their vitalities radically confined unto one part; for they are not dead when they cease to move or afford the visible evidences of life; as may be observed in Flies, who when they appear even desperate and quite forsaken of their forms; by vertue of the Sun or warm ashes will be revoked unto life, and perform its functions again.

Now whether this lustre, a while remaining after death, dependeth not still upon the first impression, and light communicated or raised from an inward spirit, subsisting a while in a moist and apt recipient, nor long continuing in this, or the more remarkable *Indian* Glow-worm; or whether it be of another Nature, and proceedeth from different causes of illumination; yet since it confessedly subsisteth so little a while after their lives, how to make perpetual lights, and sublunary moons thereof as is pretended, we rationally doubt, though not so sharply deny, with *Scaliger* and *Muffetus*.

13. The wisdom of the Pismire is magnified by all, and in the Panegyricks of their providence we alwaies meet with this, that to prevent the growth of Corn which they store up, they bite off the end thereof: And some have conceived that from hence they have their name in Hebrew: Nemalah à Namal circumcidit. From whence ariseth a conceit that Corn will not grow if the extreams be cut or broken. But herein we find no security to prevent its germination; as having made trial in grains, whose ends cut off have notwithstanding suddenly sprouted, and accordingly to the Law of their kinds; that is, the roots of barley and oats at contrary ends, of wheat and rye at the same. And therefore some have delivered that after rainy weather they dry these grains in the Sun; which if effectual, we must conceive to be made in a high degree and above the progression of Malt; for that Malt will grow, this year hath informed us, and that unto a perfect ear.

A natural vicissitude of generation in Homogeneous things.

And if that be true which is delivered by many, and we shall further experiment, that a decoction of Toad-stools if poured upon earth, will produce the same again: If Sow-thistles will abound in places manured with dung of Hogs, which feeds much upon that plant: If Horse-dung reproduceth oats: If winds and rains will transport the seminals of plants; it will not be easie to determine where the power of generation ceaseth. The forms of things may lie deeper then we conceive them; seminal principles may not be dead in the divided atoms of plants: but wandering in the ocean of nature, when they hit upon proportionable materials, may unite, and return to their visible selves again.

But the prudence of this Animal is by knawing, piercing, or otherwise, to destroy the little nebbe or principle of germination. Which notwithstanding is not easily discoverable; it being no ready business to meet with such grains in Ant-hils; and he must dig deep, that will seek them in the Winter.

CHAPTER XXVIII
Of some others.

Of the Chicken.

That a Chicken is formed out of the yelk of the Egg, was the opinion of some Ancient Philosophers. Whether it be not the nutriment of the Pullet, may also be considered: Since umbilical vessels are carried unto it: Since much of the yelk remaineth after the Chicken is formed: Since in a Chicken newly hatched, the stomack is tincted yellow, and the belly full of yelk, which is drawn in at the navel or vessels towards the vent, as may be discerned in Chickens within a day or two before exclusion.

Whether the Chicken be made out of the white, or that be not also its aliment, is likewise very questionable: Since an umbilical vessel is derived unto it: Since after the formation and perfect shape of the Chicken, much of the white remaineth.

Whether it be not made out of the grando, gallature, germ or tred of the Egg, as, *Aquapendente* informeth us, seemed to many of doubt: for at the blunter end it is not discovered after the Chicken is formed; by this also the yelk and white are continued, whereby it may conveniently receive its nutriment from them both.

Now that from such slender materials, nature should effect this production it is no more then is observed in other animals; and even in grains and kernels, the greatest part is but the nutriment of that generative particle, so disproportionable unto it.

Of Eggs.

A greater difficulty in the doctrine of Eggs, is, how the sperm of the Cock prolificates and makes the oval conception fruitful, or how it attaineth unto every Egg, since the vitellary or place of the yelk is very high: Since the ovary or part where the white involveth it, is in the second region of the matrix, which is somewhat long and inverted: Since also a Cock will in one day fertilate the whole racemation or cluster of Eggs, which are not excluded in many weeks after.

But these at last, and how in the Cicatricula or little pale circle formation first beginneth, how the Grando or tredle, are but the poles and establishing particles of the tender membrans, firmly conserving the floating parts, in their proper places, with many other observables, that ocular Philosopher, and singular discloser of truth, Dr. *Harvey* hath discovered, in that excellent discourse of Generation; So strongly erected upon the two great pillars of truth, experience and solid reason.

That the sex is discernable from the figure of Eggs, or that Cocks or Hens proceed from long or round ones, as many contend, experiment will easily frustrate.

The *Ægyptians* observed a better way to hatch their Eggs in Ovens, then the *Babylonians* to roast them at the bottom of a sling, by swinging them round about, till heat from motion had concocted them; for that confuseth all parts without any such effect.

Though slight distinction be made between boiled and roasted Eggs, yet is there no slender difference, for the one is much drier then the other: the Egg expiring less in the elixation or boiling; whereas in the assation or roasting, it will sometimes abate a dragm; that is, threescore grains in weight. So a new laid Egg will not so easily be boiled hard, because it contains a greater stock of humid parts; which must be evaporated, before the heat can bring the inexhalable parts into consistence.

Why the Hen hatcheth not the Egg in her belly, or maketh not at least some rudiment thereof within her self, by the natural heat of inward parts, since the same is performed by incubation from an outward warmth after? Why the Egg is thinner at one extream? Why there is some cavity or emptiness at the blunter end? Why we open them at that part? Why the greater end is first excluded? Why some Eggs are all red, as the Kestrils; some only red at one end, as those of Kites and Buzzards? why some Eggs are not Oval but Round, as those of fishes? etc. are problems, whose decisions would too much enlarge this discourse.

Of Snakes, etc.

That Snakes and Vipers do sting or transmit their mischief by the tail, is a common expression not easily to be justified; and a determination of their venoms unto a part, wherein we could never find it; the poison lying about the teeth, and communicated by bite, in such are destructive. And therefore when biting Serpents are mentioned in the Scripture, they are not differentially set down from such as mischief by stings; nor can conclusions be made conformable to this opinion, because when the Rod of *Moses* was turned into a Serpent, God determinately commanded him to take up the same by the tail.

Nor are all Snakes of such empoisoning qualities, as common opinion presumeth; as is confirmable from the ordinary green Snake with us, from several histories of domestick Snakes, from Ophiophagous nations, and such as feed upon Serpents.

Surely the destructive delusion of Satan in this shape, hath much enlarged the opinion of their mischief. Which notwithstanding was not so high with the heathens, in whom the Devil had wrought a better opinion of this animal, it being sacred unto the *Egyptians*, *Greeks* and *Romans*, and the common symbole of sanity. In the shape whereof *Æsculapius* the God of health appeared unto the *Romans*, accompanied their Embassadors to *Rome* from *Epidaurus*; and the same did stand in the *Tiberine* Isle upon the Temple of *Æsculapius*.

Some doubt many have of the Tarantula, or poisonous Spider of *Calabria*, and that magical cure of the bite thereof by Musick. But since we observe that many attest it from experience: Since the learned *Kircherius* hath positively averred it, and set down the songs and tunes solemnly used for it; Since some also affirm the Tarantula it self will dance upon certain stroaks, whereby they set their instruments against its poison; we shall not at all question it.

Much wonder is made of the Boramez, that strange plant-animal or vegetable Lamb of *Tartary*, which Wolves delight to feed on, which hath the shape of a Lamb, affordeth a bloody juyce upon breaking, and liveth while the plants be consumed about it. And yet if all this be no more, then the shape of a Lamb in the flower or seed, upon the top of the stalk, as we meet with the forms of Bees, Flies and Dogs in some others; he hath seen nothing that shall much wonder at it.

It may seem too hard to question the swiftness of Tigers, which hath therefore given names unto Horses, Ships and Rivers, nor can we deny what all have thus affirmed; yet cannot but observe, that *Jacobus Bontius* late Physitian at *Java* in the East *Indies*, as an ocular and frequent witness is not afraid to deny it; to condemn *Pliny* who affirmeth it, and that indeed it is but a slow and tardigradous animal, preying upon advantage, and otherwise may be escaped.

Many more there are whose serious enquiries we must request of others, and shall only awake considerations, Whether that common opinion that Snakes do breed out of the back or spinal marrow of man, doth build upon any constant root or seed in nature; or did not arise from contingent generation, in some single bodies remembred by *Pliny* or others, and might be paralleld since in living corruptions of the guts and other parts; which regularly proceed not to putrifactions of that nature.

Whether the Story of the Remora be not unreasonably amplified; whether that of Bernacles and Goose-trees be not too much enlarged; whether the common history of Bees will hold, as large accounts have delivered; whether the brains of Cats be attended with such destructive malignities, as *Dioscorides* and others put upon them.

As also whether there be not some additional help of Art, unto the Numismatical and Musical shells, which we sometimes meet with in conchylious collections among us?

Whether the fasting spittle of man be poison unto Snakes and Vipers, as experience hath made us doubt? Whether the Nightingals setting with her breast against a thorn, be any more then that she placeth some prickels on the outside of her nest, or roosteth in thorny and prickly places, where Serpents may least approach her? Whether Mice may be bred by putrifaction as well as univocall production, as may be easily believed, if that receit to make Mice out of wheat will hold, which *Helmont* hath delivered. Helm. Imago fermenti, *etc.* Whether Quails from any idiosyncracy or peculiarity of constitution, do innocuously feed upon Hellebore, or rather sometime but medically use the same; because we perceive that Stares, which are commonly said harmlessly to feed on Hemlock, do not make good the tradition; and he that observes what vertigoes, cramps and convulsions follow thereon in these animals, will be of our belief.

THE FOURTH BOOK
Of many popular and received Tenents concerning Man, which examined, prove either false or dubious.

CHAPTER I
Of the Erectness of Man.

What figure in animals is properly erect.

That only *Man* hath an Erect figure, and for to behold and look up toward heaven, according to that of the Poet,

Pronaque cum spectant animalia cætera terram,
Os homini sublime dedit, cælumque tueri
Jussit, et erectos ad sydera tollere vultus,

is a double assertion, whose first part may be true, if we take Erectness strictly, and so as *Galen* hath defined it; for they only, saith he, have an Erect figure, whose spine and thigh-bone are carried in right lines; and so indeed of any we yet know, *Man* only is Erect. For the thighs of other animals do stand at Angles with their spine, and have rectangular positions in Birds, and perfect Quadrupeds. Nor doth the Frog, though stretched out, or swimming, attain the rectitude of *Man*, or carry its thigh without all angularity. *What seiante or sitting.* And thus is it also true, that Man only sitteth, if we define sitting to be a firmation of the body upon the *Ischias*: wherein if the position be just and natural, the Thigh-bone lieth at right angles to the Spine, and the Leg-bone or Tibia to the Thigh. For others when they seem to sit, as *Dogs, Cats,* or *Lions,* do make unto their Spine acute angles with their Thigh, and acute to the Thigh with their Shank. Thus is it likewise true, what *Aristotle* alledgeth in that Problem; why *Man* alone suffereth pollutions in the Night, ἐξονειρωκτικός. because *Man* only lyeth upon his Back; if we define not the same by every supine position, but when the Spine is in rectitude with the Thigh, and both with the arms lie parallel to the *Horizon*: so that a line through their Navel will pass through the Zenith and Centre of the Earth. And so cannot other Animals lie upon their Backs: for though the Spine lie parallel with the *Horizon*, yet will their Legs incline, and lie at angles unto it. And upon these three divers positions in *Man*, wherein the Spine can only be at right lines with the Thigh, arise those remarkable postures, prone, supine and erect; which are but differenced in situation, or in angular postures upon the Back, the Belly and the Feet.

But if Erectness be popularly taken, and as it is largely opposed unto proneness, or the posture of animals looking downwards, carrying their venters or opposite part to the Spine, directly towards the Earth, it may admit of question. For though in *Serpents* and *Lizards* we may truly allow a proneness, yet *Galen* acknowledgeth that perfect Quadrupeds, as *Horses, Oxen* and *Camels,* are but partly prone, and have some part of Erectness. And *Birds* or flying Animals, are so far from this kind of proneness, that they are almost Erect; advancing the Head and Breast in their progression, and only prone in the Act of volitation or flying. And if that be true which is delivered of the *Pengin* or *Anser Magellanicus*, often described in Maps about those *Straits*, that they go Erect like *Men*, and with their Breast and Belly do make one line perpendicular unto the axis of the Earth; it will almost make up the exact Erectness of *Man*. *Observe also the* Vrias Bellanii *and* Mergus major. Nor will that Insect come very short which we have often beheld, that is, one kind of Locust which stands not prone, or a little inclining upward, but in a large Erectness, elevating alwaies the two fore Legs, and sustaining it self in the middle of the other four: by *Zoographers* [*Describers of animals.*] called *Mantis*, and by the common people of *Provence, Prega, Dio,* the Prophet and praying Locust; as being generally found in the posture of supplication, or such as resembleth ours, when we lift up our hands to Heaven.

As for the end of this Erection; to look up toward Heaven; though confirmed by several testimonies, and the *Greek* Etymology of *Man*, it is not so readily to be admitted; and as a popular and vain conceit was Anciently rejected by *Galen*; who in his third, *De usu partium*, determines, that *Man* is Erect, because he was made with hands, and was therewith to exercise all Arts, which in any other figure he could not have performed; as he excellently declareth in that place, where he also proves that *Man* could have been made neither Quadruped nor Centaur.

And for the accomplishment of this intention, that is, to look up and behold the Heavens, *Man* hath a notable disadvantage in the Eye lid; whereof the upper is far greater than the lower, which abridgeth the sight upwards; contrary to those of *Birds*, who herein have the advantage of *Man*: Insomuch that the Learned *Plempius* [*Plemp. Ophthalmographia.*] is bold to affirm, that if he had had the formation of the Eye-lids, he would have contrived them quite otherwise.

The ground and occasion of this conceit was a literal apprehension of a figurative expression in *Plato*, as *Galen* thus delivers; To opinion that *Man* is Erect to look up and behold the Heavens, is a conceit only fit for those that never saw the *Fish* Uranoscopus, that is, the Beholder of Heaven; which hath its Eyes so placed, that it looks up directly to Heaven; which *Man* doth not, except he recline, or bend his head backward: and thus to look up to Heaven, agreeth not only unto *Men*, but *Asses*; to omit *Birds* with long necks, which look not only upwards, but round about at pleasure. And therefore *Men* of this opinion understood not *Plato* when he said that *Man* doth *Sursum aspicere*; for thereby was not meant to gape, or look upward with the Eye, but to have his thoughts sublime; and not only to behold, but speculate their Nature, with the Eye of the understanding.

Now although *Galen* in this place makes instance but in one, yet are the other fishes, whose Eyes regard the Heavens, as Plane, and Cartilagineous *Fishes*; as *Pectinals*, or such as have their bones made laterally like a Comb; for when they apply themselves to sleep or rest upon the white side, their Eyes on the other side look upward toward Heaven. For *Birds*, they generally carry their heads Erectly like *Man*, and have advantage in their upper Eye-lid; and many that have long necks, and bear their heads somewhat backward, behold far more of the Heavens, and seem to look above the æquinoxial Circle. And so also in many Quadrupeds, although their progression be partly prone, yet is the sight of their Eye direct, not respecting the Earth but Heaven; and make an higher Arch of altitude then our own. The position of a *Frog* with his head above water exceedeth these; for therein he seems to behold a large part of the Heavens, and the acies of his Eye to ascend as high as the Tropick; but he that hath beheld the posture of a *Bittor*, will not deny that it beholds almost the very *Zenith*. [*Point of heaven over our heads.*]

CHAPTER II
Of the Heart.

How a Mans heart is placed in his Body.

That the *Heart* of Man is seated in the left side, is an asseveration, which strictly taken, is refutable by inspection, whereby it appears the base and centre thereof is in the midst of the chest; true it is, that the Mucro or Point thereof inclineth unto the left; for by this position it giveth way unto the ascension of the midriff, and by reason of the hollow vein could not commodiously deflect unto the right. From which diversion, nevertheless we cannot so properly say tis placed in the left, as that it consisteth in the middle, that is, where its centre resteth; for so do we usually say a Gnomon or Needle is in the middle of a Dial, although the extreams may respect the North or South, and approach the circumference thereof.

The ground of this mistake is a general observation from the pulse or motion of the *Heart*, which is more sensible on this side; but the reason hereof is not to be drawn from the situation of the *Heart*, but the site of the left ventricle wherein the vital Spirits are laboured; and also the great Artery that conveieth them out; both which are situated on the left. Upon this reason Epithems or cordial Applications are justly applied unto the left Breast; and the Wounds under the fifth Rib may be more suddenly destructive if made on the sinister side, and the Spear of the Souldier that peirced our Saviour, is not improperly described, when Painters direct it a little towards the left.

The other ground is more particular and upon inspection; for in dead Bodies especially lying upon the Spine, the *Heart* doth seem to incline unto the left. Which happeneth not from its proper site; but besides its sinistrous gravity, is drawn that way by the great Artery, which then subsideth and haleth the *Heart* unto it. And therefore strictly taken, the *Heart* is seated in the middle of the Chest; but after a careless and inconsiderate aspection, or according to the readiest sense of pulsation, we shall not quarrel, if any affirm it is seated toward the left. And in these considerations must *Aristotle* be salved, when he affirmeth the *Heart* of Man is placed in the left side, and thus in a popular acception may we receive the Periphrasis of *Persius*; ——Leva in parte mamillæ. when he taketh the part under the left Pap for the *Heart*; and if rightly apprehended, it concerneth not this controversie, when it is said in *Ecclesiastes*: The *Heart* of a wise Man is in the right side, but that of a Fool in the left, for thereby may be implied, that the *Heart* of a wise Man delighteth in the right way, or in the path of Vertue; that of a Fool in the left or road of Vice; according to the mystery of the Letter of *Pythagoras*, or that expression in *Jonah*, concerning sixscore thousand, that could not discern between their right hand and their left, or knew not good from evil.

That assertion also that Man proportionally hath the largest brain, I did I confess somewhat doubt; and conceived it might have failed in Birds, especially such as having little Bodies, have yet large Cranies, and seem to contain much Brain, as *Snipes*, *Woodcocks*, etc. But upon trial I find it very true. The Brains of a Man, *Archangelus* and *Bauhinus* observe, to weigh four pound, and sometime five and a half. If therefore a Man weigh one hundred and fourty pounds, and his Brain but five, his Weight is 27. times as much as his brain, deducting the weight of that five pound which is allowed for it. Now in a Snipe, which weighed four ounces two dragms, I find the Brains to weigh but half a dragm; so that the weight of the Body (allowing for the Brain) exceeded the weight of the Brain, sixty seven times and an half.

More controvertible it seemeth in the Brains of Sparrows, whose Cranies are rounder, and so of larger capacity: and most of all in the Heads of Birds, upon the first formation in the Egg, wherein the Head seems larger then all the Body, and the very Eyes almost as big as either. A Sparrow in the total we found to weigh seven dragms and four and twenty grans; whereof the Head a dragm, but the Brain not fifteen grains; which answereth not fully the proportion of the brain of Man. And therefore it is to be taken of the whole Head with the Brains, when *Scaliger* Histor. Animal. lib. 1. objecteth that the Head of a Man is the fifteenth part of his Body; that of a Sparrow, scarce the fifth.

CHAPTER III
Of Pleurisies.

What a Pleurisie is.

That *Pleurisies* are only on the left side, is a popular Tenent not only absurd but dangerous. From the misapprehension hereof, men omitting the opportunity of remedies, which otherwise they would not neglect. Chiefly occasioned by the Ignorance of *Anatomy* and the extent of the part affected; which in an exquisite *Pleurisie* is determined to be the skin or membrane which invested the Ribs, for so it is defined, *Inflammatio membranæ costas succingentis*; An Inflammation, either simple, consisting only of an hot and sanguineous affluxion; or else denominable from other humours, according to the predominancy of melancholy, flegm, or choler. The membrane thus inflamed, is properly called *Pleura*; from whence the disease hath its name; and this investeth not only one side, but overspreadeth the cavity of the chest, and affordeth a common coat unto the parts contained therein.

Now therefore the *Pleura* being common unto both sides, it is not reasonable to confine the inflammation unto one, nor strictly to determine it is alwaies in the side; but sometimes before and behind, that is, inclining to the Spine or Breast-bone; for thither this Coat extendeth; and therefore with equal propriety we may affirm, that ulcers of the lungs, or Apostems of the brain do happen only in the left side; or that Ruptures are confinable unto one side, whereas the Peritoneum or Rib of the Belly may be broke, or its perforations relaxed in either.

CHAPTER IV
Of the Ring-finger.

An opinion there is, which magnifies the fourth *Finger* of the left Hand; presuming therein a cordial relation, that a particular vessel, nerve, vein or artery is conferred thereto from the heart, and therefore that especially hath the honour to bear our Rings. Which was not only the Christian practice in Nuptial contracts, but observed by Heathens, as *Alexander ab Alexandro*, *Gellius*, *Macrobius* and *Pierius* have delivered, as *Levinus Lemnius* hath confirmed, who affirms this peculiar vessel to be an artery, and not a Nerve, as Antiquity hath conceived it; adding moreover that *Rings* hereon peculiarly affect the Heart; that in Lipothymies or swoundings he used the frication of this *Finger* with saffron and gold: that the ancient Physitians mixed up their Medicines herewith; that this is seldom or last of all affected with the Gout, and when that becometh nodous, Men continue not long after. Notwithstanding all which we remain unsatisfied, nor can we think the reasons alleadged sufficiently establish the preheminency of this *Finger*.

For first, Concerning the practice of Antiquity, the custom was not general to wear their *Rings* either on this hand or *Finger*; for it is said, and that emphatically in *Jeremiah*, *Si fuerit Jeconias filius Joachim regis Judæ annulus in manu dextrâ meâ, inde evallam eum*: Though *Coniah* the son of *Joachim* King of *Judah*, were the signet on my right Hand, yet would I pluck thee thence. So is it observed by *Pliny*, that in the portraits of their Gods, the *Rings* were worn on the *Finger* next the *Thumb*; that the *Romans* wore them also upon their little Finger, as *Hero* is described in *Petronius*; some wore them on the middle *Finger*, as the ancient *Gaules* and *Britans*; and some upon the fore-*Finger*, as is deduceable from *Julius Pollux*: who names that *Ring* Corionos.

Rings anciently of Iron.

Again, That the practice of the ancients, had any such respect of cordiality or reference unto the Heart, will much be doubted, if we consider their Rings were made of iron; such was that of *Prometheus*, who is conceived the first that brought them in use. So, as *Pliny* affirmeth, for many years the Senators of *Rome* did not wear any Rings of Gold; but the slaves wore generally Iron Rings until their manumission or preferment to some dignity. That the *Lacedemonians* continued their Iron Rings unto his daies, *Pliny* also delivereth, and surely they used few of Gold; for beside that *Lycurgus* prohibited that mettal, we read in *Athenæus*, that having a desire to guild the face of *Apollo*, they enquired of the Oracle where they might purchase so much Gold; and were directed unto *Crœsus* King of *Lydia*.

Moreover whether the Ancients had any such intention, the grounds which they conceived in Vein, Nerve or Artery, are not to be justified, nor will inspection confirm a peculiar vessel in this Finger. For as *Anatomy* informeth, the Basilica vein dividing into two branches below the cubit, the outward sendeth two surcles unto the thumb, two unto the fore-finger, and one unto the middle finger in the inward side; the other branch of the Basilica sendeth one surcle unto the outside of the middle finger, two unto the Ring, and as many unto the little fingers; so that they all proceed from the Basilica, and are in equal numbers derived unto every one. In the same manner are the branches of the axillary artery distributed into the Hand; for below the cubit it divideth into two parts, the one running along the *Radius*, and passing by the wrest or place of the pulse, is at the *Fingers* subdivided into three Branches; whereof the first conveyeth two surcles unto the *Thumb*, the second as many to the fore-*Finger*, and the third one unto the middle *Finger*; the other or lower division of the artery descendeth by the ulna, and furnisheth the other *Fingers*; that is the middle with one surcle, and the *Ring* and little *Fingers* with two. *Whence the Nerves proceed.* As for the Nerves, they are disposed much after the same manner, and have their original from the Brain, and not the Heart, as many of the Ancients conceived; which is so far from affording Nerves unto other parts, that it receiveth very few it self from the sixth conjugation, or pair of Nerves in the Brain.

Lastly, These propagations being communicated unto both Hands, we have no greater reason to wear our *Rings* on the left, then on the right; nor are there cordial considerations in the one, more then the other. And therefore when *Forestus* for the stanching of blood makes use of Medical applications unto the fourth *Finger*, he confines not that practice unto the left, but varieth the side according to the nostril bleeding. So in Feavers, where the Heart primarily suffereth, we apply Medicines unto the wrests of either arm; so we touch the pulse of both, and judge of the affections of the Heart by the one as well as the other. And although in indispositions of Liver or Spleen, considerations are made in *Phlebotomy* respectively to their situation; yet when the Heart is affected, Men have thought it as effectual to bleed on the right as the left; and although also it may be thought, a nearer respect is to be had of the left, because the great artery proceeds from the left ventricle, and so is nearer that arm; it admits not that consideration. For under the channel bones the artery divideth into two great branches, from which trunk or point of division, the distance unto either Hand is equal, and the consideration also answerable.

All which with many respective Niceties, in order unto parts, sides, and veines, are now become of less consideration, by the new and noble doctrine of the circulation of the blood.

And therefore *Macrobius* discussing the point, hath alleadged another reason; affirming that the gestation of *Rings* upon this Hand and *Finger*, might rather be used for their conveniency and preservation, then any cordial relation. For at first (saith he) it was both free and usual to wear *Rings* on either Hand; but after that luxury encreased, when pretious gems and rich insculptures were added, the custom of wearing them on the right Hand was translated unto the left; for that Hand being less imployed, thereby they were best preserved. And for the same reason they placed them on this *Finger*; for the *Thumb* was too active a *Finger*, and is commonly imployed with either of the rest: the Index or fore-*Finger* was too naked whereto to commit their pretiosities, and hath the tuition of the *Thumb* scarce unto the second joint: the middle and little *Finger* they rejected as extreams, and too big or too little for their *Rings*, and of all chose out the fourth, as being least used of any, as being guarded on either side, and having in most this peculiar condition, that it cannot be extended alone and by itself, but will be accompanied by some *Finger* on either side. And to this opinion assenteth *Alexander ab Alexandro, Annulum nuptialem prior ætas in sinistrâ ferebat, crediderim ne attereretur.*

Now that which begat or promoted the common opinion, was the common conceit that the Heart was seated on the left side; but how far this is verified, we have before declared. The *Egyptian* practice hath much advanced the same, who unto this *Finger* derived a Nerve from the Heart; and therefore the Priest anointed the same with precious oyls before the Altar. But how weak *Anatomists* they were, which were so good Embalmers, we have already shewed. And though this reason took most place, yet had they another which more commended that practice: and that was the number whereof this *Finger* was an Hieroglyphick. For by holding down the fourth *Finger* of the left Hand, while the rest were extended, they signified the perfect and magnified number of six. For as *Pierius* hath graphically declared, Antiquity expressed numbers by the *Fingers* of either Hand: on the left they accounted their digits and articulate numbers unto an hundred; on the right Hand hundreds and thousands; the depressing this *Finger*, which in the left Hand implied but six, in the right indigitated six hundred. In this way of numeration, may we construe that of *Juvenal* concerning *Nestor*,

——*Qui per tot sæcula mortem*
Distulit, atque suos jam dextrâ computat annos.

And however it were intended, in this sense it will be very elegant what is delivered of Wisdom, *Prov.* 3. Length of daies is in her right Hand, and in her left Hand riches and honour.

Hand-Gouty persons.

As for the observation of *Lemnius* an eminent Physitian, concerning the Gout; however it happened in his Country, we may observe it otherwise in ours; that is, that chiragrical persons do suffer in this *Finger* as well as in the rest, and sometimes first of all, and sometimes no where else. And for the mixing up medicines herewith; it is rather an argument of opinion, then any considerable effect; and we as highly conceive of the practice in *Diapalma*, that is, in the making of that plaister, to stir it with the stick of a Palm.

CHAPTER V
Of the right and left Hand.

It is also suspicious, and not with that certainty to be received, what is generally believed concerning the right and left hand; that Men naturally make use of the right, and that the use of the other is a digression or aberration from that way which nature generally intendeth. We do not deny that almost all Nations have used this hand, and ascribed a preheminence thereto: hereof a remarkable passage there is in the 48. of *Genesis*, And *Joseph* took them both, *Ephraim* in his right hand towards *Israels* left hand, and *Manasses* in his left hand towards *Israels* right hand, and *Israel* stretched out his right hand and laid it upon *Ephraims* head, who was the younger, and his left hand upon *Manasses* head, guiding his hands wittingly, for *Manasses* was the first-born; and when *Joseph* saw that his father laid his right hand upon the head of *Ephraim*, it displeased him, and he held up his fathers hand to remove it from *Ephraims* head unto *Manasses* head, and *Joseph* said, Not so my father, for this is the first-born, put thy right hand upon his head: The like appeareth from the ordinance of *Moses* in the consecration of their Priests, Then shalt thou kill the Ram, and take of his blood, and put it upon the tip of the right ear of *Aaron*, and upon the tip of the right ear of his sons, and upon the thumb of the right hand, and upon the great toe of the right foot, and sprinkle the blood on the Altar round about. That the *Persians* were wont herewith to plight their faith, is testified by *Diodorus*: That the *Greeks* and *Romans* made use hereof, beside the testimony of divers Authors, is evident from their custom of discumbency at their meals, which was upon their left side, for so their right hand was free, and ready for all service. As also from the conjunction of the right hands and not the left observable in the *Roman* medals of concord. Nor was this only in use with divers Nations of Men, but was the custom of whole Nations of Women; as is deduceable from the Amazones in the amputation of their right breast, whereby they had the freer use of their bow. All which do seem to declare a natural preferment of the one unto motion before the other; wherein notwithstanding in submission to future information, we are unsatisfied unto great dubitation.

For first, if there were a determinate prepotency in the right, and such as ariseth from a constant root in nature, we might expect the same in other animals, whose parts are also differenced by dextrality; wherein notwithstanding we cannot discover a distinct and complying account; for we find not that *Horses*, *Buls*, or *Mules*, are generally stronger on this side. As for Animals whose forelegs more sensibly supply the use of arms, they hold, if not an equality in both, a prevalency oft-times in the other, as *Squirrels*, *Apes*, and *Monkies*; the same is also discernable in *Parrets*, who feed themselves more commonly by the left-leg, and Men observe that the Eye of a Tumbler is biggest, not constantly in one, but in the bearing side.

Whence the dextral activity in men proceeds.

That there is also in Men a natural prepotency in the right, we cannot with constancy affirm, if we make observation in children; who permitted the freedom of both, do oft-times confine unto the left, and are not without great difficulty restrained from it. And therefore this prevalency is either uncertainly placed in the laterality, or custom determines its difference. Which is the resolution of *Aristotle* in that Problem, which enquires why the right side being better then the left, is equal in the senses? because, saith he, the right and left do differ by use and custom, which have no place in the senses. For right and left as parts inservient unto the motive faculty, are differenced by degrees from use and assuefaction, according whereto the one grows stronger and oft-times bigger then the other. But in the senses it is otherwise; for they acquire not their perfection by use or custom, but at the first we equally hear and see with one Eye, as well as with another. And therefore, were this indifferency permitted, or did not constitution, but nature determine dextrality, there would be many more Scevolaes then are delivered in story; nor needed we to draw examples of the left, from the sons of the right hand; *Benjamin filius dextræ.* as we read of seven thousand in the Army of the *Benjamites*. True it is, that although there be an indifferency in either, or a prevalency indifferent in one, yet is it most reasonable for uniformity, and sundry respective uses, that Men should apply themselves to the constant use of one; for there will otherwise arise anomalous disturbances in manual actions, not only in civil and artificial, but also in Military affairs, and the several actions of war.

Secondly, The grounds and reasons alleadged for the right, are not satisfactory, and afford no rest in their decision. *Scaliger* finding a defect in the reason of *Aristotle*, introduceth one of no less deficiency himself; *Ratio materialis* (saith he) *sanguinis crassitudo simul et multitudo*; that is, the reason of the vigour of this side, is the crassitude and plenty of blood; but this is not sufficient; for the crassitude or thickness of blood affordeth no reason why one arm should be enabled before the other, and the plenty thereof, why both not enabled equally. *Fallopius* is of another conceit, deducing the reason from the Azygos or *vena sine pari*, a large and considerable vein arising out of the *cava* or hollow vein, before it enters the right ventricle of the Heart, and placed only in the right side. But neither is this perswasory; for the Azygos communicates no branches unto the arms or legs on either side, but disperseth into the Ribs on both, and in its descent doth furnish the left Emulgent with one vein, and the first vein of the loins on the right side with another; which manner of derivation doth not confer a peculiar addition unto either. *Cælius Rodiginus* undertaking to give a reason of Ambidexters and *Left-handed* Men, delivereth a third opinion: Men, saith he, are Ambidexters, and use both *Hands* alike, when the heat of the Heart doth plentifully disperse into the left side, and that of the Liver into the right, and the spleen be also much dilated; but Men are *Left-handed* when ever it happeneth that the Heart and Liver are seated on the left-side; or when the Liver is on the right side, yet so obducted and covered with thick skins, that it cannot diffuse its vertue into the right. Which reasons are no way satisfactory; for herein the spleen is injustly introduced to invigorate the sinister side, which being dilated it would rather infirm and debilitate. As for any tunicles or skins which should hinder the Liver from enabling dextral parts; we must not conceive it diffuseth its vertue by meer irradiation, but by its veins and proper vessels, which common skins and teguments cannot impede. And for the seat of the Heart and Liver in one side, whereby Men become *Left-handed*, it happeneth too rarely to countenance an effect so common; for the seat of the Liver on the left side is monstrous, and rarely to be met with in the observations of Physitians. Others not considering ambidextrous and *Left-handed* Men, do totally submit unto the efficacy of the Liver; which though seated on the right side, yet by the subclavian division doth equidistantly communicate its activity unto either Arm; nor will it salve the doubts of observation; for many are *Right-handed* whose Livers are weakly constituted, and many use the left, in whom that part is strongest; and we observe in Apes, and other animals, whose Liver is in the right, no regular prevalence therein.

And therefore the brain, especially the spinal marrow, which is but the brain prolonged, hath a fairer plea hereto; for these are the principles of motion, wherein dextrality consists; and are divided within and without the Crany. By which division transmitting Nerves respectively unto either side; according to the indifferency, or original and native prepotency, there ariseth an equality in both, or prevalency on either side. And so may it be made out, what many may wonder at, why some most actively use the contrary Arm and Leg; for the vigour of the one dependeth upon the upper part of the spine, but the other upon the lower.

And therefore many things are Philosophically delivered concerning right and left, which admit of some suspension. That a Woman upon a masculine conception advanceth her right Leg, will not be found to answer strick observation. That males are conceived in the right side of the womb, females in the left, though generally delivered, and supported by ancient testimony, will make no infallible account; it happening oft times that males and females do lie upon both sides, and Hermaphrodites for ought we know on either. It is also suspitious what is delivered concerning the right and left testicle, that males are begotten from the one, and females from the other. For though the left seminal vein proceedeth from the emulgent, and is therefore conceived to carry down a serous and feminine matter; yet the seminal Arteries which send forth the active materials, are both derived from the great Artery. Beside this original of the left vein was thus contrived, to avoid the pulsation of the great Artery, over which it must have passed to attain unto the testicle. Nor can we easily infer such different effects from the divers situation of parts which have one end and office; for in the kidneys which have one office, the right is seated lower then the left, whereby it lieth free, and giveth way unto the Liver. And therefore also that way which is delivered for masculine generation, to make a strait ligature about the left testicle, thereby to intercept the evacuation of that part, deserveth consideration. For one sufficeth unto generation, as hath been observed in semicastration, and oft times in carnous ruptures. *How an Horse or Bull may generate after they be gelt.* Beside, the seminal ejaculation proceeds not immediately from the testicle, but from the spermatick glandules; and therefore *Aristotle* affirms (and reason cannot deny) that although there be nothing diffused from the testicles, an *Horse* or *Bull* may generate after castration; that is, from the stock and remainder of seminal matter, already prepared and stored up in the Prostates or grandules of generation.

Thirdly, Although we should concede a right and left in Nature, yet in this common and received account we may err from the proper acception; mistaking one side for another; calling that in Man and other animals the right which is the left, and that the left which is the right, and that in some things right and left, which is not properly either.

For first the right and left, are not defined by Phylosophers according to common acception, that is, respectively from one Man unto another, or any constant site in each; as though that should be the right in one, which upon confront or facing, stands athwart or diagonally unto the other; but were distinguished according to the activity and predominant locomotion upon either side. Thus *Aristotle* in his excellent Tract *de incessu animalium*, ascribeth six positions unto Animals, answering the three dimensions; which he determineth not by site or position unto the Heavens, but by their faculties and functions; and these are *Imum summum, Ante Retro, Dextra et Sinistra*: that is, the superiour part, where the aliment is received, that the lower extream, where it is last expelled; so he termeth a Man a plant inverted; for he supposeth the root of a Tree the head or upper part thereof, whereby it receiveth its aliment, although therewith it respects the Center of the Earth, but with the other the Zenith; and this position is answerable unto longitude. Those parts are anteriour and measure profundity, where the senses, especially the Eyes are placed, and those posterior which are opposite hereunto. The dextrous and sinistrous parts of the body make up the latitude; and are not certain and inalterable like the other; for that, saith he, is the right side, from whence the motion of the body beginneth, that is, the active or moving side; but that the sinister which is the weaker or more quiescent part. Of the same determination were the *Platonicks* and *Pythagoreans* before him; who conceiving the heavens an animated body, named the *East*, the right or dextrous part, from whence began their motion: and thus the *Greeks*, from whence the *Latins* have borrowed their appellation, have named this hand δέξια, denominating it not from the site, but office, from δέχομαι *capio*, that is, the hand which receiveth, or is usually implied in that action.

Now upon these grounds we are most commonly mistaken, defining that by situation which they determined by motion; and giving the term of right hand to that which doth not properly admit it. For first, Many in their Infancy are sinistrously disposed, and divers continue all their life Ἀριστεροί, that is, left handed, and have but weak and imperfect use of the right; now unto these, that hand is properly the right, and not the other esteemed so by situation. Thus may *Aristotle* be made out, when he affirmeth the right claw of *Crabs* and *Lobsters* is biggest, if we take the right for the most vigorous side, and not regard the relative situation: for the one is generally bigger then the other, yet not always upon the same side. So may it be verified what is delivered by *Scaliger* in his Comment, that Palsies do oftnest happen upon the left side, if understood in this sense; the most vigorous part protecting it self, and protruding the matter upon the weaker and less resistive side. And thus the Law of Common-Weals, that cut off the right hand of Malefactors, if Philosophically executed, is impartial; otherwise the amputation not equally punisheth all.

Some are Ἀμφιδέξιοι, that is, ambidextrous or right handed on both sides; which happeneth only unto strong and Athletical bodies, whose heat and spirits are able to afford an ability unto both. *Apt for contention.* And therefore *Hippocrates* saith, that Women are not ambidextrous, that is, not so often as Men; for some are found, which indifferently make use of both. And so may *Aristotle* say, that only Men are ambidexterous; of this constitution was *Asteropæus* in *Homer*, and *Parthenopeus* the *Theban* Captain in *Statius*: and of the same, do some conceive our Father *Adam* to have been, as being perfectly framed, and in a constitution admitting least defect. Now in these Men the right hand is on both sides, and that is not the left which is opposite unto the right, according to common acception.

Again, Some are Ἀμφαριστεροὶ, as *Galen* hath expressed it; that is, ambilevous or left-handed on both sides; such as with agility and vigour have not the use of either: who are not gymnastically *Strongly or fit for corporal exercise.* composed: nor actively use those parts. Now in these there is no right hand: of this constitution are many Women, and some Men, who though they accustom themselves unto either hand, do dexterously make use of neither. And therefore although the Political advice of *Aristotle* be very good, that Men should accustom themselves to the command of either hand: yet cannot the execution or performance thereof be general: for though there be many found that can use both, yet will there divers remain that can strenuously make use of neither.

Lastly, These lateralities in Man are not only fallible, if relatively determined unto each other, but made in reference unto the heavens and quarters of the Globe: for those parts are not capable of these conditions in themselves, nor with any certainty respectively derived from us, nor from them to us again. And first in regard of their proper nature, the heavens admit not these sinister and dexter respects; there being in them no diversity or difference, but a simplicity of parts, and equiformity in motion continually succeeding each other; so that from what point soever we compute, the account will be common unto the whole circularity. And therefore though it be plausible, it is not of consequence hereto what is delivered by *Solinus*. That Man was therefore a Microcosm or little World, because the dimensions of his positions were answerable unto the greater. For as in the Heavens the distance of the North and Southern pole, which are esteemed the superior and inferior points, is equal unto the space between the East and West, accounted the dextrous and sinistrous parts thereof; so is it also in Man, for the extent of his fathome or distance betwixt the extremity of the fingers of either hand upon expansion, is equal unto the space between the sole of the foot and the crown. But this doth but petionarily infer a dextrality in the Heavens, and we may as reasonably conclude a right and left laterality in the Ark or naval edifice of *Noah*. For the length thereof was thirty cubits, the breadth fifty, and the height or profundity thirty; which well agreeth unto the proportion of Man, whose length, that is, a perpendicular from the vertex unto the sole of the foot is sextuple unto his breadth, or a right line drawn from the ribs of one side to another; and decuble unto his profundity; that is, a direct line between the breast bone and the spine.

Again, They receive not these conditions with any assurance or stability from our selves. For the relative foundations and points of denomination, are not fixed and certain, but variously designed according to imagination. The Philosopher accounts that East from whence the Heavens begin their motion. The Astronomer regarding the South and Meridian Sun, calls that the dextrous part of Heaven which respecteth his right hand; and that is the West. Poets respecting the West, assign the name of right unto the North, which regardeth their right hand; and so must that of *Ovid* be explained *utque duæ dextrâ Zonæ totidemquæ sinistrâ*. *Declarable from the original expression*, Psalm 89. 13. But Augurs or Southsayers turning their face to the East, did make the right in the South; which was also observed by the *Hebrews* and *Chaldeans*. Now if we name the quarters of Heaven respectively unto our sides, it will be no certain or invariable denomination. For if we call that the right side of Heaven which is seated Easterly unto us, when we regard the Meridian Sun; the inhabitants beyond the Æquator and Southern Tropick when they face us, regarding the Meridian, will contrarily define it; for unto them, the opposite part of Heaven will respect the left, and the Sun arise to their right.

And thus have we at large declared that although the right be most commonly used, yet hath it no regular or certain root in nature. Since it is not confirmable from other Animals: Since in Children it seems either indifferent or more favourable in the other; but more reasonable for uniformity in action, that Men accustom unto one: Since the grounds and reasons urged for it, do not sufficiently support it: Since if there be a right and stronger side in nature, yet may we mistake in its denomination; calling that the right which is the left, and the left which is the right. Since some have one right, some both, some neither. And lastly, Since these affections in Man are not only fallible in relation unto one another, but made also in reference unto the Heavens, they being not capable of these conditions in themselves, nor with any certainty from us, nor we from them again.

And therefore what admission we ow unto many conceptions concerning right and left, requireth circumspection. That is, how far we ought to rely upon the remedy in *Kiranides*, that is, the left eye of an *Hedg-hog* fried in oyl to procure sleep, and the right foot of a *Frog* in a *Dears* skin for the *Gout*; or that to dream of the loss of right or left tooth, presageth the death of male or female kindred, according to the doctrine of *Artemidorus*. What verity there is in that numeral conceit in the lateral division of Man by even and odd, ascribing the odd unto the right side, and even unto the left; and so by parity or imparity of letters in Mens names to determine misfortunes on either side of their bodies; by which account in Greek numeration, *Hephæstus* or *Vulcan* was lame in the right foot, and *Anibal* lost his right eye. And lastly, what substance there is in that Auspicial principle, and fundamental doctrine of Ariolation, that the left hand is ominous, and that good things do pass sinistrously upon us, because the left hand of man respected the right hand of the Gods, which handed their favours unto us.

CHAPTER VI
Of Swimming and Floating.

That Men swim naturally, if not disturbed by fear; that Men being drowned and sunk, do float the ninth day when their gall breaketh; that Women drowned, swim prone, but Men supine, or upon their backs; are popular affirmations, whereto we cannot assent. And first, that Man should swim naturally, because we observe it is no lesson unto other Animals, we are not forward to conclude; for other Animals swim in the same manner as they go, and need no other way of motion for natation in the water, then for progression upon the land. And this is true whether they move *per latera*, that is, two legs of one side together, which is Tollutation or ambling; or *per diametrum*, lifting one foot before, and the cross foot behind, which is succussation or trotting; or whether *per frontem* or *quadratum*, as *Scaliger* terms it, upon a square base, the legs of both sides moving together, as *Frogs* and salient Animals, which is properly called leaping. For by these motions they are able to support and impel themselves in the water, without alteration in the stroak of their legs, or position of their bodies.

But with Man it is performed otherwise; for in regard of site he alters his natural posture and swimmeth prone; whereas he walketh erect. Again, in progression the arms move parallel to the legs, and the arms and legs unto each other; but in natation they intersect and make all sorts of angles. And lastly, in progressive motion, the arms and legs do move successively, but in natation both together; all which aptly to perform, and so as to support and advance the body, is a point of Art, and such as some in their young and docile years could never attain. But although swimming be acquired by art, yet is there somewhat more of nature in it then we observe in other habits, nor will it strictly fall under that definition; for once obtained, it is not to be removed; nor is there any who from disuse did ever yet forget it.

Secondly, That persons drowned arise and float the ninth day when their gall breaketh, is a questionable determination both in the time and cause. For the time of floating, it is uncertain according to the time of putrefaction, which shall retard or accelerate according to the subject and season of the year; for as we observed, *Cats* and *Mice* will arise unequally, and at different times, though drowned at the same. Such as are fat do commonly float soonest, for their bodies soonest ferment, and that substance approacheth nearest unto air: and this is one of *Aristotles* reasons why dead *Eels* will not float, because saith he, they have but slender bellies, and little fat.

Why drowned bodies float after a time.

As for the cause, it is not so reasonably imputed unto the breaking of the gall as the putrefaction or corruptive firmentation of the body, whereby the unnatural heat prevailing, the putrifying parts do suffer a turgescence and inflation, and becoming aery and spumous affect to approach the air, and ascend unto the surface of the water. And this is also evidenced in Eggs, whereof the sound ones sink, and such as are addled swim, as do also those which are termed hypenemia or wind-eggs; and this is also a way to separate seeds, whereof such as are corrupted and steril, swim; and this agreeth not only unto the seed of plants lockt up and capsulated in their husks, but also unto the sperm and seminal humour of Man; for such a passage hath *Aristotle* upon the Inquisition and test of its fertility.

That the breaking of the gall is not the cause hereof, experience hath informed us. For opening the *abdomen*, and taking out the gall in *Cats* and *Mice*, they did notwithstanding arise. And because we had read in *Rhodiginus* of a Tyrant, who to prevent the emergency of murdered bodies, did use to cut off their lungs, and found Mens minds possessed with this reason; we committed some unto the water without lungs, which notwithstanding floated with the others. And to compleat the experiment, although we took out the guts and bladder, and also perforated the Cranium, yet would they arise, though in a longer time. From these observations in other Animals, it may not be unreasonable to conclude the same in Man, who is too noble a subject on whom to make them expressly, and the casual opportunity to rare almost to make any. Now if any should ground this effect from gall or choler, because it is the highest humour and will be above the rest; or being the fiery humour will readiest surmount the water, we must confess in the common putrescence it may promote elevation, which the breaking of the bladder of gall, so small a part in Man, cannot considerably advantage.

Lastly, That Women drowned float prone, that is, with their bellies downward, but Men supine or upward, is an assertion wherein the *hoti* or point it self is dubious; and were it true, the reason alledged for it, is of no validity. The reason yet currant was first expressed by *Pliny*, *veluti pudori defunctorum parcente naturâ*, nature modestly ordaining this position to conceal the shame of the dead; which hath been taken up by *Solinus*, *Rhodiginus*, and many more. This indeed (as *Scaliger* termeth it) is *ratio civilis non philosophica*, strong enough for morality of Rhetoricks, not for Philosophy or Physicks. For first, in nature the concealment of secret parts is the same in both sexes, and the shame of their reveal equal: so *Adam* upon the tast of the fruit was ashamed of his nakedness as well as *Eve*. And so likewise in *America* and Countries unacquainted with habits, where modesty conceals these parts in one sex, it doth it also in the other; and therefore had this been the intention of nature, not only Women but Men also had swimmed downwards; the posture in reason being common unto both, where the intent is also common.

Again, While herein we commend the modesty, we condemn the wisdom of nature: for that prone position we make her contrive unto the Woman, were best agreeable unto the Man, in whom the secret parts are very anteriour and more discoverable in a supine and upward posture. And therefore *Scaliger* declining this reason, hath recurred unto another from the difference of parts in both sexes; *Quod ventre vasto sunt mulieres plenoque intestinis, itaque minus impletur et subsidet, inanior maribus quibus nates præponderant*: If so, then Men with great bellies will float downward, and only *Callipygæ*, and Women largely composed behind, upward. But *Anatomists* observe, that to make the larger cavity for the Infant, the hanch bones in Women, and consequently the parts appendant are more protuberant then they are in Men. They who ascribe the cause unto the breasts of Women, take not away the doubt; for they resolve not why children float downward, who are included in that sex, though not in the reason alleadged. But hereof we cease to discourse, lest we undertake to afford a reason of the [1]golden tooth, that is, to invent or assign a cause when we remain unsatisfied or unassured of the effect.

That a *Mare* will sooner drown then a *Horse*, though commonly opinion'd, is not I fear experienced: nor is the same observed, in the drowning of *Whelps* and *Kitlins*. But that a Man cannot shut or open his eyes under water, easie experiment may convict. Whether Cripples and mutilated Persons, who have lost the greatest part of their thighs, will not sink but float, their lungs being abler to waft up their bodies, which are in others overpoised by the hinder legs; we have not made experiment. Thus much we observe, that Animals drown downwards, and the same is observable in *Frogs*, when the hinder legs are cut off. But in the air most seem to perish headlong from high places; however *Vulcan* thrown from Heaven, be made to fall on his feet.

Footnotes

[1]*Of the cause whereof much dispute was made, and at last proved an imposture.*

CHAPTER VII
Concerning Weight.

That Men weigh heavier dead then alive, if experiment hath not failed us, we cannot reasonably grant. For though the trial hereof cannot so well be made on the body of Man, nor will the difference be sensible in the abate of scruples and dragms, yet can we not confirm the same in lesser Animals, from whence the inference is good; and the affirmative of *Pliny* saith, that it is true in all. For exactly weighing and strangling a *Chicken* in the Scales; upon an immediate ponderation, we could discover no sensible difference in weight; but suffering it to lie eight or ten hours, untill it grew perfectly cold, it weighed most sensibly lighter; the like we attempted, and verified in *Mice*, and performed their trials in Scales, that would turn upon the eighth or tenth part of a grain.

Now whereas some alledge that spirits are lighter substances, and naturally ascending, do elevate and waft the body upward, whereof dead bodies being destitute, contract a greater gravity; although we concede that spirits are light, comparatively unto the body, yet that they are absolutely so, or have no weight at all, we cannot readily allow. For since Philosophy affirmeth, that spirits are middle substances between the soul and body, they must admit of some corporiety, which supposeth weight or gravity. Beside, in carcasses warm, and bodies newly disanimated, while transpiration remaineth, there do exhale and breath out vaporous and fluid parts, which carry away some power of gravitation. Which though we allow, we do not make answerable unto living expiration; and therefore the *Chicken* or *Mice* were not so light being dead, as they would have been after ten hours kept alive; for in that space a man abateth many ounces. Nor if it had slept, for in that space of sleep, a Man will sometimes abate fourty ounces; nor if it had been in the middle of summer, for then a Man weigheth some pounds less, then in the height of winter; according to experience, and the statick Aphorisms of *Sanctorius*.

Again, Whereas Men affirm they perceive an addition of ponderosity in dead bodies, comparing them usually unto blocks and stones, whensoever they lift or carry them; this accessional preponderancy is rather in appearance then reality. For being destitute of any motion, they confer no relief unto the Agents, or Elevators; which makes us meet with the same complaints of gravity in animated and living bodies, where the Nerves subside, and the faculty locomotive seems abolished; as may be observed in the lifting or supporting of persons inebriated, Apoplectical, or in Lypothymies and swoundings.

Many are also of opinion, and some learned Men maintain, that Men are lighter after meals then before, and that by a supply and addition of spirits obscuring the gross ponderosity of the aliment ingested; but the contrary hereof we have found in the trial of sundry persons in different sex and ages. And we conceive Men may mistake if they distinguish not the sense of levity unto themselves, and in regard of the scale or decision of trutination. For after a draught of wine, a Man may seem lighter in himself from sudden refection, although he be heavier in the balance, from a corporal and ponderous addition; but a Man in the morning is lighter in the scale, because in sleep some pounds have perspired; and is also lighter unto himself, because he is refected.

And to speak strictly, a Man that holds his breath is weightier while his lungs are full, then upon expiration. For a bladder blown is weightier then one empty, and if it contain a quart, expressed and emptied it will abate about a quarter of a grain. And therefore we somewhat mistrust the experiment of a pumice stone taken up by *Montanus*, in his Comment upon *Avicenna*, where declaring how the rarity of parts, and numerosity of pores, occasioneth a lightness in bodies, he affirms that a pumice-stone powdered, is lighter then one entire; which is an experiment beyond our satisfaction; for beside that abatement can hardly be avoided in the Trituration; if a bladder of good capacity will scarce include a grain of air, a pumice of three or four dragms, cannot be presumed to contain the hundred part thereof; which will not be sensible upon the exactest beams we use. Nor is it to be taken strictly which is delivered by the learned Lord *Verulam*, and referred unto further experiment; That a dissolution of Iron in *aqua fortis*, will bear as good weight as their bodies did before, notwithstanding a great deal of waste by a thick vapour that issueth during the working; for we cannot find it to hold neither in Iron nor Copper, which is dissolved with less ebullition; and hereof we made trial in Scales of good exactness: wherein if there be a defect, or such as will not turn upon quarter grains, there may be frequent mistakes in experiments of this nature. That also may be considered which is delivered by *Hamerus Poppius* Basilica Antimonii., that *Antimony* calcin'd or reduced to ashes by a burning glass, although it emit a gross and ponderous exhalation, doth rather exceed then abate its former gravity. Nevertheless, strange it is; how very little and almost insensible abatement there will be sometimes in such operations, or rather some encrease, as in the refining of metals, in the test of bone ashes, according to experience: and in a burnt brick, as *Monsieur de Clave* Des Pierres. affirmeth. Mistake may be made in this way of trial, when the *Antimony* is not weighed immediately upon the calcination; but permitted the air, it imbibeth the humidity thereof, and so repaireth its gravity.

CHAPTER VIII
Of the passage of Meat and Drink.

That there are different passages for Meat and Drink, the Meat or dry aliment descending by the one, the Drink or moistening vehicle by the other, is a popular Tenent in our daies, but was the assertion of learned men of old. For the same was affirmed by *Plato*, maintained by *Eustathius* in *Macrobius*, and is deducible from *Eratosthenes*, *Eupolis* and *Euripides*. Now herein Men contradict experience, not well understanding *Anatomy*, and the use of parts. For at the Throat there are two cavities or conducting parts; the one the Oesophagus or Gullet, seated next the spine, a part official unto nutrition, and whereby the aliment both wet and dry is conveied unto the stomack; the other (by which tis conceived the Drink doth pass) is the weazon, rough artery, or wind-pipe, a part inservient to voice and respiration; for thereby the air descendeth into the lungs, and is communicated unto the heart. And therefore all Animals that breath or have lungs, have also the weazon; but many have the gullet or feeding channel, which have no lungs or wind-pipe; as fishes which have gils, whereby the heart is refrigerated; for such thereof as have lungs and respiration, are not without the weazon, as Whales and cetaceous Animals.

Again, Beside these parts destin'd to divers offices, there is a peculiar provision for the wind-pipe, that is, a cartilagineous flap upon the opening of the Larinx or Throttle, which hath an open cavity for the admission of the air; but lest thereby either meat or drink should descend, Providence hath placed the *Epiglottis*, *Ligula*, or flap like an Ivy leaf, which alwaies closeth when we swallow, or when the meat and drink passeth over it into the gullet. Which part although all have not that breath, as all cetaceous and oviparous Animals, yet is the weazon secured some other way; and therefore in Whales that breath, least the water should get into the lungs, an ejection thereof is contrived by a Fistula or spout at the head. And therefore also though birds have no Epiglottis, yet can they so contract the rim or chink of their Larinx, as to prevent the admission of wet or dry ingested; either whereof getting in, occasioneth a cough, until it be ejected. Why a man cannot drink and breath at once. And this is the reason why a Man cannot drink and breath at the same time; why, if we laugh while we drink, the drink flies out at the nostrils; why, when the water enters the weazon, Men are suddenly drowned; and thus must it be understood, when we read Anacreon *the Poet, if the story be taken literally.* of one that died by the seed of a Grape, and another by an hair in milk.

Now if any shall still affirm, that some truth there is in the assertion, upon the experiment of *Hippocrates*, who killing an Hog after a red potion, found the tincture thereof in the Larinx; if any will urge the same from medical practice, because in affections both of Lungs and weazon, Physitians make use of syrupes, and lambitive medicines; we are not averse to acknowledge, that some may distil and insinuate into the wind-pipe, and medicines may creep down, as well as the rheum before them; yet to conclude from hence, that air and water have both one common passage, were to state the question upon the weaker side of the distinction, and from a partial or guttulous irrigation, to conclude a total descension.

CHAPTER IX
Of Sneezing.

Concerning Sternutation or Sneezing, and the custom of saluting or blessing upon that motion, it is pretended, and generally believed to derive its original from a disease, wherein Sternutation proved mortal, and such as Sneezed, died. And this may seem to be proved from *Carolus Sigonius*, who in his History of *Italy*, makes mention of a Pestilence in the time of *Gregory* the Great, that proved pernitious and deadly to those that Sneezed. Which notwithstanding will not sufficiently determine the grounds hereof: that custom having an elder *Æra*, then this Chronology affordeth.

For although the age of *Gregory* extend above a thousand, yet is this custom mentioned by *Apuleius*, in the Fable of the Fullers wife, who lived three hundred years before; by *Pliny* in that Problem of his, *Cur Sternutantes salutantur*; and there are also reports that *Tiberius* the Emperour, otherwise a very sower Man, would perform this rite most punctually unto others, and expect the same from others, unto himself. *Petronius Arbiter*, who lived before them both, and was Proconsul of *Bythinia* in the raign of *Nero*, hath mentioned it in these words, *Gyton collectione spiritus plenus, ter continuo ita sternutavit ut grabatum concuteret, ad quem motum Eumolpus conversus, Salvere Gytona jubet*. *Cælius Rhodiginus* hath an example hereof among the *Greeks*, far antienter than these, that is, in the time of *Cyrus* the younger; when consulting about their retreat, it chanced that one among them Sneezed; at the noise whereof, the rest of the Souldiers called upon *Jupiter Soter*. There is also in the Greek Anthology *A Collection of Greek Epigrams*, Titulo εἰς δυσειδεῖς., a remarkable mention hereof in an Epigram, upon one *Proclus*; the Latin whereof we shall deliver, as we find it often translated.

Non potis est Proclus digitis emungere nasum,
Namq; est pro nasi mole pusilla manus:
Non vocat ille Jovem sternutans, quippe, nec audit
Sternutamentum, tam procul aure sonat.
Proclus with his hand his nose can never wipe,
His hand too little is his nose to gripe;
He Sneezing calls not *Jove*, for why? he hears
Himself not Sneeze, the sound's so far from's ears.

Nor was this only an ancient custom among the *Greeks* and *Romans*, and is still in force with us, but is received at this day in remotest parts of *Africa*. *De rebus Abassinorum* For so we read in *Codignus*; that upon a Sneeze of the Emperour of *Monomotapa*, there passed acclamations successively through the City. And as remarkable an example there is of the same custom, *Buxt. Lex. Chald.* in the remotest parts of the East, recorded in the travels of *Pinto*.

But the history will run much higher, if we should take in the *Rabinical* account hereof; that Sneezing was a mortal sign even from the first Man; until it was taken off by the special supplication of *Jacob*. From whence, as a thankful acknowledgment, this salutation first began; and was after continued by the expression of *Tobim Chaiim*, or *vita bona*, by standers by, upon all occasion of Sneezing.

Whence Sternutation or Sneezing proceeds.

Now the ground of this ancient custom was probably the opinion the ancients held of sternutation, which they generally conceived, to be a good sign or a bad, and so upon this motion accordingly used, a Salve or Ζεῦ σῶσον, as a gratulation for the one, and a deprecation for the other. Now of the waies whereby they enquired and determined its signality; the first was natural, arising from Physical causes, and consequences oftentimes naturally succeeding this motion; and so it might be justly esteemed a good sign. For Sneezing being properly a motion of the brain, suddenly expelling through the nostrils what is offensive unto it, it cannot but afford some evidence of its vigour; and therefore saith *Aristotle* *Problem Sect. 33.*, they that hear it, προσκυνοῦσιν ὡς ἱερόν, honour it as somewhat sacred, and a sign of Sanity in the diviner part; and this he illustrates from the practice of Physitians, who in persons near death, do use Sternutatories, or such medicines as provoke unto Sneezing; when if the faculty awaketh, and Sternutation ensueth, they conceive hopes of life, and with gratulation receive the signs of safety. *In what cases a sign of good.* And so is it also of good signality, according to that of *Hippocrates*, that Sneezing cureth the hicket, and is profitable unto Women in hard labour; and so is it good in Lethargies, Apoplexies, Catalepsies, and Coma's *2. King 4. 35.* *In what of bad.* And in this natural way it is sometime likewise of bad effects or signs, and may give hints of deprecation; as in diseases of the chest; for therein *Hippocrates* condemneth it as too much exagitating: in the beginning of *Catarrhs* according unto *Avicenna*, as hindering concoction, in new and tender conceptions (as *Pliny* observeth) for then it endangers abortion.

The second way was superstitious and Augurial, as *Cælius Rhodiginus* hath illustrated in testimonies, as ancient as *Theocritus* and *Homer*: as appears from the *Athenian* Master, who would have retired, because a Boat-man Sneezed; and the testimony of *Austin*, that the Ancients were wont to go to bed again if they Sneezed while they put on their shoe. And in this way it was also of good and bad signification; so *Aristotle* hath a Problem, why Sneezing from noon unto midnight was good, but from night to noon unlucky? So *Eustathius* upon *Homer* observes, that Sneezing to the left hand was unlucky, but prosperous unto the right; so, as *Plutarch* relateth, when *Themistocles* sacrificed in his galley before the battle of *Xerxes*, and one of the assistants upon the right hand sneezed; *Euphrantides* the Southsayer, presaged the victory of the *Greeks*, and the overthrow of the *Persians*.

Thus we may perceive the custom is more ancient then commonly conceived; and these opinions hereof in all ages, not any one disease to have been the occasion of this salute and deprecation. Arising at first from this vehement and affrighting motion of the brain, inevitably observable unto the standers by; from whence some finding dependent effects to ensue; others ascribing hereto as a cause what perhaps but casually or inconnexedly succeeded; they might proceed unto forms of speeches, felicitating the good, or deprecating the evil to follow.

CHAPTER X
Of the Jews.

That *Jews* stink naturally, that is, that in their race and nation there is an evil savour, is a received opinion we know not how to admit; although concede many questionable points, and dispute not the verity of sundry opinions which are of affinity hereto. We will acknowledg that certain odours attend on animals, no less then certain colours; that pleasant smels are not confined unto vegetables, but found in divers animals, and some more richly then in plants. And though the Problem of *Aristotle* enquire why no animal smels sweet beside the Parde? yet later discoveries add divers sorts of *Monkeys*, the *Civet Cat* and *Gazela*, from which our Musk proceedeth. We confess that beside the smell of the species, there may be individual odours, and every Man may have a proper and peculiar savour; which although not perceptible unto Man, who hath this sense, but weak, yet sensible unto *Dogs*, who hereby can single out their masters in the dark. We will not deny that particular Men have sent forth a pleasant savour, as *Theophrastus* and *Plutarch* report of *Alexander* the great, and *Tzetzes* and *Cardan* do testifie of themselves. That some may also emit an unsavory odour, we have no reason to deny; for this may happen from the quality of what they have taken; the Fætor whereof may discover it self by sweat and urine, as being unmasterable by the natural heat of Man, not to be dulcified by concoction beyond an unsavory condition: the like may come to pass from putrid humours, as is often discoverable in putrid and malignant feavers. And sometime also in gross and humid bodies even in the latitude of sanity; the natural heat of the parts being insufficient for a perfect and through digestion, and the errors of one concoction not rectifiable by another. But that an unsavory odour is gentilitious or national unto the *Jews*, if rightly understood, we cannot well concede; nor will the information of reason or sence induce it.

For first, Upon consult of reason, there will be found no easie assurance to fasten a material or temperamental propriety upon any nation; there being scarce any condition (but what depends upon clime) which is not exhausted or obscured from the commixture of introvenient nations either by commerce or conquest; much more will it be difficult to make out this affection in the *Jews*; whose race however pretended to be pure, must needs have suffered inseparable commixtures with nations of all sorts; not only in regard of their proselytes, but their universal dispersion; some being posted from several parts of the earth, others quite lost, and swallowed up in those nations where they planted. For the tribes of *Reuben*, *Gad*, part of *Manasses* and *Naphthali*, which were taken by *Assur*, and the rest at the Sacking of *Samaria*, which were led away by *Salmanasser* into *Assyria*, and after a year and half arrived at *Arsereth*, as is delivered in *Esdras*; these I say never returned, and are by the *Jews* as vainly expected as their *Messias*. Of those of the tribe of *Judah* and *Benjamin*, which were led captive into *Babylon* by *Nebuchadnezzar*, many returned under *Zorobabel*; the rest remained, and from thence long after upon invasion of the *Saracens*, fled as far as *India*; where yet they are said to remain, but with little difference from the *Gentiles*.

The Tribes that returned to *Judea*, were afterward widely dispersed; for beside sixteen thousand which *Titus* sent to *Rome* unto the triumph of his father *Vespasian*, he sold no less then an hundred thousand for slaves. Not many years after, *Adrian* the Emperour, who ruined the whole Countrey, transplanted many thousands into *Spain*, from whence they dispersed into divers Countreys, as into *France* and *England*, but were banished after from both. From *Spain* they dispersed into *Africa*, *Italy*, *Constantinople*, and the Dominions of the *Turk*, where they remain as yet in very great numbers. And if (according to good relations) where they may freely speak it, they forbear not to boast that there are at present many thousand *Jews* in *Spane*, *France* and *England*, and some dispensed withall even to the degree of Priesthood; it is a matter very considerable, and could they be smelled out, would much advantage, not only the Church of Christ, but also the coffers of Princes.

Now having thus lived in several Countries, and alwaies in subjection, they must needs have suffered many commixtures; and we are sure they are not exempted from the common contagion of Venery contracted first from Christians. Nor as fornications unfrequent between them both; there commonly passing opinions of invitement, that their Women desire copulation with them rather then their own Nation, and affect Christian carnality above circumcised venery. It being therefore acknowledged, that some are lost, evident that others are mixed, and not assured that any are distinct, it will be hard to establish this quality upon the *Jews*, unless we also transfer the same unto those whose generations are mixed, whose genealogies are *Jewish*, and naturally derived from them.

Again, if we concede a National unsavouriness in any people, yet shall we find the *Jews* less subject hereto then any, and that in those regards which most powerfully concur to such effects, that is, their diet and generation. *The Jews generally very temperate.* As for their diet whether in obedience unto the precepts of reason, or the injunctions of parsimony, therein they are very temperate; seldom offending in ebriety or excess of drink, nor erring in gulosity or superfluity of meats; whereby they prevent indigestion and crudities, and consequently putrescence of humors. They have in abomination all flesh maimed, or the inwards any way vitiated; and therefore eat no meat but of their own killing. They observe not only fasts at certain times, but are restrained unto very few dishes at all times; so few, that whereas St. *Peters* sheet will hardly cover our Tables, their Law doth scarce permit them to set forth a Lordly feast; nor any way to answer the luxury of our times, or those of our fore-fathers. For of flesh their Law restrains them many sorts, and such as compleat our feasts: That Animal, *Propter convivia natum* Quanta est gula, quæ sibi totos ponit Apros! Animal propter convivia natum. they touch not, nor any of its preparations, or parts so much in respect at *Roman* Tables, nor admit they unto their board, *Hares, Conies, Herons, Plovers* or *Swans*. Of *Fishes* they only taste of such as have both fins and scales; which are comparatively but few in number, such only, saith *Aristotle*, whose Egg or spawn is arenaceous; whereby are excluded all cetaceous and cartilagious *Fishes*; many pectinal, whose ribs are rectilineal; many costal, which have their ribs embowed; all spinal, or such as have no ribs, but only a back bone, or somewhat analogous thereto, as *Eels, Congers, Lampries*; all that are testaceous, as *Oysters, Cocles, Wilks, Scollops, Muscles*; and likewise all crustaceous, as *Crabs, Shrimps* and *Lobsters*. So that observing a spare and simple diet, whereby they prevent the generation of crudities; and fasting often whereby they might also digest them; they must be less inclinable unto this infirmity then any other Nation, whose proceedings are not so reasonable to avoid it.

As for their generations and conceptions (which are the purer from good diet,) they become more pure and perfect by the strict observation of their Law; upon the injunctions whereof, they severely observe the times of Purification, and avoid all copulation, either in the uncleanness of themselves, or impurity of their Women. A Rule, I fear, not so well observed by Christians; whereby not only conceptions are prevented, but if they proceed, so vitiated and defiled, that durable inquinations remain upon the birth. The original or material causes of the Pox and Meazels. Which, when the conception meets with these impurities, must needs be very potent; since in the purest and most fair conceptions, learned Men derive the cause of *Pox* and *Meazels*, from principles of that nature; that is, the menstrous impurities in the Mothers blood, and virulent tinctures contracted by the Infant, in the nutriment of the womb.

Lastly, Experience will convict it; for this offensive odor is no way discoverable in their Synagogues where many are, and by reason of their number could not be concealed: nor is the same discernable in commerce or conversation with such as are cleanly in Apparel, and decent in their Houses. Surely the Viziars and *Turkish* Basha's are not of this opinion; who as Sir *Henry Blunt* informeth, do generally keep a *Jew* of their private Counsel. And were this true, the *Jews* themselves do not strictly make out the intention of their Law, for in vain do they scruple to approach the dead, who livingly are cadaverous, or fear any outward pollution, whose temper pollutes themselves. And lastly, were this true, yet our opinion is not impartial; for unto converted *Jews* who are of the same seed, no Man imputeth this unsavoury odor; as though Aromatized by their conversion, they lost their scent with their Religion, and smelt no longer then they savoured of the *Jew*.

Now the ground that begat or propagated this assertion, might be the distasteful aversness of the Christian from the *Jew*, upon the villany of that fact, which made them abominable and stink in the nostrils of all Men. Which real practise, and metaphorical expression, did after proceed into a literal construction; but was a fraudulent illation; for such an evil savour their father *Jacob* acknowledged in himself Gen. 34. when he said, his sons had made him stink in the land, that is, to be abominable unto the inhabitants thereof. Now how dangerous it is in sensible things to use metaphorical expressions unto the people, and what absurd conceits they will swallow in their literals; an impatient example we have in our profession; who having called an eaten *ulcer* by the name of a *Wolf*, common apprehension conceives a reality therein; and against our selves, ocular affirmations are pretended to confirm it.

The nastiness of that Nation, and sluttish course of life hath much promoted the opinion, occasioned by their servile condition at first, and inferiour ways of parsimony ever since; as is delivered by Mr. *Sandys*. They are generally fat, saith he, and rank of the savours which attend upon sluttish corpulency. The *Epithetes* assigned them by ancient times, have also advanced the same; for *Ammianus Marcellinus* describeth them in such language; and *Martial* more ancient, in such a relative expression sets forth unsavoury *Bassa*.

Quod jejunia Sabbatoriorum.
Mallem, quam quod oles, olere Bassa.

From whence notwithstanding we cannot infer an inward imperfection in the temper of that Nation; it being but an effect in the breath from outward observation, in their strict and tedious fasting; and was a common effect in the breaths of other Nations, became a Proverb Νηστείας ὄζειν. Iejunia olere. among the *Greeks*, and the reason thereof begot a Problem in *Aristotle*.

Lastly, If all were true, and were this savour conceded, yet are the reasons alleadged for it no way satisfactory. *Hucherius*, De sterilitate and after him *Alsarius Crucius*, Cruc. Med. Epist. imputes this effect unto their abstinence from salt or salt meats; which how to make good in the present diet of the *Jews*, we know not; nor shall we conceive it was observed of old, if we consider they seasoned every Sacrifice, and all oblations whatsoever; whereof we cannot deny a great part was eaten by the Priests. And if the offering were of flesh, it was salted no less than thrice, that is, once in the common chamber of salt, at the foot-step of the Altar, and upon the top thereof, as is at large delivered by *Maimonides*. Nor if they refrained all salt, is the illation very urgent; for many there are, not noted for ill odours, which eat no salt at all; as all carnivorous Animals, most Children, many whole Nations, and probably our Fathers after the Creation; there being indeed in every thing we eat, a natural and concealed salt, which is separated by digestions, as doth appear in our tears, sweat and urines, although we refrain all salt, or what doth seem to contain it.

Another cause is urged by *Campegius*, and much received by Christians; that this ill savour is a curse derived upon them by Christ, and stands, as a badge or brand of a generation that crucified their *Salvator*. But this is a conceit without all warrant; and an easie way to take off dispute in what point of obscurity soever. A method of many Writers, which much depreciates the esteem and value of miracles; that is, therewith to salve not only real verities, but also nonexistencies. Thus have elder times not only ascribed the immunity of *Ireland* from any venemous beast, unto the staff or rod of *Patrick*; but the long tails of *Kent*, unto the malediction of *Austin*. Thus therefore, although we concede that many opinions are true which hold some conformity unto this, yet in assenting hereto, many difficulties must arise: it being a dangerous point to annex a constant property unto any Nation, and much more this unto the *Jew*; since this quality is not verifiable by observation; since the grounds are feeble that should establish it; and lastly, since if all were true, yet are the reasons alleadged for it, of no sufficiency to maintain it.

CHAPTER XI
Of Pigmies.

By *Pigmies* we understand a dwarfish race of people, or lowest diminution of mankind, comprehended in one cubit, or as some will have it, in two foot or three spans; not taking them single, but nationally considering them, and as they make up an aggregated habitation. Whereof although affirmations be many, and testimonies more frequent then in any other point which wise men have cast into the list of fables, yet that there is, or ever was such a race or Nation, upon exact and confirmed testimonies, our strictest enquiry receives no satisfaction.

I say, exact testimonies, first, In regard of the Authors, from whom we derive the account, for though we meet herewith in *Herodotus, Philostratus, Mela, Pliny, Solinus*, and many more; yet were they derivative Relators, and the primitive Author was *Homer*; who, using often similies, as well to delight the ear, as to illustrate his matter, in the third of his Iliads, compareth the *Trojans* unto *Cranes*, when they descend against the *Pigmies*; which was more largely set out by *Oppian, Juvenal, Mantuan*, and many Poets since, and being only a pleasant figment in the fountain, became a solemn story in the stream, and current still among us.

Again, Many professed enquirers have rejected it; *Strabo* an exact and judicious Geographer, hath largely condemned it as a fabulous story, *Julius Scaliger* a diligent enquirer, accounts thereof, but as a Poetical fiction; *Ulysses Aldrovandus* a most exact Zoographer in an express discourse hereon, concludes the story fabulous, and a Poetical account of *Homer*; and the same was formerly conceived by *Eustathius*, his excellent Commentator. *Albertus Magnus* a man ofttimes too credulous, herein was more then dubious; for he affirmeth, if any such dwarfs were ever extant, they were surely some kind of *Apes*: which is a conceit allowed by *Cardan*, and not esteemed improbable by many others.

There are I confess two testimonies, which from their authority admit of consideration. The first of *Aristotle*, *Hist. animal. lib. 3.* whose words are these, ἐστὶ δὲ ὁ τόπος, etc. That is, *Hic locus est quem incolunt Pygmæi, non enim id fabula est, sed pusillum genus ut aiunt*. Wherein indeed *Aristotle* plaies the *Aristotle*, that is, the wary and evading assertor; For though with *non est fabula*, he seems at first to confirm it, yet at the last he claps in *Sciunt aiunt*, and shakes the belief he put before upon it. And therefore I observe *Scaliger* hath not translated the first; perhaps supposing it surreptitious or unworthy so great an assertor. And truly for those books of animals, or work of eight hundred talents, as *Athenæus* terms it, although ever to be admired, as containing most excellent truths; yet are many things therein delivered upon relation, and some repugnant unto the history of our senses; as we are able to make out in some, and *Scaliger* hath observed in many more, as he hath freely declared in his Comment upon that piece.

The second testimony is deduced from holy Scripture; *Ezek. 27. 12.* thus rendered in the vulgar translation, *Sed et Pygmæi qui erant in turribus tuis, pharetras suas suspenderunt in muris tuis per gyrum*: from whence notwithstanding we cannot infer this assertion, for first the Translators accord not, and the Hebrew word *Gammadim* is very variously rendered. Though *Aquila, Vetablus* and *Lyra* will have it *Pygmæi*, yet in the Septuagint, it is no more then Watchmen; and so in the *Arabick* and high *Dutch*. In the *Chalde, Cappadocians*, in *Symmachus, Medes*, and in the *French*, those of *Gamad. Theodotian* of old, and *Tremellius* of late, have retained the Textuary word; and so have the *Italian*, Low *Dutch* and *English* Translators, that is, the Men of *Arvad* were upon thy walls round about, and the *Gammadims* were in thy Towers.

Nor do men only dissent in the Translation of the word, but in the Exposition of the sense and meaning thereof; for some by *Gammadims* understand a people of *Syria*, so called from the City *Gamala*; some hereby understand the *Cappadocians*, many the *Medes* *See Mr. Fullers excellent description of Palestine.*: and hereof *Forerius* hath a singular Exposition, conceiving the Watchmen of *Tyre* might well be called *Pigmies*, the Towers of that City being so high, that unto Men below, they appeared in a cubital stature. Others expounded it quite contrary to common acception, that is not Men of the least, but of the largest size; so doth *Cornelius* construe *Pygmæi*, or *viri cubitales*, that is, not Men of a cubit high, but of the largest stature, whose height like that of Giants, is rather to be taken by the cubit then the foot; in which phrase we read the measure of *Goliah*, whose height is said to be six cubits and a span. Of affinity hereto is also the Exposition of *Jerom*; not taking *Pigmies* for dwarfs, but stout and valiant Champions; not taking the sense of πυγμὴ, which signifies the cubit measure, but that which expresseth Pugils; that is, Men fit for combat and the exercise of the fist. Thus can there be no satisfying illation from this Text, the diversity or rather contrariety of Expositions and interpretations, distracting more then confirming the truth of the story.

Again, I say, exact testimonies; in reference unto circumstantial relations so diversly or contrarily delivered. Thus the Relation of *Aristotle* placeth them above *Egypt* towards the head of *Nyle* in *Africa*; *Philostratus* affirms they are about *Ganges* in *Asia*, and *Pliny* in a third place, that is, *Gerania* in *Scythia*: some write they fight with Cranes, but *Menecles* in *Athenæus* affirms they fight with *Partridges*, some say they ride on *Partridges*, and some on the backs of *Rams*.

Lastly, I say, confirmed testimonies; for though *Paulus Jovius* delivers there are *Pigmies* beyond *Japan*; *Pigafeta*, about the *Molucca's*; and *Olaus Magnus* placeth them in *Greenland*; yet wanting frequent confirmation in a matter so confirmable, their affirmation carrieth but slow perswasion;[2] and wise men may think there is as much reality in the [3]*Pigmies* of *Paracelsus*; that is, his non-Adamical men, or middle natures betwixt men and spirits.

There being thus no sufficient confirmation of their verity, some doubt may arise concerning their possibility, wherein, since it is not defined in what dimensions the soul may exercise her faculties, we shall not conclude impossibility; or that there might not be a race of *Pigmies*, as there is sometimes of Giants. So may we take in the opinion of *Austin*, and his Comment *Ludovicus*, but to believe they should be in the stature of a foot or span, requires the preaspection of such a one as *Philetas* the Poet in *Athenæus*: who was fain to fasten lead unto his feet lest the wind should blow him away. Or that other in the same Author, who was so little *ut ad obolum accederet*; a story so strange, that we might herein excuse the PRINTER, did not the account of *Ælian* accord unto it, as *Causabone* hath observed in his learned Animadversions.

Lastly, If any such Nation there were, yet is it ridiculous what Men have delivered of them; that they fight with *Cranes* upon the backs of *Rams* or *Partridges*: or what is delivered by *Ctesias*, that they are *Negroes* in the middest of *India*; whereof the King of that Country entertaineth three thousand Archers for his guard. Which is a relation below the tale of *Oberon*; nor could they better defend him, then the Emblem saith, they offended *Hercules* whilest he slept; that is, to wound him no deeper, then to awake him.

Footnotes

[2]*The story of Pigmies rejected.*
[3]*By Pigmies intending Fairies and other spirits about the earth as by Nymphs and Salamanders, spirits of fire and water.* Lib. De Pigmæis, Nymphis, *etc.*

CHAPTER XII
Of the great Climacterical year, that is, Sixty three.

Certainly the Eyes of the understanding, and those of the sense are differently deceived in their greatest objects; the sense apprehending them in lesser magnitudes then their dimensions require; so it beholdeth the Sun, the Stars, and the Earth it self. But the understanding quite otherwise: for that ascribeth unto many things far larger horizons then their due circumscriptions require: and receiveth them with amplifications which their reality will not admit. Thus hath it fared with many Heroes and most worthy persons, who being sufficiently commendable from true and unquestionable merits, have received advancement from falshood and the fruitful stock of Fables. Thus hath it happened unto the Stars, and Luminaries of heaven: who being sufficiently admirable in themselves, have been set out by effects, no way dependent on their efficiencies, and advanced by amplifications to the questioning of their true endowments. Thus is it not improbable it hath also fared with number, which though wonderful in it self, and sufficiently magnifiable from its demonstrable affections, hath yet received adjections from the multiplying conceits of men, and stands laden with additions, which its equity will not admit.

And so perhaps hath it happened unto the number, 7 and 9, which multiplied into themselves do make up Sixty three, commonly esteemed the great Climacterical of our lives. For the daies of men are usually cast up by Septenaries, and every seventh year conceived to carry some altering character with it, either in the temper of body, mind, or both. But among all other, three are most remarkable, that is, 7 times 7 or fourty nine, 9 times 9 or eighty one, and 7 times 9 or the year of Sixty three; which is conceived to carry with it the most considerable fatality; and consisting of both the other numbers was apprehended to comprise the vertue of either: is therefore expected and entertained with fear, and esteemed a favour of fate to pass it over. *The great Climacterical, Sixty-three, no such dangerous year.* Which notwithstanding many suspect to be but a Panick terrour, and men to fear they justly know not what: and to speak indifferently, I find no satisfaction: nor any sufficiency in the received grounds to establish a rational fear.

Now herein to omit Astrological considerations (which are but rarely introduced) the popular foundation whereby it hath continued, is first, the extraordinary power and secret virtue conceived to attend these numbers: whereof we must confess there have not wanted not only especial commendations, but very singular conceptions. Among Philosophers, *Pythagoras* seems to have played the leading part; which was long after continued by his disciples, and the *Italick* School. The Philosophy of *Plato*, and most of the *Platonists* abounds in numeral considerations: above all, *Philo* the learned *Jew*, hath acted this part even to superstition; bestowing divers pages in summing up every thing, which might advantage this number. Which notwithstanding, when a serious Reader shall perpend, he will hardly find any thing that may convince his judgment, or any further perswade, then the lenity of his belief, or prejudgment of reason inclineth.

For first, Not only the number of 7 and 9 from considerations abstruse, have been extolled by most, but all or most of the other digits have been as mystically applauded. For the number of One and Three have not been only admired by the Heathens, but from adorable grounds, the unity of God, and mystery of the Trinity admired by many Christians. The number of four stands much admired, not only in the quaternity of the Elements, which are the principles of bodies, but in the letters of the Name of God, which in the *Greek, Arabian, Persian, Hebrew,* and *Egyptian*, consisteth of that number; and was so venerable among the *Pythagoreans*, that they swore by the number four. That of six hath found many leaves in its favour; not only for the daies of the Creation, but its natural consideration, as being a perfect number, and the first that is compleated by its parts; that is, the sixt, the half, and the third, 1. 2. 3. Which drawn into a sum, make six. The number of Ten hath been as highly extolled, as containing even, odd, long, plain, quadrate and cubical numbers; and *Aristotle* observed with admiration, that *Barbarians* as well as *Greeks*, did use numeration unto Ten, which being so general, was not to be judged casual, but to have a foundation in nature. So that not only 7 and 9, but all the rest have had their Elogies, as may be observed at large in *Rhodiginus*, and in several Writers since: every one extolling number, according to his subject, and as it advantaged the present discourse in hand.

Again, They have been commended not only from pretended grounds in nature, but from artificial, casual or fabulous foundations: so have some endeavoured to advance their admiration, from the 9 Muses, from the 7 Wonders of the World, from the 7 Gates of *Thebes*: in that 7 Cities contended for *Homer*, in that there are 7 Stars in *Ursa minor*, and 7 in Charles wayn, or Plaustrum of *Ursa major*. Wherein indeed although the ground be natural, yet either from constellations or their remarkable parts, there is the like occasion to commend any other number, the number 5 from the stars in *Sagitta*, 3 from the girdle of *Orion*, and 4 from *Equiculus, Crusero*, or the feet of the Centaur: yet are such as these clapt in by very good Authors, and some not omitted by *Philo*.

Nor are they only extolled from Arbitrary and Poetical grounds, but from foundations and principles, false or dubious. That Women are menstruant, and Men pubescent at the year of twice seven is accounted a punctual truth; which period nevertheless we dare not precisely determine, as having observed a variation and latitude in most, agreeable unto the heat of clime or temper; Men arising variously unto virility, according to the activity of causes that promote it. *Sanguis menstruosus ad diem, ut plurimum, septimum durat*, saith *Philo*. Which notwithstanding is repugnant unto experience, and the doctrine of *Hippocrates*, who in his book, *de diæta*, plainly affirmeth, it is thus but with few women, and only such as abound with pituitous and watery humours.

It is further conceived to receive addition, in that there are 7 heads of *Nyle*, but we have made manifest elsewhere, that by the description of Geographers, they have been sometime more, and are at present fewer.

In that there were 7 Wise men of *Greece*, which though generally received, yet having enquired into the verity thereof we cannot so readily determine it, for in the life of *Thales*, who was accounted in that number, *Diogenes Laertius* plainly saith, *Magna de eorum numero discordia est*; some holding but four, some ten, others twelve, and none agreeth in their names, though according in their number.

In that there are just 7 Planets or errant Stars in the lower orbs of Heaven, but it is now demonstrable unto sense, that there are many more; as *Galileo* Nuncius Sydereus. hath declared, that is, two more in the orb of Saturn, and no less then four more in the sphere of Jupiter. And the like may be said of the *Pleiades* or 7 Stars, which are also introduced to magnifie this number, for whereas scarce discerning six, we account them 7, by his relation, there are no less then fourty.

That the Heavens are encompassed with 7 Circles, is also the allegation of *Philo*; which are in his account, the Arctick, Antarctick, the Summer and Winter Tropicks, the Æquator, Zodiack, and the Milky circle; whereas by Astronomers they are received in greater number. For though we leave out the Lacteous circle (which *Aratus*, *Geminus*, and *Proclus*, out of him hath numbred among the rest) yet are there more by four then *Philo* mentions; that is, the Horizon, Meridian and both the Colures; circles very considerable, and generally delivered, not only by *Ptolomie*, and the Astronomers since his time, but such as flourished long before, as *Hipparchus* and *Eudoxus*. So that for ought I know, if it make for our purpose, or advance the theme in hand, with equal liberty, we may affirm there were 7 Sybils, or but 7 signs in the Zodiack circle of Heaven.

That verse in *Virgil* translated out of *Homer* Τρὶς μάκαρες Δαναοὶ καὶ τετράχις., *O terque quaterque beati*; that is as men will have it, 7 times happy, hath much advanced this number in critical apprehensions; yet is not this construction so indubitably to be received, as not at all to be questioned: for though *Rhodiginus*, *Beroaldus*, and others from the authority of *Macrobius* so interpret it, yet *Servius* his ancient commentator conceives no more thereby then a finite number for indefinite, and that no more is implied then often happy. *Strabo* Lib. 10. the ancientest of them all, conceives no more by this in *Homer*, then a full and excessive expression; whereas in common phrase and received language, he should have termed them thrice happy; herein exceeding that number, he called them four times happy, that is, more then thrice. And this he illustrates by the like expression of *Homer*, in the speech of *Circe*; who to express the dread and terrour of the Ocean, sticks not unto the common form of speech in the strict account of its reciprocations, but largely speaking, saith, it ebbs and flows no less then thrice a day, *terque die revomit fluctus iterumque resorbet*. And so when it is said by *Horace*, *fælices ter et amplius*, the exposition is sufficient, if we conceive no more then the letter fairly beareth, that is, four times, or indefinitely more then thrice.

But the main considerations which most set of this number, are observations drawn from the motions of the Moon, supposed to be measured by sevens; and the critical or decretory daies dependent on that number. As for the motion of the Moon, though we grant it to be measured by sevens, yet will not this advance the same before its fellow numbers; for hereby the motion of other Stars are not measured, the fixed Stars by many thousand years, the Sun by 365 daies, the superiour Planets by more, the inferiour by somewhat less. And if we consider the revolution of the first Movable, and the daily motion from East to West, common unto all the Orbs, we shall find it measured by another number, for being performed in four and twenty hours, it is made up of 4 times 6: and this is the measure and standard of other parts of time, of months, of years, Olympiades, Lustres, Indictions of Cycles, Jubilies, etc.

What a Solary month is.

Again, Months are not only Lunary, and measured by the Moon, but also Solary, and determined by the motion of the Sun; that is, the space wherein the Sun doth pass 30 degrees of the Ecliptick. By this month *Hippocrates* De octomestri partu. computed the time of the Infants gestation in the womb; for 9 times 30, that is, 270 daies, or compleat 9 months, make up forty weeks, the common compute of women. And this is to be understood, when he saith, 2 daies makes the fifteenth, and 3 the tenth part of a mouth. This was the month of the ancient *Hebrews* before their departure out of *Egypt*: and hereby the compute will fall out right, and the account concur, when in one place it is said, the waters of the flood prevailed an hundred and fifty daies, and in another it is delivered, that they prevailed from the seventeenth day of the second month, unto the seventeenth day of the seventh. As for hebdomadal periods or weeks, although in regard of their Sabbaths, they were observed by the *Hebrews*, yet it is not apparent the ancient *Greeks* or *Romans* used any: but had another division of their months into Ides, Nones and Calends.

Moreover, Moneths howsoever taken, are not exactly divisible into septenaries or weeks, which fully contain seven daies: whereof four times do make compleatly twenty eight. For, beside the usual or Calendary month, there are but four considerable: the month of Peragration, of Apparition, of Consecution, and the medical or Decretorial month; whereof some come short, others exceed this account. A month of Peragration, is the time of the Moons revolution from any part of the Zodiack, unto the same again; and this containeth but 27 daies, and about 8 hours: which cometh short to compleat the septenary account. The month of Consecution, or as some will term it, of progression, is the space between one conjunction of the Moon with the Sun, unto another: and this containeth 29 daies and an half: for the Moon returning unto the same point wherein it was kindled by the Sun, and not finding it there again (for in the mean time, by its proper motion it hath passed through 2 signs) it followeth after, and attains the Sun in the space of 2 daies and 4 hours more, which added unto the account of Peragration, makes 29 daies and an half: so that this month exceedeth the latitude of Septenaries, and the fourth part comprehendeth more then 7 daies. A month of Apparition, is the space wherein the Moon appeareth (deducting three daies wherein it commonly disappeareth; and being in combustion with the Sun, is presumed of less activity,) and this containeth but 26 daies and 12 hours. The medical month, not much exceedeth this, consisting of 26 daies and 22 hours, and is made up out of all the other months. For if out of 29 and an half, the month of Consecution, we deduct 3 daies of disappearance, there will remain the month of Apparition 26 daies and 12 hours: whereto if we add 27 daies and 8 hours, the month of Peragration, there will arise 53 daies and 10 hours, which divided by 2, makes 26 daies and 22 hours: called by Physitians the medical month: introduced by *Galen* against *Archigenes*, for the better compute of Decretory or Critical daies.

What a Critical day is.

As for the Critical daies (such I mean wherein upon a decertation between the disease and nature, there ensueth a sensible alteration, either to life or death,) the reasons thereof are rather deduced from Astrology, then Arithmetick: for accounting from the beginning of the disease, and reckoning on unto the seventh day, the Moon will be in a Tetragonal or Quadrate aspect, that is, 4 signs removed from that wherein the disease began: in the fourteenth day it will be in an opposite aspect: and at the end of the third septenary, Tetragonal again: as will most graphically appear in the figures of Astrologers, especially *Lucas Gauricus, De diebus decretoriis*.

Again, (Beside that computing by the Medical month, the first hebdomade or septenary consists of 6 daies, seventeen hours and an half, the second happeneth in 13 daies and eleven hours, and the third but in the twentieth natural day) what *Galen* first, and *Aben-Ezra* since observed in his Tract of Critical daies, in regard of Eccentricity and the Epicycle or lesser orb wherein it moveth, the motion of the Moon is various and unequal; whereby the Critical account must also vary. For though its middle motion be equal, and of 13 degrees, yet in the other it moveth sometimes fifteen, sometimes less then twelve. For moving in the upper part of its orb, it performeth its motion more slowly then in the lower; insomuch that being at the height, it arriveth at the Tetragonal and opposite signs sooner, and the Critical day will be in 6 and 13; and being at the lowest, the critical account will be out of the latitude of 7, nor happen before the eighth or ninth day. Which are considerations not to be neglected in the compute of decretory daies, and manifestly declare that other numbers must have a respect herein as well as 7 and fourteen.

Lastly, Some things to this intent are deduced from holy Scripture; thus is the year of *Jubile* introduced to magnifie this number, as being a year made out of 7 times 7; wherein notwithstanding there may be a misapprehension; for this ariseth not from 7 times 7, that is, 49;

but was observed the fiftieth year, as is expressed, Levit. 25., And you shall hallow the fiftieth year, a *Jubile* shall that fiftieth year be unto you. Answerable whereto is the Exposition of the *Jews* themselves, as is delivered by *Ben-Maimon*; that is, the year of *Jubile*, cometh not into the account of the years of 7, but the fourty ninth is the Release, and the fiftieth the year of *Jubile*. Thus is it also esteemed no small advancement unto this number, that the Genealogy of our Saviour is summed up by 14, that is, this number doubled; according as is expressed Mat. 1. So all the generations from *Abraham* to *David* are fourteen generations, and from *David* unto the carrying away into *Babylon*, are fourteen generations; and from the carrying away into *Babylon* unto *Christ*, are fourteen generations. Which nevertheless must not be strictly understood as numeral relations require; for from *David* unto *Jeconiah* are accounted by *Matthew* but 14 generations; whereas according to the exact account in the History of Kings, there were at least 17; and 3 in this account, that is, *Ahazias, Joas* and *Amazias* are left out. For so it is delivered by the Evangelist: And *Joram* begat *Ozias*: whereas in the regal Genealogy there are 3 successions between: for *Ozias* or *Uzziah* was the son of *Amazias, Amazias* of *Joas, Joas* of *Azariah*, and *Azariah* of *Joram*: so that in strict account, *Joram* was the *Abavus* or Grand-father twice removed, and not the Father of *Ozias*. And these second omitted descents made a very considerable measure of time, in the Royal chronology of *Judah*: for though *Azariah* reigned but one year, yet *Joas* reigned fourty, and *Amazias* no less then nine and twenty. However therefore these were delivered by the Evangelist, and carry (no doubt) an incontroulable conformity unto the intention of his delivery: yet are they not appliable unto precise numerality, nor strictly to be drawn unto the rigid test of numbers.

 Lastly, Though many things have been delivered by Authors concerning number, and they transferred unto the advantage of their nature, yet are they oft-times otherwise to be understood, then as they are vulgarly received in active and causal considerations; they being many times delivered Hieroglyphically, Metaphorically, Illustratively, and not with reference unto action or causality. True it is, that God made all things in number, weight and measure, yet nothing by them or through the efficacy of either. Indeed our daies, actions and motions being measured by time (which is but motion measured) what ever is observable in any, falls under the account of some number; which notwithstanding cannot be denominated the cause of those events. So do we injustly assign the power of Action even unto Time it self; nor do they speak properly who say that Time consumeth all things; for Time is not effective, nor are bodies destroyed by it, but from the action and passion of their Elements in it; whose account it only affordeth: and measuring out their motion, informs us in the periods and terms of their duration, rather then effecteth or physically produceth the same.

 A second consideration which promoteth this opinion, are confirmations drawn from Writers, who have made observations, or set down favourable reasons for this Climacterical year; so have *Henricus Ranzovius, Baptista Codronchus,* De annis Climactericis. and *Levinus Lemnius* De occultis naturæ miraculis. much confirmed the same; but above all, that memorable Letter of *Augustus* Bel. lib. 5. sent unto his Nephew *Caius*, wherein he encourageth him to celebrate his nativity, for he had now escaped Sixty three, the great Climacterical and dangerous year unto man: which notwithstanding rightly perpended, it can be no singularity to question it, nor any new Paradox to deny it.

 For first, It is implicitly, and upon consequence denied by *Aristotle* in his Politicks, in that discourse against *Plato*, who measured the vicissitude and mutation of States, by a periodical fatality of number. *Ptolomie* that famous Mathematician plainly saith, he will not deliver his doctrines by parts and numbers which are ineffectual, and have not the nature of causes; now by these numbers saith *Rhodiginus* and *Mirandula*, he implieth Climacterical years, that is, septenaries, and novenaries set down by the bare observation of numbers. *Censorinus* an Author of great authority, and sufficient antiquity, speaks yet more amply in his book *De die Natali*, wherein expresly treating of Climacterical daies, he thus delivereth himself. Some maintain that 7 times 7, that is, fourty nine, is most dangerous of any other, and this is the most general opinion; others unto 7 times 7, add 9 times 9, that is, the year of eighty one, both which consisting of square and quadrate numbers, were thought by *Plato* and others to be of great consideration; as for this year of Sixty three or 7 times 9, though some esteem it of most danger, yet do I conceive it less dangerous then the other; for though it containeth both numbers above named, that is, 7 and 9, yet neither of them square or quadrate; and as it is different from them both, so is it not potent in either. Nor is this year remarkable in the death of many famous men. I find indeed that *Aristotle* died this year, but he by the vigour of his mind, a long time sustained a natural infirmity of stomack; so that it was a greater wonder he attained unto Sixty three, then that he lived no longer. The Psalm of *Moses* hath mentioned a year of danger differing from all these: and that is ten times 7 or seventy; for so it is said, The daies of Man are threescore and ten. And the very same is affirmed by *Solon*, as *Herodotus* relates in a speech of his unto *Crœsus*, *Ego annis septuaginta humanæ vitæ modum definio*: and surely that year must be of greatest danger, which is the Period of all the rest; and fewest safely pass thorow that, which is set as a bound for few or none to pass. And therefore the consent of elder times, setling their conceits upon Climacters, not only differing from this of ours, but one another; though several Nations and Ages do fancy unto themselves different years of danger, yet every one expects the same event, and constant verity in each.

Again, Though *Varro* divided the daies of man into five proportions, *Hippocrates* into 7, and *Solon* into 10; yet probably their divisions were to be received with latitude, and their considerations not strictly to be confined unto their last unities. So when *Varro* extendeth *Puertia* unto 15. *Adolescentia* unto 30. *Juventus* unto 35. There is a latitude between the terms or Periods of compute, and the verity holds good in the accidents of any years between them. So when *Hippocrates* divideth our life into 7 degrees or stages, and maketh the end of the first 7. Of the second 14. Of the third 28. Of the fourth 35. Of the fift 47. Of the sixt 56. And of the seventh, the last year when ever it happeneth; herein we may observe, he maketh not his divisions precisely by 7 and 9, and omits the great Climacterical; beside there is between every one at least the latitude of 7 years, in which space or interval, that is either in the third or fourth year, what ever falleth out is equally verified of the whole degree, as though it had happened in the seventh. *Solon* divided it into ten Septenaries, because in every one thereof, a man received some sensible mutation; in the first is Dedention or falling of teeth; in the second Pubescence; in the third the beard groweth; in the fourth strength prevails; in the fift maturity for issue; in the sixt moderation of appetite; in the seventh prudence, etc. Now herein there is a tolerable latitude, and though the division proceed by 7, yet is not the total verity to be restrained unto the last year; nor constantly to be expected the beard should be compleat at 21. or wisdom acquired just in 49. and thus also though 7 times 9 contain one of those septenaries, and doth also happen in our declining years; yet might the events thereof be imputed unto the whole septenary; and be more reasonably entertained with some latitude, then strictly reduced unto the last number, or all the accidents from 56. imputed unto Sixty three.

Thirdly, Although this opinion may seem confirmed by observation, and men may say it hath been so observed, yet we speak also upon experience, and do believe that men from observation will collect no satisfaction. That other years may be taken against it, especially if they have the advantage to precede it; as sixty against sixty three, and sixty three against sixty six. For fewer attain to the latter then the former; and so surely in the first septenary do most die, and probably also in the very first year; for all that ever lived were in the account of that year; beside the infirmities that attend it are so many, and the body that receives them so tender and inconfirmed, we scarce count any alive that is not past it.

Fabritius Paduanius De catena temporis. discoursing of the great Climacterical, attempts a numeration of eminent men, who died in that year; but in so small a number, as not sufficient to make a considerable Induction. He mentioneth but four, *Diogenes Cynicus*, *Dyonysius Heracleoticus*, *Xenocrates Platonicus*, and *Plato*. As for *Dionysius*, as *Censorinus* witnesseth, he famished himself in the 82 year of his life; *Xenocrates* by the testimony of *Laertius* fell into a cauldron, and died the same year, and *Diogenes* the *Cynick*, by the same testimony lived almost unto ninety. The date of *Plato's* death is not exactly agreed on, but all dissent from this which he determineth: *Neanthes* in *Laertius* extendeth his daies unto 84. *Suidas* unto 82. But *Hermippus* defineth his death in 81. And this account seemeth most exact; for if, as he delivereth, *Plato* was born in the 88 Olympiade, and died in the first year of the 108, the account will not surpass the year of 81, and so in his death he verified the opinion of his life, and of the life of man, whose period, as *Censorinus* recordeth, he placeth in the Quadrate of 9, or 9 times 9, that is, eighty one: and therefore as *Seneca* delivereth, the *Magicians* at *Athens* did sacrifice unto him, as declaring in his death somewhat above humanity; because he died in the day of his nativity, and without deduction justly accomplished the year of eighty one. *Bodine* I confess, delivers a larger list of men that died in this year *Method. Hist.*, *Moriuntur innumerabiles anno sexagesimo tertio, Aristoteles, Chrysippus, Bocatius, Bernardus, Erasmus, Lutherus, Melancthon, Sylvius, Alexander, Jacobus Sturmius, Nicolaus Causanus, Thomas Linacer, eodem anno Cicero cæsus est.* Wherein beside that it were not difficult to make a larger Catalogue of memorable persons that died in other years, we cannot but doubt the verity of his Induction. As for *Sylvius* and *Alexander*, which of that name he meaneth I know not; but for *Chrysippus*, by the testimony of *Laertius*, he died in the 73 year, *Bocatius* in the 62, *Linacer* the 64, and *Erasmus* exceedeth 70, as *Paulus Jovius* hath delivered in his Elogy of learned men. And as for *Cicero*, as *Plutarch* in his life affirmeth, he was slain in the year of 64; and therefore sure the question is hard set, and we have no easie reason to doubt, when great and entire Authors shall introduce injustifiable examples, and authorize their assertions by what is not authentical.

Fourthly, They which proceed upon strict numerations, and will by such regular and determined waies measure out the lives of men, and periodically define the alterations of their tempers; conceive a regularity in mutations, with an equality in constitutions, and forget that variety, which Physitians therein discover. *Cholerick men commonly shorter lived.* For seeing we affirm that women do naturally grow old before men, that the cholerick fall short in longævity of the sanguine, that there is *senium ante senectum*, and many grow old before they arrive at age, we cannot affix unto them all one common point of danger, but should rather assign a respective fatality unto each. Which is concordant unto the doctrine of the numerists, and such as maintain this opinion: for they affirm that one number respecteth Men, another Women, as *Bodin* explaineth that of *Seneca Septimus quisque annus ætati signum imprimit*, subjoins *Hoc de maribus dictum oportuit, hoc primum intueri licet, perfectum numerum, id est, sextum fæminas septenarium mares immutare.*

Fiftly, Since we esteem this opinion to have some ground in nature, and that nine times seven revolutions of the Sun, imprints a dangerous Character on such as arrive unto it; it will have some doubt behind, in what subjection hereunto were the lives of our fore-fathers presently after the flood, and more especially before it; who attaining unto 8 or 900 years, had not their Climacters Computable by digits, or as we do account them; for the great Climacterical was past unto them before they begat Children, or gave any Testimony of their virility; for we read not that any begat children before the age of sixty five. And this may also afford a hint to enquire, what are the Climacters of other animated creatures; whereof the lives of some attain not so far as this of ours, and that of others extend a considerable space beyond it.

Lastly, The imperfect accounts that Men have kept of time, and the difference thereof both in the same and divers common Wealths, will much distract the certainty of this assertion. For though there were a fatality in this year, yet divers were, and others might be out in their account, aberring several waies from the true and just compute, and calling that one year, which perhaps might be another.

For first, They might be out in the commencement or beginning of their account; for every man is many months elder then he computeth. For although we begin the same from our nativity, and conceive that no arbitrary, but natural term of compute, yet for the duration of life or existence, we are liable in the Womb unto the usual distinctions of time; and are not to be exempted from the account of age and life, where we are subject to diseases, and often suffer death. And therefore *Pythagoras, Hippocrates, Diocles, Avicenna* and others, have set upon us numeral relations and temporal considerations in the womb; not only affirming the birth of the seventh month to be vital, that of the eighth mortal, but the progression thereto to be measured by rule, and to hold a proportion unto motion and formation. As what receiveth motion in the seventh, to be perfected in the Triplicities; that is, the time of conformation unto motion is double, and that from motion unto the birth, treble; So what is formed the 35 day, is moved the seventy, and born the 210 day. And therefore if any invisible causality there be, that after so many years doth evidence it self as Sixty three, it will be questionable whether its activity only set out at our nativity, and begin not rather in the womb, wherein we place the like considerations. Which doth not only entangle this assertion, but hath already embroiled the endeavours of Astrology in the erection of Schemes, and the judgment of death or diseases; for being not incontroulably determined, at what time to begin, whether at conception, animation or exclusion (it being indifferent unto the influence of Heaven to begin at either) they have invented another way, that is, to begin *ab Hora quæstionis*, as *Haly, Messahallach, Ganivetus,* and *Guido Bonatus* have delivered.

Again, In regard of the measure of time by months and years, there will be no small difficulty; and if we shall strictly consider it, many have been and still may be mistaken. For neither the motion of the Moon, whereby months are computed; nor of the Sun, whereby years are accounted, consisteth of whole numbers, but admits of fractions, and broken parts, as we have already declared concerning the Moon. That of the Sun consisteth of 365 daies, and almost 6 hours, that is, wanting eleven minutes; which 6 hours omitted, or not taken notice of, will in process of time largely deprave the compute; and this is the occasion of the Bissextile or leap-year, which was not observed in all times, nor punctually in all Common-Wealths; so that in Sixty three years there may be lost almost 18 daies, omitting the intercalation of one day every fourth year, allowed for this quadrant, or 6 hours supernumerary. And though the same were observed, yet to speak strictly a man may be somewhat out in the account of his age at Sixty three, for although every fourth year we insert one day, and so fetch up the quadrant, yet those eleven minutes whereby the year comes short of perfect 6 hours, will in the circuit of those years arise unto certain hours; and in a larger progression of time unto certain daies. Whereof at present we find experience in the Calender we observe. For the *Julian* year of 365 daies being eleven minutes larger then the annual revolution of the Sun, there will arise an anticipation in the Æquinoxes; and as *Junctinus* Comment. in Sphæram Ioh. de Sacro bosco. computeth, in every 136 year they will anticipate almost one day. And therefore those ancient men and Nestors of old times, which yearly observed their nativities, might be mistaken in the day; nor that to be construed without a grain of Salt, which is delivered by *Moses*; At the end of four hundred years, even the self same day, all the host of *Israel* went out of the land of *Egypt*. For in that space of time the Æquinoxes had anticipated, and the eleven minutes had amounted far above a day. And this compute rightly considered will fall fouler on them who cast up the lives of Kingdoms, and sum up their duration by particular numbers; as *Plato* first began, and some have endeavoured since by perfect and spherical numbers, by the square and cube of 7 and 9 and 12, the great number of *Plato*. Wherein indeed *Bodine* Mat. Histor. hath attempted a particular enumeration; but (beside the mistakes committible in the solary compute of years) the difference of Chronology disturbs the satisfaction and quiet of his computes; some adding, others detracting, and few punctually according in any one year; whereby indeed such accounts should be made up; for the variation in an unite destroys the total illation.

Thirdly, The compute may be unjust not only in a strict acception, of few daies or hours, but in the latitude also of some years; and this may happen from the different compute of years in divers Nations, and even such as did maintain the most probable way of account: their year being not only different from one another, but the civil and common account disagreeing much from the natural year, whereon the consideration is founded. Thus from the testimony of *Herodotus*, *Censorinus* and others, the *Greeks* observed the Lunary year, **The Lunary year what.** that is, twelve revolutions of the Moon, 354 daies; but the *Egyptians*, and many others adhered unto the Solary account, **The Solary year what.** that is, 365 daies, that is, eleven daies longer. Now hereby the account of the one would very much exceed the other: A man in the one would account himself 63, when one in the other would think himself but 61; and so although their nativities were under the same hour, yet did they at different years believe the verity of that which both esteemed affixed and certain unto one. The like mistake there is in a tradition of our daies; men conceiving a peculiar danger in the beginning daies of *May*, set out as a fatal period unto consumptions and Chronical diseases; wherein notwithstanding we compute by Calenders, not only different from our ancestors, but one another; the compute of the one anticipating that of the other; so that while we are in *April*, others begin *May*, and the danger is past unto one, while it beginneth with another.

Fourthly, Men were not only out in the number of some daies, the latitude of a few years, but might be wide by whole Olympiades and divers Decades of years. **The different account or measure of a year.** For as *Censorinus* relateth, the ancient *Arcadians* observed a year of three months, the *Carians* of six, the *Iberians* of four; and as *Diodorus* and *Xenophon de Æquivocis* alleadgeth, the ancient *Egyptians* have used a year of three, two, and one moneth: so that the Climacterical was not only different unto those Nations, but unreasonably distant from ours; for Sixty three will pass in their account, before they arrive so high as ten in ours.

Nor if we survey the account of *Rome* it self, may we doubt they were mistaken; and if they feared Climacterical years, might err in their numeration. For the civil year whereof the people took notice, did sometimes come short, and sometimes exceed the natural. For according to *Varro*, *Suctoninus* and *Censorinus*, their year consisted first of ten months; which comprehended but 304 daies, that is, 61 less than ours containeth; after by *Numa* or *Tarquine* from a superstitious conceit of imparity were added 51 daies, which made 355, one day more then twelve revolutions of the Moon. And thus a long time it continued, the civil compute exceeding the natural; the correction whereof, and the due ordering of the Leap year was referred unto the Pontifices; who either upon favour or malice, that some might continue their offices a longer or shorter time; or from the magnitude of the year that men might be advantaged, or endamaged in their contracts, by arbitrary intercalations depraved the whole account. Of this abuse *Cicero* accused *Verres*, which at last proceeded so far, that when *Julius Cæsar* came unto that office, before the redress hereof he was fain to insert two intercalary months unto *November* and *December*, when he had already inserted 23 daies unto *February*; so that the year consisted of 445 daies; a quarter of a year longer then that we observe; and though at the last the year was reformed, yet in the mean time they might be out wherein they summed up Climacterical observations.

Lastly, One way more there may be of mistake, and that not unusual among us, grounded upon a double compute of the year; the one beginning from the 25 of *March*, the other from the day of our birth, unto the same again which is the natural account. Now hereupon many men frequently miscast their daies; for in their age they deduce the account not from the day of their birth, but the year of our Lord, wherein they were born. So a man that was born in *January* 1582, if he live to fall sick in the latter end of *March* 1645, will sum up his age, and say I am now Sixty three, and in my Climacterical and dangerous year; for I was born in the year 1582, and now it is 1645, whereas indeed he wanteth many months of that year, considering the true and natural account unto his birth; and accounteth two months for a year: and though the length of time and accumulation of years do render the mistake insensible; yet is it all one, as if one born in *January* 1644, should be accounted a year old the 25 of *March* 1645.

All which perpended, it may be easily perceived with what insecurity of truth we adhere unto this opinion; ascribing not only effects depending on the natural period of time unto arbitrary calculations, and such as vary at pleasure; but confirming our tenets by the uncertain account of others and our selves. There being no positive or indisputable ground where to begin our compute; that if there were, men have been several waies mistaken; the best in some latitude, others in greater, according to the different compute of divers states, the short and irreconcilable years of some, the exceeding error in the natural frame of others, and the lapses and false deductions of ordinary accountants in most.

Which duly considered, together with a strict account and critical examen of reason, will also distract the witty determinations of Astrology. That Saturn the enemy of life, comes almost every seventh year, unto the quadrate or malevolent place; that as the Moon about every seventh day arriveth unto a contrary sign, so Saturn, which remaineth about as many years, as the Moon doth daies in one sign, and holdeth the same consideration in years as the Moon in daies; doth cause these periculous periods. Which together with other Planets, and profection of the Horoscope, unto the seventh house, or opposite signs every seventh year; oppresseth living natures, and causeth observable mutations, in the state of sublunary things.

Further satisfaction may yet be had from the learned discourse of *Salmasius* lately published *De annis Climactericis.*, if any desire to be informed how different the present observations are from those of the ancients; how every one hath different Climactericals; with many other observables, impugning the present opinion.

CHAPTER XIII
Of the Canicular or Dog daies.

Whereof to speak distinctly: among the Southern constellations two there are which bear the name of the Dog; the one in 16 degrees of latitude, containing on the left thigh a Star of the first magnitude, usually called Procyon or Anticanis, because say some it riseth before the other; which if truly understood, must be restrained unto those habitations, who have elevation of pole above thirty two degrees. Mention thereof there is in *Horace*, Iam Procyon fuerit et stella vesani Leonis. who seems to mistake or confound the one with the other; and after him in *Galen*, who is willing, the remarkablest Star of the other should be called by this name; because it is the first that ariseth in the constellation; which notwithstanding, to speak strictly, it is not; unless we except one of the third magnitude in the right paw in his own and our elevation, and two more on his head in and beyond the degree of Sixty. What the Dog-star is. A second and more considerable one there is, and neighbour unto the other, in 40 degrees of latitude, containing 18 Stars, whereof that in his mouth of the first magnitude, the *Greeks* call Σείριος, the *Latines canis major*, and we emphatically the Dog-Star.

Now from the rising of this Star, not cosmically, that is, with the Sun, but Heliacally, that is, its emersion from the raies of the Sun, the Ancients computed their canicular daies; concerning which there generally passeth an opinion, that during those daies, all medication or use of physick is to be declined; and the cure committed unto nature. And therefore as though there were any feriation in nature, or justitiums imaginable in professions, whose subject is natural, and under no intermissive, but constant way of mutation; this season is commonly termed the Physitians vacation, and stands so received by most men. Which conceit however general, is not only erroneous, but unnatural, and subsisting upon foundations either false, uncertain, mistaken or misapplied, deserves not of mankind that indubitable assent it findeth.

For first, which seems to be the ground of this assertion, and not to be drawn into question, that is, the magnified quality of this Star conceived to cause, or intend the heat of this season whereby these daies become more observable then the rest: We find that wiser Antiquity was not of this opinion. For, seventeen hundred years ago it was as a vulgar error rejected by *Geminus*, a learned Mathematician in his Elements of Astronomy; wherein he plainly affirmeth, that common opinion made that a cause, which was at first observed but as a sign. The rising and setting both of this Star and others being observed by the Ancients, to denote and testifie certain points of mutation rather then conceived to induce or effect the same. For our fore-fathers, saith he, observing the course of the Sun, and marking certain mutations to happen in his progress through particular parts of the Zodiack, they registred and set them down in their Parapegmes, or Astronomical Canons; and being not able to design these times by daies, months or years (the compute thereof, and the beginning of the year being different, according unto different Nations) they thought best to settle a general account unto all; and to determine these alterations by some known and invariable signs; and such did they conceive the rising and setting of the fixed Stars; not ascribing thereto any part of causality, but notice and signification. And thus much seems implied in that expression of *Homer*, when speaking of the Dog Star, he concludeth——κακὸν δέ τε σῆμα τέτυκται, *Malum autem signum est*; The same, as *Petavius* observeth, is implied in the word of *Ptolomy*, and the Ancients, περὶ ἐπισημασιῶν, that is, of the signification of Stars. The term of Scripture also favours it, as that of *Isaiah*, *Nolite timere à signis cœli*; and that in *Genesis*, *Ut sint in signa et tempora*: Let there be lights in the firmament, and let them be for signs and for seasons.

The Primative and leading magnifiers of this Star, were the *Egyptians*, the great admirers of Dogs in Earth and Heaven. *Dionysius Periegesi.* Wherein they worshipped *Anubis* or *Mercurius*, the Scribe of *Saturn*, and Counseller of *Osyris*, the great inventor of their religious rites, and Promoter of good unto *Egypt*. Who was therefore translated into this Star; by the *Egyptians* called *Sothis*, and *Siris* by the *Ethiopians*; from whence that *Sirius* or the Dog-star had its name, is by some conjectured.

And this they looked upon, not with reference unto heat, but cœlestial influence upon the faculties of man, in order to religion and all sagacious invention; and from hence derived the abundance and great fertility of *Egypt*, the overflow of *Nilus* happening about the ascent hereof. And therefore in hieroglyphical monuments, *Anubis* is described with a Dogs-head, with a Crocodile between his legs, with a sphere in his hand, with two Stars, and a water Pot standing by him; implying thereby, the rising and setting of the Dog-star, and the inundation of the River *Nilus*.

But if all were silent, *Galen* hath explained this point unto the life; who expounding the reason why *Hippocrates* declared the affections of the year by the rising and setting of Stars; it was saith he, because he would proceed on signs and principles best known unto all Nations. And upon his words in the first of the Epidemicks, *In Thaso Autumno circa Equinoxium et sub virgilias pluviæ erant multæ*, he thus enlargeth. If (saith he) the same compute of times and months were observed by all Nations, *Hippocrates* had never made any mention either of Arcturus, Pleiades or the Dog-star; but would have plainly said, in *Macedonia*, in the month Dion, thus or thus was the air disposed. But for as much as the month Dion is only known unto the *Macedonians*, but obscure unto the *Athenians* and other Nations, he found more general distinctions of time, and instead of naming months, would usually say, at the Æquinox, the rising of the Pleiades, or the Dog-star. *How the Ancients divided the seasons of the year.* And by this way did the Ancients divide the seasons of the year, the Autumn, Winter, Spring, and Summer. By the rising of the Pleiades, denoting the beginning of Summer, and by that of the Dog-star, the declination thereof. By this way *Aristotle* through all his books of Animals, distinguishing their times of generation, latitancy, migration, sanity and venation. And this were an allowable way of compute, and still to be retained, were the site of the Stars as inalterable, and their ascents as invariable as primitive Astronomy conceived them. And therefore though *Aristotle* frequently mentioneth this Star, and particularly affirmeth that Fishes in the Bosphorus are best catched from the arise of the Dog-star, we must not conceive the same a meer effect thereof. Nor though *Scaliger* from hence be willing to infer the efficacy of this Star, are we induced hereto; except because the same Philosopher affirmeth, that Tunny is fat about the rising of the Pleiades, and departs upon Arcturus, or that most insects are latent, from the setting of the 7 Stars; except, I say, he give us also leave to infer that these particular effects and alterations proceed from those Stars; which were indeed but designations of such quarters and portions of the year, wherein the same were observed. Now what *Pliny* affirmeth of the Orix, that it seemeth to adore this Star, and taketh notice thereof by voice and sternutation; until we be better assured of its verity, we shall not salve the sympathy.

Secondly, What slender opinion the Ancients held of the efficacy of this Star, is declarable from their compute. For as *Geminus* affirmeth, and *Petavius* his learned Commentator proveth, they began their account from its Heliacal emersion, and not its cosmical ascent. *What the Cosmical.* The cosmical ascention of a Star we term that, when it ariseth together with the Sun, or the same degree of the Ecliptick wherein the Sun abideth: *What the Heliacal ascent of Star is.* and that the Heliacal, when a Star which before for the vicinity of the Sun was not visible, being further removed, beginning to appear. For the annual motion of the Sun from West to East being far swifter then that of the fixed Stars, he must of necessity leave them on the East while he hasteneth forward, and obscureth others to the West: and so the Moon who performs its motion swifter then the Sun (as may be observed in their Conjunctions and Eclipses) gets Eastward out of his raies; and appears when the Sun is set. If therefore the Dog-star had this effectual heat which is ascribed unto it, it would afford best evidence thereof, and the season would be most fervent, when it ariseth in the probablest place of its activity, that is, the cosmical ascent; for therein it ariseth with the Sun, and is included in the same irradiation. But the time observed by the Ancients was long after this ascent, and in the Heliacal emersion; when it becomes at greatest distance from the Sun, neither rising with it nor near it. And therefore had they conceived any more then a bare signality in this Star, or ascribed the heat of the season therunto, they would not have computed from its Heliacal ascent, which was of inferiour efficacy; nor imputed the vehemency of heat unto those points wherein it was more remiss, and where with less probability they might make out its action.

Thirdly, Although we derive the authority of these daies from observations of the Ancients, yet are our computes very different, and such as confirm not each other. For whereas they observed it Heliacally, we seem to observe it Cosmically; for before it ariseth Heliacally unto our latitude, the Summer is even at an end. Again, we compute not only from different ascents, but also from divers Stars; they from the greater Dog-star, we from the lesser; they from *Orions* we from *Cephalus* his Dog; they from *Seirius*, we from *Procyon*; for the beginning of the Dog-daies with us is set down the 19 of *July*, about which time the lesser Dog-star ariseth with the Sun; whereas the Star of the greater Dog ascendeth not until after that month. And this mistake will yet be larger, if the compute be made stricter, and as Dr. *Bainbrigge* late professor of Astronomy in Oxford, hath set it down. *Bainb. Canicularis.* Who in the year 1629 computed, that in the Horizon of *Oxford* the Dog-star arose not before the fifteenth day of *August*; when in our Almanack accounts, those daies are almost ended. So that the common and received time not answering the true compute, it frustrates the observations of our selves. And being also different from the calculations of the Ancients, their observations confirm not ours, nor ours theirs, but rather confute each other.

Nor will the computes of the Ancients be so Authentick unto those, who shall take notice, how commonly they applied the celestial descriptions of other climes unto their own; wherein the learned *Bainbrigius* justly reprehendeth *Manilius*, who transferred the *Ægyptian* descriptions unto the *Roman* account; confounding the observation of the *Greek* and *Barbarick* Spheres.

Fourthly, (which is the Argument of *Geminus*) were there any such effectual heat in this Star, yet could it but weakly evidence the same in Summer; it being about 40 degrees distant from the Sun: and should rather manifest its warming power in the Winter, when it remains conjoyned with the Sun in its Hybernal conversion. For about the 29 of *October*, and in the 16 of *Scorpius* and so again in *January*, the Sun performs his revolution in the same parallel with the Dog-star. Again,

If we should impute the heat of this season, unto the co-operation of any Stars with the Sun, it seems more favourable for our times, to ascribe the same unto the constellation of Leo. Where besides that the Sun is in his proper house, it is conjoyned with many Stars; whereof two of the first magnitude; and in the 8{th} of *August* is corporally conjoyned with *Basilicus*; a Star of eminent name in Astrology, and seated almost in the Ecliptick.

Fifthly, If all were granted, that observation and reason were also for it, and were it an undeniable truth, that an effectual fervour proceeded from this Star; yet would not the same determine the opinion now in question; it necessarily suffering such restrictions as take off general illations. For first in regard of different latitudes, unto some the canicular daies are in the Winter; as unto such as have no latitude, but live in a right Sphere, that is, under the Equinoctial line; for unto them it ariseth when the Sun is about the Tropick of Cancer; which season unto them is Winter, and the Sun remotest from them. Nor hath the same position in the Summer, that is, in the Equinoctial points, any advantage from it; for in the one point the Sun is at the Meridian, before the Dog-star ariseth; in the other the Star is at the Meridian, before the sun ascendeth.

What latitudes have no Dog-daies at all.
Some latitudes have no canicular daies at all; as namely all those which have more then 73 degrees of Northern Elevation; as the territory of *Nova Zembla*, part of *Greenland* and *Tartary*; for unto that habitation the Dog-star is invisible, and appeareth not above the Horizon.

Unto such latitudes wherein it ariseth, it carrieth a various and very different respect; unto some it ascendeth when Summer is over, whether we compute Heliacally or Cosmically; for though unto *Alexandria* it ariseth in Cancer; yet it ariseth not unto Biarmia Cosmically before it be in Virgo, and Heliacally about the Autumnal Equinox. Even unto the latitude of 52, the efficacy thereof is not much considerable, whether we consider its ascent, Meridian, altitude or abode above the Horizon. For it ariseth very late in the year, about the eighteenth of *Leo*, that is, the 31 of *July*. Of Meridian Altitude it hath but 23 degrees, so that it plaies but obliquely upon us, and as the Sun doth about the 23 of *January*. And lastly, his abode above the Horizon is not great; for in the eighteenth of *Leo*, the 31 of *July*, although they arise together; yet doth it set above 5 hours before the Sun, that is, before two of the clock, after which time we are more sensible of heat, then all the day before.

Secondly, In regard of the variation of the longitude of the Stars, we are to consider (what the Ancients observed not) that the site of the fixed Stars is alterable, and that since elder times they have suffered a large and considerable variation of their longitudes. *What the longitude of a Star is.* The longitude of a Star, to speak plainly, is its distance from the first point of numeration toward the East; which first point unto the Ancients was the vernal æquinox. Now by reason of their motion from West to East, they have very much varied from this point: The first Star of Aries in the time of *Meton* the *Athenian* was placed in the very intersection, which is now elongated and removed Eastward 28 degrees; insomuch that now the sign of Aries possesseth the place of Taurus, and Taurus that of Gemini. Which variation of longitude must very much distract the opinion of the Dog star; not only in our daies, but in times before and after; for since the World began it hath arisen in Taurus, and if the World last, may have its ascent in Virgo; so that we must place the canicular daies, that is, the hottest time of the year in the Spring in the first age, and in the Autumn in Ages to come.

Thirdly, The Stars have not only varied their longitudes, whereby their ascents have altered; but have also changed their declinations, whereby their rising at all, that is, their appearing hath varied. *What the declination of a Star is.* The declination of a Star we call its distance from the Equator. Now though the Poles of the world and the Equator be immovable, yet because the Stars in their proper motions from West to East, do move upon the poles of the Ecliptick, distant 23 degrees and an half from the Poles of the Equator, and describe circles parallel not unto the Equator, but the Ecliptick; they must be therefore sometimes nearer, sometimes removed further from the Equator. All Stars that have their distance from the Ecliptick Northward not more then

23 degrees and an half (which is the greatest distance of the Ecliptick from the Equator) may in progression of time have declination Southward, and move beyond the Equator: but if any Star hath just this distance of 23 and an half (as hath Capella on the back of Ericthonius) it may hereafter move under the Equinoctial; and the same will happen respectively unto Stars which have declination Southward. And therefore many Stars may be visible in our Hemisphere, which are not so at present; and many which are at present, shall take leave of our Horizon, and appear unto Southern habitations. And therefore the time may come that the Dog star may not be visible in our Horizon, and the time hath been, when it hath not shewed it self unto our neighbour latitudes. So that canicular daies there have been none, nor shall be; yet certainly in all times some season of the year more notably hot then other.

Lastly, We multiply causes in vain; and for the reason hereof, we need not have recourse unto any Star but the Sun, and continuity of its action. For the Sun ascending into the Northern signs, begetteth first a temperate heat in the air; which by his approach unto the solstice he intendeth; and by continuation increaseth the same even upon declination. *Why the Dog-daies be so hot.* For running over the same degrees again, that is, in Leo, which he hath done in Taurus, in *July* which he did in *May*; he augmenteth the heat in the latter which he began in the first; and easily intendeth the same by continuation which was well promoted before. So it is observed, that they which dwell between the Tropicks and the Equator, have their second summer hotter and more maturative of fruits then the former. So we observe in the day (which is a short year) the greatest heat about two in the afternoon, when the Sun is past the Meridian (which is his diurnal solstice) and the same is evident from the Thermometer or observations of the weather-glass. So are the colds of the night sharper in the Summer about two or three after midnight, and the frosts in Winter stronger about those hours. So likewise in the year we observe the cold to augment, when the daies begin to increase, though the Sun be then ascensive, and returning from the Winter Tropick. And therefore if we rest not in this reason for the heat in the declining part of Summer, we must discover freezing Stars that may resolve the latter colds of Winter; which whoever desires to invent, let him study the Stars of *Andromeda*, or the nearer constellation of *Pegasus*, which are about that time ascendent.

It cannot therefore seem strange, or savour of singularity that we have examined this point; since the same hath been already denied by some, since the authority and observations of the Ancients rightly understood, do not confirm it, since our present computes are different from those of the Ancients, whereon notwithstanding they depend; since there is reason against it, and if all were granted, yet must it be maintained with manifold restraints, far otherwise then is received. And lastly, since from plain and natural principles, the doubt may be fairly salved, and not clapt up from petitionary foundations and principles unestablished.

But that which chiefly promoted the consideration of these daies, and medically advanced the same, was the doctrin of *Hippocrates*; a Physitian of such repute, that he received a testimony from a Christian, that might have been given unto Christ. *Qui nec fallere potest nec falli.* The first in his book, *de Acre, Aquis, et locis. Syderum ortus*, etc. That is, we are to observe the rising of Stars, especially the Dog-star, Arcturus, and the setting of the Pleiades or seven Stars. From whence notwithstanding we cannot infer the general efficacy of these Stars, or co-efficacy particular in medications. Probably expressing no more hereby then if he should have plainly said, especial notice we are to take of the hottest time in Summer, of the beginning of Autumn and Winter; for by the rising and setting of those Stars were these times and seasons defined. *Diseases commonly determined, by what seasons.* And therefore subjoyns this reason, *Quoniam his temporibus morbi finiuntur*, because at these times diseases have their ends; as Physitians well known, and he elsewhere affirmeth, that seasons determine diseases, beginning in their contraries; as the Spring the diseases of Autumn, and the Summer those of Winter. Now (what is very remarkable) whereas in the some place he adviseth to observe the times of notable mutations, as the Equinoxes, and the Solstices, and to decline Medication ten daies before and after; how precisely soever canicular cautions be considered, this is not observed by Physitians, nor taken notice of by the people. And indeed should we blindly obey the restraints both of Physitians and Astrologers, we should contract the liberty of our prescriptions, and confine the utility of Physick unto a very few daies. For observing the Dog-daies, and as is expressed, some daies before, likewise ten daies before and after the Equinoctial and Solsticial points; by this observation alone are exempted an hundred daies. Whereunto if we add the two *Egyptian* daies in every month, the interlunary and plenilunary exemptions, the Eclipses of Sun and Moon, conjunctions and oppositions Planetical, the houses of Planets, and the site of the Luminaries under the signs (wherein some would induce a restraint of Purgation or Phlebotomy) there would arise above an hundred more; so that of the whole year the use of Physick would not be secure much above a quarter. Now as we do not strictly observe these daies, so need we not the other; and although consideration be made hereof, yet must we prefer the nearer indications before those which are drawn from the time of the year; or other cælestial relations.

The second Testimony is taken out of the last piece of his Age, and after the experience (as some think) of no less then an hundred years, that is, his book of Aphorisms, or short and definitive determinations in Physick. The Aphorism alleadged is this, *Sub Cane et ante Canem difficiles sunt purgationes. Sub Cane et Anticane*, say some including both the Dog-stars; but that cannot consist with the Greek: ὑπὸ κύνα καὶ πρὸ κυνὸς, nor had that Criticism been ever omitted by *Galen*. Now how true this sentence was in the mouth of *Hippocrates*, and with what restraint it must be understood by us, will readily appear from the difference between us both, in circumstantial relations.

And first, Concerning his time and Chronology: *When* Hippocrates *lived.* he lived in the reign of *Artaxerxes Longimanus*, about the 82 Olympiade, 450 years before Christ; and from our times above two thousand. Now since that time (as we have already declared) the Stars have varied their longitudes; and having made large progressions from West to East, the time of the Dog-stars ascent must also very much alter. For it ariseth later now in the year, then it formerly did in the same latitude; and far later unto us who have a greater elevation; for in the daies of *Hippocrates* this Star ascended in Cancer, which now ariseth in Leo: and will in progression of time arise in Virgo. And therefore in regard of the time wherein he lived, the Aphorism was more considerable in his daies then in ours, and in times far past then present, and in his Countrey then ours.

The place of his nativity was *Coos*, an Island in the *Myrtoan* Sea, not far from *Rhodes*, described in Maps by the name of *Lango*, and called by the *Turks* who are Masters thereof, *Stancora*; according unto *Ptolomy* of Northern latitude 36 degrees. That he lived and writ in these parts, is not improbably collected from the Epistles that passed betwixt him and *Artaxerxes*; as also between the Citizens of *Abdera*, and *Coos*, in the behalf of *Democritus*. Which place being seated from our latitude of 52, 16 degrees Southward, there will arise a different consideration; and we may much deceive our selves if we conform the ascent of Stars in one place unto another, or conceive they arise the same day of the month in *Coos* and in *England*. For as *Petavius* computes in the first *Julian* year, at *Alexandria* of latitude 31, the Star arose cosmically in the twelfth degree of Cancer, Heliacally the 26, by the compute of *Geminus* about this time at *Rhodes* of latitude 37, it ascended cosmically the 16 of Cancer, Heliacally the first of Leo; and about that time at *Rome* of latitude 42, cosmically the 22 of Cancer, and Heliacally the first of Leo. For unto places of greater latitude it ariseth ever later; so that in some latitudes the cosmical ascent happeneth not before the twentieth degree of Virgo, ten daies before the Autumnal Equinox, and if they compute Heliacally, after it, in Libra.

Again, Should we allow all, and only compute unto the latitude of *Coos*; yet would it not impose a total omission of Physick. For if in the hottest season of that clime, all Physick were to be declined, then surely in many other none were to be used at any time whatsoever; for unto many parts, not only in the Spring and Autumn, but also in the Winter, the Sun is nearer, then unto the clime of *Coos* in the Summer.

The third consideration concerneth purging medicines, which are at present far different from those implied in this Aphorism, and such as were commonly used by *Hippocrates*. **Three degrees of purgations.** For three degrees we make of purgative medicines: The first thereof is very benign, nor far removed from the nature of Aliment, into which, upon defect of working, it is oft-times converted; and in this form do we account *Manna, Cassia, Tamarindes*, and many more; whereof we find no mention in *Hippocrates*. This second is also gentle having a familiarity with some humor, into which it is but converted if it fail of its operation: of this sort are *Aloe, Rhabarb, Senna*, etc. Whereof also few or none were known unto *Hippocrates*. The third is of a violent and venemous quality, which frustrate of its action, assumes as it were the nature of poison; such as are Scammoneum, Colocynthis, Elaterium, Euphorbium, Tithymallus, Laureola, Peplum, etc. Of this sort *Hippocrates* made use, even in Fevers, Pleurisies and Quinsies; and that composition is very remarkable which is ascribed unto *Diogenes* in *Ætius*; **Tetrab. lib. 1. Serm. 3.** that is, of Pepper, Sal Armoniac, Euphorbium, of each an ounce, the Dosis whereof four scruples and an half; which whosoever should take, would find in his bowels more then a canicular heat, though in the depth of Winter; many of the like nature may be observed in *Ætius*, or in the book *De Dinamidiis*, ascribed unto *Galen*, which is the same *verbatim* with the other.

Now in regard of the second, and especially the first degree of Purgatives, the Aphorism is not of force; but we may safely use them, they being benign and of innoxious qualities. And therefore *Lucas Gauricus*, who hath endeavoured with many testimonies to advance this consideration, at length concedeth that lenitive Physick may be used, especially when the Moon is well affected in Cancer or in the watery signs. But in regard of the third degree the Aphorism is considerable: purgations may be dangerous; and a memorable example there is in the medical Epistles of *Crucius*, of a *Roman* Prince that died upon an ounce of Diaphænicon, taken in this season. From the use whereof we refrain not only in hot seasons, but warily exhibit it at all times in hot diseases. Which when necessity requires, we can perform more safely then the Ancients, as having better waies of preparation and correction; that is, not only by addition of other bodies, but separation of noxious parts from their own.

But beside these differences between *Hippocrates* and us, the Physitians of these times and those of Antiquity; the condition of the disease, and the intention of the Physitian, hold a main consideration in what time and place soever. For Physick is either curative or preventive; Preventive we call that which by purging noxious humors, and the causes of diseases, preventeth sickness in the healthy, or the recourse thereof in the valetudinary; this is of common use at the spring and fall, and we commend not the same at this season. Therapeutick or curative Physick, we term that, which restoreth the Patient unto Sanity, and taketh away diseases actually affecting. **Diseases Chronical and Acute what they be.** Now of diseases some are cronical and of long duration, as quartane Agues, Scurvy, etc. Wherein because they admit of delay we defer the cure to more advantagious seasons; Others we term acute, that is, of short duration and danger, as Fevers, Pleurisies, etc. In which, because delay is dangerous, and they arise unto their state before the Dog-daies determine, we apply present remedies according unto Indications; respecting rather the acuteness of the disease, and precipitancy of occasion, then the rising or setting of Stars; the effects of the one being disputable, of the other assured and inevitable.

And although Astrology may here put in, and plead the secret influence of this Star; yet *Galen* in his Comment, makes no such consideration; confirming the truth of the Aphorism from the heat of the year; and the operation of Medicines exhibited. **Strong purgations not so well given in the heat of summer, and why.** In regard that bodies being heated by the Summer, cannot so well endure the acrimony of purging Medicines; and because upon purgations contrary motions ensue, the heat of the air attracting the humours outward, and the action of the Medicine retracting the same inward. But these are readily salved in the distinctions before alleadged; and particularly in the constitution of our climate and divers others, wherein the air makes no such exhaustion of spirits. And in the benignity of our Medicines; whereof some in their own natures, others well prepared, agitate not the humors, or make sensible perturbation.

A Problem.

Nor do we hereby reject or condemn a sober and regulated Astrology; we hold there is more truth therein then in Astrologers; in some more then many allow, yet in none so much as some pretend. We deny not the influence of the Stars, but often suspect the due application thereof; for though we should affirm that all things were in all things; that heaven were but earth celestified, and earth but heaven terrestrified, or that each part above had an influence upon its divided affinity below; yet how to single out these relations, and duly to apply their actions is a work oft times to be effected by some revelation, and *Cabala* from above, rather then any Philosophy, or speculation here below. What power soever they have upon our bodies, it is not requisite they should destroy our reasons, that is, to make us rely on the strength of Nature, when she is least able to relieve us; and when we conceive the heaven against us, to refuse the assistance of the earth created for us.

Upon the biting of a mad Dog there ensues an hydrophobia or fear of water. This were to suffer from the mouth of the Dog above, what others do from the teeth of Dogs below; that is, to be afraid of their proper remedy, and refuse to approach any water, though that hath often proved a cure unto their disease. There is in wise men a power beyond the Stars; and *Ptolomy* encourageth us, that by foreknowledge, we may evade their actions; for, being but universal causes, they are determined by particular agents; which being inclined, not constrained, contain within themselves the casting act, and a power to command the conclusion.

Lastly, If all be conceded, and were there in this Aphorism an unrestrained truth, yet were it not reasonable from a caution to inferr a non-usance or abolition, from a thing to be used with discretion, not to be used at all. Because the Apostle bids us beware of Philosophy, heads of extremity will have none at all; an usual fallacy in vulgar and less distinctive brains, who having once overshot the mean, run violently on, and find no rest but in the extreams.

Now hereon we have the longer insisted, because the error is material, and concerns oft-times the life of man; an error to be taken notice of by State, and provided against by Princes, who are of the opinion of *Solomon*, that their riches consists in the multitude of their subjects. An error worse then some reputed *Heresies*; and of greater danger to the body, then they unto the soul; which whosoever is able to reclaim, he shall salve more in one summer then *Themison* *A Physitian. Quot Themison ægros Autumno occiderit uno. Juvenal.* destroyed in any Autumn; he shall introduce a new way of cure, preserving by Theory, as well as practice, and men not only from death, but from destroying themselves.

THE FIFTH BOOK
Of many things questionable as they are commonly described in Pictures.

CHAPTER I
Of the Picture of the Pelecan.

And first in every place we meet with the picture of the Pelecan, opening her breast with her bill, and feeding her young ones with the blood distilling from her. Thus is it set forth not only in common Signs, but in the Crest and Schucheon of many Noble families; hath been asserted by many holy Writers, and was an Hieroglipihck of piety and pitty among the *Ægyptians*; on which consideration, they spared them at their tables.

Notwithstanding upon enquiry we find no mention hereof in Ancient Zodiographers, and such as have particularly discoursed upon Animals, as *Aristotle, Ælian, Pliny, Solinus* and many more;

who seldom forget proprieties of such a nature, and have been very punctual in less considerable Records. Some ground hereof I confess we may allow, nor need we deny a remarkable affection in Pelecans toward their young; for *Ælian* discoursing of Storks, and their affection toward their brood, whom they instruct to fly, and unto whom they re-deliver up the provision of their Bellies, concludeth at last, that Herons and Pelecans do the like.

As for the testimonies of Ancient Fathers, and Ecclesiastical Writers, we may more safely conceive therein some Emblematical than any real Story: so doth *Eucherius* confess it to be the Emblem of Christ. And we are unwilling literally to receive that account of *Jerom*, that perceiving her young ones destroyed by Serpents, she openeth her side with her bill, by the blood whereof they revive and return unto life again. By which relation they might indeed illustrate the destruction of man by the old Serpent, and his restorement by the blood of Christ: and in this sense we shall not dispute the like relations of *Austine, Isidore, Albertus*, and many more: and under an Emblematical intention, we accept it in coat-armour.

As for the Hieroglyphick of the *Egyptians*, they erected the same upon another consideration, which was parental affection; manifested in the protection of her young ones, when her nest was set on fire. For as for letting out her blood, it was not the assertion of the *Egyptians*, but seems translated unto the Pelecan from the Vulture, as *Pierius* hath plainly delivered. *Sed quod Pelicanum (ut etiam aliis plerisque persuasum est) rostro pectus dissecantem pingunt, ita ut suo sanguine filios alat, ab Ægyptiorum historiâ valde alienum est, illi enim vulturem tantum id facere tradiderunt.*

And lastly, as concerning the picture, if naturally examined, and not Hierogliphically conceived, it containeth many improprieties, disagreeing almost in all things from the true and proper description. For, whereas it is commonly set forth green or yellow, in its proper colour, it is inclining to white; excepting the extremities or tops of the wing feathers, which are brown. *The bigness of a Pelecan.* It is described in the bigness of a Hen, whereas it approacheth and sometimes exceedeth the magnitude of a Swan. It is commonly painted with a short bill; whereas that of the Pelecan attaineth sometimes the length of two spans. The bill is made acute or pointed at the end; whereas it is flat and broad, though somewhat inverted at the extream. It is described like fissipedes, or birds which have their feet or claws divided; whereas it is palmipedous, or fin-footed like Swans and Geese; according to the method of nature, in latirostrous or flat-bild birds; which being generally swimmers, the organ is wisely contrived unto the action, and they are framed with fins or oars upon their feet; and therefore they neither light, nor build on trees, if we except Cormorants, who make their nests like Herons. *Of her Crop.* Lastly, there is one part omitted more remarkable than any other, that is, the chowle or crop adhering unto the lower side of the bill, and so descending by the throat: a bag or sachel very observable, and of a capacity almost beyond credit; which notwithstanding, this animal could not want; for therein it receiveth Oysters, Cochels, Scollops, and other testaceous animals; which being not able to break, it retains them until they open, and vomiting them up, takes out the meat contained. This is that part preserved for a rarity and wherein (as *Sanctius* delivers) in one dissected, a *Negro* child was found.

A possibility there may be of opening and bleeding their breast; for this may be done by the uncous and pointed extremity of their bill: and some probability also that they sometimes do it, for their own relief, though not for their young ones; that is by nibling and biting themselves on their itching part of their breast, upon fullness or acrimony of blood. And the same may be better made out; if (as some relate) their feathers on that part are sometimes observed to be red and tincted with blood.

CHAPTER II
Of the Picture of Dolphins.

That Dolphins are crooked, is not only affirmed by the hand of the Painter, but commonly conceived their natural and proper figure; which is not only the opinion of our times, but seems the belief of elder times before us. For, beside the expressions of *Ovid* and *Pliny*, their Pourtraicts in some ancient Coyns are framed in this figure, as will appear in some thereof in *Gesner*, others in *Goltsius*, and *Lævinus Hulsius* in his discription of Coyns, from *Julius Cæsar* unto *Rhodulphus* the second.

Notwithstanding, to speak strictly in their natural figure they are streight, nor have their spine convexed, or more considerably embowed, than Sharks, Porposes, Whales, and other Cetaceous animals, as *Scaliger* plainly affirmeth: *Corpus habet non magis curvum quam reliqui pisces*. As ocular enquiry informeth; and as unto such as have not had the opportunity to behold them, their proper pourtraicts will discover in *Rondeletius*, *Gesner*, and *Aldrovandus*. And as indeed is deducible from pictures themselves; for though they be drawn repandous, or convexedly crooked in one piece, yet the Dolphin that carrieth Arion is concavously inverted, and hath its spine depressed in another. And answerably hereto may we behold them differently bowed in medals, and the Dolphins of *Tarus* and *Fulius* do make another flexure from that of *Commodus* and *Agrippa*.

And therefore what is delivered of their incurvity, must either be taken Emphatically, that is, not really but in appearance; which happeneth, when they leap above water, and suddenly shoot down again; which is a fallacy in vision, whereby straight bodies in a sudden motion protruded obliquely downward, appear unto the eye crooked; and this is the construction of *Bellonius*. Or if it be taken really, it must not universally and perpetually; that is, not when they swim and remain in their proper figures, but only when they leap, or impetuously whirl their bodies any way; and this is the opinion of *Gesnerus*. Or lastly, It may be taken neither really nor emphatically, but only Emblematically: for being the Hieroglyphick of celerity, and swifter than other animals, men best expressed their velocity by incurvity, and under some figure of a bow: and in this sense probably do Heralds also receive it, when from a Dolphin extended, they distinguish a Dolphin embowed.

And thus also must that picture be taken of a Dolphin clasping an Anchor: that is, not really, as is by most conceived out of affection unto man, conveighing the Anchor unto the ground: but emblematically, according as *Pierius* hath expressed it, The swiftest animal conjoyned with that heavy body, implying that common moral, *Festina lentè*: and that celerity should always be contempered with cunctation.

CHAPTER III
Of the Picture of a Grashopper.

There is also among us a common description and picture of a Grashopper, as may be observed in the pictures of Emblematists, in the coats of several families, and as the word *Cicada* is usually translated in Dictionaries. Wherein to speak strictly, if by this word Grashopper, we understand that animal which is implied by τέττιξ with the *Greeks*, and by *Cicada* with the *Latines*; we may with safety affirm the picture is widely mistaken, and that for ought enquiry can inform, there is no such insect in *England*. Which how paradoxical soever, upon a strict enquiry, will prove undeniable truth.

For first, That animal which the *French* term *Sauterelle*, we a Grashopper, and which under this name is commonly described by us, is named Ἄκρις by the *Greeks*, by the *Latines Locusta*, and by our selves in proper speech a Locust; as in the diet of John *Baptist*, and in our Translation, Prov. 30. the *Locusts* have no King, yet go they forth all of them by bands. Again, Between the *Cicada* and that we call a Grashopper, the differences are very many, as may be observed in themselves, or their descriptions in *Matthiolus*, *Aldrovandus* and *Muffetus*. For first, They are differently cucullated or capuched upon the head and back, and in the *Cicada* the eyes are more prominent: the Locusts have *Antennæ*: or long horns before, with a long falcation or forcipated tail behind; and being ordained for saltation, their hinder legs do far exceed the other. The Locust or our Grashopper hath teeth, the *Cicada* none at all; nor any mouth according unto *Aristotle*: the *Cicada* is most upon trees; and lastly, the fritinnitus or proper note thereof, is far more shril than that of the Locust; and its life so short in Summer, that for provision it needs not have recourse unto the providence of the Pismire in Winter.

And therefore where the *Cicada* must be understood, the pictures of Heralds and Emblematists are not exact, nor is it safe to adhere unto the interpretation of Dictionaries; and we must with candour make out our own Translations: for in the Plague of *Ægypt*, *Exodus* 10. the word Ἄκρις is translated a Locust, but in the same sense and subject, *Wisdom* 16. it is translated a Grashopper; For them the bitings of Grashoppers and flies killed: whereas we have declared before, the *Cicada* hath no teeth, but is conceived to live upon dew; and the possibility of its subsistence is disputed by *Licetus*. Hereof I perceive *Muffetus* hath taken notice, dissenting from *Langius* and *Lycostenes*, while they deliver, the *Cicada's* destroyed the fruits in *Germany*, where that insect is not found; and therefore concludeth, *Tam ipsos quam alios deceptos fuisse autumo, dum locustas cicadas esse vulgari errore crederent.*

And hereby there may be some mistake in the due dispensation of Medicines desumed from this animal; particularly of Diatettigon commended by *Ætius* in the affections of the kidneys. It must be likewise understood with some restriction what hath been affirmed by *Isidore*, and yet delivered by many, that Cicades are bred out of Cuccow spittle or Woodsear; that is, that spumous, frothy dew or exudation, or both, found upon Plants, especially about the joints of Lavender and Rosemary, observable with us about the latter end of May. For here the true *Cicada* is not bred, but certain it is, that out of this, some kind of Locust doth proceed; for herein may be discovered a little insect of a festucine or pale green, resembling in all parts a Locust, or what we call a Grashopper.

Lastly, The word it self is improper, and the term of Grashopper not appliable unto the *Cicada*; for therein the organs of motion are not contrived for saltation, nor are the hinder legs of such extension, as is observable in salient animals, and such as move by leaping. Whereto the Locust is very well conformed; for therein the legs behind are longer than all the body, and make at the second joynt acute angles, at a considerable advancement above their backs.

The mistake therefore with us might have its original from a defect in our language; for having not the insect with us, we have not fallen upon its proper name, and so make use of a term common unto it and the Locust; whereas other countries have proper expressions for it. So the *Italian* calls it *Cicada*, the *Spaniard Cigarra*, and the *French Cigale*; all which appellations conform unto the original, and properly express this animal. Whereas our word is borrowed from the Saxon Gærsthopp, which our forefathers, who never beheld the *Cicada*, used for that insect which we yet call a Grashopper.

CHAPTER IV
Of the Picture of the Serpent tempting Eve.

In the Picture of Paradise, and delusion of our first Parents, the Serpent is often described with humane visage; not unlike unto *Cadmus* or his wife, in the act of their Metamorphosis. Which is not a meer pictorial contrivance or invention of the Picturer, but an ancient tradition and conceived reality, as it stands delivered by *Beda* and Authors of some antiquity; that is, that Sathan appeared not unto *Eve* in the naked form of a Serpent, but with a Virgins head, that thereby he might become more acceptable, and his temptation find the easier entertainment. Which nevertheless is a conceit not to be admitted, and the plain and received figure, is with better reason embraced.

For first, as *Pierius* observeth from *Barcephas*, the assumption of humane shape had proved a disadvantage unto Sathan; affording not only a suspicious amazement in *Eve*, before the fact, in beholding a third humanity beside her self and *Adam*; but leaving some excuse unto the woman, which afterward the man took up with lesser reason; that is, to have been deceived by another like her self.

Again, There was no inconvenience in the shape assumed, or any considerable impediment that might disturb that performance in the common form of a Serpent. For whereas it is conceived the woman must needs be afraid thereof, and rather flie than approach it; it was not agreeable unto the condition of Paradise and state of innocency therein; if in that place as most determine, no creature was hurtful or terrible unto man, and those destructive effects they now discover succeeded the curse, and came in with thorns and briars. And therefore *Eugubinus* (who affirmeth this Serpent was a Basilisk) incurreth no absurdity, nor need we infer that *Eve* should be destroyed immediately upon that Vision. For noxious animals could offend them no more in the Garden, than *Noah* in the Ark: as they peaceably received their names, so they friendly possessed their natures: and were their conditions destructive unto each other, they were not so unto man, whose constitutions then were antidotes, and needed not fear poisons. And if (as most conceive) there were but two created of every kind, they could not at that time destroy either man or themselves; for this had frustrated the command of multiplication, destroyed a species, and imperfected the Creation. And therefore also if Cain were the first man born, with him entred not only the act, but the first power of murther; for before that time neither could the Serpent nor *Adam* destroy *Eve*; nor *Adam* and *Eve* each other; for that had overthrown the intention of the world, and put its Creator to act the sixt day over again.

Moreover, Whereas in regard of speech, and vocal conference with *Eve*, it may be thought he would rather assume an humane shape and organs, then the improper form of a serpent; it implies no material impediment. Nor need we to wonder how he contrived a voice out of the mouth of a Serpent, who hath done the like out of the belly of a Pythonissa, and the trunk of an Oak; as he did for many years at *Dodona*.

Why Eve *wondered not at the serpents speaking*.

Lastly, Whereas it might be conceived that an humane shape was fitter for this enterprise; it being more than probable she would be amazed to hear a Serpent speak; some conceive she might not yet be certain that only man was priviledged with speech; and being in the novity of the Creation, and inexperience of all things, might not be affrighted to hear a Serpent speak. Beside she might be ignorant of their natures, who was not versed in their names, as being not present at the general survey of Animals, when *Adam* assigned unto every one a name concordant unto its nature. Nor is this my opinion, but the determination of *Lombard* and *Tostatus*; and also the reply of *Cyril* unto the objection of *Julian*, who compared this story unto the fables of the *Greeks*.

CHAPTER V

Of the Picture of *Adam* and *Eve* with Navels.

Another mistake there may be in the Picture of our first Parents, who after the manner of their posterity are both delineated with a Navel. And this is observable not only in ordinary and stained pieces, but in the Authentick draughts of *Urbin*, *Angelo* and others. Which notwithstanding cannot be allowed, except we impute that unto the first cause, which we impose not on the second; or what we deny unto nature, we impute unto Naturity it self; that is, that in the first and most accomplished piece, the Creator affected superfluities, or ordained parts without use or office.

What the Navel is, and for what use.

For the use of the Navel is to continue the Infant unto the Mother, and by the vessels thereof to convey its aliment and sustentation. The vessels whereof it consisteth, are the umbilical vein, which is a branch of the Porta, and implanted in the Liver of the Infant; two Arteries likewise arising from the Iliacal branches, by which the Infant receiveth the purer portion of blood and spirits from the mother; and lastly, the Urachos or ligamental passage derived from the bottom of the bladder, whereby it dischargeth the waterish and urinary part of its aliment. Now upon the birth, when the Infant forsaketh the womb, although it dilacerate, and break the involving membranes, yet do these vessels hold, and by the mediation thereof the Infant is connected unto the womb, not only before, but a while also after the birth. These therefore the midwife cutteth off, contriving them into a knot close unto the body of the Infant; from whence ensueth that tortuosity or complicated modosity we usually call the Navel; occasioned by the colligation of vessels before mentioned. *That* Adam *and* Eve *had not Navels.* Now the Navel being a part, not precedent, but subsequent unto generation, nativity or parturition, it cannot be well imagined at the creation or extraordinary formation of *Adam*, who immediately issued from the Artifice of God; nor also that of *Eve*; who was not solemnly begotten, but suddenly framed, and anomalously proceeded from *Adam*.

And if we be led into conclusions that *Adam* had also this part, because we behold the same in our selves, the inference is not reasonable; for if we conceive the way of his formation, or of the first animals, did carry in all points a strict conformity unto succeeding productions, we might fall into imaginations that *Adam* was made without Teeth; or that he ran through those notable alterations in the vessels of the heart, which the Infant suffereth after birth: we need not dispute whether the egg or bird were first; and might conceive that Dogs were created blind, because we observe they are littered so with us. Which to affirm, is to confound, at least to regulate creation unto generation, the first Acts of God, unto the second of Nature; which were determined in that general indulgence, Encrease and Multiply, produce or propagate each other; that is, not answerably in all points, but in a prolonged method according to seminal progression. For the formation of things at first was different from their generation after; and although it had nothing to precede it, was aptly contrived for that which should succeed it. And therefore though *Adam* were framed without this part, as having no other womb than that of his proper principles, yet was not his posterity without the same: for the seminality of his fabrick contained the power thereof; and was endued with the science of those parts whose predestinations upon succession it did accomplish.

All the Navel therefore and conjunctive part we can suppose in *Adam*, was his dependency on his Maker, and the connexion he must needs have unto heaven, who was the Son of God. For holding no dependence on any preceding efficient but God; in the act of his production there may be conceived some connexion, and *Adam* to have been in a momental Navel with his Maker. And although from his carnality and corporal existence, the conjunction seemeth no nearer than of causality and effect; yet in his immortal and diviner part he seemed to hold a nearer coherence, and an umbilicality even with God himself. And so indeed although the propriety of this part be found but in some animals, and many species there are which have no Navel at all; yet is there one link and common connexion, one general ligament, and necessary obligation of all what ever unto God. Whereby although they act themselves at distance, and seem to be at loose; yet do they hold a continuity with their Maker. Which catenation or conserving union when ever his pleasure shall divide, let go, or separate, they shall fall from their existence, essence, and operations: in brief, they must retire unto their primitive nothing, and shrink into their Chaos again.

They who hold the egg was before the Bird, prevent this doubt in many other animals, which also extendeth unto them: For birds are nourished by umbilical vessels, and the Navel is manifest sometimes a day or two after exclusion. The same is probable in oviparous exclusions, if the lesser part of eggs must serve for the formation, the greater part for nutriment. The same is made out in the eggs of Snakes; and is not improbable in the generation of Porwiggles or Tadpoles, and may be also true in some vermiparous exclusions: although (as we have observed in the daily progress in some) the whole Maggot is little enough to make a Fly, without any part remaining.

CHAPTER VI
Of the Pictures of Eastern Nations, and the *Jews* at their Feasts, especially our *Saviour* at the Passover.

Concerning the Pictures of the *Jews*, and Eastern Nations at their Feasts, concerning the gesture of our Saviour at the Passover, who is usually described sitting upon a stool or bench at a square table, in the middest of the twelve, many make great doubt; and (though they concede a table-gesture) will hardly allow this usual way of Session.

Wherein restraining no mans enquiry, it will appear that accubation, or lying down at meals was a gesture used by very many Nations. That the *Persians* used it, beside the testimony of humane Writers, is deducible from that passage in *Esther*. Esther 7. That when the King returned into the place of the banquet of wine, *Haman* was fallen upon the bed whereon *Esther* was. That the *Parthians* used it, is evident from *Athenæus*, who delivereth out of *Possidonius*, that their King lay down at meals, on an higher bed than others. That *Cleopatra* thus entertained *Anthony*, the same Author manifesteth when he saith, she prepared twelve Tricliniums. That it was in use among the *Greeks*, the word Triclinium implieth, and the same is also declarable from many places in the Symposiacks of *Plutarch*. That it was not out of fashion in the days of *Aristotle*, he declareth in his politicks; when among the Institutionary rules of youth, he adviseth they might not be permitted to hear Iambicks and Tragedies before they were admitted unto discumbency or lying along with others at their meals. That the *Romans* used this gesture at repast, beside many more, is evident from *Lipsius, Mercurialis, Salmasius* and *Ciaconius*, who have expresly and distinctly treated hereof.

Now of their accumbing places, the one was called Stibadion and Sigma, carrying the figure of an half Moon, and of an uncertain capacity, whereupon it received the name of Hexaclinon, Octoclinon, according unto that of *Martial*,

Accipe Lunata scriptum testudine Sigma:
Octo capit, veniat quisquis amicus erit.

Hereat in several ages the left and right horn were the principal places, and the most honorable person, if he were not master of the feast, possessed one of those rooms. The other was termed Triclinium, that is, Three beds about a table, as may be seen in the figures thereof, and particularly in the *Rhamnusian* Triclinium, set down by *Mercurialis*. [Merc. De Arte Gymnastica.] The customary use hereof was probably deduced from the frequent use of bathing, after which they commonly retired to bed, and refected themselves with repast; and so that custom by degrees changed their cubiculary beds into discubitory, and introduced a fashion to go from the bathes unto these.

The ancient gesture or position of the body at feasts.

As for their gesture or position, the men lay down leaning on their left elbow, their back being advanced by some pillow or soft substance: the second lay so with his back towards the first, that his head attained about his bosome; and the rest in the same order. For women, they sat sometimes distinctly with their sex, sometime promiscuously with men, according to affection or favour, as is delivered by *Juvenal*,

Gremio jacuit nova nupta mariti.

And by *Suetonius* of *Caligula*, that at his feasts he placed his sisters, with whom he had been incontinent, successively in order below him.

Again, As their beds were three, so the guests did not usually exceed that number in every one; according to the ancient Laws, and proverbial observations to begin with the Graces, and make up their feasts with the Muses. And therefore it was remarkable in the Emperour *Lucius Verus*, that he lay down with twelve: which was, saith *Julius Capitolinus, præter exempla majorum*, not according to the custom of his Predecessors, except it were at publick and nuptial suppers. The regular number was also exceeded in this last supper, whereat there were no less than thirteen, and in no place fewer than ten, for, as *Josephus* delivereth, it was not lawful to celebrate the Passover with fewer than that number.

Lastly, For the disposing and ordering of the persons: The first and middle beds were for the guests, the third and lowest for the Master of the house and his family; he always lying in the first place of the last bed, that is, next the middle bed; but if the wife or children were absent, their rooms were supplied by the Umbræ, or hangers on, according to that of *Juvenal* [Who the Umbræ were at banquets.] ——*Locus est et pluribus Umbris*. For the guests, the honourablest place in every bed was the first, excepting the middle or second bed; wherein the most honourable Guest of the feast was placed in the last place, because by that position he might be next the Master of the feast. [Iul. Scalig. familiarium exercitationum Problema 1.] For the Master lying in the first of the last bed, and the principal Guest in the last place of the second, they must needs be next each other; as this figure doth plainly declare, and whereby we may apprehend the feast of *Perpenna* made unto *Sertorius*, described by *Salustius*, whose words we shall thus read with *Salmasius*: *Igitur discubuere, Sertorius inferior in medio lecto, supra Fabius; Antonius in summo; Infra Scriba Sertorii Versius; alter scriba Mæcenas in Imo, medius inter Tarquitium et Dominum Perpennam.*

		Ultimus Honoratissimus Infra	Medius	Locus Summus Supra		
		Sertorius	Locus Vacuus Medius Lectus	L. Fabius		
Locus Summus Seu Domini Supra	Perpenna Dominus				Versinis	Ultimus Infra
Medius	Mæcenas Imus Lectus				Locus Vacuus Summus Lectus	Medius
Ultimas	Tarquitius				Antonius	Primus Locus Seu Summus Supra

At this feast there were but seven; the middle places of the highest and middle bed being vacant; and hereat was *Sertorius* the General and principal guest slain. And so may we make out what is delivered by *Plutarch* in his life, that lying on his back, and raising himself up, *Perpenna* cast himself upon his stomach; which he might very well do, being Master of the feast, and lying next unto him. And thus also from this Tricliniary disposure, we may illustrate that obscure expression of *Seneca*; That the Northwind was in the middle, the North-East on the higher side, and the North-West on the lower. For as appeareth in the circle of the winds, the North-East will answer the bed of *Antonius*, and the North-West that of *Perpenna*.

That the custom of feasting upon beds was in use among the *Hebrews*, many deduce from *Ezekiel*, Ezek. 23. Thou sattest upon a stately bed, and a table prepared before it. The custom of Discalceation or putting off their shoes at meals, is conceived to confirm the same; as by that means keeping their beds clean; and therefore they had a peculiar charge to eat the Passover with their shooes on; which Injunction were needless, if they used not to put them off. However it were in times of high antiquity, probable it is that in after ages they conformed unto the fashions of the *Assyrians* and Eastern Nations, and lastly of the *Romans*, being reduced by *Pompey* unto a Provincial subjection.

That this discumbency at meals was in use in the days of our Saviour, is conceived probable from several speeches of his expressed in that phrase, even unto common Auditors, as *Luke* 14. *Cum invitatus fueris ad nuptias, non discumbas in primo loco*, and besides many more, *Matthew* 23. When reprehending the *Scribes* and *Pharises*, he saith, *Amant protoclisias, id est, primos recubitus in cænis, et protocathedrias, sive, primas cathedras, in Synagogis*: wherein the terms are very distinct, and by an Antithesis do plainly distinguish the posture of sitting, from this of lying on beds. The consent of the *Jews* with the *Romans* in other ceremonies and rites of feasting, makes probable their conformity in this. The *Romans* washed, were anointed, and wore a cenatory garment: and that the same was practised by the *Jews*, is deduceable from that expostulation of our Saviour with *Simon*, Luke 7. that he washed not his feet, nor anointed his head with oyl; the common civilities at festival entertainments; and that expression of his concerning the cenatory or wedding garment; Matth. 22. and as some conceive of the linnen garment of the young man or St. *John*; which might be the same he wore the night before at the last Supper.

That they used this gesture at the Passover, is more than probable from the testimony of *Jewish* Writers, and particularly of *Ben-maimon* recorded by *Scaliger De emendatione temporum*. After the second cup according to the Institution. Exod. 12. The Son asketh, what meaneth this service? Then he that maketh the declaration, saith, How different is this night from all other nights? for all other nights we wash but once but this night twice; all other we eat leavened or unleavened bread, but this only leavened; all other we eat flesh roasted, boyled or baked, but this only roasted, all other nights we eat together lying or sitting, but this only lying along. And this posture they used as a token of rest and security which they enjoyed, far different from that at the eating of the Passover in *Ægypt*.

That this gesture was used when our Saviour eat the Passover, is not conceived improbable from the words whereby the Evangelists express the same, that is, ἀναπίπτειν, ἀνακεῖσθαι, κατακεῖσθαι, ἀνακλειθῆναι, which terms do properly signifie this Gesture in *Aristotle, Athenæus, Euripides, Sophocles*, and all humane Authors; and the like we meet with in the paraphrastical expression of *Nonnus*.

Lastly, If it be not fully conceded, that this gesture was used at the Passover, yet that it was observed at the last supper, seems almost incontrovertible: for at this feast or cenatory convention, learned men make more than one supper, or at least many parts thereof. The first was that Legal one of the Passover, or eating of the Paschal Lamb with bitter herbs, and ceremonies described by *Moses*. Of this it is said, Matth. 26. then when the even was come he sat down with the twelve. This is supposed when it is said, John 13. that the supper being ended, our Saviour arose, took a towel and washed the disciples feet. The second was common and Domestical, consisting of ordinary and undefined provisions; of this it may be said, that our Saviour took his garment, and sat down again, after he had washed the Disciples feet, and performed the preparative civilities of suppers; at this 'tis conceived the sop was given unto *Judas*, the Original word implying some broath or decoction, not used at the Passover. The third or latter part was Eucharistical, which began at the breaking and blessing of the bread, according to that of *Matthew*, And as they were eating, Jesus took bread and blessed it.

Now although at the Passover or first supper, many have doubted this Reclining posture, and some have affirmed that our Saviour stood; yet that he lay down at the other, the same men have acknowledged, as *Chrysostom, Theophylact, Austin*, and many more. And if the tradition will hold, the position is unquestionable; for the very Triclinium is to be seen at *Rome*, brought thither by *Vespasian*, and graphically set forth by *Casalius*. De veterum ritibus.

Thus may it properly be made out; what is delivered, *John* 13. *Erat recumbens unus ex Discipulis ejus in sinu Jesu quem diligebat*; Now there was leaning on Jesus bosom one of his Disciples whom Jesus loved; which gesture will not so well agree unto the position of sitting, but is natural, and cannot be avoided in the Laws of accubation. And the very same expression is to be found in *Pliny*, concerning the Emperour *Nerva* and *Veiento* whom he favoured; *Cœnabat Nerva cum paucis, Veiento recumbebat proprius atque etiam in sinu*; and from this custom arose the word ἐπιστήθιος, that is, a near and bosom friend. And therefore *Causabon* Not in Evan. justly rejecteth *Theophylact*; who not considering the ancient manner of decumbency, imputed this gesture of the beloved Disciple unto Rusticity, or an act of incivility. And thus also have some conceived, it may be more plainly made out what is delivered of *Mary Magdalen*. Luke 7. That she stood at Christs feet behind him weeping, and began to wash his feet with tears, and did wipe them with the hairs of her head. Which actions, if our Saviour sat, she could not perform standing, and had rather stood behind his back, than at his feet. And therefore it is not allowable, what is observable in many pieces, and even of *Raphael Urbin*; wherein *Mary Magdalen* is pictured before our Saviour, washing his feet on her knees; which will not consist with the strict description and letter of the Text.

Now whereas this position may seem to be discountenanced by our Translation, which usually renders it sitting, it cannot have that illation, for the *French* and *Italian* Translations expressing neither position of session or recubation, do only say that he placed himself at the table; and when ours expresseth the same by sitting, it is in relation unto our custom, time, and apprehension. The like upon occasion is not unusual: so when it is said, *Luke* 4. πτύξας τὸ βιβλίον, and the Vulgar renders it, *Cum plicasset librum*, ours translateth it, he shut or closed the book; which is an expression proper unto the paginal books of our times, but not so agreeable unto volumes or rolling books in use among the *Jews*, not only in elder times, but even unto this day. *What* Denarius, or the penny in the Gospel is. So when it is said, the *Samaritan* delivered unto the host two pence for the provision of the *Levite*; and when our Saviour agreed with the Labourers for a penny a day, in strict translation it should be seven pence half penny; and is not to be conceived our common penny, the sixtieth part of an ounce. For the word in the Original is δηνάριον, in Latine, *Denarius*, and with the *Romans* did value the eight part of an ounce, which after five shillings the ounce amounteth unto seven pence half penny of our money.

Lastly, Whereas it might be conceived that they eat the Passover standing rather than sitting, or lying down, according to the Institution, *Exod.* 12. *Ceremonies of the Passover omitted.* Thus shall you eat, with your loins girded, your shooes on your feet, and your staff in your hand; the *Jews* themselves reply, this was not required of succeeding generations, and was not observed, but in the Passover of *Ægypt*. And so also many other injunctions were afterward omitted, as the taking up of the Paschal Lamb, from the tenth day, the eating of it in their houses dispersed; the striking of the blood on the door posts, and the eating thereof in hast. Solemnities and Ceremonies primitively enjoyned, afterward omitted; as was also this of station, for the occasion ceasing, and being in security, they applied themselves unto gestures in use among them.

Now in what order of recumbancy Christ and the Disciples were disposed, is not so easily determined. *Casalius* from the Lateran Triclinium will tell us, that there being thirteen, five lay down in the first bed, five in the last, and three in the middle bed; and that our Saviour possessed the upper place thereof. That *John* lay in the same bed seems plain, because he leaned on our Saviours bosom. That *Peter* made the third in that bed, conjecture is made, because he beckened unto *John*, as being next to him, to ask of Christ, who it was that should betray him. That *Judas* was not far off seems probable, not only because he dipped in the same dish, but because he was so near, that our Saviour could hand the sop unto him.

CHAPTER VII
Of the Picture of our Saviour with long hair.

Another Picture there is of our Saviour described with long hair, according to the custom of the *Jews*, and his description sent by *Lentulus* unto the Senate. Wherein indeed the hand of the Painter is not accusable, but the judgement of the common Spectator; conceiving he observed this fashion of his hair; because he was a *Nazarite*, and confounding a *Nazarite* by vow, with those by birth or education.

The *Nazarite* by vow is declared, *Numb.* 6. And was to refrain three things, drinking of Wine, cutting the hair, and approaching unto the dead; and such a one was *Sampson*. Now that our Saviour was a *Nazarite* after this kind, we have no reason to determine; for he drank Wine, and was therefore called by the *Pharisees*, a Wine-bibber; he approached also the dead, as when he raised from death *Lazarus*, and the daughter of *Jairus*.

The other *Nazarite* was a Topical appellation, and appliable unto such as were born in *Nazareth*, a City of *Galilee*, and in the Tribe of *Napthali*. Neither if strictly taken was our Saviour in this sense a *Nazarite*; for he was born in *Bethlehem* in the Tribe of *Judah*; but might receive that name, because he abode in that City; and was not only conceived therein, but there also passed the silent part of his life, after his return from *Ægypt*; as is delivered by *Matthew*, And he came and dwelt in a City called *Nazareth*, that it might be fulfilled which was spoken by the Prophet, He shall be called a *Nazarene*. Both which kinds of *Nazarites*, as they are distinguishable by *Zain*, and *Tsade* in the Hebrew, so in the Greek, by *Alpha* and *Omega*; for as *Jansenius* observeth, | Ians. Concordia Evangelica. | where the votary *Nazarite* is mentioned, it is written, Ναζαραῖος, as *Levit.* 6. and *Lament.* 4. Where it is spoken of our Saviour, we read it, Ναζωρεῖος, as in *Matthew, Luke* and *John*; only *Mark* who writ his Gospel at *Rome*, did Latinize, and wrote it Ναζαρηνός.

CHAPTER VIII
Of the Picture of *Abraham* sacrificing *Isaac*.

In the Picture of the Immolation of *Isaac*, or *Abraham* sacrificing his son, *Isaac* is described as a little boy; which notwithstanding is not consentaneous unto the authority of Expositors, or the circumstance of the Text. For therein it is delivered that *Isaac* carried on his back the wood for the sacrifice; which being an holocaust or burnt offering to be consumed unto ashes, we cannot well conceive a burthen for a boy; but such a one unto *Isaac*, as that which it typified was unto Christ, that is, the wood or cross whereon he suffered; which was too heavy a load for his shoulders, and was fain to be relieved therein by *Simon* of *Cyrene*.

Again, He was so far from a boy, that he was a man grown, and at his full stature, if we believe *Josephus*, who placeth him in the last of *Adolescency*, and makes him twenty five years old. And whereas in the Vulgar Translation he is termed *puer*, it must not be strictly apprehended (for that age properly endeth in puberty, and extendeth but unto fourteen) but respectively unto *Abraham*, who was at that time above sixscore. And therefore also herein he was not unlike unto him, who was after led dumb unto the slaughter, and commanded by others, who had legions at command; that is, in meekness and humble submission. For had he resisted, it had not been in the power of his aged parent to have enforced; and many at his years have performed such acts, as few besides at any. | *Men of eminent fame and prowess at 25.* | *David* was too strong for a Lion and a Bear; *Pompey* had deserved the name of Great; *Alexander* of the same cognomination was *Generalissimo* of *Greece*; and *Anibal* but one year after, succeeded *Asdruball* in that memorable war against the *Romans*.

CHAPTER IX
Of the Picture of *Moses* with horns.

In many pieces, and some of ancient Bibles, *Moses* is described with horns. The same description we find in a silver Medal; that is, upon one side *Moses* horned, and on the reverse the commandment against sculptile Images. Which is conceived to be a coynage of some *Jews*, in derision of Christians, who first began that Pourtract.

The ground of this absurdity, was surely a mistake of the Hebrew Text, in the history of *Moses* when he descended from the Mount; | Exod. 34.29, 35. | upon the affinity of *Kæren* and *Karan*, that is, an horn, and to shine, which is one quality of horn: The Vulgar Translation conforming unto the former. *Ignorabat quod cornuta esset facies ejus. Qui videbant faciem Mosis esse cornutam.* But the *Chaldee* paraphrase, translated by *Paulus Fagius*, hath otherwise expressed it. *Moses nesciebat quod multus esset splendor gloriæ vultus ejus. Et viderunt filii Israel quod multa esset claritas gloriæ faciei Moses.* The expression of the Septuagint is as large, δεδόξασται ἡ ὄψις τοῦ χρώματος τοῦ προσώπου, *Glorificatus est aspectus cutis, seu coloris faciei.*

And this passage of the Old Testament, is well explained by another of the New | 2 Cor. 3. | wherein it is delivered, that they could not stedfastly behold the face of *Moses*, Διὰ τὴν δόξαν τοῦ προσώπου; that is, for the glory of his countenance. And surely the exposition of one Text is best performed by another; men vainly interposing their constructions, where the Scripture decideth the controversie. And therefore some have seemed too active in their expositions, who in the story of *Rahab* the harlot, have given notice that the word also signifieth an Hostess; for in the Epistle to the *Hebrews*, she is plainly termed πόρνη, which signifies not an Hostess, but a pecuniary and prostituting Harlot; *What kind of Harlot she was, read* Camar. De vita Eliæ. a term applied unto *Lais* by the *Greeks*, and distinguished from ἑταιρα, or *amica*, as may appear in the thirteenth of *Athenæus*.

And therefore more allowable is the Translation of *Tremellius, Quod splendida facta esset cutis facici ejus*; or as *Estius* hath interpreted it, *facies ejus erat radiosa*, his face was radiant, and dispersing beams like many horns and cones about his head; which is also consonant unto the original signification, and yet observed in the pieces of our Saviour, and the Virgin *Mary*, who are commonly drawn with scintillations, or radient Halo's about their head; which after the *French* expression are usually termed, the Glory.

Now if besides this occasional mistake, any man shall contend a propriety in this picture, and that no injury is done unto Truth by this description, because an horn is the Hieroglyphick of authority, power and dignity, and in this Metaphor is often used in Scripture; the piece I confess in this acception is harmless and agreeable unto *Moses*: and under such emblematical constructions, we find that *Alexander* the Great, and *Attila* King of *Hunnes*, in ancient Medals are described with horns. But if from the common mistake, or any solary consideration we persist in this description, we vilify the mystery of the irradiation, and authorize a dangerous piece conformable unto that of *Jupiter Hammon*; which was the Sun, and therefore described with horns; as is delivered by *Macrobius; Hammonem quem Deum solem occidentem Lybies existimant, arietinis cornibus fingunt, quibus id animal valet, sicut radiis sol*. We herein also imitate the Picture of *Pan*, and *Pagan* emblem of Nature. And if (as *Macrobius* and very good Authors concede) *Bacchus*, (who is also described with horns) be the same Deity with the Sun; and if (as *Vossius* well contendeth *Moses and* Bacchus *supposed to be the same person*, De origine Idolatriæ.) *Moses* and *Bacchus* were the same person; their descriptions must be relative, or the Tauricornous picture of the one, perhaps the same with the other.

CHAPTER X
Of the Scutcheons of the Tribes of Israel.

We will not pass over the Scutcheons of the Tribes of *Israel*, as they are usually described in the Maps of *Canaan* and several other pieces; generally conceived to be the proper coats, and distinctive badges of their several Tribes. So *Reuben* is conceived to bear three Bars wave, *Judah* a Lyon Rampant, *Dan* a Serpent nowed, *Simeon* a sword inpale the point erected, etc. The ground whereof is the last Benediction of *Jacob*, Gen. 49. wherein he respectively draweth comparisons from things here represented.

Now herein although we allow a considerable measure of truth, yet whether as they are usually described, these were the proper cognizances, and coat-arms of the Tribes; whether in this manner applyed, and upon the grounds presumed, material doubts remain.

For first, They are not strictly made out, from the Prophetical blessing of *Jacob*; for *Simeon* and *Levi* have distinct coats, that is, a Sword, and the two Tables, yet are they by *Jacob* included in one Prophesie, *Simeon* and *Levi* are brethren, Instruments of cruelties are in their habitations. So *Joseph* beareth an Ox, whereof notwithstanding there is no mention in this Prophesie; for therein it is said *Joseph* is a fruitful bough, even a fruitful bough by a well; by which repitition are intimated the two Tribes descending from him, *Ephraim* and *Manasses*; whereof notwithstanding *Ephraim* only beareth an Ox: True it is, that many years after in the benediction of *Moses*, it is said of *Joseph*, Deut. 33. His glory is like the firstlings of his Bullock: and so we may concede, what *Vossius* learnedly declareth, that the *Ægyptians* represented *Joseph*, in the Symbole of an Ox; for thereby was best implied the dream of *Pharoah*, which he interpreted, the benefit by Agriculture, and provident provision of corn which he performed; and therefore did *Serapis* bear a bushel upon his head.

Again, If we take these two benedictions together, the resemblances are not appropriate, and *Moses* therein conforms not unto *Jacob*: for that which in the Prophesie of *Jacob* is appropriated unto one, is in the blessing of *Moses* made common unto others. So whereas *Judah* is compared unto a Lion by *Jacob*, *Judah* is a Lions whelp, the same is applied unto *Dan* by *Moses*, *Dan* is a Lions whelp, he shall leap from *Bashan*, and also unto *Gad*; he dwelleth as a Lion.

Thirdly, If a lion were the proper coat of *Judah*, yet were it not probably a Lion Rampant, as it is commonly described, but rather couchant or dormant, as some *Heralds* and *Rabbins* do determine; according to the letter of the Text, *Recumbens dormisti ut Leo*, He couched as a Lion, and as a young Lion, who shall rouse him?

Lastly, when it is said, Num. 2. Every man of the Children of *Israel* shall pitch by his own standard with the Ensign of their fathers house; upon enquiry what these standards and ensigns were there is no small incertainty; and men conform not unto the Prophesie of *Jacob*. Christian expositors are fain herein to rely upon the *Rabbins*, who notwithstanding are various in their traditions, and confirm not these common descriptions. For as for inferiour ensigns, either of particular bands or houses, they determine nothing at all; and of the four principal or Legionary standards, that is, of *Judah*, *Reuben*, *Ephraim*, and *Dan* (under every one whereof marched three Tribes) they explain them very variously. *Jonathan* who compiled the Thargum conceives the colours of these banners to answer the precious stones in the breast-plate, and upon which the names of the Tribes were engraven. The like also P. Fagius *upon the Thargum or* Chaldie *Paraphrase of* Onkelus. Num. 1. So the standard for the Camp of *Judah* was of three colours, according unto the stones, Chalcedony, Saphir and Sardonix; and therein were expressed the names of the three Tribes, Num. 10. *Judah*, *Isachar*, and *Zabulon*, and in the middest thereof was written, Rise up Lord, and let thy enemies be scattered, and let them that hate thee flee before thee; in it was also the pourtrait of a Lion. The standard of *Reuben* was also of three colours, Sardine, Topaz, and Amethyst; therein were expressed the names of *Reuben*, *Simeon*, and *Gad*, in the middest was written, Deut. 6. Hear, O *Israel*, The Lord our God, the Lord is one: Therein was also the pourtraiture of a Hart. But *Abenezra* and others, beside the colours of the field, do set down other charges, in *Reubens* the form of a man or mandrake, in that of *Judah* a Lion, in *Ephraims* an Ox, in *Dan's* the figure of an Eagle.

And thus indeed the four figures in the banners of the principal squadrons of *Israel* are answerable unto the Cherubins in the vision of *Ezekiel*; Ezek. 1. every one carrying the form of all these. As for the likeness of their faces, they four had the likeness of the face of a Man, and the face of a Lion on the right side, and they four had the face of an Ox on the left side, they four had also the face of an Eagle. The common Pictures of the 4 Evangelists explicated. And conformable hereunto the pictures of the Evangelists (whose Gospels are the Christian banners) are set forth with the addition of a man or Angel, an Ox, a Lion, and a Eagle. And these symbolically represent the office of Angels, and Ministers of Gods Will; in whom is required understanding as in a man, courage and vivacity as in the Lion, service and ministerial officiousness, as in the Ox, expedition or celerity of execution, as in the Eagle.

From hence therefore we may observe that these descriptions, the most authentick of any, are neither agreeable unto one another, nor unto the Scutcheons in question. For though they agree in *Ephraim* and *Judah*, that is, the Ox and the Lion, yet do they differ in those of *Dan*, and *Reuben*, as far as an Eagle is different from a Serpent, and the figure of a Man, Hart, or Mandrake, from three Bars wave. *The Antiquity of bearing Scutcheons.* Wherein notwithstanding we rather declare the incertainty of Arms in this particular, than any way question their antiquity; for hereof more ancient examples there are, than the Scutcheons of the Tribes, if *Osyris*, *Mizraim* or *Jupiter* the Just, were the Son of *Cham*; for of his two Sons, as *Diodorus* delivereth, the one for his Device gave a Dog, the other a Wolf. And, beside the shield of *Achilles*, and many ancient *Greeks*: if we receive the conjecture of *Vossius*, that the Crow upon *Corvinus* his head, was but the figure of that Animal upon his helmet, it is an example of Antiquity among the *Romans*.

But more widely must we walk, if we follow the doctrine of the *Cabalists*, *Ricius*[4] *de cœlesti Agricultura, lib. 4.*, who in each of the four banners inscribe a letter of the Tetragrammaton, or quadriliteral name of God: and mysterizing their ensigns, do make the particular ones of the twelve Tribes, accommodable unto the twelve signs in the Zodiack, and twelve moneths in the year: but the Tetrarchical or general banners, of *Judah*, *Reuben*, *Ephraim*, and *Dan*, unto the signs of Aries, Cancer, Libra and Capricornus: that is, the four cardinal parts of the Zodiack, and seasons of the year.

Footnotes

[4]*Recius*, 1650, 1658, 1669, 1672, 1686.

CHAPTER XI

Of the Pictures of the *Sibyls*.

The Pictures of the *Sibyls* are very common, and for their Prophesies of Christ in high esteem with Christians; described commonly with youthful faces, and in a defined number. Common pieces making twelve, and many precisely ten; observing therein the account of *Varro*, that is, *Sibylla, Delphica, Erythræa, Samia, Cumana, Cumæa,*
or *Cimmeria, Hellespontiaca, Lybica, Phrygia, Tiburtina, Persica*. In which enumeration I perceive learned men are not satisfied, and many conclude an irreconcilable incertainty; some making more, others fewer, and not this certain number. For *Suidas*, though he affirm that in divers ages there were ten, yet the same denomination he affordeth unto more; *Boysardus* in his Tract of Divination hath set forth the Icons of these Ten, yet addeth two others, *Epirotica*, and *Ægyptia*; and some affirm that Prophesying women were generally named *Sibyls*.

Others make them fewer: *Martianus Capella* two; *Pliny* and *Solinus* three; *Ælian* four; and *Salmasius* in effect but seven. For discoursing hereof in his *Plinian* Exercitations, he thus determineth; *Ridere licet hodiernos Pictores, qui tabulas proponunt Cumanæ, Cumeæ, et Erythræeæ, quasi trium diversarum Sibyllarum; cum una cademque fuerit Cumana, Cumæa, et Erythræa, ex plurium et doctissimorum Authorum sententia*. *Boysardus* gives us leave to opinion there was no more than one; for so doth he conclude, *In tanta Scriptorum varietate liberum relinquimus Lectori credere, an una et eadem in diversis regionibus peregrinata, cognomen sortita sit ab iis locis ubi oracula reddidisse comperitur, an plures extiterint*: And therefore not discovering a resolution of their number from pens of the best Writers, we have no reason to determine the same from the hand and pencil of Painters.

As touching their age, that they are generally described as young women, History will not allow; for the Sibyl whereof *Virgil* speaketh is termed by him *longæva sacerdos*, and *Servius* in his Comment amplifieth the same. The other that sold the books unto *Tarquin*, and whose History is plainer than any, by *Livie* and *Gellius* is termed *Anus*; that is, properly no woman of ordinary age, but full of years, and in the dayes of dotage, according to the Etymology of *Festus*; Anus, quasi Ἀnoûs, sine mente. and consonant unto the History; wherein it is said, that *Tarquin* thought she doted with old age. Which duly perpended, the *Licentia pictoria* is very large; with the same reason they may delineate old *Nestor* like *Adonis*, *Hecuba* with *Helens* face, and Time with *Absolons* head. But this absurdity that eminent Artist *Michael Angelo* hath avoided, in the Pictures of the *Cumean* and *Persian* Sibyls, as they stand described from the printed sculptures of *Adam Mantuanus*.

CHAPTER XII
Of the Picture describing the death of *Cleopatra*.

The Picture concerning the death of *Cleopatra* with two Asps or venemous Serpents unto her arms, or breasts, or both, requires consideration: for therein (beside that this variety is not excusable) the thing it self is questionable; nor is it indisputably certain what manner of death she died. *Plutarch* in the life of *Antony* plainly delivereth, that no man knew the manner of her death; for some affirmed she perished by poison, which she always carried in a little hollow comb, and wore it in her hair. Beside, there were never any Asps discovered in the place of her death, although two of her maids perished also with her; only it was said, two small and almost insensible pricks were found upon her arm; which was all the ground that *Cæsar* had to presume the manner of her death. *Galen* who was contemporary unto *Plutarch*, delivereth two wayes of her death: that she killed her self by the bite of an Asp, or bit an hole in her arm, and poured poison therein. *Strabo* that lived before them both hath also two opinions; that she died by the bite of an Asp, or else a poisonous ointment.

We might question the length of the Asps, which are sometimes described exceeding short; whereas the Chersæa or land-Asp which most conceive she used, is above four cubits long. Their number is not unquestionable; for whereas there are generally two described, *Augustus* (as *Plutarch* relateth) did carry in his triumph the Image of *Cleopatra* but with one Asp under her arm. As for the two pricks, or little spots in her arm, they infer not their plurality: for like the Viper, the Asp hath two teeth; whereby it left this impression, or double puncture behind it.

And lastly, We might question the place; for some apply them unto her breast, which notwithstanding will not consist with the History; and *Petrus Victorius* hath well observed the same. But herein the mistake was easie; it being the custom in capital malefactors to apply them unto the breast, as the Author *De Theriaca ad Pisonem*, an eye witness hereof in *Alexandria*, where *Cleopatra* died, determineth: I beheld, saith he, in *Alexandria*, how suddenly these Serpents bereave a man of life; for when any one is condemned to this kind of death, if they intend to use him favourably, that is, to dispatch him suddenly, they fasten an Asp unto his breast; and bidding him walk about, he presently perisheth thereby.

CHAPTER XIII
Of the Pictures of the Nine Worthies.

The Pictures of the nine Worthies are not unquestionable, and to critical spectators may seem to contain sundry improprieties. Some will enquire why *Alexander* the Great is described upon an Elephant: for, we do not find he used that animal in his armies, much less in his own person; but his horse is famous in History, and its name alive to this day. Beside, he fought but one remarkable battel, wherein there were any Elephants, and that was with *Porus* King of *India*; in which notwithstanding, as *Curtius*, *Arrianus*, and *Plutarch* report, he was on Horseback himself. And if because he fought against Elephants, he is with propriety set upon their backs; with no less or greater reason is the same description agreeable unto *Judas Maccabeus*, as may be observed from the history of the *Maccabees*; and also unto *Julius Cæsar*, whose triumph was honoured with captive Elephants, as may be observed in the order thereof, set forth by *Jacobus Laurus*. In *splendere urbis Antiquæ.* And if also we should admit this description upon an Elephant, yet were not the manner thereof unquestionable, that is, in his ruling the beast alone; for beside the Champion upon their back, there was also a guide or ruler, which sat more forward to command or guide the beast. Thus did King *Porus* ride when he was overthrown by *Alexander*; and thus are also the towred Elephants described, *Maccab.* 2. 6. Upon the beasts there were strong towers of wood, which covered every one of them, and were girt fast unto them by devices: there were also upon every one of them thirty two strong men, beside the *Indian* that ruled them.

Others will demand, not only why *Alexander* upon an Elephant, but *Hector* upon an Horse: whereas his manner of fighting, or presenting himself in battel, was in a Chariot, as did the other noble *Trojans*, who as *Pliny* affirmeth were the first inventers thereof. The same way of fight is testified by *Diodorus*, and thus delivered by Sir *Walter Rawleigh*. Of the vulgar little reckoning was made, for they fought all on foot, slightly armed, and commonly followed the success of their Captains; who rode not upon horses, but in Chariots drawn by two or three Horses. And this was also the ancient way of fight among the *Britains*, as is delivered by *Diodorus*, *Cæsar*, and *Tacitus*; and there want not some who have taken advantage hereof, and made it one argument of their original from *Troy*.

The use of stirrops not ancient.

Lastly, By any man versed in Antiquity, the question can hardly be avoided, why the Horses of these Worthies, especially of *Cæsar*, are described with the furniture of great saddles, and stirrops; for saddles largely taken, though some defence there may be, yet that they had not the use of stirrops, seemeth of lesser doubt; as *Pancirollus* hath observed, as *Polydore Virgil*, and *Petrus Victorius* have confirmed, *De inventione rerum, variæ Lectiones.* expresly discoursing hereon; as is observable from *Pliny*, and cannot escape our eyes in the ancient monuments, medals and Triumphant arches of the *Romans*. Nor is there any ancient classical word in Latine to express them. For *Staphia*, *Stapes* or *Stapeda* is not to be found in Authors of this Antiquity. And divers words which may be urged of this signification, are either later, or signified not thus much in the time of *Cæsar*. And therefore as *Lipsius* observeth, lest a thing of common use should want a common word, *Franciscus Philelphus* named them *Stapedas*, and *Bodinus Subicus* Pedaneos. And whereas the name might promise some Antiquity, because among the three small bones in the Auditory Organ, by Physitians termed *Incus*, *Malleus* and *stapes*, one thereof from some resemblance doth bear this name; these bones were not observed, much less named by *Hippocrates*, *Galen*, or any ancient Physitian. But as *Laurentius* observeth, concerning the invention of the stapes or stirrop bone, there is some contention between *Columbus* and *Ingrassias*; the one of *Sicilia*, the other of *Cremona*, and both within the compass of this Century.

The same is also deduceable from very approved Authors: *Polybius* speaking of the way which *Anibal* marched into *Italy*, useth the word βεβημάτισται, that is, saith *Petrus Victorius*, it was stored with devices for men to get upon their horses, which ascents were termed *Bemata*, and in the life of *Caius Gracchus*, *Plutarch* expresseth as much. For endevouring to ingratiate himself with the people, besides the placing of stones at every miles end, he made at nearer distances certain elevated places, and Scalary ascents, that by the help thereof they might with better ease ascend or mount their Horses. Now if we demand how Cavaliers then destitute of stirrops did usually mount their Horses; as *Lipsius* informeth the unable and softer sort of men had their ἀναβολεῖς, or Stratores, which helped them up on horse back, as in the practice of *Crassus* in *Plutarch*, and *Caracalla* in *Spartianus*, and the later example of *Valentinianus*, who because his horse rised before that he could not be setled on his back, cut off the right hand of his Strator. But how the active and hardy persons mounted, *Vegetius* *De re Milit.* resolves us, that they used to vault or leap up, and therefore they had wooden horses in their houses and abroad: that thereby young men might enable themselves in this action: wherein by instruction and practice they grew so perfect, that they could vault up on the right or left, and that with their sword in hand, according to that of *Virgil*

Poscit equos atque arma simul, saltuque superbus Emicat.

And again:

Infrænant alii currus et corpora saltu
Injiciunt in equos.

So *Julius Pollux* adviseth to teach horses to incline, dimit, and bow down their bodies, that their riders may with better ease ascend them. And thus may it more causally be made out, what *Hippocrates* affirmeth of the *Scythians*, that using continual riding, they were generally molested with the Sciatica or hip-gout. Or what *Suetonius* delivereth of *Germanicus*, that he had slender legs, but encreased them by riding after meals; that is, the humours descending upon their pendulosity, they having no support or suppedaneous stability.

Now if any shall say that these are petty errors and minor lapses, not considerably injurious unto truth, yet is it neither reasonable nor fair to contemn inferiour falsities; but rather as between falshood and truth there is no medium, so should they be maintained in their distances: nor the contagion of the one, approach the sincerity of the other.

CHAPTER XIV
Of the Picture of *Jephthah* sacryficing his daughter.

That Jephthah *did not kill his daughter.*

The hand of the Painter confidently setteth forth the Picture of *Jephthah* in the posture of *Abraham*, sacrificing his only daughter: Thus is it commonly received, and hath had the attest of many worthy Writers. Notwithstanding upon enquiry we find the matter doubtful, and many upon probable grounds to have been of another opinion: conceiving in this oblation not a natural but a civil kind of death, and a separation only unto the Lord. Judg. 11.39 For that he pursued not his vow unto a literal oblation, there want not arguments both from the Text and reason.

For first, It is evident that she deplored her Virginity, and not her death; Let me go up and down the mountains, and bewail my Virginity, I and my fellows.

Secondly, When it is said, that *Jephthah* did unto her according unto his vow, it is immediately subjoyned, *Et non cognovit virum*, and she knew no man; which as immediate in words, was probably most near in sense unto the vow.

Thirdly, It is said in the Text, that the daughters of *Israel* went yearly to talk with the daughter of *Jephthah* four dayes in the year; which had she been sacrificed, they could not have done: For whereas the word is sometime translated to lament, yet doth it also signifie to talk or have conference with one, and by *Tremellius*, who was well able to Judge of the Original, it is in this sense translated: *Ibant filii Israelitarum, ad confabulandum cum filia Jephthaci, quatuor diebus quotannis*: And so it is also set down in the marginal notes of our Translation. And from this annual concourse of the daughters of *Israel*, it is not improbable in future Ages, the daughter of *Jephthah* came to be worshipped as a Deity; and had by the *Samaritans* an annual festivity observed unto her honour, as *Epiphanius* hath left recorded in the Heresie of the *Melchidecians*.

It is also repugnant unto reason; for the offering of mankind was against the Law of God, who so abhorred humane sacrifice, that he omitted not the oblation of unclean beasts, and confined his Altars but unto few kinds of Animals, the Ox, the Goat, the Sheep, the Pigeon and its kinds: In the cleansing of the Leper, there is I confess, mention made of the Sparrow; but great dispute may be made whether it be properly rendered. And therefore the Scripture with indignation oft-times makes mention of humane sacrifice among the *Gentiles*; whose oblations scarce made scruple of any Animal, sacrificing not only Man, but Horses, Lions, Ægles; and though they come not into holocausts, yet do we read the *Syrians* did make oblations of fishes unto the goddess *Derceto*. It being therefore a sacrifice so abominable unto God, although he had pursued it, it is not probable the Priests and Wisdom of *Israel* would have permitted it; and that not only in regard of the subject or sacrifice it self, but also the sacrificator, which the Picture makes to be *Jephthah*; who was neither Priest, nor capable of that Office: for he was a *Gileadite*, and as the Text affirmeth, the son also of an harlot. And how hardly the Priesthood would endure encroachment upon their function, a notable example there is in the story of *Ozias*.

Secondly, The offering up of his daughter was not only unlawful, and entrenched upon his Religion, but had been a course that had much condemned his discretion; that is, to have punished himself in the strictest observance of his vow, when as the Law of God had allowed an evasion; that is, by way of commutation or redemption, according as is determined, *Levit.* 27. Whereby if she were between the age of five and twenty, she was to be estimated but at ten shekels, and if between twenty and sixty, not above thirty. A sum that could never discourage an indulgent Parent; it being but the value of servant slain; the inconsiderable Salary of *Judas*; and will make no greater noise than three pound fifteen shillings with us. And therefore their conceit is not to be exploded, who say that from the story of *Jephthah* sacrificing his own daughter, might spring the fable of *Agamemnon*, delivering unto sacrifice his daughter *Iphigenia*, who was also contemporary unto *Jephthah*: wherein to answer the ground that hinted it, *Iphigenia* was not sacrificed her self, but redeemed with an Hart, which *Diana* accepted for her.

Lastly, Although his vow run generally for the words, Whatsoever shall come forth, etc. Yet might it be restrained in the sense, for whatsoever was sacrificable, and justly subject to lawful immolation: and so would not have sacrificed either Horse or Dog, if they had come out upon him. Nor was he obliged by oath unto a strict observation of that which promissorily was unlawful; or could he be qualified by vow to commit a fact which naturally was abominable. Which doctrine had *Herod* understood, it might have saved *John Baptists* head; when he promised by oath to give unto *Herodias* whatsoever she would ask; that is, if it were in the compass of things, which he could lawfully grant. For his oath made not that lawful which was illegal before: and if it were unjust to murther *John*, the supervenient Oath did not extenuate the fact, or oblige the Juror unto it.

Now the ground at least which much promoted the opinion, might be the dubious words of the text, which contain the sense of his vow; most men adhering unto their common and obvious acception. Whatsoever shall come forth of the doors of my house shall surely be the Lords, and I will offer it up for a burnt offering. Now whereas it is said, *Erit Jehovæ, et offeram illud holocaustum*, the word signifying both *et* and *aut*, it may be taken disjunctively; *aut offeram*, that is, it shall either be the Lords by separation, or else, an holocaust by common oblation; even as our marginal translation advertiseth; and as *Tremellius* rendreth it, *Erit inquam Jehovæ, aut offeram illud holocaustum*: and for the vulgar translation, it useth often *et*, where *aut* must be presumed, as *Exod.* 21. *Si quis percusserit patrem et matrem*, that is, not both, but either. There being therefore two waies to dispose of her, either to separate her unto the Lord, or offer her as a sacrifice, it is of no necessity the later should be necessary; and surely less derogatory unto the sacred text and history of the people of God, must be the former.

CHAPTER XV
Of the Picture of *John* the Baptist.

The Picture of *John* the Baptist, in a Camels skin is very questionable, and many I perceive have condemned it. The ground or occasion of this description are the words of the holy Scripture, especially of *Matthew* and *Mark*, for *Luke* and *John* are silent herein; by them it is delivered, his garment was of Camels hair, and had a leather girdle about his loins. Now here it seems the Camels hair is taken by Painters for the skin or pelt with the hair upon it. But this Exposition will not so well consist with the strict acceptation of the words; for *Mark* 1. It is said, he was, ἐνδεδυμένος τρίχας καμήλου, and *Matthew* 3. εἶχε τὸ ἔνδυμα ἀπὸ τριχῶν καμήλου, that is, as the vulgar translation, that of *Beza*, that of *Sixtus Quintus*, and *Clement* the eight hath rendred it, *vestimentum habebat è pilis camelinis*; which is as ours translateth it, a garment of Camels hair; that is, made of some texture of that hair, a course garment; a cilicious or sackcloth habit; sutable to the austerity of his life; the severity of his Doctrine, Repentance; and the place thereof, the wilderness, his food and diet, locusts and wild hony. 2 Kings 3. 18. Agreeable unto the example of *Elias*, who is said to be *vir pilosus*, that is, as *Tremellius* interprets, *Veste villosa*[5] *cinctus*, answerable unto the habit of the ancient Prophets, according to that of *Zachary*. Zach. 13. In that day the Prophets shall be ashamed, neither shall they wear a rough garment to deceive; and sutable to the Cilicious and hairy Vests of the strictest Orders of Fryers, who derive the institution of their Monastick life from the example of *John* and *Elias*.

As for the wearing of skins, where that is properly intended, the expression of the Scripture is plain; so it is said, *Heb.* 11. They wandered about ἐν αἰγείοις δέρμασιν, that is, in Goats skins; and so it is said of our first Parents, *Gen.* 3. That God made them χιτῶνας δερματίνους, *Vestes pelliceas*, or coats of skins; which though a natural habit unto all, before the invention of Texture, was something more unto *Adam*, who had newly learned to die; for unto him a garment from the dead, was but a dictate of death, and an habit of mortality.

Now if any man will say this habit of *John* was neither of Camels skin, nor any course Texture of its hair, but rather some finer Weave of Camelot, Grograin or the like, in as much as these stuffs are supposed to be made of the hair of that Animal, or because that *Ælian* affirmeth, that Camels hair of *Persia*, is as fine as *Milesian* wool, wherewith the great ones of that place were cloathed; they have discovered an habit, not only unsutable unto his leathern cincture, and the coarseness of his life; but not consistent with the words of our Saviour, when reasoning with the people concerning *John*, he saith, What went you out into the wilderness to see? a man clothed in soft raiment? Behold, they that wear soft raiment, are in Kings houses.

Footnotes

[5]*villoso*, 1646, 1650, 1658, 1669, 1672.

CHAPTER XVI
Of the Picture of St. *Christopher*.

The Picture of St. *Christopher*, that is, a man of a Giantlike stature, bearing upon his shoulders our Saviour Christ, and with a staff in his hand, wading thorow the water, is known unto Children, common over all *Europe*, not only as a sign unto houses, but is described in many Churches, and stands *Colossus* like in the entrance of *Nostre Dame* in *Paris*.

Now from hence, common eyes conceive an history sutable unto this description, that he carried our Saviour in his Minority over some river or water: which notwithstanding we cannot at all make out. For we read not thus much in any good Author, nor of any remarkable *Christopher*, before the reign of *Decius*: who lived 250 years after Christ. This man indeed according unto History suffered as a Martyr in the second year of that Emperour, and in the *Roman* Calendar takes up the 21 of *July*.

The ground that begat or promoted this opinion, was, first the fabulous adjections of succeeding ages unto the veritable acts of this Martyr, who in the most probable accounts was remarkable for his staff, and a man of a goodly stature.

The second might be a mistake or misapprehension of the Picture, most men conceiving that an History which was contrived at first but as an Emblem or Symbolical fancy: as from the Annotations of *Baronius* upon the *Roman* Martyrologie, *Lipellous* Lip. De vitis Sanctorum. in the life of St. *Christopher* hath observed in these words; *Acta S. Christopheri à multis depravata inveniuntur: quod quidem non aliunde originem sumpsisse certum est, quam quod symbolicas figuras imperiti ad veritatem successu temporis transtulerint: itaque cuncta illa de Sancto Christophero pingi consueta, symbola potius, quam historiæ alicujus existimandum est esse expressam imaginem*; that is, The Acts of St. *Christopher* are depraved by many: which surely began from no other ground, then, that in process of time, unskilful men translated symbolical figures unto real verities: and therefore what is usually described in the Picture of St. *Christopher*, is rather to be received as an Emblem, or Symbolical description, then any real History. Now what Emblem this was, or what its signification, conjectures are many; *Pierius* hath set down one, that is, of the Disciple of Christ; for he that will carry Christ upon his shoulders, must rely upon the staff of his direction, whereon if he firmeth himself, he may be able to overcome the billows of resistance, and in the vertue of this staff, like that of *Jacob*, pass over the waters of *Jordan*. Or otherwise thus; He that will submit shoulders unto Christ, shall by the concurrence of his power encrease into the strength of a Giant; and being supported by the staff of his holy Spirit, shall not be overwhelmed by the waves of the world, but wade through all resistance.

Add also the mystical reasons of this pourtract alleadged by *Vida* and *Xerisanus*: and the recorded story of *Christopher*, that before his Martyrdom he requested of God, that where ever his body were, the places should be freed from pestilence and mischiefs, from infection. Anton. Castellionæi antiquitates Mediolanenses. And therefore his picture or pourtract, was usually placed in publick wayes, and at the entrance of Towns and Churches, according to the received Distich

Christophorum videas, postea tutus eris.

CHAPTER XVII
Of the Picture of St. *George*.

The Picture of St. *George* killing the Dragon, and, as most ancient draughts do run, with the daughter of a King standing by, is famous amongst Christians. And upon this description dependeth a solemn story, how by this atchievement he redeemed a Kings daughter: which is more especially believed by the *English*, whose Protector he is: and in which form and history, according to his description in the *English* Colledge at *Rome*, he is set forth in the Icons or Cuts of Martyrs by *Cevalerius*: and all this according to the *Historia Lombardica*, or golden legend of *Jacobus de Voragine*. Now of what authority soever this piece be amongst us, it is I perceive received with different beliefs: for some believe the person and the story; some the person, but not the story; and others deny both.

That such a person there was, we shall not contend: for besides others, Dr. *Heilin* hath clearly asserted it in his History of St. *George*. The indistinction of many in the community of name, or the misapplication of the acts of one unto another, hath made some doubt thereof. For of this name we meet with more then one in History, and no less then two conceived of *Cappadocia*. The one an *Arrian*, who was slain by the *Alexandrians* in the time of *Julian*; the other a valiant Souldier and Christian Martyr, beheaded in the reign of *Dioclesian*. This is the *George* conceived in this Picture, who hath his day in the *Roman* Calender, on whom so many fables are delivered, whose story is set forth by *Metaphrastes*, and his miracles by *Turonensis*.

As for the story depending hereon, some conceive as lightly thereof, as of that of *Persius* and *Andromeda*; conjecturing the one to be the father of the other; and some too highly assert it. Others with better moderation, do either entertain the same as a fabulous addition unto the true and authentick story of St. *George*; or else conceive the literal acception to be a misconstruction of the symbolical expression; apprehending a veritable History, in an Emblem or piece of Christian Poesie. And this Emblematical construction hath been received by men not forward to extenuate the acts of Saints: as from *Baronius*, *Lipellous* the *Carthusian* hath delivered in the life of St. *George*; *Picturam illam St. Georgii quâ effingitur eques armatus, qui hastæ cuspide hostem interficit, juxta quam etiam virgo posita manus supplices tendens ejus explorat auxilium, Symboli potius quam historiæ alicujus censenda expressa imago. Consuevit quidem ut equestris militiæ miles equestri imagine referri*: that is, The Picture of St. *George*, wherein he is described like a Curassier or horseman compleatly armed, etc. Is rather a symbolical image, then any proper figure.

Now in the Picture of this Saint and Souldier, might be implied the Christian Souldier and true Champion of Christ. A horseman armed *Cap a pe*, intimating the *Panoplia* or compleat armour of a Christian; combating with the Dragon, that is, with the Devil; in defence of the Kings daughter, that is, the Church of God. And therefore although the history be not made out, it doth not disparage the Knights and Noble order of St. *George*: whose cognisance is honourable in the Emblem of the Souldier of Christ, and is a worthy memorial to conform unto its mystery. Nor, were there no such person at all, had they more reason to be ashamed, then the Noble order of *Burgundy*, and Knights of the Golden Fleece; whose badge is a confessed fable.

CHAPTER XVIII
Of the Picture of *Jerom*.

Clocks no very ancient invention.

The Picture of *Jerom* usually described at his study, with a Clock hanging by, is not to be omitted; for though the meaning be allowable, and probable it is that industrious Father did not let slip his time without account; yet must not perhaps that Clock be set down to have been his measure thereof. For Clocks or Automatous organs, whereby we now distinguish of time, have found no mention in any ancient Writers but are of late invention, as *Pancirollus* observeth. And *Polydore Virgil* discoursing of new inventions whereof the authors are not known, makes instance in Clocks and Guns. Now *Jerom* is no late Writer, but one of the ancient Fathers, and lived in the fourth Century, in the reign of *Theodosius* the first.

It is not to be denied that before the daies of *Jerom* there were Horologies, and several accounts of time; for they measured the hours not only by drops of water in glasses called Clepsydræ, but also by sand in glasses called Clepsammia. There were also from great antiquity, Scioterical or Sun Dials, by the shadow of a stile or gnomon denoting the hours of the day: an invention ascribed unto *Anaximines* by *Pliny*. Hereof a memorable one there was in *Campus Martius*, from an obelisk erected, and golden figures placed horozontally about it; which was brought out of *Egypt* by *Augustus*, and described by *Jacobus Laurus*. And another of great antiquity we meet with in the story of *Ezechias*; for so it is delivered in *King*. 2. 20. That the Lord brought the shadow backward ten degrees by which it had gone down in the dial of Ahaz. *A peculiar description and particular construction hereof out of* R. Chomer, *is set down*, Curios de Caffarel. chap. 9. That is, say some, ten degrees, not lines; for the hours were denoted by certain divisions or steps in the Dial, which others distinguished by lines, according to that of *Persius*

Stertimus indomitum quod despumare Falernum
Sufficiat, quintâ dum linea tangitur umbra.

That is, the line next the Meridian, or within an hour of noon.

Doctrine of circular motions.

Of later years there succeeded new inventions, and horologies composed by Trochilick or the artifice of wheels; whereof some are kept in motion by weight, others perform without it. Now as one age instructs another, and time that brings all things to ruin, perfects also every thing; so are these indeed of more general and ready use then any that went before them. By the Water-glasses the account was not regular: for from attenuation and condensation, whereby that Element is altered, the hours were shorter in hot weather then in cold, and in Summer then in Winter. As for Scioterical Dials, whether of the Sun or Moon, they are only of use in the actual radiation of those Luminaries, and are of little advantage unto those inhabitants, which for many months enjoy not the Lustre of the Sun.

It is I confess no easie wonder how the horometry of Antiquity discovered not this Artifice, how *Architas* that contrived the moving Dove, or rather the *Helicosophie* of *Archimedes*, fell not upon this way. Surely as in many things, so in this particular, the present age hath far surpassed Antiquity; whose ingenuity hath been so bold not only to proceed below the account of minutes, but to attempt perpetual motions, and engines whose revolutions (could their substance answer the design) might out-last the exemplary mobility, and out measure time it self. For such a one is that mentioned by *John Dee*, whose words are these in his learned Preface unto *Euclide*: By Wheels strange works and incredible are done: A wondrous example was seen in my time in a certain Instrument, which by the Inventer and Artificer was sold for twenty talents of gold; and then by chance had received some injury, and one *Janellus* of *Cremona* did mend the same, and presented it unto the Emperor *Charles* the fift. *Jeronimus Cardanus* can be my witness, that therein was one Wheel that moved at such a rate, that in seven thousand years his own period should be finished; a thing almost incredible, but how far I keep within my bounds, many men yet alive can tell.

CHAPTER XIX
Of the Pictures of *Mermaids, Unicorns,* and some others.

Few eyes have escaped the Picture of *Mermaids*: that is, according to *Horace* his Monster, with womans head above, and fishy extremity below; and these are conceived to answer the shape of the ancient *Syrens* that attempted upon *Ulysses*. Which notwithstanding were of another description, containing no fishy composure, but made up of Man and Bird; the humane mediety variously placed not only above, but below; according unto *Ælian, Suidas, Servius, Boccatius,* and *Aldrovandus*, who hath referred their description unto the story of fabulous Birds; according to the description of Ovid, and the account thereof in Hyginus, that they were the daughters of *Melpomene*, and metamorphosed into the shape of man and bird by *Ceres*.

And therefore these pieces so common among us, do rather derive their original, or are indeed the very description of *Dagon*; [*Dagon the Idol, of what form.*] which was made with human figure above, and fishy shape below; whose stump, or as *Tremellius* and our margin renders it, whose fishy part only remained, when the hands and upper part fell before the Ark. [1 Sam. 5.] Of the shape of *Artergates*, or *Derceto* with the *Phœnitians*; in whose fishy and feminine mixture, as some conceive, were implied the Moon and the Sea, or the Deity of the waters; and therefore, in their sacrifices, they made oblations of fishes. From whence were probably occasioned the Pictures of *Nereides* and *Tritons* among the *Grecians*, and such as we read in *Macrobius*, to have been placed on the top of the Temple of *Saturn*.

We are unwilling to question the Royal Supporters of *England*, that is, the approved descriptions of the Lion and the Unicorn. Although, if in the Lion, the position of the pizel be proper, and that the natural situation; it will be hard to make out their retro-copulation, or their coupling and pissing backward, according to the determination of *Aristotle*; All that urine backward do copulate πυγηδὸν *clunatim*, or aversly, as Lions, Hares, Linxes.

As for the Unicorn, if it have the head of a Deer, and the tail of a Boar, as *Vartomannus* describeth it, how agreeable it is to this picture every eye may discern. If it be made bisulcous or cloven footed, it agreeth unto the description of *Vartommanus*, but scarce of any other; and *Aristotle* supposeth that such as divide the hoof, do also double the horn; they being both of the same nature, and admitting division together. And lastly if the horn have this situation and be so forwardly affixed, as is described, it will not be easily conceived, how it can feed from the ground; and therefore we observe, that Nature in other cornigerous animals, hath placed the horns higher and reclining, as in Bucks; in some inverted upwards, as in the Rhinoceros, the *Indian* Ass, and Unicornous Beetles; and thus have some affirmed it is seated in this animal.

We cannot but observe that in the Picture of *Jonah* and others, Whales are described with two prominent spouts on their heads; whereas indeed they have but one in the forehead, and terminating over the wind-pipe. Nor can we overlook the Picture of Elephants with Castles on their backs, made in the form of land Castles, or stationary fortifications, and answerable unto the Arms of *Castile*, or Sir *John* Old Castle; whereas the towers they bore were made of wood, and girt unto their bodies; as is delivered in the books of *Maccabees*, and as they were appointed in the Army of *Antiochus*.

We will not dispute the Pictures of Retiary Spiders, and their position in the web, which is commonly made lateral, and regarding the Horizon; although, if observed, we shall commonly find it downward, and their heads respecting the Center. [*Where the seven Stars be situated.*] We will not controvert the Picture of the seven Stars; although if thereby be meant the Pleiades, or subconstellation upon the back of Taurus, with what congruity they are described, either in site or magnitude, in a clear night an ordinary eye may discover, from July unto April. We will not question the tongues of Adders and Vipers, described like an Anchor; nor the Picture of the Flower *de Luce*: though how far they agree unto their natural draughts, let every spectator determine.

Whether the Cherubims about the Ark be rightly described in the common Picture, that is, only in humane heads, with two wings; or rather in the shape of Angels or young men, or somewhat at least with feet, as the Scripture seems to imply. 2 Chron. 3. 13. Whether the Cross seen in the air by *Constantine*, were of that figure wherein we represent it; or rather made out of X and P, the two first letters of χριστός. Whether the Cross of Christ did answer the common figure; whether so far advanced above his head; whether the feet were so disposed, that is, one upon another, or separately nailed, as some with reason describe it: we shall not at all contend. Much less whether the house of *Diogenes* were a Tub framed of wood, and after the manner of ours, or rather made of earth, as learned men conceive, and so more clearly make out that expression of *Juvenal*. —

—Dolia nudi non ardent Cynici, etc. We should be too critical to question the letter Y, or bicornous element of *Pythagoras*, that is, the making of the horns equal: or the left less then the right, and so destroying the Symbolical intent of the figure; confounding the narrow line of Vertue, with the larger road of Vice; answerable unto the narrow door of Heaven, and the ample gates of Hell, expressed by our Saviour, and not forgotten by *Homer*, in that Epithete of *Pluto's* house. Εὐρυπυλής.

Many more there are whereof our pen shall take no notice, nor shall we urge their enquiry; we shall not enlarge with what incongruity, and how dissenting from the pieces of Antiquity, the Pictures of their gods and goddesses are described, and how hereby their symbolical sense is lost; although herein it were not hard to be informed from *Phornutus*, Phornut. De natura deorum. *Fulgentius*, Fulg. mytho. Logia and *Albricus* Albric. De deorum imaginibus. Whether *Hercules* be more properly described strangling than tearing the Lion, as *Victorius* hath disputed; nor how the characters and figures of the Signs and Planets be now perverted, as *Salmasius* hath learnedly declared. We will dispence with Bears with long tails, such as are described in the figures of heaven; We shall tolerate flying Horses, black Swans, Hydra's, Centaur's, Harpies and Satyrs; for these are monstrosities, rarities, or else Poetical fancies, whose shadowed moralities requite their substantial falsities. Wherein indeed we must not deny a liberty; nor is the hand of the Painter more restrainable than the Poet. But where the real works of Nature, or veritable acts of storie are to be described, digressions are aberrations; and Art being but the imitator or secondary representor, it must not vary from the verity of the example; or describe things otherwise than they truly are or have been. For hereby introducing false Idea's of things it perverts and deforms the face and symmetry of truth.

CHAPTER XX
Of the Hieroglyphical Pictures of the *Egyptians*.

Certainly of all men that suffered from the confusion of *Babel*, the *Ægyptians* found the best evasion; for, though words were confounded, they invented a language of things, and spake unto each other by common notions in Nature. Whereby they discoursed in silence, and were intuitively understood from the theory of their Expresses. For they assumed the shapes of animals common unto all eyes; and by their conjunctions and compositions were able to communicate their conceptions, unto any that co-apprehended the Syntaxis of their Natures. This many conceive to have been the primitive way of writing, and of greater antiquity than letters; and this indeed might *Adam* well have spoken, who understanding the nature of things, had the advantage of natural expressions. Which the *Egyptians* but taking upon trust, upon their own or common opinion; from conceded mistakes they authentically promoted errors; describing in their Hieroglyphicks creatures of their own invention; or from known and conceded animals, erecting significations not inferrible from their natures.

And first, Although there were more things in Nature than words which did express them; yet even in these mute and silent discourses, to express complexed significations, they took a liberty to compound and piece together creatures of allowable forms into mixtures inexistent. Thus began the descriptions of Griphins, Basilicks, Phœnix, and many more; which Emblematists and Heralds have entertained with significations answering their institutions; Hieroglyphically adding Martegres, Wivernes, Lion fishes, with divers others. Pieces of good and allowable invention unto the prudent Spectator, but are lookt on by vulgar eyes as literal truths, or absurd impossibilities; whereas indeed, they are commendable inventions, and of laudable significations.

Again, Beside these pieces fictitiously set down, and having no Copy in Nature; they had many unquestionable drawn, of inconsequent signification, nor naturally verifying their intention. We shall instance but in few, as they stand recorded by *Orus*. The male sex they expressed by a Vulture, because of Vultures all are females, and impregnated by the wind; which authentically transmitted hath passed many pens, and became the assertion of *Ælian, Ambrose, Basil, Isidore, Tzetzes, Philes*, and others. Wherein notwithstanding what injury is offered unto the Creation in this confinement of sex, and what disturbance unto Philosophy in the concession of windy conceptions, we shall not here declare. By two dragms they thought it sufficient to signifie an heart; because the heart at one year weigheth two dragms, that is, a quarter of an ounce, and unto fifty years annually encreaseth the weight of one dragm, after which in the same proportion it yearly decreaseth; so that the life of a man doth not naturally extend above an hundred. And this was not only a popular conceit, but consentaneous unto their Physical principles, as *Heurnius* hath accounted it. *In his* Philosophia Barbarica.

A Woman that hath but one Child, they express by a Lioness; for that conceiveth but once. Fecundity they set forth by a Goat, because but seven daies old, it beginneth to use coition. The abortion of a Woman they describe by an Horse kicking a Wolf; because a Mare will cast her foal if she tread in the track of that animal. Deformity they signifie by a Bear; and an unstable Man by an Hyæna, because that animal yearly exchangeth its sex. A Woman delivered of a female Child, they imply by a Bull looking over his left shoulder; because if in coition a Bull part from a Cow on that side, the Calf will prove a female.

All which, with many more, how far they consent with truth, we shall not disparage our Reader to dispute; and though some way allowable unto wiser conceits, who could distinctly receive their significations: yet carrying the majesty of Hicroglyphicks, and so transmitted by Authors: they crept into a belief with many, and favourable doubt with most. And thus, I fear, it hath fared with the Hieroglyphical Symboles of Scripture: which excellently intended in the species of things sacrificed, in the prohibited meats, in the dreams of *Pharoah, Joseph*, and many other passages: are oft-times wrackt beyond their symbolizations, and inlarg'd into constructions disparaging their true intentions.

CHAPTER XXI
Of the Picture of *Haman* hanged.

In common draughts, *Haman* is hanged by the Neck upon an high Gibbet, after the usual and now practised way of suspension, but whether this description truly answereth the Original, Learned pens consent not, and good grounds there are to doubt. For it is not easily made out that this was an ancient way of Execution, in the publick punishment of Malefactors among the *Persians*; but we often read of Crucifixion in their Stories. So we find that *Oroetes*[6] a *Persian* Governour crucified *Polycrates* the *Samian* Tyrant. And hereof we have an example in the life of *Artaxerxes* King of *Persia*; (whom some will have to be *Ahasuerus* in this Story) that his Mother *Parysatis* flead and crucified her *Eunuch*. The same also seems implied in the letters patent of King *Cyrus*. *In* Ezra 6. *Omnis qui hanc mutaverit jussionem, tollatur lignum de domo ejus, et erigatur et configatur in eo.*

The same kind of punishment was in use among the *Romans, Syrians, Egyptians, Carthaginians* and *Grecians*. For though we find in *Homer*, that *Ulysses* in a fury hanged the strumpets of those who courted *Penelope*, yet is it not so easie to discover, that this was the publick practice or open course of justice among the *Greeks*.

And even that the *Hebrews* used this present way of hanging, by illaqueation or pendulous suffocation in publick justice and executions; the expressions and examples in scripture conclude not beyond good doubt.

That the King of *Hai* was hanged, or destroyed by the common way of suspension, is not conceded by the learned *Masius* in his comment upon that text; who conceiveth thereby rather some kind of crucifixion; at least some patibulary affixion after he was slain; and so represented unto the people untill toward the evening.

Though we read in our translation, that *Pharaoh* hanged the chief Baker, yet learned expositors understand hereby some kind of crucifixion, according to the mode of *Egypt*, whereby he exemplarily hanged out till the fowls of the air fed on his head or face, the first part of their prey being the eyes. And perhaps according to the signal draught hereof in a very old manuscript of *Genesis*, now kept in the Emperors Library at *Vienna*; and accordingly set down by the learned *Petrus Zamberius*, in the second Tome of the description of that Library.

When the *Gibeonites* hanged the bodies of those of the house of *Saul*, thereby was intended some kind of crucifying, according unto good expositors, and the vulgar translation: *crucifixerunt eos in monte coram domino*; many both in Scripture and humane writers might be said to be crucified, though they did not perish immediately by crucifixion: But however otherwise destroyed, their bodies might be afterward appended or fastned unto some elevated engine, as exemplary objects unto the eyes of the people: So sometimes we read of the crucifixion of only some part, as of the Heads of *Julianus* and *Albinus*, though their bodies were cast away.

That legal Text Deut. 21. which seems to countenance the common way of hanging, if a man hath committed a sin worthy of Death, and they hang him on a Tree; is not so received by Christian and Jewish expositors. And as a good Annotator of ours Ainsworth. delivereth, out of *Maimonides*: The *Hebrews* understand not this of putting him to death by hanging, but of hanging of a Man after he was stoned to death; and the manner is thus described. After he is stoned to death, they fasten a piece of timber in the Earth, and out of it there commeth a piece of wood, and then they tye both his hands one to another, and hang him unto the setting of the Sun.

Beside, the original word *Hakany* determineth not the doubt. For that by *Lexicographers* or *Dictionarie* interpreters, is rendred suspension and crucifixion; there being no *Hebrew* word peculiarly and fully expressing the proper word of crucifixion, as it was used by the *Romans*; nor easie to prove it the custom of the *Jewish* Nation to nail them by distinct parts unto a Cross, after the manner of our SAVIOUR crucified: wherein it was a special favour indulged unto *Joseph* to take down the Body.

Lipsius[7] lets fall a good caution to take off doubts about suspension delivered by ancient Authors, and also the ambiguous sence of κρεμάσαι among the *Greeks*. *Tale apud Latinos ipsum suspendere, quod in crucem referendum moneo juventutem*, as that also may be understood of *Seneca*. *Latrocinium fecit aliquis, quid ergo meruit? ut suspendatur*. And this way of crucifying he conceiveth to have been in general use among the *Romans*, until the latter daies of *Constantine*, who in reverence unto our SAVIOUR abrogated that opprobrious and infamous way of crucifixion. Whereupon succeeded the common and now practised way of suspension.

But long before this abrogation of the Cross, the *Jewish* Nation had known the true sense of crucifixion; whereof no Nation had a sharper apprehension, while *Adrian* crucified five hundred of them every day, until Wood was wanting for that service. So that they which had nothing but *crucifie* in their mouths, were therewith paid home in their own bodies: Early suffering the reward of their imprecations, and properly in the same kind.

Footnotes

[6]*Oroetes*, 1672, 1686, etc.
[7]*Zipsias*, 1672.

CHAPTER XXII

Compendiously of many questionable Customs, Opinions, Pictures, Practices, and Popular Observations.

The ground of many vain observations.

1. If an Hare cross the high way, there are few above threescore years that are not perplexed thereat: which notwithstanding is but an Augurial terror, according to that received expression, *Inauspicatum dat iter oblatus Lepus.* And the ground of the conceit was probably no greater than this, that a fearful animal passing by us, portended unto us some thing to be feared: as upon the like consideration, the meeting of a Fox presaged some future imposture; which was a superstitious observation prohibited unto the *Jews*, as is expressed in the Idolatry of *Maimonides*, and is referred unto the sin of an observer of Fortunes, or one that abuseth events unto good or bad signs; forbidden by the Law of *Moses* [Deut. 18.]; which notwithstanding sometimes succeeding, according to fears or desires, have left impressions and timerous expectations in credulous minds for ever.

The Emblem of superstition.

2. That Owls and Ravens are ominous appearers, and pre-signifying unlucky events, as Christians yet conceit, was also an Augurial conception. Because many Ravens were seen when *Alexander* entred *Babylon*, they were thought to pre-ominate his death; and because an Owl appeared before the battle, it presaged the ruin of *Crassus.* Which though decrepite superstitions, and such as had their nativity in times beyond all history, are fresh in the observation of many heads, and by the credulous and feminine party still in some Majesty among us. And therefore the Emblem of Superstition was well set out by *Ripa* [Iconologia de Cæsare Ripa.], in the picture of an Owl, an Hare, and an Old Woman. And it no way confirmeth the Augurial consideration, that an Owl is a forbidden food in the Law of *Moses*; or that *Jerusalem* was threatned by the Raven and the Owl, in that expression of *Esay* 34. That it should be a court for Owls, that the Cormorant and the Bittern should possess it, and the Owl and the Raven dwell in it. For thereby was only implied their ensuing desolation, as is expounded in the words succeeding; He shall draw upon it the line of confusion, and the stones of emptiness.

3. The falling of Salt is an authentick presagement of ill luck, nor can every temper contemn it; from whence notwithstanding nothing can be naturally feared: nor was the same a general prognostick of future evil among the Ancients, but a particular omination concerning the breach of friendship. For Salt as incorruptible, was the Symbole of friendship, and before the other service was offered unto their guests; which if it casually fell, was accounted ominous, and their amity of no duration. But whether Salt were not only a Symbole of friendship with man, but also a figure of amity and reconciliation with God, and was therefore observed in sacrifices, is an higher speculation.

4. To break the egg shell after the meat is out, we are taught in our childhood, and practise it all our lives; which nevertheless is but a superstitious relict, according to the judgment of *Pliny*, *Huc pertinet ovorum, ut exorbuerit quisq; calices protinus frangi, aut eosdem coclearibus perforari*; and the intent hereof was to prevent witchcraft; for lest witches should draw or prick their names therein, and veneficiously mischief their persons, they broke the shell, as *Dalecampius* hath observed.

5. The true Lovers knot is very much magnified, and still retained in presents of Love among us; which though in all points it doth not make out, had perhaps its original from the *Nodus Herculanus*, or that which was called *Hercules* his knot, resembling the snaky complication in the caduceus or rod of *Hermes*; and in which form the Zone or woollen girdle of the Bride was fastned, as *Turnebus* observeth in his *Adversaria*.

6. When our cheek burneth or ear tingleth, we usually say that some body is talking of us, which is an ancient conceit, and ranked among superstitious opinions by *Pliny. Absentes tinnitu aurium præsentire sermones de se receptum est*, according to that distick noted by *Dalecampius*.

Garrula quid totis resonas mihi noctibus auris?
Nescio quem dicis nunc meminisse mei.

Which is a conceit hardly to be made out without the concession of a signifying *Genius*, or universal *Mercury*; conducting sounds unto their distant subjects, and teaching us to hear by touch.

The original of the proverb, Under the Rose be it, *etc.*

7. When we desire to confine our words, we commonly say they are spoken under the Rose; which expression is commendable, if the Rose from any natural property may be the Symbole of silence, as *Nazianzene* seems to imply in these translated verses:

Utq; latet Rosa Verna suo putamine clausa,
Sic os vincla ferat, validisq; arctetur habenis,
Indicatq; suis prolixa silentia labris:

And is also tolerable, if by desiring a secrecy to words spoke under the Rose, we only mean in society and compotation, from the ancient custom in Symposiack meetings, to wear chaplets of Roses about their heads: and so we condemn not the *German* custom, which over the Table describeth a Rose in the cieling. But more considerable it is, if the original were such as *Lemnius*, and others have recorded; that the Rose was the flower of *Venus*, which *Cupid* consecrated unto *Harpocrates* the God of silence, and was therefore an Emblem thereof, to conceal the pranks of Venery; as is declared in this Tetrastick;

Est Rosa flos veneris, cujus quo facta laterent,
Harpocrati matris, dona dicavit Amor;
Inde Rosam mensis hospes suspendit Amicis.
Convivæ ut sub eâ dicta tacenda sciant.

8. That smoak doth follow the fairest, is an usual saying with us, and in many parts of *Europe*; whereof although there seem no natural ground, yet it is the continuation of a very ancient opinion, as *Petrus Victorius* and *Causabon* have observed from a passage in *Athenæus*: wherein a *Parasite* thus describeth himself:

To every Table first I come,
Whence Porridge I am cal'd by some:
A Capaneus at Stares I am,
To enter any Room a Ram;
Like whips and thongs to all I ply,
Like smoake unto the Fair I fly.

9. To sit cross leg'd, or with our fingers pectinated or shut together, is accounted bad, and friends will perswade us from it. The same conceit religiously possessed the Ancients, as is observable from *Pliny*. *Poplites alternis genibus imponere nefas olim*; and also from *Athenæus*, that it was an old veneficious practice, and *Juno* is made in this posture to hinder the delivery of *Alcmena*. And therefore, as *Pierius* observeth, in the Medal of *Julia Pia*, the right hand of *Venus* was made extended with the inscription of *Venus, Genetrix*; for the complication or pectination of the fingers was an Hieroglyphick of impediment, as in that place he declareth.

10. The set and statary times of pairing of nails, and cutting of hair, is thought by many a point of consideration; which is perhaps but the continuation of an ancient superstition. For piaculous it was unto the *Romans* to pare their nails upon the Nundinæ, observed every ninth day; and was also feared by others in certain daies of the week; according to that of *Ausonius*, *Ungues Mercurio, Barbam Jove, Cypride Crines*; and was one part of the wickedness that filled up the measure of 2 Chron.33. *Manasses*, when 'tis delivered that he observed times.

11. A common fashion it is to nourish hair upon the mouls of the face; which is the perpetuation of a very ancient custom; and though innocently practised among us, may have a superstitious original, according to that of *Pliny, Nævos in facie tondere religiosum habent nunc multi*. From the like might proceed the fears of poling Elvelocks or complicated hairs of the head, and also of locks longer than the other hair; they being votary at first, and dedicated upon occasion; preserved with great care, and accordingly esteemed by others, as appears by that of *Apuleius, Adjuro per dulcem capilli tui nodulum*.

12. A custom there is in most parts of *Europe* to adorn Aqueducts, spouts and Cisterns with Lions heads: which though no illaudable ornament, is of an *Egyptian* genealogy,[8] who practised

the same under a symbolical illation. For because the Sun being in Leo, the flood of *Nilus* was at the full, and water became conveyed into every part, they made the spouts of their Aqueducts through the head of a Lion. And upon some cœlestial respects it is not improbable the great Mogul or *Indian* King doth bear for his Arms a Lion and the Sun.

Symbolical significations of the girdle.

13. Many conceive there is somewhat amiss, and that as we usually say, they are unblest until they put on their girdle. Wherein (although most know not what they say) there are involved unknown considerations. For by a girdle or cincture are symbolically implied Truth, Resolution, and Readiness unto action, which are parts and vertues required in the service of God. According whereto we find that the *Israelites* did eat the Paschal Lamb with their loins girded; and the Almighty challenging *Job*, bids him gird up his loins like a man. So runneth the expression of *Peter*, Gird up the loins of your minds, be sober and hope to the end: so the high Priest was girt with the girdle of fine linnen: so is it part of the holy habit to have our lines girt about with truth; Isa. 11. and so is it also said concerning our Saviour, Righteousness shall be the girdle of his loins, and faithfulness the girdle of his reins.

Moreover by the girdle, the heart and parts which God requires are divided from the inferior and concupiscential organs; implying thereby a memento unto purification and cleanness of heart, which is commonly denied from the concupiscence and affection of those parts; and therefore unto this day the *Jews* do bless themselves when they put on their zone or cincture. And thus may we make out the doctrin of *Pythagoras*, to offer sacrifice with our feet naked, that is, that our inferiour parts and farthest removed from reason might be free, and of no impediment unto us. Thus *Achilles*, though dipped in Styx, yet having his heel untouched by that water; although he were fortified elsewhere, he was slain in that part, as only vulnerable in the inferiour and brutal part of Man. This is that part of *Eve* and her posterity the devil still doth bruise, that is, that part of the soul which adhereth unto earth, and walks in the paths thereof. And in this secundary and symbolical sense it may be also understood, when the Priests in the Law washed their feet before the sacrifice; when our Saviour washed the feet of his Disciples, and said unto *Peter*, If I wash not thy feet thou hast no part in me. And thus is it symbolically explainable, and implyeth purification and cleanness, when in the burnt offerings the Priest is commanded to wash the inwards and legs thereof in water; and in the peace and sin-offerings, to burn the two kidneys, the fat which is about the flanks, and as we translate it, the Caul above the Liver. But whether the *Jews* when they blessed themselves, had any eye unto the words of *Jeremy*, Jer. 13. wherein God makes them his Girdle; or had therein any reference unto the Girdle, which the Prophet was commanded to hide in the hole of the rock of *Euphrates*, and which was the type of their captivity, we leave unto higher conjecture.

Certain Hereticks *who ascribed humane figure unto God, after which they conceived he created man in his likeness.*

14. The Picture of the Creator, or God the Father in the shape of an old Man, is a dangerous piece, and in this Fecundity of sects may revive the Anthropomorphites. Which although maintained from the expression of *Daniel*, I beheld where the Ancient of dayes did sit, whose hair of his head was like the pure wool; yet may it be also derivative from the Hieroglyphical description of the *Ægyptians*; who to express their Eneph, or Creator of the world, described an old man in a blew mantle, with an egg in his mouth; which was the Emblem of the world. Surely those heathens, that notwithstanding the exemplary advantage in heaven, would endure no pictures of Sun or Moon, as being visible unto all the world, and needing no representation; do evidently accuse the practice of those pencils, that will describe invisibles. And he that challenged the boldest hand unto the picture of an Echo, must laugh at this attempt, not only in the description of invisibility, but circumscription of Ubiquity, and fetching under lines incomprehensible circularity.

The Pictures of the *Ægyptians* were more tolerable, and in their sacred letters more veniably expressed the apprehension of Divinity. For though they implied the same by an eye upon a Scepter, by an Ægles head, a Crocodile, and the like: yet did these manual descriptions pretend no corporal representations; nor could the people misconceive the same unto real correspondencies.

So though the Cherub carried some apprehension of Divinity, yet was it not conceived to be the shape thereof: and so perhaps because it is metaphorically predicated of God, that he is a consuming fire, he may be harmlessly described by a flaming representation; Yet if, as some will have it, all mediocrity of folly is foolish, and because an unrequitable evil may ensue, an indifferent convenience must be omitted; we shall not urge such representments; we could spare the holy Lamb for the picture of our Saviour, and the Dove or fiery Tongues to represent the holy Ghost.

15. The Sun and Moon are usually described with humane faces; whether herein there be not a *Pagan* imitation, and those visages at first implied *Apollo* and *Diana*, we may make some doubt; and we find the statua of the Sun was framed with raies about the head, which were the indiciduous and unshaven locks of *Apollo*. We should be too Iconomical [*Or quarrelsom with Pictures.*] to question the pictures of the winds, as commonly drawn in humane heads, and with their cheeks distended; which notwithstanding we find condemned by *Minutius*, as answering poetical fancies, and the gentile description of *Æolus*, *Boreas*, and the feigned Deities of winds.

16. We shall not, I hope, disparage the Resurrection of our Redeemer, if we say the Sun doth not dance on Easter day. And though we would willingly assent unto any sympathetical exultation, yet cannot conceive therein any more than a Tropical expression. Whether any such motion there were in that day wherein Christ arised, Scripture hath not revealed, which hath been punctual in other records concerning solary miracles: and the Areopagite [*Dion. Ep. 7. a. ad Policar. et Pet. Hall not. in vit. S. Dionys*] that was amazed at the Eclipse, took no notice of this. And if metaphorical expressions go so far, we may be bold to affirm, not only that one Sun danced, but two arose that day: That light appeared at his nativity, and darkness at his death, and yet a light at both; for even that darkness was a light unto the *Gentiles*, illuminated by that obscurity. That 'twas the first time the Sun set above the Horizon; that although there were darkness above the earth, there was light beneath it, nor dare we say that hell was dark if he were in it.

17. Great conceits are raised of the involution or membranous covering, commonly called the Silly-how, that sometimes is found about the heads of children upon their birth; and is therefore preserved with great care, not only as medical in diseases, but effectual in success, concerning the Infant and others; which is surely no more than a continued superstition. For hereof we read in the life of *Antoninus* delivered by *Spartianus*, that children are born sometimes with this natural cap; which Midwives were wont to sell unto credulous Lawyers, who had an opinion it advantaged their promotion.

But to speak strictly, the effect is natural, and thus may be conceived: Animal conceptions have largely taken three teguments, or membranous films which cover them in the womb, that is, the Corion, Amnios, and Allantois; the Corion is the outward membrane wherein are implanted the Veins, Arteries and umbilical vessels, whereby its nourishment is conveyed: the Allantois a thin coat seated under the Corion, wherein are received the watery separations conveyed by the Urachus, that the acrimony thereof should not offend the skin. [*De formato fœtu.*] The Amnios is a general investment, containing the sudorus or thin serosity perspirable through the skin. Now about the time when the Infant breaketh these coverings, it sometimes carrieth with it about the head a part of the Amnios or nearest coat; which saith *Spiegelius*, either proceedeth from the toughness of the membrane or weakness of the Infant that cannot get clear thereof. And therefore herein significations are natural and concluding upon the Infant, but not to be extended unto magical signalities, or any other person.

18. That 'tis good to be drunk once a moneth, is a common flattery of sensuality, supporting it self upon Physick, and the healthful effects of inebriation. This indeed seems plainly affirmed by *Avicenna*, a Physitian of great authority, and whose religion prohibiting Wine, could less extenuate ebriety. But *Averroes* a man of his own faith was of another belief; restraining his ebriety unto hilarity, and in effect making no more thereof than *Seneca* commendeth, and was allowable in *Cato*; that is, a sober incalescence and regulated æstuation from wine; or what may

be conceived between *Joseph* and his brethren, when the text expresseth they were merry, or drank largely, and whereby indeed the commodities set down by *Avicenna*, that is, alleviation of spirits, resolution of superfluities, provocation of sweat and urine may also ensue. But as for dementation, sopition of reason, and the diviner particle from drink; though *American* religion approve, and *Pagan* piety of old hath practised it, even at their sacrifices; Christian morality and the doctrine of Christ will not allow. And surely that religion which excuseth the fact of *Noah*, in the aged surprizal of six hundred years, and unexpected inebriation from the unknown effects of wine, will neither acquit ebriosity nor ebriety, in their known and intended perversions.

And indeed, although sometimes effects succeed which may relieve the body, yet if they carry mischief or peril unto the soul, we are therein restrainable by Divinity, which circumscribeth Physick, and circumstantially determines the use thereof. From natural considerations, Physick commendeth the use of venery; and happily, incest, adultery, or stupration may prove as Physically advantagious, as conjugal copulation; which notwithstanding must not be drawn into practise. And truly effects, consequents, or events which we commend, arise oft-times from wayes which we all condemn. Thus from the fact of *Lot*, we derive the generation of *Ruth*, and blessed Nativity of our Saviour; which notwithstanding did not extenuate the incestuous ebriety of the generator. And if, as is commonly urged, we think to extenuate ebriety from the benefit of vomit oft succeeding, *Egyptian* sobriety will condemn us, which purged both wayes twice a moneth, without this perturbation: and we foolishly contemn the liberal hand of God, and ample field of medicines which sobriety produce that action.

Why the devil is commonly said to appear with a cloven foot.

19. A conceit there is, that the Devil commonly appeareth with a cloven hoof; wherein although it seem excessively ridiculous, there may be somewhat of truth; and the ground thereof at first might be his frequent appearing in the shape of a Goat, which answers that description. This was the opinion of ancient Christians concerning the apparition of Panites, Fauns and Satyres; and in this form we read of one that appeared unto *Antony* in the wilderness. The same is also continued from expositions of holy Scripture; for whereas it is said, Levit. 17. Thou shalt not offer unto Devils, the Original word is *Seghnirim*, that is, rough and hairy Goats, because in that shape the Devil most often appeared; as is expounded by the *Rabbins*, as *Tremellius* hath also explained; and as the word *Ascimah*, the god of *Emath* is by some conceived. Nor did he only assume this shape in elder times, but commonly in later dayes, especially in the place of his worship, if there be any truth in the confession of Witches, and as in many stories it stands confirmed by *Bodinus*. In his *Dæmonomania*. And therefore a Goat is not improperly made the Hieroglyphick of the devil, as *Pierius* hath expressed it. So might it be the Emblem of sin, as it was in the sin-offering; and so likewise of wicked and sinful men, according to the expression of Scripture in the method of the last distribution; when our Saviour shall separate the Sheep from the Goats, that is, the Sons of the Lamb from the children of the devil.

Footnotes

[8] geneologie, 1658, 1669, geneology, 1672.

CHAPTER XXIII
Of some others.

1. That temperamental dignotions, and conjecture of prevalent humours, may be collected from spots in our nails, we are not averse to concede. But yet not ready to admit sundry divinations, vulgarly raised upon them. Nor do we observe it verified in others, what *Cardan* De varietate rerum. discovered as a property in himself: to have found therein some signs of most events that ever happened unto him. Or that there is much considerable in that doctrine of Cheiromancy, that spots in the top of the nails do signifie things past; in the middle, things present; and at the bottom, events to come. That white specks presage our felicity, blew ones our misfortunes. That

those in the nail of the thumb have significations of honour, those in the forefinger, of riches, and so respectively in other fingers, (according to Planetical relations, from whence they receive their names) as *Tricassus* hath taken up, [De inspectione manus.] and *Picciolus* well rejecteth.

We shall not proceed to querie, what truth there is in Palmistry, or divination from those lines in our hands, of high denomination. Although if any thing be therein, it seems not confinable unto man; but other creatures are also considerable; as is the fore-foot of the Moll, and especially of the Monkey; wherein we have observed the table line, that of life, and of the liver.

2. That Children committed unto the school of Nature, without institution would naturally speak the primitive language of the world, was the opinion of ancient heathens, and continued since by Christians: who will have it our *Hebrew* tongue, as being the language of *Adam*. That this were true, were much to be desired, not only for the easie attainment of that useful tongue, but to determine the true and primitive Hebrew. For whether the present Hebrew, be the unconfounded language of *Babel*, and that which remaining in *Heber* was continued by *Abraham* and his posterity, or rather the language of *Phœnicia* and *Canaan*, wherein he lived, some learned men I perceive do yet remain unsatisfied. Although I confess probability stands fairest for the former: nor are they without all reason, who think that at the confusion of tongues, there was no constitution of a new speech in every family: but a variation and permutation of the old; out of one common language raising several Dialects: the primitive tongue remaining still intire. Which they who retained, might make a shift to understand most of the rest. [*How Abraham might understand the language of several Nations.*] By vertue whereof in those primitive times and greener confusions, *Abraham* of the family of *Heber* was able to converse with the *Chaldeans*, to understand *Mesopotamians, Cananites, Philistins,* and *Egyptians*: whose several Dialects he could reduce unto the Original and primitive tongue, and so be able to understand them.

3. Though useless unto us, and rather of molestation, we commonly refrain from killing Swallows, and esteem it unlucky to destroy them: whether herein there be not a *Pagan* relique, we have some reason to doubt. For we read in *Ælian*, that these birds were sacred unto the *Penates* or houshold gods of the ancients, and therefore were preserved. The same they also honoured as the nuncio's of the spring; and we find in *Athenæus* [*The same is extant in the* 8th *of* Athenæus.] that the *Rhodians* had a solemn song to welcome in the Swallow.

Why candles may burn blew, before the apparition of a spirit.

4. That Candles and Lights burn dim and blew at apparition of spirits, may be true, if the ambient ayr be full of sulphurious spirits, as it happeneth oft-times in mines; where damps and acide exhalations are able to extinguish them. And may be also verified, when spirits do make themselves visible by bodies of such effluviums. But of lower consideration is the common foretelling of strangers, from the fungous parcels about the weeks of Candles: which only signifieth a moist and pluvious ayr about them, hindering the avolation of the light and favillous particles: whereupon they are forced to settle upon the Snast.

5. Though Coral doth properly preserve and fasten the Teeth in men, yet is it used in Children to make an easier passage for them: and for that intent is worn about their necks. But whether this custom were not superstitiously founded, as presumed an amulet or defensative against fascination, is not beyond all doubt. For the same is delivered by *Pliny*. [Lib. 32.] *Aruspices religiosum Coralli gestamen amoliendis periculis arbitrantur; et surculi infantiæ alligati, tutelam habere creduntur.*

6. A strange kind of exploration and peculiar way of Rhabdomancy is that which is used in mineral discoveries; that is, with a forked hazel, commonly called *Moses* his Rod, which freely held forth, will stir and play if any mine be under it. And though many there are who have attempted to make it good, yet until better information, we are of opinion with *Agricola* [*De re metallica, lib.*]

2. that in it self it is a fruitless exploration, strongly scenting of *Pagan* derivation, and the *virgula Divina*, proverbially magnified of old. The ground whereof were the Magical rods in Poets that of *Pallas* in *Homer*, that of *Mercury* that charmed *Argus*, and that of *Circe* which transformed the followers of *Ulysses*. Too boldly usurping the name of *Moses* rod, from which notwithstanding, and that of *Aaron*, were probably occasioned the fables of all the rest. For that of *Moses* must needs be famous unto the *Ægyptians*; and that of *Aaron* unto many other Nations, as being preserved in the Ark, until the destruction of the Temple built by *Solomon*.

7. A practise there is among us to determine doubtful matters, by the opening of a book, and letting fall a staff; which notwithstanding are ancient fragments of *Pagan* divinations. The first an imitation of *Sortes Homericæ*; or *Virgilianæ*, drawing determinations from verses casually occurring. The same was practised by *Severus*, who entertained ominous hopes of the Empire, from that verse in *Virgil, Tu regere imperio populos, Romane, memento*; and *Cordianus* who reigned but few dayes was discouraged by another, that is, *Ostendunt terris hunc tantum fata, nec ultra esse sinunt*. Nor was this only performed in heathen Authors, but upon the sacred text of Scripture, as *Gregorius Turonensis* hath left some account, and as the practise of the Emperour *Heraclius*, before his Expedition into *Asia* minor, is delivered by *Cedrenus*.

As for the Divination or decision from the staff; it is an Augurial relique, and the practise thereof is accused by God himself Hosea 4. ; My people ask counsel of their stocks, and their staff declareth unto them. Of this kind of Rhabdomancy was that practised by *Nabuchadonozor* in that *Caldean* miscellany, delivered by *Ezekiel*; Ezek. 24. the king of *Babylon* stood at the parting of the way, at the head of two wayes to use divination, he made his arrows bright, he consulted with Images, he looked in the Liver; at the right hand were the divinations of *Jerusalem*. That is, as *Estius* expounded it, the left way leading unto *Rabbah*, the chief City of the *Ammonites*, and the right unto *Jerusalem*, he consulted *Idols* and entrails, he threw up a bundle of arrows to see which way they would light; and falling on the right hand he marched towards *Jerusalem*. A like way of Belomancy or Divination by arrows hath been in request with *Scythians, Alanes, Germans*, with the *Africans* and *Turks* of *Algier*. But of another nature was that which was practised by *Elisha*, 2 King. 13.15. when by an arrow shot from an Eastern window, he pre-signified the destruction of *Syria*; or when according unto the three stroaks of *Joash*, with an arrow upon the ground, he foretold the number of his victories. For thereby the spirit of God particular'd the same; and determined the stroaks of the King unto three, which the hopes of the Prophet expected in twice that number.

8. We cannot omit to observe the tenacity of ancient customs, in the nominal observation of the several dayes of the week, according to *Gentile* and *Pagan* appellations Dion. Cassii. lib. 37. : for the Original is very high, and as old as the ancient *Ægyptians*, who named the same according to the seven Planets, the admired stars of heaven, and reputed Deities among them. Unto every one assigning a several day; not according to their cœlestial order, or as they are disposed in heaven; but after a diatesseron or musical fourth. For beginning Saturday with Saturn, the supremest Planet, they accounted by Jupiter and Mars unto Sol, making Sunday. From Sol in like manner by Venus and Mercury unto Luna, making Munday; and so through all the rest. And the same order they confirmed by numbering the hours of the day unto twenty four, according to the natural order of the Planets. For beginning to account from Saturn, Jupiter, Mars, and so about unto twenty four, the next day will fall unto Sol; whence accounting twenty four, the next will happen unto Luna, making Munday. And so with the rest, according to the account and order observed still among us.

The *Jews* themselves in their Astrological considerations, concerning Nativities, and Planetary hours, observe the same order, upon as witty foundations. Because by an equal interval, they make seven triangles, the bases whereof are the seven sides of a septilateral figure, described within a circle. That is, If a figure of seven sides be described in a circle, and at the angles thereof the names of the Planets be placed in their natural order on it: if we begin with Saturn, and successively draw lines from angle to angle, until seven equicrural triangles be described, whose bases are the seven sides of the septilateral figure; the triangles will be made by this order. The first being made by Saturn, Sol and Luna, that is, Saturday, Sunday, and Munday; and so the rest in the order still retained. Cujus Icon apud doct. Iaffarel. chap. 11. Et Fabrit. Paduantum.

But thus much is observable, that however in coelestial considerations they embraced the received order of the Planets, yet did they not retain either characters, or names in common use amongst us; but declining humane denominations, they assigned them names from some remarkable qualities; as is very observable in their red and splendent Planets, that is, of Mars Maadim. and Venus. Nogah. But the change of their names disparaged not the consideration of their natures; nor did they thereby reject all memory of these remarkable Stars; which God himself admitted in his Tabernacle, if conjecture will hold concerning the Golden Candlestick, whose shaft resembled the Sun, and six branches the Planets about it.

9. We are unwilling to enlarge concerning many other; only referring unto sober examination, what natural effects can reasonably be expected, when to prevent the Ephialtes or night-Mare we hang up an hollow stone in our stables; when for amulets against Agues we use the chips of Gallows and places of execution. When for Warts we rub our hands before the Moon, or commit any maculated part unto the touch of the dead. What truth there is in those common female Doctrines, that the first Rib of Roast Beef powdered is a peculiar remedy against Fluxes. That to urine upon earth newly cast up by a Moll, bringeth down the menses in Women. That if a Child dieth, and the neck becommeth not stiff, but for many howers remaineth Lythe and Flaccid, some other in the same house will dye not long after. That if a woman with child looketh upon a dead body, her child will be of a pale complexion, our learned Philosophers and critical Philosophers might illustrate, whose exacter performances our adventures do but solicite; mean while, I hope, they will plausibly receive our attempts, or candidly correct our misconjectures.

Disce, sed ira cadat naso, rugosaque sanna,
Dum veteres avias tibi de pulmone recello.

THE SIXTH BOOK
Of sundry common opinions Cosmographical and Historical
The first Discourse comprehended in several Chapters.

CHAPTER I
Concerning the beginning of the World, that the time thereof is not precisely to be known, as men generally suppose: Of mens enquiries in what season or point of the Zodiack it began. That as they are generally made they are in vain, and as particularly applied uncertain. Of the division of the seasons and four quarters of the year, according to Astronomers and Physitians. That the common compute of the Ancients, and which is yet retained by most, is unreasonable and erroneous. Of some Divinations and ridiculous diductions from one part of the year to another. And of the Providence and Wisdom of God in the site and motion of the Sun.

The age of the world not certainly determinable.

Concerning the World and its temporal circumscriptions, who ever shall strictly examine both extreams, will easily perceive there is not only obscurity in its end, but its beginning; that as its period is inscrutable, so is its nativity indeterminable: That as it is presumption to enquire after the one, so is there no rest or satisfactory decision in the other. And hereunto we shall more readily assent, if we examine the informations, and take a view of the several difficulties in this point; which we shall more easily do, if we consider the different conceits of men, and duly perpend the imperfections of their discoveries.

And first, The histories of the *Gentiles* afford us slender satisfaction, nor can they relate any story, or affix a probable point to its beginning. For some thereof (and those of the wisest amongst them) are so far from determining its beginning, that they opinion and maintain it never had any at all; as the doctrin of *Epicurus* implieth, and more positively *Aristotle* in his books *De Cœlo* declareth. Endeavouring to confirm it with arguments of reason, and those appearingly demonstrative; wherein his labours are rational, and uncontroulable upon the grounds assumed, that is, of Physical generation, and a Primary or first matter, beyond which no other hand was apprehended. But herein we remain sufficiently satisfied from *Moses*, and the Doctrin delivered of the Creation; that is, a production of all things out of nothing, a formation not only of matter, but of form, and a materiation even of matter it self.

Others are so far from defining the Original of the World or of mankind, that they have held opinions not only repugnant unto Chronology, but Philosophy; that is, that they had their beginning in the soil where they inhabited; assuming or receiving appellations conformable unto such conceits. *Why the Athenians did wear a golden Insect upon their head.* So did the *Athenians*, term themselves αὐτοχθόνες or *Aborigines*, and in testimony thereof did wear a golden Insect on their heads: the same name is also given unto the Inlanders, or *Midland* inhabitants of this Island by *Cæsar*. But this is a conceit answerable unto the generation of the Giants; not admittable in Philosophy, much less in Divinity, which distinctly informeth we are all the seed of *Adam*, that the whole world perished unto eight persons before the flood, and was after peopled by the *Colonies* of the sons of *Noah*. There was therefore never any *Autochthon*, or man arising from the earth but *Adam*; for the Woman being formed out of the rib, was once removed from earth, and framed from that Element under incarnation. And so although her production were not by copulation, yet was it in a manner seminal: For if in every part from whence the seed doth flow, there be contained the Idea of the whole; there was a seminality and contracted *Adam* in the rib, which by the information of a soul, was individuated into *Eve*. And therefore this conceit applied unto the Original of man, and the beginning of the world, is more justly appropriable unto its end. For then indeed men shall rise out of the earth: the graves shall shoot up their concealed seeds, and in that great Autumn, men shall spring up, and awake from their Chaos again.

Others have been so blind in deducing the Original of things, or delivering their own beginnings, that when it hath fallen into controversie, they have not recurred unto Chronologie or the Records of time: but betaken themselves unto probabilities, and the conjecturalities of Philosophy. Thus when the two ancient Nations, *Egyptians* and *Scythians*, contended for antiquity, the *Egyptians* pleaded their antiquity from the fertility of their soil, Diodor. Justin. inferring that men there first inhabited, where they were with most facility sustained; and such a land did they conceive was *Egypt*.

The *Scythians*, although a cold and heavier Nation urged more acutely, deducing their arguments from the two active Elements and Principles of all things, Fire and Water. For if of all things there was first an union, and that Fire over-ruled the rest: surely that part of earth which was coldest, would first get free, and afford a place of habitation. But if all the earth were first involved in Water, those parts would surely first appear, which were most high, and of most elevated situation, and such was theirs. These reasons carried indeed the antiquity from the *Egyptians*, but confirmed it not in the *Scythians*: for as *Herodotus* relateth from *Pargitaus*, their first King unto *Darius*, they accounted but two thousand years.

That men speak not by natural instinct, but by instruction and imitation.

As for the *Egyptians* they invented another way of trial; for as the same Author relateth, *Psammitichus* their King attempted this decision by a new and unknown experiment, bringing up two Infants with Goats, and where they never heard the voice of man; concluding that to be the ancientest Nation, whose language they should first deliver. But herein he forgot that speech was by instruction not instinct, by imitation, not by nature, that men do speak in some kind but like Parrets, and as they are instructed, that is, in simple terms and words, expressing the open notions of things; which the second act of Reason compoundeth into propositions, and the last into Syllogisms and Forms of ratiocination. And howsoever the account of *Manethon* the *Egyptian* Priest run very high, and it be evident that *Mizraim* peopled that Country (whose name with the *Hebrews* it beareth unto this day) and there be many things of great antiquity related in Holy Scripture, yet was their exact account not very ancient; for *Ptolomy* their Country-man beginning his Astronomical compute no higher than *Nabonasser*, who is conceived by some the same with *Salmanasser*. As for the argument deduced from the Fertility of the soil, duly enquired, it rather overthroweth than promoteth their antiquity; if that Country whose Fertility they so advance, was in ancient times no firm or open land, but some vast lake or part of the Sea, and became a gained ground by the mud and limous matter brought down by the River *Nilus*, which setled by degrees into a firm land. According as is expressed by *Strabo*, and more at large by *Herodotus*, both from the *Egyptian* tradition and probable inducements from reason, called therefore *fluvii donum*, an accession of earth, or tract of land acquired by the River.

Lastly, Some indeed there are, who have kept Records of time, and a considerable duration, yet do the exactest thereof afford no satisfaction concerning the beginning of the world, or any way point out the time of its creation. The most authentick Records and best approved antiquity are those of the *Chaldeans*; yet in the time of *Alexander* the Great, they attained not so high as the flood. For as *Simplicius* relateth, *Aristotle* required of *Calisthenes*, who accompanied that Worthy in his Expedition, that at his arrive at *Babylon*, he would enquire of the antiquity of their Records; and those upon compute he found to amount unto 1903 years; which account notwithstanding ariseth no higher than 95 years after the flood. The *Arcadians* I confess, were esteemed of great antiquity, and it was usually said they were before the Moon, according unto that of *Seneca*, *Sydus post veteres Arcades editum*; and that of *Ovid*, *Lunâ gens prior illa fuit*. But this as *Censorinus* observeth, must not be taken grosly, as though they were existent before that Luminary; but were so esteemed, because they observed a set course of year, before the *Greeks* conformed their year unto the course and motion of the Moon.

Thus the Heathens affording no satisfaction herein, they are most likely to manifest this truth, who have been acquainted with Holy Scripture, and the sacred Chronology delivered by *Moses*, who distinctly sets down this account, computing by certain intervails, by memorable *Æras*, *Epoches*, or terms of time. As from the Creation unto the flood, from thence unto *Abraham*, from *Abraham* unto the departure from *Egypt*, etc. Now in this number have only been *Samaritans*, *Jews* and *Christians*. **Different accounts upon Scripture concerning the Age of the World.** For the *Jews* they agree not in their accounts, as *Bodine* in his method of History hath observed out of *Baal Seder*, *Rabbi Nassom*, *Gersom*, and others; in whose compute the age of the World is not yet 5400 years. The same is more evidently observable from the two most learned *Jews*, *Philo* and *Josephus*; who very much differ in the accounts of time, and variously sum up these Intervails assented unto by all. Thus *Philo* from the departure out of *Egypt* unto the building of the Temple, accounts but 920 years, but *Josephus* sets down 1062. *Philo* from the building of the Temple to its destruction 440. *Josephus* 470. *Philo* from the Creation to the Destruction of the Temple 3373, but *Josephus* 3513. *Philo* from the Deluge to the Destruction of the Temple 1718, but *Josephus* 1913. In which Computes there are manifest disparities, and such as much divide the concordance and harmony of times.

For the *Samaritans*; their account is different from these or any others; for they account from the Creation to the Deluge, but 1302 years; which cometh to pass upon the different account of the ages of the Patriarchs set down when they begat children. For whereas the *Hebrew*, *Greek* and *Latin* texts account *Jared* 162 when he begat *Enoch*, they account but 62, and so in others. Now the *Samaritans* were no incompetent Judges of times and the Chronology thereof; for they embraced the five books of *Moses*, and as it seemeth, preserved the Text with far more integrity then the *Jews*; who as *Tertullian*, *Chrysostom*, and others observe, did several wayes corrupt the same, especially in passages concerning the prophesies of Christ; So that as *Jerom* professeth, in his translation he was fain sometime to relieve himself by the *Samaritan* Pentateuch; as amongst others in that Text, *Deuteronomy* 27. *Maledictus omnis qui non permanserit in omnibus quæ scripta sunt in libro Legis.* From hence Saint *Paul* [Gal. 3.] inferreth there is no justification by the Law, and urgeth the Text according to the Septuagint. Now the Jews to afford a latitude unto themselves, in their copies expunged the word בל or Syncategorematical term *omnis*: wherein lieth the strength of the Law, and of the Apostles argument; but the *Samaritan* Bible retained it right, and answerable unto what the Apostle had urged.

As for Christians from whom we should expect the exactest and most concurring account, there is also in them a manifest disagreement, and such as is not easily reconciled. For first, the Latins accord not in their account: to omit the calculation of the Ancients, of *Austin, Bede,* and others, the Chronology of the Moderns doth manifestly dissent. *Josephus Scaliger,* whom *Helvicus* seems to follow, accounts the Creation in 765 of the *Julian* period; and from thence unto the Nativity of our Saviour alloweth 3947 years; but *Dionysius Petavius* a learned Chronologer dissenteth from this compute almost 40 years; placing the Creation in the 730 of the *Julian* period, and from thence unto the Incarnation accounteth 3983 years.

For the Greeks; their accounts are more anomalous: for if we recur unto ancient computes, we shall find that *Clemens Alexandrinus,* an ancient Father and *Præceptor* unto *Origen,* accounted from the Creation unto our Saviour, 5664 years; for in the first of his Stromaticks, he collecteth the time from *Adam* unto the death of *Commodus* to be 5858 years; now the death of *Commodus* he placeth in the year after Christ 194, which number deducted from the former, there remaineth 5664. *Theophilus* Bishop of *Antioch* accounteth unto the Nativity of Christ 5515, deduceable from the like way of compute, for in his first book *ad Autolychum,* he accounteth from *Adam* unto *Aurelius Verus* 5695 years; now that Emperour died in the year of our Lord 180, which deducted from the former sum, there remaineth 5515. *Julius Africanus,* an ancient Chronologer, accounteth somewhat less, that is, 5500. *Eusebius, Orosius* and others dissent not much from this, but all exceed five thousand.

The latter compute of the Greeks, as *Petavius* observeth, hath been reduced unto two or three accounts. The first accounts unto our Saviour 5501, and this hath been observed by *Nicephorus, Theophanes,* and *Maximus.* [By what account the world hath lasted 7154 years.] The other accounts 5509; and this of all at present is generally received by the Church of *Constantinople,* observed also by the *Moscovite,* as I have seen in the date of the Emperors letters; wherein this year of ours 1645 is from the year of the world 7154, which doth exactly agree unto this last account 5509, for if unto that sum be added 1645, the product will be 7154, by this Chronology are many Greek Authors to be understood; and thus is *Martinus Crusius* to be made out, when in his Turcogrecian history he delivers, the City of *Constantinople* was taken by the Turks in the year ϛϡξα; that is, 6961. Now according unto these Chronologists, the Prophecy of *Elias* the Rabbin, so much in request with the Jews, and in some credit also with Christians, that the world should last but six thousand years; unto these I say, it hath been long and out of memory disproved, for the Sabbatical and 7000 year wherein the world should end (as did the Creation on the seventh day) unto them is long ago expired; they are proceeding in the eight thousand year, and numbers exceeding those days which men have made the types and shadows of these. But certainly what *Marcus Leo* the Jew conceiveth of the end of the heavens, exceedeth the account of all that ever shall be; for though he conceiveth the Elemental frame shall end in the Seventh or Sabbatical Millenary, yet cannot he opinion the heavens and more durable part of the Creation shall perish before seven times seven, or 49, that is, the Quadrant of the other seven, and perfect Jubilee of thousands.

Thus may we observe the difference and wide dissent of mens opinions, and thereby the great incertainty in this establishment. The Hebrews not only dissenting from the Samaritans, the Latins from the Greeks, but every one from another. Insomuch that all can be in the right it is impossible; that any one is so, not with assurance determinable. And therefore as *Petavius* confesseth, to effect the same exactly without inspiration it is impossible, and beyond the Arithmetick of any but God himself. And therefore also what satisfaction may be obtained from those violent disputes, and eager enquirers in what day of the month the world began either of March or October; likewise in what face or position of the Moon, whether at the prime or full, or soon after, let our second and serious considerations determine.

The cause of so different accounts about the age of the world.

Now the reason and ground of this dissent, is the unhappy difference between the Greek and Hebrew Editions of the Bible, for unto these two Languages have all translations conformed; the holy Scripture being first delivered in Hebrew, and first translated into Greek. For the Hebrew; it seems the primitive and surest text to rely on, and to preserve the same entire and uncorrupt there hath been used the highest caution humanity could invent. For as *R. Ben. Maimon* hath declared, if in the copying thereof one letter were written twice, or if one letter but touched another, that copy was not admitted into their Synagogues, but only allowable to be read in Schools and private families. Neither were they careful only in the exact number of their Sections of the Law, but had also the curiosity to number every word, and affixed the account unto their several books. *Corruption even in the Hebrew Text of the Bible.* Notwithstanding all which, divers corruptions ensued, and several depravations slipt in, arising from many and manifest grounds, as hath been exactly noted by *Morinus* in his preface unto the Septuagint.

As for the Septuagint, it is the first and most ancient Translation; and of greater antiquity than the Chaldee version; occasioned by the request of *Ptolomeus Philadelphus*, King of *Egypt*, for the ornament of his memorable Library; unto whom the high Priest addressed six Jews out of every Tribe, which amounteth unto 72; and by these was effected that Translation we usually term the Septuagint, or Translation of seventy. *The Credit of the Septuagint translation.* Which name, however it obtain from the number of their persons, yet in respect of one common Spirit, it was the Translation but as it were of one man; if as the story relateth, although they were set apart and severed from each other, yet were their Translations found to agree in every point, according as is related by *Philo* and *Josephus*; although we find not the same in *Aristæas*, *Aristeas ad Philocratorem de 72 interpretibus.* who hath expresly treated thereof. But of the Greek compute there have passed some learned dissertations not many years ago, wherein the learned *Isacius Vossius* makes the nativity of the world to anticipate the common account one thousand four hundred and forty years.

This Translation in ancient times was of great authority, by this many of the Heathens received some notions of the Creation and the mighty works of God; This in express terms is often followed by the Evangelists, by the Apostles, and by our Saviour himself in the quotations of the Old Testament. This for many years was used by the Jews themselves, that is, such as did Hellenize and dispersedly dwelt out of Palestine with the Greeks; and this also the succeeding Christians and ancient Fathers observed; although there succeeded other Greek versions, that is, of *Aquila, Theodosius* and *Symmachus*; for the Latin translation of *Jerom*, called now the Vulgar, was about 800 years after the Septuagint; although there was also a Latin translation before, called the Italick version. Which was after lost upon the general reception of the translation of Saint *Jerom*. *Præfat. in Paralipom.* Which notwithstanding (as he himself acknowledgeth) had been needless, if the Septuagint copys had remained pure, and as they were first translated. But, (beside that different copys were used, that *Alexandria* and *Egypt* followed the copy of *Hesychius, Antioch* and *Constantinople* that of *Lucian* the Martyr, and others that of *Origen*) the Septuagint was much depraved, not only from the errors of Scribes, and the emergent corruptions of time, but malicious contrivance of the Jews; as *Justin Martyr* hath declared, in his learned dialogue *Tryphon*, and *Morinus* hath learnedly shewn from many confirmations.

De Hebræi et Græci textus sinceritate.

Whatsoever Interpretations there have been since, have been especially effected with reference unto these, that is, the Greek and Hebrew text, the Translators sometimes following the one, sometimes adhering unto the other, according as they found them consonant unto truth, or most correspondent unto the rules of faith. Now however it cometh to pass, these two are very different in the enumeration of Genealogies, and particular accounts of time; for in the second intervail, that is, between the Flood and *Abraham*, there is by the Septuagint introduced one *Cainan* to be the son of *Arphaxad* and father of *Salah*; whereas in the Hebrew there is no mention of such a person, but *Arphaxad* is set down to be the father of *Salah*. But in the first intervail, that is, from the Creation unto the Flood, their disagreement is more considerable; for therein the Greek exceedeth the Hebrew, and common account almost 600 years. And 'tis indeed a thing not very strange, to be at the difference of a third part, in so large and collective an account, if we consider how differently they are set forth in minor and less mistakable numbers. So in the Prophesie of *Jonah*, both in the Hebrew and Latin text, it is said, Yet forty dayes and *Ninevy* shall be overthrown: But the Septuagint saith plainly, and that in letters at length, τρεῖς ἡμέρας that is, yet three dayes and *Ninevy* shall be destroyed. Which is a difference not newly crept in, but an observation very ancient, discussed by *Austin* and *Theodoret*, and was conceived an error committed by the Scribe. Men therefore have raised different computes of time, according as they have followed their different texts; and so have left the history of times far more perplexed than Chronology hath reduced.

Again, However the texts were plain, and might in their numerations agree, yet were there no small difficulty to set down a determinable Chronology, or establish from whence any fixed point of time. For the doubts concerning the time of the Judges are inexplicable; that of the Reigns and succession of Kings is as perplexed; it being uncertain whether the years both of their lives and reigns ought to be taken as compleat, or in their beginning and but currant accounts. Nor is it unreasonable to make some doubt whether in the first ages and long lives of our fathers, *Moses* doth not sometime account by full and round numbers, whereas strictly taken they might be some few years above or under; as in the age of *Noah*, it is delivered to be just five hundred when he begat *Sem*; whereas perhaps he might be somewhat above or below that round and compleat number. For the same way of speech is usual in divers other expressions: Thus do we say the Septuagint, and using the full and articulate number, do write the Translation of Seventy; whereas we have shewn before, the precise number was Seventy two. So is it said that Christ was three days in the grave; according to that of *Mathew*, as *Jonas* was three days and three nights in the Whales belly, so shall the Son of man be three days and three nights in the heart of the earth: which notwithstanding must be taken Synecdochically; or by understanding a part for an whole day; for he remained but two nights in the grave; for he was buried in the afternoon of the first day, and arose very early in the morning on the third; that is, he was interred in the eve of the Sabbath, and arose in the morning after it.

Moreover although the number of years be determined and rightly understood, and there be without doubt a certain truth herein; yet the text speaking obscurely or dubiously, there is ofttimes no slender difficulty at what point to begin or terminate the account. So when it is said *Exod.* 12. the sojourning of the children of *Israel* who dwelt in *Egypt* was 430 years, it cannot be taken strictly, and from their first arrival into Egypt, for their habitation in that land was far less; but the account must begin from the Covenant of God with *Abraham*, and must also comprehend their sojourn in the land of *Canaan*, according as is expressed, *Gal.* 3. The Covenant that was confirmed before of God in Christ, the Law which was 430 years after cannot disanul. Thus hath it also happened in the account of the 70 years of their captivity, according to that of *Jeremy*, Chap. 20. This whole land shall be a desolation, and these nations shall serve the King of *Babylon* 70 years. Now where to begin or end this compute, ariseth no small difficulties; for there were three remarkable captivities and deportations of the Jews. The first was in the third or fourth year of *Joachim*, and first of *Nabuchodonozor*, when *Daniel* was carried away; the second in the reign of *Ieconiah*, and the eighth year of the same King; the third and most deplorable to the reign of *Zedechias* and in the nineteenth year of *Nabuchodonozor*, whereat both the Temple and City were burned. Now such is the different conceit of these times, that men have computed from all; but the probablest account and most concordant unto the intention of *Ieremy*, is from the first of *Nabuchodonozor* unto the first of King *Cyrus* over *Babylon*; although the Prophet *Zachary* Chap. 1. 12. accounteth from the last. O Lord of hosts, How Long! Wilt thou not have mercy on *Ierusalem*, against which thou hast had indignation these threescore and ten years? for he maketh this expostulation in the second year of *Darius Histaspes*, wherein he prophesied, which is about eighteen years in account after the other.

The difficulties of Daniels 70 Weeks.

Thus also although there be a certain truth therein, yet is there no easie doubt concerning the seventy weeks, or seventy times seven years of *Daniel*; whether they have reference unto the nativity or passion of our Saviour, and especially from whence, or what point of time they are to be computed. For thus is it delivered by the Angel *Gabriel*: Seventy weeks are determined upon the people; and again in the following verse: Know therefore and understand, that from the going forth of the Commandment to restore and to build *Ierusalem* unto the Messias the Prince, shall be seven weeks, and threescore and two weeks, the street shall be built again, and the wall even in troublesome times; and after threescore and two weeks shall Messiah be cut off. Now the going out of the Commandment to build the City, being the point from whence to compute, there is no slender controversie when to begin. For there are no less than four several Edicts to this effect, the one in the first year of *Cyrus*, the other in the second of *Darius*, the third and fourth in the seventh, and in the twentieth of *Artaxerxes Longimanus*; although as *Petavius* accounteth, it best accordeth unto the twenty year of *Artaxerxes*, from whence *Nehemiah* deriveth his Commission. Of our Bless. Saviours age at his Passion. Now that computes are made uncertainly with reference unto Christ, it is no wonder, since I perceive the time of his Nativity is in controversie, and no less his age at his Passion. For *Clemens* and *Tertullian* conceive he suffered at thirty; but *Irenæus* a Father neerer his time, is further off in his account, that is, between forty and fifty.

Longomontanus a late Astronomer, endeavours to discover this secret from Astronomical grounds, that is, the Apogeum of the Sun; conceiving the Excentricity invariable, and the Apogeum yearly to move one scruple, two seconds, fifty thirds, etc. Wherefore if in the time of *Hipparchus*, that is, in the year of the *Iulian* period 4557 it was in the fifth degree of *Gemini*, and in the daies of *Tycho Brahe*, that is in the year of our Lord 1588, or of the world 5554, the same was removed unto the fift degree of *Cancer*; by the proportion of its motion, it was at the Creation first in the beginning of *Aries*, and the Perigeum or nearest point in *Libra*. But this conceit how ingenious or subtile soever, is not of satisfaction; it being not determinable, or yet agreed in what time precisely the Apogeum absolveth one degree, as *Petavius* De Doctrina temporum 1.4. hath also delivered.

Lastly, However these or other difficulties intervene, and that we cannot satisfie our selves in the exact compute of time, yet may we sit down with the common and usual account; nor are these differences derogatory unto the Advent or Passion of Christ, unto which indeed they all do seem to point, for the Prophecies concerning our Saviour were indefinitely delivered before that of *Daniel*; so was that pronounced unto *Eve* in paradise, that after of *Balaam*, those of *Isaiah* and the Prophets, and that memorable one of *Iacob*, the Scepter shall not depart from *Israel* untill *Shilo* come; which time notwithstanding it did not define at all. In what year therefore soever, either from the destruction of the Temple, from the re-edifying thereof, from the flood, or from the Creation he appeared, certain it is, that in the fulness of time he came. When he therefore came is not so considerable, as that he is come: in the one there is consolation, in the other no satisfaction. The greater Quere is, when he will come again; and yet indeed it is no Quere at all: for that is never to be known, and therefore vainly enquired: 'tis a professed and authentick obscurity, unknown to all but to the omniscience of the Almighty. Certainly the ends of things are wrapt up in the hands of God, he that undertakes the knowledge thereof, forgets his own beginning, and disclaims his principles of earth. No man knows the end of the world, nor assuredly of any thing in it: God sees it, because unto his Eternity it is present; he knoweth the ends of us, but not of himself: and because he knows not this, he knoweth all things, and his knowledge is endless, even in the object of himself.

CHAPTER II
Of mens Enquiries in what season or Point of the Zodiack it began, that as they are generally made, they are in vain, and as particularly, uncertain.

The world began in all the four quarters of the year.

Concerning the Seasons, that is, the quarters of the year, some are ready to enquire, others to determine, in what season, whether in the Autumn, Spring, Winter or Summer the World had its beginning. Wherein we affirm, that as the question is generally, and in respect of the whole earth proposed, it is with manifest injury unto reason in any particular determined; because when ever the world had its beginning it was created in all these four. For, as we have elsewhere delivered, whatsoever sign the Sun possesseth (whose recess or vicinity defineth the quarters of the year) those four seasons were actually existent; it being the nature of that Luminary to distinguish the several seasons of the year; all which it maketh at one time in the whole earth, and successively in any part thereof. Thus if we suppose the Sun created in Libra, in which sign unto some it maketh Autumn; at the same time it had been Winter unto the Northern-pole, for unto them at that time the Sun beginneth to be invisible, and to shew it self again unto the Pole of the South. Unto the position of a right Sphere or directly under the Æquator, it had been Summer; for unto that situation the Sun is at that time vertical. Unto the latitude of Capricorn, or the Winter Solstice it had been Spring; for unto that position it had been in a middle point, and that of ascent, or approximation, but unto the latitude of Cancer or the Summer Solstice it had been Autumn; for then had it been placed in a middle point, and that of descent, or elongation.

And if we shall take it literally what *Moses* described popularly, this was also the constitution of the first day. For when it was evening unto one longitude, it was morning unto another; when night unto one, day unto another. And therefore that question, whether our Saviour shall come again in the twilight (as is conceived he arose) or whether he shall come upon us in the night, according to the comparison of a thief, or the *Jewish* tradition, that he will come about the time of their departure out of *Ægypt*, when they eat the Passover, and the Angel passed by the doors of their houses; this Quere I say needeth not further dispute. For if the earth be almost every where inhabited, and his coming (as Divinity affirmed) must needs be unto all; then must the time of his appearance be both in the day and night. For if unto *Jerusalem*, or what part of the world soever he shall appear in the night, at the same time unto the *Antipodes*, it must be day; if twilight unto them, broad day unto the *Indians*; if noon unto them, yet night unto the *Americans*: and so with variety according unto various habitations, or different positions of the Sphere, as will be easily conceived by those who understand the affections of different habitations, and the conditions of *Antæci*, *Periæci*, and *Antipodes*. And so although he appear in the night, yet may the day of Judgement or Dooms-day well retain that name; for that implieth one revolution of the Sun, which maketh the day and night, and that one natural day. Νυχθήμερον And yet to speak strictly, if (as the Apostle affirmeth) we shall be changed in the twinckling of an eye (and as the Schools determine) the destruction of the world shall not be successive but in an instant; we cannot properly apply thereto the usual distinctions of time; called that twelve hours, which admits not the parts thereof, or use at all the name of time, when the nature thereof shall perish.

But if the enquiry be made unto a particular place, and the question determined unto some certain Meridian; as namely, unto *Mesopotamia* wherein the seat of paradice is presumed, the Query becomes more reasonable, and is indeed in nature also determinable. Yet positively to define that season, there is no slender difficulty; for some contend that it began in the Spring; as (beside *Eusebius*, *Ambrose*, *Bede*, and *Theodoret*) some few years past *Henrico Philippi* in his Chronology of the Scripture. Others are altogether for Autumn; and from hence do our Chronologers commence their compute; as may be observed in *Helvicus*, *Jo. Scaliger*, *Calvisius*, and *Petavius*.

CHAPTER III

Of the Divisions of the seasons and four Quarters of the year, according unto Astronomers and Physitians; that the common compute of the Ancients, and which is still retained by some is very questionable.

As for the divisions of the year, and the quartering out this remarkable standard of time, there have passed especially two distinctions; the first in frequent use with Astronomers, according to the cardinal intersections of the Zodiack, that is, the two Æquinoctials and both the Solstitial points; defining that time to be the Spring of the year, wherein the Sun doth pass from the Æquinox of Aries unto the Solstice of Cancer; the time between the Solstice and the Æquinox of Libra, Summer; from thence unto the Solstice of Capricornus, Autumn; and from thence unto the Æquinox of Aries again, Winter. Now this division although it be regular and equal, is not universal; for it includeth not those latitudes which have the seasons of the year double; as have the inhabitants under the Equator, or else between the Tropicks. *Between the Tropicks two Summers in a year.* For unto them the Sun is vertical twice a year, making two distinct Summers in the different points of verticality. So unto those which live under the Æquator, when the sun is in the Æquinox it is Summer, in which points it maketh Spring or Autumn unto us; and unto them it is also Winter when the Sun is in either Tropick; whereas unto us it maketh always Summer in the one. And the like will happen unto those habitations, which are between the Tropicks and the Æquator.

A second and more sensible division there is observed by *Hippocrates*, and most of the ancient *Greeks*, according to the rising and setting of divers stars; dividing the year, and establishing the account of seasons from usual alterations, and sensible mutations in the air, discovered upon the rising and setting of those stars, accounting the Spring from the Æquinoxial point of Aries; from the rising of the Pleiades, or the several stars on the back of Taurus, Summer; from the rising of Arcturus, a star between the thighs of Bootes, Autumn; and from the setting of the Pleiades, Winter. Of these divisions because they were unequal, they were fain to subdivide the two larger portions, that is of the Summer and Winter quarters; the first part of the Summer they named θέρος, the second unto the rising of the Dog-star, ὥρα, from thence unto the setting of Arcturus, ὀπώρα. The Winter they divided also into three parts; the first part, or that of seed time they named σπόρετον, the middle or proper Winter, χειμών, the last, which was their planting or grafting time φυταλίαν. This way of division was in former ages received, is very often mentioned in Poets, translated from one Nation to another; from the *Greeks* unto the *Latines* as is received by good Authors; and delivered by Physitians, even unto our times.

Now of these two, although the first in some latitude may be retained, yet is not the other in any to be admitted. For in regard of time (as we elsewhere declare) the stars do vary their longitudes, and consequently the times of their ascension and descension. That star which is the term of numeration, or point from whence we commence the account, altering his site and longitude in process of time, and removing from West to East, almost one degree in the space of 72 years, so that the same star, since the age of *Hippocrates* who used this account, is removed in *consequentia* about 27 degrees. Which difference of their longitudes, doth much diversifie the times of their ascents, and rendereth the account unstable which shall proceed thereby.

Again, In regard of different latitudes, this cannot be a setled rule, or reasonably applied unto many Nations. For whereas the setting of the Pleiades or seven stars, is designed the term of Autumn, and the beginning of Winter; unto some latitudes these stars do never set, as unto all beyond 67 degrees. And if in several and far distant latitudes we observe the same star as a common term of account unto both, we shall fall upon an unexpected, but an unsufferable absurdity; and by the same account it will be Summer unto us in the North, before it be so unto those, which unto us are Southward, and many degrees approaching nearer the Sun. For if we consult the Doctrine of the sphere, and observe the ascension of the Pleiades, which maketh the beginning of Summer, we shall discover that in the latitude of 40, these stars arise in the 16 degree of Taurus; but in the latitude of 50, they ascend in the eleventh degree of the same sign, that is, 5 dayes sooner; so shall it be Summer unto *London*, before it be unto *Toledo*, and begin to scorch in *England*, before it grow hot in *Spain*.

This is therefore no general way of compute, nor reasonable to be derived from one Nation unto another; the defect of which consideration hath caused divers errors in Latine poets, translating these expressions from the *Greeks*; and many difficulties even in the *Greeks* themselves; which living in divers latitudes, yet observed the same compute. So that to make them out, we are fain to use distinctions; sometime computing cosmically what they intended heliacally: and sometime in the same expression accounting the rising heliacally, the setting cosmically. Otherwise it will be hardly made out, what is delivered by approved Authors; and is an observation very considerable unto those which meet with such expressions, as they are very frequent in the poets of elder times, especially *Hesiod, Aratus, Virgil, Ovid, Manilius*; and Authors Geoponical, or which have treated *de re rustica*, as *Constantine, Marcus Cato, Columella, Palladius* and *Varro*.

Lastly, The absurdity in making common unto many Nations those considerations whose verity is but particular unto some, will more evidently appear, if we examine the Rules and Precepts of some one climate, and fall upon consideration with what incongruity they are transferrible unto others. Thus is it advised by *Hesiod*.

Pleiadibus Atlante natis orientibus
Incipe messem, Arationem vero occidentibus.

Implying hereby the Heliacal ascent and Cosmical descent of those stars. Now herein he setteth down a rule to begin harvest at the arise of the Pleiades; which in his time was in the beginning of *May*. This indeed was consonant unto the clime wherein he lived, and their harvest began about that season: but is not appliable unto our own, for therein we are so far from expecting an harvest, that our Barley-seed is not ended. Again, correspondent unto the rule of *Hesiod*, *Virgil* affordeth another,

Ante tibi Eoæ Atlantides abscondantur,
Debita quam sulcis committas semina.

Understanding hereby their Cosmical descent, or their setting when the Sun ariseth, and not their Heliacal obscuration, or their inclusion in the lustre of the Sun, as *Servius* upon this place would have it; for at that time these stars are many signs removed from that luminary. Now herein he strictly adviseth, not to begin to sow before the setting of these stars; which notwithstanding without injury to agriculture, cannot be observed in *England*; for they set unto us about the 12 of November, when our Seed-time is almost ended.

And this diversity of clime and cœlestial observations, precisely observed unto certain stars and moneths, hath not only overthrown the deductions of one Nation to another, but hath perturbed the observation of festivities and statary Solemnities, even with the *Jews* themselves. For unto them it was commanded that at their entrance into the land of *Canaan*, in the fourteenth of the first moneth (that is *Abib* or *Nisan* which is Spring with us) they should observe the celebration of the Passover; and on the morrow after, which is the fifteenth day, the feast of unleavened bread; and in the sixteenth of the same moneth, that they should offer the first sheaf of the harvest. Now all this was feasible and of an easie possibility in the land of *Canaan*, or latitude of *Jerusalem*; for so it is observed by several Authors in later times; and is also testified by holy Scripture in times very far before. For when the children of *Israel* passed the river *Jordan*, Josh. 3. it is delivered by way of parenthesis, that the river overfloweth its banks in the time of harvest; which is conceived the time wherein they passed; and it is after delivered, Josh. 5. that in the fourteenth day they celebrated the Passover: which according to the Law of *Moses* was to be observed in the first moneth, or moneth of *Abib*.

And therefore it is no wonder, what is related by *Luke*, that the Disciples upon the *Deuteroproton*, as they passed by, plucked the ears of corn. What the Sabbaton *Deuteroproton*, Luk. 6. was. For the *Deuteroproton* or second first Sabbath, was the first

Sabbath after the Deutera or second of the Passover, which was the sixteenth of *Nisan* or *Abib*. And this is also evidenced from the received construction of the first and latter rain. I will give you the rain of your land in his due season, the first rain and the latter rain. *Deut.* 11. For the first rain fell upon the seed-time about October, and was to make the seed to root, the latter was to fill the ear, and fell in Abib or March, the first moneth: according as is expressed. *Joel* 2. And he will cause to come down for you the rain, the former rain and the latter rain in the first moneth; that is the moneth of *Abib* wherein the Passover was observed. This was the Law of *Moses*, and this in the land of *Canaan* was well observed, according to the first institution: but since their dispersion and habitation in Countries, whose constitutions admit not such tempestivity of harvests; and many not before the latter end of Summer; notwithstanding the advantage of their Lunary account, and intercalary moneth Veader, affixed unto the beginning of the year, there will be found a great disparity in their observations; nor can they strictly and at the same season with their forefathers observe the commands of God.

To add yet further, those Geoponical rules and precepts of Agriculture which are delivered by divers Authors, are not to be generally received; but respectively understood unto climes whereto they are determined. For whereas one adviseth to sow this or that grain at one season, a second to set this or that at another, it must be conceived relatively, and every Nation must have its Country Farm; for herein we may observe a manifest and visible difference, not only in the seasons of harvest, but in the grains themselves. For with us Barley-harvest is made after wheat-harvest, but with the *Israelites* and *Ægyptians* it was otherwise; so is it expressed by way of priority, *Ruth* the 2. So *Ruth* kept fast by the maidens of *Boaz* to glean unto the end of Barley-harvest and of Wheat-harvest, which in the plague of hayl in *Ægypt* is more plainly delivered, *Exod.* 9. And the Flax and the Barley were smitten, for the Barley was in the ear and the Flax was bolled, but the Wheat and the Rye were not smitten, for they were not grown up.

And thus we see the account established upon the arise or descent of the stars can be no reasonable rule unto distant Nations at all, and by reason of their retrogression but temporary unto any one. Nor must these respective expressions be entertained in absolute considerations; for so distinct is the relation, and so artificial the habitude of this inferiour globe unto the superiour, and even of one thing in each unto the other, that general rules are dangerous, and applications most safe that run with security of circumstance. Which rightly to effect, is beyond the subtlety of sense, and requires the artifice of reason.

CHAPTER IV
Of some computation of days and deductions of one part of the year unto another.
That the days decrease and increase unequally.

Fourthly, There are certain vulgar opinions concerning days of the year, and conclusions popularly deduced from certain days of the moneth: men commonly believing the days increase and decrease equally in the whole year: which notwithstanding is very repugnant unto truth. For they increase in the moneth of March, almost as much as in the two moneths of January and February: and decrease as much in September, as they do in July and August. For the days increase or decrease according to the declination of the Sun, that is, its deviation Northward or Southward from the Æquator. Now this digression is not equal but near the Æquinoxial intersections, it is right and greater, near the Solstices more oblique and lesser. So from the eleventh of March the vernal Æquinox, unto the eleventh of April the Sun declineth to the North twelve degrees; from the eleventh of April unto the eleventh of May but eight, from thence unto the fifteenth of June, or the Summer Solstice but three and a half: all which make twenty two degrees and an half, the greatest declination of the Sun.

And this inequality in the declination of the Sun in the Zodiack or line of life, is correspondent unto the growth or declination of man. For setting out from infancy we increase not equally, or regularly attain to our state or perfection: nor when we descend from our state, is our declination equal, or carrieth us with even paces unto the grave. For as *Hippocrates* affirmeth, a man is hottest in the first day of his life, and coldest in the last: his natural heat setteth forth most vigorously at first, and declineth most sensibly at last. *The natural proportion of humane growth, etc. In the world,* And so though the growth of man end not perhaps until twenty one, yet is his stature more advanced in the first septenary than in the second, and in the second, more than in the third, and more indeed in the first seven years, than in the fourteen succeeding; for what stature we attain unto at seven years, we do sometimes but double, most times come short of at one and twenty. And so do we decline again: For in the latter age upon the Tropick and first descension from our solstice, we are scarce sensible of declination: but declining further, our decrement accelerates, we set apace, and in our last days precipitate into our graves. *and in the womb.* And thus are also our progressions in the womb, that is, our formation, motion, our birth or exclusion. For our formation is quickly effected, our motion appeareth later, and our exclusion very long after: if that be true which *Hippocrates* and *Avicenna* have declared, that the time of our motion is double unto that of formation, and that of exclusion treble unto that of motion. As if the Infant be formed at thirty five days, it moveth at seventy, and is born the two hundred and tenth day, that is, the seventh month; or if it receives not formation before forty five days, it moveth the ninetieth day, and is excluded in the two hundred and seventy, that is, the ninth month.

There are also certain popular prognosticks drawn from festivals in the Calender, and conceived opinions of certain days in months; so is there a general tradition in most parts of *Europe*, that inferreth the coldness of succeeding winter from the shining of the Sun upon *Candlemas* day, or the Purification of the Virgin *Mary*, according to the proverbial distich,

Si Sol splendescat Mariâ purificante,
Major erit glacies post festum quam fuit ante.

So is it usual among us to qualifie and conditionate the twelve months of the year, answerably unto the temper of the twelve days in *Christmas*; and to ascribe unto March certain borrowed days from April; all which men seem to believe upon annual experience of their own, and the received traditions of their fore-fathers.

Now it is manifest, and most men likewise know, that the Calenders of these computers, and the accounts of these days are very different; the Greeks dissenting from the Latins, and the Latins from each other; the one observing the *Julian* or ancient account, as great *Britain* and part of *Germany*; the other adhering to the *Gregorian* or new account, as *Italy*, *France*, *Spain*, and the united Provinces of the Netherlands. Now this later account by ten days at least anticipateth the other; so that before the one beginneth the account, the other is past it; yet in the several calculations, the same events seem true, and men with equal opinion of verity, expect and confess a confirmation from them all. Whereby is evident the Oraculous authority of tradition, and the easie seduction of men, neither enquiring into the verity of the substance, nor reforming upon repugnance of circumstance.

And thus may divers easily be mistaken who superstitiously observe certain times, or set down unto themselves an observation of unfortunate months, or dayes, or hours; As did the *Egyptians*, two in every month, and the *Romans*, the days after the Nones, Ides and Calends. And thus the Rules of Navigators must often fail, setting down, as *Rhodiginus* observeth, suspected and ominous days in every month, as the first and seventh of March, the fift and sixt of April, the sixt, the twelfth and fifteenth of February. For the accounts hereof in these months are very different in our days, and were different with several Nations in Ages past; and how strictly soever the account be made, and even by the self-same Calender, yet is it possible that Navigators may be out. For so were the Hollanders, who passing Westward through *fretum le Mayre*, and compassing the Globe, upon their return into their own Country, found that they had lost a day. For if two men at the same time travel from the same place, the one Eastward, the other Westward round about the earth, and meet in the same place from whence the first set forth; it will so fall out, that he which hath moved Eastward against the diurnal motion of the Sun, by anticipating dayly something of its circle with his own motion, will gaine one day; but he that travelleth Westward, with the motion of the Sun, by seconding its revolution, shall lose or come short a day. And therefore also upon these grounds that *Delos* was seated in the middle of the earth, it was no exact decision, because two Eagles let fly East and West by *Jupiter*, their meeting fell out just in the Island *Delos*.

CHAPTER V
A Digression of the wisdom of God in the site and motion of the Sun.

Having thus beheld the ignorance of man in some things, his error and blindness in others, that is, in the measure of duration both of years and seasons, let us a while admire the Wisdom of God in this distinguisher of times, and visible Deity (as some have termed it) the Sun. Which though some from its glory adore, and all for its benefits admire, we shall advance from other considerations, and such as illustrate the artifice of its Maker. Nor do we think we can excuse the duty of our knowledge, if we only bestow the flourish of Poetry hereon, or those commendatory conceits which popularly set forth the eminency of this creature; except we ascend unto subtiler considerations, and such as rightly understood, convincingly declare the wisdom of the Creator. Which since a Spanish Physitian *Valerius de Philos. Sacr.* hath begun, we will enlarge with our deductions; and this we shall endeavour from two considerations; its proper situation, and wisely ordered motion.

And first we cannot pass over his providence, in that it moveth at all; for had it stood still, and were it fixed like the earth, there had been then no distinction of times, either of day or year, of Spring, of Autumn, of Summer, or of Winter; for these seasons are defined by the motions of the Sun; when that approacheth neare our Zenith, or vertical Point, we call it Summer, when furthest off, Winter, when in the middle spaces, Spring or Autumn, whereas remaining in one place these distinctions had ceased, and consequently the generation of all things depending on their vicissitudes; making in one hemisphere a perpetual Summer, in the other a deplorable and comfortless Winter. *What the natural day is.* And thus had it also been continual day unto some, and perpetual night unto others; for the day is defined by the abode of the Sun above the Horizon, and the night by its continuance below; so should we have needed another Sun, one to illustrate our Hemisphere, a second to enlighten the other; which inconvenience will ensue in what site soever we place it, whether in the Poles, or the Æquator, or between them both; no spherical body of what bigness soever illuminating the whole sphere of another, although it illuminate something more than half of a lesser, according unto the doctrine of the Opticks.

Every part of the Earth habitable.

His wisdom is again discernable, not only in that it moveth at all, and in its bare motion, but wonderful in contriving the line of its revolution; which is so prudently effected, that by a vicissitude in one body and light it sufficeth the whole earth, affording thereby a possible or pleasurable habitation in every part thereof; and this is the line Eclipthick; all which to effect by any other circle it had been impossible. For first, if we imagine the Sun to make his course out of the Eclipthick, and upon a line without any obliquity, let it be conceived within that Circle, that is either on the Æquator, or else on either side: (For if we should place it either in the Meridian or Colures, beside the subversion of its course from East to West, there would ensue the like incommodities.) Now if we conceive the sun to move between the obliquity of this Eclipthick in a line upon one side of the Æquator, then would the Sun be visible but unto one pole, that is the same which was nearest unto it. So that unto the one it would be perpetual day; unto the other perpetual night; the one would be oppressed with constant heat, the other with insufferable cold; and so the defect of alternation would utterly impugn the generation of all things; which naturally require a vicissitude of heat to their production, and no less to their increase and conservation.

But if we conceive it to move in the Æquator; first unto a parallel sphere, or such as have the pole for their Zenith, it would have made neither perfect day nor night. For being in the Æquator it would intersect their Horizon, and be half above and half beneath it: or rather it would have made perpetual night to both; for though in regard of the rational Horizon, which bisecteth the Globe into equal parts, the Sun in the Æquator would intersect the Horizon: yet in respect of the sensible Horizon (which is defined by the eye) the Sun would be visible unto neither. For if as ocular witnesses report, and some also write, by reason of the convexity of the Earth, the eye of man under the Æquator cannot discover both the poles; neither would the eye under the poles discover the Sun in the Æquator. Thus would there nothing fructifie either near or under them: The Sun being Horizontal to the poles, and of no considerable altitude unto parts a reasonable distance from them. Again, unto a right sphere, or such as dwell under the Æquator, although it made a difference in day and night, yet would it not make any distinction of seasons: for unto them it would be constant Summer, it being alwaies vertical, and never deflecting from them: So had there been no fructification at all, and the Countries subjected would be as uninhabitable, as indeed antiquity conceived them.

Lastly, It moving thus upon the Æquator, unto what position soever, although it had made a day, yet could it have made no year: for it could not have had those two motions now ascribed unto it, that is, from East to West, whereby it makes the day, and likewise from West to East, whereby the year is computed. For according to received Astronomy, the poles of the Æquator are the same with those of the *Primum Mobile*. Now it is impossible that on the same circle, having the same poles, both these motions from opposite terms should be at the same time performed; all which is salved, if we allow an obliquity in his annual motion, and conceive him to move upon the Poles of the Zodiack, distant from these of the world 23 degrees and an half. Thus may we discern the necessity of its obliquity, and how inconvenient its motion had been upon a circle parallel to the Æquator, or upon the Æquator it self.

Now with what Providence this obliquity is determined, we shall perceive upon the ensuing inconveniences from any deviation. For first, if its obliquity had been less (as instead of twenty three degrees, twelve or the half thereof) the vicissitude of seasons appointed for the generation of all things, would surely have been too short; for different seasons would have hudled upon each other; and unto some it had not been much better than if it had moved on the Æquator.

But had the obliquity been greater than now it is, as double, or of 40 degrees; several parts of the earth had not been able to endure the disproportionable differences of seasons, occasioned by the great recess, and distance of the Sun. For unto some habitations the Summer would have been extream hot, and the Winter extream cold; likewise the Summer temperate unto some, but excessive and in extremity unto others, as unto those who should dwell under the Tropick of Cancer, as then would do some part of *Spain*, or ten degrees beyond, as *Germany*, and some part of *England*; who would have Summers as now the *Moors* of *Africa*. For the Sun would sometime be vertical unto them: but they would have Winters like those beyond the Artick Circle; for in that season the Sun would be removed above 80 degrees from them. Again, it would be temperate to some habitations in the Summer, but very extream in the Winter: temperate to those in two or three degrees beyond the Artick Circle, as now it is unto us; for they would be equidistant from that Tropick, even as we are from this at present. But the Winter would be extream, the Sun being removed above an hundred degrees, and so consequently would not be visible in their Horizon, no position of sphere discovering any star distant above 90 degrees, which is the distance of every Zenith from the Horizon. And thus if the obliquity of this Circle had been less, the vicissitude of seasons had been so small as not to be distinguished; if greater, so large and disproportionable as not to be endured.

A competent distinction of seasons necessary, and why.

Now for its situation, although it held this Ecliptick line, yet had it been seated in any other Orb, inconveniences would ensue of condition like the former; for had it been placed in the lowest sphere of the Moon, the year would have consisted but of one month; for in that space of time it would have passed through every part of the Ecliptick: so would there have been no reasonable distinction of seasons required for the generation and fructifying of all things; contrary seasons which destroy the effects of one another, so suddenly succeeding. Besides by this vicinity unto the earth, its heat had been intollerable; for if (as many affirm) there is a different sense of heat from the different points of its proper Orb, and that in the Apogeum or highest point (which happeneth in Cancer) it is not so hot under that Tropick, on this side the Æquator, as unto the other side in the Perigeum or lowest part of the Eccentrick (which happeneth in Capricornus) surely being placed in an Orb far lower, its heat would be unsufferable, nor needed we a fable to set the world on fire.

But had it been placed in the highest Orb, or that of the eighth sphere, there had been none but *Platoes* year, and a far less distinction of seasons; for one year had then been many, and according unto the slow revolution of that Orb which absolveth not his course in many thousand years, no man had lived to attain the account thereof. These are the inconveniences ensuing upon its situation in the extream orbs, and had it been placed in the middle orbs of the Planets, there would have ensued absurdities of a middle nature unto them.

Now whether we adhere unto the hypothesis of *Copernicus*, affirming the earth to move, and the Sun to stand still; or whether we hold, as some of late have concluded, from the spots in the Sun, which appear and disappear again; that besides the revolution it maketh with its Orbs, it hath also a dinetical motion, and rowls upon its own Poles, whether I say we affirm these or no, the illations before mentioned are not thereby infringed. We therefore conclude this contemplation, and are not afraid to believe, it may be literally said of the wisdom of God, what men will have but figuratively spoken of the works of Christ; that if the wonders thereof were duly described, the whole world, that is, all within the last circumference, would not contain them. For as his Wisdom is infinite, so cannot the due expressions thereof be finite, and if the world comprise him not, neither can it comprehend the story of him.

CHAPTER VI
Concerning the vulgar opinion, that the Earth was slenderly peopled before the Flood.

Beside the slender consideration men of latter times do hold of the first ages, it is commonly opinioned, and at first thought generally imagined, that the earth was thinly inhabited, at least not remotely planted before the flood; whereof there being two opinions, which seem to be of some extremity, the one too largely extending, the other too narrowly contracting the populosity of those times; we shall not pass over this point without some enquiry into it.

Now for the true enquiry thereof, the means are as obscure as the matter, which being naturally to be explored by History, Humane or Divine, receiveth thereby no small addition of obscurity. For as for humane relations, they are so fabulous in *Deucalions* flood, that they are of little credit about *Ogyges* and *Noahs*. For the Heathens (as *Varro* accounteth) make three distinctions of time: the first from the beginning of the world unto the general Deluge of *Ogyges*, they term *Adelon*, that is, a time not much unlike that which was before time, immanifest and unknown; because thereof there is almost nothing or very obscurely delivered: for though divers Authors have made some mention of the Deluge, as *Manethon* the *Egyptian* Priest, *Xenophon* de æquivocis, *Fabius Pictor* de Aureo seculo, *Mar. Cato* de originibus, and *Archilochus* the Greek, who introduceth also the Testimony of *Moses* in his fragment *de temporibus*: yet have they delivered no account of what preceded or went before. *Josephus* I confess in his Discourse against *Appion* induceth the antiquity of the *Jews* unto the flood, and before from the testimony of humane Writers; insisting especially upon *Maseus* of *Damascus*, *Jeronimus Ægyptius*, and *Berosus*; and confirming the long duration of their lives, not only from these, but the authority of *Hesiod*, *Erathius*, *Hellanicus* and *Agesilaus*. *Berosus* the *Chaldean* Priest, writes most plainly, mentioning the city of *Enos*, the name of *Noah* and his Sons, the building of the Ark, and also the place of its landing. And *Diodorus Siculus* hath in his third book a passage, which examined, advanceth as high as *Adam*: for the *Chaldeans*, saith he, derive the Original of their Astronomy and letters forty three thousand years before the Monarchy of *Alexander* the Great: now the years whereby they computed the antiquity of their letters, being as *Xenophon* interprets to be accounted Lunary: the compute will arise unto the time of *Adam*. For forty three thousand Lunary years make about three thousand six hundred thirty four years, which answereth the Chronology of time from the beginning of the world unto the reign of *Alexander*, as *Annius* of *Viterbo* computeth in his Comment upon *Berosus*.

The second space or interval of time is accounted from the flood unto the first Olympiad, that is, the year of the world 3174, which extendeth unto the days of *Isaiah* the Prophet, and some twenty years before the foundation of *Rome*: this they term *Mythicon* or fabulous, because the account thereof, especially of the first part, is fabulously or imperfectly delivered. Hereof some things have been briefly related by the Authors above mentioned: more particularly by *Dares*

Phrygius, Dictys Cretensis, Herodotus, Diodorus Siculus, and *Trogus Pompeius*; the most famous *Greek* Poets lived also in this interval, as *Orpheus, Linus, Musæus, Homer, Hesiod*; and herein are comprehended the grounds and first inventions of Poetical fables, which were also taken up by historical Writers, perturbing the *Chaldean* and *Egyptian* Records with fabulous additions; and confounding their names and stories, with their own inventions.

The third time succeeding until their present ages, they term *Historicon*, that is, such wherein matters have been more truly historified, and may therefore be believed. Of these times also have been written *Herodotus, Thucydides, Xenophon, Diodorus*; and both of these and the other preceding such as have delivered universal Histories or Chronologies; as (to omit *Philo*, whose Narrations concern the *Hebrews*) *Eusebius, Julius Africanus, Orosius, Ado* of *Vienna, Marianus Scotus, Historia tripartita, Urspergensis, Carion, Pineda, Salian,* and with us Sir *Walter Raleigh*.

Now from the first hereof that most concerneth us, we have little or no assistance; the fragments and broken records hereof inforcing not at all our purpose. And although some things not usually observed, may be from thence collected, yet do they not advantage our discourse, nor any way make evident the point in hand. For the second, though it directly concerns us not, yet in regard of our last medium and some illustrations therein, we shall be constrained to make some use thereof. As for the last, it concerns us not at all; for treating of times far below us, it can no way advantage us. And though divers in this last Age have also written of the first, as all that have delivered the general accounts of time, yet are their Tractates little auxiliary unto ours, nor afford us any light to detenebrate and clear this Truth.

As for holy Scripture and divine revelation, there may also seem therein but slender information, there being only left a brief narration hereof by *Moses*, and such as affords no positive determination. For the Text delivereth but two genealogies, that is, of *Cain* and *Seth*; in the line of *Seth* there are only ten descents, in that of *Cain* but seven, and those in a right line with mention of father and son; excepting that of *Lamech*, where is also mention of wives, sons, and a daughter. Notwithstanding if we seriously consider what is delivered therein, and what is also deducible, it will be probably declared what is by us intended, that is, the populous and ample habitation of the earth before the flood. Which we shall labour to induce not from postulates and entreated Maxims, but undeniable Principles declared in holy Scripture; that is, the length of mens lives before the flood, and the large extent of time from Creation thereunto.

We shall only first crave notice, that although in the relation of *Moses* there be very few persons mentioned, yet are there many more to be presumed; nor when the Scripture in the line of *Seth* nominates but ten persons, are they to be conceived all that were of this generation: The Scripture singly delivering the holy line, wherein the world was to be preserved, first in *Noah*, and afterward in our Saviour. For in this line it is manifest there were many more born than are named, for it is said of them all, that they begat sons and daughters. And whereas it is very late before it is said they begat those persons which are named in the Scripture, the soonest at 65, it must not be understood that they had none before; but not any in whom it pleased God the holy line should be continued. And although the expression that they begat sons and daughters be not determined to be before or after the mention of these, yet must it be before in some; for before it is said that *Adam* begat *Seth* at the 130 year, it is plainly affirmed that *Cain* knew his wife, and had a son; which must be one of the daughters of *Adam*, one of those whereof it is after said, he begat sons and daughters. And so for ought can be disproved there might be more persons upon earth then are commonly supposed, when *Cain* slew *Abel*; nor the fact so hainously to be aggravated in the circumstance of the fourth person living. And whereas it is said upon the nativity of *Seth*, God hath appointed me another seed instead of *Abel*, it doth not imply he had no other all this while; but not any of that expectation, or appointed (as his name applies) to make a progression in the holy line; in whom the world was to be saved, and from whom he should be born, that was mystically slain in *Abel*.

Now our first ground to induce the numerosity of people before the flood, is the long duration of their lives, beyond 7, 8, and 9, hundred years. Which how it conduceth unto populosity we shall make but little doubt, if we consider there are two main causes of numerosity in any kind or species, that is, a frequent and multiparous way of breeding, whereby they fill the world with others, though they exist not long themselves; or a long duration and subsistence, whereby they do not only replenish the world with a new annumeration of others, but also maintain the former account in themselves. From the first cause we may observe examples in creatures oviparous, as Birds and Fishes; in vermiparous, as Flies, Locusts, and Gnats; in animals also viviparous, as Swine and Conies. Of the first there is a great example in the herd of Swine in *Galilee*; although an unclean beast, and forbidden unto the *Jews*. Of the other a remarkable one in *Athenus*, in the Isle *Astipalea*, one of the Cyclades now called *Stampalia*, wherein from two that were imported, the number so increased, that the Inhabitants were constrained to have recourse unto the Oracle *Delphos*, for an invention how to destroy them.

Others there are which make good the paucity of their breed with the length and duration of their daies, whereof there want not examples in animals uniparous: *A Million of Beeves yearly killed in England.* First, in bisulcous or cloven-hooft, as Camels, and Beeves, whereof there is above a million annually slain in *England*. It is also said of *Job*, that he had a thousand yoak of Oxen, and six thousand Camels; and of the children of *Israel* passing into the land of *Canaan*, that they took from the *Midianites* threescore and ten thousand Beeves; and of the Army of *Semiramis*, that there were therein one hundred thousand Camels. For Solipeds or firm-hoofed animals, as Horses, Asses, Mules, etc., they are also in mighty numbers, so it is delivered that *Job* had a thousand she Asses: that the *Midianites* lost sixty one thousand Asses. For Horses it is affirmed by *Diodorus*, that *Ninus* brought against the *Bactrians* two hundred eighty thousand Horses; after him *Semiramis* five hundred thousand Horses, and Chariots one hundred thousand. Even in creatures steril and such as do not generate, the length of life conduceth much unto the multiplicity of the species; for the number of Mules which live far longer then their Dams or Sires, in Countries where they are bred, is very remarkable, and far more common then Horses.

For Animals multifidous, or such as are digitated or have several divisions in their feet, there are but two that are uniparous, that is, Men and Elephants; who though their productions be but single, are notwithstanding very numerous. The Elephant (as *Aristotle* affirmeth) carrieth the young two years, and conceiveth not again (as *Edvardus Lopez* affirmeth) in many after, yet doth their age requite this disadvantage; they living commonly one hundred, sometime two hundred years. Now although they be rare with us in *Europe*, and altogether unknown unto *America*, yet in the two other parts of the world they are in great abundance, as appears by the relation of *Gorcias ab Horto*, Physitian to the Viceroy at *Goa*, who relates that at one venation the King of *Sion* took four thousand; and is of opinion they are in other parts in greater number then herds of Beeves in *Europe*. And though this delivered from a *Spaniard* unacquainted with our Northern droves, may seem very far to exceed; yet must we conceive them very numerous, if we consider the number of teeth transported from one Country to another; they having only two great teeth, and those not falling or renewing.

As for man, the disadvantage in his single issue is the same with these, and in the lateness of his generation somewhat greater then any; yet in the continual and not interrupted time thereof, and the extent of his days, he becomes at present, if not then any other species, at least more numerous then these before mentioned. Now being thus numerous at present, and in the measure of threescore, fourscore or an hundred years, if their dayes extended unto six, seven, or eight hundred, their generations would be proportionably multiplied; their times of generation being not only multiplied, but their subsistence continued. For though the great Grand-child went on, the *Petrucius* *The term for that person from whom consanguineal relations are accounted, as in the Arbor civilis.* and first Original would subsist and make one of the world; though he outlived all the terms of consanguinity, and became a stranger unto his proper progeny. So by compute of Scripture *Adam* lived unto the ninth generation, unto the days of *Lamech* the Father of *Noah*; *Methuselah* unto the year of the flood; and *Noah* was contemporary unto all from *Enoch* unto *Abraham*. So that although some died, the father beholding so many descents, the number of Survivers must still be very great; for if half the men were now alive, which lived in the last Century, the earth would scarce contain their number. Whereas in our abridged and Septuagesimal Ages, it is very rare, and deserves a Distick Mater ait natæ dic natæ filia, etc. to behold the fourth generation. *Xerxes* complaint still remaining; and what he lamented in his Army, being almost deplorable in the whole world: men seldom arriving unto those years whereby *Methuselah* exceeded nine hundred, and what *Adam* came short of a thousand, was defined long ago to be the age of man.

Now although the length of days conduceth mainly unto the numerosity of mankind, and it be manifest from Scripture they lived very long, yet is not the period of their lives determinable, and some might be longer livers, than we account that any were. For (to omit that conceit of some, that *Adam* was the oldest man, in as much as he is conceived to be created in the maturity of mankind, that is, at 60, (for in that age it is set down they begat children) so that adding this number unto his 930, he was 21 years older than any of his posterity) that even *Methuselah* was the longest liver of all the children of *Adam*, we need not grant; nor is it definitively set down by *Moses*. Indeed of those ten mentioned in Scripture, with their severall ages it must be true; but whether those seven of the line of *Cain* and their progeny, or any of the sons or daughters posterity after them out-lived those, is not expressed in holy Scripture; and it will seem more probable, that of the line of *Cain* some were longer lived than any of *Seth*; if we concede that seven generations of the one lived as long as nine of the other. As for what is commonly alledged, that God would not permit the life of any unto a thousand, because (alluding unto that of *David*) no man should live one day in the sight of the Lord; although it be urged by divers, yet is it methinks an inference somewhat Rabbinicall; and not of power to perswade a serious examiner.

Having thus declared how powerfully the length of lives conduced unto populosity of those times, it will yet be easier acknowledged if we descend to particularities, and consider how many in seven hundred years might descend from one man; wherein considering the length of their dayes, we may conceive the greatest number to have been alive together. And this that no reasonable spirit may contradict, we will declare with manifest disadvantage; for whereas the duration of the world unto the flood was above 1600 years, we will make our compute in less then half that time. Nor will we begin with the first man, but allow the earth to be provided of women fit for marriage the second or third first Centuries; and will only take as granted, that they might beget children at sixty, and at an hundred years have twenty, allowing for that number forty years. Nor will we herein single out *Methuselah*, or account from the longest livers, but make choice of the shortest of any we find recorded in the Text, excepting *Enoch*; who after he had lived as many years as there be days in the year, was translated at 365. And thus from one stock of seven hundred years, multiplying still by twenty, we shall find the product to be one thousand, three hundred forty seven millions, three hundred sixty eight thousand, four hundred and twenty.

	1	20.
	2	400.
	3	8000.
Century	4	160,000.
	5	3,200,000.
	6	46,000,000.
	7	1,280,000,000.
Product		1,347,368,420.

Now if this account of the learned *Petavius* will be allowed, it will make an unexpected encrease, and a larger number than may be found in *Asia, Africa* and *Europe*; especially if in *Constantinople*, the greatest City thereof, there be no more of Europe than *Botero* accounteth, seven hundred thousand souls. Which duly considered, we shall rather admire how the earth contained its inhabitants, then doubt its inhabitation; and might conceive the deluge not simply penall, but in some way also necessary, as many have conceived of translations, if *Adam* had not sinned, and the race of man had remained upon earth immortal.

Now whereas some to make good their longevity, have imagined that the years of their compute were Lunary; unto these we must reply: That if by a Lunary year they understand twelve revolutions of the Moon, that is 354 days, eleven fewer then in the Solary year; there will be no great difference; at least not sufficient to convince or extenuate the question. But if by a Lunary year they mean one revolution of the Moon, that is, a moneth, they first introduce a year never used by the Hebrews in their Civil accompts; and what is delivered before of the Chaldean years (as *Xenophon* gives a caution) was only received in the Chronology of their Arts. Secondly, they contradict the Scripture, which makes a plain enumeration of many moneths in the account of the Deluge; for so is it expressed in the Text. In the tenth moneth, in the first day of the moneth were the tops of the mountains seen: Concordant whereunto is the relation of humane Authors, *Inundationes plures fuere, prima novimestris inundatio terrarum sub prisco Ogyge.* *Xenophon de Æquivocis.* *Meminisse hoc loco par est post primum diluvium Ogygi temporibus notatum, cum novem et amplius mensibus diem continua nox inumbrasset, Delon ante omnes terras radiis solis illuminatum sortitumque ex eo nomen.* Solinus. And lastly, they fall upon an absurdity, for they make *Enoch* to beget children about six years of age. For whereas it is said he begat *Methuselah* at 65, if we shall account every moneth a year, he was at that time some six years and an half, for so many moneths are contained in that space of time.

Having thus declared how much the length of mens lives conduced unto the populosity of their kind, our second foundation must be the large extent of time, from the Creation unto the Deluge, that is (according unto received computes about 1655 years) almost as long a time as hath passed since the nativity of our Saviour: and this we cannot but conceive sufficient for a very large increase, if we do but affirm what reasonable enquirers will not deny: That the earth might be as populous in that number of years before the flood, as we can manifest it was in the same number after. And whereas there may be conceived some disadvantage, in regard that at the Creation the original of mankind was in two persons, but after the flood their propagation issued at least from six; against this we might very well set the length of their lives before the flood, which were abbreviated after, and in half this space contracted into hundreds and threescores. Notwithstanding to equalize accounts, we will allow three hundred years, and so long a time as we can manifest from the Scripture. There were four men at least that begat children, *Adam, Cain, Seth*, and *Enos*; So shall we fairly and favourably proceed, if we affirm the world to have been as populous in sixteen hundred and fifty before the flood, as it was in thirteen hundred after. Now how populous and largely inhabited it was within this period of time, we shall declare from probabilities, and several testimonies of Scripture and humane Authors.

And first, To manifest the same neer those parts of the earth where the Ark is presumed to have rested, we have the relation of holy Scripture accounting the genealogy of *Japhet, Cham* and *Sem*, and in this last, four descents unto the division of the earth in the days of *Peleg*, which time although it were not upon common compute much above an hundred years, yet were men at this time mightily increased. Nor can we well conceive it otherwise, if we consider they began already to wander from their first habitation, and were able to attempt so mighty a work as the building of a City and a Tower, whose top should reach unto the heavens. Whereunto there was required no slender number of persons, if we consider the magnitude thereof, expressed by some, and conceived to be *Turris Beli* in *Herodotus*; and the multitudes of people recorded at the erecting of the like or inferiour structures: for at the building of *Solomons* Temple there were threescore and ten thousand that carried burdens, and fourscore thousand hewers in the mountains, beside the chief of his officers three thousand and three hundred; and at the erecting of the Piramids in the reign of King *Cheops*, as *Herodotus* reports, there were *decem myriads*, that is an hundred thousand *men*. And though it be said of the *Egyptians, Porrum et cæpe nefas violare et frangere morsu;* Juvenal. yet did the summes expended in Garlick and Onyons amount unto no less then one thousand six hundred Talents.

Who Nimrod *and* Assur *were.*

The first Monarchy or Kingdom of *Babylon* is mentioned in Scripture under the foundation of *Nimrod*, which is also recorded in humane history; as beside *Berosus*, in *Diodorus* and *Justine*, for *Nimrod* of the Scriptures is *Belus* of the Gentiles, and *Assur* the same with *Ninus* his successour. There is also mention of divers Cities, particularly of *Ninivey* and *Resen* expressed emphatically in the Text to be a great City.

That other Countries round about were also peopled, appears by the Wars of the Monarchs of *Assyria* with
the *Bactrians, Indians, Scythians, Ethiopians, Armenians, Hyrcanians, Parthians, Persians, Su sians*; they vanquishing (as *Diodorus* relateth) *Egypt, Syria*, and all *Asia* minor, even from *Bosphorus* unto *Tanais*. And it is said, that *Semiramis* in her expedition against the *Indians* brought along with her the King of *Arabia*. About the same time of the *Assyrian* Monarchy, do Authors place that of the *Sycionians* in *Greece*, and soon after that of the *Argives*, and not very long after, that of the *Athenians* under *Cecrops*; and within our period assumed are historified many memorable actions of the Greeks, as the expedition of the *Argonautes*, with the most famous Wars of *Thebes* and *Troy*.

That *Canaan* also and *Egypt* were well peopled far within this period, besides their plantation by *Canaan* and *Misraim*, appeareth from the history of *Abraham*, who in less then 400 years after the Flood, journied from *Mesopotamia* unto *Canaan* and *Egypt*, both which he found well peopled and policied into Kingdoms: wherein also in 430 years, from threescore and ten persons which came with *Jacob* into *Egypt*, he became a mighty Nation; for it is said, at their departure, there journeyed from *Rhamesis* to *Succoth* about six hundred thousand on foot, that were men, besides children. Now how populous the land from whence they came was, may be collected not only from their ability in commanding such subjections and mighty powers under them, but from the several accounts of that Kingdom delivered by *Herodotus*. And how soon it was peopled, is evidenced from the pillar of their King *Osyris*, with this inscription in *Diodorus*; *Mihi pater est Saturnus deorum junior, sum vero Osyris rex qui totum peragravi orbem usq; ad Indorum fines, ad eos quoq; sum profectus qui septentrioni subjacent usq; ad Istri fontes, et alias partes usq; ad Occanum.* Who *Osyris and* Saturnus *Ægyptius were.* Now according unto the best determinations *Osyris* was *Misraim*, and *Saturnus Egyptius* the same with *Cham*; after whose name *Egypt* is not only called in Scripture the laud of *Ham*, but thus much is also testified by *Plutarch*; for in his Treatise *de Osyride*, he delivereth that *Egypt* was called *Chamia a Chamo Noe filio*, that is from *Cham* the son of *Noah*. And if according to the consent of ancient Fathers, *Adam* was buried in the same place where Christ was crucified, that is Mount *Calvary*, the first man ranged far before the Flood, and laid his bones many miles from that place, where its presumed he received them. And this migration was the greater, if as the text expresseth, he was cast out of the East-side of Paradise to till the ground; and as the Position of the Cherubines implieth, who were placed at the east end of the garden to keep him from the tree of life.

That the remoter parts of the earth were in this time inhabited is also induceable from the like testimonies; for (omitting the numeration of *Josephus*, and the genealogies of the Sons of *Noah*) that *Italy* was inhabited, appeareth from the Records of *Livie*, and *Dionysius Halicarnasscus*, the story of *Æneas, Evander* and *Janus*, whom *Annius* of *Viterbo*, and the Chorographers of *Italy*, do make to be the same with *Noah*. That *Sicily* was also peopled, is made out from the frequent mention thereof in *Homer*, the Records of *Diodorus* and others; but especially from a remarkable passage touched by *Aretius* and *Ranzanus* Bishop of *Lucerium*, but fully explained by *Thomas Fazelli* in his accurate History of *Sicily*; that is, from an ancient inscription in a stone at *Panormo*, expressed by him in its proper characters, and by a *Syrian* thus translated, *Non est alius Deus præter unum Deum, non est alius potens præter eundem Deum, neq; est alius victor præter eundem quem colimus Deum: Hujus turris præfectus est* Sapha *filius* Eliphat, *filii* Esau, *fratris* Jacob, *filii* Isaac, *filii* Abraham: *et turri quidem ipsi nomen est* Baych, *sed turri huic proximæ nomen est* Pharath. The antiquity of the inhabitation of *Spain* is also confirmable, not only from *Berosus* in the plantation of *Tubal*, and a City continuing yet in his name, but the story of *Gerion*, the travels of *Hercules* and his pillars: and especially a passage in *Strabo*, which advanceth unto the time of *Ninus*, thus delivered in his fourth book. The *Spaniards* (saith he) affirm that they have had Laws and Letters above six thousand years. Now the *Spaniards* or *Iberians* observing (as *Xenophon* hath delivered) *Annum quadrimestrem,* four moneths unto a year, this compute will make up 2000 solary years, which is about the space of time from *Strabo,* who lived in the days of *Augustus,* unto the reign of *Ninus.*

That *Mauritania* and the coast of *Africa* were peopled very soon, is the conjecture of many wise men, and that by the *Phœnicians,* who left their Country upon the invasion of *Canaan* by the *Israelites.* For beside the conformity of the *Punick* or *Carthaginian* language with that of *Phœnicia,* there is a pregnant and very remarkable testimony hereof in *Procopius,* who in his second *de bello Vandalico,* recordeth, that in a town of *Mauritania Tingitana,* there was to be seen upon two white Columns in the *Phœnician* language these ensuing words; *Nos Maurici sumus qui fugimus a facie Jehoschua filii Nunis prædatoris.* The fortunate Islands or *Canaries* were not unknown; for so doth *Strabo* interpret that speech in *Homer* of *Proteus* unto *Menelaus,*

Sed te qua terræ postremus terminus extat,
Elysium in Campum cœlestia numina ducunt.

The like might we affirm from credible histories both of *France* and *Germany,* and perhaps also of our own Country. For omitting the fabulous and *Trojan* original delivered by *Jeofrey* of *Monmouth,* and the express text of Scripture; that the race of *Japhet* did people the Isles of the *Gentiles;* the *Brittish* Original was so obscure in *Cæsars* time, that he affirmeth the Inland inhabitants were *Aborigines,* that is, such as reported that they had their beginning in the Island. That *Ireland* our neighbour Island was not long time without Inhabitants, may be made probable by sundry accounts; although we abate the Traditions of *Bartholanus* the *Scythian,* who arrived there three hundred years after the flood, or the relation of *Giraldus*; that *Cæsaria* the daughter of *Noah* dwelt there before.

Now should we call in the learned account of *Bochartus,* [Bochart. Geog. Sacr. part. 2.] deducing the ancient names of Countries from *Phœnicians,* who by their plantations, discoveries, and sea negotiations, have left unto very many Countries, *Phœnician* denominations; the enquiry would be much shorter, and if *Spain* in the *Phœnician* Original, be but the region of *Conies, Lusitania,* or *Portugal* the Countrey of Almonds, if *Brittanica* were at first *Baratanaca,* or the land of Tin, and *Ibernia* or *Ireland,* were but *Ibernae,* or the farthest habitation; and these names imposed and dispersed by *Phœnician* Colonies in their several navigations; the Antiquity of habitations might be more clearly advanced.

Thus though we have declared how largely the world was inhabited within the space of 1300 years, yet must it be conceived more populous then can be clearly evinced; for a greater part of the earth hath ever been peopled, then hath been known or described by Geographers, as will appear by the discoveries of all Ages. For neither in *Herodotus* or *Thucydides* do we find any mention of *Rome,* nor in *Ptolomy* of many parts of *Europe, Asia* or *Africa.* And because many places we have declared of long plantations of whose populosity notwithstanding or memorable actions we have no ancient story; if we may conjecture of these by what we find related of others, we shall not need many words, nor assume the half of 1300 years. And this we might illustrate from the mighty acts of the *Assyrians* performed not long after the flood; recorded by *Justine* and *Diodorus*; who makes relation of expeditions by Armies more numerous then have been ever since. For *Ninus* King of *Assyria* brought against the *Bactrians* 700000 foot, 200000 horse, 10600 Chariots. *Semiramis* his successor led against the *Indians* 1300000 foot, 500000 horse, 100000 Chariots, and as many upon Camels: And it is said, *Staurobates* the *Indian* King, met her with greater forces then she brought against him. All which was performed within less then four hundred years after the flood.

Now if any imagine the unity of their language did hinder their dispersion before the flood, we confess it some hindrance at first, but not much afterward. For though it might restrain their dispersion, it could not their populosity; which necessarily requireth transmigration and emission of Colonies; as we read of *Romans, Greeks, Phœnicians* in ages past, and have beheld examples thereof in our days. We may also observe that after the flood before the confusion of tongues, men began to disperse: for it is said, they journeyed towards the East: and the Scripture it self expresseth a necessity conceived of their dispersion, for the intent of erecting the Tower is so delivered in the text, Lest we be scattered abroad upon the face of the earth.

Whether any Islands before the Flood.

Again, If any apprehend the plantation of the earth more easie in regard of Navigation and shipping discovered since the flood, whereby the Islands and divided parts of the earth are now inhabited; he must consider, that whether there were Islands or no before the flood, is not yet determined, and is with probability denied by very learned Authors.

Lastly, If we shall fall into apprehension that it was less inhabited, because it is said in the sixt of *Genesis* about a 120 years before the flood, and it came to pass that when men began to multiply upon the face of the earth. Beside that this may be only meant of the race of *Cain*, it will not import they were not multiplied before, but that they were at that time plentifully encreased; for so is the same word used in other parts of Scripture. And so is it afterward in the 9 Chapter said, that *Noah* began to be an husbandman, that is, he was so, or earnestly performed the Acts thereof; so it is said of our Saviour, that he began to cast them out that bought and sold in the Temple, that is, he actually cast them out, or with alacrity effected it.

Thus have I declared some private and probable conceptions in the enquiry of this truth; but the certainty hereof let the Arithmetick of the last day determine; and therefore expect no further belief than probability and reason induce. Only desire men would not swallow dubiosities for certainties, and receive as Principles points mainly controvertible; for we are to adhere unto things doubtful in a dubious and opinative way. It being reasonable for every man to vary his opinion according to the variance of his reason, and to affirm one day what he denied another. Wherein although at last we miss of truth; we die notwithstanding in harmless and inoffensive errors; because we adhere unto that, whereunto the examen of our reasons, and honest enquiries induce us.

CHAPTER VII
Of East, and West.

The next shall be of East and West; that is, the proprieties and conditions ascribed unto Regions respectively unto those situations; which hath been the obvious conception of Philosophers and Geographers, magnifying the condition of *India*, and the Eastern Countries, above the setting and occidental Climates, some ascribing hereto the generation of gold, precious stones and spices, others the civility and natural endowments of men; conceiving the bodies of this situation to receive a special impression from the first salutes of the Sun, and some appropriate influence from his ascendent and oriental radiations. But these proprieties affixed unto bodies, upon considerations deduced from East, West, or those observable points of the sphere, how specious and plausible so ever, will not upon enquiry be justified from such foundations.

For to speak strictly, there is no East and West in nature, nor are those absolute and invariable, but respective and mutable points, according unto different longitudes, or distant parts of habitation, whereby they suffer many and considerable variations. For first, unto some the same part will be East or West in respect of one another, that is, unto such as inhabit the same parallel, or differently dwell from East to West. Thus as unto *Spain*, *Italy* lyeth East, unto *Italy Greece*, unto *Greece Persia*, and unto *Persia China*; so again unto the Country of *China*, *Persia* lyeth West, unto *Persia Greece*, unto *Greece Italy*, and unto *Italy Spain*. So that the same Countrey is sometimes East and sometimes West; and *Persia* though East unto *Greece*, yet is it West unto *China*.

Unto other habitations the same point will be both East and West; as unto those that are *Antipodes* or seated in points of the Globe diametrically opposed. So the *Americans* are Antipodal unto the *Indians*, and some part of *India* is both East and West unto *America*, according as it shall be regarded from one side or the other, to the right or to the left; and setting out from any middle point, either by East or West, the distance unto the place intended is equal, and in the same space of time in nature also performable.

To a third that have the Poles for their vertex, or dwell in the position of a parallel sphere, there will be neither East nor West, at least the greatest part of the year. For if (as the name *Oriental* implyeth) they shall account that part to be East where ever the Sun ariseth, or that West where the Sun is occidental or setteth: almost half the year they have neither the one nor the other. For half the year it is below their Horizon, and the other half it is continually above it, and circling round about them intersecting not the Horizon, nor leaveth any part for this compute. And if (which will seem very reasonable) that part should be termed the Eastern point, where the Sun at Æquinox, and but once in the year ariseth, yet will this also disturb the cardinal accounts, nor will it with propriety admit that appellation. For that surely cannot be accounted East which hath the South on both sides; which notwithstanding this position must have. For if unto such as live under the Pole, that he only North which is above them, that must be Southerly which is below them, which is all the other portion of the by Globe, beside that part possessed them. And thus these points of East and West being not absolute in any, respective in some, and not at all relating unto others; we cannot hereon establish so general considerations, nor reasonably erect such immutable assertions, upon so unstable foundations.

Now the ground that begat or promoted this conceit, was first a mistake in the apprehension of East and West, considering thereof as of the North and South, and computing by these as invariably as by the other; but herein, upon second thoughts there is a great disparity. *What the Northern and Southern Poles be.* For the North and Southern Pole, are the invariable terms of that Axis whereon the heavens do move; and are therefore incommunicable and fixed points; wherof the one is not apprehensible in the other. But with East and West it is quite otherwise: for the revolution of the Orbs being made upon the Poles of North and South, all other points about the Axis are mutable; and wheresoever therein the East point be determined, by succession of parts in one revolution every point becometh East. And so if where the Sun ariseth, that part be termed East, every habitation differing in longitude, will have this point also different; in as much as the Sun successively ariseth unto every one.

The second ground, although it depend upon the former, approacheth nearer the effect; and that is the efficacy of the Sun, set out and divided according to priority of ascent; whereby his influence is conceived more favourable unto one Countrey than another, and to felicitate *India* more than any after. But hereby we cannot avoid absurdities, and such as infer effects controulable by our senses. For first, by the same reason that we affirm the *Indian* richer than the *American*, the *American* will also be more plentiful than the *Indian*, and *England* or *Spain* more fruitful than *Hispaniola* or golden Castle: in as much as the Sun ariseth unto the one sooner than the other: and so accountably unto any Nation subjected unto the same parallel, or with a considerable diversity of longitude from each other.

Secondly, An unsufferable absurdity will ensue: for thereby a Country may be more fruitful than it self: For *India* is more fertile than *Spain*, because more East, and that the Sun ariseth first unto it: *Spain*, likewise by the same reason more fruitful than *America*, and *America* than *India*: so that *Spain* is less fruitful than that Countrey, which a less fertile Country than it self excelleth.

Lastly, If we conceive the Sun hath any advantage by priority of ascent, or makes thereby one Country more happy than another, we introduce injustifiable determinations, and impose a natural partiality on that Luminary, which being equidistant from the earth, and equally removed in the East as in the West, his Power and Efficacy in both places must be equal, as *Boetius* hath taken notice, and *Scaliger* *De gemmis exercitat.* hath graphically declared. Some have therefore forsaken this refuge of the Sun, and to salve the effect have recurred unto the influence of the Stars, making their activities National, and appropriating their Powers unto particular regions. So *Cardan* conceiveth the tail of *Ursa Major* peculiarly respecteth *Europe*: whereas indeed once in 24 hours it also absolveth its course over *Asia* and *America*. And therefore it will not be easie to apprehend those stars peculiarly glance on us, who must of necessity carry a common eye and regard unto all Countries, unto whom their revolution and verticity is also common.

The effects therefore or different productions in several Countries, which we impute unto the action of the Sun, must surely have nearer and more immediate causes than that Luminary. And these if we place in the propriety of clime, or condition of soil wherein they are produced, we shall more reasonably proceed, than they who ascribe them unto the activity of the Sun. Whose revolution being regular, it hath no power nor efficacy peculiar from its orientality, but equally disperseth his beams unto all, which equally, and in the same restriction, receive his lustre. And being an universal and indefinite agent, the effects or productions we behold, receive not their circle from his causality, but are determined by the principles of the place, or qualities of that region which admits them. And this is evident not only in gemms, minerals, and mettals, but observable in plants and animals; whereof some are common unto many Countries, some peculiar unto one, some not communicable unto another. *Whence proceed the different commodities of several Countries.* For the hand of God that first created the earth, hath with variety disposed the principles of all things; wisely contriving them in their proper seminaries, and where they best maintain the intention of their species; whereof if they have not a concurrence, and be not lodged in a convenient matrix, they are not excited by the efficacy of the Sun; or failing in particular causes, receive a relief or sufficient promotion from the universal. For although superiour powers co-operate with inferiour activities, and may (as some conceive) carry a stroke in the plastick and formative draught of all things, yet do their determinations belong unto particular agents, and are defined from their proper principles. Thus the Sun which with us is fruitful in the generation of Frogs, Toads and Serpents, to this effect proves impotent in our neighbour Island; wherein as in all other carrying a common aspect, it concurreth but unto predisposed effects; and only suscitates those forms, whose determinations are seminal, and proceed from the *Idea* of themselves.

Why Astrological judgments upon Nativities be taken from the Ascendent.

Now whereas there be many observations concerning East, and divers considerations of Art which seem to extol the quality of that point, if rightly understood they do not really promote it. That the Astrologer takes account of nativities from the Ascendent, that is, the first house of the heavens, whose beginning is toward the East, it doth not advantage the conceit. For, he establisheth not his Judgment upon the orientality thereof, but considereth therein his first ascent above the Horizon; at which time its efficacy becomes observable, and is conceived to have the signification of life, and to respect the condition of all things, which at the same time arise from their causes, and ascend to their Horizon with it. Now this ascension indeed falls out respectively in the East: but as we have delivered before, in some positions there is no Eastern point from whence to compute these ascentions. So is it in a parallel sphere: for unto them six houses are continually depressed, and six never elevated: and the planets themselves, whose revolutions are of more speed, and influences of higher consideration, must find in that place a very imperfect regard; for half their period they absolve above, and half beneath the Horizon. And so for six years, no man can have the happiness to be born under *Jupiter*: and for fifteen together all must escape the ascendent dominion of *Saturn*.

That *Aristotle* in his Politicks, commends the situation of a City which is open towards the East, and admitteth the raies of the rising Sun, thereby is implied no more particular efficacy than in the West: But that position is commended, in regard the damps and vaporous exhalations ingendered in the absence of the Sun, are by his returning raies the sooner dispelled; and men thereby more early enjoy a clear and healthy habitation. Upon the like considerations it is, that *Marcus Varro* *De re Rustica.* commendeth the same situation, and exposeth his farm unto the equinoxial ascent of the Sun, and that *Palladius* adviseth the front of his edifice should so respect the South, that in the first angle it receive the rising raies of the Winter Sun, and decline a little from the Winter setting thereof. And concordant hereunto is the instruction of *Columella De positione villæ*: which he contriveth into Summer and Winter habitations, ordering that the Winter lodgings regard the Winter ascent of the Sun, that is South-East; and the rooms of repast at supper, the Æquinoxial setting thereof, that is the West: that the Summer lodgings regard the Æquinoxial Meridian: but the rooms of cænation in the Summer, he obverts unto the Winter ascent, that is, South-East; and the Balnearies or bathing places, that they may remain under the Sun until evening, he exposeth unto the Summer setting, that is, North-West, in all which although the Cardinal points be introduced, yet is the consideration Solary, and only determined unto the aspect or visible reception of the Sun.

Jews and *Mahometans* in these and our neighbour parts are observed to use some gestures towards the East, as at their benediction, and the killing of their meat. And though many ignorant spectators, and not a few of the Actors conceive some Magick or Mysterie therein, yet is the Ceremony only Topical, and in a memorial relation unto a place they honour. So the *Jews* do carry a respect and cast an eye upon *Jerusalem*: for which practice they are not without the example of their fore-fathers, and the encouragement of their wise King; For so it is said that *Daniel* [Dan. 6.] went into his house, and his windows being opened towards *Jerusalem*, he kneeled upon his knees three times a day, and prayed. So is it expressed in the prayer of *Solomon*, what prayer or supplication soever be made by any man, which shall spread forth his hands towards this house: if thy people go out to battle, and shall pray unto the Lord towards the City which thou hast chosen, and towards the house which I have chosen to build for thy Name, then hear thou in heaven their prayer and their supplication, and maintain their cause. Now the observation hereof, unto the Jews that are dispersed Westward, and such as most converse with us, directeth their regard unto the East: But the words of *Solomon* are appliable unto all quarters of Heaven: and by the Jews of the East and South must be regarded in a contrary position. So *Daniel* in *Babylon* looking toward *Jerusalem* had his face toward the West. So the Jews in their own land looked upon it from all quarters. For the Tribe of *Judah* beheld it to the North: *Manasses, Zabulon*, and *Napthali* unto the South: *Reuben* and *Gad* unto the West; only the Tribe of *Dan* regarded it directly or to the due East. So when it is said, [Luke 12.] when you see a cloud rise out of the West, you say there cometh a shower, and so it is: the observation was respective unto *Judea*: nor is this a reasonable illation in all other Nations whatsoever: For the Sea lay West unto that Country, and the winds brought rain from that quarter; But this consideration cannot be transferred unto *India* or *China*, which have a vast Sea Eastward, and a vaster Continent toward the West. So likewise when it is said [Job.] in the vulgar Translation, Gold cometh out of the North, it is no reasonable inducement unto us and many other Countries, from some particular mines septentrional unto his situation, to search after that mettal in cold and Northern regions, which we most plentifully discover in hot and Southern habitations.

For the *Mahometans*, as they partake with all Religions in something, so they imitate the *Jew* in this. For in their observed gestures, they hold a regard unto *Mecha* and *Medina Talnabi*, two Cities in *Arabia fælix*, where their Prophet was born and buried; whither they perform their pilgrimages: and from whence they expect he should return again. And therefore they direct their faces unto these parts, which unto the *Mahometans* of *Barbary* and *Egypt* lie East, and are in some point thereof unto many other parts of *Turkie*. Wherein notwithstanding there is no Oriental respect; for with the same devotion on the other side they regard these parts toward the West, and so with variety wheresoever they are seated, conforming unto the ground of their conception.

Fourthly, Whereas in the ordering of the Camp of *Israel*, the East quarter is appointed unto the noblest Tribe, that is the Tribe of *Judah*, according to the command of God, [Num. 3.] in the East-side toward the rising of the Sun shall the Standard of the Tribe of *Judah* pitch: it doth not peculiarly extol that point. For herein the East is not to be taken strictly, but as it signifieth or implieth the foremost place; for *Judah* had the Van, and many Countries through which they passed were seated Easterly unto them. Thus much is implied by the Original, and expressed by Translations which strictly conform thereto: So *Tremelius, Castra habentium ab anteriore parte Orientem versus, vexillum esto castrorum Judæ*; so hath *R. Solomon Jarchi* expounded it, the foremost or before, is the East quarter, and the West is called behind. And upon this interpretation may all be salved that is alleageable against it. For if the Tribe of *Judah* were to pitch before the Tabernacle at the East, and yet to march first, as is commanded, *Numb*. 10. there must ensue a disorder in the Camp, nor could they conveniently observe the execution thereof: For when they set out from *Mount Sinah* where the Command was delivered, they made Northward unto *Rithmah*; from *Rissah* unto *Eziongaber* about fourteen stations they marched South: From *Almon Diblathaim* through the mountains of *Yabarim* and plains of *Moab* towards *Jordan* the face of their march was West: So that if *Judah* were strictly to pitch in the East of the Tabernacle, every night he encamped in the Rear: and if (as some conceive) the whole Camp could not be less than twelve miles long, it had been preposterous for him to have marched foremost; or set out first who was most remote from the place to be approached.

Fiftly, That Learning, Civility and Arts had their beginning in the East, it is not imputable either to the action of the Sun, or its Orientality, but the first plantation of Man in those parts, which unto *Europe* do carry the respect of East. *Where the Ark rested as some think.* For on the mountains of *Ararat*, that is part of the hill *Taurus*, between the *East Indies* and *Scythia*, as Sir *W. Raleigh* accounts it, the Ark of *Noah* rested; from the East they travelled that built the Tower of *Babel*: from thence they were dispersed and successively enlarged, and Learning, good Arts, and all Civility communicated. The progression whereof was very sensible; and if we consider the distance of time between the confusion of *Babel*, and the Civility of many parts now eminent therein, it travelled late and slowly into our quarters. For notwithstanding the learning of *Bardes* and *Druides* of elder times, he that shall peruse that work of *Tacitus de moribus Germanorum*, may easily discern how little Civility two thousand years had wrought upon that Nation: the like he may observe concerning our selves, from the same Author in the life of *Agricola*, and more directly from *Strabo*; who to the dishonour of our Predecessors, and the disparagement of those that glory in the Antiquity of their Ancestors, affirmeth the *Britains* were so simple, that though they abounded in Milk, they had not the Artifice of Cheese.

Lastly, That the Globe it self is by Cosmographers divided into East and West, accounting from the first Meridian, it doth not establish this conceit. For that division is not naturally founded, but artificially set down, and by agreement; as the aptest terms to define or commensurate the longitude of places. Thus the ancient Cosmographers do place the division of the East and Western Hemisphere, that is the first term of longitude in the Canary or fortunate Islands; conceiving these parts the extreamest habitations Westward: But the Moderns have altered that term, and translated it unto the Azores or Islands of St. *Michael*; and that upon a plausible conceit of the small or insensible variation of the Compass in those parts, wherein nevertheless, and though upon second invention, they proceed upon a common and no appropriate foundation; for even in that Meridian farther North or South the Compass observably varieth; and there are also other places wherein it varieth not, as *Alphonso* and *Rodoriges de Lago* will have it about *Capo de las Agullas* in *Africa*; as *Maurolycus* affirmeth in the shore of *Peleponesus* in *Europe*: and as *Gilbertus* averreth, in the midst of great regions, in most parts of the earth.

CHAPTER VIII
Of the River *Nilus*.

Hereof uncontroulably and under general consent many opinions are passant, which notwithstanding upon due examination, do admit of doubt or restriction. It is generally esteemed, and by most unto our days received, that the River of *Nilus* hath seven ostiaries; that is, by seven Channels disburdeneth it self into the Sea. Wherein notwithstanding, beside that we find no concurrent determination of ages past, and a positive and undeniable refute of these present, the affirmative is mutable, and must not be received without all limitation.

For some, from whom we receive the greatest illustrations of Antiquity, have made no mention hereof: So *Homer* hath given no number of its Channels, nor so much as the name thereof in use with all Historians. *Eratosthenes* in his description of *Egypt* hath likewise passed them over. *How Egypt first became firm land.* *Aristotle* is so indistinct in their names and numbers, that in the first *of Meteors* he plainly affirmeth the Region of *Egypt* (which we esteem the ancientest Nation in the world) was a meer gained ground, and that by the setling of mud and limous matter brought down by the River *Nilus*, that which was at first a continued Sea, was raised at last into a firm and habitable Country. The like opinion he held of *Mæotis Palus*, that by the floods of *Tanais* and earth brought down thereby, it grew observably shallower in his days, and would in process of time become a firm land. And though his conjecture be not as yet fulfilled, yet is the like observable in the River *Gihon*, a branch of *Euphrates* and River of Paradise; which having in former Ages discharged it self into the *Persian* Sea, doth at present fall short; being lost in the lakes of *Chaldea*, and hath left between the Sea, a large and considerable part of dry land.

Others expresly treating hereof, have diversly delivered themselves; *Herodotus* in his Euterpe makes mention of seven; but carelesly of two thereof; that is *Bolbitinum*, and *Bucolicum*; for these, saith he, were not the natural currents, but made by Art for some occasional convenience. *Strabo* in his Geography naming but two, *Peleusiacum* and *Canopicum*, plainly affirmeth there were many more than seven; *Inter hæc alia quinque*, etc. There are (saith he) many remarkable towns within the currents of Nile, especially such which have given the names unto the ostiaries thereof, not unto all, for they are eleven, and four besides, but unto seven and most considerable; that is *Canopicum, Bolbitinum, Selenneticum, Sebenneticum, Pharniticum, Mendesium, Taniticum* and *Pelusium*: wherein to make up the number, one of the artificial chanels of *Herodotus* is accounted. *Ptolomy* an *Egyptian*, and born at the *Pelusian* mouth of *Nile*, in his Geography maketh nine: and in the third Map of *Africa*, hath unto their mouths prefixed their several names; *Heracleoticum, Bolbitinum, Sebenneticum, Pineptum, Diolcos, Pathmeticum, Mendesium, Taniticum, Peleusiacum*: wherein notwithstanding there are no less then three different names from those delivered by *Pliny*. All which considered, we may easily discern that Authors accord not either in name or number; and must needs confirm the Judgement of *Maginus, de Ostiorum Nili numero et nominibus, valde antiqui scriptores discordant.*

Modern Geographers and travellers do much abate of this number, for as *Maginus* and others observe, there are now but three or four mouths thereof; as *Gulielmus Tyrius* long ago, and *Bellonius* since, both ocular enquirers, with others have attested. For below *Cairo*, the River divides it self into four branches, whereof two make the chief and navigable streams, the one running to *Pelusium* of the Ancients, and now *Damiata*; the other unto *Canopium*, and now *Roscetta*; the other two, saith Mr. *Sandys*, [Sand. Relation.] do run between these; but poor in water. Of those seven mentioned by *Herodotus*, and those nine by *Ptolomy*, these are all I could either see or hear of. Which much confirmeth the testimony of the Bishop of *Tyre* a diligent and ocular Enquirer; who in his holy war doth thus deliver himself. We wonder much at the Ancients, who assigned seven mouths unto *Nilus*; which we can no otherwise salve, then that by process of time, the face of places is altered, and the river hath lost his chanels; or that our fore-fathers did never obtain a true account thereof.

And therefore when it is said in holy Scripture, [Isa. 11. 15, 16.] The Lord shall utterly destroy the tongue of the *Egyptian* sea, and with his mighty wind he shall shake his hand over the river, and shall smite it in the seven streams, and make men go over dry-shod. If this expression concerneth the river *Nilus*, it must only respect the seven principal streams. But the place is very obscure, and whether thereby be not meant the river *Euphrates*, is not without some controversie; as is collectible from the subsequent words; And there shall be an high way for the remnant of his people, that shall be left from *Assyria*; and also from the bare name *River*, emphatically signifying *Euphrates*, and thereby the division of the *Assyrian* Empire into many fractions, which might facilitate their return: [Gr. Not in Isaiam.] as *Grotius* hath observed; and is more plainly made out, [Esdr. 2. 13, 43, 47.] if the Apocrypha of *Esdras*, and that of the *Apocalyps* [Apoc. 16. 12.] have any relation hereto.

Lastly, Whatever was or is their number, the contrivers of Cards and Maps afford us no assurance or constant description therein. For whereas *Ptolemy* hath set forth nine, *Hondius* in his Map of *Africa* makes but eight, and in that of *Europe* ten. *Ortelius* in the Map of the *Turkish* Empire, setteth down eight, in that of *Egypt* eleven; and *Maginus* in his Map of that

Country hath observed the same number. And if we enquire farther, we shall find the same diversity and discord in divers others.

Thus may we perceive that this account was differently related by the Ancients, that it is undeniably rejected by the Moderns, and must be warily received by any. For if we receive them all into account, they were more then seven, if only the natural sluces, they were fewer; and however we receive them, there is no agreeable and constant description thereof. And therefore how reasonable it is to draw continual and durable deductions from alterable and uncertain foundations; let them consider who make the gates of *Thebes*, and the mouths of this River a constant and continued periphrasis for this number, and in their Poetical expressions do give the River that Epithite unto this day.

The same River is also accounted the greatest of the earth, called therefore *Fluviorum pater*, and *totius Orbis maximus*, by *Ortelius*: If this be true, many Maps must be corrected, or the relations of divers good Authors renounced.

For first, In the deliniations of many Maps of *Africa*, the River *Niger* exceedeth it about ten degrees in length, that is, no less then six hundred miles. For arising beyond the Æquator it maketh Northward almost 15 degrees, and deflecting after Westward, without Meanders, continueth a strait course about 40 degrees; and at length with many great currents disburdeneth it self into the Occidental Ocean. Again, if we credit the descriptions of good Authors, other Rivers excell it in length, or breadth, or both. *Arrianus* in his history of *Alexander*, assigneth the first place unto the River *Ganges*; which truly according unto latter relations, if not in length, yet in breadth and depth may be granted to excell it. For the magnitude of *Nilus* consisteth in the dimension of longitude, and is inconsiderable in the other; what stream it maintaineth beyond *Syene* or *Asna*, and so forward unto its original, relations are very imperfect; but below these places, and farther removed from the head, the current is but narrow, and we read in the History of the *Turks*, the *Tartar* horsemen of *Selimus* swam over the *Nile* from *Cairo*, to meet the forces of *Tonumbeus*.

Baptista Scortia expresly treating hereof, *De natura et incremento Nili.* preferreth the River of *Plate* in *America*; for that as *Maffeus* hath delivered, falleth into the Ocean in the latitude of forty leagues; and with that source and plenty that men at Sea do tast fresh water, before they approach so near as to discover the land. So is it exceeded by that which by *Cardan* is termed the greatest in the world, that is the River *Oregliana* in the same continent; which as *Maginus* delivereth, hath been navigated 6000 miles; and opens in a chanel of ninety leagues broad; so that, as *Acosta*, an ocular witness recordeth, they that sail in the middle, can make no land of either side.

Now the ground of this assertion was surely the magnifying esteem of the Ancients, arising from the indiscovery of its head. For as things unknown seem greater then they are, and are usually received with amplifications above their nature; so might it also be with this River, whose head being unknown and drawn to a proverbial obscurity, the opinion thereof became without bounds; and men must needs conceit a large extent of that to which the discovery of no man had set a period. And this an usual way to give the superlative unto things of eminency in any kind; and when a thing is very great, presently to define it to be the greatest of all. Whereas indeed Superlatives are difficult; whereof there being but one in every kind, their determinations are dangerous, and must not be made without great circumspection. *The greatest Cities of the World.* So the City of Rome is magnified by the *Latines* to be the greatest of the earth; but time and Geography informs us, that *Cairo* is bigger, and *Quinsay* in *China* far exceedeth both. *The highest Hills.* So is *Olympus* extolled by the *Greeks*, as an hill attaining unto heaven; but the enlarged Geography of aftertimes makes slight account hereof, when they discourse of *Andes* in *Peru*, or *Teneriffa* in the *Canaries*. And we understand by a person who hath lately had a fair opportunity to behold the magnified mount *Olympus*, that it is exceeded by some peakes of the *Alpes*. So have all Ages conceived, and most are still ready to swear, the Wren is the least of Birds; yet the discoveries of *America*, and even of our own Plantations have shewed us one far less; that is, the Humbird, Tomineio. not much exceeding a Beetle. And truly, for the least and greatest, the highest and the lowest of every kind, as it is very difficult to define them in visible things, so is it to understand in things invisible. Thus is it no easie lesson to comprehend the first matter, and the affections of that which is next neighbour unto nothing, but impossible truly to comprehend God, who indeed is all in all. For things as they arise unto perfection, and approach unto God, or descend to imperfection, and draw nearer unto nothing, fall both imperfectly into our apprehensions; the one being too weak for our conceptions, our conceptions too weak for the other.

Thirdly, Divers conceptions there are concerning its increment or inundation. The first unwarily opinions, that this encrease or annual overflowing is proper unto *Nile*, and not agreeable unto any other River; which notwithstanding is common unto many Currents of *Africa*. For about the same time the River *Niger* and *Zaire* do overflow; and so do the Rivers beyond the mountains of the Moon, as *Suama*, and *Spirito Santo*. And not only these in *Africa*, but some also in *Europe* and *Asia*; for so it is reported of *Menan* in *India*, and so doth *Botero* report of *Duina* in *Livonia*; and the same is also observable in the River *Jordan* in *Judea*; for so is it delivered, that *Jordan* overfloweth all his banks in the time of harvest.

The effect indeed is wonderful in all, and the causes surely best resolvable from observations made in the Countries themselves, the parts through which they pass, or whence they take their Original. That of *Nilus* hath been attempted by Many, and by some to that despair of resolution, that they have only referred it unto the Providence of God, and his secret manuduction of all things unto their ends. The cause of the overflowing of Nilus. But divers have attained the truth, and the cause alledged by *Diodorus*, *Seneca*, *Strabo*, and others, is allowable; that the inundation of *Nilus* in *Egypt* proceeded from the rains in *Æthiopia*, and the mighty source of waters falling towards the fountains thereof. For this inundation unto the *Egyptians* happeneth when it is winter unto the *Æthiopians*; which habitations, although they have no cold Winter (the Sun being no farther removed from them in Cancer, then unto us in Taurus) yet is the fervour of the air so well remitted, as it admits a sufficient generation of vapors, and plenty of showers ensuing thereupon. This Theory of the Ancients is since confirmed by experience of the Moderns; by *Franciscus Alvarez*, who lived long in those parts, and left a description of *Æthiopia*; affirming that from the middle of June unto September, there fell in his time continual rains. As also *Antonius Ferdinandus*, who in an Epistle written from thence, and noted by *Codignus*, affirmeth, that during the winter, in those Countries there passed no day without rain.

Now this is also usual, to translate a remarkable quality into a propriety, and where we admire an effect in one, to opinion there is not the like in any other. With these conceits do common apprehensions entertain the antidotal and wondrous condition of *Ireland*; conceiving only in that land an immunity from venemous creatures: but unto him that shall further enquire, the same will be affirmed of *Creta*, memorable in ancient stories, even unto fabulous causes, and benediction from the birth of *Jupiter*. The same is also found in *Ebusus* or *Evisa*, an Island near *Majorca* upon the coast of *Spain*. With these apprehensions do the eyes of neighbour Spectators behold *Ætna*, the flaming mountain in *Sicilia*; but Navigators tell us there is a burning mountain in Island, a more remarkable one in *Teneriffa* of the *Canaries*, and many Vulcano's or fiery Hils elsewhere. Thus Crocodiles were thought to be peculiar unto *Nile*, and the opinion so possessed *Alexander*, that when he had discovered some in *Ganges*, he fell upon a conceit he had found the head of *Nilus*; but later discoveries affirm they are not only in *Asia* and *Africa*, but very frequent in some rivers of *America*.

Another opinion confineth its Inundation, and positively affirmeth, it constantly encreaseth the seventeenth day of June; wherein perhaps a larger form of speech were safer, then that which punctually prefixeth a constant day thereto. For this expression is different from that of the Ancients, as *Herodotus*, *Diodorus*, *Seneca*, etc. delivering only that it happeneth about the entrance of the Sun into Cancer; wherein they warily deliver themselves, and reserve a reasonable latitude. So when *Hippocrates* saith, *Sub Cane et ante Canem difficiles sunt purgationes*: There is a latitude of days comprised therein; for under the Dog-star he containeth not only the day of its ascent, but many following, and some ten days preceeding. So *Aristotle* delivers the affections of animals: with the wary terms of *Circa, et magna ex parte*: and when *Theodorus* translateth that part of his, *Coeunt Thunni et Scombri mense Februario post Idus, pariunt Junio ante Nonas*: *Scaliger* for *ante Nonas*, renders it *Junii initio*; because that exposition affordeth the latitude of divers days: For affirming it happeneth before the Nones, he alloweth but one day; that is the Calends; for in the *Roman* account, the second day is the fourth of the Nones of June.

Again, Were the day definitive, it had prevented the delusion of the devil, nor could he have gained applause by its prediction; who notwithstanding (as *Athanasius* in the life of *Anthony* relateth) to magnifie his knowledge in things to come, when he perceived the rains to fall in *Æthiopia*, would presage unto the *Egyptians* the day of its inundation. And this would also make useless that natural experiment observed in earth or sand about the River; by the weight whereof (as good Authors report) they have unto this day a knowledge of its encrease.

Lastly, It is not reasonable from variable and unstable causes, to derive a fixed and constant effect, and such are the causes of this inundation, which cannot indeed be regular, and therefore their effects not prognosticable like Eclipses. For depending upon the clouds and descent of showers in *Æthiopia*, which have their generation from vaporous exhalations, they must submit their existence unto contingencies, and endure anticipation and recession from the movable condition of their causes. And therefore some years there hath been no encrease at all, as some conceive in the years of Famin under *Pharaoh*, as *Seneca*, and divers relate of the eleventh year of *Cleopatra*; nor nine years together, as is testified by *Calisthenes*. Some years it hath also retarded, and came far later then usually it was expected, as according to *Sozomen* and *Nicephorus* it happened in the days of *Theodosius*; whereat the people were ready to mutiny, because they might not sacrifice unto the River, according to the custom of their Predecessors.

Now this is also an usual way of mistake, and many are deceived who too strictly construe the temporal considerations of things. Thus books will tell us, and we are made to believe that the fourteenth year males are seminifical and pubescent; but he that shall enquire into the generality, will rather adhere unto the cautelous assertion of *Aristotle*, that is, *bis septem annis exactis*, and then but *magna ex parte*. That Whelps are blind nine days, and then begin to see, is generally believed, but as we have elsewhere declared, it is exceeding rare, nor do their eye-lids usually open until the twelfth, and sometimes not before the fourteenth day. And to speak strictly, an hazardable determination it is unto fluctuating and indifferent effects, to affix a positive Type or Period. For in effects of far more regular causalities, difficulties do often arise, and even in time it self, which measureth all things, we use allowance in its commensuration. Thus while we conceive we have the account of a year in 365 days, exact enquirers and Computists will tell us, that we escape 6 hours, that is a quarter of a day. And so in a day which every one accounts 24 hours, or one revolution of the Sun, in strict account we must allow the addition of such a part as the Sun doth make in his proper motion, from West to East, whereby in one day he describeth not a perfect Circle.

Fourthly, It is affirmed by many, and received by most, that it never raineth in *Egypt*, the river supplying that defect, and bountifully requiting it in its inundation: but this must also be received in a qualified sense, that is, that it rains but seldom at any time in the Summer, and very rarely in the Winter. *That Egypt hath rain.* But that great showers do sometimes fall upon that Region, beside the Assertion of many Writers, *Sir William Paston Baronet.*, we can confirm from honourable and ocular testimony, and that not many years past, it rained in Grand *Cairo* divers days together.

The same is also attested concerning other parts of *Egypt*, by *Prosper Alpinus*, who lived long in that Country, and hath left an accurate Treaty of the medical practise thereof. *Cayri raro decidunt pluviæ, Alexandriæ, Pelusiiq; et in omnibus locis mari adjacentibus, pluit largissime et sæpe*; that is, it raineth seldom at *Cairo*, but at *Alexandria*, *Damiata*, and places near the Sea, it raineth plentifully and often. Whereto we might add the latter testimony of Learned Mr. *Greaves*, in his accurate description of the *Pyramids*.

Beside, Men hereby forget the relation of holy Scripture. *Exod. 9.* *Behold I will cause it to rain a very great hail, such as hath not been in* Egypt *since the foundation thereof, even untill now*. Wherein God threatning such a rain as had not happened, it must be presumed they had been acquainted with some before, and were not ignorant of the substance, the menace being made in the circumstance. The same concerning hail is inferrible from *Prosper Alpinus. Rarissime nix, grando*, it seldom snoweth or haileth. Where by we must concede that snow and hail do sometimes fall, because they happen seldom.

Now this mistake ariseth from a misapplication of the bounds or limits of time, and an undue transition from one unto another; which to avoid, we must observe the punctual differences of time, and so distinguish thereof, as not to confound or lose the one in the other. For things may come to pass, *Semper, Plerumq; Sæpe, aut Nunquam, Aliquando, Raro*; that is, Always, or Never, For the most part, or Sometimes, Ofttimes, or Seldom. Now the deception is usual which is made by the mis-application of these; men presently concluding that to happen often, which happeneth but sometimes: that never, which happeneth but seldom; and that alway, which happeneth for the most part. So is it said, the Sun shines every day in Rhodes, because for the most part it faileth not. So we say and believe that a Camelion never eateth, but liveth only upon air, whereas indeed it is seen to eat very seldom, but many there are who have beheld it to feed on Flyes. And so it is said, that children born in the eighth moneth live not, that is, for the most part, but not to be concluded alwaies: nor it seems in former ages in all places: for it is otherwise recorded by *Aristotle* concerning the births of *Egypt*.

Lastly, It is commonly conceived that divers Princes hath attempted to cut the Isthmus or tract of land *Lingua maris Ægyptii. Isa. 11. 15.* which parteth the *Arabian* and *Mediterranean* Sea: but upon enquiry I find some difficulty concerning the place attempted; many with good authority affirming, that the intent was not immediately to unite these Seas, but to make a navigable chanel between the Red Sea and the Nile, the marks whereof are extant to this day; it was first attempted by *Sesostris*, after by *Darius*, and in a fear to drown the Country, deserted by them both; but was long after re-attempted and in some manner effected by *Philadelphus*. And so the grand Signior who is Lord of the Country, conveyeth his Gallies into the Red Sea by the Nile; for he bringeth them down to Grand *Cairo* where they are taken in pieces, carried upon Camels backs, and rejoyned together at Sues, his port and Naval station for that Sea; whereby in effect he acts the design of *Cleopatra*, who after the battle of *Actium* in a different way would have conveyed her Gallies into the Red Sea.

And therefore that proverb to cut an Isthmus, *Isthmum perfodere.* that is, to take great pains, and effect nothing, alludeth not unto this attempt; but is by *Erasmus* applyed unto several other, as that undertaking of the Cnidians to cut their Isthmus, but especially that of *Corinth* so unsuccessfully attempted by many Emperours. The Cnidians were deterred by the peremptory disswasion of *Apollo*, plainly commanding them to desist; for if God had thought it fit, he would have made that Country an Island at first. But this perhaps will not be thought a reasonable discouragement unto the activity of those spirits which endeavour to advantage nature by Art, and upon good grounds to promote any part of the universe; nor will the ill success of some be made a sufficient determent unto others; who know that many learned men affirm, that Islands were not from the beginning, that many have been made since by Art, that some Isthmus have been eat through by the Sea, and others cut by the spade: And if policy would permit, that of *Panama* in *America* were most worthy the attempt: it being but few miles over, and would open a shorter cut unto the East Indies and China.

CHAPTER IX
Of the Red Sea.

Contrary apprehensions are made of the Erythræan or Red Sea; most apprehending a material redness therein, from whence they derive its common denomination; and some so lightly conceiving hereof, as if it had no redness at all, are fain to recur unto other originals of its appellation. *What the Red Sea is.* Wherein to deliver a distinct account, we first observe that without consideration of colour it is named the *Arabian Gulph*: The Hebrews who had best reason to remember it, do call it *Zuph*, or the weedy Sea; because it was full of sedge, or they found it so in their passage; the *Mahometans* who are now lords thereof do know it by no other name then the *Gulph* of *Mecha* a City of *Arabia*.

The stream of Antiquity deriveth its name from King *Erythrus*; so sleightly conceiving of the nominal deduction from Redness, that they plainly deny there is any such accident in it. The words of *Curtius* are plain beyond Evasion, *Ab Erythro rege inditum est nomen, propter quod ignari rubere aquas credunt*: Of no more obscurity are the words of *Philostratus*, and of later times, *Sabellicus; Stulte persuasam est vulgo rubras alicubi esse maris aquas, quin ab Erythro rege nomen pelago inditum.* *More exactly hereof* Bochartus *and* Mr. Dickinson. Of this opinion was *Andræas Corsalius, Pliny, Solinus, Dio Cassius*, who although they denied not all redness, yet did they rely upon the original from King *Erythrus*.

Others have fallen upon the like, or perhaps the same conceit under another appellation; deducing its name not from King *Erythrus*, but *Esau* or *Edom*, whose habitation was upon the coasts thereof. Now *Edom* is as much as *Erythrus*, and the red Sea no more then the *Idumean*; from whence the posterity of *Edom* removing towards the Mediterranean coast, according to their former nomination by the Greeks were called Phœnicians or red men: and from a plantation and colony of theirs, an Island near Spain was by the Greek describers termed *Erithra*, as is declared by *Strabo* and *Solinus*.

Very many omitting the nominal derivation, do rest in the gross and literal conception thereof, apprehending a real redness and constant colour of parts. Of which opinion are also they which hold the Sea receiveth a red and minious tincture from springs, wells, and currents that fall into it; and of the same belief are probably many Christians, who conceiving the passage of the *Israelites* through this Sea to have been the type of Baptism, according to that of the Apostle, *1 Cor. 10. 2.* All were baptized unto *Moses* in the cloud, and in the Sea: for the better resemblance of the blood of Christ, they willingly received it in the apprehension of redness, and a colour agreeable unto its mystery: according unto that of *Austin*, *Aug. in Johannem.* *Significat mare illud rubrum Baptismum Christi; unde nobis Baptismus Christi nisi sanguine Christi consecratus?*

But divers Moderns not considering these conceptions, and appealing unto the Testimony of sense, have at last determined the point: concluding a redness herein, but not in the sense received. Sir *Walter Raleigh* from his own and *Portugal* observations, doth place the redness of the Sea in the reflection from red Islands, and the redness of the earth at the bottom: wherein Coral grows very plentifully, and from whence in great abundance it is transported into *Europe*. The observations of *Alberquerque* and *Stephanus de Gama* (as from *Johannes de Bairros, Fernandius de Cordova* relateth) derive this redness from the colour of the sand and argillous earth at the bottom; for being a shallow Sea, while it rowleth to and fro, there appeareth a redness upon the water, which is most discernable in sunny and windy weather. But that this is no more than a seeming redness, he confirmeth by an experiment; for in the reddest part taking up a vessel of water, it differed not from the complexion of other Seas. Nor is this colour discoverable in every place of that Sea, for as he also observeth, in some places it is very green, in others white and yellow, according to the colour of the earth or sand at the bottom. And so may *Philostratus* be made out, when he saith, this Sea is blew; or *Bellonius* denying this redness, because he beheld not that colour about Sues; or when *Corsalius* at the mouth thereof could not discover the same.

Now although we have enquired the ground of redness in this Sea, yet are we not fully satisfied: for what is forgot by many, and known by few, there is another Red Sea whose name we pretend not to make out from these principles; that is, the *Persian* Gulph or Bay, which divideth the *Arabian* and *Persian* shore, as *Pliny* hath described it. *Mare rubrum in duos dividitur sinus, is qui ab Oriente est, Persicus appellatur*; or as *Solinus* expresseth it, *Qui ab Oriente est Persicus appellatur, ex adverso unde Arabia est, Arabicus*: whereto assenteth *Suidas, Ortelius*, and many more. And therefore there is no absurdity in *Strabo* when he delivereth that *Tigris* and *Euphrates* do fall into the Red Sea, and *Fernandius de Cordova* justly defendeth his Countryman *Seneca* in that expression;

Et qui renatum prorsus excipiens diem
Tepidum Rubenti Tigrin immiscet freto.

Nor hath only the *Persian* Sea received the same name with the *Arabian*, but what is strange, and much confounds the distinction, the name thereof is also derived from King *Erythrus*; who was conceived to be buried in an Island of this Sea, as *Dionysius Afer, Curtius* and *Suidas* do deliver. Which were of no less probability than the other, if (as with the same authors *Strabo* affirmeth) he was buried neer *Caramania* bordering upon the *Persian* Gulph. And if his Tomb was seen by *Nearchus*, it was not so likely to be in the *Arabian* Gulph; for we read that from the River *Indus* he came unto *Alexander* at *Babylon*, some few days before his death. Now *Babylon* was seated upon the River *Euphrates*, which runs into the *Persian* Gulph. And therefore however the Latin expresseth it in *Strabo*, that *Nearchus* suffered much in the *Arabian Sinus*, yet is the original κόλπος πέρσικος, that is, the Gulf of *Persia*.

That therefore the Red Sea or *Arabian* Gulph received its name from personal derivation, though probable, is but uncertain; that both the Seas of one name should have one common denominator, less probable; that there is a gross and material redness in either, not to be affirmed: that there is an emphatical or appearing redness in one, not well to be denied. And this is sufficient to make good the Allegory of the Christians: and in this distinction may we justifie the name of the Black Sea, given unto *Pontus Euxinus*: the name of *Xanthus*, or the yellow River of *Phrygia*: and the name of *Mar Vermeio*, or the Red Sea in *America*.

CHAPTER X
Of the Blackness of *Negroes*.

It is evident not only in the general frame of Nature, that things most manifest unto sense, have proved obscure unto the understanding: But even in proper and appropriate Objects, wherein we affirm the sense cannot err, the faculties of reason most often fail us. Thus of colours in general, under whose gloss and vernish all things are seen, few or none have yet beheld the true nature; or positively set down their incontroulable causes. Which while some ascribe unto the mixture of the Elements, others to the graduality of Opacity and Light; they have left our endeavours to grope them out by twi-light, and by darkness almost to discover that whose existence is evidenced by Light. *The Principles of Colour according to the Chymists.* The *Chymists* have laudably reduced their causes unto Sal, Sulphur, and Mercury; and had they made it out so well in this, as in the objects of smell and taste, their endeavours had been more acceptable: For whereas they refer Sapor unto Salt, and Odor unto Sulphur, they vary much concerning colour; some reducing it unto Mercury, some to Sulphur; others unto Salt. Wherein indeed the last conceit doth not oppress the former; and though Sulphur seem to carry the master-stroak, yet Salt may have a strong co-operation. For beside the fixed and terrestrious Salt, there is in natural bodies a *Sal niter* referring unto Sulphur; there is also a volatile or Ammoniack Salt, retaining unto Mercury; by which Salts the colours of bodies are sensibly qualified, and receive degrees of lustre or obscurity, superficiality or profundity, fixation or volatility.

Their general or first Natures being thus obscure, there will be greater difficulties in their particular discoveries; for being farther removed from their simplicities, they fall into more complexed considerations; and so require a subtiler act of reason to distinguish and call forth their natures. Thus although a man understood the general nature of colours, yet were it no easie Problem to resolve, Why Grass is green? Why Garlick, Molyes, and Porrets have white roots, deep green leaves, and black seeds? Why several docks and sorts of Rhubarb with yellow roots, send forth purple flowers? Why also from Lactary or milky plants which have a white and lacteous juyce dispersed through every part, there arise flowers blew and yellow? Moreover, beside the specifical and first digressions ordained from the Creation, which might be urged to salve the variety in every species; Why shall the marvail of *Peru* produce its flowers of different colours, and that not once, or constantly, but every day, and variously? Why Tulips of one colour produce some of another, and running through almost all, should still escape a blew? And lastly, Why some men, yea and they a mighty and considerable part of mankind, should first acquire and still retain the gloss and tincture of blackness? Which whoever strictly enquires, shall find no less of darkness in the cause, than in the effect it self; there arising unto examination no such satisfactory and unquarrelable reasons, as may confirm the causes generally received; which are but two in number. The heat and scorch of the Sun; or the curse of God on *Cham* and his Posterity.

The first was generally received by the Ancients, who in obscurities had no higher recourse than unto Nature, as may appear by a Discourse concerning this point in *Strabo*. By *Aristotle* it seems to be implied in those Problems which enquire why the Sun makes men black, and not the fire? Why it whitens wax, yet blacks the skin? By the word *Æthiops* it self, applied to the memorablest Nations of *Negroes*, that is of a burnt and torrid countenance. The fancy of the Fable infers also the Antiquity of the opinion; which deriveth this complexion from the deviation of the Sun, and the conflagration of all things under *Phaeton*. But this opinion though generally embraced, was I perceive rejected by *Aristobulus* a very ancient Geographer; as is discovered by *Strabo*. It hath been doubted by several modern Writers, particularly by *Ortelius*; but amply and satisfactorily discussed as we know by no man. We shall therfore endeavour a full delivery hereof, declaring the grounds of doubt, and reasons of denial, which rightly understood, may, if not overthrow, yet shrewdly shake the security of this Assertion.

And first, Many which countenance the opinion in this reason, do tacitly and upon consequence overthrow it in another. For whilst they make the River *Senaga* to divide and bound the *Moors*, so that on the South side they are black, on the other only tawny; they imply a secret causality herein from the air, place or river; and seem not to derive it from the Sun. The effects of whose activity are not precipitously abrupted, but gradually proceed to their cessations.

Secondly, If we affirm that this effect proceeded, or as we will not be backward to concede, it may be advanced and fomented from the fervour of the Sun; yet do we not hereby discover a principle sufficient to decide the question concerning other animals; nor doth he that affirmeth the heat makes man black, afford a reason why other animals in the same habitations maintain a constant and agreeable hue unto those in other parts, as Lions, Elephants, Camels, Swans, Tigers, Estriges. Which though in *Æthiopia*, in the disadvantage of two Summers, and perpendicular Rayes of the Sun, do yet make good the complexion of their species, and hold a colourable correspondence unto those in milder regions. Now did this complexion proceed from heat in man, the same would be communicated unto other animals which equally participate the Influence of the common Agent. For thus it is in the effects of cold, in Regions far removed from the Sun; for therein men are not only of fair complexions, gray-eyed, and of light hair; but many creatures exposed to the air, deflect in extremity from their natural colours; from brown, russet and black, receiving the complexion of Winter, and turning perfect white. Thus *Olaus Magnus* relates, that after the Autumnal Æquinox, Foxes begin to grow white; thus *Michovius* reporteth, and we want not ocular confirmation, that Hares and Partridges turn white in the Winter; and thus a white Crow, a proverbial rarity with us, is none unto them; but that inseparable accident of *Porphyrie* is separated in many hundreds.

Thirdly, If the fervour of the Sun, or intemperate heat of clime did solely occasion this complexion, surely a migration or change thereof might cause a sensible, if not a total mutation; which notwithstanding experience will not admit. For *Negroes* transplanted, although into cold and phlegmatick habitations, continue their hue both in themselves, and also their generations; except they mix with different complexions; whereby notwithstanding there only succeeds a remission of their tinctures; there remaining unto many descents a strong shadow of their

Originals; and if they preserve their copulations entire, they still maintain their complexions. As is very remarkable in the dominions of the Grand Signior, and most observable in the *Moors* in *Brasilia*, which transplanted about an hundred years past, continue the tinctures of their fathers unto this day. And so likewise fair or white people translated in hotter Countries receive not impressions amounting to this complexion, as hath been observed in many *Europeans* who have lived in the land of *Negroes*: and as *Edvardus Lopes* testifieth of the *Spanish* plantations, that they retained their native complexions unto his days.

Fourthly, If the fervour of the Sun were the sole cause hereof in *Ethiopia* or any land of *Negroes*, it were also reasonable that inhabitants of the same latitude, subjected unto the same vicinity of the Sun, the same diurnal arch, and direction of its rayes, should also partake of the same hue and complexion, which notwithstanding they do not. For the Inhabitants of the same latitude in *Asia* are of a different complexion, as are the Inhabitants of *Cambogia* and *Java*, insomuch that some conceive the *Negro* is properly a native of *Africa*, and that those places in *Asia* inhabited now by *Moors*, are but the intrusions of *Negroes* arriving first from *Africa*, as we generally conceive of *Madagascar*, and the adjoyning Islands, who retain the same complexion unto this day. But this defect is more remarkable in *America*; which although subjected unto both the Tropicks, yet are not the Inhabitants black between, or near, or under either; neither to the Southward in *Brasilia*, *Chili*, or *Peru*; nor yet to the Northward in *Hispaniola*, *Castilia*, *del Oro*, or *Nicaragua*. And although in many parts thereof there be at present swarms of *Negroes* serving under the *Spaniard*, yet were they all transported from *Africa*, since the discovery of *Columbus*; and are not indigenous or proper natives of *America*.

Fifthly, We cannot conclude this complexion in Nations from the vicinity or habitude they hold unto the Sun; for even in *Africa* they be *Negroes* under the Southern Tropick, but are not all of this hue either under or near the Northern. So the people of *Gualata*, *Agades*, *Garamantes*, and of *Goaga*, all within the Northern Tropicks are not *Negroes*; but on the other side about *Capo Negro*, *Cefala*, and *Madagascar*, they are of a jetty black.

Now if to salve this Anomaly we say the heat of the Sun is more powerful in the Southern Tropick, because in the sign of Capricorn fals out the Perigeum or lowest place of the Sun in his Excentrick, whereby he becomes nearer unto them than unto the other in Cancer, we shall not absolve the doubt. And if any insist upon such niceties, and will presume a different effect of the Sun, from such a difference of place or vicinity, we shall ballance the same with the concernment of its motion, and time of revolution, and say he is more powerful in the Northern Hemisphere, and in the Apogeum; for therein his motion is slower, and so his heat respectively unto those habitations, as of duration, so also of more effect. For, though he absolve his revolution in 365 days, odd hours and minutes, yet by reason of Excentricity, his motion is unequal, and his course far longer in the Northern Semicircle, than in the Southern; for the latter he passeth in a 178 days, but the other takes him a 187, that is, eleven days more. So is his presence more continued unto the Northern Inhabitants; and the longer day in Cancer is longer unto us, than that in Capricorn unto the Southern Habitator. Beside, hereby we only infer an inequality of heat in different Tropicks, but not an equality of effects in other parts subjected to the same. For, in the same degree, and as near the earth he makes his revolution unto the *American*, whose Inhabitants notwithstanding partake not of the same effect. And if herein we seek a relief from the Dog-star, we shall introduce an effect proper unto a few, from a cause common unto many; for upon the same grounds that Star should have as forcible a power upon *America* and *Asia*; and although it be not vertical unto any part of *Asia*, but only passeth by *Beach*, *in terra incognita*; yet is it so unto *America*, and vertically passeth over the habitations of *Peru* and *Brasilia*.

Sixthly, And which is very considerable, there are *Negroes* in *Africa* beyond the Southern Tropick, and some so far removed from it, as Geographically the clime is not intemperate, that is, near the Cape of good Hope, in 36 of the Southern Latitude. Whereas in the same elevation Northward, the Inhabitants of *America* are fair; and they of *Europe* in *Candy*, *Sicily*, and some parts of *Spain*, deserve not properly so low a name as *Tawny*.

Lastly, Whereas the *Africans* are conceived to be more peculiarly scorched and torrified from the Sun, by addition of driness from the soil, from want and defect of water, it will not excuse the doubt. For the parts which the *Negroes* possess, are not so void of Rivers and moisture, as is presumed; for on the other side the mountains of the Moon, in that great tract called *Zanzibar*, there are the mighty Rivers of *Suama* and *Spirito Santo*; on this side, the great River *Zaire*, the mighty *Nile* and *Niger*; which do not only moisten and contemperate the air by their exhalations, but refresh and humectate the earth by their annual Inundations. Beside, in that part of *Africa*, which with all disadvantage is most dry, that is, in situation between the Tropicks, defect of Rivers and inundations, as also abundance of Sands, the people are not esteemed *Negroes*; and that is *Lybia*, which with the *Greeks* carries the name of all *Africa*. A region so desert, dry and sandy, that Travellers (as *Leo* reports) are fain to carry water on their Camels; whereof they find not a drop sometime in six or seven days. Yet is this Country accounted by Geographers no part of *terra Nigritarum*, and *Ptolomy* placeth herein the *Leuco Æthiops*, or pale and Tawny *Moors*.

Now the ground of this opinion might be the visible quality of Blackness observably produced by heat, fire and smoak; but especially with the Ancients the violent esteem they held of the heat of the Sun, in the hot or torrid Zone; conceiving that part unhabitable, and therefore that people in the vicinities or frontiers thereof, could not escape without this change of their complexions. But how far they were mistaken in this apprehension, modern Geography hath discovered: And as we have declared, there are many within this Zone whose complexions descend not so low as unto blackness. And if we should strictly insist hereon, the possibility might fall into question; that is, whether the heat of the Sun, whose fervour may swart a living part, and even black a dead or dissolving flesh, can yet in animals, whose parts are successive and in continual flux, produce this deep and perfect gloss of Blackness.

The particular causes of the Negroes blackness probably.

Thus having evinced, at least made dubious, the Sun is not the Author of this Blackness, how, and when this tincture first began is yet a Riddle, and positively to determine, it surpasseth my presumption. Seeing therefore we cannot discover what did effect it, it may afford some piece of satisfaction to know what might procure it. It may be therefore considered, whether the inward use of certain waters or fountains of peculiar operations, might not at first produce the effect in question. For, of the like we have records in *Aristotle*, *Strabo* and *Pliny*, who hath made a collection hereof, as of two fountains in *Bœotia*, the one making Sheep white, the other black; of the water of *Siberis* which made Oxen black, and the like effect it had also upon men, dying not only the skin, but making their hairs black and curled. This was the conceit of *Aristobulus*, who received so little satisfaction from the other, or that it might be caused by heat, or any kind of fire, that he conceived it as reasonable to impute the effect unto water.

Secondly, It may be perpended whether it might not fall out the same way that *Jacobs* cattle became speckled, spotted and ring-straked, that is, by the Power and Efficacy of Imagination; which produceth effects in the conception correspondent unto the phancy of the Agents in generation; and sometimes assimilates the Idea of the Generator into a reality in the thing ingendred. For, hereof there pass for current many indisputed examples; so in *Hippocrates* we read of one, that from an intent view of a Picture conceived a *Negro*; And in the History of *Heliodore* of a Moorish Queen, who upon aspection of the Picture of *Andromeda*, conceived and brought forth a fair one. *Vide plura apud Tho. Fienum, de viribus imaginationis.* And thus perhaps might some say was the beginning of this complexion: induced first by Imagination, which having once impregnated the seed, found afterward concurrent co-operation, which were continued by Climes, whose constitution advantaged the first impression. *Why Beares etc. white in some places.* Thus *Plotinus* conceiveth white Peacocks first came in. Thus many opinion that from aspection of the Snow, which lieth long in Northern Regions, and high mountains. Hawks, Kites, Beares, and other creatures become white; and by this way *Austin* conceiveth the devil provided, they never wanted a white spotted Ox in *Egypt*; for such an one they worshipped, and called *Apis*.

Thirdly, It is not indisputable whether it might not proceed from such a cause and the like foundation of Tincture, as doth the black Jaundise, which meeting with congenerous causes might settle durable inclinations, and advance their generations unto that hue, which were naturally before but a degree or two below it. And this transmission we shall the easier admit in colour, if we remember the like hath been effected in organical parts and figures; the Symmetry whereof being casually or purposely perverted; their morbosities have vigorously descended to their posterities, and that in durable deformities. This was the beginning of *Macrocephali*, or people with long heads, whereof *Hippocrates* De Aere, Aquis, et Locis. hath clearly delivered himself: *Cum primum editus est Infans, caput ejus tenellum manibus effingunt, et in logitudine adolescere cogunt; hoc institutum primum hujusmodi, naturæ dedit vitium, successu vero temporis in naturam abiit, ut proinde instituto nihil amplius opus esset; semen enim genitale ex omnibus corporis partibus provenit, ex sanis quidem sanum, ex morbosis morbosum. Si igitur ex calvis calvi, ex cæciis cæcii, et ex distortis, ut plurimum, distorti gignuntur, eademque in cæteris formis valet ratio, quid prohibet cur non ex macrocephalis macrocephali gignantur?* Thus as *Aristotle* observeth, the Deers of *Arginusa* had their ears divided; occasioned at first by slitting the ears of Deers. Thus have the *Chineses* little feet, most *Negroes* great Lips and flat Noses; And thus many *Spaniards*, and *Mediterranean* Inhabitants, which are of the Race of *Barbary Moors* (although after frequent commixture) have not worn out the *Camoys* Nose Flat Nose. unto this day.

Artificial *Negroes*, or *Gypsies* acquire their complexion by anointing their bodies with Bacon and fat substances, and so exposing them to the Sun. In *Guiny Moors* and others, it hath been observed, that they frequently moisten their skins with fat and oyly materials, to temper the irksom driness thereof from the parching rayes of the Sun. Whether this practise at first had not some efficacy toward this complexion, may also be considered.

How sundry kinds of Animals come to be found in Islands.

Lastly, If we still be urged to particularities, and such as declare how, and when the seed of *Adam* did first receive this tincture; we may say that men became black in the same manner that some Foxes, Squirrels, Lions, first turned of this complexion, whereof there are a constant sort in divers Countries; that some Chaughs came to have red Legs and Bils, that Crows became pyed: All which mutations however they began, depend on durable foundations; and such as may continue for ever. And if as yet we must farther define the cause and manner of this mutation, we must confess, in matters of Antiquity, and such as are decided by History, if their Originals and first beginnings escape a due relation, they fall into great obscurities, and such as future Ages seldom reduce unto a resolution. Thus if you deduct the administration of Angels, and that they dispersed the creatures into all parts after the flood, as they had congregated them into *Noahs* Ark before; it will be no easie question to resolve, how several sorts of animals were first dispersed into Islands, and almost how any into *America*: How the venereal Contagion began in that part of the earth, since history is silent, is not easily resolved by Philosophy. For whereas it is imputed unto Anthropophagy, or the eating of mans flesh; that cause hath been common unto many other Countries, and there have been Canibals or men eaters in the three other parts of the world, if we credit the relations of *Ptolomy*, *Strabo* and *Pliny*. And thus if the favourable pen of *Moses* had not revealed the confusion of tongues, and positively declared their division at *Babel*, our disputes concerning their beginning had been without end; Elias cum venerit solvet dubium. and I fear we must have left the hopes of that decision unto *Elias*.

And if any will yet insist, and urge the question farther still upon me, I shall be enforced unto divers of the like nature, wherein perhaps I shall receive no greater satisfaction. I shall demand how the Camels of *Bactria* came to have two bunches on their backs, whereas the Camels of *Arabia* in all relations have but one? How Oxen in some Countries began and continue gibbous or bunch-back'd? what way those many different shapes, colours, hairs, and natures of Dogs came in? how they of some Countries became depilous, and without any hair at all, whereas some sorts in excess abound therewith? How the Indian Hare came to have a long tail, whereas that part in others attains no higher than a scut? How the hogs of *Illyria* which *Aristotle* speaks of, became solipedes or whole-hoofed, whereas in other parts they are bisulcous, and described cloven-hoofed by God himself? All which with many others must needs seem strange unto those that hold there were but two of the unclean sort in the ark; and are forced to reduce these varieties to unknown originals.

How the complexion of the Negroes may be propagated.

However therefore this complexion was first acquired, it is evidently maintained by generation, and by the tincture of the skin as a spermatical part traduced from father unto Son; so that they which are strangers contract it not, and the Natives which transmigrate, omit it not without commixture, and that after divers generations. And this affection (if the story were true) might wonderfully be confirmed, by what *Maginus* and others relate of the Emperour of *Æthiopia*, or *Prester John*, who derived from *Solomon* is not yet descended into the hue of his Country, but remains a *Mulatto*, that is, of a Mongril complexion unto this day. Now although we conceive this blackness to be seminal, yet are we not of *Herodotus* conceit, that their seed is black. An opinion long ago rejected by *Aristotle*, and since by sense and enquiry. His assertion against the Historian was probable, that all seed was white; that is without great controversie in viviparous Animals, and such as have Testicles, or preparing vessels wherein it receives a manifest dealbation. And not only in them, but (for ought I know) in Fishes not abating the seed of Plants; whereof at least in most though the skin and covering be black, yet is the seed and fructifying part not so; as may be observed in the seeds of *Onyons*, *Pyonie* and *Basil*. Most controvertible it seems in the spawn of Frogs, and Lobsters, whereof notwithstanding at the very first the spawn is white, contracting by degrees a blackness, answerable in the one unto the colour of the shell, in the other unto the Porwigle or Tadpole; that is that Animall which first proceedeth from it. And thus may it also be in the generation and sperm of Negroes; that being first and in its naturals white, but upon separation of parts, accidents before invisible become apparent; there arising a shadow or dark efflorescence in the outside; whereby not only their legitimate and timely births, but their abortions are also dusky, before they have felt the scorch and fervor of the Sun.

CHAPTER XI
Of the same.

A Second opinion there is, that this complexion was first a curse of God derived unto them from *Cham*, upon whom it was inflicted for discovering the nakedness of *Noah*. Which notwithstanding is sooner affirmed then proved, and carrieth with it sundry improbabilities. For first, if we derive the curse on *Cham*, or in general upon his posterity, we shall denigrate a greater part of the earth then was ever so conceived; and not only paint the Æthiopians and reputed sons of *Cush*, but the people also of *Egypt*, *Arabia*, *Assyria* and *Chaldea*; for by this race were these Countries also peopled. And if concordantly unto *Berosus*, the fragment of *Cato de Originibus*, some things of *Halicarnasseus*, *Macrobius*, and out of them of *Leandro* and *Annius*, we shall conceive of the travels of *Camese* or *Cham*; we may introduce a generation of *Negroes* as high as *Italy*; which part was never culpable of deformity, but hath produced the magnified examples of beauty.

Secondly, The curse mentioned in Scripture was not denounced upon *Cham*, but *Canaan* his youngest son, and the reasons thereof are divers. The first, from the Jewish Tradition, whereby it is conceived that *Canaan* made the discovery of the nakedness of *Noah*, and notified it unto *Cham*. Secondly, to have cursed *Cham* had been to curse all his posterity, whereof but one was guilty of the fact. And lastly, he spared *Cham*, because he had blessed him before. Cap. 9. Now if we confine this curse unto *Canaan*, and think the same fulfilled in his posterity; then do we induce this complexion on the Sidonians, then was the promised land a tract of Negroes; For from *Canaan* were descended the *Canaanites*, *Jebusites*, *Amorites*, *Gergazites* and *Hivites*, which were possessed of that land.

Thirdly, Although we should place the original of this curse upon one of the sons of *Cham*, yet were it not known from which of them to derive it. For the particularity of their descents is imperfectly set down by accountants, nor is it distinctly determinable from whom thereof the *Æthiopians* are proceeded. For whereas these of *Africa* are generally esteemed to be the Issue of *Chus*, the elder son of *Cham*, it is not so easily made out. For the land of *Chus*, which the Septuagint translates *Æthiopia*, makes no part of *Africa*, nor is it the habitation of Blackmores, but the Country of *Arabia*, especially the Happy and Stony possessions and Colonies of all the sons of *Chus*, excepting *Nimrod* and *Havilah*: possessed and planted wholly by the children of *Chus*, that is, by *Sabtah* and *Raamah*, *Sabtacha*, and the sons of *Raamah*, *Dedan*, and *Sheba*, according unto whose names the Nations of those parts have received their denominations, as may be collected from *Pliny* and *Ptolemy*; and as we are informed by credible Authors, they hold a fair Analogy in their names, even unto our days. So the wife of *Moses* translated in Scripture an *Æthiopian*, and so confirmed by the fabulous relation of *Josephus*, was none of the daughters of *Africa*, nor any Negroe of *Æthiopia*, but the daughter of *Jethro*, Prince and Priest of *Madian*, which was a part of *Arabia* the stony, bordering upon the Red Sea. So the Queen of *Sheba* came not unto *Solomon* out of *Æthiopia*, but from *Arabia*, and that part thereof which bore the name of the first planter, the son of *Chus*. So whether the Eunuch which *Philip* the Deacon baptised, were servant unto *Candace* Queen of the *African Æthiopia* (although *Damianus a Goes*, *Codignus*, and the Æthiopick relations averr) is yet by many, and with strong suspitions doubted. So that Army of a million, which *Zerah* King of *Æthiopia* is said to bring against *Asa*, was drawn out of *Arabia*, and the plantations of *Chus*; not out of *Æthiopia*, and the remote habitations of the Moors. For it is said that *Asa* pursuing his victory, took from him the City *Gerar*; now *Gerar* was no City in or near *Æthiopia*, but a place between *Cadesh* and *Zur*, where *Abraham* formerly sojourned. Since thereof these *African Æthiopians* are not convinced by the common acception to be the sons of *Chus*, whether they be not the posterity of *Phut* or *Mizraim*, or both, it is not assuredly determined. For *Mizraim*, he possessed *Egypt*, and the East parts of *Africa*. From *Lubym* his son came the *Lybians*, and perhaps from them the *Æthiopians*. *Phut* possessed *Mauritania*, and the Western parts of *Africa*, and from these perhaps descended the Moors of the West, of *Mandinga*, *Meleguette* and *Guinie*. But from *Canaan*, upon whom the curse was pronounced, none of these had their originall; for he was restrained unto *Canaan* and *Syria*; although in after Ages many Colonies dispersed, and some thereof upon the coasts of *Africa*, and prepossessions of his elder brothers.

Fourthly, To take away all doubt or any probable divarication, the curse is plainly specified in the Text, nor need we dispute it, like the mark of *Cain*; *Servus servorum erit fratribus suis*, Cursed be *Canaan*, a servant of servants shall he be unto his brethren; which was after fulfilled in the conquest of *Canaan*, subdued by the *Israelites*, the posterity of *Sem*. Which Prophecy *Abraham* well understanding, took an oath of his servant not to take a wife for his son *Isaac* out of the daughters of the *Canaanites*; and the like was performed by *Isaac* in the behalf of his Son *Jacob*. As for *Cham* and his other sons, this curse attained them not; for *Nimrod* the son of *Chus* set up his kingdom in *Babylon*, and erected the first great Empire; *Mizraim* and his posterity grew mighty Monarchs in *Egypt*; and the Empire of the *Æthiopians* hath been as large as either. Nor did the curse descend in generall upon the posterity of *Canaan*: for the *Sidonians*, *Arkites*, *Hamathites*, *Sinites*, *Arvadites*, and *Zemerites* seem exempted. But why there being eleven Sons, five only were condemned and six escaped the malediction, is a secret beyond discovery.

Lastly, Whereas men affirm this colour was a Curse, I cannot make out the propriety of that name, it neither seeming so to them, nor reasonably unto us; for they take so much content therein, that they esteem deformity by other colours, describing the Devil, and terrible objects, white. And if we seriously consult the definitions of beauty, and exactly perpend what wise men determine thereof, we shall not apprehend a curse, or any deformity therein. For first, some place the essence thereof in the proportion of parts, conceiving it to consist in a comely commensurability of the whole unto the parts, and the parts between themselves: which is the determination of the best and learned Writers. Now hereby the Moors are not excluded from beauty: there being in this description no consideration of colours, but an apt connexion and frame of parts and the whole. Others there be, and those most in number, which place it not only in proportion of parts, but also in grace of colour. But to make Colour essential unto Beauty, there will arise no slender difficulty: For *Aristotle* in two definitions of pulchritude, and *Galen* in one, have made no mention of colour.

Neither will it agree unto the Beauty of Animals: wherein notwithstanding there is an approved pulchritude. Thus horses are handsome under any colour, and the symmetry of parts obscures the consideration of complexions. Thus in concolour animals and such as are confined unto one colour, we measure not their Beauty thereby: For if a Crow or Black-bird grow white, we generally account it more pretty; and in almost a monstrosity descend not to opinion of deformity. By this way likewise the Moors escape the curse of deformity: there concurring no stationary colour, and sometimes not any unto Beauty.

The Platonick contemplators reject both these descriptions founded upon parts and colours, or either: as *M. Leo* the Jew hath excellently discoursed in his Genealogy of Love, defining beauty a formal grace, which delights and moves them to love which comprehend it. This grace say they, discoverable outwardly, is the resplendor and Ray of some interiour and invisible Beauty, and proceedeth from the forms of compositions amiable. Whose faculties if they can aptly contrive their matter, they beget in the subject an agreeable and pleasing beauty; if over-ruled thereby, they evidence not their perfections, but run into deformity. For seeing that out of the same materials, *Thersites* and *Paris*, Beauty and monstrosity may be contrived; the forms and operative faculties introduce and determine their perfections. Which in natural bodies receive exactness in every kind, according to the first *Idea* of the Creator, and in contrived bodies the phancy of the Artificer. And by this consideration of Beauty, the Moors also are not excluded, but hold a common share therein with all mankind.

Lastly, In whatsoever its *Theory* consisteth, or if in the general, we allow the common conceit of symmetry and of colour, yet to descend unto singularities, or determine in what symmetry or colour it consisted, were a slippery designation. For Beauty is determined by opinion, and seems to have no essence that holds one notion with all; that seeming beauteous unto one, which hath no favour with another; and that unto every one, according as custome hath made it natural, or sympathy and conformity of minds shall make it seem agreeable. Thus flat noses seem comely unto the Moor, an Aquiline or hawked one unto the *Persian*, a large and prominent nose unto the Romane; but none of all these are acceptable in our opinion. Thus some think it most ornamental to wear their Bracelets on their Wrests, others say it is better to have them about their Ancles; some think it most comely to wear their Rings and Jewels in the Ear, others will have them about their Privities; a third will not think they are compleat except they hang them in their lips, cheeks, or noses. Thus *Homer* to set off *Minerva*, calleth her γλαυκῶπις, that is, gray or light-blew eyed: now this unto us seems far less amiable then the black. Thus we that are of contrary complexions accuse the blackness of the Moors as ugly: But the Spouse in the *Canticles* excuseth this conceit, in that description of hers, I am black, but comely. And howsoever *Cerberus*, and the furies of hell be described by the Poets under this complexion, yet in the beauty of our Saviour blackness is commended, when it is said, his locks are bushie and black as a Raven. So that to inferr this as a curse, or to reason it as a deformity, is no way reasonable; the two foundations of beauty, Symmetry and complexion receiving such various apprehensions, that no deviation will be expounded so high as a curse or undeniable deformity, without a manifest and confessed degree of monstrosity.

Lastly, It is a very injurious method unto Philosophy, and a perpetual promotion of ignorance, in points of obscurity; nor open unto easie considerations, to fall upon a present refuge unto Miracles; or recurr unto immediate contrivance, from the insearchable hands of God. Thus in the conceit of the evil odor of the Jews, Christians without a further research into the verity of the thing, or inquiry into the cause, draw up a judgement upon them from the passion of their Saviour. Thus in the wondrous effects of the clime of *Ireland*, and the freedom from all venemous creatures, the credulity of common conceit imputes this immunity unto the benediction of S. *Patrick*, as *Beda* and *Gyraldus* have left recorded. Thus the Ass having a peculiar mark of a cross made by a black list down his back, and another athwart, or at right angles down his shoulders; common opinion ascribes this figure unto a peculiar signation; since that beast had the honour to bear our Saviour on his back. Certainly this is a course more desperate then Antipathies, Sympathies, or occult qualities; wherein by a final and satisfactive discernment of faith, we lay the last and particular effects upon the first and general cause of all things; whereas in the other, we do but palliate our determinations, untill our advanced endeavours do totally reject, or partially salve their evasions.

CHAPTER XII
A Digression concerning Blackness.

There being therefore two opinions repugnant unto each other, it may not be presumptive or skeptical to doubt of both. And because we remain imperfect in the general Theory of colours, we shall deliver at present a short discovery of blackness; wherein although perhaps we afford no greater satisfaction then others, yet shall we Emperically and sensibly discourse hereof; deducing the causes of Blackness from such Originals in nature, as we do generally observe things are denigrated by Art. And herein I hope our progression will not be thought unreasonable, for Art being the imitation of Nature, or Nature at the second hand, it is but a sensible expression of effects dependant on the same, though more removed causes: and therefore the works of the one may serve to discover the other. And though colours of bodies may arise according to the receptions, refraction, or modification of Light; yet are there certain materialls which may dispose them unto such qualities.

And first, Things become black by a sooty and fuliginous matter proceeding from the Sulphur of bodies torrified; not taking *fuligo* strictly, but in opposition unto ἀτμὸς, that is any kind of vaporous or madefying excretion; and comprehending ἀναθυμίασις, that is as *Aristotle* defines it, a separation of moist and dry parts made by the action of heat or fire, and colouring bodies objected. Hereof in his Meteors, from the qualities of the subject he raiseth three kinds; the exhalations from ligneous and lean bodies, as bones, hair, and the like he calleth κάπνος, *fumus*, from fat bodies, and such as have not their fatness conspicuous or separated he termeth λίγνυς, *fuligo*, as wax, rosin, pitch, or turpentine; that from unctuous bodies, and such whose oyliness is evident, he named κνίση or *nidor*. Now everyone of these do black bodies objected unto them, and are to be conceived in the sooty and fuliginous matter expressed.

I say, proceeding from the sulphur of bodies torrified, that is the oylie fat, and unctuous parts wherein consist the principles of flammability. Not pure and refined sulphur, as in the Spirits of wine often rectified; but containing terrestrious parts, and carrying with it the volatile salt of the body, and such as is distinguishable by taste in soot; nor vulgar and usual sulphur, for that leaves none or very little blackness, except a metalline body receive the exhalation.

I say, torrified, sindged, or suffering some impression from fire; thus are bodies casually or artificially denigrated, which in their naturals are of another complexion; thus are Charcoals made black by an infection of their own suffitus, so is it true what is affirmed of combustible bodies. *Adusta nigra, perusta alba*; black at first from the fuliginous tincture, which being exhaled they become white, as is perceptible in ashes. And so doth fire cleanse and purifie bodies, because it consumes the sulphureous parts, which before did make them foul: and therefore refines those bodies which will never be mundified by water. Thus Camphire of a white substance, by its *fuligo* affordeth a deep black. So is pitch black, although it proceed from the same tree with Rosin, the one distilling forth, the other forced by fire. So of the suffitus of a torch, do Painters make a velvet black: so is lamp-black made: so of burnt Harts-horn a sable; so is Bacon denigrated in chimnies: so in Feavers and hot distempers from choler adust is caused a blackness in our tongues, teeth and excretions: so are ustilago, brant corn and trees black by blasting; so parts cauterized, gangrenated, siderated and mortified, become black, the radical moisture, or vital sulphur suffering an extinction, and smothered in the part effected. So not only actual but potential fire: not burning fire, but also corroding water will induce a blackness.

Why the smoak of pure Sulphur blacks not. So are Chimnies and Furnaces generally black, except they receive a clear and manifest sulphur: for the smoak of sulphur will not black a paper, and is commonly used by women to whiten Tiffinies, which it performeth by an acide vitriolous, and penetrating spirit ascending from it, by reason whereof it is not apt to kindle any thing nor will it easily light a Candle, untill that spirit be spent, and the flame approacheth the match. This is that acide and piercing spirit which with such activity and compunction invadeth the brains and nostrils of those that receive it. And thus when *Bellonius* affirmeth that Charcoals made out of the wood of Oxycedar are white, Dr. *Jordan* in his judicious Discourse of mineral waters yeeldeth the reason, because their vapors are rather sulphureous then of any other combustible substance. So we see that *Tinby* coals will not black linnen being hanged in the smoak thereof, but rather whiten it, by reason of the drying and penetrating quality of sulphur, which will make Red roses white. And therefore to conceive a general blackness in Hell, and yet therein the pure and refined flames of sulphur, is no Philosophical conception, nor will it well consist with the real effects of its nature.

These are the advenient and artificial wayes of denigration, answerably whereto may be the natural progress. These are the wayes whereby culinary and common fires do operate, and correspondent hereunto may be the effects of fire elemental. So may Bitumen, Coals, Jet, Black-lead, and divers mineral earths become black; being either fuliginous concretions in the earth, or suffering a scorch from denigrating Principles in their formation. So men and other animals receive different tinctures from constitution and complexional efflorescences, and descend still lower, as they partake of the fuliginous and denigrating humour. And so may the *Æthiopians* or *Negroes* become coal-black, from fuliginous efflorescences and complexional tinctures arising from such probabilities, as we have declared before.

The second way whereby bodies become black, is an Atramentous condition or mixture, that is a vitriolate or copperose quality conjoyning with a terrestrious and astringent humidity; for so is *Atramentum Scriptorium*, or writing Ink commonly made by copperose cast upon a decoction or infusion of galls. I say a vitriolous or copperous quality; for vitriol is the active or chief ingredient in Ink, and no other salt that I know will strike the colour with galls; neither Alom, Sal-gem, Nitre, nor Armoniack. *What the common Copperose is.* Now artificial copperose, and such as we commonly use, is a rough and acrimonious kind of salt drawn out of ferreous and eruginous earths, partaking chiefly of Iron and Copper; the blew of Copper, the green most of Iron: Nor is it unusual to dissolve fragments of Iron in the liquor thereof, for advantage in the concretion. I say, a terrestrious or astringent humidity; for without this there will ensue no tincture; for Copperose in a decoction of Lettuce or Mallows affords no black, which with an astringent mixture it will do, though it be made up with oyl, as in printing and painting Ink. But whereas in this composition we use only Nut-gals, that is an excrescence from the Oak, therein we follow and beat upon the old receit; for any plant of austere and stiptick parts will suffice, as I have experimented in *Bistorte, Myrobolans, Myrtus Brabantica, Balaustium* and Red Roses. And indeed, most decoctions of astringent plants, of what colour soever, do leave in the Liquor a deep and Muscadine red: which by addition of vitriol descends into a black: and so *Dioscorides* in his receit of Ink, leaves out gall, and with copperose makes use of soot.

Now if we enquire in what part of vitriol this Atramental and denigrating condition lodgeth, it will seem especially to lie in the more fixed salt thereof; for the phlegm or aqueous evaporation will not denigrate; nor yet spirits of vitriol, which carry with them volatile and nimbler Salt: For if upon a decoction of Copperose and gall, be poured the spirits or oyl of vitriol, the liquor will relinquish his blackness; the gall and parts of the copperose precipitate unto the bottom, and the Ink grow clear again; which it will not so easily do in common Ink, because that gum is dissolved therein which hindereth the separation. But Colcothar or vitriol burnt, though unto a redness containing the fixed salt, will make good Ink; and so will the Lixivium, or Lye made thereof with warm water; but the Terra or Insipid earth remaining, affords no black at all, but serves in many things for a gross and useful red. And though Spirits of vitriol, projected upon a decoction of gals, will not raise a black, yet if these spirits be any way fixed, or return into vitriol again, the same will act their former parts and denigrate as before.

And if we yet make a more exact enquiry, by what this salt of vitriol more peculiarly gives this colour, we shall find it to be from a metalline condition, and especially an Iron Property or ferreous participation. For blew Copperose which deeply partakes of the copper will do it but weakly, Verdigrise which is made of Copper will not do it at all, but the filings of Iron infused in vinegar, will with a decoction of gals make good Ink, without any Copperose at all; and so will infusion of Load-stone; which is of affinity with Iron. And though more conspicuously in iron, yet such a Calcanthous or Atramentous quality, we will not wholly reject in other mettals; whereby we often observe black tinctures in their solutions. Thus a Lemmon, Quince or sharp Apple cut with a knife becomes immediately black: And from the like cause, Artichokes; so sublimate beat up with whites of eggs, if touched with a knife, becomes incontinently black. So *Aqua fortis*, whose ingredient is vitriol, will make white bodies black. So leather dressed with the bark of Oak, is easily made black by a bare solution of Copperose. So divers Mineral waters and such as participate of Iron, upon an infusion of gals, become of a dark colour, and entering upon black. So steel infused, makes not only the liquor duskie, but in bodies wherein it concurs with proportionable tinctures makes also the excretions black. And so also from this vitriolous quality *Mercurius dulcis*, and vitriol vomitive occasion black ejections. But whether this denigrating quality in Copperose proceedeth from an Iron participation, or rather in Iron from a vitriolous communication; or whether black tinctures from metallical bodies be not from vitriolous parts contained in their sulphur, since common sulphur containeth also much vitriol, may admit consideration. However in this way of tincture, it seemeth plain, that Iron and Vitriol are the powerful Denigrators.

Such a condition there is naturally in some living creatures. Thus that black humour by *Aristotle* named θόλος, and commonly translated *Atramentum*, may be occasioned in the Cuttle-fish. Such a condition there is naturally in some Plants, as Black-berries, Walnut-rinds, Black-cherries; whereby they extinguish inflammations, corroborate the stomack, and are esteemed specifical in the Epilepsie. Such an atramentous condition there is to be found sometime in the blood, when that which some call *Acetum*, others *Vitriolum*, concurs with parts prepared for this tincture. And so from these conditions the Moors might possibly become Negroes, receiving Atramentous impressions in some of those wayes, whose possibility is by us declared.

How a vitriolous quality may be in living bodies.

Nor is it strange that we affirm there are vitriolous parts, qualities, and even at some distance Vitriol it self in living bodies; for there is a sower stiptick salt diffused through the Earth, which passing a concoction in plants, becometh milder and more agreeable unto the sense, and this is that vegetable vitriol, whereby divers plants contain a gratefull sharpness, as Lemmons, Pomegranats, Cherries, or an austere and inconcocted roughness, as Sloes, Medlars and Quinces. And that not only vitriol is a cause of blackness, but that the salts of natural bodies do carry a powerfull stroke in the tincture and vernish of all things, we shall not deny, if we contradict not experience, and the visible art of Dyars; who advance and graduate their colours with Salts. For the decoctions of simples which bear the visible colours of bodies decocted, are dead and evanid, without the commixtion of Alum, Argol, and the like. And this is also apparent in Chymical preparations. So Cinaber becomes red by the acide exhalation of sulphur, which otherwise presents a pure and niveous white. So spirits of Salt upon a blew paper make an orient red. So Tartar or vitriol upon an infusion of violets affords a delightfull crimson.

Whence the colours of Plants, etc. may arise.

Thus it is wonderful what variety of colours the spirits of Saltpeter, and especially, if they be kept in a glass while they pierce the sides thereof; I say, what Orient greens they will project: from the like spirits in the earth the plants thereof perhaps acquire their verdure. And from such salary irradiations may those wondrous varieties arise, which are observable in Animals, as Mallards heads, and Peacocks feathers, receiving intention or alteration according as they are presented unto the light. Thus Saltpeter, Ammoniack and Mineral spirits emit delectable and various colours; and common *Aqua fortis* will in some green and narrow mouthed glasses, about the verges thereof, send forth a deep and Gentianella blew.

Thus have we at last drawn our conjectures unto a period; wherein if our contemplations afford no satisfaction unto others, I hope our attempts will bring no condemnation on our selves (for besides that adventures in knowledge are laudable, and the assayes of weaker heads afford oftentimes improveable hints unto better) although in this long journey we miss the intended end; yet are there many things of truth disclosed by the way; and the collaterall verity may unto reasonable speculations some what requite the capital indiscovery.

CHAPTER XIII
Of Gypsies.

Great wonder it is not we are to seek in the original of *Æthiopians* and natural Negroes, being also at a loss concerning the Original of Gypsies and counterfeit Moors, observable in many parts of *Europe*, *Asia*, and *Africa*.

Opinions concerning the original of Gypsies.

Common opinion deriveth them from *Egypt*, and from thence they derive themselves, according to their own account hereof, as *Munster* discovered in the letters and pass which they obtained from *Sigismund* the Emperour; that they first came out of lesser *Egypt*, that having defected from the Christian rule, and relapsed unto Pagan rites, some of every family were enjoyned this penance to wander about the world; or as *Aventinus* delivereth, they pretend for this vagabond course, a judgement of God upon their fore-fathers, who refused to entertain the Virgin *Mary* and Jesus, when she fled into their Country.

Which account notwithstanding is of little probability: for the generall stream of writers, who enquire into their originall, insist not upon this; and are so little satisfied in their descent from *Egypt*, that they deduce them from several other nations: *Fernand. de Cordua didascal. multipl.* *Polydore Virgil* accounting them originally *Syrians*, *Philippus Bergomas* fetcheth them from *Chaldæa*, *Æneas Sylvius* from some part of *Tartary*, *Bellonius* no further then *Walachia* and *Bulgaria*, nor *Aventinus* then the confines of *Hungaria*.

That they are no *Egyptians*, *Bellonius* *Observat. l. 2.* maketh evident: who met great droves of Gypsies in *Egypt*, about Gran Cairo, Matærea, and the villages on the banks of *Nilus*, who notwithstanding were accounted strangers unto that Nation, and wanderers from foreign parts, even as they are esteemed with us.

Gypsies first known in Germany.

That they came not out of *Egypt* is also probable, because their first appearance was in *Germany*, since the year 1400, nor were they observed before in other parts of *Europe*, as is deducible from *Munster, Genebrard, Crantsius* and *Ortilius*.

But that they first set out not far from *Germany*, is also probable from their language, which was the Sclavonian tongue; and when they wandred afterward into *France*, they were commonly called *Bohemians*, which name is still retained for Gypsies. And therefore when *Crantsius* delivereth, they first appeared about the Baltick Sea, when *Bellonius* deriveth them from *Bulgaria* and *Walachia*, and others from about *Hungaria*, they speak not repugnantly hereto: for the language of those Nations was Sclavonian, at least some dialect thereof.

What use the Grand Signior maketh of Gypsies.

But of what nation soever they were at first, they are now almost of all; associating unto them some of every country where they wander: when they will be lost, or whether at all again, is not without some doubt: for unsetled nations have out-lasted others of fixed habitations: and though Gypsies have been banished by most Christian Princes, yet have they found some countenance from the great Turk, who suffereth them to live and maintain publick Stews near the Imperial City in *Pera*, *Bellon. observat. l. 2.* of whom he often maketh a politick advantage, imploying them as spies into other nations, under which title they were banished by *Charles* the fift.

CHAPTER XIV
Of some others.

We commonly accuse the phancies of elder times in the improper figures of heaven assigned unto Constellations, which do not seem to answer them, either in Greek or Barbarick Spheres: yet equall incongruities have been commonly committed by Geographers and Historians, in the figurall resemblances of several regions on earth; While by *Livy* and *Julius*, *Rusticus* the Island of *Britain* is made to resemble a long dish or two-edged ax; *Italy* by *Numatianus* to be like an Oak-leaf: and *Spain* an Ox-hide; while the phancy of *Strabo* makes the habitated earth like a cloak, and *Dionysius Afer* will have it like a sling: with many others observable in good writers [Tacit. de vita Jul. Agric.], yet not made out from the letter or signification; acquitting Astronomy in their figures of the Zodiack: wherein they are not justified unto strict resemblances, but rather made out from the effects of Sun or Moon in these several portions of heaven, or from peculiar influences of those constellations, which some way make good their names [Junctin. in Sph. l. de Sacro bosco cap. 2.].

Which notwithstanding being now authentick by prescription, may be retained in their naked acceptions, and names translated from substances known on earth. And therefore the learned *Hevelius* in his accurate Selenography, or description of the Moon, hath well translated the known appellations of Regions, Seas and Mountains, unto the parts of that Luminary: and rather then use invented names or humane denominations, with witty congruity hath placed *Mount Sinai, Taurus, Mæotis Palus,* the Mediterranean Sea, *Mauritania, Sicily* and *Asia* Minor in the Moon.

More hardly can we find the Hebrew letters in the heavens, made out of the greater and lesser Stars which put together do make up words, wherein Cabalisticall Speculators conceive they read the events of future things; [The Cabala of the Stars.] and how from the Stars in the head of *Medusa,* to make out the word *Charab;* and thereby desolation presignified unto *Greece* or *Javan,* numerally characterized in that word, requireth no rigid reader [Greffarel *out of R.* Chomer.].

It is not easie to reconcile the different accounts of longitude, while in modern tables the hundred and eighty degree is more then thirty degrees beyond that part, where *Ptolomy* placeth an 180. Nor will the wider and more Western term of Longitude, from whence the Moderns begin their commensuration, sufficiently salve the difference [Athan. Kircher. in prooemio.]. The ancients began the measure of Longitude from the fortunate Islands or Canaries, the Moderns from the Azores or Islands of S. *Michael;* but since the Azores are but fifteen degrees more West, why the Moderns should reckon 180, where *Ptolomy* accounteth above 220, or though they take in 15 degrees at the West, why they should reckon 30 at the East, beyond the same measure, is yet to be determined; nor would it be much advantaged, if we should conceive that the compute of *Ptolomy* were not so agreeable unto the Canaries, as the Hesperides or Islands of *Cabo Verde* [Robertus Hues de globis.].

Whether the compute of moneths from the first appearance of the Moon, which divers nations have followed, be not a more perturbed way, then that which accounts from the conjunction, may seem of reasonable doubt [Hevel. Selenog. cap. 9.]; not only from the uncertainty of its appearance in foul and cloudy weather, but unequal time in any; [When the Moon will be seen on the first day of the change.] that is sooner or later, according as the Moon shall be in the signs of long descention, as *Pisces, Aries, Taurus,* in the Perigeum or swiftest motion, and in the Northern Latitude: whereby sometimes it may be seen the very day of the change, as will observably happen 1654, in the moneths of April and May? or whether also the compute of the day be exactly made, from the visible arising or setting of the Sun, because the Sun is sometimes naturally set, and under the Horizon, when visibly it is above it; *Why the Sun is seen after it is set, or naturally under the Horizon.* from the causes of refraction, and such as make us behold a piece of silver in a basin, when water is put upon it, which we could not discover before, as under the verge thereof.

Whether the globe of the earth be but a point, in respect of the Stars and Firmament, or how if the rayes thereof do fall upon a point, they are received in such variety of Angles, appearing greater or lesser from differences of refraction?

To what the motion of the Heavens serveth, Met. Lib.

Whether if the motion of the Heavens should cease a while, all things would instantly perish? and whether this assertion doth not make the frame of sublunary things to hold too loose a dependency upon the first and conserving cause? at least impute too much unto the motion of the heavens, whose eminent activities are by heat, light and influence, the motion it self being barren, or chiefly serving for the due application of celestial virtues unto sublunary bodies as *Cabeus* hath learnedly observed?

Whether Comets or blazing Stars be generally of such terrible effects, as elder times have conceived them; for since it is found that many, from whence these predictions are drawn, have been above the Moon; why they may not be qualified from their positions, and aspects which they hold with stars of favourable natures; or why since they may be conceived to arise from the effluviums of other Stars, they may not retain the benignity of their Originals; or since the natures of the fixed Stars are astrologically differenced by the Planets, and are esteemed Martial or Jovial, according to the colours whereby they answer these Planets; why although the red Comets do carry the portensions of Mars, the brightly-white should not be of the Influence of Jupiter or Venus, answerably unto *Cor Scorpii* and Arcturus, is not absurd to doubt.

VOL. III
PREFATORY NOTE

In concluding the present edition of Sir Thomas Browne's works, attention may be drawn to the reprint of the *Hydriotaphia*, from the first edition of 1658. The copy collated was the one preserved in the Library of Trinity College, Cambridge. In this, in addition to the corrections made at the time of publication on the printed label attached, there are a few others made by a contemporary hand, which deserve consideration. Among these is the excision of a sentence hitherto preserved in the text, and now relegated to the margin (p. 205). If further sanction were needed for the change indicated, it may be gathered from the inscription on the title-page, 'Ex dono Auctoris.' The text of the *Christian Morals* of 1716 has been collated with the copy in the same Library.

For the account of Birds and Fishes found in Norfolk (pp. 513-539), Professor Alfred Newton generously placed his annotated copy at the disposal of the editor. As those actual pages were in the press, Professor Newton passed away, and Death has deprived us of the pleasure of placing this volume in his hands. In this edition Professor Newton's readings have been in the main followed, with the additional help of the valuable recension, published by Mr. Thomas Southwell of Norwich, in 1902, to which every serious student of this treatise must always refer.

For further assistance in questions of identification, I am again indebted to the kindness of Mr. W. Aldis Wright; and for one correction to Mr. A. R. Waller.

Sir Thomas Browne's Latin treatises and his correspondence are not included in these volumes. It was the determination of the original publisher of this edition that they should be omitted; and indeed they do not form the most characteristic part of Sir Thomas Browne's work. His erudition, and the resources from which he drew, his amazing industry, his marvellous diction, and natural piety—all these are apparent to the general reader of his English text; and it is to such that the present edition of Sir Thomas Browne's works, as they originally appeared, will primarily appeal.

C. S.

16th June 1907.

THE SEVENTH BOOK
Concerning many Historical Tenents generally received, and some deduced from the history of holy Scripture.

CHAPTER I
Of the Forbidden Fruit.

Opinions, of what kind the forbidden fruit was.

That the Forbidden fruit of Paradise was an Apple, is commonly believed, confirmed by Tradition, perpetuated by Writings, Verses, Pictures; and some have been so bad *Prosodians*, as from thence to derive the Latine word *malum*, because that fruit was the first occasion of evil; wherein notwithstanding determinations are presumptuous, and many I perceive are of another belief. For some have, conceived it a Vine; in the mystery of whose fruit lay the expiation of the transgression: *Goropius Becanus* reviving the conceit of *Barcephas*, peremptorily concludeth it to be the *Indian* Fig-tree; and by a witty Allegory labours to confirm the same. Again, some fruits pass under the name of *Adams* apples, which in common acception admit not that appellation; the one described by *Mathiolus* under the name of *Pomum Adami*, a very fair fruit, and not unlike a Citron, but somewhat rougher, chopt and cranied, vulgarly conceived the marks of *Adams* teeth. Another, the fruit of that plant which *Serapion* termeth *Musa*, but the Eastern Christians commonly the Apples of Paradise; not resembling an apple in figure, and in taste a Melon or Cowcomber. Which fruits although they have received appellations suitable unto the tradition, yet can we not from thence infer they were this fruit in question: No more then *Arbor vitæ*, so commonly called, to obtain its name from the tree of life in Paradise, or *Arbor Judæ*, to be the same which supplied the gibbet unto *Judas*.

Again, There is no determination in the Text; wherein is only particulared that it was the fruit of a tree good for food, and pleasant unto the eye, in which regards many excell the Apple; and therefore learned men do wisely conceive it inexplicable; and *Philo* puts determination unto despair, when he affirmeth the same kind of fruit was never produced since. Surely were it not requisite to have been concealed, it had not passed unspecified; nor the tree revealed which concealed their nakedness, and that concealed which revealed it; for in the same chapter mention is made of fig-leaves. And the like particulars, although they seem uncircumstantial, are oft set down in holy Scripture; so is it specified that *Elias* sat under a juniper tree, *Absalom* hanged by an Oak, and *Zacheus* got up into a Sycomore.

And although to condemn such Indeterminables unto him that demanded on what hand *Venus* was wounded, the Philosopher thought it a sufficient resolution to re-inquire upon what leg King *Philip* halted; and the *Jews* not undoubtedly resolved of the Sciatica-side of *Jacob*, [Jacobs *Sciatica*, see *Gen.* 32. 25, 31, 32.] do cautelously in their diet abstain from the sinews of both: yet are there many nice particulars which may be authentically determined. That *Peter* cut off the right ear of *Malchus*, is beyond all doubt. That our Saviour eat the Passover in an upper room, we may determine from the Text. And some we may concede which the Scripture plainly defines not. That the Dyal of *Ahaz* was placed upon the West side of the Temple, we will not deny, or contradict the description of *Adricomius*. That *Abrahams* servant put his hand under his right thigh, we shall not question; and that the Thief on the right hand was saved, and the other on the left reprobated, to make good the Method of the last judicial dismission, we are ready to admit. But surely in vain we enquire of what wood was *Moses* rod, or the tree that sweetned the waters. Or though tradition or humane History might afford some light, whether the Crown of thorns was made of *Paliurus*; Whether the cross of Christ were made of those four woods in the Distick of *Durantes*, [*Pes ceorus est, truncus cupressus, oliva supremum, palmaq; transversum Christi sunt in cruce lignum.*] or only of Oak, according unto *Lipsius* and *Goropius*, we labour not to determine. For though hereof prudent Symbols and pious Allegories be made by wiser Conceivers; yet common heads will flie unto superstitious applications, and hardly avoid miraculous or magical expectations.

Now the ground or reason that occasioned this expression by an Apple, might be the community of this fruit, and which is often taken for any other. So the Goddess of Gardens is termed *Pomona*; so the Proverb expresseth it to give Apples unto *Alcinous;* so the fruit which *Paris* decided was called an Apple; so in the garden of *Hesperides* (which many conceive a fiction drawn from Paradise) we read of golden Apples guarded by the Dragon. And to speak strictly in this appellation, they placed it more safely then any other; for beside the great variety of Apples, the word in Greek comprehendeth Orenges, Lemmons, Citrons, Quinces; and as *Ruellius* defineth, [*Ruel. de stirpium natura.*] such fruits as have no stone within, and a soft covering without; excepting the Pomegranate. And will extend much farther in the acception of *Spigelius*, [*Isagoge in rem Herbariam.*] who comprehendeth all round fruits under the name of apples, not excluding Nuts and Plumbs.

It hath been promoted in some constructions from a passage in the *Canticle*, [*Can.* 8.] as it runs in the vulgar translation, *Sub arbore malo suscitavi te, ibi corrupta est mater tua, ibi violata est genetrix tua*; Which words notwithstanding parabolically intended, admit no literal inference, and are of little force in our translation, I raised thee under an Apple-tree, there thy mother brought thee forth, there she brought thee forth that bare thee. So when from a basket of summer fruits or apples, as the vulgar rendreth them, God by *Amos* foretold the destruction of his people, we cannot say they had any reference unto the fruit of Paradise, which was the destruction of man; but thereby was declared the propinquity of their desolation, and that their tranquility was of no longer duration then those horary or soon decaying fruits of Summer. Nor when it is said in the same translation, [*Fructus horæi.*] *Poma desiderii animæ tuæ discesserunt à te*, the apples that thy soul lusted after are departed from thee, is there any allusion therein unto the fruit of Paradise. But thereby is threatned unto *Babylon*, that the pleasures and delights of their Palate should forsake them. And we read in *Pierius*, that an Apple was the Hieroglyphick of Love, and that the Statua of *Venus* was made with one in her hand. So the little Cupids in the figures of *Philostratus* [*Philostrat.* figur. 6. De amoribus.] do play with apples in a garden; and there want not some who have symbolized the Apple of Paradise unto such constructions.

Since therefore after this fruit, curiosity fruitlessly enquireth, and confidence blindly determineth, we shall surcease our Inquisition; rather troubled that it was tasted, then troubling our selves in its decision; this only we observe, when things are left uncertain, men will assure them by determination. Which is not only verified concerning the fruit, but the Serpent that perswaded; many defining the kind or species thereof. *Opinions of what kind the Serpent was, etc.* So *Bonaventure* and *Comestor* affirm it was a Dragon, *Eugubinus* a Basilisk, *Delrio* a Viper, and others a common snake. Wherein men still continue the delusion of the Serpent, who having deceived *Eve* in the main, sets her posterity on work to mistake in the circumstance, and endeavours to propagate errors at any hand. And those he surely most desireth which concern either God or himself; for they dishonour God who is absolute truth and goodness; but for himself, who is extreamly evil, and the worst we can conceive, by aberration of conceit they may extenuate his depravity, and ascribe some goodness unto him.

CHAPTER II
That a Man hath one Rib less then a Woman.

That a Man hath one Rib less then a Woman, is a common conceit derived from the History of *Genesis*, wherein it stands delivered, that *Eve* was framed out of a Rib of *Adam*; whence 'tis concluded the sex of man still wants that rib our Father lost in *Eve*. And this is not only passant with the many, but was urged against *Columbus* in an Anatomy of his at *Pisa*, where having prepared the Sceleton of a woman that chanced to have thirteen ribs on one side, there arose a party that cried him down, and even unto oaths affirmed, this was the rib wherein a woman exceeded. Were this true, it would ocularly silence that dispute out of which side *Eve* was framed; it would determine the opinion of *Oleaster*, that she was made out of the ribs of both sides, or such as from the expression of the Text [Os ex ossibus meis.] maintain there was a plurality of ribs required; and might indeed decry the parabolical exposition of *Origen*, *Cajetan*, and such as fearing to concede a monstrosity, or mutilate the integrity of *Adam*, preventively conceive the creation of thirteen ribs.

How many ribs commonly in men and women.

But this will not consist with reason or inspection. For if we survey the Sceleton of both sexes, and therein the compage of bones, we shall readily discover that men and women have four and twenty ribs, that is, twelve on each side, seven greater annexed unto the Sternon, and five lesser which come short thereof. Wherein if it sometimes happen that either sex exceed, the conformation is irregular, deflecting from the common rate or number, and no more inferrible upon mankind, then the monstrosity of the son of *Rapha*, or the vitious excess in the number of fingers and toes. And although some difference there be in figure and the female *os inominatum* be somewhat more protuberant, to make a fairer cavity for the Infant; the coccyx sometime more reflected to give the easier delivery, and the ribs themselves seem a little flatter, yet are they equal in number. And therefore while *Aristotle* doubteth the relations made of Nations, which had but seven ribs on a side, and yet delivereth, that men have generally no more than eight; as he rejecteth their history, so can we not accept of his Anatomy.

Again, Although we concede there wanted one rib in the Sceleton of *Adam*, yet were it repugnant unto reason and common observation that his posterity should want the same. For we observe that mutilations are not transmitted from father unto son; the blind begetting such as can see, men with one eye children with two, and cripples mutilate in their own persons do come out perfect in their generations. For the seed conveyeth with it not only the extract and single Idea of every part, whereby it transmits their perfections or infirmities; but double and over again; whereby sometimes it multipliciously delineates the same, as in Twins, in mixed and numerous generations. Parts of the seed do seem to contain the Idea and power of the whole; so parents deprived of hands, beget manual issues, and the defect of those parts is supplied by the Idea of others. So in one grain of corn appearing similary and insufficient for a plural germination, there lyeth dormant the virtuality of many other; and from thence sometimes proceed above an hundred ears. And thus may be made out the cause of multiparous productions; for though the seminal materials disperse and separate in the matrix, the formative operator will not delineate a part, but endeavour the formation of the whole; effecting the same as far as the matter will permit, and from dividing materials attempt entire formations. And therefore, though wondrous strange, it may not be impossible what is confirmed at *Lausdun* concerning the Countess of *Holland*, nor what *Albertus* reports of the birth of an hundred and fifty. And if we consider the magnalities of generation in some things, we shall not controvert its possibilities in others: nor easily question that great work, whose wonders are only second unto those of the Creation, and a close apprehension of the one, might perhaps afford a glimmering light, and crepusculous glance of the other.

CHAPTER III
Of *Methuselah*.

What hath been every where opinioned by all men, and in all times, is more then paradoxical to dispute; and so that *Methuselah* was the longest liver of all the posterity of *Adam*, we quietly believe: but that he must needs be so, is perhaps below paralogy to deny. For hereof there is no determination from the Text; wherein it is only particulared he was the longest Liver of all the Patriarchs whose age is there expressed; but that he out-lived all others, we cannot well conclude. For of those nine whose death is mentioned before the flood, the Text expresseth that *Enoch* was the shortest Liver; who saw but three hundred sixty-five years. But to affirm from hence, none of the rest, whose age is not expressed, did die before that time, is surely an illation whereto we cannot assent.

Again, Many persons there were in those days of longevity, of whose age notwithstanding there is no account in Scripture; as of the race of *Cain*, the wives of the nine Patriarchs, with all the sons and daughters that every one begat: whereof perhaps some persons might out-live *Methuselah*; the Text intending only the masculine line of *Seth*, conduceable unto the Genealogy of our Saviour, and the antediluvian Chronology. And therefore we must not contract the lives of those which are left in silence by *Moses*; for neither is the age of *Abel* expressed in the Scripture, yet is he conceived far elder then commonly opinioned; and if we allow the conclusion of his Epitaph as made by *Adam*, and so set down by *Salian*, *Posuit mœrens pater, cui à filio justius positum foret, Anno ab ortu rerum 130. Ab Abele nato 129*, we shall not need to doubt. Which notwithstanding *Cajetan* and others confirm, nor is it improbable, if we conceive that *Abel* was born in the second year of *Adam*, and *Seth* a year after the death of *Abel*: for so it being said, that *Adam* was an hundred and thirty years old when he begat *Seth*, *Abel* must perish the year before, which was one hundred twenty nine.

And if the account of *Cain* extend unto the Deluge, it may not be improbable that some thereof exceeded any of *Seth*. Nor is it unlikely in life, riches, power and temporal blessings, they might surpass them in this world, whose lives related unto the next. For so when the seed of *Jacob* was under affliction and captivity, that of *Ismael* and *Esau* flourished and grew mighty, there proceeding from the one twelve Princes, from the other no less then fourteen Dukes and eight Kings. And whereas the age of *Cain* and his posterity is not delivered in the Text, some do salve it from the secret method of Scripture, which sometimes wholly omits, but seldom or never delivers the entire duration of wicked and faithless persons, as is observable in the history of *Esau*, and the Kings of *Israel* and *Judah*. And therefore when mention is made that *Ismael* lived 137 years, some conceive he adhered unto the faith of *Abraham*; *Job thought by some to be of the race of* Esau. for so did others who were not descended from *Jacob*; for *Job* is thought to be an *Idumean*, and of the seed of *Esau*.

Lastly (although we rely not thereon) we will not omit that conceit urged by learned men, that *Adam* was elder then *Methuselah*; inasmuch as he was created in the perfect age of man, which was in those days 50 or 60 years, for about that time we read that they begat children; so that if unto 930 we add 60 years, he will exceed *Methuselah*. And therefore if not in length of days, at least in old age he surpassed others; he was older then all, who was never so young as any. For though he knew old age, he was never acquainted with puberty, youth or Infancy; and so in a strict account he begat children at one year old. And if the usual compute will hold, that men are of the same age which are born within compass of the same year, *Eve* was as old as her husband and parent *Adam*, and *Cain* their son coetaneous unto both.

Now that conception, that no man did ever attain unto a thousand years, because none should ever be one day old in the sight of the Lord, unto whom according to that of *David*, A thousand years are but one day, doth not advantage *Methuselah*. And being deduced from a popular expression, which will not stand a *Metaphysical* and strict examination, is not of force to divert a serious enquirer. For unto God a thousand years are no more then one moment, and in his sight *Methuselah* lived no nearer one day then *Abel*, for all parts of time are alike unto him, unto whom none are referrible; and all things present, unto whom nothing is past or to come. And therefore, although we be measured by the Zone of time, and the flowing and continued instants thereof, do weave at last a line and circle about the eldest: yet can we not thus commensurate the sphere of *Trismegistus*; or sum up the unsuccessive and stable duration of God.

CHAPTER IV
That there was no Rain-bow before the Flood.

That there shall no Rain-bow appear forty years before the end of the world, and that the preceding drought unto that great flame shall exhaust the materials of this Meteor, was an assertion grounded upon no solid reason: but that there was not any in sixteen hundred years, that is, before the flood, seems deduceable from holy Scripture, *Gen.* 9. I do set my bow in the clouds, and it shall be for a token of a Covenant between me and the earth. From whence notwithstanding we cannot conclude the nonexistence of the Rain-bow; nor is that Chronology naturally established, which computeth the antiquity of effects arising from physical and setled causes, by additionall impositions from voluntary determinators. Now by the decree of reason and Philosophy, the Rain-bow hath its ground in Nature, as caused by the rays of the Sun, falling upon a roride and opposite cloud: whereof some reflected, others refracted, beget that semi-circular variety we generally call the Rain-bow; which must succeed upon concurrence of causes and subjects aptly predisposed. And therefore, to conceive there was no Rain-bow before, because God chose this out as a token of the Covenant, is to conclude the existence of things from their signalities, or of what is objected unto the sense, a coexistence with that which is internally presented unto the understanding. With equall reason we may infer there was no water before the institution of Baptism, nor bread and wine before the holy Eucharist.

That there is a Rain-bow of the Moon.

Again, while men deny the antiquity of one Rain-bow, they anciently concede another. For, beside the solary Iris which God shewed unto *Noah*, there is another Lunary, whose efficient is the Moon, visible only in the night, most commonly at full Moon, and some degrees above the Horizon. Now the existence hereof men do not controvert, although effected by a different Luminary in the same way with the other. And probably appeared later, as being of rare appearance and rarer observation, and many there are which think there is no such thing in Nature. And therefore by casual spectators they are lookt upon like prodigies, and significations made, not signified by their natures.

Lastly, We shall not need to conceive God made the Rain-bow at this time, if we consider that in its created and predisposed nature, it was more proper for this signification then any other Meteor or celestial appearancy whatsoever. Thunder and lightning had too much terrour to have been tokens of mercy; Comets or blazing Stars appear too seldom to put us in mind of a Covenant to be remembred often: and might rather signifie the world should be once destroyed by fire, then never again by water. The Galaxia or milky Circle had been more probable; for (beside that unto the latitude of thirty, it becomes their Horizon twice in four and twenty hours, and unto such as live under the Æquator, in that space the whole Circle appeareth) part thereof is visible unto any situation; but being only discoverable in the night, and when the ayr is clear, it becomes of unfrequent and comfortless signification. A fixed Star had not been visible unto all the Globe, and so of too narrow a signality in a Covenant concerning all. But Rain-bows are seen unto all the world, and every position of sphere. Unto our own elevation they may appear in the morning, while the Sun hath attained about forty five degrees above the Horizon (which is conceived the largest semi-diameter of any Iris) and so in the afternoon when it hath declined unto that altitude again; which height the Sun not attaining in winter, rain-bows may happen with us at noon or any time. Unto a right position of sphere they may appear three hours after the rising of the Sun, and three before its setting; for the Sun ascending fifteen degrees an hour, in three attaineth forty five of altitude. Even unto a parallel sphere, and such as live under the pole, for half a year some segments may appear at any time and under any quarter, the Sun not setting, but walking round about them.

The natural signification of the rain-bow.

But the propriety of its Election most properly appeareth in the natural signification and prognostick of it self; as containing a mixt signality of rain and fair weather. For being in a roride cloud and ready to drop, it declareth a pluvious disposure in the air; but because when it appears the Sun must also shine, there can be no universal showrs, and consequently no Deluge. Thus when the windows of the great deep were open, in vain men lookt for the Rain-bow: for at that time it could not be seen, which after appeared unto *Noah*. It might be therefore existent before the flood, and had in nature some ground of its addition. Unto that of nature God superadded an assurance of his Promise, that is, never to hinder its appearance, or so to replenish the heavens again, as that we should behold it no more. And thus without disparaging the promise, it might rain at the same time when God shewed it unto *Noah*; thus was there more therein then the heathens understood, when they called it the *Nuncia* of the gods, and the laugh of weeping Heaven; Risus plorantis Olympi. and thus may it be elegantly said; I put my bow, not my arrow in the clouds, that is, in the menace of rain the mercy of fair weather.

Cabalistical heads, who from that expression in *Esay*, Isa. 34. 4. do make a book of heaven, and read therein the great concernments of earth, do literally play on this, and from its semicircular figure, resembling the Hebrew letter כ Caph, whereby is signified the uncomfortable number of twenty, at which years *Joseph* was sold, which *Jacob* lived under *Laban*, and at which men were to go to war: do note a propriety in its signification; as thereby declaring the dismal Time of the Deluge. And Christian conceits do seem to strain as high, while from the irradiation of the Sun upon a cloud, they apprehend the mysterie of the Sun of Righteousness in the obscurity of flesh; by the colours green and red, the two destructions of the world by fire and water; or by the colours of blood and water, the mysteries of Baptism, and the holy Eucharist.

Laudable therefore is the custom of the *Jews*, who upon the appearance of the Rain-bow, do magnifie the fidelity of God in the memory of his Covenant; according to that of *Syracides*, look upon the Rain-bow, and praise him that made it. And though some pious and Christian pens have only symbolized the same from the mysterie of its colours, yet are there other affections which might admit of Theological allusions. Nor would he find a more improper subject, that should consider that the colours are made by refraction of Light, and the shadows that limit that light; that the Center of the Sun, the Rain-bow, and the eye of the Beholder must be in one right line, that the spectator must be between the Sun and the Rain-bow; that sometime there appear, sometime one reversed. With many others, considerable in Meteorological Divinity, which would more sensibly make out the Epithite of the Heathens; Thaumancias. and the expression of the son of *Syrach*. Very beautifull is the Rain-bow, it compasseth the heaven about with a glorious circle, and the hands of the most High have bended it.

CHAPTER V
Of *Sem*, *Ham* and *Japhet*.

Concerning the three sons of *Noah*, *Sem, Ham* and *Japhet*, that the order of their nativity was according to that of numeration, and *Japhet* the youngest son, as most believe, as *Austin* and others account, the sons of *Japhet*, and *Europeans* need not grant: nor will it so well concord unto the letter of the Text, and its readiest interpretations. For so is it said in our Translation, *Sem* the father of all the sons of *Heber* the brother of *Japhet* the elder: so by the Septuagint, and so by that of *Tremelius*. And therefore when the Vulgar reads it, *Fratre Japhet majore*, the mistake as *Junius* observeth, might be committed by the neglect of the Hebrew account; which occasioned *Jerom* so to render it, and many after to believe it. Nor is that Argument contemptible which is deduced from their Chronology: for probable it is that *Noah* had none of them before, and begat them from that year when it is said he was five hundred years old, and begat *Sem, Ham* and *Japhet*. Again it is said he was six hundred years old at the flood, and that two years after *Sem* was but an hundred; therefore *Sem* must be born when *Noah* was five hundred and two, and some other before in the year of five hundred and one.

Now whereas the Scripture affordeth the priority of order unto *Sem*, we cannot from thence infer his primogeniture. For in *Sem* the holy line was continued: and therefore however born, his genealogy was most remarkable. So is it not unusuall in holy Scripture to nominate the younger before the elder: so is it said, That *Tarah* begat *Abraham*, Gen. 11. *Nachor* and *Haram*: whereas *Haram* was the eldest. So *Rebecca* Gen. 28. is termed the mother of *Jacob* and *Esau*. Nor is it strange the younger should be first in nomination, who have commonly had the priority in the blessings of God, and been first in his benediction. *In divine benedictions the younger often preferred.* So *Abel* was accepted before *Cain*, *Isaac* the younger preferred before *Ishmael* the elder, *Jacob* before *Esau*, *Joseph* was the youngest of twelve, and *David* the eleventh son and minor cadet of *Jesse*.

Lastly, though *Japhet* were not elder then *Sem*, yet must we not affirm that he was younger then *Cham*, for it is plainly delivered, that after *Sem* and *Japhet* had covered *Noah*, he awaked, and knew what his youngest son had done unto him υἱὸς ὁ νεώτερος, is the expression of the Septuagint, *Filius minor* of *Jerom*, and *minimus* of *Tremelius*. And upon these grounds perhaps *Josephus* doth vary from the Scripture enumeration, and nameth them *Sem, Japhet* and *Cham*; which is also observed by the *Annian Berosus*; *Noah cum tribus filiis, Semo, Japeto, Cham*. And therefore although in the priority of *Sem* and *Japhet*, there may be some difficulty, though *Cyril, Epiphanius* and *Austin* have accounted *Sem* the elder, and *Salian* the *Annalist*, and *Petavius* the Chronologist contend for the same, yet *Cham* is more plainly and confessedly named the youngest in the Text.

That Noah *and* Saturn *were the same person.*

And this is more conformable unto the Pagan history and Gentile account hereof, unto whom *Noah* was *Saturn*, whose symbol was a ship, as relating unto the Ark, and who is said to have divided the world between his three sons. *Ham* is conceived to be *Jupiter*, who was the youngest son: worshipped by the name of *Hamon*, which was the *Egyptian* and *African* name for *Jupiter*, who is said to have cut off the genitals of his father, derived from the history of *Ham* Gen. 9. 22. , who beheld the nakednes of his, and by no hard mistake; *Reading* Veiaggod et abscidit, *for* Veiegged et nunciavit. might be confirmed from the Text, as *Bochartus* Bochartus de Geographia sacrâ. hath well observed.

CHAPTER VI
That the Tower of *Babel* was erected against a second Deluge.

An opinion there is of some generality, that our fathers after the flood attempted the Tower of *Babel* to secure themselves against a second Deluge. Which however affirmed by *Josephus* and others, hath seemed improbable unto many who have discoursed hereon. For (beside that they could not be ignorant of the Promise of God never to drown the world again, and had the Rainbow before their eyes to put them in mind thereof) it is improbable from the nature of the Deluge; which being not possibly causable from natural showers above, or watery eruptions below, but requiring a supernatural hand, and such as all acknowledg irresistible; must needs disparage their knowledg and judgment in so succesless attempts.

Again, They must probably hear, and some might know, that the waters of the flood ascended fifteen cubits above the highest mountains. Now, if as some define, the perpendicular altitude of the highest mountains be four miles; or as others, but fifteen furlongs, it is not easily conceived how such a structure could be effected. Although we allowed the description of *Herodotus* concerning the Tower of *Belus*; whose lowest story was in height and bredth one furlong, and seven more built upon it; abating that of the Annian *Berosus*, the traditional relation of *Jerom*, and fabulous account of the *Jews*. Probable it is that what they attempted was feasible, otherwise they had been amply fooled in fruitless success of their labours, nor needed God to have hindred them, saying, Nothing will be restrained from them, which they begin to do.

History of the world.

It was improbable from the place, that is a plain in the land of *Shinar*. And if the situation of *Babylon* were such at first as it was in the days of *Herodotus*, it was rather a feat of amenity and pleasure, than conducing unto this intention. It being in a very great plain, and so improper a place to provide against a general Deluge by Towers and eminent structures, that they were fain to make provisions against particular and annual inundations by ditches and trenches, after the manner of *Egypt*. And therefore Sir *Walter Raleigh* accordingly objecteth: If the Nations which followed *Nimrod*, still doubted the surprise of a second flood, according to the opinions of the ancient *Hebrews*, it soundeth ill to the ear of Reason, that they would have spent many years in that low and overflown valley of *Mesopotamia*. And therefore in this situation, they chose a place more likely to have secured them from the worlds destruction by fire, then another Deluge of water: and as *Pierius* observeth, some have conceived that this was their intention.

Lastly, The reason is delivered in the Text. Let us build us a City and a Tower, whose top may reach unto heaven, and let us make us a name, lest we be scattered abroad upon the whole earth; as we have already began to wander over a part. These were the open ends proposed unto the people; but the secret design of *Nimrod* was to settle unto himself a place of dominion, and rule over his Brethren, as it after succeeded, according to the delivery of the Text, the beginning of his kingdom was *Babel*.

CHAPTER VII
Of the Mandrakes of *Leah*.

We shall not omit the Mandrakes of *Leah*, according to the History of *Genesis*. And *Reuben* went out in the daies of Wheat-harvest, and found Mandrakes in the field, and brought them unto his mother *Leah*; then *Rachel* said unto *Leah*, give me, I pray thee, of thy sons Mandrakes: and she said unto her, is it a small matter that thou hast taken my husband, and wouldest thou take my sons Mandrakes also? and *Rachel* said, Therefore he shall lie with thee this night for thy sons Mandrakes. From whence hath arisen a common conceit, that *Rachel* requested these plants as a medicine of fecundation, or whereby she might become fruitfull. Which notwithstanding is very questionable, and of incertain truth.

For first from the comparison of one Text with another, whether the Mandrakes here mentioned, be the same plant which holds that name with us, there is some cause to doubt. The word is used in another place of Scripture, *Cant. 7.* when the Church inviting her beloved into the fields, among the delightfull fruits of Grapes and Pomegranates, it is said, The Mandrakes give a smell, and at our gates are all manner of pleasant fruits. Now instead of a smell of Delight, our Mandrakes afford a papaverous and unpleasant odor, whether in the leaf or apple, as is discoverable in their simplicity or mixture. The same is also dubious from the different interpretations: for though the Septuagint and *Josephus* do render it the Apples of Mandrakes in this Text, yet in the other of the *Canticles*, the *Chaldy* Paraphrase termeth it Balsame. R. *Solomon*, as *Drusius* observeth, conceives it to be that plant the *Arabians* named Jesemin. *Oleaster*, and *Georgius Venetus*, the Lilly, and that the word *Dudaim* may comprehend any plant that hath a good smell, resembleth a womans breast, and flourisheth in wheat harvest. *Tremelius* interprets the same for any amiable flowers of a pleasant and delightfull odor: but the *Geneva* Translators have been more wary then any: for although they retain the word Mandrake in the Text, they in effect retract it in the Margin: wherein is set down the word in the original is *Dudaim*, which is a kind of fruit or Flower unknown.

The vegetables in H. Scripture how variously expounded.

Nor shall we wonder at the dissent of exposition, and difficulty of definition concerning this Text, if we perpend how variously the vegetables of Scripture are expounded, and how hard it is in many places to make out the *species* determined. Thus are we at variance concerning the plant that covered *Jonas*; which though the Septuagint doth render Colocynthis, the *Spanish* Calabaca, and ours accordingly a Gourd: yet the vulgar translates it Hedera or Ivy; and as *Grotius* observeth, *Jerom* thus translated it, not as the same plant, but best apprehended thereby. The Italian of *Diodati*, and that of *Tremelius* have named it *Ricinus*, and so hath ours in the Margin, for *palma Christi* is the same with *Ricinus*. The *Geneva* Translators have herein been also circumspect, for they have retained the Original word *Kikaion*, and ours hath also affixed the same unto the Margin.

Nor are they indeed always the same plants which are delivered under the same name, and appellations commonly received amongst us. So when it is said of *Solomon*, that he writ of plants from the Cedar of Lebanus, unto the Hysop that groweth upon the wall, that is, from the greatest unto the smallest, it cannot be well conceived our common Hysop; for neither is that the least of vegetables, nor observed to grow upon wals; but rather as *Lemnius* well conceiveth, some kind of the capillaries, which are very small plants, and only grow upon wals and stony places. Nor are the four species in the holy oyntment, Cinnamon, Myrrhe, Calamus and Cassia, nor the other in the holy perfume, Frankincense, Stacte, Onycha and Galbanum, so agreeably expounded unto those in use with us, as not to leave considerable doubts behind them. Nor must that perhaps be taken for a simple unguent, which *Matthew* only termeth a precious oyntment; but rather a composition as *Mark* and *John* imply by pistick Nard, *V. Mathioli. Epist.* that is faithfully dispensed, and may be that famous composition described by *Dioscorides*, made of oyl of Ben, Malabathrum, Juncus Odoratus, Costus, Amomum, Myrrhe, Balsam and Nard; which *Galen* affirmeth to have been in use with the delicate Dames of *Rome*; and that the best thereof was made at *Laodicea*; from whence by Merchants it was conveyed unto other parts. But how to make out that Translation concerning the Tithe of Mint, Anise and Cumin, we are still to seek; for we find not a word in the Text that can properly be rendred Anise; the Greek being ἄνηθον, which the Latines call *Anethum*, and is properly Englished Dill. Lastly, What meteor that was, that fed the *Israelites* so many years, they must rise again to inform us. Nor do they make it out, *V. Doctissimum Chrysostom. Magnenum de Manna.* who will have it the same with our Manna; nor will any one kind thereof, or hardly all kinds we read of, be able to answer the qualities thereof, delivered in the Scripture;

that is, to fall upon the ground, to breed worms, to melt with the Sun, to taste like fresh oyl, to be grounded in Mils, to be like Coriander seed, and of the colour of Bdellium.

Again, It is not deducible from the Text or concurrent sentence of Comments, that *Rachel* had any such intention, and most do rest in the determination of *Austin*, that she desired them for rarity, pulchritude or suavity. Nor is it probable she would have resigned her bed unto *Leah*, when at the same time she had obtained a medicine to fructifie her self. And therefore *Drusius* who hath expresly and favourable treated hereof, is so far from conceding this intention, that he plainly concludeth, *Hoc quo modo illis in mentem venerit conjicere nequeo*; how this conceit fell into mens minds, it cannot fall into mine; for the Scripture delivereth it not, nor can it be clearly deduced from the Text.

Thirdly, If *Rachel* had any such intention, yet had they no such effect, for she conceived not many years after of *Joseph*; whereas in the mean time *Leah* had three children, *Isachar*, *Zebulon* and *Dinah*.

Lastly, Although at that time they failed of this effect, yet is it mainly questionable whether they had any such vertue either in the opinions of those times, or in their proper nature. That the opinion was popular in the land of *Canaan*, it is improbable, and had *Leah* understood thus much, she would not surely have parted with fruits of such a faculty; especially unto *Rachel*, who was no friend unto her. As for its proper nature, the Ancients have generally esteemed in Narcotick or stupefactive, and it is to be found in the list of poysons, set down by *Dioscorides*, *Galen*, *Ætius*, *Ægineta*, and several Antidotes delivered by them against it. It was I confess from good Antiquity, and in the days of *Theophrastus* accounted a philtre, or plant that conciliates affection; and so delivered by *Dioscorides*. And this intent might seem most probable, had they not been the wives of holy *Jacob*: had *Rachel* presented them unto him, and not requested them for her self.

Now what *Dioscorides* affirmeth in favour of this effect, that the grains of the apples of Mandrakes mundifie the matrix, and applied with Sulphur, stop the fluxes of women, he overthrows again by qualities destructive unto conception; affirming also that the juice thereof purgeth upward like Hellebore; and applied in pessaries provokes the menstruous flows, and procures abortion. *Petrus Hispanus*, or Pope *John* the twentieth speaks more directly in his *Thesaurus pauperum*: wherein among the receits of fecundation, he experimentally commendeth the wine of Mandrakes given with *Triphera magna*. But the soul of the medicine may lie in *Triphera magna*, an excellent composition, and for this effect commended by *Nicolaus*. And whereas *Levinus Lemnius* that eminent Physitian doth also concede this effect, it is from manifest causes and qualities elemental occasionally producing the same. For he imputeth the same unto the coldness of that simple, and is of opinion that in hot climates, and where the uterine parts exceed in heat, by the coldness hereof they may be reduced into a conceptive constitution, and Crasis accommodable unto generation; whereby indeed we will not deny the due and frequent use may proceed unto some effect, from whence notwithstanding we cannot infer a fertilitating condition or property of fecundation. For in this way all vegetables do make fruitful according unto the complexion of the Matrix; if that excel in heat, plants exceeding in cold do rectifie it; if it be cold, simples that are hot reduce it; if dry moist, if moist dry correct it; in which division all plants are comprehended. But to distinguish thus much is a point of Art, and beyond the Method of *Rachels* or feminine Physick. Again, Whereas it may be thought that Mandrakes may fecundate, since Poppy hath obtained the Epithite of fruitful, and that fertility was Hieroglyphically described by *Venus* with an head of Poppy in her hand; the reason hereof was the multitude of seed within it self, and no such multiplying in humane generation. And lastly, whereas they may seem to have this quality, since Opium it self is conceived to extimulate unto venery, and for that intent is sometimes used by *Turks*, *Persians*, and most oriental Nations; although *Winclerus* doth seem to favour the conceit, yet *Amatus Lusitanus*, and *Rodericus à Castro* are against it; *Garcias ab horto* refutes it from experiment; and they speak probably who affirm the intent and effect of eating Opium, *Opium, of what effect in venery.* it not so much to invigorate themselves in coition, as to prolong the Act, and spin out the motions of carnality.

CHAPTER VIII
Of the three Kings of *Collein*.

Three magi or wise men (Mat. 2.) *What manner of Kings they were.*

A common conceit there is of the three Kings of *Collein*, conceived to be the wise men that travelled unto our Saviour by the direction of the Star, Wherein (omitting the large Discourses of *Baronius*, *Pineda* and *Montacutius*,) that they might be Kings, beside the Ancient Tradition and Authority of many Fathers, the Scripture also implieth. The Gentiles shall come to thy light, and Kings to the brightness of thy rising. The Kings of *Tharsis* and the Isles, the Kings of *Arabia* and *Saba* shall offer gifts, which places most Christians and many *Rabbins* interpret of the *Messiah*. Not that they are to be conceived potent monarchs, or mighty Kings; but Toparks, Kings of Cities or narrow Territories; such as were the Kings of *Sodom* and *Gomorrah*, the Kings of *Jericho* and *Ai*, the one and thirty which *Joshuah* subdued, and such as some conceive the Friends of *Job* to have been.

But although we grant they were Kings, yet can we not be assured they were three. For the Scripture maketh no mention of any number; and the numbers of their presents, Gold, Myrrhe and Frankincense, concludeth not the number of their persons; for these were the commodities of their Country, and such as probably the Queen of *Sheba* in one person had brought before unto *Solomon*. So did not the sons of *Jacob* divide the present unto *Joseph*, but are conceived to carry one for them all, according to the expression of their Father—Take of the best fruits of the land in your vessels, and carry down the man a present. And therefore their number being uncertain, what credit is to be given unto their names, *Gasper, Melchior, Balthazar*, what to the charm thereof against the falling sickness, Gaspar fert myrrham, *etc.* or what unto their habits, complexions, and corporal accidents, we must rely on their uncertain story, and received pourtraits of *Collein*.

Lastly, Although we grant them Kings, and three in number, yet could we not conceive that they were Kings of *Collein*. For though *Collein* were the chief City of the *Ubii*, then called *Ubiopolis*, and afterwards *Agrippina*, yet will no History inform us there were three Kings thereof. Beside, these being rulers in their Countries, and returning home, would have probably converted their subjects: but according unto *Munster*, their conversion was not wrought until seventy years after by *Maternus* a disciple of *Peter*. And lastly, it is said that the wise men came from the East; but *Collein* is seated West-ward from *Jerusalem*; for *Collein* hath of longitude thirty four degrees, but *Jerusalem* seventy two.

And why of Collein.

The ground of all was this. These wise men or Kings, were probably of *Arabia*, and descended from *Abraham* by *Keturah*, who apprehending the mystery of this Star, either by the Spirit of God, the prophesie of *Balaam*, the prophesie which *Suetonius* mentions, received and constantly believed through all the East, that out of Jury one should come that should rule the whole world: or the divulged expectation of the *Jews* from the expiring prediction of *Daniel*: were by the same conducted unto *Judea*, returned unto their Country, and were after baptized by *Thomas*. From whence about three hundred years after, by *Helena* the Empress their bodies were translated to *Constantinople*. From thence by *Eustatius* unto Millane, and at last by *Renatus* the Bishop unto *Collein*: where they are believed at present to remain, their monuments shewn unto strangers, and having lost their *Arabian* titles, are crowned Kings of *Collein*.

CHAPTER IX
Of the food of *John Baptist*, Locusts and Wild-honey.

Concerning the food of *John Baptist* in the wilderness, Locusts and Wild-honey, lest popular opiniatrity should arise, we will deliver the chief opinions. The first conceiveth the Locusts here mentioned to be that fruit which the Greeks name κεράτιον mentioned by *Luke* in the diet of the Prodigal son, the Latins *Siliqua*, and some *Panis Sancti Johannis*; included in a broad Cod, and indeed a taste almost as pleasant as Honey. But this opinion doth not so truly impugn that of the Locusts: and might rather call into controversie the meaning of Wild-honey.

Opinions concerning ἀκρίδες, *or the Locusts of S.* John Baptist.

The second affirmeth that they were the tops or tender crops of trees: for so *Locusta* also signifieth: which conceit is plausible in Latin, but will not hold in Greek, wherein the word is ἀκρὶς, except for ἀκρίδες, we read ἀκρόδυα, or ἀκρέμονες, which signifie the extremities of trees, of which belief have divers been: more confidently *Isidore Peleusiota*, who in his Epistles plainly affirmeth they think unlearnedly who are of another belief. And this so wrought upon *Baronius*, that he concludeth in neutrality; *Hæc cum scribat Isidorus definiendum nobis non est et totum relinquimus lectoris arbitrio; nam constat Græcam dictionem* ἀκρίδες, *et Locustam, insecti genus, et arborum summitates significare. Sed fallitur*, saith Montacutius, *nam constat contrarium,* Ἀκρίδα *apud nullum authorem classicum* Ἀκρόδρυα *significare*. But above all *Paracelsus* with most animosity promoteth this opinion, and in his book *de melle*, spareth not his Friend Erasmus. *Hoc à nonnullis ita explicatur ut dicant Locastus aut cicadas Johanni pro cibo fuisse; sed hi stultitiam dissimulare non possunt, veluti Jeronimus, Erasmus, et alii Prophetæ Neoterici in Latinitate immortui.*

The more probable what.

A third affirmeth that they were properly Locusts: that is, a sheath-winged and six-footed insect, such as is our Grashopper. And this opinion seems more probable than the other. For beside the authority of *Origen, Jerom, Chrysostom, Hillary* and *Ambrose* to confirm it: this is the proper signification of the word, thus used in Scripture by the Septuagint, Greek vocabularies thus expound it. *Suidas* on the word Ακρὶς observes it to be that animal whereon the Baptist fed in the desert; in this sense the word is used by *Aristotle, Dioscorides, Galen*, and several humane Authors. And lastly, there is no absurdity in this interpretation, or any solid reason why we should decline it, it being a food permitted unto the *Jews*, whereof four kinds are reckoned up among clean meats. Beside, not only the *Jews*, but many other Nations long before and since, have made an usual food thereof. That the *Æthiopians, Mauritanians* and *Arabians* did commonly eat them, is testified by *Diodorus, Strabo, Solinus, Ælian* and *Pliny*: that they still feed on them is confirmed by *Leo, Cadamustus* and others. *John* therefore as our Saviour saith, came neither eating nor drinking: that is, far from the diet of *Jerusalem* and other Riotous places: but fared coursly and poorly according unto the apparel he wore, that is of Camels hair: the place of his abode, the wilderness; and the doctrin he preached, humiliation and repentance.

CHAPTER X
That *John* the Evangelist should not die.

The conceit of the long-living, or rather not dying of *John* the Evangelist, although it seem inconsiderable, and not much weightier than that of *Joseph* the wandring *Jew*: yet being deduced from Scripture, and abetted by Authors of all times, it shall not escape our enquiry. It is drawn from the speech of our Saviour unto *Peter* after the prediction of his Martyrdom; *Peter* saith unto Jesus. *John 21.* Lord what shall this man do? Jesus saith unto him, If I will that he tarry until I come, what is that to thee? Follow thou me; then went this saying abroad among the brethren, that this disciple should not die.

Now the belief hereof hath been received either grosly and in the general, that is not distinguishing the manner or particular way of this continuation, in which sense probably the grosser and undiscerning party received it. Or more distinctly apprehending the manner of his immortality; that is, that *John* should never properly die, but be translated into Paradise, there to remain with *Enoch* and *Elias* until about the coming of Christ; and should be slain with them under Antichrist, according to that of the Apocalyps. I will give power unto my two witnesses, and they shall prophesie a thousand two hundred and threescore days cloathed in sack-cloth, and when they shall have finished their Testimony, the beast that ascendeth out of the bottomless pit, shall make war against them, and shall overcome them, and kill them. Hereof, as *Baronius* observeth, within three hundred years after Christ, *Hippolytus* the Martyr was the first assertor, but hath been maintained by *Metaphrastes*, by *Freculphus*, but especially by *Georgius Trapezuntius*, who hath expresly treated upon this Text, and although he lived but in the last Century, did still affirm that *John* was not yet dead.

The same is also hinted by the learned Italian Poet *Dante*, who in his Poetical survey of Paradise, meeting with the soul of St. *John*, and desiring to see his body; received answer from him that his body was in earth, and there should remain with other bodys, until the number of the blessed were accomplished.

In terra è terra il mio corpo, et saragli
Tanto con gli altri, che l' numero nostro
Con l' eterno proposito s' agguagli.

As for the gross opinion that he should not die, it is sufficiently refuted by that which first occasioned it, that is the Scripture it self, and no further off than the very subsequent verse: Yet Jesus said unto him, he should not die, but if I will that he tarry till I come, What is that to thee? And this was written by *John* himself, whom the opinion concerned; and as is conceived many years after, when *Peter* had suffered and fulfilled the prophesie of Christ.

For the particular conceit, the foundation is weak, nor can it be made out from the Text alledged in the Apocalyps: for beside that therein two persons are only named, no mention is made of *John*, a third Actor in this Tragedy. *The death of St.* John *Evangelist, where and when.* The same is also overthrown by History, which recordeth not only the death of *John*, but assigneth the place of his burial, that is *Ephesus*, a City in *Asia* minor, whither after he had been banished into *Patmos* by *Domitian*, he returned in the reign of Nerva, there deceased, and was buried in the days of *Trajan*. And this is testified by *Jerom*, *De Scriptor. Ecclesiast.* by *Tertullian*, *De Anima.* by *Chrysostom* and *Eusebius*, in whose days his Sepulchre was to be seen; and by a more ancient Testimony alleadged also by him, that is of *Polycrates* Bishop of *Ephesus*, not many successions after *John*; whose words are these in an Epistle unto *Victor* Bishop of *Rome*, *Johannes ille qui supra pectus Domini recumbebat, Doctor optimus, apud Ephesum dormivit*; many of the like nature are noted by *Baronius*, *Jansenius*, *Estius*, *Lipellous*, and others.

Now the main and primitive ground of this error, was a gross mistake in the words of Christ, and a false apprehension of his meaning; understanding that positively which was but conditionally expressed, or receiving that affirmatively which was but concessively delivered. For the words of our Saviour run in a doubtful strain, rather reprehending than satisfying the curiosity of *Peter*; as though he should have said, Thou hast thy own doom, why enquirest thou after thy Brothers? What relief unto thy affliction, will be the society of anothers? Why pryest thou into the secrets of Gods will? If he stay until I come, what concerneth it thee, who shalt be sure to suffer before that time? And such an answer probably he returned, because he fore-knew *John* should not suffer a violent death, but go unto his grave in peace. Which had *Peter* assuredly known, it might have cast some water on his flames, and smothered those fires which kindled after unto the honour of his Master.

Of all the Apostles St. John *only is thought to have suffered a natural death: And why?*

Now why among all the rest *John* only escaped the death of a Martyr, the reason is given; because all others fled away or withdrew themselves at his death, and he alone of the Twelve beheld his passion on the Cross. Wherein notwithstanding, the affliction that he suffered could not amount unto less than Martyrdom: for if the naked relation, at least the intentive consideration of that Passion, be able still, and at this disadvantage of time, to rend the hearts of pious Contemplators; surely the near and sensible vision thereof must needs occasion Agonies beyond the comprehension of flesh; and the trajections of such an object more sharply pierce the Martyred soul of *John*, than afterward did the nails the crucified body of *Peter*.

Again, They were mistaken in the Emphatical apprehension, placing the consideration upon the words, If I will: whereas it properly lay in these, when I come. Which had they apprehended as some have since, that is, not for his ultimate and last return, but his coming in Judgment and destruction upon the *Jews*; or such a coming, as it might be said, that that generation should not pass before it was fulfilled; they needed not, much less need we suppose such diuturnity. For after the death of *Peter*, *John* lived to behold the same fulfilled by *Vespasian*: nor had he then his *Nunc dimittis*, or went out like unto *Simeon*; but old in accomplisht obscurities, and having seen the expire of *Daniels* prediction, as some conceive, he accomplished his Revelation.

But besides this original and primary foundation, divers others have made impressions according unto different ages and persons by whom they were received. For some established the conceit in the disciples and brethren, which were contemporary unto him, or lived about the same time with him; and this was first the extraordinary affection our Saviour bare unto this disciple, who hath the honour to be called the disciple whom Jesus loved. Now from hence they might be apt to believe their Master would dispense with his death, or suffer him to live to see him return in glory, who was the only Apostle that beheld him to die in dishonour. Another was the belief and opinion of those times, that Christ would suddenly come; for they held not generally the same opinion with their successors, or as descending ages after so many Centuries; but conceived his coming would not be long after his passion, according unto several expressions of our Saviour grosly understood, and as we find the same opinion not long after reprehended by St. *Paul*: *Thes. 2.* and thus conceiving his coming would not be long, they might be induced to believe his favorite should live unto it. *Saint John, how long surviving our B. Saviour.* Lastly, the long life of *John* might much advantage this opinion; for he survived the other twelve, he was aged 22 years when he was called by Christ, and 25 that is the age of Priesthood at his death, and lived 93 years, that is 68 after his Saviour, and died not before the second year of *Trajan*. Now having out lived all his fellows, the world was confirmed he might live still, and even unto the coming of his Master.

The grounds which promoted it in succeeding ages, were especially two. The first his escape of martyrdom: for whereas all the rest suffered some kind of forcible death, we have no history that he suffered any; and men might think he was not capable thereof: For as History informeth, by the command of *Domitian* he was cast into a Caldron of burning oyl, and came out again unsinged. Now future ages apprehending he suffered no violent death, and finding also the means that tended thereto could take no place, they might be confirmed in their opinion that death had no power over him, that he might live always who could not be destroyed by fire, and was able to resist the fury of that element which nothing shall resist. The second was a corruption crept into the Latin Text, reading for *Si, Sic eum manere volo*; whereby the answer of our Saviour becometh positive, or that he will have it so; which way of reading was much received in former ages, and is still retained in the vulgar Translation; but in the Greek and original the word is ἐάν, signifying *Si* or if, which is very different from οὕτως, and cannot be translated for it: and answerable hereunto is the translation of *Junius*, and that also annexed unto the Greek by the authority of *Sixtus Quintus*.

The third confirmed it in ages farther descending, and proved a powerfull argument unto all others following; because in his tomb at *Ephesus* there was no corps or relique thereof to be found; whereupon arose divers doubts, and many suspitious conceptions; some believing he was not buried, some that he was buried but risen again, others that he descended alive into his tomb, and from thence departed after. But all these proceeded upon unveritable grounds, as *Baronius* hath observed; who alledgeth a letter of *Celestine* Bishop of *Rome*, unto the Council of *Ephesus*, wherein he declareth the reliques of *John* were highly honoured by that City; and by a passage also of *Chrysostome* in the Homilies of the Apostles, That *John* being dead, did cures in *Ephesus*, as though he were still alive. And so I observe that *Esthius* discussing this point concludeth hereupon, *Quod corpus ejus nunquam reperiatur, hoc non dicerent si veterum scripta diligenter perlustrassent*.

Now that the first ages after Christ, those succeeding, or any other should proceed into opinions so far divided from reason, as to think of immortality after the fall of *Adam*, or conceit a man in these later times should out-live our fathers in the first; although it seem very strange, yet is it not incredible. For the credulity of men hath been deluded into the like conceits; and as *Ireneus* and *Tertullian* mention, one *Menander* a *Samaritan* obtained belief in this very point; whose doctrin it was, that death should have no power on his disciples, and such as received his baptism should receive immortality therewith. Twas surely an apprehension very strange; nor usually falling either from the absurdities of Melancholy or vanities of ambition. Some indeed have been so affectedly vain, as to counterfeit Immortality, and have stoln their death, in a hope to be esteemed immortal; and others have conceived themselves dead; but surely few or none have fallen upon so bold an errour, as not to think that they could die at all. The reason of those mighty ones, whose ambition could suffer them to be called gods, would never be flattered into immortality; but the proudest thereof have by the daily dictates of corruption convinced the impropriety of that appellation. And surely although delusion may run high, and possible it is that for a while a man may forget his nature, yet cannot this be durable. For the inconcealable imperfections of our selves, or their daily examples in others, will hourly prompt us our corruption, and loudly tell us we are the sons of earth.

CHAPTER XI
More compendiously of some others.

Many others there are which we resign unto Divinity, and perhaps deserve not controversie. Whether *David* were punished only for pride of heart in numbring the people, as most do hold, or whether as *Josephus* and many maintain, he suffered also for not performing the Commandment of God concerning capitation; that when the people were numbred, for every head they should pay unto God a shekell, we shall not here contend. Surely, if it were not the occasion of this plague, we must acknowledge the omission thereof was threatned with that punishment, according to the words of the Law. *Exod. 30.* When thou takest the sum of the children of *Israel*, then shall they give every man a ransom for his soul unto the Lord, that there be no plague amongst them. Now how deeply hereby God was defrauded in the time of *David*, and opulent State of Israel, will easily appear by the sums of former lustrations. For in the first, *Exod. 38.* the silver of them that were numbred was an hundred Talents, and a thousand seven hundred three-score and fifteen shekels; a Bekah for every man, that is, half a shekel, after the shekel of the sanctuary; for every one from twenty years old and upwards, for six hundred thousand, and three thousand and five hundred and fifty men. Answerable whereto we read in *Josephus*, *Vespasian* ordered that every man of the *Jews* should bring into the Capital two dragms; which amounts unto fifteen pence, or a quarter of an ounce of silver with us: and is equivalent unto a Bekah, or half a shekel of the Sanctuary. *What the Attick dragm is. What the didrachmum and the stater*, Mat. 17. 27. For an Attick dragm is seven pence halfpeny or a quarter of a shekel, and a didrachmum or double dragm, is the word for Tribute money, or half a shekel; and a stater the money found in the fishes mouth was two Didrachmums, or an whole shekel, and tribute sufficient for our Saviour and for *Peter*.

We will not question the Metamorphosis of *Lots* wife, or whether she were transformed into a real statua of Salt: though some conceive that expression Metaphorical, and no more thereby then a lasting and durable column, according to the nature of Salt, which admitteth no corruption: in which sense the Covenant of God is termed a Covenant of Salt; and it is also said, God gave the Kingdom unto *David* for ever, or by a Covenant of Salt.

That *Absalom* was hanged by the hair of the head, and not caught up by the neck, as *Josephus* conceiveth, and the common argument against long hair affirmeth, we are not ready to deny. Although I confess a great and learned party there are of another opinion; although if he had his Morion or Helmet on, I could not well conceive it; although the translation of *Jerom* or *Tremelius* do not prove it, and our own seems rather to overthrow it.

How Judas *might die.*

That *Judas* hanged himself, much more, that he perished thereby, we shall not raise a doubt. Although *Jansenius* discoursing the point, produceth the testimony of *Theophylact* and *Euthimius*, that he died not by the Gallows, but under a cart wheel, and *Baronius* also delivereth, this was the opinion of the *Greeks*, and derived as high as *Papias*, one of the Disciples of *John*. Although also how hardly the expression of *Matthew* is reconcilable unto that of *Peter*, and that he plainly hanged himself, with that, that falling head-long he burst asunder in the midst, with many other, the learned *Grotius* plainly doth acknowledge. And lastly, Although as he also urgeth, the word ἀπήγξατο in *Matthew*, doth not only signifie suspension or pendulous illaqueation, as the common picture discribeth it, but also suffocation, strangulation or interception of breath, which may arise from grief, despair, and deep dejection of spirit, Strangulat inclusus dolor. in which sense it is used in the History of *Tobit* concerning *Sara*, ἐλυπήθη σφόδρα ὥστε ἀπάγξασθαι. *Ita tristata est ut strangulatione premeretur*, saith *Junius*; and so might it happen from the horrour of mind unto *Judas*. So do many of the *Hebrews* affirm, that *Achitophel* was also strangled, that is, not from the rope, but passion. For the Hebrew and Arabick word in the Text, not only signifies suspension, but indignation, as *Grotius* hath also observed.

Many more there are of indifferent truths, whose dubious expositions worthy Divines and Preachers do often draw into wholesome and sober uses whereof we shall not speak; with industry we decline such Paradoxes, and peaceably submit unto their received acceptions.

CHAPTER XII
Of the Cessation of Oracles.

That Oracles ceased or grew mute at the coming of Christ, is best understood in a qualified sense, and not without all latitude, as though precisely there were none after, nor any decay before. For (what we must confess unto relations of Antiquity) some pre-decay is observable from that of *Cicero*, urged by *Baronius*; *Cur isto modo jam oracula Delphis non eduntur, non modo nostra ætate, sed jam diu, ut nihil possit esse contemptius*. That during his life they were not altogether dumb, is deduceable from *Suetonius* in the life of *Tiberius*, who attempting to subvert the Oracles adjoyning unto *Rome*, was deterred by the Lots or chances which were delivered at *Preneste*. After his death we meet with many; *Suetonius* reports, that the Oracle of *Antium* forewarned *Caligula* to beware of *Cassius*, who was one that conspired his death. *Plutarch* enquiring why the Oracles of *Greece* ceased, excepteth that of *Lebadia*: and in the same place *Demetrius* affirmeth the Oracles of *Mopsus* and *Amphilochus* were much frequented in his days. In brief, Histories are frequent in examples, and there want not some even to the reign of *Julian*.

What therefore may consist with history, by cessation of Oracles with *Montacutius* we may understand their intercision, not abscission or consummate desolation; their rare delivery, not total dereliction, and yet in regard of divers Oracles, we may speak strictly, and say there was a proper cessation. Thus may we reconcile the accounts of times, and allow those few and broken divinations, whereof we read in story and undeniable Authors. For that they received this blow from Christ, and no other causes alledged by the heathens, from oraculous confession they cannot deny; whereof upon record there are some very remarkable. The first that Oracle of *Delphos* delivered unto *Augustus*.

Me puer Hebræus Divos Deus ipse gubernans
Cedere sede jubet, tristemq; redire sub orcum;
Aris ergo dehinc tacitus discedito nostris.
An Hebrew child, a God all gods excelling,
To hell again commands me from this dwelling.
Our Altars leave in silence, and no more
A Resolution e're from hence implore.

A second recorded by *Plutarch*, of a voice that was heard to cry unto Mariners at the sea, *Great Pan is dead*; which is a relation very remarkable, and may be read in his defect of Oracles. A third reported by *Eusebius* in the life of his magnified *Constantine*, that about that time *Apollo* mourned, declaring his Oracles were false and that the righteous upon earth did hinder him from speaking truth. And a fourth related by *Theodoret*, and delivered by *Apollo Daphneus* unto *Julian* upon his *Persian* expedition, that he should remove the bodies about him before he could return an answer, and not long after his Temple was burnt with lightning.

All which were evident and convincing acknowledgements of that Power which shut his lips, and restrained that delusion which had reigned so many Centuries. But as his malice is vigilant, and the sins of men do still continue a toleration of his mischiefs, he resteth not, nor will he ever cease to circumvent the sons of the first deceived. *The devils retreat when expelled the Oracles.* And therefore expelled from Oracles and solemn Temples of delusion, he runs into corners, exercising minor trumperies, and acting his deceits in Witches, Magicians, Diviners, and such inferiour seducers. And yet (what is deplorable) while we apply our selves thereto, and affirming that God hath left to speak by his Prophets, expect in doubtfull matters a resolution from such spirits, while we say the devil is mute, yet confess that these can speak; while we deny the substance, yet practise the effect and in the denied solemnity maintain the equivalent efficacy; in vain we cry that Oracles are down; *Apollos* Altar still doth smoak; nor is the fire of *Delphos* out unto this day.

Impertinent it is unto our intention to speak in general of Oracles, and many have well performed it. The plainest of others was that of *Apollo Delphicus* recorded by *Herodotus*, and delivered unto *Crœsus*; who as a trial of their omniscience sent unto distant Oracles; and so contrived with the Messengers, that though in several places, yet at the same time they should demand what *Crœsus* was then a doing. Among all others the Oracle of *Delphos* only hit it, returning answer, he was boyling a Lamb with a Tortoise, in a brazen vessel, with a cover of the same metal. The stile is haughty in Greek, though somewhat lower in Latine.

Æquoris est spatium et numerus mihi notus arenæ
Mutum percipio, fantis nihil audio vocem.
Venit ad hos sensus nidor testudinis acris,
Quæ semel agninâ coquitur cum carne labete,
Aere infra strato, et stratum cui desuper æs est.
I know the space of Sea, the number of the sand,
I hear the silent, mute I understand.
A tender Lamb joined with Tortoise flesh,
Thy Master King of *Lydia* now doth dress.
The scent thereof doth in my nostrils hover,
From brazen pot closed with brazen cover.

Hereby indeed he acquired much wealth and more honour, and was reputed by *Crœsus* as a Diety: and yet not long after, by a vulgar fallacy he deceived his favourite and greatest friend of Oracles into an irreparable overthrow by *Cyrus*. And surely the same success are likely all to have that rely or depend upon him. 'Twas the first play he practised on mortality; and as time hath rendred him more perfect in the Art, so hath the inveterateness of his malice more ready in the execution. 'Tis therefore the soveraign degree of folly, and a crime not only against God, but also our own reasons, to expect a favour from the devil; whose mercies are more cruel than those of *Polyphemus*; for he devours his favourites first, and the nearer a man approacheth, the sooner he is scorched by *Moloch*. In brief, his favours are deceitfull and double-headed, he doth apparent good, for real and convincing evil after it; and exalteth us up to the top of the Temple, but to humble us down from it.

CHAPTER XIII
Of the death of *Aristotle*.

That *Aristotle* drowned himself in *Euripus*, as despairing to resolve the cause of its reciprocation, or ebb and flow seven times a day, with this determination, *Si quidem ego non capio te, tu capies me*, was the assertion of *Procopius, Nazianzen, Justin Martyr*, and is generally believed amongst us. Wherein, because we perceive men have but an imperfect knowledge, some conceiving *Euripus* to be a River, others not knowing where or in what part to place it; we first advertise, it generally signifieth any strait, fret, or channel of the Sea, running between two shoars, as *Julius Pollux* hath defined it; *What an Euripus is generally.* as we read of *Euripus Hellespontiacus, Pyrrhæus*, and this whereof we treat, *Euripus Euboicus* or *Chalcidicus*, that is, a narrow passage of Sea dividing *Attica*, and the Island of *Euboea*, now called *Golfo de Negroponte*, from the name of the Island and chief City thereof; famous in the wars of *Antiochus*, and taken from the *Venetians* by *Mahomet* the Great.

Touching the death of Aristotle.

Now that in this *Euripe* or fret of *Negropont*, and upon the occasion mentioned, *Aristotle* drowned himself, as many affirm, and almost all believe, we have some room to doubt. For without any mention of this, we find two ways delivered of his death by *Diogenes Laertius*, who expresly treateth thereof; the one from *Eumolus* and *Phavorimus*, that being accused of impiety for composing an Hymn unto *Hermias* (upon whose Concubine he begat his son *Nichomachus*) he withdrew into *Chalcis*, where drinking poison he died; the Hymn is extant in *Laertius*, and the fifteenth book of *Athenæus*. Another by *Apollodorus*, that he died at *Chalcis* of a natural death and languishment of stomach, in his sixty third, or great Climacterical year; and answerable hereto is the account of *Suidas* and *Censorinus*. And if that were clearly made out, which *Rabbi Ben Joseph* affirmeth, he found in an *Egyptian* book of *Abraham Sapiens Perizol*; that *Aristotle* acknowledged all that was written in the Law of *Moses*, and became at last a Proselyte; *Licetus de quæsitis, epist.* it would also make improbable this received way of his death.

Again, Beside the negative of Authority, it is also deniable by reason; nor will it be easie to obtrude such desperate attempts upon *Aristotle*, from unsatisfaction of reason, who so often acknowledged the imbecillity thereof. Who in matters of difficulty, and such which were not without abstrusities, conceived it sufficient to deliver conjecturalities. And surely he that could sometimes sit down with high improbabilities, that could content himself, and think to satisfie others, that the variegation of Birds was from their living in the Sun, or erection made by deliberation of the Testicles; would not have been dejected unto death with this. He that was so well acquainted with ἢ ὅτι, and πότερον *utrum*, and *An Quia*, as we observe in the Queries of his Problems: with ἴσως and ἐπὶ τὸ πολὺ, *fortasse* and *plerumque*, as is observable through all his Works: had certainly rested with probabilities, and glancing conjectures in this: Nor would his resolutions have ever run into that mortal Antanaclasis, and desperate piece of Rhetorick, to be compriz'd in that he could not comprehend. Nor is it indeed to be made out that he ever endeavoured the particular of *Euripus*, or so much as to resolve the ebb and flow of the Sea. For, as *Vicomercatus* and others observe, he hath made no mention hereof in his Works, although the occasion present it self in his Meteors, wherein he disputeth the affections of the Sea: nor yet in his Problems, although in the twenty-third Section, there be no less than one and forty Queries of the Sea. Some mention there is indeed in a Work of the propriety of Elements, ascribed unto *Aristotle*: which notwithstanding is not reputed genuine, *De placitis Philosophorum.* and was perhaps the same whence this was urged by *Plutarch*.

Lastly, the thing it self whereon the opinion dependeth, that is, the variety of the flux and the reflux of *Euripus*, or whether the same do ebb and flow seven times a day, is not incontrovertible. For though *Pomponius Mela*, and after him *Solinus* and *Pliny* have affirmed it, yet I observe *Thucydides*, who speaketh often of *Euboea*, hath omitted it. *Pausanias* an ancient Writer, who hath left an exact description of *Greece*, and in as particular a way as *Leandro* of *Italy*, or *Cambden* of great *Britain*, describing not only the Country Towns, and Rivers; but Hills, Springs and Houses, hath left no mention hereof. *Æschines* in *Ctesiphon* only alludeth unto it; and *Strabo* that accurate Geographer speaks warily of it, that is, ὡς φασὶ, and as men commonly reported. And so doth also *Maginus*, *Velocis ac varii fluctus est mare, ubi quater in die, aut septies, ut alii dicunt, reciprocantur æstus*. *Botero* more plainly, *Il mar cresce e cala con un impeto mirabile quatra volte il di, ben che communimente si dica sette volte*, etc. This Sea with wondrous impetuosity ebbeth and floweth four times a day, although it be commonly said seven times, and generally opinioned, that *Aristotle* despairing of the reason, drowned himself therein. In which description by four times a day, it exceeds not in number the motion of other Seas, taking the words properly, that is, twice ebbing and twice flowing in four and twenty hours. And is no more than what *Thomaso Porrcacchi* affirmeth in his description of famous Islands, that twice a day it hath such an impetuous flood, as is not without wonder. *Livy* speaks more particularly, *Haud facile infestior classi statio est et fretum ipsum Euripi, non septies die (ficut fama fert) temporibus certis reciprocat, sed temere in modum venti, nunc hunc nunc illuc verso mari, velut monte præcipiti devolutus torrens rapitur.* There is hardly a worse harbour, the fret or channel of *Euripus* not certainly ebbing or flowing seven times a day, according to common report: but being uncertainly, and in the manner of a wind carried hither and thither, is whirled away as a torrent down a hill. But the experimental testimony of *Gillius* is most considerable of any: who having beheld the course thereof, and made enquiry of Millers that dwelt upon its shore, received answer, that it ebbed and flowed four times a day, that is, every six hours, according to the Law of the Ocean: but that indeed sometimes it observed not that certain course. And this irregularity, though seldom happening, together with its unruly and tumultuous motion, might afford a beginning unto the common opinion. Thus may the expression in *Ctesiphon* be made out: And by this may *Aristotle* be interpreted, when in his Problems he seems to borrow a Metaphor from *Euripus*: while in the five and twentieth Section he enquireth, why in the upper parts of houses the air doth Euripize, that is, is whirled hither and thither.

A later and experimental testimony is to be found in the travels of Monsieur *Duloir*; who about twenty years ago, remained sometime at *Negroponte*, or old *Chalcis*, and also passed and repassed this *Euripus*; who thus expresseth himself. I wonder much at the Error concerning the flux and reflux of *Euripus*; and I assure you that opinion is false. I gave a Boat-man a Crown, to set me in a convenient place, where for a whole day I might observe the same. It ebbeth and floweth by six hours, even as it doth at *Venice*, but the course thereof is vehement.

Now that which gave life unto the assertion, might be his death at *Chalcis*, the chief City of *Eubœa*, and seated upon *Euripus*, where 'tis confessed by all he ended his days. That he emaciated and pined away in the too anxious enquiry of its reciprocations, although not drowned therein, as *Rhodiginus* relateth, some conceived, was a half confession thereof not justifiable from Antiquity. Surely the Philosophy of flux and reflux was very imperfect of old among the Greeks and Latins; nor could they hold a sufficient theory thereof, who only observed the Mediterranean, which in some places hath no ebb, and not much in any part. Nor can we affirm our knowledg is at the height, who have now the Theory of the Ocean and narrow Seas beside. While we refer it unto the Moon, we give some satisfaction for the Ocean, but no general salve for Creeks, and Seas which know no flood; nor resolve why it flows three or four foot at *Venice* in the bottom of the Gulf, yet scarce at all at *Ancona, Durazzo,* or *Corcyra*, which lie but by the way. And therefore old abstrusities have caused new inventions; and some from the Hypotheses of *Copernicus*, or the Diurnal and annual motion of the earth, endeavour to salve flows and motions of these Seas, *Rog. Bac. doctis, Cabeus Met. 2.* illustrating the same by water in a boal, that rising or falling to either side, according to the motion of the vessel; the conceit is ingenuous, salves some doubts, and is discovered at large by *Galileo*.

How the Moon may cause the ebbing and flowing of the Sea.

But whether the received principle and undeniable action of the Moon may not be still retained, although in some difference of application, is yet to be perpended; that is, not by a simple operation upon the surphace or superiour parts, but excitation of the nitro-sulphureous spirits, and parts disposed to intumescency at the bottom; not by attenuation of the upper part of the Sea, (whereby ships would draw more water at the flow than at the ebb) but inturgescencies caused first at the bottom, and carrying the upper part before them: subsiding and falling again, according to the Motion of the Moon from the Meridian, and languor of the exciting cause: *Why Rivers and Lakes ebb and flow not. Why some Seas flow higher than others, and continue longer.* and therefore Rivers and Lakes who want these fermenting parts at the bottom, are not excited unto æstuations; and therefore some Seas flow higher than others, according to the Plenty of these spirits, in their submarine constitutions. And therefore also the periods of flux and reflux are various, nor their increase or decrease equal: according to the temper of the terreous parts at the bottom: who as they are more hardly or easily moved, do variously begin, continue or end their intumescencies.

Whence the violent flows proceed in some Estuaries and Rivers.

From the peculiar disposition of the earth at the bottom, wherein quick excitations are made, may arise those Agars and impetuous flows in some æstuaries and Rivers, as is observable about *Trent* and *Humber* in *England*; which may also have some effect in the boisterous tides of *Euripus*, not only from ebullitions at the bottom, but also from the sides and lateral parts, driving the streams from either side, which arise or fall according to the motion in those parts, and the intent or remiss operation of the first exciting causes, which maintain their activities above and below the Horizon; even as they do in the bodies of plants and animals, and in the commotion of *Catarrhes*.

However therefore *Aristotle* died, what was his end, or upon what occasion, although it be not altogether assured, yet that his memory and worthy name shall live, no man will deny, nor grateful Scholar doubt, and if according to the Elogy of *Solon*, a man may be only said to be happy after he is dead, and ceaseth to be in the visible capacity of beatitude, or if according unto his own Ethicks, sense is not essential unto felicity, but a man may be happy without the apprehension thereof; surely in that sense he is pyramidally happy; nor can he ever perish but in the Euripe of Ignorance, or till the Torrent or Barbarism overwhelmeth all.

Homers *death.*

A like conceit there passeth of *Melisigenes, alias Homer*, the Father Poet, that he pined away upon the Riddle of the fishermen. But *Herodotus* who wrote his life hath cleared this point; delivering, that passing from *Samos* unto Athens, he went sick ashore upon the Island *Ios*, where he died, and was solemnly interred upon the Sea side; and so decidingly concludeth, *Ex hac ægritudine extremum diem clausit Homerus in Io, non, ut arbitrantur aliqui, Ænigmatis perplexitate enectus, sed morbo.*

CHAPTER XIV
Of the Wish of *Philoxenus*.

That Relation of *Aristotle*, and conceit generally received concerning *Philoxenus*, who wished the neck of a Crane, that thereby he might take more pleasure in his meat, although it pass without exception, upon enquiry I find not only doubtful in the story, but absurd in the desire or reason alledged for it. For though his Wish were such as is delivered, yet had it not perhaps that end, to delight his gust in eating; but rather to obtain advantage thereby in singing, as is declared by *Mirandula. Aristotle* (saith he) in his Ethicks and Problems, accuseth *Philoxenus* of sensuality, for the greater pleasure of gust desiring the neck of a Crane; which desire of his, assenting unto *Aristotle*, I have formerly condemned: But since I perceive that *Aristotle* for this accusation hath been accused by divers Writers. For *Philoxenus* was an excellent Musician, and desired the neck of a Crane, not for any pleasure at meat; but fancying thereby an advantage in singing or warbling, and dividing the notes in musick. And many Writers there are which mention a Musician of that name, as *Plutarch* in his book against usury, and *Aristotle* himself in the eighth of his Politicks, speaks of one *Philoxenus* a Musician, that went off from the Dorick Dithyrambicks unto the Phrygian Harmony.

Again, Be the story true or false, rightly applied or not, the intention is not reasonable, and that perhaps neither one way nor the other. For if we rightly consider the Organ of tast, we shall find the length of the neck to conduce but little unto it. For the tongue being the instrument of tast, and the tip thereof the most exact distinguisher, it will not advantage the gust to have the neck extended; Wherein the Gullet and conveying parts are only seated, which partake not of the nerves of gustation, or appertaining unto sapor, but receive them only from the sixth pair; whereas the nerves of tast descend from the third and fourth propagations, and so diffuse themselves into the tongue. And therefore Cranes, Herns and Swans have no advantage in taste beyond Hawks, Kites, and others of shorter necks.

Nor, if we consider it, had Nature respect unto the taste in the different contrivance of necks, but rather unto the parts contained, the composure of the rest of the body, and the manner whereby they feed. Thus animals of long legs, have generally long necks; that is, for the conveniency of feeding, as having a necessity to apply their mouths unto the earth. So have Horses, Camels, Dromedaries long necks, and all tall animals, except the Elephant, who in defect thereof is furnished with a Trunk, without which he could not attain the ground. So have Cranes, Herns, Storks and Shovelards long necks: and so even in Man, whose figure is erect, the length of the neck followeth the proportion of other parts: and such as have round faces or broad chests and shoulders, have very seldom long necks. For, the length of the face twice exceedeth that of the neck, and the space betwixt the throat-pit and the navell, is equall unto the circumference thereof. Again, animals are framed with long necks, according unto the course of their life or feeding: so many with short legs have long necks, because they feed in the water, as Swans, Geese, Pelicans, and other fin-footed animals. But Hawks and birds of prey have short necks and trussed leggs; for that which is long is weak and flexible, and a shorter figure is best accomodated unto that intention. Lastly, the necks of animals do vary, according to the parts that are contained in them, which are the weazon and the gullet. Such as have no weazon and breath not, have scarce any neck, as most sorts of fishes; and some none at all, as all sorts of pectinals, Soals, Thornback, Flounders; and all crustaceous animals, as Crevises, Crabs and Lobsters.

All which considered, the Wish of *Philoxenus* will hardly consist with reason. More excusable had it been to have wished himself an Ape, which if common conceit speak true, is exacter in taste then any. Rather some kind of granivorous bird then a Crane, for in this sense they are so exquisite that upon the first peck of their bill, they can distinguish the qualities of hard bodies; which the sense of man discerns not without mastication. Rather some ruminating animal, that he might have eat his meat twice over; or rather, as *Theophilus* observed in *Athenæus*, his desire had been more reasonable, had he wished himself an Elephant, or an Horse; for in these animals the appetite is more vehement, and they receive their viands in large and plenteous manner. And this indeed had been more sutable, if this were the same *Philoxenus* whereof *Plutarch* speaketh who was so uncivilly greedy, that to engross the mess, he would preventively deliver his nostrils in the dish.

As for the musical advantage, although it seem more reasonable, yet do we not observe that Cranes and birds of long necks have any musical, but harsh and clangous throats. But birds that are canorous, and whose notes we most commend, are of little throats and short necks, as Nightingales, Finches, Linnets, Canary birds and Larks. And truly, although the weazon, throtle and tongue be the instruments of voice, and by their agitations do chiefly concurr unto these delightfull modulations, yet cannot we distinctly and peculiarly assign the cause unto any particular formation; and I perceive the best thereof, the nightingale, hath some disadvantage in the tongue; which is not accuminate and pointed as in the rest, but seemeth as it were cut off, which perhaps might give the hint unto the fable of *Philomela*, and the cutting off her tongue by *Tereus*.

CHAPTER XV
Of the Lake Asphaltites.

Concerning the Lake *Asphaltites*, the Lake of *Sodom*, or the dead Sea, that heavy bodies cast therein sink not, but by reason of a salt and bituminous thickness in the water float and swim above, narrations already made are of that variety, we can hardly from thence deduce a satisfactory determination; and that not only in the story it self, but in the cause alledged. As for the story, men deliver it variously: some I fear too largely, as *Pliny*, who affirmeth that bricks will swim therein. *Mandevil* goeth farther, that Iron swimmeth, and feathers sink. *Munster* in his Cosmography hath another relation, although perhaps derived from the Poem of *Tertullian,* that a candle Burning swimmeth, but if extinguished sinketh. Some more moderately, as *Josephus*, and many others: affirming only that living bodies float, nor peremptorily averring they cannot sink, but that indeed they do not easily descend. Most traditionally, as *Galen, Pliny, Solinus* and *Strabo*, who seems to mistake the Lake *Serbonis* for it. Few experimentally, most contenting themselves in the experiment of *Vespasian*, by whose command some captives bound were cast therein, and found to float as though they could have swimmed: divers contradictorily, or contrarily, quite overthrowing the point. *Aristotle* in the second of his Meteors speaks lightly thereof, ὥσπερ μυθολογοῦσι, which word is variously rendred, by some as a fabulous account, by some as a common talk. *Biddulphus* divideth the common accounts of *Judea* in three parts, the one saith he, are apparent Truths, the second apparent falshoods, the third are dubious or between both; in which form he ranketh the relation of this Lake. Biddulphi intinerarium Anglice. But *Andrew Thevet* in his Cosmography doth ocularly overthrow it; for he affirmeth, he saw an Ass with his Saddle cast therein and drowned. Now of these relations so different or contrary unto each other, the second is most moderate and safest to be embraced, which saith, that living bodies swim therein, that is, they do not easily sink: and this, untill exact experiment further determine, may be allowed, as best consistent with this quality, and the reasons alledged for it.

As for the cause of this effect, common opinion conceives it to be the salt and bituminous thickness of the water. This indeed is probable, and may be admitted as far as the second opinion concedeth. For certain it is that salt water will support a greater burden then fresh; and we see an egg will descend in salt water, which will swim in brine. But that Iron should float therein, from this cause is hardly granted; for heavy bodies will only swim in that liquor, wherein the weight of their bulk exceedeth not the weight of so much water as it occupieth or taketh up. But surely no water is heavy enough to answer the ponderosity of Iron, and therefore that metal will sink in any kind thereof, and it was a perfect Miracle which was wrought this way by *Elisha*. Thus we perceive that bodies do swim or sink in different liquors, according unto the tenuity or gravity of those liquors which are to support them. So salt water beareth that weight which will sink in vineger, vineger that which will fall in fresh water, fresh water that which will sink in spirits of Wine, and that will swim in spirits of Wine which will sink in clear oyl; as we made experiment in globes of wax pierced with light sticks to support them. So that although it be conceived an hard matter to sink in oyl, I believe a man should find it very difficult, and next to flying, to swim therein. And thus will Gold sink in Quick-silver, wherein Iron and other metals swim; for the bulk of Gold is only heavier then that space of Quick-silver which it containeth: and thus also in a solution of one ounce of Quick-silver in two of *Aqua fortis*, the liquor will bear Amber, Horn, and the softer kinds of stones, as we have made triall in each.

But a private opinion there is which crosseth the common conceit, maintained by some of late, and alleadged of old by *Strabo*, that the floating of bodies in this Lake proceeds not from the thickness of the water, but a bituminous ebullition from the bottom, whereby it wafts up bodies injected, and suffereth them not easily to sink. The verity thereof would be enquired by ocular exploration, for this way is also probable. So we observe, it is hard to wade deep in baths where springs arise; and thus sometime are bals made to play upon a spouting stream.

And therefore, until judicious and ocular experiment confirm or distinguish the assertion, that bodies do not sink herein at all, we do not yet believe; that they not easily, or with more difficulty descend in this than other water, we shall readily assent. But to conclude an impossibility from a difficulty, or affirm whereas things not easily sink, they do not drown at all; beside the fallacy, is a frequent addition in humane expression, and an amplification not unusual as well in opinions as relations; which oftentimes give indistinct accounts of proximities, and without restraint transcend from one another. Thus, forasmuch as the torrid Zone was conceived exceeding hot, and of difficult habitation, the opinions of men so advanced its constitution, as to conceive the same unhabitable, and beyond possibility for man to live therein. Thus, because there are no Wolves in *England*, nor have been observed for divers generations, common people have proceeded into opinions, and some wise men into affirmations, they will not live therein, although brought from other Countries. Thus most men affirm, and few here will believe the contrary, that there be no Spiders in *Ireland*; but we have beheld some in that Country; and though but few, some Cob-webs we behold in Irish wood in *England*. Thus the Crocodile from an egg growing up to an exceeding magnitude, common conceit, and divers Writers deliver, it hath no period of encrease, but groweth as long as it liveth. And thus in brief, in most apprehensions the conceits of men extend the considerations of things, and dilate their notions beyond the propriety of their natures.

In the Mapps of the dead Sea or Lake of *Sodom*, we meet with the destroyed Cities, and in divers the City of *Sodom* placed about the middle, or far from the shore of it; but that it could not be far from *Segor*, which was seated under the mountains neer the side of the Lake, seems inferrible from the sudden arrival of *Lot*, who coming from *Sodom* at day break, attained *Segor* at Sun rising; and therefore *Sodom* to be placed not many miles from it, and not in the middle of the Lake, which is accounted about eighteen miles over; and so will leave about nine miles to be passed in too small a space of time.

CHAPTER XVI
Of divers other Relations.

1. The relation of *Averroes*, and now common in every mouth, of the woman that conceived in a bath, by attracting the sperm or seminal effluxion of a man admitted to bath in some vicinity unto her, I have scarce faith to believe; and had I been of the Jury, should have hardly thought I had found the father in the person that stood by her. 'Tis a new and unseconded way in History to fornicate at a distance, and much offendeth the rules of Physick, which say, there is no generation without a joynt emission, nor only a virtual, but corporal and carnal contaction. And although *Aristotle* and his adherents do cut off the one, who conceive no effectual ejaculation in women, yet in defence of the other they cannot be introduced. For, if as he believeth, the inordinate longitude of the organ, though in its proper recipient, may be a means to inprolificate the seed; surely the distance of place, with the commixture of an aqueous body, must prove an effectual impediment, and utterly prevent the success of a conception. And therefore that conceit concerning the daughters of *Lot*, that they were impregnated by their sleeping father, or conceived by seminal pollution received at distance from him, will hardly be admitted. *Generations by the Devil very improbable.* And therefore what is related of devils, and the contrived delusions of spirits, that they steal the seminal emissions of man, and transmit them into their votaries in coition, is much to be suspected; and altogether to be denied, that there ensue conceptions thereupon; however husbanded by Art, and the wisest menagery of that most subtile imposter. And therefore also that our magnified *Merlin* was thus begotten by the devil, is a groundless conception; and as vain to think from thence to give the reason of his prophetical spirit. For if a generation could succeed, yet should not the issue inherit the faculties of the devil, who is but an auxiliary, and no univocal Actor; Nor will his nature substantially concur to such productions.

And although it seems not impossible, that impregnation may succeed from seminal spirits, and vaporous irradiations containing the active principle, without material and gross immissions; as it happeneth sometimes in imperforated persons, and rare conceptions of some much under pubertie or fourteen. As may be also conjectured in the coition of some insects, wherein the female makes intrusion into the male; and from the continued ovation in Hens, from one single tread of a cock, and little stock laid up near the vent, sufficient for durable prolification. And although also in humane generation the gross and corpulent seminal body may return again, and the great business be acted by what it caryeth with it: yet will not the same suffice to support the story in question, wherein no corpulent immission is acknowledged; answerable unto the fable of the *Talmudists*, in the storie of *Benzira*, begotten in the same manner on the daughter of the Prophet *Jeremie*.

2. The Relation of *Lucillius*, and now become common, concerning *Crassus* the grand-father of *Marcus* the wealthy *Roman*, that he never laughed but once in all his life, and that was at an Ass eating thistles, is something strange. For, if an indifferent and unridiculous object could draw his habitual austereness unto a smile, it will be hard to believe he could with perpetuity resist the proper motives thereof. *Laughter. What kind of Passion it is.* For the act of Laughter which is evidenced by a sweet contraction of the muscles of the face, and a pleasant agitation of the vocal Organs, is not meerly voluntary, or totally within the jurisdiction of our selves: but as it may be constrained by corporal contaction in any, and hath been enforced in some even in their death, so the new unusual or unexpected jucundities, which present themselves to any man in his life, at some time or other will have activity enough to excitate the earthiest soul, and raise a smile from most composed tempers. Certainly the times were dull when these things happened, and the wits of those Ages short of these of ours; when men could maintain such immutable faces, as to remain

like statues under the flatteries of wit and persist unalterable at all efforts of Jocularity. The spirits in hell, and *Pluto* himself, whom *Lucian* makes to laugh at passages upon earth, will plainly condemn these Saturnines, and make ridiculous the magnified *Heraclitus*, who wept preposterously, and made a hell on earth; for rejecting the consolations of life, he passed his days in tears, and the uncomfortable attendments of hell.

3. The same conceit there passeth concerning our blessed Saviour, and is sometimes urged as an high example of gravity. And this is opinioned, because in holy Scripture it is recorded he sometimes wept, but never that he laughed. Which howsoever granted, it will be hard to conceive how he passed his younger years and child-hood without a smile, if as Divinity affirmeth, for the assurance of his humanity unto men, and the concealment of his Divinity from the devil, he passed this age like other children, and so proceeded untill he evidenced the same. And surely herein no danger there is to affirm the act or performance of that, whereof we acknowledge the power and essential property; and whereby indeed he most nearly convinced the doubt of his humanity. Nor need we be afraid to ascribe that unto the incarnate Son, which sometimes is attributed unto the uncarnate Father; of whom it is said, He that dwelleth in the heavens shall laugh the wicked to scorn. For a laugh there is of contempt or indignation, as well as of mirth and Jocosity; and that our Saviour was not exempted from the ground hereof, that is, the passion of anger, regulated and rightly ordered by reason, the schools do not deny: and besides the experience of the money-changers and Dove-sellers in the Temple, is testified by St. *John*, when he saith, the speech of *David* *Zelus domus tuæ comedit me.* was fulfilled in our Saviour.

Now the Alogie of this opinion consisteth in the illation; it being not reasonable to conclude from Scripture negatively in points which are not matters of faith, and pertaining unto salvation. And therefore although in the description of the creation there be no mention of fire, Christian Philosophy did not think it reasonable presently to annihilate that element, or positively to decree there was no such thing at all. Thus whereas in the brief narration of *Moses* there is no record of wine before the flood, we cannot satisfactorily conclude that *Noah* was the first that ever tasted thereof. *Only in the vulgar Latin.* Judg. 9. 53. And thus because the word *Brain* is scarce mentioned once, but *Heart* above an hundred times in holy Scripture; Physitians that dispute the principality of parts are not from hence induced to bereave the animal Organ of its priority. Wherefore the Scriptures being serious, and commonly omitting such Parergies, it will be unreasonable from hence to condemn all Laughter, and from considerations inconsiderable to discipline a man out of his nature. For this is by a rustical severity to banish all urbanity; whose harmless and confined condition, as it stands commended by morality, so is it consistent with Religion, and doth not offend Divinity.

4. The custom it is of Popes to change their name at their creation; and the Author thereof is commonly said to be *Bocca di porco*, or swines face; who therefore assumed the stile of *Sergius* the second, as being ashamed so foul a name should dishonour the chair of *Peter*; wherein notwithstanding, from *Montacutius* and others I find there may be some mistake. For *Massonius* who writ the lives of Popes, acknowledgeth he was not the first that changed his name in that Sea; nor as *Platina* affirmeth, have all his Successors precisely continued that custom; for *Adrian* the sixt, and *Marcellus* the second, did still retain their Baptismal denomination. Nor is it proved, or probable, that *Sergius* changed the name of *Bocca di Porco*, for this was his sirname or gentilitious appellation: nor was it the custom to alter that with the other; but be commuted his Christian name *Peter* for *Sergius*, because he would seem to decline the name of *Peter* the second. A scruple I confess not thought considerable in other Seas, whose Originals and first Patriarchs have been less disputed; nor yet perhaps of that reality as to prevail in points of the same nature. For the names of the Apostles, Patriarchs and Prophets have been assumed even to affectation; the name of Jesus hath not been appropriate; but some in precedent ages have born that name, and many since have not refused the Christian name of *Emmanuel*. Thus are there few names more frequent then *Moses* and *Abraham* among the *Jews*; The *Turks* without scruple affect the name of *Mahomet*, and with gladness receive so honourable cognomination.

And truly in humane occurrences there ever have been many well directed intentions, whose rationalities will never bear a rigid examination, and though in some way they do commend their Authors, and such as first began them, yet have they proved insufficient to perpetuate imitation in such as have succeeded them. Thus was it a worthy resolution of *Godfrey*, and most Christians have applauded it, That he refused to wear a Crown of Gold where his Saviour had worn one of thorns. Yet did not his Successors durably inherit that scruple, but some were anointed, and solemnly accepted the Diadem of regality. Thus *Julius*, *Augustus* and *Tiberius* with great humility or popularity refused the name of *Imperator*, but their Successors have challenged that title, and retain the same even in its titularity. And thus to come nearer our subject, the humility of *Gregory* the Great would by no means admit the stile of universal Bishop; but the ambition of *Boniface* made no scruple thereof, nor of more queasie resolutions have been their Successors ever since.

Turkish *History*.

5. That *Tamerlane* was a *Scythian* Shepherd, from Mr. *Knolls* and others, from *Alhazen* a learned *Arabian* who wrote his life, and was Spectator of many of his exploits, we have reasons to deny. Not only from his birth, for he was of the blood of the *Tartarian* Emperours, whose father *Og* had for his possession the Country of *Sagathy*; which was no slender Territory, but comprehended all that tract wherein were contained *Bactriana*, *Sogdiana*, *Margiana*, and the nation of the *Massagetes*, whose capital City was *Samarcand*; a place though now decaid, of great esteem and trade in former ages. But from his regal Inauguration, for it is said, that being about the age of fifteen, his old father resigned the Kingdom and men of war unto him. And also from his education, for as the storie speaks it, he was instructed in the *Arabian* learning, and afterward exercised himself therein. Now *Arabian* learning was in a manner all the liberal Sciences, especially the Mathematicks, and natural Philosophy; wherein not many ages before him there flourished *Avicenna*, *Averroes*, *Avenzoar*, *Geber*, *Almanzor* and *Alhazen*, cognominal unto him that wrote his History, whose Chronology indeed, although it be obscure, yet in the opinion of his Commentator, he was contemporary unto *Avicenna*, and hath left sixteen books of Opticks, of great esteem with ages past, and textuary unto our days.

Now the ground of this mistake was surely that which the Turkish Historian declareth. Some, saith he, of our Historians will needs have *Tamerlane* to be the Son of a Shepherd. But this they have said, not knowing at all the custom of their Country; wherein the principal revenews of the King and Nobles consisteth in cattle; who despising gold and silver, abound in all sorts thereof. And this was the occasion that some men call them Shepherds, and also affirm this Prince descended from them. Now, if it be reasonable, that great men whose possessions are chiefly in cattle, should bear the name of Shepherds, and fall upon so low denominations; then may we say that *Abraham* was a Shepherd, although too powerful for four Kings: that *Job* was of that condition, who beside Camels and Oxen had seven thousand Sheep: and yet is said to be the greatest man in the East. Thus was *Mesha* King of *Moab* a Shepherd, who annually paid unto the Crown of *Israel* an hundred thousand Lambs, and as many Rams. Surely it is no dishonourable course of life which *Moses* and *Jacob* have made exemplary: 'tis a profession supported upon the natural way of acquisition, and though contemned by the *Egyptians*, much countenanced by the Hebrews, whose sacrifices required plenty of Sheep and Lambs. And certainly they were very numerous; for, at the consecration of the Temple, beside two and twenty thousand Oxen, King *Solomon* sacrificed an hundred and twenty thousand Sheep: and the same is observable from the daily provision of his house: which was ten fat Oxen, twenty Oxen out of the pastures, and an hundred Sheep, beside row Buck, fallow Deer, and fatted Fowls. *Description of the Turkish Seraglio, since printed. The daily provision of the Seraglio.* Wherein notwithstanding (if a punctual relation thereof do rightly inform us) the grand Seignior doth exceed: the daily provision of whose Seraglio in the reign of *Achmet*, beside Beeves, consumed two hundred Sheep, Lambs and Kids when they were in season one hundred, Calves ten, Geese fifty, Hens two hundred, Chickens one hundred, Pigeons an hundred pair.

And therefore this mistake concerning the noble *Tamerlane*, was like that concerning *Demosthenes*, who is said to be the Son of a Black-smith, according to common conceit, and that handsome expression of *Juvenal*.

Quem pater ardentis massæ fuligine lippus,
A carbone et forcipibus, gladiosq; parante
Incude, et luteo Vulcano ad Rhetora misit.
Thus Englished by Sir Robert *Stapleton*.
Whom's Father with the smoaky forg half blind,
From blows on sooty Vulcans anvil spent.
In ham'ring swords, to study Rhet'rick sent.

But *Plutarch* who writ his life hath cleared this conceit, plainly affirming he was most nobly descended, and that this report was raised, because his father had many slaves that wrought Smiths work, and brought the profit unto him.

CHAPTER XVII
Of some others.

1. We are sad when we read the story of *Belisarius* that worthy Chieftain of *Justinian*; who, after his Victories over *Vandals*, *Goths*, *Persians*, and his Trophies in three parts of the World, had at last his eyes put out by the Emperour, and was reduced to that distress, that he begged relief on the high-way, in that uncomfortable petition, *Date obolum Belisario*. And this we do not only hear in Discourses, Orations and Themes, but find it also in the leaves of *Petrus Crinitus*, *Volaterranus*, and other worthy Writers.

But, what may somewhat consolate all men that honour vertue, we do not discover the latter Scene of his Misery in Authors of Antiquity, or such as have expresly delivered the stories of those times. For, *Suidas* is silent herein, *Cedrenus* and *Zonaras*, two grave and punctual Authors, delivering only the confiscation of his goods, omit the History of his mendication. *Paulus Diaconus* goeth farther, not only passing over this act, but affirming his goods and dignities were restored. *Agathius* who lived at the same time, declareth he suffered much from the envy of the Court: but that he descended thus deep into affliction, is not to be gathered from his pen. The same is also omitted by *Procopius* a contemporary and professed enemy unto *Justinian* and *Belisarius*, who hath left an opprobrious book Ἀνέκδοτα, *or Arcana historia*. against them both.

And in this opinion and hopes we are not single, but *Andreas Alciatus* the Civilian in his *Parerga*, and *Franciscus de Cordua* in his *Didascalia*, have both declaratorily confirmed the same, which is also agreeable unto the judgment of *Nicolaus Alemannus*, in his notes upon the bitter History of *Procopius*. Certainly sad and Tragical stories are seldom drawn within the circle of their verities; but as their Relators do either intend the hatred or pitty of the persons, so are they set forth with additional amplifications. Thus have some suspected it hath happened unto the story of *Oedipus*; and thus do we conceive it hath fared with that of *Judas*, who having sinned beyond aggravation, and committed one villany which cannot be exasperated by all other: is also charged with the murther of his reputed brother, parricide of his father, and Incest with his own mother, as *Florilegus* or *Matthew* of *Westminster* hath at large related. And thus hath it perhaps befallen the noble *Belisarius*; who, upon instigation of the Empress, having contrived the exile, and very hardly treated Pope *Serverius*, Latin pens, as a judgment of God upon this fact, have set forth his future sufferings: and omitting nothing of amplification, they have also delivered this: which notwithstanding *Johannes* the Greek makes doubtful, as may appear from his Iambicks in *Baronius*, and might be a mistake or misapplication, translating the affliction of one man upon another, for the same befell unto *Johannes Cappadox*, Procop. Bell. Persic. 1. Ἄρτον ἢ ὀβολὸν αἰτεῖσθαι. contemporary unto *Belisarius*, and in great favour with *Justinian*; who being afterward banished into *Egypt*, was fain to beg relief on the high-way.

2. That *fluctus Decumanus*, or the tenth wave is greater and more dangerous than any other, some no doubt will be offended if we deny; and hereby we shall seem to contradict Antiquity; for, answerable unto the litteral and common acception, the same is averred by many Writers, and plainly described by Ovid.

Qui venit hic fluctus, fluctus supereminet omnes,
Posterior nono est, undecimoq; prior.

Which notwithstanding is evidently false; nor can it be made out by observation either upon the shore or the Ocean, as we have with diligence explored in both. And surely in vain we expect a regularity in the waves of the Sea, or in the particular motions thereof, as we may in its general reciprocations whose causes are constant, and effects therefore correspondent. Whereas its fluctuations are but motions subservient; which winds, storms, shores, shelves, and every interjacency irregulates. With semblable reason we might expect a regularity in the winds; whereof though some be statary, some anniversary, and the rest do tend to determinate points of heaven, yet do the blasts and undulary breaths thereof maintain no certainty in their course; nor are they numerally feared by Navigators.

Of affinity hereto is that conceit of *Ovum Decumanum*, so called, because the tenth egg is bigger than any other, according unto the reason alledged by *Festus, Decumana ova dicuntur, quia ovum decimum majus nascitur*. For the honour we bear unto the Clergy, we cannot but wish this true: but herein will be found no more of verity than in the other: and surely few will assent hereto without an implicite credulity, or Pythagorical submission unto every conception of number.

For, surely the conceit is numeral, and though not in the sense apprehended, relateth unto the number of ten, as *Franciscus Sylvius* hath most probably declared. For, whereas amongst simple numbers or Digits, the number of ten is the greatest: therefore whatsoever was the greatest in every kind, might in some sense be named from this number. Now, because also that which was the greatest, was metaphorically by some at first called *Decumanus*; therefore whatsoever passed under this name, was literally conceived by others to respect and make good this number.

The conceit is also Latin; for the Greeks to express the greatest wave, do use the number of three, that is, the word τρικυμία, which is a concurrence of three waves in one, whence arose the proverb, τρικυμία κακῶν, or a trifluctuation of evils, which *Erasmus* doth render, *Malorum fluctus Decumanus*. And thus, although the terms be very different, yet are they made to signifie the self-same thing; the number of ten to explain the number of three, and the single number of one wave the collective concurrence of more.

3. The poyson of *Parysatis* reported from *Ctesias* by *Plutarch* in the life of *Artaxerxes*, whereby anointing a knife on the one side, and therewith dividing a bird; with the one half she poysoned *Statira*, and safely fed her self on the other, was certainly a very subtile one, and such as our ignorance is well content it knows not. But surely we had discovered a poyson that would not endure *Pandoraes* box, could we be satisfied in that which for its coldness nothing could contain but an Asses hoof, and wherewith some report that *Alexander* the great was poysoned. Had men derived so strange an effect from some occult or hidden qualities, they might have silenced contradiction; but ascribing it unto the manifest and open qualities of cold, they must pardon our belief, who perceive the coldest and most Stygian waters may be included in glasses; and by *Aristotle* who saith, that glass is the perfectest work of Art, we understand they were not then to be invented.

And though it be said that poyson will break a Venice glass, yet have we not met with any of that nature. Were there a truth herein, it were the best preservative for Princes and persons exalted unto such fears: and surely far better than divers now in use. And though the best of China dishes, and such as the Emperour doth use, be thought by some of infallible vertue unto this effect; yet will they not, I fear, be able to elude the mischief of such intentions. *In what sense God Almighty hath created all things double.* And though also it be true, that God made all things double, and that if we look upon the works of the most High, there are two and two, one against another; that one contrary hath another, and poyson is not without a poyson unto it self; yet hath the curse so far prevailed, or else our industry defected that poysons are better known than their

Antidotes, and some thereof do scarce admit of any. And lastly, although unto every poyson men have delivered many Antidotes, and in every one is promised an equality unto its adversary, yet do we often find they fail in their effects: Moly will not resist a weaker cup then that of Circe; a man may be poysoned in a Lemnian dish; without the miracle of *John*, there is no confidence in the earth of *Paul*; [Terra Melitea.] and if it be meant that no poyson could work upon him, we doubt the story, and expect no such success from the diet of *Mithridates*.

A story there passeth of an Indian King, that sent unto *Alexander* a fair woman fed with Aconites and other poysons, with this intent, either by converse or copulation complexionally to destroy him. For my part, although the design were true, I should have doubted the success. For, though it be possible that poysons may meet with tempers whereto they may become Aliments, and we observe from fowls that feed on fishes, and others fed with garlick and onyons, that simple aliments are not always concocted beyond their vegetable qualities; and therefore that even after carnall conversion, poysons may yet retain some portion of their natures; yet are they so refracted, cicurated and subdued, as not to make good their first and destructive malignities. And therefore the Stork that eateth Snakes, and the Stare that feedeth upon Hemlock, though no commendable aliments, are not destructive poysons. For, animals that can innoxiously digest these poysons, become antidotall unto the poyson digested. And therefore whether their breath be attracted, or their flesh ingested, the poysonous reliques go still along with their Antidote: whose society will not permit their malice to be destructive. And therefore also animals that are not mischieved by poysons which destroy us, may be drawn into Antidote against them; the blood or flesh of Storks against the venom of Serpents, the Quail against Hellebore, and the diet of Starlings against the drought of *Socrates*. [Hemlock.] Upon like grounds are some parts of Animals Alexipharmacall unto others; and some veins of the earth, and also whole regions, not only destroy the life of venemous creatures, but also prevent their productions. For though perhaps they contain the seminals of Spiders and Scorpions, and such as in other earths by suscitiation of the Sun may arise unto animation; yet lying under command of their Antidote, without hope of emergency they are poysoned in their matrix by powers easily hindring the advance of their originals, whose confirmed forms they are able to destroy.

5. The story of the wandring Jew is very strange, and will hardly obtain belief; yet is there a formall account thereof set down by *Mathew Paris*, from the report of an Armenian Bishop; who came into this kingdom about four hundred years ago, and had often entertained this wanderer at his Table. That he was then alive, was first called *Cartaphilus*, was keeper of the Judgement Hall, whence thrusting out our Saviour with expostulation of his stay, was condemned to stay untill his return; [Vade quid moraris? Ego vado, tu autem morare donec venio.] was after baptized by *Ananias*, and by the name of *Joseph*; was thirty years old in the dayes of our Saviour, remembred the Saints that arised with him, the making of the Apostles Creed, and their several peregrinations. Surely were this true, he might be an happy arbitrator in many Christian controversies; but must impardonably condemn the obstinacy of the Jews, who can contemn the Rhetorick of such miracles, and blindly behold so living and lasting conversions.

6. Clearer confirmations must be drawn for the history of Pope *Joan*, who succeeded *Leo* the fourth, and preceeded *Benedict* the third, then many we yet discover. And since it is delivered with *aiunt* and *ferunt* by many; [Confutatio fabulæ de Joanna Papissa cum Nihusio.] since the learned *Leo Allatius* hath discovered, that ancient copies of *Martinus Polonus*, who is chiefly urged for it, had not this story in it; since not only the stream of Latine Historians have omitted it, but *Photius* the Patriarch, *Metrophanes Smyrnæus*, and the exasperated Greeks have made no mention of it, but conceded *Benedict* the third to bee Successor unto *Leo* the fourth; he wants not grounds that doubts it.

Many things historicall which seem of clear concession, want not affirmations and negations, according to divided pens: as is notoriously observable in the story of *Hildebrand* or *Gregory* the seventh, repugnantly delivered by the Imperiall and Papal party. In such divided records partiality hath much depraved history, wherein if the equity of the reader do not correct the iniquity of the writer, he will be much confounded with repugnancies, and often find in the same person, *Numa* and *Nero*. *Of* Luther, Calvin, Beza. In things of this nature moderation must intercede; and so charity may hope, that Roman Readers will construe many passages in *Bolsech, Fayus, Schlusselberg* and *Cochlæus*.

7. Every ear is filled with the story of Frier *Bacon*, Rog. Bacon. minor ita. Oxoniensis vir doctissimus. that made a brazen head to speak these words, *Time is*, Which though there want not the like relations, is surely too literally received, and was but a mystical fable concerning the Philosophers great work, wherein he eminently laboured: implying no more by the copper head, then the vessel wherein it was wrought, and by the words it spake, then the opportunity to be watched, about the *Tempus ortus*, or birth of the mystical child, or Philosophical King of *Lullius*: the rising of the *Terra foliata* of *Arnoldus*, when the earth sufficiently impregnated with the water, ascendeth white and splendent. Which not observed, the work is irrecoverably lost; according to that of *Petrus Bonus*. Margarita pretiosa. *Ibi est operis perfectio aut annihilatio; quoniam ipsa die, immo horâ, oriuntur elementa simplicia depurata, quæ egent statim compositione, antequam volent ab igne.*

Now letting slip this critical opportunity, he missed the intended treasure. Which had he obtained, he might have made out the tradition of making a brazen wall about *England*. That is, the most powerfull defence, and strongest fortification which Gold could have effected.

8. Who can but pity the vertuous *Epicurus*, who is commonly conceived to have placed his chief felicity in pleasure and sensual delights, and hath therefore left an infamous name behind him? How true, let them determine who read that he lived seventy years, and wrote more books then any Philosopher but *Chrysippus*, and no less then three hundred, without borrowing from any Author. That he was contented with bread and water, and when he would dine with *Jove*, and pretend unto epulation, he desired no other addition then a piece of *Cytheridian* cheese. That shall consider the words of *Seneca, Non dico, quod pleriq; nostrorum, sectam Epicuri flagitiorum magistrum esse: sed illud dico, malè audit infamis est, et immerito*. Or shall read his life, his Epistles, his Testament in *Laertius*, who plainly names them Calumnies, which are commonly said against them.

The ground hereof seems a mis-apprehension of his opinion, who placed his Felicity not in the pleasures of the body, but the mind, and tranquility thereof, obtained by wisdom and vertue, as is clearly determined in his Epistle unto *Menœceus*. Now how this opinion was first traduced by the *Stoicks*, how it afterwards became a common belief, and so taken up by Authors of all ages, by *Cicero, Plutarch, Clemens, Ambrose* and others, De vita et moribus Epicuri. the learned Pen of *Gassendus* hath discovered.

CHAPTER XVIII
More briefly of some others.

Other relations there are, and those in very good Authors, which though we do not positively deny, yet have they not been unquestioned by some, and at least as improbable truths have been received by others. Unto some it hath seemed incredible what *Herodotus* reporteth of the great Army of *Xerxes*, that drank whole rivers dry. And unto the Author himself it appeared wondrous strange, that they exhausted not the provision of the Countrey, rather then the waters thereof. For as he maketh the account, and *Budeus de Asse* correcting the mis-compute of *Valla*, delivereth it; if every man of the Army had had a chenix of Corn a day, that is, a sextary and half; or about two pints and a quarter, the Army had daily expended ten hundred thousand and forty Medimna's, or measures containing six Bushels. Which rightly considered, the *Abderites* had reason to bless the

Heavens, that *Xerxes* eat but one meal a day; and *Pythius* his noble Host, might with less charge and possible provision entertain both him and his Army. And yet may all be salved, if we take it hyperbolically, as wise men receive that expression in *Job*, concerning *Behemoth* or the Elephant; Behold, he drinketh up a river and hasteth not, he trusteth that he can draw up *Jordan* into his mouth.

2. That *Annibal* eat or brake through the Alps with Vinegar, may be too grosly taken and the Author of his life annexed unto *Plutarch* affirmeth only, he used this artifice upon the tops of some of the highest mountains. For as it is vulgarly understood, that he cut a passage for his Army through those mighty mountains, it may seem incredible, not only in the greatness of the effect, but the quantity of the efficient and such as behold them, may think an Ocean of Vinegar too little for that effect. 'Twas a work indeed rather to be expected from earthquakes and inundations, then any corrosive waters, and much condemneth the Judgement of *Xerxes*, that wrought through Mount *Athos* with Mattocks.

3. That *Archimedes* burnt the ships of *Marcellus*, with speculums of parabolical figures, at three furlongs, or as some will have it, at the distance of three miles, sounds hard unto reason, and artificial experience: and therefore justly questioned by *Kircherus*, *De luce et umbra.* who after long enquiry could find but one made by *Manfredus Septalius* that fired at fifteen paces. And therefore more probable it is, that the ships were nearer the shore, or about some thirty paces: at which distance notwithstanding the effect was very great. But whereas men conceive the ships were more easily set on flame by reason of the pitch about them, it seemeth no advantage. Since burning glasses will melt pitch or make it boyle, not easily set it on fire.

4. The story of the *Fabii*, whereof three hundred and six marching against the *Veientes*, were all slain, and one child alone to support the family remained; is surely not to be paralleld, nor easie to be conceived, except we can imagine, that of three hundred and six, but one had children below the service of war; that the rest were all unmarried, or the wife but of one impregnated.

5. The received story of *Milo*, who by daily lifting a Calf, attained an ability to carry it being a Bull, is witty conceit, and handsomly sets forth the efficacy of Assuefaction. But surely the account had been more reasonably placed upon some person not much exceeding in strength, and such a one as without the assistance of custom could never have performed that act; which some may presume that *Milo* without precedent artifice or any other preparative, had strength enough to perform. For as relations declare, he was the most pancratical man of *Greece*, and as *Galen* reporteth, and *Mercurialis* in his Gymnasticks representeth, he was able to persist erect upon an oyled plank, and not to be removed by the force or protrusion of three men. And if that be true which *Atheneus* reporteth, he was little beholding to custom for this ability. For in the Olympick games, for the space of a furlong, he carried an Ox of four years upon his shoulders; and the same day he carried it in his belly: for as it is there delivered he eat it up himself. Surely he had been a proper guest at *In Rabelais.* *Grandgousiers* feast, and might have matcht his throat that eat six pilgrims for a Salad.

6. It much disadvantageth the Panegyrick of *Synesius*, *Who writ in the praise of baldness.* and is no small disparagement unto baldness, if it be true what is related by *Ælian* concerning *Æschilus*, whose bald-pate was mistaken for a rock, and so was brained by a Tortoise which an *Æagle* let fall upon it. *An argument or instance against the motion of the earth.* Certainly it was a very great mistake in the perspicacy of that Animal. Some men critically disposed, would from hence confute the opinion of *Copernicus*, never conceiving how the motion of the earth below should not wave him from a knock perpendicularly directed from a body in the air above.

7. It crosseth the Proverb, and *Rome* might well be built in a day; if that were true which is traditionally related by *Strabo*; that the great Cities *Anchiale* and *Tarsus*, were built by *Sardanapalus* both in one day, according to the inscription of his monument, *Sardanapalus Anacyndaraxis filius, Anchialem et Tarsum unâ die edificavi, Tu autem hospes Ede, Lude, Bibe,* etc. Which if strictly taken, that is, for the finishing thereof, and not only for the beginning; for an artificial or natural day, and not one of *Daniels* weeks, that is, seven whole years; surely their hands were very heavy that wasted thirteen years in the private house of *Solomon*: It may be wondred how forty years were spent in the erection of the Temple of *Jerusalem*, and no less than an hundred in that famous one of *Ephesus*. Certainly it was the greatest Architecture of one day, since that great one of six; an Art quite lost with our Mechanicks, a work not to be made out, but like the wals of *Thebes*, and such an Artificer as *Amphion*.

The Syracusia or King Hiero's Galleon, of what Bulk.

8. It had been a sight only second unto the Ark to have beheld the great *Syracusia*, or mighty ship of *Hiero*, described in *Athenæus*; and some have thought it a very large one, wherein were to be found ten stables for horses, eight Towers, besides Fish-ponds, Gardens, Tricliniums, and many fair rooms paved with Agath, and precious Stones. But nothing was impossible unto *Archimedes*, the learned Contriver thereof; nor shall we question his removing the earth, when he finds an immoveable base to place his Engine upon it.

9. That the *Pamphilian* Sea gave way unto *Alexander* in his intended March toward *Persia*, many have been apt to credit, and *Josephus* is willing to believe, to countenance the passage of the *Israelites* through the Red Sea. But *Strabo* who writ before him delivereth another account; that the Mountain *Climax* adjoyning to the *Pamphilian* Sea, leaves a narrow passage between the Sea and it, which passage at an ebb and quiet Sea all men take; but *Alexander* coming in the Winter, and eagerly pursuing his affairs, would not wait for the reflux or return of the Sea; and so was fain to pass with his Army in the water, and march up to the navel in it.

A List of some historical Errata's in this and the following Sections.

10. The relation of *Plutarch* of a youth of *Sparta*, that suffered a Fox concealed under his robe to tear out his bowels, before he would either by voice or countenance betray his theft; and the other of the Spartan Lad, that with the same resolution suffered a coal from the Altar to burn his arm, although defended by the Author that writes his life, is I perceive mistrusted by men of Judgment, and the Author with an *aiunt*, is made to salve himself. Assuredly it was a noble Nation that could afford an hint to such inventions of patience, and upon whom, if not such verities, at least such verisimilities of fortitude were placed. Were the story true, they would have made the only Disciples for *Zeno* and the *Stoicks*, and might perhaps have been perswaded to laugh in *Phaleris* his Bull.

11. If any man shall content his belief with the speech of *Balaams* Ass, without a belief of that of *Mahomets* Camel, or *Livies* Ox: If any man make a doubt of *Giges* ring in *Justinus*, or conceives he must be a *Jew* that believes the Sabbatical river in *Josephus*. If any man will say he doth not apprehend how the tayl of an *African* Weather out-weigheth the body of a good Calf, that is, an hundred pound, according unto *Leo Africanus*, or desires before belief, to behold such a creature as is the Ruck in *Paulus Venetus*, for my part I shall not be angry with his incredulity.

12. If any one shall receive as stretcht or fabulous accounts what is delivered of *Cocles*, *Scævola* and *Curtius*, the sphere of *Archimedes*, the story of the *Amazons*, the taking of the City of *Babylon*, not known to some therein three days after; that the nation was deaf which dwelt at the fall of *Nilus*, the laughing and weeping humour of *Heraclitus* and *Democritus*, Farsalloni Historici. with many more, he shall not want some reason and the authority of *Lancelotti*.

13. If any man doubt of the strange Antiquities delivered by Historians, as of the wonderful corps of *Antæus* untombed a thousand years after his death by *Sertorius*. Whether there were no deceit in those fragments of the Ark so common to be seen in the days of *Berosus*; whether the Pillar which *Josephus* beheld long ago, *Tertullian* long after, and *Bartholomeus de Saligniaco*, and *Borchardus* long since, be the same with that of *Lots* wife; whether this were the hand of *Paul*, or that which is commonly shewn the head of *Peter*, if any doubt, I shall not much dispute with

their suspicions. If any man shall not believe the Turpentine Tree, betwixt *Jerusalem* and *Bethlem*, under which the Virgin suckled our Saviour, as she passed between those Cities; or the fig-tree of *Bethany* shewed to this day, whereon *Zacheus* ascended to behold our Saviour; I cannot tell how to enforce his belief, nor do I think it requisite to attempt it. *To compel Religion, somewhat contrary to Reason.* For, as it is no reasonable proceeding to compel a religion, or think to enforce our own belief upon another, who cannot without the concurrence of Gods spirit have any indubitable evidence of things that are obtruded: So is it also in matters of common belief; whereunto neither can we indubitably assent, without the co-operation of our sense or reason, wherein consists the principles of perswasion. For, as the habit of Faith in Divinity is an Argument of things unseen, and a stable assent unto things inevident, upon authority of the Divine Revealer: So the belief of man which depends upon humane testimony is but a staggering assent unto the affirmative, not without some fear of the negative. And as there is required the Word of God, or infused inclination unto the one, so must the actual sensation of our senses, at least the non-opposition of our reasons procure our assent and acquiescence in the other. So when *Eusebius* an holy Writer affirmeth, there grew a strange and unknown plant near the statue of Christ, erected by his Hæmorrhoidal patient in the Gospel, which attaining unto the hem of his vesture, acquired a sudden faculty to cure all diseases. Although he saith he saw the statue in his days, yet hath it not found in many men so much as humane belief? Some believing, others opinioning, a third suspective it might be otherwise. For indeed, in matters of belief the understanding assenting unto the relation, either for the authority of the person, or the probability of the object, although there may be a confidence of the one, yet if there be not a satisfaction in the other, there will arise suspensions; nor can we properly believe until some argument of reason, or of our proper sense convince or determine our dubitations.

And thus it is also in matters of certain and experimented truth: for if unto one that never heard thereof, a man should undertake to perswade the affections of the Load-stone, or that Jet and Amber attracteth straws and light bodies, there would be little Rhetorick in the authority of *Aristotle*, *Pliny*, or any other. Thus although it be true that the string of a Lute or Viol will stir upon the stroak of an Unison or Diapazon in another of the same kind; that Alcanna being green, will suddenly infect the nails and other parts with a durable red; that a Candle out of a Musket will pierce through an Inch-board, or an urinal force a nail through a Plank; yet can few or none believe thus much without a visible experiment. Which notwithstanding fals out more happily for knowledge; for these relations leaving unsatisfaction in the Hearers, do stir up ingenuous dubiosities unto experiment, and by an exploration of all, prevent delusion in any.

CHAPTER XIX
Of some Relations whose truth we fear.

Lastly, As there are many Relations whereto we cannot assent, and make some doubt thereof, so there are divers others whose verities we fear, and heartily wish there were no truth therein.

1. It is an unsufferable affront unto filiall piety, and a deep discouragement unto the expectation of all aged Parents, who shall but read the story of that barbarous Queen, who after she had beheld her royall Parents ruin, lay yet in the arms of his assassine, and carowsed with him in the skull of her father. For my part, I should have doubted the operation of antimony, where such a potion would not work; 'twas an act me thinks beyond Anthropophagy, and a cup fit to be served up only at the table of *Atreus*.

2. While we laugh at the story of *Pygmaleon*, and receive as a fable that he fell in love with a statue; we cannot but fear it may be true, what is delivered by *Herodotus* concerning *Egyptian* Pollinctors, or such as annointed the dead; that some thereof were found in the act of carnality with them. From wits that say 'tis more then incontinency for *Hylas* to sport with *Hecuba*, and youth to flame in the frozen embraces of age, we require a name for this: wherein *Petronius* or *Martial* cannot relieve us. *Who tied dead and living bodies*

together. The tyrannie of *Mezentius* did never equall the vitiosity of this *Incubus*, that could embrace corruption, and make a Mistress of the grave; that could not resist the dead provocations of beauty, whose quick invitements scarce excuse submission. Surely, if such depravities there be yet alive, deformity need not despair; nor will the eldest hopes be ever superannuated, since death hath spurs, and carcasses have been courted.

3. I am heartily sorry, and wish it were not true, what to the dishonour of Christianity is affirmed of the *Italian*, who after he had inveigled his enemy to disclaim his faith for the redemption of his life, did presently poyniard him, to prevent repentance, and assure his eternal death. The villany of this Christian exceedeth the persecution of Heathens, whose malice was never so Longimanous *Long-handed.* as to reach the soul of their enemies; or to extend unto the exile of their *Elysiums*. And though the blindness of some ferities have savaged on the bodies of the dead, and been so injurious unto worms, as to disinter the bodies of the deceased; yet had they therein no design upon the soul: and have been so far from the destruction of that, or desires of a perpetual death, that for the satisfaction of their revenge they wisht them many souls, and were it in their power would have reduced them unto life again. It is a great depravity in our natures, and surely an affection that somewhat savoureth of hell, to desire the society, or comfort our selves in the fellowship of others that suffer with us; but to procure the miseries of others in those extremities, wherein we hold an hope to have no society our selves, is me thinks a strain above *Lucifer*, and a project beyond the primary seduction of hell.

4. I hope it is not true, and some indeed have probably denied, what is recorded of the Monk that poysoned *Henry* the Emperour, in a draught of the holy Eucharist. 'Twas a scandalous wound unto Christian Religion, and I hope all Pagans will forgive it, when they shall read that a Christian was poysoned in a cup of Christ, and received his bane in a draught of his salvation. Had he believed Transubstantiation, he would have doubted the effect; and surely the sin it self received an aggravation in that opinion. It much commendeth the innocency of our forefathers, and the simplicity of those times, whose Laws could never dream so high a crime as parricide: whereas this at the least may seem to out-reach that fact, and to exceed the regular distinctions of murder. I will not say what sin it was to act it; yet may it seem a kind of martyrdom to suffer by it. For, although unknowingly, he died for Christ his sake, and lost his life in the ordained testimony of his death. Certainly, had they known it, some noble zeales would scarcely have refused it; rather adventuring their own death, then refusing the memorial of his.

Many other accounts like these we meet sometimes in history, *Hujus farinæ multa in historia horribili.* scandalous unto Christianity, and even unto humanity; whose verities not only, but whose relations honest minds do deprecate. For of sins heteroclital, and such as want either name or president, there is oft times a sin even in their histories. We desire no records of such enormities; sins should be accounted new, that so they may be esteemed monstrous. They omit of monstrosity as they fall from their rarity; for men count it veniall to err with their forefathers, and foolishly conceive they divide a sin in its society. The pens of men may sufficiently expatiate without these singularities of villany; For, as they encrease the hatred of vice in some, so do they enlarge the theory of wickedness in all. And this is one thing that may make latter ages worse then were the former; For, the vicious examples of Ages past, poyson the curiosity of these present, affording a hint of sin unto seduceable spirits, and soliciting those unto the imitation of them, whose heads were never so perversly principled as to invent them. In this kind we commend the wisdom and goodness of *Galen*, who would not leave unto the world too subtile a Theory of poisons; unarming thereby the malice of venemous spirits, whose ignorance must be contented with Sublimate and Arsenick. For, surely there are subtiler venenations, such as will invisibly destroy, and like the Basilisks of heaven. In things of this nature silence commendeth history: 'tis the veniable part of things lost; wherein there must never rise a Pancirollus, *Who writ* De Antiquis deperditis, *or of inventions lost.* nor remain any Register but that of hell.

And yet, if as some Stoicks opinion, and *Seneca* himself disputeth, these unruly affections that make us sin such prodigies, and even sins themselves be animals; there is an history of *Africa* and story of Snakes in these. And if the transanimation of *Pythagoras* or method thereof were true, that the souls of men transmigrated into species answering their former natures; some men must surely live over many Serpents, and cannot escape that very brood whose sire Satan entered. And though the objection of *Plato* should take place, that bodies subjected unto corruption, must fail at last before the period of all things, and growing fewer in number, must leave some souls apart unto themselves; the spirits of many long before that time will find but naked habitations: and meeting no assimilables wherein to react their natures, must certainly anticipate such natural desolations.

Lactant.
Primus sapientiæ gradus est, falsa intelligere.
FINIS.

HYDRIOTAPHIA
URNE-BURIALL
OR A DISCOURSE OF THE

SEPULCHRALL URNES

LATELY FOUND

IN NORFOLK
TOGETHER WITH
THE GARDEN OF CYRUS

TO MY WORTHY AND HONOURED FRIEND
THOMAS LE GROS
Of *Crostwick* Esquire.

When the Funerall pyre was out, and the last valediction over, men took a lasting adieu of their interred Friends, little expecting the curiosity of future ages should comment upon their ashes, and having no old experience of the duration of their Reliques, held no opinion of such after-considerations.

But who knows the fate of his bones, or how often he is to be buried? who hath the Oracle of his ashes, or whether they are to be scattered? The Reliques of many lie like the ruines of [A]*Pompeys*, in all parts of the earth; And when they arrive at your hands, these may seem to have wandred farre, who in a [B] direct and *Meridian* Travell, have but few miles of known Earth between your selfe and the Pole.

That the bones of *Theseus* should be seen again [C]in *Athens*, was not beyond conjecture, and hopeful expectation; but that these should arise so opportunely to serve your self, was an hit of fate and honour beyond prediction.

We cannot but wish these Urnes might have the effect of Theatrical vessels, and great [D]*Hippodrome* Urnes in *Rome*; to resound the acclamations and honour due unto you. But these are sad and sepulchral Pitchers, which have no joyfull voices; silently expressing old mortality, the ruines of forgotten times, and can only speak with life, how long in this corruptible frame, some parts may be uncorrupted; yet able to out-last bones long unborn, and noblest [E]pyle among us.

We present not these as any strange sight or spectacle unknown to your eyes, who have beheld the best of Urnes, and noblest variety of Ashes; Who are your self no slender master of Antiquities, and can daily command the view of so many Imperiall faces; Which raiseth your thoughts unto old things, and consideration of times before you, when even living men were Antiquities; when the living might exceed the dead, and to depart this world, could not be properly said, to go unto the [F]greater number. And so run up your thoughts upon the ancient of dayes, the Antiquaries truest object, unto whom the eldest parcels are young, and earth it self an Infant; and without [G]Ægyptian account makes but small noise in thousands.

We were hinted by the occasion, not catched the opportunity to write of old things, or intrude upon the Antiquary. We are coldly drawn unto discourses of Antiquities, who have scarce time before us to comprehend new things, or make out learned Novelties. But seeing they arose as they lay, almost in silence among us, at least in short account suddenly passed over; we were very unwilling they should die again, and be buried twice among us.

Beside, to preserve the living, and make the dead to live, to keep men out of their Urnes, and discourse of humane fragments in them, is not impertinent unto our profession; whose study is life and death, who daily behold examples of mortality, and of all men least need artificial *memento's*, or coffins by our bed side, to minde us of our graves.

'Tis time to observe Occurrences, and let nothing remarkable escape us; The Supinity of elder dayes hath left so much in silence, or time hath so martyred the Records, that the most industrious[H] heads do finde no easie work to erect a new *Britannia*.

'Tis opportune to look back upon old times, and contemplate our Forefathers. Great examples grow thin, and to be fetched from the passed world. Simplicity flies away, and iniquity comes at long strides upon us. We have enough to do to make up our selves from present and passed times, and the whole stage of things scarce serveth for our instruction. A compleat peece of vertue must be made up from the *Centos* of all ages, as all the beauties of *Greece* could make but one handsome *Venus*.

When the bones of King *Arthur* were digged up[I], the old Race might think, they beheld therein some Originals of themselves; Unto these of our Urnes none here can pretend relation, and can only behold the Reliques of those persons, who in their life giving the Laws unto their predecessors, after long obscurity, now lye at their mercies. But remembring the early civility they brought upon these Countreys, and forgetting long passed mischiefs; We mercifully preserve their bones, and pisse not upon their ashes.

In the offer of these Antiquities we drive not at ancient Families, so long out-lasted by them; We are farre from erecting your worth upon the pillars of your Fore-fathers, whose merits you illustrate. We honour your old Virtues, conformable unto times before you, which are the Noblest Armoury. And having long experience of your friendly conversation, void of empty Formality, full of freedome, constant and Generous Honesty, I look upon you as a Gemme of the Old Rock[J], and must professe my self even to Urne and Ashes,

Your ever faithfull Friend,
  and Servant

THOMAS BROWNE.

Norwich, May 1.

TO MY WORTHY AND HONOURED FRIEND
NICHOLAS BACON
Of *Gillingham* Esquire.

Had I not observed that [K]*Purblinde men have discoursed well of sight, and some* [L]*without issue, excellently of Generation; I that was never master of any considerable garden, had not attempted this Subject. But the Earth is the Garden of Nature, and each fruitfull Countrey a Paradise. Dioscorides made most of his Observations in his march about with* Antonius; *and* Theophrastus *raised his generalities chiefly from the field.*

Beside, we write no Herball, nor can this Volume deceive you, who have handled the [M]*massiest thereof: who know that thre* [N]*Folio's are yet too little, and how New Herbals fly from* America *upon us, from persevering Enquirers, and* [O]*old in those singularities, we expect such Descriptions. Wherein* [P]*England is now so exact, that it yeelds not to other Countreys.*

We pretend not to multiply vegetable divisions by Quincuncial and Reticulate plants; or erect a new Phytology. The Field of knowledge hath been so traced, it is hard to spring any thing new. Of old things we write something new, If truth may receive addition, or envy will have any thing new; since the Ancients knew the late Anatomicall discoveries, and Hippocrates *the Circulation.*

You have been so long out of trite learning, that 'tis hard to finde a subject proper for you; and if you have met with a Sheet upon this, we have missed our intention. In this multiplicity of writing, bye and barren Themes are best fitted for invention; Subjects so often discoursed confine the Imagination, and fix our conceptions unto the notions of fore-writers. Beside, such Discourses allow excursions, and venially admit of collaterall truths, though at some distance from their principals. Wherein if we sometimes take wide liberty, we are not single, but erre by great [Q]*example.*

He that will illustrate the excellency of this order, may easily fail upon so spruce a Subject, wherein we have not affrighted the common Reader with any other Diagramms, then of it self; and have industriously declined illustrations from rare and unknown plants.

Your discerning judgement so well acquainted with that study, will expect herein no mathematicall truths, as well understanding how few generalities and [R]*Vfinita's there are in nature. How* Scaliger *hath found exceptions in most Universals of* Aristotle *and* Theophrastus. *How Botanicall Maximes must have fair allowance, and are tolerably currant, if not intolerably over-ballanced by exceptions.*

You have wisely ordered your vegetable delights, beyond the reach of exception. The Turks who passt their dayes in Gardens here, will have Gardens also hereafter, and delighting in Flowers on earth, must have Lillies and Roses in Heaven. In Garden Delights 'tis not easie to hold a Mediocrity; that insinuating pleasure is seldome without some extremity. The Antients venially delighted in flourishing Gardens; Many were Florists that knew not the true use of a Flower; And in Plinies *dayes none had directly treated of that subject. Some commendably affected Plantations of venemous Vegetables, some confined their delights unto single plants, and Cato seemed to dote upon Cabbadge; While the Ingenuous delight of Tulipists, stands saluted with hard language, even by their own* [S]*Professors.*

That in this Garden Discourse, we range into extraneous things, and many parts of Art and Nature, we follow herein the example of old and new Plantations, wherein noble spirits contented not themselves with Trees, but by the attendance of Aviaries, Fish-Ponds, and all variety of Animals, they made their gardens the Epitome of the earth, and some resemblance of the secular shows of old.

That we conjoyn these parts of different Subjects, or that this should succeed the other; Your judgement will admit without impute of incongruity; Since the delightfull World comes after death, and Paradise succeeds the Grave. Since the verdant state of things is the Symbole of the Resurrection, and to flourish in the state of Glory, we must first be sown in corruption. Beside the ancient practise of Noble Persons, to conclude in Garden-Graves, and Urnes themselves of old, to be wrapt up flowers and garlands.

Nullam sine venia placuisse eloquium, *is more sensibly understood by Writers, then by Readers; nor well apprehended by either, till works have hanged out like* Apelles *his Pictures; wherein even common eyes will finde something for emendation.*

To wish all Readers of your abilities, were unreasonably to multiply the number of Scholars beyond the temper of these times. But unto this ill-judging age, we charitably desire a portion of your equity, judgement, candour, and ingenuity; wherein you are so rich, as not to lose by diffusion. And being a flourishing branch of that [T]*Noble Family, unto which we owe so much observance, you are not new set, but long rooted in such perfection; whereof having had so lasting confirmation in your worthy conversation, constant amity, and expression; and knowing you a serious Student in the highest* arcana's *of Nature; with much excuse we bring these low delights, and poor maniples to your Treasure.*

    Your affectionate Friend,
        and Servant

Norwich, May 1.

Footnotes

[A]Pompeios juvenes Asia, atque Europa, sed ipsum terra tegit *Lybies*.
[B]*Little directly, but Sea between your house and* Greenland.
[C]*Brought back by* Cimon. *Plutarch.*
[D]*The great Urnes in the* Hippodrome *at* Rome *conceived to resound the voices of people at their shows.*
[E]*Worthily possessed by that true Gentleman Sir* Horatio Townshend *my honored Friend.*
[F]Abiit ad plures.
[G]*Which makes the world so many years old.*
[H]*Wherein M.* Dugdale *hath excellently well endeavoured, and worthy to be countenanced by ingenuous and noble persons.*
[I]*In the time of* Henry *the second*, Cambden.
[J]Adamas de rupe veteri præstantissimus.
[K]Plempius, Cabeus, *etc.*
[L]*D.* Harvy.
[M]*Besleri* Hortus Eystetensis.
[N]*Bauhini* Theatrum Botanicum, *etc.*
[O]*My worthy friend M.* Goodier *an ancient and learned Botanist.*
[P]*As in* London *and divers parts, whereof we mention none, lest we seem to omit any.*
[Q]Hippocrates de superfœtatione, de dentitione.
[R]*Rules without exceptions.*
[S]Tulipo mania, Narrencruiid, Laurenberg. Pet. Hondius. in lib. *Belg.*
[T]*Of the most worthy Sr* Edmund Bacon *prime Baronet, my true and noble Friend.*

HYDRIOTAPHIA: URNE BURIAL
Or, a brief Discourse of the Sepulchrall Urnes lately found in Norfolk.

CHAPTER I

In the deep discovery of the Subterranean world, a shallow part would satisfie some enquirers; who, if two or three yards were open about the surface, would not care to wrack the bowels of *Potosi*,[1] regions towards the Centre. Nature hath furnished one part of the Earth, and man another. The treasures of time lie high, in Urnes, Coynes, and Monuments, scarce below the roots of some vegetables. Time hath endlesse rarities, and shows of all varieties; which reveals old things in heaven, makes new discoveries in earth, and even earth it self a discovery. That great antiquity *America* lay buried for thousands of years; and a large part of the earth is still in the Urne unto us.

Though if *Adam* were made out of an extract of the Earth, all parts might challenge a restitution, yet few have returned their bones far lower then they might receive them; not affecting the graves of Giants under hilly and heavy coverings, but content with lesse then their own depth, have wished their bones might lie soft, and the earth be light upon them; Even such as hope to rise again, would not be content with central interrment, or so desperately to place their reliques as to lie beyond discovery, and in no way to be seen again; which happy contrivance hath made communication with our forefathers, and left unto our view some parts, which they never beheld themselves.

Though earth hath engrossed the name yet water hath proved the smartest grave; which in fourty dayes swallowed almost mankinde, and the living creation; Fishes not wholly escaping, except the salt Ocean were handsomly contempered by a mixture of the fresh Element.

Many have taken voluminous pains to determine the state of the soul upon disunion; but men have been most phantastical in the singular contrivances of their corporall dissolution: whilest the soberest Nations have rested in two wayes, of simple inhumation and burning.

That carnal interrment or burying, was of the elder date, the old examples of *Abraham* and the Patriarches are sufficient to illustrate; And were without competition, if it could be made out, that *Adam* was buried near *Damascus*, or Mount *Calvary*, according to some Tradition. God himself that buried but one, was pleased to make choice of this way, collectible from Scripture-expression, and the hot contest between Satan and the Arch-Angel, about discovering the body of *Moses*. But the practice of Burning was also of great Antiquity, and of no slender extent. For (not to derive the same from *Hercules*) noble descriptions there are hereof in the Grecian Funerale of *Homer*, in the formal Obsequies of *Patroclus*, and *Achilles*; and somewhat elder in the *Theban* war, and solemn combustion of *Meneceus*, and *Archemorus*, contemporary unto *Jair* the Eighth Judge of *Israel*. Confirmable also among the *Trojans*, from the Funeral Pyre of *Hector*, burnt before the gates of *Troy*, and the burning[2] of *Penthisilea* the *Amazonian Queen*: and long continuance of that practice in the inward Countries of *Asia*; while as low as the Reign of *Julian*, we finde that the King of *Chionia*[3] burnt the body of his Son, and interred the ashes in a silver Urne.

The same practice extended also far West,[4] and besides *Herulians*, *Getes*, and *Thracians*, was in use with most of the *Celtæ*, *Sarmatians*, *Germans*, *Gauls*, *Danes*, *Swedes*, *Norwegians*; not to omit some use thereof among *Carthaginians* and *Americans*: Of greater antiquity among the *Romans* then most opinion, or *Pliny* seems to allow. For (beside the old Table Laws of burning[5] or burying within the City, of making the Funeral fire with plained wood, or quenching the fire with wine) *Manlius* the Consul burnt the body of his son: *Numa* by special clause of his will, was not burnt but buried; And *Remus* was solemnly buried, according to the description of *Ovid*.[6]

Cornelius Sylla was not the first whose body was burned in *Rome*, but of the *Cornelian* Family, which being indifferently, not frequently used before; from that time spread and became the prevalent practice. Not totally pursued in the highest run of Cremation; For when even Crows were funerally burnt, *Poppæa* the wife of *Nero* found a peculiar grave enterment. Now as all customs were founded upon some bottom of Reason, so there wanted not grounds for this; according to several apprehensions of the most rational dissolution. Some being of the opinion of *Thales*, that water was the original of all things, thought it most equal to submit unto the principle of putrifaction, and conclude in a moist relentment. Others conceived it most natural to end in fire, as due unto the master principle in the composition, according to the doctrine of *Heraclitus*.

And therefore heaped up large piles, more actively to waft them toward that Element, whereby they also declined a visible degeneration into worms, and left a lasting parcel of their composition.

Some apprehended a purifying virtue in fire, refining the grosser commixture, and firing out the Æthereal particles so deeply immersed in it. And such as by tradition or rational conjecture held any hint of the final pyre of all things; or that this Element at last must be too hard for all the rest; might conceive most naturally of the fiery dissolution. Others pretending no natural grounds, politickly declined the malice of enemies upon their buried bodies. Which consideration led *Sylla* unto this practice; who having thus served the body of *Marius*, could not but fear a retaliation upon his own; entertained after in the Civil wars, and revengeful contentions of *Rome*.

But as many Nations embraced, and many left it indifferent, so others too much affected, or strictly declined this practice. The *Indian Brachmans* seemed too great friends unto fire, who burnt themselves alive, and thought it the noblest way to end their dayes in fire; according to the expression of the Indian, burning himself at *Athens*,[7] in his last words upon the pyre unto the amazed spectators, *Thus I make my self immortal*.

But the *Chaldeans* the great Idolaters of fire, abhorred the burning of their carcasses, as a polution of that Deity. The *Persian Magi* declined it upon the like scruple, and being only solicitous about their bones, exposed their flesh to the prey of Birds and Dogs. And the *Persees* now in *India*, which expose their bodies unto Vultures, and endure not so much as *feretra* or Beers of Wood; the proper Fuell of fire, are led on with such nicities. But whether the ancient *Germans* who burned their dead, held any such fear to pollute their Deity of *Herthus*, or the earth, we have no Authentick conjecture.

The Ægyptians were afraid of fire, not as a Deity, but a devouring Element, mercilesly consuming their bodies, and leaving too little of them; and therefore by precious Embalments, depositure in dry earths, or handsome inclosure in glasses, contrived the notablest wayes of integrall conservation. And from such Ægyptian scruples imbibed by *Pythagoras*, it may be conjectured that *Numa* and the Pythagorical Sect first waved the fiery solution.

The *Scythians* who swore by winde and sword, that is, by life and death, were so far from burning their bodies, that they declined all interrment, and made their grave in the ayr: And the *Ichthyophagi* or fish-eating Nations about Ægypt, affected the Sea for their grave: Thereby declining visible corruption, and restoring the debt of their bodies. Whereas the old Heroes in *Homer*, dreaded nothing more than water or drowning; probably upon the old opinion of the fiery substance of the soul, onely extinguishable by that Element; And therfore the Poet emphatically implieth the total destruction in this kinde of death, which happened to *Ajax Oileus*.[8]

The old *Balearians*[9] had a peculiar mode, for they used great Urnes and much wood, but no fire in their burials; while they bruised the flesh and bones of the dead, crowded them into Urnes, and laid heaps of wood upon them. And the *Chinois*[10] without cremation or urnal interrment of their bodies, make use of trees and much burning, while they plant a Pine-tree by their grave, and burn great numbers of printed draughts of slaves and horses over it, civilly content with their companies in effigie, which barbarous Nations exact unto reality.

Christians abhorred this way of obsequies, and though they stickt not to give their bodies to be burnt in their lives, detested that mode after death; affecting rather a depositure than absumption, and properly submitting unto the sentence of God, to return not unto ashes but unto dust again, conformable unto the practice of the Patriarches, the interrment of our Saviour, of *Peter*, *Paul*, and the ancient Martyrs. And so far at last declining promiscuous enterrment with Pagans, that some[11] have suffered Ecclesiastical censures, for making no scruple thereof.

The *Musselman* beleevers will never admit this fiery resolution. For they hold a present trial from their black and white Angels in the grave; which they must have made so hollow, that they may rise upon their knees.

The Jewish Nation, though they entertained the old way of inhumation, yet sometimes admitted this practice. For the men of *Jabesh* burnt the body of *Saul*. And by no prohibited practice to avoid contagion or pollution, in time of pestilence, burnt the bodies of their friends.[12] And when they burnt not their dead bodies, yet sometimes used great burnings near and about them, deducible from the expressions concerning *Jehoram*, *Sedechias*, and the sumptuous pyre of Asa; And were so little averse from Pagan[13] burning, that the Jews lamenting the death of *Cæsar* their friend, and revenger on *Pompey*, frequented the place where his body was burnt for many nights together. And as they raised noble Monuments and *Mausolæums* for their own Nation,[14] so they were not scrupulous in erecting some for others, according to the practice of *Daniel*, who left that lasting sepulchral pyle in *Echbatana*, for the *Median* and *Persian* Kings.[15]

But even in times of subjection and hottest use, they conformed not unto the *Romane* practice of burning; whereby the Prophecy was secured concerning the body of Christ, that it should not see corruption, or a bone should not be broken; which we beleeve was also providentially prevented, from the Souldiers spear and nailes that past by the little bones both in his hands and feet: Nor of ordinary contrivance, that it should not corrupt on the crosse, according to the Law of *Romane* Crucifixion, or an hair of his head perish, though observable in Jewish customes, to cut the haires of Malefactors.

Nor in their long co-habitation with the Ægyptians, crept into a custome of their exact embalming, wherein deeply slashing the muscles, and taking out the braines and entrailes, they had broken the subject of so entire a Resurrection, nor fully answered the tipes of *Enoch*, *Eliah*, or *Jonah*, which yet to prevent or restore, was of equall facility unto that rising power, able to break the fasciations and bands of death, to get clear out of the Cere-cloth, and an hundred pounds of oyntment, and out of the Sepulchre before the stone was rolled from it.

But though they embraced not this practice of burning, yet entertained they many ceremonies agreeable unto *Greek* and *Romane* obsequies, And he that observeth their funeral Feasts, their Lamentations at the grave, their musick, and weeping mourners; how they closed the eyes of their friends, how they washed, anointed, and kissed the dead; may easily conclude these were not meer Pagan Civilities. But whether that mournful burthen, and treble calling out after *Absalom*, had any reference unto the last conclamation, and triple valediction, used by other nations, we hold but a wavering conjecture.

Civilians make sepulture but of the Law of nations, others do naturally found it and discover it also in animals. They that are so thick skinned as still to credit the story of the *Phœnix*, may say something for animal burning: More serious conjectures finde some examples of sepulture in Elephants, Cranes, the Sepulchral Cells of Pismires and practice of Bees; which civil society carrieth out their dead, and hath exequies, if not interrments.

Footnotes

[1]*The rich mountain of Peru.*
[2]*Q. Calaber lib.* 1.
[3]*Ammianus Marcellinus, Gumbrates King of* Chionia *a Countrey near* Persia.
[4]*Arnoldis Montanis not in* Cæs. Commentar. L. L. Gyraldus. Kirkmannus.
[5]*12 Tabul. part. 1 de jure sacro. Hominem mortuum in urbe ne sepelito, neve urito. tom. 2. Rogum asciâ ne polito. to. 4 Item vigeneri Annottat in Livium, et Alex. ab Alex. cum Tiraquello Roscinus cum dempstero.*
[6]*Ultima prolato subditu flamma rogo. De Fast. lib. 4. cum Car. Neapol. anaptyxi.*
[7]*And therefore the Inscription of his Tomb was made accordingly.* Nic. Damasc.
[8]*Which* Magius *reads* ἐξαπόλωλε.
[9]Diodorus Siculus.
[10]Ramusius *in* Navigat.
[11]*Martialis the Bishop.* Cyprian.
[12]*Amos* 6. 10.
[13]*Sueton. in vita.* Jul. Cæs.
[14]*As that magnificent sepulchral Monument erected by Simon. Mach. 1. 13.*
[15]Κατασκεύασμα θαυμασίως πεποιημένον, *whereof a Jewish Priest had alwayes the custody unto* Josephus *his dayes.* Jos. Lib. 10. Antiq.

CHAPTER II

The Solemnities, Ceremonies, Rites of their Cremation or enterrment, so solemnly delivered by Authours, we shall not disparage our Reader to repeat. Only the last and lasting part in their Urns, collected bones and Ashes, we cannot wholly omit, or decline that Subject, which occasion lately presented, in some discovered among us.

In a Field of old *Walsingham*, not many months past, were digged up between fourty and fifty Urnes, deposited in a dry and sandy soile, not a yard deep, nor far from one another: Not all strictly of one figure, but most answering these described; Some containing two pounds of bones, distinguishable in skulls, ribs, jawes, thigh-bones, and teeth, with fresh impressions of their combustion. Besides the extraneous substances, like peeces of small boxes, or combs handsomely wrought, handles of small brasse instruments, brazen nippers, and in one some kinde of *Opale*[16].

Near the same plot of ground, for about six yards compasse were digged up coals and incinerated substances, which begat conjecture that this was the *Ustrina* or place of burning their bodies, or some sacrificing place unto the *Manes*, which was properly below the surface of the ground, as the *Aræ* and *Altars* unto the gods and *Heroes* above it.

That these were the Urnes of *Romanes* from the common custome and place where they were found, is no obscure conjecture, not far from a *Romane* Garrison, and but five mile from *Brancaster*, set down by ancient Record under the name of *Brannodunum*. And where the adjoyning Town, containing seven Parishes, in no very different sound, but Saxon termination, still retaines the Name of *Burnham*, which being an early station, it is not improbable the neighbour parts were filled with habitations, either of *Romanes* themselves, or *Brittains Romanised*, which observed the *Romane* customes.

Nor is it improbable that the *Romanes* early possessed this Countrey; for though we meet not with such strict particulars of these parts, before the new Institution of *Constantine*, and military charge of the Count of the *Saxon* shore, and that about the *Saxon* Invasions, the *Dalmatian* Horsemen were in the Garrison of *Brancaster*: Yet in the time of *Claudius Vespasian*, and *Severus*, we finde no lesse then three Legions dispersed through the Province of *Brittain*. And as high as the Reign of *Claudius* a great overthrow was given unto the *Iceni*, by the *Romane* Lieutenant *Ostorius*. Not long after the Countrey was so molested, that in hope of a better state *Prasatagus* bequeathed his Kingdom unto *Nero* and his Daughters; and *Boadicea* his Queen fought the last decisive Battle with *Paulinus*. After which time and Conquest of *Agricola* the Lieutenant of *Vespasian*, probable it is they wholly possessed this Countrey, ordering it into Garrisons or Habitations, best suitable with their securities. And so some *Romane* habitations, not improbable in these parts, as high as the time of *Vespasian*, where the *Saxons* after seated, in whose thin-fill'd Mappes we yet finde the Name of *Walsingham*. Now if the *Iceni* were but *Gammadims*, *Anconians*, or men that lived in an Angle wedge or Elbow of *Brittain*, according to the Original Etymologie, this country will challenge the Emphatical appellation, as most properly making the Elbow or Iken of *Icenia*.

That *Britain* was notably populous is undeniable, from that expression of *Cæsar*[17]. That the *Romanes* themselves were early in no small numbers, Seventy Thousand with their associats slain by *Boadicea*, affords a sure account. And though many *Roman* habitations are now unknown, yet some by old works, Rampiers, Coynes, and Urnes do testifie their Possessions. Some Urnes have been found at Castor, some also about *Southcreake* and not many years past, no lesse then ten in a field at *Buxton*,[18] not near any recorded Garrison. Nor is it strange to finde *Romane* Coynes of Copper and Silver among us; of *Vespasian*, *Trajan*, *Adrian*, *Commodus*, *Antoninus*, *Severus*, etc. But the greater number of *Dioclesian*, *Constantine*, *Constans*, *Valens*, with many of *Victorinus Posthumius*, *Tetricus*, and the thirty Tyrants in the Reigne of *Gallienus*; and some as high as *Adrianus* have been found about *Thetford*, or *Sitomagus*, mentioned in the itinerary of *Antoninus*, as the way from *Venta* or *Castor* unto *London*.[19] But the most frequent discovery is made at the two *Casters* by *Norwich* and *Yarmouth*[20] at *Burghcastle* and *Brancaster*.[21]

Besides, the *Norman*, *Saxon* and *Danish* peeces of *Cuthred*, *Canutus*, *William Matilda*,[22] and others, some *Brittish* Coynes of gold have been dispersedly found; And no small number of silver peeces neer *Norwich*[23]; with a rude head upon the obverse, and an ill formed horse on the reverse, with inscriptions *Ic. Duro T*. whether implying *Iceni*, *Duroriges*, *Tascia*, or *Trinobantes*, we leave to higher conjecture. Vulgar Chronology will have *Norwich* Castle as old as *Julius Cæsar*, but his distance from these parts, and its *Gothick* form of structure, abridgeth such Antiquity. The *British* Coyns afford conjecture of early habitation in these parts, though the City of *Norwich* arose from the ruines of *Venta*, and though perhaps not without some habitation before, was enlarged, builded, and nominated by the *Saxons*. In what bulk or populosity it stood in the old East-angle Monarchy, tradition and history are silent. Considerable it was in the *Danish* Eruptions, when *Sueno* burnt *Thetford* and *Norwich*,[24] and *Ulfketel* the Governour thereof was able to make some resistance, and after endeavoured to burn the *Danish* Navy.

How the *Romanes* left so many Coynes in Countreys of their Conquests, seemes of hard resolution, except we consider how they buried them under ground, when upon barbarous invasions they were fain to desert their habitations in most part of their Empire, and the strictnesse of their laws forbiding to transfer them to any other uses; Wherein the *Spartans*[25] were singular, who to make their copper money uselesse, contempered it with vinegar. That the *Britains* left any, some wonder; since their money was iron, and Iron rings before *Cæsar*; and those of after stamp by permission, and but small in bulk and bignesse; that so few of the *Saxons* remain, because overcome by suceeding Conquerours upon the place, their Coynes by degrees passed into other stamps, and the marks of after ages.

Then the time of these Urnes deposited, or precise Antiquity of these Relicks, nothing of more uncertainty. For since the Lieutenant of *Claudius* seems to have the first progresse into these parts, since *Boadicea* was overthrown by the Forces of *Nero*, and *Agricola* put a full end to these Conquests; it is not probable the Country was fully garrisoned or planted before; and therefore however these Urnes might be of later date, not likely of higher Antiquity.

And the succeeding Emperours desisted not from their conquests in these and other parts; as testified by history and medal inscription yet extant. The Province of *Britain* in so divided a distance from *Rome*, beholding the faces of many Imperial persons, and in large account no fewer than *Cæsar, Claudius, Britannicus, Vespasian, Titus, Adrian, Severus, Commodus, Geta,* and *Caracalla.*

A great obscurity herein, because, no medall or Emperours coyne enclosed, which might denote the dates of their enterrments, observable in many Urnes, and found in those of *Spittle* Fields by *London*,[26] which contained the Coynes of *Claudius, Vespasian, Commodus, Antoninus,* attended with Lacrymatories, Lamps, Bottles of Liquor, and other appurtenances of affectionate superstition, which in these rurall interrments were wanting.

Some uncertainty there is from the period or term of burning, or the cessation of that practise. *Macrobius* affirmeth it was disused in his dayes. But most agree, though without authentick record, that it ceased with the *Antonini*. Most safely to be understood after the Reigne of those Emperours, which assumed the name of *Antoninus*, extending unto *Heliogabalus*. Not strictly after *Marcus*; For about fifty years later we finde the magnificent burning, and consecration of *Severus*; and if we so fix this period or cessation, these Urnes will challenge above thirteen hundred yeers.

But whether this practise was onely then left by Emperours and great persons, or generally about *Rome*, and not in other Provinces, we hold no authentick account. For after *Tertullian*, in the dayes of *Minucius* it was obviously objected upon Christians, that they condemned the practise of burning.[27] And we finde a passage in *Sidonius*,[28] which asserteth that practise in France unto a lower account. And perhaps not fully disused till Christianity fully established, which gave the final extinction to these Sepulchral Bonefires.

Whether they were the bones of men or women or children, no authentick decision from ancient custome in distinct places of burial. Although not improbably conjectured, that the double Sepulture or burying place of *Abraham*, had in it such intension. But from exility of bones, thinnesse of skulls, smallnesse of teeth, ribbes, and thigh-bones; not improbable that many thereof were persons of *minor* age, or women. Confirmable also from things contained in them: In most were found substances resembling Combes, Plates like Boxes, fastened with Iron pins, and handsomely overwrought like the necks or Bridges of Musicall Instruments, long brasse plates overwrought like the handles of neat implements, brazen nippers to pull away hair, and in one a kinde of *Opale* yet maintaining a blewish colour.

Now that they accustomed to burn or bury with them, things wherein they excelled, delighted, or which were dear unto them, either as farewells unto all pleasure, or vain apprehension that they might use them in the other world, is testified by all Antiquity. Observable from the Gemme or Beril Ring upon the finger of *Cynthia*, the Mistress of *Propertius*, when after her Funeral Pyre her Ghost appeared unto him. And notably illustrated from the Contents of that *Roman* Urne preserved by Cardinal *Farnese*,[29] wherein besides great number of Gemmes with heads of Gods and Goddesses, were found an Ape of *Agath*, a Grashopper, an Elephant of Ambre, a Crystal Ball, three glasses, two Spoons, and six Nuts of Crystall. And beyond the content of Urnes, in the Monument of *Childerick* the first,[30] and fourth King from *Pharamond*, casually discovered three years past at *Tournay*, restoring unto the world much gold richly adorning his Sword, two hundred Rubies, many hundred Imperial Coyns, three hundred Golden Bees, the bones and horseshoe of his horse enterred with him, according to the barbarous magnificence of those dayes in their sepulchral Obsequies. Although if we steer by the conjecture of many and Septuagint expression; some trace thereof may be found even with the ancient Hebrews, not only from the Sepulcral treasure of *David*, but the circumcision knives which *Josuah* also buried.

Some men considering the contents of these Urnes, lasting peeces and toyes included in them, and the custome of burning with many other Nations, might somewhat doubt whether all Urnes found among us, were properly *Romane* Reliques, or some not belonging unto our *Brittish, Saxon,* or *Danish* Forefathers.

In the form of Burial among the ancient *Brittains*, the large Discourses of *Cæsar, Tacitus,* and *Strabo* are silent: For the discovery whereof, with other particulars, we must deplore the loss of that Letter which *Cicero* expected or received from his Brother *Quintus*, as a resolution of *Brittish* customes; or the account which might have been made by *Scribonius Largus* the Physician, accompanying the Emperor *Claudius*, who might have also discovered that frugal Bit[31] of the Old *Brittains*, which in the bigness of a Bean could satisfie their thirst and hunger.

But that the *Druids* and ruling Priests used to burn and bury, is expressed by *Pomponius*; That *Bellinus* the Brother of *Brennus*, and King of *Brittains* was burnt, is acknowledged by *Polydorus*, as also by *Amandus Zierexensis* in *Historia*, and *Pineda* in his *Universa historia*. Spanish. That they held that practise in *Gallia, Cæsar* expressly delivereth. Whether the Brittains (probably descended from them, of like Religion, Language and Manners) did not sometimes make use of burning; or whether at least such as were after civilized unto the *Romane* life and manners, conformed not unto this practise, we have no historical assertion or denial. But since from the account of *Tacitus* the *Romanes* early wrought so much civility upon the Brittish stock, that they brought them to build Temples, to wear the Gown, and study the *Romane* Laws and Language, that they conformed also unto their Religious rites and customes in burials, seems no improbable conjecture.

That burning the dead was used in *Sarmatia*, is affirmed by *Gaguinus*, that the *Sueons* and *Gothlanders* used to burn their Princes and great persons, is delivered by *Saxo* and *Olaus*; that this was the old *Germane* practise, is also asserted by *Tacitus*. And though we are bare in historical particulars of such obsequies in this Island, or that the *Saxons*, *Jutes*, and *Angles* burnt their dead, yet came they from parts where 'twas of ancient practise; the *Germanes* using it, from whom they were descended. And even in *Jutland* and *Sleswick* in *Anglia Cymbrica*, Urnes with bones were found not many years before us.

Roisold, Brendetiide. Ild tyde.

But the *Danish* and Northern Nations have raised an *Æra* or point of compute from their Custome of burning their dead: Some deriving it from *Unguinus*, some from *Frotho* the great; who ordained by Law, that Princes and Chief Commanders should be committed unto the fire, though the common sort had the common grave enterrment. So *Starkatterus* that old *Heroe* was burnt, and *Ringo* royally burnt the body of *Harald* the King slain by him.

What time this custome generally expired in that Nation, we discern no assured period; whether it ceased before Christianity, or upon their Conversion, by *Ansgurius* the Gaul in the time of *Ludovicus Pius* the Son of *Charles* the Great, according to good computes; or whether it might not be used by some persons, while for a hundred and eighty years Paganisme and Christianity were promiscuously embraced among them, there is no assured conclusion. About which times the *Danes* were busie in *England*, and particularly infested this Countrey: Where many Castles and strong holds were built by them, or against them, and great number of names and Families still derived from them. But since this custome was probably disused before their Invasion or Conquest, and the *Romanes* confessedly practised the same, since their possession of this Island, the most assured account will fall upon the *Romanes*, or *Brittains Romanized*.

However certain it is, that Urnes conceived of no *Romane* Original, are often digged up both in *Norway* and *Denmark*, handsomely described, and graphically represented by the Learned Physician *Wormius*,[32] And in some parts of *Denmark* in no ordinary number, as stands delivered by Authors exactly describing those Countreys.[33] And they contained not only bones, but many other substances in them, as Knives, peeces of Iron, Brass and Wood, and one of *Norway* a brasse guilded Jewes harp.

Nor were they confused or carelesse in disposing the noblest sort, while they placed large stones in circle about the Urnes, or bodies which they interred: Somewhat answerable unto the Monument of *Rollrich* stones in *England*,[34] or sepulcral Monument probably erected by *Rollo*, who after conquered *Normandy*. Where 'tis not improbable somewhat might be discovered. Mean while to what Nation or person belonged that large Urne found at *Ashburie*,[35] containing mighty bones, and a Buckler; what those large Urnes found at little *Massingham*,[36] or why the *Anglesea* Urnes are placed with their mouths downwards, remains yet undiscovered.

Footnotes

[16]*In one sent me by my worthy friend Dr*. Thomas Witherley *of* Walsingham.

[17]Hominum infinita multitudo est, creberrimaque ædificia ferè Gallicis consimilia. Cæs. de bello Gal. *l*. 5.

[18]*In the ground of my worthy Friend* Rob. Jegon, *Esq., wherein some things contained were preserved by the most worthy Sir* William Paston, *Bt*.

[19]*From Castor to Thetford the Romans accounted thirty-two miles, and from thence observed not our common road to* London, *but passed by* Combretonium ad Ansam, Canonium, Cæsaromagus, etc., by Bretenham, Coggeshall, Chelmeford, Burntwood, *etc.*

[20]*Most at* Caster *by* Yarmouth, *found in a place called* East-bloudyburgh furlong, *belonging to Mr.* Thomas Wood, *a person of civility, industry and knowledge in this way, who hath made observation of remarkable things about him, and from whom we have received divers Silver and Copper Coynes.*

[21]*Belonging to that Noble Gentleman, and true example of worth Sir* Ralph Hare, *Baronet, my honoured Friend.*

[22]*A peece of* Maud *the Empresse said to be found in* Buckenham Castle *with this inscription,* Elle n'a elle.

[23]*At* Thorpe.

[24]*Brampton* Abbas Jorvallensis.

[25]*Plut.* in vita Lycurg.

[26]Stowes *Survey of* London.

[27]Execrantur rogos, et damnant ignium sepulturam. *Min. in Oct.*

[28]Sidon. Apollinaris.

[29]Vigeneri Annot. in 4. Liv.

[30]Chifflet in Anast. Childer.

[31]Dionis excerpta per Xiphilin. in Severo.

[32]Olai Wormii monumenta et Antiquitat. Dan.

[33]Adolphus Cyprius in Annal. Sleswic. urnis adeo abundabat collis, *etc.*

[34]*In Oxfordshire*; Cambden.

[35]*In Cheshire*, Twinus de rebus Albionicis.

[36]*In Norfolk*, Hollingshead.

CHAPTER III

Playstered and whited Sepulchres, were anciently affected in cadaverous, and corruptive Burials; And the rigid Jews were wont to garnish the Sepulchres of the righteous;[37] Ulysses in *Hecuba*[38] cared not how meanly he lived, so he might finde a noble Tomb after death. Great Princes affected great Monuments, and the fair and larger Urnes contained no vulgar ashes, which makes that disparity in those which time discovereth among us. The present Urnes were not of one capacity, the largest containing above a gallon, Some not much above half that measure; nor all of one figure, wherein there is no strict conformity, in the same or different Countreys; Observable from those represented by *Casalius, Bosio,* and others, though all found in *Italy*: While many have handles, ears, and long necks, but most imitate a circular figure, in a spherical and round composure; whether from any mystery, best duration or capacity, were but a conjecture. But the common form with necks was a proper figure, making our last bed like our first; nor much unlike the Urnes of our Nativity, while we lay in the nether part of the Earth,[39] and inward vault of our Microcosme. Many Urnes are red, these but of a black colour, somewhat smooth, and dully sounding, which begat some doubt, whether they were burnt, or only baked in Oven or Sun: According to the ancient way, in many bricks, tiles, pots, and testaceous works; and as the word *testa* is properly to be taken, when occurring without addition: And chiefly intended by *Pliny,* when he commendeth bricks and tiles of two years old, and to make them in the spring. Nor only these concealed peeces, but the open magnificence of Antiquity, ran much in the Artifice of Clay. Hereof the house of *Mausolus* was built, thus old *Jupiter* stood in the Capitol, and the *Statua* of *Hercules* made in the Reign of *Tarquinius Priscus*, was extant in *Plinies* dayes. And such as declined burning or Funeral Urnes, affected Coffins of Clay, according to the mode of *Pythagoras,* and way preferred by *Varro*. But the spirit of great ones was above these circumscriptions, affecting Copper, Silver, Gold, and *Porphyrie* Urnes, wherein *Severus* lay, after a serious view and sentence on that which should contain him.[40] Some of these Urnes were thought to have been silvered over, from sparklings in several pots, with small Tinsel parcels; uncertain whether from the earth, or the first mixture in them.

Among these Urnes we could obtain no good account of their coverings; only one seemed arched over with some kinde of brickwork. Of those found at *Buxton* some were covered with flints, some in other parts with Tiles, those at *Yarmouth Caster*, were closed with *Romane* bricks. And some have proper earthen covers adapted and fitted to them. But in the *Homerical* Urne of *Patroclus*, whatever was the solid Tegument, we finde the immediate covering to be a purple peece of silk: And such as had no covers might have the earth closely pressed into them, after which disposure were probably some of these, wherein we found the bones and ashes half mortered unto the sand and sides of the Urne; and some long roots of Quich, or Dogs-grass wreathed about the bones.

No Lamps, included Liquors, Lachrymatories, or Tear-Bottles attended these rural Urnes, either as sacred unto the *Manes*, or passionate expressions of their surviving friends. While with rich flames, and hired teares they solemnized their Obsequies, and in the most lamented Monuments made one part of their Inscriptions.[41] Some finde sepulchral Vessels containing liquors, which time hath incrassated into gellies. For beside these Lachrymatories, notable Lamps, with Vessels of Oyles and Aromatical Liquors attended noble Ossuaries. And some yet retaining a Vinosity[42] and spirit in them, which if any have tasted they have far exceeded the Palats of Antiquity. Liquors not to be computed by years of annual Magistrates, but by great conjunctions and the fatal periods of Kingdoms.[43] The draughts of Consulary date, were but crude unto these, and *Opimian*[44] Wine but in the muste unto them.

In sundry graves and Sepulchres, we meet with Rings, Coynes, and Chalices; Ancient frugality was so severe, that they allowed no gold to attend the Corps, but onely that which served to fasten their teeth.[45] Whether the *Opaline* stone in this Urne were burnt upon the finger of the dead, or cast into the fire by some affectionate friend, it will consist with either custome. But other incinerable substances were found so fresh, that they could feel no sindge from fire. These upon view were judged to be wood, but sinking in water and tried by the fire, we found them to be bone or Ivory. In their hardnesse and yellow colour they most resembled Box, which in old expressions found the Epithete[46] of Eternal, and perhaps in such conservatories might have passed uncorrupted.

That Bay-leaves were found green in the Tomb of S. *Humbert*,[47] after an hundred and fifty yeers, was looked upon as miraculous. Remarkable it was unto old Spectators, that the Cypresse of the Temple of *Diana*, lasted so many hundred years: The wood of the Ark and Olive Rod of *Aaron* were older at the Captivity. But the Cypresse of the Ark of *Noah*, was the greatest vegetable Antiquity, if *Josephus* were not deceived, by some fragments of it in his dayes. To omit the Moore-logs, and Firre-trees found underground in some parts of *England*; the undated ruines of winds, flouds or earthquakes; and which in *Flanders* still shew from what quarter they fell, as generally lying in the North-East position.[48]

But though we found not these peeces to be Wood, according to first apprehension, yet we missed not altogether of some woody substance; for the bones were not so clearly pickt, but some coals were found amongst them; A way to make wood perpetual, and a fit associat for metal, whereon was laid the foundation of the great *Ephesian* Temple, and which were made the lasting tests of old boundaries, and Landmarks; Whilest we look on these we admire not observations of Coals found fresh, after four hundred years.[49] In a long deserted habitation,[50] even Egge-shels have been found fresh, not tending to corruption.

In the Monument of King *Childerick*, the Iron Reliques were found all rusty and crumbling into peeces. But our little Iron pins which fastened the ivory works, held well together, and lost not their Magneticall quality, though wanting a tenacious moisture for the firmer union of parts, although it be hardly drawn into fusion, yet that metal soon submitteth unto rust and dissolution. In the brazen peeces we admired not the duration but the freedom from rust, and ill savour; upon the hardest attrition, but now exposed unto the piercing Atomes of aire; in the space of a few moneths, they begin to spot and betray their green entrals. We conceive not these Urns to have descended thus naked as they appear, or to have entred their graves without the old habit of flowers. The Urne of *Philopœmen* was so laden with flowers and ribbons, that it afforded no sight of it self. The rigid *Lycurgus* allowed Olive and Myrtle. The *Athenians* might fairely except against the practise of *Democritus* to be buried up in honey; as fearing to embezzle a great commodity of their Countrey, and the best of that kinde in *Europe*. But *Plato* seemed too frugally politick, who allowed no larger monument then would contain four Heroick verses, and designed the most barren ground for sepulture: Though we cannot commend the goodnesse of that sepulchral ground, which was set at no higher rate then the mean salary of *Judas*. Though the earth had confounded the ashes of these Ossuaries, yet the bones were so smartly burnt, that some thin plates of brasse were found half melted among them: whereby we apprehended they were not of the meanest carcasses, perfunctorily fired as sometimes in military, and commonly in pestilence, burnings; or after the manner of abject corps, hudled forth and carelessly burnt, without the Esquiline Port at *Rome*; which was an affront continued upon *Tiberius*, while they but half burnt his body,[51] and in the Amphitheatre, according to the custome in notable Malefactors; whereas *Nero* seemed not so much to fear his death, as that his head should be cut off and his body not burnt entire.

Some finding many fragments of sculs in these Urnes, suspected a mixture of bones; In none we searched was there cause of such conjecture, though sometimes they declined not that practise; The ashes of *Domitian*[52] were mingled with those of *Julia*, of *Achilles* with those of *Patroclus*: All Urnes contained not single ashes; Without confused burnings they affectionately compounded their bones; passionately endeavouring to continue their living Unions. And when distance of death denied such conjunctions, unsatisfied affections conceived some satisfaction to be neighbours in the grave, to lye Urne by Urne, and touch but in their names. And many were so curious to continue their living relations, that they contrived large, and family Urnes, wherein the Ashes of their nearest friends and kindred might successively be received,[53] at least some parcels thereof, while their collateral memorials lay in *minor* vessels about them.

Antiquity held too light thoughts from Objects of mortality, while some drew provocatives of mirth from Anatomies,[54] and Juglers shewed tricks with Skeletons. When Fidlers made not so pleasant mirth as Fencers, and men could sit with quiet stomacks while hanging was plaied before them.[55] Old considerations made few *memento's* by sculs and bones upon their monuments. In the Ægyptian Obelisks and Hieroglyphical figures, it is not easie to meet with bones. The sepulchral Lamps speak nothing lesse then sepulture; and in their literal draughts prove often obscene and antick peeces: Where we finde *D. M.*[56] it is obvious to meet with sacrificing *patera's*, and vessels of libation, upon old sepulchral Monuments. In the Jewish *Hypogæum*[57] and subterranean Cell at *Rome*, was little observable beside the variety of Lamps, and frequent draughts of the holy Candlestick. In authentick draughts of *Anthony* and *Jerome*, we meet with thigh-bones and deaths heads; but the cœmiterial Cels of ancient Christians and Martyrs, were filled with draughts of Scripture Stories; not declining the flourishes of Cypresse, Palms, and Olive; and the mystical Figures of Peacocks, Doves and Cocks. But iterately affecting the pourtraits of *Enoch*, *Lazarus*, *Jonas*, and the vision of *Ezechiel*, as hopeful draughts, and hinting imagery of the Resurrection; which is the life of the grave, and sweetens our habitations in the Land of *Moles* and *Pismires*.

Gentile inscriptions precisely delivered the extent of mens lives, seldome the manner of their deaths, which history it self so often leaves obscure in the records of memorable persons. There is scarce any Philosopher but dies twice or thrice in *Laertius*; Nor almost any life without two or three deaths in *Plutarch*; which makes the tragical ends of noble persons more favourably resented by compassionate Readers, who finde some relief in the Election of such differences.

The certainty of death is attended with uncertainties, in time, manner, places. The variety of Monuments hath often obscured true graves: and *Cenotaphs* confounded Sepulchres. For beside their real Tombs, many have found honorary and empty Sepulchres. The variety of *Homers* Monuments made him of various Countreys. *Euripides*[58] had his Tomb in *Africa*, but his sepulture in *Macedonia*. And *Severus*[59] found his real Sepulchre in *Rome*, but his empty grave in *Gallia*.

He that lay in a golden Urne[60] eminently above the earth, was not like to finde the quiet of these bones. Many of these Urnes were broke by a vulgar discoverer in hope of inclosed treasure. The ashes of *Marcellus*[61] were lost above ground, upon the like account. Where profit hath prompted, no age hath wanted such miners. The Commission of *the* Gothish *King* Theodoric *for finding out sepulchrall treasure.* Cassiodor. Var. *l.* 4. For which the most barbarous Expilators found the most civil Rhetorick. Gold once out of the earth is no more due unto it; What was unreasonably committed to the ground is reasonably resumed from it: Let Monuments and rich Fabricks, not Riches adorn mens ashes. The commerce of the living is not to be transferred unto the dead: It is no injustice to take that which none complains to lose, and no man is wronged where no man is possessor.

What virtue yet sleeps in this *terra damnata* and aged cinders, were petty magick to experiment; These crumbling reliques and long-fired particles superannuate such expectations: Bones, hairs, nails, and teeth of the dead, were the treasures of old Sorcerers. In vain we revive such practices; Present superstition too visibly perpetuates the folly of our fore-fathers, wherein unto old Observation this Island was so compleat, that it might have instructed *Persia*.[62]

Plato's historian of the other world, lies twelve dayes incorrupted, while his soul was viewing the large stations of the dead. How to keep the corps seven dayes from corruption by anointing and washing, without exenteration, were an hazardous peece of art, in our choisest practise. How they made distinct separation of bones and ashes from fiery admixture, hath found no historical solution. Though they seemed to make a distinct collection, and overlooked not *Pyrrhus* his toe. Some provision they might make by fictile Vessels, Coverings, Tiles, or flat stones, upon and about the body. And in the same Field, not far from these Urnes, many stones were found under ground, as also by careful separation of extraneous matter, composing and raking up the burnt bones with forks, observable in that notable lamp of *Galuanus. Martianus*,[63] who had the sight of the *Vas Ustrinum*, or vessel wherein they burnt the dead, found in the Esquiline Field at *Rome*, might have afforded clearer solution. But their insatisfaction herein begat that remarkable invention in the Funeral Pyres of some Princes, by incombustible sheets made with a texture of *Asbestos*, incremable flax, or Salamanders wool, which preserved their bones and ashes[64] incommixed.

How the bulk of a man should sink into so few pounds of bones and ashes, may seem strange unto any who considers not its constitution, and how slender a mass will remain upon an open and urging fire of the carnal composition. Even bones themselves reduced into ashes, do abate a notable proportion. And consisting much of a volatile salt, when that is fired out, make a light kind of cinders. Although their bulk be disproportionable to their weight, when the heavy principle of Salt is fired out, and the Earth almost onely remaineth; Observable in sallow, which makes more Ashes then Oake; and discovers the common fraud of selling Ashes by measure, and not by ponderation.

Some bones make best Skeletons,[65] some bodies quick and speediest ashes: Who would expect a quick flame from Hydropical *Heraclitus*? The poisoned Souldier when his Belly brake, put out two pyres in *Plutarch*.[66] But in the plague of *Athens*,[67] one private pyre served two or three Intruders; and the *Saracens* burnt in large heaps, by the King of *Castile*,[68] shewed how little Fuel sufficeth. Though the Funeral pyre of *Patroclus* took up an hundred foot,[69] a peece of an old boat burnt *Pompey*; And if the burthen of *Isaac* were sufficient for an holocaust, a man may carry his own pyre.

From animals are drawn good burning lights, and good medicines[70] against burning; Though the seminal humor seems of a contrary nature to fire, yet the body compleated proves a combustible lump, wherein fire findes flame even from bones, and some fuel almost from all parts. Though the Metropolis[71] of humidity seems least disposed unto it, which might render the sculls of these Urnes less burned then other bones. But all flies or sinks before fire almost in all bodies. When the common ligament is dissolved, the attenuable parts ascend, the rest subside in coal, calx or ashes.

To burn the bones of the King of *Edom*[72] for Lyme, seems no irrational ferity; But to drink of the ashes of dead relations,[73] a passionate prodigality. He that hath the ashes of his friend, hath an everlasting treasure: where fire taketh leave, corruption slowly enters; In bones well burnt, fire makes a wall against it self, experimented in copels, and tests of metals, which consist of such ingredients. What the Sun compoundeth, fire analyseth, not transmuteth. That devouring agent leaves almost always a morsel for the Earth, whereof all things are but a colony; and which, if time permits, the mother Element will have in their primitive mass again.

He that looks for Urnes and old sepulchral reliques, must not seek them in the ruines of Temples: where no Religion anciently placed them. These were found in a Field, according to ancient custome, in noble or private burial; the old practise of the *Canaanites*, the Family of *Abraham*, and the burying place of *Josua*, in the borders of his possessions; and also agreeable unto *Romane* practise to bury by highwayes, whereby their Monuments were under eye: Memorials of themselves, and *memento's* of mortality into living passengers; whom the Epitaphs of great ones were fain to beg to stay and look upon them. A language though sometimes used, not so proper in Church-Inscriptions.[74] The sensible Rhetorick of the dead, to exemplarity of good life, first admitted the bones of pious men, and Martyrs within Church-wals; which in succeeding ages crept into promiscuous practise. While *Constantine* was peculiarly favoured to be admitted unto the Church Porch; and the first thus buried in *England* was in the dayes of *Cuthred*.

Christians dispute how their bodies should lye in the grave.[75] In urnal enterrment they clearly escaped this Controversie: Though we decline the Religious consideration, yet in cemiterial and narrower burying places, to avoid confusion and crosse position, a certain posture were to be admitted; which even Pagan civility observed, The *Persians* lay North and South, The *Megarians* and *Phœnicians* placed their heads to the East: The *Athenians*, some think, towards the West, which Christians still retain. And *Beda* will have it to be the posture of our Saviour. That he was crucified with his face towards the West, we will not contend with tradition and probable account; But we applaud not the hand of the Painter, in exalting his Cross so high above those on either side; since hereof we finde no authentick account in history, and even the crosses found by *Helena* pretend no such distinction from longitude or dimension.

To be gnawd out of our graves, to have our sculs made drinking-bowls, and our bones turned into Pipes, to delight and sport our Enemies, are Tragical abominations, escaped in burning Burials.

Urnal enterrments, and burnt Reliques lye not in fear of worms, or to be an heritage for Serpents; In carnal sepulture, corruptions seem peculiar unto parts, and some speak of snakes out of the spinal marrow. But while we suppose common wormes in graves, 'tis not easie to finde any there; few in Church-yards above a foot deep, fewer or none in Churches, though in fresh decayed bodies. Teeth, bones, and hair, give the most lasting defiance to corruption. In an Hydropical body ten years buried in a Church yard, we met with a fat concretion, where the nitre of the Earth, and the salt and lixivious liquor of the body, had coagulated large lumps of fat, into the consistence of the hardest castle-soap; whereof part remaineth with us. After a battle with the *Persians*, the *Romane* Corps decayed in few dayes, while the *Persian* bodies remained dry and uncorrupted. Bodies in the same ground do not uniformly dissolve, nor bones equally moulder; whereof in the opprobrious disease we expect no long duration. The body of the Marquess of *Dorset* seemed sound and handsomely cereclothed, that after seventy eight years was found uncorrupted.[76] Common Tombs preserve not beyond powder: A firmer consistence and compage of parts might be expected from Arefaction, deep burial or Charcoal. The greatest Antiquities of mortal bodies may remain in petrified bones, whereof, though we take not in the pillar of *Lots* wife, or Metamorphosis of *Ortelius*,[77] some may be older then Pyramids, in the petrified Reliques of the general inundation. When *Alexander* opened the Tomb of *Cyrus*, the remaining bones discovered his proportion, whereof urnal fragments afford but a bad conjecture, and have this disadvantage of grave enterrments, that they leave us ignorant of most personal discoveries. For since bones afford not only rectitude and stability, but figure unto the body; It is no impossible Physiognomy to conjecture at fleshly appendencies; and after what shape the muscles and carnous parts might hang in their full consistences. A full spread *Cariola* shews a well-shaped horse behinde, handsome formed sculls, give some analogy of flesh resemblance. A critical view of bones makes a good distinction of sexes. Even colour is not beyond conjecture, since it is hard to be deceived in the distinction of *Negro's* sculls. *Dantes*[78] Characters are to be found in sculls as well as faces. *Hercules* is not onely known by his foot. Other parts make out their comproportions, and inferences upon whole, or parts. And since the dimensions of the head measure the whole body, and the figure thereof gives conjecture of the principal faculties; Physiognomy out-lives our selves, and ends not in our graves.

Severe contemplators observing these lasting reliques, may think them good monuments of persons past, little advantage to future beings. And considering that power which subdueth all things unto it self, that can resume the scattered Atomes, or identifie out of any thing, conceive it superfluous to expect a resurrection out of Reliques. But the soul subsisting, other matter clothed with due accidents, may salve the individuality: Yet the Saints we observe arose from graves and monuments, about the holy City. Some think the ancient Patriarchs so earnestly desired to lay their bones in *Canaan*, as hoping to make a part of that Resurrection, and though thirty miles from Mount *Calvary*, at least to lie in that Region, which should produce the first-fruits of the dead. And if according to learned conjecture, the bodies of men shall rise where their greatest Reliques remain, many are not like to erre in the Topography of their Resurrection, though their bones or bodies be after translated by Angels into the field of *Ezechiels* vision, or as some will order it, into the Valley of Judgement, or *Jehosaphat*.[79]

Footnotes

[37]*Matt*. 23.
[38]Euripides.
[39]*Psa*. 63.
[40]Χωρήσεις τον ἄνθρωπον ὅν ἡ οἰκουμένη οὐκ ἠχώρησεν. Dion.
[41]Cum lacrymis posuere.
[42]Lazius.
[43]*About five hundred years*. Plato.
[44]Vinum Opiminianum annorum centum. *Petron*.
[45]12. Tabul. *l. xi*. de Jure sacro. Neve aurum addito, ast quoi auro dentes vincti erunt, im cum illo sepelire et utere, se fraude esto.
[46]*Plin*. 1. xvi. Inter ξύλα ἀσαπῆ numerat Theophrastus.
[47]Surius.
[48]Gorop. Becanus in Niloscopio.
[49]*Of* Beringuccio nella pyrotechnia.
[50]*At* Elmeham.
[51]*Sueton*. in vitâ Tib. et in Amphitheatro semiustulandum, *not*. Casaub.
[52]Sueton. in vitâ Domitian
[53]*S. the most learned and worthy Mr*. M. Casaubon *upon* Antoninus.
[54]Sic erimus cuncti, *etc*. Ergo dum vivimus vivamus.
[55]Ἀγχόνην παίζειν. *A barbarous pastime at Feasts, when men stood upon a rolling Globe, with their necks in a Rope, and a knife in their hands, ready to cut it when the stone was rolled away, wherein if they failed, they lost their lives to the laughter of their spectators*. Athenæus.
[56]Diis manibus.
[57]Bosio.
[58]Pausan. in Atticis.
[59]*Lamprid*. in vit. Alexand. Severi.
[60]*Trajanus*. Dion.
[61]*Plut*. in vit. Marcelli.
[62]Britannia hodie eam attonitè celebrat tantis ceremoniis, ut dedisse Persis videri possit. *Plin. l. 29*.
[63]Topographiæ Roma ex Martiano. Erat et vas ustrinum appellatum quod in eo cadavera comburerenur. *Cap*. de Campo Esquilino.
[64]*To be seen in* Licet. de reconditis veterum lucernis.
[65]*Old bones according to* Lyserus. *Those of young persons not tall nor fat according to* Columbus.
[66]In vita. *Gracc*.
[67]Thucydides.
[68]Laurent. Valla.
[69]Ἑκατόμπεδον ἔνθα ἤ ἔνθα.
[70]Sperm ran. Alb. Ovor.

[71]*The brain.* Hippocrates.
[72]*Amos* 2. 1.
[73]*As* Artemisia *of her Husband* Mausolus.
[74]Siste viator.
[75]Kirckmannus de funer.
[76]*Of* Thomas *Marquesse of* Dorset, *whose body being buried 1530, was 1608 upon the cutting open of the Cerecloth found perfect and nothing corrupted, the flesh not hardened, but in colour, proportion, and softnesse like an ordinary corps newly to be interred.* Burtons *descript. of* Leicestershire.
[77]*In his Map of* Russia.
[78]*The Poet* Dante *in his view of Purgatory, found gluttons so meagre, and extenuated, that he conceived them to have been in the siege of* Jerusalem, *and that it was easie to have discovered* Homo *or* Omo *in their faces: M being made by the two lines of their cheeks, arching over the Eye-brows to the nose, and their sunk eyes making O O which makes up* Omo. Parean l'occhiaie anella senza gemme che nel viso de gli huomini legge huomo Ben'hauria quiui conosciuto l'emme.
[79]Tirin. *in Ezek.*

CHAPTER IV

Christians have handsomely glossed the deformity of death, by careful consideration of the body, and civil rites which take off brutal terminations. And though they conceived all reparable by a resurrection, cast not off all care of enterrment. And since the ashes of Sacrifices burnt upon the Altar of God, were carefully carried out by the Priests, and deposed in a clean field; since they acknowledged their bodies to be the lodging of Christ, and temples of the holy Ghost, they devolved not all upon the sufficiency of soul existence; and therefore with long services and full solemnities concluded their last Exequies, wherein[80] to all distinctions the Greek devotion seems most pathetically ceremonious.

Christian invention hath chiefly driven at Rites, which speak hopes of another life, and hints of a Resurrection. And if the ancient Gentiles held not the immortality of their better part, and some subsistence after death; in several rites, customes, actions and expressions, they contradicted their own opinions: wherein *Democritus* went high, even to the thought of a resurrection,[81] as scoffingly recorded by *Pliny*. What can be more express than the expression of *Phocyllides*?[82] Or who would expect from *Lucretius*[83] a sentence of *Ecclesiastes*? Before *Plato* could speak, the soul had wings in *Homer*, which fell not, but flew out of the body into the mansions of the dead; who also observed that handsome distinction of *Demas* and *Soma*, for the body conjoyned to the soul and body separated from it. *Lucian* spoke much truth in jest, when he said, that part of *Hercules* which proceeded from *Alchmena* perished, that from *Jupiter* remained immortal. Thus *Socrates*[84] was content that his friends should bury his body, so they would not think they buried *Socrates*, and regarding only his immortal part, was indifferent to be burnt or buried. From such Considerations *Diogenes* might contemn Sepulture. And being satisfied that the soul could not perish, grow careless of corporal enterrment. The *Stoicks* who thought the souls of wise men had their habitation about the *Moon*, might make slight account of subterraneous deposition; whereas the *Pythagorians* and transcorporating Philosophers, who were to be often buried, held great care of their enterrment. And the Platonicks rejected not a due care of the grave, though they put their ashes to unreasonable expectations, in their tedious term of return and long set revolution.

Men have lost their reason in nothing so much as their Religion, wherein stones and clouts make Martyrs; and since the Religion of one seems madness unto another, to afford an account or rational of old Rites, requires no rigid Reader; That they kindled the pyre aversly, or turning their face from it, was an handsome Symbole of unwilling ministration; That they washed their bones with wine and milk, that the mother wrapt them in Linnen, and dryed them in her bosome, the first fostering part, and place of their nourishment; That they opened their eyes towards heaven, before they kindled the fire, as the place of their hopes or original, were no improper Ceremonies. Their last valediction[85] thrice uttered by the attendants was also very solemn, and somewhat answered by Christians, who thought it too little, if they threw not the earth thrice upon the enterred body. That in strewing their Tombs the *Romanes* affected the Rose, the Greeks *Amaranthus* and myrtle; that the Funeral pyre consisted of sweet fuel, Cypress, Firre, Larix, Yewe, and Trees perpetually verdant, lay silent expressions of their surviving hopes: Wherein Christians which deck their Coffins with Bays have found a more elegant Embleme. For that tree seeming dead, will restore it self from the root, and its dry and exuccous leaves resume their verdure again; which if we mistake not, we have also observed in Furze. Whether the planting of Yewe in Churchyards, hold not its original from ancient Funeral Rites, or as an Embleme of Resurrection from its perpetual verdure, may also admit conjecture.

They made use of Musick to excite or quiet the affections of their friends, according to different harmonies. But the secret and symbolical hint was the harmonical nature of the soul; which delivered from the body, went again to enjoy the primitive harmony of heaven, from whence it first descended; which according to its progresse traced by antiquity, came down by *Cancer*, and ascended by *Capricornus*.

They burnt not children before their teeth appeared, as apprehending their bodies too tender a morsel for fire, and that their gristly bones would scarce leave separable reliques after the pyral combustion. That they kindled not fire in their houses for some dayes after, was a strict memorial of the late afflicting fire. And mourning without hope, they had an happy fraud against excessive lamentation, by a common opinion that deep sorrows disturbed their ghosts.[86]

That they buried their dead on their backs, or in a supine position, seems agreeable unto profound sleep, and common posture of dying; contrary to the most natural way of birth; Nor unlike our pendulous posture, in the doubtful state of the womb. *Diogenes* was singular, who preferred a prone situation in the grave, and some Christians[87] like neither, who decline the figure of rest, and make choice of an erect posture.

That they carried them out of the world with their feet forward, not inconsonant unto reason: As contrary unto the native posture of man, and his production first into it. And also agreeable unto their opinions, while they bid adieu unto the world, not to look again upon it; whereas *Mahometans* who think to return to a delightful life again, are carried forth with their heads forward, and looking towards their houses.

They closed their eyes as parts which first die or first discover the sad effects of death. But their iterated clamations to excite their dying or dead friends, or revoke them unto life again, was a vanity of affection; as not presumably ignorant of the critical tests of death, by apposition of feathers, glasses, and reflexion of figures, which dead eyes represent not; which however not strictly verifiable in fresh and warm *cadavers*, could hardly elude the test, in corps of four or five dayes.

That they suck'd in the last breath of their expiring friends, was surely a practice of no medicall institution, but a loose opinion that the soul passed out that way, and a fondnesse of affection from some *Pythagoricall*[88] foundation, that the spirit of one body passed into another; which they wished might be their own.

That they powred oyle upon the pyre, was a tolerable practise, while the intention rested in facilitating the accension; But to place good *Omens* in the quick and speedy burning, to sacrifice unto the winds for a dispatch in this office, was a low form of superstition.

The *Archimime* or *Jester* attending the Funeral train, and imitating the speeches, gesture, and manners of the deceased, was too light for such solemnities, contradicting their funerall Orations, and dolefull rites of the grave.

That they buried a peece of money with them as a Fee of the *Elysian Ferriman*, was a practise full of folly. But the ancient custome of placing coynes in considerable Urnes, and the present practice of burying medals in the Noble Foundations of *Europe*, are laudable wayes of historicall discoveries, in actions, persons, Chronologies; and posterity will applaud them.

We examine not the old Laws of Sepulture, exempting certain persons from burial or burning. But hereby we apprehend that these were not the bones of persons Planet-struck or burnt with fire from Heaven: No Reliques of Traitors to their Countrey, Self-killers, or Sacrilegious Malefactors; Persons in old apprehension unworthy of the *earth*; condemned unto the *Tartara's* of Hell, and bottomlesse pit of *Pluto*, from whence there was no redemption.

Nor were only many customes questionable in order to their Obsequies, but also sundry practises, fictions, and conceptions, discordant or obscure, of their state and future beings; whether unto eight or ten bodies of men to adde one of a woman, as being more inflammable, and unctuously constituted for the better pyrall combustion, were any rational practise: Or whether the complaint of *Perianders* Wife be tolerable, that wanting her Funerall burning she suffered intolerable cold in Hell, according to the constitution of the infernal house of *Pluto*, wherein cold makes a great part of their tortures; it cannot passe without some question.

Why the Female Ghosts appear unto *Ulysses*, before the *Heroes* and masculine spirits? Why the *Psyche* or soul of *Tiresias* is of the masculine gender; who being blinde on earth sees more then all the rest in hell; Why the Funeral Suppers consisted of Egges, Beans, Smallage, and Lettuce, since the dead are made to eat *Asphodels* about the *Elysian* medows? Why since there is no Sacrifice acceptable, nor any propitiation for the Covenant of the grave: men set up the Deity of *Morta*, and fruitlesly adored Divinities without ears? it cannot escape some doubt.

The dead seem all alive in the humane *Hades* of *Homer*, yet cannot we speak, prophesie, or know the living, except they drink blood, wherein is the life of man. And therefore the souls of *Penelope's* Paramours conducted by *Mercury* chiriped like bats, and those which followed *Hercules* made a noise but like a flock of birds.

The departed spirits know things past and to come, yet are ignorant of things present. *Agememnon* fortels what should happen unto *Ulysses*, yet ignorantly enquires what is become of his own Son. The ghosts are afraid of swords in *Homer*, yet *Sybilla* tells *Æneas* in *Virgil*, the thin habit of spirits was beyond the force of weapons. The spirits put off their malice with their bodies, and *Cæsar* and *Pompey* accord in Latine Hell, yet *Ajax* in *Homer* endures not a conference with *Ulysses*: And *Deiphobus* appears all mangled in *Virgils* Ghosts, yet we meet with perfect shadows among the wounded ghosts of *Homer*.

Since *Charon* in *Lucian* applauds his condition among the dead, whether it be handsomely said of *Achilles*, that living contemner of death, that he had rather be a Plowmans servant then Emperour of the dead? How *Hercules* his soul is in hell, and yet in heaven, and *Julius* his soul in a Star, yet seen by *Æneas* in hell, except the Ghosts were but images and shadows of the soul, received in higher mansions, according to the ancient division of body, soul, and image or *simulachrum* of them both. The particulars of future beings must needs be dark unto ancient Theories, which Christian Philosophy yet determines but in a Cloud of opinions. A Dialogue between two Infants in the womb concerning the state of this world, might handsomly illustrate our ignorance of the next, whereof methinks we yet discourse in *Platoes* denne, and are but *Embryon* Philosophers.

Pythagoras escapes in the fabulous hell of *Dante*,[89] among that swarm of Philosophers, wherein whilest we meet with *Plato* and *Socrates*, *Cato* is to be found in no lower place then Purgatory. Among all the set, *Epicurus* is most considerable, whom men make honest without an *Elyzium*, who contemned life without encouragement of immortality, and making nothing after death, yet made nothing of the King of terrours.

Were the happinesse of next world as closely apprehended as the felicities of this, it were a martyrdome to live; and unto such as consider none hereafter, it must be more then death to die, which makes us amazed at those audacities, that durst be nothing, and return into their *Chaos* again. Certainly such spirits as could contemn death, when they expected no better being after, would have scorned to live had they known any. And therefore we applaud not the judgment of *Machiavel*, that Christianity makes men cowards, or that with the confidence of but half dying, the dispised virtues of patience and humility, have abased the spirits of men, which Pagan principles exalted, but rather regulated the wildenesse of audacities, in the attempts, grounds, and eternal sequels of death; wherein men of the boldest spirits are often prodigiously temerarious. Nor can we extenuate valour of ancient Martyrs, who contemned death in the uncomfortable scene of their lives, and in their decrepit Martyrdomes did probably lose not many monethes of their dayes, or parted with life when it was scarce worth the living. For (beside that long time past holds no consideration unto a slender time to come) they had no small disadvantage from the constitution of old age, which naturally makes men fearful; And complexionally superannuated from the bold and courageous thoughts of youth and fervent years. But the contempt of death from corporal animosity, promoteth not our felicity. They may set in the *Orchestra*, and noblest Seats of Heaven, who have held up shaking hands in the fire, and humanely contended for glory.

Mean while *Epicurus* lies deep in *Dante's* hell, wherin we meet with Tombs enclosing souls which denied their immortalities. But whether the virtuous heathen, who lived better then he spake, or erring in the principles of himself, yet lived above Philosophers of more specious Maximes, lye so deep as he is placed; at least so low as not to rise against Christians, who beleeving or knowing that truth, have lastingly denied it in their practise and conversation, were a quæry too sad to insist on.

But all or most apprehensions rested in Opinions of some future being, which ignorantly or coldly beleeved, beget those perverted conceptions, Ceremonies, Sayings, which Christians pity or laugh at. Happy are they, which live not in that disadvantage of time, when men could say little for futurity, but from reason. Whereby the noblest mindes fell often upon doubtful deaths, and melancholly Dissolutions; With these hopes *Socrates* warmed his doubtful spirits, against that cold potion, and *Cato* before he durst give the fatal stroak, spent part of the night in reading the immortality of *Plato*, thereby confirming his wavering hand unto the animosity of that attempt.

It is the heaviest stone that melancholy can throw at a man, to tell him he is at the end of his nature; or that there is no further state to come, unto which this seemes progressional, and otherwise made in vaine; Without this accomplishment the natural expectation and desire of such a state, were but a fallacy in nature; unsatisfied Considerators would quarrel the justice of their constitutions, and rest content that *Adam* had fallen lower; whereby by knowing no other Original, and deeper ignorance of themselves, they might have enjoyed the happinesse of inferiour Creatures; who in tranquillity possess their Constitutions, as having not the apprehension to deplore their own natures. And being framed below the circumference of these hopes, or cognition of better being, the wisedom of God hath necessitated their Contentment: But the superiour ingredient and obscured part of our selves, whereto all present felicities afford no resting contentment, will be able at last to tell us we are more then our present selves; and evacuate such hopes in the fruition of their own accomplishments.

Footnotes

[80]Rituale Græcum opera J. Goar in officio exequiarum.

[81]Similis reviviscendi promissa Democrito vanitas, qui non revixit ipse. Quæ, malùm, ista dementia est; iterari vitam morte. *Plin. l. 7 c. 55.*

[82]Καὶ τάχα δ' ἐκ γαίης ἐλπίζομεν ἐς φάος ἐλθεῖν λείψαν ἀποιχομένων.

[83]Cedit enim retro de terra quod fuit ante In terram, *etc. Lucret.*

[84]Plato *in* Phæd.

[85]Vale, vale, vale, nos te ordine quo natura permittet sequemur.

[86]Tu manes ne læde meos.

[87]Russians, *etc.*

[88]Francesco Perucci Pompe funebr.

[89]Del inferno. *cant. 4.*

CHAPTER V

Now since these dead bones have already out-lasted the living ones of *Methuselah*, and in a yard under ground, and thin walls of clay, out-worn all the strong and specious buildings above it; and quietly rested under the drums and tramplings of three conquests; What Prince can promise such diuturnity unto his Reliques, or might not gladly say,

Sic ego componi versus in ossa velim.[90]

Time which antiquates Antiquities, and hath an art to make dust of all things, hath yet spared these *minor* Monuments. In vain we hope to be known by open and visible conservatories, when to be unknown was the means of their continuation and obscurity their protection: If they dyed by violent hands, and were thrust into their Urnes, these bones become considerable, and some old Philosophers would honour them,[91] whose soules they conceived most pure, which were thus snatched from their bodies; and to retain a stronger propension unto them: whereas they weariedly left a languishing corps, and with faint desires of reunion. If they fell by long and aged decay, yet wrapt up in the bundle of time, they fall into indistinction, and make but one blot with Infants. If we begin to die when we live, and long life be but a prolongation of death; our life is a sad composition; we live with death, and die not in a moment. How many pulses made up the life of *Methuselah*, were work for *Archimedes*: Common Counters sum up the life of *Moses* his man.[92] Our dayes become considerable like petty sums by minute accumulations; where numerous fractions make up but small round numbers; and our dayes of a span long make not one little finger.[93]

If the nearnesse of our last necessity, brought a nearer conformity unto it, there were a happinesse in hoary hairs, and no calamity in half senses. But the long habit of living indisposeth us for dying; When Avarice makes us the sport of death; When even *David* grew politickly cruel; and *Solomon* could hardly be said to be the wisest of men. But many are to early old, and before the date of age. Adversity stretcheth our dayes, misery makes *Alcmenas* nights,[94] and time hath no wings unto it. But the most tedious being is that which can unwish it self, content to be nothing, or never to have been, which was beyond the *male*-content of *Job*, who cursed not the day of his life, but his Nativity; Content to have so far been, as to have a title to future being; Although he had lived here but in an hidden state of life, and as it were an abortion.

The puzling questions of Tiberius *unto Grammarians. Marcel. Donatus in Suet.* Κλυτὰ ἔθνεα νεκρῶν Hom. Job.

What Song the *Syrens* sang, or what name *Achilles* assumed when he hid himself among women, though puzling questions are not beyond all conjecture. What time the persons of these Ossuaries entred the famous Nations of the dead, and slept with Princes and Counsellors, might admit a wide solution. But who were the proprietaries of these bones, or what bodies these ashes made up, were a question above Antiquarism. Not to be resolved by man, nor easily perhaps by spirits, except we consult the Provincial Guardians, or tutelary Observators. Had they made as good provision for their names, as they have done for their Reliques, they had not so grosly erred in the art of perpetuation. But to subsist in bones, and be but Pyramidally extant, is a fallacy in duration. Vain ashes, which in the oblivion of names, persons, times, and sexes, have found unto themselves a fruitlesse continuation, and only arise unto late posterity, as Emblemes of mortal vanities; Antidotes against pride, vainglory, and madding vices. Pagan vain glories which thought the world might last for ever, had encouragement for ambition, and finding no *Atropos* unto the immortality of their Names, were never dampt with the necessity of oblivion. Even old ambitions had the advantage of ours, in the attempts of their vain-glories, who acting early, and before the probable Meridian of time, have by this time found great accomplishment of their designes, whereby the ancient *Heroes* have already out-lasted their Monuments, and Mechanical preservations. But in this latter Scene of time we cannot expect such Mummies unto our memories, when ambition may fear the Prophecy of *Elias*,[95] and *Charles* the fift can never hope to live within two *Methusela's* of *Hector*.[96]

And therefore restlesse inquietude for the diuturnity of our memories unto present considerations, seemes a vanity almost out of date, and superannuated peece of folly. We cannot hope to live so long in our names, as some have done in their persons, one face of *Janus* holds no proportion to the other. 'Tis to late to be ambitious. The great mutations of the world are acted, or time may be too short for our designes. To extend our memories by Monuments, whose death we dayly pray for, and whose duration we cannot hope, without injury to our expectations, in the advent of the last day, were a contradiction to our beliefs. We whose generations are ordained in this setting part of time, are providentially taken off from such imaginations. And being necessitated to eye the remaining particle of futurity, are naturally constituted unto thoughts of the next world, and cannot excusably decline the consideration of that duration, which maketh Pyramids pillars of snow, and all that's past a moment.

Circles and right lines limit and close all bodies, and the mortal right-lined-circle[97] must conclude and shut up all. There is no antidote against the *Opium* of time, which temporally considereth all things; Our Fathers finde their graves in our short memories, and sadly tell us how we may be buried in our Survivors. Grave-stones tell truth scarce fourty yeers:[98] Generations passe while some trees stand, and old Families last not three Oakes. To be read by bare inscriptions like many in *Gruter*,[99] to hope for Eternity by Ænigmatical Epithetes, or first letters of our names, to be studied by Antiquaries, who we were, and have new Names given us like many of the Mummies, are cold consolations unto the Students of perpetuity, even by everlasting Languages.

To be content that times to come should only know there was such a man, not caring whether they knew more of him, was a frigid ambition in *Cardan*:[100] disparaging his horoscopal inclination and judgement of himself, who cares to subsist like *Hippocrates* Patients, or *Achilles* horses in *Homer*, under naked nominations, without deserts and noble acts, which are the balsame of our memories, the *Entelechia* and soul of our subsistences. To be namelesse in worthy deeds exceeds an infamous history. The *Canaanitish* woman lives more happily without a name, then *Herodias* with one. And who had not rather have been the good theef, then *Pilate*?

But the iniquity of oblivion blindly scattereth her poppy, and deals with the memory of men without distinction to merit of perpetuity. Who can but pity the founder of the Pyramids? *Herostratus* lives that burnt the Temple of *Diana*, he is almost lost that built it; Time hath spared the Epitaph of *Adrians* horse, confounded that of himself. In vain we compute our felicities by the advantage of our good names, since bad have equal durations; and *Thersites* is like to live as long as *Agamemnon*. Who knows whether the best of men be known? or whether there be not more remarkable persons forgot, then any that stand remembred in the known account of time? Without the favour of the everlasting Register the first man had been as unknown as the last, and *Methuselahs* long life had been his only Chronicle.

Oblivion is not to be hired: The greater part must be content to be as though they had not been, to be found in the register of God, not in the record of man. Twenty seven names make up the first story, and the recorded names ever since contain not one living Century. The number of the dead long exceedeth all that shall live. The night of time far surpasseth the day, and who knows when was the Æquinox? Every houre addes unto that current Arithmetique, which scarce stands one moment. And since death must be the *Lucina* of life, and even Pagans could doubt whether thus to live, were to die; Since our longest Sun sets at right descensions, and makes but winter arches, and therefore it cannot be long before we lie down in darknesse, and have our light in ashes; Since the brother of death daily haunts us with dying *memento's*, and time that grows old it self, bids us hope no long duration: Diuturnity is a dream and folly of expectation.

Darknesse and light divide the course of time, and oblivion shares with memory, a great part even of our living beings; we slightly remember our felicities, and the smartest strokes of affliction leave but short smart upon us. Sense endureth no extremities, and sorrows destroy us or themselves. To weep into stones are fables. Afflictions induce callosities, miseries are slippery, or fall like snow upon us, which notwithstanding is no stupidity. To be ignorant of evils to come, and forgetful of evils past, is merciful provision in nature, whereby we digest the mixture of our few and evil dayes, and our delivered senses not relapsing into cutting remembrances, our sorrows are not kept raw by the edge of repetitions. A great part of Antiquity contented their hopes of subsistency with a transmigration of their souls. A good way to continue their memories, while having the advantage of plural successions, they could not but act something remarkable in such variety of beings, and enjoying the fame of their passed selves, make accumulation of glory unto their last durations. Others rather then be lost in the uncomfortable night of nothing, were content to recede into the common being, and make one particle of the publick soul of all things, which was no more then to return into their unknown and divine Original again. Ægyptian ingenuity was more unsatisfied, contriving their bodies in sweet consistences, to attend the return of their souls. But all was vanity, feeding the winde,[101] and folly. The Ægyptian Mummies, which *Cambyses* or time hath spared, avarice now consumeth. Mummie is become Merchandise, *Mizraim* cures wounds, and *Pharaoh* is sold for balsoms.

In vain do individuals hope for immortality, or any patent from oblivion, in preservations below the Moon: Men have been deceived even in their flatteries above the Sun, and studied conceits to perpetuate their names in heaven. The various Cosmography of that part hath already varied the names of contrived constellations; *Nimrod* is lost in *Orion*, and *Osyris* in the Dogge-starre. While we look for incorruption in the heavens, we finde they are but like the Earth; Durable in their main bodies, alterable in their parts: whereof beside Comets and new Stars, perspectives begin to tell tales. And the spots that wander about the Sun, with *Phaetons* favour, would make clear conviction.

There is nothing strictly immortal, but immortality; whatever hath no beginning may be confident of no end. All others have a dependent being, and within the reach of destruction, which is the peculiar of that necessary essence that cannot destroy it self; And the highest strain of omnipotency to be so powerfully constituted, as not to suffer even from the power of it self. But the sufficiency of Christian Immortality frustrates all earthly glory, and the quality of either state after death makes a folly of posthumous memory. God who can only destroy our souls, and hath assured our resurrection, either of our bodies or names hath directly promised no duration. Wherein there is so much of chance that the boldest Expectants have found unhappy frustration; and to hold long subsistence, seems but a scape in oblivion. But man is a Noble Animal, splendid in ashes, and pompous in the grave, solemnizing Nativities and Deaths with equal lustre, nor omitting Ceremonies of bravery, in the infamy of his nature.

Life is a pure flame, and we live by an invisible Sun within us. A small fire sufficeth for life, great flames seemed too little after death, while men vainly affected precious pyres, and burn like *Sardanapalus*, but the wisedom of funeral Laws found the folly of prodigal blazes, and reduced undoing fires, unto the rule of sober obsequies, wherein few could be so mean as not to provide wood, pitch, a mourner, and an Urne.

Five Languages secured not the Epitaph of *Gordianus;* The man of God lives longer without a Tomb then any by one, invisibly interred by Angels, and adjudged to obscurity, though not without some marks directing humane discovery. *Enoch* and *Elias* without either tomb or burial, in an anomalous state of being, are the great Examples of perpetuity, in their long and living memory, in strict account being still on this side death, and having a late part yet to act upon this stage of earth. If in the decretory term of the world we shall not all die but be changed, according to received translation; the last day will make but few graves; at least quick Resurrections will anticipate lasting Sepultures; Some Graves will be opened before they be quite closed, and *Lazarus* be no wonder. When many that feared to die shall groan that they can die but once, the dismal state is the second and living death, when life puts despair on the damned; when men shall wish the coverings of Mountaines, not of Monuments, and annihilation shall be courted.

While some have studied Monuments, others have studiously declined them: and some have been so vainly boisterous, that they durst not acknowledge their Graves; wherein *Alaricus*[102] seems most subtle, who had a Rever turned to hide his bones at the bottome. Even *Sylla* that thought himself safe in his Urne, could not prevent revenging tongues, and stones thrown at his Monument. Happy are they whom privacy makes innocent, who deal so with men in this world, that they are not afraid to meet them in the next, who when they die, make no commotion among the dead, and are not toucht with that poeticall taunt of *Isaiah*.[103]

Pyramids, *Arches*, *Obelisks*, were but the irregularities of vain-glory, and wilde enormities of ancient magnanimity. But the most magnanimous resolution rests in the Christian Religion, which trampleth upon pride, and sets on the neck of ambition, humbly pursuing that infallible perpetuity, unto which all others must diminish their diameters and be poorly seen in Angles of contingency.[104]

Pious spirits who passed their dayes in raptures of futurity, made little more of this world, then the world that was before it, while they lay obscure in the Chaos of preordination, and night of their fore-beings. And if any have been so happy as truly to understand Christian annihilation, extasis, exolution, liquefaction, transformation, the kisse of the Spouse, gustation of God, and ingression into the divine shadow, they have already had an handsome anticipation of heaven; the glory of the world is surely over, and the earth in ashes unto them.

To subsist in lasting Monuments, to live in their productions, to exist in their names, and prædicament of *Chymera's*, was large satisfaction unto old expectations and made one part of their *Elyziums*. But all this is nothing in the Metaphysicks of true belief. To live indeed is to be again our selves, which being not only an hope but an evidence in noble beleevers; 'Tis all one to lie in St. *Innocents* Church-yard,[105] as in the Sands of *Ægypt*: Ready to be any thing, in the extasie of being ever, and as content with six foot as the Moles of *Adrianus*.[106]

Lucan
——Tabesne cadavera solvat
An rogus haud refert.——

Footnotes

[90]Tibullus.

[91]Oracula Chaldaica cum scholiis Pselli et Phethonis. Βίη λιπόντων σῶμα ψυχαὶ καθαρώταται. Vi corpus relinquentium animæ purissimæ.

[92]*In the Psalme of* Moses.

[93]*According to the ancient Arithmetick of the hand wherein the little finger of the right hand contracted, signified an hundred.* Pierius in Hieroglyph.

[94]*One night as long as three.*

[95]*That the world may last but six thousand years.*

[96]*Hectors fame lasting above two lives of* Methuselah, *before that famous Prince was extant.*

[97]Θ *The character of death.*

[98]*Old ones being taken up, and other bodies laid under them.*

[99]Gruteri Inscriptiones Antiquæ

[100]Cuperem notum esse quod sim, non opto ut sciatur qualis sim. *Card.* in vita propria.

[101]Omnia vanitas et pastio venti, νομὴ ἀνέμου, βόσκησις ut olim Aquila et Symmachus. V. Drus. Eccles.

[102]Jornandes de rebus Geticis.

[103]*Isa.* 14.

[104]Angulus contingentiæ, *the least of Angles.*

[105]*In* Paris *where bodies soon consume.*

[106]*A stately* Mausoleum *or sepulchral pyle built by* Adrianus *in* Rome, *where now standeth the Castle of* St. Angelo.

THE GARDEN OF CYRUS
OR, THE QUINCUNCIAL, LOZENGE OR NET-WORK PLANTATIONS OF

THE ANCIENTS, ARTIFICIALLY

NATURALLY, MYSTICALLY

CONSIDERED
BY
THOMAS BROWN D. OF PHYSICK
Printed in the Year, 1658

THE GARDEN OF CYRUS
Or, The Quincuncial, Lozenge, or Net-work Plantations of the Ancients, Artificially, Naturally, Mystically considered.

CHAPTER I

That *Vulcan* gave arrows unto *Apollo* and *Diana* the fourth day after their Nativities, according to Gentile Theology, may passe for no blinde apprehension of the Creation of the Sunne and Moon, in the work of the fourth day; When the diffused light contracted into Orbes, and shooting rayes, of those Luminaries. Plainer Descriptions there are from Pagan pens, of the creatures of the fourth day; While the divine Philosopher[107] unhappily omitteth the noblest part of the third; And *Ovid* (whom many conceive to have borrowed his description from *Moses*) coldly deserting the remarkable account of the text, in three words,[108] describeth this work of the third day; the vegetable creation, and first ornamental Scene of nature; the primitive food of animals, and first story of Physick, in Dietetical conservation.

For though Physick may pleade high, from the medicall act of God, in casting so deep a sleep upon our first Parent; And Chirurgery[109] finde its whole art, in that one passage concerning the Rib of *Adam*, yet is there no rivality with Garden contrivance and Herbery. For if Paradise were planted the third day of the Creation, as wiser Divinity concludeth, the Nativity thereof was too early for Horoscopie; Gardens were before Gardiners, and but some hours after the earth.

Of deeper doubt is its Topography, and locall designation, yet being the primitive garden, and without much controversie[110] seated in the East; it is more then probable the first curiosity, and cultivation of plants, most nourished in those quarters. And since the Ark of *Noah* first toucht upon some mountains of *Armenia,* the planting art arose again in the East, and found its revolution not far from the place of its Nativity, about the Plains of those Regions. And if *Zoroaster* were either *Cham*, *Chus*, or *Mizraim*, they were early proficients therein, who left (as *Pliny* delivereth) a work of Agriculture.

However the account of the Pensill or hanging gardens of *Babylon*, if made by *Semiramis*, the third or fourth from *Nimrod*, is of no slender antiquity; which being not framed upon ordinary level of ground, but raised upon pillars admitting under-passages, we cannot accept as the first *Babylonian* Gardens; But a more eminent progress and advancement in that art, then any that went before it: Somewhat answering or hinting the old Opinion concerning Paradise it self, with many conceptions elevated above the plane of the Earth.

Nebuchodonosor, whom some will have to be the famous *Syrian* King of *Diodorus*, beautifully repaired that City; and so magnificently built his hanging gardens;[111] that from succeeding Writers he had the honour of the first. From whence over-looking *Babylon*, and all the Region about it, he found no circumscription to the eye of his ambition, till over-delighted with the bravery of this Paradise; in his melancholy metamorphosis, he found the folly of that delight, and a proper punishment, in the contrary habitation, in wilde plantations and wandrings of the fields.

The *Persian* Gallants who destroyed this Monarchy, maintained their Botanicall bravery. Unto whom we owe the very name of Paradise: wherewith we meet not in Scripture before the time of *Solomon*, and conceived originally *Persian*. The word for that disputed Garden, expressing in the Hebrew no more then a Field enclosed, which from the same Root is content to derive a garden and a Buckler.

Cyrus the elder brought up in Woods and Mountains, when time and power enabled, pursued the dictate of his education, and brought the treasures of the field into rule and circumscription, So nobly beautifying the hanging Gardens of *Babylon*, that he was also thought to be the authour thereof.

Ahasuerus (whom many conceive to have been *Artaxerxes Longimanus*) in the Countrey and City of Flowers,[112] and in an open Garden, entertained his Princes and people, while *Vasthi* more modestly treated the Ladies within the Palace thereof.

But if (as some opinion) [Plutarch *in the life of* Artaxerxes.] King *Ahasuerus* were *Artaxerxes Mnemon*, that found a life and reign answerable unto his great memory, our magnified *Cyrus* was his second brother: who gave the occasion of that memorable work, and almost miraculous retrait of *Xenophon*. A person of high spirit and honour, naturally a King, though fatally prevented by the harmlesse chance of *post*-geniture: Not only a Lord of Gardens, but a manuall planter thereof: disposing his trees like his armies in regular ordination. So that while old *Laertas* hath found a name in *Homer* for pruning hedges, and clearing away thorns and bryars; while King *Attalus* lives for his poysonous plantations of *Aconites*, Henbane, Hellebore, and plants hardly admitted within the walls of Paradise; While many of the Ancients do poorly live in the single names of Vegetables; All stories do look upon *Cyrus*, as the splendid and regular planter.

According whereto *Xenophon*[113] describeth his gallant plantation at *Sardis*, thus rendered by *Stobæus, Arbores pari intervallo sitas, rectos ordines, et omnia perpulchrè in Quincuncem directa*.[114] Which we shall take for granted as being accordingly rendered by the most elegant of the Latines;[115] and by no made term, but in use before by *Varro*. That is, the rows and orders so handsomely disposed; or five trees so set together, that a regular angularity, and through prospect, was left on every side. Owing this name not only unto the Quintuple number of Trees, but the figure declaring that number, which being doubled at the angle, makes up the Letter X, that is the Emphatical decussation, or fundamental figure.

Now though in some ancient and modern practice the *area* or decussated plot, might be a perfect square, answerable to a *Tuscan Pedestal*, and the *Quinquernio* or Cinque-point of a die; wherein by Diagonal lines the intersection was regular; accommodable unto Plantations of large growing Trees; and we must not denie our selves the advantage of this order; yet shall we chiefly insist upon that of *Curtius*[116] and *Porta*, in their brief description hereof. Wherein the *decussis* is made within a longilateral square, with oposite angles, acute and obtuse at the intersection; and so upon progression making a *Rhombus* or Lozenge figuration, which seemeth very agreeable unto the Original figure; Answerable whereunto we observe the decussated characters in many consulary coynes, and even in those of *Constantine* and his Sons, which pretend their pattern in the Sky; the crucigerous Ensigne carried this figure, not transversly or rectangularly intersected, but in a decussation, after the form of an *Andrean* or *Burgundian* cross, which answereth this description.

Where by the way we shall decline the old Theme, so traced by antiquity of crosses and crucifixion: Whereof some being right, and of one single peece without traversion or transome, do little advantage our subject. Nor shall we take in the mystical *Tau*, or the Crosse of our blessed Saviour, which having in some descriptions an *Empedon* or crossing foot-stay, made not one single transversion. And since the Learned *Lipsius* hath made some doubt even of the crosse of St. *Andrew*, since some Martyrological Histories deliver his death by the general Name of a crosse, and *Hippolitus* will have him suffer by the sword; we should have enough to make out the received Crosse of that Martyr. Nor shall we urge the *labarum*, and famous Standard of *Constantine*, or make further use thereof, then as the first letters in the Name of our Saviour Christ, in use among Christians, before the dayes of *Constantine*, to be observed in Sepulchral Monuments of Martyrs,[117] in the Reign of *Adrian*, and *Antoninus*; and to be found in the Antiquities of the Gentiles, before the advent of Christ, as in the Medal of King *Ptolomy*, signed with the same characters, and might be the beginning of some word or name, which Antiquaries have not hit on.

We will not revive the mysterious crosses of *Ægypt*, with circles on their heads, in the breast of *Serapis*, and the hands of their Geniall spirits, not unlike the character of *Venus*, and looked on by ancient Christians, with relation unto Christ. Since however they first began, the Ægyptians thereby expressed the processe and motion of the spirit of the world, and the diffusion thereof upon the Celestiall and Elementall nature; implyed by a circle and right-lined intersection. A secret in their Telesmes and magicall Characters among them. Though he that considereth the plain crosse[118] upon the head of the Owl in the Laterane Obelisk, or the crosse[119] erected upon a pitcher diffusing streams of water into two basins, with sprinkling branches in them, and all described upon a two-footed Altar, as in the Hieroglyphicks of the brazen Table of *Bembus*: will hardly decline all thought of Christian signality in them.

We shall not call in the Hebrew *Tenapha*, or ceremony of their Oblations, waved by the priest unto the four quarters of the world, after the form of a cross; as in the peace-offerings. And if it were clearly made out what is remarkably delivered from the Traditions of the Rabbins, that as the Oyle was powred coronally or circularly upon the head of Kings, so the High-Priest was anointed decussatively or in the form of a X; though it could not escape a typical thought of Christ, from mystical considerators; yet being the conceit is Hebrew, we should rather expect its verification from Analogy in that language, then to confine the same unto the unconcerned Letters of *Greece*, or make it out by the characters of *Cadmus* or *Palamedes*.

Of this Quincuncial Ordination the Ancients practised, much discoursed little; and the Moderns have nothing enlarged; which he that more nearly considereth, in the form of its square *Rhombus*, and decussation, with the several commodities, mysteries, parallelismes, and resemblances, both in Art and Nature, shall easily discern the elegancy of this order.

That this was in some wayes of practice in diverse and distant Nations, hints or deliveries there are from no slender Antiquity. In the hanging Gardens of *Babylon*, from *Abydenus*, *Eusebius*, and others, *Curtius*[120] describeth this rule of decussation. In the memorable Garden of *Alcinous* anciently conceived an original phancy, from Paradise, mention there is of well contrived order; For so hath *Didymus* and *Eustachius* expounded the emphatical word. *Diomedes* describing the Rurall possessions of his Father, gives account in the same Language of Trees orderly planted. And *Ulysses* being a boy was promised by his father fourty Fig-trees, and fifty rows of vines,[121] producing all kind of grapes.

That the Eastern Inhabitants of *India*, made use of such order, even in open Plantations, is deducible from *Theophrastus*; who describing the trees whereof they made their garments, plainly delivereth that they were planted κατ' ὄρχους, and in such order that at a distance men would mistake them for Vineyards. The same seems confirmed in *Greece* from a singular expression in *Aristotle*[122] concerning the order of Vines, delivered by a military term representing the orders of Souldiers, which also confirmeth the antiquity of this form yet used in vineal plantations.

That the same was used in Latine plantations is plainly confirmed from the commending penne of *Varro, Quintilian*, and handsome Description of *Virgil*.[123]

That the first Plantations not long after the Floud were disposed after this manner, the generality and antiquity of this order observed in Vineyards, and Wine Plantations, affordeth some conjecture. And since from judicious enquiry, *Saturn* who divided the world between his three sonnes, who beareth a Sickle in his hand, who taught the Plantations of Vines, the setting, grafting of trees, and the best part of Agriculture, is discovered to be *Noah*, whether this early dispersed Husbandry in Vineyards, had not its Original in that Patriarch, is no such Paralogical doubt.

And if it were clear that this was used by *Noah* after the Floud, I could easily beleeve it was in use before it; Not willing to fix such ancient inventions no higher original then *Noah*; Nor readily conceiving those aged *Heroes*, whose diet was vegetable, and only, or chiefly consisted in the fruits of the earth, were much deficient in their splendid cultivations; or after the experience of fifteen hundred years, left much for future discovery in Botanical Agriculture. Nor fully perswaded that Wine was the invention of *Noah*, that fermented Liquors, which often make themselves, so long escaped their Luxury or experience; that the first sinne of the new world was no sin of the old. That *Cain* and *Abel* were the first that offered Sacrifice; or because the Scripture is silent that *Adam* or *Isaac* offered none at all.

Whether *Abraham* brought up in the first planting Countrey, observed not some rule hereof, when he planted a grove at *Beer-sheba*; or whether at least a like ordination were not in the Garden of *Solomon*, probability may contest. Answerably unto the wisedom of that eminent Botanologer, and orderly disposer of all his other works. Especially since this was one peece of Gallantry, wherein he pursued the specious part of felicity, according to his own description. I made me Gardens and Orchards, and planted Trees in them of all kindes of fruit. I made me Pools of water, to water therewith the wood that bringeth forth Trees,[124] which was no ordinary plantation, if according to the *Targum*, or *Chaldee Paraphrase*, it contained all kindes of Plants, and some fetched as far as *India*; And the extent thereof were from the wall of *Jerusalem* unto the water of *Siloah*.

And if *Jordan* were but *Jaar Eden*, that is, the River of *Eden, Genesar* but *Gansar* or the prince of Gardens; and it could be made out, that the Plain of *Jordan* were watered not comparatively, but causally, and because it was the Paradise of God, as the learned *Abramas*[125] hinteth, he was not far from the Prototype and originall of Plantations. And since even in Paradise it self, the tree of knowledge was placed in the middle of the Garden, whatever was the ambient figure; there wanted not a centre and rule of decussation. Whether the groves and sacred Plantations of Antiquity, were not thus orderly placed, either by *quaternio's*, or quintuple ordinations, may favourably be doubted. For since they were so methodical in the constitutions of their temples, as to observe the due scituation, aspect, manner, form, and order in Architectonicall relations, whether they were not as distinct in their groves and Plantations about them, in form and *species* respectively unto their Deities, is not without probability of conjecture. And in their groves of the Sunne this was a fit number, by multiplication to denote the dayes of the year; and might Hieroglyphically speak as much, as the mystical *Statua* of *Janus*[126] in the Language of his fingers. And since they were so critical in the number of his horses, the strings of his Harp, and rayes about his head, denoting the orbes of heaven, the Seasons and Moneths of the Yeare: witty Idolatry would hardly be flat in other appropriations.

Footnotes

[107]Plato in Timæo.

[108]fronde tegi silvas.

[109]διαίρεσις *in opening the flesh.* ἐξαίρεσις, *in taking out the rib.* σύνθεσις, *in closing up the part again.*

[110]*For some there is from the ambiguity of the word* Mikedem, *whether* ab oriente *or* a principio.

[111]Josephus.

[112]Sushan in Susiana.

[113]Xenophon in Oeconomico.

[114]Καλὰ μὲν τὰ δένδρα, δι' ἴσου δὲ τὰ πεφυτευμένα, ὀρθοὶ δὲ οἱ στίχοι τῶν δένδρον, εὐγώνεα δὲ πάντα καλῶς.]

[115]Cicero iæ Cat. Major.

[116]Benedict Curtius de Hortis. Bapt. Portainvilla.

[117]*Of* Marius, Alexander, Roma Sotterranea.

[118]*Wherein the lower part is some what longer, as defined by* Upton de studio militari, *and* Johannes de Bado Aureo, cum comment. clariss. et doctiss. Bi sæi.

[119]Casal. de Ritibus. Bosio nella Trionfante croce.

[120]Decussatio ipsa jucundum ac peramænum conspectum præbuit. *Cart.* Hortar. l. 6.

[121]ὄρχοι, στίχοι ἀμπελῶν, φυτῶν στίχος, ἡ κατὰ τάξιν φυτεία. Phavorinus ὄρχοι, στίχοι ἀμπελῶν, φυτῶν στίχος, ἡ κατὰ τάξιν φυτείαPhiloxenus.

[122]συστάδας ἀμπέλων. Polit. 7.

[123]Indulge ordinibus, nec secius omnis in unguem Arboribus positis, secto via limite quadret. *Georg. 2.*

[124]*Eccles.* 2.

[125]Vet. Testamenti Pharus.

[126]*Which King* Numa *set up with his fingers so disposed that they numerically denoted 365.* Pliny.

CHAPTER II

Nor was this only a form of practise in Plantations, but found imitation from high Antiquity, in sundry artificial contrivances and manual operations. For to omit the position of squared stones, *cuncatim* or *wedgwise* in the walls of *Roman* and *Gothick* buildings; and the *lithostrata* or figured pavements of the ancients, which consisted not all of square stones, but were divided into triquetrous segments, honeycombs, and sexangular figures, according to *Vitruvius*; The squared stones and bricks in ancient fabricks, were placed after this order. And two above or below conjoyned by a middle stone or *Plinthus*, observable in the ruines of *Forum Nervæ*, the *Mausoleum* of *Augustus*, the Pyramid of *Cestius*, and the sculpture draughts of the larger Pyramids of Ægypt. And therefore in the draughts of eminent fabricks, Painters do commonly imitate this order in the lines of their description.

In the Laureat draughts of sculpture and picture, the leaves and foliate works are commonly thus contrived, which is but in imitation of the *Pulvinaria*, and ancient pillow-work, observable in *Ionick* peeces, about columns, temples and altars. To omit many other analogies, in Architectonicall draughts, which art itself is founded upon fives,[127] as having its subject, and most gracefull peeces divided by this number.

The Triumphal Oval, and Civicall Crowns of Laurel, Oake, and Myrtle, when fully made, were pleated after this order. And to omit the Crossed Crowns of Christian Princes; what figure that was which *Anastatius* described upon the head of *Leo* the third; or who first brought in the Arched Crown; That of Charles the great, (which seems the first remarkably closed Crown), was framed after this manner;[128] with an intersection in the middle from the main crossing barres, and the interspaces, unto the frontal circle, continued by handsome network-plates, much after this order. Whereon we shall not insist, because from greater Antiquity, and practice of consecration, we meet with the radiated, and starry Crown, upon the head of *Augustus*, and many succeeding Emperors. Since the Armenians and Parthians had a peculiar royall Capp; And the Grecians from *Alexander* another kinde of diadem. And even Diadems themselves were but fasciations, and handsome ligatures, about the heads of Princes; nor wholly omitted in the mitrall Crown, which common picture seems to set too upright and forward upon the head of *Aaron*: Worne[129] sometimes singly, or doubly by Princes, according to their Kingdomes; and no more to be expected from two Crowns at once, upon the head of *Ptolomy*. And so easily made out when historians tell us, some bound up wounds, some hanged themselves with diadems.

The beds of the antients were corded somewhat after this fashion: That is not directly, as ours at present, but obliquely, from side to side, and after the manner of network; whereby they strengthened the spondæ or bedsides, and spent less cord in the work: as is demonstrated by *Blancanus*.[130]

And as they lay in crossed beds, so they sat upon seeming crosse legg'd seats: in which form the noblest thereof were framed; Observable in the triumphall seats, the *sella curulis*, or *Ædyle Chayres*, in the coyns of *Cestius*, *Sylla*, and *Julius*. That they sat also crosse legg'd many noble draughts declare; and in this figure the sitting gods and goddesses are drawn in medalls and medallions. And beside this kinde of work in Retiarie and hanging tectures, in embroderies, and eminent needle-works; the like is obvious unto every eye in glass-windows. Nor only in Glassie contrivances, but also in Lattice and Stone-work, conceived in the Temple of *Solomon*; wherein the windows are termed *fenestræ reticulatæ*, or lights framed like nets.[131] And agreeable unto the Greek expression concerning Christ in the *Canticles*,[132] looking through the nets, which ours hath rendered, he looketh forth at the windows, shewing himselfe through the lattesse; that is, partly seen and unseen, according to the visible and invisible side of his nature. To omit the noble reticulate work, in the chapters of the pillars of *Solomon*, with Lillies, and Pomegranats upon a network ground; and the *Craticula* or grate through which the ashes fell in the altar of burnt offerings.

That the networks and nets of antiquity were little different in the form from ours at present, is confirmable from the nets in the hands of the Retiarie gladiators, the proper combatants with the secutores. To omit the ancient Conopcion or gnatnet of the Ægyptians, the inventors of that Artifice: the rushey labyrinths of *Theocritus*; the nosegaynets, which hung from the head under the nostrils of Princes; and that uneasie metaphor of *Reticulum Jecoris*, which some expound the lobe, we the caule above the liver. As for that famous network[133] of *Vulcan*, which inclosed *Mars* and *Venus*, and caused that unextinguishable laugh in heaven; since the gods themselves could not discern it, we shall not prie into it; Although why *Vulcan* bound them, *Neptune* loosed them, and *Apollo* should first discover them, might afford no vulgar mythologie. Heralds have not omitted this order or imitation thereof, whiles they Symbollically adorn their Scuchions with Mascles, Fusils and Saltyrs,[134] and while they disposed the figures of Ermins, and vaired coats in this Quincuncial method.

The same is not forgot by Lapidaries while they cut their gemms pyramidally, or by æquicrural triangles. Perspective pictures, in their Base, Horison, and lines of distances, cannot escape these Rhomboidall decussations. Sculptors in their strongest shadows, after this order doe draw their double Haches. And the very *Americans* do naturally fall upon it, in their neat and curious textures, which is also observed in the elegant artifices of *Europe*. But this is no law unto the wool of the neat *Retiarie* Spider, which seems to weave without transversion, and by the union of right lines to make out a continued surface, which is beyond the common art of Textury, and may still nettle *Minerva* the goddesse of that mystery.[135] And he that shall hatch the little seeds, either found in small webs, or white round Egges, carried under the bellies of some Spiders, and behold how at their first production in boxes, they will presently fill the same with their webbs, may observe the early, and untaught finger of nature, and how they are natively provided with a stock, sufficient for such Texture.

The Rurall charm against *Dodder*, *Tetter*, and strangling weeds, was contrived after this order, while they placed a chalked Tile at the four corners, and one in the middle of their fields, which though ridiculous in the intention, was rationall in the contrivance, and a good way to diffuse the magick through all parts of the *Area*.

Somewhat after this manner they ordered the little stones in the old game of *Pentalithismus*, or casting up five stones to catch them on the back of their hand. And with some resemblance hereof, the *Proci* or Prodigal Paramours disposed their men, when they played *Penelope*.[136] For being themselves an hundred and eight, they set fifty four stones on either side, and one in the middle, which they called *Penelope*, which he that hit was Master of the game.

In Chesse-boards and Tables we yet finde Pyramids and Squares, I wish we had their true and ancient description, far different from ours, or the *Chet mat* of the *Persians*, and might continue some elegant remarkables, as being an invention as High as *Hermes* the Secretary of *Osyris*,[137] figuring the whole world, the motion of the Planets, with Eclipses of Sunne and Moon.

Physicians are not without the use of this decussation in several operations, in ligatures and union of dissolved continuities. Mechanicks make use hereof in forcipal Organs, and Instruments of incision; wherein who can but magnifie the power of decussation, inservient to contrary ends, solution and consolidation, union, and division, illustrable from *Aristotle* in the old *Nucifragium* or Nutcraker, and the Instruments of Evulsion, compression or incision; which consisting of two *Vectes* or armes, converted towards each other, the innitency and stresse being made upon the *hypomochlion* or fulciment in the decussation, the greater compression is made by the union of two impulsors.

The *Romane Batalia*[138] was ordered after this manner, whereof as sufficiently known *Virgil* hath left but an hint, and obscure intimation. For thus were the maniples and cohorts of the *Hastiti*, *Principes* and *Triarii* placed in their bodies, wherein consisted the strength of the *Romane battle*. By this Ordination they readily fell into each other; the *Hastati* being pressed, handsomely retired into the intervals of the *principes*, these into that of the *Triarii*, which making as it were a new body, might joyntly renew the battle, wherein consisted the secret of their successes. And therefore it was remarkably singular[139] in the battle of *Africa*, that *Scipio* fearing a rout from the Elephants the Enemy, left not the *Principes* in their alternate distances, whereby the Elephants passing the vacuities of the *Hastati*, might have run upon them, but drew his battle into right order, and leaving the passages bare, defeated the mischief intended by the Elephants. Out of this figure were made two remarkable forms of Battle, the *Cuneus* and *Forceps*, or the Sheare and wedge Battles, each made of half a *Rhombus*, and but differenced by position. The wedge invented to break or worke into a body, the *forceps* to environ and defeat the power thereof composed out of selectest Souldiery and disposed into the form of an V, wherein receiving the wedge, it inclosed it on both sides. After this form the famous *Narses*[140] ordered his battle against the *Franks*, and by this figure the *Almans* were enclosed, and cut in peeces.

The *Rhombus* or Lozenge figure so visible in this order, was also a remarkable form of battle in the *Grecian* Cavalry,[141] observed by the *Thessalians*, and *Philip* King of *Macedon*, and frequently by the *Parthians*, As being most ready to turn every way, and best to be commanded, as having its ductors, or Commanders at each Angle.

The *Macedonian Phalanx* (a long time thought invincible) consisted of a long square. For though they might be sixteen in Rank and file, yet when they shut close, so that the sixt pike advanced before the first, though the number might be square, the figure was oblong, answerable unto the Quincuncial quadrate of *Curtius*. According to this square *Thucydides* delivers, the *Athenians* disposed their battle against the *Lacedemonians* brickwise,[142] and by the same word the Learned *Guellius* expoundeth the quadrat of *Virgil*[143] after the form of a brick or tile.

And as the first station and position of trees, so was the first habitation of men, not in round Cities, as of later foundation; For the form of *Babylon* the first City was square, and so shall also be the last, according to the description of the holy City in the Apocalyps. The famous pillars of *Seth* before the floud had also the like foundation, if they were but *antidiluvian* Obelisks, and such as *Cham* and his *Ægyptian* race, imitated after the Floud.

But *Nineveh* which Authours acknowledge to have exceeded *Babylon*, was of a longilaterall[144] figure, ninety five Furlongs broad, and an hundred and fifty long, and so making about sixty miles in circuit, which is the measure of three dayes journey, according unto military marches, or castrensiall mansions. So that if *Jonas* entred at the narrower side, he found enough for one dayes walk to attain the heart of the City, to make his Proclamation, And if we imagine a City extending from *Ware* to *London*, the expression will be moderate of six score thousand Infants, although we allow vacuities, fields, and intervals of habitation, as there needs must be when the monument of *Ninus* took up no lesse then ten furlongs.

And, though none of the seven wonders, yet a noble peece of Antiquity, and made by a Copy exceeding all the rest, had its principal parts disposed after this manner, that is, the Labyrinth of *Crete*, built upon a long quadrate, containing five large squares, communicating by right inflections, terminating in the centre of the middle square, and lodging of the *Minotaur*, if we conform unto the description of the elegant medal thereof in *Agostino*.[145] And though in many accounts we reckon grosly by the square, yet is that very often to be accepted as a long-sided quadrate which was the figure of the Ark of the Covenant, the table of the Shew-bread, and the stone wherein the names of the twelve Tribes were engraved, that is, three in a row, naturally making a longilateral Figure, the perfect quadrate being made by nine.

What figure the stones themselves maintained, tradition and Scripture are silent, yet Lapidaries in precious stones affect a Table or long square, and in such proportion, that the two laterall, and also the three inferiour Tables are equall unto the superiour, and the angles of the laterall Tables, contain and constitute the *hypothenusæ*, or broder sides subtending.

That the Tables of the Law were of this figure, general imitation and tradition hath confirmed; yet are we unwilling to load the shoulders of *Moses* with such massie stones, as some pictures lay upon them, since 'tis plainly delivered that he came down with them in his hand; since the word strictly taken implies no such massie hewing, but cutting, and fashioning of them into shape and surface; since some will have them Emeralds, and if they were made of the materials of Mount *Sina*, not improbable that they were marble: since the words were not many, the letters short of seven hundred, and the Tables written on both sides required no such capacity.

The beds of the Ancients were different from ours at present, which are almost square, being framed oblong, and about a double unto their breadth; not much unlike the *area*, or bed of this Quincuncial quadrate. The single beds of *Greece* were six foot,[146] and a little more in length, three in breadth; the Giant-like bed of *Og*, which had four cubits of bredth, nine and a half in length, varied not much from this proportion. The Funeral bed of King *Cheops*, in the greater Pyramid, which holds seven in length, and four foot in bredth, had no great deformity from this measure; And whatsoever were the bredth, the length could hardly be lesse, of the tyrannical bed of *Procrustes*, since in a shorter measure he had not been fitted with persons for his cruelty of extension. But the old sepulchral bed, or *Amazonian* Tomb[147] in the market-place of *Megara*, was in the form of a Lozenge; readily made out by the composure of the body. For the armes not lying fasciated or wrapt up after the *Grecian* manner but in a middle distention, the including lines will strictly make out that figure.

Footnotes

[127]*Of a structure five parts*, Fundamentum, parietes, Aperturæ, Compartitio tectum, *Leo. Alberti. Five Columes*, Tuscan, Dorick, Ionick, Corinthian, Compound. *Five different intercolumniations*, Pycnostylos, dystylos, Systylos, Areostylos, Eustylos. *Vitru.*

[128]Uti constat ex pergamena apud Chifflet; in *B. R.* Bruxelli, et Icon. *f.* Stradæ.

[129]Macc, 1. 11.

[130]Aristot. Mechan. Quæst.

[131]δικτυοτά.

[132]*Cant.* 2.

[133]Ἄσβεστος δ' ἄρ' ἐνῶρτο γελως. Hom.

[134]De armis Scaccatis, Masculatis, invectis fuselatis vide Spelm. Aspilog. et Upton. cum erudit. Bissæo.

[135]*As in the contention between* Minerva *and* Arachne.

[136]*In* Eustachius.

[137]Plato.

[138]*In the disposure of the Legions in the Wars of the Republike, before the division of the Legion into ten cohorts by the Emperours.* Salmas. *in his Epistle a Mounsieur de Peyresc. & de Re militari Romanorum.*

[139]Polybius Appianus.

[140]Agathius Ammianus.

[141]Ælian. Tact.

[142]ἐν πλασίω.

[143]Secto via limite quadret. *Comment.* in Virgil.

[144]Diod. Sic.

[145]Antonio Agostino delle medaglie.

[146]Aristot. Mechan.

[147]*Plut.* in vit. Thes.

CHAPTER III

Now although this elegant ordination of vegetables, hath found coincidence or imitation in sundry works of Art, yet is it not also destitute of natural examples, and though overlooked by all, was elegantly observable, in severall works of nature.

Could we satisfie our selves in the position of the lights above, or discover the wisedom of that order so invariably maintained in the fixed Stars of heaven; Could we have any light, why the stellary part of the first masse, separated into this order, that the Girdle of *Orion* should ever maintain its line, and the two Stars in *Charles's* Wain never leave pointing at the Pole-Starre, we might abate the *Pythagoricall* Musick of the Spheres, the sevenfold Pipe of *Pan*; and the strange Cryptography of *Gaffarell* in his Starrie Book of Heaven.

But not to look so high as Heaven or the single Quincunx of the *Hyades* upon the neck of *Taurus*, the Triangle, and remarkable *Crusero* about the foot of the *Centaur*; observable rudiments there are hereof in subterraneous concretions, and bodies in the Earth; in the *Gypsum* or *Talcum Rhomboides*, in the Favaginites or honey-comb-stone, in the *Asteria* and *Astroites*, and in the crucigerous stone of S. *Iago* of *Gallicia*.

The same is observably effected in the *Julus, Catkins*, or pendulous excrescencies of severall Trees, of Wallnuts, Alders, and Hazels, which hanging all the Winter, and maintaining their Network close, by the expansion thereof are the early foretellers of the spring, discoverable also in long Pepper, and elegantly in the *Julus* of *Calamus Aromaticus*, so plentifully growing with us in the first palms of Willowes, and in the flowers of Sycamore, Petasites, Asphodelus, and *Blattaria*, before explication. After such order stand the flowery Branches in our best spread *Verbascum*, and the seeds about the spicous head or torch of *Tapsus Barbatus*, in as fair a regularity as the circular and wreathed order will admit, which advanceth one side of the square, and makes the same Rhomboidall.

In the squamous heads of *Scabious, Knapweed*, and the elegant *Jacea Pinea*, and in the Scaly composure of the Oak-Rose,[148] which some years most aboundeth. After this order hath Nature planted the Leaves in the Head of the common and prickled Artichoak: wherein the black and shining Flies do shelter themselves, when they retire from the purple Flower about it; The same is also found in the pricks, sockets, and impressions of the seeds, in the pulp or bottome thereof; wherein do elegantly stick the Fathers of their Mother. To omit the Quincunciall Specks on the top of the Miscle-berry, especially that which grows upon the *Tilia* or Lime-Tree. And the remarkable disposure of those yellow fringes about the purple Pestill of *Aaron*, and elegant clusters of Dragons, so peculiarly secured by nature, with an *umbrella* or skreening Leaf about them.

The Spongy leaves of some Sea-wracks, Fucus, Oaks, in their several kindes, found about the shoar,[149] with ejectments of the Sea, are overwrought with Net-work *Especially the* porus cervinus Imperati, Sporosa, Alga πλατυκέρως. Bauhini. elegantly containing this order, which plainly declareth the naturality of this texture; And how the needle of nature delighteth to work, even in low and doubtful vegetations.

The *Arbustetum* or Thicket on the head of the Teazell, may be observed in this order: And he that considereth that fabrick so regularly palisadoed, and stemm'd with flowers of the royal colour; in the house of the solitary maggot, may finde the Seraglio of *Solomon*. And contemplating the calicular shafts, and uncous disposure of their extremities, so accommodable unto the office of abstersion, not condemn as wholly improbable the conceit of those who accept it, for the herb *Borith*.[150] Where by the way, we could with much inquiry never discover any transfiguration, in this abstemious insect, although we have kept them long in their proper houses, and boxes. Where some wrapt up in their webbs, have lived upon their own bowels, from *September* unto *July*.

In such a grove doe walk the little creepers about the head of the burre. And such an order is observed in the aculeous prickly plantation, upon the heads of several common thistles, remarkably in the notable palisados about the flower of the milk-thistle; And he that inquireth into the little bottome of the globe-thistle, may finde that gallant bush arise from a scalpe of like disposure.

The white umbrella or medicall bush of Elder, is an Epitome of this order: arising from five main stemms Quincuncially disposed, and tollerably maintained in their subdivisions. To omit the lower observations in the seminal spike of Mercurie weld, and Plantane.

Thus hath nature ranged the flowers of Santfoyne, and French honey suckle; and somewhat after this manner hath ordered the bush in *Jupiters* beard, or house-leek; which old superstition set on the tops of houses, as a defensative against lightening and thunder. The like in Fenny Seagreen or the water Souldier;[151] which, though a military name from Greece, makes out the Roman order.

A like ordination there is in the favaginous Sockets, and Lozenge seeds of the noble flower of the Sunne. Wherein in Lozenge figured boxes nature shuts up the seeds, and balsame which is about them.

But the Firre and Pinetree from their fruits doe naturally dictate this position. The Rhomboidall protuberances in Pineapples maintaining this Quincuncial order unto each other, and each Rhombus in it self. Thus are also disposed the triangular foliations, in the conicall fruit of the firre tree, orderly shadowing and protecting the winged seeds below them.

The like so often occurreth to the curiosity of observers, especially in spicated seeds and flowers, that we shall not need to take in the single Quincunx of Fuchsius in the grouth of the masle fearn, the seedie disposure of Gramen Ischemon, and the trunck or neat Reticulate work in the codde of the Sachell palme.

For even in very many round stalk plants, the leaves are set after a Quintuple ordination, the first leaf answering the fift, in lateral disposition. Wherein the leaves successively rounding the stalk, in foure at the furthest the compasse is absolved, and the fifth leafe or sprout, returns to the position of the other fift before it; as in accounting upward is often observable in furze pellitorye, Ragweed, the sproutes of Oaks, and thorns upon pollards, and very remarkably in the regular disposure of the rugged excrescencies in the yearly shoots of the Pine.

But in square stalked plants, the leaves stand respectively unto each other, either in crosse or decussation to those above or below them, arising at crosse positions; whereby they shadow not each other, and better resist the force of winds, which in a parallel situation, and upon square stalkes would more forcibly bear upon them.

And to omit, how leaves and sprouts which compasse not the stalk, are often set in a Rhomboides, and making long and short Diagonals, do stand like the leggs of Quadrupeds when they goe: Nor to urge the thwart enclosure and furdling of flowers, and blossomes, before explication, as in the multiplied leaves of Pionie; And the Chiasmus in five leaved flowers, while one lies wrapt about the staminous beards, the other foure obliquely shutting and closing upon each other; and how even flowers which consist of foure leaves, stand not ordinarily in three and one, but two, and two crosse wise unto the Stilus; even the Autumnal budds, which awaite the return of the Sun, doe after the winter solstice multiply their calicular leaves, making little Rhombuses, and network figures, as in the Sycamore and Lilac.

The like is discoverable in the original production of plants which first putting forth two leaves, those which succeed, bear not over each other, but shoot, obliquely or crossewise, untill the stalk appeareth; which sendeth not forth its first leaves without all order unto them; and he that from hence can discover in what position the two first leaves did arise, is no ordinary observator.

Where by the way, he that observeth the rudimental spring of seeds, shall finde strict rule, although not after this order. How little is required unto effectual generation, and in what deminutives the plastick principle lodgeth, is exemplified in seeds, wherein the greater mass affords so little comproduction. In beans the leaf and root sprout from the Germen, the main sides split, and lye by, and in some pull'd up near the time of blooming, we have found the pulpous sides intire or little wasted. In Acorns the nebb dilating splitteth the two sides, which sometimes lye whole, when the Oak is sprouted two handfuls. In Lupins these pulpy sides do sometimes arise with the stalk in a resemblance of two fat leaves. Wheat and Rye will grow up, if after they have shot some tender roots, the adhering pulp be taken from them. Beanes will prosper though a part be cut away, and so much set as sufficeth to contain and keep the Germen close. From this superfluous pulp in unkindely, and wet years, may arise that multiplicity of little insects, which infest the Roots and Sprouts of tender Graines and pulses.

In the little nebbe or fructifying principle, the motion is regular, and not transvertible, as to make that ever the leaf, which nature intendeth the root; observable from their conversion, until they attain their right position, if seeds be set inversedly.

In vain we expect the production of plants from different parts of the seed, from the same *corculum* or little original proceed both germinations; and in the power of this slender particle lye many Roots and Spoutings, that though the same be pull'd away, the generative particle will renew them again, and proceed to a perfect plant; And malt may be observed to grow, though the Cummes be fallen from it.

The seminal nebbe hath a defined and single place, and not extended unto both extremes. And therefore many too vulgarly conceive that Barley and Oats grow at both ends; For they arise from one *punctilio* or generative nebbe, and the Speare sliding under the husk, first appeareth nigh the toppe. But in Wheat and Rye being bare the sprouts are seen together. If Barley unhulled would grow, both would appear at once. But in this and Oat-meal the nebbe is broken away, which makes them the milder food, and lesse apt to raise fermentation in Decoctions.

Men taking notice of what is outwardly visible, conceive a sensible priority in the Root. But as they begin from one part, so they seem to start and set out upon one signall of nature. In Beans yet soft, in Pease while they adhere unto the Cod, the rudimentall Leafe and Root are discoverable. In the Seeds of Rocket and Mustard, sprouting in Glasses of water, when the one is manifest the other is also perceptible. In muddy waters apt to breed *Duckweed*, and Periwinkles, if the first and rudimentall stroaks of *Duckweed* be observed, the Leaves and Root anticipate not each other. But in the Date-stone the first sprout is neither root nor leaf distinctly, but both together; For the

Germination being to passe through the narrow navel and hole about the midst of the stone, the generative germ is faine to enlengthen it self, and shooting out about an inch, at that distance divideth into the ascending and descending portion.

And though it be generally thought that Seeds will root at that end, where they adhere to their Originals, and observable it is that the nebbe sets most often next the stalk, as in Grains, Pulses, and most small Seeds, yet is it hardly made out in many greater plants. For in Acornes, Almonds, Pistachios, Wallnuts, and acuminated shells, the germ puts forth at the remotest part of the pulp. And therefore to set Seeds in that posture, wherein the Leaf and Roots may shoot right without contortion, or forced circumvolution, which might render them strongly rooted, and straighter, were a Criticisme in Agriculture. And nature seems to have made some provision hereof in many from their figure, that as they fall from the Tree they may lye in Positions agreeable to such advantages.

Beside the open and visible Testicles of plants, the seminall powers lie in great part invisible, while the Sun findes polypody in stone-wals, the little stinging Nettle, and nightshade in barren sandy High-wayes, *Scurvy-grasse* in *Greeneland*, and unknown plants in earth brought from remote Countries. Beside the known longevity of some Trees, what is the most lasting herb, or seed, seems not easily determinable. Mandrakes upon known account have lived near an hundred yeares. Seeds found in Wilde-Fowls Gizards have sprouted in the earth. The Seeds of Marjorane and *Stramonium* carelessly kept, have grown after seven years. Even in Garden-Plots long fallow, and digged up, the seeds of *Blattaria* and yellow henbane, and after twelve years burial have produced themselves again.

That bodies are first spirits *Paracelsus* could affirm, which in the maturation of Seeds and fruits, seems obscurely implied by [152]*Aristotle*, when he delivereth, that the spirituous parts are converted into water, and the water into earth, and attested by observation in the maturative progresse of Seeds, wherein at first may be discerned a flatuous distention of the husk, afterwards a thin liquor, which longer time digesteth into a pulp or kernell observable in Almonds and large Nuts. And some way answered in the progressionall perfection of animall semination, in its spermaticall maturation, from crude pubescency unto perfection. And even that seeds themselves in their rudimentall discoveries, appear in foliaceous surcles, or sprouts within their coverings, in a diaphanous gellie, before deeper incrassation, is also visibly verified in Cherries, Acorns, Plums.

From seminall considerations, either in reference unto one mother, or distinction from animall production, the holy Scripture describeth the vegetable creation; And while it divideth plants but into Herb and Tree, though it seemeth to make but an accidental division, from magnitude, it tacitely containeth the naturall distinction of vegetables, observed by Herbarists, and comprehending the four kinds. For since the most naturall distinction is made from the production of leaf or stalk, and plants after the two first seminall leaves, do either proceed to send forth more leaves, or a stalk, and the folious and stalky emission distinguisheth herbs and trees, in a large acception it compriseth all Vegetables, for the frutex and suffrutex are under the progression of trees, and stand Authentically differenced, but from the accidents of the stalk.

The Æquivocal production of things under undiscerned principles, makes a large part of generation, though they seem to hold a wide univocacy in their set and certain Originals, while almost every plant breeds its peculiar insect, most a Butterfly, moth or fly, wherein the Oak seemes to contain the largest seminality, while the Julus, Oak, apple, dill, woolly tuft, foraminous roundles upon the leaf, and grapes under ground make a Fly with some difference. The great variety of Flyes lyes in the variety of their Originals, in the Seeds of Caterpillars or Cankers there lyeth not only a Butterfly or Moth, but if they be sterill or untimely cast, their production is often a Fly, which we have also observed from corrupted and mouldred Egges, both of Hens and Fishes; To omit the generation of Bees out of the bodies of dead Heifers, or what is strange yet well attested, the production of Eeles[153] in the backs of living Cods and Perches.

The exiguity and smallnesse of some seeds extending to large productions is one of the magnalities of nature, somewhat illustrating the work of the Creation, and vast production from nothing. The true seeds of Cypresse[154] and Rampions are indistinguishable by old eyes. Of the seeds of Tobacco a thousand make not one grain, The disputed seeds of Harts tongue, and Maidenhair, require a greater number. From such undiscernable seminalities arise spontaneous productions. He that would discern the rudimentall stroak of a plant, may behold it in the Originall of Duckweed, at the bignesse of a pins point, from convenient water in glasses, wherein a watchfull eye may also discover the puncticular Originals of Periwincles and Gnats.

That seeds of some Plants are lesse then any animals, seems of no clear decision; That the biggest of Vegetables exceedeth the biggest of Animals, in full bulk, and all dimensions, admits exception in the Whale, which in length and above ground measure, will also contend with tall Oakes. That the richest odour of plants surpasseth that of Animals, may seem of some doubt, since animall-musk, seems to excell the vegetable, and we finde so noble a scent in the Tulip-Fly, and Goat-Beetle.[155]

Now whether seminall nebbes hold any sure proportion unto seminall enclosures, why the form of the germe doth not answer the figure of the enclosing pulp, why the nebbe is seated upon the solid, and not the channeld side of the seed as in grains, why since we often meet with two yolks in one shell, and sometimes one Egge within another, we do not oftener meet with two nebbes in one distinct seed: why since the Egges of a Hen laid at one course, do commonly outweigh the bird, and some moths coming out of their cases, without assistance of food, will lay so many Egges as to outweigh their bodies, trees rarely bear their fruit, in that gravity or proportion: Whether in the germination of seeds according to *Hippocrates*, the lighter part ascendeth, and maketh the sprout, the heaviest tending downward frameth the root; Since we observe that the first shoot of seeds in water, will sink or bow down at the upper and leafing end: Whether it be not more rational Epicurisme to contrive whole dishes out of the nebbes and spirited particles of plants, then from the Gallatures and treddles of Egges; since that part is found to hold no seminall share in Oval Generation, are quæries which might enlarge but must conclude this digression.

And though not in this order, yet how nature delighteth in this number, and what consent and coordination there is in the leaves and parts of flowers, it cannot escape our observation in no small number of plants. For the calicular or supporting and closing leaves, do answer the number of the flowers, especially in such as exceed not the number of Swallows Egges; as in Violets, Stichwort, Blossomes, and flowers of one leaf have often five divisions, answered by a like number of calicular leaves; as *Gentianella, Convolvulus*, Bell-flowers. In many the flowers, blades, or staminous shoots and leaves are all equally five, as in cockle, mullein and *Blattaria*; Wherein the flowers before explication are pentagonally wrapped up, with some resemblance of the *blatta* or moth from whence it hath its name; But the contrivance of nature is singular in the opening and shutting of Bindeweeds, performed by five inflexures, distinguishable by pyramidicall figures, and also different colours.

The rose at first is thought to have been of five leaves, as it yet groweth wilde among us; but in the most luxuriant, the calicular leaves do still maintain that number. But nothing is more admired then the five Brethren of the Rose, and the strange disposure of the Appendices or Beards, in the calicular leaves thereof, which in despair of resolution is tolerably salved from this contrivance, best ordered and suited for the free closure of them before explication. For those two which are smooth, and of no beard are contrived to lye undermost, as without prominent parts, and fit to be smoothly covered, the other two which are beset with Beards on either side, stand outward and uncovered, but the fifth or half-bearded leaf is covered on the bare side but on the open side stands free, and bearded like the other.

Besides a large number of leaves have five divisions, and may be circumscribed by a *Pentagon* or figure of five Angles, made by right lines from the extremity of their leaves, as in Maple, Vine, Figge-Tree: But five-leaved flowers are commonly disposed circularly about the *Stylus*; according to the higher Geometry of Nature, dividing a circle by five *Radii*, which concurre not to make Diameters, as in Quadrilaterall and sexangular Intersections.

Now the number of five is remarkable in every Circle, not only as the first sphærical Number, but the measure of sphærical motion. For sphærical bodies move by fives, and every globular Figure placed upon a plane, in direct volutation, returns to the first point of contaction in the fift touch, accounting by the Axes of the Diameters or Cardinall points of the four quarters thereof. And before it arriveth unto the same point again, it maketh five circles equall unto it self, in each progresse from those quarters, absolving an equall circle.

By the same number doth nature divide the circle of the Sea-starre, and in that order and number disposeth those elegant Semi-circles, or dentall sockets and egges in the Sea Hedge-hogge. And no mean Observations hereof there is in the Mathematicks of the neatest Retiary Spider, which concluding in fourty four Circles, from five Semidiameters beginneth that elegant texture.

And after this manner doth lay the foundation of the Circular branches of the Oak, which being five-cornered, in the tender annual sprouts, and manifesting upon incision the signature of a Starre, is after made circular, and swel'd into a round body: Which practice of nature is become a point of art, and makes two Problemes in *Euclide*.[156] But the Bryar which sends forth shoots and prickles from its angles, maintains its pentagonall figure, and the unobserved signature of a handsome porch within it. To omit the five small buttons dividing the Circle of the Ivy-berry, and the five characters in the Winter stalk of the Walnut, with many other Observables, which cannot escape the eyes of signal discerners; Such as know where to finde *Ajax* his name in *Gallitricum*, or *Arons* Mitre in Henbane.

Quincuncial forms and ordinations are also observable in animal figurations. For to omit the hioides or throat bone of animals, the *furcula* or *merry-thought* in birds; which supporteth the *scapulæ*, affording a passage for the winde-pipe and the gullet, the wings of Flyes, and disposure of their legges in their first formation from maggots, and the position of their horns, wings and legges, in their *Aurelian* cases and swadling clouts: The back of the *Cimex Arboreus*, found often upon Trees and lesser plants, doth elegantly discover the *Burgundian* decussation; And the like is observable in the belly of the *Notonecton*, or water-Beetle, which swimmeth on its back, and the handsome Rhombusses of the Sea-poult, or Weazell, on either side the Spine.

The sexangular Cels in the Honey-combs of Bees are disposed after this order, much there is not of wonder in the confused Houses of Pismires; though much in their busie life and actions, more in the edificial Palaces of Bees and Monarchical spirits; who make their combs six-corner'd, declining a circle, whereof many stand not close together, and compleatly fill the *area* of the place; But rather affecting a six-sided figure, whereby every cell affords a common side unto six more, and also a fit receptacle for the Bee it self, which gathering into a Cylindrical Figure, aptly enters its sexangular house, more nearly approaching a circular figure, then either doth the Square or Triangle. And the Combes themselves so regularly contrived, that their mutual intersections make three Lozenges at the bottom of every Cell; which severally regarded make three Rows of neat Rhomboidall Figures, connected at the angles, and so continue three several chaines throughout the whole comb.

As for the *Favago* found commonly on the Sea-shoar, though named from an honey-comb, it but rudely makes out the resemblance, and better agrees with the round Cels of humble Bees. He that would exactly discern the shop of a Bees mouth, need observing eyes, and good augmenting glasses; wherein is discoverable one of the neatest peeces in nature, and must have a more piercing eye then mine; who findes out the shape of Buls heads, in the guts of Drones pressed out behinde, according to the experiment of *Gomesius*[157]; wherein notwithstanding there seemeth somewhat which might incline a pliant fancy to credulity of similitude.

A resemblance hereof there is in the orderly and rarely disposed Cels, made by Flyes and Insects, which we have often found fastened about small sprigs, and in those cottonary and woolly pillows, which sometimes we meet with fastened unto Leaves, there is included an elegant Net-work Texture, out of which come many small Flies. And some resemblance there is of this order in the Egges of some Butterflies and moths, as they stick upon leaves, and other substances; which being dropped from behinde, nor directed by the eye, doth neatly declare how nature Geometrizeth, and observeth order in all things.

A like correspondency in figure is found in the skins and outward teguments of animals, whereof a regardable part are beautiful by this texture. As the backs of several Snakes and Serpents, elegantly remarkable in the *Aspis*, and the Dart-snake, in the Chiasmus, and larger decussations upon the back of the Rattlesnake, and in the close and finer texture of the *Mater formicarum*, or snake that delights in Anthils; whereby upon approach of outward injuries, they can raise a thicker Phalanx on their backs, and handsomely contrive themselves into all kindes of flexures: Whereas their bellies are commonly covered with smooth semicircular divisions, as best accommodable unto their quick and gliding motion.

This way is followed by nature in the peculiar and remarkable tayl of the Bever, wherein the scaly particles are disposed, somewhat after this order, which is the plainest resolution of the wonder of *Bellonius*, while he saith, with incredible Artifice hath Nature framed the tayl or Oar of the Bever: where by the way we cannot but wish a model of their houses, so much extolled by some Describers: wherein since they are so bold as to venture upon three stages, we might examine their Artifice in the contignations, the rule and order in the compartitions; or whether that magnified structure be any more then a rude rectangular pyle or meer hovell-building.

Thus works the hand of nature in the feathery plantation about birds. Observable in the skins of the breast,[158] legs and Pinions of Turkies, Geese, and Ducks, and the Oars or finny feet of Water-Fowl: And such a naturall net is the scaly covering of Fishes, of Mullets, Carps, Tenches, *etc.* even in such as are excoriable and consist of smaller scales, as Bretts, Soals, and Flounders. The like Reticulate grain is observable in some *Russia* Leather. To omit the ruder Figures of the ostracion, the triangular or cunny fish, or the pricks of the Sea-Porcupine.

The same is also observable in some part of the skin of man, in habits of neat texture, and therefore not unaptly compared unto a Net: We shall not affirm that from such grounds, the Ægyptian Embalmers imitated this texture, yet in their linnen folds the same is still observable among their neatest Mummies, in the figures of *Isis* and *Osyris*, and the Tutelary spirits in the Bembine Table. Nor is it to be over-looked how *Orus*, the Hieroglyphick of the world is described in a Net-work covering, from the shoulder to the foot. And (not to enlarge upon the cruciated Character of *Trismegistus*, or handed crosses, so often occurring in the Needles of *Pharaoh*, and Obelisks of Antiquity) the *Statuæ Isiacæ*, Teraphims, and little Idols, found about the Mummies, do make a decussation or *Jacobs* Crosse, with their armes, like that on the head of *Ephraim* and *Manasses*, and this *decussis* is also graphically described between them.

This Reticulate or Net-work was also considerable in the inward parts of man, not only from the first *subtegmen* or warp of his formation, but in the netty *fibres* of the veines and vessels of life; wherein according to common Anatomy the right and transverse *fibres* are decussated by the oblique *fibres*; and so must frame a Reticulate and Quincuncial Figure by their Obliquations, Emphatically extending that Elegant expression of Scripture. Thou hast curiously embroydered me, thou hast wrought me up after the finest way of texture, and as it were with a Needle.

Nor is the same observable only in some parts, but in the whole body of man, which upon the extension of arms and legges, doth make out a square, whose intersection is at the genitals. To omit the phantastical Quincunx, in *Plato* of the first Hermaphrodite or double man, united at the Loynes, which *Jupiter* after divided.

A rudimental resemblance hereof there is in the cruciated and rugged folds of the *Reticulum*, or Net-like Ventricle of ruminating horned animals, which is the second in order, culinarily called the Honey-comb. For many divisions there are in the stomach of severall animals; what number they maintain in the *Scarus* and ruminating Fish, common description, or our own experiment hath made no discovery. But in the Ventricle of *Porpuses* there are three divisions. In many Birds a crop, Gizard, and little receptacle before it; but in Cornigerous animals, which chew the cudd, there are no lesse then four of distinct position and office.

The *Reticulum* by these crossed cels, makes a further digestion, in the dry and exuccous part of the Aliment received from the first Ventricle. For at the bottome of the gullet there is a double Orifice; What is first received at the mouth descendeth into the first and greater stomack, from whence it is returned into the mouth again; and after a fuller mastication, and salivous mixture, what part thereof descendeth again, in a moist and succulent body, it slides down the softer and more permeable Orifice, into the Omasus or third stomack; and from thence conveyed into the fourth, receives its last digestion. The other dry and exuccous part after rumination by the larger and stronger Orifice beareth into the first stomack, from thence into the *Reticulum*, and so progressively into the other divisions. And therefore in Calves newly calved, there is little or no use of the two first Ventricles, for the milk and liquid aliment slippeth down the softer Orifice, into the third stomack; where making little or no stay, it passeth into the fourth, the seat of the *Coagulum*, or Runnet, or that division of stomach which seems to bear the name of the whole, in the Greek translation of the Priests Fee, in the Sacrifice of Peace-offerings.

As for those Rhomboidal Figures made by the Cartilagineous parts of the Wezon, in the Lungs of great Fishes, and other animals, as *Rondeletius* discovered, we have not found them so to answer our Figure as to be drawn into illustration; Something we expected in the more discernable texture of the lungs of frogs, which notwithstanding being but two curious bladders not weighing above a grain, we found interwoven with veins, not observing any just order. More orderly situated are those cretaceous and chalky concretions found sometimes in the bignesse of a small fech on either side their spine; which being not agreeable unto our order, nor yet observed by any, we shall not here discourse on.

But had we found a better account and tolerable Anatomy of that prominent jowle of the *Sperma Ceti* Whale,[159] then questuary operation, or the stench of the last cast upon our shoar, permitted, we might have perhaps discovered some handsome order in those Net-like seases and sockets, made like honey-combs, containing that medicall matter.

Lastly, The incession or locall motion of animals is made with analogy unto this figure, by decussative diametrals, Quincunciall Lines and angles. For to omit the enquiry how Butterflies and breezes move their four wings, how birds and fishes in ayre and water move by joynt stroaks of opposite wings and Finnes, and how salient animals in jumping forward seem to arise and fall upon a square base; As the station of most Quadrupeds is made upon a long square, so in their motion they make a Rhomboides; their common progression being performed Diametrally, by decussation and crosse advancement of their legges, which not observed begot that remarkable absurdity in the position of the legges of *Castors* horse in the Capitoll. The Snake which moveth circularly makes his spires in like order, the convex and concave spirals answering each other at alternate distances; In the motion of man the armes and legges observe this thwarting position, but the legges alone do move Quincuncially by single angles with some resemblance of an V measured by successive advancement from each foot, and the angle of indenture great or lesse, according to the extent or brevity of the stride.

Studious Observators may discover more analogies in the orderly book of nature, and cannot escape the Elegancy of her hand in other correspondencies. The Figures of nails and crucifying appurtenances, are but precariously made out in the *Granadilla* or flower of Christs passion; And we despair to behold in these parts that handsome draught of crucifixion in the fruit of the *Barbado* Pine. The seminal Spike of *Phalaris*, or great shaking grasse, more nearly answers the tayl of a Rattle-Snake, then many resemblances in Porta: And if the man *Orchis*[160] of *Culumna* be well made out, it excelleth all analogies. In young Wall-nuts cut athwart, it is not hard to apprehend strange characters; and in those of somewhat elder growth, handsome ornamental draughts about a plain crosse. In the root of *Osmond* or Water-fern, every eye may discern the form of a Half Moon, Rain-bow, or half the character of *Pisces*. Some finde Hebrew, Arabick, Greek, and Latine Characters in Plants; In a common one among us we seem to read *Acaia, Viviu, Lilil*.

Right lines and circles make out the bulk of plants; In the parts thereof we finde Helicall or spirall roundles, voluta's, conicall Sections, circular Pyramids, and frustums of *Archimedes*; And cannot overlook the orderly hand of nature, in the alternate succession of the flat and narrower sides in the tender shoots of the Ashe, or the regular inequality of bignesse in the five leaved flowers of Henbane, and something like in the calicular leaves of *Tutson*. How the spots of *Persicaria* do manifest themselves between the sixth and tenth ribbe. How the triangular capp in the stemme or *stylus* of Tuleps doth constantly point at three outward leaves. That spicated flowers do open first at the stalk. That white flowers have yellow thrums or knops. That the nebbe of Beans and Pease do all look downward, and so presse not upon each other; And how the seeds of many pappous or downy flowers lockt up in sockets after a gomphosis or *mortis*-articulation, diffuse themselves circularly into branches of rare order, observable in *Tragopogan* or Goats-beard, conformable to the Spiders web, and the *Radii* in like manner telarely inter-woven.

And how in animall natures, even colours hold correspondencies, and mutuall correlations. That the colour of the Caterpillar will shew again in the Butterfly, with some latitude is allowable. Though the regular spots in their wings seem but a mealie adhesion, and such as may be wiped away, yet since they come in this variety, out of their cases, there must be regular pores in those parts and membranes, defining such Exudations.

That *Augustus*[161] had native notes on his body and belly, after the order and number in the Starre of *Charles wayne*, will not seem strange unto astral Physiognomy, which accordingly considereth moles in the body of man, or Physicall Observators, who from the position of moles in the face, reduce them to rule and correspondency in other parts. Whether after the like method medicall conjecture may not be raised, upon parts inwardly affected; since parts about the lips are the criticall seats of Pustules discharged in Agues; And scrophulous tumours about the neck do so often speak the like about the Mesentery, may also be considered.

The russet neck in young Lambs seems but adventitious, and may owe its tincture to some contaction in the womb; But that if sheep have any black or deep russet in their faces, they want not the same about their legges and feet; That black Hounds have mealy months and feet; That black Cows which have any white in their tayls, should not misse of some in their bellies; and if all white in their bodies, yet if black-mouth'd, their ears and feet maintain the same colour, are correspondent tinctures not ordinarily failing in nature, which easily unites the accidents of extremities, since in some generations she transmutes the parts themselves, while in the *Aurelian Metamorphosis* the head of the canker becomes the Tayl of the Butterfly. Which is in some way not beyond the contrivance of Art, in submersions and Inlays, inverting the extremes of the plant, and fetching the root from the top, and also imitated in handsome columnary work, in the inversion of the extremes; wherein the Capitel, and the Base, hold such near correspondency.

In the motive parts of animals may be discovered mutuall proportions; not only in those of Quadrupeds, but in the thigh-bone, legge, foot-bone, and claws of Birds. The legs of Spiders are made after a sesquitertian proportion, and the long legs of some locusts, double unto some others. But the internodial parts of Vegetables, or spaces between the joints, are contrived with more uncertainty; though the joints themselves in many Plants, maintain a regular number.

In vegetable composure, the unition of prominent parts seems most to answer the *Apophyses* or processes of Animall bones, whereof they are the produced parts or prominent explantations. And though in the parts of plants which are not ordained for motion, we do not expect correspondent Articulations; yet in the setting on of some flowers, and seeds in their sockets, and the lineall commissure of the pulp of severall seeds, may be observed some shadow of the Harmony; some show of the *Gomphosis* or *mortis*-articulation.

As for the *Diarthrosis* or motive Articulation, there is expected little Analogy, though long-stalked leaves doe move by long lines, and have observable motions, yet are they made by outward impulsion, like the motion of pendulous bodies, while the parts themselves are united by some kinde of *symphysis* unto the stock.

But standing Vegetables, void of motive-Articulations, are not without many motions. For beside the motion of vegetation upward, and of radiation unto all quarters, that of contraction, dilatation, inclination, and contortion, is discoverable in many plants. To omit the rose of *Jericho*, the ear of Rye, which moves with change of weather, and the Magical spit, made of no rare plants, which windes before the fire, and rosts the bird without turning.

Even Animals near the Classis of plants, seem to have the most restlesse motions. The Summer-worm of Ponds and plashes makes a long waving motion; the hair-worm seldome lies still. He that would behold a very anomalous motion, may observe it in the Tortile and tiring stroaks of Gnatworms.[162]

Footnotes

[148]Capitula squammata Quercum Bauhini, *whereof though he saith* perraro reperiuntur bis tantum invenimus, *yet we finde them commonly with us and in great numbers.*

[149]Antho. Græc. inter Epigrammata γριφῶδη ἐνδον ἐμῶν μητρὸς λαγονων ἔχω πατέρα.

[150]*Jer.* 2, 22.

[151]Stratiotes.

[152]In met. cum Gabeo.

[153]Schoneveldus de Pisc.

[154]Doctissim. Laurenburg horr.

[155]*The long and tender green* Capricornus *rarely found, we could never meet with but two.*

[156]Elem. *li.* 4.

[157]Gom. de Sale.

[158]*Elegantly conspicuous on the inside of the striped skins of Dive-Fowl, of the cormorant, Goshonder, Weasell, Loon, etc.*

[159]1652. *described in our* Pseudo Epidem. *Edit.* 3.

[160]Orchis Anthropophora, Fabii Columnæ.

[161]Suet. in vit. Aug.

[162]*Found often in some form of redmaggot in the standing waters of Cisterns in the Summer.*

CHAPTER IV

As for the delights, commodities, mysteries, with other concernments of this order, we are unwilling to fly them over, in the short deliveries of *Virgil, Varro,* or others, and shall therefore enlarge with additionall ampliations.

By this position they had a just proportion of Earth, to supply an equality of nourishment. The distance being ordered, thick or thin, according to the magnitude or vigorous attraction of the plant, the goodnesse, leannesse, or propriety of the soyl, and therefore the rule of *Solon*, concerning the territory of *Athens*, not extendible unto all; allowing the distance of six foot unto common Trees, and nine for the Figge and Olive.

They had a due diffusion of their roots on all or both sides, whereby they maintained some proportion to their height, in Trees of large radication. For that they strictly make good their profundeur or depth unto their height, according to common conceit, and that expression of *Virgil*,[163] though confirmable from the plane Tree in *Pliny*, and some few examples, is not to be expected from the generation of Trees almost in any kinde, either of side-spreading or tap-roots: Except we measure them by lateral and opposite diffusions; nor commonly to be found in *minor* or hearby plants; If we except Sea-holly, Liquorish, Sea-rush, and some others.

They had a commodious radiation in their growth; and a due expansion of their branches, for shadow or delight. For trees thickly planted, do runne up in height and branch with no expansion, shooting unequally or short, and thinne upon the neighbouring side. And therefore Trees are inwardly bare, and spring, and leaf from the outward and Sunny side of their branches.

Whereby they also avoided the perill of συνολεθρισμὸς or one tree perishing with another, as it happeneth ofttimes from the sick *effluviums* or entanglements of the roots, falling foul with each other. Observable in Elmes set in hedges, where if one dieth the neighbouring Tree prospereth not long after.

In this situation divided into many intervals and open unto six passages, they had the advantage of a fair perflation from windes, brushing and cleansing their surfaces; relaxing and closing their pores unto due perspiration. For that they afford large *effluviums* perceptible from odours, diffused at great distances, is observable from Onyons out of the Earth; which though dry, and kept until the spring, as they shoot forth large and many leaves, do notably abate of their weight. And mint growing in glasses of water, until it arriveth unto the weight of an ounce, in a shady place, will sometimes exhaust a pound of water.

And as they send forth much, so may they receive somewhat in: For beside the common way and road of reception by the root, there may be a refection and imbibition from without; For gentle showrs refresh plants, though they enter not their roots; And the good and bad *effluviums* of Vegetables, promote or debilitate each other. So *Epithymum* and *Dodder*, rootlesse and out of the ground, maintain themselves upon Thyme, Savory, and plants, whereon they hang. And *Ivy* divided from the root, we have observed to live some years, by the cirrous parts commonly conceived but as tenacles and holdfasts unto it. The stalks of mint cropt from the root stripped from the leaves, and set in *glasses* with the root end upward, and out of the water, we have observed to send forth sprouts and leaves without the aid of roots, and *scordium* to grow in like manner, the leaves set downward in water. To omit severall Sea-plants, which grow on single roots from stones, although in very many there are side-shoots *fibres*, beside the fastening root.

By this open position they were fairly exposed unto the rayes of Moon and Sunne, so considerable in the growth of Vegetables. For though Poplars, Willows, and severall Trees be made to grow about the brinks of *Acharon*, and dark habitations of the dead; Though some plants are content to grow in obscure Wells; wherein also old Elme pumps afford sometimes long bushy sprouts, not observable in any above ground: And large fields of Vegetables are able to maintain their verdure at the bottome and shady part of the Sea; yet the greatest number are not content without the actual rayes of the Sun, but bend, incline, and follow them; As large lists of solisequious and Sun-following plants. And some observe the method of its motion in their own growth and conversion twining towards the West by the South, as Bryony, Hops, Woodbine, and several kindes of Bindeweed, which we shall more admire; when any can tell us, they observe another motion, and Twist by the North at the *Antipodes*. The same plants rooted against an erect North-wall full of holes, will finde a way through them to look upon the Sun. And in tender plants from mustard-seed, sown in the winter, and in a plot of earth placed inwardly against a South-window, the tender stalks of two leaves arose not erect, but bending towards the window, nor looking much higher then the Meridian Sun. And if the pot were turned they would work themselves into their former declinations, making their conversion by the East. That the Leaves of the Olive and some other Trees solstitially turn, and precisely tell us, when the Sun is entred *Cancer*, is scarce expectable in any Climate; and *Theophrastus* warily observes it; Yet somewhat thereof is observable in our own, in the leaves of Willows and Sallows, some weeks after the Solstice. But the great *Convolvulus* or white-flower'd *Bindweed* observes both motions of the Sunne, while the flower twists Æquinoctionally from the left hand to the right according to the daily revolution; The stalk twineth ecliptically from the right to the left, according to the annual conversion.

Some commend the exposure of these orders unto the Western gales, as the most generative and fructifying breath of heaven. But we applaud the Husbandry of *Solomon*, whereto agreeth the doctrine of *Theophrastus*. Arise O North-winde, and blow thou South upon my garden, that the spices thereof may flow out; For the North-winde closing the pores, and shutting up the *effluviums*, when the South doth after open and relax them; the Aromatical gummes do drop, and sweet odours fly actively from them. And if his garden had the same situation, which mapps and charts afford it, on the East side of *Jerusalem*, and having the wall on the West; these were the winds, unto which it was well exposed.

By this way of plantation they encreased the number of their trees, which they lost in *Quaternio's*, and square-orders, which is a commodity insisted on by *Varro*, and one great intent of nature, in this position of flowers and seeds in the elegant formation of plants, and the former Rules observed in naturall and artificiall Figurations.

Whether in this order and one Tree in some measure breaking the cold, and pinching gusts of windes from the other, trees will not better maintain their inward circles, and either escape or moderate their excentricities, may also be considered. For the circles in Trees are naturally concentricall, parallel unto the bark, and unto each other, till frost and piercing windes contract and close them on the weatherside, the opposite semi-circle widely enlarging, and at a comely distance, which hindreth oftentimes the beauty and roundnesse of Trees, and makes the Timber lesse serviceable; whiles the ascending juyce not readily passing, settles in knots and inequalities. And therefore it is no new course of Agriculture, to observe the native position of Trees according to North and South in their transplantations.

The same is also observable underground in the circinations and sphærical rounds of Onyons, wherein the circles of the Orbes are ofttimes larger, and the meridionall lines stand wider upon one side then the other. And where the largenesse will make up the number of planetical Orbes, that of *Luna*, and the lower planets excede the dimensions of *Saturne*, and the higher: Whether the like be not verified in the Circles of the large roots of Briony and Mandrake, or why in the knotts of Deale or Firre the Circles are often eccentrical, although not in a plane, but vertical and right position, deserves a further enquiry.

Whether there be not some irregularity of roundnesse in most plants according to their position? Whether some small compression of pores be not perceptible in parts which stand against the current of waters, as in Reeds, Bull-rushes, and other vegetables toward the streaming quarter, may also be observed, and therefore such as are long and weak, are commonly contrived into a roundnesse of figure, whereby the water presseth lesse, and slippeth more smoothly from them, and even in flags or flat-figured leaves, the greater part obvert their sharper sides unto the current in ditches.

But whether plants which float upon the surface of the water, be for the most part of cooling qualities, those which shoot above it of heating vertues, and why? whether *Sargasso* for many miles floating upon the Western Ocean, or Sea-lettuce, and Phasganium at the bottom of our Seas, make good the like qualities? Why Fenny waters afford the hottest and sweetest plants, as Calamus, Cyperus, and Crowfoot, and mudd cast out of ditches most naturally produceth Arsmart? Why plants so greedy of water so little regard oyl? Why since many seeds contain much oyl within them, they endure it not well without, either in their growth or production? Why since Seeds shoot commonly under ground, and out of the aire, those which are let fall in shallow glasses, upon the surface of the water, will sooner sprout then those at the bottom? And if the water be covered with oyle, those at the bottom will hardly sprout at all, we have not room to conjecture.

Whether Ivy would not lesse offend the Trees in this clean ordination, and well kept paths, might perhaps deserve the question. But this were a quæry only unto some habitations, and little concerning *Cyrus* or the Babylonian territory; wherein by no industry *Harpalus* could make Ivy grow: And *Alexander* hardly found it about those parts to imitate the pomp of *Bacchus*. And though in these Northern Regions we are too much acquainted with one Ivy, we know too little of another, whereby we apprehend not the expressions of Antiquity, the Splenetick[164] medicine of *Galen*, and the Emphasis of the Poet, in the beauty of the white Ivy.[165]

The like concerning the growth of Missetoe, which dependeth not only of the *species*, or kinde of Tree, but much also of the Soil. And therefore common in some places, not readily found in others, frequent in *France*, not so common in *Spain*, and scarce at all in the Territory of *Ferrara*: Nor easily to be found where it is most required upon Oakes, lesse on trees continually verdant. Although in some places the Olive escapeth it not, requiting its detriment, in the delightful view of its red Berries; as *Clusius* observed in *Spain*, and *Bellonius* about *Hierusalem*. But this Parasitical plant suffers nothing to grow upon it, by any way of art; nor could we ever make it grow where nature had not planted it; as we have in vain attempted by inocculation and incision, upon its native or forreign stock, and though there seem nothing improbable in the seed, it hath not succeeded by sation in any manner of ground, wherein we had no reason to despair since we reade of vegetable horns, Linschoten. and how Rams horns will root about *Goa*.

But besides these rural commodities, it cannot be meanly delectable in the variety of Figures, which these orders open, and closed do make. Whilest every inclosure makes a *Rhombus*, the figures obliquely taken a Rhomboides, the intervals bounded with parallel lines, and each intersection built upon a square, affording two Triangles or Pyramids vertically conjoyned; which in the strict Quincuncial order do oppositely make acute and blunt Angles.

And though therein we meet not with right angles, yet every Rhombus containing four Angles equal unto two right, it virtually contains two right in every one. Nor is this strange unto such as observe the natural lines of Trees, and parts disposed in them. For neither in the root doth nature affect this angle, which shooting downward for the stability of the plant, doth best effect the same by Figures of Inclination; Nor in the Branches and stalky leaves, which grow most at acute angles; as declining from their head the root, and diminishing their Angles with their altitude: Verified also in lesser Plants, whereby they better support themselves, and bear not so heavily upon the stalk: So that while near the root they often make an Angle of seventy parts, the sprouts near the top will often come short of thirty. Even in the nerves and master veines of the leaves the acute angle ruleth; the obtuse but seldome found, and in the backward part of the leaf, reflecting and arching about the stalk. But why ofttimes one side of the leaf is unequal unto the other, as in Hazell and Oaks, why on either side the master vein the lesser and derivative channels stand not directly opposite, nor at equal angles, respectively unto the adverse side, but those of one part do often exceed the other, as the Wallnut and many more, deserves another enquiry.

Now if for this order we affect coniferous and tapering Trees, particularly the Cypresse, which grows in a conical figure; we have found a tree not only of great Ornament, but in its Essentials of affinity unto this order. A solid Rhombus being made by the conversion of two Equicrural Cones, as *Archimedes* hath defined. And these were the common Trees about *Babylon*, and the East, whereof the Ark was made; and *Alexander* found no Trees so accommodable to build his Navy;

And this we rather think to be the tree mentioned in the Canticles, which stricter Botanology will hardly allow to be Camphire.

And if delight or ornamentall view invite a comely disposure by circular amputations, as is elegantly performed in Hawthorns; then will they answer the figures made by the conversion of a Rhombus, which maketh two concentrical Circles; the greater circumference being made by the lesser angles, the lesser by the greater.

The Cylindrical figure of trees is virtually contained and latent in this order. A Cylinder or long round being made by the conversion or turning of a Parallelogram, and most handsomely by a long square, which makes an equal, strong, and lasting figure in trees, agreeable unto the body and motive parts of animals, the greatest number of Plants, and almost all roots, though their stalks be angular, and of many corners, which seem not to follow the figure of their Seeds; Since many angular Seeds send forth round stalks, and sphæricall seeds arise from angular spindles, and many rather conform unto their roots, as the round stalks of bulbous Roots, and in tuberous Roots stemmes of like figure. But why since the largest number of Plants maintain a circular Figure, there are so few with teretous or long round leaves; why coniferous Trees are tenuifolious or narrow leafed, why Plants of few or no joynts have commonly round stalks, why the greatest number of hollow stalks are round stalks; or why in this variety of angular stalks the quadrangular most exceedeth, were too long a speculation; Mean while obvious experience may finde, that in Plants of divided leaves above, nature often beginneth circularly in the two first leaves below, while in the singular plant of Ivy, she exerciseth a contrary Geometry, and beginning with angular leaves below, rounds them in the upper branches.

Nor can the rows in this order want delight, as carrying an aspect answerable unto the *dipteros hypœthros*, or double order of columns open above; the opposite ranks of Trees standing like pillars in the *Cavedia* of the Courts of famous buildings, and the *Portico's* of the *Templa subdialia* of old; Somewhat imitating the *Peristylia* or Cloyster buildings, and the *Exedræ* of the Ancients, wherein men discoursed, walked and exercised; For that they derived the rule of Columnes from trees, especially in their proportionall diminutions, is illustrated by *Vitruvius* from the shafts of Firre and Pine. And though the inter-arboration do imitate the *Areostylos*, or thin order, not strictly answering the proportion of intercolumniations; yet in many trees they will not exceed the intermission of the Columnes in the court of the Tabernacle; which being an hundred cubits long, and made up by twenty pillars, will afford no lesse then intervals of five cubits.

Beside, in this kinde of aspect the sight being not diffused but circumscribed between long parallels and the ἐπισκιασμὸς and adumbration from the branches, it frameth a penthouse over the eye, and maketh a quiet vision: And therefore in diffused and open aspects, men hollow their hand above their eye, and make an artificiall brow, whereby they direct the dispersed rayes of sight, and by this shade preserve a moderate light in the chamber of the eye; keeping the *pupilla* plump and fair, and not contracted or shrunk as in light and vagrant vision.

And therefore providence hath arched and paved the great house of the world, with colours of mediocrity, that is, blew and green, above and below the sight, moderately terminating the *acies* of the eye. For most plants, though green above-ground, maintain their original white below it, according to the candour of their seminall pulp, and the rudimental leaves do first appear in that colour; observable in Seeds sprouting in water upon their first foliation. Green seeming to be the first supervenient, or above-ground complexion of Vegetables, separable in many upon ligature or inhumation, as Succory, Endive, Artichoaks, and which is also lost upon fading in the Autumn.

And this is also agreeable unto water it self, the alimental vehicle of plants, which first altereth into this colour; And containing many vegetable seminalities, revealeth their Seeds by greennesse; and therefore soonest expected in rain or standing water, not easily found in distilled or water strongly boiled; wherein the seeds are extinguished by fire and decoction, and therefore last long and pure without such alteration, affording neither uliginous coats, gnatworms, Acari, hairworms, like crude and common water; And therefore most fit for wholsome beverage, and with malt makes Ale and Beer without boyling. What large water-drinkers some Plants are, the Canary-tree and Birches in some Northern Countries, drenching the fields about them do sufficiently demonstrate. How water it self is able to maintain the growth of Vegetables, and without extinction of their generative or medicall vertues; Beside the experiment of *Helmonts* tree, we have found in some which have lived six years in glasses. The seeds of Scurvy-grasse growing in water-pots, have been fruitful in the Land; and *Asarum* after a years space, and once casting its leaves in water in the second leaves, hath handsomely performed its vomiting operation.

Nor are only dark and green colours, but shades and shadows contrived through the great Volume of nature, and trees ordained not only to protect and shadow others, but by their shades and shadowing parts, to preserve and cherish themselves. The whole radiation or branchings shadowing the stock and the root, the leaves, the branches and fruit, too much exposed to the windes and scorching Sunne. The calicular leaves inclose the tender flowers, and the flowers themselves lye wrapt about the seeds, in their rudiment and first formations, which being advanced the flowers fall away; and are therefore contrived in variety of Figures, best satisfying the intention; Handsomely observable in hooded and gaping flowers, and the Butterfly bloomes of leguminous plants, the lower leaf closely involving the rudimental Cod, and the alary or wingy divisions embracing or hanging over it.

But Seeds themselves do lie in perpetual shades, either under the leaf, or shut up in coverings; and such as lye barest, have their husks, skins, and pulps about them, wherein the nebbe and generative particle lyeth moist and secured from the injury of Aire and Sunne. Darknesse and light hold interchangeable dominions, and alternately rule the seminal state of things. Light unto *Pluto*[166] is darknesse unto *Jupiter*. Legions of seminall *Idæa's* lye in their second Chaos and *Orcus* of *Hippocrates*; till putting on the habits of their forms, they shew themselves upon the stage of the world, and open dominion of *Jove*. They that held the Stars of heaven were but rayes and flashing glimpses of the Empyreall light, through holes and perforations of the upper heaven, took of the natural shadows of stars, while according to better discovery the poor Inhabitants of the Moon[167] have but a polary life, and must passe half their dayes in the shadow of that Luminary.

Light that makes things seen, makes some things invisible, were it not for darknesse and the shadow of the earth, the noblest part of the Creation had remained unseen, and the Stars in heaven as invisible as on the fourth day, when they were created above the Horizon, with the Sun, or there was not an eye to behold them. The greatest mystery of Religion is expressed by adumbration, and in the noblest part of Jewish Types, we finde the Cherubims shadowing the Mercy-seat: Life it self is but the shadow of death, and souls departed but the shadows of the living: All things fall under this name. The Sunne it self is but the dark *simulachrum*, and light but the shadow of God.

Lastly, It is no wonder that this Quincunciall order was first and still affected as gratefull unto the Eye: For all things are seen Quincuncially; For at the eye the Pyramidal rayes from the object, receive a decussation, and so strike a second base upon the *Retina* or hinder coat, the proper organ of Vision; wherein the pictures from objects are represented, answerable to the paper, or wall in the dark chamber; after the decussation of the rayes at the hole of the hornycoat, and their refraction upon the Christalline humour, answering the *foramen* of the window, and the *convex* or burning-glasses, which refract the rayes that enter it. And if ancient Anatomy would hold, a like disposure there was of the optick or visual nerves in the brain, wherein Antiquity conceived a concurrence by decussation. And this not only observable in the Laws of direct Vision, but in some part also verified in the reflected rayes of sight. For making the angle of incidence equal to that of reflexion, the visuall ray returneth Quincuncially, and after the form of a V, and the line of reflexion being continued unto the place of vision, there ariseth a semi-decussation which makes the object seen in a perpendicular unto it self, and as farre below the reflectent, as it is from it above, observable in the Sun and Moon beheld in water.

And this is also the law of reflexion in moved bodies and sounds, which though not made by decussation, observe the rule of equality between incidence and reflexion; whereby whispering places are framed by Elliptical arches laid side-wise; where the voice being delivered at the *focus* of one extremity, observing an equality unto the angle of incidence, it will reflect unto the *focus* of the other end, and so escape the ears of the standers in the middle.

A like rule is observed in the reflection of the vocall and sonorous line in Ecchoes, which cannot therefore be heard in all stations. But hapning in woody plantations, by waters, and able to return some words; if reacht by a pleasant and well-dividing voice, there may be heard the softest notes in nature.

And this not only verified in the way of sense, but in animall and intellectual receptions. Things entring upon the intellect by a Pyramid from without, and thence into the memory by another from within, the common decussation being in the understanding as is delivered by *Bovillus*.[168] Whether the intellectual and phantastical lines be not thus rightly disposed, but magnified, diminished, distorted, and ill placed in the Mathematicks of some brains, whereby they have irregular apprehensions of things, perverted notions, conceptions, and incurable hallucinations, were no unpleasant speculation.

And if Ægyptian Philosophy may obtain, the scale of influences was thus disposed, and the geniall spirits of both worlds, do trace their way in ascending and descending Pyramids, mystically apprehended in the Letter X, and the open Bill and stradling Legges of a Stork, which was imitated by that Character.

Of this Figure *Plato* made choice to illustrate the motion of the soul, both of the world and man; while he delivered that God divided the whole conjunction length-wise, according to figure of a Greek X, and then turning it about reflected it into a circle; By the circle implying the uniform motion of the first Orb, and by the right lines, the planetical and various motions within it. And this also with application unto the soul of man, which hath a double aspect, one right, whereby it beholdeth the body, and objects without; another circular and reciprocal, whereby it beholdeth it self. The circle declaring the motion of the indivisible soul, simple, according to the divinity of its nature, and returning into it self; the right lines respecting the motion pertaining unto sense, and vegetation, and the central decussation, the wonderous connexion of the severall faculties conjointly in one substance. And so conjoyned the unity and duality of the soul, and made out the three substances so much considered by him; That is, the indivisible or divine, the divisible or corporeal, and that third, which was the *Systasis* or harmony of those two, in the mystical decussation.

And if that were clearly made out which *Justin Martyr* took for granted, this figure hath had the honour to characterise and notifie our blessed Saviour, as he delivereth in that borrowed expression from *Plato: Decussavit eum in universo*, the hint whereof he would have *Plato* derive from the figure of the brazen Serpent, and to have mistaken the Letter X for T, whereas it is not improbable, he learned these and other mystical expressions in his Learned Observations of Ægypt, where he might obviously behold the Mercurial characters, the handed crosses, and other mysteries not throughly understood in the sacred Letter X, which being derivative from the Stork, one of the ten sacred animals, might be originally Ægyptian, and brought into *Greece* by *Cadmus* of that Countrey.

Footnotes

[163]Quantum vertice ad auras Æthereas, tantum radice ad tartara tendit.
[164]Galen. de med. secundum loc.
[165]Hedera formosior alba.
[166]Lux orco, tenebræ Jovi, tenebræ orco, lux Jovi. *Hippocr.* de diæta.
[167]S. Hevelii Selenographia.
[168]Car. Bovillus de intellectu.

CHAPTER V

To enlarge this contemplation unto all the mysteries and secrets, accommodable unto this number, were inexcusable Pythagorisme, yet cannot omit the ancient conceit of five surnamed the number of justice[169]; as justly dividing between the digits, and hanging in the centre of Nine, described by square numeration, which angularly divided will make the decussated number; and so agreeable unto the Quincunciall Ordination, and rowes divided by Equality, and just *decorum*, in the whole complantation; And might be the Originall of that common game among us, wherein the fifth place is Soveraigne, and carrieth the chief intention. The Ancients wisely instructing youth, even in their recreations unto virtue, that is, early to drive at the middle point and Central Seat of justice.

Nor can we omit how agreeable unto this number an handsome division is made in Trees and Plants, since *Plutarch* and the Ancients have named it the Divisive Number, justly dividing the Entities of the world, many remarkable things in it, and also comprehending the generall[170] division of Vegetables. And he that considers how most blossomes of Trees, and greatest number of Flowers, consist of five Leaves; and therein doth rest the setled rule of nature; So that in those which exceed there is often found, or easily made a variety; may readily discover how nature rests in this number, which is indeed the first rest and pause of numeration in the fingers, the natural Organs thereof. Nor in the division of the feet of perfect animals doth nature exceed this account. And even in the joynts of feet, which in birds are most multiplied, surpasseth not this number; So progressionally making them out in many, that from five in the foreclaw she descendeth unto two in the hindemost. And so in fower feet makes up the number of joynts, in the five fingers or toes of man.

Not to omit the Quintuple Section of a Cone,[171] of handsome practise in Ornamentall Garden-plots, and in some way discoverable in so many works of Nature; In the leaves, fruits, and seeds of Vegetables, and scales of some Fishes, so much considerable in glasses, and the optick doctrine; wherein the learned may consider the Crystalline humour of the eye in the cuttle-fish and *Loligo*.

He that forgets not how Antiquity named this the Conjugall or wedding Number, and made it the Embleme of the most remarkable conjunction, will conceive it duely appliable unto this handsome Oeconomy, and vegetable combination; May hence apprehend the allegoricall sence of that obscure expression of *Hesiod*,[172] and afford no improbable reason why *Plato* admitted his Nuptiall guests by fives, in the kindred of the married[173] couple.

And though a sharper mystery might be implied in the Number of the five wise and foolish Virgins, which were to meet the Bridegroom, yet was the same agreeable unto the Conjugall Number, which ancient Numerists made out by two and three, the first parity and imparity, the active and passive digits, the materiall and formall principles in generative Societies. And not discordant even from the customes of the *Romans*, who admitted but five[174] Torches in their Nuptiall Solemnities. Whether there were any mystery or not implied, the most generative animals were created on this day, and had accordingly the largest benediction; And under a Quintuple consideration, wanton Antiquity considered the Circumstances of generation, while by this number of five they naturally divided the Nectar of the fifth Planet.

The same number in the Hebrew Mysteries and Cabalistical Accounts was the Character[175] of Generation; declared by the Letter *He*, the fifth in their Alphabet; According to that Cabalisticall *Dogma*: If *Abram* had not had this Letter added unto his Name, he had remained fruitlesse, and without the power of Generation: Not onely because hereby the number of his Name attained two hundred fourty eight, the number of the affirmative precepts, but because as in created natures there is a male and female, so in divine and intelligent productions, the mother of Life and Fountain of souls in Cabalisticall Technology is called *Binah*; whose Seal and Character was *He*. So that being sterill before, he received the power of generation from that measure and mansion in the Archetype; and was made conformable unto *Binah*. And upon such involved considerations, the ten[176] of *Sarai* was exchanged into five. If any shall look upon this as a stable number, and fitly appropriable unto Trees, as Bodies of Rest and Station, he hath herein a great Foundation in nature, who observing much variety in legges and motive Organs of Animals, as two, four, six, eight, twelve, fourteen, and more, hath passed over five and ten, and assigned them unto none.[177] And for the stability of this Number, he shall not want the sphericity of its nature, which multiplied in it self, will return into its own denomination, and bring up the reare of the account. Which is also one of the Numbers that makes up the mysticall Name of God, which consisting of Letters denoting all the sphæricall Numbers, ten, five, and six; Emphatically sets forth the notion of *Trismegistus*, and that intelligible Sphear which is the Nature of God.

Many Expressions by this Number occurre in Holy Scripture, perhaps unjustly laden with mysticall Expositions, and little concerning our order. That the Israelites were forbidden to eat the fruit of their new planted Trees, before the fifth yeare, was very agreeable unto the naturall Rules of Husbandry; Fruits being unwholsome, and lash, before the fourth, or fifth Yeare. In the second day or Feminine part of five, there was added no approbation. For in the third or masculine day, the same is twice repeated; and a double benediction inclosed both Creations, whereof the one in some part was but an accomplishment of the other. That the Trespasser[178] was to pay a fifth part above the head or principall, makes no secret in this Number, and implied no more then one part above the principall; which being considered in four parts, the additionall forfeit must bear the

Name of a fift. The five golden mice had plainly their determination from the number of the Princes; That five should put to flight an hundred might have nothing mystically implyed; considering a rank of Souldiers could scarce consist of a lesser number. Saint *Paul* had rather speak five words in a known then ten thousand in an unknown tongue: That is as little as could well be spoken. A simple proposition consisting of three words, and a complexed one, not ordinarily short of five.

More considerable there are in this mysticall account, which we must not insist on. And therefore why the radicall Letters in the Pentateuch should equall the number of the Souldiery of the Tribes; Why our Saviour in the Wildernesse fed five thousand persons with five Barley Loaves, and again, but four thousand with no lesse then seven of Wheat? Why *Joseph* designed five changes of Rayment unto *Benjamin*? and *David* took just five pibbles[179] out of the Brook against the Pagan Champion? We leave it unto Arithmeticall Divinity, and Theologicall explanation.

Yet if any delight in new Problemes, or think it worth the enquiry, whether the Criticall Physician hath rightly hit the nominall notation of Quinque; Why the Ancients mixed five or three but not four parts of water unto their Wine: And *Hippocrates* observed a fifth proportion in the mixture of water with milk, as in *Dysenteries* and bloudy fluxes. Under what abstruse foundation Astrologers do figure the good or bad Fate from our Children, in good Fortune,[180] or the fifth house of their Celestial Schemes. Whether the Ægyptians described a Starre by a Figure of five points, with reference unto the five[181] Capitall aspects, whereby they transmit their Influences, or abstruser Considerations? Why the Cabalisticall Doctors, who conceive the whole *Sephiroth*, or divine Emanations to have guided the ten-stringed Harp of *David*, whereby he pacified the evil spirit of *Saul*, in strict numeration doe begin with the Perihypate Meson, or ff fa ut, and so place the Tiphereth answering C sol fa ut, upon the fifth string: Or whether this number be oftner applied unto bad things and ends, then good in holy Scripture, and why? He may meet with abstrusities of no ready resolution.

If any shall question the rationality of that Magick, in the cure of the blinde man by *Serapis*, commanded to place five fingers on his Altar, and then his hand on his Eyes? Why since the whole Comœdy is primarily and naturally comprised in four[182] parts; and Antiquity permitted not so many persons to speak in one Scene, yet would not comprehend the same in more or lesse then five acts? Why amongst Sea-starres nature chiefly delighteth in five points? And since there are found some of no fewer then twelve, and some of seven and nine, there are few or none discovered of six or eight? If any shall enquire why the Flowers of Rue properly consist of four Leaves, The first and third Flower have five? Why since many Flowers have one leaf or none,[183] as *Scaliger* will have it, diverse three, and the greatest number consist of five divided from their bottomes; there are yet so few of two: or why nature generally beginning or setting out with two opposite leaves at the Root, doth so seldome conclude with that order and number at the Flower? he shall not passe his hours in vulgar speculations.

If any shall further quæry why magneticall Philosophy excludeth decussations, and needles transversly placed do naturally distract their verticities. Why Geomancers do imitate the Quintuple Figure, in their Mother Characters of Acquisition and Amission, *etc.* somewhat answering the Figures in the Lady or speckled Beetle? With what Equity, Chiromantical conjecturers decry these decussations in the Lines and Mounts of the hand? What that decussated Figure intendeth in the medall of *Alexander* the Great? Why the Goddesses sit commonly crosse-legged in ancient draughts, Since *Juno* is described in the same as a venefical posture to hinder the birth of *Hercules*? If any shall doubt why at the Amphidromicall Feasts, on the fifth day after the Childe was born, presents were sent from friends, of *Polipusses*, and Cuttle fishes? Why five must be only left in that Symbolicall mutiny among the men of *Cadmus*? Why *Proteus* in *Homer* the Symbole of the first matter, before he setled himself in the midst of his Sea-Monsters, doth place them out by fives? Why the fifth years Oxe was acceptable Sacrifice unto *Jupiter*? Or why the Noble *Antoninus* in some sence doth call the soul it self a Rhombus? He shall not fall on trite or triviall disquisitions. And these we invent and propose unto acuter enquirers, nauseating crambe verities and questions over-queried. Flat and flexible truths are beat out by every hammer; But *Vulcan* and his whole forge sweat to work out *Achilles* his armour. A large field is yet left unto sharper discerners to enlarge upon this order, to search out the *quaternio's* and figured draughts of this nature, and moderating the study of names, and meer nomenclature of plants, to erect generalities, disclose unobserved proprieties, not only in the vegetable shop, but the whole volume of nature; affording delightfull Truths, confirmable by sense and ocular Observation, which seems to me the surest path, to trace the Labyrinth of truth. For though discursive enquiry and rationall conjecture, may leave handsome gashes and flesh-wounds; yet without conjunction of this expect no mortal or dispatching blows unto errour.

But the Quincunx[184] of Heaven runs low, and 'tis time to close the five ports of knowledge; We are unwilling to spin out our awaking thoughts into the phantasmes of sleep, which often continueth præcogitations; making Cables of Cobwebbes and Wildernesses of handsome Groves. Beside *Hippocrates*[185] hath spoke so little and the Oneirocriticall Masters,[186] have left such frigid Interpretations from plants, that there is little encouragement to dream of Paradise it self. Nor will the sweetest delight of Gardens afford much comfort in sleep; wherein the dulnesse of that sense shakes hands with delectable odours; and though in the Bed[187] of *Cleopatra*, can hardly with any delight raise up the ghost of a Rose.

Night, which Pagan Theology could make the daughter of *Chaos*, affords no advantage to the description of order: Although no lower then that Masse can we derive its Genealogy. All things began in order, so shall they end, and so shall they begin again; according to the ordainer of order and mystical Mathematicks of the City of heaven.

Though *Somnus* in *Homer* be sent to rowse up *Agamemnon*, I finde no such effects in the drowsy approaches of sleep. To keep our eyes open longer were but to act our *Antipodes*. The Huntsmen are up in *America*, and they are already past their first sleep in *Persia*. But who can be drowsie at that howr which freed us from everlasting sleep? or have slumbring thoughts at that time, when sleep it self must end, and as some conjecture all shall awake again?

FINIS
Footnotes

[169]δίκη

.

.

.

...

[170]Δενδρον, Θάμνος, Φρύγανον, Πόα, Arbor, frutex, suffrutex, herba, *and that fifth which comprehendeth the* fungi *and* tubera, *whether to be named* Ἄσχιον *or* γύμνον, *comprehending also* conserva marina salsa, *and Sea-cords, of so many yards length.*

[171]Elleipsis, parabola, Hyperbole, Circulus, Triangulum.

[172]πεμπτας id est nuptias multas. *Rhodig.*

[173]*Plato* de leg. 6.

[174]Plutarch problem. Rom. 1.

[175]Archang. dog. Cabal.

[176]Jod *into* He.

[177]Or very few, as the *Phalangium monstrosum Brasilianum, Clusii et Jac de Laet. Cur. poster. Americæ, Descript.* If perfectly described.

[178]Lev. 6.

[179]τέσσαρα ἕν κε *four and one, or five*. Scalig.

[180]Ἀγαθὴ τυχὴ, *or* bona fortuna *the name of the fifth house.*

[181]*Conjunct, opposite, sextile, trigonal, tetragonal.*

[182]Πρότασις, ἐπίτασις, κατάστασις, καταστροφή.

[183]Unifolium nullifolima.

[184]Hyades *near the Horizon about midnight, at that time.*

[185]De insomniis.

[186]Artemodorus et Apomazar.

[187]*Strewed with roses.*

THE STATIONER TO THE READER

I cannot omit to advertise, that a Book was published not long since, Entituled, *Natures Cabinet Unlockt*, bearing the Name of this Authour: If any man have been benefited thereby this Authour is not so ambitious as to challenge the honour thereof, as having no hand in that Work. To distinguish of true and spurious Peeces was the Originall Criticisme, and some were so handsomely counterfeited, that the Entitled Authours needed not to disclaime them. But since it is so, that either he must write himself, or Others will write for him, I know no better Prevention then to act his own part with lesse intermission of his Pen.

CERTAIN

MISCELLANY

TRACTS.

Written by
***THOMAS BROWN*, K**[t]**,**
and Doctour of Physick;
late of *NORWICH*.
***LONDON*,**
Printed for *Charles Mearne*, and are to be sold
by *Henry Bonwick*, at the *Red Lyon*,
in St. *Paul's* Church-Yard,
MDCLXXXIV.

THE PUBLISHER TO THE READER

The Papers from which these *Tracts* were printed, were, a while since, deliver'd to me by, those worthy persons, the *Lady* and *Son* of the excellent Authour. He himself gave no charge concerning his *Manuscripts*, either for the suppressing or the publishing of them. Yet, seeing he had procured *Transcripts* of them, and had kept those *Copies* by him, it seemeth probable that He designed them for publick use.

Thus much of his Intention being presumed, and many who had tasted of the fruits of his former studies being covetous of more of the like kind; Also these *Tracts* having been perused and much approv'd of by some Judicious and Learned men; I was not unwilling to be instrumental in fitting them for the Press.

To this end, I selected them out of many disordred Papers, and dispos'd them into such a method as They seem'd capable of; beginning first with *Plants*, going on to *Animals*, proceeding farther to things relating to *Men*, and concluding with *matters* of a *various nature*.

Concerning the *Plants*, I did, on purpose, forbear to range them (as some advised) according to their *Tribes* and *Families*; because, by so doing, I should have represented that as a studied and formal work, which is but a Collection of *occasional Essaies*. And, indeed, both this *Tract*, and those which follow, were rather the *diversions* than the *Labours* of his Pen: and, because He did, as it were, drop down his Thoughts of a sudden, in those little spaces of vacancy which he snatch'd from those very many occasions which gave him hourly interruption; If there appears, here and there, any uncorrectness in the style, a small degree of Candour sufficeth to excuse it.

If there be any such errours in the words, I'm sure the Press has not made them fewer; but I do not hold my self oblig'd to answer for That which I could not perfectly govern. However, the matter is not of any great moment: such errours will not mislead a Learned Reader; and He who is not such in some competent degree, is not a fit Peruser of these LETTERS. Such these *Tracts* are; but, for the Persons to whom they were written, I cannot well learn their *Names* from those few obscure marks which the Authour has set at the beginning of them. And these Essaies being *Letters*, as many as take offence at some few familiar things which the Authour hath mixed with them, find fault with decence. Men are not wont to set down Oracles in every line they write to their Acquaintance.

There, still, remain other brief Discourses written by this most Learned and ingenious Authour. Those, also, may come forth, when some of his Friends shall have sufficient leisure; and at such due distance from these Tracts, that They may follow rather than stifle them.

Amongst these Manuscripts there is one which gives a brief Account of all the *Monuments* of the *Cathedral* of *Norwich*. It was written merely for private use: and the Relations of the Authour expect such Justice from those into whose hands some imperfect Copies of it are fallen; that, without their Consent first obtain'd, they forbear the publishing of It.

The truth is, matter equal to the skill of the Antiquary was not, there, afforded: had a fit Subject of that nature offer'd it self, He would scarce have been guilty of an oversight like to that of *Ausonius*, who, in the description of his native City of *Burdeaux*, omitted the two famous Antiquities of it, *Palais de Tutele*, and, *Palais de Galien*.

Concerning the *Authour himself*, I chuse to be silent, though I have had the happiness to have been, for some years, known to him. There is on foot a design of writing his *Life*: and there are, already, some Memorials collected by one of his ancient Friends. Till that work be perfected, the Reader may content himself with these present *Tracts*; all which commending themselves by their *Learning, Curiosity* and *Brevity*, if He be not pleased with them, he seemeth to me to be distemper'd with such a niceness of Imagination as no wise man is concern'd to humour.

THO. TENISON.

OBSERVATIONS
Upon several
PLANTS mention'd in SCRIPTURE.
TRACT I

The Introduction.

SIR,

Though many ordinary Heads run smoothly over the Scripture, yet I must acknowledge, it is one of the hardest Books I ever met with: and therefore well deserveth those numerous Comments, Expositions and Annotations which make up a good part of our Libraries.

However so affected I am therewith, that I wish there had been more of it: and a larger Volume of that Divine Piece which leaveth such welcome impressions, and somewhat more, in the Readers, than the words and sense after it. At least, who would not be glad that many things barely hinted were at large delivered in it? The particulars of the Dispute between the Doctours and our Saviour could not but be welcome to them, who have every word in honour which proceeded from his mouth, or was otherwise delivered by him: and so would be glad to be assured what he wrote with his Finger on the ground: But especially to have a particular of that instructing Narration or Discourse which he made unto the Disciples after his resurrection, where 'tis said: Luke 24. 27. *And beginning at Moses, and all the Prophets, he expounded unto them in all the Scriptures the things concerning himself.*

But to omit Theological obscurities, you must needs observe that most Sciences do seem to have something more nearly to consider in the expressions of the Scripture.

Astronomers find therein the Names but of few Stars, scarce so many as in *Achilles* his *Buckler* in *Homer*, and almost the very same. But in some passages of the Old Testament they think they discover the Zodiacal course of the Sun: and they, also, conceive an Astronomical sense in that elegant expression of S. James Jam. 1. 17. concerning *the father of lights, with whom there is no variableness, neither shadow of turning*: and therein an allowable allusion unto the tropical conversion of the Sun, whereby ensueth a variation of heat, light, and also of shadows from it. But whether the *Stellæ erraticæ*, or wandring Stars in S. *Jude*, may be referr'd to the celestial Planets, or some meteorological wandring Stars, *Ignes fatui, Stellæ cadentes et erraticæ*, or had any allusion unto the Impostour *Barchochebas*, or *Stellæ Filius*, who afterward appeared, and wandred about in the time of *Adrianus*, they leave unto conjecture.

Chirurgions may find their whole Art in that one passage, concerning the Rib which God took out of *Adam*, that is their διαίρεσις in opening the Flesh, ἐξαίρεσις in taking out the Rib, and σύνθεσις in closing and healing the part again.

Rhetoricians and Oratours take singular notice of very many excellent passages, stately metaphors, noble tropes and elegant expressions, not to be found or parallel'd in any other Authour.

Mineralists look earnestly into the twenty eighth of *Job*, take special notice of the early artifice in Brass and Iron under *Tubal-Cain*: And find also mention of Gold, Silver, Brass, Tin, Lead, Iron; beside Refining, Sodering, Dross, Nitre, Saltpits, and in some manner also of Antimony.[188]

Gemmarie Naturalists reade diligently the pretious Stones in the holy City of the *Apocalypse*: examine the Breast-plate of *Aaron*, and various Gemms upon it, and think the second Row the nobler of the four: they wonder to find the Art of Ingravery so ancient upon pretious Stones and Signets; together with the ancient use of Ear-rings and Bracelets. And are pleased to find Pearl, Coral, Amber and Crystal in those sacred Leaves, according to our Translation. And when they often meet with Flints and Marbles, cannot but take notice that there is no mention of the Magnet or Loadstone, which in so many similitudes, comparisons, and allusions, could hardly have been omitted in the Works of *Solomon*: if it were true that he knew either the attractive or directive power thereof, as some have believed.

Navigatours consider the Ark, which was pitched without and within, and could endure the Ocean without Mast or Sails: They take special notice of the twenty seventh of *Ezekiel*; the mighty Traffick and great Navigation of *Tyre*, with particular mention of their Sails, their Masts of Cedar, Oars of Oak, their skilfull Pilots, Mariners and Calkers; as also of the long Voyages of the Fleets of *Solomon*; of *Jehosaphat's* Ships broken at *Ezion-Geber*; of the notable Voyage and Shipwreck of S. *Paul*, so accurately delivered in the *Acts*.

Oneirocritical Diviners apprehend some hints of their knowledge, even from Divine Dreams; while they take notice of the Dreams of *Joseph, Pharaoh, Nebuchadnezzar*, and the Angels on *Jacob's* Ladder; and find, in *Artemidorus* and *Achmetes*, that Ladders signifie Travels, and the Scales thereof Preferment; and that Oxen Lean and Fat naturally denote Scarcity or Plenty, and the successes of Agriculture.

Physiognomists will largely put in from very many passages of Scripture. And when they find in *Aristotle, quibus frons quadrangula, commensurata, fortes, referuntur ad leones*, cannot but take special notice of that expression concerning the Gadites; *mighty men of war, fit for battel, whose faces were as the faces of lyons*.

Geometrical and Architectonical Artists look narrowly upon the description of the Ark, the fabrick of the Temple, and the holy City in the *Apocalypse*.

But the Botanical Artist meets every where with Vegetables, and from the Figg Leaf in *Genesis* to the Star Wormwood in the *Apocalypse*, are variously interspersed expressions from Plants, elegantly advantaging the significancy of the Text: Whereof many being delivered in a Language proper unto *Judæa* and neighbour Countries are imperfectly apprehended by the common Reader, and now doubtfully made out, even by the Jewish Expositour.

And even in those which are confessedly known, the elegancy is often lost in the apprehension of the Reader, unacquainted with such Vegetables, or but nakedly knowing their natures: whereof holding a pertinent apprehension, you cannot pass over such expressions without some doubt or want of satisfaction in your judgment. Hereof we shall onely hint or discourse some few which I could not but take notice of in the reading of holy Scripture.

Many Plants are mention'd in Scripture which are not distinctly known in our Countries, or under such Names in the Original, as they are fain to be rendred by analogy, or by the name of Vegetables of good affinity unto them, and so maintain the textual sense, though in some variation from identity.

The Observations. Kikaion.

1. The Plant which afforded a shade unto *Jonah*,[189] mention'd by the name of Kikaion, and still retained at least marginally in some Translations, to avoid obscurity *Jerome* rendred *Hedera* or Ivy; which notwithstanding (except in its scandent nature) agreed not fully with the other, that is,

to *grow up in a night*, or be consumed with a Worm; Ivy being of no swift growth, little subject unto Worms, and a scarce Plant about *Babylon*.

Hyssope.

2. That Hyssope is taken for that Plant which cleansed the Leper, being a well scented, and very abstersive Simple, may well be admitted; so we be not too confident, that it is strictly the same with our common Hyssope: The Hyssope of those parts differing from that of ours; as *Bellonius* hath observed in the Hyssope which grows in *Judæa*, and the Hyssope of the Wall mention'd in the Works of *Solomon*, no kind of our Hyssope; and may tolerably be taken for some kind of minor Capillary, which best makes out the Antithesis with the Cedar. Nor when we meet with *Libanotis*, is it to be conceived our common Rosemary, which is rather the first kind thereof among several others, used by the Ancients.

Hemlock. Hosea 10. 4. Amos 6. 2.

3. That it must be taken for Hemlock, which is twice so rendred in our Translation, will hardly be made out, otherwise than in the intended sense, and implying some Plant, wherein bitterness or a poisonous quality is considerable.

Paliurus.

4. What *Tremelius* rendreth *Spina*, and the Vulgar Translation *Paliurus*, and others make some kind of *Rhamnus*, is allowable in the sense; and we contend not about the species, since they are known Thorns in those Countries, and in our Fields or Gardens among us: and so common in *Judæa*, that men conclude the thorny Crown of our Saviour was made either of *Paliurus* or *Rhamnus*.

Rubus.

5. Whether the Bush which burnt and consumed not, were properly a *Rubus* or Bramble, was somewhat doubtfull from the Original and some Translations, had not the Evangelist, and S. *Paul* express'd the same by the Greek word Bátos, which from the description of *Dioscorides*, Herbarists accept for *Rubus*; although the same word Bátos expresseth not onely the *Rubus* or kinds of Bramble, but other Thorn-bushes, and the Hipp-briar is also named Κυνοσβάτος, or the Dog-briar or Bramble.

Myrica. Cant. 1. 14.

6. That *Myrica* is rendred, Heath, sounds instructively enough to our ears, who behold that Plant so common in barren Plains among us: But you cannot but take notice that *Erica*, or our Heath is not the same Plant with *Myrica* or Tammarice, described by *Theophrastus* and *Dioscorides*, and which *Bellonius* declareth to grow so plentifully in the Desarts of *Judæa* and *Arabia*.

Cypress. Cant. 1. 14.

7. That the βότρυς τῆς Κύπρου, *botrus Cypri*, or Clusters of Cypress, should have any reference to the Cypress Tree, according to the original *Copher*, or Clusters of the noble Vine of *Cyprus*, which might be planted into *Judæa*, may seem to others allowable in some latitude. But there seeming some noble Odour to be implied in this place, you may probably conceive that the expression drives at the Κύπρος of *Dioscorides*, some oriental kind of *Ligustrum* or *Alcharma*, which *Dioscorides* and *Pliny* mention under the name of Κύπρος and *Cyprus*, and to grow about *Ægypt* and *Ascalon*, producing a sweet and odorate bush of Flowers, and out of which was made the famous *Oleum Cyprinum*.

But why it should be rendred Camphyre your judgment cannot but doubt, who know that our Camphyre was unknown unto the Ancients, and no ingredient into any composition of great Antiquity: that learned men long conceived it a bituminous and fossile Body, and our latest experience discovereth it to be the resinous substance of a Tree, in *Borneo* and *China*; and that the Camphyre that we use is a neat preparation of the same.

Shittah Tree, etc. Isa. 41. 19.

8. When 'tis said in *Isaiah 41. I will plant in the wilderness the Cedar, the Shittah Tree, and the Myrtle and the Oil Tree, I will set in the Desart, the Firre Tree, and the Pine, and the Box Tree*: Though some doubt may be made of the Shittah Tree, yet all these Trees here mentioned being such as are ever green, you will more emphatically apprehend the mercifull meaning of God in this mention of no fading, but always verdant Trees in dry and desart places.

Grapes of Eshcol. Num. 13. 23.

9. *And they cut down a Branch with one cluster of Grapes, and they bare it between two upon a Staff, and they brought Pomegranates and Figgs.* This cluster of Grapes brought upon a Staff by the Spies, was an incredible sight, in *Philo Judæus*,[190] seem'd notable in the eyes of the Israelites, but more wonderfull in our own, who look onely upon Northern Vines. But herein you are like to consider, that the Cluster was thus carefully carried to represent it entire, without bruising or breaking; that this was not one Bunch but an extraordinary Cluster, made up of many depending upon one gross stalk. And however, might be parallel'd with the Eastern Clusters of *Margiana* and *Caramania*, if we allow but half the expressions of *Pliny* and *Strabo*, whereof one would lade a Curry or small Cart; and may be made out by the clusters of the Grapes of *Rhodes* presented unto Duke *Radzivil*,[191] each containing three parts of an Ell in compass, and the Grapes as big as Prunes.

Ingred. of holy Perfume. Stacte, etc. Exod. 30.34, 35.

10. Some things may be doubted in the species of the holy Ointment and Perfume. With Amber, Musk and Civet we meet not in the Scripture, nor any Odours from Animals; except we take the Onycha of that Perfume for the Coverclé of a Shell-fish called *Unguis Odoratus*, or *Blatta Byzantina*, which *Dioscorides* affirmeth to be taken from a Shell-fish of the Indian Lakes, which feeding upon the Aromatical Plants is gathered when the Lakes are drie. But whether that which we now call *Blatta Byzantina*, or *Unguis Odoratus*, be the same with that odorate one of Antiquity, great doubt may be made; since *Dioscorides* saith it smelled like *Castoreum*, and that which we now have is of an ungratefull odour.

No little doubt may be also made of Galbanum prescribed in the same Perfume, if we take it for Galbanum which is of common use among us, approaching the evil scent of *Assa Fœtida*; and not rather for Galbanum of good odour, as the adjoining words declare, and the original *Chelbena* will bear; which implies a fat or resinous substance, that which is commonly known among us being properly a gummous body and dissoluble also in Water.

The holy Ointment of Stacte or pure Myrrh, distilling from the Plant without expression or firing, of Cinnamon, Cassia and Calamus, containeth less questionable species, if the Cinnamon of the Ancients were the same with ours, or managed after the same manner. For thereof *Dioscorides* made his noble Unguent. And Cinnamon was so highly valued by Princes, that *Cleopatra* carried it unto her Sepulchre with her Jewels; which was also kept in wooden Boxes among the rarities of Kings: and was of such a lasting nature, that at his composing of Treacle for the Emperor *Severus*, *Galen* made use of some which had been laid up by *Adrianus*.

Husks eaten by the Prodigal. Luke 15. 16.

11. That the Prodigal Son desired *to eat of Husks* given unto Swine, will hardly pass in your apprehension for the Husks of Pease, Beans, or such edulious Pulses; as well understanding that the textual word Κεράτιον or *Ceration*, properly intendeth the Fruit of the *Siliqua* Tree so common in *Syria*, and fed upon by Men and Beasts; called also by some the Fruit of the Locust Tree, and *Panis Sancti Johannis*, as conceiving it to have been part of the Diet of the *Baptist* in the Desart. The Tree and Fruit is not onely common in *Syria* and the Eastern parts, but also well known in *Apuglia*, and the Kingdom of *Naples*, growing along the *Via Appia*, from *Fundi* unto *Mola*; the hard Cods or Husks making a rattling noise in windy weather, by beating against one another: called by the Italians *Carobe* or *Carobole*, and by the French *Carouges*. With the sweet Pulp hereof some conceive that the Indians preserve Ginger, Mirabolans and Nutmegs. Of the same (as *Pliny* delivers) the Ancients made one kind of Wine, strongly expressing the Juice thereof; and so they might after give the expressed and less usefull part of the Cods, and remaining Pulp unto their Swine: which being no gustless or unsatisfying Offal, might be well desired by the Prodigal in his hunger.

Cucumbers etc. *of Ægypt.*

12. No marvel it is that the Israelites having lived long in a well watred Country, and been acquainted with the noble Water of *Nilus*, should complain for Water in the dry and barren Wilderness. More remarkable it seems that they should extoll and linger after the Cucumbers and Leeks, Onions and Garlick in *Ægypt*: wherein notwithstanding lies a pertinent expression of the Diet of that Country in ancient times, even as high as the building of the Pyramids,

when *Herodotus* delivereth, that so many Talents were spent in Onions and Garlick, for the Food of Labourers and Artificers; and is also answerable unto their present plentifull Diet in Cucumbers, and the great varieties thereof, as testified by *Prosper Alpinus*, who spent many years in *Ægypt*.

Forbidden Fruit. Gen. 2. 17. etc.

13. What Fruit that was which our first Parents tasted in Paradise, from the disputes of learned men seems yet indeterminable. More clear it is that they cover'd their nakedness or secret parts with Figg Leaves; which when I reade, I cannot but call to mind the several considerations which Antiquity had of the Figg Tree, in reference unto those parts, particularly how Figg Leaves by sundry Authours are described to have some resemblance unto the Genitals, and so were aptly formed for such contection of those parts; how also in that famous Statua of *Praxiteles*, concerning *Alexander* and *Bucephalus*, the Secret Parts are veil'd with Figg Leaves; how this Tree was sacred unto *Priapus*, and how the Diseases of the Secret Parts have derived their Name from Figgs.

Balsam. Oil. Luke 10. 34.

14. That the good Samaritan coming from *Jericho* used any of the Judean Balsam upon the wounded Traveller, is not to be made out, and we are unwilling to disparage his charitable Surgery in pouring Oil into a green Wound; and therefore when 'tis said he used Oil and Wine, may rather conceive that he made an *Oinelæum* or medicine of Oil and Wine beaten up and mixed together, which was no improper Medicine, and is an Art now lately studied by some so to incorporate Wine and Oil that they may lastingly hold together, which some pretend to have, and call it *Oleum Samaritanum*, or Samaritans Oil.

Pulse of Daniel. Dan. 1. 12.

15. When *Daniel* would not pollute himself with the Diet of the Babylonians, he probably declined Pagan commensation, or to eat of Meats forbidden to the Jews, though common at their Tables, or so much as to taste of their Gentile Immolations, and Sacrifices abominable unto his Palate.

But when 'tis said that he made choice of the Diet of Pulse and Water, whether he strictly confined unto a leguminous Food, according to the Vulgar Translation, some doubt may be raised, from the original word *Zeragnim*, which signifies *Seminalia*, and is so set down in the Margin of *Arias Montanus*; and the Greek word *Spermata*, generally expressing Seeds, may signifie any edulious or cerealious Grains besides ὄσπρια or leguminous Seeds.

Yet if he strictly made choice of a leguminous Food, and Water instead of his portion from the King's Table, he handsomely declined the Diet which might have been put upon him, and particularly that which was called the *Potibasis* of the King, which as *Athenæus* informeth implied the Bread of the King, made of Barley, and Wheat, and the Wine of *Cyprus*, which he drank in an oval Cup. And therefore distinctly from that he chose plain Fare of Water, and the gross Diet of Pulse, and that perhaps not made into Bread, but parched, and tempered with Water.

Now that herein (beside the special benediction of God) he made choice of no improper Diet to keep himself fair and plump and so to excuse the Eunuch his Keeper, Physicians will not deny, who acknowledge a very nutritive and impinguating faculty in Pulses, in leguminous Food, and in several sorts of Grains and Corns, is not like to be doubted by such who consider that this was probably a great part of the Food of our Forefathers before the Floud, the Diet also of *Jacob*: and that the Romans (called therefore *Pultifagi*) fed much on Pulse for six hundred years; that they had no Bakers for that time: and their Pistours were such as, before the use of Mills, beat out and cleansed their Corn. As also that the Athletick Diet was of Pulse, *Alphiton*, *Maza*, Barley and Water; whereby they were advantaged sometimes to an exquisite state of health, and such as was not without danger. And therefore though *Daniel* were no Eunuch, and of a more fatning and thriving temper, as some have phancied, yet was he by this kind of Diet, sufficiently maintained in a fair and carnous state of Body, and accordingly his Picture not improperly drawn, that is, not meagre and lean, like *Jeremy's*, but plump and fair, answerable to the most authentick draught of the *Vatican*, and the late German *Luther's* Bible.

The Cynicks in *Athenæus* make iterated Courses of Lentils, and prefer that Diet before the Luxury of *Seleucus*. The present Ægyptians, who are observed by *Alpinus* to be the fattest Nation, and Men to have breasts like Women, owe much, as he conceiveth, unto the Water of *Nile*, and their Diet of Rice, Pease, Lentils and white Cicers. The Pulse-eating Cynicks and Stoicks, are all very long livers in *Laertius*. And *Daniel* must not be accounted of few years, who, being carried away Captive in the Reign of *Joachim*, by King *Nebuchadnezzar*, lived, by Scripture account, unto the first year of *Cyrus*.

Jacob's *Rods*. Gen. 30. 31.

16. *And Jacob took Rods of green Poplar, and of the Hazel and the Chesnut Tree, and pilled white streaks in them, and made the white appear which was in the Rods*, etc. Men multiply the Philosophy of *Jacob*, who, beside the benediction of God, and the powerfull effects of imagination, raised in the Goats and Sheep from pilled and party-coloured objects, conceive that he chose out these particular Plants above any other, because he understood they had a particular virtue unto the intended effects, according unto the conception of *Georgius Venetus*.[192]

Whereto you will hardly assent, at least till you be better satisfied and assured concerning the true species of the Plants intended in the Text, or find a clearer consent and uniformity in the Translation: For what we render Poplar, Hazel and Chesnut, the Greek translateth *Virgam styracinam, nucinam, plataninam*, which some also render a Pomegranate: and so observing this variety of interpretations concerning common and known Plants among us, you may more reasonably doubt, with what propriety or assurance others less known be sometimes rendred unto us.

Lilies of the Field. Matt. 6. 28.

17. Whether in the Sermon of the Mount, the *Lilies of the Field* did point at the proper Lilies, or whether those Flowers grew wild in the place where our Saviour preached, some doubt may be made: because Κρίνον the word in that place is accounted of the same signification with Λείριον, and that in *Homer* is taken for all manner of specious Flowers: so received by *Eustachius*, *Hesychius*, and the Scholiast upon *Apollonius Rhodius*, Καθόλου τὰ ἄνθη Λείρια λέγεται. And Κρίνον is also received in the same latitude, not signifying onely Lilies, but applied unto Daffodils, Hyacinths, Iris's, and the Flowers of *Colocynthis*.

Under the like latitude of acception, are many expressions in the *Canticles* to be received. And when it is said *he feedeth among the Lilies*, therein may be also implied other specious Flowers, not excluding the proper Lilies. But in that expression, *the Lilies drop forth Myrrhe*, neither proper Lilies nor proper Myrrhe can be apprehended, the one not proceeding from the other, but may be received in a Metaphorical sense: and in some latitude may be also made out from the roscid and honey drops observable in the Flowers of Martagon, and inverted flowred Lilies, and, 'tis like, is the standing sweet Dew on the white eyes of the Crown Imperial, now common among us.

And the proper Lily may be intended in that expression of 1 *Kings* 7. that the brazen Sea was of the thickness of a hand breadth, and the brim like a Lily. For the figure of that Flower being round at the bottom, and somewhat repandous, or inverted at the top, doth handsomely illustrate the comparison.

But that the Lily of the Valley, mention'd in the *Canticles*, Cant. 2. *I am the Rose of Sharon, and the Lily of the Valleys*, is that Vegetable which passeth under the same name with us, that is *Lilium convallium*, or the *May* Lily, you will more hardly believe, who know with what insatisfaction the most learned Botanists reduce that Plant unto any described by the Ancients; that *Anguillara* will have it to be the *Oenanthe* of *Athenæus*, *Cordus* the *Pothos* of *Theophrastus*; and *Lobelius* that the Greeks had not described it; who find not six Leaves in the Flower agreeably to all Lilies, but onely six small divisions in the Flower, who find it also to have a single, and no bulbous Root, nor Leaves shooting about the bottom, nor the Stalk round, but angular. And that the learned *Bauhinus* hath not placed it in the Classis of Lilies, but nervifolious Plants.

Fitches, Cummin, &c. in Isa. 28. 25

18. *Doth he not cast abroad the Fitches, and scatter the Cummin Seed, and cast in the principal Wheat, and the appointed Barley, and the Rye in their place*: Herein though the sense may hold under the names assigned, yet is it not so easie to determine the particular Seeds and Grains, where the obscure original causeth such differing Translations. For in the Vulgar we meet

with *Milium* and Gith, which our Translation declineth, placing Fitches for Gith, and Rye for *Milium* or Millet, which notwithstanding is retained by the Dutch.

That it might be *Melanthium, Nigella*, or Gith, may be allowably apprehended, from the frequent use of the Seed thereof among the Jews and other Nations, as also from the Translation of *Tremellius*; and the Original implying a black Seed, which is less than Cummin, as, out of *Aben Ezra, Buxtorfius* hath expounded it.

But whereas *Milium* or Κέγχρος of the Septuagint is by ours rendred Rye, there is little similitude or affinity between those Grains; For *Milium* is more agreeable unto *Spelta* or Espaut, as the Dutch and others still render it.

That we meet so often with Cummin Seed in many parts of Scripture in reference unto *Judæa*, a Seed so abominable at present unto our Palates and Nostrils, will not seem strange unto any who consider the frequent use thereof among the Ancients, not onely in medical but dietetical use and practice: For their Dishes were filled therewith, and the noblest festival preparations in *Apicius* were not without it: And even in the *Polenta*, and parched Corn, the old Diet of the Romans, (as *Pliny* recordeth) unto every Measure they mixed a small proportion of Lin-seed and Cummin-seed.

And so Cummin is justly set down among things of vulgar and common use, when it is said in *Matthew* 23. v. 23. *You pay Tithe of Mint, Annise and Cummin*: but how to make out the translation of Annise we are still to seek, there being no word in that Text which properly signifieth Annise: the Original being Ἄνηθον, which the Latins call *Anethum*, and is properly englished Dill.

That among many expressions, allusions and illustrations made in Scripture from Corns, there is no mention made of Oats, so usefull a Grain among us, will not seem very strange unto you, till you can clearly discover that it was a Grain of ordinary use in those parts; who may also find that *Theophrastus*, who is large about other Grains, delivers very little of it. That *Dioscorides* is also very short therein. And *Galen* delivers that it was of some use in *Asia minor*, especially in *Mysia*, and that rather for Beasts than Men: And *Pliny* affirmeth that the *Pulticula* thereof was most in use among the Germans. Yet that the Jews were not without all use of this Grain seems confirmable from the Rabbinical account, who reckon five Grains liable unto their Offerings, whereof the Cake presented might be made; that is, Wheat, Oats, Rye, and two sorts of Barley.

Ears of Corn. Matt. 12. 1.

19. Why the Disciples being hungry pluck'd the Ears of Corn, it seems strange to us, who observe that men half starved betake not themselves to such supply; except we consider the ancient Diet of *Alphiton* and *Polenta*, the Meal of dried and parched Corn, or that which was Ὠμήλυσις, or Meal of crude and unparched Corn, wherewith they being well acquainted, might hope for some satisfaction from the Corn yet in the Husk; that is, from the nourishing pulp or mealy part within it.

Stubble of Ægypt Exod. 5.7, etc.

20. The inhumane oppression of the Ægyptian Task-masters, who, not content with the common tale of Brick, took also from the Children of Israel their allowance of *Straw*, and forced them to gather *Stubble* where they could find it, will be more nearly apprehended, if we consider how hard it was to acquire any quantity of Stubble in *Ægypt*, where the Stalk of Corn was so short, that to acquire an ordinary measure, it required more than ordinary labour; as is discoverable from that account, which *Pliny*[193] hath happily left unto us. In the Corn gather'd in *Ægypt* the Straw is never a Cubit long: because the Seed lieth very shallow, and hath no other nourishment than from the Mudd and Slime left by the River; For under it is nothing but Sand and Gravel.

So that the expression of Scripture is more Emphatical than is commonly apprehended, when 'tis said, *The people were scattered abroad through all the Land of Ægypt to gather Stubble instead of Straw*. For the Stubble being very short, the acquist was difficult; a few Fields afforded it not, and they were fain to wander far to obtain a sufficient quantity of it.

Flowers of the Vine. Cant. 2. 13.

21. It is said in the *Song of Solomon*, that *the Vines with the tender Grape give a good smell*. That the Flowers of the Vine should be Emphatically noted to give a pleasant smell, seems hard unto our Northern Nostrils, which discover not such Odours, and smell them not in full Vineyards; whereas in hot Regions, and more spread and digested Flowers, a sweet savour may be allowed,

denotable from several humane expressions, and the practice of the Ancients, in putting the dried Flowers of the Vine into new Wine to give it a pure and flosculous race or spirit, which Wine was therefore called Οἰνάθινον, allowing unto every *Cadus* two pounds of dried Flowers.

And, therefore, the Vine flowering but in the Spring, it cannot but seem an impertinent objection of the Jews, that the Apostles were *full of new Wine* at *Pentecost* when it was not to be found. Wherefore we may rather conceive that the word Γλεύκυ[194] in that place implied not *new Wine* or *Must*, but some generous strong and sweet Wine, wherein more especially lay the power of inebriation.

But if it be to be taken for some kind of *Must*, it might be some kind of Ἀεγίλευκος, or long-lasting *Must*, which might be had at any time of the year, and which, as *Pliny* delivereth, they made by hindring, and keeping the *Must* from fermentation or working, and so it kept soft and sweet for no small time after.

The Olive Leaf in Gen. 8. 11.

22. When the *Dove*, sent out of the Ark, return'd with *a green Olive Leaf*, according to the Original: how the Leaf, after ten Months, and under water, should still maintain a verdure or greenness, need not much amuse the Reader, if we consider that the Olive Tree is Ἀείφυλλον, or continually green; that the Leaves are of a bitter taste, and of a fast and lasting substance. Since we also find fresh and green Leaves among the Olives which we receive from remote Countries; and since the Plants at the bottom of the Sea, and on the sides of Rocks, maintain a deep and fresh verdure.

How the Tree should stand so long in the Deluge under Water, may partly be allowed from the uncertain determination of the Flows and Currents of that time, and the qualification of the saltness of the Sea, by the admixture of fresh Water, when the whole watery Element was together.

And it may be signally illustrated from the like examples in *Theophrastus*[195] and *Pliny*[196] in words to this effect: Even the Sea affordeth Shrubs and Trees; In the red Sea whole Woods do live, namely of Bays and Olives bearing Fruit. The Souldiers of *Alexander*, who sailed into *India*, made report, that the Tides were so high in some Islands, that they overflowed, and covered the Woods, as high as Plane and Poplar Trees. The lower sort wholly, the greater all but the tops, whereto the Mariners fastned their Vessels at high Waters, and at the root in the Ebb; That the Leaves of these Sea Trees while under water looked green, but taken out presently dried with the heat of the Sun. The like is delivered by *Theophrastus*, that some Oaks do grow and bear Acrons under the Sea.

Grain of Mustard-seed in S. Matt 13. 31, 32.

23. *The Kingdom of Heaven is like to a grain of Mustard-seed, which a Man took and sowed in his Field, which indeed is the least of all Seeds; but when 'tis grown is the greatest among Herbs, and becometh a Tree, so that the Birds of the Air come and lodge in the Branches thereof.*

Luke 13. 19. *It is like a grain of Mustard-seed, which a Man took and cast it into his Garden, and it waxed a great Tree, and the Fowls of the Air lodged in the Branches thereof.*

This expression by a grain of Mustard-seed, will not seem so strange unto you, who well consider it. That it is simply the least of Seeds, you cannot apprehend, if you have beheld the Seeds of *Rapunculus*, Marjorane, Tobacco, and the smallest Seed of *Lunaria*.

But you may well understand it to be the smallest Seed among Herbs which produce so big a Plant, or the least of herbal Plants, which arise unto such a proportion, implied in the expression; *the smallest of Seeds*, and *becometh the greatest of Herbs*.

And you may also grant that it is the smallest of Seeds of Plants apt to δενδρίζειν, *arborescere, fruticescere*, or to grow unto a ligneous substance, and from an herby and oleraceous Vegetable, to become a kind of Tree, and to be accounted among the *Dendrolachana*, or *Arboroleracea*; as upon strong Seed, Culture and good Ground, is observable in some Cabbages, Mallows, and many more, and therefore expressed by γίνεται τὸ δένδρον, and γίνεται εἰς τὸν δένδρον, it becometh a Tree, or *arborescit*, as *Beza* rendreth it.

Nor if warily considered doth the expression contain such difficulty. For the Parable may not ground it self upon generals, or imply any or every grain of Mustard, but point at such a grain as from its fertile spirit, and other concurrent advantages, hath the success to become arboreous, shoot into such a magnitude, and acquire the like tallness. And unto such a Grain the Kingdom of Heaven is likened which from such slender beginnings shall find such increase and grandeur.

The expression also that it might grow into such dimensions that Birds might lodge in the Branches thereof, may be literally conceived; if we allow the luxuriancy of plants in *Judæa*, above our Northern Regions; If we accept of but half the Story taken notice of by Tremellius, from the *Jerusalem Talmud*, of a Mustard Tree that was to be climbed like a Figg Tree; and of another, under whose shade a Potter daily wrought: and it may somewhat abate our doubts, if we take in the advertisement of *Herodotus* concerning lesser Plants of *Milium* and *Sesamum* in the Babylonian Soil: *Milium ac Sesamum in proceritatem instar arborum crescere, etsi mihi compertum, tamen memorare supersedeo, probè sciens eis qui nunquam Babyloniam regionem adierunt perquam incredibile visum iri.* We may likewise consider that the word κατασκηνῶσαι doth not necessarily signifie *making a Nest*, but rather sitting, roosting, covering and resting in the Boughs, according as the same word is used by the *Septuagint* in other places[197] as the Vulgar rendreth it in this, *inhabitant*, as our Translation, *lodgeth*, and the Rhemish, *resteth* in the Branches.

The Rod of Aaron. Numb. 17. 8.

24. *And it came to pass that on the morrow Moses went into the Tabernacle of witness, and behold the Rod of Aaron for the House of Levi was budded, and brought forth Buds, and bloomed Blossomes, and yielded Almonds.* In the contention of the Tribes and decision of priority and primogeniture of *Aaron*, declared by the Rod, which in a night budded, flowred and brought forth Almonds, you cannot but apprehend a propriety in the Miracle from that species of Tree which leadeth in the Vernal germination of the year, unto all the Classes of Trees; and so apprehend how properly in a night and short space of time the Miracle arose, and somewhat answerable unto its nature the Flowers and Fruit appeared in this precocious Tree, and whose original Name[198] implies such speedy efflorescence, as in its proper nature flowering in *February*, and shewing its Fruit in *March*.

This consideration of that Tree maketh the expression in *Jeremy* Jer. 1. 11. more Emphatical, when 'tis said, *What seest thou? and he said, A Rod of an Almond Tree. Then said the Lord unto me, Thou hast well seen, for I will hasten the Word to perform it.* I will be quick and forward like the Almond Tree, to produce the effects of my word, and hasten to display my judgments upon them.

And we may hereby more easily apprehend the expression in *Ecclesiastes*, Eccles. 12. 5. *When the Almond Tree shall flourish.* That is when the Head, which is the prime part, and first sheweth it self in the world, shall grow white, like the Flowers of the Almond Tree, whose Fruit, as *Athenæus* delivereth, was first called Κάρηνον, or the Head, from some resemblance and covering parts of it.

How properly the priority was confirmed by a Rod or Staff, and why the Rods and Staffs of the Princes were chosen for this decision, Philologists will consider. For these were the badges, signs and cognisances of their places, and were a kind of Sceptre in their hands, denoting their supereminencies. The Staff of Divinity is ordinarily described in the hands of Gods and Goddesses in old draughts. Trojan and Grecian Princes were not without the like, whereof the Shoulders of *Thersites* felt from the hands of *Ulysses*. *Achilles* in *Homer*, as by a desperate Oath, swears by his wooden Sceptre, which should never bud nor bear Leaves again; which seeming the greatest impossibility to him, advanceth the Miracle of *Aaron's* Rod. And if it could be well made out that *Homer* had seen the Books of *Moses*, in that expression of *Achilles*, he might allude unto this Miracle.

That power which proposed the experiment by Blossomes in the Rod, added also the Fruit of Almonds; the Text not strictly making out the Leaves, and so omitting the middle germination: the Leaves properly coming after the Flowers, and before the Almonds. And therefore if you have well perused Medals, you cannot but observe how in the impress of many Shekels, which pass among us by the name of the *Jerusalem* Shekels, the Rod of *Aaron* is improperly laden with many Leaves, whereas that which is shewn under the name of the Samaritan Shekel seems most conformable unto the Text, which describeth the Fruit without Leaves.

The Vine in Gen. 49. 11.

25. *Binding his Foal unto the Vine, and his Asses Colt unto the choice Vine.*

That Vines, which are commonly supported, should grow so large and bulky, as to be fit to fasten their Juments, and Beasts of labour unto them, may seem a hard expression unto many: which notwithstanding may easily be admitted, if we consider the account of *Pliny*, that in many places out of *Italy* Vines do grow without any stay or support: nor will it be otherwise conceived of lusty Vines, if we call to mind how the same Authour[199] delivereth, that the *Statua* of *Jupiter* was made out of a Vine; and that out of one single Cyprian Vine a Scale or Ladder was made that reached unto the Roof of the Temple of *Diana* at *Ephesus*.

Rose of Jericho. Ecclus. 24. 14.

26. *I was exalted as a Palm Tree in Engaddi, and as a Rose Plant in Jericho.* That the Rose of *Jericho*, or that Plant which passeth among us under that denomination, was signified in this Text, you are not like to apprehend with some, who also name it the *Rose of S. Mary*, and deliver, that it openeth the Branches, and Flowers upon the Eve of our Saviour's Nativity: But rather conceive it some proper kind of Rose, which thrived and prospered in *Jericho* more than in the neighbour Countries. For our Rose of *Jericho* is a very low and hard Plant, a few inches above the ground; one whereof brought from *Judæa* I have kept by me many years, nothing resembling a Rose Tree, either in Flowers, Branches, Leaves or Growth; and so, improper to answer the Emphatical word of exaltation in the Text: growing not only about *Jericho*, but other parts of *Judæa* and *Arabia*, as *Bellonius* hath observed: which being a drie and ligneous Plant, is preserved many years, and though crumpled and furdled up, yet, if infused in Water, will swell and display its parts.

Turpentine Tree in Ecclus. 24. 16.

27. *Quasi Terebinthus extendi ramos*, when it is said in the same Chapter, *as a Turpentine Tree have I stretched out my Branches*: it will not seem strange unto such as have either seen that Tree, or examined its description: For it is a Plant that widely displayeth its Branches: and though in some European Countries it be but of a low and fruticeous growth, yet *Pliny*[200] observeth that it is great in *Syria*, and so allowably, or at least not improperly mentioned in the expression of *Hosea*[201] according to the Vulgar Translation. *Super capita montium sacrificant,* etc. *sub quercu, populo et terebintho, quoniam bona est umbra ejus.* And this diffusion and spreading of its Branches, hath afforded the Proverb of *Terebintho stultior*, applicable unto arrogant or boasting persons, who spread and display their own acts, as *Erasmus* hath observed.

Pomegranate in 1 Sam. 14. 2.

28. It is said in our Translation. *Saul tarried in the uppermost parts of Gibeah, under a Pomegranate Tree which is in Migron: and the people which were with him were about six hundred men.* And when it is said in some Latin Translations, *Saul morabatur fixo tentorio sub Malogranato*, you will not be ready to take in the common literal sense, who know that a Pomegranate Tree is but low of growth, and very unfit to pitch a Tent under it; and may rather apprehend it as the name of a place, or the Rock of *Rimmon*, or Pomegranate; so named from Pomegranates which grew there, and which many think to have been the same place mentioned in *Judges*.[202]

A Green Field in Wisd. 19. 7.

29. It is said in the Book of *Wisedom, Where water stood before, drie land appeared, and out of the red Sea a way appeared without impediment, and out of the violent streams a green Field*; or as the Latin renders it, *Campus germinans de profundo*: whereby it seems implied that the Israelites passed over a green Field at the bottom of the Sea: and though most would have this but a Metaphorical expression, yet may it be literally tolerable; and so may be safely apprehended by those that sensibly know what great number of Vegetables (as the several varieties of *Alga's, Sea Lettuce, Phasganium, Conferua, Caulis Marina, Abies, Erica, Tamarice*, divers sorts of *Muscus, Fucus, Quercus Marina* and *Corallins*) are found at the bottom of the Sea. Since it is also now well known, that the Western Ocean, for many degrees, is covered with *Sargasso* or *Lenticula Marina*, and found to arise from the bottom of that Sea; since, upon

the coast of *Provence* by the Isles of *Eres*, there is a part of the *Mediterranean Sea*, called *la Prairie*, or the *Meadowy Sea*, from the bottom thereof so plentifully covered with Plants: since vast heaps of Weeds are found in the Bellies of some Whales taken in the Northern Ocean, and at a great distance from the Shore: And since the providence of Nature hath provided this shelter for minor Fishes; both for their spawn, and safety of their young ones. And this might be more peculiarly allowed to be spoken of the Red Sea, since the Hebrews named it *Suph*, or the *Weedy Sea*: and, also, seeing *Theophrastus* and *Pliny*, observing the growth of Vegetables under water, have made their chief illustrations from those in the Red Sea.

Sycamore.

30. You will readily discover how widely they are mistaken, who accept the Sycamore mention'd in several parts of Scripture for the Sycamore, or Tree of that denomination, with us: which is properly but one kind or difference of *Acer*, and bears no Fruit with any resemblance unto a Figg.

But you will rather, thereby, apprehend the true and genuine Sycamore, or *Sycaminus*, which is a stranger in our parts. A Tree (according to the description of *Theophrastus*, *Dioscorides* and *Galen*) resembling a Mulberry Tree in the Leaf, but in the Fruit a Figg; which it produceth not in the Twiggs but in the Trunck or greater Branches, answerable to the Sycamore of *Ægypt*, the Ægyptian Figg or Giamez of the Arabians, described by *Prosper Alpinus*, with a Leaf somewhat broader than a Mulberry, and in its Fruit like a Figg. Insomuch that some have fancied it to have had its first production from a Figg Tree grafted on a Mulberry.

It is a Tree common in *Judæa*, whereof they made frequent use in Buildings; and so understood, it explaineth that expression in *Isaiah*:[203] *Sycamori excisi sunt, Cedros substituemus. The Bricks are fallen down, we will build with hewen Stones: The Sycamores are cut down, but we will change them into Cedars.*

It is a broad spreading Tree, not onely fit for Walks, Groves and Shade, but also affording profit. And therefore it is said that King *David*[204] appointed *Baalhanan* to be over his Olive Trees and Sycamores, which were in great plenty; and it is accordingly delivered,[205] that *Solomon made Cedars to be as the Sycamore Trees that are in the Vale for abundance.* That is, he planted many, though they did not come to perfection in his days.

And as it grew plentifully about the Plains, so was the Fruit good for Food; and, as *Bellonius* and late accounts deliver, very refreshing unto Travellers in those hot and drie Countries: whereby the expression of *Amos*[206] becomes more intelligible, when he said he was *an Herdsman, and a gatherer of Sycamore Fruit*. And the expression of *David*[207] also becomes more Emphatical; *He destroyed their Vines with Hail, and their Sycamore Trees with Frost.* That is, their *Sicmoth* in the Original, a word in the sound not far from the Sycamore.

Thus when it is said,[208] *If ye had Faith as a grain of Mustard-seed, ye might say unto this Sycamine Tree, Be thou plucked up by the roots, and be thou placed in the Sea, and it should obey you*: it might be more significantly spoken of this Sycamore; this being described to be *Arbor vasta*, a large and well rooted Tree, whose removal was more difficult than many others. And so the instance in that Text, is very properly made in the Sycamore Tree, one of the largest and less removable Trees among them. A Tree so lasting and well rooted, that the Sycamore which *Zacheus* ascended, is still shewn in *Judæa* unto Travellers; as also the hollow Sycamore at *Maturæa* in *Ægypt*, where the blessed Virgin is said to have remained: which though it relisheth of the Legend, yet it plainly declareth what opinion they had of the lasting condition of that Tree, to countenance the Tradition; for which they might not be without some experience, since the learned describer of the *Pyramides*[209] observeth, that the old Ægyptians made Coffins of this Wood, which he found yet fresh and undecayed among divers of their Mummies.

And thus, also, when *Zacheus* climbed up into a Sycamore above any other Tree, this being a large and fair one, it cannot be denied that he made choice of a proper and advantageous Tree to look down upon our Saviour.

Increase of Seed 100. fold in Matt. 13. 23.

31. Whether the expression of our Saviour in the Parable of the Sower, and the increase of the Seed *unto thirty, sixty and a hundred fold*, had any reference unto the ages of Believers, and measures of their Faith, as Children, Young and Old Persons, as to beginners, well advanced and strongly confirmed Christians, as learned men have hinted; or whether in this progressional assent

there were any latent Mysteries, as the mystical Interpreters of Numbers may apprehend, I pretend not to determine.

But, how this multiplication may well be conceived, and in what way apprehended, and that this centesimal increase is not naturally strange, you that are no stranger in Agriculture, old and new, are not like to make great doubt.

That every Grain should produce an Ear affording an hundred Grains, is not like to be their conjecture who behold the growth of Corn in our Fields, wherein a common Grain doth produce far less in number. For barley consisting but of two *Versus* or Rows, seldom exceedeth twenty Grains, that is, ten upon each Στοῖχος, or Row; Rye, of a square figure, is very fruitfull at forty: Wheat, besides the *Frit* and *Uruncus*, or imperfect Grains of the small Husks at the top and bottom of the Ear, is fruitfull at ten treble *Glumæ* or Husks in a Row, each containing but three Grains in breadth, if the middle Grain arriveth at all to perfection; and so maketh up threescore Grains in both sides.

Yet even this centesimal fructification may be admitted in some sorts of *Cerealia*, and Grains from one Ear: if we take in the *Triticum centigranum*, or *fertilissimum Plinii*, Indian Wheat, and *Panicum*; which, in every Ear, containeth hundreds of Grains.

But this increase may easily be conceived of Grains in their total multiplication, in good and fertile ground, since, if every Grain of Wheat produceth but three Ears, the increase will arise above that number. Nor are we without examples of some grounds which have produced many more Ears, and above this centesimal increase: As *Pliny* hath left recorded of the *Byzacian* Field in *Africa*. *Misit ex eo loco Procurator ex uno quadraginta minus germina. Misit et Neroni pariter tercentum quadraginta stipulos, ex uno grano. Cum centessimos quidem Leontini Siciliæ campi fundunt, aliique, et tota Bœtica, et imprimis Ægyptus.* And even in our own Country, from one Grain of Wheat sowed in a Garden, I have numbred many more than an hundred.

And though many Grains are commonly lost which come not to sprouting or earing, yet the same is also verified in measure; as that one Bushel should produce a hundred, as is exemplified by the Corn in *Gerar*;[210] *Then Isaac sowed in that Land, and received in that year an hundred fold*. That is, as the Chaldee explaineth it, *a hundred for one*, when he measured it. And this *Pliny* seems to intend, when he saith of the fertile Byzacian Territory before mentioned, *Ex uno centeni quinquaginta modii redduntur*. And may be favourably apprehended of the fertility of some grounds in *Poland*; wherein, after the account of *Gaguinus*, from Rye sowed in *August*, come thirty or forty Ears, and a Man on Horseback can scarce look over it. In the Sabbatical Crop of *Judæa*, there must be admitted a large increase, and probably not short of this centesimal multiplication: For it supplied part of the sixth year, the whole seventh, and eighth untill the Harvest of that year.

The *seven years of plenty in Ægypt* must be of high increase; when, by storing up but the fifth part, they supplied the whole Land, and many of their neighbours after: for it is said,[211] the Famine was in all the Land about them. And therefore though the causes of the Dearth in *Ægypt* be made out from the defect of the overflow of *Nilus*, according to the Dream of *Pharaoh*; yet was that no cause of the scarcity of the Land of *Canaan*, which may rather be ascribed to the want of the former and latter rains, for some succeeding years, if their Famine held time and duration with that of *Ægypt*; as may be probably gather'd from that expression of *Joseph*,[212] *Come down unto me [into Ægypt] and tarry not, and there will I nourish you: (for yet there are five years of Famine) lest thou and thy Household, and all that thou hast come to poverty*.

How they preserved their Corn so long in *Ægypt* may seem hard unto Northern and moist Climates, except we consider the many ways of preservation practised by antiquity, and also take in that handsome account of *Pliny*; What Corn soever is laid up in the Ear, it taketh no harm keep it as long as you will; although the best and most assured way to keep Corn is in Caves and Vaults under ground, according to the practice of *Cappadocia* and *Thracia*.

In *Ægypt* and *Mauritania* above all things they look to this, that their Granaries stand on high ground; and how drie so ever their Floor be, they lay a course of Chaff betwixt it and the ground. Besides, they put up their Corn in Granaries and Binns together with the Ear. And *Varro* delivereth that Wheat laid up in that manner will last fifty years; Millet an hundred; and Beans so conserved in a Cave of *Ambracia*, were known to last an hundred and twenty years; that is, from the time of King *Pyrrhus*, unto the Pyratick War under the conduct of *Pompey*.

More strange it may seem how, after seven years, the Grains conserved should be fruitfull for a new production. For it is said that *Joseph delivered Seed unto the Ægyptians, to sow their Land for the eighth year*: and Corn after seven years is like to afford little or no production, according to *Theophrastus*;[213] *Ad Sementem semen anniculum optimum putatur, binum deterius et trinum; ultra sterile fermè est, quanquam ad usum cibarium idoneum.*

Yet since, from former exemplifications, Corn may be made to last so long, the fructifying power may well be conceived to last in some good proportion, according to the region and place of its conservation, as the same *Theophrastus* hath observed, and left a notable example from *Cappadocia*, where Corn might be kept sixty years, and remain fertile at forty; according to his expression thus translated; *In Cappadociæ loco quodam petra dicto, triticum ad quadraginta annos fœcundum est, at ad sementem percommodum durare proditum est, sexagenos aut septuagenos ad usum cibarium servari posse idoneum.* The situation of that Conservatory, was, as he delivereth, ὑψηλὸν, εὔπνουν, εὔαυρον, *high, airy and exposed to several favourable winds*. And upon such consideration of winds and ventilation, some conceive the Ægyptian Granaries were made open, the Country being free from rain. Howsoever it was, that contrivance could not be without some hazard:[214] for the great Mists and Dews of that Country might dispose the Corn unto corruption.

More plainly may they mistake, who from some analogy of name (as if *Pyramid* were derived from Πὐρον, *Triticum*), conceive the Ægyptian Pyramids to have been built for Granaries; or look for any settled Monuments about the Desarts erected for that intention; since their Store-houses were made in the great Towns, according to Scripture expression,[215] *He gathered up all the Food of seven years, which was in the Land of Ægypt, and laid up the Food in the Cities: the Food of the Field which was round about every City, laid he up in the same.*

Olive Tree in Rom. 11. 24.

32. *For if thou wert cut out of the Olive Tree, which is wild by nature, and wert grafted, contrary to nature, into a good Olive Tree, how much more shall these, which be the natural Branches, be grafted into their own Olive Tree?* In which place, how answerable to the Doctrine of Husbandry this expression of S. *Paul* is, you will readily apprehend who understand the rules of insition or grafting, and that way of vegetable propagation; wherein that is contrary to nature, or natural rules which Art observeth: *viz.* to make use of a Cyons more ignoble than the Stock, or to graft wild upon domestick and good Plants, according as *Theophrastus*[216] hath anciently observed, and, making instance in the Olive, hath left this Doctrine unto us; *Urbanum Sylvestribus ut satis Oleastris inserere. Nam si è contrario Sylvestrem in Urbanos severis, etsi differentia quædam erit, tamen*[217] *bonæ frugis Arbor nunquam profecto reddetur*: which is also agreeable unto our present practice, who graft Pears on Thorns, and Apples upon Crabb Stocks, not using the contrary insition. And when it is said, *How much more shall these, which are the natural Branches, be grafted into their own natural Olive Tree?* this is also agreeable unto the rule of the same Author; Ἔστι δὲ βελτίων ἐγκεντρισμὸς, ὁμοίων εἰς ὅμοια, *Insitio melior est similium in similibus*: For the nearer consanguinity there is between the Cyons and the Stock, the readier comprehension is made, and the nobler fructification. According also unto the later caution of *Laurenbergius*;[218] *Arbores domesticæ insitioni destinatæ, semper anteponendæ Sylvestribus.* And though the success be good, and may suffice upon Stocks of the same denomination; yet, to be grafted upon their own and Mother Stock, is the nearest insition: which way, though less practised of old, is now much imbraced, and found a notable way for melioration of the Fruit; and much the rather, if the Tree to be grafted on be a good and generous Plant, a good and fair Olive, as the Apostle seems to imply by a peculiar word[219] scarce to be found elsewhere.

It must be also considered, that the *Oleaster*, or wild Olive, by cutting, transplanting and the best managery of Art, can be made but to produce such Olives as (*Theophrastus* saith) were particularly named *Phaulia*, that is, but *bad Olives*; and that it was reckon'd among Prodigies, for the *Oleaster* to become an Olive Tree.

And when insition and grafting, in the Text, is applied unto the Olive Tree, it hath an Emphatical sense, very agreeable unto that Tree which is best propagated this way; not at all by surculation, as *Theophrastus* observeth, nor well by Seed, as hath been observed. *Omne semen simile genus perficit, præter oleam, Oleastrum enim generat, hoc est sylvestrem oleam, et non oleam veram.*

"If, therefore, thou Roman and Gentile Branch, which wert cut from the wild Olive, art now, by the signal mercy of God, beyond the ordinary and commonly expected way, grafted into the true Olive, the Church of God; if thou, which neither naturally nor by humane art canst be made to produce any good Fruit, and, next to a Miracle, to be made a true Olive, art now by the benignity of God grafted into the proper Olive; how much more shall the Jew, and natural Branch, be grafted into its genuine and mother Tree, wherein propinquity of nature is like, so readily and prosperously, to effect a coalition? And this more especially by the expressed way of insition or implantation, the Olive being not successfully propagable by Seed, nor at all by surculation."

Stork nesting on Firre Trees in Psal. 104. 17.

33. *As for the Stork, the Firre Trees are her House.* This expression, in our Translation, which keeps close to the Original *Chasidah*, is somewhat different from the Greek and Latin Translation; nor agreeable unto common observation, whereby they are known commonly to build upon Chimneys, or the tops of Houses, and high Buildings, which notwithstanding, the common Translation may clearly consist with observation, if we consider that this is commonly affirmed of the black Stork, and take notice of the description of *Ornithologus* in *Aldrovandus*, that such Storks are often found in divers parts, and that they do *in Arboribus nidulari, præsertim in abietibus*; Make their Nests on Trees, especially upon Firre Trees. Nor wholly disagreeing unto the practice of the common white Stork, according unto *Varro, nidulantur in agris*: and the concession of *Aldrovandus* that sometimes they build on Trees: and the assertion of *Bellonius*,[220] that men dress them Nests, and place Cradles upon high Trees, in Marish regions, that Storks may breed upon them: which course some observe for Herns and Cormorants with us. And this building of Storks upon Trees, may be also answerable unto the original and natural way of building of Storks before the political habitations of men, and the raising of Houses and high Buildings; before they were invited by such conveniences and prepared Nests, to relinquish their natural places of nidulation. I say, before or where such advantages are not ready; when Swallows found other places than Chimneys, and Daws found other places than holes in high Fabricks to build in.

Balm, in Gen. 43. 11.

34. *And, therefore, Israel said carry down the man a present, a little Balm, a little Honey, and Myrrhe, Nuts and Almonds.* Now whether this, which *Jacob* sent, were the proper Balsam extolled by humane Writers, you cannot but make some doubt, who find the Greek Translation to be Ῥητίνη, that is, *Resina*, and so may have some suspicion that it might be some pure distillation from the Turpentine Tree, which grows prosperously and plentifully in *Judæa*, and seems so understood by the Arabick; and was indeed esteemed by *Theophrastus* and *Dioscorides*, the chiefest of resinous Bodies, and the word *Resina* Emphatically used for it.

That the Balsam Plant hath grown and prospered in *Judæa* we believe without dispute. For the same is attested by *Theophrastus*, *Pliny*, *Justinus*, and many more; from the commendation that *Galen* affordeth of the Balsam of *Syria*, and the story of *Cleopatra*, that she obtain'd some Plants of Balsam from *Herod* the Great to transplant into *Ægypt*. But whether it was so anciently in *Judæa* as the time of *Jacob*; nay, whether this Plant was here before the time of *Solomon*, that great collectour of Vegetable rarities, some doubt may be made from the account of *Josephus*, that the Queen of *Sheba*, a part of *Arabia*, among presents unto *Solomon*, brought some Plants of the Balsam Tree, as one of the peculiar estimables of her Country.

Whether this ever had its natural growth, or were an original native Plant of *Judæa*, much more that it was peculiar unto that Country, a greater doubt may arise: while we reade in *Pausanias*, *Strabo* and *Diodorus,* that it grows also in *Arabia*, and find in *Theophrastus*,[221] that it grew in two Gardens about *Jericho* in *Judæa*. And more especially whiles we seriously consider that notable discourse between *Abdella*, *Abdachim* and *Alpinus*, concluding the natural and original place of this singular Plant to be in *Arabia*, about *Mecha* and *Medina*, where it still plentifully groweth, and Mountains abound therein. From whence it hath been carefully transplanted by the *Basha's* of *Grand Cairo*, into the Garden of *Matarea*; where, when it dies, it is repaired again from those parts of *Arabia*, from whence the *Grand Signior* yearly receiveth a present of Balsam from the *Xeriff* of *Mecha*, still called by the Arabians *Balessan*; whence they believe arose the Greek appellation *Balsam*. And since these Balsam-plants are not now to be found in *Judæa*, and though purposely cultivated, are often lost in *Judæa*, but everlastingly live, and naturally renew in *Arabia*; They probably concluded, that those of *Judæa* were foreign and transplanted from these parts.

All which notwithstanding, since the same Plant may grow naturally and spontaneously in several Countries, and either from inward or outward causes be lost in one Region, while it continueth and subsisteth in another, the Balsam Tree might possibly be a native of *Judæa* as well as of *Arabia*; which because *de facto* it cannot be clearly made out, the ancient expressions of Scripture become doubtfull in this point. But since this Plant hath not, for a long time, grown in *Judæa*, and still plentifully prospers in *Arabia*, that which now comes in pretious parcels to us, and still is called the Balsam of *Judæa*, may now surrender its name, and more properly be called the Balsam of *Arabia*.

Barley Flax, &c. in Exod. 9. 31.

35. *And the Flax and the Barley was smitten; for the Barley was in the Ear, and the Flax was bolled, but the Wheat and the Rye was not smitten, for they were not grown up.*[222] How the Barley and the Flax should be smitten in the plague of Hail in *Ægypt*, and the Wheat and Rye escape, because they were not yet grown up, may seem strange unto English observers, who call Barley Summer Corn sown so many months after Wheat, and, beside *hordeum Polystichon*, or big Barley, sowe not Barley in the Winter, to anticipate the growth of Wheat.

And the same may also seem a preposterous expression unto all who do not consider the various Agriculture, and different Husbandry of Nations, and such as was practised in *Ægypt*, and fairly proved to have been also used in *Judæa*, wherein their Barley Harvest was before that of Wheat; as is confirmable from that expression in *Ruth*, that she *came into Bethlehem at the beginning of Barley Harvest*, and staid unto the end of Wheat Harvest; from the death of *Manasses* the Father of *Judith*, Emphatically expressed to have happened in the Wheat Harvest, and more advanced heat of the Sun; and from the custom of the Jews, to offer the Barley Sheaf of the first fruits in *March*, and a Cake of Wheat Flower but at the end of *Pentecost*. Consonant unto the practice of the Ægyptians, who (as *Theophrastus* delivereth) sowed their Barley early in reference to their first Fruits; and also the common rural practice, recorded by the same Authour, *Maturè seritur Triticum, Hordeum, quod etiam maturius seritur; Wheat and Barley are sowed early, but Barley earlier of the two*.

Flax was also an early Plant, as may be illustrated from the neighbour Country of *Canaan*. For the Israelites kept the Passover in *Gilgal* in the fourteenth day of the first Month, answering unto part of our *March*, having newly passed *Jordan*: And the Spies which were sent from *Shittim* unto *Jericho*, not many days before, were hid by *Rahab* under the stalks of Flax, which lay drying on the top of her House; which sheweth that the Flax was already and newly gathered. For this was the first preparation of Flax, and before fluviation or rotting, which, after *Pliny's* account, was after Wheat Harvest.

But the Wheat and the Rye were not smitten, for they were not grown up. The Original signifies that it was *hidden*, or *dark*, the Vulgar and Septuagint that it was *serotinous* or *late*, and our old Translation that it was *late sown*. And so the expression and interposition of *Moses*, who well understood the Husbandry of *Ægypt*, might Emphatically declare the state of Wheat and Rye in that particular year; and if so, the same is solvable from the time of the floud of *Nilus*, and the measure of its inundation. For if it were very high, and over-drenching the ground, they were forced to later Seed-time; and so the Wheat and the Rye escaped; for they were more slowly growing Grains, and, by reason of the greater inundation of the River, were sown later than ordinary that year, especially in the Plains near the River, where the ground drieth latest.

Some think the plagues of *Ægypt* were acted in one Month, others but in the compass of twelve. In the delivery of Scripture there is no account, of what time of the year or particular Month they fell out; but the account of these grains, which were either smitten or escaped, make the plague of Hail to have probably hapned in *February*: This may be collected from the new and old account of the Seed time and Harvest in *Ægypt*. For, according to the account of *Radzevil*,[223] the river rising in *June*, and the Banks being cut in *September*, they sow about S. *Andrews*, when the Floud is retired, and the moderate driness of the ground permitteth. So that the Barley anticipating the Wheat, either in time of sowing or growing, might be in Ear in *February*.

The account of *Pliny*[224] is little different. They cast the Seed upon the Slime and Mudd when the River is down, which commonly happeneth in the beginning of *November*. They begin to reap and cut down a little before the Calends of *April*, about the middle of *March*, and in the Month of *May* their Harvest is in. So that Barley anticipating Wheat, it might be in Ear in *February*, and Wheat not yet grown up, at least to the Spindle or Ear, to be destroyed by the Hail. For they cut down about the middle of *March*, at least their forward Corns, and in the Month of *May* all sorts of Corns were in.

The *turning of the River into Bloud* shews in what Month this happened not. That is, not when the River had overflown; for it is said, *the Ægyptians digged round about the River for Water to drink*, which they could not have done, if the River had been out, and the Fields under Water.

In the same Text you cannot, without some hesitation, pass over the translation of Rye, which the Original nameth *Cassumeth*, the Greek rendreth *Olyra*, the French and Dutch *Spelta*, the Latin *Zea*, and not *Secale* the known word for Rye. But this common Rye so well understood at present, was not distinctly described, or not well known from early Antiquity. And therefore, in this uncertainty, some have thought it to have been the *Typha* of the Ancients. *Cordus* will have it to be *Olyra*, and *Ruellius* some kind of *Oryza*. But having no vulgar and well known name for those Grains, we warily embrace an appellation of near affinity, and tolerably render it *Rye*.

While Flax, Barley, Wheat and Rye are named, some may wonder why no mention is made of Ryce, wherewith, at present, *Ægypt* so much aboundeth. But whether that Plant grew so early in that Country, some doubt may be made: for Ryce is originally a Grain of *India*, and might not then be transplanted into *Ægypt*.

Sheaves of Grass, in Psal. 12. 6, 7.

36. *Let them become as the Grass growing upon the House top, which withereth before it be plucked up, whereof the mower filleth not his hand, nor he that bindeth Sheaves his bosome*. Though the *filling of the hand*, and mention of *Sheaves of Hay*, may seem strange unto us, who use neither handfulls nor Sheaves in that kind of Husbandry, yet may it be properly taken, and you are not like to doubt thereof, who may find the like expressions in the Authours *de Re rustica*, concerning the old way of this Husbandry.

Columella,[225] delivering what Works were not to be permitted upon the Roman *Feriæ*, or Festivals, among others sets down, that upon such days, it was not lawfull to carry or bind up Hay, *nec fœnum vincire nec vehere, per religiones Ponteficum licet*.

Marcus Varro[226] is more particular; *Primum de pratis herbarum cum crescere desiit, subsecari falcibus debet, et quoad peracescat furcillis versari, cum peracuit, de his manipulos fieri et vehi in villam*.

And their course of mowing seems somewhat different from ours. For they cut not down clear at once, but used an after section, which they peculiarly called *Sicilitium*, according as the word is expounded by *Georgius Alexandrinus*, and *Beroaldus* after *Pliny*; *Sicilire est falcibus consectari quæ fœnisecæ præterierunt, aut ea secare quæ fœnisecæ præterierunt*.

Juniper Tree, in 1 King. 19. 5, etc.

37. When 'tis said that *Elias* lay and slept under a Juniper Tree, some may wonder how that Tree, which in our parts groweth but low and shrubby, should afford him shade and covering. But others know that there is a lesser and a larger kind of that Vegetable; that it makes a Tree in its proper soil and region. And may find in *Pliny* that in the Temple of *Diana Saguntina* in *Spain*, the Rafters were made of Juniper.

In that expression of *David*,[227] *Sharp Arrows of the mighty, with Coals of Juniper*; Though Juniper be left out in the last Translation, yet may there be an Emphatical sense from that word; since Juniper abounds with a piercing Oil, and makes a smart Fire. And the rather, if that quality be half true, which *Pliny* affirmeth, that the Coals of Juniper raked up will keep a glowing Fire for the space of a year. For so the expression will Emphatically imply, not onely the *smart burning*, but the *lasting fire of their malice*.

That passage of *Job*,[228] wherein he complains that poor and half famished fellows despised him, is of greater difficulty; *For want and famine they were solitary, they cut up Mallows by the Bushes, and Juniper roots for meat.* Wherein we might at first doubt the Translation, not onely from the Greek Text but the assertion of *Dioscorides*, who affirmeth that the roots of Juniper are of a venomous quality. But *Scaliger* hath disproved the same from the practice of the African Physicians, who use the decoction of Juniper roots against the Venereal Disease. The Chaldee reads it *Genista*, or some kind of Broom, which will be also unusual and hard Diet, except thereby we understand the *Orobanche*, or Broom Rape, which groweth from the roots of Broom; and which, according to *Dioscorides*, men used to eat raw or boiled in the manner of *Asparagus*.

And, therefore, this expression doth highly declare the misery, poverty and extremity of the persons who were now mockers of him; they being so contemptible and necessitous, that they were fain to be content, not with a mean Diet, but such as was no Diet at all, the roots of Trees, the roots of Juniper, which none would make use of for Food, but in the lowest necessity, and some degree of famishing.

Scarlet Tincture, in Gen. 38. 28. Exod. 25. 4, etc.

38. While some have disputed whether *Theophrastus* knew the Scarlet Berry, others may doubt whether that noble tincture were known unto the Hebrews, which notwithstanding seems clear from the early and iterated expressions of Scripture concerning the Scarlet Tincture, and is the less to be doubted because the Scarlet Berry grew plentifully in the Land of *Canaan*, and so they were furnished with the Materials of that Colour. For though *Dioscorides* saith it groweth in *Armenia* and *Cappadocia*, yet that it also grew in *Judæa*, seems more than probable from the account of *Bellonius*, who observed it to be so plentifull in that Country, that it afforded a profitable Commodity, and great quantity thereof was transported by the Venetian Merchants.

How this should be fitly expressed by the word *Tolagnoth, Vermis*, or *Worm*, may be made out from *Pliny*, who calls it *Coccus Scolecius*, or the *Wormy Berry*; as also from the name of that Colour called *Vermilion*, or the *Worm Colour*; and which is also answerable unto the true nature of it. For this is no proper Berry containing the fructifying part, but a kind of Vessicular excrescence, adhering commonly to the Leaf of the *Ilex Coccigera*, or dwarf and small kind of Oak, whose Leaves are always green, and its proper seminal parts Acrons. This little Bagg containeth a red Pulp, which, if not timely gathered, or left to it self, produceth small red Flies, and partly a red powder, both serviceable unto the tincture. And therefore, to prevent the generation of Flies, when it is first gathered, they sprinkle it over with Vinegar, especially such as make use of the fresh Pulp for the confection of *Alkermes*; which still retaineth the Arabick name, from the *Kermesberry*; which is agreeable unto the description of *Bellonius* and *Quinqueranus*. And the same we have beheld in *Provence* and *Languedock*, where it is plentifully gathered, and called *Manna Rusticorum*, from the considerable profit which the Peasants make by gathering of it.

Oaks, in Gen. 35. 4, 8. Josh. 24. 26. Isa. 1. 29. Ezek. 27. 6. Hosea. 4. 13, etc.

39. Mention is made of Oaks in divers parts of Scripture, which though the Latin sometimes renders a Turpentine Tree, yet surely some kind of Oak may be understood thereby; but whether our common Oak as is commonly apprehended, you may well doubt; for the common Oak, which prospereth so well with us, delighteth not in hot regions. And that diligent Botanist *Bellonius*, who took such particular notice of the Plants of *Syria* and *Judæa*, observed not the vulgar Oak in those parts. But he found the *Ilex, Chesne Vert*, or Ever-green Oak, in many places; as also that kind of Oak which is properly named *Esculus*: and he makes mention thereof in places about *Jerusalem*, and in his Journey from thence unto *Damascus*, where he found *Montes Ilice, et Esculo virentes*; which, in his Discourse of *Lemnos*, he saith are always green. And therefore when it is said[229] of *Absalom*, that his *Mule went under the thick Boughs of a great Oak, and his Head caught hold of the Oak, and he was taken up between the Heaven and the Earth*, that Oak might be some *Ilex*, or rather *Esculus*. For that is a thick and bushy kind, in *Orbem comosa*, as *Dalechampius*; *ramis in orbem dispositis comans*, as *Renealmus* describeth it. And when it is said[230] that *Ezechias broke down the Images, and cut down the Groves*, they might much consist of Oaks, which were sacred unto Pagan Deities, as this more particularly, according to that of *Virgil*,

Nemorúmque Jovi quæ maxima frondet Esculus.

And, in *Judæa*, where no hogs were eaten by the Jews, and few kept by others, 'tis not unlikely that they most cherished the *Esculus*, which might serve for Food of men. For the Acrons thereof are the sweetest of any Oak, and taste like Chesnuts; and so producing an edulious or esculent Fruit, is properly named *Esculus*.

They which know the *Ilex*, or Ever-green Oak, with somewhat prickled leaves, named Πρίνος, will better understand the irreconcileable answer of the two Elders, when the one accused *Susanna* of incontinency under a Πρίνος, or Ever-green Oak, the other under a Σχῖνος, *Lentiscus*, or Mastick Tree, which are so different in Bigness, Boughs, Leaves and Fruit, the one bearing Acrons, the other Berries: And, without the knowledge hereof, will not Emphatically or distinctly understand that of the Poet,

Flaváque de viridi stillabant Ilice mella.

Cedars of Libanus.

40. When we often meet with the Cedars of *Libanus*, that expression may be used not onely because they grew in a known and neighbour Country, but also because they were of the noblest and largest kind of that Vegetable, and we find the Phœnician Cedar magnified by the Ancients. The Cedar of *Libanus* is a *coniferous* Tree, bearing *Cones* or Cloggs; (not Berries) of such a vastness, that *Melchior Lussy*, a great Traveller, found one upon *Libanus* as big as seven men could compass. Some are now so curious as to keep the Branches and *Cones* thereof among their rare Collections. And, though much Cedar Wood be now brought from *America*, yet 'tis time to take notice of the true Cedar of *Libanus*, imployed in the Temple of *Solomon*; for they have been much destroyed and neglected, and become at last but thin. *Bellonius* could reckon but twenty eight, *Rowolfius* and *Radzevil* but twenty four, and *Bidulphus* the same number. And a later account[231] of some English Travellers saith, that they are now but in one place, and in a small compass, in *Libanus*.

Uncircumcised Fruit, in Levit. 19. 23.

Quando ingressi fueritis terram, et Plantaveritis in illa ligna Pomifera, auferetis præputia eorum. Poma quæ germinant immunda erunt vobis, nec edetis ex eis. Quarto autem anno, omnis fructus eorum sanctificabitur, laudabilis Domino. Quinto autem anno comedetis fructus. By this Law they were injoyned not to eat of the Fruits of the Trees which they planted for the *first three years*: and, as the Vulgar expresseth it, to take away the Prepuces, from such Trees, during that time; the Fruits of *the fourth year being holy unto the Lord*, and those of the fifth allowable unto others. Now if *auferre præputia* be taken, as many learned men have thought, to pluck away the bearing Buds, before they proceed unto Flowers or Fruit, you will readily apprehend the Metaphor, from the analogy and similitude of those Sprouts and Buds, which, shutting up the fruitfull particle, resembleth the preputial part.

And you may also find herein a piece of Husbandry not mentioned in *Theophrastus*, or *Columella*. For by taking away of the Buds, and hindering fructification, the Trees become more vigorous, both in growth and future production. By such a way King *Pyrrhus* got into a lusty race of Beeves, and such as were desired over all *Greece*, by keeping them from Generation untill the ninth year.

And you may also discover a physical advantage of the goodness of the Fruit, which becometh less crude and more wholsome, upon the fourth or fifth years production.

Partition of Plants into Herb and Tree, in Gen. 1. 11.

41. While you reade in *Theophrastus*, or modern Herbalists, a strict division of Plants, into *Arbor, Frutex, Suffrutex et Herba*, you cannot but take notice of the Scriptural division at the Creation, into *Tree* and *Herb*: and this may seem too narrow to comprehend the Classis of Vegetables; which, notwithstanding, may be sufficient, and a plain and intelligible division thereof. And therefore in this difficulty concerning the division of Plants, the learned Botanist, *Cæsalpinus*, thus concludeth. *Clarius agemus si alterâ divisione neglectâ, duo tantùm Plantarum genera substituamus, Arborem scilicet, et Herbam, conjungentes cum Arboribus Frutices, et cum Herba Suffrutices*; *Frutices* being the lesser Trees, and *Suffrutices* the larger, harder and more solid Herbs.

And this division into Herb and Tree, may also suffice, if we take in that natural ground of the division of perfect Plants, and such as grow from Seeds. For Plants, in their first production, do send forth two Leaves adjoining to the Seed; and then afterwards, do either produce two other Leaves, and so successively before any Stalk; and such go under the name of Πόα, Βοτάνη, or *Herb*; or else, after the first Leaves succeeding to the Seed Leaves, they send forth a Stalk, or rudiment of a Stalk before any other Leaves, and such fall under the Classis of Δένδρον, or *Tree*. So that, in this natural division, there are but two grand differences, that is, *Tree* and *Herb*. The *Frutex* and *Suffrutex* have the way of production from the Seed, and in other respects the *Suffrutices*, or *Cremia*, have a middle and participating nature, and referable unto Herbs.

The Bay Tree, in Psal. 37. 35

42. *I have seen the ungodly in great power, and flourishing like a green Bay Tree.* Both Scripture and humane Writers draw frequent illustrations from Plants. *Scribonius Largus* illustrates the old Cymbals from the *Cotyledon Palustris*, or *Umbelicus Veneris*. Who would expect to find *Aaron's* Mitre in any Plant? yet *Josephus* hath taken some pains to make out the same in the seminal knop of *Hyoscyamus*, or Henbane. The Scripture compares the Figure of Manna unto the Seed of Coriander. In *Jeremy*[232] we find the expression, *Streight as a Palm Tree*: And here the wicked in their flourishing state are likened unto a Bay Tree. Which, sufficiently answering the sense of the Text, we are unwilling to exclude that noble Plant from the honour of having its name in Scripture. Yet we cannot but observe, that the Septuagint renders it *Cedars*, and the Vulgar accordingly, *Vidi impium superexaltatum, et elevatum sicut Cedros Libani*; and the Translation of *Tremelius* mentions neither Bay nor Cedar; *Sese explicantem tanquam Arbor indigena virens*; which seems to have been followed by the last Low Dutch Translation. A private Translation renders it like *a green self-growing*[233] *Laurel*, The High Dutch of *Luther's* Bible, retains the word *Laurel*; and so doth the old Saxon and Island Translation; so also the French, Spanish; and Italian of *Diodati*: yet his Notes acknowledge that some think it rather a Cedar, and others any large Tree in a prospering and natural Soil.

But however these Translations differ, the sense is allowable and obvious unto apprehension: when no particular Plant is named, any proper to the sense may be supposed; where either Cedar or Laurel is mentioned, if the preceding words [*exalted and elevated*] be used, they are more appliable unto the Cedar; where the word [*flourishing*] is used, it is more agreeable unto the Laurel, which, in its prosperity, abounds with pleasant flowers, whereas those of the Cedar are very little, and scarce perceptible, answerable to the Firre, Pine and other coniferous Trees.

The Figg Tree, in S. Mark. 11. 13, etc.

43. *And in the morning, when they were come from Bethany, he was hungry; and seeing a Figg Tree afar off having Leaves, he came, if haply he might find any thing thereon; and when he came to it, he found nothing but leaves: for the time of Figgs was not yet.* Singular conceptions have passed from learned men to make out this passage of S. *Mark*, which S. *Matthew*[234] so plainly delivereth; most men doubting why our Saviour should curse the Tree for bearing no Fruit, when the time of Fruit was not yet come; or why it is said that *the time of Figgs was not yet*, when, notwithstanding, Figgs might be found at that season.

Heinsius,[235] who thinks that *Elias* must salve the doubt, according to the received Reading of the Text, undertaketh to vary the same, reading οὕ γὰρ ἦν, καιρὸς σύκων, that is, *for where he was, it was the season or time of Figgs*.

A learned Interpreter[236] of our own, without alteration of accents or words, endeavours to salve all, by another interpretation of the same, Οὐ γὰρ καιρὸς σύκων, *For it was not a good or seasonable year for Figgs*.

But, because men part not easily with old beliefs, or the received construction of words, we shall briefly set down what may be alledged for it.

And, first, for the better comprehension of all deductions hereupon, we may consider the several differences and distinctions both of Figg Trees and their Fruits. *Suidas* upon the word Ἰσχὰς makes four divisions of Figgs, Ὄλυνθος, Φήληξ, Σῦκον and Ἰσχὰς and Ἰσχὰς. But because Φήληξ makes no considerable distinction, learned men do chiefly insist upon the three others; that is, Ὄλυνθος, or *Grossus*, which are the Buttons, or small sort of Figgs, either not ripe, or not ordinarily proceeding to ripeness, but fall away at least in the greatest part, and especially in sharp Winters; which are also named Συκάδες, and distinguished from the Fruit of the wild Figg, or *Caprificus*, which is named Ἐρινεὸς, and never cometh unto ripeness. The second is called

Σῦκον, or *Ficus*, which commonly proceedeth unto ripeness in its due season. A third the ripe Figg dried, which maketh the Ἰσχάδες, or *Carrier*.

Of Figg Trees there are also many divisions; For some are *prodromi*, or precocious, which bear Fruit very early, whether they bear once, or oftner in the year; some are *protericæ*, which are the most early of the precocious Trees, and bear soonest of any; some are *æstivæ*, which bear in the common season of the Summer, and some *serotinæ* which bear very late.

Some are *biferous* and *triferous*, which bear twice or thrice in the year, and some are of the ordinary standing course, which make up the expected season of Figgs.

Again some Figg Trees, either in their proper kind, or fertility in some single ones, do bear Fruit or rudiments of Fruit all the year long; as is annually observable in some kind of Figg Trees in hot and proper regions; and may also be observed in some Figg Trees of more temperate Countries, in years of no great disadvantage, wherein, when the Summer-ripe Figg is past, others begin to appear, and so, standing in Buttons all the Winter, do either fall away before the Spring, or else proceed to ripeness.

Now, according to these distinctions, we may measure the intent of the Text, and endeavour to make out the expression. For, considering the diversity of these Trees, and their several fructifications, probable or possible it is, that some thereof were implied, and may literally afford a solution.

And first, though it was not the season for Figgs, yet some Fruit might have been expected, even in ordinary bearing Trees. For the *Grossi* or Buttons appear before the Leaves, especially before the Leaves are well grown. Some might have stood during the Winter, and by this time been of some growth: Though many fall off, yet some might remain on, and proceed towards maturity. And we find that good Husbands had an art to make them hold on, as is delivered by *Theophrastus*.

The Σῦκον or common Summer Figg was not expected; for that is placed by *Galen* among the *Fructus Horarii*, or *Horæi*, which ripen in that part of Summer, called Ὥρα, and stands commended by him above other Fruits of that season. And of this kind might be the Figgs which were brought unto *Cleopatra* in a Basket together with an Asp, according to the time of her death on the nineteenth of *August*. And that our Saviour expected not such Figgs, but some other kind, seems to be implied in the indefinite expression, *if haply he might find any thing thereon*; which in that Country, and the variety of such Trees, might not be despaired of, at this season, and very probably hoped for in the first precocious and early bearing Trees. And that there were precocious and early bearing Trees in *Judæa*, may be illustrated from some expressions in Scripture concerning precocious Figgs;[237] *Calathus unus habebat Ficus bonas nimis, sicut solent esse Ficus primi temporis*; *One Basket had very good Figgs, even like the Figgs that are first ripe*. And the like might be more especially expected in this place, if this remarkable Tree be rightly placed in some Mapps of *Jerusalem*; for it is placed, by *Adrichomius*, in or near *Bethphage*, which some conjectures will have to be the *House of Figgs*: and at this place Figg Trees are still to be found, if we consult the Travels of *Bidulphus*.

Again, in this great variety of Figg Trees, as precocious, proterical, biferous, triferous, and always bearing Trees, something might have been expected, though the time of common Figgs was not yet. For some Trees bear in a manner all the year; as may be illustrated from the Epistle of the Emperour *Julian*, concerning his Present of *Damascus* Figgs, which he commendeth from their successive and continued growing and bearing, after the manner of the Fruits which *Homer* describeth in the Garden of *Alcinous*. And though it were then but about the eleventh of *March*, yet, in the Latitude of *Jerusalem*, the Sun at that time hath a good power in the day, and might advance the maturity of precocious often-bearing or ever-bearing Figgs. And therefore when it is said that S. *Peter*[238] stood and warmed himself by the Fire in the Judgment Hall, and the reason is added [*for it was cold*[239]] that expression might be interposed either to denote the coolness in the Morning, according to hot Countries, or some extraordinary and unusual coldness, which happened at that time. For the same *Bidulphus*, who was at that time of the year at *Jerusalem*, saith, that it was then as hot as at *Midsummer* in *England*: and we find in Scripture, that the first Sheaf of Barley was offer'd in *March*.

Our Saviour therefore, seeing a Figg Tree with Leaves well spread, and so as to be distinguished a far off, went unto it, and when he came, found nothing but Leaves; he found it to be no precocious, or always-bearing Tree: And though it were not the time for Summer Figgs, yet he found no rudiments thereof: and though he expected not common Figgs, yet something might happily have been expected of some other kind, according to different fertility, and variety of production; but, discovering nothing, he found a Tree answering the State of the Jewish Rulers, barren unto all expectation.

And this is consonant unto the mystery of the Story, wherein the Figg Tree denoteth the Synagogue and Rulers of the Jews, whom God having peculiarly cultivated, singularly blessed and cherished, he expected from them no ordinary, slow, or customary fructification, but an earliness in good Works, a precocious or continued fructification, and was not content with common after-bearing; and might justly have expostulated with the Jews, as God by the Prophet *Micah*[240] did with their Forefathers; *Præcoquas Ficus desideravit Anima mea, My Soul longed for*, (or desired) *early ripe Fruits, but ye are become as a Vine already gathered, and there is no cluster upon you.*

Lastly, In this account of the Figg Tree, the mystery and symbolical sense is chiefly to be looked upon. Our Saviour, therefore, taking a hint from his hunger to go unto this specious Tree, and intending, by this Tree, to declare a Judgment upon the Synagogue and people of the Jews, he came unto the Tree, and, after the usual manner, inquired, and looked about for some kind of Fruit, as he had done before in the Jews, but found nothing but Leaves and specious outsides, as he had also found in them; and when it bore no Fruit like them, when he expected it, and came to look for it, though it were not the time of ordinary Fruit, yet failing when he required it, in the mysterious sense, 'twas fruitless longer to expect it. For he had come unto them, and they were nothing fructified by it, his departure approached, and his time of preaching was now at an end.

Now, in this account, besides the Miracle, some things are naturally considerable. For it may be question'd how the Figg Tree, naturally a fruitfull Plant, became barren, for it had no shew or so much as rudiment of Fruit: And it was in old time, a signal Judgment of God, that *the Figg Tree should bear no Fruit*: and therefore this Tree may naturally be conceived to have been under some Disease indisposing it to such fructification. And this, in the Pathology of Plants, may be the Disease of φυλλομανία ἐμφυλλισμὸς; or superfolliation mention'd by *Theophrastus*; whereby the fructifying Juice is starved by the excess of Leaves; which in this Tree were already so full spread, that it might be known and distinguished a far off. And this was, also, a sharp resemblance of the hypocrisie of the Rulers, made up of specious outsides, and fruitless ostentation, contrary to the Fruit of the Figg Tree, which, filled with a sweet and pleasant pulp, makes no shew without, not so much as of any Flower.

Some naturals are also considerable from the propriety of this punishment settled upon a Figg Tree: For infertility and barrenness seems more intolerable in this Tree than in any, as being a Vegetable singularly constituted for production; so far from bearing no Fruit that it may be made to bear almost any. And therefore the Ancients singled out this as the fittest Tree whereon to graft and propagate other Fruits, as containing a plentifull and lively Sap, whereby other Cyons would prosper: And, therefore, this Tree was also sacred unto the Deity of Fertility: and the *Statua* of *Priapus* was made of the Figg Tree.

Olim Truncus eram Ficulnus inutile Lignum.

It hath also a peculiar advantage to produce and maintain its Fruit above all other Plants, as not subject to miscarry in Flowers and Blossomes, from accidents of Wind and Weather. For it beareth no Flowers outwardly, and such as it hath, are within the Coat, as the later examination of Naturalists hath discovered.

Lastly, It was a Tree wholly constituted for Fruit, wherein if it faileth, it is in a manner useless, the Wood thereof being of so little use, that it affordeth proverbial expressions,

Homo Ficulneus, argumentum Ficulneum,

for things of no validity.

The Palm Tree, in Cant. 7. 8.

44. *I said I will go up into the Palm Tree, and take hold of the Boughs thereof.* This expression is more agreeable unto the Palm than is commonly apprehended, for that it is a tall bare Tree bearing its Boughs but at the top and upper part; so that it must be ascended before its Boughs or Fruit can be attained: And the going, getting or climbing up, may be Emphatical in this Tree; for

the Trunk or Body thereof is naturally contrived for ascension, and made with advantage for getting up, as having many welts and eminencies, and so as it were a natural Ladder, and Staves, by which it may be climbed, as *Pliny*[241] observeth, *Palmæ teretes atque proceres, densis quadratisque pollicibus faciles se ad scandendum præbent*, by this way men are able to get up into it. And the Figures of Indians thus climbing the same are graphically described in the Travels of *Linschoten*. This Tree is often mentioned in Scripture, and was so remarkable in *Judæa*, that in after-times it became the Emblem of that Country, as may be seen in that Medal of the Emperour *Titus*, with a Captive Woman sitting under a Palm, and the Inscription of *Judæa Capta*. And *Pliny* confirmeth the same when he saith, *Judæa Palmis inclyta*.

Lilies, in Cant. 2. 1, 2, 16.

45. Many things are mention'd in Scripture, which have an Emphasis from this or the neighbour Countries: For besides the Cedars, the Syrian Lilies are taken notice of by Writers. That expression in the *Canticles*,[242] *Thou art fair, thou art fair, thou hast Doves eyes*, receives a particular character, if we look not upon our common Pigeons, but the beauteous and fine ey'd Doves of Syria.

When the Rump is so strictly taken notice of in the Sacrifice of the Peace Offering, in these words,[243] *The whole Rump, it shall be taken off hard by the Back-bone*, it becomes the more considerable in reference to this Country, where Sheep had so large Tails; which, according to *Aristotle*,[244] were a Cubit broad; and so they are still, as *Bellonius* hath delivered.

When 'tis said in the *Canticles*,[245] *Thy Teeth are as a Flock of Sheep, which go up from the washing, whereof every one beareth Twins, and there is not one barren among them*; it may seem hard unto us of these parts to find whole Flocks bearing Twins, and not one barren among them; yet may this be better conceived in the fertile Flocks of those Countries, where Sheep have so often two, sometimes three, and sometimes four, and which is so frequently observed by Writers of the neighbour Country of *Ægypt*. And this fecundity, and fruitfulness of their Flocks, is answerable unto the expression of the Psalmist,[246] *That our Sheep may bring forth thousands and ten thousands in our Streets*. And hereby, besides what was spent at their Tables, a good supply was made for the great consumption of Sheep in their several kinds of Sacrifices; and of so many thousand Male unblemished yearling Lambs, which were required at their Passeovers.

Nor need we wonder to find so frequent mention both of Garden and Field Plants; since *Syria* was notable of old for this curiosity and variety, according to *Pliny*, *Syria hortis operosissima*; and since *Bellonius* hath so lately observed of *Jerusalem*, that its hilly parts did so abound with Plants, that they might be compared unto Mount *Ida* in *Crete* or *Candia*: which is the most noted place for noble Simples yet known.

Trees and Herbs not expresly nam'd in Scripture.

46. Though so many Plants have their express Names in Scripture, yet others are implied in some Texts which are not explicitly mention'd. In the Feast of *Tabernacles* or *Booths*, the Law was this,[247] *Thou shalt take unto thee Boughs of goodly Trees, Branches of the Palm, and the Boughs of thick Trees, and Willows of the Brook*. Now though the Text descendeth not unto particulars of the *goodly Trees*, and *thick Trees*; yet *Maimonides* will tell us that for a *goodly Tree* they made use of the Citron Tree, which is fair and goodly to the eye, and well prospering in that Country: And that for the *thick Trees* they used the Myrtle, which was no rare or infrequent Plant among them. And though it groweth but low in our Gardens, was not a little Tree in those parts; in which Plant also the Leaves grew thick, and almost covered the Stalk. And *Curtius*[248] *Symphorianus* in his description of the *Exotick* Myrtle, makes it, *Folio densissimo senis in ordinem versibus*. The Paschal Lamb was to be eaten with bitterness or bitter Herbs, not particularly set down in Scripture: but the Jewish Writers declare, that they made use of Succory, and wild Lettuce, which Herbs while some conceive they could not get down, as being very bitter, rough and prickly, they may consider that the time of the Passeover was in the Spring, when these Herbs are young and tender, and consequently less unpleasant: besides, according to the Jewish custom, these Herbs were dipped in the *Charoseth* or Sawce made of Raisins stamped with Vinegar, and were also eaten with Bread; and they had four Cups of Wine allowed unto them; and it was sufficient to take but a pittance of Herbs, or the quantity of an Olive.

Reeds in Scripture.

47. Though the famous paper Reed of *Ægypt*, be onely particularly named in Scripture; yet when Reeds are so often mention'd, without special name or distinction, we may conceive their differences may be comprehended, and that they were not all of one kind, or that the common Reed was onely implied. For mention is made in *Ezekiel*[249] of *a measuring Reed of six Cubits*: we find that they smote our Saviour on the Head with a Reed,[250] and put a Sponge with Vinegar on a Reed, which was long enough to reach to his mouth, while he was upon the Cross; And with such differences of Reeds, *Vallatory*, *Sagittary*, *Scriptory*, and others, they might be furnished in *Judæa*: For we find in the portion of *Ephraim*,[251] *Vallis arundineti*; and so set down in the Mapps of *Adricomius*, and in our Translation the River *Kana*, or Brook of *Canes*. And *Bellonius* tells us that the River *Jordan* affordeth plenty and variety of Reeds; out of some whereof the Arabs make Darts, and light Lances, and out of others, Arrows; and withall that there plentifully groweth the fine *Calamus, arundo Scriptoria*, or writing Reed, which they gather with the greatest care, as being of singular use and commodity at home and abroad; a hard Reed about the compass of a Goose or Swans Quill, whereof I have seen some polished and cut with a Webb; which is in common use for writing throughout the Turkish Dominions, they using not the Quills of Birds.

And whereas the same Authour with other describers of these parts affirmeth, that the River *Jordan* not far from *Jerico*, is but such a Stream as a youth may throw a Stone over it, or about eight fathoms broad, it doth not diminish the account and solemnity of the miraculous passage of the Israelites under *Joshua*; For it must be considered, that they passed it in the time of Harvest, when the River was high, and the Grounds about it under Water, according to that pertinent parenthesis, *As the Feet of the Priests, which carried the Ark, were dipped in the brim of the Water, (for Jordan*[252] *overfloweth all its Banks at the time of Harvest.)* In this consideration it was well joined with the great River *Euphrates*, in that expression in *Ecclesiasticus*,[253] *God maketh the understanding to abound like Euphrates, and as Jordan in the time of Harvest*.

Zizania, in S. Matt. 13. 24, 25, etc.

48. *The Kingdom of Heaven is likened unto a man which sowed good Seed in his Field, but while men slept, his Enemy came and sowed Tares* (or, as the Greek, *Zizania*) *among the Wheat*.

Now, how to render *Zizania*, and to what species of Plants to confine it, there is no slender doubt; for the word is not mention'd in other parts of Scripture, nor in any ancient Greek Writer: it is not to be found in *Aristotle, Theophrastus*, or *Dioscorides*. Some Greek and Latin Fathers have made use of the same, as also *Suidas* and *Phavorinus*; but probably they have all derived it from this Text.

And therefore this obscurity might easily occasion such variety in Translations and Expositions. For some retain the word *Zizania*, as the Vulgar, that of *Beza*, of *Junius*, and also the Italian and Spanish. The Low Dutch renders it *Oncruidt*, the German *Oncraut*, or *Herba Mala*, the French *Turoye* or *Lolium*, and the English *Tares*.

Besides, this being conceived to be a Syriack word, it may still add unto the uncertainty of the sense. For though this Gospel were first written in Hebrew, or Syriack, yet it is not unquestionable whether the true Original be any where extant: And that Syriack Copy which we now have, is conceived to be of far later time than S. *Matthew*.

Expositours and Annotatours are also various. *Hugo Grotius* hath passed the word *Zizania* without a Note. *Diodati*, retaining the word *Zizania*, conceives that it was some peculiar Herb growing among the Corn of those Countries, and not known in our Fields. But *Emanuel de Sa* interprets it, *Plantas semini noxias*, and so accordingly some others.

Buxtorfius, in his Rabbinical Lexicon, gives divers interpretations, sometimes for degenerated Corn, sometimes for the black Seeds in Wheat, but withall concludes, *an hæc sit eadem vox aut species, cum Zizaniâ apud Evangelistam, quærant alii*. But Lexicons and Dictionaries by *Zizania* do almost generally understand *Lolium*, which we call *Darnel*, and commonly confine the signification to that Plant: Notwithstanding, since *Lolium* had a known and received Name in Greek, some may be apt to doubt, why, if that Plant were particularly intended, the proper Greek word was not used in the Text. For *Theophrastus*[254] named *Lolium* Αἶρα, and hath often mentioned that Plant; and in one place saith that Corn doth sometimes *Loliescere* degenerate into *Darnel*. *Dioscorides*, who travelled over *Judæa*, gives it the same name, which is also to be found in *Galen*, *Ætius* and *Ægineta*; and *Pliny* hath sometimes latinized that word into *Æra*.

Besides, *Lolium* or Darnel shews it self in the Winter, growing up with the Wheat; and *Theophrastus* observed that it was no Vernal Plant, but came up in the Winter; which will not well answer the expression of the Text, *And when the Blade came up, and brought forth Fruit*, or gave evidence of its Fruit, *the Zizania* appeared. And if the Husbandry of the Ancients were agreeable unto ours, they would not have been so earnest to weed away the Darnel; for our Husbandmen do not commonly weed it in the Field, but separate the Seeds after Thrashing. And therefore *Galen* delivereth, that in an unseasonable year, and great scarcity of Corn, when they neglected to separate the Darnel, the Bread proved generally unwholsome, and had evil effects on the Head.

Our old and later Translation render *Zizania*, Tares, which name our English Botanists give unto *Aracus*, *Cracca*, *Vicia sylvestris*, calling them Tares, and strangling Tares. And our Husbandmen by Tares understand some sorts of wild Fitches, which grow amongst Corn, and clasp upon it, according to the Latin Etymology, *Vicia à Vinciendo*. Now in this uncertainty of the Original, Tares as well as some others, may make out the sense, and be also more agreeable unto the circumstances of the Parable. For they come up and appear what they are, when the Blade of the Corn is come up, and also the Stalk and Fruit discoverable. They have likewise little spreading Roots, which may intangle or rob the good Roots, and they have also tendrils and claspers, which lay hold of what grows near them, and so can hardly be weeded without endangering the neighbour Corn.

However, if by *Zizania* we understand *Herbas segeti noxias*, or *vitia segetum*, as some Expositours have done, and take the word in a more general sense, comprehending several Weeds and Vegetables offensive unto Corn, according as the Greek word in the plural Number may imply, and as the learned *Laurenbergius*[255] hath expressed, *Runcare quod apud nostrates Weden dicitur, Zizanias inutiles est evellere*. If, I say, it be thus taken, we shall not need to be definitive, or confine unto one particular Plant, from a word which may comprehend divers: And this may also prove a safer sense, in such obscurity of the Original.

And therefore since in this Parable the sower of the *Zizania* is the Devil, and the *Zizania* wicked persons; if any from this larger acception, will take in Thistles, Darnel, Cockle, wild strangling Fitches, Bindweed, *Tribulus*, Restharrow and other *Vitia Segetum*; he may, both from the natural and symbolical qualities of those Vegetables, have plenty of matter to illustrate the variety of his mischiefs, and of the wicked of this world.

Cockle, in Job 31. 40.

49. When 'tis said in *Job*, *Let Thistles grow up instead of Wheat, and Cockle instead of Barley*, the words are intelligible, the sense allowable and significant to this purpose: but whether the word *Cockle* doth strictly conform unto the Original, some doubt may be made from the different Translations of it; For the Vulgar renders it *Spina*, Tremelius *Vitia Frugum*, and the *Geneva Turoye* or Darnel. Besides, whether Cockle were common in the ancient Agriculture of those parts, or what word they used for it, is of great uncertainty. For the Elder Botanical Writers have made no mention thereof, and the Moderns have given it the Name of *Pseudomelanthium*, *Nigellastrum*, *Lychnoeides Segetum*, names not known unto Antiquity: And therefore our Translation hath warily set down [*noisome Weeds*] in the Margin.

Footnotes

[188]*Depinxit oculos stibio*. 2 Kings 9. 30. Jerem. 4. 30. Ezek. 23. 40.
[189]Jona 4. 6. *a Gourd*.
[190]ἄπιστος θέα. Philo.
[191]Radzivil *in his Travels*.
[192]G. Venetus *Problem* 200.
[193]*Lib. 18. Nat. Hist.*
[194]Acts 2. 13.
[195]Theophrast. *Hist. Lib. 4. Cap. 7. 8.*
[196]Plin. *lib. 13. cap. ultimo.*
[197]Dan. 4. 9. Ps. 1. 14. 12.

[198] Sbacher *from* Sbachar festinus fuit *or* maturuit.
[199] Plin. *lib. 14.*
[200] Terebinthus in Macedonia fruticat, in Syria, magna est. *Lib. 13.* Plin.
[201] Hosea. 4. 13.
[202] Judges 20. 45, 47. *Ch.* 21. 13.
[203] Isa. 9. 10
[204] 1 Chron. 27. 28.
[205] 1 King. 10. 27.
[206] Amos 7. 14.
[207] Psal. 78 47.
[208] Luk. 17. 6.
[209] D. Greaves.
[210] Gen. 26. 12.
[211] Gen. 41. 56.
[212] Gen. 45. 9, 11.
[213] Theoph. *Hist. l. 8.*
[214] Ægypt ὀμιχλώδης, καὶ δρόσερος *Vid.* Theophrastum
[215] Gen. 41. 48.
[216] De causis Plant. *Lib. 1. Cap. 7.*
[217] Καλλικαρπεῖν οὐκ ἔξει.
[218] De horticultura.
[219] Καλλιέλαιον Rom. 11. 42.
[220] Bellonius *de Avibus.*
[221] Theophrast. *l. 9. c. 6.*
[222] Linum folliculos germinavit, σπερματίζον *Septuag.* Serotina, *Lat.* ὄψιμα, *Gr.*
[223] Radzevil's *Travels.*
[224] Plin. *lib. 18. cap. 18.*
[225] Columella *lib. 2 cap. 22.*
[226] Varro *lib. 1. cap. 49.*
[227] Psal. 120. 4.
[228] Job 30. 3, 4.
[229] 2 Sam. 18. 9, 14.
[230] 2 King. 18. 4.
[231] *A journey to* Jerusalem, 1672.
[232] Jer. 10. 5.
[233] Ainsworth.
[234] Matt. 21. 19.
[235] Heinsius *in* Nonnum.
[236] D. Hammond.
[237] Jer. 24. 2.
[238] *S.* Mark 14. 67. *S.* Luke 22. 55, 56.
[239] *S.* John 18. 18.
[240] Micah 7. 1.
[241] Plin. 13. *cap. 4.*
[242] Cant. 4. 1.
[243] Levit. 3. 9.
[244] Aristot. *Hist. Animal. lib. 8.*
[245] Cant. 4. 2.
[246] Psal. 144. 13.
[247] Levit. 23. 40.
[248] Curtius *de Hortis.*
[249] Ezek. 40. 5.
[250] *S.* Matt 27. 30, 48.
[251] Josh. 16. 17.

[252] Josh. 3. 13.
[253] Ecclus. 24. 26.
[254] ἐξαιρῆσθαι. Theophrast. *Hist. Plant. l. 8.*
[255] De Horticultura.

OF GARLANDS
and Coronary or Garden-plants.
TRACT II

SIR,

The use of flowry Crowns and Garlands is of no slender Antiquity, and higher than I conceive you apprehend it. For, besides the old Greeks and Romans, the Ægyptians made use hereof; who, beside the bravery of their Garlands, had little Birds upon them to peck their Heads and Brows, and so to keep them sleeping at their Festival compotations. This practice also extended as far as *India*: for at the Feast with the Indian King, it is peculiarly observed by *Philostratus* that their custom was to wear Garlands, and come crowned with them unto their Feast.

The Crowns and Garlands of the Ancients were either Gestatory, such as they wore about their Heads or Necks; Portatory, such as they carried at solemn Festivals; Pensile or Suspensory, such as they hanged about the Posts of their Houses in honour of their Gods, as of *Jupiter Thyræus* or *Limeneus*; or else they were Depository, such as they laid upon the Graves and Monuments of the dead. And these were made up after all ways of Art, Compactile, Sutile, Plectile; for which Work there were στεφανοπλόκοι or expert Persons to contrive them after the best grace and property.

Though we yield not unto them in the beauty of flowry Garlands, yet some of those of Antiquity were larger than any we lately meet with: for we find in *Athenæus* that a Myrtle Crown of one and twenty foot in compass was solemnly carried about at the Hellotian Feast in *Corinth*, together with the Bones of *Europa*.

And Garlands were surely of frequent use among them; for we reade in *Galen*[256] that when *Hippocrates* cured the great Plague of *Athens* by Fires kindled in and about the City; the fuel thereof consisted much of their Garlands. And they must needs be very frequent and of common use, the ends thereof being many. For they were convivial, festival, sacrificial, nuptial, honorary, funebrial. We who propose unto our selves the pleasure of two Senses, and onely single out such as are of Beauty and good Odour, cannot strictly confine our selves unto imitation of them.

For, in their convivial Garlands, they had respect unto Plants preventing drunkenness, or discussing the exhalations from Wine; wherein, beside Roses, taking in Ivy, Vervain, Melilote, *etc.* they made use of divers of small Beauty or good Odour. The solemn festival Garlands were made properly unto their Gods, and accordingly contrived from Plants sacred unto such Deities; and their sacrificial ones were selected under such considerations. Their honorary Crowns triumphal, ovary, civical, obsidional, had little of Flowers in them: and their funebrial Garlands had little of beauty in them beside Roses, while they made them of Myrtle, Rosemary, Apium, *etc.* under symbolical intimations: but our florid and purely ornamental Garlands, delightfull unto sight and smell, nor framed according to mystical and symbolical considerations, are of more free election, and so may be made to excell those of the Ancients; we having *China*, *India*, and a new world to supply us, beside the great distinction of Flowers unknown unto Antiquity, and the varieties thereof arising from Art and Nature.

But, beside Vernal, Æstival and Autumnal made of Flowers, the Ancients had also Hyemal Garlands; contenting themselves at first with such as were made of Horn died into several Colours, and shaped into the Figures of Flowers, and also of *Æs Coronarium* or *Clincquant* or Brass thinly wrought out into Leaves commonly known among us. But the curiosity of some Emperours for such intents had Roses brought from *Ægypt* untill they had found the art to produce late Roses in *Rome*, and to make them grow in the Winter, as is delivered in that handsome Epigramme of *Martial*,

At tu Romanæ jussus jam cedere Brumæ
Mitte tuas messes, Accipe, Nile, Rosas.

Some American Nations, who do much excell in Garlands, content not themselves onely with Flowers, but make elegant Crowns of Feathers, whereof they have some of greater radiancy and lustre than their Flowers: and since there is an Art to set into shapes, and curiously to work in choicest Feathers, there could nothing answer the Crowns made of the choicest Feathers of some *Tomineios* and Sun Birds.

The Catalogue of Coronary Plants is not large in *Theophrastus, Pliny, Pollux,* or *Athenæus*: but we may find a good enlargement in the Accounts of Modern Botanists; and additions may still be made by successive acquists of fair and specious Plants, not yet translated from foreign Regions or little known unto our Gardens: he that would be complete may take notice of these following,
Flos Tigridis.
Flos Lyncis.
Pinea Indica Recchi, Talama Ouiedi.
Herba Paradisea.
Volubilis Mexicanus.
Narcissus Indicus Serpentarius.
Helichrysum Mexicanum.
Xicama.
Aquilegia novæ Hispaniæ Cacoxochitli Recchi.
Aristochæa Mexicana.
Camaratinga sive Caragunta quarta Pisonis.
Maracuia Granadilla.
Cambay sive Myrtus Americana.
Flos Auriculæ Flor de la Oreia.
Floripendio novæ Hispaniæ.
Rosa Indica.
Zilium Indicum.
Fula Magori Garciæ.
Champe Garciæ Champacca Bontii.
Daullontas frutex odoratus seu Chamæmelum arborescens Bontii.
Beidelsar Alpini.
Sambuc.
Amberboi Turcarum.
Nuphar Ægyptium.
Lilionarcissus Indicus.
Bamma Ægyptiacum.
Hiucca Canadensis horti Farnesiani.
Bupthalmum novæ Hispaniæ Alepocapath.
Valeriana seu Chrysanthemum Americanum Acocotlis.
Flos Corvinus Coronarius Americanus. Capolin Cerasus dulcis Indicus Floribus racemosis.
Asphodelus Americanus.
Syringa Lutea Americana.
Bulbus unifolius.
Moly latifolium Flore luteo.
Conyza Americana purpurea.
Salvia Cretica pomifera Bellonii.
Lausus Serrata Odora.
Ornithogalus Promontorii Bonæ Spei.
Fritallaria crassa Soldanica Promontorii Bonæ Spei.
Sigillum Solomonis Indicum.
Tulipa Promontorii Bonæ Spei.
Iris Uvaria.
Nopolxoch sedum elegans novæ Hispaniæ.

More might be added unto this List; and I have onely taken the pains to give you a short Specimen of those many more which you may find in respective Authours, and which time and future industry may make no great strangers in *England*. The Inhabitants of *Nova Hispania*, and a great part of *America*, Mahometans, Indians, Chineses, are eminent promoters of these coronary and specious Plants: and the annual tribute of the King of *Bisnaguer* in *India*, arising out of Odours and Flowers, amounts unto many thousands of Crowns.

Thus, in brief, of this matter. I am, *etc.*

Footnotes

[256]*De Theriaca ad Pisonem.*

OF THE
FISHES EATEN BY OUR SAVIOUR
with His Disciples after His Resurrection from the Dead.
TRACT III

SIR,

I have thought, a little, upon the Question proposed by you [viz. *What kind of Fishes those were of which our Saviour ate with his Disciples after his Resurrection?*[257]] and I return you such an Answer, as, in so short time for study, and in the midst of my occasions, occurs to me.

The Books of Scripture (as also those which are Apocryphal) are often silent, or very sparing, in the particular Names of Fishes; or in setting them down in such manner as to leave the kinds of them without all doubt and reason for farther inquiry. For, when it declareth what Fishes were allowed the Israelites for their Food, they are onely set down in general which have Finns and Scales; whereas, in the account of *Quadrupeds* and Birds, there is particular mention made of divers of them. In the Book of *Tobit* that Fish which he took out of the River is onely named a great Fish, and so there remains much uncertainty to determine the Species thereof. And even the Fish which swallowed *Jonah*, and is called a *great Fish*, and commonly thought to be a great Whale, is not received without all doubt; while some learned men conceive it to have been none of our Whales, but a large kind of *Lamia*.

And, in this narration of S. *John*, the Fishes are onely expressed by their Bigness and Number, not their Names, and therefore it may seem undeterminable what they were: notwithstanding, these Fishes being taken in the great Lake or Sea of *Tiberias*, something may be probably stated therein. For since *Bellonius*, that diligent and learned Traveller, informeth us, that the Fishes of this Lake were Trouts, Pikes, Chevins and Tenches; it may well be conceived that either all or some thereof are to be understood in this Scripture. And these kind of Fishes become large and of great growth, answerable unto the expression of Scripture, *One hundred and fifty-three great Fishes*; that is, large in their own kinds, and the largest kinds in this Lake and fresh Water, wherein no great variety, and of the larger sort of Fishes, could be expected. For the River *Jordan*, running through this Lake, falls into the Lake of *Asphaltus*, and hath no mouth into the Sea, which might admit of great Fishes or greater variety to come up into it.

And out of the mouth of some of these forementioned Fishes might the *Tribute money* be taken, when our Saviour, at *Capernaum*, seated upon the same Lake, said unto *Peter, Go thou to the Sea, and cast an Hook, and take up the Fish that first cometh; and when thou hast opened his mouth thou shalt find a piece of money; that take and give them for thee and me.*

And this makes void that common conceit and tradition of the Fish called *Fabermarinus*, by some, a *Peter* or *Penny Fish*; which having two remarkable round spots upon either side, these are conceived to be the marks of S. *Peter's* Fingers or signatures of the Money: for though it hath these marks, yet is there no probability that such a kind of Fish was to be found in the Lake of *Tiberias, Geneserah* or *Galilee*, which is but sixteen miles long and six broad, and hath no communication with the Sea; for this is a mere Fish of the Sea and salt Water, and (though we meet with some thereof on our Coast) is not to be found in many Seas.

Thus having returned no improbable Answer unto your Question, I shall crave leave to ask another of your self concerning that Fish mentioned by *Procopius*,[258] which brought the famous King *Theodorick* to his end: his words are to this effect: "The manner of his Death was this, *Symmachus* and his Son-in-law *Boëthius*, just men and great relievers of the poor, Senatours and Consuls, had many enemies, by whose false accusations *Theodorick* being perswaded that they plotted against him, put them to death and confiscated their Estates. Not long after his Waiters set before him at Supper a great Head of a Fish, which seemed to him to be the Head of *Symmachus* lately murthered; and with his Teeth sticking out, and fierce glaring eyes to threaten him: being frighted, he grew chill, went to Bed, lamenting what he had done to *Symmachus* and *Boëthius*; and soon after died.' What Fish do you apprehend this to have been? I would learn of you; give me your thoughts about it.

I am, etc.

Footnotes

[257] *S.* Joh. 21. 9, 10, 11, 13.
[258] *De Bello Gothico, lib. 1.*

AN ANSWER TO CERTAIN QUERIES
relating to Fishes, Birds, Insects.
TRACT IV

SIR,

I return the following Answers to your Queries which were these,

[1. What Fishes are meant by the Names, *Halec* and *Mugil*?

2. What is the Bird which you will receive from the Bearer? and what Birds are meant by the Names *Halcyon*, *Nysus*, *Ciris*, *Nycticorax*?

3. What Insect is meant by the word *Cicada*?]

Answer to Query 1.

The word *Halec* we are taught to render an *Herring*, which, being an ancient word, is not strictly appropriable unto a Fish not known or not described by the Ancients; and which the modern Naturalists are fain to name *Harengus*; the word *Halecula* being applied unto such little Fish out of which they were fain to make Pickle; and *Hulec* or *Alec*, taken for the Liquamen or Liquor itself, according to that of the Poet,

——*Ego fæcem primus et Alec*
Primus et inveni piper album——

And was a conditure and Sawce much affected by Antiquity, as was also *Muria* and *Garum*.

In common constructions, *Mugil* is rendred a *Mullet*, which, notwithstanding, is a different Fish from the *Mugil* described by Authours; wherein, if we mistake, we cannot so closely apprehend the expression of *Juvenal*,

——*Quosdam ventres et Mugilis intrat.*

And misconceive the Fish, whereby Fornicatours were so opprobriously and irksomely punished; for the *Mugil* being somewhat rough and hard skinned, did more exasperate the gutts of such offenders: whereas the Mullet was a smooth Fish, and of too high esteem to be imployed in such offices.

Answer to Query 2.

I cannot but wonder that this Bird you sent should be a stranger unto you, and unto those who had a sight thereof: for, though it be not seen every day, yet we often meet with it in this Country. It is an elegant Bird, which he that once beholdeth can hardly mistake any other for it. From the proper Note it is called an *Hoopebird* with us; in Greek *Epops*, in Latin *Upupa*. We are little obliged unto our School instruction, wherein we are taught to render *Upupa*, a *Lapwing*, which Bird our natural Writers name *Vannellus*; for thereby we mistake this remarkable Bird, and apprehend not rightly what is delivered of it.

We apprehend not the Hieroglyphical considerations which the old Ægyptians made of this observable Bird; who considering therein the order and variety of Colours, the twenty six or twenty eight Feathers in its Crest, his latitancy, and mewing this handsome outside in the Winter; they made it an Emblem of the varieties of the World, the succession of Times and Seasons, and signal mutations in them. And therefore *Orus*, the Hieroglyphick of the World, had the Head of an Hoopebird upon the top of his Staff.

Hereby we may also mistake the *Duchiphath*, or Bird forbidden for Food in *Leviticus*, and, not knowing the Bird, may the less apprehend some reasons of that prohibition; that is, the magical virtues ascribed unto it by the Ægyptians, and the superstitious apprehensions which that Nation held of it, whilst they precisely numbred the Feathers and Colours thereof, while they placed it on the Heads of their Gods, and near their Mercurial Crosses, and so highly magnified this Bird in their sacred Symbols.

> Levit. 11. 19.

Again, not knowing or mistaking this Bird, we may misapprehend, or not closely apprehend, that handsome expression of *Ovid*, when *Tereus* was turned into an *Upupa*, or Hoopebird.

Vertitur in volucrem cui sunt pro vertice Cristæ,
Protinus immodicum surgit pro cuspide rostrum
Nomen Epops volucri, facies armata videtur.

For, in this military shape, he is aptly phancied even still revengefully to pursue his hated Wife *Progne*: in the propriety of his Note crying out, *Pou, pou, ubi, ubi*, or *Where are you?*

Nor are we singly deceived in the nominal translation of this Bird: in many other Animals we commit the like mistake. So *Gracculus* is rendred a *Jay*, which Bird notwithstanding must be of a dark colour according to that of *Martial*,

Sed quandam volo nocte nigriorem
Formica, pice, Gracculo, cicada.

Halcyon[259] is rendred a *King-fisher*, a Bird commonly known among us, and by Zoographers and Naturals the same is named *Ispida*, a well coloured Bird frequenting Streams and Rivers, building in holes of Pits, like some Martins, about the end of the Spring; in whose Nests we have found little else than innumerable small Fish Bones, and white round Eggs of a smooth and polished surface, whereas the true *Alcyon* is a Sea Bird, makes an handsome Nest floating upon the Water, and breedeth in the Winter.

That *Nysus* should be rendred either an *Hobby* or a *Sparrow Hawk*, in the Fable of *Nysus* and *Scylla* in *Ovid*, because we are much to seek in the distinction of Hawks according to their old denominations, we shall not much contend, and may allow a favourable latitude therein: but that the *Ciris* or Bird into which *Scylla* was turned should be translated a *Lark*, it can hardly be made out agreeable unto the description of *Virgil* in his Poem of that name,

Inde alias volucres mimóque infecta rubenti
Crura——

But seems more agreeable unto some kind of *Hæmantopus* or Redshank; and so the *Nysus* to have been some kind of Hawk, which delighteth about the Sea and Marishes, where such prey most aboundeth, which sort of Hawk while *Scaliger* determineth to be a Merlin, the French Translatour warily expoundeth it to be some kind of Hawk.

Nycticorax we may leave unto the common and verbal translation of a *Night Raven*, but we know no proper kind of Raven unto which to confine the same, and therefore some take the liberty to ascribe it unto some sort of Owls, and others unto the Bittern; which Bird in its common Note, which he useth out of the time of coupling and upon the Wing, so well resembleth the croaking of a Raven that I have been deceived by it.

Answer to Query 3.

While *Cicada* is rendred a *Grashopper*, we commonly think that which is so called among us to be the true *Cicada*; wherein, as we have elsewhere declared,[260] there is a great mistake: for we have not the *Cicada* in *England*, and indeed no proper word for that Animal, which the French nameth *Cigale*. That which we commonly call a Grashopper, and the French *Saulterelle* being one kind of Locust, so rendred in the Plague of *Ægypt*, and, in old Saxon named *Gersthop*.

I have been the less accurate in these Answers, because the Queries are not of difficult Resolution, or of great moment: however, I would not wholly neglect them or your satisfaction, as being, Sir,

Yours, etc.

Footnotes

[259] *See Vulg. Err. B. 3. c. 10.*
[260] *Vulg. Err. B. 5. c. 3.*

OF HAWKS AND FALCONRY
Ancient and Modern.
TRACT V

Sir,

In vain you expect much information, *de Re Accipitraria*, of Falconry, Hawks or Hawking, from very ancient Greek or Latin Authours; that Art being either unknown or so little advanced among them, that it seems to have proceeded no higher than the daring of Birds: which makes so little thereof to be found in *Aristotle*, who onely mentions some rude practice thereof in *Thracia*; as also in *Ælian*, who speaks something of Hawks and Crows among the Indians; little or nothing of true Falconry being mention'd before *Julius Firmicus*, in the days of *Constantius*, Son to *Constantine* the Great.

Yet if you consult the accounts of later Antiquity left by *Demetrius* the Greek, by *Symmachus* and *Theodosius*, and by *Albertus Magnus*, about five hundred years ago, you, who have been so long acquainted with this noble Recreation, may better compare the ancient and modern practice, and rightly observe how many things in that Art are added, varied, disused or retained in the practice of these days.

In the Diet of Hawks, they allowed of divers Meats which we should hardly commend. For beside the Flesh of Beef, they admitted of Goat, Hog, Deer, Whelp and Bear. And how you will approve the quantity and measure thereof, I make some doubt; while by weight they allowed half a pound of Beef, seven ounces of Swines Flesh, five of Hare, eight ounces of Whelp, as much of Deer, and ten ounces of He-Goats Flesh.

In the time of *Demetrius* they were not without the practice of Phlebotomy or Bleeding, which they used in the Thigh and Pounces; they plucked away the Feathers on the Thigh, and rubbed the part, but if the Vein appeared not in that part, they opened the Vein of the fore Talon.

In the days of *Albertus*, they made use of Cauteries in divers places: to advantage their sight they seared them under the inward angle of the eye; above the eye in distillations and diseases of the Head; in upward pains they seared above the Joint of the Wing, and at the bottom of the Foot, against the Gout; and the chief time for these cauteries they made to be the month of *March*.

In great coldness of Hawks they made use of Fomentations, some of the steam or vapour of artificial and natural Baths, some wrapt them up in hot Blankets, giving them Nettle Seeds and Butter.

No Clysters are mention'd, nor can they be so profitably used; but they made use of many purging Medicines. They purged with Aloe, which, unto larger Hawks, they gave in the bigness of a Great Bean; unto less, in the quantity of a *Cicer*, which notwithstanding I should rather give washed, and with a few drops of Oil of Almonds: for the Guts of flying Fowls are tender and easily scratched by it; and upon the use of Aloe both in Hawks and Cormorants I have sometimes observed bloody excretions.

In phlegmatick causes they seldom omitted *Stave-saker*, but they purged sometimes with a Mouse, and the Food of boiled Chickens, sometimes with good Oil and Honey.

They used also the Ink of Cuttle Fishes, with Smallage, Betony, Wine and Honey. They made use of stronger Medicines than present practice doth allow. For they were not afraid to give *Coccus Baphicus*; beating up eleven of its Grains unto a Lentor, which they made up into five Pills wrapt up with Honey and Pepper: and, in some of their old Medicines, we meet with Scammony and *Euphorbium*. Whether, in the tender Bowels of Birds, infusions of Rhubarb, Agaric and Mechoachan be not of safer use, as to take of Agary two Drachms, of Cinnamon half a Drachm, of

Liquorish a Scruple, and, infusing them in Wine, to express a part into the mouth of the Hawk, may be considered by present practice.

Few Mineral Medicines were of inward use among them: yet sometimes we observe they gave filings of Iron in the straitness of the Chest, as also Lime in some of their pectoral Medicines.

But they commended Unguents of Quick-silver against the Scab: and I have safely given six or eight Grains of *Mercurius Dulcis* unto Kestrils and Owls, as also crude and current Quick-silver, giving the next day small Pellets of Silver or Lead till they came away uncoloured: and this, if any, may probably destroy that obstinate Disease of the *Filander* or Back-worm.

A peculiar remedy they had against the Consumption of Hawks. For, filling a Chicken with Vinegar, they closed up the Bill, and hanging it up untill the Flesh grew tender, they fed the Hawk therewith: and to restore and well Flesh them, they commonly gave them Hogs Flesh, with Oil, Butter and Honey; and a decoction of Cumfory to bouze.

They disallowed of salt Meats and Fat; but highly esteemed of Mice in most indispositions; and in the falling Sickness had great esteem of boiled Batts: and in many Diseases, of the Flesh of Owls which feed upon those Animals. In Epilepsies they also gave the Brain of a Kid drawn thorough a gold Ring; and, in Convulsions, made use of a mixture of Musk and *Stercus humanum aridum*.

For the better preservation of their Health they strowed Mint and Sage about them; and for the speedier mewing of their Feathers, they gave them the Slough of a Snake, or a Tortoise out of the Shell, or a green Lizard cut in pieces.

If a Hawk were unquiet, they hooded him, and placed him in a Smith's Shop for some time, where, accustomed to the continual noise of hammering, he became more gentle and tractable.

They used few terms of Art, plainly and intelligibly expressing the parts affected, their Diseases and Remedies. This heap of artificial terms first entring with the French Artists: who seem to have been the first and noblest Falconers in the Western part of *Europe*; although, in their Language, they have no word which in general expresseth an Hawk.

They carried their Hawks in the left hand, and let them flie from the right. They used a Bell, and took great care that their Jesses should not be red, lest Eagles should flie at them. Though they used Hoods, we have no clear description of them, and little account of their Lures.

The ancient Writers left no account of the swiftness of Hawks or measure of their flight: but *Heresbachius*[261] delivers that *William* Duke of *Cleve* had an Hawk which, in one day, made a flight out of *Westphalia* into *Prussia*. And, upon good account, an Hawk in this Country of *Norfolk*, made a flight at a Woodcock near thirty miles in one hour. How far the Hawks, Merlins and wild Fowl which come unto us with a North-west wind in the Autumn, flie in a day, there is no clear account; but coming over Sea their flight hath been long, or very speedy. For I have known them to light so weary on the coast, that many have been taken with Dogs, and some knock'd down with Staves and Stones.

Their Perches seem not so large as ours; for they made them of such a bigness that their Talons might almost meet: and they chose to make them of Sallow, Poplar or Lime Tree.

They used great clamours and hollowing in their flight, which they made by these words, *ou loi, la, la, la*; and to raise the Fowls, made use of the sound of a Cymbal.

Their recreation seemed more sober and solemn than ours at present, so improperly attended with Oaths and Imprecations. For they called on God at their setting out, according to the account of *Demetrius*, τὸν Θεὸν ἐπικαλέσαντες, *in the first place calling upon God*.

The learned *Rigaltius* thinketh, that if the Romans had well known this airy Chase, they would have left or less regarded their Circensial Recreations. The Greeks understood Hunting early, but little or nothing of our Falconry. If *Alexander* had known it, we might have found something of it and more of Hawks in *Aristotle*; who was so unacquainted with that way, that he thought that Hawks would not feed upon the Heart of Birds. Though he hath mention'd divers Hawks, yet *Julius Scaliger*, an expert Falconer, despaired to reconcile them unto ours. And 'tis well if, among them, you can clearly make out a Lanner, a Sparrow Hawk and a Kestril, but must not hope to find your Gier Falcon there, which is the noble Hawk; and I wish you one no worse than that of *Henry* King of *Navarre*; which, *Scaliger* saith, he saw strike down a Buzzard, two wild Geese, divers Kites, a Crane and a Swan.

Nor must you expect from high Antiquity the distinctions of Eyess and Ramage Hawks, of Sores and Entermewers, of Hawks of the Lure and the Fist; nor that material distinction into short and long winged Hawks; from whence arise such differences in their taking down of Stones; in their flight, their striking down or seizing of their Prey, in the strength of their Talons, either in the Heel and fore-Talon, or the middle and the Heel: nor yet what Eggs produce the different Hawks, or when they lay three Eggs, that the first produceth a Female and large Hawk, the second of a midler sort, and the third a smaller Bird Tercellene or Tassel of the Masle Sex; which Hawks being onely observed abroad by the Ancients, were looked upon as Hawks of different kinds and not of the same Eyrie or Nest. As for what *Aristotle* affirmeth that Hawks and Birds of prey drink not; although you know that it will not strictly hold, yet I kept an Eagle two years, which fed upon Kats, Kittlings, Whelps and Ratts, without one drop of Water.

If any thing may add unto your knowledge in this noble Art, you must pick it out of later Writers than those you enquire of. You may peruse the two Books of Falconry writ by that renowned Emperour *Frederick* the Second; as also the Works of the noble Duke *Belisarius*, of *Tardiffe*, *Francherius*, of *Francisco Sforzino* of *Vicensa*; and may not a little inform or recreate your self with that elegant Poem of *Thuanus*.[262] I leave you to divert your self by the perusal of it, having, at present, no more to say but that I am, *etc.*

Footnotes

[261]*De Re Accipitraria, in 3 Books.*
[262]*De Re Rustica.*

OF CYMBALS, Etc.
TRACT VI

Sir,

With what difficulty, if possibility, you may expect satisfaction concerning the Musick, or Musical Instruments of the Hebrews, you will easily discover if you consult the attempts of learned men upon that Subject: but for Cymbals, of whose Figure you enquire, you may find some described in *Bayfius*, in the Comment of *Rhodius* upon *Scribonius Largus*, and others.

As for Κύμβαλον ἀλαλάζον mentioned by S. *Paul*,[263] and rendred a *Tinckling Cymbal*, whether the translation be not too soft and diminutive some question may be made: for the word ἀλαλάζον implieth no small sound, but a strained and lofty vociferation, or some kind of hollowing sound, according to the Exposition of *Hesychius*, Ἀλαλάξατε ἐνυψώσατε τὴν φωνήν. A word drawn from the lusty shout of Souldiers, crying Ἀλαλὰ at the first charge upon their Enemies, according to the custom of Eastern Nations, and used by Trojans in *Homer*; and is also the Note of the Chorus in *Aristophanes* Ἀλαλαὶ ἰὴ παιών. In other parts of Scripture we reade of loud and high sounding Cymbals; and in *Clemens Alexandrinus* that the Arabians made use of Cymbals in their Wars instead of other military Musick; and *Polyænus* in his *Stratagemes* affirmeth that *Bacchus* gave the signal of Battel unto his numerous Army not with Trumpets but with Tympans and Cymbals.

And now I take the opportunity to thank you for the new Book sent me containing the Anthems sung in our Cathedral and Collegiate Churches: 'tis probable there will be additions, the Masters of Musick being now active in that affair. Beside my naked thanks I have yet nothing to return you but this enclosed, which may be somewhat rare unto you, and that is a Turkish Hymn translated into French out of the Turkish Metre, which I thus render unto you.

O what praise doth he deserve, and how great is that Lord, all whose Slaves are as so many Kings!

Whosoever shall rub his Eyes with the dust of his Feet, shall behold such admirable things that he shall fall into an ecstasie.

He that shall drink one drop of his Beverage, shall have his Bosome like the Ocean filled with Gems and pretious Liquours.

Let not loose the Reins unto thy Passions in this world: he that represseth them shall become a true Solomon in the Faith.

Amuse not thy self to adore Riches, nor to build great Houses and Palaces.

The end of what thou shall build is but ruine.

Pamper not thy Body with delicacies and dainties; it may come to pass one day that this Body may be in Hell.

Imagine not that he who findeth Riches findeth Happiness; he that findeth Happiness is he that findeth God.

All who prostrating themselves in humility shall this day believe in Velè,[264] *if they were Poor shall be Rich, and if Rich shall become Kings.*

After the Sermon ended which was made upon a Verse in the Alcoran containing much Morality, the *Deruices* in a Gallery apart sung this Hymn, accompanied with Instrumental Musick, which so affected the Ears of Monsieur *du Loyr*, that he would not omit to set it down, together with the Musical Notes, to be found in his first Letter unto Monsieur *Bouliau*, Prior of *Magny*.

Excuse my brevity: I can say but little where I understand but little.

I am, etc.

Footnotes

[263]Cor. 13. 1
[264]Velè *the Founder of the Convent.*

OF ROPALIC
or Gradual Verses, Etc.
Mens mea sublimes rationes præmeditatur.
TRACT VII

SIR,

Though I may justly allow a good intention in this Poem presented unto you, yet I must needs confess, I have no affection for it; as being utterly averse from all affectation in Poetry, which either restrains the phancy, or fetters the invention to any strict disposure of words. A poem of this nature is to be found in *Ausonius* beginning thus,

Spes Deus æternæ stationis conciliator.

These are Verses *Ropalici* or *Clavales*, arising gradually like the Knots in a Ῥοπάλη or Clubb; named also *Fistulares* by *Priscianus*, as *Elias Vinetus*[265] hath noted. They consist properly of five words, each thereof encreasing by one syllable. They admit not of a *Spondee* in the fifth place, nor can a Golden or Silver Verse be made this way. They run smoothly both in Latin and Greek, and some are scatteringly to be found in *Homer*; as,

Ὦ μάκαρ Ἀτρείδη μοιρηγενὲς ὀλβιοδαῖμον,

Liberè dicam sed in aurem, ego versibus hujusmodi Ropalicis, longo syrmate protractis, Ceraunium affigo.

He that affecteth such restrained Poetry, may peruse the Long Poem of *Hugbaldus* the Monk, wherein every word beginneth with a C penned in the praise of *Calvities* or Baldness, to the honour of *Carolus Calvus* King of *France*,

Carmina clarisonæ calvis cantate Camænæ.

The rest may be seen at large in the *adversaria* of *Barthius*: or if he delighteth in odd contrived phancies may he please himself with *Antistrophes, Counterpetories, Retrogrades, Rebusses, Leonine* Verses, etc. to be found in *Sieur des Accords*. But these and the like are to be look'd upon, not pursued, odd works might be made by such ways; and for your recreation I propose these few lines unto you,

Arcu paratur quod arcui sufficit.
Misellorum clamoribus accurrere non tam humanum quam sulphureum est.
Asino teratur quæ Asino teritur.
Ne Asphodelos comedas, phœnices manduca.
Cœlum aliquid potest, sed quæ mira præstat Papilio est.

Not to put you unto endless amusement, the Key hereof is the homonomy of the Greek made use of in the Latin words, which rendreth all plain. More ænigmatical and dark expressions might be made if any one would speak or compose them out of the numerical Characters or characteristical Numbers set down by *Robertus de Fluctibus*.[266]

As for your question concerning the contrary expressions of the Italian and Spaniards in their common affirmative answers, the Spaniard answering *cy Sennor*, the Italian *Signior cy*, you must be content with this Distich,

Why saith the Italian Signior cy, the Spaniard cy Sennor?
Because the one puts that behind, the other puts before.

And because you are so happy in some Translations, I pray return me these two verses in English,

Occidit heu tandem multos quæ occidit amantes,
Et cinis est hodie quæ fuit ignis heri.

My occasions make me to take off my Pen. I am, *etc.*

Footnotes

[265]El Vinet. *in* Auson.
[266]Tract 2. Part lib. 1.

OF LANGUAGES
And particularly of the Saxon Tongue.
TRACT VIII

SIR,

The last Discourse we had of the Saxon Tongue recalled to my mind some forgotten considerations. Though the Earth were widely peopled before the Flood, (as many learned men conceive) yet whether after a large dispersion, and the space of sixteen hundred years, men maintained so uniform a Language in all parts, as to be strictly of one Tongue, and readily to understand each other, may very well be doubted. For though the World preserved in the Family of *Noah* before the confusion of Tongues might be said to be of one Lip, yet even permitted to themselves their humours, inventions, necessities, and new objects, without the miracle of Confusion at first, in so long a tract of time, there had probably been a Babel. For whether *America* were first peopled by one or several Nations, yet cannot that number of different planting Nations, answer the multiplicity of their present different Languages, of no affinity unto each other; and even in their Northern Nations and incommunicating Angles, their Languages are widely differing. A native Interpreter brought from *California* proved of no use unto the Spaniards upon the neighbour Shore. From *Chiapa*, to *Guatemala*, *S. Salvador*, *Honduras*, there are at least eighteen several languages; and so numerous are they both in the Peruvian and Mexican Regions, that the great Princes are fain to have one common Language, which besides their vernaculous and Mother Tongues, may serve for commerce between them.

And since the confusion of Tongues at first fell onely upon those which were present in *Sinaar* at the work of *Babel*, whether the primitive Language from *Noah* were onely preserved in the Family of *Heber*, and not also in divers others, which might be absent at the same, whether all came away and many might not be left behind in their first Plantations about the foot of the Hills, whereabout the Ark rested and *Noah* became an Husbandman, is not absurdly doubted.

For so the primitive Tongue might in time branch out into several parts of *Europe* and *Asia*, and thereby the first or Hebrew Tongue which seems to be ingredient into so many Languages, might have larger originals and grounds of its communication and traduction than from the Family of *Abraham*, the Country of *Canaan* and words contained in the Bible which come short of the full of that Language. And this would become more probable from the Septuagint or Greek Chronology strenuously asserted by *Vossius*; for making five hundred years between the Deluge and the days of *Peleg*, there ariseth a large latitude of multiplication and dispersion of People into several parts, before the descent of that Body which followed *Nimrod* unto *Sinaar* from the East.

They who derive the bulk of European Tongues from the Scythian and the Greek, though they may speak probably in many points, yet must needs allow vast difference or corruptions from so few originals, which however might be tolerably made out in the old Saxon, yet hath time much confounded the clearer derivations. And as the knowledge thereof now stands in reference unto our selves, I find many words totally lost, divers of harsh sound disused or refined in the pronunciation, and many words we have also in common use not to be found in that Tongue, or venially derivable from any other from whence we have largely borrowed, and yet so much still remaineth with us that it maketh the gross of our Language.

The religious obligation unto the Hebrew Language hath so notably continued the same, that it might still be understood by *Abraham*, whereas by the *Mazorite* Points and Chaldee Character the old Letter stands so transformed, that if *Moses* were alive again, he must be taught to reade his own Law.

The Chinoys, who live at the bounds of the Earth, who have admitted little communication, and suffered successive incursions from one Nation, may possibly give account of a very ancient Language; but consisting of many Nations and Tongues; confusion, admixtion and corruption in length of time might probably so have crept in as without the virtue of a common Character, and lasting Letter of things, they could never probably make out those strange memorials which they pretend, while they still make use of the Works of their great *Confutius* many hundred years before Christ, and in a series ascend as high as *Poncuus*, who is conceived our *Noah*.

The present Welch, and remnant of the old Britanes, hold so much of that ancient Language, that they make a shift to understand the Poems of *Merlin*, *Enerin*, *Telesin*, a thousand years ago, whereas the Herulian *Pater Noster*, set down by *Wolfgangus Lazius*, is not without much criticism made out, and but in some words; and the present Parisians can hardly hack out those few lines of the League between *Charles* and *Lewis*, the Sons of *Ludovicus Pius*, yet remaining in old French.

The Spaniards, in their corruptive traduction and Romance, have so happily retained the terminations from the Latin, that notwithstanding the Gothick and Moorish intrusion of words, they are able to make a Discourse completely consisting of Grammatical Latin and Spanish, wherein the Italians and French will be very much to seek.

The learned *Casaubon* conceiveth that a Dialogue might be composed in Saxon onely of such words as are derivable from the Greek, which surely might be effected, and so as the learned might not uneasily find it out. *Verstegan* made no doubt that he could contrive a Letter which might be understood by the English, Dutch and East Frislander, which, as the present confusion standeth, might have proved no very clear Piece, and hardly to be hammer'd out: yet so much of the Saxon still remaineth in our English, as may admit an orderly discourse and series of good sense, such as not onely the present English, but *Ælfric*, *Bede* and *Alured* might understand after so many hundred years.

Nations that live promiscuously, under the Power and Laws of Conquest, do seldom escape the loss of their Language with their Liberties, wherein the Romans were so strict that the Grecians were fain to conform in their judicial Processes; which made the Jews loose more in seventy years dispersion in the Provinces of *Babylon*, than in many hundred in their distinct habitation in *Ægypt*; and the English which dwelt dispersedly to loose their Language in *Ireland*, whereas more tolerable reliques there are thereof in *Fingall*, where they were closely and almost solely planted; and the Moors which were most huddled together and united about *Granada*, have yet left their *Arvirage* among the Granadian Spaniards.

But shut up in Angles and inaccessible corners, divided by Laws and Manners, they often continue long with little mixture, which hath afforded that lasting life unto the Cantabrian and British Tongue, wherein the Britanes are remarkable, who, having lived four hundred years together with the Romans, retained so much of the British as it may be esteemed a Language; which either they resolutely maintained in their cohabitation with them in Britane, or retiring after in the time of the Saxons into Countries and parts less civiliz'd and conversant with the Romans, they found the People distinct, the Language more intire, and so fell into it again.

But surely no Languages have been so straitly lock'd up as not to admit of commixture. The Irish, although they retain a kind of a Saxon Character, yet have admitted many words of Latin and English. In the Welch are found many words from Latin, some from Greek and Saxon. In what parity and incommixture the Language of that People stood which were casually discovered in the heart of *Spain*, between the Mountains of *Castile*, no longer ago than in the time of Duke *D'Alva*, we have not met with a good account any farther than that their words were Basquish or Cantabrian: but the present Basquensa one of the minor Mother Tongues of *Europe*, is not without commixture of Latin and Castilian, while we meet with *Santifica, tentationeten, Glaria, puissanea,* and four more in the short Form of the Lord's

Prayer, set down by *Paulus Merula*: but although in this brief Form we may find such commixture, yet the bulk of their Language seems more distinct, consisting of words of no affinity unto others, of numerals totally different, of differing Grammatical Rule, as may be observed in the Dictionary and short *Basquensa* Grammar, composed by *Raphael Nicoleta*, a Priest of *Bilboa*.

And if they use the auxiliary Verbs of *Equin* and *Ysan*, answerable unto *Hazer* and *Ser*, to Have, and Be, in the Spanish, which Forms came in with the Northern Nations into the Italian, Spanish and French, and if that Form were used by them before, and crept not in from imitation of their neighbours, it may shew some ancienter traduction from Northern Nations, or else must seem very strange; since the Southern Nations had it not of old, and I know not whether any such mode be found in the Languages of any part of *America*.

The Romans, who made the great commixture and alteration of Languages in the World, effected the same, not onely by their proper Language, but those also of their military Forces, employed in several Provinces, as holding a standing *Militia* in all Countries, and commonly of strange Nations; so while the cohorts and Forces of the Britanes were quartered in *Ægypt*, *Armenia*, *Spain*, *Illyria*, etc. the Stablæsians and Dalmatians here, the Gauls, Spaniards and Germans in other Countries, and other Nations in theirs, they could not but leave many words behind them, and carry away many with them, which might make that in many words of very distinct Nations some may still remain of very unknown and doubtfull Genealogy.

And if, as the learned *Buxhornius* contendeth, the Scythian Language as the Mother Tongue runs through the Nations of *Europe*, and even as far as *Persia*, the community in many words between so many Nations, hath a more reasonable original traduction, and were rather derivable from the common Tongue diffused through them all, than from any particular Nation, which hath also borrowed and holdeth but at second hand.

The Saxons settling over all *England*, maintained an uniform Language, onely diversified in Dialect, Idioms, and minor differences, according to their different Nations which came in to the common Conquest, which may yet be a cause of the variation in the speech and words of several parts of *England*, where different Nations most abode or settled, and having expelled the Britanes, their Wars were chiefly among themselves, with little action with foreign Nations untill the union of the Heptarchy under *Egbert*; after which time although the Danes infested this Land and scarce left any part free, yet their incursions made more havock in Buildings, Churches and Cities, than the Language of the Country, because their Language was in effect the same, and such as whereby they might easily understand one another.

And if the Normans, which came into *Neustria* or *Normandy* with *Rollo* the Dane, had preserved their Language in their new acquists, the succeeding Conquest of *England*, by Duke *William* of his race, had not begot among us such notable alterations; but having lost their Language in their abode in *Normandy* before they adventured upon *England*, they confounded the English with their French, and made the grand mutation, which was successively encreased by our possessions in *Normandy*, *Guien* and *Aquitain*, by our long Wars in France, by frequent resort of the French, who to the number of some thousands came over with *Isabel* Queen to *Edward* the Second, and the several Matches of *England* with the Daughters of *France* before and since that time.

But this commixture, though sufficient to confuse, proved not of ability to abolish the Saxon words; for from the French we have borrowed many Substantives, Adjectives and some Verbs, but the great Body of Numerals, auxiliary Verbs, Articles, Pronouns, Adverbs, Conjunctions and Prepositions, which are the distinguishing and lasting part of a Language, remain with us from the Saxon, which, having suffered no great alteration for many hundred years, may probably still remain, though the English swell with the inmates of Italian, French and Latin. An Example whereof may be observ'd in this following.

English I.

The first and formost step to all good Works is the dread and fear of the Lord of Heaven and Earth, which thorough the Holy Ghost enlightneth the blindness of our sinfull hearts to tread the ways of wisedom, and leads our feet into the Land of Blessing.

Saxon I.

The erst and fyrmost stæp to eal gode Weorka is the dræd and feurt of the Lauord of Heofan and Eorth, whilc thurh the Heilig Gast onlihtneth the blindnesse of ure sinfull heorte to træd the wæg of wisdome, and thone læd ure fet into the Land of Blessung.

English II.

For to forget his Law is the Door, the Gate and Key to let in all unrighteousness, making our Eyes, Ears and Mouths to answer the lust of Sin, our Brains dull to good Thoughts, our Lips dumb to his Praise, our Ears deaf to his Gospel, and our Eyes dim to behold his Wonders, which witness against us that we have not well learned the word of God, that we are the Children of wrath, unworthy of the love and manifold gifts of God, greedily following after the ways of the Devil and witchcraft of the World, doing nothing to free and keep our selves from the burning fire of Hell, till we be buried in Sin and swallowed in Death, not to arise again in any hope of Christ's Kingdom.

Saxon II.

For to fuorgytan his Laga is the Dure, the Gat and Cæg to let in eal unrightwisnysse, makend ure Eyge, Eore and Muth to answare the lust of Sin, ure Brægan dole to gode Theoht, ure Lippan dumb to his Preys, ure Earen deaf to his Gospel, and ure Eyge dim to behealden his Wundra, whilc ge witnysse ongen us that wee œf noht wel gelæred the weord of God, that wee are the Cilda of ured, unwyrthe of the lufe and mænigfeald gift of God, grediglice felygend æfter the wægen of the Deoful and wiccraft of the Weorld, doend nothing to fry and cæp ure saula from the byrnend fyr of Hell, till we be geburied in Synne and swolgen in Death not to arise agen in ænig hope of Christes Kynedome.

English III.

Which draw from above the bitter doom of the Almighty of Hunger, Sword, Sickness, and brings more sad plagues than those of Hail, Storms, Thunder, Bloud, Frogs, swarms of Gnats and Grashoppers, which ate the Corn, Grass and Leaves of the Trees in *Ægypt*.

Saxon III.

Whilc drag from buf the bitter dome of the Almagan of Hunger, Sweorde, Seoknesse, and bring mere sad plag, thone they of Hagal, Storme, Thunner, Blode, Frog, swearme of Gnæt and Gærsupper, whilc eaten the Corn, Gærs and Leaf of the Treowen in *Ægypt*.

English IV.

If we reade his Book and holy Writ, these among many others, we shall find to be the tokens of his hate, which gathered together might mind us of his will, and teach us when his wrath beginneth, which sometimes comes in open strength and full sail, oft steals like a Thief in the night, like Shafts shot from a Bow at midnight, before we think upon them.

Saxon IV.

Gyf we ræd his Boc and heilig Gewrit, these gemong mænig othern, we sceall findan the tacna of his hatung whilc gegatherod together miht gemind us of his willan, and teac us whone his ured onginneth, whilc sometima come in open strength and fill seyle, oft stæl gelyc a Theof in the niht, gelyc Sceaft scoten fram a Boge at midneoht, beforan we thinck uppen them.

English V.

And though they were a deal less, and rather short than beyond our sins, yet do we not a whit withstand or forbear them, we are wedded to, not weary of our misdeeds, we seldom look upward, and are not ashamed under sin, we cleanse not our selves from the blackness and deep hue of our guilt; we want tears and sorrow, we weep not, fast not, we crave not forgiveness from the mildness, sweetness and goodness of God, and with all livelihood and stedfastness to our uttermost will hunt after the evil of guile, pride, cursing, swearing, drunkenness, overeating, uncleanness, all idle lust of the flesh, yes many uncouth and nameless sins, hid in our inmost Breast and Bosomes, which stand betwixt our forgiveness, and keep God and Man asunder.

Saxon V.

And theow they wære a dæl lesse, and reither scort thone begond oure sinnan, get do we naht a whit withstand and forbeare them, we eare bewudded to, noht werig of ure agen misdeed, we seldon loc upweard, and ear not ofschæmod under sinne, we cleans noht ure selvan from the blacnesse and dæp hue of ure guilt; we wan teare and sara, we weope noht, fæst noht, we craf noht foregyfnesse fram the mildnesse, sweetnesse and goodnesse of God, and mit eal lifelyhood and stedfastnesse to ure uttermost witt hunt æfter the ufel of guile, pride, cursung, swearung, druncennesse, overeat, uncleannesse and eal idle lust of the flæsc, vis mænig uncuth and nameleas sinnan, hid in ure inmæst Brist and Bosome, whilc stand betwixt ure foregyfnesse, and cæp God and Man asynder.

English VI.

Thus are we far beneath and also worse than the rest of God's Works; for the Sun and Moon, the King and Queen of Stars, Snow, Ice, Rain, Frost, Dew, Mist, Wind, fourfooted and creeping things, Fishes and feathered Birds, and Fowls either of Sea or Land do all hold the Laws of his will.

Saxon VI.

Thus eare we far beneoth and ealso wyrse thone the rest of Gods Weorka; for the Sune and Mone, the Cyng and Cquen of Stearran, Snaw, Ise, Ren, Frost, Deaw, Miste, Wind, feower fet and crypend dinga, Fix yefetherod Brid, and Fælan auther in Sæ or Land do eal heold the Lag of his willan.

Thus have you seen in few words how near the Saxon and English meet.

Now of this account the French will be able to make nothing; the modern Danes and Germans, though from several words they may conjecture at the meaning, yet will they be much to seek in the orderly sense and continued construction thereof, whether the Danes can continue such a series of sense out of their present Language and the old Runick, as to be intelligible unto present and ancient times, some doubt may well be made; and if the present French would attempt a Discourse in words common unto their present Tongue and the old *Romana Rustica* spoken in Elder times, or in the old Language of the Francks, which came to be in use some successions after *Pharamond*, it might prove a Work of some trouble to effect.

It were not impossible to make an Original reduction of many words of no general reception in *England* but of common use in *Norfolk*, or peculiar to the East Angle Countries; as, *Bawnd, Bunny, Thurck, Enemmis, Sammodithee, Mawther, Kedge, Seele, Straft, Clever, Ma tchly, Dere, Nicked, Stingy, Noneare, Feft, Thepes, Gosgood, Kamp, Sibrit, Fangast, Sap, Cothis h, Thokish, Bide owe, Paxwax*: of these and some others of no easie originals, when time will permit, the resolution may be attempted; which to effect, the Danish Language new and more ancient may prove of good advantage: which Nation remained here fifty years upon agreement, and have left many Families in it, and the Language of these parts had surely been more commixed and perplex, if the Fleet of *Hugo de Bones* had not been cast away, wherein threescore thousand Souldiers out of *Britany* and *Flanders* were to be wafted over, and were by King *John's* appointment to have a settled habitation in the Counties of *Norfolk* and *Suffolk*.

But beside your laudable endeavours in the Saxon, you are not like to repent you of your studies in the other European and Western Languages, for therein are delivered many excellent Historical, Moral and Philosophical Discourses, wherein men merely versed in the learned Languages are often at a loss: but although you are so well accomplished in the French, you will not surely conceive that you are master of all the Languages in *France*, for to omit the Briton, Britonant or old British, yet retained in some part of *Britany*, I shall onely propose this unto your construction.

Chavalisco d' aquestes Boemes chems an freitado lou cap cun taules Jargonades, ero necy chi voluiget bouta sin tens embè aquelles. Anin à lous occells, che dizen tat prou ben en ein voz L' ome nosap comochodochi yen ay jes de plazer, d' ausir la mitat de paraulles en el mon.

This is a part of that Language which *Scaliger* nameth *Idiotismus Tectosagicus*, or *Langue d' oc*, counterdistinguishing it unto the *Idiotismus Francicus*, or *Langue d'ouy*, not understood in a petty corner or between a few Mountains, but in parts of early civility, in *Languedoc, Provence* and *Catalonia*, which put together will make little less than *England*.

Without some knowledge herein you cannot exactly understand the Works of *Rablais*: by this the French themselves are fain to make out that preserved relique of old French, containing the League between *Charles* and *Lewis* the Sons of *Ludovicus Pius*. Hereby may tolerably be understood the several Tracts written in the Catalonian Tongue; and in this is published the Tract of Falconry written by *Theodosius* and *Symmachus*: in this is yet conserved the Poem *Vilhuardine* concerning the French expedition in the Holy War, and the taking of *Constantinople*, among the Works of *Marius Æquicola* an Italian Poet. You may find, in this Language, a pleasant Dialogue of Love: this, about an hundred years ago, was in high esteem, when many Italian Wits flocked into *Provence*; and the famous *Petrarcha* wrote many of his Poems in *Vaucluse* in that Country.

For the word [*Dread*] in the Royal Title [*Dread Sovereign*] of which you desire to know the meaning, I return answer unto your question briefly thus.

Most men do vulgarly understand this word *Dread* after the common and English acception, as implying *Fear, Awe* or *Dread*.

Others may think to expound it from the French word *Droit* or *Droyt*. For, whereas in elder times, the *Presidents* and *Supremes* of Courts were termed *Sovereigns*, men might conceive this a distinctive Title and proper unto the King as eminently and by right the Sovereign.

A third exposition may be made from some Saxon Original, particularly from *Driht, Domine,* or *Drihten, Dominus,* in the Saxon Language, the word for *Dominus* throughout the Saxon Psalms, and used in the expression of the year of our Lord in the Decretal Epistle of Pope *Agatho* unto *Athelred* King of the Mercians, *Anno*, 680.

Verstegan would have this term *Drihten* appropriate unto God. Yet, in the Constitutions of *Withred*[267] *King of Kent*, we find the same word used for a Lord or Master, *Si in vesperâ præcedente solem servus ex mandato Domini aliquod opus servile egerit, Dominus (Drihten) 80 solidis luito*. However therefore, though *Driht, Domine*, might be most eminently applied unto the Lord of Heaven, yet might it be also transferred unto Potentates and Gods on Earth, unto whom fealty is given or due, according unto the Feudist term *Ligeus à Ligando* unto whom they were bound in fealty. And therefore from *Driht, Domine, Dread Sovereign*, may, probably, owe its Original.

I have not time to enlarge upon this Subject: 'Pray let this pass, as it is, for a Letter and not for a Treatise. I am

Yours, etc.

Footnotes

[267] V. Cl. Spelmanni *Concil*.

OF ARTIFICIAL HILLS, MOUNTS OR BURROWS
In many parts of England.
What they are, to what end raised, and by what Nations.
TRACT IX

My honoured Friend Mr. *E. D.*[268] his *Quære*.

'In my last Summer's Journey through *Marshland, Holland* and a great part of the *Fenns*, I observed divers artificial heaps of Earth of a very large magnitude, and I hear of many others which are in other parts of those Countries, some of them are at least twenty foot in direct height from the level whereon they stand. I would gladly know your opinion of them, and whether you think not that they were raised by the Romans or Saxons to cover the Bones or Ashes of some eminent persons?'

My Answer.

Worthy Sir,

Concerning artificial Mounts and Hills, raised without Fortifications attending them, in most parts of *England*, the most considerable thereof I conceive to be of two kinds; that is, either Signal Boundaries and Land-Marks, or else sepulchral Monuments or Hills of Interrment for remarkable and eminent persons, especially such as died in the Wars.

As for such which are sepulchral Monuments, upon bare and naked view they are not appropriable unto any of the three Nations of the Romans, Saxons or Danes, who, after the Britaines, have possessed this Land; because upon strict account, they may be appliable unto them all.

For that the Romans used such hilly Sepultures, beside many other testimonies, seems confirmable from the practice of *Germanicus*, who thus interred the unburied Bones of the slain Souldiers of *Varus*; and that expression of *Virgil*, of high antiquity among the Latins,

––*facit ingens monte sub alto*
Regis Dercenni terreno ex aggere Bustum.

That the Saxons made use of this way is collectible from several Records, and that pertinent expression of *Lelandus*,[269] *Saxones gens Christi ignara, in hortis amœnis, si domi forte ægroti moriebantur; sin foris et bello occisi, in egestis per campos terræ tumulis (quos Burgos appellabant) sepulti sunt.*

That the Danes observed this practice, their own Antiquities do frequently confirm, and it stands precisely delivered by *Adolphus Cyprius*, as the learned *Wormius*[270] hath observed. *Dani olim in memoriam Regum et Heroum, ex terra coacervata ingentes moles, Montium instar eminentes, erexisse, credibile omnino ac probabile est, atque illis in locis ut plurimum, quo sæpe homines commearent, atque iter haberent, ut in viis publicis posteritati memoriam consecrarent, et quodammodo immortalitati mandarent.* And the like Monuments are yet to be observed in *Norway* and *Denmark* in no small numbers.

So that upon a single view and outward observation they may be the Monuments of any of these three Nations: Although the greatest number, not improbably, of the Saxons; who fought many Battels with the Britaines and Danes, and also between their own Nations, and left the proper name of Burrows for these Hills still retained in many of them, as the seven Burrows upon *Salisbury* Plain, and in many other parts of *England*.

But of these and the like Hills there can be no clear and assured decision without an ocular exploration, and subterraneous enquiry by cutting through one of them either directly or crosswise. For so with lesser charge discovery may be made what is under them, and consequently the intention of their erection.

For if they were raised for remarkable and eminent Boundaries, then about their bottom will be found the lasting substances of burnt Bones of Beasts, of Ashes, Bricks, Lime or Coals.

If Urns be found, they might be erected by the Romans before the term of Urn-burying or custom of burning the dead expired: but if raised by the Romans after that period; Inscriptions, Swords, Shields, and Arms after the Roman mode, may afford a good distinction.

But if these Hills were made by Saxons or Danes, discovery may be made from the fashion of their Arms, Bones of their Horses, and other distinguishing substances buried with them.

And for such an attempt there wanteth not encouragement. For a like Mount or Burrow was opened in the days of King *Henry* the Eighth upon *Barham* Down in *Kent*, by the care of Mr. *Thomas Digges* and charge of Sir *Christopher Hales*; and a large Urn with Ashes was found under it, as is delivered by *Thomas Twinus De Rebus Albionicis*, a learned Man of that Country, *Sub incredibili Terræ acervo, Urna cinere ossium magnorum fragmentis plena, cùm galeis, clypeis æneis et ferreis rubigine ferè consumptis, inusitatæ magnitudinis, eruta est: sed nulla inscriptio nomen, nullum testimonium tempus, aut fortunam exponebant*: and not very long ago, as *Cambden*[271] delivereth, in one of the Mounts of *Barklow* Hills in *Essex*, being levelled there were found three Troughs, containing broken Bones, conceived to have been of Danes: and in later time we find, that a Burrow was opened in the Isle of *Man*, wherein fourteen Urns were found with burnt Bones in them; and one more neat than the rest, placed in a Bed of fine white Sand, containing nothing but a few brittle Bones, as having passed the Fire; according to the particular account thereof in the description[272] of the Isle of *Man*. Surely many noble Bones and Ashes have been contented with such hilly Tombs; which neither admitting Ornament, Epitaph or Inscription, may, if Earthquakes spare them, out last all other Monuments. *Suæ sunt Metis metæ*. Obelisks have their term, and Pyramids will tumble, but these mountainous Monuments may stand, and are like to have the same period with the Earth.

More might be said, but my business, of another nature, makes me take off my hand. I am

Yours, etc.

Footnotes

[268][Sir William Dugdale.—ED.]
[269]Leland. *in Assertione Regis* Arthuri.
[270]Wormius *in Monumentis Danicis*.
[271]Cambd. Brit. *p. 326.*
[272]*Published* 1656, by Dan. King.

OF TROAS
What place is meant by that Name.
Also, of the situations of *Sodom*, *Gomorrha*, *Admah*, *Zeboim*, in the dead Sea.
TRACT X

Sir,
To your Geographical Queries, I answer as follows.

In sundry passages of the new Testament, in the *Acts of the Apostles*, and Epistles of S. *Paul*, we meet with the word *Troas*; how he went from *Troas* to *Philippi* in *Macedonia*, from thence unto *Troas* again: how he remained seven days in that place; from thence on foot to *Assos*, whither the Disciples had sailed from *Troas*, and there, taking him in, made their Voyage unto *Cæsarea*.

Now, whether this *Troas* be the name of a City or a certain Region seems no groundless doubt of yours: for that 'twas sometimes taken in the signification of some Country, is acknowledged by *Ortelius*, *Stephanus* and *Grotius*; and it is plainly set down by *Strabo*, that a Region of *Phrygia* in *Asia minor* was so taken in ancient times; and that, at the Trojan War, all the Territory which comprehended the nine Principalities subject unto the King of *Ilium*, Τροίη λεγομένη, was called by the name of *Troja*. And this might seem sufficiently to salve the intention of the description, when he came or went from *Troas*, that is, some part of that Region; and will otherwise seem strange unto many how he should be said to go or come from that City which all Writers had laid in the Ashes about a thousand years before.

All which notwithstanding, since we reade in the Text a particular abode of seven days, and such particulars as leaving of his Cloak, Books and Parchments at *Troas*: And that S. *Luke* seems to have been taken in to the Travels of S. *Paul* in this place, where he begins in the *Acts* to write in the first person, this may rather seem to have been some City or special Habitation, than any Province or Region without such limitation.

Now that such a City there was, and that of no mean note, is easily verified from historical observation. For though old *Ilium* was anciently destroyed, yet was there another raised by the relicts of that people, not in the same place, but about thirty Furlongs westward, as is to be learned from *Strabo*.

Of this place *Alexander* in his expedition against *Darius* took especial notice, endowing it with sundry Immunities, with promise of greater matters at his return from *Persia*; inclined hereunto from the honour he bore unto *Homer*, whose earnest Reader he was, and upon whose Poems, by the help of *Anaxarchus* and *Callisthenes*, he made some observations. As also much moved hereto upon the account of his cognation with the *Æacides* and Kings of *Molossus*, whereof *Andromache* the Wife of *Hector* was Queen. After the death of *Alexander*, *Lysimachus* surrounded it with a Wall, and brought the inhabitants of the neighbour Towns unto it, and so it bore the name of *Alexandria*; which, from *Antigonus*, was also called *Antigonia*, according to the inscription of that famous Medal in *Goltsius*, *Colonia Troas Antigonia Alexandrea, Legio vicesima prima*.

When the Romans first went into *Asia* against *Antiochus* 'twas but a Κωμόπολις and no great City; but, upon the Peace concluded, the Romans much advanced the same. *Fimbria*, the rebellious Roman, spoiled it in the Mithridatick War, boasting that he had subdued *Troy* in eleven days which the Grecians could not take in almost as many years. But it was again rebuilt and countenanced by the Romans, and became a Roman Colony, with great immunities conferred on it; and accordingly it is so set down by *Ptolomy*. For the Romans, deriving themselves from the Trojans, thought no favour too great for it; especially *Julius Cæsar*, who, both in imitation of *Alexander*, and for his own descent from *Julus*, of the posterity of *Æneas*, with much passion affected it, and, in a discontented humour,[273] was once in mind to translate the Roman wealth unto it; so that it became a very remarkable place, and was, in *Strabo's* time, ἐλλογίμων πόλεων, one of the noble Cities of *Asia*.

And, if they understood the prediction of *Homer* in reference unto the Romans, as some expound it in *Strabo*, it might much promote their affection unto that place; which being a remarkable prophecy, and scarce to be parallel'd in Pagan story, made before *Rome* was built, and concerning the lasting Reign of the progeny of *Æneas*, they could not but take especial notice of it. For thus is *Neptune* made to speak, when he saved *Æneas* from the fury of *Achilles*.

> *Verum agite hunc subito præsenti à morte trahamus*
> *Ne Cronides ira flammet si fortis Achilles*
> *Hunc mactet, fati quem Lex evadere jussit.*
> *Ne genus intereat de læto semine totum*
> *Dardani ab excelso præ cunctis prolibus olim,*
> *Dilecti quos è mortali stirpe creavit,*
> *Nunc etiam Priami stirpem Saturnius odit,*
> *Trojugenum posthæc Æneas sceptra tenebit*
> *Et nati natorum et qui nascentur ab illis.*

The Roman favours were also continued unto S. *Paul's* days; for *Claudius*,[274] producing an ancient Letter of the Romans unto King *Seleucus* concerning the Trojan Privileges, made a Release of their Tributes; and *Nero* [Tacit. *l. 13.*] elegantly pleaded for their Immunities, and remitted all Tributes unto them.

And, therefore, there being so remarkable a City in this Territory, it may seem too hard to loose the same in the general name of the Country; and since it was so eminently favoured by Emperours, enjoying so many Immunities, and full of Roman Privileges, it was probably very populous, and a fit abode for S. *Paul*, who being a Roman Citizen, might live more quietly himself, and have no small number of faithfull well-wishers in it.

Yet must we not conceive that this was the old *Troy*, or re-built in the same place with it: for *Troas* was placed about thirty Furlongs West, and upon the Sea shore; so that, to hold a clearer apprehension hereof than is commonly delivered in the Discourses of the Ruines of *Troy*, we may consider one Inland *Troy* or old *Ilium*, which was built farther within the Land, and so was removed from the Port where the Grecian Fleet lay in *Homer*; and another Maritime *Troy*, which was upon the Sea Coast placed in the Maps of *Ptolomy*, between *Lectum* and *Sigæum* or Port *Janizam*, Southwest from the old City, which was this of S. *Paul*, and whereunto are appliable the particular accounts of *Bellonius*, when, not an hundred years ago, he described the Ruines of *Troy* with their Baths, Aqueducts, Walls and Towers, to be seen from the Sea as he sailed between it and *Tenedos*; and where, upon nearer view, he observed some signs and impressions of his conversion in the ruines of Churches, Crosses, and Inscriptions upon Stones.

Nor was this onely a famous City in the days of S. *Paul*, but considerable long after. For, upon the Letter of *Adrianus*, [Philostrat. *in Vita* Herodis Attici.] *Herodes Atticus*, at a great charge, repaired their Baths, contrived Aqueducts and noble Water-courses in it. As is also collectible from the Medals of *Caracalla*, of *Severus*, and *Crispina*; with Inscriptions, *Colonia Alexandria Troas*, bearing on the Reverse either an Horse, a Temple, or a Woman; denoting their destruction by an Horse, their prayers for the Emperour's safety, and, as some conjecture, the memory of *Sibylla*, *Phrygia* or *Hellespontica*.

Nor wanted this City the favour of Christian Princes, but was made a Bishop's See under the Archbishop of *Cyzicum*; but in succeeding discords was destroyed and ruined, and the nobler Stones translated to *Constantinople* by the Turks to beautifie their Mosques and other Buildings.

Concerning the Dead Sea, accept of these few Remarks.

In the Map of the Dead Sea we meet with the Figure of the Cities which were destroyed: of *Sodom*, *Gomorrha*, *Admah* and *Zeboim*; but with no uniformity; men placing them variously, and, from the uncertainty of their situation, taking a fair liberty to set them where they please.

For *Admah*, *Zeboim* and *Gomorrha*, there is no light from the Text to define their situation. But, that *Sodom* could not be far from *Segor* which was seated under the Mountains near the side of the Lake, seems inferrible from the sudden arrival of *Lot*, who, coming from *Sodom* at day break, attained to *Segor* at Sun rising; and therefore *Sodom* is to be placed not many miles from it, not in the middle of the Lake, which against that place is about eighteen miles over, and so will leave nine miles to be gone in so small a space of time.

The Valley being large, the Lake now in length about seventy English miles, the River *Jordan* and divers others running over the Plain, 'tis probable the best Cities were seated upon those Streams: but how the *Jordan* passed or winded, or where it took in the other Streams, is a point too old for Geography to determine.

For, that the River gave the fruitfulness unto this Valley by over watring that low Region, seems plain from that expression in the Text,[275] that it was watered, *sicut Paradisus et Ægyptus*, like *Eden* and the Plains of *Mesopotamia*, where *Euphrates* yearly overfloweth; or like *Ægypt* where *Nilus* doth the like: and seems probable also from the same course of the River not far above this Valley where the Israelites passed *Jordan*, where 'tis said that *Jordan overfloweth its Banks in the time of Harvest*.

That it must have had some passage under ground in the compass of this Valley before the creation of this Lake, seems necessary from the great current of *Jordan*, and from the Rivers *Arnon*, *Cedron*, *Zaeth*, which empty into this Valley; but where to place that concurrence of Waters or place of its absorbition, there is no authentick decision.

The probablest place may be set somewhat Southward, below the Rivers that run into it on the East or Western Shore: and somewhat agreeable unto the account which *Brocardus* received from the Sarazens which lived near it, *Jordanem ingredi Mare Mortuum et rursum egredi, sed post exiguum intervallum à Terra absorberi*.

Strabo speaks naturally of this Lake, that it was first caused by Earthquakes, by sulphureous and bituminous eruptions, arising from the Earth. But the Scripture makes it plain to have been from a miraculous hand, and by a remarkable expression, *pluit Dominus ignem et Sulphur à Domino*. See also *Deut. 29. in ardore Salis*: burning the Cities and destroying all things about the Plain, destroying the vegetable nature of Plants and all living things, salting and making barren the whole Soil, and, by these fiery Showers, kindling and setting loose the body of the bituminous Mines, which shewed their lower Veins before but in some few Pits and openings, swallowing up the Foundation of their Cities; opening the bituminous Treasures below, and making a smoak like a Furnace able to be discerned by *Abraham* at a good distance from it.

If this little may give you satisfaction, I shall be glad, as being, Sir,

Yours, etc.

Footnotes

[273]Sueton.
[274]Sueton.
[275]Gen. 13. 10.

OF THE ANSWERS
of the Oracle of Apollo at Delphos to
Croesus King of Lydia.
TRACT XI

Sir,

Among the Oracles[276] of *Appollo* there are none more celebrated than those which he delivered unto *Crœsus* King of *Lydia*,[277] who seems of all Princes to have held the greatest dependence on them. But most considerable are his plain and intelligible replies which he made unto the same King, when he sent his Chains of Captivity unto *Delphos*, after his overthrow by *Cyrus*, with sad expostulations why he encouraged him unto that fatal War by his Oracle, saying,[278] Crœsus, *if he Wars against the Persians, shall dissolve a great Empire*. Why, at least, he prevented not that sad infelicity of his devoted and bountifull Servant, and whether it were fair or honourable for the Gods of *Greece* to be ingratefull: which being a plain and open delivery of *Delphos*, and scarce to be parallel'd in any ancient story, it may well deserve your farther consideration.

1. His first reply was, *That* Crœsus *suffered not for himself*; but paid the transgression of his fifth predecessour, who kill'd his Master and usurp'd the dignity unto which he held no title.

Now whether *Crœsus* suffered upon this account or not, hereby he plainly betrayed his insufficiency to protect him; and also obliquely discovered he had a knowledge of his misfortune; for knowing that wicked act lay yet unpunished, he might well divine some of his successours might smart for it: and also understanding he was like to be the last of that race, he might justly fear and conclude this infelicity upon him.

Hereby he also acknowledged the inevitable justice of God; that though Revenge lay dormant, it would not always sleep; and consequently confessed the just hand of God punishing unto the third and fourth generation, nor suffering such iniquities to pass for ever unrevenged.

Hereby he flatteringly encouraged him in the opinion of his own merits, and that he onely suffered for other mens transgressions: mean while he concealed *Crœsus* his pride, elation of mind and secure conceit of his own unparallel'd felicity, together with the vanity, pride and height of luxury of the Lydian Nation, which the Spirit of *Delphos* knew well to be ripe and ready for destruction.

2. A Second excuse was, *That it is not in the power of God to hinder the Decree of Fate*. A general evasion for any falsified prediction founded upon the common opinion of Fate, which impiously subjecteth the power of Heaven unto it; widely discovering the folly of such as repair unto him concerning future events: which, according unto this rule, must go on as the Fates have ordered, beyond his power to prevent or theirs to avoid; and consequently teaching that his Oracles had onely this use to render men more miserable by foreknowing their misfortunes; whereof *Crœsus* himself had a sensible experience in that Dæmoniacal Dream concerning his eldest Son, *That he should be killed by a Spear*, which, after all care and caution, he found inevitably to befall him.

3. In his Third Apology he assured him that he endeavoured to transfer the evil Fate and to pass it upon his Children; and did however procrastinate his infelicity, and deferred the destruction of *Sardis* and his own Captivity three years longer than was fatally decreed upon it.

Wherein while he wipes off the stain of Ingratitude, he leaves no small doubt whether, it being out of his power to contradict or transfer the Fates of his Servants, it be not also beyond it to defer such signal events, and whereon the Fates of whole Nations do depend.

As also, whether he intended or endeavoured to bring to pass what he pretended, some question might be made. For that he should attempt or think he could translate his infelicity upon his Sons, it could not consist with his judgment, which attempts not impossibles or things beyond his power; nor with his knowledge of future things, and the Fates of succeeding Generations: for he understood that Monarchy was to expire in himself, and could particularly foretell the infelicity of his Sons, and hath also made remote predictions unto others concerning the fortunes of many succeeding descents; as appears in that answer unto *Attalus*,

Be of good courage, Attalus, *thou shalt reign*
And thy Sons Sons, but not their Sons again.

As also unto *Cypselus* King of Corinth.

Happy is the Man who at my Altar stands,
Great Cypselus *who* Corinth *now commands.*
Happy is he, his Sons shall happy be,
But for their Sons, unhappy days they'll see.

Now, being able to have so large a prospect of future things, and of the fate of many Generations, it might well be granted he was not ignorant of the Fate of *Crœsus* his Sons, and well understood it was in vain to think to translate his misery upon them.

4. In the Fourth part of his reply, he clears himself of Ingratitude which Hell it self cannot hear of; alledging that he had saved his life when he was ready to be burnt, by sending a mighty Showre, in a fair and cloudless day, to quench the Fire already kindled, which all the Servants of *Cyrus* could not doe. Though this Shower might well be granted, as much concerning his honour, and not beyond his power; yet whether this mercifull Showre fell not out contingently or were not contrived by an higher power, which hath often pity upon Pagans, and rewardeth their vertues sometimes with extraordinary temporal favours; also, in no unlike case, who was the authour of those few fair minutes, which, in a showry day, gave onely time enough for the burning of *Sylla's* Body, some question might be made.

5. The last excuse devolveth the errour and miscarriage of the business upon *Crœsus*, and that he deceived himself by an inconsiderate misconstruction of his Oracle, that if he had doubted, he should not have passed it over in silence, but consulted again for an exposition of it. Besides, he

had neither discussed, nor well perpended his Oracle concerning *Cyrus*, whereby he might have understood not to engage against him.

Wherein, to speak indifferently, the deception and miscarriage seems chiefly to lie at *Crœsus* his door, who, if not infatuated with confidence and security, might justly have doubted the construction: besides, he had received two Oracles before, which clearly hinted an unhappy time unto him: the first concerning *Cyrus*.

When ever a Mule shall o'er the Medians reign,
Stay not, but unto Hermus *fly amain.*

Herein though he understood not the *Median Mule* of *Cyrus*, that is, of his mixed descent, and from Assyrian and Median Parents, yet he could not but apprehend some misfortune from that quarter.

Though this prediction seemed a notable piece of Divination, yet did it not so highly magnifie his natural sagacity or knowledge of future events as was by many esteemed; he having no small assistance herein from the Prophecy of *Daniel* concerning the Persian Monarchy, and the Prophecy of *Jeremiah* and *Isaiah*, wherein he might reade the name of *Cyrus* who should restore the Captivity of the Jews, and must, therefore, be the great Monarch and Lord of all those Nations.

The same misfortune was also foretold when he demanded of *Apollo* if ever he should hear his dumb Son speak.

O foolish Crœsus *who hast made this choice,*
To know when thou shalt hear thy dumb Son's voice;
Better he still were mute, would nothing say,
When he first speaks, look for a dismal day.

This, if he contrived not the time and the means of his recovery, was no ordinary divination: yet how to make out the verity of the story some doubt may yet remain. For though the causes of deafness and dumbness were removed, yet since words are attained by hearing, and men speak not without instruction, how he should be able immediately to utter such apt and significant words, as Ἄνθρωπε, μὴ κτεῖνε Κροῖσον,[279] *O Man slay not* Crœsus, it cannot escape some doubt, since the Story also delivers, that he was deaf and dumb, that he then first began to speak, and spake all his life after.

Now, if *Crœsus* had consulted again for a clearer exposition of what was doubtfully delivered, whether the Oracle would have spake out the second time or afforded a clearer answer, some question might be made from the examples of his practice upon the like demands.

So when the Spartans had often fought with ill success against the *Tegeates*, they consulted the Oracle what God they should appease, to become victorious over them. The answer was, *that they should remove the Bones of* Orestes. Though the words were plain, yet the thing was obscure, and like finding out the Body of *Moses*. And therefore they once more demanded in what place they should find the same; unto whom he returned this answer,

When in the Tegean Plains a place thou find'st
Where blasts are made by two impetuous Winds,
Where that that strikes is struck, blows follow blows,
There doth the Earth Orestes *Bones enclose.*

Which obscure reply the wisest of *Sparta* could not make out, and was casually unriddled by one talking with a Smith who had found large Bones of a Man buried about his House; the Oracle importing no more than a Smith's Forge, expressed by a Double Bellows, the Hammer and Anvil therein.

Now, why the Oracle should place such consideration upon the Bones of *Orestes* the Son of *Agamemnon*, a mad man and a murtherer, if not to promote the idolatry of the Heathens, and maintain a superstitious veneration of things of no activity, it may leave no small obscurity.

Or why, in a business so clear in his knowledge, he should affect so obscure expressions it may also be wondred; if it were not to maintain the wary and evasive method in his answers: for, speaking obscurely in things beyond doubt within his knowledge, he might be more tolerably dark in matters beyond his prescience.

Though **EI** were inscribed over the Gate of *Delphos*, yet was there no uniformity in his deliveries. Sometimes with that *obscurity* as argued a fearfull prophecy; sometimes so *plainly* as might confirm a spirit of divinity; sometimes *morally*, deterring from vice and villany; another time *vitiously*, and in the spirit of bloud and cruelty: observably modest in his civil enigma and periphrasis of that part which old *Numa* would plainly name,[280] and *Medea* would not understand, when he advised *Ægeus* not to draw out his foot before, untill he arriv'd upon the Athenian ground; whereas another time he seemed too literal in that unseemly epithet unto *Cyanus* King of *Cyprus*,[281] and put a beastly trouble upon all *Ægypt* to find out the Urine of a true Virgin. Sometimes, more beholding unto memory than invention, he delighted to express himself in the bare Verses of *Homer*. But that he principally affected Poetry, and that the Priest not onely or always composed his prosal raptures into Verse, seems plain from his necromantical Prophecies, whilst the dead Head in *Phlegon* delivers a long Prediction in Verse; and at the raising of the Ghost of *Commodus* unto *Caracalla*, when none of his Ancestours would speak, the divining Spirit versified his infelicities; corresponding herein to the apprehensions of elder times, who conceived not onely a Majesty but something of Divinity in Poetry, and as in ancient times the old Theologians delivered their inventions.

Some critical Readers might expect in his oraculous Poems a more than ordinary strain and true spirit of *Apollo*; not contented to find that Spirits make Verses like Men, beating upon the filling Epithet, and taking the licence of dialects and lower helps, common to humane Poetry; wherein, since *Scaliger*, who hath spared none of the Greeks, hath thought it wisedom to be silent, we shall make no excursion.

Others may wonder how the curiosity of elder times, having this opportunity of his Answers, omitted Natural Questions; or how the old Magicians discovered no more Philosophy; and if they had the assistance of Spirits, could rest content with the bare assertions of things, without the knowledge of their causes; whereby they had made their Acts iterable by sober hands, and a standing part of Philosophy. Many wise Divines hold a reality in the wonders of the Ægyptian Magicians, and that those *magnalia* which they performed before *Pharaoh* were not mere delusions of Sense. Rightly to understand how they made Serpents out of Rods; Froggs and Bloud of Water, were worth half *Porta's* Magick.

Hermolaus Barbarus was scarce in his wits, when, upon conference with a Spirit, he would demand no other question than the explication of *Aristotle's Entelecheia*. *Appion* the Grammarian, that would raise the Ghost of *Homer* to decide the Controversie of his Country, made a frivolous and pedantick use of Necromancy. *Philostratus* did as little, that call'd up the Ghost of *Achilles* for a particular of the Story of *Troy*. Smarter curiosities would have been at the great Elixir, the Flux and Reflux of the Sea, with other noble obscurities in Nature; but probably all in vain: in matters cognoscible and framed for our disquisition, our Industry must be our Oracle, and Reason our *Apollo*.

Not to know things without the Arch of our intellectuals, or what Spirits apprehend, is the imperfection of our nature not our knowledge, and rather inscience than ignorance in man. Revelation might render a great part of the Creation easie which now seems beyond the stretch of humane indagation, and welcome no doubt from good hands might be a true *Almagest*, and great celestial construction: a clear Systeme of the planetical Bodies of the invisible and seeming useless Stars unto us, of the many Suns in the eighth Sphere, what they are, what they contain and to what more immediately those Stupendous Bodies are serviceable. But being not hinted in the authentick Revelation of God, nor known how far their discoveries are stinted; if they should come unto us from the mouth of evil Spirits, the belief thereof might be as unsafe as the enquiry.

This is a copious Subject; but, having exceeded the bounds of a letter, I will not, now, pursue it farther. I am

Yours, etc.

Footnotes

[276] *See* Vulg. Err. *l.* 7. c. 12.
[277] Herod. *l.* 1. 46, 47, etc. 90, 91.
[278] Προλέγουσαι Κροίσω, ἢν στρατεύηται ἐπὶ Πέρσας, μεγάλην ἀρχήν μιν καταλύσειν. Herod. *Ibid.* 54.
[279] Herod. *l.* 1. 85.
[280] Plut. *in* Thes.

A PROPHECY
Concerning the future state of several Nations, In a Letter written upon occasion of an old Prophecy sent to the Authour from a Friend, with a Request that he would consider it.
TRACT XII

SIR,

I take no pleasure in Prophecies so hardly intelligible, and pointing at future things from a pretended spirit of Divination; of which sort this seems to be which came unto your hand, and you were pleased to send unto me. And therefore, for your easier apprehension, divertisement and consideration, I present you with a very different kind of prediction: not positively or peremptorily telling you what shall come to pass; yet pointing at things not without all reason or probability of their events; not built upon fatal decrees, or inevitable designations, but upon conjectural foundations, whereby things wished may be promoted, and such as are feared, may more probably be prevented.

THE PROPHECY

When New England *shall trouble* New Spain.
When Jamaica *shall be Lady of the Isles and the Main.*
When Spain *shall be in* America *hid,*
And Mexico *shall prove a* Madrid.
When Mahomet's *Ships on the* Baltick *shall ride,*
And Turks shall labour to have Ports on that side.
When Africa *shall no more sell out their Blacks*
To make Slaves and Drudges to the American Tracts.
When Batavia *the Old shall be contemn'd by the New.*
When a new Drove of Tartars shall China *subdue.*
When America *shall cease to send out its Treasure,*
But employ it at home in American Pleasure.
When the new World shall the old invade,
Nor count them their Lords but their fellows in Trade.
When Men shall almost pass to Venice *by Land,*
Not in deep Water but from Sand to Sand.
When Nova Zembla *shall be no stay*
Unto those who pass to or from Cathay.
Then think strange things are come to light,
Whereof but few have had a foresight.

THE EXPOSITION OF THE PROPHECY

When New England *shall trouble* New Spain.

That is, When that thriving Colony, which hath so much encreased in our days, and in the space of about fifty years, that they can, as they report, raise between twenty and thirty thousand men upon an exigency, shall in process of time be so advanced, as to be able to send forth Ships and Fleets, as to infest the American Spanish Ports and Maritime Dominions by depredations or assaults; for which attempts they are not like to be unprovided, as abounding in the Materials for Shipping, Oak and Firre. And when length of time shall so far encrease that industrious people, that the neighbouring Country will not contain them, they will range still farther and be able, in time, to set forth great Armies, seek for new possessions, or make considerable and conjoined migrations, according to the custom of swarming Northern Nations; wherein it is not likely that they will move Northward, but toward the Southern and richer Countries, which are either in the

Dominions or Frontiers of the Spaniards: and may not improbably erect new Dominions in places not yet thought of, and yet, for some Centuries, beyond their power or Ambition.

When Jamaica *shall be Lady of the Isles and the Main.*

That is, When that advantageous Island shall be well peopled, it may become so strong and potent as to over-power the neighbouring Isles, and also a part of the main Land, especially the Maritime parts. And already in their infancy they have given testimony of their power and courage in their bold attempts upon *Campeche* and *Santa Martha*; and in that notable attempt upon *Panama* on the Western side of *America*: especially considering this Island is sufficiently large to contain a numerous people, of a Northern and warlike descent, addicted to martial affairs both by Sea and Land, and advantageously seated to infest their neighbours both of the Isles and the Continent, and like to be a receptacle for Colonies of the same originals from *Barbadoes* and the neighbour Isles.

When Spain *shall be in* America *hid;*
And Mexico *shall prove a* Madrid.

That is, When *Spain*, either by unexpected disasters, or continued emissions of people into *America*, which have already thinned the Country, shall be farther exhausted at home: or when, in process of time, their Colonies shall grow by many accessions more than their Originals, then *Mexico* may become a *Madrid*, and as considerable in people, wealth and splendour; wherein that place is already so well advanced, that accounts scarce credible are given of it. And it is so advantageously seated, that, by *Acapulco* and other Ports on the South Sea, they may maintain a communication and commerce with the Indian Isles and Territories, and with *China* and *Japan*, and on this side, by *Porto Belo* and others, hold correspondence with *Europe* and *Africa*.

When Mahomet's *Ships in the Baltick shall ride.*

Of this we cannot be out of all fear; for, if the Turk should master *Poland*, he would be soon at this Sea. And from the odd constitution of the Polish Government, the divisions among themselves, jealousies between their Kingdom and Republick; vicinity of the Tartars, treachery of the Cossacks, and the method of Turkish Policy, to be at Peace with the Emperour of *Germany* when he is at War with the Poles, there may be cause to fear that this may come to pass. And then he would soon endeavour to have Ports upon that Sea, as not wanting Materials for Shipping. And, having a new acquist of stout and warlike men, may be a terrour unto the confiners on that Sea, and to Nations which now conceive themselves safe from such an Enemy.

When Africa *shall no more sell out their Blacks.*

That is, When African Countries shall no longer make it a common Trade to sell away the people to serve in the drudgery of American Plantations. And that may come to pass when ever they shall be well civilized, and acquainted with Arts and Affairs sufficient to employ people in their Countries: if also they should be converted to Christianity, but especially unto Mahometism; for then they would never sell those of their Religion to be Slaves unto Christians.

When Batavia *the Old shall be contemn'd by the New.*

When the Plantations of the Hollanders at *Batavia* in the *East Indies*, and other places in the *East Indies*, shall, by their conquests and advancements, become so powerfull in the Indian Territories; Then their Original Countries and States of *Holland* are like to be contemned by them, and obeyed onely as they please. And they seem to be in a way unto it at present by their several Plantations, new acquists and enlargements: and they have lately discovered a part of the Southern Continent, and several places which may be serviceable unto them, when ever time shall enlarge them unto such necessities.

And a new Drove of Tartars shall China *subdue.*

Which is no strange thing if we consult the Histories of *China*, and successive Inundations made by Tartarian Nations. For when the Invaders, in process of time, have degenerated into the effeminacy and softness of the Chineses, then they themselves have suffered a new Tartarian Conquest and Inundation. And this hath happened from time beyond our Histories: for, according to their account, the famous Wall of *China*, built against the irruptions of the Tartars, was begun above a hundred years before the Incarnation.

When America *shall cease to send forth its treasure,*
But employ it at home for American Pleasure.

That is, When *America* shall be better civilized, new policied and divided between great Princes, it may come to pass that they will no longer suffer their Treasure of Gold and Silver to be sent out to maintain the Luxury of *Europe* and other parts: but rather employ it to their own advantages, in great Exploits and Undertakings, magnificent Structures, Wars or Expeditions of their own.

When the new World shall the old invade.

That is, When *America* shall be so well peopled, civilized and divided into Kingdoms, they are like to have so little regard of their Originals, as to acknowledge no subjection unto them: they may also have a distinct commerce between themselves, or but independently with those of *Europe*, and may hostilely and pyratically assault them, even as the Greek and Roman Colonies after a long time dealt with their Original Countries.

When Men shall almost pass to Venice *by Land,*
Not in deep Waters but from Sand to Sand.

That is, When, in long process of time, the Silt and Sands shall so choak and shallow the Sea in and about it. And this hath considerably come to pass within these fourscore years; and is like to encrease from several causes, especially by the turning of the River *Brenta*, as the learned *Castelli* hath declared.

When Nova Zembla *shall be no stay*
Unto those who pass to or from Cathay.

That is, When ever that often sought for Northeast passage unto *China* and *Japan* shall be discovered; the hindrance whereof was imputed to *Nova Zembla*; for this was conceived to be an excursion of Land shooting out directly, and so far Northward into the Sea that it discouraged from all Navigation about it. And therefore Adventurers took in at the Southern part at a strait by *Waygatz* next the Tartarian Shore: and, sailing forward they found that Sea frozen and full of Ice, and so gave over the attempt. But of late years, by the diligent enquiry of some Moscovites, a better discovery is made of these parts, and a Map or Chart made of them. Thereby *Nova Zembla* is found to be no Island extending very far Northward; but, winding Eastward, it joineth to the Tartarian Continent, and so makes a *Peninsula*: and the Sea between it which they entred at *Waygatz*, is found to be but a large Bay, apt to be frozen by reason of the great River of *Oby*, and other fresh Waters, entring into it: whereas the main Sea doth not freez upon the North of *Zembla* except near unto Shores; so that if the Moscovites were skilfull Navigatours they might, with less difficulties, discover this passage unto *China*: but however the English, Dutch and Danes are now like to attempt it again.

But this is Conjecture, and not Prophecy: and so (I know) you will take it. I am,

Sir, etc.

MUSÆUM CLAUSUM
or
Bibliotheca Abscondita:
Containing some remarkable Books, Antiquities, Pictures and Rarities of several kinds, scarce or never seen by any man now living.
TRACT XIII

Sir,

With many thanks I return that noble Catalogue of Books, Rarities and Singularities of Art and Nature, which you were pleased to communicate unto me. There are many Collections of this kind in *Europe*. And, besides the printed accounts of the *Musæum Aldrovandi, Calceolarianum, Moscardi, Wormianum*; the *Casa Abbellitta* at *Loretto*, and *Threasor* of S. *Dennis*, the *Repository* of the Duke of *Tuscany*, that of the Duke of *Saxony*, and that noble one of the Emperour at *Vienna*, and many more are of singular note. Of what in this kind I have by me I shall make no repetition, and you having already had a view thereof, I am bold to present you with the List of a Collection, which I may justly say you have not seen before.

The Title is, as above,

Musæum Clausum, or *Bibliotheca Abscondita:* containing some remarkable Books, Antiquities, Pictures and Rarities of several kinds, scarce or never seen by any man now living.

1. Rare and generally unknown Books.

1. A poem of *Ovidius Naso*, written in the Getick Language,[282] during his exile at *Tomos*, found wrapt up in Wax at *Sabaria*, on the Frontiers of *Hungary*, where there remains a tradition that he died, in his return towards *Rome* from *Tomos*, either after his pardon or the death of *Augustus*.

2. The Letter of *Quintus Cicero*, which he wrote in answer to that of his Brother *Marcus Tullius*, desiring of him an account of *Britany*, wherein are described the Country, State and Manners of the Britains of that Age.

3. An Ancient British Herbal, or description of divers Plants of this Island, observed by that famous Physician *Scribonius Largus*, when he attended the Emperour *Claudius* in his expedition into *Britany*.

4. An exact account of the Life and Death of *Avicenna* confirming the account of his Death by taking nine Clysters together in a fit of the Colick; and not as *Marius* the Italian Poet delivereth, by being broken upon the Wheel; left with other Pieces by *Benjamin Tudelensis*, as he travelled from *Saragossa* to *Jerusalem*, in the hands of *Abraham Jarchi*, a famous Rabbi of *Lunet* near *Montpelier*, and found in a Vault when the Walls of that City were demolished by *Lewis* the Thirteenth.

5. A punctual relation of *Hannibal's* march out of *Spain* into *Italy*, and far more particular than that of *Livy*, where about he passed the River *Rhodanus* or *Rhosne*; at what place he crossed the *Isura* or *L'isere*; when he marched up toward the confluence of the *Sone* and the *Rhone*, or the place where the City *Lyons* was afterward built; how wisely he decided the difference between King *Brancus* and his Brother, at what place he passed the *Alpes*, what Vinegar he used, and where he obtained such quantity to break and calcine the Rocks made hot with Fire.

6. A learned Comment upon the *Periplus* of *Hanno* the Carthaginian, or his Navigation upon the Western Coast of *Africa*, with the several places he landed at; what Colonies he settled, what Ships were scattered from his Fleet near the Æquinoctial Line, which were not afterward heard of, and which probably fell into the Trade Winds, and were carried over into the Coast of *America*.

7. A particular Narration of that famous Expedition of the English into *Barbary* in the ninety fourth year of the *Hegira*, so shortly touched by *Leo Africanus*, whither called by the Goths they besieged, took and burnt the City of *Arzilla* possessed by the Mahometans, and lately the seat of *Gayland*; with many other exploits delivered at large in Arabick, lost in the Ship of Books and Rarities which the King of *Spain* took from *Siddy Hamet* King of *Fez*, whereof a great part were carried into the *Escurial*, and conceived to be gathered out of the relations of *Hibnu Nachu*, the best Historian of the African Affairs.

8. A Fragment of *Pythæas* that ancient Traveller of *Marseille*; which we suspect not to be spurious, because, in the description of the Northern Countries, we find that passage of *Pythæas* mentioned by *Strabo*, that all the Air beyond *Thule* is thick, condensed and gellied, looking just like Sea Lungs.

9. A *Sub Marine* Herbal, describing the several Vegetables found on the Rocks, Hills, Valleys, Meadows at the bottom of the Sea, with many sorts of *Alga*, *Fucus*, *Quercus*, *Polygonum*, *Gramens* and others not yet described.

10. Some Manuscripts and Rarities brought from the Libraries of *Æthiopia*, by *Zaga Zaba*, and afterward transported to *Rome*, and scattered by the Souldiers of the Duke of *Bourbon*, when they barbarously sacked that City.

11. Some Pieces of *Julius Scaliger*, which he complains to have been stoln from him, sold to the Bishop of *Mende* in *Languedock*, and afterward taken away and sold in the Civil Wars under the Duke of *Rohan*.

12. A Comment of *Dioscorides* upon *Hyppocrates*, procured from *Constantinople* by *Amatus Lusitanus*, and left in the hands of a Jew of *Ragusa*.

13. *Marcus Tullius Cicero* his Geography; as also a part of that magnified Piece of his *De Republica*, very little answering the great expectation of it, and short of Pieces under the same name by *Bodinus* and *Tholosanus*.

14. King *Mithridates* his *Oneirocritica*.

Aristotle de *Precationibus*.

Democritus *de his quæ fiunt apud Orcum, et Oceani circumnavigatio*.

Epicurus *de Pietate*.

A Tragedy of *Thyestes*, and another of *Medea*, writ by *Diogenes* the Cynick.

King *Alfred* upon *Aristotle de Plantis*.

Seneca's Epistles to S. *Paul*.

King *Solomon de Umbris Idæarum*, which *Chicus Asculænus*, in his Comment upon *Johannes de Sacrobosco*, would make us believe he saw in the Library of the Duke of *Bavaria*.

15. Artemidori *Oneirocritici Geographia*.

Pythagoras *de Mari Rubro*.

The Works of *Confutius* the famous Philosopher of *China*, translated into Spanish.

16. *Josephus* in Hebrew, written by himself.

17. The Commentaries of *Sylla* the Dictatour.

18. A Commentary of *Galen* upon the Plague of *Athens* described by *Thucydides*.

19. *Duo Cæsaris Anti-Catones*, or the two notable Books writ by *Julius Cæsar* against *Cato*; mentioned by *Livy*, *Salustius* and *Juvenal*; which the Cardinal of *Liege* told *Ludovicus Vives* were in an old Library of that City.

Mazhapha Einok, or, the Prophecy of *Enoch*, which *Ægidius Lochiensis*, a learned Eastern Traveller, told *Peireschius* that he had found in an old Library at *Alexandria* containing eight thousand Volumes.

20. A Collection of Hebrew Epistles, which passed between the two learned Women of our age *Maria Molinea* of *Sedan*, and *Maria Schurman* of *Utrecht*.

A wondrous Collection of some Writings of *Ludovica Saracenica*, Daughter of *Philibertus Saracenicus* a Physician of *Lyons*, who at eight years of age had made a good progress in the Hebrew, Greek and Latin Tongues.

2. Rarities in Pictures.

1. A picture of the three remarkable Steeples or Towers in *Europe* built purposely awry and so as they seem falling. *Torre Pisana* at *Pisa*, *Torre Garisenda* in *Bononia*, and that other in the City of *Colein*.

2. A Draught of all sorts of Sistrums, Crotaloes, Cymbals, Tympans, *etc.* in use among the Ancients.

3. Large *Submarine* Pieces, well delineating the bottom of the Mediterranean Sea, the Prerie or large Sea-meadow upon the Coast of *Provence*, the Coral Fishing, the gathering of Sponges, the Mountains, Valleys and Desarts, the Subterraneous Vents and Passages at the bottom of that Sea. Together with a lively Draught of *Cola Pesce*, or the famous Sicilian Swimmer, diving into the *Voragos* and broken Rocks by *Charybdis*, to fetch up the Golden Cup, which *Frederick*, King of *Sicily*, had purposely thrown into that Sea.

4. A Moon Piece, describing that notable Battel between *Axalla*, General of *Tamerlane*, and *Camares* the Persian, fought by the light of the Moon.

5. Another remarkable Fight of *Inghimmi* the Florentine with the Turkish Galleys by Moon-light, who being for three hours grappled with the *Basha* Galley, concluded with a signal Victory.

6. A delineation of the great Fair of *Almachara* in *Arabia*, which, to avoid the great heat of the Sun, is kept in the Night, and by the light of the Moon.

7. A Snow Piece, of Land and Trees covered with Snow and Ice, and Mountains of Ice floating in the Sea, with Bears, Seals, Foxes, and variety of rare Fowls upon them.

8. An Ice Piece describing the notable Battel between the Jaziges and the Romans, fought upon the frozen *Danubius*, the Romans settling one foot upon their Targets to hinder them from slipping, their fighting with the Jaziges when they were fallen, and their advantages therein by their art in volutation and rolling contention or wrastling, according to the description of *Dion*.

9. *Socia*, or a Draught of three persons notably resembling each other. Of King *Henry* the Fourth of *France*, and a Miller of *Languedock*; of *Sforza* Duke of *Milain* and a Souldier; of *Malatesta* Duke of *Rimini* and *Marchesinus* the Jester.

10. A Picture of the great Fire which happened at *Constantinople* in the Reign of *Sultan Achmet*. The Janizaries in the mean time plundring the best Houses, *Nassa Bassa* the Vizier riding about with a Cimetre in one hand and a Janizary's Head in the other to deter them; and the Priests attempting to quench the Fire, by Pieces of *Mahomet's* Shirt dipped in holy Water and thrown into it.

11. A Night Piece of the dismal Supper and strange Entertain of the Senatours by *Domitian*, according to the description of *Dion*.

12. A Vestal Sinner in the Cave with a Table and a Candle.

13. An Elephant dancing upon the Ropes with a *Negro* Dwarf upon his Back.

14. Another describing the mighty Stone falling from the Clouds into *Ægospotamos* or the Goats River in *Greece*, which Antiquity could believe that *Anaxagoras* was able to foretell half a year before.

15. Three noble Pieces; of *Vercingetorix* the Gaul submitting his person unto *Julius Cæsar*; of *Tigranes* King of *Armenia* humbly presenting himself unto *Pompey*; and of *Tamerlane* ascending his Horse from the Neck of *Bajazet*.

16. Draughts of three passionate Looks; of *Thyestes* when he was told at the Table that he had eaten a piece of his own Son; of *Bajazet* when he went into the Iron Cage; of *Oedipus* when he first came to know that he had killed his Father, and married his own Mother.

17. Of the Cymbrian Mother in *Plutarch* who, after the overthrow by *Marius*, hanged her self and her two Children at her feet.

18. Some Pieces delineating singular inhumanities in Tortures. The *Scaphismus* of the Persians. The living truncation of the Turks. The hanging Sport at the Feasts of the Thracians. The exact method of flaying men alive, beginning between the Shoulders, according to the description of *Thomas Minadoi*, in his Persian War. Together with the studied tortures of the French Traitours at *Pappa* in *Hungaria*: as also the wild and enormous torment invented by *Tiberius*, designed according unto the description of *Suetonius*. *Excogitaverunt inter genera cruciatûs, ut largâ meri potione per falluciam oneratos repentè veretris deligatis fidicularum simul urinæque tormento distenderet.*

19. A Picture describing how *Hannibal* forced his passage over the River *Rhosne* with his Elephants, Baggage and mixed Army; with the Army of the Gauls opposing him on the contrary Shore, and *Hanno* passing over with his Horse much above to fall upon the Rere of the Gauls.

20. A neat Piece describing the Sack of *Fundi* by the Fleet and Souldiers of *Barbarossa* the Turkish Admiral, the confusion of the people and their flying up to the Mountains, and *Julia Gonzaga* the beauty of *Italy* flying away with her Ladies half naked on Horseback over the Hills.

21. A noble Head of *Franciscus Gonzaga*, who, being imprisoned for Treason, grew grey in one night, with this Inscription,

O nox quam longa est quæ facit una senem.

22. A large Picture describing the Siege of *Vienna* by *Solyman* the Magnificent, and at the same time the Siege of *Florence* by the Emperour *Charles* the Fifth and Pope *Clement* the Seventh, with this Subscription,

Tum vacui capitis populum Phæaca *putares?*

23. An exquisite Piece properly delineating the first course of *Metellus* his Pontifical Supper, according to the description of *Macrobius*; together with a Dish of *Pisces Fossiles*, garnished about with the little Eels taken out of the backs of Cods and Perches; as also with the Shell Fishes found in Stones about *Ancona*.

24. A Picture of the noble Entertain and Feast of the Duke of *Chausue* at the Treaty of *Collen*, 1673, when in a very large Room, with all the Windows open, and at a very large Table he sate himself, with many great persons and Ladies; next about the Table stood a row of Waiters, then a row of Musicians, then a row of Musketiers.

25. *Miltiades*, who overthrew the Persians at the Battel of *Marathon* and delivered *Greece*, looking out of a Prison Grate in *Athens*, wherein he died, with this Inscription,

Non hoc terribiles Cymbri non Britones unquam,
Sauromatæve truces aut immanes Agathyrsi.

26. A fair English Lady drawn *Al Negro*, or in the Æthiopian hue excelling the original White and Red Beauty, with this Subscription,
Sed quondam volo nocte Nigriorem.

27. Pieces and Draughts in *Caricatura*, of Princes, Cardinals and famous men; wherein, among others, the Painter hath singularly hit the signatures of a Lion and a Fox in the face of Pope *Leo* the Tenth.

28. Some Pieces *A la ventura*, or Rare Chance Pieces, either drawn at random, and happening to be like some person, or drawn for some and happening to be more like another; while the Face, mistaken by the Painter, proves a tolerable Picture of one he never saw.

29. A Draught of famous Dwarfs with this Inscription,
Nos facimus Bruti puerum nos Lagona vivum.

30. An exact and proper delineation of all sorts of Dogs upon occasion of the practice of *Sultan Achmet*; who in a great Plague at *Constantinople* transported all the Dogs therein unto *Pera*, and from thence into a little Island, where they perished at last by Famine: as also the manner of the Priests curing of mad Dogs by burning them in the forehead with Saint *Bellin's Key*.

31. A noble Picture of *Thorismund* King of the Goths as he was killed in his Palace at *Tholouze*, who being let bloud by a Surgeon, while he was bleeding, a stander by took the advantage to stab him.

32. A Picture of rare Fruits with this Inscription,
Credere quæ possis surrepta sororibus Afris.

33. An handsome Piece of Deformity expressed in a notable hard Face, with this Inscription,
——*Ora*
Julius in Satyris qualia Rufus habet.

34. A noble Picture of the famous Duel between *Paul Manessi* and *Caragusa* the Turk in the time of *Amurath* the Second; the Turkish Army and that of *Scanderbeg* looking on; wherein *Manessi* slew the Turk, cut off his Head and carried away the Spoils of his Body.

3. Antiquities and Rarities of several sorts.

1. Certain ancient Medals with Greek and Roman Inscriptions, found about *Crim Tartary*; conceived to be left in those parts by the Souldiers of *Mithridates*, when overcome by *Pompey*, he marched round about the North of the *Euxine* to come about into *Thracia*.

2. Some ancient Ivory and Copper Crosses found with many others in *China*; conceived to have been brought and left there by the Greek Souldiers who served under *Tamerlane* in his Expedition and Conquest of that Country.

3. Stones of strange and illegible Inscriptions, found about the great ruines which *Vincent le Blanc* describeth about *Cephala* in *Africa*, where he opinion'd that the Hebrews raised some Buildings of old, and that *Solomon* brought from thereabout a good part of his Gold.

4. Some handsome Engraveries and Medals, of *Justinus* and *Justinianus*, found in the custody of a Bannyan in the remote parts of *India*, conjectured to have been left there by the Friers mentioned in *Procopius*, who travelled those parts in the reign of *Justinianus*, and brought back into *Europe* the discovery of Silk and Silk Worms.

5. An original Medal of *Petrus Aretinus*, who was called *Flagellum Principum*, wherein he made his own Figure on the Obverse part with this Inscription,
Il Divino Aretino.
On the Reverse sitting on a Throne, and at his Feet Ambassadours of Kings and Princes bringing presents unto him, with this Inscription,
I Principi tributati da i Popoli tributano il Servitor loro.

6. *Mummia Tholosana*; or, The complete Head and Body of Father *Crispin*, buried long ago in the Vault of the Cordeliers at *Tholouse*, where the Skins of the dead so drie and parch up without corrupting that their persons may be known very long after, with this Inscription,
Ecce iterum Crispinus.

7. A noble *Quandros* or Stone taken out of a Vulture's Head.

8. A large *Ostridges* Egg, whereon is neatly and fully wrought that famous Battel of *Alcazar*, in which three Kings lost their lives.

9. An *Etiudros Alberti* or Stone that is apt to be always moist: usefull unto drie tempers, and to be held in the hand in Fevers instead of Crystal, Eggs, Limmons, Cucumbers.

10. A small Viol of Water taken out of the Stones therefore called *Enhydri*, which naturally include a little Water in them, in like manner as the *Ætites* or *Aëgle* Stone doth another Stone.

11. A neat painted and gilded Cup made out of the *Confiti di Tivoli* and formed up with powder'd Egg-shells; as *Nero* is conceived to have made his *Piscina admirabilis*, singular against Fluxes to drink often therein.

12. The Skin of a Snake bred out of the Spinal Marrow of a Man.

13. Vegetable Horns mentioned by *Linschoten*, which set in the ground grow up like Plants about *Goa*.

14. An extract of the Inck of Cuttle Fishes reviving the old remedy of *Hippocrates* in Hysterical Passions.

15. Spirits and Salt of *Sargasso* made in the Western Ocean covered with that Vegetable; excellent against the Scurvy.

16. An extract of *Cachundè* or *Liberans* that famous and highly magnified Composition in the *East Indies* against Melancholy.

17. *Diarhizon mirificum*; or an unparallel'd Composition of the most effectual and wonderfull Roots in Nature.

☐ Rad. Butuæ Cuamensis.
Rad. Moniche Cuamensis.
Rad. Mongus Bazainensis.
Rad. Casei Baizanensis.
Rad. Columbæ Mozambiguensis.
Gim Sem Sinicæ.
Fo Lim lac Tigridis dictæ.
Fo seu.
Cort. Rad. Soldæ.
Rad. Ligni Solorani.
Rad. Malacensis madrededios dictæ an. ʒij.
M. fiat pulvis, qui cum gelatinâ Cornu cervi Moschati Chinensis formetur in massas oviformes.

18. A transcendent Perfume made of the richest Odorates of both the *Indies*, kept in a Box made of the Muschie Stone of *Niarienburg*, with this Inscription,
——*Deos rogato*
Totum ut te faciant, Fabulle, Nasum.

19. A *Clepselæa*, or Oil Hour-glass, as the Ancients used those of Water.

20. A Ring found in a Fishes Belly taken about *Gorro*; conceived to be the same wherewith the Duke of *Venice* had wedded the Sea.

21. A neat Crucifix made out of the cross Bone of a Frogs Head.

22. A large Agath containing a various and careless Figure, which looked upon by a Cylinder representeth a perfect Centaur. By some such advantages King *Pyrrhus* might find out *Apollo* and the nine Muses in those Agaths of his whereof *Pliny* maketh mention.

23. *Batrachomyomachia*, or the Homerican Battel between Frogs and Mice, neatly described upon the Chizel Bone of a large Pike's Jaw.

24. *Pyxis Pandoræ*, or a Box which held the *Unguentum Pestiferum*, which by anointing the Garments of several persons begat the great and horrible Plague of *Milan*.

25. A Glass of Spirits made of Æthereal Salt, Hermetically sealed up, kept continually in Quick-silver; of so volatile a nature that it will scarce endure the Light, and therefore onely to be shown in Winter, or by the light of a Carbuncle, or Bononian Stone.

He who knows where all this Treasure now is, is a great *Apollo*. I'm sure I am not He. However, I am,

Sir, Yours, etc.

Footnotes

[282]*Ah pudet et scripsi Getico sermone Libellum.*

A LETTER to a FRIEND upon occasion of the DEATH OF HIS Intimate Friend
1690

A LETTER TO A FRIEND,
Upon Occasion of the
Death of his Intimate Friend.

Give me leave to wonder that News of this Nature should have such heavy Wings that you should hear so little concerning your dearest Friend, and that I must make that unwilling Repetition to tell you, *Ad portam rigidos calces extendit*, that he is Dead and Buried, and by this time no Puny among the mighty Nations of the Dead; for tho' he left this World not very many Days past, yet every Hour you know largely addeth unto that dark Society; and considering the incessant Mortality of Mankind, you cannot conceive there dieth in the whole Earth so few as a thousand an Hour.

Altho' at this distance you had no early Account or Particular of his Death; yet your Affection may cease to wonder that you had not some secret Sense or Intimation thereof by Dreams, thoughtful Whisperings, Mercurisms, Airy Nuncio's, or sympathetical Insinuations, which many seem to have had at the Death of their dearest Friends: for since we find in that famous Story, that Spirits themselves were fain to tell their Fellows at a distance, that the great *Antonio* was dead; we have a sufficient Excuse for our Ignorance in such Particulars, and must rest content with the common Road, and *Appian* way of Knowledge by Information. Tho' the uncertainty of the End of this World hath confounded all Human Predictions; yet they who shall live to see the Sun and Moon darkned, and the Stars to fall from Heaven, will hardly be deceiv'd in the Advent of the last Day; and therefore strange it is, that the common Fallacy of consumptive Persons, who feel not themselves dying, and therefore still hope to live, should also reach their Friends in perfect Health and Judgment. That you should be so little acquainted with *Plautus's* sick Complexion, or that almost an *Hippocratical* Face should not alarum you to higher fears, or rather despair of his Continuation in such an emaciated State, wherein medical Predictions fail not, as sometimes in acute Diseases, and wherein 'tis as dangerous to be sentenc'd by a Physician as a Judge.

Upon my first Visit I was bold to tell them who had not let fall all Hopes of his Recovery, that in my sad Opinion he was not like to behold a Grashopper, much less to pluck another Fig; and in no long time after seem'd to discover that odd mortal Symptom in him not mention'd by *Hippocrates*, that is, to lose his own Face, and look like some of his near Relations; for he maintain'd not his proper Countenance, but look'd like his Uncle, the Lines of whose Face lay deep and invisible in his healthful Visage before: For as from our beginning we run through Variety of Looks, before we come to consistent and setled Faces; so before our End, by sick and languishing alterations, we put on new Visages: and in our Retreat to Earth, may fall upon such Looks which from Community of seminal Originals were before latent in us.

He was fruitlesly put in hope of advantage by change of Air, and imbibing the pure Aerial Nitre of these Parts; and therefore being so far spent, he quickly found *Sardinia* in *Tivoli*,[283] and the most healthful Air of little effect, where Death had set her broad Arrow; for he lived not unto the middle of *May*, and confirmed the Observation of *Hippocrates*[284] of that mortal time of the Year when the Leaves of the Fig-tree resemble a Daw's Claw. He is happily seated who lives in Places whose Air, Earth and Water, promote not the Infirmities of his weaker Parts, or is early removed into Regions that correct them. He that is tabidly inclin'd, were unwise to pass his Days in *Portugal*: Cholical Persons will find little Comfort in *Austria* or *Vienna*: He that is weak-legg'd must not be in Love with *Rome*, nor an infirm Head with *Venice* or *Paris*. Death hath not only particular Stars in Heaven, but malevolent Places on Earth, which single out our Infirmities, and strike at our weaker Parts; in which Concern, passager and migrant Birds have the great Advantages; who are naturally constituted for distant Habitations, whom no Seas nor Places limit, but in their appointed Seasons will visit us from *Greenland* and Mount *Atlas*, and as some think, even from the *Antipodes*.[285]

Tho' we could not have his Life, yet we missed not our desires in his soft Departure, which was scarce an Expiration; and his End not unlike his Beginning, when the salient Point scarce affords a sensible Motion, and his Departure so like unto Sleep, that he scarce needed the civil Ceremony of closing his Eyes; contrary unto the common way wherein Death draws up, Sleep let fall the Eye-lids. With what Strift and Pains we came into the World we know not; but 'tis commonly no easie matter to get out of it: yet if it could be made out, that such who have easie Nativities have commonly hard Deaths, and contrarily; his Departure was so easie, that we might justly suspect his Birth was of another nature, and that some *Juno* sat cross-legg'd at his Nativity.

Besides his soft Death, the incurable state of his Disease might somewhat extenuate your Sorrow, who know that Monsters[286] but seldom happen, Miracles more rarely, in Physick. *Angelus Victorius*[287] gives a serious Account of a Consumptive, Hectical, Pthysical Woman, who was suddenly cured by the Intercession of *Ignatius*. We read not of any in Scripture who in this case applied unto our Saviour, tho' some may be contain'd in that large Expression, that he went about *Galilee* healing all manner of Sickness, and all manner of Diseases. Amulets, Spells, Sigils and Incantations, practised in other Diseases, are seldom pretended in this; and we find no Sigil in the Archidoxis of *Paracelsus* to cure an extreme Consumption or *Marasmus*, which if other Diseases fail, will put a period unto long Livers, and at last makes Dust of all. And therefore the *Stoicks* could not but think that the fiery Principle would wear out all the rest, and at last make an end of the World, which notwithstanding without such a lingring period the Creator may effect at his Pleasure: and to make an end of all things on Earth, and our Planetical System of the World, he need but put out the Sun.

I was not so curious to entitle the Stars unto any Concern of his Death, yet could not but take notice that he died when the Moon was in motion from the Meridian; at which time, an old *Italian* long ago would perswade me that the greatest Part of Men died: but herein I confess I could never satisfie my Curiosity; altho' from the time of Tides in Places upon or near the Sea, there may be considerable Deductions; and *Pliny*[288] hath an odd and remarkable Passage concerning the Death of Men and Animals upon the Recess or Ebb of the Sea. However, certain it is he died in the dead and deep part of the Night, when *Nox* might be most apprehensibly said to be the Daughter of *Chaos*, the Mother of Sleep and Death, according to old Genealogy; and so went out of this World about that hour when our blessed Saviour entred it, and about what time many conceive he will return again unto it. *Cardan*[289] hath a peculiar and no hard Observation from a Man's Hand to know whether he was born in the Day or Night, which I confess holdeth in my own. And *Scaliger* to that purpose hath another from the tip of the Ear: Most Men are begotten in the Night, Animals in the Day; but whether more Persons have been born in the Night or the Day, were a Curiosity undecidable, tho' more have perished by violent Deaths in the Day; yet in natural Dissolutions both Times may hold an Indifferency, at least but contingent Inequality. The whole Course of Time runs out in the Nativity and Death of Things; which whether they happen by Succession or Coincidence, are best computed by the natural not artificial Day.

That *Charles* the Vth was crown'd upon the Day of his Nativity, it being in his own Power so to order it, makes no singular Animadversion; but that he should also take King *Francis* Prisoner upon that Day, was an unexpected Coincidence, which made the same remarkable. *Antipater* who had an Anniversary Fever every Year upon his Birth-day, needed no Astrological Revolution to know what Day he should dye on. When the fixed Stars have made a Revolution unto the Points from whence they first set out, some of the Ancients thought the World would have an end; which was a kind of dying upon the Day of its Nativity. Now the Disease prevailing and swiftly advancing about the time of his Nativity, some were of Opinion that he would leave the World on the Day he entred into it: but this being a lingring Disease, and creeping softly on, nothing critical was found or expected, and he died not before fifteen Days after. Nothing is more common with Infants than to die on the Day of their Nativity, to behold the worldly Hours, and but the Fractions thereof; and even to perish before their Nativity in the hidden World of the Womb, and before their good Angel is conceived to undertake them. But in Persons who out-live many Years, and when there are no less than three hundred sixty five days to determine their Lives in every Year; that the first day should make the last, that the Tail of the Snake should return into its Mouth precisely at that time, and they should wind up upon the day of their Nativity,[290] is indeed a remarkable Coincidence, which, tho' Astrology hath taken witty Pains to salve, yet hath it been very wary in making Predictions of it.

In this consumptive Condition and remarkable Extenuation he came to be almost half himself, and left a great Part behind him which he carried not to the Grave. And tho' that Story of Duke *John Ernestus Mansfield*[291] be not so easily swallow'd, that at his Death his Heart was found not to be so big as a Nut; yet if the Bones of a good Skeleton weigh little more than twenty Pounds, his Inwards and Flesh remaining could make no Bouffage, but a light Bit for the Grave. I never more lively beheld the starved Characters of *Dante*[292] in any living Face; an *Aruspex* might have read a Lecture upon him without Exenteration, his Flesh being so consumed, that he might, in a manner, have discerned his Bowels without opening of him: so that to be carried *sextâ cervice*, to the Grave, was but a civil Unnecessity; and the Complements of the Coffin might out-weigh the Subject of it.

Omnibonus Ferrarius[293] in mortal Dysenteries of Children looks for a Spot behind the Ear; in consumptive Diseases some eye the Complexion of Moles; *Cardan* eagerly views the Nails, some the Lines of the Hand, the Thenar or Muscle of the Thumb; some are so curious as to observe the depth of the Throat-pit, how the Proportion varieth of the Small of the Legs unto the Calf, or the compass of the Neck unto the Circumference of the Head: but all these, with many more, were so drown'd in a mortal Visage, and last Face of *Hippocrates*, that a weak Physiognomist might say at first Eye, This was a Face of Earth, and that *Morta*[294] had set her hard Seal upon his Temples, easily perceiving what *Caricatura*[295] Draughts Death makes upon pined Faces, and unto what an unknown degree a Man may live backward.

Tho' the Beard be only made a Distinction of Sex, and Sign of masculine Heat by *Ulmus*, yet the Precocity and early Growth thereof in him, was not to be liked in reference unto long Life. *Lewis*, that virtuous but unfortunate King of *Hungary*, who lost his Life at the Battle of *Mohacz*, was said to be born without a Skin, to have bearded at fifteen,[296] and to have shewn some grey Hairs about twenty; from whence the Diviners conjectur'd, that he would be spoiled of his Kingdom, and have but a short Life: But Hairs make fallible Predictions, and many Temples early grey have out-liv'd d the Psalmist's Period.[297] Hairs which have most amused me have not been in the Face or Head, but on the Back, and not in Men but Children, as I long ago observed in that Endemial Distemper of little Children in *Languedock*, call'd the *Morgellons*,[298] wherein they critically break out with harsh Hairs on their Backs, which takes off the unquiet Symptoms of the Disease, and delivers them from Coughs and Convulsions.

The *Egyptian* Mummies that I have seen, have had their Mouths open, and somewhat gaping, which affordeth a good Opportunity to view and observe their Teeth, wherein 'tis not easie to find any wanting or decay'd; and therefore in *Egypt*, where one Man practised but one Operation, or the Diseases but of single Parts, it must needs be a barren Profession to confine unto that of drawing of Teeth, and little better than to have been Tooth-drawer unto King *Pyrrhus*,[299] who had but two in his Head. How the *Bannyans* of *India* maintain the Integrity of those Parts, I find not particularly observed; who notwithstanding have an Advantage of their Preservation by abstaining from all Flesh, and employing their Teeth in such Food unto which they may seem at first framed, from their Figure and Conformation: but sharp and corroding Rheums had so early mouldred those Rocks and hardest parts of his Fabrick, that a Man might well conceive that his Years were never like to double or twice tell over his Teeth.[300] Corruption had dealt more severely with them than sepulchral Fires and smart Flames with those of burnt Bodies of old; for in the burnt Fragments of Urnes which I have enquired into, altho' I seem to find few Incisors or Shearers, yet the Dog Teeth and Grinders do notably resist those Fires.

In the Years of his Childhood he had languish'd under the Disease of his Country, the Rickets; after which notwithstanding many have been become strong and active Men; but whether any have attain'd unto very great Years, the Disease is scarce so old as to afford good Observation. Whether the Children of the *English* Plantations be subject unto the same Infirmity, may be worth the

Observing. Whether Lameness and Halting do still encrease among the Inhabitants of *Rovigno* in *Istria*, I know not; yet scarce twenty Years ago Monsieur *du Loyr* observed, that a third part of that People halted: but too certain it is, that the Rickets encreaseth among us; the Small-Pox grows more pernicious than the Great: the King's Purse knows that the King's Evil grows more common. *Quartan* Agues are become no Strangers in *Ireland*; more common and mortal in *England*: and tho' the Ancients gave that Disease[301] very good Words, yet now that Bell makes no strange sound which rings out for the Effects thereof.

Some think there were few Consumptions in the Old World, when Men lived much upon Milk; and that the ancient Inhabitants of this Island were less troubled with Coughs when they went naked, and slept in Caves and Woods, than Men now in Chambers and Feather-beds. *Plato* will tell us, that there was no such Disease as a Catarrh in *Homer's* time, and that it was but new in *Greece* in his Age. *Polydore Virgil* delivereth that Pleurisies were rare in *England*, who lived but in the Days of *Henry* the Eighth. Some will allow no Diseases to be new, others think that many old ones are ceased and that such which are esteem'd new, will have but their time: However, the Mercy of God hath scatter'd the Great Heap of Diseases, and not loaded any one Country with all: some may be new in one Country which have been old in another. New Discoveries of the Earth discover new Diseases: for besides the common Swarm, there are endemial and local Infirmities proper unto certain Regions, which in the whole Earth make no small Number: and if *Asia*, *Africa*, and *America* should bring in their List, *Pandora's* Box would swell, and there must be a strange Pathology.

Most Men expected to find a consumed Kell, empty and bladder-like Guts, livid and marbled Lungs, and a wither'd *Pericardium* in this exuccous Corps: but some seemed too much to wonder that two Lobes of his Lungs adher'd unto his Side; for the like I had often found in Bodies of no suspected Consumptions or difficulty of Respiration. And the same more often happeneth in Men than other Animals; and some think in Women than in Men; but the most remarkable I have met with, was in a Man, after a Cough of almost fifty Years, in whom all the Lobes adhered unto the Pleura,[302] and each Lobe unto another; who having also been much troubled with the Gout, brake the Rule of *Cardan*,[303] and died of the Stone in the Bladder. *Aristotle* makes a Query, Why some Animals cough, as Man; some not, as Oxen. If Coughing be taken as it consisteth of a natural and voluntary motion, including Expectoration and spitting out, it may be as proper unto Man as bleeding at the Nose; otherwise we find that *Vegetius* and rural Writers have not left so many Medicines in vain against the Coughs of Cattel; and Men who perish by Coughs die the Death of Sheep, Cats and Lions: and tho' Birds have no Midriff, yet we meet with divers Remedies in *Arrianus* against the Coughs of Hawks. And tho' it might be thought that all Animals who have Lungs do cough; yet in cetaceous Fishes, who have large and strong Lungs, the same is not observed; nor yet in oviparous Quadrupeds: and in the greatest thereof, the Crocodile, altho' we read much of their Tears, we find nothing of that Motion.

From the Thoughts of Sleep, when the Soul was conceived nearest unto Divinity, the Ancients erected an Art of Divination, wherein while they too widely expatiated in loose and inconsequent Conjectures, *Hippocrates*[304] wisely considered Dreams as they presaged Alterations in the Body, and so afforded hints toward the Preservation of Health, and prevention of Diseases; and therein was so serious as to advise Alteration of Diet, Exercise, Sweating, Bathing and Vomiting; and also so religious, as to order Prayers and Supplications unto respective Deities, in good Dreams unto *Sol, Jupiter cœlestis, Jupiter opulentus, Minerva, Mercurius* and *Apollo*; in bad unto *Tellus* and the Heroes.

And therefore I could not but take notice how his Female Friends were irrationally curious so strictly to examine his Dreams, and in this low State to hope for the Fantasms of Health. He was now past the healthful Dreams of the Sun, Moon and Stars, in their Clarity and proper Courses. 'Twas too late to dream of Flying, of Limpid Fountains, smooth Waters, white Vestments, and fruitful green Trees, which are the Visions of healthful Sleeps, and at good Distance from the Grave.

And they were also too deeply dejected that he should dream of his dead Friends, inconsequently divining, that he would not be long from them; for strange it was not that he should sometimes dream of the dead, whose Thoughts run always upon Death; beside, to dream of the dead, so they appear not in dark Habits, and take nothing away from us, in *Hippocrates* his Sense was of good Signification: for we live by the dead, and every thing is or must be so before it becomes our Nourishment. And *Cardan*, who dream'd that he discoursed with his dead Father in the Moon, made thereof no mortal Interpretation: and even to dream that we are dead, was no condemnable Fantasm in old *Oneirocriticism*, as having a Signification of Liberty, vacuity from Cares, Exemption and Freedom from Troubles unknown unto the dead.

Some Dreams I confess may admit of easie and feminine Exposition; he who dream'd that he could not see his right Shoulder, might easily fear to lose the Sight of his right Eye; he that before a Journey dream'd that his Feet were cut off, had a plain Warning not to undertake his intended Journey. But why to dream of Lettuce should presage some ensuing Disease, why to eat Figs should signifie foolish Talk, why to eat Eggs great Trouble, and to dream of Blindness should be so highly commended, according to the *Oneirocritical* Verses of *Astrampsychus* and *Nicephorus*, I shall leave unto your Divination.

He was willing to quit the World alone and altogether, leaving no Earnest behind him for Corruption or After-grave, having small content in that common Satisfaction to survive or live in another, but amply satisfied that his Disease should die with himself, nor revive in a Posterity to puzzle Physick, and make sad *Memento's* of their Parent hereditary. Leprosie awakes not sometimes before forty, the Gout and Stone often later; but consumptive and tabid[305] Roots sprout more early, and at the fairest make seventeen Years of our Life doubtful before that Age. They that enter the World with original Diseases as well as Sin, have not only common Mortality but sick Traductions to destroy them, make commonly short Courses, and live not at length but in Figures; so that a sound *Cæsarean*[306] Nativity may out-last a Natural Birth, and a Knife may sometimes make Way for a more lasting Fruit than a Midwife; which makes so few Infants now able to endure the old Test of the River,[307] and many to have feeble Children who could scarce have been married at *Sparta*, and those provident States who studied strong and healthful Generations; which happen but contingently in mere *pecuniary* Matches, or Marriages made by the Candle, wherein notwithstanding there is little redress to be hoped from an Astrologer or a Lawyer, and a good discerning Physician were like to prove the most successful Counsellor.

Julius Scaliger, who in a sleepless Fit of the Gout could make two hundred Verses in a Night, would have but five[308] plain Words upon his Tomb. And this serious Person, tho' no *minor* Wit, left the Poetry of his Epitaph unto others; either unwilling to commend himself, or to be judg'd by a Distich, and perhaps considering how unhappy great Poets have been in versifying their own Epitaphs: wherein *Petrarcha*, *Dante*, and *Ariosto*, have so unhappily failed, that if their Tombs should outlast their Works, Posterity would find so little of *Apollo* on them, as to mistake them for *Ciceronian* Poets.

In this deliberate and creeping Progress unto the Grave, he was somewhat too young, and of too noble a Mind, to fall upon that stupid Symptom observable in divers Persons near their Journey's End, and which may be reckoned among the mortal Symptoms of their last Disease; that is, to become more narrow minded, miserable and tenacious, unready to part with any thing, when they are ready to part with all, and afraid to want when they have no Time to spend; mean while Physicians, who know that many are mad but in a single depraved Imagination, and one prevalent Decipiency; and that beside and out of such single Deliriums a Man may meet with sober Actions and good Sense in *Bedlam*; cannot but smile to see the Heirs and concern'd Relations, gratulating themselves in the sober Departure of their Friends; and tho' they behold such mad covetous Passages, content to think they die in good Understanding, and in their sober Senses.

Avarice, which is not only Infidelity but Idolatry, either from covetous Progeny or questuary Education, had no Root in his Breast, who made good Works the Expression of his Faith, and was big with Desires unto publick and lasting Charities; and surely where good Wishes and charitable Intentions exceed Abilities, Theorical Beneficency may be more than a Dream. They build not Castles in the Air who would build Churches on Earth; and tho' they leave no such Structures here, may lay good Foundations in Heaven. In brief, his Life and Death were such, that I could not blame them who wished the like, and almost to have been himself; almost, I say; for tho' we may wish the prosperous Appurtenances of others, or to be an other in his happy Accidents; yet so intrinsecal is every Man unto himself, that some doubt may be made, whether any would exchange his Being, or substantially become another Man.

He had wisely seen the World at home and abroad, and thereby observed under what variety Men are deluded in the pursuit of that which is not here to be found. And altho' he had no Opinion of reputed Felicities below, and apprehended Men widely out in the Estimate of such Happiness; yet his sober Contempt of the World wrought no *Democratism* or *Cynicism*, no laughing or snarling at it, as well understanding there are not Felicities in this World to satisfy a serious Mind; and therefore to soften the Stream of our Lives, we are fain to take in the reputed Contentations of this World, to unite with the Crowd in their Beatitudes, and to make ourselves happy by Consortion, Opinion, or Co-existimation: for strictly to separate from received and customary Felicities, and to confine unto the Rigor of Realities, were to contract the Consolation of our Beings unto too uncomfortable Circumscriptions.

Not to fear Death,[309] nor Desire it, was short of his Resolution: to be dissolved, and be with Christ, was his dying Ditty. He conceived his Thred long, in no long course of Years, and when he had scarce out-liv'd the second Life of *Lazarus*;[310] esteeming it enough to approach the Years of his Saviour, who so order'd his own human State, as not to be old upon Earth.

But to be content with Death may be better than to desire it: a miserable Life may make us wish for Death, but a virtuous one to rest in it; which is the Advantage of those resolved Christians, who looking on Death not only as the Sting, but the Period and End of Sin, the Horizon and Isthmus between this Life and a better, and the Death of this World but as Nativity of another, do contentedly submit unto the common Necessity, and envy not *Enoch* or *Elias*.

Not to be content with Life is the unsatisfactory State of those which destroy themselves;[311] who being afraid to live, run blindly upon their own Death, which no Man fears by Experience: And the Stoicks had a notable Doctrine to take away the Fear thereof; that is, in such Extremities, to desire that which is not to be avoided, and wish what might be feared; and so made Evils voluntary, and to suit with their own Desires, which took off the Terror of them.

But the ancient Martyrs were not encouraged by such Fallacies; who, tho' they feared not Death, were afraid to be their own Executioners; and therefore thought it more Wisdom to crucify their Lusts than their Bodies, to circumcise than stab their Hearts, and to mortify than kill themselves.

His Willingness to leave this World about that Age, when most men think they may best enjoy it, tho' paradoxical unto worldly Ears, was not strange unto mine, who have so often observed, that many, tho' old, oft stick fast unto the World, and seem to be drawn like *Cacus's* Oxen, backward, with great Struggling and Reluctancy unto the Grave. The long Habit of Living makes meer men more hardly to part with Life, and All to be Nothing, but what is to come. To live at the rate of the old World, when some could scarce remember themselves young, may afford no better digested Death than a more moderate Period. Many would have thought it an Happiness to have had their Lot of Life in some notable Conjunctures of Ages past; but the Uncertainty of future Times hath tempted few to make a Part in Ages to come. And surely, he that hath taken the true Altitude of things, and rightly calculated the degenerate State of this Age, is not like to envy those that shall live in the next, much less three or four hundred Years hence, when no Man can comfortably imagine what Face this World will carry: And therefore since every Age makes a Step unto the End of all things, and the Scripture affords so hard a Character of the last Times; quiet Minds will be content with their Generations, and rather bless Ages past, than be ambitious of those to come.

Tho' Age had set no Seal upon his Face, yet a dim Eye might clearly discover Fifty in his Actions; and therefore since Wisdom is the grey Hair, and an unspotted Life old Age; altho' his Years came short he might have been said to have held up with longer Livers, and to have been *Solomon's*[312] Old Man. And surely if we deduct all those Days of our Life which we might wish unliv'd, and which abate the Comfort of those we now live; if we reckon up only those Days which God hath accepted of our Lives, a Life of good Years will hardly be a Span long: the Son in this Sense may out-live the Father, and none be climacterically old. He that early arriveth unto the Parts and Prudence of Age, is happily old without the uncomfortable Attendants of it; and 'tis superfluous to live unto grey Hairs, when in a precocious Temper we anticipate the Virtues of them. In brief, he cannot be accounted young who out-liveth the old Man. He that hath early arrived unto the measure of a perfect Stature in Christ, hath already fulfilled the prime and longest Intention of his Being: and one Day lived after the perfect Rule of Piety, is to be preferr'd before sinning Immortality.

Altho' he attain'd not unto the Years of his Predecessors, yet he wanted not those preserving Virtues which confirm the Thread of weaker Constitutions. Cautelous Chastity and crafty Sobriety were far from him; those Jewels were Paragon, without Flaw, Hair, Ice, or Cloud in him: which affords me an Hint to proceed in these good Wishes, and few *Memento's* unto you.

Tread softly and circumspectly in this funambulous Track, and narrow Path of Goodness: pursue Virtue virtuously; be sober and temperate, not to preserve your Body in a sufficiency to wanton Ends; not to spare your Purse; not to be free from the Infamy of common Transgressors that way, and thereby to ballance or palliate obscure and closer Vices; nor simply to enjoy Health: By all which you may leaven good Actions, and render Virtues disputable: but in one Word, that you may truly serve God; which every Sickness will tell you, you cannot well do without health. The sick Man's Sacrifice is but a lame Oblation. Pious Treasures laid up in healthful Days, excuse the Defect of sick Non-performances; without which we must needs look back with Anxiety upon the lost Opportunities of Health; and may have cause rather to envy than pity the Ends of penitent Malefactors, who go with clear Parts unto the last Act of their Lives; and in the Integrity of their Faculties return their Spirit unto God that gave it.

Consider whereabout thou art in *Cebes* his Table, or that old philosophical Pinax of the Life of Man; whether thou art still in the Road of Uncertainties; whether thou hast yet entred the narrow Gate, got up the Hill and asperous Way which leadeth unto the House of Sanity, or taken that purifying Potion from the Hand of sincere Erudition, which may send the clear and pure away unto a virtuous and happy Life.

In this virtuous voyage let not Disappointment cause Despondency, nor Difficulty Despair: Think not that you are sailing from *Lima*[313] to *Manillia*, wherein thou may'st tye up the Rudder, and sleep before the Wind; but expect rough Seas, Flaws, and contrary Blasts; and 'tis well if by many cross Tacks and Veerings thou arrivest at thy Port. Sit not down in the popular Seats, and common Level of Virtues, but endeavour to make them Heroical. Offer not only Peace-Offerings but Holocausts unto God. To serve him singly to serve our selves, were too partial a Piece of Piety, nor likely to place us in the highest Mansions of Glory.

He that is chaste and continent, not to impair his Strength, or terrified by Contagion, will hardly be heroically virtuous. Adjourn not that Virtue unto those Years when *Cato* could lend out his Wife, and impotent *Satyrs* write Satyrs against Lust: but be chaste in thy flaming Days, when *Alexander* dared not trust his Eyes upon the fair Daughters of *Darius*, and when so many Men think there is no other Way but *Origen's*.[314]

Be charitable before Wealth makes thee covetous, and lose not the Glory of the Mitre. If Riches increase, let thy Mind hold Pace with them; and think it not enough to be liberal, but munificent. Tho' a Cup of cold Water from some hand may not be without its Reward; yet stick not thou for Wine and Oyl for the Wounds of the distressed: and treat the poor as our Saviour did the Multitude, to the Relicks of some Baskets.

Trust not to the Omnipotency of Gold, or say unto it, Thou art my Confidence: kiss not thy Hand when thou beholdest that terrestrial Sun, nor bore thy Ear unto its Servitude. A Slave unto Mammon makes no Servant unto God: Covetousness cracks the Sinews of Faith, numbs the Apprehension of any thing above Sense, and only affected with the Certainty of Things present, makes a Peradventure of things to come; lives but unto one World, nor hopes but fears another; makes our own Death sweet unto others, bitter unto our selves; gives a dry Funeral, Scenical Mourning, and no wet Eyes at the Grave.

If Avarice be thy Vice, yet make it not thy Punishment: Miserable Men commiserate not themselves, bowelless unto themselves, and merciless unto their own Bowels. Let the Fruition of things bless the Possession of them, and take no Satisfaction in dying but living rich: for since thy good Works, not thy Goods, will follow thee; since Riches are an Appurtenance of Life, and no dead Man is rich, to famish in Plenty, and live poorly to die rich, were a multiplying Improvement in Madness, and Use upon Use in Folly.

Persons lightly dip'd, not grain'd in generous Honesty, are but pale in Goodness, and faint hued in Sincerity: but be thou what thou virtuously art, and let not the Ocean wash away thy Tincture: stand magnetically upon that Axis where prudent Simplicity hath fix'd thee, and let no Temptation invert the Poles of thy Honesty: and that Vice may be uneasie, and even monstrous unto thee, let iterated good Acts, and long confirm'd Habits make Vertue natural, or a second Nature in thee. And since few or none prove eminently vertuous but from some advantageous Foundations in their Temper, and natural Inclinations; study thy self betimes, and early find what Nature bids thee to be, or tells thee what thou may'st be. They who thus timely descend into themselves, cultivating the good Seeds which Nature hath set in them, and improving their prevalent Inclinations to Perfection, become not Shrubs, but Cedars in their Generation; and to be in the form of the best of the Bad, or the worst of the Good, will be no Satisfaction unto them.

Let not the Law of thy Country be the *non ultra* of thy Honesty, nor think that always good enough which the Law will make good. Narrow not the Law of Charity, Equity, Mercy; joyn Gospel Righteousness with Legal Right; be not a meer *Gamaliel* in the Faith; but let the Sermon in the Mount be thy *Targum* unto the Law of *Sinai*.

Make not the Consequences of Vertue the Ends thereof: be not beneficent for a Name or Cymbal of Applause, nor exact and punctual in Commerce, for the Advantages of Trust and Credit which attend the Reputation of just and true Dealing; for such Rewards, tho' unsought for, plain Vertue will bring with her, whom all Men honour, tho' they pursue not. To have other bye Ends in good Actions, sowers laudable Performances, which must have deeper Roots, Motions, and Instigations, to give them the Stamp of Vertues.

Tho' human Infirmity may betray thy heedless Days into the popular Ways of Extravagancy, yet let not thine own Depravity, or the Torrent of vicious Times, carry thee into desperate Enormities in Opinions, Manners, or Actions: if thou hast dip'd thy Foot in the River, yet venture not over *Rubicon*; run not into Extremities from whence there is no Regression, nor be ever so closely shut up within the Holds of Vice and Iniquity, as not to find some Escape by a Postern of Resipiscency.

Owe not thy Humility unto Humiliation by Adversity, but look humbly down in that State when others look upward upon thee: be patient in the Age of Pride and Days of Will and Impatiency, when Men live but by Intervals of Reason, under the Sovereignty of Humor and Passion, when 'tis in the Power of every one to transform thee out of thy self, and put thee into the short Madness. If you cannot imitate *Job*, yet come not short of *Socrates*,[315] and those patient Pagans, who tir'd the Tongues of their Enemies while they perceiv'd they spet their Malice at brazen Walls and Statues.

Let Age, not Envy, draw Wrinkles on thy Cheeks: be content to be envied, but envy not. Emulation may be plausible, and Indignation allowable; but admit no Treaty with that Passion which no Circumstance can make good. A Displacency at the Good of others, because they enjoy it, altho' we do not want it, is an absurd Depravity, sticking fast unto human Nature from its primitive Corruption; which he that can well subdue, were a Christian of the first Magnitude, and for ought I know, may have one Foot already in Heaven.

While thou so hotly disclaim'st the Devil, be not guilty of Diabolism; fall not into one Name with that unclean Spirit, nor act his Nature whom thou so much abhorrest; that is, to accuse, calumniate, backbite, whisper, detract, or sinistrously interpret others; degenerous Depravities and narrow-minded Vices, not only below S. *Paul's* noble Christian, but *Aristotle's*[316] true Gentleman. Trust not with some, that the Epistle of S. *James* is Apocryphal, and so read with less Fear that Stabbing Truth, that in company with this Vice thy Religion is in vain. *Moses* broke the Tables without breaking of the Law; but where Charity is broke the Law it self is shatter'd, which cannot be whole without Love, that is the fulfilling of it. Look humbly upon thy Vertues, and tho' thou art rich in some, yet think thy self poor and naked, without that crowning Grace, which thinketh no Evil, which envieth not, which beareth, believeth, hopeth, endureth all things. With these sure Graces, while busie Tongues are crying out for a Drop of cold Water, Mutes may be in Happiness, and sing the *Trisagium*[317] in Heaven.

Let not the Sun in *Capricorn* go down upon thy Wrath, but Write thy Wrongs in Water: draw the Curtain of Night upon Injuries; shut them up in the Tower of Oblivion,[318] and let them be as tho' they had not been. Forgive thine Enemies totally, and without any Reserve of Hope, that however, God will revenge thee.

Be substantially great in thy self, and more than thou appearest unto others; and let the World be deceived in thee, as they are in the Lights of Heaven. Hang early Plummets upon the Heels of Pride, and let Ambition have but an Epicycle or narrow Circuit in thee. Measure not thy self by thy Morning Shadow, but by the Extent of thy Grave; and reckon thy self above the Earth by the Line thou must be contented with under it. Spread not into boundless Expansions either to Designs or Desires. Think not that Mankind liveth but for a few, and that the rest are born but to serve the Ambition of those, who make but Flies of Men, and Wildernesses of whole Nations. Swell not into Actions which embroil and confound the Earth; but be one of those violent ones which *force the Kingdom of Heaven.*[319] If thou must needs reign, be *Zeno*, King, and enjoy that Empire which every Man gives himself. Certainly, the iterated Injunctions of Christ unto Humility, Meekness, Patience, and that despised Train of Vertues, cannot but make pathetical Impressions upon those who have well consider'd the Affairs of all Ages, wherein Pride, Ambition, and Vain glory, have led up the worst of Actions, and whereunto Confusion, Tragedies, and Acts denying all Religion, do owe their Originals.

Rest not in an Ovation,[320] but a Triumph over thy Passions; chain up the unruly Legion of thy Breast; behold thy Trophies within thee, not without thee: Lead thine own Captivity captive, and be *Cæsar* unto thy self.

Give no quarter unto those Vices which are of thine inward Family; and having a Root in thy Temper, plead a Right and Property in thee. Examine well thy complexional Inclinations. Raise early Batteries against those strong Holds built upon the Rock of Nature, and make this a great Part of the Militia of thy Life. The politick Nature of Vice must be oppos'd by Policy, and therefore wiser Honesties project and plot against Sin; wherein notwithstanding we are not to rest in Generals, or the trite Stratagems of Art: that may succeed with one Temper which may prove successless with another. There is no Community or Common-wealth of Virtue; every Man must study his own Oeconomy, and erect these Rules unto the Figure of himself.

Lastly, If Length of Days be thy Portion, make it not thy Expectation: Reckon not upon long Life, but live always beyond thy Account. He that so often surviveth his Expectation, lives many Lives, and will hardly complain of the Shortness of his Days. Time past is gone like a Shadow; make Times to come present; conceive that near which may be far off; approximate thy last Times by present Apprehensions of them: Live like a Neighbour unto Death, and think there is but little to come. And since there is something in us that must still live on, join both Lives together; unite them in thy Thoughts and Actions, and live in one but for the other. He who thus ordereth the Purposes of this Life, will never be far from the next, and is in some manner already in it, by an happy Conformity, and close Apprehension of it.

FINIS

Footnotes

[283]*Cum mors venerit, in medio Tibure Sardinia est.*

[284]In the King's Forests they set the Figure of a broad Arrow upon Trees that are to be cut down. *Hippoc. Epidem.*

[285]Bellonius *de Avibus.*

[286]*Monstra contingunt in Medicina Hippoc.*

[287]Strange and rare Escapes there happen sometimes in Physick. *Angeli Victorii Consultationes.* Matth. iv. 25.

[288]*Aristoteles nullum animal nisi æstu recedente expirare affirmat: observatum id multum in Gallico Oceano et duntaxat in Homine comertum,* lib. 2. cap. 101.

[289]*Auris pars pendula Lobus dicitur, non omnibus ea pars est auribus; non enim iis qui noctu nati sunt, sed qui interdiu, maxima ex parte. Com. in Aristot. de Animal.* lib. 1.

[290]According to the *Egyptian* Hieroglyphick.

[291]*Turkish* History.

[292]In the Poet *Dante* his Discription.

[293]*De Morbis Puerorum.*

[294]*Morta*, the Deity of Death or Fate.

[295]When Men's Faces are drawn with Resemblance to some other Animals, the *Italians* call it, to be drawn in *Caricatura.*

[296]*Ulmus de usu barbæ humanæ.*

[297]The Life of a Man is threescore and ten.

[298]See *Picotus de Rheumatismo.*

[299]His upper and lower Jaw being solid, and without distinct Rows of Teeth.

[300]Twice tell over his Teeth, never live to threescore Years.

[301]Ἀσφαλέστατος καὶ ῥήιστος, *securissima et facillima*. Hippoc. Pro Febre quartana raro sonat campana.

[302]So *A. F.*

[303]*Cardan* in his *Encomium Podagræ* reckoneth this among the *Dona Podagræ*, that they are deliver'd thereby from the Phthysis and Stone in the Bladder.

[304]*Hippoc. de Insomniis.*

[305]*Tabes maxime contingunt ab anno decimo octavo ad trigesimum quintum*, Hippoc.

[306]A sound Child cut out of the Body of the Mother.

[307]*Natos ad flumina primum deserimus sævoque gelu duramus et undis.*

[308]*Julii Cæsaris Scaligeri, quod fuit.* Joseph. Scaliger in vita patris.

[309]*Summum nec metuas diem nec optes.*

[310]Who upon some Accounts, and Tradition, is said to have lived 30 Years after he was raised by our Saviour. *Baronius.*

[311]In the Speech of *Vulteius in Lucan*, animating his Souldiers in a great Struggle to kill one another. *Decernite Lethum et metus omnis abest, cupias quodcunque necesse est.* All Fear is over, do but resolve to die, and make your Desires meet Necessity.

[312]*Wisdom*, cap. iv.

[313]Through the Pacifick Sea, with a constant Gale from the East.

[314]Who is said to have castrated himself.

[315]*Ira furor brevis est.*

[316]See *Arist. Ethicks* Chapt. of Magnanimity.

[317]Holy, Holy, Holy.

[318]Even when the Days are shortest; alluding to the Tower of *Oblivion* mentioned by *Procopius*, which was the Name of a Tower of Imprisonment among the *Persians*: whosoever was put therein he was as it were buried alive, and it was Death for any but to name it.

[319]*Matthew* xi.

[320]*Ovation*, a petty and minor kind of Triumph.

POSTHUMOUS WORKS
1712

REPERTORIUM:
Or, some Account of the Tombs and Monuments in the Cathedral Church of Norwich, in 1680.

In the Time of the late Civil Wars, there were about an hundred Brass Inscriptions stol'n and taken away from Grave-Stones, and Tombs, in the Cathedral Church of *Norwich*; as I was inform'd by *John Wright*, one of the Clerks, above Eighty Years old, and Mr. *John Sandlin*, one of the Choir, who lived Eighty nine Years; and, as I remember, told me that he was a Chorister in the Reign of Queen *Elizabeth*.

Hereby the distinct Places of the Burials of many noble and considerable Persons become unknown; and, lest they should be quite buried in Oblivion, I shall, of so many, set down only these following that are most noted to Passengers, with some that have been erected since those unhappy Times.

First, in the Body of the Church, between the Pillars of the South Isle, stands a Tomb, cover'd with a kind of Touch-stone; which is the Monument of MILES SPENCER, LL.D. and Chancellor of *Norwich*, who lived unto Ninety Years. The Top Stone was entire, but now quite broken, split, and depress'd by Blows: There was more special Notice taken of this Stone, because Men used to try their Money upon it; and that the Chapter demanded certain Rents to be paid on it. He was Lord of the Mannor of *Bowthorp* and *Colney*, which came unto the *Yaxley's* from him; also Owner of *Chappel*, in the Field.

The next Monument is that of Bishop RICHARD NICKS, *alias* Nix, or the Blind Bishop, being quite dark many Years before he died. He sat in this *See* Thirty Six Years, in the Reigns of

King *Henry* VII. and *Henry* VIII. The Arches are beautified above and beside it, where are to be seen the Arms of the *See* of *Norwich, impaling* his own, *viz.* a *Chevron* between three *Leopards* Heads. The same Coat of Arms is on the Roof of the *North* and *South Cross Isle*; which Roofs he either rebuilt, or repair'd. The Tomb is low, and broad, and 'tis said there was an Altar at the bottom of the Eastern Pillar: The Iron-work, whereon the Bell hung, is yet visible on the Side of the Western Pillar.

Then the Tomb of Bishop JOHN PARKHURST, with a legible Inscription on the Pillar, set up by Dean *Gardiner*, running thus.

Johannes Parkhurst, *Theol. Professor*, Guilfordiæ *natus*,
Oxoniæ *educatus, temporibus* Mariæ *Reginæ pro*
Nitida conscientia tuenda Tigurinæ *vixit exul*
Voluntarius: Postea presul factus, sanctissime
Hanc rexit Ecclesiam per 16 an. Obiit secundo die
Febr. 1574.

A Person he was of great Esteem and Veneration in the Reign of Queen *Elizabeth*. His Coat of Arms is on the Pillars, visible, at the going out of the Bishop's Hall.

Between the two uppermost Pillars, on the same Side, stood a handsom Monument of Bishop EDMUND SCAMLER, thus.

Natus apud Gressingham, *in Com.* Lanc. SS. *Theol. Prof. apud* Cantabrigienses. *Obiit Ætat.* 85. *an.* 1594 *nonis* Maii.

He was Houshold Chaplain to the Archbishop of *Canterbury*, and died 1594. The Monument was above a yard and half high, with his Effigies in Alabaster, and all enclosed with a high Iron Grate. In the late Times the Grate was taken away, the Statue broken, and the Free-stone pulled down as far as the inward Brick-work; which being unsightly, was afterwards taken away, and the Space between the Pillars left void, as it now remaineth.

In the South-side of this Isle, according as the Inscription denoteth, was buried GEORGE GARDINER, sometime Dean.

Georgius Gardiner Barvici *natus*, Cantabrigiæ *educatus*,
Primo minor Canonicus, secundo Præbendarius, tertio Archidiaconus.
Nordovici, *et demum* 28 Nov. An. 1573. *factus est Sacellanus*
Dominæ Reginæ, et Decanus hujus Ecclesiæ, in quo loco per 16
Annos rexit.

Somewhat higher is a Monument for Dr. EDMUND PORTER, a learned Prebendary, sometime of this Church.

Between two Pillars of the North Isle in the Body of the Church, stands the Monument of Sir JAMES HOBART, Attorney-General to King *Henry* VII. and VIII. He built *Loddon* Church, St. *Olave's* Bridge, and made the Causeway adjoining upon the South-side. On the upper Part is the Atchievement of the *Hobarts*, and below are their Arms; as also of the *Nantons, viz.* (*three Martlets*) his second Lady being of that Family. It is a close Monument, made up of handsom Stone-work: And this Enclosure might have been employ'd as an Oratory. Some of the Family of the *Hobarts* have been buried near this Monument; as Mr. *James Hobart* of *Holt*. On the South-side, two young Sons, and a Daughter of Dean *Herbert Astley*, who married *Barbara*, Daughter of *John*, only Son of Sir *John Hobart* of *Hales*.

In the Middle Isle, under a very large Stone, almost over which a Branch for Lights hangeth, was buried Sir FRANCIS SOUTHWELL, descended from those of great Name and Estate in *Norfolk*, who formerly possessed *Woodrising*.

Under a fair Stone, by Bishop *Parkhurst's* Tomb, was buried Dr. MASTERS, Chancellor.

Gul. Maister, *LL*. Doctor Curiæ Cons. Epatus Norwicen. *Officialis principalis. Obiit* 2 *Feb.* 1589.

At the upper End of the Middle Isle, under a large Stone, was buried Bishop WALTER de HART, *alias le* HART, or LYGHARD. He was Bishop 26 Years, in the Times of *Henry* VI. and *Edward* IV. He built the Transverse Stone Partition, or Rood Loft, on which the great Crucifix was placed, beautified the Roof of the Body of the Church, and paved it. Towards the North-side of the Partition-Wall are his Arms the *Bull* and towards the South-side, *a Hart in*

Water, as a *Rebus* of his Name, *Walter Hart*. Upon the Door, under the Rood Loft, was a Plate of Brass, containing these Verses.

Hic jacet absconsus sub marmore presul honestus
Anno milleno C quater cum septuageno
Annexis binis instabat ei prope finis
Septima cum decima lux Maij sit numerata
Ipsius est anima de corpore tunc separata.

Between this Partition and the Choir on the North-side, is the Monument of Dame ELIZABETH CALTHORPE, Wife of Sir *Francis Calthorpe*, and afterwards Wife of *John Colepepper*, Esq.

In the same Partition, behind the Dean's Stall, was buried JOHN CROFTS, lately Dean, Son of Sir *Henry Crofts* of *Suffolk*, and Brother to the Lord *William Crofts*. He was sometime Fellow of *All-Souls* College in *Oxford*, and the first Dean after the Restauration of his Majesty King *Charles* II. whose Predecessor, Dr. *John Hassal*, who was Dean many Years, was not buried in this Church, but in that of *Creek*. He was of *New* College in *Oxford*, and Chaplain to the Lady *Elizabeth*, Queen of *Bohemia*, who obtain'd this Deanry for him.

On the South-side of the Choir, between two Pillars, stands the Monument of Bishop JAMES GOLDWELL, Dean of Salisbury, and Secretary to King *Edward* IV. who sat in this *See* Twenty five Years. His Effigies is in Stone, with a *Lion* at his Feet, which was his Arms, as appears on his Coat above the Tomb. On the Choir Side, his Arms are also to be seen in the sixth Escocheon, in the West-side over the Choir; as also in S. *Andrew's* Church, at the Deanry in a Window; at *Trowes*, *Newton-Hall*, and at *Charta-magna* in *Kent*, the Place of his Nativity; where he also built, or repair'd the Chappel. He is said to have much repair'd the East End of this Church; did many good Works, lived in great Esteem, and died *Ann*. 1498 or 1499.

Next above Bishop *Goldwell*, where the Iron Grates yet stand, Bishop JOHN WAKERING is said to have been buried. He was Bishop in the Reign of King *Henry* V. and was sent to the Council of *Constance*: He is said also to have built the Cloister in the Bishop's Palace, which led into it from the Church Door, which was cover'd with a handsom Roof, before the late Civil War. Also reported to have built the Chapter-house, which being ruinous, is now demolish'd, and the decay'd Parts above and about it handsomly repair'd, or new built. The Arms of the *See* impaling his own Coat, the Three *Fleur des Lys*, are yet visible upon the Wall by the Door. He lived in great Reputation, and died 1426, and is said to have been buried before S. *George's* Altar.

On the North-side of the Choir, between the two Arches, next to Queen *Elizabeth's* Seat, were buried Sir THOMAS ERPINGHAM, and his Wives the Lady JOAN, *etc.* whose Pictures were in the Painted-Glass Windows, next unto this Place, with the Arms of the *Erpingham's*. The Insides of both the Pillars were painted in red Colours, with divers Figures and Inscriptions, from the top almost to the bottom, which are now washed out by the late whiting of the Pillars. He was a Knight of the Garter in the Time of *Hen.* IV. and some Part of *Hen.* V. and I find his Name in the List of the Lord Wardens of the Cinque-Ports. He is said to have built the *Black Friars* Church, or Steeple, or both, now called *New-Hall Steeple*. His Arms are often on the Steeple, which are an Escocheon within an *Orle of Martlets*, and also upon the out-side of the Gate, next the School-House. There was a long Brass Inscription about the Tomb-stone, which was torn away in the late Times, and the Name of *Erpingham* only remaining. *Johannes Dominus de Erpingham Miles*, was buried in the Parish Church of *Erpingham*, as the Inscription still declareth.

In the North Isle, near to the Door, leading towards *Jesus Chappel*, was buried Sir WILLIAM DENNY, Recorder of *Norwich*, and one of the Counsellors at Law to King *Charles* I.

In *Jesus Chappel* stands a large Tomb (which is said to have been translated from our Ladies Chappel, when that grew ruinous, and was taken down) whereof the Brass Inscription about it is taken away; but old Mr. *Spendlow*, who was a Prebendary 50 Years, and Mr. *Sandlin*, used to say, that it was the Tombstone of the *Windham's*; and in all Probability, might have belonged to Sir *Thomas Windham*, one of King *Henry* VIII.'s Counsellors, of his Guard, and Vice-Admiral; for I find that there hath been such an Inscription upon the Tomb of a *Windham* in this Church.

Orate pro aia Thome Windham, *militis,* Elianore, *et* Domine Elizabethe, *uxorum ejus, etc. qui quidem* Thomas *fuit unus consiliariorum Regis* Henrici VIII. *et unus militum pro corpore, ejusdem Domini, nec non Vice-Admirallus.*

And according to the Number of the Three Persons in the Inscription, there are Three Figures upon the Tomb.

On the North Wall of *Jesus Chappel* there is a legible Brass Inscription in Latin Verses; and at the last Line *Pater Noster*. This was the Monument of *Randulfus Pulvertoft custos caronelle*. Above the Inscription was his Coat of Arms, *viz. Six Ears of Wheat with a Border of Cinque-foils*; but now washed out, since the Wall was whiten'd.

At the Entrance of St. *Luke's Chappel*, on the Left Hand, is an arched Monument, said to belong to one of the Family of the *Bosvile's* or *Boswill*, sometime Prior of the Convent. At the East End of the Monument are the Arms of the Church (*the Cross*) and on the West End another (*three Bolt Arrows*,) which is supposed to be his Paternal Coat. The same Coat is to be seen in the sixth Escocheon of the South-side, under the Belfry. Some Inscriptions upon this Monument were washed out when the Church was lately whiten'd; as among the rest, *O morieris! O morieris! O morieris!* The *three Bolts* are the known Arms of the *Bosomes*, an ancient Family in *Norfolk*; but whether of the *Bosviles*, or no, I am uncertain.

Next unto it is the Monument of RICHARD BROME, Esq. whose Arms thereon are *Ermyns*; and for the Crest, *a Bunch or Branch of Broom with Golden Flowers*. This might be *Richard Brome*, Esq. whose Daughter married the Heir of the *Yaxley's of Yaxley*, in the Time of *Henry* VII. And one of the same Name founded a Chappel in the Field in *Norwich*.

There are also in St. *Luke's Chappel*, amongst the Seats on the South-side, two substantial Marble and cross'd Tombs, very ancient, said to be two Priors of this Convent.

At the Entrance into the Cloister, by the upper Door on the Right Hand, next the Stairs, was a handsom Monument on the Wall, which was pulled down in the late Times, and a Void Place still remaineth. Upon this Stone were the Figures of two Persons in a praying Posture, on their Knees. I was told by Mr. *Sandlin*, that it was said to be the Monument for one of the *Bigots*, who built or beautified that Arch by it, which leadeth into the Church.

In the Choir towards the high Altar, and below the Ascents, there is an old Tomb, which hath been generally said to have been the Monument of Bishop WILLIAM HERBERT, Founder of the Church, and commonly known by the Name of the Founder's Tomb. This was above an Ell high; but when the Pulpit, in the late Confusion, was placed at the Pillar, where Bishop *Overall's* Monument now is, and the Aldermen's Seats were at the East End, and the Mayor's Seat in the middle at the high Altar, the height of the Tomb being a Hindrance unto the People, it was taken down to such a Lowness as it now remains in. He was born at *Oxford*, in good Favour with King *William Rufus*, and King *Henry* I. removed the Episcopal *See* from *Thetford* to *Norwich*, built the Priory for 60 Monks, the Cathedral Church, the Bishop's Palace, the Church of S. *Leonard*, whose Ruins still remain upon the Brow of *Mushold-Hill*; the Church of S. *Nicolas* at *Yarmouth*, of S. *Margaret* at *Lynn*, of S. *Mary* at *Elmham*, and instituted the *Cluniack* Monks at *Thetford*. *Malmsbury* saith he was, *Vir pecuniosus*, which his great Works declare, and had always this good Saying of S. *Hierom* in his Mouth, *Erravimus juvenes, emendemus senes*.

Many Bishops of old might be buried about, or not far from the Founder, as *William Turbus*, a *Norman*, the third Bishop of *Norwich*, and *John* of *Oxford* the fourth, accounted among the learned Men of his Time, who built *Trinity* Church in *Ipswich*, and died in the Reign of King *John*; and it is deliver'd, that these two Bishops were buried near to Bishop *Herbert*, the Founder.

In the same Row, or not far off, was buried Bishop HENRY le SPENCER, as lost Brass Inscriptions have declar'd. And Mr. *Sandlin* told me, that he had seen an Inscription on a Gravestone thereabouts, with the Name of *Henricus de*, or *le Spencer*: He came young unto the *See*, and sat longer in it than any before or after him: But his Time might have been shorter, if he had not escaped in the Fray at *Lennam*, (a Town of which he was Lord) where forcing the Magistrate's Tipstaff to be carried before him, the People with Staves, Stones, and Arrows, wounded, and put his Servants to Flight. He was also wounded, and left alone, as *John Fox* hath set it down out of the Chronicle of S. *Albans*.

In the same Row, of late Times, was buried Bishop RICHARD MONTAGUE, as the Inscription, *Depositum Montacutii Episcopi*, doth declare.

For his eminent Knowledge in the *Greek* Language, he was much countenanc'd by Sir *Henry Savile*, Provost of *Eaton* College, and settled in a Fellowship thereof: Afterwards made Bishop of *Chichester*; thence translated unto *Norwich*, where he lived about three Years. He came unto *Norwich* with the evil Effects of a quartan Ague, which he had about a Year before, and which accompany'd him to his Grave; yet he studied, and writ very much, had an excellent Library of Books, and Heaps of Papers, fairly written with his own Hand, concerning the Ecclesiastical History. His Books were sent to *London*; and, as it was said, his Papers against *Baronius*, and others transmitted to *Rome*; from whence they were never return'd.

On the other Side was buried Bishop JOHN OVERALL, Fellow of *Trinity* College in *Cambridge*, Master of *Katherine* Hall, *Regius* Professor, and Dean of St. *Pauls*; and had the Honour to be nominated one of the first Governours of *Sutton* Hospital, by the Founder himself, a Person highly reverenc'd and belov'd; who being buried without any Inscription, had a Monument lately erected for him by Dr. *Cosin*, Lord Bishop of *Durham*, upon the next Pillar.

Under the large Sandy-colour'd Stone was buried Bishop RICHARD CORBET, a Person of singular Wit, and an eloquent Preacher, who lived Bishop of this See but three Years, being before Dean of *Christ* Church, then Bishop of *Oxford*. The Inscription is as follows:

Richardus Corbet *Theologiæ Doctor,*
Ecclesiæ Cathedralis Christi Oxoniensis
Primum alumnus inde Decanus, exinde
Episcopus, illinc huc translatus, et
Hinc in cœlum, Jul. 28. Ann. 1635.

The Arms on it, are the *See* of *Norwich*, impaling, *Or a Raven sab.* Corbet.

Towards the upper End of the Choir, and on the South-side, under a fair large Stone, was interred Sir WILLIAM BOLEYN, or BULLEN, Great Grandfather to Queen *Elizabeth*. The Inscription hath been long lost, which was this:

Hic jacet corpus Willelmi Boleyn, *militis,*
Qui obiit x *Octobris, Ann. Dom.* MCCCCCV.

And I find in a good Manuscript of the Ancient Gentry of *Norfolk* and *Suffolk* these Words. *Sir* William Boleyn, *Heir unto Sir* Tho. Boleyn, *who married* Margaret, *Daughter and Heir of* Tho. Butler, *Earl of* Ormond, *died in the Year* 1505, *and was buried on the South-side of the Chancel of Christ Church in* Norwich. And surely the Arms of few Families have been more often found in any Church, than those of the *Boleyn's*, on the Walls, and in the Windows of the East Part of this Church. Many others of this noble Family were buried in *Bleckling* Church.

Many other Bishops might be buried in this Church, as we find it so asserted by some Historical Accounts; but no History or Tradition remaining of the Place of their Interment, in vain we endeavour to design and point out the same.

As of Bishop JOHANNES de GRAY, who, as it is delivered, was interr'd in this Church, was a Favourite of King *John*, and sent by him to the Pope: He was also Lord Deputy of *Ireland*, and a Person of great Reputation, and built *Gaywood Hall* by *Lynn*.

As also of Bishop ROGER SKEREWYNG, in whose Time happened that bloody Contention between the Monks and Citizens, begun at a Fair kept before the Gate, when the Church was fir'd: To compose which King *Henry* III. came to *Norwich*, and *William de Brunham*, Prior, was much to blame. See *Holingshead, etc.*

Or, of Bishop WILLIAM MIDDLETON, who succeeded him, and was buried in this Church; in whose Time the Church that was burnt while *Skerewyng* sat was repair'd and consecrated, in the Presence of King *Edward* I.

Or, of Bishop JOHN SALMON, sometime Lord Chancellor of *England*, who died 1325, and was here interr'd, his Works were noble. He built the great Hall in the Bishop's Palace; the Bishop's long Chappel on the East-side of the Palace, which was no ordinary Fabrick; and a strong handsom Chappel at the West End of the Church, and appointed four Priests for the daily Service therein: Unto which great Works he was the better enabled, by obtaining a Grant of the first Fruits from Pope *Clement*.

Or, of Bishop THOMAS PERCY, Brother to the Earl of *Northumberland*, in the reign of *Richard* II. who gave unto a Chantry the Lands about *Carlton*, *Kimberly*, and *Wicklewood*; in whose Time the Steeple and Belfry were blown down, and rebuilt by him, and a Contribution from the Clergy.

Or, of Bishop ANTHONY *de* BECK, a Person of an unquiet Spirit, very much hated, and poison'd by his Servants.

Or likewise, of Bishop THOMAS BROWNE, who being Bishop of *Rochester*, was chosen Bishop of *Norwich*, while he was at the Council of *Basil*, in the reign of King *Henry* VI. was a strenuous Assertor of the Rights of the Church against the Citizens.

Or, of Bishop WILLIAM RUGGE, in whose last Year happen'd *Kett's* Rebellion, in the Reign of *Edward* VI. I find his Name, *Guil. Norwicensis*, among the Bishops, who subscribed unto a Declaration against the Pope's Supremacy, in the Time of *Henry* VIII.

Or, of Bishop JOHN HOPTON, who was Bishop in the Time of Queen *Mary*, and died the same Year with her. He is often mentioned, together with his Chancellor *Dunning*, by *John Fox* in his Martyrology.

Or lastly, of Bishop WILLIAM REDMAN, of *Trinity College* in *Cambridge*, who was Archdeacon of *Canterbury*. His Arms are upon a Board on the North-side of the Choir, near to the Pulpit.

Of the four Bishops in Queen *Elizabeth's* Reign, *Parkhurst, Freake, Scamler* and *Redman*, Sir *John Harrington*, in his *History of the Bishops* in her Time, writeth thus; *For the four Bishops in the Queen's Days, they liv'd as Bishops should do, and were not Warriours like Bishop* Spencer, *their Predecessor.*

Some Bishops were buried neither in the Body of the Church, nor in the Choir; but in our Ladies Chappel, at the East End of the Church, built by Bishop WALTER *de* SUTHFEILD, (in the Reign of *Henry* III.) wherein he was buried, and Miracles said to be wrought at his Tomb, he being a Person of great Charity and Piety.

Wherein also was buried Bishop SIMON *de* WANTON, *vel* WALTON, and Bishop *Alexander*, who had been Prior of the Convent; and also, as some think, Bishop *Roger Skerewyng*, and probably other Bishops, and Persons of Quality, whose Tombs and Monuments we now in vain enquire after in the Church.

This was a handsom Chappel; and there was a fair Entrance into it out of the Church, of a considerable Height also, as may be seen by the out-side, where it adjoined unto the Wall of the Church. But being ruinous, it was, as I have heard, demolished in the Time of Dean *Gardiner*: But what became of the Tombs, Monuments, and Grave-stones, we have no Account: In this Chappel, the Bishop's Consistory, or Court, might be kept in old Time, for we find in *Fox's Martyrology*, that divers Persons accused of Heresy were examined by the Bishop, or his Chancellor, in St. *Mary's* Chappel. This famous Bishop, *Walter de Suthfeild*, who built this Chappel, is also said to have built the Hospital not far off.

Again, divers Bishops sat in this *See*, who left not their Bones in this Church; for some died not here, but at distant Places; some were translated to other Bishopricks; and some, tho' they lived and died here, were not buried in this Church.

Some died at distant Places; as Bishop Richard Courtney, Chancellor of *Oxford*, and in great Favour with King *Henry* V. by whom he was sent unto the King of *France*, to challenge his Right unto that Crown; but he dying in *France*, his Body was brought into *England*, and interr'd in *Westminster-Abbey* among the Kings.

Bishop WILLIAM BATEMAN, LL.D. born in *Norwich*, who founded *Trinity-Hall*, in *Cambridge*, and persuaded *Gonvil* to build *Gonvil-College*, died at *Avignon* in *France*, being sent by the King to *Rome*, and was buried in that City.

Bishop WILLIAM AYERMIN died near *London*.

Bishop THOMAS THIRLBY, Doctor of Law, died in Archbishop *Matthew Parker's* House, and was buried at *Lambeth*, with this inscription:

[*Hic jacet* Thomas Thirlby, *olim Episcopus Eliensis, qui obiit 26 die Augusti, Anno Domini, 1570.*]

Bishop THOMAS JANN, who was Prior of *Ely*, died at *Folkston-Abbey*, near *Dover* in *Kent*.

Some were translated unto other Bishopricks; as Bishop WILLIAM RALEGH was remov'd unto *Winchester*, by King *Henry* III.

Bishop RALPH *de* WALPOLE was translated to *Ely*, in the time of *Edward* I. He is said to have begun the building of the Cloister, which is esteemed the fairest in *England*.

Bishop WILLIAM ALNWICK built the Church Gates at the West End of the Church, and the great Window, and was translated to *Lincoln*, in the Reign of *Henry* VI.

And of later time, Bishop EDMUND FREAKE, who succeeded Bishop *Parkhurst*, was removed unto *Worcester*, and there lieth entomb'd.

Bishop SAMUEL HARSNET, Master of *Pembroke-Hall*, in *Cambridge*, and Bishop of *Chichester*, was thence translated to *York*.

Bishop FRANCIS WHITE, Almoner unto the King, formerly Bishop of *Carlisle*, translated unto *Ely*.

Bishop MATTHEW WREN, Dean of the Chappel, translated also to *Ely*, and was not buried here.

Bishop JOHN JEGON, who died 1617, was buried at *Aylesham*, near *Norwich*. He was Master of *Bennet College*, and Dean of *Norwich*, whose Arms, *Two Chevrons with an Eagle on a Canton*, are yet to be seen on the West Side of the Bishop's Throne.

My honour'd Friend Bishop JOSEPH HALL, Dean of *Worcester*, and Bishop of *Exon*, translated to *Norwich*, was buried at *Heigham*, near *Norwich*, where he hath a Monument. When the Revenues of the Church were alienated, he retired unto that Suburbian Parish, and there ended his Days, being above 80 Years of Age. A Person of singular Humility, Patience, and Piety; his own Works are the best Monument and Character of himself, which was also very lively drawn in his excellent Funeral Sermon, preach'd by my learned and faithful old Friend, *John Whitefoot*, Rector of *Heigham*, a very deserving Clerk of the Convocation of *Norwich*. His Arms in the Register Office of *Norwich* are, *Sable three Talbots Heads erased Argent*.

My honour'd Friend also, Bishop EDWARD REYNOLDS, was not buried in the Church but in the Bishop's Chappel; which was built by himself. He was born at *Southampton*, brought up at *Merton Colledge* in *Oxford*, and the first Bishop of *Norwich* after the King's Restauration: A Person much of the Temper of his Predecessor, Dr. *Joseph Hall*, of singular Affability, Meekness and Humility; of great Learning; a frequent Preacher, and constant Resident: He sat in this *See* about 17 Years; and though buried in his private Chappel, yet his Funeral Sermon was preached in the Cathedral, by Mr. *Benedict Rively*, now Minister of S. *Andrews*: He was succeeded by Dr. *Anthony Sparrow*, our worthy and honoured Diocesan.

It is thought that some Bishops were buried in the old Bishops Chappel, said to be built by Bishop *John Salmon* [demolish'd in the Time of the late War] for therein were many Gravestones, and some plain Monuments. This old Chappel was higher, broader, and much larger than the said new Chappel built by Bishop *Reynolds*; but being covered with Lead, the Lead was sold, and taken away in the late rebellious Times; and the Fabrick growing ruinous and useless, it was taken down, and some of the Stones partly made use of in the building of the new Chappel.

Now, whereas there have been so many noble and ancient Families in these Parts, yet we find not more of them to have been buried in this the Mother Church. It may be consider'd, that no small numbers of them were interred in the Churches and Chappels of the Monasteries and religious Houses of this City, especially in three thereof; the *Austin-Fryars*, the *Black-Fryars*, the *Carmelite,* or *White Fryars*; for therein were buried many Persons of both Sexes, of great and good Families, whereof there are few or no Memorials in the Cathedral. And in the best preserved Registers of such Interments of old, from Monuments and Inscriptions, we find the Names of Men and Women of many ancient Families; as of *Ufford, Hastings, Radcliffe, Morley, Windham, Geney, Clifton, Pigot, Hengrave, Garney, Ho well, Ferris, Bacon, Boys, Wichingham, Soterley*;

of *Falstolph, Ingham, Felbrigge, Talbot, Harsick, Pagrave, Berney, Woodhowse, Howldich*;

of *Argenton, Somerton, Gros, Benhall, Banyard, Paston, Crunthorpe, Withe, Colet, Gerbrigge, Berry, Calthorpe, Everard, Hetherset, Wachesham*: All Lords, Knights, and Esquires, with divers others. Beside the great and noble Families of the *Bigots, Mowbrays, Howards*, were the most part interr'd at *Thetford*, in the Religious Houses of which they were Founders, or Benefactors. The *Mortimers* were buried at *Attleburgh*; the *Aubeneys* at *Windham*, in the Priory or Abbey founded by them. And *Camden* says, *That a great part of the Nobility and Gentry of those Parts were buried at Pentney* Abbey: Many others were buried dispersedly in Churches, or Religious

Houses, founded or endowed by themselves; and therefore it is the less to be wonder'd at, that so many great and considerable Persons of this Country were not interr'd in this Church.

There are Twenty-four Escocheons, *viz.* six on a Side on the inside of the Steeple over the Choir, with several Coats of Arms, most whereof are Memorials of Things, Persons, and Families, Wellwishers, Patrons, Benefactors, or such as were in special Veneration, Honour, and Respect, from the Church. As particularly the Arms of *England*, of *Edward* the Confessor; an Hieroglyphical Escocheon of the Trinity, unto which this Church was dedicated. *Three Cups within a Wreath of Thorns*, the Arms of *Ely*, the Arms of the *See* of *Canterbury*, quartered with the Coat of the famous and magnified *John Morton*, Archbishop of *Canterbury*, who was Bishop of *Ely* before; of Bishop *James Goldwell*, that honoured Bishop of *Norwich*. *The three Lions of* England, S. *George's* Cross, the Arms of the Church impaled with Prior *Bosviles* Coat, the Arms of the Church impaled with the private Coats of three Priors, the Arms of the City of *Norwich*.

There are here likewise the Coats of some great and worthy Families; as of *Vere, Stanley, De la Pole, Wingfield, Heyden, Townshend, Bedingfield, Bruce, Clere*; which being little taken notice of, and Time being still like to obscure, and make them past Knowledge, I would not omit to have a Draught thereof set down, which I keep by me.

There are also many Coats of Arms on the Walls, and in the Windows of the East End of the Church; but none so often as those of the *Boleyns, viz.* in a Field *Arg. a Chev. Gul. between three Bulls Heads couped sab. armed or*; whereof some are quartered with the Arms of noble Families. As also about the Church, the Arms of *Hastings, De la Pole, Heyden, Stapleton, Windham, Wichingham, Clifton, Heveningham, Bokenham, Inglos*.

In the North Window of *Jesus* Chappel are the Arms of *Radcliff* and *Cecil*; and in the East Window of the same Chappel the Coats of *Branch*, and of *Beale*.

There are several Escocheon Boards fastened to the upper Seats of the Choir: Upon the three lowest on the South-side are the Arms of Bishop *Jegon*, of the *Pastons*, and of the *Hobarts*; and in one above the Arms of the *Howards*. On the Board on the North-side are the Arms of Bishop *Redmayn*; and of the *Howards*.

Upon the outside of the Gate, next to the School, are the Escocheons and Arms of *Erpingham*, being an Escocheon within an *Orle of Martlets*; impaled with the Coats of *Clopton* and *Bavent*, or such Families who married with the *Erpinghams* who built the Gates. The Word, *Pœna*, often upon the Gates, shews it to have been built upon Pennance.

At the West End of the Church are chiefly observable the Figure of King *William Rufus*, or King *Henry* I. and a Bishop on his Knees receiving the Charter from him: Or else of King *Henry* VI. in whose Reign this Gate and fair Window was built. Also the maimed Statues of Bishops, whose Copes are garnished and charged with a Cross *Moline*: And at their Feet, Escocheons, with the Arms of the Church; and also Escocheons with Crosses *Molines*. That these, or some of them, were the Statues of Bishop *William Alnwyck*, seems more than probable; for he built the three Gates, and the great Window at the West End of the Church; and where the Arms of the *See* are in a Roundele, are these Words,—*Orate pro anima Domini Willelmi Alnwyk*.—Also in another Escocheon, charged with Cross *Molines*, there is the same Motto round about it.

Upon the wooden Door on the outside, there are also the *Three Miters*, which are the Arms of the *See* upon one Leaf, and a Cross *Moline* on the other.

Upon the outside of the End of the North Cross Isle, there is a Statue of an old Person; which, being formerly covered and obscured by Plaister and Mortar over it, was discovered upon the late Reparation, or whitening of that End of the Isle. This may probably be the Statue of Bishop *Richard Nicks*, or the blind Bishop; for he built the Isle, or that Part thereof; and also the Roof, where his Arms are to be seen, *A Chevron* between *three Leopards Heads Gules*.

The Roof of the Church is noble, and adorn'd with Figures. In the Roof of the Body of the Church there are no Coats of Arms, but Representations from Scripture Story, as the Story of *Pharaoh*; of *Sampson* towards the East End. Figures of the last Supper, and of our Saviour on the Cross, towards the West End; besides others of Foliage, and the like ornamental Figures.

The North Wall of the Cloister was handsomly beautified, with the Arms of some of the Nobility in their proper Colours, with their Crests, *Mantlings, Supporters*, and the whole Atchivement quartered with the several Coats of their Matches, drawn very large from the upper Part of the

Wall, and took up about half of the Wall. They are Eleven in Number; particularly these. 1. An empty Escocheon. 2. The Atchievement of *Howard*, Duke of *Norfolk*. 3. Of *Clinton*. 4. *Russel.* 5. *Cheyney.* 6. The Queen's Atchievement. 7. *Hastings.* 8. *Dudley.* 9. *Cecill.* 10. *Carey.* 11. *Hatton.*

They were made soon after Queen *Elizabeth* came to *Norwich, Ann. 1578,* where she remained a Week, and lodged at the Bishop's Palace in the Time of Bishop *Freake*, attended by many of the Nobility; and particularly by those, whose Arms are here set down.

They made a very handsome Show, especially at that Time, when the Cloister Windows were painted unto the Cross-Bars. The Figures of those Coats, in their distinguishable and discernable Colours, are not beyond my Remembrance. But in the late Times, when the Lead was faulty, and the Stone-work decayed, the Rain falling upon the Wall, washed them away.

The Pavement also of the Cloister on the same Side was broken, and the Stones taken away, a Floor of Dust remaining: But that Side is now handsomly paved by the Beneficence of my worthy Friend *William Burleigh*, Esq.

At the Stone Cistern in the Cloister, there yet perceivable *a Lyon Rampant, Argent, in a field Sable*, which Coat is now quartered in the Arms of the *Howards*.

In the Painted Glass in the Cloister, which hath been above the Cross-Bars, there are several Coats. And I find by an Account taken thereof, and set down in their proper Colours, that here were these following, *viz.* the Arms of *Morley, Shelton, Scales, Erpingham, Gournay, Mowbray, Savage*, now *Rivers*, three Coats of *Thorpe's*, and one of *a Lyon Rampant, Gules in a Field Or*, not well known to what Family it belongeth.

Between the lately demolish'd Chapter-House and S. *Luke's* Chappel, there is an handsom Chappel, wherein the Consistory, or Bishop's Court is kept, with a noble Gilded Roof. This goeth under no Name, but may well be call'd *Beauchampe's* Chappel, or the Chappel of our *Lady* and *All-Saints*, as being built by *William Beauchampe*, according to this Inscription. *In honore Beate Marie Virginis, et omnium sanctorum* Willelmus Beauchampe *capellam hanc ordinavit, et ex propriis sumptibus construxit.* This Inscription is in old Letters on the outside of the Wall, at the South-side of the Chappel, and almost obliterated; He was buried under an Arch in the Wall, which was richly gilded; and some part of the Gilding is yet to be perceived, tho' obscured and blinded by the Bench on the inside. I have heard there is a Vault below gilded like the Roof of the Chappel. The Founder of this Chappel, *William Beauchampe*, or *de Bello Campo*, might be one of the *Beauchampe's*, who were Lords of *Abergevenny*; for *William* Lord *Abergevenny* had Lands and Mannors in this Country. And in the Register of Institutions it is to be seen, that *William Beauchampe*, Lord of *Abergevenny* was Lord Patron of *Berg cum Apton*, five Miles distant from *Norwich*, and presented Clerks to that Living, 1406, and afterward: So that, if he lived a few Years after, he might be buried in the latter End of *Henry* IV. or in the Reign of *Henry* V. or in the Beginning of *Henry* VI. Where to find *Heydon's* Chappel is more obscure, if not altogether unknown; for such a Place there was, and known by the Name of *Heydon's* Chappel, as I find in a Manuscript concerning some ancient Families of *Norfolk*, in these Words, *John Heydon of Baconsthorpe, Esq.; died in the Reign of* Edward IV. *Ann. 1479. He built a Chappel on the South side of the Cathedral Church of* Norwich, *where he was buried. He was in great Favour with King* Henry VI. *and took part with the House of* Lancaster *against that of* York.

HEN. HEYDON, Kt. his Heir, built the Church of *Salthouse*, and made the Causey between *Thursford* and *Walsingham* at his own Charge: He died in the Time of *Henry* VII. and was buried in *Heydon's* Chappel, joining to the Cathedral aforesaid. The Arms of the *Heydon's* are Quarterly *Argent*, and *Gules a Cross engrailed counter-changed*, make the third Escocheon in the North-Row over the Choir, and are in several Places in the Glass-Windows, especially on the South-side, and once in the Deanry.

There was a Chappel to the South-side of the Goal, or Prison, into which there is one Door out of the Entry of the Cloister; and there was another out of the Cloister itself, which is now made up of Brickwork: The Stone-work which remaineth on the inside is strong and handsom. This seems to have been a much frequented Chappel of the Priory by the wearing of the Steppings unto it, which are on the Cloister Side.

Many other Chappels there were within the Walls and Circuit of the Priory; as of S. *Mary* of the *Marsh*; of S. *Ethelbert*, and others. But a strong and handsom Fabrick of one is still remaining, which is the Chappel of St. *John* the Evangelist, said to have been founded by Bishop *John Salmon*, who died *Ann*. 1325, and four Priests were entertained for the daily Service therein: That which was properly the Chappel, is now the Free-School: The adjoining Buildings made up the Refectory, Chambers, and Offices of the Society.

Under the Chappel, there was a Charnell-House, which was a remarkable one in former Times, and the Name is still retained. In an old Manuscript of a Sacrist of the Church, communicated to me by my worthy Friend Mr. *John Burton*, the Learned, and very deserving Master of the Free-School, I find that the Priests had a Provisional Allowance from the Rectory of *Westhall* in *Suffolk*. And of the Charnell-House it is delivered, that with the Leave of the Sacrist, the Bones of such as were buried in *Norwich* might be brought into it. *In carnario subtus dictam capellam sancti Johannis constituto, ossa humana in civitate* Norwici *humata, de licentia sacristæ, qui dicti carnarii clavem et custodiam habebit specialem utusque ad resurrectionem generalem honeste conserventur a carnibus integre demulata reponi volumus et obsignari*. Probably the Bones were piled in good Order, the Sculls, Arms, and Leg-Bones, in their distinct Rows and Courses, as in many Charnell-Houses. How these Bones were afterwards disposed of, we have no Account; or whether they had not the like Removal with those in the Charnell-House of S. *Paul* kept under a Chappel on the North-side of S. *Paul's* Church-yard: For when the Chappel was demolish'd, the Bones which lay in the Vault, amounting to more than a Thousand Cart-Loads, were conveyed into *Finnesbury* Fields, and there laid in a moorish Place, with so much Soil to cover them, as raised the Ground for three Wind-mills to stand on, which have since been built there, according as *John Stow* hath delivered, in his Survey of *London*.

There was formerly a fair and large, but plain Organ in the Church, and in the same Place with this at present. (It was agreed in a Chapter by the Dean and Prebends, that a new Organ be made, and Timber fitted to make a Loft for it, *June* 6. *Ann*. *1607*. repaired 1626. and 10*l*. which *Abel Colls* gave to the Church, was bestowed upon it.) That in the late tumultuous Time was pulled down, broken, sold, and made away. But since his Majesty's Restauration, another fair, well-tuned, plain Organ, was set up by Dean *Crofts* and the Chapter, and afterwards painted, and beautifully adorned, by the Care and Cost of my honoured Friend Dr. *Herbert Astley*, the present worthy Dean. There were also five or six Copes belonging to the Church; which, tho' they look'd somewhat old, were richly embroider'd. These were formerly carried into the Market-Place; some blowing the Organ-pipes before them, and were cast into a Fire provided for that purpose, with shouting and rejoicing: So that, at present, there is but one Cope belonging to the Church, which was presented thereunto by *Philip Harbord*, Esq. the present High Sheriff of *Norfolk*, my honoured Friend.

Before the late Times, the Combination Sermons were preached in the Summer Time at the Cross in the Green-Yard, where there was a good Accommodation for the Auditors. The Mayor, Aldermen, with their Wives and Officers, had a well-contriv'd Place built against the Wall of the Bishop's Palace, cover'd with Lead; so that they were not offended by Rain. Upon the North-side of the Church, Places were built Gallery-wise, one above another; where the Dean, Prebends, and their Wives, Gentlemen, and the better Sort, very well heard the Sermon: The rest either stood, or sat in the Green, upon long Forms provided for them, paying a Penny, or Halfpenny apiece, as they did at S. *Paul's* Cross in *London*. The Bishop and Chancellor heard the Sermons at the Windows of the Bishop's Palace: The Pulpit had a large Covering of Lead over it, and a Cross upon it; and there were eight or ten Stairs of Stone about it, upon which the Hospital-Boys and others stood. The Preacher had his Face to the South, and there was a painted Board, of a Foot and a half broad, and about a Yard and a half long, hanging over his Head before, upon which were painted the Arms of the Benefactors towards the Combination Sermon, which he particularly commemorated in his Prayer, and they were these; Sir *John Suckling*, Sir *John Pettus*, *Edward Nuttel*, *Henry Fasset*, *John Myngay*. But when the Church was sequester'd, and the Service put down, this Pulpit was taken down, and placed in *New-Hall* Green, which had been the Artillery-Yard, and the Public Sermon was there preached. But the Heirs of the Benefactors denying to pay the wonted Beneficence for any Sermon out of *Christ*-Church, (the Cathedral being now commonly so call'd) some other Ways were found to provide a Minister, at a yearly Sallary, to preach every Sunday, either in that Pulpit in the Summer, or elsewhere in the Winter.

I must not omit to say something of the Shaft, or Spire of this Church, commonly called the Pinacle, as being a handsom and well proportioned Fabrick, and one of the highest in *England*, higher than the noted Spires of *Litchfield*, *Chichester*, or *Grantham*, but lower than that at *Salisbury*, [at a general Chapter, holden June 4. 1633, it was agreed that the Steeple should be mended] for that Spire being raised upon a very high Tower, becomes higher from the Ground; but this Spire, considered by itself, seems, at least, to equal that. It is an Hundred and five Yards and two Foot from the Top of the Pinacle unto the Pavement of the Choir under it. The Spire is very strongly built, tho' the Inside be of Brick. The upper Aperture, or Window, is the highest Ascent inwardly; out of which, sometimes a long Streamer hath been hanged, upon the Guild, or Mayor's Day. But at His Majesty's Restauration, when the Top was to be mended, and a new gilded Weather-Cock was to be placed upon it, there were Stayings made at the upper Window, and divers Persons went up to the Top of the Pinacle. They first went up into the Belfry, and then by eight Ladders, on the Inside of the Spire, till they came to the upper Hole, or Window; then went out unto the Outside, where a Staying was set, and so ascended up unto the Top-Stone, on which the Weather-Cock standeth.

The Cock is three quarters of a Yard high, and one Yard and two Inches long; as is also the Cross-Bar, and Top-Stone of the Spire, which is not flat, but consists of a half Globe, and Channel about it; and from thence are eight Leaves of Stone spreading outward, under which begin the eight Rows of Crockets, which go down the Spire at five Foot distance.

From the Top there is a Prospect all about the Country. *Mourshold-Hill* seems low, and flat Ground. The *Castle-Hill*, and high Buildings, do very much diminish. The River looks like a Ditch. The City, with the Streets, make a pleasant Show, like a Garden with several Walks in it.

Tho' this Church, for its Spire, may compare, in a manner, with any in *England*, yet in its Tombs and Monuments it is exceeded by many.

No Kings have honour'd the same with their Ashes, and but few with their Presence. And it is not without some Wonder, that *Norwich* having been for a long Time so considerable a Place, so few Kings have visited it: Of which Number, among so many Monarchs since the Conquest, we find but Four, viz. King *Henry* III. *Edward* I. Queen *Elizabeth*, and our Gracious Sovereign now reigning; King *Charles* II. of which I had particular Reason to take Notice.[321]

The Castle was taken by the Forces of King *William* the Conqueror; but we find not, that he was here. King *Henry* VII. by the Way of *Cambridge*, made a Pilgrimage unto *Walsingham*; but Records tell us not, that he was at *Norwich*. King *James* I. came sometimes to *Thetford* for his Hunting Recreation, but never vouchsafed to advance twenty Miles farther.

Not long after the writing of these Papers, Dean *Herbert Astley* died, a civil, generous, and public-minded Person, who had travell'd in *France*, *Italy*, and *Turkey*, and was interr'd near the Monument of Sir *James Hobart*: Unto whom succeeded my honoured Friend Dr. *John Sharpe*, a Prebend of this Church, and Rector of St. *Giles's* in the Fields, *London*; a Person of singular Worth, and deserv'd Estimation, the Honour and Love of all Men; in the first Year of whose Deanery, 1681, the Prebends were these:

Mr. *Joseph Loveland*,	Dr. *William Smith*,
Dr. *Hezekiah Burton*, } {	Mr. *Nathaniel Hodges*,
Dr. *William Hawkins*,	Mr. *Humphrey Prideaux*.

(But Dr. *Burton* dying in that Year, Mr. *Richard Kidder* succeeded,) worthy Persons, learned Men, and very good Preachers.

ADDENDA

I have by me the Picture of Chancellor SPENCER, drawn when he was Ninety Years old, as the Inscription doth declare, which was sent unto me from *Colney*.

Tho' Bishop NIX sat long in the *See* of *Norwich*, yet is not there much deliver'd of him: *Fox* in his *Martyrology* hath said something of him in the Story of THOMAS BILNEY, who was burnt in *Lollard's* Pit without *Bishopgate*, in his Time.

Bishop SPENCER lived in the Reign of RICHARD II. and HENRY IV. sat in the *See* of *Norwich* 37 Years: Of a Soldier made a Bishop, and sometimes exercising the Life of a Soldier in his Episcopacy; for he led an Army into *Flanders* on the Behalf of Pope *Urban* VI. in Opposition to *Clement* the Anti-Pope; and also over-came the Rebellious Forces of *Litster* the *Dyer*, in *Norfolk*, by *North-Walsham*, in the Reign of King RICHARD II.

Those that would know the Names of the Citizens who were chief Actors in the Tumult in Bishop SKEREWYNG'S Time, may find 'em set down in the Bull of Pope *Gregory* XI.

Some Bishops, tho' they liv'd and died here, might not be buried in this Church, as some Bishops probably of old, more certainly of later Time.

HERE CONCLUDES SIR Thomas Browne's *MS.*
Footnotes
[321]Sir *Thomas* being then Knighted.

MISCELLANIES
**An Account of Island, alias Ice-land,
In the Year 1662.**

Great Store of Drift-wood, or Float-wood, is every Year cast up on their Shores, brought down by the Northern Winds, which serveth them for Fewel, and other Uses, the greatest Part whereof is *Firr*.

Of *Bears* there are none in the Country, but sometimes they are brought down from the North upon Ice, while they follow *Seales*, and so are carried away. Two in this Manner came over, and landed in the North of *Island* this last Year, 1662.

No *Conies*, or *Hares*, but of *Foxes* great Plenty, whose White Skins are much desired, and brought over into this Country.

The last Winter, 1662, so cold, and lasting with us in *England*, was the mildest they have had for many Years in *Island*.

Two new Eruptions with Slime and Smoak, were observed the last Year in some Mountains about Mount *Hecla*.[322]

Some hot Mineral Springs they have, and very effectual, but they make but rude Use thereof.

The Rivers are large, swift, and rapid, but have many Falls, which render them less Commodious; they chiefly abound with *Salmons*.

They sow no Corn, but receive it from Abroad.

They have a kind of large *Lichen*, which dried, becometh hard and sticky, growing very plentifully in many Places; whereof they make use for Food, either in Decoction, or Powder, some whereof I have by me, different from any with us.

In one Part of the Country, and not near the Sea, there is a large black Rock, which Polished, resembleth Touchstone, as I have seen in Pieces thereof, of various Figures.

There is also a Rock, whereof I received one Fragment, which seems to make it one kind of *Pisolithes*, or rather *Orobites*, as made up of small Pebbles, in the Bigness and Shape of the Seeds of *Eruum*, or *Orobus*.

They have some large Well-grained White Pebbles, and some kind of White *Cornelian*, or *Agath* Pebbles, on the Shore, which Polish well. Old Sir *Edmund Bacon*, of these Parts, made Use thereof in his peculiar Art of Tinging and Colouring of Stones.

For Shells found on the Sea-shore, such as have been brought unto me are but coarse, nor of many Kinds, as ordinary *Turbines*, *Chamas*, *Aspers*, *Laves*, etc.

I have received divers Kinds of Teeth, and Bones of Cetaceous Fishes, unto which they could assign no Name.

An exceeding fine Russet Downe is sometimes brought unto us, which their great Number of Fowls afford, and sometimes store of Feathers, consisting of the Feathers of small Birds.

Beside *Shocks*, and little Hairy *Dogs*, they bring another sort over, Headed like a *Fox*, which they say are bred betwixt *Dogs* and *Foxes*; these are desired by the Shepherds of this Country.

Green *Plovers*, which are Plentiful here in the Winter, are found to breed there in the beginning of Summer.

Some *Sheep* have been brought over, but of coarse Wooll, and some *Horses* of mean Stature, but strong and Hardy: one whereof kept in the Pastures by *Yarmouth*, in the Summer, would often take the Sea, swimming a great Way, a Mile or Two, and return the same, when its Provision fail'd in the Ship wherein it was brought, for many Days fed upon Hoops and Cask; nor at the Land would, for many Months, be brought to feed upon Oats.

These Accounts I received from a Native of *Island*, who comes Yearly into *England*; and by Reason of my long Acquaintance, and Directions I send unto some of his Friends against the *Elephantiasis*, (*Leprosie*,) constantly visits me before his Return; and is ready to perform for me what I shall desire in his Country; wherein, as in other Ways, I shall be very Ambitious to serve the Noble Society, whose most Honouring Servant I am,

THOMAS BROWNE.

Norwich, Jan.
15, 1663.

Concerning some Urnes found in Brampton-Field, in Norfolk, Ann. 1667.

I thought I had taken Leave of URNES, when I had some Years past given a short Account of those found at *Walsingham*,[323] but a New Discovery being made, I readily obey your Commands in a brief Description thereof.

In a large Arable Field, lying between *Buxton* and *Brampton*, but belonging to *Brampton*, and not much more than a Furlong from *Oxnead Park*, divers *Urnes* were found. A Part of the Field being designed to be inclosed, while the Workmen made several Ditches, they fell upon divers *Urnes*, but earnestly, and carelesly digging, they broke all they met with, and finding nothing but Ashes, or burnt Cinders, they scattered what they found. Upon Notice given unto me, I went unto the Place, and though I used all Care with the Workmen, yet they were broken in the taking out, but many, without doubt, are still remaining in that Ground.

Of these Pots none were found above Three Quarters of a Yard in the Ground, whereby it appeareth, that in all this Time the Earth hath little varied its Surface, though this Ground hath been Plowed to the utmost Memory of Man. Whereby it may be also conjectured, that this hath not been a *Wood-Land*, as some conceive all this Part to have been; for in such Lands they usually made no common Burying-places, except for some special Persons in Graves, and likewise that there hath been an Ancient Habitation about these Parts; for at *Buxton* also, not a Mile off, *Urnes* have been found in my Memory, but in their Magnitude, Figure, Colour, Posture, *etc.* there was no small Variety, some were large and capacious, able to contain above Two Gallons, some of a middle, others of a smaller Size; the great ones probably belonging to greater Persons, or might be Family *Urnes*, fit to receive the Ashes successively of their Kindred and Relations, and therefore of these, some had Coverings of the same Matter, either fitted to them, or a thin flat Stone, like a Grave Slate, laid over them; and therefore also great Ones were but thinly found, but others in good Number; some were of large wide Mouths, and Bellies proportionable, with short Necks, and bottoms of Three Inches *Diameter*, and near an Inch thick; some small, with Necks like Juggs, and about that Bigness; the Mouths of some few were not round, but after the Figure of a Circle compressed; though some had small, yet none had pointed Bottoms, according to the Figures of those which are to be seen in *Roma Soteranea*, *Viginerus*, or *Mascardus*.

In the Colours also there was great Variety, some were Whitish, some Blackish, and inclining to a Blue, others Yellowish, or dark Red, arguing the Variety of their Materials. Some Fragments, and especially Bottoms of Vessels, which seem'd to be handsome neat Pans, were also found of a fine *Coral*-like Red, somewhat like *Portugal* Vessels, as tho' they had been made out of some fine *Bolary* Earth, and very smooth; but the like had been found in divers Places, as Dr. *Casaubon* hath observed about the Pots found at *Newington* in *Kent*, and as other Pieces do yet testifie, which are to be found at *Burrow* Castle, an Old *Roman* Station, not far from *Yarmouth*.

Of the *Urnes*, those of the larger Sort, such as had Coverings, were found with their Mouths placed upwards, but great Numbers of the others were, as they informed me, (and One I saw my self,) placed with their Mouths downward, which were probably such as were not to be opened again, or receive the Ashes of any other Person; though some wonder'd at this Position, yet I saw no Inconveniency in it; for the Earth being closely pressed, and especially in *Minor* Mouth'd Pots, they stand in a Posture as like to continue as the other, as being less subject to have the Earth fall in, or the Rain to soak into them; and the same Posture has been observed in some found in other Places, as *Holingshead* delivers, of divers found in *Anglesea*.

Some had Inscriptions, the greatest Part none; those with Inscriptions were of the largest Sort, which were upon the reverted Verges thereof; the greatest part of those which I could obtain were somewhat obliterated; yet some of the Letters to be made out: The Letters were between Lines, either Single or Double, and the Letters of some few after a fair *Roman* Stroke, others more rudely and illegibly drawn, wherein there seemed no great Variety. NUON being upon very many of them; only upon the inside of the bottom of a small Red Pan-like Vessel, were legibly set down in embossed Letters, CRACUNA. F. which might imply *Cracuna figuli*, or the Name of the Manufactor, for Inscriptions commonly signified the Name of the Person interr'd, the Names of Servants Official to such Provisions, or the Name of the Artificer, or Manufactor of such Vessels; all which are particularly exemplified by the Learned *Licetus*,[324] where the same inscription is often found, it is probably, of the Artificer, or where the Name also is in the *Genitive* Case, as he also observeth.

Out of one was brought unto me a Silver *Denarius*, with the Head of *Diva Faustina* on the Obverse side, on the Reverse the Figures of the Emperor and Empress joining their Right Hands, with this Inscription, *Concordia*; the same is to be seen in *Augustino*; I also received from some Men and Women then present Coins of *Posthumus*, and *Tetricus*, Two of the Thirty Tyrants in the Reign of *Gallienus*, which being of much later Date, begat an Inference, that *Urne-Burial* lasted longer, at least in this Country, than is commonly supposed. Good Authors conceive, that this Custom ended with the Reigns of the *Antonini*, whereof the last was *Antoninus Heliogabalus*, yet these Coins extend about Fourscore Years lower; and since the Head of *Tetricus* is made with a radiated Crown, it must be conceived to have been made after his Death, and not before his Consecration, which as the Learned *Tristan* Conjectures, was most probably in the Reign of the Emperor *Tacitus*, and the Coin not made, or at least not issued Abroad, before the Time of the Emperor *Probus*, for *Tacitus* Reigned but Six Months and an Half, his Brother *Florianus* but Two Months, unto whom *Probus* succeeding, Reigned Five Years.

There were also found some pieces of Glass, and finer Vessels, which might contain such Liquors as they often Buried in, or by, the *Urnes*; divers Pieces of Brass, of several Figures; and in one *Urne* was found a Nail Two Inches long; whither to declare the Trade or Occupation of the Person, is uncertain. But upon the Monuments of *Smiths* in *Gruter*, we meet with the Figures of *Hammers*, *Pincers*, and the like; and we find the Figure of a *Cobler's* Awl on the Tomb of one of that Trade, which was in the Custody of *Berini*, as *Argulus* hath set it down in his Notes upon ONUPHRIUS, *Of the Antiquities of* VERONA.

Now, though *Urnes* have been often discovered in former Ages, many think it strange there should be many still found, yet assuredly there may be great Numbers still concealed. For tho' we should not reckon upon any who were thus buried before the Time of the *Romans*, [altho' that the *Druids* were thus buried, it may be probable, and we read of the *Urne of Chindonactes*, a *Druid*, found near *Dijon* in *Burgundy*, largely discoursed of by *Licetus*,] and tho, I say, we take not in any Infant which was *Minor igne rogi*, before Seven Months, or Appearance of Teeth, nor should account this Practice of burning among the *Britains* higher than *Vespasian*, when it is said by Tacitus, that they conformed unto the Manners and Customs of the *Romans*, and so both Nations might have one Way of Burial: yet from his Days, to the Dates of these *Urnes*, were about Two Hundred Years. And therefore if we fall so low, as to conceive there were buried in this Nation but Twenty Thousand Persons, the Account of the buried Persons would amount unto Four Millions, and consequently so great a Number of *Urnes* dispersed through the Land, as may still satisfy the Curiosity of succeeding Times, and arise unto all Ages.

The Bodies, whose Reliques these *Urnes* contained, seemed thoroughly burned; for beside pieces of Teeth, there were found few Fragments of Bones, but rather Ashes in hard Lumps, and pieces of Coals, which were often so fresh, that one sufficed to make a good Draught of its *Urne*, which still remaineth with me.

Some Persons digging at a little Distance from the *Urne* Places, in hopes to find something of Value, after they had digged about Three Quarters of a Yard deep, fell upon an observable Piece of Work, whose Description this Figure affordeth. The Work was Square, about Two Yards and a Quarter on each Side. The Wall, or outward Part, a Foot thick, in Colour Red, and looked like Brick; but it was solid, without any Mortar or Cement, or figur'd Brick in it, but of an whole Piece, so that it seemed to be Framed and Burnt in the same Place where it was found. In this kind of Brick-work were Thirty-two Holes, of about Two Inches and an Half *Diameter*, and Two above a Quarter of a Circle in the East and West Sides. Upon Two of these Holes, on the East Side, were placed Two Pots, with their Mouths downward; putting in their Arms they found the Work hollow below, and the Earth being clear'd off, much Water was found below them, to the Quantity of a Barrel, which was conceived to have been the Rain-water which soaked in through the Earth above them.

The upper Part of the Work being broke, and opened, they found a Floor about Two Foot below, and then digging onward, Three Floors successively under one another, at the Distance of a Foot and Half, the Stones being of a Slatty, not Bricky, substance; in these Partitions some Pots were found, but broke by the Workmen, being necessitated to use hard Blows for the breaking of the Stones; and in the last Partition but one, a large Pot was found of a very narrow Mouth, short Ears, of the Capacity of Fourteen Pints, which lay in an enclining Posture, close by, and somewhat under a kind of Arch in the solid Wall, and by the great Care of my worthy Friend, Mr. *William Masham*, who employed the Workmen, was taken up whole, almost full of Water, clean, and without Smell, and insipid, which being poured out, there still remains in the Pot a great Lump of an heavy crusty Substance. What Work this was we must as yet reserve unto better Conjecture. Mean while we find in *Gruter* that some Monuments of the Dead had divers Holes successively to let in the Ashes of their Relations, but Holes in such a great Number to that Intent, we have not anywhere met with.

About Three Months after, my Noble and Honoured Friend, Sir *Robert Paston*, had the Curiosity to open a Piece of Ground in his Park at *Oxnead*, which adjoined unto the former Field, where Fragments of Pots were found, and upon one the Figure of a well-made Face; but probably this Ground had been opened and digged before, though out of the Memory of Man, for we found divers small Pieces of Pots, *Sheeps* Bones, sometimes an *Oyster*-shell a Yard deep in the Earth, an unusual *Coin* of the Emperor *Volusianus*, having on the Obverse the Head of the Emperor, with a Radiated Crown, and this Inscription, *Imp. Cæs. C. Volusiano Aug.* that is, *Imperatori Cæsari Caio Vibio Volusiano Augusto*. On the Reverse an Human Figure, with the Arms somewhat extended, and at the Right Foot an Altar, with the Inscription, *Pietas*. This Emperor was Son unto *Caius Vibius Tribonianus Gallus*, with whom he jointly reigned after the *Decii*, about the Year 254; both he, himself, and his Father, were slain by the Emperor *Æmilianus*. By the Radiated Crown this Piece should be Coined after his Death and Consecration, but in whose Time it is not clear in History.

Concerning the too nice Curiosity of censuring the Present, or judging into Future Dispensations.

We have enough to do rightly to apprehend and consider things as they are, or have been, without amusing our selves how they might have been otherwise, or what Variations, Consequences and Differences might have otherwise arose upon a different Face of things, if they had otherwise fallen out in the State or Actions of the World.

If SCANDERBERG had joined his Forces with HUNNIADES, as might have been expected before the Battel in the Plains of *Cossoan*, in good probability they might have ruin'd MAHOMET, if not the *Turkish* Empire.

If ALEXANDER had march'd Westward, and warr'd with the *Romans*, whether he had been able to subdue that little but valiant People, is an uncertainty: We are sure he overcame *Persia*; Histories attest, and Prophecies foretel the same. It was decreed that the *Persians* should be conquered by ALEXANDER, and his Successors by the *Romans*, in whom Providence had determin'd to settle the fourth Monarchy, which neither PYRRHUS nor HANNIBAL must prevent;

tho' HANNIBAL came so near it, that he seem'd to miss it by fatal Infatuation: which if he had effected, there had been such a traverse and confusion of Affairs, as no Oracle could have predicted. But the *Romans* must reign, and the Course of Things was then moving towards the Advent of CHRIST, and blessed Discovery of the Gospel: Our Saviour must suffer at *Jerusalem*, and be sentenc'd by a *Roman* Judge; St. PAUL, a *Roman* Citizen, must preach in the *Roman* Provinces, and St. PETER be Bishop of *Rome*, and not of *Carthage*.

Upon Reading Hudibras.

The way of *Burlesque* POEMS is very Ancient, for there was a ludicrous mock way of transferring Verses of Famous Poets into a Jocose Sense and Argument, and they were call'd Ὠδέαι or *Parodiæ*; divers Examples of which are to be found in ATHENÆUS.

The first Inventer hereof was HIPPONACTES, but HEGEMON SOPATER and many more pursu'd the same Vein; so that the *Parodies* of OVID'S *Buffoon Metamorphoses Burlesques*, *Le Eneiade Travastito*, are no new Inventions, but old Fancies reviv'd.

An Excellent *Parodie* there is of both the SCALIGERS upon an Epigram of CATULLUS, which STEPHENS hath set down in his *Discourse of Parodies*: a remarkable one among the *Greeks* is that of MATRON, in the Words and Epithites of HOMER describing the Feast of XENOCLES the *Athenian* Rhetorician, to be found in the fourth Book of *Athenæus*, pag. 134. Edit. *Casaub.*

Footnotes

[322]*A Burning Mountain in* Island.

[323]*See* Hydriotaphia, *Urne-Burial: or, A Discourse of the Sepulchral Urnes lately found in* Norfolk, *8vo*. Lond. *printed* 1658.

[324]Vid. *Licet.* de Lucernis.

**CHRISTIAN
MORALS,
BY
S**R **THOMAS BROWN,
OF NORWICH,** *M.D.*
And AUTHOR **of
RELIGIO MEDICI**

**Published from the Original and Correct
Manuscript of the Author;
by** *JOHN JEFFERY*, **D.D.**
ARCH-DEACON of NORWICH.

CAMBRIDGE:

Printed at the UNIVERSITY-PRESS,
For *Cornelius Crownfield*, Printer to the UNIVERSITY;
And are to be sold by Mr. *Knapton* at the Crown
in St. *Paul's* Churchyard; and Mr. *Morphew* near
Stationers-Hall, LONDON, 1716.

TO THE RIGHT HONOURABLE

DAVID EARL OF BUCHAN.

VISCOUNT AUCHTERHOUSE, LORD CARDROSS
AND GLENDOVACHIE,
ONE OF THE LORDS COMMISSIONERS OF POLICE, AND LORD

LIEUTENANT OF THE COUNTIES OF STIRLING
AND CLACKMANNAN IN NORTH-BRITTAIN.

MY LORD,

The Honour you have done our Family Obligeth us to make all just Acknowledgments of it: and there is no Form of Acknowledgment in our power, more worthy of Your Lordship's Acceptance, than this Dedication of the last Work of our Honoured and Learned Father. Encouraged hereunto by the Knowledge we have of Your Lordship's Judicious Relish of universal Learning, and sublime Virtue, we beg the Favour of Your Acceptance of it, which will very much Oblige our Family in general, and Her in particular, who is,

MY LORD,
Your Lordship's
most humble Servant,
ELIZABETH LITTELTON.

THE PREFACE

If any One, after he has read Religio Medici, *and the ensuing Discourse, can make Doubt, whether the same Person was the Author of them both, he may be Assured by the Testimony of Mrs.* LITTELTON, *Sr.* THOMAS BROWN'S *Daughter, who Lived with her Father when it was composed by Him; and who, at the time, read it written by his own Hand: and also by the Testimony of Others (of whom I am One), who read the MS. of the Author, immediately after his Death, and who have since Read the Same; from which it hath been faithfully and exactly Transcribed for the Press. The Reason why it was not Printed sooner is, because it was unhappily Lost, by being Mislay'd among Other MSS. for which Search was lately made in the Presence of the Lord Arch-bishop of Canterbury, of which his Grace, by Letter, Informed M*rs. LITTELTON, *when he sent the MS to Her. There is nothing printed in the Discourse, or in the short notes, but what is found in the original MS of the Author, except only where an Oversight had made the Addition or transposition of some words necessary.*

JOHN JEFFERY

Arch-Deacon

of Norwich.

CHRISTIAN MORALS

PART I

SECT. 1

Tread softly and circumspectly in this funambulatory Track and narrow Path of Goodness: Pursue Virtue virtuously: Leven not good Actions, nor render Virtues disputable. Stain not fair Acts with foul Intentions: Maim not Uprightness by halting Concomitances, nor circumstantially deprave substantial Goodness.

Consider whereabout thou art in *Cebes's* Table, or that old Philosophical Pinax of the Life of Man: whether thou art yet in the Road of uncertainties; whether thou hast yet entred the narrow Gate, got up the Hill and asperous way, which leadeth unto the House of Sanity; or taken that purifying Potion from the hand of sincere Erudition, which may send Thee clear and pure away unto a virtuous and happy Life.

In this virtuous Voyage of thy Life hall not about like the Ark, without the use of Rudder, Mast, or Sail, and bound for no Port. Let not Disappointment cause Despondency, nor difficulty despair. Think not that you are Sailing from *Lima* to *Manillia*, when you may fasten up the Rudder, and sleep before the Wind; but expect rough Seas, Flaws, and contrary Blasts: and 'tis well, if by many cross Tacks and Veerings you arrive at the Port; for we sleep in Lyons Skins in our Progress unto Virtue, and we slide not, but climb unto it.

Sit not down in the popular Forms and common Level of Virtues. Offer not only Peace Offerings but Holocausts unto God: where all is due make no reserve, and cut not a Cummin Seed with the

Almighty: To serve Him singly to serve ourselves were too partial a piece of Piety; not like to place us in the illustrious Mansions of Glory.

SECT. 2

Rest not in an Ovation[325] but a Triumph over thy Passions. Let Anger walk hanging down the head; Let Malice go Manicled, and Envy fetter'd after thee. Behold within thee the long train of thy Trophies not without thee. Make the quarrelling Lapithytes sleep, and Centaurs within lye quiet. Chain up the unruly Legion of thy breast. Lead thine own captivity captive, and be *Cæsar* within thy self.

SECT. 3

He that is Chast and Continent not to impair his strength, or honest for fear of Contagion, will hardly be Heroically virtuous. Adjourn not this virtue untill that temper, when *Cato* could lend out his Wife, and impotent Satyrs write Satyrs upon Lust: But be chast in thy flaming Days, when *Alexander* dar'd not trust his eyes upon the fair sisters of *Darius*, and when so many think there is no other way but *Origen's*.[326]

SECT. 4

Show thy Art in Honesty, and loose not thy Virtue by the bad Managery of it. Be Temperate and Sober, not to preserve your body in an ability for wanton ends; not to avoid the infamy of common transgressors that way, and thereby to hope to expiate or palliate obscure and closer vices; not to spare your purse, nor simply to enjoy health: but in one word, that thereby you may truly serve God, which every sickness will tell you you cannot well do without health. The sick Man's Sacrifice is but a lame Oblation. Pious Treasures lay'd up in healthful days plead for sick non-performances: without which we must needs look back with anxiety upon the lost opportunities of health; and may have cause rather to envy than pity the ends of penitent publick Sufferers, who go with healthful prayers unto the last Scene of their lives, and in the Integrity of their faculties return their Spirit unto God that gave it.

SECT. 5

Be charitable before wealth make thee covetous, and loose not the glory of the Mite. If Riches encrease let thy mind hold pace with them; and think it not enough to be Liberal, but Munificent. Though a Cup of cold water from some hand may not be without it's reward, yet stick not thou for Wine and Oyl for the Wounds of the Distressed, and treat the poor, as our Saviour did the Multitude, to the reliques of some baskets. Diffuse thy beneficence early, and while thy Treasures call thee Master: there may be an Atropos of thy Fortunes before that of thy Life, and thy wealth cut off before that hour, when all Men shall be poor; for the Justice of Death looks equally upon the dead, and *Charon* expects no more from *Alexander* than from *Irus*.

SECT. 6

Give not only unto seven, but also unto eight,[327] that is, unto more than many. Though to give unto every one that asketh may seem severe advice,[328] yet give thou also before asking; that is, where want is silently clamorous, and mens Necessities not their Tongues do loudly call for thy Mercies. For though sometimes necessitousness be dumb, or misery speak not out, yet true Charity is sagacious, and will find out hints for beneficence. Acquaint thyself with the Physiognomy of Want, and let the Dead colours and first lines of necessity suffice to tell thee there is an object for thy bounty. Spare not where thou canst not easily be prodigal, and fear not to be undone by mercy. For since he who hath pity on the poor lendeth unto the Almighty Rewarder, who observes no Ides but every day for his payments; Charity becomes pious Usury, Christian Liberality the most thriving industry; and what we adventure in a Cockboat may return in a Carrack unto us. He who thus casts his bread upon the Water shall surely find it again; for though it falleth to the bottom, it sinks but like the Ax of the Prophet, to rise again unto him.

SECT. 7

If Avarice be thy Vice, yet make it not thy Punishment. Miserable men commiserate not themselves, bowelless unto others, and merciless unto their own bowels. Let the fruition of things bless the possession of them, and think it more satisfaction to live richly than dye rich. For since thy good works, not thy goods, will follow thee; since wealth is an appertinance of life, and no dead Man is Rich; to famish in Plenty, and live poorly, to dye Rich, were a multiplying improvement in Madness, and use upon use in Folly.

SECT. 8
Trust not to the Omnipotency of Gold, and say not unto it Thou art my Confidence. Kiss not thy hand to that Terrestrial Sun, nor bore thy ear unto its servitude. A Slave unto Mammon makes no servant unto God. Covetousness cracks the sinews of Faith; nummes the apprehension of any thing above sense; and only affected with the certainty of things present, makes a peradventure of things to come; lives but unto one World, nor hopes but fears another; makes their own death sweet unto others, bitter unto themselves; brings formal sadness, scenical mourning, and no wet eyes at the grave.

SECT. 9
Persons lightly dipt, not grain'd in generous Honesty, are but pale in Goodness, and faint hued in Integrity. But be thou what thou vertuously art, and let not the Ocean wash away thy Tincture. Stand magnetically upon that Axis, when prudent simplicity hath fixt there; and let no attraction invert the Poles of thy Honesty. That Vice may be uneasy and even monstrous unto thee, let iterated good Acts and long confirmed habits make Virtue almost natural, or a second nature in thee. Since virtuous superstructions have commonly generous foundations, dive into thy inclinations, and early discover what nature bids thee to be, or tells thee thou may'st be. They who thus timely descend into themselves, and cultivate the good seeds which nature hath set in them, prove not shrubs but Cedars in their generation. And to be in the form of the best of the Bad, or the worst of the Good,[329] will be no satisfaction unto them.

SECT. 10
Make not the consequence of Virtue the ends thereof. Be not beneficent for a name or Cymbal of applause, nor exact and just in Commerce for the advantages of Trust and Credit, which attend the reputation of true and punctual dealing. For these Rewards, though unsought for, plain Virtue will bring with her. To have other by-ends in good actions sowers Laudable performances, which must have deeper roots, motives, and instigations, to give them the stamp of Virtues.

SECT. 11
Let not the Law of thy Country be the non ultra of thy Honesty; nor think that always good enough which the law will make good. Narrow not the Law of Charity, Equity, Mercy. Joyn Gospel Righteousness with Legal Right. Be not a mere *Gamaliel* in the Faith, but let the Sermon in the Mount be thy *Targum* unto the law of *Sinah*.

SECT. 12
Live by old Ethicks and the classical Rules of Honesty. Put no new names or notions upon Authentick Virtues and Vices. Think not that Morality is Ambulatory; that Vices in one age are not Vices in another; or that Virtues, which are under the everlasting Seal of right Reason, may be Stamped by Opinion. And therefore though vicious times invert the opinions of things, and set up a new Ethicks against Virtue, yet hold thou unto old Morality; and rather than follow a multitude to do evil, stand like *Pompey's* pillar conspicuous by thyself, and single in Integrity. And since the worst of times afford imitable Examples of Virtue; since no Deluge of Vice is like to be so general but more than eight will escape; Eye well those Heroes who have held their Heads above Water, who have touched Pitch, and not been defiled, and in the common Contagion have remained uncorrupted.

SECT. 13
Let Age not Envy draw wrinkles on thy cheeks, be content to be envy'd, but envy not. Emulation may be plausible and Indignation allowable, but admit no treaty with that passion which no circumstance can make good. A displacency at the good of others because they enjoy it, though not unworthy of it, is an absurd depravity, sticking fast unto corrupted nature, and often too hard for Humility and Charity, the great Suppressors of Envy. This surely is a Lyon not to be strangled but by *Hercules* himself, or the highest stress of our minds, and an Atom of that power which subdueth all things unto it self.

SECT. 14
Owe not thy Humility unto humiliation from adversity, but look humbly down in that State when others look upwards upon thee. Think not thy own shadow longer than that of others, nor delight to take the Altitude of thyself. Be patient in the age of Pride, when Men live by short intervals of Reason under the dominion of Humor and Passion, when it's in the Power of every one

to transform thee out of thy self, and run thee into the short madness. If you cannot imitate *Job*, yet come not short of *Socrates*, and those patient Pagans who tired the Tongues of their Enemies, while they perceived they spit their malice at brazen Walls and Statues.

SECT. 15

Let not the Sun in Capricorn[330] go down upon thy wrath, but write thy wrongs in Ashes. Draw the Curtain of night upon injuries, shut them up in the Tower of Oblivion[331] and let them be as though they had not been. To forgive our Enemies, yet hope that God will punish them, is not to forgive enough. To forgive them our selves, and not to pray God to forgive them, is a partial piece of Charity. Forgive thine enemies totally, and without any reserve that however God will revenge thee.

SECT. 16

While thou so hotly disclaimest the Devil, be not guilty of Diabolism. Fall not into one name with that unclean Spirit, nor act his nature whom thou so much abhorrest; that is to Accuse, Calumniate, Backbite, Whisper, Detract, or sinistrously interpret others. Degenerous depravities, and narrow minded vices! not only below St. *Paul's* noble Christian but *Aristotle's* true Gentleman.[332] Trust not with some that the Epistle of St. *James* is Apocryphal, and so read with less fear that Stabbing Truth, that in company with this vice thy religion is in vain. *Moses* broke the Tables without breaking of the Law; but where Charity is broke, the Law it self is shattered, which cannot be whole without Love, which is the fulfilling of it. Look humbly upon thy Virtues, and though thou art Rich in some, yet think thyself Poor and Naked without that Crowning Grace, which thinketh no evil, which envieth not, which beareth, hopeth, believeth, endureth all things. With these sure Graces, while busy Tongues are crying out for a drop of cold Water, mutes may be in happiness, and sing the *Trisagion*[333] in heaven.

SECT. 17

However thy understanding may waver in the Theories of True and False, yet fasten the Rudder of thy Will, steer strait unto good and fall not foul on evil. Imagination is apt to rove, and conjecture to keep no bounds. Some have run out so far, as to fancy the Stars might be but the light of the Crystalline Heaven shot through perforations on the bodies of the Orbs. Others more Ingeniously doubt whether there hath not been a vast tract of land in the *Atlantick* ocean, which Earthquakes and violent causes have long ago devoured. Speculative Misapprehensions may be innocuous, but immorality pernicious; Theoretical mistakes and Physical Deviations may condemn our Judgments, not lead us into Judgment. But perversity of Will, immoral and sinfull enormities walk with *Adraste* and *Nemesis* at their Backs, pursue us unto Judgment, and leave us viciously miserable.

SECT. 18

Bid early defiance unto those Vices which are of thine inward Family, and having a root in thy Temper plead a right and propriety in thee. Raise timely batteries against those strong holds built upon the Rock of Nature, and make this a great part of the Militia of thy life. Delude not thyself into iniquities from participation or community, which abate the sense but not the obliquity of them. To conceive sins less, or less of sins, because others also Transgress, were Morally to commit that natural fallacy of Man, to take comfort from Society, and think adversities less, because others also suffer them. The politick nature of Vice must be opposed by Policy; and therefore wiser Honesties project and plot against it. Wherein notwithstanding we are not to rest in generals, or the trite Stratagems of Art. That may succeed with one which may prove successless with another: There is no community or commonweal of Virtue: Every man must study his own œconomy, and adapt such rules unto the figure of himself.

SECT. 19

Be substantially great in thy self, and more than thou appearest unto others; and let the World be deceived in thee, as they are in the Lights of Heaven. Hang early plummets upon the heels of Pride, and let Ambition have but an Epicycle and narrow circuit in thee. Measure not thy self by thy morning shadow, but by the extent of thy grave, and Reckon thy self above the Earth by the line thou must be contented with under it. Spread not into boundless Expansions either of designs or desires. Think not that mankind liveth but for a few, and that the rest are born but to serve those Ambitions, which make but flies of Men and wildernesses of whole Nations. Swell not into vehement actions which imbroil and confound the Earth; but be one of those violent ones which force the Kingdom of Heaven.[334] If thou must needs Rule, be *Zeno's* king, and enjoy that empire which every Man gives himself. He who is thus his own Monarch contentedly sways the Scepter of himself, not envying the Glory of Crowned Heads and Elohims of the Earth. Could the World unite in the practise of that despised train of Virtues, which the Divine Ethicks of our Saviour hath so inculcated upon us, the furious face of things must disappear, Eden would be yet to be found, and the Angels might look down not with pity, but Joy upon us.

SECT. 20

Though the Quickness of thine Ear were able to reach the noise of the Moon, which some think it maketh in it's rapid revolution; though the number of thy Ears should equal *Argus* his Eyes; yet stop them all with the wise man's wax, and be deaf unto the suggestions of Tale-bearers, Calumniators, Pickthank or Malevolent Delators, who while quiet Men sleep, sowing the Tares of discord and division, distract the tranquillity of Charity and all friendly Society. These are the Tongues that set the world on fire, cankers of reputation, and, like that of *Jonas* his gourd, wither a good name in a night. Evil Spirits may sit still, while these Spirits walk about, and perform the business of Hell. To speak more strictly, our corrupted hearts are the Factories of the Devil, which may be at work without his presence. For when that circumventing Spirit hath drawn Malice, Envy, and all unrighteousness unto well rooted habits in his disciples, iniquity then goes on upon its own legs, and if the gate of Hell were shut up for a time, Vice would still be fertile and produce the fruits of Hell. Thus when God forsakes us, Satan also leaves us. For such offenders he looks upon as sure and sealed up, and his temptations then needless unto them.

SECT. 21

Annihilate not the Mercies of God by the Oblivion of Ingratitude. For Oblivion is a kind of Annihilation, and for things to be as though they had not been, is like unto never being. Make not thy Head a Grave, but a Repository of God's Mercies. Though thou hadst the Memory of *Seneca*, or *Simonides*, and Conscience, the punctual Memorist within us, yet trust not to thy Remembrance in things which need Phylacteries. Register not only strange but merciful occurrences: Let *Ephemerides* not *Olympiads* give thee account of his mercies. Let thy Diaries stand thick with dutiful Mementos and Asterisks of acknowledgment. And to be compleat and forget nothing, date not his mercy from thy nativity, Look beyond the World, and before the *Æara* of *Adam*.

SECT. 22

Paint not the Sepulcher of thy self, and strive not to beautify thy corruption. Be not an Advocate for thy Vices, nor call for many Hour-Glasses to justify thy imperfections. Think not that always good which thou thinkest thou canst always make good, nor that concealed which the Sun doth not behold. That which the Sun doth not now see, will be visible when the Sun is out, and the Stars are fallen from Heaven. Mean while there is no darkness unto Conscience; which can see without Light, and in the deepest obscurity give a clear Draught of things, which the Cloud of dissimulation hath conceal'd from all eyes. There is a natural standing Court within us, examining, acquitting, and condemning at the Tribunal of ourselves, wherein iniquities have their natural Theta's and no nocent is absolved by the verdict of himself. And therefore although our transgressions shall be tryed at the last bar, the process need not be long: for the Judge of all knoweth all, and every Man will nakedly know himself. And when so few are like to plead not Guilty, the Assize must soon have an end.

SECT. 23

Comply with some humours, bear with others, but serve none. Civil complacency consists with decent honesty: Flattery is a Juggler, and no Kin unto Sincerity. But while thou maintainest the plain path, and scornest to flatter others, fall not into self Adulation, and become not thine own Parasite. Be deaf unto thy self, and be not betrayed at home. Self-credulity, pride, and levity lead unto self-Idolatry. There is no *Damocles* like unto self opinion, nor any *Siren* to our own fawning Conceptions. To magnify our minor things, or hug ourselves in our apparitions; to afford a credulous Ear unto the clawing suggestions of fancy; to pass our days in painted mistakes of our selves; and though we behold our own blood, to think ourselves the sons of *Jupiter*;[335] are blandishments of self love, worse than outward delusion. By this Imposture Wise Men sometimes are Mistaken in their Elevation, and look above themselves. And Fools, which are Antipodes unto the Wise, conceive themselves to be but their *Periœci*, and in the same parallel with them.

SECT. 24

Be not a *Hercules furens* abroad, and a Poltron within thy self. To chase our Enemies out of the Field, and be led captive by our Vices; to beat down our Foes, and fall down to our Concupiscences; are Solecisms in Moral Schools, and no Laurel attends them. To well manage our Affections, and wild Horses of *Plato*, are the highest Circenses; and the noblest Digladiation is in the Theater of our selves; for therein our inward Antagonists, not only like common Gladiators, with ordinary Weapons and down right Blows make at us, but also like Retiary and Laqueary Combatants, with Nets, Frauds, and Entanglements, fall upon us. Weapons for such combats are not to be forged at *Lipara*: *Vulcan's* Art doth nothing in this internal Militia; wherein not the Armour of *Achilles*, but the Armature of *St. Paul*, gives the Glorious day, and Triumphs not Leading up into Capitols, but up into the highest Heavens. And therefore while so many think it the only valour to command and master others, study thou the Dominion of thy self, and quiet thine own Commotions. Let Right Reason be thy *Lycurgus*, and lift up thy hand unto the Law of it; move by the Intelligences of the superiour Faculties, not by the Rapt of Passion, nor merely by that of Temper and Constitution. They who are merely carried on by the Wheel of such Inclinations, without the Hand and Guidance of Sovereign Reason, are but the Automatous part of mankind, rather lived than living, or at least under-living themselves.

SECT. 25

Let not Fortune, which hath no name in Scripture, have any in thy Divinity. Let Providence, not Chance, have the honour of thy acknowledgments, and be thy *Œdipus* in Contingences. Mark well the Paths and winding Ways thereof; but be not too wise in the Construction, or sudden in the Application. The Hand of Providence writes often by Abbreviatures, Hieroglyphicks or short Characters, which, like the Laconism on the Wall, are not to be made out but by a Hint or Key from that Spirit which indited them. Leave future occurrences to their uncertainties, think that which is present thy own; And since 'tis easier to foretell an Eclipse, than a foul Day at some distance, Look for little Regular below. Attend with patience the uncertainty of Things, and what lieth yet unexerted in the Chaos of Futurity. The uncertainty and ignorance of Things to come makes the World new unto us by unexpected Emergences; whereby we pass not our days in the trite road of affairs affording no Novity; for the novellizing Spirit of Man lives by variety, and the new Faces of Things.

SECT. 26

Though a contented Mind enlargeth the dimension of little things; and unto some 'tis Wealth enough not to be Poor; and others are well content, if they be but Rich enough to be Honest, and to give every Man his due: yet fall not into that obsolete Affectation of Bravery to throw away thy Money, and to reject all Honours or Honourable stations in this courtly and splendid World. Old Generosity is superannuated, and such contempt of the World out of date. No Man is now like to refuse the favour of great ones, or be content to say unto Princes, stand out of my Sun. And if any there be of such antiquated Resolutions, they are not like to be tempted out of them by great ones; and 'tis fair if they escape the name of Hypocondriacks from the Genius of latter times, unto whom contempt of the World is the most contemptible opinion, and to be able, like *Bias*, to carry all they have about them were to be the eighth Wise-man. However, the old tetrick Philosophers look'd always with Indignation upon such a Face of Things; and observing the unnatural current of Riches, Power, and Honour in the World, and withal the imperfection and demerit of persons often advanced unto them, were tempted into angry Opinions, that Affairs were ordered more by Stars than Reason, and that things went on rather by Lottery, than Election.

SECT. 27

If thy Vessel be but small in the Ocean of this World, if Meanness of Possessions be thy allotment upon Earth, forget not those Virtues which the great disposer of all bids thee to entertain from thy Quality and Condition, that is, Submission, Humility, Content of mind, and Industry. Content may dwell in all Stations. To be low, but above contempt, may be high enough to be Happy. But many of low Degree may be higher than computed, and some Cubits above the common Commensuration; for in all States Virtue gives Qualifications, and Allowances, which make out defects. Rough Diamonds are sometimes mistaken for Pebbles, and Meanness may be Rich in Accomplishments, which Riches in vain desire. If our merits be above our Stations, if our intrinsecal Value be greater than what we go for, or our Value than our Valuation, and if we stand higher in God's, than in the Censor's Book; it may make some equitable balance in the inequalities of this World, and there may be no such vast Chasm or Gulf between disparities as common Measures determine. The Divine Eye looks upon high and low differently from that of Man. They who seem to stand upon *Olympus*, and high mounted unto our eyes, may be but in the Valleys, and low Ground unto his; for he looks upon those as highest who nearest approach his Divinity, and upon those as lowest who are farthest from it.

SECT. 28

When thou lookest upon the Imperfections of others, allow one Eye for what is Laudable in them, and the balance they have from some excellency, which may render them considerable. While we look with fear or hatred upon the Teeth of the Viper, we may behold his Eye with love. In venemous Natures something may be amiable: Poysons afford Antipoysons: nothing is totally, or altogether uselessly bad. Notable Virtues are sometimes dashed with notorious Vices, and in some vicious tempers have been found illustrious Acts of Virtue; which makes such observable worth in some actions of king *Demetrius*, *Antonius*, and *Ahab*, as are not to be found in the same kind in *Aristides*, *Numa*, or *David*. Constancy, Generosity, Clemency, and Liberality, have been highly conspicuous in some Persons not markt out in other concerns for Example or Imitation. But since Goodness is exemplary in all, if others have not our Virtues, let us not be wanting in theirs, nor scorning them for their Vices whereof we are free, be condemned by their Virtues, wherein we are deficient. There is Dross, Alloy, and Embasement in all human Temper; and he flieth without Wings, who thinks to find Ophyr or pure Metal in any. For perfection is not like Light center'd in any one body, but like the dispersed Seminalities of Vegetables at the Creation scattered through the whole Mass of the Earth, no place producing all and almost all some. So that 'tis well, if a perfect Man can be made out of many Men, and to the Perfect Eye of God even out of Mankind. Time, which perfects some Things, imperfects also others. Could we intimately apprehend the Ideated Man, and as he stood in the intellect of God upon the first exertion by Creation, we might more narrowly comprehend our present Degeneration, and how widely we are fallen from the pure Exemplar and Idea of our Nature: for after this corruptive Elongation from a primitive and pure Creation, we are almost lost in Degeneration; and *Adam* hath not only fallen from his Creator, but we ourselves from *Adam*, our Tycho and primary Generator.

SECT. 29

Quarrel not rashly with Adversities not yet understood; and overlook not the Mercies often bound up in them. For we consider not sufficiently the good of Evils, nor fairly compute the Mercies of Providence in things afflictive at first hand. The famous *Andreas Doria* being invited to a feast by *Aloysio Fieschi* with design to Kill him, just the night before, fell mercifully into a fit of the Gout and so escaped that mischief. When *Cato* intended to Kill himself, from a blow which he gave his servant, who would not reach his Sword unto him, his Hand so swell'd that he had much ado to Effect his design. Hereby any one but a resolved Stoick might have taken a fair hint of consideration, and that some merciful Genius would have contrived his preservation. To be sagacious in such intercurrences is not Superstition, but wary and pious Discretion: and to contemn such hints were to be deaf unto the speaking hand of God, wherein *Socrates* and *Cardan* would hardly have been mistaken.

SECT. 30

Break not open the gate of Destruction, and make no haste or bustle unto Ruin. Post not heedlessly on unto the *non ultra* of Folly, or precipice of Perdition. Let vicious ways have their Tropicks and Deflexions, and swim in the Waters of Sin but as in the *Asphaltick* Lake, though smeared and defiled, not to sink to the bottom. If thou hast dipt thy foot in the Brink, yet venture not over *Rubicon*. Run not into Extremities from whence there is no regression. In the vicious ways of the World it mercifully falleth out that we become not extempore wicked, but it taketh some time and pains to undo ourselves. We fall not from Virtue, like *Vulcan* from Heaven, in a day. Bad Dispositions require some time to grow into bad Habits, bad Habits must undermine good, and often repeated acts make us habitually evil: so that by gradual depravations, and while we are but staggeringly evil, we are not left without Parentheses of considerations, thoughtful rebukes, and merciful interventions, to recal us unto ourselves. For the Wisdom of God hath methodiz'd the course of things unto the best advantage of goodness, and thinking Considerators overlook not the tract thereof.

Sect. 31

Since Men and Women have their proper Virtues and Vices, and even Twins of different sexes have not only distinct coverings in the Womb, but differing qualities and Virtuous Habits after; transplace not their Proprieties, and confound not their Distinctions. Let Masculine and feminine accomplishments shine in their proper Orbs, and adorn their Respective subjects. However unite not the Vices of both Sexes in one; be not Monstrous in Iniquity, nor Hermaphroditically Vitious.

Sect. 32

If generous Honesty, Valour, and plain Dealing, be the Cognisance of thy Family or Characteristick of thy Country, hold fast such inclinations suckt in with thy first Breath, and which lay in the Cradle with thee. Fall not into transforming degenerations, which under the old name create a new Nation. Be not an Alien in thine own Nation; bring not *Orontes* into *Tiber*; learn the Virtues not the Vices of thy foreign Neighbours, and make thy imitation by discretion not contagion. Feel something of thyself in the noble Acts of thy Ancestors, and find in thine own Genius that of thy Predecessors. Rest not under the Expired merits of others, shine by those of thy own. Flame not like the central fire which enlightneth no Eyes, which no Man seeth, and most men think there's no such thing to be seen. Add one Ray unto the common Lustre; add not only to the Number but the Note of thy Generation; and prove not a Cloud but an Asterisk in thy Region.

SECT. 33

Since thou hast an Alarum in thy Breast, which tells thee thou hast a Living Spirit in thee above two thousand times in an hour; dull not away thy Days in sloathful supinity and the tediousness of doing nothing. To strenuous Minds there is an inquietude in overquietness, and no laboriousness in labour; and to tread a mile after the slow pace of a Snail, or the heavy measures of the Lazy of Brazilia, were a most tiring Pennance, and worse than a race of some furlongs at the Olympicks. The rapid courses of the heavenly bodies are rather imitable by our Thoughts, than our corporeal Motions; yet the solemn motions of our lives amount unto a greater measure than is commonly apprehended. Some few men have surrounded the Globe of the Earth; yet many in the set Locomotions and movements of their days have measured the circuit of it, and twenty thousand miles have been exceeded by them. Move circumspectly not meticulously, and rather carefully sollicitous than anxiously sollicitudinous. Think not there is a Lyon in the way, nor walk with Leaden Sandals in the paths of Goodness; but in all Virtuous motions let Prudence determine thy measures. Strive not to run like *Hercules* a furlong in a breath: Festination may prove Precipitation; Deliberating delay may be wise cunctation, and slowness no sloathfulness.

SECT. 34

Since virtuous actions have their own Trumpets, and without any noise from thy self will have their resound abroad; busy not thy best Member in the Encomium of thy self. Praise is a debt we owe unto the Virtues of others, and due unto our own from all, whom Malice hath not made Mutes, or Envy struck Dumb. Fall not however into the common prevaricating way of self commendation and boasting, by denoting the imperfections of others. He who discommendeth others obliquely commendeth himself. He who whispers their infirmities proclaims his own Exemption from them; and consequently says, I am not as this Publican, or *Hic Niger*,[336] whom I talk of. Open ostentation and loud vain-glory is more tolerable than this obliquity, as but containing some Froath, no Ink, as but consisting of a personal piece of folly, nor complicated with uncharitableness. Superfluously we seek a precarious applause abroad: every good Man hath his plaudite within himself; and though his Tongue be silent, is not without loud Cymbals in his Breast. Conscience will become his Panegyrist, and never forget to crown and extol him unto himself.

SECT. 35

Bless not thy self only that thou wert born in *Athens*;[337] but among thy multiplyed acknowledgments lift up one hand unto Heaven, that thou wert born of Honest Parents, that Modesty, Humility, Patience, and Veracity lay in the same Egg, and came into the World with thee. From such foundations thou may'st be Happy in a Virtuous precocity, and make an early and long walk in Goodness; so may'st thou more naturally feel the contrariety of Vice unto Nature, and resist some by the Antidote of thy Temper. As Charity covers, so Modesty preventeth a multitude of sins; withholding from noon day Vices and brazen-brow'd Iniquities, from sinning on the house-top, and painting our follies with the rays of the Sun. Where this Virtue reigneth, though Vice may show its Head, it cannot be in its Glory: where shame of sin sets, look not for Virtue to arise; for when Modesty taketh Wing, *Astræa*[338] goes soon after.

SECT. 36

The Heroical vein of Mankind runs much in the Souldiery, and couragious part of the World; and in that form we oftenest find Men above Men. History is full of the gallantry of that Tribe; and when we read their notable Acts, we easily find what a difference there is between a Life in *Plutarch* and in *Laërtius*. Where true Fortitude dwells, Loyalty, Bounty, Friendship, and Fidelity, may be found. A man may confide in persons constituted for noble ends, who dare do and suffer, and who have a Hand to burn for their Country and their Friend. Small and creeping things are the product of petty Souls. He is like to be mistaken, who makes choice of a covetous Man for a Friend, or relieth upon the Reed of narrow and poltron Friendship. Pityful things are only to be found in the cottages of such Breasts; but bright Thoughts, clear Deeds, Constancy, Fidelity, Bounty, and generous Honesty are the Gems of noble Minds; wherein, to derogate from none, the true Heroick English Gentleman hath no Peer.

Footnotes

[325]Ovation, a petty and minor kind of Triumph.
[326]Who is said to have Castrated himself.
[327]Ecclesiasticus.
[328]Luke.
[329]Optimi malorum pessimi bonorum.
[330]Even when the Days are shortest.
[331]Alluding unto the Tower of Oblivion mentioned by *Procopius*, which was the name of a Tower of Imprisonment among the *Persians*: whoever was put therein was as it were buried alive, and it was death for any but to name him.
[332]See *Aristotle's* Ethicks, chapter of Magnanimity.
[333]Holy, holy, holy.
[334]Matthew xi.
[335]As *Alexander* the Great did.
[336]Hic niger est, hunc tu Romane caveto. *Horace*.
[337]As *Socrates* did. *Athens* a place of Learning and Civility.
[338]*Astræa* Goddess of justice and consequently of all virtue.

PART II

SECT. 1

Punish not thy self with Pleasure; Glut not thy sense with palative Delights; nor revenge the contempt of Temperance by the penalty of Satiety. Were there an Age of delight or any pleasure durable, who would not honour *Volupia*? but the Race of Delight is short, and Pleasures have mutable faces. The pleasures of one age are not pleasures in another, and their Lives fall short of our own. Even in our sensual days, the strength of delight is in its seldomness or rarity, and sting in its satiety: Mediocrity is its Life, and immoderacy its Confusion. The Luxurious Emperors of old inconsiderately satiated themselves with the dainties of Sea and Land, till, wearied through all varieties, their refections became a study unto them, and they were fain to feed by Invention. Novices in true Epicurism! which by mediocrity, paucity, quick and healthful Appetite, makes delights smartly acceptable; whereby *Epicurus* himself found *Jupiter's* brain[339] in a piece of Cytheridian Cheese, and the Tongues of Nightingals in a dish of Onyons. Hereby healthful and temperate poverty hath the start of nauseating Luxury; unto whose clear and naked appetite every meal is a feast, and in one single dish the first course of *Metellus*;[340] who are cheaply hungry, and never loose their hunger, or advantage of a craving appetite, because obvious food contents it; while *Nero*,[341] half famish'd, could not feed upon a piece of Bread, and lingring after his snowed water, hardly got down an ordinary cup of Calda.[342] By such circumscriptions of pleasure the contemned Philosophers reserved unto themselves the secret of Delight, which the *Helluo's* of those days lost in their exorbitances. In vain we study Delight: It is at the command of every sober Mind, and in every sense born with us: but Nature, who teacheth us the rule of pleasure, instructeth also in the bounds thereof, and where its line expireth. And therefore Temperate Minds, not pressing their pleasures until the sting appeareth, enjoy their contentations contentedly, and without regret, and so escape the folly of excess, to be pleased unto displacency.

SECT. 2

Bring candid Eyes unto the perusal of mens works, and let not *Zoilism* or Detraction blast well intended labours. He that endureth no faults in mens writings must only read his own, wherein for the most part all appeareth White. Quotation mistakes, inadvertency, expedition, and human Lapses may make not only Moles but Warts in Learned Authors, who notwithstanding being judged by the capital matter admit not of disparagement. I should unwillingly affirm that Cicero was but slightly versed in *Homer*, because in his work *de Gloria* he ascribed those verses unto *Ajax*, which were delivered by *Hector*. What if *Plautus* in the account of *Hercules* mistaketh nativity for conception? Who would have mean thoughts of *Apollinaris Sidonius*, who seems to mistake the river *Tigris* for *Euphrates*; and though a good Historian and learned Bishop of *Auvergne* had the misfortune to be out in the Story of *David*, making mention of him when the Ark was sent back by the *Philistins* upon a Cart; which was before his time. Though I have no great opinion of *Machiavel's* learning, yet I shall not presently say, that he was but a Novice in Roman History, because he was mistaken in placing *Commodus* after the Emperour *Severus*. Capital Truths are to be narrowly eyed, collateral Lapses and circumstantial deliveries not to be too strictly sifted. And if the substantial subject be well forged out, we need not examine the sparks, which irregularly fly from it.

SECT. 3

Let well weighed Considerations, not stiff and peremptory Assumptions, guide thy discourses, Pen, and Actions. To begin or continue our works like *Trismegistus* of old, *verum certè verum atque verissimum est*,[343] would sound arrogantly unto present Ears in this strict enquiring Age, wherein, for the most part, Probably, and Perhaps, will hardly serve to mollify the Spirit of captious Contradictors. If *Cardan* saith that a Parrot is a beautiful Bird, *Scaliger* will set his Wits o' work to prove it a deformed Animal. The Compage of all Physical Truths is not so closely jointed, but opposition may find intrusion, nor always so closely maintained, as not to suffer attrition. Many Positions seem quodlibetically constituted, and like a *Delphian* blade will cut on both sides. Some Truths seem almost Falshoods, and some Falshoods almost Truths; wherein Falshood and Truth seem almost æquilibriously stated, and but a few grains of distinction to bear down the ballance. Some have digged deep, yet glanced by the Royal Vein; and a man may come unto the *Pericardium*, but not the Heart of Truth. Besides, many things are known, as some are seen, that is by Parallaxis, or at some distance from their true and proper beings, the superficial regard of things having a different aspect from their true and central Natures. And this moves sober Pens unto suspensory and timorous assertions, nor presently to obtrude them as *Sibyls* leaves, which after considerations may find to be but folious apparances, and not the central and vital interiors of truth.

SECT. 4

Value the Judicious, and let not mere acquests in minor parts of Learning gain thy preexistimation. 'Tis an unjust way of compute to magnify a weak Head for some Latin abilities, and to undervalue a solid Judgment, because he knows not the genealogy of *Hector*. When that notable King of *France*[344] would have his son to know but one sentence in Latin, had it been a good one, perhaps it had been enough. Natural parts and good Judgments rule the World. States are not governed by Ergotisms. Many have Ruled well who could not perhaps define a Commonwealth, and they who understand not the Globe of the Earth command a great part of it. Where natural Logick prevails not, Artificial too often faileth. Where Nature fills the Sails, the Vessel goes smoothly on, and when Judgment is the Pilot, the Ensurance need not be high. When Industry builds upon Nature, we may expect Pyramids: where that foundation is wanting, the structure must be low. They do most by Books, who could do much without them; and he that chiefly ows himself unto himself is the substantial Man.

SECT. 5

Let thy Studies be as free as thy Thoughts and Contemplations: but fly not only upon the wings of Imagination; Joyn Sense unto Reason, and Experiment unto Speculation, and so give life unto Embryon Truths, and Verities yet in their Chaos. There is nothing more acceptable unto the Ingenious World, than this noble Eluctation of Truth; wherein, against the tenacity of Prejudice and Prescription, this Century now prevaileth. What Libraries of new Volumes aftertimes will behold, and in what a new World of Knowledge the eyes of our posterity may be happy, a few Ages may joyfully declare; and is but a cold thought unto those, who cannot hope to behold this Exantlation of Truth, or that obscured Virgin half out of the Pit. Which might make some content with a commutation of the time of their lives, and to commend the Fancy of the *Pythagorean* metempsychosis; whereby they might hope to enjoy this happiness in their third or fourth selves, and behold that in *Pythagoras*, which they now but foresee in *Euphorbus*.[345] The World, which took but six days to make, is like to take six thousand to make out: mean while old Truths voted down begin to resume their places, and new ones arise upon us; wherein there is no comfort in the happiness of *Tully's* Elizium,[346] or any satisfaction from the Ghosts of the Ancients, who knew so little of what is now well known. Men disparage not Antiquity, who prudently exalt new Enquiries, and make not them the Judges of Truth, who were but fellow Enquirers of it. Who can but magnify the Endeavors of *Aristotle*, and the noble start which Learning had under him; or less than pitty the slender progression made upon such advantages? While many Centuries were lost in repetitions and transcriptions sealing up the Book of Knowledge. And therefore rather than to swell the leaves of Learning by fruitless Repetitions, to sing the same Song in all Ages, nor adventure at Essays beyond the attempt of others, many would be content that some would write like *Helmont* and *Paracelsus*; and be willing to endure the monstrosity of some opinions, for divers singular notions requiting such aberrations.

SECT. 6

Despise not the obliquities of younger ways, nor despair of better things whereof there is yet no prospect. Who would imagine that *Diogenes*, who in his younger days was a falsifier of Money, should in the after course of his life be so great a contemner of Metal? Some Negros who believe the Resurrection, think that they shall Rise white.[347] Even in this life Regeneration may imitate Resurrection, our black and vitious tinctures may wear off, and goodness cloath us with candour. Good admonitions Knock not always in vain. There will be signal Examples of God's mercy, and the Angels must not want their charitable Rejoyces for the conversion of lost Sinners. Figures of most Angles do nearest approach unto Circles, which have no Angles at all. Some may be near unto goodness, who are conceived far from it, and many things happen, not likely to ensue from any promises of Antecedencies. Culpable beginnings have found commendable conclusions, and infamous courses pious retractations. Detestable Sinners have proved exemplary Converts on Earth, and may be Glorious in the Apartment of *Mary Magdalen* in Heaven. Men are not the same through all divisions of their Ages. Time, Experience, self Reflexions, and God's mercies make in some well-temper'd minds a kind of translation before Death, and Men to differ from themselves as well as from other Persons. Hereof the old World afforded many Examples to the infamy of latter Ages, wherein Men too often live by the rule of their inclinations; so that, without any astral prediction, the first day gives the last,[348] Men are commonly as they were, or rather, as bad dispositions run into worser habits, the Evening doth not crown, but sowerly conclude the Day.

SECT. 7

If the Almighty will not spare us according to his merciful capitulation at *Sodom*, if his Goodness please not to pass over a great deal of Bad for a small pittance of Good, or to look upon us in the Lump; there is slender hope for Mercy, or sound presumption of fulfilling half his Will, either in Persons or Nations: they who excel in some Virtues being so often defective in others; few Men driving at the extent and amplitude of Goodness, but computing themselves by their best parts, and others by their worst, are content to rest in those Virtues, which others commonly want. Which makes this speckled Face of Honesty in the World; and which was the imperfection of the old Philosophers and great pretenders unto Virtue, who well declining the gaping Vices of

Intemperance, Incontinency, Violence and Oppression, were yet blindly peccant in iniquities of closer faces, were envious, malicious, contemners, scoffers, censurers, and stufft with Vizard Vices, no less depraving the Ethereal particle and diviner portion of Man. For Envy, Malice, Hatred, are the qualities of *Satan*, close and dark like himself; and where such brands smoak the Soul cannot be White. Vice may be had at all prices; expensive and costly iniquities, which make the noise, cannot be every Man's sins: but the soul may be foully inquinated at a very low rate, and a Man may be cheaply vitious, to the perdition of himself.

SECT. 8

Opinion rides upon the neck of Reason, and Men are Happy, Wise, or Learned, according as that Empress shall set them down in the Register of Reputation. However weigh not thyself in the scales of thy own opinion, but let the Judgment of the Judicious be the Standard of thy Merit. Self-estimation is a flatterer too readily intitling us unto Knowledge and Abilities, which others sollicitously labour after, and doubtfully think they attain. Surely such confident tempers do pass their days in best tranquility, who, resting in the opinion of their own abilities, are happily gull'd by such contentation; wherein Pride, Self-conceit, Confidence, and Opiniatry will hardly suffer any to complain of imperfection. To think themselves in the right, or all that right, or only that, which they do or think, is a fallacy of high content; though others laugh in their sleeves, and look upon them as in a deluded state of Judgment. Wherein notwithstanding 'twere but a civil piece of complacency to suffer them to sleep who would not wake, to let them rest in their securities, nor by dissent or opposition to stagger their contentments.

SECT. 9

Since the Brow speaks often true, since Eyes and Noses have Tongues, and the countenance proclaims the Heart and inclinations; let observation so far instruct thee in Physiognomical lines, as to be some Rule for thy distinction, and Guide for thy affection unto such as look most like Men. Mankind, methinks, is comprehended in a few Faces, if we exclude all Visages, which any way participate of Symmetries and Schemes of Look common unto other Animals. For as though Man were the extract of the World, in whom all were *in coagulato*, which in their forms were *in soluto*, and at Extension; we often observe that Men do most act those Creatures, whose constitution, parts, and complexion do most predominate in their mixtures. This is a corner-stone in Physiognomy, and holds some Truth not only in particular Persons but also in whole Nations. There are therefore Provincial Faces, National Lips and Noses, which testify not only the Natures of those Countries, but of those which have them elsewhere. Thus we may make *England* the whole Earth, dividing it not only into *Europe, Asia, Africa*, but the particular Regions thereof, and may in some latitude affirm, that there are *Ægyptians, Scythians, Indians* among us; who though born in *England*, yet carry the Faces and Air of those Countries, and are also agreeable and correspondent unto their Natures. Faces look uniformly unto our Eyes: How they appear unto some Animals of a more piercing or differing sight, who are able to discover the inequalities, rubbs, and hairiness of the Skin, is not without good doubt. And therefore in reference unto Man, *Cupid* is said to be blind. Affection should not be too sharp-Eyed, and Love is not to be made by magnifying Glasses. If things were seen as they truly are, the beauty of bodies would be much abridged. And therefore the wise Contriver hath drawn the pictures and outsides of things softly and amiably unto the natural Edge of our Eyes, not leaving them able to discover those uncomely asperities, which make Oyster-shells in good Faces, and Hedghoggs even in *Venus's* moles.

SECT. 10

Court not Felicity too far, and weary not the favorable hand of Fortune. Glorious actions have their times, extent, and *non ultra's*. To put no end unto Attempts were to make prescription of Successes, and to bespeak unhappiness at the last. For the Line of our Lives is drawn with white and black vicissitudes, wherein the extremes hold seldom one complexion. That *Pompey* should obtain the sirname of Great at twenty five years, that Men in their young and active days should be fortunate and perform notable things, is no observation of deep wonder, they having the strength of their fates before them, nor yet acted their parts in the World, for which they were brought into it: whereas Men of years, matured for counsels and designs, seem to be beyond the vigour of their active fortunes, and high exploits of life, providentially ordained unto Ages best agreeable unto them. And therefore many brave men finding their fortune grow faint, and feeling its declination, have timely withdrawn themselves from great attempts, and so escaped the ends of mighty Men, disproportionable to their beginnings. But magnanimous thoughts have so dimmed the Eyes of many, that forgetting the very essence of Fortune, and the vicissitude of good and evil, they apprehend no bottom in felicity; and so have been still tempted on unto mighty Actions, reserved for their destructions. For Fortune lays the Plot of our Adversities in the foundation of our Felicities, blessing us in the first quadrate, to blast us more sharply in the last. And since in the highest felicities there lieth a capacity of the lowest miseries, she hath this advantage from our happiness to make us truly miserable. For to become acutely miserable we are to be first happy. Affliction smarts most in the most happy state, as having somewhat in it of *Bellisarius* at Beggers bush, or *Bajazet* in the grate. And this the fallen Angels severely understand, who having acted their first part in Heaven, are made sharply miserable by transition, and more afflictively feel the contrary state of Hell.

SECT. 11

Carry no careless Eye upon the unexpected scenes of things; but ponder the acts of Providence in the publick ends of great and notable Men, set out unto the view of all for no common *memorandums*. The Tragical Exits and unexpected periods of some eminent Persons cannot but amuse considerate Observators; wherein notwithstanding most men seem to see by extramission, without reception or self-reflexion, and conceive themselves unconcerned by the fallacy of their own Exemption: Whereas the Mercy of God hath singled out but few to be the signals of his Justice, leaving the generality of Mankind to the pædagogy of Example. But the inadvertency of our Natures not well apprehending this favorable method and merciful decimation, and that he sheweth in some what others also deserve; they entertain no sense of his Hand beyond the stroak of themselves. Whereupon the whole becomes necessarily punished, and the contracted Hand of God extended unto universal Judgments: from whence nevertheless the stupidity of our tempers receives but faint impressions, and in the most Tragical state of times holds but starts of good motions. So that to continue us in goodness there must be iterated returns of misery, and a circulation in afflictions is necessary. And since we cannot be wise by warnings, since Plagues are insignificant, except we be personally plagued, since also we cannot be punish'd unto Amendment by proxy or commutation, nor by vicinity, but contaction; there is an unhappy necessity that we must smart in our own Skins, and the provoked arm of the Almighty must fall upon ourselves. The capital sufferings of others are rather our monitions than acquitments. There is but one who died salvifically for us, and able to say unto Death, hitherto shalt thou go and no farther; only one enlivening Death, which makes Gardens of Graves, and that which was sowed in Corruption to arise and flourish in Glory: when Death it self shall dye, and living shall have no Period, when the damned shall mourn at the funeral of Death, when Life not Death shall be the wages of sin, when the second Death shall prove a miserable Life, and destruction shall be courted.

SECT. 12

Although their Thoughts may seem too severe, who think that few ill natur'd Men go to heaven; yet it may be acknowledged that good natur'd Persons are best founded for that place; who enter the World with good Dispositions, and natural Graces, more ready to be advanced by impressions from above, and christianized unto pieties; who carry about them plain and down right dealing Minds, Humility, Mercy, Charity, and Virtues acceptable unto God and Man. But whatever success they may have as to Heaven, they are the acceptable Men on Earth, and happy is he who hath his quiver full of them for his Friends. These are not the Dens wherein Falshood lurks, and Hypocrisy hides its Head, wherein Frowardness makes its Nest, or where Malice, Hard-heartedness, and Oppression love to dwell; not those by whom the Poor get little, and the Rich some time loose all; Men not of retracted Looks, but who carry their Hearts in their Faces, and need not to be look'd upon with perspectives; not sordidly or mischievously ingrateful; who cannot learn to ride upon the neck of the afflicted, nor load the heavy laden, but who keep the temple of *Janus* shut by peaceable and quiet tempers; who make not only the best Friends, but the best Enemies, as easier to forgive than offend, and ready to pass by the second offence, before they avenge the first; who make natural Royalists, obedient Subjects, kind and merciful Princes, verified in our own, one of the best natur'd Kings of this Throne. Of the old Roman Emperours the best were the best natur'd; though they made but a small number, and might be writ in a Ring. Many of the rest were as bad

Men as Princes; Humorists rather than of good humors, and of good natural parts, rather than of good natures: which did but arm their bad inclinations, and make them wittily wicked.

SECT. 13

With what shift and pains we come into the World we remember not; but 'tis commonly found no easy matter to get out of it. Many have studied to exasperate the ways of Death, but fewer hours have been spent to soften that necessity. That the smoothest way unto the grave is made by bleeding, as common opinion presumeth, beside the sick and fainting Languors which accompany that effusion, the experiment in *Lucan* and *Seneca* will make us doubt; under which the noble Stoick so deeply laboured, that, to conceal his affliction, he was fain to retire from the sight of his Wife, and not ashamed to implore the merciful hand of his Physician to shorten his misery therein. *Ovid*,[349] the old Heroes, and the Stoicks, who were so afraid of drowning, as dreading thereby the extinction of their Soul, which they conceived to be a Fire, stood probably in fear of an easier way of Death; wherein the Water, entring the possessions of Air, makes a temperate suffocation, and kills as it were without a fever. Surely many, who have had the Spirit to destroy themselves, have not been ingenious in the contrivance thereof. 'Twas a dull way practised by *Themistocles*,[350] to overwhelm himself with Bulls-blood, who, being an *Athenian*, might have held an easier Theory of Death from the state potion of his Country; from which *Socrates* in *Plato* seemed not to suffer much more than from the fit of an Ague. *Cato* is much to be pitied, who mangled himself with poyniards; and *Hannibal* seems more subtle, who carried his delivery, not in the point but the pummel[351] of his Sword.

The *Egyptians* were merciful contrivers, who destroyed their malefactors by Asps, charming their senses into an invincible sleep, and killing as it were with *Hermes* his Rod. The Turkish Emperour,[352] odious for other Cruelty, was herein a remarkable Master of Mercy, killing his Favorite in his sleep, and sending him from the shade into the house of darkness. He who had been thus destroyed would hardly have bled at the presence of his destroyer; when Men are already dead by metaphor, and pass but from one sleep unto another, wanting herein the eminent part of severity, to feel themselves to dye, and escaping the sharpest attendant of Death, the lively apprehension thereof. But to learn to dye is better than to study the ways of dying. Death will find some ways to unty or cut the most Gordian Knots of Life, and make men's miseries as mortal as themselves: whereas evil Spirits, as undying Substances, are unseparable from their calamities; and therefore they everlastingly struggle under their *Angustia's*, and bound up with immortality can never get out of themselves.

Footnotes

[339]*Cerebrum Jovis*, for a delicious bit.

[340]*Metellus* his riotous Pontifical Supper, the great variety whereat is to be seen in *Macrobius*.

[341]*Nero* in his flight. *Sueton*.

[342]*Caldæ gelidæque minister*.

[343]*In Tabula Smaragdina*.

[344]Lewis the Eleventh. *Qui nescit dissimulare nescit Regnare*.

[345]
Ipse ego, nam memini, Trojani in tempore belli
Panthoides Euphorbus eram.

[346]Who comforted himself that he should there converse with the old Philosophers.

[347]Mandelslo.

[348]*Primusque dies dedit extremum.*

[349]*Demito naufragium, mors mihi munus erit.*

[350]Plutarch.

[351]Pummel, wherein he is said to have carried something, whereby upon a struggle or despair he might deliver himself from all misfortunes.

[352]*Solyman*. Turkish history.

PART III

SECT. 1

'Tis hard to find a whole Age to imitate, or what Century to propose for Example. Some have been far more approveable than others: but Virtue and Vice, Panegyricks and Satyrs, scatteringly to be found in all. History sets down not only things laudable, but abominable; things which should never have been, or never have been known: So that noble patterns must be fetched here and there from single Persons, rather than whole Nations, and from all Nations, rather than any one. The World was early bad, and the first sin the most deplorable of any. The younger World afforded the oldest Men, and perhaps the Best and the Worst, when length of days made virtuous habits Heroical and immoveable, vitious, inveterate, and irreclaimable. And since 'tis said the imaginations of their hearts were evil, only evil, and continually evil; it may be feared that their sins held pace with their lives; and their Longevity swelling their Impieties, the Longanimity of God would no longer endure such vivacious abominations. Their Impieties were surely of a deep dye, which required the whole Element of Water to wash them away, and overwhelmed their memories with themselves; and so shut up the first Windows of Time, leaving no Histories of those longevous generations, when Men might have been properly Historians, when *Adam* might have read long Lectures unto *Methuselah*, and *Methuselah* unto *Noah*. For had we been happy in just Historical accounts of that unparallel'd World, we might have been acquainted with Wonders; and have understood not a little of the Acts and undertakings of *Moses* his mighty Men, and Men of renown of old; which might have enlarged our Thoughts, and made the World older unto us. For the unknown part of time shortens the estimation, if not the compute of it. What hath escaped our Knowledge falls not under our Consideration, and what is and will be latent is little better than non existent.

SECT. 2

Some things are dictated for our Instruction, some acted for our Imitation, wherein 'tis best to ascend unto the highest conformity, and to the honour of the Exemplar. He honours God who imitates him. For what we virtuously imitate we approve and Admire; and since we delight not to imitate Inferiors, we aggrandize and magnify those we imitate; since also we are most apt to imitate those we love, we testify our affection in our imitation of the Inimitable. To affect to be like may be no imitation. To act, and not to be what we pretend to imitate, is but a mimical conformation, and carrieth no Virtue in it. *Lucifer* imitated not God, when he said he would be like the Highest, and he imitated not *Jupiter*, who counterfeited Thunder. Where Imitation can go no farther, let Admiration step on, whereof there is no end in the wisest form of Men. Even Angels and Spirits have enough to admire in their sublimer Natures, Admiration being the act of the Creature and not of God, who doth not Admire himself. Created Natures allow of swelling Hyperboles; nothing can be said Hyperbolically of God, nor will his Attributes admit of expressions above their own Exuperances. *Trismegistus* his Circle, whose center is every where, and circumference no where, was no Hyperbole. Words cannot exceed, where they cannot express enough. Even the most winged Thoughts fall at the setting out, and reach not the portal of Divinity.

SECT. 3

In Bivious Theorems, and *Janus*-faced Doctrines, let Virtuous considerations state the determination. Look upon Opinions as thou dost upon the Moon, and chuse not the dark hemisphere for thy contemplation. Embrace not the opacous and blind side of Opinions, but that which looks most Luciferously or influentially unto Goodness. 'Tis better to think that there are Guardian Spirits, than that there are no Spirits to Guard us; that vicious Persons are Slaves, than that there is any servitude in Virtue; that times past have been better than times present, than that times were always bad, and that to be Men it sufficeth to be no better than Men in all Ages, and so promiscuously to swim down the turbid stream, and make up the grand confusion. Sow not thy understanding with Opinions, which make nothing of Iniquities, and fallaciously extenuate Transgressions. Look upon Vices and vicious Objects with Hyperbolical Eyes, and rather enlarge their dimensions, that their unseen Deformities may not escape thy sense, and their Poysonous parts and stings may appear massy and monstrous unto thee; for the undiscerned Particles and Atoms of Evil deceive us, and we are undone by the Invisibles of seeming Goodness. We are only deceived in what is not discerned, and to Err is but to be Blind or Dim-sighted as to some Perceptions.

SECT. 4

To be Honest in a right Line,[353] and Virtuous by Epitome, be firm unto such Principles of Goodness, as carry in them Volumes of instruction and may abridge thy Labour. And since instructions are many, hold close unto those, whereon the rest depend. So may we have all in a few, and the Law and the Prophets in a Rule, the Sacred Writ in Stenography, and the Scripture in a Nut-Shell. To pursue the osseous and solid part of Goodness, which gives Stability and Rectitude to all the rest; To settle on fundamental Virtues, and bid early defiance unto Mother-vices, which carry in their Bowels the seminals of other Iniquities, makes a short cut in Goodness, and strikes not off an Head but the whole Neck of *Hydra*. For we are carried into the dark Lake, like the *Ægyptian* River into the Sea, by seven principal Ostiaries. The Mother-Sins of that number are the Deadly engins of Evil Spirits that undo us, and even evil Spirits themselves, and he who is under the Chains thereof is not without a possession. *Mary Magdalene* had more than seven Devils, if these with their Imps were in her, and he who is thus possessed, may literally be named *Legion*. Where such Plants grow and prosper, look for no Champain or Region void of Thorns, but productions like the Tree of *Goa*,[354] and Forrests of abomination.

SECT. 5

Guide not the Hand of God, nor order the Finger of the Almighty, unto thy will and pleasure; but sit quiet in the soft showers of Providence, and Favourable distributions in this World, either to thyself or others. And since not only Judgments have their Errands, but Mercies their Commissions; snatch not at every Favour, nor think thy self passed by if they fall upon thy Neighbour. Rake not up envious displacences at things successful unto others, which the wise Disposer of all thinks not fit for thy self. Reconcile the events of things unto both beings, that is, of this World and the next: So will there not seem so many Riddles in Providence, nor various inequalities in the dispensation of things below. If thou dost not anoint thy Face, yet put not on sackcloth at the felicities of others. Repining at the Good draws on rejoicing at the evils of others, and so falls into that inhumane Vice,[355] for which so few Languages have a name. The blessed Spirits above rejoice at our happiness below: but to be glad at the evils of one another, is beyond the malignity of Hell, and falls not on evil Spirits, who, though they rejoice at our unhappiness, take no pleasure at the afflictions of their own Society or of their fellow Natures. Degenerous Heads! who must be fain to learn from such Examples, and to be Taught from the School of Hell.

SECT. 6

Grain not thy vicious stains, nor deepen those swart Tinctures, which Temper, Infirmity, or ill habits have set upon thee; and fix not by iterated depravations what time might Efface, or Virtuous washes expunge. He, who thus still advanceth in Iniquity deepneth his deformed hue; turns a Shadow into Night, and makes himself a *Negro* in the black Jaundice; and so becomes one of those Lost ones, the disproportionate pores of whose Brains afford no entrance unto good Motions, but reflect and frustrate all Counsels, Deaf unto the Thunder of the Laws, and Rocks unto the Cries of charitable Commiserators. He who hath had the Patience of *Diogenes*, to make Orations unto Statues, may more sensibly apprehend how all Words fall to the Ground, spent upon such a surd and Earless Generation of Men, stupid unto all Instruction, and rather requiring an Exorcist, than an Orator for their Conversion.

SECT. 7

Burden not the back of *Aries, Leo*, or *Taurus*, with thy faults; nor make *Saturn, Mars*, or *Venus*, guilty of thy Follies. Think not to fasten thy imperfections on the Stars, and so despairingly conceive thy self under a fatality of being evil. Calculate thy self within, seek not thy self in the Moon, but in thine own Orb or Microcosmical Circumference. Let celestial aspects admonish and advertise, not conclude and determine thy ways. For since good and bad stars moralize not our Actions, and neither excuse or commend, acquit or condemn our Good or Bad Deeds at the present or last Bar, since some are Astrologically well disposed who are morally highly vicious; not Celestial Figures, but Virtuous Schemes must denominate and state our Actions. If we rightly understood the Names whereby God calleth the Stars, if we knew his Name for the Dog-Star, or by what appellation *Jupiter, Mars*, and *Saturn* obey his Will; it might be a welcome accession unto Astrology, which speaks great things, and is fain to make use of appellations from Greek and Barbarick Systems. Whatever Influences, Impulsions, or Inclinations there be from the Lights above, it were a piece of wisdom to make one of those Wise men who overrule their

Stars,[356] and with their own Militia contend with the Host of Heaven. Unto which attempt there want not Auxiliaries from the whole strength of Morality, supplies from Christian Ethicks, influences also and illuminations from above, more powerfull than the Lights of Heaven.

SECT. 8

Confound not the distinctions of thy Life which Nature hath divided: that is, Youth, Adolescence, Manhood, and old Age, nor in these divided Periods, wherein thou art in a manner Four, conceive thyself but One. Let every division be happy in its proper Virtues, nor one Vice run through all. Let each distinction have its salutary transition, and critically deliver thee from the imperfections of the former, so ordering the whole, that Prudence and Virtue may have the largest section. Do as a Child but when thou art a Child, and ride not on a Reed at twenty. He who hath not taken leave of the follies of his Youth, and in his maturer state scarce got out of that division, disproportionately divideth his Days, crowds up the latter part of his Life, and leaves too narrow a corner for the Age of Wisdom, and so hath room to be a Man scarce longer than he hath been a Youth. Rather than to make this confusion, anticipate the Virtues of Age, and live long without the infirmities of it. So may'st thou count up thy Days as some do *Adams*,[357] that is, by anticipation; so may'st thou be coetaneous unto thy Elders, and a Father unto thy contemporaries.

SECT. 9

While others are curious in the choice of good Air, and chiefly sollicitous for healthful habitations, Study thou Conversation, and be critical in thy Consortion. The aspects, conjunctions, and configurations of the Stars, which mutually diversify, intend, or qualify their influences, are but the varieties of their nearer or farther conversation with one another, and like the Consortion of Men, whereby they become better or worse, and even Exchange their Natures. Since men live by Examples, and will be imitating something; order thy imitation to thy Improvement, not thy Ruin. Look not for Roses in *Attalus*[358] His Garden, or wholesome Flowers in a venemous Plantation. And since there is scarce any one bad, but some others are the worse for him; tempt not Contagion by proximity, and hazard not thy self in the shadow of Corruption. He who hath not early suffered this Shipwreck, and in his Younger Days escaped this *Charybdis*, may make a happy Voyage, and not come in with black Sails into the port. Self conversation, or to be alone, is better than such Consortion. Some School-men tell us, that he is properly alone, with whom in the same place there is no other of the same Species. *Nabuchodonozor* was alone, though among the Beasts of the field; and a Wise Man may be tolerably said to be alone though with a Rabble of People, little better than Beasts about him. Unthinking Heads, who have not learn'd to be alone, are in a Prison to themselves, if they be not also with others: Whereas on the contrary, they whose thoughts are in a fair, and hurry within, are sometimes fain to retire into Company, to be out of the crowd of themselves. He who must needs have Company, must needs have sometimes bad Company. Be able to be alone. Loose not the advantage of Solitude, and the Society of thy self, nor be only content, but delight to be alone and single with Omnipresency. He who is thus prepared, the Day is not uneasy nor the Night black unto him. Darkness may bound his Eyes, not his Imagination. In his Bed he may ly, like *Pompey*[359] and his Sons, in all quarters of the Earth, may speculate the Universe, and enjoy the whole World in the Hermitage of himself. Thus the old *Ascetick* Christians found a Paradise in a Desert, and with little converse on Earth held a conversation in Heaven; thus they Astronomiz'd in Caves, and though they beheld not the Stars, had the Glory of Heaven before them.

SECT. 10

Let the Characters of good things stand indelibly in thy Mind, and thy Thoughts be active on them. Trust not too much unto suggestions from Reminiscential Amulets, or artificial *Memorandums*. Let the mortifying *Janus* of *Covarrubias*[360] be in thy daily Thoughts, not only on thy Hand and Signets. Rely not alone upon silent and dumb remembrances. Behold not Death's Heads till thou doest not see them, nor look upon mortifying Objects till thou overlook'st them. Forget not how assuefaction unto any thing minorates the passion from it, how constant Objects loose their hints, and steal an inadvertisement upon us. There is no excuse to forget what every thing prompts unto us. To thoughtful Observators the whole World is a Phylactery, and every thing we see an Item of the Wisdom, Power, or Goodness of God. Happy are they who verify their Amulets, and make their Phylacteries speak in their Lives and Actions. To run on in despight of the Revulsions and Pul-backs of such Remora's aggravates our transgressions. When Death's Heads on our Hands have no influence upon our Heads, and fleshless Cadavers abate not the exorbitances of the Flesh; when Crucifixes upon Mens Hearts suppress not their bad commotions, and his Image who was murdered for us with-holds not from Blood and Murder; Phylacteries prove but formalities, and their despised hints sharpen our condemnations.

SECT. 11

Look not for *Whales* in the *Euxine* Sea, or expect great matters where they are not to be found. Seek not for Profundity in Shallowness, or Fertility in a Wilderness. Place not the expectation of great Happiness here below, or think to find Heaven on Earth; wherein we must be content with Embryon-felicities, and fruitions of doubtful Faces. For the Circle of our felicities makes but short Arches. In every clime we are in a periscian state, and with our Light our Shadow and Darkness walk about us. Our Contentments stand upon the tops of Pyramids ready to fall off, and the insecurity of their enjoyments abrupteth our Tranquillities. What we magnify is Magnificent, but like to the *Colossus*, noble without, stuft with rubbidge and coarse Metal within. Even the Sun, whose Glorious outside we behold, may have dark and smoaky Entrails. In vain we admire the Lustre of any thing seen: that which is truly glorious is invisible. *Paradise* was but a part of the Earth, lost not only to our Fruition but our Knowledge. And if, according to old Dictates, no Man can be said to be happy before Death, the happiness of this Life goes for nothing before it be over, and while we think ourselves happy we do but usurp that Name. Certainly true Beatitude groweth not on Earth, nor hath this World in it the Expectations we have of it. He Swims in Oyl, and can hardly avoid sinking, who hath such light Foundations to support him. 'Tis therefore happy that we have two Worlds to hold on. To enjoy true happiness we must travel into a very far Countrey, and even out of our selves; for the Pearl we seek for is not to be found in the *Indian*, but in the *Empyrean* Ocean.

SECT. 12

Answer not the Spur of Fury, and be not prodigal or prodigious in Revenge. Make not one in the *Historia Horribilis*;[361] Flay not thy Servant for a broken Glass, nor pound him in a Mortar who offendeth thee; supererogate not in the worst sense, and overdo not the necessities of evil; humour not the injustice of Revenge. Be not Stoically mistaken in the equality of sins, nor commutatively iniquous in the valuation of transgressions; but weigh them in the Scales of Heaven, and by the weights of righteous Reason. Think that Revenge too high, which is but level with the offence. Let thy Arrows of Revenge fly short, or be aimed like those of *Jonathan*, to fall beside the mark. Too many there be to whom a Dead Enemy smells well, and who find Musk and Amber in Revenge. The ferity of such minds holds no rule in Retaliations, requiring too often a Head for a Tooth, and the Supreme revenge for trespasses which a night's rest should obliterate. But patient Meekness takes injuries like Pills, not chewing but swallowing them down, Laconically suffering, and silently passing them over, while angered Pride makes a noise, like *Homerican Mars*[362], at every scratch of offences. Since Women do most delight in Revenge, it may seem but feminine manhood to be vindicative. If thou must needs have thy Revenge of thine Enemy, with a soft Tongue break his Bones,[363] heap Coals of Fire on his Head, forgive him, and enjoy it. To forgive our Enemies is a charming way of Revenge, and a short *Cæsarian* Conquest overcoming without a blow; laying our Enemies at our Feet, under sorrow, shame, and repentance; leaving our Foes our Friends, and solicitously inclined to grateful Retaliations. Thus to Return upon our Adversaries is a healing way of Revenge, and to do good for evil a soft and melting ultion, a method Taught from Heaven to keep all smooth on Earth. Common forceable ways make not an end of Evil, but leave Hatred and Malice behind them. An Enemy thus reconciled is little to be trusted, as wanting the foundation of Love and Charity, and but for a time restrained by disadvantage or inability. If thou hast not Mercy for others, yet be not Cruel unto thy self. To ruminate upon evils, to make critical notes upon injuries, and be too acute in their apprehensions, is to add unto our own Tortures, to feather the Arrows of our Enemies, to lash our selves with the Scorpions of our Foes, and to resolve to sleep no more. For injuries long dreamt on take away at last all rest; and he sleeps but like *Regulus*, who busieth his Head about them.

SECT. 13

Amuse not thyself about the Riddles of future things. Study Prophecies when they are become Histories, and past hovering in their causes. Eye well things past and present, and let conjectural sagacity suffice for things to come. There is a sober Latitude for prescience in contingences of discoverable Tempers, whereby discerning Heads see sometimes beyond their Eyes, and Wise Men become Prophetical. Leave Cloudy predictions to their Periods, and let appointed Seasons have the lot of their accomplishments. 'Tis too early to study such Prophecies before they have been long made, before some train of their causes have already taken Fire, laying open in part what lay obscure and before buryed unto us. For the voice of Prophecies is like that of Whispering-places: They who are near or at a little distance hear nothing, those at the farthest extremity will understand all. But a Retrograde cognition of times past, and things which have already been, is more satisfactory than a suspended Knowledge of what is yet unexistent. And the Greatest part of time being already wrapt up in things behind us; it's now somewhat late to bait after things before us; for futurity still shortens, and time present sucks in time to come. What is Prophetical in one Age proves Historical in another, and so must hold on unto the last of time; when there will be no room for Prediction, when *Janus* shall loose one Face, and the long beard of time shall look like those of *David's* Servants, shorn away upon one side, and when, if the expected *Elias* should appear, he might say much of what is past, not much of what's to come.

SECT. 14

Live unto the Dignity of thy Nature, and leave it not disputable at last, whether thou hast been a Man, or since thou art a composition of Man and Beast, how thou hast predominantly passed thy days, to state the denomination. Un-man not therefore thy self by a Beastial transformation, nor realize old Fables. Expose not thy self by four-footed manners unto monstrous draughts, and *Caricatura* representations. Think not after the old *Pythagorean* conceit, what Beast thou may'st be after death. Be not under any Brutal *metempsychosis* while thou livest, and walkest about erectly under the scheme of Man. In thine own circumference, as in that of the Earth, let the Rational Horizon be larger than the sensible, and the Circle of Reason than of Sense. Let the Divine part be upward, and the Region of Beast below. Otherwise, 'tis but to live invertedly, and with thy Head unto the Heels of thy *Antipodes*. Desert not thy title to a Divine particle and union with invisibles. Let true Knowledge and Virtue tell the lower World thou art a part of the higher. Let thy Thoughts be of things which have not entred into the Hearts of Beasts: Think of things long past, and long to come: Acquaint thy self with the *Choragium* of the Stars, and consider the vast expansion beyond them. Let Intellectual Tubes give thee a glance of things, which visive Organs reach not. Have a glimpse of incomprehensibles, and Thoughts of things, which Thoughts but tenderly touch. Lodge immaterials in thy Head: ascend unto invisibles: fill thy Spirit with Spirituals, with the mysteries of Faith, the magnalities of Religion, and thy Life with the Honour of God; without which, though Giants in Wealth and Dignity, we are but Dwarfs and Pygmies in Humanity, and may hold a pitiful rank in that triple division of mankind into Heroes, Men, and Beasts. For though human Souls are said to be equal, yet is there no small inequality in their operations; some maintain the allowable Station of Men; many are far below it; and some have been so divine, as to approach the *Apogeum* of their Natures, and to be in the *Confinium* of Spirits.

SECT. 15

Behold thy self by inward Opticks and the Crystalline of thy Soul. Strange it is that in the most perfect sense there should be so many fallacies, that we are fain to make a doctrine, and often to see by Art. But the greatest imperfection is in our inward sight, that is, to be Ghosts unto our own Eyes, and while we are so sharp sighted as to look thorough others, to be invisible unto our selves; for the inward Eyes are more fallacious than the outward. The Vices we scoff at in others laugh at us within our selves. Avarice, Pride, Falshood lye undiscerned and blindly in us, even to the Age of blindness: and therefore to see our selves interiourly, we are fain to borrow other Mens Eyes; wherein true Friends are good Informers, and Censurers no bad Friends. Conscience only, that can see without Light, sits in the *Areopagy* and dark Tribunal of our Hearts, surveying our Thoughts and condemning their obliquities. Happy is that State of Vision that can see without Light, though all should look as before the Creation, when there was not an Eye to see, or Light to actuate a Vision: wherein notwithstanding obscurity is only imaginable respectively unto Eyes; for unto God there was none, Eternal Light was ever, created Light was for the creation, not himself, and as he saw before the Sun, may still also see without it. In the City of the new *Jerusalem* there is neither Sun nor Moon; where glorifyed Eyes must see by the *Archetypal* Sun, or the Light of God, able to illuminate Intellectual Eyes, and make unknown Visions. Intuitive perceptions in Spiritual beings may perhaps hold some Analogy unto Vision: but yet how they see us, or one another, what Eye, what Light, or what perception is required unto their intuition, is yet dark unto our apprehension; and even how they see God, or how unto our glorified Eyes the Beatifical Vision will be celebrated, another World must tell us, when perceptions will be new, and we may hope to behold invisibles.

SECT. 16

When all looks fair about, and thou seest not a cloud so big as a Hand to threaten thee, forget not the Wheel of things: Think of sullen vicissitudes, but beat not thy brains to fore-know them. Be armed against such obscurities, rather by submission than fore-knowledge. The Knowledge of future evils mortifies present felicities, and there is more content in the uncertainty or ignorance of them. This favour our Saviour vouchsafed unto *Peter*, when he fore-told not his Death in plain terms, and so by an ambiguous and cloudy delivery dampt not the Spirit of his Disciples. But in the assured fore-knowledge of the deluge, *Noah* lived many Years under the affliction of a Flood; and *Jerusalem* was taken unto *Jeremy*, before it was besieged. And therefore the Wisdom of Astrologers, who speak of future things, hath wisely softned the severity of their Doctrines; and even in their sad predictions, while they tell us of inclination not coaction from the Stars, they Kill us not with *Stygian* oaths and merciless necessity, but leave us hopes of evasion.

SECT. 17

If thou hast the brow to endure the Name of Traytor, Perjur'd, or Oppressor, yet cover thy Face when Ingratitude is thrown at thee. If that degenerous Vice possess thee, hide thy self in the shadow of thy shame, and pollute not noble society. Grateful Ingenuities are content to be obliged within some compass of Retribution, and being depressed by the weight of iterated favours may so labour under their inabilities of Requital, as to abate the content from Kindnesses. But narrow self-ended Souls make prescription of good Offices, and obliged by often favours think others still due unto them: whereas, if they but once fail, they prove so perversely ungrateful, as to make nothing of common courtesies, and to bury all that's past. Such tempers pervert the generous course of things; for they discourage the inclinations of noble minds, and make Beneficency cool unto acts of obligation, whereby the grateful World should subsist, and have their consolation. Common gratitude must be kept alive by the additionary fewel of new courtesies: but generous Gratitudes, though but once well obliged, without quickening repetitions or expectation of new Favours, have thankful minds for ever; for they write not their obligations in sandy but marble memories, which wear not out but with themselves.

SECT. 18

Think not Silence the wisdom of Fools, but, if rightly timed, the honour of Wise Men, who have not the Infirmity, but the Virtue of Taciturnity, and speak not out of the abundance, but the well weighted thoughts of their Hearts. Such silence may be Eloquence, and speak thy worth above the power of Words. Make such a one thy friend, in whom Princes may be happy, and great Councels successful. Let him have the Key of thy Heart, who hath the Lock of his own, which no Temptation can open; where thy Secrets may lastingly ly, like the lamp in *Olybius* his Urn,[364] alive, and light, but close and invisible.

SECT. 19

Let thy Oaths be sacred, and Promises be made upon the Altar of thy Heart. Call not *Jove*[365] to witness with a Stone in one Hand, and a Straw in another, and so make Chaff and Stubble of thy Vows. Worldly Spirits, whose interest is their belief, make Cobwebs of Obligations, and, if they can find ways to elude the Urn of the *Prætor*, will trust the Thunderbolt of *Jupiter*: And therefore if they should as deeply swear as *Osman* to *Bethlem Gabor*:[366] yet whether they would be bound by those chains, and not find ways to cut such *Gordian* Knots, we could have no just assurance. But Honest Mens Words are *Stygian* Oaths, and Promises inviolable. These are not the Men for whom the fetters of Law were first forged: they needed not the solemness of Oaths; by keeping their Faith they swear,[367] and evacuate such confirmations.

SECT. 20

Though the World be Histrionical, and most Men live Ironically, yet be thou what thou singly art, and personate only thy self. Swim smoothly in the stream of thy Nature, and live but one Man. To single Hearts doubling is discruciating: such tempers must sweat to dissemble, and prove but hypocritical Hypocrites. Simulation must be short: Men do not easily continue a counterfeiting Life, or dissemble unto Death. He who counterfeiteth, acts a part; and is as it were out of himself: which, if long, proves so irksome, that Men are glad to pull of their Vizards, and resume themselves again; no practice being able to naturalize such unnaturals, or make a Man rest content not to be himself. And therefore since Sincerity is thy Temper, let veracity be thy Virtue in Words, Manners, and Actions. To offer at iniquities, which have so little foundations in thee, were to be vitious up hill, and strain for thy condemnation. Persons vitiously inclined, want no Wheels to make them actively vitious, as having the Elater and Spring of their own Natures to facilitate their Iniquities. And therefore so many, who are sinistrous unto Good Actions, are Ambi-dexterous unto bad; and *Vulcans* in virtuous paths, *Achilleses* in vitious motions.

SECT. 21

Rest not in the high strain'd Paradoxes of old Philosophy supported by naked Reason, and the reward of mortal Felicity, but labour in the Ethicks of Faith, built upon Heavenly assistance, and the happiness of both beings. Understand the Rules, but swear not unto the doctrines of *Zeno* or *Epicurus*. Look beyond *Antoninus*, and terminate not thy morals in *Seneca* or *Epictetus*. Let not the twelve, but the two Tables be thy Law: Let *Pythagoras* be thy Remembrancer, not thy textuary and final Instructer; and learn the Vanity of the World rather from *Solomon* than *Phocylides*. Sleep not in the Dogma's of the *Peripatus*, Academy, or *Porticus*. Be a moralist of the Mount, an *Epictetus* in the *Faith*, and christianize thy Notions.

SECT. 22

In seventy or eighty years a Man may have a deep Gust of the World, Know what it is, what it can afford, and what 'tis to have been a Man. Such a latitude of years may hold a considerable corner in the general Map of Time; and a Man may have a curt Epitome of the whole course thereof in the days of his own life, may clearly see he hath but acted over his Fore-fathers; what it was to live in Ages past, and what living will be in all ages to come.

He is like to be the best judge of Time who hath lived to see about the sixtieth part thereof. Persons of short times may Know what 'tis to live, but not the life of Man, who, having little behind them, are but *Januses* of one face, and Know not singularities enough to raise Axioms of this World: but such a compass of Years will shew new Examples of old Things, Parallelisms of occurrences through the whole course of Time, and nothing be monstrous unto him; who may in that time understand not only the varieties of Men, but the variation of himself, and how many Men he hath been in that extent of time.

He may have a close apprehension what it is to be forgotten, while he hath lived to find none who could remember his Father, or scarce the friends of his youth, and may sensibly see with what a face in no long time oblivion will look upon himself. His Progeny may never be his Posterity; he may go out of the World less related than he came into it; and considering the frequent mortality in Friends and Relations, in such a Term of Time, he may pass away divers years in sorrow and black habits, and leave none to mourn for himself; Orbity may be his inheritance, and Riches his Repentance.

In such a thred of Time, and long observation of Men, he may acquire a *Physiognomical* intuitive Knowledge, Judge the interiors by the outside, and raise conjectures at first sight; and knowing what Men have been, what they are, what Children probably will be, may in the present Age behold a good part, and the temper of the next; and since so many live by the Rules of Constitution, and so few overcome their temperamental Inclinations, make no improbable predictions.

Such a portion of Time will afford a large prospect backward, and Authentick Reflections how far he hath performed the great intention of his Being, in the Honour of his Maker; whether he hath made good the Principles of his Nature, and what he was made to be; what Characteristick and special Mark he hath left, to be observable in his Generation; whether he hath Lived to purpose or in vain, and what he hath added, acted, or performed, that might considerably speak him a Man.

In such an Age Delights will be undelightful and Pleasures grow stale unto him; Antiquated Theorems will revive, and *Solomon's* Maxims be Demonstrations unto him; Hopes or presumptions be over, and despair grow up of any satisfaction below. And having been long tossed in the Ocean of this World, he will by that time feel the In-draught of another, unto which this seems but preparatory, and without it of no high value. He will experimentally find the Emptiness of all things, and the nothing of what is past; and wisely grounding upon true Christian Expectations, finding so much past, will wholly fix upon what is to come. He will long for Perpetuity, and live as though he made haste to be happy. The last may prove the prime part of his Life, and those his best days which he lived nearest Heaven.

SECT. 23

Live happy in the *Elizium* of a virtuously composed Mind, and let Intellectual Contents exceed the Delights wherein mere Pleasurists place their Paradise. Bear not too slack reins upon Pleasure, nor let complexion or contagion betray thee unto the exorbitancy of Delight. Make Pleasure thy Recreation or intermissive Relaxation, not thy *Diana*, Life and Profession. Voluptuousness is as insatiable as Covetousness. Tranquillity is better than Jollity, and to appease pain than to invent pleasure. Our hard entrance into the world, our miserable going out of it, our sicknesses, disturbances, and sad Rencounters in it, do clamorously tell us we come not into the World to run a Race of Delight, but to perform the sober Acts and serious purposes of Man; which to omit were foully to miscarry in the advantage of humanity, to play away an uniterable Life, and to have lived in vain. Forget not the capital end, and frustrate not the opportunity of once Living. Dream not of any kind of *Metempsychosis* or transanimation, but into thine own body, and that after a long time, and then also unto wail or bliss, according to thy first and fundamental Life. Upon a curricle in this World depends a long course of the next, and upon a narrow Scene here an endless expansion hereafter. In vain some think to have an end of their Beings with their Lives. Things cannot get out of their natures, or be or not be in despite of their constitutions. Rational existences in Heaven perish not at all, and but partially on Earth: That which is thus once will in some way be always: The first Living human Soul is still alive, and all *Adam* hath found no Period.

SECT. 24

Since the Stars of Heaven do differ in Glory; since it hath pleased the Almighty hand to honour the North Pole with Lights above the South; since there are some Stars so bright that they can hardly be looked on, some so dim that they can scarce be seen, and vast numbers not to be seen at all even by Artificial Eyes; Read thou the Earth in Heaven, and things below from above. Look contentedly upon the scattered difference of things, and expect not equality in lustre, dignity, or perfection, in Regions or Persons below; where numerous numbers must be content to stand like *Lacteous* or *Nebulous* Stars, little taken notice of, or dim in their generations. All which may be contentedly allowable in the affairs and ends of this World, and in suspension unto what will be in the order of things hereafter, and the new Systeme of Mankind which will be in the World to come; when the last may be the first and the first the last; when *Lazarus* may sit above *Cæsar*, and the just obscure on Earth shall shine like the Sun in Heaven; when personations shall cease, and Histrionism of happiness be over; when Reality shall rule, and all shall be as they shall be for ever.

SECT. 25

When the *Stoick* said that life would not be accepted if it were offered unto such as knew it,[368] he spoke too meanly of that state of being which placeth us in the form of Men. It more depreciates the value of this life, that Men would not live it over again; for although they would still live on, yet few or none can endure to think of being twice the same Men upon Earth, and some had rather never have lived than to tread over their days once more. *Cicero* in a prosperous state had not the patience to think of beginning in a cradle again. *Job* would not only curse the day of his Nativity, but also of his Renascency, if he were to act over his Disasters, and the miseries of the Dunghil. But the greatest under-weening of this Life is to undervalue that, unto which this is but Exordial or a Passage leading unto it. The great advantage of this mean life is thereby to stand in a capacity of a better; for the Colonies of Heaven must be drawn from Earth, and the Sons of the first *Adam* are only heirs unto the second. Thus *Adam* came into this World with the power also of another, nor only to replenish the Earth, but the everlasting Mansions of Heaven. Where we were when the foundations of the earth were lay'd, when the morning Stars sang together,[369] and all the Sons of God shouted for Joy, He must answer who asked it; who understands Entities of preordination, and beings yet unbeing; who hath in his Intellect the Ideal Existences of things, and Entities before their Extances. Though it looks but like an imaginary kind of existency to be before we are; yet since we are under the decree or prescience of a sure and Omnipotent Power, it may be somewhat more than a non-entity to be in that mind, unto which all things are present.

SECT. 26

If the end of the World shall have the same foregoing Signs, as the period of Empires, States, and Dominions in it, that is, Corruption of Manners, inhuman degenerations, and deluge of iniquities; it may be doubted whether that final time be so far of, of whose day and hour there can be no prescience. But while all men doubt, and none can determine how long the World shall last, some may wonder that it hath spun out so long and unto our days. For if the Almighty had not determin'd a fixed duration unto it, according to his mighty and merciful designments in it, if he had not said unto it, as he did unto a part of it, hitherto shalt thou go and no farther; if we consider the incessant and cutting provocations from the Earth, it is not without amazement how his patience hath permitted so long a continuance unto it, how he, who cursed the Earth in the first days of the first Man, and drowned it in the tenth Generation after, should thus lastingly contend with Flesh and yet defer the last flames. For since he is sharply provoked every moment, yet punisheth to pardon, and forgives to forgive again; what patience could be content to act over such vicissitudes, or accept of repentances which must have after penitences, his goodness can only tell us. And surely if the patience of Heaven were not proportionable unto the provocations from Earth; there needed an Intercessor not only for the sins, but the duration of this World, and to lead it up unto the present computation. Without such a merciful Longanimity, the Heavens would never be so aged as to grow old like a Garment; it were in vain to infer from the Doctrine of the Sphere, that the time might come when *Capella*, a noble Northern Star, would have its motion in the *Æquator*, that the Northern *Zodiacal* Signs would at length be the Southern, the Southern the Northern, and *Capricorn* become our *Cancer*. However therefore the Wisdom of the Creator hath ordered the duration of the World, yet since the end thereof brings the accomplishment of our happiness, since some would be content that it should have no end, since Evil Men and Spirits do fear it may be too short, since Good Men hope it may not be too long; the prayer of the Saints under the Altar will be the supplication of the Righteous World. That his mercy would abridge their languishing Expectation and hasten the accomplishment of their happy state to come.

SECT. 27

Though Good Men are often taken away from the Evil to come, though some in evil days have been glad that they were old, nor long to behold the iniquities of a wicked World, or Judgments threatened by them; yet is it no small satisfaction unto honest minds to leave the World in virtuous well temper'd times, under a prospect of good to come, and continuation of worthy ways acceptable unto God and Man. Men who dye in deplorable days, which they regretfully behold, have not their Eyes closed with the like content; while they cannot avoid the thoughts of proceeding or growing enormities, displeasing unto that Spirit unto whom they are then going, whose honour they desire in all times and throughout all generations. If *Lucifer* could be freed from his dismal place, he would little care though the rest were left behind. Too many there may be of *Nero's* mind, who, if their own turn were served, would not regard what became of others, and, when they dye themselves, care not if all perish. But good Mens wishes extend beyond their lives, for the happiness of times to come, and never to be known unto them. And therefore while so many question prayers for the dead, they charitably pray for those who are not yet alive; they are not so enviously ambitious to go to Heaven by themselves: they cannot but humbly wish, that the little Flock might be greater, the narrow Gate wider, and that, as many are called, so not a few might be chosen.

SECT. 28

That a greater number of Angels remained in Heaven, than fell from it, the School-men will tell us; that the number of blessed Souls will not come short of that vast number of fallen Spirits, we have the favorable calculation of others. What Age or Century hath sent most Souls unto Heaven, he can tell who vouchsafeth that honour unto them. Though the Number of the blessed must be compleat before the World can pass away, yet since the World it self seems in the wane, and we have no such comfortable prognosticks of Latter times, since a greater part of time is spun than is to come, and the blessed Roll already much replenished; happy are those pieties, which solicitously look about, and hasten to make one of that already much filled and abbreviated List to come.

SECT. 29

Think not thy time short in this World since the World it self is not long. The created World is but a small *Parenthesis* in Eternity; and a short interposition for a time between such a state of duration, as was before it and may be after it. And if we should allow of the old Tradition that the world should last Six Thousand years, it could scarce have the name of old, since the first Man lived near a sixth part thereof, and seven *Methusela's* would exceed its whole duration. However, to palliate the shortness of our Lives, and somewhat to compensate our brief term in this World, it's good to know as much as we can of it; and also, so far as possibly in us lieth, to hold such a *Theory* of times past, as though we had seen the same. He who hath thus considered the World, as also how therein things long past have been answered by things present, how matters in one Age have been acted over in another, and how there is nothing new under the Sun, may conceive himself in some manner to have lived from the beginning, and to be as old as the World; and if he should still live on 'twould be but the same thing.

SECT. 30

Lastly, if length of Days be thy Portion, make it not thy Expectation. Reckon not upon long Life: think every day the last, and live always beyond thy account. He that so often surviveth his Expectation lives many Lives, and will scarce complain of the shortness of his days. Time past is gone like a Shadow; make time to come present. Approximate thy latter times by present apprehensions of them: be like a neighbour unto the Grave, and think there is but little to come. And since there is something of us that will still live on, join both lives together, and live in one but for the other. He who thus ordereth the purposes of this Life will never be far from the next, and is in some manner already in it, by a happy conformity, and close apprehension of it. And if, as we have elsewhere declared, any have been so happy as personally to understand Christian Annihilation, Extasy, Exolution, Transformation, the Kiss of the Spouse, and Ingression into the Divine Shadow, according to Mystical Theology, they have already had an handsome Anticipation of Heaven; the World is in a manner over, and the Earth in Ashes unto them.

Footnotes

[353]*Linea recta brevissima.*

[354]*Arbor Goa de Ruyz*, or *ficus Indica*, whose branches send down shoots which root in the ground, from whence there successively rise others, till one Tree becomes a wood.

[355]Ἐπιχαιρεκακία.

[356]*Sapiens dominabitur Astris.*

[357]*Adam* thought to be created in the State of Man, about thirty years Old.

[358]*Attalus* made a Garden which contained only venemous plants.

[359]*Pompeios Juvenes Asia atque Europa, sed ipsum Terra tegit Libyes.*

[360]*Don Sebastian de Covarrubias*, writ 3 Centuries of moral Emblems in *Spanish*. In the 88th of the second Century he sets down two Faces averse, and conjoined *Janus*-like; the one a Gallant Beautiful Face, the other a Death's-Head Face, with this Motto out of *Ovid's Metamorphosis, Quid fuerim quid simque vide.*

[361]A Book so intitled wherein are sundry horrid accounts.

[362]
Tu miser exclamas, ut Stentora vincere possis,
Vel potius quantum Gradivus Homericus. Juvenal.

[363]A soft tongue breaketh the bones. *Proverbs* 25. 15.

[364]Which after many hundred years was found burning under ground, and went out as soon as the air came to it.

[365]*Jovem lapidem jurare.*

[366]See the oath of *Sultan Osman* in his life, in the addition to *Knolls* his Turkish history.

[367]*Colendo fidem jurant.*—Curtius.

[368]*Vitam nemo acciperet si daretur scientibus.*—Seneca.

[369]Job 38.

NOTES ON CERTAIN BIRDS AND FISHES FOUND IN NORFOLK

NOTES ON CERTAIN BIRDS FOUND IN NORFOLK.

I willingly obey your commands in setting down such birds fishes and other animals which for many years I have observed in Norfolk.

Beside the ordinarie birds which keep constantly in the country many are discouerable both in winter and summer which are of a migrant nature and exchange their seats according to the season. Those which come in the spring coming for the most part from the southward those which come in the Autumn or winter from the northward. So that they are obserued to come in great flocks with a north east wind and to depart with a south west. Nor to come only in flocks of one kind butt teals woodcocks felfars thrushes and small birds to come and light together, for the most part some hawkes and birds of pray attending them.

The great and noble kind of Agle calld Aquila Gesneri I have not seen in this country but one I met with in this country brought from Ireland which I kept 2 yeares, feeding it with whelpes cattes ratts and the like, in all that while not giving it any water which I afterwards presented unto my worthy friend Dr Scarburgh.

Of other sorts of Agles there are severall kinds especially of the Halyætus or fenne Agles some of 3 yards and a quarter from the extremitie of the wings, whereof one being taken aliue grewe so tame that it went about the yard feeding on fish redherrings flesh and any offells without the least trouble.

There is also a lesser sort of Agle called an ospray which houers about the fennes and broads and will dippe his claws and take up a fish oftimes for which his foote is made of an extraordinarie roughnesse for the better fastening and holding of it and the like they will do unto cootes.

Aldrovandus takes particular notice of the great number of Kites about London and about the Thames. Wee are not without them heare though not in such numbers. There are also the gray and bald Buzzard of all which the great number of broad waters and warrens makes no small number and more than in woodland counties.

Cranes are often seen here in hard winters especially about the champian and feildie part it seems they have been more plentifull for in a bill of fare when the maior entertaind the duke of norfolk I meet with Cranes in a dish.

In hard winters elkes a kind of wild swan are seen in no small numbers, in whom and not in common swans is remarkable that strange recurvation of the windpipe through the sternon, and the same is also obseruable in cranes. Tis probable they come very farre for all the northern discouerers have obserued them in the remotest parts and like diuers other northern birds if the winter bee mild they commonly come no further southward then Scotland; if very hard they go lower and seeke more southern places. Which is the cause that sometimes wee see them not before christmas or the hardest time of winter.

A white large and strong billd fowle called a Ganet which seemes to bee the greater sort of Larus, whereof I met with one kild by a greyhound neere Swaffam another in marshland while it fought and would not bee forced to take wing, another intangled in an herring net which taken aliue was fed with herrings for a while. It may be named Larus maior Leucophæopterus as being white and the top of the wings browne.

In hard winters I have also met with that large and strong billd fowle which Clusius describeth by the name of Skua Hoyeri sent him from the Faro Island by Hoierus a physitian, one whereof was shot at Hickling while 2 thereof were feeding upon a dead horse.

As also that large and strong billd fowle spotted like a starling which Clusius nameth Mergus maior farrœnsis as frequently the Faro islands seated above Shetland, one whereof I sent unto my worthy friend Dr Scarburgh.

Here is also the pica marina or seapye, many sorts of Lari, seamewes and cobs; the Larus maior in great abundance in herring time about Yarmouth.

Larus alba or puets in such plentie about Horsey that they sometimes bring them in carts to Norwich and sell them at small rates, and the country people make use of their egges in puddings and otherwise. Great plentie thereof haue bred about Scoulton meere, and from thence sent to London.

Larus cinereus greater and smaller, butt a coars meat; commonly called sternes.

Hirundo marina or sea swallowe a neat white and forked tayle bird butt longer then a swallowe.

The ciconia or stork I have seen in the fennes and some haue been shot in the marshes between this and Yarmouth.

The platea or shouelard, which build upon the topps of high trees. They haue formerly built in the Hernerie at Claxton and Reedham now at Trimley in Suffolk. They come in March and are shot by fowlers not for their meat butt the handsomenesse of the same, remarkable in their white colour copped crowne and spoone or spatule like bill.

Corvus marinus, cormorants, building at Reedham upon trees from whence King Charles the first was wont to bee supplyed. Beside the Rock cormorant which breedeth in the rocks in northerne countries and cometh to us in the winter, somewhat differing from the other in largenesse and whitenesse under the wings.

A sea fowl called a shearwater, somewhat billed like a cormorant butt much lesser a strong and feirce fowle houering about shipps when they cleanse their fish. 2 were kept 6 weekes cramming them with fish which they would not feed on of themselues. The seamen told mee they had kept them 3 weekes without meat, and I giuing ouer to feed them found they liued 16 dayes without taking any thing.

Barnacles Brants Branta are common sheldrakes sheledracus jonstoni.

Barganders a noble coloured fowle vulpanser which breed in cunny burrowes about Norrold and other places.

Wild geese Anser ferus.

Scoch goose Anser scoticus.

Goshander. merganser.

Mergus acutirostris speciosus or Loone an handsome and specious fowle cristated and with diuided finne feet placed very backward and after the manner of all such which the Duch call Arsvoote. They haue a peculiar formation in the leggebone which hath a long and sharpe processe extending aboue the thigh bone. They come about April and breed in the broad waters so making their nest on the water that their egges are seldom drye while they are sett on.

Mergus acutarostris cinereus which seemeth to bee a difference of the former.

Mergus minor the smaller diuers or dabchicks in riuers and broade waters.

Mergus serratus the saw billd diuer bigger and longer than a duck distinguished from other diuers by a notable sawe bill to retaine its slipperie pray as liuing much upon eeles whereof we haue seldome fayled to find some in their bellies.

Diuers other sorts of diuefowle more remarkable the mustela fusca and mustela variegata the graye dunne and the variegated or partie coloured wesell so called from the resemblance it beareth vnto a wesell in the head.

Many sorts of wild ducks which passe under names well knowne unto the fowlers though of no great signification as smee widgeon Arts ankers noblets.

The most remarkable are Anas platyrinchos a remarkably broad bild duck.

And the sea phaysant holding some resemblance unto that bird in some fethers in the tayle.

Teale Querquedula, wherein scarce any place more abounding, the condition of the country and the very many decoys especially between Norwich and the sea making this place very much to abound in wild fowle.

Fulicæ cottæ cootes in very great flocks upon the broad waters. Upon the appearance of a Kite or buzzard I have seen them vnite from all parts of the shoare in strange numbers when if the Kite stoopes neare them they will fling up spred such a flash of water up with there wings that they will endanger the Kite, and so keepe him of agayne and agayne in open opposition, and an handsome prouision they make about their nest agaynst the same bird of praye by bending and twining the rushes and reedes so about them that they cannot stoope at their yong ones or the damme while she setteth.

Gallinula aquatica more hens.

And a kind of Ralla aquatica or water Rayle.

An onocrotalus or pelican shott upon Horsey fenne 1663 May 22 which stuffed and cleansed I yet retaine. It was 3 yards and half between the extremities of the wings the chowle and beake answering the vsuall description the extremities of the wings for a spanne deepe browne the rest of the body white, a fowle which none could remember upon this coast. About the same time I heard one of the kings pellicans was lost at St James', perhaps this might bee the same.

Anas Arctica clusii which though hee placeth about the Faro Islands is the same wee call a puffin common about Anglisea in Wales and sometimes taken upon our seas not sufficiently described by the name of puffinus the bill being so remarkably differing from other ducks and not horizontally butt meridionally formed to feed in the clefts of the rocks of insecks, shell-fish and others.

The great number of riuers riuulets and plashes of water makes hernes and herneries to abound in these parts, yong hensies being esteemed a festiuall dish and much desired by some palates.

The Ardea stellaris botaurus, or bitour is also common and esteemed the better dish. In the belly of one I found a frog in an hard frost at christmas. another I kept in a garden 2 yeares feeding it with fish mice and frogges, in defect whereof making a scrape for sparrowes and small birds, the bitour made shifft to maintaine herself upon them.

Bistardæ or Bustards are not vnfrequent in the champain and feildie part of this country a large Bird accounted a dayntie dish, obseruable in the strength of the brest bone and short heele layes an egge much larger then a Turkey.

Morinellus or Dotterell about Thetford and the champain which comes vnto us in September and March staying not long, and is an excellent dish.

There is also a sea dotterell somewhat lesse butt better coloured then the former.

Godwyts taken chiefly in marshland, though other parts not without them accounted the dayntiest dish in England and I think for the bignesse, of the biggest price.

Gnats or Knots a small bird which taken with netts grow excessively fatt. If being mewed and fed with corne a candle lighted in the roome they feed day and night, and when they are at their hight of fattnesse they beginne to grow lame and are then killed or as at their prime and apt to decline.

Erythropus or Redshanck a bird common in the marshes and of common food butt no dayntie dish.

A may chitt a small dark gray bird litle bigger then a stint of fatnesse beyond any. It comes in May into marshland and other parts and abides not aboue a moneth or 6 weekes.

Another small bird somewhat larger than a stint called a churre and is commonly taken amongst them.

Stints in great numbers about the seashore and marshes about Stifkey Burnham and other parts.

Pluuialis or plouer green and graye in great plentie about Thetford and many other heaths. They breed not with us butt in some parts of Scotland, and plentifully in Island [Iceland].

The lapwing or vannellus common ouer all the heaths.

Cuccowes of 2 sorts the one farre exceeding the other in bignesse. Some have attempted to keepe them in warme roomes all the winter butt it hath not succeeded. In their migration they range very farre northward for in the summer they are to bee found as high as Island.

Avis pugnax. Ruffes a marsh bird of the greatest varietie of colours euery one therein somewhat varying from other. The female is called a Reeve without any ruffe about the neck, lesser then the other and hardly to bee got. They are almost all cocks and putt together fight and destroy each other, and prepare themselues to fight like cocks though they seeme to haue no other offensive part butt the bill. They loose theire Ruffes about the Autumne or beginning of winter as wee haue obserued keeping them in a garden from may till the next spring. They most abound in Marshland butt are also in good number in the marshes between Norwich and Yarmouth.

Of picus martius or woodspeck many kinds. The green the Red the Leucomelanus or neatly marked black and white and the cinereus or dunne calld little [bird calld] a nuthack, remarkable in the larger are the hardnesse of the bill and skull and the long nerues which tend vnto the tongue whereby it strecheth out the tongue aboue an inch out of the mouth and so licks up insecks. They make the holes in trees without any consideration of the winds or quarters of heauen butt as the rottenesse thereof best affordeth conuenience.

Black heron black on both sides the bottom of the neck white gray on the outside spotted all along with black on the inside a black coppe of small feathers some a spanne long, bill poynted and yallowe 3 inches long.

Back heron coloured intermixed with long white fethers.

The flying fethers black.

The brest black and white most black.

The legges and feet not green but an ordinarie dark cork colour.

The number of riuulets becks and streames whose banks are beset with willowes and Alders which giue occasion of easier fishing and slooping to the water makes that handsome coulered bird abound which is calld Alcedo Ispida or the King fisher. They bild in holes about grauell pitts wherein is to bee found great quantitie of small fish bones. and lay very handsome round and as it were polished egges.

An Hobby bird so calld becaus it comes in ether with or a litle before the Hobbies in the spring, of the bignesse of a Thrush coloured and paned like an hawke maruellously subiet to the vertigo and are sometimes taken in those fitts.

Upupa or Hoopebird so named from its note a gallant marked bird which I have often seen and tis not hard to shoote them.

Ringlestones a small white and black bird like a wagtayle and seemes to bee some kind of motacilla marina common about Yarmouth sands. They lay their egges in the sand and shingle about June and as the eryngo diggers tell mee not sett them flat butt upright like egges in salt.

The Arcuata or curlewe frequent about the sea coast.

There is also an handsome tall bird Remarkably eyed and with a bill not aboue 2 inches long commonly calld a stone curlewe butt the note thereof more resembleth that of a green plouer and breeds about Thetford about the stones and shingle of the Riuers.

Auoseta calld shoohinghorne a tall black and white bird with a bill semicircularly reclining or bowed upward so that it is not easie to conceiue how it can feed answerable vnto the Auoseta Italorum in Aldrovandus a summer marsh bird and not unfrequent in Marshland.

A yarwhelp so thought to bee named from its note a gray bird intermingled with some whitish fethers somewhat long legged and the bill about an inch and half. Esteemed a dayntie dish.

Loxias or curuirostra a bird a litle bigger than a Thrush of fine colours and prittie note differently from other birds, the upper and lower bill crossing each other, of a very tame nature, comes about the beginning of summer. I have known them kept in cages butt not to outliue the winter.

A kind of coccothraustes calld a coble bird bigger than a Thrush, finely coloured and shaped like a Bunting it is chiefly seen in sumer about cherrie time.

A small bird of prey calld a birdcatcher about the bignesse of a Thrush and linnet coloured with a longish white bill and sharpe of a very feirce and wild nature though kept in a cage and fed with flesh. A kind of Lanius.

A Dorhawke or kind of Accipiter muscarius conceiued to haue its name from feeding upon flies and beetles, of a woodcock colour but paned like an Hawke a very litle poynted bill, large throat, breedeth with us and layes a maruellous handsome spotted egge. Though I haue opened many I could neuer find anything considerable in their mawes. Caprimulgus.

Auis Trogloditica or Chock a small bird mixed of black and white and breeding in cony borrouges whereof the warrens are full from April to September, at which time they leaue the country. They are taken with an Hobby and a net and are a very good dish.

Spermologus. Rookes which by reason of the great quantitie of corn feilds and Rooke groues are in great plentie the yong ones are commonly eaten sometimes sold in Norwich market and many are killd for their Liuers in order to cure of the Rickets.

Crowes as euerywhere and also the coruus variegatus or pyed crowe with dunne and black interchangeably, they come in the winter and depart in the summer and seeme to bee the same which Clusius discribeth in the Faro Islands from whence perhaps these come, and I have seen them very common in Ireland, butt not known in many parts of England.

Coruus maior Rauens in good plentie about the citty which makes so few Kites to bee seen hereabout, they build in woods very early and lay egges in Februarie.

Among the many monedulas or Jackdawes I could neuer in these parts obserue the pyrrhocorax or cornish chough with red leggs and bill to bee commonly seen in Cornwall, and though there bee heere very great store of partridges yet the french Red legged partridge is not to bee met with. The Ralla or Rayle wee haue counted a dayntie dish, as also no small number of Quayles. The Heathpoult common in the north is vnknown heere as also the Grous, though I haue heard some haue been seen about Lynne. The calandrier or great great crested lark Galerita I haue not met with heere though with 3 other sorts of Larkes the ground lark woodlark and titlark.

Stares or starlings in great numbers, most remarkable in their numerous flocks which I haue obserued about the Autumne when they roost at night in the marshes in safe places upon reeds and alders, which to obserue I went to the marshes about sunne set, where standing by their vsuall place of resort I obserued very many flocks flying from all quarters, which in lesse than an howers space came all in and settled in innumerable numbers in a small compasse.

Great varietie of finches and other small birds whereof one very small calld a whinne bird marked with fine yellow spotts and lesser than a wren. There is also a small bird called a chipper somewhat resembling the former which comes in the spring and feeds upon the first buddings of birches and other early trees.

A kind of Anthus Goldfinch or fooles coat commonly calld a drawe water, finely marked with red and yellowe and a white bill, which they take with trap cages in Norwich gardens and fastning a chaine about them tyed to a box of water it makes a shift with bill and legge to draw up the water unto it from the litle pot hanging by the chaine about a foote belowe.

On the xiiii of May 1664 a very rare bird was sent mee kild about Crostwick which seemed to bee some kind of Jay. The bill was black strong and bigger then a Jayes somewhat yellowe clawes tippd black, 3 before and one clawe behind the whole bird not so bigge as a Jaye.

The head neck and throat of a violet colour the back upper parts of the wing of a russet yellowe the fore and part of the wing azure succeeded downward by a greenish blewe then on the flying feathers bright blewe the lower parts of the wing outwardly of a browne inwardly of a merry blewe the belly a light faynt blewe the back toward the tayle of a purple blewe the tayle eleuen fethers of a greenish coulour the extremities of the outward fethers thereof white wth an eye of greene. Garrulus Argentoratensis.

NOTES ON CERTAIN FISHES AND MARINE ANIMALS FOUND IN NORFOLK.

It may well seeme no easie matter to giue any considerable account of fishes and animals of the sea wherein tis sayd that there are things creeping innumerable both small and great beasts because they liue in an element wherein they are not so easely discouerable. Notwithstanding probable it is that after this long nauigation search of the ocean bayes creeks Estuaries and riuers there is scarce any fish butt hath been seen by some man, for the large and breathing sort thereof do sometimes discouer themselues aboue water and the other are in such numbers that some at one time or other they are discouered and taken, euen the most barbarous nations being much addicted to fishing: and in America and the new discouered world the people were well acquantd with fishes of sea and rivers, and the fishes thereof haue been since described by industrious writers.

Pliny seemes to short in the estimate of their number in the ocean, who recons up butt one hundred and seuentic six species; butt the seas being now farther known and searched Bellonius much enlargeth, and in his booke of Birds thus deliuereth himself allthough I think it impossible to reduce the same vnto a certain number yet I may freelie say that tis beyond the power of man to find out more than fiue hundred sorts of fishes, three hundred sorts of birds, more than three hundred sorts of fourfoted animalls and fortie diversities of serpents.

Of fishes sometimes the larger sort are taken or come ashoar. A spermaceti whale of 62 foote long neere Welles, another of the same kind 20 yeares before at Hunstanton, and not farre of 8 or nine came ashoare and 2 had yong ones after they were forsaken by ye water.

A grampus aboue 16 foot long taken at Yarmouth 4 yeares agoe.

The Tursio or porpose is common, the Dolphin more rare though sometimes taken which many confound with the porpose, butt it hath a more waued line along the skinne sharper toward ye tayle the head longer and nose more extended which maketh good the figure of Rondeletius; the flesh more red and well cooked of very good taste to most palates and exceedeth that of porpose.

The vitulus marinus seacalf or seale which is often taken sleeping on the shoare. 5 yeares agoe one was shot in the riuer of Norwich about Surlingham ferry having continued in the riuer for diuers moneths before being an Amphibious animal it may bee caryed about aliue and kept long if it can bee brought to feed. Some haue been kept many moneths in ponds. The pizzell the bladder the cartilago ensiformis the figure of the Throttle the clusterd and racemous forme of the kidneys the flat and compressed heart are remarkable in it. In stomaks of all that I have opened I have found many wormes.

I haue also obserued a scolopendra cetacea of about ten foot long answering to the figure in Rondeletius which the mariners told me was taken in these seas.

A pristes or serra saw fish taken about Lynne commonly mistaken for a sword fish and answers the figure in Rondeletius.

A sword fish or Xiphias or Gladius intangled in the Herring netts at Yarmouth agreable unto the Icon in Johnstonus with a smooth sword not vnlike the Gladius of Rondeletius about a yard and half long, no teeth, eyes very remarkable enclosed in an hard cartilaginous couercle about ye bignesse of a good apple. ye vitreous humor plentifull the crystalline larger then a nutmegge remaining cleare sweet and vntainted when the rest of the eye was vnder a deepe corruption wch wee kept clear and limpid many moneths vntill an hard frost split it and manifested the foliations thereof.

It is not vnusuall to take seuerall sorts of canis or doggefishes great and small which pursue the shoale of herrings and other fish, butt this yeare 1662 one was taken intangled in the Herring netts about 9 foot in length, answering the last figure of Johnstonus lib 7 vnder the name of *canis carcherias alter* and was by the teeth and 5 gills one kind of shark particularly remarkable in the vastnesse of the optick nerves and 3 conicall hard pillars which supported the extraordinarie elevated nose which wee haue reserued with the scull; the seamen called this kind a scrape.

Sturio or Sturgeon so common on the other side of the sea about the mouth of the Elbe come seldome into our creekes though some haue been taken at Yarmouth and more in the great Owse by Lynne butt their heads not so sharpe as represented in the Icons of Rondeletius and Johnstonus.

Sometimes wee meet with a mola or moonefish so called from some resemblance it hath of a crescent in the extreme part of the body from one finne vnto another one being taken neere the shoare at Yarmouth before breake of day seemed to shiuer and grunt like an hogge as Authors deliuer of it, the flesh being hard and neruous it is not like to afford a good dish butt from the Liuer which is large white and tender somewhat may bee expected; the gills of these fishes wee found thick beset with a kind of sea-lowse. In the yeare 1667 a mola was taken at Monsley which weighed 2 hundred pound.

The Rana piscatrix or frogge fish is sometimes found in a very large magnitude and wee haue taken the care to haue them clend and stuffed, wherein wee obserued all the appendices whereby they cach fishes butt much larger then are discribed in the Icons of Johnstonus tab xi fig 8.

The sea wolf or Lupus nostras of Schoneueldus remarkable for its spotted skinne and notable teeth incisors Dogteeth and grinders the dogteeth both in the jawes and palate scarce answerable by any fish of that bulk for the like disposure strength and soliditie.

Mustela marina called by some a wesell ling which salted and dryed becomes a good Lenten dish.

A Lump or Lumpus Anglorum so named by Aldrouandus by some esteemed a festiuall dish though it affordeth butt a glutinous jellie and the skinne is beset with stony knobs after no certaine order. Ours most answereth the first figure in the xiii table of Johnstonus butt seemes more round and arcuated then that figure makes it.

Before the herrings there commonly cometh a fish about a foot long by the fishman called an horse resembling in all poynts the Trachurus of Rondeletius of a mixed shape between a mackerell and an herring, obseruable from its greene eyes rarely skye colored back after it is kept a day, and an oblique bony line running on ye outside from the gills vnto ye tayle. A drye and hard dish butt makes an handsome picture.

The Rubelliones or Rochets butt thinly met with on this coast, the gornart cuculus or Lyræ species more often which they seldome eat butt bending the back and spredding the finnes into a liuely posture do hang up in their howses.

Beside the common mullus or mullet there is another not vnfrequent which some call a cunny fish butt rather a red muellett of a flosculous redde and somewhat rough on the scales answering the discription of Icon of Rondeletius vnder the name of mullus ruber asper butt not the tast of the vsually knowne mullet as affording butt a drye and leane bitt.

Seuerall sorts of fishes there are which do or may beare the names of seawoodcocks as the Acus maior scolopax and saurus. The saurus wee sometimes meet with yonge. Rondeletius confesseth it a very rare fish somewhat resembling the Acus or needlefish before and a makerell behind. Wee have kept one dryed many yeares agoe.

The Acus maior calld by some a garfish and greenback answering the figure of Rondeletius under the name of Acus prima species remarkable for its quadrangular figure and verdigreece green back bone.

A lesser sort of Acus maior or primæ specæei wee meet with much shorter then the common garfish and in taking out the spine wee found it not green as in the greater and much answering the saurus of Rondeletius.

A scolopax or sea woodcock of Rondeletius was giuen mee by a seaman of these seas, about 3 inches long and seemes to bec one kind of Acus or needlefish answering the discription of Rondeletius.

The Acus of Aristotle lesser thinner corticated and sexangular by diuers calld an addercock and somewhat resembling a snake ours more plainly finned then Rondeletius discribeth it.

A little corticated fish about 3 or 4 inches long, ours answering that which is named piscis octangularis by Wormius, cataphractus by Schoneueldeus; octagonius versus caput, versus caudam hexagonius.

The faber marinus sometimes found very large answering the figure of Rondeletius, which though hee mentioneth as a rare fish and to be found in the Atlantick and Gaditane ocean yet wee often meet with it in these seas commonly calld a peterfish hauing one black spot on ether side the body conceued the perpetuall signature from the impression of St Peters fingers or to resemble the 2 peeces of money which St Peter tooke out of this fish remarkable also from its disproportionable mouth and many hard prickles about other parts.

A kind of scorpius marinus a rough prickly and monstrous headed fish 6 8 or 12 inches long answerable vnto the figure of Schoneueldeus.

A sting fish wiuer or kind of ophidion or Araneus slender, narrowe headed about 4 inches long with a sharpe small prickly finne along the back which often venemouslv pricketh the hands of fishermen.

Aphia cobites marina or sea Loche.

Blennus a sea millars thumb.

Funduli marini sea gogions.

Alosæ or chads to bee met with about Lynne.

Spinachus or smelt in greatest plentie about Lynne butt where they haue also a small fish calld a primme answering in tast and shape a smelt and perhaps are butt the yonger sort thereof.

Aselli or cods of seuerall sorts. Asellus albus or whitings in great plentie. Asellus niger carbonarius or coale fish. Asellus minor Schoneueldei, callarias Pliny, or Haydocks with many more also a weed fish somewhat like an haydock butt larger and dryer meat. A Basse also much resembling a flatter kind of Cod.

Scombri are makerells in greate plentie a dish much desired butt if as Rondeletius affirmeth they feed upon sea starres and squalders there may bee some doubt whether their flesh bee without some ill qualitie. Sometimes they are of a very large size and one was taken this yeare 1668 which was by measure an ell long and of the length of a good salmon, at Lestoffe.

Herrings departed sprats or sardæ not long after succeed in great plentie which are taken with smaller nets and smoakd and dryed like herrings become a sapid bitt and vendible abroad.

Among these are found Bleakes or bliccæ a thinne herring like fishe which some will also think to bee young herrings. And though the sea aboundeth not with pilchards, yet they are commonly taken among herrings, butt few esteeme thereof or eat them.

Congers are not so common on these coasts as on many seas about England, butt are often found upon the north coast of Norfolk, and in frostie wether left in pulks and plashes upon the ebbe of the sea.

The sand eels Anglorum of Aldrouandus, or Tobianus of Schoneueldeus commonly called smoulds taken out of the sea sands with forks and rakes about Blakeney and Burnham a small round slender fish about 3 or 4 inches long as bigge as a small Tobacco pipe a very dayntie dish.

Pungitius marinus or sea bausticle hauing a prickle one each side the smallest fish of the sea about an inch long sometimes drawne ashoare with netts together with weeds and pargaments of the sea.

Many sorts of flat fishes. The pastinaca oxyrinchus with a long and strong aculeus in the tayle conceued of speciall venome and virtues.

Severall sorts of Raia's skates and Thornebacks the Raia clauata oxyrinchus, raia oculata, aspera, spinosa fullonica.

The great Rhombus or Turbot aculeatus and leuis.

The passer or place.

Butts of various kinds.

The passer squamosus Bret Bretcock and skulls comparable in taste and delicacy vnto the soale.

The Buglossus solea or soale plana and oculata as also the Lingula or small soale all in very great plentie.

Sometimes a fish aboue half a yard long like a butt or soale called asprage which I haue known taken about Cromer.

Sepia or cuttle fish and great plentie of the bone or shellie substance which sustaineth the whole bulk of that soft fishe found commonly on the shoare.

The Loligo sleue or calamar found often upon the shoare from head to tayle sometimes aboue an ell long, remarkable for its parretlike bill, the gladiolus or calamus along the back and the notable crystallyne of the eye which equalleth if not exceedeth the lustre of orientall pearle.

A polypus another kind of the mollia sometimes wee haue met with.

Lobsters in great number about Sheringham and Cromer from whence all the country is supplyed.

Astacus marinus pediculi marini facie found also in that place, with the aduantage of ye long foreclawes about 4 inches long.

Crabs large and well tasted found also in the same coast.

Another kind of crab taken for cancer fluuiatilis litle slender and of a very quick motion found in the Riuer running through Yarmouth, and in Bliburgh riuer.

Oysters exceeding large about Burnham and Hunstanton like those of Poole St Mallowes or Ciuita Vechia whereof many are eaten rawe the shells being broakin with cleuers the greater part pickled and sent weekly to London and other parts.

Mituli or muscles in great quantitie as also chams or cochles about Stiskay and the northwest coast.

Pectines pectunculi varij or scallops of the lesser sort.

Turbines or smaller wilks, leues, striati, as also Trochi, Trochili, or scaloppes finely variegated and pearly. Lewise purpuræ minores, nerites, cochleæ, Tellinæ.

Lepades, patellæ Limpets, of an vniualue shell wherein an animal like a snayle cleauing fast unto the rocks.

Solenes cappe lunge venetorum commonly a razor fish the shell thereof dentalia.

Dentalia by some called pinpaches because pinmeat thereof is taken out with a pinne or needle.

Cancellus Turbinum et neritis Barnard the Hermite of Rondeletius a kind of crab or astacus liuing in a forsaken wilk or nerites.

Echinus echinometrites sea hedghogge whose neat shells are common on the shoare the fish aliue often taken by the dragges among the oysters.

Balani a smaller sort of vniualue growing commonly in clusters, the smaller kinds thereof to bee found oftimes upon oysters wilks and lobsters.

Concha anatifera or Ansifera or Barnicleshell whereof about 4 yeares past were found upon the shoare no small number by Yarmouth hanging by slender strings of a kind of Alga vnto seuerall splinters or cleauings of firre boards vnto which they were seuerally fastned and hanged like ropes of onyons: their shell flat and of a peculiar forme differing from other shelles, this being of four diuisions, containing a small imperfect animal at the lower part diuided into many shootes or streames which prepossed spectators fancy to bee the rudiment of the tayle of some goose or duck to bee produced from it; some whereof in ye shell and some taken out and spred upon paper we shall keepe by us.

Stellæ marinæ or sea starres in great plentie especially about Yarmouth. Whether they bee bred out of the vrticæ squalders or sea gellies as many report wee cannot confirme butt the squalderes in the middle seeme to haue some lines or first draughts not unlike. Our starres exceed not 5 poynts though I haue heard that some with more haue been found about Hunstanton and Burnham, where are also found stellæ marinæ testacæ or handsome crusted and brittle sea starres much lesse.

The pediculus and culex marinus the sea lowse and flie are also no strangeres.

Physsalus Rondeletij or eruca marina physsaloides according to the icon of Rondeletius of very orient green and purple bristles.

Urtica marina of diuers kinds some whereof called squalderes, of a burning and stinging qualitie if rubbed in the hand; the water thereof may afford a good cosmetick.

Another elegant sort that is often found cast up by shoare in great numbers about the bignesse of a button cleere and welted and may bee called fibula marina crystallina.

Hirudines marini or sea Leaches.

Vermes marini very large wormes digged a yarde deepe out of the sands at the ebbe for bayt. Tis known where they are to be found by a litle flat ouer them on the surface of the sand; as also vermes in tubulis testacei. Also Tethya or sea dugges some whereof resemble fritters the vesicaria marina also and fanago sometimes very large conceaued to proceed from some testaceous animals, and particularly from the purpura butt ours more probably from other testaceous wee hauing not met with any large purpura upon this coast.

Many riuer fishes also and animals. Salmon no common fish in our riuers though many are taken in the Owse, in the Bure or north riuer, in ye Waueney or south riuer, in ye Norwich river butt seldome and in the winter butt 4 yeares ago 15 were taken at Trowes mill in Xtmas, whose mouths were stuck with small wormes or horsleaches no bigger than fine threads. Some of these I kept in water 3 moneths: if a few drops of blood were putt to the water they would in a litle time looke red. They sensibly grewe bigger then I first found them and were killed by an hard froast freezing the water. Most of our Salmons haue a recurued peece of flesh in the end of the lower iawe which when they shutt there mouths deepely enters the upper, as Scaliger hath noted in some.

The Riuers lakes and broads abound in the Lucius or pikes of very large size where also is found the Brama or Breme large and well tasted the Tinca or Tench the Rubecula Roach as also Rowds and Dare or Dace perca or pearch great and small: whereof such as are in Braden on this side Yarmouth in the mixed water make a dish very dayntie and I think scarce to bee bettered in England. Butt the Blea[k] the chubbe the barbell to bee found in diuers other Riuers in England I haue not obserued in these. As also fewer mennowes then in many other riuers.

The Trutta or trout the Gammarus or crawfish butt scarce in our riuers butt frequently taken in the Bure or north riuer and in the seuerall branches thereof, and very remarkable large crawfishes to bee found in the riuer which runnes by Castleaker and Nerford.

The Aspredo perca minor and probably the cernua of Cardan commonly called a Ruffe in great plentie in Norwich Riuers and euen in the streame of the citty, which though Camden appropriates vnto this citty yet they are also found in the riuers of Oxforde and Cambridge.

Lampetra Lampries great and small found plentifully in Norwich riuer and euen in the Citty about May whereof some are very large and well cooked are counted a dayntie bitt collard up butt especially in pyes.

Mustela fluuiatilis or eele poult to bee had in Norwich riuer and between it and Yarmouth as also in the riuers of marshland resembling an eele and a cod, a very good dish and the Liuer thereof well answers the commendations of the Ancients.

Godgions or funduli fluuiatiles, many whereof may bee taken within the Riuer in the citty.

Capitones fluuiatilis or millers thumbs, pungitius fluuiatilis or stanticles. Aphia cobites fluuiatilis or Loches. In Norwich riuers in the runnes about Heueningham heath in the north riuer and streames thereof.

Of eeles the common eele and the glot which hath somewhat a different shape in the bignesse of the head and is affirmed to have yong ones often found within it, and wee haue found a vterus in the same somewhat answering the icon thereof in Senesinus.

Carpiones carpes plentifull in ponds and sometimes large ones in broads: 2 the largest I euer beheld were taken in Norwich Riuer.

Though the woods and dryelands abound with adders and vipers yet there are few snakes about our riuers or meadowes, more to bee found in Marsh land; butt ponds and plashes abound in Lizards or swifts.

The Gryllotalpa or fencricket common in fenny places butt wee haue met with them also in dry places dung-hills and church yards of this citty.

Beside horseleaches and periwinkles in plashes and standing waters we haue met with vermes setacei or hardwormes butt could neuer conuert horsehayres into them by laying them in water: as also the great Hydrocantharus or black shining water Beetle the forficula, sqilla, corculum and notonecton that swimmeth on its back.

Camden reports that in former time there haue been Beuers in the Riuer of Cardigan in Wales. This wee are to sure of that the Riuers great Broads and carres afford great store of otters with us, a great destroyer of fish as feeding butt from ye vent downewards, not free from being a prey it self for their yong ones haue been found in Buzzards nests. They are accounted no bad dish by many, are to bee made very tame and in some howses haue serued for turnespitts.

ON THE OSTRICH.

The ostrich hath a compounded name in Greek and Latin—*Struthio-Camelus*, borrowed from a bird and a beast, as being a feathered and biped animal, yet in some ways like a camel; somewhat in the long neck; somewhat in the foot; and, as some imagine, from a camel-like position in the part of generation.

It is accounted the largest and tallest of any winged and feathered fowl; taller than the gruen or cassowary. This ostrich, though a female, was about seven feet high, and some of the males were higher, either exceeding or answerable unto the stature of the great porter unto king Charles the First. The weight was a[370] [ ] in grocer's scales.

Whosoever shall compare or consider together the ostrich and the tomineio, or humbird, not weighing twelve grains, may easily discover under what compass or latitude the creation of birds hath been ordained.

The head is not large, but little in proportion to the whole body. And, therefore, Julius Scaliger, when he mentioned birds of large heads (comparatively unto their bodies), named the sparrow, the owl, and the woodpecker; and, reckoning up birds of small heads, instanceth in the hen, the peacock, and the ostrich.

The head is looked upon by discerning spectators to resemble that of a goose rather than any kind of στροῦθος, or *passer*: and so may be more properly called *cheno-camelus*, or *ansero-camelus*.

There is a handsome figure of an ostrich in Mr. Willoughby's and Ray's *Ornithologia*: another in Aldrovandus and Jonstonus, and Bellonius; but the heads not exactly agreeing. 'Rostrum habet exiguum, sed acutum,' saith Jonstoun; 'un long bec et poinctu,' saith Bellonius; men describing such as they have an opportunity to see, and perhaps some the ostriches of very different countries, wherein, as in some other birds, there may be some variety.

In Africa, where some eat elephants, it is no wonder that some also feed upon ostriches. They flay them with their feathers on, which they sell, and eat the flesh. But Galen and physicians have condemned that flesh, as hard and indigestible. The emperor Heliogabalus had a fancy for the brains, when he brought six hundred ostriches' heads to one supper, only for the brains' sake; yet Leo Africanus saith that he ate of young ostriches among the Numidians with a good gust; and, perhaps, boiled, and well cooked, after the art of Apicius, with peppermint, dates, and other good things, they might go down with some stomachs.

I do not find that the strongest eagles, or best-spirited hawks, will offer at these birds; yet, if there were such gyrfalcons as Julius Scaliger saith the duke of Savoy and Henry, king of Navarre, had, it is like they would strike at them, and, making at the head, would spoil them, or so disable them, that they might be taken.

If these had been brought over in June, it is, perhaps, likely we might have met with eggs in some of their bellies, whereof they lay very many: but they are the worst of eggs for food, yet serviceable unto many other uses in their country; for, being cut transversely, they serve for drinking cups and skull-caps; and, as I have seen, there are large circles of them, and some painted and gilded, which hang up in Turkish mosques, and also in Greek churches. They are preserved with us for rarities; and, as they come to be common, some use will be found of them in physic, even as of other eggshells and other such substances.

When it first came into my garden, it soon ate up all the gilliflowers, tulip-leaves, and fed greedily upon what was green, as lettuce, endive, sorrell; it would feed on oats, barley, peas, beans; swallow onions; eat sheep's lights and livers.—Then you mention what you know more.

When it took down a large onion, it stuck awhile in the gullet, and did not descend directly, but wound backward behind the neck; whereby I might perceive that the gullet turned much; but this is not peculiar unto the ostrich; but the same hath been observed in the stork, when it swallows down frogs and pretty big bits.

It made sometimes a strange noise; had a very odd note, especially in the morning, and, perhaps, when hungry.

According to Aldrovandus, some hold that there is an antipathy between it and a horse, which an ostrich will not endure to see or be near; but, while I kept it, I could not confirm this opinion; which might, perhaps, be raised because a common way of hunting and taking them is by swift horses.

It is much that Cardanus should be mistaken with a great part of men, that the coloured and dyed feathers of ostriches were natural; as red, blue, yellow, and green; whereas, the natural colours in this bird were white and greyish. Of the fashion of wearing feathers in battles or wars by men, and women, see Scaliger, *Contra Cardan. Exercitat. 220.*

If wearing of feather-fans should come up again, it might much increase the trade of plumage from Barbary. Bellonius saith he saw two hundred skins with the feathers on in one shop of Alexandria.

Footnotes

[370] Undecipherable in the original.

BOULIMIA CENTENARIA.

There is a woman now living in Yarmouth, named Elizabeth Michell, an hundred and two years old; a person of four feet and half high, very lean, very poor, and living in a mean room with pitiful accommodation. She had a son after she was past fifty. Though she answers well enough unto ordinary questions, yet she apprehends her eldest daughter to be her mother; but what is most remarkable concerning her is a kind of *boulimia* or dog-appetite; she greedily eating day and night what her allowance, friends, and charitable persons afford her, drinking beer or water, and making little distinction or refusal of any food, either of broths, flesh, fish, apples, pears, and any coarse food, which she eateth in no small quantity, insomuch that the overseers of the poor have of late been fain to augment her weekly allowance. She sleeps indifferently well, till hunger awakes her; then she must have no ordinary supply whether in the day or night. She vomits not, nor is very laxative. This is the oldest example of the *sal esurinum chymicorum*, which I have taken notice of; though I am ready to afford my charity unto her, yet I should be loth to spend a piece of ambergris

I have upon her, and to allow six grains to every dose till I found some effect in moderating her appetite: though that be esteemed a great specific in her condition.

UPON THE DARK THICK MIST HAPPENING ON THE 27TH OF NOVEMBER, 1674.

Though it be not strange to see frequent mists, clouds, and rains, in England, as many ancient describers of this country have noted, yet I could not but take notice of a very great mist which happened upon the 27th of the last November, and from thence have taken this occasion to propose something of mists, clouds, and rains, unto your candid considerations.

Herein mists may well deserve the first place, as being, if not the first in nature, yet the first meteor mentioned in Scripture, and soon after the creation, for it is said, Gen. ii. that 'God had not yet caused it to rain upon the earth, but a mist went up from the earth, and watered the whole face of the ground,' for it might take a longer time for the elevation of vapours sufficient to make a congregation of clouds able to afford any store of showers and rain in so early days of the world.

Thick vapours, not ascending high but hanging about the earth and covering the surface of it, are commonly called mists; if they ascend high they are called clouds. They remain upon the earth till they either fall down or are attenuated, rarified, and scattered.

The great mist was not only observable about London, but in remote parts of England, and as we hear, in Holland, so that it was of larger extent than mists are commonly apprehended to be; most men conceiving that they reach not much beyond the places where they behold them. Mists make an obscure air, but they beget not darkness, for the atoms and particles thereof admit the light, but if the matter thereof be very thick, close, and condensed, the mist grows considerably obscure and like a cloud, so the miraculous and palpable darkness of Egypt is conceived to have been effected by an extraordinary dense and dark mist or a kind of cloud spread over the land of Egypt, and also miraculously restrained from the neighbour land of Goshen.

Mists and fogs, containing commonly vegetable spirits, when they dissolve and return upon the earth, may fecundate and add some fertility unto it, but they may be more unwholesome in great cities than in country habitations: for they consist of vapours not only elevated from simple watery and humid places, but also the exhalations of draughts, common sewers, and fœtid places, and decoctions used by unwholesome and sordid manufactures: and also hindering the sea-coal smoke from ascending and passing away, it is conjoined with the mist and drawn in by the breath, all which may produce bad effects, inquinate the blood, and produce catarrhs and coughs. Sereins, well known in hot countries, cause headache, toothache, and swelled faces; but they seem to have their original from subtle, invisible, nitrous, and piercing exhalations, caused by a strong heat of the sun, which falling after sunset produce the effects mentioned.

There may be also subterraneous mists, when heat in the bowels of the earth, working upon humid parts, makes an attenuation thereof and consequently nebulous bodies in the cavities of it.

There is a kind of a continued mist in the bodies of animals, especially in the cavous parts, as may be observed in bodies opened presently after death, and some think that in sleep there is a kind of mist in the brain; and upon exceeding motion some animals cast out a mist about them.

When the cuttle fish, polypus, or loligo, make themselves invisible by obscuring the water about them; they do it not by any vaporous emission, but by a black humour ejected, which makes the water black and dark near them: but upon excessive motion some animals are able to afford a mist about them, when the air is cool and fit to condense it, as horses after a race, so that they become scarce visible.

ACCOUNT OF A THUNDER STORM AT NORWICH, 1665.

June 28, 1665.

After seven o'clock in the evening there was almost a continued thunder until eight, wherein the *tonitru* and *fulgur*, the noise and lightning, were so terrible, that they put the whole city into an amazement, and most unto their prayers. The clouds went low, and the cracks seemed near over our heads during the most part of the thunder. About eight o'clock, an *ignis fulmineus, pila ignea fulminans, telum igneum fulmineum*, or fire-ball, hit against the little wooden pinnacle of the high leucome window of my house, toward the market-place, broke the flue boards, and carried pieces thereof a stone's cast off; whereupon many of the tiles fell into the street, and the windows

in adjoining houses were broken. At the same time either a part of that close-bound fire, or another of the same nature, fell into the court-yard, and whereof no notice was taken till we began to examine the house, and then we found a freestone on the outside of the wall of the entry leading to the kitchen, half a foot from the ground, fallen from the wall; a hole as big as a foot-ball bored through the wall, which is about a foot thick, and a chest which stood against it, on the inside, split and carried about a foot from the wall. The wall also, behind the leaden cistern, at five yards distance from it, broken on the inside and outside; the middle seeming entire. The lead on the edges of the cistern turned a little up; and a great washing-bowl, that stood by it, to recover the rain, turned upside down, and split quite through. Some chimneys and tiles were struck down in other parts of the city. A fire-ball also struck down the wall in the market-place. And all this, God be thanked! without mischief unto any person. The greatest terror was from the noise, answerable unto two or three cannon. The smell it left was strong, like that after the discharge of a cannon. The balls that flew were not like fire in the flame, but the coal; and the people said it was like the sun. It was *discutiens, terebrans,* but not *urens.* It burnt nothing, nor any thing it touched smelt of fire; nor melted any lead of window or cistern, as I found it do in the great storm, about nine years ago, at Melton-hall, four miles off, at that time when the hail broke three thousand pounds worth of glass in Norwich, in half-a-quarter of an hour. About four days after, the like fulminous fire killed a man in Erpingham church, by Aylsham, upon whom it broke, and beat down divers which were within the wind of it. One also went off in Sir John Hobart's gallery, at Blickling. He was so near that his arm and thigh were numbed about an hour after. Two or three days after, a woman and horse were killed near Bungay; her hat so shivered that no piece remained bigger than a groat, whereof I had some pieces sent unto me. Granades, crackers, and squibs, do much resemble the discharge, and *aurum fulminans* the fury thereof. Of other thunderbolts or *lapides fulminei,* I have little opinion. Some I have by me under that name, but they are *è genere fossilium.*
THOMAS BROWNE.

Norwich, 1665.

ON DREAMS.

Half our days we pass in the shadow of the earth; and the brother of death exacteth a third part of our lives. A good part of our sleep is peered out with visions and fantastical objects, wherein we are confessedly deceived. The day supplieth us with truths; the night with fictions and falsehoods, which uncomfortably divide the natural account of our beings. And, therefore, having passed the day in sober labours and rational enquiries of truth, we are fain to betake ourselves unto such a state of being, wherein the soberest heads have acted all the monstrosities of melancholy, and which unto open eyes are no better than folly and madness.

Happy are they that go to bed with grand music, like Pythagoras, or have ways to compose the fantastical spirit, whose unruly wanderings take off inward sleep, filling our heads with St. Anthony's quo;s visions, and the dreams of Lipara in the sober chambers of rest.

Virtuous thoughts of the day lay up good treasures for the night; whereby the impressions of imaginary forms arise into sober similitudes, acceptable unto our slumbering selves and preparatory unto divine impressions. Hereby Solomon's sleep was happy. Thus prepared, Jacob might well dream of angels upon a pillow of stone. And the best sleep of Adam might be the best of any after.

That there should be divine dreams seems unreasonably doubted by Aristotle. That there are demoniacal dreams we have little reason to doubt. Why may there not be angelical? If there be guardian spirits, they may not be inactively about us in sleep; but may sometimes order our dreams: and many strange hints, instigations, or discourses, which are so amazing unto us, may arise from such foundations.

But the phantasms of sleep do commonly walk in the great road of natural and animal dreams, wherein the thoughts or actions of the day are acted over and echoed in the night. Who can therefore wonder that Chrysostom should dream of St. Paul, who daily read his epistles; or that Cardan, whose head was so taken up about the stars, should dream that his soul was in the moon! Pious persons, whose thoughts are daily busied about heaven, and the blessed state thereof, can hardly escape the nightly phantasms of it, which though sometimes taken for illuminations, or divine dreams, yet rightly perpended may prove but animal visions, and natural night-scenes of their awaking contemplations.

Many dreams are made out by sagacious exposition, and from the signature of their subjects; carrying their interpretation in their fundamental sense and mystery of similitude, whereby, he that understands upon what natural fundamental every notion dependeth, may, by symbolical adaptation, hold a ready way to read the characters of Morpheus. In dreams of such a nature, Artemidorus, Achmet, and Astrampsichus, from Greek, Egyptian, and Arabian oneirocriticism, may hint some interpretation: who, while we read of a ladder in Jacob's dream, will tell us that ladders and scalary ascents signify preferment; and while we consider the dream of Pharaoh, do teach us that rivers overflowing speak plenty, lean oxen, famine and scarcity; and therefore it was but reasonable in Pharaoh to demand the interpretation from his magicians, who, being Egyptians, should have been well versed in symbols and the hieroglyphical notions of things. The greatest tyrant in such divinations was Nabuchodonosor, while, besides the interpretation, he demanded the dream itself; which being probably determined by divine immission, might escape the common road of phantasms, that might have been traced by Satan.

When Alexander, going to besiege Tyre, dreamt of a Satyr, it was no hard exposition for a Grecian to say, 'Tyre will be thine.' He that dreamed that he saw his father washed by Jupiter and anointed by the sun, had cause to fear that he might be crucified, whereby his body would be washed by the rain, and drop by the heat of the sun. The dream of Vespasian was of harder exposition; as also that of the emperor Mauritius, concerning his successor Phocas. And a man might have been hard put to it, to interpret the language of Æsculapius, when to a consumptive person he held forth his fingers; implying thereby that his cure lay in dates, from the homonomy of the Greek, which signifies dates and fingers.

We owe unto dreams that Galen was a physician, Dion an historian, and that the world hath seen some notable pieces of Cardan; yet, he that should order his affairs by dreams, or make the night a rule unto the day, might be ridiculously deluded; wherein Cicero is much to be pitied, who having excellently discoursed of the vanity of dreams, was yet undone by the flattery of his own, which urged him to apply himself unto Augustus.

However dreams may be fallacious concerning outward events, yet may they be truly significant at home; and whereby we may more sensibly understand ourselves. Men act in sleep with some conformity unto their awaked senses; and consolations or discouragements may be drawn from dreams which intimately tell us ourselves. Luther was not like to fear a spirit in the night, when such an apparition would not terrify him in the day. Alexander would hardly have run away in the sharpest combats of sleep, nor Demosthenes have stood stoutly to it, who was scarce able to do it in his prepared senses. Persons of radical integrity will not easily be perverted in their dreams, nor noble minds do pitiful things in sleep. Crassus would have hardly been bountiful in a dream, whose fist was so close awake. But a man might have lived all his life upon the sleeping hand of Antonius.

There is an art to make dreams, as well as their interpretation; and physicians will tell us that some food makes turbulent, some gives quiet, dreams. Cato, who doated upon cabbage, might find the crude effects thereof in his sleep; wherein the Egyptians might find some advantage by their superstitious abstinence from onions. Pythagoras might have calmer sleeps, if he totally abstained from beans. Even Daniel, the great interpreter of dreams, in his leguminous diet, seems to have chosen no advantageous food for quiet sleeps, according to Grecian physic.

To add unto the delusion of dreams, the fantastical objects seem greater than they are; and being beheld in the vaporous state of sleep, enlarge their diameters unto us; whereby it may prove more easy to dream of giants than pigmies. Democritus might seldom dream of atoms, who so often thought of them. He almost might dream himself a bubble extending unto the eighth sphere. A little water makes a sea; a small puff of wind a tempest. A grain of sulphur kindled in the blood may make a flame like Ætna; and a small spark in the bowels of Olympias a lightning over all the chamber.

But, beside these innocent delusions, there is a sinful state of dreams. Death alone, not sleep, is able to put an end unto sin; and there may be a night-book of our iniquities; for beside the transgressions of the day, casuists will tell us of mortal sins in dreams, arising from evil precogitations; meanwhile human law regards not noctambulos; and if a night-walker should break his neck, or kill a man, takes no notice of it.

Dionysius was absurdly tyrannical to kill a man for dreaming that he had killed him; and really to take away his life, who had but fantastically taken away his. Lamia was ridiculously unjust to sue a young man for a reward, who had confessed that pleasure from her in a dream which she had denied unto his awaking senses: conceiving that she had merited somewhat from his fantastical fruition and shadow of herself. If there be such debts, we owe deeply unto sympathies; but the common spirit of the world must be ready in such arrearages.

If some have swooned, they may also have died in dreams, since death is but a confirmed swooning. Whether Plato died in a dream, as some deliver, he must rise again to inform us. That some have never dreamed, is as improbable as that some have never laughed. That children dream not the first half-year; that men dream not in some countries, with many more, are unto me sick men's dreams; dreams out of the ivory gate, and visions before midnight.

OBSERVATIONS ON GRAFTING.

In the doctrine of all insitions, those are esteemed most successful which are practised under these rules:—

That there be some consent or similitude of parts and nature between the plants conjoined.

That insition be made between trees not of very different barks; nor very differing fruits or forms of fructification; nor of widely different ages.

That the scions or buds be taken from the south or east part of the tree.

That a rectitude and due position be observed; not to insert the south part of the scions unto the northern side of the stock, but according to the position of the scions upon his first matrix.

Now, though these rules be considerable in the usual and practised course of insitions, yet were it but reasonable for searching spirits to urge the operations of nature by conjoining plants of very different natures in parts, barks, lateness, and precocities, nor to rest in the experiments of hortensial plants in whom we chiefly intend the exaltation or variety of their fruit and flowers, but in all sorts of shrubs and trees applicable unto physic and mechanical uses, whereby we might alter their tempers, moderate or promote their virtues, exchange their softness, hardness, and colour, and so render them considerable beyond their known and trite employments.

To which intent curiosity may take some rule or hint from these or the like following, according to the various ways of propagation:—

Colutea upon anagris—arbor judæ upon anagris—cassia poetica upon cytisus—cytisus upon periclymenum rectum—woodbine upon jasmine—cystus upon rosemary—rosemary upon ivy—sage or rosemary upon cystus—myrtle upon gall or rhus myrtifolia—whortleberry upon gall, heath, or myrtle—coccygeia upon alaternus—mezereon upon an almond—gooseberry and currants upon mezereon, barberry, or blackthorn—barberry upon a currant tree—bramble upon gooseberry or raspberry—yellow rose upon sweetbrier—phyllerea upon broom—broom upon furze—anonis lutea upon furze—holly upon box—bay upon holly—holly upon pyracantha—a fig upon chestnut—a fig upon mulberry—peach upon mulberry—mulberry upon buckthorn—walnut upon chesnut—savin upon juniper—vine upon oleaster, rosemary, ivy—an arbutus upon a fig—a peach upon a fig—white poplar upon black poplar—asp upon white poplar—wych elm upon common elm—hazel upon elm—sycamore upon wych elm—cinnamon rose upon hipberry—a whitethorn upon a blackthorn—hipberry upon a sloe, or skeye, or bullace—apricot upon a mulberry—arbutus upon a mulberry—cherry upon a peach—oak upon a chesnut—katherine peach upon a quince—a warden upon a quince—a chesnut upon a beech—a beech upon a chesnut—an hornbeam upon a beech—a maple upon an hornbeam—a sycamore upon a maple—a medlar upon a service tree—a sumack upon a quince or medlar—an hawthorn upon a service tree—a quicken tree upon an ash—an ash upon an asp—an oak upon an ilex—a poplar upon an elm—a black cherry tree upon a tilea or lime tree—tilea upon beech—alder upon birch or poplar—a filbert upon an almond—an almond upon a willow—a nux vesicaria upon an almond or pistachio—a cerasus avium upon a nux vesicaria—a cornelian upon a cherry tree—a cherry tree upon a cornelian—an hazel upon a willow or sallow—a lilac upon a sage tree—a syringa upon lilac or tree-mallow—a rose elder upon syringa—a water elder upon rose elder—buckthorn upon elder—frangula upon buckthorn—hirga sanguinea upon privet—phyllerea upon vitex—vitex upon evonymus—evonymus upon viburnum—ruscus upon pyracantha—paleurus upon hawthorn—tamarisk upon birch—erica upon tamarisk—polemonium upon genista hispanica—genista hispanica upon colutea.

Nor are we to rest in the frustrated success of some single experiments, but to proceed in attempts in the most unlikely unto iterated and certain conclusions, and to pursue the way of ablactation or inarching. Whereby we might determine whether, according to the ancients, no fir, pine, or picea, would admit of any incision upon them; whether yew will hold society with none; whether walnut, mulberry, and cornel cannot be propagated by insition, or the fig and quince admit almost of any, with many others of doubtful truths in the propagations.

And while we seek for varieties in stocks and scions, we are not to admit the ready practice of the scion upon its own tree. Whereby, having a sufficient number of good plants, we may improve their fruits without translative conjunction, that is, by insition of the scion upon his own mother, whereby an handsome variety or melioration seldom faileth—we might be still advanced by iterated insitions in proper boughs and positions. Insition is also made not only with scions and buds, but seeds, by inserting them in cabbage stalks, turnips, onions, etc., and also in ligneous plants.

Within a mile of this city of Norwich, an oak groweth upon the head of a pollard willow, taller than the stock, and about half a foot in diameter, probably by some acorn falling or fastening upon it. I could show you a branch of the same willow which shoots forth near the stock which beareth both willow and oak twigs and leaves upon it. In a meadow I use in Norwich, beset with willows and sallows, I have observed these plants to grow upon their heads; bylders, currants, gooseberries, *cynocrambe*, or dog's mercury, barberries, bittersweet, elder, hawthorn.

CORRIGENDA

Vol.	Page	line	
I.	4,	24.	*For* than *read* that.
	97,	10.	*For* fell in love *read* carnal'd.
	227,	4.	*For* Capio *read* Capo.
	300,	8.	*For* Apicus *read* a Picus.
	301,	30.	*For* Caterpillaries *read* capillaries.
II.	111,	14.	*Prega, Dio* omit comma.
	206,	1.	*For* Tarus and Fulius *read* Varus and Julius.

Made in the USA
Coppell, TX
15 September 2021